Brazil

a Lonely Planet travel survival kit

Andrew Draffen
Chris McAsey
Leonardo Pinheiro
Robyn Jones

ROBYN JONES

Brazil

3rd edition

Published by
Lonely Planet Publications
Head Office: PO Box 617, Hawthorn, Vic 3122, Australia
Branches: 155 Filbert St, Suite 251, Oakland, CA 94607, USA
10 Barley Mow Passage, Chiswick, London W4 4PH, UK
71 bis rue du Cardinal Lemoine, 75005 Paris, France

Printed by
SNP Printing Pte Ltd, Singapore

Photographs by

Greg Caire	Andrew Draffen
Robyn Jones	John Maier, Jr
Chris McAsey	Guy Moberly

Front cover: John Maier, Jr

First Published
August 1989

This Edition
January 1996

Although the authors and publisher have tried to make the information as accurate as possible, they accept no responsibility for any loss, injury or inconvenience sustained by any person using this book.

National Library of Australia Cataloguing in Publication Data

Brazil.

3rd ed.
Includes index.
ISBN 0 86442 317 9.

1. Brazil – Guidebooks. 1. Draffen, Andrew.
II. Draffen, Andrew. Brazil III. Title: Brazil.
(Series: Lonely Planet travel survival kit).

918.10463

Andrew Draffen

Australian-born Andrew has travelled and worked his way around Australia, Asia, North America and the Caribbean, settling just long enough in Melbourne to complete an Arts degree, majoring in history. During his first trip to South America in 1984, Andrew fell in love with both Brazil and his future wife, Stella. They have since toured extensively in Brazil, Europe and Asia, and today travel with their young children, Gabriela and Christopher, whose great-great-grandfather introduced football to Brazil.

Chris McAsey

After being weeded out of law school, Chris had varying levels of success as kitchenhand, professional footballer and clothing wholesaler. He left Australia in 1988 and travelled, worked and studied in Western and Eastern Europe, Russia, the USA and Japan. He returned to Australia in 1991 to complete an Arts degree majoring in professional writing, and in 1993 published a guidebook on Australia for Japanese people. He has recently worked on Lonely Planet's *Indonesia*.

Leonardo Pinheiro

Leonardo was born and raised in Rio de Janeiro. Brazil. At 15, curious to roam further than Rio city, he jumped on a bus to the Northeast coast. From then on he travelled as much as his pocket money and time would allow throughout Brazil. After tertiary studies in agricultural science he came to Sydney to do a Masters degree in biotechnology and to check out the Australian surf. He met Robyn and has now relocated to Melbourne.

Robyn Jones

Robyn grew up in rural Victoria, Australia. She traded farm life for a year as an exchange student in the metropolis of São Paulo. She fell in love with travel and in particular with Brazil. While studying for her degree in architecture, she tripped around Australia and Europe, and later returned to Brazil to live in Rio de Janeiro for six months. Robyn works as an architect in Melbourne.

From the Authors

From Andrew Special thanks to my Brazilian family in São Paulo, especially Vera Miller – my favourite mother-in-law; Iara Costa da Pinto (São Paulo) for her hospitality on many Brazil trips; Ivana and Portugues, *nossa superpadrinhos*; Mari from Regina Turismo (São Paulo) for her Paulistana efficiency; Peter Bolgarow (Australia) for his excellent driving and radical mood swings which made for an entertaining trip; Eduardo Peterson (Porto Alegre) for his *gaúcho* hospitality; John and Masai (Rio); Beatriz Rondon (Aquidauana); Frank & Helen Draffen (Australia) for their support over the years; and Stella, Gabriela & Christopher Draffen, who make it all worthwhile.

From Chris Thanks to Valéria Moura and Daniela Pinheiro (Empetur, Recife); Mary, Luís and my tutor Wellington (Olinda); Leif, Suzanne and the Vikings (Jacumã); Simon Mortimer (England) for the company and roof; Ivone Facci and Marco António (São Paulo); Maria Aperecida Azevêdo França (Salvador); Suzanne von Davidson (Sítio); François Wolf (France); and John Zenari (Guayamerin). At home, thanks to Gina, Jenny, Michael, Ross and Jackie for their love and support.

From Robyn & Leonardo Thanks to Izane, Nazarene, Daniela and Orlando of Emamtur in Manaus; Lindalva and Socorro of Paratur in Belém; Rosana of Santarém tur; Leozildo of IBAMA in Macapá; and Déa Lucia of Embratur in Rio. Special thanks to Leo's family in Rio de Janeiro and Marj & Alex Jones and family for their support over the years; to *familias* Gonçalves Arruda and Prado in São Paulo for their hospitality back in 1981.

This Book

The 1st edition of *Brazil – a travel survival kit* was written by Mitchell Schoen & William Herzberg. The 2nd edition was written by Andrew Draffen, Deanna Swaney & Robert Strauss. For this 3rd edition, Andrew Draffen covered the Southeast, South and Central West, Chris McAsey covered the Northeast and Robyn Jones & Leonardo Pinheiro covered the North. All four writers covered overlapping sections of these regions.

Thanks to Krzysztof Dydyński for information for the sections on Leticia, Colombian and Peruvian borders and for Santa Elena, Venezuela, taken from Lonely Planet's *South America on a shoestring*.

From the Publisher

This 3rd edition of *Brazil* was edited and proofed by Rowan McKinnon and Alison White with assistance from Katie Cody, Nick Tapp, Brigitte Barta, Steve Womersley and Mary Neighbour. Sharon Wertheim produced the index. The mapping and design were done by Matt King and he was assisted by Chris Lee Ack, Kay Dancey, Jacqui Saunders, Ann Jeffree, Andrew Smith, Chris Klep, Maliza Kruh and Jane Hart. The illustrations were done by Tamsin Wilson and Carl Alexander, and the cartoons were drawn by Peter Morris.

Special thanks to contrary Mary Neighbour and 'Scalpel' Jane Hart for exhortation, expostulation and abetment. All power to the packers!

Thanks to those who wrote to us about their experiences in Brazil. These people's names appear at the end of this book.

Warning & Request

Things change – prices go up, schedules change, good places go bad and bad places go bankrupt – nothing stays the same. So if you find things better or worse, recently opened or long since closed, please write and tell us and help make the next edition better.

Your letters will be used to help update future editions and, where possible, important changes will also be included in reprints.

We greatly appreciate all information that is sent to us by travellers. Back at Lonely Planet we employ a hard-working readers' letters team to sort through the many letters we receive. The best ones will be rewarded with a free copy of the next edition or another Lonely Planet guide if you prefer. We give away lots of books, but, unfortunately, not every letter/postcard receives one.

Contents

Map Legend

BOUNDARIES

.... International Boundary

.... Regional Boundary

ROUTES

.... Freeway

.... Highway

.... Major Road

.... Unsealed Road or Track

.... City Road

.... City Street

.... Railway

.... Underground Railway

.... Tram

.... Walking Track

.... Walking Tour

.... Ferry Route

.... Cable Car or Chairlift

AREA FEATURES

.... Parks

.... Built-Up Area

.... Pedestrian Mall

.... Market

.... Cemetery

.... Reef

.... Beach or Desert

.... Mountain Ranges

HYDROGRAPHIC FEATURES

.... Coastline

.... River, Creek

.... Intermittent River or Creek

.... Rapids, Waterfalls

.... Lake, Intermittent Lake

.... Canal

.... Swamp

SYMBOLS

✪ CAPITAL		.... National Capital
◉ Capital		.... Regional Capital
◍ CITY		.... Major City
● City		.... City
● Town		.... Town
● Village		.... Village
■	▼	.... Place to Stay, Place to Eat
☒	☗	.... Cafe, Pub or Bar
✉	☎	.... Post Office, Telephone
❶	❸	.... Tourist Information, Bank
◕	℗	.... Transport, Parking
🏛	⚑	.... Museum, Youth Hostel
⚘	⚠	Caravan Park, Camping Ground
✝	✚	.... Church, Cathedral
☪	✡	.... Mosque, Synagogue
卍	🛕	Buddhist Temple, Hindu Temple
✛	★	.... Hospital, Police Station

◔	⛽	.... Embassy, Petrol Station
✈	✝	.... Airport, Airfield
▭	✿	.... Swimming Pool, Gardens
❖	🐘	.... Shopping Centre, Zoo
❦	⛱	...Winery or Vineyard, Picnic Site
←	A25	One Way Street, Route Number
🏛	⚱	.... Stately Home, Monument
🏰	■	.... Castle, Tomb
⌒	⌂	.... Cave, Hut or Chalet
▲	☀	.... Mountain or Hill, Lookout
🗼	⚓	.... Lighthouse, Shipwreck
)(	◎	.... Pass, Spring
⚲	⚑	.... Beach, Surf Beach
	∴	.... Archaeological Site or Ruins
		.... Ancient or City Wall
		.... Cliff or Escarpment, Tunnel
		.... Railway Station

Note: not all symbols displayed above appear in this book

Introduction

For hundreds of years Brazil has symbolised the great escape into a primordial, tropical paradise. No country ignites the Western imagination as Brazil does. From the mad passion of Carnival to the enormity of the dark Amazon, Brazil is a country of mythical proportions.

Roughly the size of the USA excluding Alaska, Brazil is a vast country encompassing nearly half of South America, and bordering all of the continent's other nations with the exceptions of Ecuador and Chile. After 40 years of internal migration and population growth, Brazil is also an urban country; more than two out of every three Brazilians live in a city. São Paulo, with more than 17 million inhabitants, is one of the most populous megalopolises in the world. Brazil's population is clustered along the Atlantic coast and much of the country, including the massive Amazon Basin, remains scarcely populated and inaccessible.

For most, the Brazilian journey begins in Rio de Janeiro. For some it goes no further. One of the world's great tourist cities, Rio has developed a highly advanced culture of pleasure. It revolves around the famous beaches of Copacabana and Ipanema, and is fuelled by the music and dance of samba, the beauty of Corcovado and Pão de Açúcar (Sugar Loaf Mountain), the athleticism of football, the happiness to be found in an ice-cold *cerveja* (beer), the camaraderie of *papo* (chitchat) and the cult of the body-beautiful. This hedonism reaches its climax in the big bang of ecstasy that is Carnival – four days of revelry and debauchery, unrivalled by any other party on the globe.

The state of Rio de Janeiro is blessed with some of the country's best beaches: from the world-renowned Búzios to the unknown and undeveloped Ilha Grande. Inland, the coastal mountains rise rapidly from under a blanket of lush, green, tropical forest, culminating in spectacular peaks. The mountains are punctuated by colonial cities and national parks

that are home to Brazil's best hiking and climbing.

The Amazon is the world's largest tropical rainforest, fed by the world's largest river, and home to the richest and most diverse ecosystem on the earth. It is a naturalist's ultimate fantasy! Though it is threatened by rapid and senseless deforestation, the Brazilian Amazon still offers years of exploration for the adventurous traveller.

South of the Amazon, in the centre of the continent, is Brazil's best kept secret – the Pantanal. The world's largest wetlands, the Pantanal is home to the greatest concentration of fauna in South America. When the floodwaters recede in March, the Pantanal becomes an ornithologist's playground, with over 200 bird species displaying their stuff:

macaws, parrots, toucans, rheas and jaburú storks are just a few of the more exotic species to be seen. Caimans (alligators), deer, capybaras, anteaters, anacondas, river otters, and the rare jaguar also thrive in the Pantanal, although several of these species are severely threatened by poaching.

The Iguaçu Falls, at the border of Argentina, Paraguay and Brazil, may be Brazil's most dazzling spectacle. The mighty waterfalls are one of the natural wonders of the world, and are superior, in size and grandeur, to both Niagara and Victoria.

Wherever the traveller goes in Brazil, from the standing-room only crowds of Copacabana to the quieter white-sand beaches along the banks of the Amazon, Brazilians are at their beaches playing. In Brazil, the beach is the national passion – everything and everyone goes there. Fortunately, with over 8000 km of coastline, there are loads of superb beaches, so you should have no problem finding your own tropical hideaway.

The mixing of races in Brazil – Indian, black and white – is most pronounced in the historic Northeast. Miscegenation and the tenacity of the traditional way of life have created a unique and wonderful civilisation, with much of Brazil's most beautiful music, dance and art, and a series of fascinating 16th and 17th-century cities like Recife, Olinda, Fortaleza, São Luís and, of course, Salvador.

Once the capital of Brazil, and one of the richest cities of the New World, Salvador is today the centre of Afro-Brazilian culture. Against a backdrop of 17th-century colonial houses, gilded churches and lively beaches, Salvador de Bahia breathes Africa: the rhythms of *afoxé*; the dance of *capoeira*; the spirituality of Candomblé, the Afro-Brazilian religion; and the many colourful pageants and festivals, particularly from December to Carnival.

Perhaps Brazil is not the paradise on earth that many travellers once imagined, but it is a land of often unimaginable beauty. There are stretches of unexplored rainforest, islands with pristine tropical beaches, and endless rivers. And there are the people themselves, who delight the visitor with their energy, fantasy and joy.

STOP PRESS
Some prices in Brazil have increased dramatically since this book was researched. The strength of the Brazilian currency, the real, is a major factor; after many years of steady decline against the US dollar, the real has actually been appreciating. In Rio de Janeiro, for instance, prices have increased by about 50% on average. ■

Facts about the Country

HISTORY
Indians
Anthropologists believe that at least 20,000 years ago American Indians migrated across the Bering Strait from north-eastern Asia. They were hunter-gatherers who followed the animals across the land bridge connecting Asia and North America. The tribes were highly mobile and, once they crossed into Alaska, they moved south to warmer climates. Eventually, they reached the Amazon Basin in Brazil and spread out from there. It's also likely that a separate, later migration took place across the oceans, jumping from island to island.

The Brazilian Indians never developed an advanced, centralised civilisation like the Inca or Maya. They left little for archaeologists to discover; only some pottery, shell mounds and skeletons. The shell mounds (*sambaquis*) are curious. They are found on the island of Marajó, the home of Brazil's most advanced pre-Columbian civilisation, and along the coast in the south. Typically as tall as a human and about 50 metres long, the mounds are naturally formed by the sea and were used as burial sites and sometimes as dwellings.

The Indian population was quite diverse. At the time of the Portuguese conquest, the Tupi people were most prevalent on the coast and best known to the white conquerors. Today, most of the animals in Brazil, nearly all the rivers and mountains, and many of the towns have Tupi names.

There were an estimated two to five million Indians living in the territory that is now Brazil when the Portuguese first arrived. Today there are fewer than 200,000. Most of them live in the hidden jungles of the Brazilian interior.

The Indians of Brazil, as the Portuguese were to learn, were divided into many groups and were primarily hunter-gatherers. The women did most of the work while the men, who were magnificent archers and fishers, went to war. They lived in long communal huts. Music, dance and games played a very important role in their culture. Little surplus was produced and they had very few possessions. Every couple of years the village packed up and moved on to richer hunting grounds.

This lifestyle, which came to symbolise the ideal of the noble savage in European minds and inspired many social thinkers such as Rousseau and Defoe, was punctuated by frequent tribal warfare and ritual cannibalism. After battles the captured enemies were ceremonially killed and eaten.

Early Colonisation
In 1500, Pedro Cabral sailed from Lisbon, bound for India, with 13 ships and 1200 men. Following Indies trailblazer Vasco da Gama's directions, his fleet sailed on a south-westerly course in order to exploit the favourable westerly trade winds in the southern hemisphere. The slow sailing ships of the fleet were vulnerable to the strong equatorial current, which took them further west than intended. Some historians say it was Cabral's secret destination all along, and his official 'discovery' was reported to the king in such matter-of-fact terms that it seems that the existence of Brazil was already well known to mariners. In fact, Portuguese records dating from 1530 suggest that the country had been colonised for more than 40 years.

Cabral landed at present-day Porto Seguro on 22 April. He and his crew were immediately greeted by some of the many Indians living along the coast. Staying only nine days, the Portuguese built a cross and held the first Christian service in the land they dubbed Terra de Vera Cruz (Land of the True Cross). The Indians watched with apparent amazement and then, complying with the exhortations of their guests, knelt before the cross. But it wasn't Catholicism that grabbed their attention. It was the building of the cross. The Indians, living in a Stone Age culture, had never seen iron tools.

Cabral sailed on, leaving behind two convicts to learn the Indians' ways and taking some logs of the *pau brasil* – brazil wood, which produces a red dye. Subsequent Portuguese expeditions were disappointed by what they found in Brazil. They had little interest in colonisation; instead they sought the riches of India and Africa where they established trading stations to obtain spices and ivory. Brazil offered the merchants little: the Indians' Stone Age culture produced nothing for the European market, and the land was heavily forested, barely passable and very wild.

However, the red dye from brazil wood provoked the interest of a few Portuguese merchants and the king granted them the rights to the brazil-wood trade. They soon began sending a few ships each year to harvest the trees. This trade depended entirely on Indian labour which they procured in exchange for metal axes and knives – objects that are used to this day by Brazilians contacting unknown Indians.

Brazil wood remained the only exportable commodity for the first half of the 16th century – long enough for the colony to change its name from Terra de Vera Cruz to Brazil, an act that was later interpreted, as reports of Brazilian godlessness reached superstition-ridden Portugal, as the work of the devil. But the brazil-wood trade was already in jeopardy. It was never terribly profitable and the most accessible trees were rapidly depleted. French competition for the trees intensified and fighting broke out. The Indians stopped volunteering their labour.

In 1531, King João III of Portugal sent the first settlers to Brazil. Martim Afonso de Sousa was placed at the head of five ships and a crew of 400. After exploring the coastline he chose São Vicente, near the modern port of Santos in São Paulo state, as the first settlement. In 1534, fearing the ambitions of other European countries, the king divided the coast into 12 parallel captaincies. These hereditary estates were given to friends of the Crown (*donatários*) who became lords of

their land. Each captaincy comprised 50 leagues (about 300 km) of coastline and unlimited territory inland.

This was one of the earliest European attempts to set up a colony in the tropics. The king's scheme was designed to minimise the cost to the Crown while securing the vast coastline through settlement. He wanted to give the captaincies to Portuguese nobility, but the wealthy nobles were interested in the riches of Asia. So instead the captaincies were given to common *fidalgos* (gentry), who lacked the means to overcome the obstacles of settling Brazil. They were hampered by the climate, hostility from the Indians and competition from the Dutch and French. One of the donatários, Duarte Coelho, wrote to the king: 'We are obliged to conquer by inches, the land that your Majesty has granted us by leagues.' Four captaincies were never settled and four were destroyed by Indians. Only Pernambuco and São Vicente were profitable.

In 1549 the king sent Tomé de Sousa to be the first governor of Brazil, to centralise authority and to save the few remaining captaincies. Despite the fact that the Indians had recently driven the Portuguese from the area, the king chose Bahia for Sousa to rule from; the Baía de Todos os Santos (Bay of All Saints) was one of Brazil's best bays, as was the land surrounding it.

Ten ships and 1000 settlers arrived safely. On board were Portuguese officials, soldiers, exiled prisoners, New Christians (converted Jews) and the first six Jesuit priests. The great Caramuru, a Portuguese living among the Indians and married to a chief's daughter, selected a spot on high ground for Salvador da Bahia, the new capital of Portuguese Brazil, a position it held until the colonial capital was transferred to Rio in 1763.

The colonists soon discovered that the land and climate were ideal for growing sugar cane. Sugar was coveted by a hungry European market that used it initially for medicinal purposes and as a condiment for almost all foods and even wine. To produce the sugar cane, all the colonists needed were workers. Growing and processing the cane was hard work. The Portuguese didn't want to do the work themselves so they attempted to enslave the Indians.

Up and down the coast, the Indians' response to the Portuguese was similar. First, they welcomed and offered the strangers food, labour and women in exchange for iron tools and liquor. They then became wary of the whites, who abused their customs and beliefs, and took the best land. Finally, when voluntary labour became slavery and the use of land became wholesale displacement, the Indians fought back and won many victories.

The capture and sale of Indian slaves became Brazil's second largest enterprise. Organised expeditions from São Paulo hunted the Indians into the Brazilian interior, exploring and claiming vast lands for the Portuguese and making fortunes supplying the sugar estates with Indian slaves. These expeditions were called *bandeiras* (flags). Each group had its own flag, and the men who followed them came to be known as *bandeirantes* (flag-bearers). Their bravery was eclipsed only by their brutality.

The Jesuit priests went to great lengths to save the Indians from the slaughter. They inveighed against the evils of Indian slavery in their sermons, though they said little about black slaves. They pleaded with the king of Portugal. They set up *aldeias* (missions) to settle, protect and Christianise the Indians.

Fear of God failed to deter the colonists. The monarchy was ambivalent about Indian slavery and too weak to do anything about it. Most of the Indians not killed by the guns of the bandeirantes or the work on the sugar plantations died from introduced European diseases and the alien life in the missions. The Jesuits may have delayed the destruction of the Brazilian Indians, but they certainly didn't prevent it. Nonetheless, the Jesuits battled heroically to save the Indians. One Brazilian statesman wrote: 'Without the Jesuits, our colonial history would be little more than a chain of nameless atrocities.'

By the end of the 16th century about 30,000 Portuguese settlers and 20,000 black slaves lived in isolated coastal towns surrounded by often hostile Indians. There were about 200 prosperous sugar mills, mostly in Pernambuco and Bahia. In an often quoted passage, a historian lamented in 1620 that the Brazilian settlers were satisfied with 'sidling like crabs along the coastline from one sugar plantation to another'.

But there were good reasons for this. The export economy looked only to Europe, not inland where the forests were dense, the rivers were wild and hostile Indians prevailed. Sugar was extremely lucrative, whereas the legendary gold of El Dorado was elusive. The sugar trade needed the rich coastal soil and access to European markets. Thus the Portuguese settled almost exclusively at the mouths of rivers on navigable bays. Where sugar grew – mainly Bahia, Pernambuco and Rio – so did the fledgling colony.

The captaincy system failed, but the sugar trade succeeded. The sparse settlements that would eventually encompass half the continent already had the elements that were to define it even into the 19th century: sugar and slavery.

Sugar & Slaves

The sugar plantations were self-sufficient economic enclaves. They were geared to large-scale production that required vast tracts of land and specialised equipment to process the sugar cane. In Brazil this meant the sugar baron needed land, a fair amount of capital and many workers, typically 100 to 150 slaves, both skilled and unskilled.

By the 1550s the wealthier sugar barons began to buy African slaves instead of Indians. The Africans were better workers and more immune to the European diseases that were killing the Indians faster than the Portuguese guns. Soon tremendous profits were being made by merchants in the slave trade. The infamous triangular trade brought slaves and elephant tusks from Africa, sugar, sugar-cane liquor and tobacco from Brazil, and guns and luxury goods from Europe.

Throughout the 17th century, blacks replaced Indians on the plantations. In the early 1600s about 1500 slaves were arriving each year. From 1550 through to 1850, when the slave trade was abolished, about 3½ million African slaves were shipped to Brazil – 38% of the total that came to the New World.

Those Africans who didn't die on the slave ships generally had short and brutal lives. The work on the plantations was hard and tedious. During the busy season slaves worked 15 to 17 hours a day. But it was the working and living conditions, not the amount of work itself, that were largely responsible for the high mortality rate of Brazil's slaves. Disease was rampant in Brazil; many succumbed to dysentery, typhus, yellow fever, malaria, syphilis, tuberculosis and scurvy.

The plantation owners ruled colonial Brazil. Their control over free whites who worked as share-croppers was almost total, and over slaves it was absolute. Slaves were dependent on their masters. Some were kind, but most were cruel and often sadistic.

Slave families were routinely broken up. Masters mixed slaves from different tribes to prevent collective rebellion. The slaves from Islamic Africa, who were themselves culturally sophisticated, were particularly feared by the white masters.

Resistance to slavery took many forms. The misery of some slaves manifested in *banzo*, the longing for Africa, which culminated in a slow suicide. Documents of the period refer to slaves who would stop eating and just fade away. Many slaves fled, mothers killed their babies and sabotage and theft were frequent, as were work slow-downs, stoppages and revolts.

Those that survived life on the plantations sought solace in their African religion and culture, in their dance and song. The slaves were given perfunctory indoctrination into Catholicism. Except for the Islamic element, a syncretic religion rapidly emerged. Spiritual elements from many of the African tribes, such as the Yoruba, Bantu and Fon were preserved and made palatable to the slave masters with a facade of Catholic saints and ritual objects. These are the roots of modern Macumba and Candomblé, prohibited by law until very recently.

Portugal was not an overpopulated country. There was no capitalist revolution and no enclosures, as in England, forcing the peasantry off the land. Consequently, the typical Brazilian settler emigrated by choice with the hope of untold riches. These settlers were notoriously indisposed to work. They came to Brazil to make others work for them, not to toil in the dangerous tropics. Even poor whites had a slave or two. There was a popular saying that 'the slaves are the hands and the feet of the whites'.

The sugar barons lived on the plantation part time and escaped to their second houses in the cities, where they often kept mulatto (of mixed black and European parentage) mistresses. The white women led barren, cloistered lives inside the walls of the *casa grande* (big house). Secluded from all but their family and servants, the women married young – usually at 14 or 15 years of age – and often died early.

Sexual relations between masters and slaves were so common that a large mulatto population soon emerged. Off the plantations there was a shortage of white women, and so many poorer settlers lived with black and Indian women. Prostitution was prevalent. Many of the free mixed-race women could only survive by working as concubines or prostitutes. Brazil was famous for its sexual permissiveness. By the beginning of the 18th century it was known as the land of syphilis; the disease had reportedly wrought devastation even in the monasteries.

The church was tolerant of any coupling that helped populate the colony. Many priests had mistresses and illegitimate children. As Gilberto Freyre, Brazil's most famous social scientist, said of the priests, 'a good part if not the majority of them assisted in the work of procreation, and their cooperation was so gratefully accepted that the courts did not arrest or issue warrants for any cleric or friar on the charge of keeping a concubine'.

In the poorer regions of Pará, Maranhão, Ceará and São Paulo, the settlers couldn't afford black slaves, and so Indian slaves were more common. Here, miscegenation

ALL PHOTOS BY JOHN MAIER, JR

Faces of Brazil

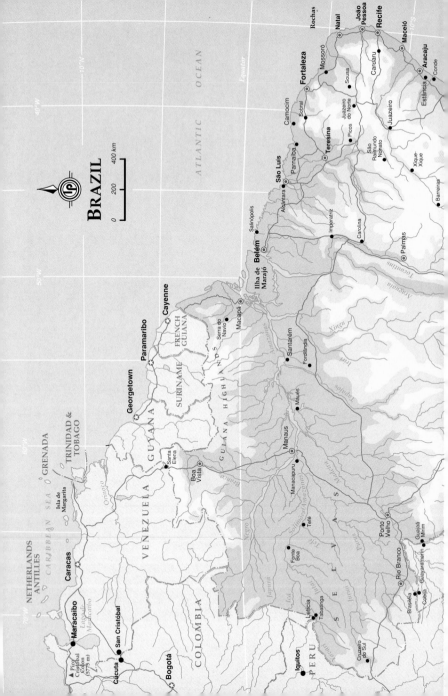

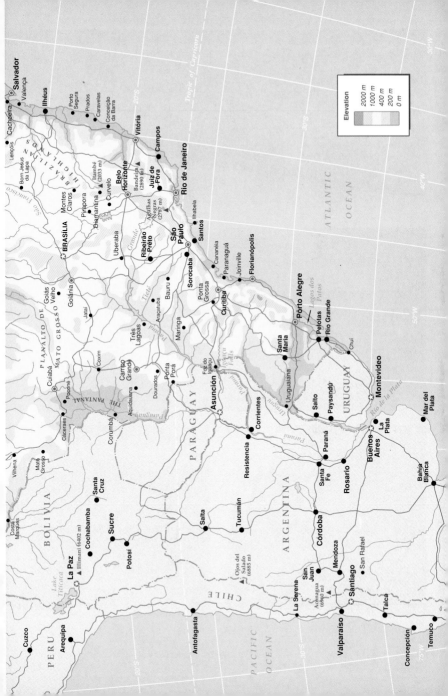

ANDREW DRAFFEN

GUY MOBERLY

JOHN MAIER, JR

JOHN MAIER, JR

ROBYN JONES

A	
B	C
D	E

A: Jacaré
B: Piranha
C: Squirrel

D: Blue Macaws
E: Spider Monkey

was more prevalent between whites and Indians and just as tolerated (this is evident in the racial mix in those states today). As in the rest of the colony, sexual relations were rather licentious. As the Bishop of Pará summed it up: 'the wretched state of manners in this country puts me in mind of the end that befell the five cities, and makes me think that I am living in the suburbs of Gomorrah, very close indeed, and in the vicinity of Sodom'.

17th Century

Sugar plantations were the first attempt at large-scale agricultural production, not just extraction, in the New World. Thanks to a virtual monopoly and increasing European demand, they were highly profitable. The sugar trade made the Portuguese colonisation of Brazil possible. In later years, as Portugal's Asian empire declined, the tax revenues from the sugar trade kept the Portuguese ship of state afloat.

Although Spain and Portugal had divided the New World exclusively between themselves with the Treaty of Tordesillas, competing European powers – principally France and Holland – were not deterred from South America. France had successfully operated trading stations in Brazil for many years and had friendly relations with many Indians, who saw the French as a lesser evil than the hated Portuguese.

In 1555 three boatloads of French settlers led by Admiral Nicolas Durand de Villegagnon landed on a small island in Baía de Guanabara. They intended to add a large part of southern Brazil to their empire, which was to be called Antarctic France. After some bloody battles they were finally expelled by the governor-general of Brazil, Mem de Sá, in 1567. In a second attempt in 1612 the French took São Luís but were driven out by the Portuguese a few years later.

The Dutch posed a more serious threat to Portuguese Brazil. Dutch merchants had profited from the Brazilian sugar trade for many years, but when Portugal was unified with Spain, the traditional enemy of the Dutch, peaceful trade quickly collapsed. The Dutch set up the Dutch West India Company to gain control of part of Brazil. A large expedition took Bahia in 1624. A year later, after bloody and confused fighting, the Portuguese retook the city. They repulsed two more attacks in 1627.

The Dutch next conquered Pernambuco in 1630, and from there took control of a major part of the Northeast from Sergipe to Maranhão and founded what they called New Holland. With their superior sea power the Dutch sailed to Africa and captured part of Portuguese-held Angola to supply slaves for their new colony. In 1637, the Dutch prince, Maurice of Nassau, took over as the governor of New Holland. An enlightened administrator, he was successful.in increasing the number of sugar plantations, creating large cattle farms and re-establishing the discipline of his troops and civil administrators. Hospitals and orphanages were founded and freedom of worship was guaranteed in an attempt to win over the local population.

But Nassau was undermined and frustrated by a lack of support from Holland. When he returned home in 1644, the rot set in. The Pernambucan merchants, resenting the Protestant invaders, funded black and Indian soldiers who fought the Dutch on land. The Portuguese governor of Rio de Janeiro and Angola, Salvador de Sá, sailed from Rio and expelled the Dutch from Angola. Finally, when provisions failed to arrive, the Dutch troops mutinied and returned to Europe. A peace treaty was signed in 1654.

Bandeirantes

Throughout the 17th and 18th centuries, bandeirantes from São Paulo continued to march off into the interior to capture Indians. Most bandeirantes, born of Indian mothers and Portuguese fathers, spoke both Tupi-Guaraní and Portuguese. They also learned the survival skills of the Indians and the use of European weaponry, and wore heavily padded cotton jackets that deflected Indian arrows. Travelling light in bands that ranged from a dozen to a couple of hundred, they would go off for months or years at a time, living off the land and plundering Indian villages. By the mid-1600s they had traversed the interior as far as the peaks of the Peruvian Andes and the lowlands of the Amazon forest. These super-human exploits, more than any treaty, secured the huge interior of South America for Portuguese Brazil.

The bandeirantes were ruthlessly effective Indian hunters. The Jesuits, who sought desperately to protect their flock of Indians – who had come to the missions to escape bandeirante attacks – built missions in the remote interior, near the present-day borders with Paraguay and Argentina. Far from São Paulo, the Jesuits hoped that they were beyond the grasp of the bandeirantes. They were wrong, and this was to be their last stand. The Jesuits armed the Indians and desperate battles took place. The bandeirantes were slowed but they were never stopped. Finally, with the collusion of the Portuguese and Spanish crowns, the missions fell and the Jesuits were expelled from Brazil in 1759.

Gold

El Dorado and other South American legends of vast deposits of gold and precious stones clouded European minds and spurred on the roving bandeirantes. Despite incessant searching, riches failed to materialise until the 1690s, when bandeirantes discovered a magical lustre in the rivers of the Serra do Espinhaço, Brazil's oldest geological formation, an inaccessible and unsettled region inland from Rio de Janeiro.

Soon the gold rush was on. People dropped everything to go to what is now the southern central part of Minas Gerais. Unaware of the hazardous journey, many died on the way. In the orgy to pan, no one bothered to plant, and in the early years terrible famines swept through the gold towns. The price of basic provisions was always outrageous and the majority suffered. But the gold was there – more than seemed possible.

When gold was first discovered, there were no white settlers in the territory of Minas Gerais. By 1710 the population was 30,000 and by the end of the 18th century it was half a million.

For 50 years, until the mines began to decline, Brazilian gold caused major demographic shifts in three continents. Paulistas came from São Paulo, followed by other Brazilians, who had failed to strike it rich in commercial agriculture. Some 400,000 Portuguese arrived in Brazil in the 18th century, many headed for the gold fields. Countless slaves were stolen away from Africa, to dig and die in Minas.

Fuelled by competition over scarce mining rights, a Brazilian species of nativism arose. Old-time Brazilians, particularly the combative Paulistas, resented the flood of recent Portuguese immigrants who were cashing in on their gold discoveries. The recent arrivals, numerically superior, loathed the favourable treatment they saw the Paulistas receiving. Gold stakes were more often settled by guns, not by judges, and armed confrontations broke out in 1708. The colonial government was faced with a virtual civil war which lasted over a year, with miners carrying pans in one hand and guns in the other, before government intervention slowed the hostilities.

Most of the gold mining was done by black slaves. An estimated third of the two million slaves who reached Brazil in the 18th century went to the gold fields, where their lives were worse than in the sugar fields. Most slave owners put their slaves on an incentive system, allowing the slaves to keep a small percentage of the gold they found. A few slaves who found great quantities of gold were able to buy their own freedom, but for the majority disease and death came quickly.

Wild boom towns arose in the mountain valleys; Sabara, Mariana, São João del Rei, and the greatest, Vila Rica de Ouro Prêto (Rich Town of Black Gold). Wealthy merchants built opulent mansions and churches. Crime, gambling, drinking and prostitution ruled the streets. A class of educated artisans created some stunning baroque church architecture. Portuguese officials provided a sense of European civilisation. The absence of white women led to a large number of mulatto offspring.

Most of Brazil's gold wealth was squandered. A few merchants and miners became incredibly rich and lived on imported European luxury goods. But the gold did little to develop Brazil's economy, create a middle class or better the common worker. Most of the wealth went to Portuguese merchants and the king, until it was ultimately traded for English goods.

By 1750, after a half-century boom, the mining regions were in decline, the migration to the interior was over and coastal Brazil was returning to centre stage. Apart from some public works and many beautiful churches, the only important legacy of Brazil's gold rush was the shift in population, from the Northeast to the Southeast. Some stayed in Minas Gerais and raised cattle on its rich lands. Many ended up in Rio, whose population and economy grew rapidly as gold and supplies passed through its ports.

19th Century

On November 29, 1807 Napoleon's army marched on Lisbon. Two days before the invasion, 40 ships carrying the Portuguese prince regent (later known as Dom João VI) and his entire court of 15,000 had set sail for Brazil under the protection of British warships. When the prince regent arrived in Rio his Brazilian subjects celebrated wildly, dancing in the streets. He immediately took over rule of Brazil from his viceroy.

As foreigners have been doing ever since, Dom João fell in love with Brazil. A great lover of nature, he founded Rio's botanical gardens and introduced the habit of sea bathing to the water-wary inhabitants of Rio. Expected to return to Portugal after Napoleon's Waterloo in 1815, he stayed in Brazil. The following year his mother, mad Queen Dona Maria I, died and Dom João VI became king. Despite demands to return to Portugal and rule, he refused and declared Rio the capital of the United Kingdom of Portugal, Brazil and the Algarves. Brazil became the only New World colony to ever have a European monarch ruling on its soil.

Five years later he finally relented to political pressures and returned to Portugal, leaving his son, Pedro, in Brazil as prince regent.

According to legend, in 1822, Pedro pulled out his sword and yelled 'Independendência ou morte!' (Independence or death), putting himself at the country's head as Emperor Dom Pedro I. Portugal was too weak to fight its favourite son, not to mention the British, who had the most to gain from Brazilian independence and would have come to the aid of the Brazilians. The Brazilian Empire was born. Without spilling blood, Brazil had attained its independence and Dom Pedro I became the first emperor of Brazil.

Dom Pedro I only ruled for nine years. From all accounts he was a bumbling incompetent who scandalised even the permissive Brazilians by siring several soccer teams of illegitimate children. He was forced to abdicate, paving the way for his five-year-old son to become emperor.

Until Dom Pedro II reached adolescence, Brazil suffered a period of civil war under the rule of a weak triple regency. In 1840, the nation rallied behind the emperor, and his 50-year reign is regarded as the most prosperous period in Brazilian history. He nurtured an increasingly powerful parliamentary system, went to war with Paraguay, interfered in Argentine, Paraguayan and Uruguayan affairs, abolished slavery, encouraged mass immigration and became the first man in Brazil to have his photograph taken and to speak on the telephone (though not at the same time). Ultimately, he forged a nation that would do away with the monarchy forever.

In 1889 a military coup supported by the coffee aristocracy and a popular wave of republican sentiment toppled the antiquated Brazilian Empire. The emperor went into exile and died in Paris a couple of years later. A military clique ruled Brazil for four years until elections were held, but because of land and literacy requirements, ignorance and threats, only about 2% of the adult population voted. Little changed, except that power of the military and the coffee growers increased, while it diminished for the sugar barons.

A New Empire

At the beginning of the 19th century Brazil was a country of masters and slaves. There were about three million people, not including the Indians, and roughly one million of them were African slaves. In the poorer areas there were fewer black slaves, more poor whites and more Indians. The central west region – Minas, Goiás, the Mato Grosso – was only settled in isolated pockets where precious metals had been found. The Northeastern interior, the *sertão*, was the most settled inland part of the country. Although the arid sertão was unable to sustain much agriculture, cattle could graze and survive. It was a poor business, constantly threatened by drought, but the hardy *sertanejo* (inhabitant of the sertão) – often of mixed Portuguese and Indian extraction – was able to eke out a living.

The south was another story. Settled by farmers from the Portuguese Azores who brought their wives with them, the area was economically backward. Few could afford slaves. The Indians had been clustered in the Jesuit missions far to the west to save them from the bandeirantes. The south was, and remains, Brazil's most European region.

Slave Revolts & Abolition

Slavery in Brazil was not abolished until 1888, 25 years after the USA and 80 years behind Britain. Resistance to slavery grew throughout the 19th century and the spectre of Haiti – the site of the first successful slave revolt – haunted the Brazilian planters who, as a result, became more brutal towards their slaves.

In Bahia there were several urban insurrections between 1807 and 1835. Most were led by Muslim blacks – those who were free and those in slavery. The uprising of 1807 in Bahia was carefully planned so that slaves from the sugar plantations would meet the city slaves at the entrance to the city and

together attack the whites, seize ships and flee to Africa. However, the plot was betrayed and the leaders killed. The following year, a similar plan was carried out and the blacks were defeated in battle. In Minas Gerais, 15,000 slaves congregated in Ouro Prêto and 6000 in São João do Morro, demanding freedom and a constitution. The last big slave revolt in Bahia was in 1835, and was almost successful.

Slaves fought their oppressors in many ways, and many managed to escape from their masters. *Quilombos*, communities of runaway slaves, scattered throughout the countryside, were common throughout the colonial period. The quilombos ranged from small groups hidden in the forests, called *mocambos*, to the most famous, the great republic of Palmares, which survived through much of the 17th century.

Palmares covered a broad tract of lush tropical forest near the coast of northern Alagoas and southern Pernambuco states. At its height, 20,000 people lived under its protection. Most were black, but there were also Indians, mulattos, *mestiços* (of mixed European and Indian parentage) and bandits. They lived off the land, growing mostly corn. Agriculture was produced as a collective and productivity was higher than on the slave plantations.

Palmares was really a collection of semi-independent quilombos united under the rule of one king to fight off the Portuguese forces. Led by Zumbí, who had been a king in Africa, the citizens of Palmares became pioneers of guerrilla warfare and defeated many Portuguese attacks. Fearing Palmares' example, the government desperately tried to crush it. Between 1670 and 1695 Palmares was attacked on an average of every 15 months, until it finally fell to a force led by Paulista bandeirantes.

Palmares is now the stuff of movies and myths, but there were many quilombos in every state. As abolitionist sentiment grew in the 19th century, the quilombos received more support and ever greater numbers of slaves fled. Only abolition itself in 1888 stopped the quilombos.

Insurrections

With the settlements separated by enormous distances, with few transportation or communication links and an economy oriented toward European markets rather than local ones, the Brazilian nation was weak and there was little sense of national identity. Throughout the 19th century the Brazilian Empire was plagued with revolts by local ruling élites demanding greater autonomy from the central government, or even fighting to secede. Rio Grande do Sul was torn by a civil war, called the Farrapos Rebellion. There were insurrections in São Paulo and Minas Gerais, and others swept through the North and Northeast in the 1830s and '40s.

The bloodiest and most radical was the Cabanagem in the state of Pará. The rebels laid siege to the capital of Belém, appropriating and distributing supplies. They held the city for a year before their defeat at the hands of a large government force. The peasants fled to the jungle with the army in pursuit and eventually 40,000 of the state's 100,000 people were killed.

The most serious insurrections, like the Cabanagem, spread to the oppressed peasants and urban poor. The empire always struck back and the revolts all failed, in part because the upper and middle classes, who led the revolts feared the mobilised poor as much as they feared the government.

The 19th century was also a period of messianic popular movements amongst Brazil's poor. Most of the movements took place in the economically depressed back-

---

Lampião

Every country has famous bad guys somewhere in its history. The USA has its Western outlaws, the UK has its highwaymen, Australia has its bushrangers and Brazil has its *cangaceiros* (bandits).

At the end of the 19th century, the harsh poverty and social injustice in the drought-plagued sertão of the Northeast caused the formation of gangs of outlaws known as *cangaços*, who attacked towns, fazendas (ranches) and army outposts. The most famous cangaceiro was Lampião, who terrorised the sertão for more than 20 years.

Lampião was a cowboy until his parents were killed by a cruel landowner. He and his brothers swore revenge and headed for the sertão to join the roaming outlaw bands.

Around 1920, two years after he had become a cangaceiro, Lampião became head of his own gang. He gained his nickname, the Lamp, because of the bright flashes given off by his rifle when he fought the police. Unlike other cangaço leaders, who were known for their generosity to the suffering people of the sertão, Lampião was renowned for his cruelty.

With his band, that numbered between 15 and 50 men, he roamed the backlands of Pernambuco, Paraíba, Alagoas and Ceará. His fame grew as stories and songs of his deeds spread throughout the Northeast.

In 1929 he met Maria Bonita, who became his lover and the first woman to join the cangaço. For another nine years the cangaço continued to be a thorn in the side of the state and federal governments, who tried many times to bring Lampião to justice. Protected by the frightened general population and scared landowners, the cangaceiros became careless. One night in July 1938, they were surrounded by a group of *polícia militar* from Sergipe. Lampião and Maria Bonita were both killed, along with nine other gang members. Their heads were cut off and for almost 30 years remained on display in the Salvador Medical Institute. They were finally buried in 1969.

The last cangaceiro and surviving member of Lampião's band, Corisco, was killed in 1940, and the era of the cangaços came to an end. ■

lands of the Northeast. Canudos is the most famous of these movements. From 1877 to 1887, Antônio Conselheiro wandered through the backlands preaching and prophesising the appearance of the Antichrist and the coming end of the world. He railed against the new republican government, and eventually gathered his followers (who called him the Counsellor) in Canudos, a settlement in the interior of Bahia.

In Canudos, the government sensed dissenting plots to return Brazil to the Portuguese monarchy. They set out to subdue the rebels, but miraculously, a force of state police and then two attacks by the federal army were defeated.

Hysterical demonstrations in the cities demanded that the republic be saved from the revolutionary-monarchist followers of the Counsellor, and Canudos was again besieged. A federal force of 4000 well-supplied soldiers took the settlement after ferocious house-to-house and hand-to-hand fighting. The military was disgraced and suffered heavy casualties and the federal government was embarrassed, but Canudos was wiped out. The military killed every man, woman and child, and then burned the town to the ground to erase it from the nation's memory.

The epic struggle has been memorialised in what is considered the masterpiece of Brazilian literature, *Os Sertões* (Rebellion in the Backlands) by Euclides de Cunha. More recently, Mario Vargas Llosa wrote of Canudos in *The War of the End of the World*.

Coffee & Rubber

Popular legend has it that the coffee bean was introduced to Brazil in the early 18th century by Francisco de Mello Palheta, an officer from Maranhão, who went to Cayenne in French Guiana in order to settle a border dispute. He reputedly won the heart of the governor's wife, who put some coffee beans into his cup as a parting gift. On his return to Brazil, he planted them. It was to be another 100 years, however, until coffee rose to become Brazil's new monoculture.

The international sugar market began a rapid decline in the 1820s. The sugar planters had depleted much of their best soil, they had failed to modernise and were unable to compete with the newly mechanised sugar mills in the West Indies. As rapidly as sugar exports fell, coffee production rose.

Coffee grew poorly in the harsh northern climate, but flourished on the low mountain slopes of the Paraíba valley from north-east of São Paulo city up to Rio de Janeiro state and along the border with Minas Gerais. As these lands were snatched up, the coffee plantations moved westward into Minas Gerais and western São Paulo.

Coffee production was labour intensive. Because of the large investment needed to employ so many workers, production excluded the small farmer and favoured large enterprises using slave labour. The master-slave sugar plantation system, complete with the big house and slave quarters, was reproduced on the coffee *fazendas* of São Paulo and Minas Gerais.

Coffee exports increased rapidly throughout the 19th century and profits soared with the introduction of mechanisation and Brazil's first railroads. In 1889 it totalled two-thirds of the country's exports. The modernisation of coffee production also eased the coffee plantations' transition to a free labour force with the end of slavery in 1888. During the next decade 800,000 European immigrants, mostly Italians, came to work on the coffee fazendas. Millions more immigrants – Japanese, German, Spanish and Portuguese – flooded into the cities from 1890 to 1916.

Brazil was still a rural society – only 10% of the population lived in cities in 1890 – but cities were growing rapidly. São Paulo and Rio in particular were the main beneficiaries of the coffee boom.

In the last decades of the 19th century and the first of the 20th, the Amazon region was the scene of another incredible economic boom. It was *Hevea brasiliensis* – the rubber tree – a native of the American tropics that was the bringer of this good fortune. Things started to inflate in 1842 with the discovery of the vulcanisation process which turned rubber into an important industrial material. Demand really increased in 1890, with the invention of the pneumatic tyre and the expansion of the fledgling automobile industry in the USA. The price of rubber skyrocketed bringing huge wealth and rapid progress to the main Amazonian cities of Belém, Manaus and Iquitos, as well as a large population increase to the region.

In 1912, Manaus boasted electric lights, trams and a magnificent opera house. Rubber production that year reached its peak, when 42,000 tonnes of latex were exported; nearly 40% of Brazilian export revenue. It was second only to coffee on the list of most valuable export commodities.

Then the puncture occurred. Unfortunately for Brazil, in 1876, seeds from the rubber tree had been smuggled out of the Amazon and sent to Kew Gardens in England. The seedlings quickly found their way to the British colonies in South-East

Henry Wickham – Executioner of Amazonas

Henry Alexander Wickham was the man who punctured the Brazilian rubber boom. A classic Victorian character, it's surprising that no film has ever been made about his famous 'seed snatch' from the Amazon.

The idea of establishing rubber plantations in the British colonies in Ceylon, Malaya and the Dutch East Indies was one which had not escaped the crafty British botanists, but they believed that the seeds or seedlings of the *Hevea brasiliensis* would never survive the very long journey to England.

In 1876, Wickham, who had been drifting through South America for some time, made a deal with Sir Joseph Hooker at Kew Gardens who assured him he'd get £10 for every 1000 rubber seeds he could provide.

As luck would have it, on March 1 a 1000-tonne liner, the SS *Amazonas*, had its entire cargo stolen from the docks in Manaus. Wickham chartered the ship and instructed the captain to sail at once and meet him in Santarém. Wickham himself went up river by canoe to a spot already chosen for the large numbers of rubber trees that grew there.

For the next week he and his Indian helpers collected seeds by listening for the sharp crack of the exploding seed capsules that scatter the seeds up to 50 metres from the tree. He then packed the precious cargo between dried banana leaves and stored them in cane baskets. When he boarded the *Amazonas* in Santarém he had 70,000 rubber tree seeds with him.

As they reached the Brazilian Customs House in Belém, the captain held the ship in the harbour under a full head of steam while Wickham visited the customs officials, declaring: 'All we have here are exceedingly delicate botanical specimens specially designated for delivery to Her Majesty's own Royal Gardens of Kew'.

Immediately on arrival in Le Havre, en route to Liverpool, Wickham jumped ashore and caught a fast boat across the Channel. He finally arrived at Kew Gardens at 3 am, and woke up a surprised Sir Joseph Hooker, who sent a goods train to Liverpool to meet the *Amazonas* and ordered workers to clear the hothouse of its other tropical plants in anticipation of the shipment.

The speed of the whole operation succeeded in bringing live rubber seeds to England, and in August of the same year, the first seedlings were shipped to Ceylon – thus ensuring the collapse of the Brazilian rubber industry.

Wickham was nicknamed the 'Executioner of Amazonas' by the Brazilian rubber barons. He went off to spend his £700 trying to grow tobacco and coffee in northern Queensland, Australia. In 1920 he was knighted by King George V for services to the plantation industry. ■

Asia, where large rubber plantations were established. These plantations started to yield in 1910 and proved to be extremely efficient. The price of latex plummeted on the world market. The Brazilian rubber boom became a blowout.

Brazil's place in the world economy remained that of an exporter of agricultural commodities and importer of manufactured goods. Some seeds of modernisation had been planted, but there was no economic take-off, no qualitative leap forward. In 1917, after repeated sinkings of Brazilian ships by Germans, Brazil entered WW I on the Allied side. The production of foodstuffs during the war years restored a brief period of prosperity, but after the war there were continuing economic crises and local political revolts.

Vargas Era

Coffee was king until the global economic crisis of 1929 put a big hole in the bottom of the coffee market and badly damaged the Brazilian economy. The coffee growers of São Paulo, who controlled the government, were badly weakened. In opposition to the pro-coffee policies of the government, a liberal alliance formed around the élites of Minas Gerais and Rio Grande do Sul and nationalist military officers. When their presidential candidate, Getúlio Vargas, lost the 1930 elections, the military took power by force, handing over the reins to Vargas.

Vargas proved to be a gifted political manoeuvrer and was to dominate the political scene for the next 20 years. He skilfully played off one sector of the ruling élite against another, but was careful not to alienate the military. His popular support came from the odd bit of social reform combined with large slabs of demagoguery and nationalism.

In 1937, on the eve of a new election, Vargas sent in the military to shut down congress and took complete control of the country. His regime was inspired by Mussolini's and Salazar's fascist states. Vargas banned political parties, imprisoned political opponents and censored the press.

When WW II struck, Vargas sided with the Allies, but when the war ended, the contradiction between fighting for democracy in Europe while operating a quasi-fascist state at home was too glaring. Vargas was forced to step down by the military authorities but he remained popular.

In 1951 he was legitimately elected to the presidency and, with the economic opportunities afforded by the war in Europe, Brazil began its fitful march towards industrialisation and urbanisation. A large network of state corporations, including national petroleum and steel companies, was established, the first minimum wage was set and peasants flocked to the cities for a better life. But Vargas' administration was plagued by corruption. The press, especially a young journalist named Carlos Lacerda, attacked him viciously and the military withdrew their support. In August of the same year, Vargas' bodyguards made an attempt to murder Lacerda, but instead killed an air force major who was with him. In the resulting scandal, the military demanded Vargas' resignation. He responded melodramatically by shooting himself in the heart. Popular reaction proved extremely sympathetic to the dead president. Anti-government newspapers were burned and the US Embassy was attacked. Lacerda was forced into exile, but later returned to become a dynamic governor of Rio.

Late 20th Century

Juscelino Kubitschek, popularly known as JK, was elected president in 1956. His motto was '50 years' progress in five'. His critics responded with '40 years' inflation in four'. The critics were closer to the mark, although industrial production did increase by 80% during Kubitschek's five years.

The dynamic Kubitschek was the first of Brazil's big spenders. Deficit spending and large loans funded roads and hydroelectric projects. Foreign capital was encouraged to invest and Brazil's automotive industry was started. Kubitschek built Brasília, a new capital which was supposed to be the catalyst for development of Brazil's vast interior.

In the 1961 elections, former São Paulo governor Janio Quadros took over the presidency on a wave of public euphoria. He gained 48% of the vote, the highest majority ever. Quadros had huge plans for political reform, but a moralistic streak saw him trying to prohibit the wearing of bathing costumes at beauty contests, bikinis on the beaches and the use of amyl nitrate at Carnival – an uphill battle indeed. He then decorated Che Guevara in a public ceremony in Brasília, a move which upset the right-wing military, who started to plot. A few days later Quadros resigned after only six months in office, claiming that 'occult forces' were at work.

João 'Jango' Goulart, his vice-president and the labour minister under Vargas, took over the presidency. Opposition to Goulart's leftist policies and the fact that he hadn't been elected led to his overthrow by the military in 1964. Within hours of the coup, President Johnson cabled his warmest good wishes. The USA immediately extended diplomatic relations to the military regime and suspicions ran deep that the USA had masterminded the coup.

Much of the middle class welcomed the military and the Revolution of 1964, as it was called at first. Brazil's military regime was not as brutal as those of Chile or Argentina; the repression tended to come and go in cycles. But at its worst, around 1968 and 1969, the use of torture and the murder of political opponents were widespread. For almost 20 years political parties were outlawed and freedom of speech was curtailed.

Borrowing heavily from international banks, the generals benefited from the Brazilian economic miracle; year after year in the late '60s and early '70s Brazil's economy grew by over 10%. The transformation to an urban and semi-industrialised country accelerated.

Spurred on by the lack of any effective rural land reform, millions came to the cities, and *favelas* (shanty towns) filled the open spaces. The middle class grew, as did the bureaucracy and military.

More mega-projects were undertaken to exploit Brazil's natural resources, to provide quick fixes to underdevelopment and to divert attention from much needed social reforms. The greatest of these was the opening of the Amazon, which has brought great wealth to a few but little to most Brazilians, while helping to turn attention away from the issue of land reform.

The military's honeymoon didn't last. Opposition grew in 1968 as students, and then many in the Church – which had been generally supportive of the coup – began to protest against the regime. Inspired by liberation theology, the Church had begun to examine Brazilian misery. Church leaders established base communities among the poor to fight for social justice. They were appalled by the military's flagrant abuse of human rights, which broke all religious and moral tenets.

In 1980 a militant working-class movement, centred around the São Paulo automotive industry, exploded onto the scene with a series of strikes under the charismatic leadership of Lula, the workers' champion.

With the economic miracle petering out and popular opposition picking up steam, the military announced the so-called *abertura* (opening): a slow and cautious process of returning the government to civilian rule.

A presidential election was held in 1985, under an electoral college system designed to ensure the victory of the military's candidate.

Surprisingly, the opposition candidate, Tancredo Neves, was elected. Millions of Brazilians took to the streets in a spontaneous outburst of joy at the end of military rule. Tragically, Tancredo died of heart failure the day before assuming the presidency and was succeeded by the vice-president, José Sarney, a relative unknown who had supported the military until 1984.

During Sarney's term the economy was hampered by severe inflation, and by 1990 Brazil had run up a US$25 billion domestic deficit and a US$115 billion foreign debt. However, the congress did, during this period, manage to hammer out a new, more liberal constitution that guaranteed human rights.

The first democratic presidential election since the military takeover was held in 1989. In a hard-fought campaign, Fernando Collor de Mello, ex-Brazilian karate champion and former governor of the small state of Alagoas, narrowly gained victory over the Workers' Party candidate, Lula. Lula's campaign was not helped by the fact that a few days before the election his ex-lover revealed on national TV that Lula had offered her money for an abortion 16 years before.

Collor gained office promising to reduce inflation and fight corruption, but by the end of 1992, the man who once reminded George Bush of Indiana Jones had been removed from office and was being indicted by Federal Police on charges of corruption – accused of being the leader of a gang which used extortion and bribery to suck more than US$1 billion from the economy. Collor joined the long list (11 out of 25) of Brazilian presidents who have left office before the end of their presidential term.

'Collorgate' had a positive side. It proved to the Brazilian people that the constitution of their fragile democracy is capable of removing a corrupt president from office without military interference. Many were disappointed that Collor escaped prison: he was found 'not guilty' of 'passive corruption' in a 4 to 3 vote by the judges of the Supreme Court in December 1994. Pictures of him enjoying his 'retirement' while shopping in New York or skiing in Colorado, still appear in the Brazilian newspapers.

Vice President Itamar Franco became president in December 1992 after Collor's resignation. Considered provincial and unprepared to take office, Itamar surprised his critics with an honest and competent administration. His greatest achievement was to begin the long-awaited stabilisation of the economy with the introduction of the Plano Real, the most successful economic plan in a decade.

The year 1994 was an emotional one for Brazilians. Grief gripped the country on the 1st of May with the death of Formula One hero Ayrton Senna, beginning a process that turned him from living legend into a Brazilian sporting god. Two months later, sorrow turned to joy as the Brazilian football team became *tetracampeão*. Brazil became the first country to win the World Cup four times. Another hero was created in the process: Romário de Souza Faria. Known simply as Romário, the champion Brazilian striker scored six of the 14 goals that took his team to victory.

It was also an election year in Brazil. Early favourite was Lula, back for a second attempt after losing to Collor in 1991. His downfall was the Plano Real, which he criticised early. The architect of the plan, Itamar's finance minister Fernando Henrique Cardoso, became known as 'Father of the Real' and rode its success all the way to a landslide victory in the presidential elections in October.

An ex-sociology professor from São Paulo, FHC (as he's known in the press – the people call him Fernando Henrique) is a social democrat, committed to economic progress and growth, as well as tackling Brazil's social problems.

But social justice and economic growth don't always coincide, especially in a country as volatile as Brazil. With the approach of the 21st century, many lingering problems remain – corruption, violence, urban overcrowding, lack of essential health and education facilities, environmental abuse and dramatic extremes of wealth and poverty.

Brazil has long been known as a land of the future. But the future never seems to arrive.

GEOGRAPHY

Brazil is the world's fifth largest country after Russia, Canada, China and the USA. It borders every country in South America, except Chile and Ecuador, and its 8.5 million sq km occupy almost half the continent. Gigantic Brazil is larger than the USA excluding Alaska, 2½ times the size of India, and larger than Europe excluding Russia. It spans three time zones and is closer to Africa than it is to Europe or the USA.

As amazing as the size of this enormous expanse, is its inaccessibility and inhospitality to humans. Much of Brazil is scarcely populated; 36% of the nation's territory is in the Amazon Basin which, along with the enormous Mato Grosso to its south, has large regions with population densities of less than one person per sq km. Most of this land was not thoroughly explored by Europeans until this century. New mountains, new rivers and new Indian tribes are still being discovered. The Amazon is being rapidly settled, lumbered and depleted.

Brazil's geography can be reduced to four primary regions: the long, narrow Atlantic coastal band that stretches from the Uruguayan border to the state of Maranhaõ; the large highlands – called the Planalto Brasileiro or Central Plateau – which extend over most of Brazil's interior south of the Amazon Basin; and two great depressions – the Amazon Basin and the Paraguay Basin in the Southeast.

The coastal band, stretching for 7408 km, is bordered by the Atlantic Ocean and the coastal mountain ranges that lie between it and the Central Plateau. From Rio Grande do Sul all the way up to Bahia the mountains are right on the coast. Sheer mountainsides, called the Great Escarpment, make rivers impossible to navigate. Especially in Rio and Espírito Santo, the littoral is rocky and irregular, with many islands, bays and sudden granite peaks, like Pão de Açucar in Rio.

North of Bahia, the coastal lands are flatter and the transition to the highlands more gradual. Rounded hills signal the beginning of the central plateau. There are navigable rivers and the coast is smooth and calm, well protected by offshore reefs.

The Planalto Brasileiro is an enormous plateau that covers a part of almost every Brazilian state. It is punctuated by several small mountain ranges that reach no more than 3000 metres – the highest of these are centred in Minas Gerais – and is sliced by several large rivers. The average elevation of the Planalto is only 500 metres.

From Minas Gerais the Planalto descends slowly to the north. The great Rio São Francisco, called the River of National Unity or more informally Velho Chico, which begins in the mountains of Minas, follows this northerly descent. There are several other rivers slicing through the Planalto. The large tablelands or plains between these river basins are called *chapadões*.

From the Planalto Brasileiro to the south, the Andes to the west and the Guyana shield to the north, the waters descend to the great depression of the Amazon Basin. In the far west the basin is 1300 km wide, to the east, between the Guyana massif and the Planalto Brasileiro, it narrows to less than 100 km wide.

There are an estimated 1100 tributaries flowing into the Amazon River, 10 of which carry more water than the Mississippi River. The 6275-km-long Amazon is the world's largest river. With its tributaries it carries an estimated 20% of the world's fresh water. The Amazon forest contains 30% of the remaining forest in the world.

In the south, there's the Paraná-Paranagua Basin. This depression, which is not as low-lying as the Amazon, includes the Pantanal and runs into the neighbouring countries of Paraguay and Argentina. It is characterised by open forest, low woods and scrubland. Its two principal rivers, the Rio Paraguai and the Rio Paraná, run south through Paraguay and Argentina.

For political and administrative purposes, Brazil is generally divided into five regions: the North, the Northeast, the Central West, the Southeast and the South.

The North is the Amazon forest. It encompasses 42% of Brazil's land and includes the states of Amazonas, Pará, Rondônia, Acre, Tocantins and the territories of Amapá and Roraima. This is Brazil's least populated region and contains most of the country's Indian people. The two major cities are Manaus and Belém, the former on the Rio Negro, and the latter on the Amazon River.

The Northeast, Brazil's poorest region, has retained much of Brazil's colonial past. It's also the region where the African influence is most evident. It contains 18% of Brazil's area and includes, moving up the coast, the states of Bahia, Sergipe, Alagoas, Pernambuco, Paraíba, Rio Grande do Norte, Ceará, Piauí and Maranhão. These states are divided into a littoral, a *zona da mata*, and the sertão (the dry interior).

In the old days the Central West was called the *mato grosso* (thick forest). It includes the states of Goiás, Mato Grosso, Mato Grosso do Sul and the federal district of Brasília: 22% of the national territory. Only recently opened to road transport, this is Brazil's fastest growing region.

The Southeast is developed, urban Brazil. The states of Rio de Janeiro, São Paulo, Minas Gerais and Espírito Santo make up 10% of the national territory but have 43% of the population and contribute 63% of all industrial production.

In the South, Brazil feels more European, and it comprises the prosperous states of Paraná (the location of the magnificent Iguaçu Falls), Santa Catarina with its very visible German presence, and Rio Grande do Sul.

FLORA & FAUNA
The richness and diversity of Brazilian flora and fauna are astounding, and the country ranks first in the world for its variety of primate, amphibian and plant species; third for bird species; and fourth for butterfly and reptile species.

The following is a rough overview of this extraordinary diversity which, for ease of reference, is divided into general vegetation zones with a few examples of the flora and fauna.

The Pantanal
A vast wetlands area in the centre of South America, the Pantanal is about half the size of France – some 230,000 sq km spread across Brazil, Bolivia and Paraguay. Something less than 100,000 sq km is in Bolivia and Paraguay; the rest is in Brazil, split between the states of Mato Grosso and Mato Grosso do Sul.

The Pantanal – 2000 km from the Atlantic Ocean yet only 100 to 200 metres above sea level – is bounded by higher lands: the mountains of the Serra de Maracaju to the east; the Serra da Bodoquena to the south; the Paraguayan and Bolivian Chaco to the west; and the Serra dos Parecis and the Serra do Roncador to the north. From these highlands the rains flow into the Pantanal to form the Rio Paraguai and its tributaries, which flow south and then east, draining into the Atlantic Ocean between Argentina and Uruguay.

During the rainy season, from October to March, the rivers flood their banks – inundating much of the low-lying Pantanal for half the year and creating *cordilheiras*, patches of dry land where the animals cluster together. The waters reach their high mark, as much as three metres, in January or February, then start to recede in March, and don't stop until the rainy season returns six months later.

This seasonal flooding has made systematic farming impossible and severely limited human incursions into the area. It has also provided an enormously rich feeding ground for wildlife.

The flood waters replenish the soil's nutrients, which would otherwise be very poor due to the excessive drainage. The waters teem with fish, and the ponds provide excellent ecological niches for many animals and plants. Enormous flocks of wading birds gather in rookeries several sq km in size.

Later in the dry season, the water recedes, the lagoons and marshes dry out, and fresh grasses emerge on the savannah (Pantanal vegetation includes savannah, forest and meadows which blend together, often with no clear divisions). The hawks and *jacaré* (caimans) compete for fish in the remaining ponds. The ponds shrink and dry up and the jacaré crawl around for water, sweating it out until the rains return.

The food economy of the extremely diverse and abundant marshland birdlife is based on snails, insects and fish. All three abound in the Pantanal and support around 270 bird species including kites and hawks, limpkins, cardinals, herons and egrets, woodpeckers, ibises and storks, woodrails, kingfishers, cuckoos, hummingbirds, parakeets, thornbirds, shrikes, wrens, jays, blackbirds, finches, toucans and macaws.

A mere list doesn't do justice to the colour of a flock of parakeets in flight or the clumsiness of the *tuiuiu* (jabiru stork), the metre-high, black-hooded, scarlet-collared symbol of the Pantanal, nor can it suggest the beauty of *ninha* birds settling like snow in the trees or the speed of a sprinting herd of *emas* (rheas). Keep an ear open for the call of the Southern Lapwing, named *quero-quero* (I want, I want) in Brazil for its sound to Brazilian ears.

Birds are the most frequently seen wildlife, but the Pantanal is also a sanctuary for giant river otters, anacondas and iguanas, jaguars, ocelots, cougars, thousands upon thousands of jacaré, pampas and swamp deer, giant and lesser anteaters, black howler monkeys, zebu bulls and capybaras, the world's largest rodents.

The capybara is the most visible mammal in the Pantanal. These rodents have guinea pig faces and bear-like coats. They grow up to 63 kg and can be seen waddling in the swampy half of the Transpantaneira, where they feed on aquatic plants. They are equally at home on land or in water and are often seen in family groups of two adults and four or five young, or in large herds.

The two species of anteater in the Pantanal are endangered and not easily seen. The hairy giant anteater roams the dry savannah ground in search of the hard termite mounds which it'll excavate for 10 to 15 minutes at a time. The lesser anteater, smaller and lighter coloured than the giant, spends most of its time in trees eating ants, termites and larvae. Both are slow footed, with poor vision, but an excellent sense of smell.

The anteater's strong arms and claws, which keep even the jaguars at bay, offer no protection from the local Pantaneiros, who prize their meat. The killing of anteaters has led to an increase in ants and termites in the last decade, and many Pantaneiros now use deadly pesticides to try to destroy the mounds, ignoring the fact that the pesticides are absorbed by cattle and wildlife feeding in the area.

With thousands of jacaré sunning themselves on the edge of each and every body of water, it's hard to believe that they are endangered by poachers, who slaughter an estimated one to two million each year.

The jacaré feed mainly on fish, and are the primary check on the growth of the piranha population, which has been growing rapidly due to the jacaré slaughter. The size of an adult jacaré is determined by the abundance of food, and varies noticeably: jacaré on the river's edge are often considerably larger than those that feed in small ponds. Although they eat young or injured animals, jacaré rarely attack people or capybara, and many birds mingle amongst the jacaré in complete peace and harmony.

Visitors to the Pantanal are always fascinated by the passivity of the jacaré. I've seen Pantaneiros swimming in rivers lined with jacaré, but there are times to be on guard. It's not safe to enter the water where there is only one jacaré. It could be a female guarding her eggs or her young. She can attack and, for short distances, run faster than a horse.

During the rainy season you must be careful walking in the water. The jacarés are not aggressive and will usually swim away before you get close. But if stepped on, the jacaré will grab a leg and roll. This has probably never happened to a tourist, and only once in a blue moon does a Pantaneiro suffer this unpleasant end, but the rare jacaré attack is used nonetheless to justify their slaughter.

The jacaré, not known for its voice, makes one of the strangest sounds in the Pantanal. Every now and then a jacaré will curl its body, with head and tail stretching to the sky, open its mouth and let out a weird, deep rattle-roar. Then, suddenly, thin lines of water shoot up from the jacaré's back, and soon after it returns to its normal state of inactivity.

The cattle that live side by side with all this wildlife graze during the dry season and gather on the little islets that form during the

Jaguar

wet season. Amazingly, the cattle live in harmony with the wildlife, as have humans until recently.

Jaguars only attack sick or injured cattle, and some eat only their natural prey, capybara and tapir. Nevertheless, many cattle ranchers kill jaguars to protect their cattle. Jaguars are also killed for their skins. They are a highly endangered species and are threatened with extinction, as are the swamp deer and the giant river otter (the 'jaguar of the waters').

The Pantaneiros believe that eating jaguar meat boosts masculine qualities like strength and virility, qualities the traditional hunter of the jaguar, the *zagaeiro*, has in abundance. Using only a *zagara*, a wooden spear with a metal tip, the zagaeiro chases the jaguar up a tree and then taunts the cat until it is ready to leap and attack. At the last moment the zagaeiro plants the spear in the ground and when the jaguar jumps on the man it impales itself, dying instantly.

See the Pantanal section in the Mato Grosso chapter for more details about the region.

The Amazon

This is the largest equatorial forest in the world and occupies approximately 42% of Brazil's area.

The rainforest ecosystem is stratified into four layers of plant and animal life. Most of the activity takes place in the canopy layer, 20 to 40 metres above ground, where plants compete for sunshine and the majority of birds and monkeys live. The dense foliage of the canopy layer blots out the sunlight at lower levels, while a few tall trees poke above the canopy and dominate the forest skyline. A poorly defined middle layer or understorey merges with the canopy from below. Epiphytes hang at this level.

Bushes and saplings up to five metres in height constitute the shrub layer, while the ground layer is composed of ferns, seedlings and herbs – plants adapted to very little light. Ants and termites, the so-called social insects, live here. The *saubas* (leaf-cutter ants) are farmers and use leaves to build underground nests for raising fungus gardens, while army ants swarm through the jungle in huge masses, eating everything in their path. Fungi and bacteria, the decomposers, keep the forest floor clear. It's tidy in comparison to temperate forests.

The forest is not homogeneous; plant species vary with the land and its exposure to water. Plants of the *igapó* and flooded lowlands are mostly palms and trees with elevated roots. The valuable hardwoods and the brazil nut tree prefer land that is high and dry. The rubber trees and other plants of the *várzea*, land by the river's edge, have adapted to spending half of the year below water and half the year dry. Then there are the aquatic plants of the river itself like the giant *Vitória regia* water lilies (named after Queen Victoria), *mureru*, *camarans* and *manbeca*. There are floating marshes with amphibious grasses that have both earth and aquatic roots, depending on the season and local conditions.

The forest still keeps many of its secrets: to this day major tributaries of the Amazon are unexplored. Of the estimated 15,000 species of Amazon creatures, thousands of birds and fish and hundreds of mammals have not been classified, and after each foray into the jungle botanists still manage to bring back dozens of unclassified plants.

A cursory sampling of known species of animals found in the forest – some common, some rare, some virtually extinct – would include the jaguar, tapir, peccary, capybara, spider monkey, howler monkey, sloth, armadillo, caiman, alligator, river dolphin, manatee and turtle; and various species of snakes such as the boa constrictor and anaconda. Typical bird species of the forest include the toucan, parrot, macaw, hummingbird, woodpecker and hawk. Insect life is well represented with over 1800 species of butterfly and more than 200 species of mosquito. Fish species include piranha, *tucunaré*, *pirarucu*, *surubim*, *pintado* and electric eel. The enormous diversity of fish

in the Amazon means that biologists are unable to catalogue or identify 30% of the catch they come across in the markets of Belém.

Unfortunately, deforestation is taking place on such a vast scale that countless unknown species of animals and plants will be destroyed. We will lose a genetic library that has already given us so much: rubber, manioc, cocoa, anti-malarial drugs, cancer drugs and thousands more medicinal plants.

For more details about the problems facing the Amazon rainforest, see the Ecology & Environment section in this chapter.

Mata Atlântica

Reduced by sugar-cane farming, logging, coffee cultivation and acid rain to between 2 and 5% of its original size, the surviving coastal rainforest, known as the Mata Atlântica, now only occurs in isolated pockets. The largest, the Estação Ecológica da Jureia, on the southern coastal escarpment in São Paulo state, owes its survival to the shelving of plans to build a nuclear power plant.

Separated from the Amazon by non-rainforest terrain, the Mata Atlântica is much older (60 million years compared to the Amazon's 40 million) and evolved independently, with only a limited overlap of species. It has an even richer biodiversity than the

Jabiru

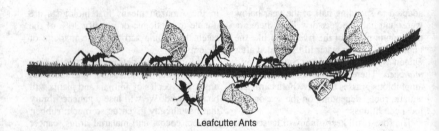

Leafcutter Ants

Amazon, and contains many unique and endangered animals, such as the spider monkey (the largest primate in the Americas), howler monkey, puma, marmoset and the golden-lion tamarin. Its distinctive flora includes many large trees; brazil wood, iron wood, Bahian jacaranda and cedar, as well as a number of rare tree ferns. The Mata Atlântica is also home to more than 500 bird species, many of which are unique. These include harpy and black-hawk eagles, tinamous and large numbers of the vibrant tanagers.

See the Ecology & the Environment section in this chapter for more details.

Mata da Araucaria

The mountainous regions of south-west and southern Brazil were once covered by coniferous forests which were dominated by the prehistoric-looking araucaria, or parana pine tree. It grows to a height of 30 to 40 metres, has clear trunks and candelabra-like heads of upturned branches that form flattened crowns. Its seeds, *pinhões*, are edible.

Decimated by timber cutters, the araucaria forests are now more scattered, but are much in evidence in the south, where their animal inhabitants include foxes, tree squirrels, skunks, spotted cats and monkeys.

Caatingas

These are dry areas, such as those of the sertão in the Northeast, where vegetation consists mainly of cacti and thorny shrubs which have adapted to lack of water and extreme heat. Much of the wildlife in these areas – anteaters and armadillos for example – has been severely depleted by hunting and habitat destruction. Currently, these areas are being exploited without control. Wood and coal from the *caatingas* are a primary energy source for a large percentage of the region's inhabitants. It's also used to fuel 30% of the Northeast's industries, generates 114,000 jobs directly, and contributes 15% of the income on rural properties. Recent studies show that continuing destruction of the caatingas at its present rate will see them disappear in Paraiba in 28 years, 40 years in Pernambuco, 50 years in Ceará and 65 years in Rio Grande do Norte. The list of endangered species for the caatingas includes the Spix and Lear's macaws, and the three-banded armadillo.

Cerrados

These open lands, which also occur in the form of savannah, are usually grassy plains dotted with small trees such as the *mangaba* and *carobeira*. This landscape extends from the borders of Maranhão in the Northeast down through Minas Gerais and as far as the Southwest. Armadillos, foxes and rheas are some of the well-known species in these areas. The *cerrados* are disappearing fast. The use of this land for agricultural purposes, such as soya farming, has reduced available habitat for wildlife, such as the maned wolf and giant anteater, which are native to this region and are now endangered species.

Further Reading

See the Books & Maps section in the Facts for the Visitor chapter.

ECOLOGY & ENVIRONMENT

In the 1970s, the military government attempted to tame the Amazon with an ambitious plan entitled Plano de Integração National (PIN). Long roads, like the 3000-km Transamazônica, were cleared from the jungle and settlers from the Northeast soon followed in the tracks of the bulldozers. The roads were said to be safety valves to ease the social tensions and overpopulation of the drought-stricken Northeast. Thousands left the Northeast to build homesteads in the newly cleared forest. The majority of these hopeful settlers failed to establish a foothold and either perished or abandoned the land for the favelas of Manaus and Belém.

During the '80s, the Brazilian government acted as if the forests were an impediment to progress, an asset to be used to pay back the debt incurred during the 20 years of military dictatorship. Encouraged by the IMF (International Monetary Fund) and the World Bank, the Brazilian government provided large incentives to coax multinational timber and mining firms to exploit the Amazon. These gigantic projects were designed to yield short-term profits and pay off the foreign debt regardless of environmental and social consequences. The economic plan was launched with purely extractive goals, and the forests and precious metals were perceived as resources to be exploited at top speed until they were gone.

Many of the loans for these gigantic projects worsened Brazil's foreign debt, which plagued the economy for more than a decade. Despite increasing criticism at home and abroad, this plan is still being maintained and will eventually exhaust Brazil's resources.

The early '90s saw a dramatic surge in international and domestic interest in Brazil's ecological progress and environmental attitudes. This was demonstrated by the choice of Brazil as the venue for ECO-92, a mega environmental and ecological bash organised by the United Nations to thrash out appropriate priorities for the environment and economic development.

Although the international media generally centres its attention on destruction of the Amazon rainforest, there are a number of other environmental issues in Brazil which are very serious.

The Mata Atlântica, a region of forest which, in the 16th century, covered 1.5 million sq km and stretched from the states now known as Rio Grande do Norte and Rio Grande do Sul, has been reduced to a mere 10,000 sq km. Some Brazilian sources, such as Fundação SOS Mata Atlântica, believe that even these remnants will be finished in 15 years, along with more than 300 species of wildlife that are already on the brink of extinction.

The Pantanal is threatened by pollution and poaching – described in more detail at the end of this section. The Northeast region, already experiencing extreme poverty and social breakdown, is literally losing ground to desertification; and beaches throughout Brazil (particularly those near industrial areas) are threatened by indiscriminate dumping of major pollutants or malfunctioning sanitation systems. Further problems involve the burning of huge tracts of land in parks and reserves; widespread and unchecked use of dangerous pesticides; and the concomitant reduction or extinction of hundreds of plant and wildlife species – an irretrievable genetic loss.

Poaching & Pollution in the Pantanal

According to Dr Maria Padua, a well-known biologist and conservationist, poachers are doing more damage to the Pantanal than the Amazon. The Brazilian government has not

Piranha

done much to stem the slaughter of the animals.

Anywhere from 500,000 to two million animals are killed each year in the Pantanal, smuggled over the Bolivian border (where poaching is also illegal, but requisite laws are not even tokenly enforced) and exchanged for cocaine, guns and cash.

The slow and fearless jacarés are easily shot at short range. A jacaré skin commands a price of US$200, but only a fraction of it is used – the supple, small-scaled skin of the jacaré's flanks is sought after to make fashionable wallets, belts, purses and shoes. The rest of the carcass is useless to poachers and is discarded.

A park ranger told us of the hundreds of jacaré carcasses, their skulls in neat piles, crates of handguns and rifles, bags of cocaine, and the many jaguar and ocelot pelts which were found in a raid on some poachers, who worked two hours by boat from Porto Jofre.

Just as poachers supply the fashion industry with skins, they supply American pet shops with rare tropical fish and birds. A hyacinth macaw will sell for US$5000 in the USA; compare that to the minimum monthly wage of a Brazilian and it's easy to see the great temptation for farmers, truckers, government officials, in fact anyone in the area, to get involved in poaching. The depletion in the numbers of jacaré is causing unchecked growth in the piranha population, which, in turn, will affect the numbers of different fish and bird populations.

As well as the threat posed by poachers, the delicate environment is also threatened by mercury in gold slurries and ever-expanding farm and ranch lands. Sediments from erosion caused by intensive soya and rice farming flow into the area. Sugar mills and factories that produce *álcool* (sugar-cane fuel) in São Paulo and Mato Grosso dump poisonous waste into rivers that drain into the Pantanal. Scientists have also detected use of the defoliant Thordon, a component of Agent Orange.

Large projects are begun without any environmental impact study. The latest is the proposed construction of a *hidrovia*, an aquatic freeway on the Rio Paraguai aimed at improving the transport of goods from the interior to the new Mercosul partners, Paraguay and Argentina. Experts predict it will cause the water level in the Pantanal to drop by up to 10 metres, with disastrous consequences for the ecology of the area.

The Fate of the Amazon

The Amazon, a very large, complex and fragile ecosystem – comprising one-tenth of the planet's entire plant and animal species, producing a fifth of the world's oxygen and containing a fifth of the world's fresh water – is endangered. Unless things change, the rainforests will be cleared for more ranches and industrial sites, the land will be stripped for mines and the rivers will be dammed for electricity. Already jaguars, caimans, dolphins, monkeys and a host of other wildlife and plant species are threatened with extinction. As in the past, the Indians will die with their forests, and the invaluable, irreplaceable Amazon may be lost forever.

The construction of roads is a prerequisite for exploiting the Amazon. This process was initiated with the construction of the Transamazônica highway in 1970. The ensuing decades saw over US$10 billion thrown into gargantuan projects and schemes offering financial incentives to exploit resources regardless of the effects on the environment. Those involved included the World Bank, the IMF, US and other international banks, and a variety of Brazilian corporations, politicians, and military figures. According to calculations made using Landsat photos, the damming of rivers, burning, and clearing of the forests between 1970 and 1989 destroyed about 400,000 sq km or around 10% of the Amazon forest.

At the end of 1988, Chico Mendes, a rubber tapper and opponent of rainforest destruction, was assassinated in the town of Xapurí (Acre state) by a local landowner. This sparked an international reaction which eventually pressured the World Bank and the IMF to declare that they would no longer fund destruction of the rainforest. For more on Chico Mendes, see the Rondônia & Acre chapter.

Despite this commitment, it seems there will be no appreciable slackening in the forest destruction. The Perimetral Norte, a highway which is projected to stretch in a huge loop from Macapá (Amapá state) via Boa Vista (Roraima state) all the way to Cruzeiro do Sul (Acre state), is still being touted as a viable project. In the state of Acre, the extension of BR-364 from Rio Branco to Cruzeiro do Sul is being supported by Japanese finance. Local politician João Toto recently stressed that this road will be 'the salvation of Acre'. The stretch between Rio Branco and Sena Madureira (about 125 km) has been completed. The inevitable conclusion is that new highway projects such as these will follow the old pattern of development and open up the Brazilian Amazon to even more destruction.

The military recently claimed in all seriousness that the environmental issues surrounding the Amazon had been exaggerated by foreigners intent on invading the region! Gilberto Mestrinho is into his third term as governor of Amazonas state, and is responsible for over 1.5 million sq km of the Brazilian Amazon. The following are samples of his pearls of ecological wisdom:

I like trees and plants, but they are not indispensable. After all, men have managed to live in space for almost a year without trees...

Man is the centre of the environment and I will be the governor of men, not of animals and the forest...

There are hardly any healthy trees in Amazônia and they should be used before woodworm gets to them.

Much of what is being promised overseas and in Brazil appears to be 'greenspeak', a type of lip service whereby the speaker certifies green intentions for a hazy point in the future without putting these into deeds.

Exploitation of the Amazon Most biologists doubt that the Amazon can support large-scale agriculture; the lushness of the jungle is deceptive. Apart from volcanic lands and flood plains which can support continuous growth, the jungle topsoil is thin and infertile; most of it is acidic and contains insufficient calcium, phosphorus and potassium for crops.

Small-scale slash and burn, a traditional agricultural technique adopted by nomadic Indians, seemed to work best at supporting small populations on such fragile lands without ecological compromises. Indians would fell trees in a four or 5-hectare plot of land and burn off remaining material. The resulting ash would support a few years of crops: squash, corn, manioc, plantains and beans. After a few seasons, however, the nutrients would be spent and the Indians would move on. The clearings were small in size and number and the land was left fallow long enough for the jungle to recover.

In contrast, modern agricultural techniques are enormous in scale, directed to the production of animal protein rather than vegetable protein, and fail to give the jungle an opportunity to recover. Nowadays ranchers clear huge areas of land – some cattle ranches are larger than European nations. These lands are never left fallow, so that nutrients contained at one point in the biomass of the forest and a thin topsoil are permanently squandered.

Farming and ranching is almost incidental to the deforestation process. Vast tracts of land are bought so that the buyers can speculate for the treasures buried beneath the earth, not those growing on it. Since Brazilian law requires that one third of the land be put to use, the owners set fire to the land (killing wildlife indiscriminately), plant some grasses and raise cattle. The government then approves the land rights and the important mineral rights are secured.

Effects of Development The Indian tribes in the Brazilian Amazon have borne the brunt of the destruction which has systematically wiped out their lands and the forest, their sole livelihood. New roads have attracted settlers and *garimpeiros* (miners) into the last refuges of these tribes, which have been virtually wiped out by introduced diseases, violent disputes over land, pollution from mining or the construction of huge dams which simply flood them out of the area. For more details about the Indians see the History and Population & People sections in this chapter.

Giant hydroelectric schemes, such as Balbina (Amazonas state) and Tucuruí (Pará state), are also a source of controversy. In the case of Balbina, a US$750 million project funded by the World Bank, there are doubts as to the usefulness of flooding over 2000 sq km. Apart from the loss of wildlife and wastage of valuable timber, the possible chemical effects of such large quantities of submerged, decomposing, vegetal matter on the water quality and the surrounding region have not been sufficiently researched. Over 70 major hydroelectric schemes are planned for completion in the Brazilian Amazon by the year 2010.

Thousands of garimpeiros have swarmed into the region to mine the streams and rivers. Unfortunately, their principal mining technique involves the use of mercury separation to extract gold from ore. Large quantities of mercury, a highly poisonous substance, are washed into the water, where they become a major health hazard for local Indians, wildlife and the garimpeiros themselves.

One of the most dramatic and disturbing sights in the forest is the burning of immense tracts to clear the area for agriculture or cattle ranching. Whilst travelling in the region we noticed that many airports – Porto Velho, Cuiabá, Imperatriz, and Açailândia are just a few examples – were regularly closed to air traffic because of the smoke. During broad daylight, we found ourselves sitting outside in semi-gloom (induced by huge clouds of smoke obscuring the sun) at a restaurant in Porto Velho, whilst a light rain of vegetal ash descended on the tables.

It is quite obvious that no attention whatsoever is being paid to legislation which restricts the number of fires on any one day; and it would be a Herculean task to enforce such a law.

According to meteorologists, the smoke cloud has already reached Africa and Antarctica. Scientists generally agree that the torching of the forest on such a massive scale contributes to the greenhouse effect, but opinions differ as to how much.

Scientists are becoming increasingly concerned by the regional and global climatic changes caused by massive deforestation.

The water cycle, which depends on transpiration from the forest canopy, has been interrupted and neighbouring lands, such as eastern Pará, are receiving less rainwater than usual, while the spent soils of the surrounding areas and deforested zones are being baked by the sun into desert wastelands.

Perhaps the most devastating long-term effect is the annual loss of thousands of forest species which disappear into extinction and thereby reduce the genetic pool which is vital (as a source of foods, medicines and chemicals) for sustaining life on earth.

The Search for Solutions

It is only fair to point out that many of the countries which have criticised Brazil's development of the Amazon were once actively encouraging such development, and have only recently been reminded that their own treatment of the environment was hardly exemplary. The general consensus for the '90s, however, is that a series of different approaches must be tried to halt and remedy the destruction. The following are a few samples of what's being attempted.

Debt-for-nature swaps are international agreements whereby a portion of a country's external debt is cancelled in exchange for local funding of conservation initiatives. Negotiation of such swaps requires that the sovereignty of recipient countries is kept intact, and that inflationary effects on their economies are avoided. Brazil is saddled with an enormous external debt and has shown interest in such a swap, but the sovereignty issue is controversial, especially with the military, and the inflationary track record of its economy is well known.

These extractive reserves gained the world's attention when Chico Mendes, an enthusiastic advocate of these reserves, was assassinated in Acre state. The aim of this concept is to set aside reserves for the sustainable harvesting of brazil nuts, rubber, and other non-timber products. The idea is to use the forest as a renewable resource, without destroying it.

Alternatives are also being researched to stop wasteful clear-cutting of timber. In many cases, huge tracts of forest are wiped out in order to extract only a few commercially valuable tree species, whilst the rest is considered waste. Different methods are being tried to control the type of timber cut, the size of the area that is logged, and the manner in which forests are harvested – preferably as part of an overall management

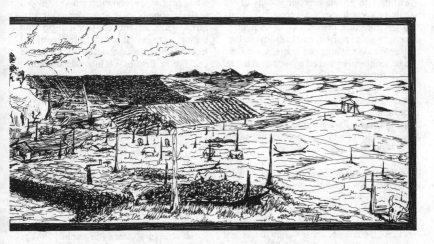

Destruction of the Amazon

Explore the rainforests of the Amazon

scheme to retain forests as a sustainable resource.

If any success is to be achieved, these schemes will have to be underpinned with finance and enforcement. A number of foreign organisations are eyeing the idea of providing finance for Brazil's environmental needs, but experience has shown that any funds provided should be watched carefully. Much of what is currently promised in Brazil exists only on paper, and funds have a strange habit of missing their destination or drifting into private accounts. Many of the country's environmental protection units suffer from lack of funds, staff and equipment, and a consequent inability to act. Depredation of parks and reserves will have to be stringently guarded against by reliable, well-informed and committed 'green rangers'. Otherwise, there will be no change in the sort of situation where, for example, the Parque Nacional da Amazônia in the state of Pará has only a handful of park guards responsible for physically protecting nearly 1,000,000 hectares.

Environmental Movements

Brazil's environmental movement is about 20 years behind those in Europe, Japan and the USA. Rallying behind the slogan 'Vamos a preservar a natureza' (let's preserve nature), the nascent conservation movement is beginning to make inroads. The environ-

mentalists have demonstrated the benefits to industry of not polluting, and industry is beginning to respond. Nowadays environmental impact studies accompany all major industrial projects, but this does not mean that the companies concerned will feel compelled to act on recommendations made in such studies.

If Brazil's environment is to be preserved it will be through the efforts of groups like these within Brazil and abroad – groups that can educate the public and enlist its support to control consumption of tropical-forest products; to pressure domestic and international banks and institutions to stop financing destructive development projects; and to persuade the Brazilian government to adopt more rational uses for the Amazon.

Ecotourism is also being considered as a powerful tool to encourage countries such as Brazil to earn more from preserving the environment than from destroying it. It is important that the organisations which proclaim an interest in ecotourism prove they are not just jumping onto the 'green' bandwagon, but also actively preserving the environment.

An example of active involvement is the growing pressure exerted by consumers, who can change economic trends on a global scale by simply changing purchasing patterns. Contact the environmental and ecological organisations in the following list for more information about environment and ecology in Brazil. For more details about tour operators, see Tours in the Facts for the Visitor chapter.

Australia
  Friends of the Earth/Aust, 312 Smith St, Fitzroy, 3065 (☎ (03) 9419-8700)
  Greenpeace Australia Ltd, 3/389 Lonsdale St, Melbourne, 3000 (☎ (03) 9670-1633)
Brazil
  Fundação SOS Mata Atlântica, Rua Manoel da Nóbrega, 456, São Paulo (SP), CEP 04001
  União dos Defensores da Terra Oikos, Avenida Brig Luís Antônio, 4442, São Paulo (SP), CEP 01402
  Centro de Estudos e Atividades de Conservação da Natureza (Ceacon), Rua Augusta, 2690, cj. 217, São Paulo (SP), CEP 01412

Associação de Defesa da Juréia, Rua Cardoso de Almeida, 1479, Casa 2, São Paulo (SP), CEP 05013

União Protetora do Ambiente Natural (Upan), Rua Lindolfo Collor, 560, Caixa Postal 189, São Leopoldo (RS), CEP 93001

Associação Capixaba de Proteção ao Meio Ambiente (Acapema), Caixa Postal 2304, Vitória (ES), CEP 29000

Associação Gaúcha de Proteção ao Ambiente Natural (Agapan), Rua João Telles, 524, Porto Alegre (RS), CEP 90020

Associação Paraíbana de Amigos da Natureza, Rua Empresário João Rogrigues Alves, 103, conj. UPFB, João Pessoa (PB), CEP 58000

Associação Pernambucana de Defesa da Natureza (Aspan), Rua Conselheiro Aguiar, 3686/206, Recife (PE), CEP 51020

Grupo Ambientalista da Bahia (Gamba), Rua Itabuna, 217, Salvador (BA), CEP 41910

Fundação Bio Diversitas, Avenida Otacílio Negrão de Lima, 8210, Belo Horizonte (MG), CEP 31390

Associação Mineira de Defesa Ambiental (AMDA), Rua Campos Gerais, 23, Belo Horizonte (MG), CEP 30710

Fundação Chico Mendes, Rua Dr Batista de Moraes, 180, Xapuri (AC), CEP 69920

Fundação Brasileira para a Conservação da Natureza (FBCN), Rua Miranda Valverde, 103, Rio de Janeiro (RJ), CEP 22281

Fundação Pró-Natura (Funatura), SCLN 107, Ed Gemini Center II, Bloco B, salas 201/13, Brasília (DF), CEP 70743

Instituto de Estudos Amazônicos (IEA),Rua Leopoldo Machado 178, 68.908.120. Bairro Jesus de Nazaré Macapá (☎ & fax (096) 223-3339)

Grupo de Estudos e Defesa dos Ecosistemas do Baixo e Médio Amazonas (Gedebam), Avenida Almeida Barroso, 71, s/28, Belém (PA), CEP 66050

UK

Friends of the Earth/UK, 26/28 Underwood St, London N17JU (☎ (0171) 490-155)

Survival International, 310 Edgeware Road, London W2 1DY (☎ (0171) 723-5535)

USA

The Rainforest Action Network (RAN), 301 Broadway, Suite A, San Francisco CA 94133 (☎ (415) 398-4404)

Conservation International, 1015 18th St, NW, Suite 1000, Washington, DC 20036 (☎ (202) 4295660)

Cultural Survival, 11 Divinity Avenue, Cambridge, MA 03128

The Nature Conservancy, 1815 Lynn Street, Arlington, VA 22209 (☎ (703) 841-5300)

Survival International USA, 2121 Decatur Place, NW, Washington, DC 20006

Friends of the Earth/USA, 218 D St, SE, Washington, DC 20003 (☎ (202) 544-2600)

Greenpeace, 1436 U St, NW, Washington, DC 20009 (☎ (202) 462-8817)

Earthwatch, 680 Mt Auburn St (PO Box 403), Watertown, MA 02272 (☎ (617) 926-8200)

The Chico Mendes Fund, Environmental Defence Fund, 257 Park Ave South, New York, NY 10010 (☎ (212) 505 2100)

Rainforest Alliance, 270 Lafayette St, Suite 512, New York, NY 10012 (☎ (071) 941 1900)

The Rainforest Foundation Inc, 1776 Broadway 14th floor, New York, NY 10019 (☎ (212) 431 9098)

Further Reading

Refer to Books and Maps in the Facts for the Visitor chapter.

NATIONAL PARKS

On a federal and state level, there are 350 parks and ecological stations, ensuring the protection of over 300,000 sq km – roughly 5% of the national territory. Unfortunately, about 70% of them exist only on paper. Only 33% of Brazilian natural reserves have a minimum infrastructure (warden offices and fences) and only 19.5% have vehicles, equipment, weapons and personnel on an appropriate level. Of all national parks, the government has managed to regulate only 22% of them. To pay out the owners of the land would cost US$1 billion. The Brazilian Environment & Natural Resources Institute (IBAMA) still hasn't expropriated any land, so ranchers continue to use it.

IBAMA makes the distinction between *parques nacionais* (national parks), *reservas biológicas* (biological reserves) and *estações ecológicas* (ecological stations). Only *parques nacionais* are open to the public for recreational use. Reservas biológicas and estações ecológicas are only open to re-searchers. To visit them you need permission from IBAMA.

Despite all this, there are some fantastic parks to visit. IBAMA has a minuscule budget which only allows it to publish a small amount of literature in Portuguese and even less in English. We have tried to locate and make available in this book as much information as possible. Any feedback from readers regarding visits to these parks would be much appreciated.

If you're prepared to rough it a bit and do some camping, you'll experience some spectacular places. The following is a quick overview of Brazil's main national parks, divided for ease of reference into regions. See the regional chapters for more detailed information.

The Southeast

In Rio, the Parque Nacional da Tijuca, surrounded by the city, is a popular day trip and offers magnificent panoramic views. The Parque Nacional do Itatiaia, 155 km to the south-east of the city, is a favourite with trekkers and climbers, its big attraction being the Agulhas Negras mountain with a 2787-metre peak. Another climbing mecca is the Parque Nacional da Serra dos Órgãos, 86 km from Rio. As well as its spectacular peaks it offers some great walks. These last two parks both possess a well-developed tourist infrastructure.

On the border of Rio and São Paulo states, close to Parati, the Parque Nacional da Serra da Bocaina is where the coastal escarpment meets the sea, and the Atlantic rainforest

quickly changes to high-altitude araucaria forest as you move up from the coast. There doesn't, as yet, exist any infrastructure for tourists.

In Minas Gerais, there are some great parks to visit. The Parque Nacional de Caparaó in the east of the state, on the border with Espírito Santo, contains the third highest peak in the country: O Pico do Bandeira, at 2890 metres, and you don't have to be a climber to get up there. The tourist infrastructure is well developed, especially for campers. In the south-west of the state, 350 km from Belo Horizonte, the Parque

Nacional da Serra da Canastra is where the Rio São Francisco begins. The area is very beautiful and contains the spectacular Cascada d'Anta waterfall. The park is also home to many endangered species, such as the maned wolf, giant anteater, pampas deer, giant armadillo and thin-spined porcupine. Camping is permitted.

The Parque Nacional da Serra do Cipó, 100 km from Belo Horizonte, is an area that is full of mountains, waterfalls and open countryside. Its highlands are an arm of the Serra do Espinhaço. The 70-metre waterfall, Cachoeira da Farofa, and the Canyon das

---

◉ NATIONAL PARKS

1 Parque Nacional de Cabo Orange
6 Parque Nacional da Amazônia
8 Parque Nacional do Jaú
11 Parque Nacional de Monte Roraima
13 Parque Nacional do Pico da Neblina
16 Parque Nacional da Serra do Divisor
19 Parque Nacional de Pacaás Novos
23 Parque Nacional da Chapada dos Guimarães
25 Parque Nacional do Pantanal Matogrossense
26 Parque Nacional das Emas
27 Parque Nacional de Brasília
28 Parque Nacional da Chapada dos Veadeiros
29 Parque Nacional do Araguaia
32 Parque Nacional dos Lençóis Maranhenses
33 Parque Nacional de Sete Cidades
34 Parque Nacional de Ubajara
38 Parque Nacional da Serra da Capivara
41 Parque Nacional da Chapada Diamantina
42 Parque Nacional de Grande Sertão Veredas
44 Parque Nacional de Monte Pascoal
45 Parque Nacional Marinho dos Abrolhos
51 Parque Nacional de Caparaó
52 Parque Nacional da Serra do Cipó
53 Parque Nacional da Serra da Canastra
55 Parque Nacional do Itatiaia
57 Parque Nacional da Serra dos Órgãos
59 Parque Nacional da Tijuca
60 Parque Nacional da Serra da Bocaina
63 Parque Nacional do Superagui
65 Parque Nacional do Iguaçu
67 Parque Nacional de São Joaquim
69 Parque Nacional de Aparados da Serra
70 Parque Nacional da Lagoa do Peixe

● BIOLOGICAL RESERVES

3 Reserva Biológica do Lago Piratuba
5 Reserva Biológica do Rio Trombetas
15 Reserva Biológica do Abufari
18 Reserva Biológica do Jarú
20 Reserva Biológica do Guaporé
30 Reserva Biológica de Tapirapé
31 Reserva Biológica do Gurupi
36 Reserva Biológica de Saltinho
37 Reserva Biológica de Serra Negra
40 Reserva Biológica de Santa Isabel
43 Reserva Biológica de Una
46 Reserva Biológica do Córrego Grande
47 Reserva Biológica do Córrego do Veado
48 Reserva Biológica de Sooretama
49 Reserva Biológica de Comboios
50 Reserva Biológica Nova Lombardia
56 Reserva Biológica do Tinguá
58 Reserva Biológica do Poço das Antas

★ ECOLOGICAL STATIONS

2 Estação Ecológica de Maracá-Jipioca
4 Estação Ecológica do Jari
7 Estação Ecológica de Anavilhanas
9 Estação Ecológica de Niquiã
10 Estação Ecológica de Caracaraí
12 Estação Ecológica da Ilha de Maracá
14 Estação Ecológica de Juami-Japurá
17 Estação Ecológica do Rio Acre
21 Estação Ecológica de Iqué
22 Estação Ecológica da Serra das Araras
24 Estação Ecológica de Taiamã
35 Estação Ecológica de Seridó
39 Estação Ecológica de Uruçui-Una
54 Estação Ecológica de Parapitinga
61 Estação Ecológica de Tupinambás
62 Estação Ecológica dos Tupiniquins
64 Estação Ecológica de Guaraqueçaba
66 Estação Ecológica de Carijós
68 Estação Ecológica de Aracuri/Esmeralda
71 Estação Ecológica do Taim

Bandeirinhas are its two principal attractions, but the park contains no tourist infrastructure.

Also in Minas, near its borders with Bahia and Goiás, the Parque Nacional Grande Sertão Veredas is made up of cerrado, caatinga, *veredas* (swampy plains between hills and rivers), and a few stands of wine-palms. Inhabitants of the park include the maned wolf, giant armadillo, banded ant-eater and rhea. Once again, this is another park with no tourist infrastructure and access is difficult.

The South

In the southern region, the most famous national park is Iguaçu, which contains the falls. Also in Paraná, but near the coast, is the Parque Nacional do Superagui, which consists of the Peças and Superagui islands. Notable attractions of the park include the huge number of wild orchids and the abundant marine life. Created in 1989, it contains no infrastructure for tourists.

Santa Catarina boasts the Parque Nacional de São Joaquim, in the highlands of the Serra do Mar, where it even snows sometimes. As yet, it contains no tourist infrastructure.

Rio Grande do Sul contains one of the most unforgettable parks in Brazil, the Parque Nacional de Aparados da Serra, with its famous Itaimbézinho Canyon. Camping is permitted inside the park. Close to the town of Rio Grande, in the south of the state, the Parque Nacional da Lagoa do Peixe is an important stopover for many species of migratory birds. It also contains the largest saltwater lagoon in the state. A visitors' centre is still on the drawing board.

The Central West

This region has its share of parks too. Just 10 km from the national capital, Brasília, is the Parque Nacional de Brasília, a favourite weekend spot with the city's inhabitants. It contains a visitors' centre, and a leisure area with natural swimming pools. Parque Nacional da Chapada dos Veadeiros, 200 km north of Brasília, in the state of Goiás, contains some rare fauna and flora, as well as some

very spectacular waterfalls and canyons. Camping is the only accommodation option here. In the extreme south-west of the state is the Parque Nacional das Emas. Its main attraction is its great abundance of wildlife and the ease with which you can spot it in the open country, especially in the dry season. Accommodation is available inside the park, and camping is permitted.

Close to the city of Cuiabá is another popular park, the Parque Nacional da Chapada dos Guimarães, with its waterfalls, huge valleys and strange rock formations. Accommodation inside the park is limited to camping, but there are hotels in the nearby town of the same name.

Halfway between Cuiabá and Corumbá, near the fork of the Paraguai and Cuiabá rivers, the Parque Nacional do Pantanal Matogrossense is deep in the Pantanal and can only be reached by river or by air. Porto Jofre, 100 km upriver, is the closest you'll get by land. Permission from IBAMA in Cuiabá is required to visit this park. Camping is the only accommodation option here.

The Northeast

In Bahia, the Parque Nacional da Chapada Diamantina has a network of trails, and great hiking to peaks, waterfalls and rivers. See the Bahia chapter for full details about this easily accessible park and the attractive old mining town of Lençóis which functions as its hub.

On the southern border of the state is the Parque Nacional de Monte Pascoal, which contains a variety of ecosystems ranging from Atlantic rainforest to mangrove swamps, beaches and reefs, and rare fauna and flora. A visitors' centre has been in the planning stage for several years.

Approximately 80 km offshore in the extreme south of the state is Parque Nacional Marinho dos Abrolhos, which was designated in 1983 as Brazil's first marine park. The attractions are the coral reefs, which can be visited on organised scuba-diving tours, and the birdlife on the numerous reefs and islets.

The state of Pernambuco recently incorporated the archipelago of Fernando de

Noronha, which lies approximately 525 km east of Recife. A section of this archipelago has been designated as the Parque Nacional Marinho de Fernando de Noronha. The attractions here are the exceptionally varied and abundant marine life and birdlife. Package tours to the archipelago are available and independent travel is possible. The tourist infrastructure is rapidly being developed.

The state of Ceará contains the Parque Nacional de Ubajara, which is renowned for its limestone caves. Tourist infrastructure is developed, and access to the caves has been re-established with a new cable car which replaced the old system destroyed by landslides in 1987.

In the northern region of the state of Piauí is the Parque Nacional de Sete Cidades. The park's interesting set of rock formations resembling 'seven cities' (*sete cidades*) are accessible via a hiking trail. Tourist facilities, including transport and accommodation, are established.

In the southern region of the state, the Parque Nacional da Serra da Capivara contains prehistoric sites and rock paintings which are still being researched. Over 300 sites have been discovered so far, and this park is already considered one of the top prehistoric monuments in South America. Tourism is still very limited, since it is difficult to combine ongoing research with public access, but a museum and guided tours are planned.

In the state of Maranhão, the Parque Nacional dos Lençóis Maranhenses has a spectacular collection of beaches, mangroves, dunes and fauna. Infrastructure is limited, but transport and basic accommodation are available.

The North

The national parks in the northern region of Brazil are best known for their diverse types of forests harbouring an astounding variety of fauna and flora. Most of these parks require that visitors obtain permits before arrival. They provide few tourist services, and access normally entails lengthy and difficult travel by plane and/or boat.

The Parque Nacional de Cabo Orange extends along the coastline at the northern tip of Amapá state. This park has retained a diverse variety of wildlife, including rare or endangered species such as the manatee, sea turtle, jaguar, anteater, armadillo and flamingo. At present, there isn't any tourist infrastructure available for transport or accommodation in the park.

In the state of Pará, the vast forests enclosed by the Parque Nacional da Amazônia are being rapidly eroded by illegal encroachment and destruction. The wildlife includes a wide variety of rainforest species, but poaching is making rapid inroads into their numbers. And it's difficult to see any change in this situation when only four park guards are responsible for nearly one million hectares. Limited services for accommodation and transport of visitors are provided.

The Parque Nacional de Monte Roraima lies on the northern boundary of Roraima state. Established in 1989, this park contains Monte Roraima (2875 metres), one of Brazil's highest peaks.

In the state of Amazonas, the Parque Nacional do Pico da Neblina adjoins the Venezuelan border and contains Brazil's highest peaks: Pico da Neblina (3014 metres) and Pico 31 de Março (2992 metres). Visitors normally require a permit from the

Green Tree Boa

IBAMA office in Brasília. No standard tourist infrastructure is established, however visitors can arrange access by using a combination of air and river transport.

Brazil's largest national park, Parque Nacional do Jaú, lies close to the centre of Amazonas state. Visitors normally require a permit from the IBAMA office in Brasília. No standard tourist infrastructure exists, but visitors can arrange access by using a combination of air and river transport.

The Parque Nacional de Pacaás Novas lies close to the town of Ji-Parana in the state of Rondônia. The principal rivers of the state, the Madeira and the Guaporé, originate within the park, where small communities of indigenous Indians have sought refuge from the massive deforestation and destruction that is still raging through the state. See the chapter on Rondônia for details about visiting the biological reserves of Guaporé and Jaru.

The Parque Nacional da Serra do Divisor lies in the extreme western part of the state of Acre and adjoins the border with Peru. Established in 1989, it has very limited tourist infrastructure.

The Parque Nacional do Araguaia now lies in the recently created state of Tocantins. The park area covers the northern end of the Ilha do Bananal, the world's largest river island, formed by the splitting of the Rio Araguaia. The park has no standard tourist infrastructure, but visitors may be able to make arrangements in Santa Teresinha (Mato Grosso state) or Gurupi (Tocantins).

CLIMATE

Many travel guides suggest a certain sameness to the weather in Brazil. This is misleading. It's true that only the south has extreme seasonal changes experienced in Europe and the USA, but most of the country does have noticeable seasonal variations in rainfall, temperature and humidity. In general, as you go from north to south, the seasonal changes are more defined.

The Brazilian winter lasts from June to August. It doesn't get cold in Brazil – except in the southern states of Rio Grande do Sul,

Santa Catarina, Paraná and São Paulo, where the average temperature during the winter months of June, July and August is between 13°C and 18°C. There are even a few towns that can get snow, which is very strange to most Brazilians, who have never touched the white flakes. The rest of the country boasts moderate temperatures all year long.

The summer season is from December to February. With many Brazilians on vacation, travel is difficult and expensive, while from Rio to the south the humidity can be oppressive. It's also the most festive time of year, as Brazilians escape their small, hot apartments and take to the beaches and streets. School vacation, corresponding with the hot season, begins sometime in mid-December and goes through to Carnival, usually in late February.

In summer, Rio is hot and humid; temperatures in the high 30°Cs are common and sometimes reach the low 40s. Frequent, short rains cool things off a bit, but the summer humidity makes things uncomfortable for people from cooler climes. The rest of the year Rio is cooler with temperatures generally in the mid 20°Cs, sometimes reaching the low 30s. If you are in Rio in the winter and the weather's lousy (the rain can continue for days nonstop), or you want more heat, head to the Northeast.

The Northeast coast gets about as hot as Rio during the summer, but due to a wonderful tropical breeze and less humidity, it's rarely stifling. Generally, from Bahia to Maranhão, temperatures are a bit warmer year-round than in Rio, rarely far from 28°C. All in all, it's hard to imagine a better climate.

The highlands or *planalto*, such as Minas Gerais and Brasília, are usually a few degrees cooler than the coast and not as humid. Here summer rains are frequent, while along the coast the rains tend to come intermittently.

Although there are variations in rainfall (see climate charts), throughout Brazil rain is a year-round affair. The general pattern is for short, tropical rains that come at all times. These rains rarely alter or interfere with

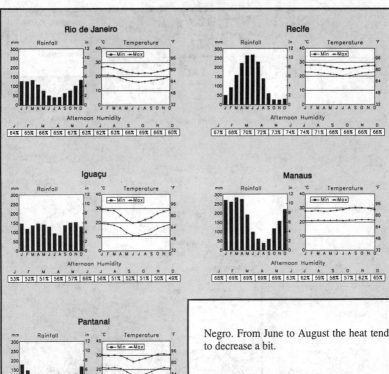

Rio de Janeiro

Recife

Iguaçu

Manaus

Pantanal

Negro. From June to August the heat tends to decrease a bit.

GOVERNMENT
Brazil slowly returned to democracy in the 1980s. In 1988 a new constitution guaranteed freedom of speech, the right to strike and outlawed the use of torture. It also gave 16 year olds and illiterates the right to vote.

In 1995, Fernando Henrique Cardoso became only the second president elected by popular vote in 32 years to take office. The 1988 constitution allows him to choose ministers of state, initiate pieces of legislation and maintain foreign relations. It also names him as commander-in-chief of the armed forces and gives him the power of total veto. These presidential powers are balanced by a bicameral legislature, which consists of a 72-seat senate and a 487-seat chamber of deputies. Presidential elections are slated to be held every five years, with congressional elections every four. State government elec-

travel plans. The sertão is a notable exception – here the rains fall heavily within a few months and periodic droughts devastate the region.

The Amazon Basin receives the most rain in Brazil, and Belém is one of the most rained on cities in the world, but the refreshing showers are usually seen as a godsend. Actually, the Amazon is not nearly as hot as most people presume – the average temperature is 27°C – but it is humid. The hottest part of the basin is between the Rio Solimões and Rio

NUMBERED STATES
1 Rio Grande
  do Notre
2 Paraíba
3 Pernambuco
4 Alagoas
5 Sergipe

The States of Brazil

tions are also held every four years, and municipal elections every three years.

Government elections are colourful affairs, regarded by the democracy-starved Brazilians as yet another excuse for a party. Posters cover every available wall space and convoys of cars cruise through the cities creating as much noise as possible in support of their chosen candidate.

Politics itself remains largely the preserve of the wealthy. In the 1994 elections for state governors and senators, several candidates were forced to drop out because of costs. Inducements to voters are common.

Corruption is still rife at all levels, though not so much at the top these days after Collorgate.

ECONOMY

Since WW II Brazil has seen tremendous growth and modernisation, albeit in fits and starts. Today, Brazil's economy is the 10th largest in the world. It's called a developing country. The military dictators had visions of Brazil joining the ranks of the advanced, industrialised nations by the year 2000. No one believes that is possible now, but no one denies that tremendous development has occurred.

Brazil is a land of fantastic economic contrasts. Travelling through the country, you will witness incredibly uneven development. Production techniques that have barely changed from the colonial era dominate many parts of the Northeast and Amazonia, while São Paulo's massive, high-tech automobile, steel, arms and chemical industries successfully compete on the world market.

Brazil's rulers, at least since President Kubitschek invented Brasília, have had a penchant for building things big and they have, of course, been encouraged to do so by the IMF and the World Bank. The government borrowed heavily to finance Brasília's construction. The country's external debt began to take off exponentially and a couple of years later inflation followed.

Economic development is slow, but there always seem to be some highly visible megaprojects under way. Many of these are economically ill-advised and some never get completed. The funding dries up, is pocketed by corrupt bureaucrats, or the politician who started it leaves office and the political enemy who takes over decides to abandon the project. Whatever the reason, huge amounts of money are wasted. The megaprojects which do get finished may produce wealth, but they don't create many jobs, at least once they are built. Utilising the latest technology, much of Brazil's new development is capital intensive. Few jobs are created – not nearly enough to employ the millions of urban poor who have come from the countryside.

Brazil now has an estimated 64 million working people and a third are women; 17% of people work in agriculture, most as landless peasants, and 12% work in industry. The majority of the rest cannot find decent work and are forced to sell their labour dirt cheap in jobs that are economically unproductive for society and a dead end for the individual.

Cheap labour and underemployment abound in Brazil. Middle-class families commonly hire two or more live-in maids. This contrasts with five-year-old kids, who will never go to school, selling chewing gum or shining shoes. People are hired just to walk dogs, to watch cars or to deliver groceries. Large crews of street cleaners work with home-made brooms. Hawkers on the beaches sell everything and earn almost nothing. Restaurants seem to have more waiters than customers.

Unlike Mexico or Turkey, the poor in Brazil have no rich neighbours where they can go for jobs. With the exception of some minor agrarian reforms, there is no relief in sight. The *fazendeiros* (estate owners), with their massive land holdings, are very influential with the government. Apart from the occasional token gesture they are unlikely to be interested in parting with their land.

Instead of land reform, the government built roads into the Amazon, the road between Belém and Brasília in 1960 and the Transamazônica and the Cuiabá to Porto Velho roads in the '70s. The idea was to open up the Amazon to mineral and agricultural development, and also encourage settlement by the rural poor.

The mineral-poor Amazonian soil proved hard for the peasants to farm. After cutting down forest and opening up the land the peasants were forced off by the hired guns of big cattle ranchers. The settlement of the Amazon continues today, particularly along the strip between Cuiabá, Porto Velho and Rio Branco, where violent boom towns, deforestation and malaria follow in the wake of the settlers.

Over 50% of Brazil's industry is clustered in and around São Paulo city. Most important is the car industry. Labour relations with the workers at Volkswagen, General Motors and Ford were managed by a system modelled on fascist Italy: government-approved unions backed by the power of the military state. From 1968 to 1978 the workers were silent and passive, until the day 100 workers at a bus factory went to work and sat down in front of their machines. Within two weeks 78,000 metalworkers were on strike in the São Paulo industrial belt.

Rapidly, the strikes spread to other industries. There were mass assemblies of workers in soccer stadiums, and the government-sponsored unions were replaced. At the invitation of the Catholic Church, union offices were moved to the cathedral of São Bernardo. Caught by surprise, the corporations and military gave in to substantial wage increases. Both sides prepared for the next time.

In 1980 there was a new wave of strikes. They were better organised, with greater rank-and-file control. Demands were made to democratise the workplace, with shop-floor union representation and factory and safety committees. Many improvements were won, many have since been lost, but the industrial working class had flexed its muscles and no one has forgotten.

Brazilian economists call the '80s the Lost Decade. Wild boom-and-bust cycles decimated the economy. Record-breaking industrial growth fuelled by foreign capital was followed by negative growth and explosive hyperinflation.

Until 1994, the only certainty in the economy was its uncertainty. Then came the Plano Real, that stabilised the currency, ended the inflation that had corroded the salaries of the lowest wage earners, and pro-voked a rise in consumption. Out of the seven economic plans introduced in the last eight years, the Real was the first without shocks or broken contracts. The death of the previous monetary unit, the cruzeiro real, was announced 52 days before the Plano Real introduced a new currency, the real. Backed by the record volume of international reserves (achieved after a healthy 4.2% increase in the gross national product in 1993), the real began on a one-for-one parity with the US dollar. Then the unthinkable happened: the Brazilian currency became worth more than the dollar.

What happened? Brazilians went shopping. In the first three months after the introduction of the plan, economic activity grew by 8%, and industrial sales rose by more than 12%. The gross national product for 1994 grew 5.7% in relation to 1993. By the summer of 1995, a new optimism had swept through Brazil. Was this the beginning of the long-awaited economic miracle that everyone was waiting for?

We'd love to say yes, but as we go to press, it's too hard to predict. The equilibrium is unstable, especially as imports increase. Economists predict that without constitu-

Mercosul

By the year 2000, all products made in Argentina, Brazil, Paraguay and Uruguay – the countries that comprise Mercosul (Mercado Comun do Sul) – will cross the borders with no tariffs.

By 2006, all imports from other places will be subject to the same tariffs in each of the Mercosul countries. It'll be known as the TEC (Tarifa Externa Comun), with tariffs varying between 0% and 20%.

Initiated in January 1995, it's a cumulative process. Already 85% of imports that enter the Mercosul countries are subject to a TEC.

Mercosul has an even bigger objective: to create a true free market, with free circulation of capital and people. With 190 million inhabitants and a combined gross product of US$700 billion, Mercosul forms the fourth largest economic block on the planet.

But there are obstacles. The two principal partners, Brazil and Argentina, are still looking to stabilise their economies. Poverty, cultural differences and lack of infrastructure also conspire against the union. It's not by accident that the main projects being studied are in the area of infrastructure, like the hidrovia Paraguai-Paraná (see Ecology & Environment).

Attempts at integration in Latin America have, in the past, generated more public servants than business opportunities. A new type of public servant has already been created – the 'Mercocrat'. Recruited from other ministries, the mercocrat is bilingual, has studied economics, is politically sensitive and knows how to negotiate.

Can mercocrats do what Bolivar failed to – unite South America? ∎

tional changes, the government deficit will soon blow out. There's no law to prevent the government from printing reais to pay for large budget deficits. If that happens, the inflation dragon will be back.

The Plano Real has at least shown that the Brazilian economy has great potential. All the ingredients for progress are there: a large labour force, the means of production, transport systems and markets for the products. The question is whether or not they can be co-ordinated efficiently. The harsh reality is that seven out of 10 Brazilians still live in poverty.

Social Conditions

The richest 10% of Brazilians control a whopping 54% of the nation's wealth; the poorest 10% have just 0.6% – and the gap is widening. Sixty million live in squalor without proper sanitation, clean water or decent housing. Over 60% of the people who work make less than twice the minimum wage. Unemployment and underemployment are rampant.

Wealthy Brazilians live closed, First World existences in luxurious houses behind high walls protected by armed guards and guard dogs.

In this developing country of almost 155 million people, 40 million people are malnourished; 25 million live in favelas; 12 million children are abandoned and more than seven million between the ages of seven and 14 don't attend school. Brazil, with its dreams of greatness, has misery that compares with the poorest countries in Africa and Asia.

As always, these ills hit some groups much harder than others. If you are a woman, a black, an Indian or from the North or Northeast the odds against escaping poverty are high. One third of the women employed in Brazil work as maids and nannies, and most earn less than the minimum wage. Of Brazil's 21 million illiterates, 13 million are black. Life expectancy in the Northeast is 56 years, compared to 66 in the rest of the country.

The Indians are fighting for survival; less

Rio favela

than 200,000 remain from an estimated five million when the Portuguese arrived. They still suffer violent attacks from ranchers and gold prospectors laying claim to their land.

The killing of peasant leaders, trade unionists and church workers involved in land disputes and strikes continues.

Even though torture has been outlawed by the constitution, reports of death in custody after its use as a means of obtaining a confession continue, although there are very few eyewitnesses. The killing of criminal suspects by uniformed and off-duty police in 'death-squad' operations, especially in Baixada Fluminense, on the outskirts of Rio de Janeiro, is widely reported.

The federal government is aware of the scale of human-rights violations and the chronic failure to administer justice at state and local levels, but will not accept responsibility for matters it deems beyond its jurisdiction.

All these facts illustrate the obvious: for the majority, Brazil is, as it has always been, a country of poverty and inequality, where reforms are as elusive as the wind.

POPULATION & PEOPLE

Brazil's population is almost 155 million, making it the world's sixth most populous country. The population has been rising rapidly over the last 45 years, although in the last 10 years it seems to have slowed a little. There were only 14 million Brazilians in 1890, 33 million in 1930, 46 million in 1945, and 71 million in 1960. The population has more than doubled in the last 35 years.

Still, Brazil is one of the least densely populated nations in the world, averaging only 15 people per sq km. The USA, by comparison, averages 25 people per sq km. The population in Brazil is concentrated along the coastal strip and in the cities. There are around 10 million in the enormous expanses of the North and less than 10 million in the Central West, while there are over 65 million in the Southeast and over 42 million in the Northeast. Brazil also has a young population: half its people are less than 20 years old, 27% under 10.

There are 12 million *abandonados*, children without parents or home. Many are hunted by the so-called 'death squads' made up of vigilantes who take it upon themselves to torture and murder the children under the pretence that 'they grow up to become criminals anyway, so why not get rid of them now?' The fate of these children is one of the most pressing social problems facing Brazil today.

Brazil is now an urban country whereas 40 years ago it was still a predominantly rural society. Due to internal migration, two-thirds of Brazilians now live in nine large urban areas: São Paulo city, Rio de Janeiro, Belo Horizonte, Porto Alegre, Salvador, Recife, Fortaleza, Brasília and Belém. Greater São Paulo has over 17 million residents, greater Rio over 10 million.

Some 500 years ago Cabral landed in Brazil. When he departed, only nine days later, he left behind two convicts who subsequently married natives. Thus, colonisation through miscegenation was how the Portu-

guese managed to control Brazil. This strategy was pursued, often consciously and semi-officially, for hundreds of years. First with native Indians, then with the black slaves and finally between Indians and blacks, miscegenation thoroughly mixed the three races. Brazilians use literally dozens of terms to describe people's various racial compositions and skin tones. Most Brazilians have some combination of European, African, Amerindian, Asian and Middle Eastern ancestry.

Accurate statistics on racial composition are difficult to obtain in Brazil. Many people who are counted as white have at least some black or Indian blood, but the 1980 census showed about 55% of the population were technically white, 6% black and 38% mulatto. Anyone who has travelled in Brazil knows these figures are ridiculous. They reflect what people want to think rather than reality. Whiteness in Brazil, they often say, is as much a reflection of one's social standing as the colour of one's skin.

Brazil has had several waves of voluntary immigration. After the end of slavery in 1887, millions of Europeans were recruited to work in the coffee fields. The largest contingent was from Italy, but there were also many Portuguese and Spaniards, with smaller groups of Germans and Russians. Japanese immigration began in 1908 and today São Paulo has the largest Japanese community outside of Japan.

Some 50,000 Portuguese came to Brazil from Africa in 1974 and 1975 with the liberation of Portugal's African colonies. During the '70s many Latin Americans fleeing military dictatorships in Argentina, Chile, Uruguay and Paraguay settled in Brazil.

Indians

The government Indian agency, Fundação Nacional do Indio (FUNAI), has documented 174 different Indian languages and dialects. Customs and belief systems vary widely.

Growing international concern over the destruction of the Amazon rainforest has also highlighted the plight of the region's Brazilian Indians, who are facing extinction early next century – if not sooner. At present the number of Indians in Brazil is estimated at less than 200,000. Of the several hundred tribes already identified, most are concentrated in the Amazon region and virtually all Brazilian Indians face a host of problems which threaten to destroy their environment and way of life. An estimated 40 tribes have never been in contact with outsiders. For more details about Indians and their status in Brazil refer to the following separate sections in this chapter: History, Ecology & Environment, Indian Art, and Culture.

Indian Policy During the 20th century, the general thrust of official Brazilian policy towards the Indians and their lands has concentrated on pacification, integration, and dispossession.

In 1910, Marechal Cândido Rondon (1865-1958), who favoured a humane and dignified Indian policy, founded the Serviço de Proteção ao Indio (SPI) as an attempt to protect the Indians against massacres and land dispossession. Unfortunately, Rondon's good intentions were swept aside and SPI became notorious as a tool for corrupt and greedy officialdom to physically eliminate Indians or force them off their lands. By the late '60s, SPI had become the target of fierce national and international criticism.

In 1967, SPI was replaced by FUNAI which was intended to redress the SPI wrongs. FUNAI was set the ambitious and controversial tasks of protecting Indian reserves, administering the medical and educational needs of the Indians, and contacting and pacifying hitherto unknown tribes.

FUNAI has been criticised for adopting a patronising attitude toward Indians, and for manipulating against Indian interests in favour of other claims to Indian lands. It's difficult to see how this grossly underfunded and understaffed organisation can escape contradictions when it represents the interests of the Indians and simultaneously acts on behalf of the government and military, which have both been expropriating Indian lands for industry and settlement.

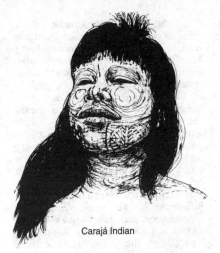

Carajá Indian

Religious organisations, such as Conselho Indígenista Missionário (CIM) and Centro Ecumênico de Documentação e Informação (CEDI) have attempted to right the imbalance, but there appears to be little interest in changing patronising attitudes or giving the Indians a chance to represent their rights as decreed by Brazilian law. The Brazilian constitution recognises Indian rights to their traditional lands, which cover approximately 87 million hectares (about 10% of Brazil's territory).

FUNAI recently started using a computer network and satellite photographs to secure the borders of large and remote tracts of land from invading lumber workers and prospectors. The system is composed of many reservations and posts plus five major parks: Xingu and Aripuanâ parks in Mato Grosso, Araguaia Park on Ilha do Bananal in Tocantins, Tumucumaque Park on the Guyanese border of Pará and the Yanomami Park in Roraima.

Recent Developments During the '80s, Indian tribes which had seen their people and lands destroyed by development projects (particularly highway construction) in the '70s were stung into independent action to protect themselves.

In 1980, nearly 1000 Xavante Indians, who had tired of FUNAI inactivity, started marking the boundaries of their reserve in Mato Grosso state. When a fierce conflict arose with encroaching ranchers, 31 Xavante leaders paid a surprise visit to the president of FUNAI in Brasília and demanded immediate boundary demarcation. Further pressure was exerted on FUNAI when Txucarramãe Indians killed 11 agricultural workers whom they had caught trespassing on their Xingu reserve and clearing the forest. In 1982, over 200 Indian leaders assembled in Brasília to debate land ownership at the First National Assembly of Indigenous Nations.

Subsequent years saw a spate of hostage takings and confiscations by Indians, who were thereby able to force rapid decisions from the government. As an attempt to deflect criticism and placate public opinion, the government hired and fired FUNAI officials in quick succession; a convenient scapegoat technique which continues to be employed in the '90s, changing names and little else. In 1989, the First Meeting of the Indigenous Nations of Xingu included a huge cast of Brazilian Indians, foreign environmentalists, and even the rock star Sting. Two Kayapo chiefs, Raoni and Megaron, then accompanied Sting on a world tour to raise funds for the preservation of the Amazon rainforest.

During the '90s, international attention has focused on the plight of the Yanomami (see the next section). Environmentalists and ecologists who attended ECO-92 pressed for practical changes to benefit the Indians and their environment – nobody wants to be fobbed off any more with speeches and papers which are simply public relations exercises to be filed and forgotten.

The Yanomami The Yanomami are one of the newly discovered Indian peoples of the Amazon. Until some Yanomami were given metal tools by visitors, all their implements were made of stone, ceramic, animal hides and plants. They are literally a Stone Age people rapidly confronting the 20th century.

The plight of the Yanomami has aroused considerable foreign interest, since the problems experienced by the Yanomami are considered typical of those encountered by other Indians in Brazil.

In 1973 the Yanomami had their first contact with Westerners; Brazilian Air Force pilots and religious missionaries. In 1974 and 1975 as BR-210 (Perimetral Norte) and BR-174 roads were cut through the Catramani and Ajarani tributaries of the Rio Negro, people from several Yanomami villages mixed with the construction workers and contracted and died from measles, influenza and venereal disease. Over a dozen villages were wiped out.

In 1988, the government instituted an absurd plan to create 19 separate pockets of land for the Yanomami, thereby depriving the Indians of 70% of their territory. Thousands of garimpeiros swarmed into the area and ignored all boundaries. Two years later, growing international and national criticism of the genocide being perpetrated on the Yanomami forced the authorities to backtrack and declare only a handful of designated zones open for mining. The garimpeiros continued to prospect at random and resisted all efforts, even force, to dislodge them.

In 1991, the Venezuelan government officially recognised the Yanomami territory on the Venezuelan side of the Brazilian border as a special Indian reserve; a few months later President Collor defied opposition and followed suit on the Brazilian side. The Brazilian military continues to oppose the decision and prefers instead to encourage development and settlement of the border areas as a buffer against possible foreign intrusions.

The Yanomami are a slight people, with Oriental features. Their estimated 18,000 seminomadic tribespeople are scattered over 320 villages on either side of the Brazilian-Venezuelan border. They speak one of four related languages: Yanomam, Yanam, Yanomamo and Sanumá.

The centre of each community is the Yano, a large circular structure where each family has its own section facing directly onto an open central area used for communal dance and ceremony. The Yano is built with palm-leaf thatch and timber posts. Each family arranges its own section by slinging hammocks around a fire which burns constantly and forms the centre of family life.

Inter-tribal visits are an opportunity to eat well – if the hunt has been successful everyone gets to eat monkey, which is a delicacy. Otherwise tapir, wild pig and a variety of insects make up the protein component of the meal, which is balanced with garden fruits, yams, plantains and manioc. The Yanomami also grow cotton and tobacco. Once their garden soils and hunting grounds are exhausted, the village moves on to a new site.

The Yanomami hold elaborate ceremonies and rituals and place great emphasis on inter-tribal alliances. The latter are intended to minimise any feuds or violence which, as has often happened in the past, can escalate into full-scale wars. Inter-tribal hostility is thought to manifest in disease that comes from evil spirits sent by the shamans of enemy tribes. Disease is cured with various herbs, shaman dances and healing hands. Sometimes the village shaman will enlist the good spirits to fight the evil spirits by using *yakoana*, a hallucinogenic herbal powder.

The Yanomami have some curious practices. When a tribal person dies, the body is hung from a tree until dry, then burned to ashes. The ashes are mixed with bananas, which are then eaten by friends and family of the deceased to incorporate and preserve the spirit. The mourning ritual is elaborate and includes having one member of the tribe assigned to cry for a month (as determined by the phases of the moon, since the Yanomami have no calendar and the only number they have greater than two is 'many'). Friends or allies from other communities will travel three to four days to join the mourning tribe.

These days even such remote tribes are exposed to encroaching civilisation in the shape of clearance roads for the Perimetral Norte, illegal airstrips built by garimpeiros, and FUNAI posts. Despite the latest positive moves from the Brazilian government, the Yanomami lands are not adequately protected against encroachment and dispossession by brute force. More details about providing support for the Yanomami can be obtained from Survival International – for the address refer to the Ecology & Environment section in this chapter.

Information & Further Reading There are several governmental and religious organisations which publish information about Brazilian Indians. *Poratim* is a newsletter published by the Conselho Indígenista Missionário (CIM) (☎ (061) 225-9457), Edifício Venâncio III, Sala 310, Caixa Postal 11.1159, CEP 70084, Brasília, DF . In the past, FUNAI's own publication, *Jornal da Funai*, was produced at the same address as CIM, but future publishing plans for it are unclear. *Aconteceu* is a bi-weekly journal (with a strong ecological emphasis) published by the Centro Ecumênico de Documentação e Informação (CEDI) (☎ (021) 224-6713), Rua Santo Amaro, 129, Rio de Janeiro, CEP 22211, RJ.

There are also various individuals or small groups working on alternative projects for tribes such as the Ticuna and Wapichana. In the state of Amazonas, there's Alírio Mendes Moraes (Ticuna), Coordenação das Organizações Indígenas da Amazônia Brasileira (COIAB) (☎ (092) 624-2511), Avenida Leopoldo Peres, 373, Caixa Postal 3264, Manaus, CEP 69000, AM. In the same state, education is the main emphasis of the Organização Geral dos Professores Ticuna Bilingüe (☎ (092) 415-5494), Avenida Castelo Branco, 594, Projeto Alto Solimões, Benjamin Constant, CEP 69630, AM. In the state of Roraima, another group has been set up by Clovis Ambrósio (Wapichana), Conselho Indígena de Roraima (CIR) (☎ (095) 224-5761), Avenida Sebastião Diniz, 1672 W, Bairro São Vicente, Boa Vista, CEP 69300, RR.

If you contact any of these organisations, groups or individuals, remember that they operate on minimal budgets, so you should at least pay return postage and material costs in advance. It is also worth pointing out that truth and facts about the Indians are hard to pinpoint, and official information is often presented in a flexible manner to suit the political, financial, or cultural agenda of those involved.

Outside Brazil, one of the most active and reputable organisations providing information on Indian affairs in Brazil is Survival International, which has campaigned especially hard for the Yanomami Indians and has members and offices worldwide (for address details see the Ecology & Environment section in this chapter). Survival International members receive a regular newsletter, *Urgent Action Bulletins*, campaign documents, and an annual review.

For suggested reading, see the Books & Maps section in the Facts for the Visitor chapter.

Visiting a Reservation If you're a physician, anthropologist or sociologist with an authentic scholarly interest, you can make an application to FUNAI for authorisation to visit a reservation.

If you are not a Brazilian citizen you must first submit a research proposal together with your curriculum vitae, a letter of introduction from your research institute, a letter from the Brazilian researcher or research institute taking responsibility for you and your work and who agrees to accompany you into the field, a declaration that you speak Portuguese and know Brazilian law, vaccination certificates for yellow fever, typhoid and tetanus and an X-ray to show that you are free from tuberculosis.

All documentation must be in Portuguese and must first be presented to the embassy or consulate of your home country. They must send it to the Ministry of Foreign Relations in Brasília, which will in turn forward it to CNPQ (National Centre for Research). CNPQ will take a minimum of 90 days to consider your proposal. If they agree to authorise your project, the file is passed to the FUNAI office in Rio at the Museu do Índio (Indian Museum) where Professor Neyland further processes it and Dra Claúdia scribbles the final signature.

The procedure is intentionally difficult. It is intended to protect the Indians from the inadvertent spread of diseases to which they have no natural immunity as well as from overexposure to alien cultural ideals. Nevertheless, many applicants make it through all the obstacles, and as many as 60 projects have been approved in one three-month period.

EDUCATION

The government claims a literacy rate of 80% but according to EDUCAR, the government department for adult education, only 40% of Brazilians old enough to be in the workforce are capable of reading a newspaper with comprehension. The government considers literate those who can write their names, know the alphabet and sound out a few words. In the workplace it has become obvious that these people are functionally illiterate. According to the government, half of the nation's pupils do not pass the first school year and many do not attempt to repeat it. Only two out of every 10 students make it through elementary school. The remainder drop out to support themselves and their family.

Education in Brazil is based on class. Public schools are so bad that anyone with the means sends their children to private schools. Almost all university students are from private schools, so very few poor children reach university and the poverty cycle is renewed. Many poor children must work to eat and never attend school. Even for those who are able to go, there aren't enough schools, teachers or desks to go around.

The Brizola government of Rio de Janeiro was one of the first to understand and act upon the connections between poverty, hunger and illiteracy, and set up food programmes in schools. The kids come to school for the food and stay for the lessons. Some schools have classes at night for those children who work during the day.

Mass media has also been used in Brazil with some success. Since 1972, TV and radio educational programmes have been on the air. They concentrate on primary (*primeiro grau*) and secondary (*segunda grau*) students, but not exclusively. One course consists of 235 radio and TV programmes, with the objective of qualifying primary teachers. In 1989 Universidade Aberta (Open University), a tertiary education programme, was introduced. You'll often see the workbooks on newsstands.

While these measures are not enough – many primary school students still have only three hours of classes per day – they show that some programmes are successful.

ARTS
Music
Brazilians are among the most musical people on the planet. Wherever you go, you'll find people playing, singing and dancing. Perhaps because of its African roots, Brazilian music is a collective act, a celebration, a festa.

Brazilian popular music has always been characterised by great diversity. Shaped by the mixing of a variety of musical influences from three different continents, the music of the people is still creating new and original forms.

Thus *samba canção*, for example, is a mixture of Spanish bolero with the cadences and rhythms of African music. *Bossa nova* was influenced by North American music, particularly jazz, and samba. And the music called *tropicalismo* is a mix of musical influences that arrived in Brazil in the '60s, including Italian ballads and bossa nova.

Samba *Tudo dá samba*: everything makes for a samba. The most popular Brazilian rhythm, samba, was first performed at the Rio Carnival in 1917, though its origins go back much further.

It is intimately linked with African rhythms; notably the Angolan tam-tam, which provided the basis for its music and distinctive dance steps. It caught on quickly after the advent of radio and records and has since become a national symbol. It is the music of the masses.

The 1930s are known as the Golden Age of Samba. By then, samba canção had also evolved, as had *choro*, a romantic, intimate music with a ukulele or guitar as its main instrument, playing off against a recorder or flute.

The most famous Brazilian singer of this period, perhaps of all time, is Carmen Miranda. A star of many Hollywood musicals of the period, she was known for her fiery, Latin temperament and her 'fruity' costumes. She has since become a cult figure among Rio's gay community, and Carnival in Rio sees many of them impersonating her.

Bossa Nova In the '50s came bossa nova, and the democratic nature of Brazilian music was altered. Bossa nova was new, modern and intellectual. It also became internationally popular. The middle class stopped listening to the old interpretations of samba and other regional music like the *forró* of the Northeast.

Bossa nova initiated a new style of playing instruments and singing. The more operatic, florid style of singing was replaced by a quieter, more relaxed sound; remember the soft sound of 'The Girl from Ipanema' composed by the late Antônio Carlos (Tom) Jobim and Vinicius Moraes? João Gilberto is the founding father of bossa nova, and leading figures, like Baden Powell and Nara Leão, are still playing in Rio. Another bossa nova voice, who became Brazil's most beloved singer, was Elis Regina.

Bossa nova was associated with the rising middle class of urban, university-educated Brazil. It was a musical response to other modernist movements of the '50s and '60s such as the Cinema Novo, the Brazilian Modern Architecture of Oscar Niemeyer et al, and other aspects of the cultural life of the nation during the optimistic presidency of Juscelino Kubitschek from 1956 to 1960.

Tropicalismo At the end of the '60s the movement known as tropicalismo burst onto the scene. Tropicalismo provoked a kind of general amnesty for all the forgotten musical traditions of the past. The leading figures – Gilberto Gil, Caetano Veloso, Rita Lee, Macalé, Maria Betânia and Gal Costa – believed that all musical styles were important and relevant. All the styles and traditions in Brazilian music could be freely mixed. This kind of open thinking led to innovations like the introduction of the electric guitar and the sound of electric samba.

Música Popular Brasileira Paralleling these musical movements are several incredibly popular musicians who are hard to categorise: they are simply known as exponents of MPB – Música Popular Brasileira (Popular Brazilian Music).

Chico Buarque de Holanda, who mixes traditional samba with a modern, universal flavour, is immensely popular, as is Paulinho da Viola, a master *sambista* who also bridges the gap between traditional samba and pop music. Jorge Bem comes from a particular black musical tradition of the Rio suburbs, but plays an original pop samba without losing the characteristic black rhythms. Another example is Luís Melodia, who combines the samba rhythms of the Rio hills with more modern forms from the '70s and '80s, always with beautiful melody.

Milton Nascimento, also from Minas, was elected by readers of *DownBeat* magazine as the number one exponent of world music. He has long been famous in Brazil for his fine voice, stirring anthems and ballads which reflect the spirituality of the Mineiro (someone from Minas).

Brazilian Rock Derived more from English than American rock, this is the least Brazilian of all Brazilian music. It's all the rage with the youngsters. Groups like Titãs, Kid Abelha, Legião Urbana, Capital Inicial and Plebe Rude are all worth a listen if you like rock music. Heavy metal bands like Sepultura and Ratos do Porão have huge domestic followings. Sepultura are now very famous amongst head bangers worldwide. Brazilian rap music is also popular, with groups like MRN (Movimento e Ritmo Negro) and Racionais MC with their hard-edged lyrics about life in the favelas.

Regional Music Samba, tropicalismo and bossa nova are all national musical forms. But wherever you go in Brazil you'll hear regional specialities.

The Northeast has perhaps the most regional musical styles and accompanying dances. The most important is the forró, a mix of Northeastern music with Mexican music – maybe introduced via Paraguay – with nuances of the music of the Brazilian frontier region. The forró incorporates the European accordion, the harmonica, and the *zabumba* (an African drum).

Another distinctive type of music is the wonderful Bumba Meu Boi festival sound from São Luís in Maranhão. *Frevo* is a music specific to Recife. The *trio elétrico*, also called *frevo baiano*, began much more recently and is more of a change in technology than music. It began as a family joke when, during Carnival in Salvador, Dodô, Armandinho and Osmar got up on top of a truck and played frevo with electric guitars. The trio elétrico is not necessarily a trio, but it is still the backbone of Salvador's Carnival, when trucks piled high with speakers with musicians perched on top, drive through the city surrounded by dancing mobs. But it wasn't popularised until

Caetano Veloso, during the period of tropicalismo, began writing songs about the trio elétrico.

Afoxé is another important type of black music of Brazil. Religious in origin, it is closely tied to Candomblé (Afro-Brazilian religion), and primarily found in Bahia. Afoxé is the most African-sounding music in Brazil. It has been rejuvenated by the strong influence of reggae and the growth of a black-consciousness movement in Bahia.

The influence of the music of the Indians was absorbed and diluted, as was so much of the various Indian cultures in Brazil. In musical terms, several whites have idealised what they thought those influences were. The *carimbó*, the music of the Amazon region – where the majority of Indians live today – is influenced primarily by the blacks of the littoral. Maybe the forró is the Brazilian music most influenced by the Indians, via Nordestinos (people from the Northeast) who have occupied a good part of the Amazon region since the end of last century.

Recent Trends *Pagode*, a type of samba that has existed for some time, was recently picked up and promoted by record producers. For some of the best pagode, listen to Bezerra da Silva, who was popular in the favelas before ever recording. Pagode, samba, frevo and forró all have corresponding dances – perhaps a reflection of the African influence on Brazilian music and the Brazilian use of music as a celebration of communication.

Lambada is a rhythm with a sensual dance that has become another international success story. Originating in Belém, and influenced by various Caribbean rhythms like rumba, merengue and salsa, lambada became really popular in Porto Seguro, which today is considered its home. From there it spread to the cities of Brazil and eventually to Europe and the USA. It even inspired a couple of terrible Hollywood movies.

The most successful lambada artist is Beto Barbosa and her group Kaoma, made up of Brazilian, Argentine and French musicians.

Other Brazilian musicians who have recorded lambada tracks include Lulu Santos, Pepeu Gomes and Moraes Moreira, and even Caetano Veloso.

Also hugely popular is *sertanejo*, a kind of Brazilian country and western music. It has long been a favourite with truck drivers and cowboys, but has only recently entered the mainstream of popular Brazilian music. Usually sung by male duets wearing cowboy hats, fringed jackets and large belt buckles, sertanejo is characterised by its soaring harmonies and, of course, its lyrics about broken hearts, life on the road, etc. Some of the popular exponents are: José Rico and Millionario, Chitãozinho and Xororó, and Leandro e Leonardo.

Axé, a samba-inspired, pop/rock/reggae/funk fusion from Salvador, has also become well known thanks to the music of the flamboyant Daniela Mercury.

If you want to have a listen to some Brazilian music before you arrive, the 'Brazil Classics' series, compiled by David Byrne and distributed by Warner Brothers, is a good starting point. These records are readily available, and cover samba and forró, and feature some individuals like Bahian Tom Zé. Bossa nova records are reasonably plentiful, especially the Grammy-winning collaborations between Brazilian and American artists, like João Gilberto and Stan Getz. *The Rhythm of the Saints*, an album by Paul Simon, was heavily influenced by Brazilian music. It included backing by Milton Nascimento and the popular Grupo Cultural Olodum from Bahia.

Purchasing Records & Tapes The widest selection of records can be found in the large Brazilian cities, like São Paulo and Rio. Regional music enthusiasts should check out the selection available at the Museu Folclorico Edson Carneiro in Rio.

Records and tapes (called K7 in Brazil) cost around US$8. Compact discs are available in Brazil, but there are doubts as to their quality compared to 'imported' CDs. They cost around US$12 to US$15.

Painting & Sculpture

The first painters of the colonial period were the Jesuit and Benedictine missionaries, who painted their churches and sacred objects in a European baroque style. The Dutch invasion in the north brought with it some important Flemish artists, such as Frans Post, who painted the flora and fauna in their tropical surroundings.

Brazilian baroque art peaked in the 18th century, when the wealth provided by the gold rush allowed talented artists to reach their full potential and create many beautiful works. The acknowledged genius of this period is the sculptor and architect Antônio Francisco Lisboa, better known as Aleijadinho (see the Minas Gerais chapter for details of his life and works).

In the 19th and 20th centuries, Brazilian artists have followed the international trends of neo-classicism, romanticism, impressionism, academicism and modernism.

The internationally best known Brazilian painter is Candido Portinari. Early in his career he made the decision to paint only Brazil and its people. Strongly influenced by the Mexican muralists like Diego Rivera, he managed to fuse native, expressionist influences into a powerful, socially conscious and sophisticated style.

Indian Art In its original form, Indian art was created for religious or utilitarian purposes and was considered part of the Indian way of life.

After first contacts with Europeans had been made, Indians were soon visited by traders who perceived their art as valuable items to be acquired by bartering and then sold as curiosities or collectables in Brazil and abroad. Today many Indians produce art items for sale as tourist curios – the income pays their keep on the margin of a society which has destroyed their environment, their way of life, and left no other purpose for their art.

The Indians are renowned for a wide range of artistic handicrafts. The plumage of forest birds is used to create necklaces, bracelets, earrings, headdresses, capes and blankets.

Some tribes pluck the original feathers from a bird such as a macaw, and smear the plucked area of the bird's skin with a vegetable dye which changes the colour of the new plumage. Members of some tribes use dyes and tattoos to decorate their bodies with intricate designs of great beauty.

Ceramic arts were a speciality of the Marajó Indians who flourished long before the arrival of the Portuguese, and today the Carajás tribe in the state of Tocantins is famed for its skilfully painted figurines. Grasses, leaves and bark from the forests are used in highly developed Indian handicrafts such as weaving and basketry. The Kaxinawá tribe in the state of Acre is especially skilled at producing woven bags and baskets to transport or store forest foods. For more details about the Indians of Brazil, refer to the Population & People section in this chapter.

Architecture

There are many examples of outstanding Brazilian architecture that have been proclaimed by UNESCO as part of the world's cultural heritage.

Representing the colonial period are Olinda, in Pernambuco, and the historic centre of Salvador, which is considered to be the finest example of Portuguese colonial architecture in the world.

In Minas Gerais, the town of Ouro Prêto and Aleijadinho's masterpiece, the church of Bom Jesus de Matzinhos in Congonhas, represent the golden age of Brazilian baroque architecture.

The remains of the 17th-century Jesuit missions in Rio Grande do Sul, on the border between Brazil, Argentina and Paraguay, are notable for the fine woodcarving and masonry of the Guaraní Indians, who achieved their own distinct style.

The central urban plan of the capital, Brasília, also earns a UNESCO rating as a striking example of modern architecture.

Literature

There are a few dozen excellent Brazilian works of fiction translated into English but, sadly, many of today's best writers have not been translated.

Machado de Assis is simply world class. The son of a freed slave, Assis worked as a typesetter and journalist in late 19th-century Rio. A tremendous stylist, with a great sense of humour, Assis had an understanding of human relations which was both subtle and deeply cynical, as the terse titles of books like *Epitaph of a Small Winner* (Avon Bard, 1977) and *Philosopher or Dog* (Avon Bard, 1982) might suggest. He wrote five major novels; my favourite is *Dom Casmurro* (Avon Bard, 1980).

The most famous writer in Brazil is Jorge Amado. Born near Ilhéus, Bahia, in 1912, and a long-time resident of Salvador, Amado has written colourful romances of Bahia's people and places. Strongly influenced by Communism during his early work, Amado's later books are better, although the subjects are lighter. His books are widely translated and easy to obtain. The best are *Gabriela, Clove and Cinnamon* (Avon Bard, 1974), which is set in Ilhéus, and *Dona Flor and her Two Husbands* (Avon Bard, 1977), whose antics occur in Salvador. Amado's *Tent of Miracles* (Avon Bard, 1978) explores racial relations in Brazil and *Pen, Sword and Camisole* (Avon Bard, 1986) laughs its way through the petty worlds of military and academic politics. *The Violent Land* (Avon Bard, 1979) is another of Amado's classics. The three short stories about a group of Bahian characters that make up *Shepherds of the Night* (Avon Bard, 1980) inspired our first visit to Brazil.

Without a word to waste, Graciliano Ramos tells of peasant life in the sertão in his best book, *Barren Lives* (University of Texas Press, 1965). The stories are powerful portraits – strong stuff. Autran Dourado's *The Voices of the Dead* (Taplinger, 1981) goes into the inner world of a small town in Minas Gerais. He has penned another couple of books about Minas Gerais, his home state. Read anything you can find by Mário de Andrade, one of Brazil's pre-eminent authors. His *Macunaíma* is comic and could only take place in Brazil.

Clarice Lispector has several collections of short stories, all of which are excellent. Lídia Fagundes Telles' books contain psychologically rich portraits of women in today's Brazil. Dinah Silveira de Queiroz's *The Women of Brazil* is about a Portuguese girl who goes to 17th-century Brazil to meet her betrothed.

Márcio Souza is a modern satirist based in Manaus. His biting humour captures the horror of the Amazon and his imaginative parodies of Brazilian history reveal the stupidity of personal and governmental endeavours to conquer the rainforest. Both the *Emperor of the Amazon* (Avon Bard, 1980), his first book, and *Mad Maria* (Avon Bard, 1985) shouldn't be missed if you're going to the Amazon, but his latest farce, *The Order of the Day* (Avon Bard, 1986), is disappointing. *The Impostors* (Avon Bard, 1987) by Pablo Vierci is a humorous novel about Amazon mayhem.

The bizarre and brutal *Zero* (Avon Bard, 1983), by Ignácio de Loyola Brandão, had the honour of being banned by the military government until a national protest helped lift the ban. *The Tower of Glass* (Avon Bard, 1982), by Ivan Ângelo, is all São Paulo: an absurdist look at big-city life where nothing that matters, matters. It's a revealing and important view of modern Brazil, 'where all that's solid melts into air'. João Ubaldo Ribeiro's *Sergeant Getúlio* (Avon Bard, 1980) is a story of a military man in Brazil's Northeast. No book tells better of the sadism, brutality and patriarchy which run through Brazil's history.

CULTURE

Brazilian culture has been shaped not only by the Portuguese, who gave the country its language and religion, but also by native Indians, black Africans, and other settlers from Europe, the Middle East and Asia.

Although often ignored, denigrated or feared by urban Brazilians, Indian culture has helped shape modern Brazil and its legends, dance and music. Many native foods and beverages, such as tapioca, manioc, potatoes, maté and *guaraná*, have become Brazilian staples. The Indians also gave the colonisers numerous objects and skills which are now in daily use in Brazil, such as hammocks, dugout canoes, thatched roofing, and weaving techniques. For more details about the Indians refer to the sections on Indian Art and Population & People in this chapter.

The influence of African culture is also very powerful in Brazil, especially the Northeast. The slaves imported by the Portuguese brought with them their religion, music and cuisine, all of which have profoundly influenced Brazilian identity.

All these elements have combined to produce a nation of people well known for their spontaneity, friendliness and lust for life. As you would expect from such a diverse population mix, there are many regional differences and accents. One of the funniest aspects of this regional diversity is the rivalry between the citizens of Rio and São Paulo. Talk to Paulistas (inhabitants of São Paulo state) and they will tell you that Cariocas (inhabitants of Rio) are hedonistic, frivolous and irresponsible. Cariocas think of Paulistas as materialistic, neurotic workaholics. Both Paulista and Carioca agree that the Nordestinos, from the Northeast, do things more slowly and simply, and are the worst drivers! Mineiros, from the state of Minas Gerais, are considered the thriftiest and most religious of Brazilians – Cariocas claim they're saving up for their tombs!

In Brazil time is warped. The cities and their 20th-century urban inhabitants exist only a short distance from fisherfolk, cowboys and forest dwellers whose lifestyles have varied little in 300 years. In the forests, the ancient traditions of the native Brazilians remain untouched by TV soap operas – for the time being.

Brazilians have an excellent sense of humour. They adore telling jokes about the Portuguese, in the same way that Americans tell Polish jokes and Australians and Brits tell Irish jokes.

If you manage to get a grasp of the language, listen to Brazilians when a group of them get together on the beach or in a corner bar. If you can get past the fact that they all talk at once, you'll discover that the conversation almost always turns to football, criticism of the government, family matters or the latest twist in the current soap opera.

So what unifies the Brazilians? The Portuguese language, love of football, Carnival and the sound of samba. Listen and watch their expressive way of communicating; go to a football game and watch the intensity and variety of emotions, both on the field and in the stands; experience the bacchanalia of Carnival and attempt to dance the samba and you may begin to understand what it is to be Brazilian.

RELIGION

Officially, Brazil is a Catholic country and claims the largest Catholic population of any country in the world. However, Brazil is also noted for the diversity and syncretism of its many sects and religions, which offer great flexibility to their followers. For example, without much difficulty you can find people from Catholic backgrounds who frequent the church and have no conflict appealing for help at a *terreiro de umbanda*, the house of one of the Afro-Brazilian cults.

Historically, the principal religious influences have been Indian animism, Catholicism and African cults brought by the blacks during the period of slavery. The slaves were prohibited from practising their religions by the colonists in the same way that they were kept from other elements of their culture, such as music and dance, for fear that it would reinforce their group identity. Religious persecution led to religious syncretism. To avoid persecution the slaves gave Catholic names and figures to all their African gods. This was generally done by finding the similarities between the Catholic images and the *orixás* (gods) of Candomblé (described later in this section). Thus, the slaves worshipped their own gods behind the representations of the Catholic saints.

Under the influence of liberalism in the 19th century, Brazilians wrote into their constitution the freedom to worship all religions. But the African cults continued to suffer persecution for many years. Candomblé was seen by the white élites as charlatanism that showed the ignorance of the poorest classes. The spectrum of Brazilian religious life was gradually broadened by the addition of Indian animism to Afro-Catholic syncretism, and by the increasing fascination of whites with the spiritualism of Kardecism (also described later in this section).

Today Catholicism retains its status as the official religion, but it is declining in popularity. Throughout Brazil, churches are closing or falling into disrepair for lack of funds and priests, and attendances at church services are dwindling such that people now merely turn up for the basics: baptism, marriage, and burial. The largest numbers of converts are being attracted to the Afro-Brazilian cults, and spiritist or mystic sects. Nowadays, the intense religious fervour of Brazilians extends across gradations and subdivisions of numerous sects; from purist cults to groups that worship Catholic saints, African deities and the Cabóclos of the Indian cults simultaneously.

Note that in this book, we use the abbreviation NS for 'Nossa Senhora' (Our Lady) or 'Nosso Senhor' (Our Lord): eg, NS do Pilar.

Afro-Brazilian Cults

These cults do not follow the ideas of major European or Asian religions; neither do they use doctrines to define good and evil. One of the things that was most shocking to Europeans in their first contact with the African images and rituals was the cult of Exú. This entity was generally represented by combined human and animal images, complete with a horn and an erect penis. Seeking parallels between their own beliefs and African religions, European Catholics and Puritans identified Exú as the devil. For Africans, however, Exú represents the transition between the material and the spiritual worlds. In the ritual of Candomblé, Exú acts as a messenger between the gods and human beings. For example, everything related to money, love, and protection against thieves

comes under the watchful eye of Exú. Ultimately, Exú's responsibility is the temporal world.

Candomblé This is the most orthodox of the cults brought from Africa by the Nago, Yoruba, and Jeje peoples. Candomblé, which is an African word denoting a dance in honour of the gods, is a general term for the cult in Bahia. Elsewhere in Brazil the cult is known by different names: in Rio it's known as Macumba; in Amazonas and Pará it's Babassuê; in Pernambuco and Alagoas it's Xangô; in Rio Grande do Sul it's either Pará or Batuque; and the term Tambor is used in Maranhão. For suggested reading on Candomblé, see the Books & Maps section in the Facts for the Visitor chapter.

The Afro-Brazilian rituals are practised in a *casa-de-santo* or *terreiro* directed by a *pai* or *mãe de santo* (literally father or mother of the saint – the Candomblé priest or priestess). This is where the initiation of novices takes place as well as consultations and rituals. The ceremonies are conducted in the Yoruba tongue. The religious hierarchy and structure is clearly established and consistent

Candomblé participant

from one terreiro to the next. Not all ceremonies are open to the public.

If you attend a Candomblé ceremony, it's best to go as the invited guest of a knowledgeable friend or commercial guide. If your request to visit is declined, you should accept the decision. Some ceremonies are only open to certain members of a terreiro, and there is genuine concern that visitors may not know the customs involved and thereby interrupt the rituals.

Although the rules for Candomblé ceremonies are not rigidly fixed, there are some general points which apply to most of these ceremonies. If in doubt, ask the person who has taken you to the ceremony. Dress for men and women can be casual, but shorts should not be worn. White is the preferred colour; black, purple, and brown should be avoided. Hats should not be worn inside the terreiro; and if you wish to smoke, you should only do so outside.

On arrival at the terreiro, make sure you do not stand blocking the doorway. There's usually someone inside who is responsible for directing people to their seats – men are often seated on the right, women on the left. The seating pattern is important, so make sure you only sit where indicated. Watch respectfully and follow the advice of your friend or guide as to what form of participation is expected of you. Sometimes drinks and food are distributed. Depending on the ritual involved, these may be intended only as offerings, or else for your consumption. In the case of the latter, there's no offence taken if you don't eat or drink what's offered. For a description of An Evening of Candomblé see the Bahia chapter.

According to Candomblé, each person has an orixá (god) which attends from birth and provides protection throughout life. The orixá for each person is identified after a pai or mãe de santo makes successive throws with a handful of *búzios* (shells). In a divination ritual known as Jogo dos Búzios (Casting of Shells) the position of the shells is used to interpret your luck, your future and your past relation with the gods.

The Jogo dos Búzios can be traced back to numerology and cabalism. It is a simple version of the Ifa ceremony in which the orixá Ifa is invoked to transmit the words of the deities to the people. The mãe de santo casts 16 seashells on a white towel. She interprets the number and arrangement of face-up and face-down shells to predict the future.

The Jogo dos Búzios is a serious, respected force in Bahia. In 1985 it was used by many politicians to forecast the election results. In Salvador, visitors can consult a mãe de santo for Candomblé-style fortune telling any day of the week, except for Friday and Monday, but Thursday is best.

Like the gods in Greek mythology, each orixá has a personality and particular history. Power struggles and rulership conflicts amongst the many orixá are part of the history of Candomblé.

Although orixá are divided into male and female types, there are some which can switch from one sex to the other. One example is Logunedé, son of two male gods, Ogun and Oxoss. Another example is Oxumaré who is male for six months of the year and female for the other months. Oxumaré is represented by the river that runs from the mainland to the sea or by the rainbow. These bisexual gods are generally, but not necessarily, the gods of homosexuals. Candomblé is very accepting of homosexuality and this may explain the foundation of these practices and why they are legitimised by the cult's mythology.

To keep themselves strong and healthy, followers of Candomblé always give food to their respective orixá. In the ritual, Exú is the first to be given food because he is the messenger for the individual to make contact with the orixá. Exú likes *cachaça* and other alcoholic drinks, cigarettes, cigars, strong perfumes and meats. The offering to the orixá depends on their particular preferences. For example, to please Iemanjá, the goddess/queen of the sea, one should give perfumes, white and blue flowers, rice and fried fish. Oxalá, the greatest god, the god and owner of the sun, eats cooked white corn. Oxúm, god of fresh waters and waterfalls, is famous for his vanity. He should be honoured with earrings, necklaces, mirrors, perfumes, champagne and honey.

Each orixá is worshipped at a particular time and place. For example, Oxósse, who is the god of the forests, should be revered in a forest or park, but Xangô, the god of stone and justice, receives his offering in rocky places.

In Bahia and Rio, followers of Afro-Brazilian cults turn out in huge numbers to attend a series of festivals at the year's end – especially those held during the night of 31 December and on New Year's Day. Millions of Brazilians go to the beach to pay homage to Iemanjá, the queen of the sea. Flowers, perfumes, fruits and even jewellery are tossed into the sea to please the mother of the waters, or to gain protection and good luck in the new year.

Umbanda Umbanda, or white magic, is a mixture of Candomblé and spiritism. It traces its origins from various sources, but in its present form it is a religion native to Brazil. The African influence is more Angolan/Bantu. The ceremony, conducted in Portuguese, incorporates figures from all of the Brazilian races: *preto velho*, the old black slave, *o caboclo* and other Amerindian deities, *o guerreiro*, the white warrior, etc. In comparison to Candomblé, Umbanda is less organised and each pai or mãe de santo modifies the religion.

Quimbanda is the evil counterpart to Umbanda. It involves lots of blood, animal sacrifice and nasty deeds. The practice of Quimbanda is illegal.

Kardecism

During the 19th century, Allan Kardec, the French spiritual master, introduced spiritism to Brazilian whites in a palatable form. Kardec's teachings, which incorporated some Eastern religious ideas into a European framework, are now followed by large numbers of Brazilians. Kardecism emphasises spiritism associated with parlour seances, multiple reincarnations and speak-

ing to the dead. Kardec wrote about his teachings in *The Book of Spirits* and *The Book of Mediums*.

Other Cults

Brasília has become the capital of the new cults. In the Planaltina neighbourhood, visit Tia Neiva and the Vale do Amanhecer, and Eclética de Mestro Yocanan (see the Brasília chapter).

A few of the Indian rites have been popularised among Brazilians without becoming part of Afro-Brazilian cults. Two such cults are União da Vegetal in Brasília, São Paulo and the South; and Santo Daime in Rondônia and Acre. A hallucinogenic drink called *ayahuasca*, made from the root and vine of two plants, *cipó jagube* and *folha chacrona*, has been used for centuries by the indigenous peoples of South America. This drink is central to the practices of these cults, which are otherwise very straight – hierarchy, moral behaviour and dress follow a strict code. The government tolerates the use of ayahuasca in the religious ceremonies of these cults, which also tightly control the production and supply.

The cult of Santo Daime was founded in 1930 in Rio Branco, Acre, by Raimundo Irineu Serra. Today it claims around 10,000 members, including notable Brazilian figures such as the flamboyant singer Ney Matogrosso, the cartoonist Glauco, and the anthropologist Edward Macrae. The cult, led by Luís Felipe Belmonte, has 10 churches and communities in Brazil. The two major communities are Ceú da Mapiá in Amazonas, and Colônia Cinco Mil in Rio Branco, Acre.

LANGUAGE

Quem tem boca vai á Roma.
(If you can speak you can get to Rome.)

When they settled Brazil in the 16th century, the Portuguese encountered the diverse languages of the Indians. These, together with the various idioms and dialects spoken by the Africans brought in as slaves, extensively changed the Portuguese spoken by the early settlers.

Along with Portuguese, Tupi-Guaraní (language), written down and simplified by the Jesuits, became a common language which was understood by the majority of the population. It was spoken by the general public until the middle of the 18th century, but its usage diminished with the great number of Portuguese gold-rush immigrants and a royal proclamation in 1757 prohibiting its use. With the expulsion of the Jesuits in 1759, Portuguese was well and truly established as the national language.

Still, many words remain from the Indian and African languages. From Tupi-Guaraní come lots of place names (eg Guanabara, Carioca, Tijuca and Niterói), animal names (eg *piranha*, *capivara* and *urubu*) and plant names (eg *mandioca*, *abacaxí*, *caju* and *jacarandá*). Words from the African dialects, mainly those from Nigeria and Angola, are used in Afro-Brazilian religious ceremonies (eg *Orixá*, *Exú* and *Iansã*), cooking (eg *vatapá*, *acarajé* and *abará*) and in general conversation (eg *samba*, *mocambo* and *moleque*).

Within Brazil, accents, dialects and slang (*gíria*) vary regionally. The Carioca inserts the 'sh' sound in place of 's'. The *gaúcho* speak a Spanish-sounding Portuguese, the Baiano (from Bahia) speak slowly and the accents of the Cearense (from Ceará) are often incomprehensible to outsiders.

Portuguese is similar to Spanish on paper, but sounds completely different. You will do quite well if you speak Spanish in Brazil. Brazilians will understand what you say, but you won't get much of what they say. So don't think studying Portuguese is a waste of time. Listen to language tapes and develop an ear for Portuguese – it's a beautiful-sounding language.

Brazilians are very easy to befriend, but unfortunately the vast majority of them speak little or no English. This is changing, however, as practically all Brazilians in school are learning English. All the same, don't count on finding an English speaker, especially out of the cities. The more Portu-

guese you speak, the more you will get out of your trip.

Most phrasebooks are not very helpful. Their vocabulary is often dated and they contain the Portuguese spoken in Portugal, not Brazil. Notable exceptions are Lonely Planet's *Brazilian Phrasebook*, and a Berlitz phrasebook for travel in Brazil. Make sure any English-Portuguese dictionary is a Brazilian Portuguese one.

If you're more intent on learning the language, try the US Foreign Service Institute (FSI) tape series. It comes in two volumes. Volume 1, which includes 23 cassettes and accompanying text, costs US$130 and covers pronunciation, verb tenses and essential nouns and adjectives. Volume 2 includes 22 tapes with text and sells for US$115. It includes some useful phrases and a travel vocabulary.

For fluent Spanish speakers, FSI also has 'Portuguese – From Spanish to Portuguese', which consists of two tapes and a text explaining similarities and differences between these languages. This one costs US$20. To get hold of these, write to or call the National Audiovisual Centre (☎ (301) 763-1896), Information Services PF, 8700 Edgeworth Drive, Capitol Heights, Maryland, USA, 20743-3701.

In Australia, most foreign-language and travel bookstores stock a range of material, from the basic 'Travel Pack' with a phrasebook and two tapes for A$35, to a condensed version of the FSI tapes. A condensed version of the FSI tapes is available from Learn Australia Pty Ltd (☎ (008) 338-183), 726 High St, East Kew, Victoria, 3102. Twelve 90-minute tapes cost A$195. The 'Living Language' course is in-between, and it includes phrases, vocabulary, grammar and conversation. The manual and CD cost A$50.

Combine these with a few Brazilian samba tapes and some Jorge Amado novels and you're ready to begin the next level of instruction on the streets of Brazil. If that doesn't suffice, it's easy to arrange tutorial instruction through any of the Brazilian-American institutes where Brazilians go to learn English, or at the IBEU (Instituto Brazil Estados Unidos) in Rio.

Portuguese has masculine and feminine forms of nouns and adjectives. Alternative gender endings to words appear separated by a slash, the masculine form first. Generally, 'o' indicates masculine and 'a' indicates feminine.

Greetings & Civilities

Hello.	*Oi.*
Goodbye.	*Tchau.*
Good morning.	*Bom dia.*
Good afternoon.	*Boa tarde.*
Good evening.	*Boa noite.*
Please.	*Por favor.*
Thank you (very much).	*(Muito) obrigado.* (males)
	(Muita) obrigada. (females)
Yes.	*Sim.*
No.	*Não.*
Maybe.	*Talvez.*
Excuse me.	*Com licença.*
I am sorry.	*Desculpe (me perdoe).* (lit: forgive me)
How are you?	*Como vai você/Tudo bem?*
I'm fine thanks.	*Vou bem, obrigado/a.*
	Tudo bem, obrigado/a.

Language Difficulties

Please write it down.
   Escreva por favor.
Please show me (on the map).
   Por favor, me mostre (no mapa).
I (don't) understand.
   Eu (não) entendo.
I (don't) speak Portuguese.
   Eu (não) falo português.
Do you speak English?
   Você fala inglês?
Does anyone speak English?
   Alguem fala inglês?
How do you say ... in Portuguese?
   Como você fala ... em Português?
I have a visa/permit.
   Eu tenho um visto/uma licença.

Paperwork

Passport	*Passaporte*
Surname	*Sobrenome*
Given name	*Nome*
Date of birth	*Data de nascimento*
Place of birth	*Local de nascimento*
Nationality	*Nacionalidade*
Male/Female	*Masculino/Feminino*

Small Talk

What is your name?
   Qual é seu nome?
My name is ...
   Meu nome é ...
I'm a tourist/student.
   Eu sou um turista/estudante.
Where/What country are you from?
   Aonde/Da onde você é?
I am from ...
   Eu sou ...
How old are you?
   Quantos anos você tem?
I am ... years old.
   Eu tenho ... anos.
Are you married?
   Você é casado/a?
Do you like ...?
   Você gosta de ...?
I (don't) like ...
   Eu (não) gosta de ...
I like it very much.
   Eu gosta muito.
May I?
   Posso?
It's all right/No problem.
   Está tudo bem/Não há problema.

Getting Around

I want to go to ...
   Eu quero ir para ...
I want to book a seat for ...
   Eu quero reservar um assento para ...

What time does the ... leave/arrive?	*A que horas ... sai/chega?*
Where does the ... leave from?	*Da onde o/a ... sai?*
bus	*onibus*
tram	*bonde*
train	*trem*

boat	*barco*
ferry	*ferry* (sometimes called *balsa*)
aeroplane	*avião*

The train is ...	*O trem está ...*
delayed	*atrasado*
cancelled	*cancelado*
on time	*na hora*
early	*adiantado*

How long does the trip take?
Quanto tempo a viagem demora?
Do I need to change?
Eu precisa trocar?
You must change trains/platform.
Você precisa trocar de trem/plataforma.

one-way (ticket)	*passagem de ida*
return (ticket)	*passagem de volta*
station	*estação*
ticket	*passagem*
ticket office	*bilheteria*
timetable	*horário*

I would like to hire a ...	*Eu gostaria de alugar um/uma ...*
bicycle	*bicicleta*
motorcycle	*moto*
car	*carro*
guide	*guia*
horse	*cavalo*

Directions
How do I get to ...?
Como eu chego a ...?
Where is ...?
Aonde é ...?
Is it near/far?
É perto/longe?

What ... is this?	*O que é ... isto?*
street/road	*rua/estrada*
house number	*numero da casa*
suburb	*bairro*
town	*cidade*

Go straight ahead.	*Vá em frente.*
Turn left.	*Vire a esquerda.*
Turn right.	*Vire a direita.*

at the traffic lights	*no farol*
at the next corner	*na próxima esquina*

up/down	*acima/abaixo*
behind/opposite	*atrás/em frente*
here/there	*aqui/lá*
east	*leste*
west	*oeste*
north	*norte*
south	*sul*

Accommodation

I'm looking for the ...	*Eu estou procurando o/a ...*
youth hostel	*albergue da juventude*
camping ground	*camping*
hotel	*hotel*
guesthouse	*pousada*
manager	*gerente*
owner	*dono*

What is the address?
Qual é o endereço?

Do you have a ... available?	*Você tem um/uma ... para alugar?*
bed	*cama*
cheap room	*quarto barato*
single room	*quarto de solteiro*
double room	*quarto de casado*
room with two beds	*quarto com duas camas*

for one/two nights	*para uma/duas noites*

How much is it per night/per person?
Quanto é por noite/por pessoa?
Is service/breakfast included?
O serviço/café de manha está incluído?
Can I see the room?
Posso ver o quarto?

It is very ...	*É muito ...*
dirty	*sujo*
noisy	*barulhento*
expensive	*caro*

Where is the toilet?
Aonde é o banheiro?
I am/We are leaving now.
Eu estou/Nós estamos saindo agora.

Do you have ...? | *Você tem ...?*
a clean sheet | *um lençol limpo*
hot water | *água quente*
a key | *uma chave*
a shower | *um chuveiro*

Around Town

Where is the/a ...? | *Aonde é o/a ...?*
bank | *banco*
exchange office | *casa de câmbio*
city centre | *centro da cidade*
embassy | *embaixada*
hospital | *hospital*
market | *mercado/feira*
post office | *correio*
public toilet | *banheiro público*
restaurant | *restaurante*
telephone centre | *telefônica*

Signs

CAMPING	CAMPING GROUND
ENTRADA	ENTRANCE
SAIDA	EXIT
CHEIO	FULL
ABERTO	OPEN
FECHADO	CLOSED
HOMENS	GENTS'
MULHERES	LADIES'
POUSADA	GUESTHOUSE
HOTEL	HOTEL
INFORMAÇÃO	INFORMATION
POLÍCIA	POLICE
DELEGACIA	POLICE STATION
PROIBIDO	PROHIBITED
QUARTOS PARA ALUGAR	ROOMS AVAILABLE
BANHEIROS	TOILETS
ESTAÇÃO DE TREM	TRAIN STATION
ALBERGUE DA JUVENTUDE	YOUTH HOSTEL

---

tourist office | *posto de informações turísticas*

I'd like to change some ... | *Eu gostaria de trocar um pouco de ...*
money | *dinheiro*
travellers' cheques | *cheques de viagem*

bridge | *ponte*
cathedral | *catedral*
church | *igreja*
fort | *forte*
lake | *lago*
main square | *praça principal*
old city | *cidade velha*
palace | *palácio*
ruins | *ruínas*
square | *praça*
tower | *torre*

Food

breakfast | *café da manhã*
lunch | *almoço*
dinner | *jantar*
set menu | *refeição*
food stall | *barraca de comida*
grocery store | *mercearia*
delicatessen | *confeitaria*
restaurant | *restaurante*

I am hungry/thirsty.
Eu estou com fome/sede.
I would like the set lunch please.
Eu gostaria do prato feito por favor.
Is service included in the bill?
O serviço esta incluído na conta?
I am a vegetarian.
Eu sou vegetariano/a.
I would like some.
Eu gostaria de algumo/a.
Another ..., please.
Outro/a ..., por favor.
I don't eat ...
Eu não como ...

beer | *cerveja*
bread | *pão*

chicken	*frango*
coffee	*café*
eggs	*ovos*
fish	*peixe*
food	*comida*
fruit	*frutas*
meat	*carne*
milk	*leite*
mineral water	*água mineral*
pepper	*pimenta*
salt	*sal*
soup	*sopa*
sugar	*açucar*
tea	*chá*
vegetables	*verduras*
wine	*vinho*

Shopping

How much does it cost?
Quanto custa?
I would like to buy it.
Eu gostaria de comprar.
It's too expensive for me.
É muito caro para mim.
Can I look at it?
Posso ver?
I'm just looking.
Só estou olhando.

I'm looking for ...	*Estou procurando ...*
a chemist	*uma farmácia*
clothing	*roupas*
souvenirs	*lembranças*

Do you take travellers' cheques/credit cards?
Você aceita cheques de viagem/cartões de crédito?
Do you have another colour/size?
Você tem outra cor/tamanho?

big/bigger	*grande/maior*
small/smaller	*pequeno/menor*
more/less	*mais/menos*
cheap/cheaper	*barato/mais barato*

Times & Dates

What time is it?
Que horas são?

It's ...	*São ...*
1.15	*uma e quinze*
1.30	*uma e meia*
1.45	*uma e quarenta e cinco*

o'clock	*horas*
in the morning	*da manhã*
in the evening	*da noite*
When?	*Quando?*
yesterday	*ontem*
today	*hoje*
tonight	*hoje de noite*
tomorrow	*amanhã*
day after tomorrow	*depois de amanhã*
morning	*a manhã*
afternoon	*a tarde*
night	*a noite*
all day	*todos o dia*
every day	*todos os dias*

Sunday	*domingo*
Monday	*segunda-feira*
Tuesday	*terça-feira*
Wednesday	*quarta-feira*
Thursday	*quinta-feira*
Friday	*sexta-feira*
Saturday	*sábado*

January	*janeiro*
February	*fevereiro*
March	*março*
April	*abril*
May	*maio*
June	*junho*
July	*julho*
August	*agosto*
September	*setembro*
October	*outubro*
November	*novembro*
December	*dezembro*

Numbers

0	*zero*
1	*um/uma*
2	*dois/duas*
3	*três*
4	*quatro*
5	*cinco*

6	*seis* (when quoting telephone or house numbers, Brazilians will often say *meia* instead of *seis*)
7	*sete*
8	*oito*
9	*nove*
10	*dez*
11	*onze*
12	*doze*
13	*treze*
14	*catorze*
15	*quinze*
16	*dezesseis*
17	*dezessete*
18	*dezoito*
19	*dezenove*
20	*vinte*
30	*trinta*
40	*quarenta*
50	*cinqüenta*
60	*sessenta*
70	*setenta*
80	*oitenta*
90	*noventa*
100	*cem*
1000	*mil*
one million	*um milhão*
first	*primeiro*
last	*último*

Health

I'm allergic to penicillin/antibiotics.
Eu sou allergico/a a penicilina/antibiôticos

I'm ...	*Eu sou ...*
diabetic	*diabético/a*
epileptic	*epilético/a*
asthmatic	*asmático/a*

antiseptic	*antiséptico*
aspirin	*aspirina*
condoms	*camisinhas*
contraceptive	*contraceptivo*
diarrhoea	*diarréia*
medicine	*remédio*
nausea	*nausea*

| sunblock cream | *creme de proteção solar* |
| tampons | *absorventes internos* |

Emergencies

Help!	*Socorro!*
Go away!	*Va embora!*
Call a doctor!	*Chame o médico!*
Call the police!	*Chame a polícia!*

Slang

Brazilians pepper their language with strange oaths and odd expressions. Literal translations are in brackets:

Hello!	*Oi!*
Everything OK?	*Tudo bem?*
Everything's OK	*Tudo bom.*
That's great/Cool!	*Chocante!*
That's bad/Shit!	*Merda!*
Great/Cool/OK!	*'ta lógico/'ta ótimo/'ta legal!*
My God!	*Meu deus!*
It's crazy/You're crazy!	*'ta louco!*
Gosh!	*Nossa!* (Our Lady!)
Whoops!	*Opa!*
Wow!	*Oba!*
You said it!	*Falou!*
I'm mad at ...	*Eu estou chateado com ...*
Is there a way?	*Tem jeito?*
There's always a way.	*Sempre tem jeito.*
(curse word)	*Palavrão!*
shooting the breeze	*batendo um papo*
marijuana	*fumo* (smoke)
guy	*cara*
girl	*garota*
money	*grana*
bum	*bum-bum/bunda*
bald	*careca*
a mess	*bagunça*
a fix/troublesome problem	*abacaxí*
the famous 'Brazilian bikini'	*fio dental* (dental floss)

Body Language

Brazilians accompany their speech with a rich body language, a sort of parallel dialogue. The thumbs up of *tudo bem* is used as a greeting, or to signify 'OK' or 'Thank you'. The authoritative *não, não* finger-wagging is most intimidating when done right under someone's nose, but it's not a threat. The sign of the *figa*, a thumb inserted between the first and second fingers of a clenched fist, is a symbol of good luck that has been derived from an African sexual charm. It's more commonly used as jewellery than in body language.

To indicate *rápido* (speed and haste), thumb and middle finger touch loosely while rapidly shaking the wrist. If you don't want something (*não quero*), slap the back of your hands as if ridding yourself of the entire affair.

Touching a finger to the lateral corner of the eye means 'I'm wise to you'.

Facts for the Visitor

VISAS & EMBASSIES

At the time of writing, Brazilian visas were necessary for visitors who were citizens of countries which required visas for visitors from Brazil. American, Canadian, French, Australian and New Zealand citizens required visas, but UK citizens did not. Tourist visas are issued by Brazilian diplomatic offices and are valid for arrival in Brazil within 90 days of issue and then for a 90-day stay in Brazil. They are renewable in Brazil for an additional 90 days.

It should only take about three hours to issue a visa, but you need a passport valid for at least six months, a single passport photograph (either B&W or colour) and either a round-trip ticket or a statement from a travel agent, addressed to the Brazilian diplomatic office, stating that you have the required ticketing. If you only have a one-way ticket they may accept a document from a bank or similar organisation proving that you have sufficient funds to stay and buy a return ticket, but it's probably easier to get a letter from a travel agent stating that you have a round-trip ticket.

Visitors under 18 years of age must submit a notarised letter of authorisation from their parents or a legal guardian.

Tourist Card

When you enter Brazil, you will be asked to fill out a tourist card, which has two parts. Immigration officials will keep one part, and the other will be attached to your passport. When you leave Brazil, this will be detached from your passport by immigration officials. Make sure you don't lose your part of the card whilst travelling around Brazil. If you do lose your portion, your departure could be delayed until officials have checked your story. For added security, make a photocopy of your section of the tourist card and keep this in a safe place, separate from your passport.

Whilst researching we crossed the Brazil- ian border many times. At one stage, whilst travelling from Brazil to Uruguay, we missed the fact that the requisite part of our tourist card had not been collected on departure. Several weeks later, when we arrived at Ponta Porã on the Paraguay-Brazil border, the immigration authorities explained that we had not technically left Brazil! After considerable cogitation and some friendly banter, the officials asked us to make a certified deposition concerning the details of our 'disappearance'. Then the old cards were doctored, and we were issued with new cards.

Visa Extensions

The Polícia Federal handles visa extensions and they have offices in the major Brazilian cities. You must go to them before your visa lapses, or suffer the consequences. Don't leave it until the last minute either. Go for an extension about 15 days before your current visa expires. The tourist office can tell you where they are. In most cases a visa extension seems to be pretty automatic, but sometimes they'll only give you 60 days. The police may require a ticket out of the country and proof of sufficient funds, but this seems to be entirely at the discretion of the police officer.

When applying for an extension, you will be told to go to a *papelaria* (stationery shop) and buy a DARF form. (Sometimes this isn't necessary; it depends on the office you go to.) After filling it out, you must then go to a Banco do Brasil (or another bank nearby) and pay a fee of about US$12. You then return to the Polícia Federal with the DARF form stamped by the bank. The extension should then be routinely issued.

If you opt for the maximum 90-day extension and then leave the country before the end of that period, you cannot return until the full 90 days have elapsed. So if you plan to leave and re-enter Brazil you must schedule your dates carefully.

Brazilian Embassies & Consulates

Brazilian embassies and consulates are maintained in the following countries:

Australia
  19 Forster Crescent, Yarralumla, ACT 2600 (☎ (062) 732-372)
Canada
  255 Albert St, Suite 900, Ottawa, Ontario K1P-6A9 (☎ (613) 237-1090)
France
  34 Cours Albert, 1er, 75008 Paris (☎ (1) 259-9250)
Germany
  Kurfürstendamm 11, 1 Stock, 1 Berlin 15 (☎ (30) 883-1208)
UK
  32 Green St, London W1Y 4AT (☎ (0171) 499-0877)
USA
  630 Fifth Ave, Suite 2720, New York, NY 10111 (☎ (212) 757-3080); there are also consulates in Chicago (☎ (312) 372-2179), Houston (☎ (713) 961-3065), Los Angeles (☎ (213) 651-2664), Miami (☎ (305) 285-6200), and San Francisco (☎ (212) 981-1870)

New Zealanders must apply to the Brazilian Embassy in Australia for their visas; this can be done easily through a travel agent.

Visas for Adjoining Countries

The following information is intended as a rough guide only. Visa regulations are notoriously quick to change, so check them before you travel. For details of the relevant embassies and consulates, refer to individual cities mentioned.

Argentina
  Australians and New Zealanders require visas. Citizens of most West European countries, Canada and the USA do not. There are Argentine consulates in Porto Alegre, Foz do Iguaçu, Rio, São Paulo and Brasília.
Bolivia
  Australians, New Zealanders, Dutch, French, and Canadian citizens require visas. Citizens of the UK and the USA do not require visas. There are Bolivian consulates in Brasília, Rio, São Paulo, Corumbá, Campo Grande, Manaus and Guajará-Mirim.

Colombia
  Visas are no longer required to enter Colombia, except if you are a Chinese national. There are consulates in Brasília, Manaus, Rio, São Paulo, and Tabatinga.
Guyana
  Most visitors require visas. Guyana has consulates in Brasília and São Paulo.
French Guiana
  Citizens of the USA, Canada and the European Union do not require visas. Australians and New Zealanders require visas which can be obtained at French consulates in Brasília, Belém, Recife, Rio, São Paulo and Salvador.
Paraguay
  Australians and New Zealanders require visas. There are Paraguayan consulates in Brasília, Campo Grande, Corumbá, Curitiba, Foz do Iguaçu, Porto Alegre, Ponta Porã, Rio and São Paulo.
Peru
  Australians, New Zealanders and South Africans require visas. There are Peruvian consulates in Brasília, Manaus, Rio Branco, Belém, Rio and São Paulo.
Surinam
  Visas are not required by UK or Canadian citizens. There is an embassy for Surinam in Brasília.
Uruguay
  Australians and New Zealanders require visas. There are Uruguayan consulates in Brasília, Chuí, Jaguarão, Porto Alegre, Rio and São Paulo.
Venezuela
  All overland travellers require visas. There are Venezuelan consulates in Brasília, Manaus, Belém, Boa Vista, Porto Alegre, Rio and São Paulo.

DOCUMENTS

The only documents you really need are your passport and visa, an airline ticket and a yellow World Health Organisation health certificate and money.

By law you must carry a passport with you at all times, but many travellers opt to carry a photocopy (preferably certified). A credit card is quite handy, as is a Hostelling International card if you plan to use the *albergues de juventude* (youth hostels). The International Student Identity Card is practically useless. To rent a car you must be at least 25 years old, and have a credit card and a valid driver's licence. You should also carry an

International Driver's Permit or Inter-Americas licence.

It's convenient to have several extra passport photographs for any documents or visas you might acquire in Brazil. As a backup for emergencies, it's handy to have photocopies of the following: your passport (including relevant visas), tourist card (provided when entering Brazil), travellers' cheque numbers, and airline tickets. For more hints on safety, see the Security section under Dangers & Annoyances in this chapter.

CUSTOMS

Travellers entering Brazil are allowed to bring in one radio, tape player, typewriter, video and still camera. Personal computers are allowed.

At airport customs, they use the random check system. After collecting your luggage you pass a post with two buttons; if you have nothing to declare, you push the appropriate button. A green light means walk straight out; a red light means you've been selected for a baggage search.

Customs searches at land borders are more thorough, especially if you're coming from Bolivia.

MONEY
Currency

Since 1986 the name of the currency has changed five times, from cruzeiro to cruzado to cruzado novo and back to cruzeiro. Then it became the cruzeiro real and, in July 1994, the real.

At the moment, the monetary unit of Brazil is the real (pronounced HAY-ow); the plural is reais (pronounced HAY-ice). It's made up of 100 centavos. The frustratingly similar coins are: one, five, 10, 25 and 50 centavos. There's also a one-real coin as well as a one-real note. The notes are different colours, so there's no mistaking them. As well as the green one-real note there's a blue/purple five, a red 10, a brown 50 and a blue 100.

Exchange Rates

There are currently three types of exchange rate operating in Brazil: official (also known as *comercial* or *câmbio livre*), *turismo* and *paralelo*.

Until recently, the official rate has always been much lower than the parallel rate. A few years ago, all dollars exchanged at banks were changed at the official rate as were all credit card transactions, making it an extremely unfavourable transaction. But thanks to a certain amount of deregulation in an attempt to wipe out black-market trading it's now possible to change cash dollars and travellers' cheques at banks using the turismo rate, which is only slightly less than the parallel rate.

Since the introduction of the Plano Real, the difference between the official and parallel rates has been minimal. Full parallel rates are usually available only at borders and in the larger cities like Rio and São Paulo.

Exchange rates are written up every day on the front page and in the business sections of the major daily papers: *O Globo*, *Jornal do Brasil* and the *Folha de São Paulo*. The rates are always announced on the evening TV news.

Approximate bank rates as at July 1995 were as follows:

Australia	A$1	=	R$0.66
Canada	C$1	=	R$0.67
France	FFr1	=	R$0.19
Germany	DM1	=	R$0.67
Japan	Y100	=	R$1.09
New Zealand	NZ$1	=	R$0.62
Switzerland	SwFr1	=	R$0.81
United Kingdom	UK£1	=	R$1.49
USA	US$1	=	R$0.92

Cash & Travellers' Cheques

US cash dollars are easier to trade and are worth a bit more on the parallel market, but travellers' cheques are an insurance against loss. Now that they can be exchanged at the turismo rate, they are good value and it's good sense to use them. They can be hard to change sometimes, and that's why you might prefer to carry a Visa card (see Credit Cards).

American Express is the most recognised

credit card, but they charge 1% of the face value of the cheque (on top of the interest that your money makes while sitting in their banks). Sometimes, with lost cheques they can be a little reluctant to give your money back on the spot. American Express has offices in Rio de Janeiro, Salvador, Recife, Maceió, Natal, Fortaleza, Belém, Manaus, Campo Grande, Brasília, Floranópolis, Curitiba, Belo Horizonte and São Paulo. Thomas Cook, Barclays and First National City Bank travellers' cheques are also good. Get travellers' cheques in US dollars and carry some small denominations for convenience. Have some emergency US cash to use when the banks are closed.

Learn in advance how to get refunds from your travellers' cheque company. Keep a close, accurate and current record of your travellers' cheque expenditures. This speeds up the refund process. Guard your travellers' cheques – they are valuable to thieves even without your counter signature.

Changing Money

Changing money in Brazil is easy in the large cities. Almost anyone can direct you to a *casa de câmbio* (money exchange house). Many casas de câmbio sprang up in response to the deregulation of foreign currency by the federal government a few years ago.

Most large banks now have a foreign section where you can change money at the slightly lower turismo rate, but sometimes this may involve a bit of time-wasting bureaucracy. At present, the two banks officially allowed to change travellers' cheques are Banco do Brasil and Banco Econômico, but you can also exchange travellers' cheques at most casas de câmbio. Make sure you ask them before you sign the cheque.

In small towns without a bank, you'll have to ask around. Someone will usually be able to direct you to someone who buys cash dollars.

Changing money at weekends, even in the big cities, can be extremely difficult, so make sure you have enough to last until Monday. If you do get stuck, the best places to try are the large hotels, expensive restaurants, travel agents, jewellery stores or souvenir shops. Be prepared to lose a few dollars on the transaction.

Don't change money on the streets, follow exchangers into unfamiliar areas or give money or unsigned cheques up front.

Small Change

There is a chronic shortage of change in Brazil. When you change money, for example at the Banco do Brasil, ask for lots of small bills – and take very few notes in denominations larger than the equivalent of US$10. Change, variously referred to as *troco* or *miúdo*, is often unobtainable at newsagents, restaurants, street stalls, in taxis, on buses, etc. Although the shortage clearly exists, it is also commonly used as an excuse to simply retain a fat tip. If you encounter this problem, insist that the seller finds change and hang around until it is procured. If you want to find out if the seller has change – preferably *before* you purchase – ask *'tem troco?'* (do you have change?). If you want to convey that you don't have change, say *'não tem troco'* (there is no change) which makes it clear that you neither have change nor have been able to find any in the vicinity – thus heading off the seller's inevitable request that you hunt around the vicinity! Sometimes sweets are used instead of small change.

Credit Cards

International credit cards like Visa, American Express and MasterCard are accepted by many expensive hotels, restaurants and shops. But it's surprising how many don't accept credit cards. Make sure you ask first if you plan to use one.

Visa is the most versatile credit card in Brazil, and getting cash advances with a Visa card is becoming easier. International Visa card holders can even use the Bradesco bank's automatic teller machines. Get hold of a list of ATM locations from one of their branches. Banco do Brasil also gives cash advances on Visa, and according to them, it won't be long before Visa card holders will be able to use the 24-hour ATM system that has distinctive red booths in almost every sizeable town.

Visa cash advances are widely available at the Banco do Brasil, Banco Econômico and Bradesco, even in some small towns with no other exchange facilities. Using Visa cash withdrawals can be a useful backup in these situations, or a good alternative to carrying travellers' cheques, which can be hard to change.

Many travellers to Brazil are now using this system instead of travellers' cheques or cash (though it's good to carry cash for emergencies). Simply put your travelling money into your Visa account so it's in credit, and you won't even have to worry about getting someone at home to pay your bills.

American Express card holders can purchase US-dollar travellers' cheques from Amex offices in the large cities.

MasterCard holders can pay for many goods and services with their card, but cash advances are difficult.

At present, you get billed at the turismo rate in reais. Sometimes, the hotel, restaurant or store will try to add an extra charge for using the card. It's illegal to do this, and you can make a complaint to the relevant credit card company, which may decide to terminate its contract with the offending establishment. Vote for fair play with your credit card!

New-style credit card coupons do not have carbon paper inserts and offer more protection against misuse. If you sign an old-style coupon, be sure to ask for the carbon inserts and destroy them after use; a worthwhile precaution against duplication.

Buying Foreign Cash

Brazilians and foreigners can buy and sell dollars with no restriction. Many casas de câmbio have appeared in the cities and larger towns to cater for the market.

Costs

Because of wild fluctuations in the economy, it's difficult to make any solid predictions about how much you'll spend. During our first couple of trips to Brazil in 1984 and '85,

prices were frozen in an attempt to halt inflation and budget travel was ridiculously cheap, as the value of the dollar kept rising on the black market. Then, on another trip in early 1990, just after Collor froze everyone's bank accounts, prices skyrocketed and budget travellers headed for the borders as fast as they could. During one research trip, there was a price freeze which caused the cheap hotels (which don't take much notice of price freezes anyway) to become relatively expensive and the more expensive hotels to be relatively cheap.

Now for the bad news. Since the introduction of the real, inflation has fallen to less than 2% per month, and although this inflation rate is still well above the US level, the real has appreciated by about 15% against the US dollar because of increased US-dollar flow into Brazil. As a result, Brazil has become a somewhat expensive destination for foreign travellers.

Since our last edition, prices have risen anywhere from 30 to 100%. How long it will stay this way is uncertain, though prices should drop off a bit from their current 'unreal' levels.

If you're travelling on buses every couple of days, staying in hotels for US$10 a night, and eating in restaurants and/or drinking in bars every night, US$30 to US$40 a day is a rough estimate of what you would need. It's possible to do it for less of course. If you plan to lie on a beach for a month, eating rice, beans and fish every day, US$15 to US$20 would be enough. You should also bear in mind that during the holiday season (December to February) accommodation costs generally increase by around 25 to 30%, sometimes more in popular resorts.

Brazil is not among the kinder destinations for solo travellers. The cost of a single room in a hotel is not much less than for a double, and when you eat, you'll find most dishes in restaurants are priced for two people.

Tipping

Most services get tipped 10%, and as the people in these services make the minimum wage – which is not enough to live on – you can be sure they need the money. In restaurants the service charge will usually be included in the bill and is mandatory. If a waiter is friendly and helpful you can give more. Even when it is not included, it's still customary to leave a 10% tip; unless the service is atrocious, the waiter shouldn't be punished for giving you the option. There are many places where tipping is not customary but is a welcome gesture. The local juice stands, bars, coffee corners, street and beach vendors are all tipped on occasion.

Because of the massive amount of unemployment in Brazil, some services that may seem superfluous are customarily tipped anyway. Parking assistants are the most notable, as they receive no wages and are dependent on tips, usually the equivalent of 25c to 50c. Petrol-station attendants, shoe shiners and barbers are also frequently tipped.

Taxi drivers are not usually tipped. Most people round the price up, but tipping is not expected.

Bargaining
Bargaining for hotel rooms should become second nature. Before you agree to take a room, ask for a better price. '*Tem desconto?*' (Is there a discount?) and '*Pode fazer um melhor preço?*' (Can you give a better price?) are the phrases to use. There's often a discount for paying *á vista* (cash) or for staying during the *baixa estação* or *época baixa* (low season) when hotels need guests to cover running costs. It's also possible to reduce the price if you state that you don't want a TV, private bath, or air-con. If you're staying longer than a couple of days, ask for a discount. Once a discount has been quoted, make sure it is noted on your bill at the same time – this avoids misunderstandings at a later date. Bargain also in markets and in unmetered taxis.

WHEN TO GO
See the Climate section in the Facts about the Country chapter for details of seasonal factors that may influence your decision on when to visit the country. There are few regions that can't be comfortably visited all year round.

WHAT TO BRING
The happiest travellers are those who can slip all their luggage under their plane seats. Pack light. Backpacks with detachable daypacks make a versatile combination. Travel packs are backpacks which can be converted into more civilised-looking suitcases. They are cleverly compartmentalised, and have internal frames and special padding.

Use small padlocks to secure your pack, particularly if you have to leave it unattended in one of the more down-market hotels that you are bound to encounter. For more details about security, refer to the section on Dangers & Annoyances in this chapter.

What you bring will be determined by what you do. If you're planning a river or jungle trip read the Amazon chapter in advance. If you're travelling cheap, a cotton sheet sleeping-sack will come in handy.

With its warm climate and informal dress standards, you don't need to bring many clothes to Brazil. Except for the South and Minas Gerais, where it gets cold in the winter, the only weather you need to contend with is heat and rain, and whatever you're lacking you can purchase while travelling. Buying clothes in Brazil is easy and has the added advantage of helping you appear less like a tourist – if you like to stand out in a crowd try wearing Birkenstock sandals and an American-style bathing suit on Brazil's beaches. The only exception is if you wear big sizes, which can be difficult to find, particularly for shoes.

However, you should be aware that unlike other basic necessities, clothing is not particularly cheap in Brazil. Shoes are the notable exception. You can get some good deals on leather shoes. Tennis shoes are the norm in Brazil, as are light jeans. Bring a pair of comfortable shorts and a light rain jacket. Bring your smallest bathing suit – men and women – which will certainly be much too modest for Brazil's beaches. So plan on buying a Brazilian suit (*maiô*) anyway. There are many funny T-shirts that are practical garments to buy along the way, and are also good souvenirs.

You don't need to pack more than a pair of shorts, trousers, a couple of T-shirts, a long-sleeved shirt, bathing suit, towel, underwear, walking shoes, thongs and some rain gear. Quick-drying, light cotton clothes are the most convenient. Suntan lotion and sun-protection cream are readily available in Brazil. Most other toiletries (even the same brand names) are also easy to get.

Usually, one set of clothes to wear and one to wash is adequate. It's probably a good idea if one set of clothes is somewhat presentable or could pass as dress-up for a good restaurant or club (or to renew your visa at the federal police station). While dress is informal, many Brazilians are very fashion conscious and pay close attention to both their own appearance and yours.

For information regarding compiling a basic medical kit, see the Health section in this chapter.

TOURIST OFFICES
Local Tourist Offices
Embratur, the Brazilian Tourist Board, has moved its headquarters to Brasília, but still maintains an office in Rio de Janeiro at Rua Mariz e Barros 13 on the 14th floor (☎ 273-2212; fax 273-9290).

In Brasília, their address is: Embratur, Setor Comercial Norte, Quadra 2, Bloco G, Brasília, DF, CEP 70710 (☎ 224-2872).

Tourist offices elsewhere in Brazil are generally sponsored by individual states and municipalities. In many places, these offices rely on shoestring budgets which are chopped or maintained according to the whims (or feuds!) of regional and local politicians. Some tourist offices clearly function only as a sinecure for the family and relatives of politicians; others have dedicated and knowledgeable staff who are interested in providing information. Some offices are conveniently placed in the centre of town; others are so far out of range that you'll spend an entire day getting there. Keep your

sense of humour, prepare for pot luck and don't expect too much!

Overseas Reps
Brazilian consulates and embassies are able to provide limited tourist information.

USEFUL ORGANISATIONS
One of the most useful sources for visitors to South America is the South American Explorers Club, 126 Indian Creek Road, Ithaca, New York, USA 14850. This club provides services, information and support to travellers, scientific researchers, mountaineers and explorers. It also sells a wide range of books, guides, and maps for South America, and publishes a quarterly journal and a mail-order catalogue. If you're travelling elsewhere in South America, the club maintains clubhouses in Ecuador and Peru. Considering the massive package of benefits offered, membership is quite a bargain.

The Brazilian American Cultural Center (BACC) (☎ (212) 7301010; or toll-free (1-800) 222-2746), 16 West 46th St, New York, NY 10036, USA, is a tourism organisation which offers its members discounted flights and tours. Members also receive a monthly newspaper about Brazil and the Brazilian community in the USA, and can send money to South America using BACC's remittance service. The organisation can also secure tourist visas for members through the Brazilian Consulate in New York.

For information about the growing network of Brazilian youth hostels, contact the Federação Brasileira dos Albergues de Juventude (FBAJ) (☎ (021) 252-4829), Rua da Assembléia 10, sala 1211 Centro, Rio de Janeiro, CEP 20011, RJ. Include an envelope and postage.

Disabled travellers in the USA might like to contact the Society for the Advancement of Travel for the Handicapped (☎ (718) 858-5483), 26 Court St, Brooklyn, New York, NY 11242. In the UK, a useful contact is the Royal Association for Disability & Rehabilitation (☎ (0171) 242-3882), 25 Mortimer St, London W1N 8AB.

BUSINESS HOURS & HOLIDAYS
Business Hours

Most shops and government services (eg post offices) are open Monday to Friday from 9 am to 6 pm and Saturday from 9 am to 1 pm. Because many Brazilians have little free time during the week, Saturday morning is usually spent shopping. Some shops stay open later than 6 pm in the cities and the huge shopping malls often stay open until 10 pm and open on Sunday as well. Banks, always in their own little world, are generally open from 10 am to 4.30 pm. Câmbios often open an hour later, when the daily dollar rates are available. Business hours vary by region and are taken less seriously in remote locations.

Holidays

National holidays fall on the following dates:

1 January
New Year's Day
6 January
Epiphany
February or March (four days before Ash Wednesday)
Carnival
March or April
Easter & Good Friday
21 April
Tiradentes Day
1 May
May Day
June
Corpus Christi
7 September
Independence Day
12 October
Our Lady of Aparecida Day
2 November
All Souls' Day
15 November
Proclamation Day
25 December
Christmas Day

Most states have several additional local holidays when everyone goes fishing.

FESTIVALS & CULTURAL EVENTS
Major festivals include:

January
Torneio de Repentistas (Olinda, Pernambuco)
Festa de São Lázaro (Salvador, Bahia)

1 January
New Year & Festa de Iemanjá (Rio de Janeiro)
Procissão do Senhor Bom Jesus dos Navegantes (Salvador, Bahia)
1 to 20 January
Folia de Reis (Parati, Rio de Janeiro)
3 to 6 January
Festa do Reis (Carpina, Pernambuco)
6 to 15 January
Festa de Santo Amaro (Santo Amaro, Bahia)
Second Sunday in January
Bom Jesus dos Navegantes (Penedo, Alagoas)
Second Thursday in January
Lavagem do Bonfim (Salvador, Bahia)
24 January to 2 February
NS de Nazaré (Nazaré, Bahia)
February
Grande Vaquejada do Nordeste (Natal, Rio Grande do Norte)
2 February
Festa de Iemanjá (Salvador, Bahia)
First Saturday in February
Buscada de Itamaracá (Itamaracá, Pernambuco)
February or March
Lavagem da Igreja de Itapoã (Itapoã, Bahia)
Shrove Tuesday (and the preceding three days to two weeks, depending on the place)
March
Procissão do Encontro (Salvador, Bahia)
After Easter Week (usually April)
Feiras dos Caxixis (Nazaré, Bahia)
Mid-April
Drama da Paixão de Cristo (Brejo da Madre de Deus, Pernambuco)
15 days after Easter (April or May)
Cavalhadas (Pirenópolis, Goiás)
45 days after Easter (between 6 May and 9 June)
Micareta (Feira de Santana, Bahia)
Late May or early June
Festa do Divino Espírito Santo (Parati, Rio de Janeiro)
June
Festas Juninas & Bumba Meu Boi (celebrated throughout June in much of the country, particularly São Luís, Belém and throughout Pernambuco and Rio states)
Festival Folclórico do Amazonas (Manaus, Amazonas)
22 to 24 June
São João (Cachoeira, Bahia & Campina Grande, Paraíba)
July
Festa do Divino (Diamantina, Minas Gerais)
Regata de Jangadas Dragão do Mar (Fortaleza, Ceará)
17 to 19 July
Missa do Vaqueiro (Serrita, Pernambuco)
Mid-August
Festa da NS de Boa Morte (Cachoeira, Bahia)

Balloons & Festa Junina

Festa Junina is the party celebrated during June throughout Brazil. Streets are closed to traffic and ornamented with flags and lanterns to imitate an *arraial* (village street). Stalls sell traditional country-style food and *quentão* (hot spiced wine), and a bonfire is lit in the evening. People, in *caipira* (daggy, hick-style dress), perform square dances and a mock wedding to Brazilian country music.

During this time *baloeiros* (balloon makers) get together to construct gigantic paper balloons, some up to 30 metres high. The balloons rise filled with hot air produced by a giant blazing cloth soaked in wax and kerosene. Although many of the balloons are launched from the favelas, much money and energy goes into their materials and construction. Some carry elaborate lighting frames with illuminated pictures and slogans and dozens of kg in fireworks! Although officially banned, one night in Rio we counted twenty such balloons in the sky simultaneously! The fire brigade is kept busy and a local bus in Rio was recently set alight by someone taking fireworks home for Festa Junina. ∎

15 August
    Festa de Iemanjá (Fortaleza, Ceará)
September
    Festival de Cirandas (Itamaracá, Pernambuco)
    Cavalhada (Caeté, Minas Gerais)
12 & 13 September
    Vaquejada de Surubim (Surubim, Pernambuco)
October (second half)
    NS do Rosário (Cachoeira, Bahia)
12 October
    Festa de Nossa Senhora Aparecida (Aparecida, São Paulo)
Starting second Sunday in October
    Círio de Nazaré (Belém, Pará)
November
    NS da Ajuda (Cachoeira, Bahia)
1 & 2 November
    Festa do Padre Cícero (Juazeiro do Norte, Ceará)
4 to 6 December
    Festa de Santa Barbara (Salvador, Bahia)
8 December
    Festa de Nossa Senhora da Conceição (Salvador, Bahia)
    Festa de Iemanjá (Belém, Pará & João Pessoa, Paraíba)
31 December
    Celebração de Fim de Ano & Festa do Iemanjá (Rio de Janeiro)

POST & TELECOMMUNICATIONS

Postal Rates

Postal services are pretty good in Brazil, although one of the authors had about a 50% success rate in receiving letters, and a parcel he sent to Lonely Planet in Australia took 6 weeks and had been torn open.

Most mail seems to get through, and airmail letters to the USA and Europe usually arrive in a week or so. For Australia, allow two weeks. The cost, however, is ridiculously high for mail leaving Brazil, around US$1 for an international letter or postcard. Rates are raised very frequently, and are now amongst the highest in the world.

There are mail boxes on the street but it's a better idea to go to a post office. Most post offices (*correios*) are open 9 am to 6 pm Monday to Friday, and Saturday morning.

Receiving Mail

The *posta restante* system seems to function reasonably well and they will hold mail for 30 days. A reliable alternative for American Express customers is to have mail sent to one of its offices.

Telephone

International Calls Phoning abroad from Brazil is very expensive, and charges continue to be revised upwards at frequent intervals. To the USA and Canada it costs approximately US$2.50 a minute. Prices are 25% lower from 8 pm to 6 am daily and all day Sunday. To the UK and France the charge is US$3 a minute, and to Australia and New Zealand US$4 a minute. There are no cheaper times to these last two countries.

Every town has a *posto telefônico* (phone company office) for long-distance calls, which require a large deposit. If you're calling direct from a private phone dial 00, then the country code, then the area code, then the phone number. So to call New York, you dial 001-212-phone number. For information on international calls dial 000333. Country codes include: UK 44, USA 1, Australia 61, New Zealand 64, Canada 1, France 33, Argentina 54, Chile 56, Peru 51, Paraguay 595.

Embratel, the Brazilian telephone monopoly, now offers Home Country Direct Services for Australia (☎ 000-8061), Canada (☎ 000-8014), France (☎ 000-8033), Germany (☎ 000-8049), Israel (☎ 000-8097), Italy (☎ 000-8039), Japan (☎ 000-8081), the Netherlands (☎ 000-8031), the UK (☎ 000-8044) and the USA (☎ 000-8010 for AT&T, 000-8012 for MCI and 000-8016 for Sprint)

International collect calls (*a cobrar*) can be made from any phone. To get the international operator dial 000111 or 107 and ask for the *telefonista internacional*. If they don't speak English you could experiment with some of the following phrases:

I would like to make an international call to...
   Quero fazer uma ligação internacional para...
I would like to reverse the charges.
   Quero fazê-la a cobrar.
I am calling from a public (private) telephone in Rio de Janeiro.
   Estou falando dum telefone público (particular) no Rio de Janeiro.
My name is...
   Meu nôme é...
The area code is...
   O código é...
The number is...
   O número é...

If you're having trouble, reception desks at the larger hotels can be helpful. Also, the phone books explain all this, but in Portuguese (although some have English translations).

National Calls National long-distance calls can also be made at the local phone company

office, unless you're calling collect. All you need is the area code and phone number, and a few dollars. For calling collect within Brazil, dial 9 – area code – phone number. A recorded message in Portuguese will ask you to say your name and where you're calling from, after the beep. The person at the other end then decides if they will accept the call.

Area codes for the major cities are as follows:

Aracaju – 079
Belém – 091
Belo Horizonte – 031
Boa Vista – 095
Brasília – 061
Campo Grande – 067
Cuiabá – 065
Curitiba – 041
Florianópolis – 0482
Fortaleza – 085
Goiânia – 062
Macapá – 096
Maceió – 082
Manaus – 092
Natal – 084
Porto Alegre – 0512
Porto Velho – 069
Recife – 081
Rio Branco – 068
Rio de Janeiro – 021
Salvador – 071
São Luís – 098
São Paulo – 011
Teresina – 086
Vitória – 027

Local Calls Brazilian public phones are nicknamed *orelhões* (big ears). They use *fichas*, coin-like tokens, which can be bought at many newsstands, pharmacies, etc. They cost less than US$0.05, but it's a good idea to buy a few extra fichas as phones often consume them liberally.

On almost all phones in Brazil you wait for a dial tone and then deposit the ficha and dial your number. Each ficha is generally good for a couple of minutes, but the time can vary considerably. When your time is up, you will be disconnected without warning, so it's a good idea to deposit an extra ficha. To call the operator dial 100, and for information call 102.

Phonecards are now widely available. They cost US$1.20 and are good for around 20 local calls. They're a good alternative to carrying round a pocket full of fichas.

Phone Books There are several kinds of *lista telefônica* (telephone book) available. In larger cities there are two types of lista: *assinantes*, which lists names in alphabetical order; and *endereço*, which lists street names in alphabetical order followed by house numbers, and the householder's name and phone number. The Brazilian equivalent of yellow pages is called Páginas Amarelas. Phone books for other parts of the country can be found at the larger telephone offices. Recently, telephone companies have been including excellent maps in phone books – see the Books & Maps section later in this chapter.

Fax, Telex & Telegraph
Post offices send and receive telegrams and the larger branches also have fax services. Faxes cost US$13 per page to the USA and Canada, US$20 to Australia and New Zealand, and US$16 to the UK.

TIME
'Delay in Brazil is a climate. You live in it. You can't get away from it. There is nothing to be done about it...a man in a hurry will be miserable in Brazil.'
(*Brazilian Adventure* by Peter Fleming)

Brazil has four official time zones, generally depicted on maps as a neat series of lines. However, in the real world, these lines are subject to administrative convenience. This means that travellers are subject to the vagaries (and inconvenience) of geodesic demarcation, state boundaries, and the euphemistic term that saves the bacon of all officials – *acidentes geográficos* (geographical accidents). The Brazilian time system rewards unhurried travellers moving short distances – most other travellers have a few tales to tell about connections missed due to temporal ignorance.

The standard time zone for Brazil covers the eastern, north-eastern, southern, and south-eastern parts of Brazil, including Brasília, Amapá, Goiás, Tocantins, and a portion of Pará. This zone is three hours behind GMT. So when it is noon in Brazil it is 3 pm in London; 10 am in New York; 7 am in San Francisco; 1 am the next day in Sydney or Melbourne and 11 pm in New Zealand.

Moving westwards, the next time zone covers Roraima, Rondônia, Mato Grosso, Mato Grosso do Sul, part of Pará and all but the far western fringe of Amazonas. This zone is one hour behind Brazilian standard time, and four hours behind GMT.

The time zone for the far west covers Acre and the western fringe of Amazonas, which are two hours behind Brazilian standard time, and five hours behind GMT.

The island of Fernando de Noronha, far to the east of the Brazilian mainland, has its own time zone, which is one hour ahead of standard Brazilian time, and two hours behind GMT.

Finally, connoisseurs of Brazilian time-keeping will be thrilled to hear that all these time zones may vary if Brazil continues to adopt daylight-savings time, which requires clocks to be set one hour ahead in October, and one hour back in March or April.

Brazilians, by the way, are not noted for their punctuality! Don't be surprised, or angry, if they arrive a couple of hours later than expected. To them it is acceptable, and they always have the most inventive reasons for not arriving on time. If you find yourself arriving late, you might like to blame it on an accident – geographical perhaps?

ELECTRICITY
Electrical current is not standardised in Brazil, so it's a good idea to carry an adaptor if you can't travel without your hair drier. In Rio de Janeiro and São Paulo, the current is almost exclusively 110 or 120 volts, 60 cycles AC. Salvador and Manaus have 127-volt service. Recife, Brasília and various other cities have 220-volt service. Check before you plug in.

Speaking of plugs, the most common power points have two round sockets.

LAUNDRY

If you own the kind of clothes we do, it's cheaper to buy new ones than to have them cleaned at many city laundromats. While all other services are cheap in Brazil, oddly, washing clothes isn't, at least if you send out. Most Brazilians wash their own clothes or have domestics do it. If you don't wish to wash your own, enquire at your hotel, as often the housekeepers will wash clothes at home to make a few extra reais.

WEIGHTS & MEASURES

Brazil uses the metric system. There is a metric conversion table at the back of this book.

BOOKS
History

Brazil has a fascinating and fantastic history, but for some reason none of the good surveys of Brazilian history have been translated into English. So the best way to go, if you want to understand the flow of Brazilian history in English, is via several of the excellent narratives.

John Hemming's *Red Gold: The Conquest of the Brazilian Indians* follows the colonists and Indians from 1500 to 1760, when the great majority of Indians were effectively either eliminated or pacified. Hemming, a founder of Survival International and eloquent campaigner for Indian rights, has extended his analysis of Indian history in *Amazon Frontier: The Defeat of the Brazilian Indians* (Harvard University Press, 1987).

Caio Prado Junior, Brazil's leading economic historian, presents a descriptive analysis of the legacy of Brazil's colonial past in *The Colonial Background of Modern Brazil*. It's probably the single best interpretation of the colonial period in English. Prado presents a sweeping view of Brazil's lack of development, which he blames on the export-based economy and the social relations of slavery.

Celso Furtado, a leading economist and the current Minister of Culture in Brazil, has written a good introductory economic history of the country titled *The Economic Growth of Brazil* (Greenwood, 1984).

Charles R Boxer is from the good old school of British economic history, which took writing seriously. All his books are fine reading and illuminating history. His *Golden Age of Brazil, 1695-1750* (University of California Press, 1962) has an excellent introductory chapter summarising life in 17th-century Brazil, and then focuses on the gold rush in Minas Gerais and its consequences in the rest of the colony. Boxer has also written *Salvador de Sá & the Struggle for Brazil & Angola, 1602-1686* and *The Dutch in Brazil, 1624-1654*.

The most famous book on Brazil's colonial period is Gilberto Freyre's *The Masters & the Slaves: A Study in the Development of Brazilian Civilization* (University of California Press, 1986). There's a new paperback edition from the University of California Press, which also publishes Freyre's other works: *The Mansions & the Shanties: The Making of Modern Brazil* (University of California Press, 1986) and *Order & Progress: Brazil from Monarchy to Republic* (University of California Press, 1986).

Freyre's argument that Brazilian slavery was less harsh than in the USA and that through miscegenation Brazil has avoided the racial problems of the USA is deeply flawed. It contributed to the myth of racial democracy in Brazil and has been severely rebuked by academics over the last 20 years. Still, Freyre's books can be read on many levels, including social history, and there are fascinating comments on folklore, myths and superstition, religion and sexuality.

Emília Viotti da Costa has a collection of well-written essays in English which is one of the best treatments of 19th-century Brazil. *The Brazilian Empire: Myths & Histories* (University of Chicago Press, 1986) interweaves the ideological and economic components of Brazilian history, and the results are illuminating and suggestive. Her essays, particularly on slavery and the landless poor, explode many of the harmony myths that hide the realities of oppression and poverty.

The English narratives on 20th-century Brazilian history are less satisfying. Peter Flynn's *Brazil: A Political Analysis* presents a political history from 1889 to 1977. Thomas Skidmore's *Politics in Brazil, 1930-1964* is good. And Irving L Horowitz covers the Goulart era in *Revolution in Brazil*.

Alfred Stepan has edited a collection of essays called *Authoritarian Brazil: Origins, Policies & Future* (Yale University Press, 1973). These are often heavy with theory, but quite interesting, particularly the essays by Fishlow, Cardoso and Schmitter.

Finally, the not-to-be-believed rebellion in Canudos by the followers of the mystic Antônio Conselheiro has been immortalised in *Rebellion in the Backlands* (University of Chicago Press, 1985), by Euclides da Cunha. Mixing history, geography and philosophy, *Os Sertões* (in Portuguese) is considered the masterpiece of Brazilian literature. It's an incredible story about the outcasts of the Northeast, and is a sort of meditation on Brazilian civilisation. The story of the author and the rebellion is told by Mário Vargas Llosa in his novel *The War of the End of the World* (Avon Bard, 1985); entertaining, light reading for the traveller.

Fiction

For a description of Brazilian literature and suggested reading, refer to the Arts section (Literature) in the Facts about the Country chapter.

Travel

Peter Fleming's *Brazilian Adventure* (Penguin, 1978) is about the young journalist's expedition into Mato Grosso in search of Colonel Fawcett, who had disappeared. At the time this area was the world's last, vast unexplored region. What Fleming found is less important than the telling: written with the humour of the disenchanted Briton, travel adventures don't get any funnier than this. Highly recommended.

While it's not all about Brazil, Peter Mattheissen's *The Cloud Forest* (Collins Harvill, 1960), an account of his 30,000-km journey across the South American wilder-ness from the Amazon to Tierra del Fuego, is well worth a read. Mattheissen is a master at describing the environment that surrounds him. Moritz Thomsen's *The Saddest Pleasure: A Journey on Two Rivers* (Graywolf Press, 1990) is a highly recommended book – skip the sickly introduction – about the author's experiences in South America, including journeys through Brazil and along the Amazon.

Although currently out of print, *Valley of the Latin Bear* by Alexander Lenard merits reading if you're interested in village life in the interior of southern Brazil. The Hungarian author is best known for his *Winnie ille Pu*, a Latin translation of the famous Edward Bear book.

For readers who like their history with a dose of fiction, *Brazil* (Simon & Schuster, 1986) by Errol Lincoln Uys, is an interesting novel that traces the history of two Brazilian families from pre-Cabral times to the foundation of Brasília.

In the 19th century, practically every Westerner who visited Brazil seems to have written a travelogue, and some, with their keen powers of observation, are quite good. Maria Graham's *Journal of a Voyage to Brazil & Residence there During Part of the Years 1821, 1822, 1823* is as precise as the title suggests. Henry Koster wrote *Travels in Brazil* in 1816; Herbert H Smith wrote *Brazil, the Amazon & the Coast* in 1880.

The Amazon & Indians

The first and last word on the history of the Portuguese colonisation, the warring and the enslavement of the Indians is *Red Gold* (Harvard University Press, 1978) by John Hemming. Hemming has brought Indian history up to date in *Amazon Frontier: The Defeat of the Brazilian Indians* (Harvard University Press, 1987).

Other interesting titles are *The Last Indians: South America's Cultural Heritage* by Fritz Tupp, *Aromeri Brazilian Indian Feather Art* by Norberto Nícola and Sónia Ferraro and *Aborigines of the Amazon Rain Forest: The Yanomami* (Time Life Books, 1982) by Robin Hanbury-Tenison.

Amazonia (1991), by Loren McIntyre, the renowned explorer and photographer, records in magnificent photographs the gradual demise of the region and its original inhabitants. To learn more about McIntyre's many journeys in search of the source of the Amazon and his extraordinary psychic experiences with indigenous tribes, pick up a copy of *Amazon Beaming* (1991) by Petru Popescu.

The works of Márcio Souza (see Literature in the Facts about the Country chapter), a skilful Brazilian satirist, are set in the Amazon. Anthropologist Darcy Ribeiro's interesting novel *Maíra* (Random House, 1983) is about the clash between Indian animism and Catholicism.

Alex Shoumatoff has written three excellent Amazon books, all of them entertaining combinations of history, myth and travelogue. His latest work, *The World is Burning* (Little Brown, 1990), recounts the Chico Mendes story.

Armchair adventurers will enjoy Spix & Martius' *Travels Brazil*, a three-volume chronology of the pair's 3½-year journey from 1817 to 1820. Illustrated with wonderful etchings, it is a biologist's record of customs, social life, ethnology and a description of flora and fauna. You may still be able to find second-hand copies of George Woodcock's *Henry Walter Bates, Naturalist of the Amazons* (Faber & Faber, 1969), a fascinating account of Bates' many years spent in pursuit of plantlife during the mid-19th century.

Those interested in *yagé*, the hallucinogenic drug used by certain tribes of the upper Amazon, will find *Wizard of the Upper Amazon – the Story of Manuel Córdova-Rios* (Houghton Mifflin, 1975) and the sequel *Rio Tigre and Beyond* by F Bruce Lamb interesting reading.

The Fate of the Forest: Developers, Destroyers, and Defenders of the Amazon (Verso, 1989) by Susanna Hecht & Alexander Cockburn is one of the best analyses of the complex web of destruction, and provides ideas on ways to mend the damage. Arnold Newman's *Tropical Rainforest: A*

World Survey of Our Most Valuable and Endangered Habitat with a Blueprint for its Survival is a massive analysis of rainforest destruction and possible strategies for sound forest management. *People of the Tropical Rainforest* (University of California Press & Smithsonian Institute, 1988) is a compilation of writings about the rainforest by experts on the subject. Augusta Dwyer delivers a fierce indictment of corruption and mismanagement in the Amazon in *Into the Amazon: The Struggle for the Amazon.*

The Rainforest Book (Living Planet, 1990) by Scott Lewis is a concise analysis of rainforest problems and remedies. It's packed with examples which link consumer behaviour with rainforest development; listings of organisations to contact; and advice on individual involvement. A similar publication compiled by the Seattle Audubon Society and the Puget Consumers Co-operative is the booklet entitled *Rainforests Forever: Consumer Choices to Help Preserve Tropical Rainforests* (1990).

Flora & Fauna Guides

Rainforests – A Guide to Tourist and Research Facilities at Selected Tropical Forest Sites in Central and South America by James L Castner is full of information and well worth getting hold of if you want to do some research or even just visit the rainforest.

Margaret Mee's *In Search of the Flowers of the Amazon Forest* is beautifully illustrated, and highly recommended for anyone (not just botanists) interested in the Amazon.

Neotropical Rainforest Mammals: A Field Guide by Louise Emmons & François Feer provides colour illustrations to identify mammals of the rainforest. For a reference work, rather than a field guide, you could consult the *World of Wildlife: Animals of South America* (Orbis Publishing, 1975) by F R de la Fuente.

Birders in the Amazon region of Brazil often use field guides for adjacent countries – many species overlap. Amateur interests should be satisfied with titles such as *South*

American Birds: A Photographic Aid to Identification (1987) by John S Dunning; or *A Guide to the Birds of Venezuela* by Rodolphe de Schauensee & William Phelps. For a definitive tome, rather than a lightweight guide, you could start with *A Guide to the Birds of South America* (Academy of Natural Science, Philadelphia).

Last, but not least, for some fascinating oddities you should dip into *Ecology of Tropical Rainforests: An Introduction for Eco-Tourists* (Free University Amsterdam, 1990) by Piet van Ipenburg & Rob Boschhuizen. This mini-booklet is packed with intriguing and bizarre scientific minutiae about sloths, bats, the strangling fig, etc; and more extraordinary details of rainforest ecology. Available in the UK from J Forrest, 64 Belsize Park, London NW3 4EH; or in the USA from M Doolittle, 32 Amy Rd, Falls Village, CT 06031. All proceeds from sales of this booklet go to the Tambopata Reserve Society, which is funding research in the Tambopata Reserve in the rainforests of south-eastern Peru.

Travel Guides

A Brazilian travel guide is published annually by Quatro Rodas. Called *Quatro Rodas: Guia Brasil*, it's readily available at most newsagents and contains a wealth of information about accommodation, restaurants, transport, sights, etc. If you buy it in Brazil it also comes with an excellent fold-out map of the country. It doesn't cover budget options. For details of additional mapping published by Quatro Rodas, see the section on maps later in this chapter.

Viajar Bem e Barato: O Superguia de Viagens Econômicas, also published by Quatro Rodas, is an excellent budget travel guide. It covers accommodation from the rock-bottom options (*dormitórios* etc usually only used by locals) to the better-value budget places, even though some of them are a fair hike out of town. Not much detail on transport though, and little on history and cultural highlights.

Quartro Rodas Guia das Praias has some impressive glossy satellite pictures, but

seems to be geared towards beach freaks on driving tours.

The *South American Handbook* (Trade & Travel Publications, 1995) contains a huge volume of information. It is useful for travel in Brazil, but haphazard updating has resulted in contradictions and a confusing layout. Travellers planning river trips on their own will find practical advice in *South American River Trips* (Bradt Publications, 1982) and *Up the Creek* (Bradt Publications, 1986). *Backcountry Brazil* (Bradt Publications, 1990) provides useful supplementary information if you want to skip the cities.

Religion

The strength and cultural richness of Candomblé has attracted and inspired a number of perceptive Western authors, several of whom were converted. *Orixás* by Pierre Fatumbi Verger is a photo book comparing the Brazilian and African religions. *The African Religions of Brazil* (John Hopkins, 1978), by the well-known French anthropologist Roger Bastide, is a scholarly look at the social forces which shaped Candomblé. Ruth Landes' *The City of Women* is about Candomblé in Bahia. For a quick overview in Portuguese, dip into *ABC do Candomblé* by Vasconcelos Maia. Edison Carneiro, a famous student of Candomblé, has written about the subject in *Candomblé da Bahia*. For light reading, try Jorge Amado's novel *Dona Flor and Her Two Husbands*, which is available in English translation.

Other Books

Florestan Fernandes' *The Negro in Brazilian Society* was one of the first books to challenge the myth of racial democracy. Thomas Skidmore's *Black into White: Race & Nationality in Brazilian Thought* is an intellectual history of the racial issue.

Carolina Maria de Jesus lived and wrote in the slums of São Paulo. Her book *Child of the Dark* (NAL, 1965) is strong and compelling. It was published in the UK and Australia under the title *Beyond All Pity*. In *The Myth of Marginality: Urban Politics &*

Poverty in Rio de Janeiro (University of California Press, 1976) Janice Perlman debunks some of the myths about life in the favelas.

MAPS

Given the size of Brazil, it's essential to be armed with decent mapping which gives a clear idea of scale. It's very easy to underestimate distances and the time required for travel, particularly if you plan to visit several regions using the roads rather than the airports.

In the USA, Maplink (☎ (805) 965-4402), 25 E Mason St, Dept G, Santa Barbara, CA 93101, is an excellent and exhaustive source for maps of Brazil and just about anywhere else in the world. A similarly extensive selection of mapping is available in the UK from Stanfords (☎ (0171) 836-1321), 12-14 Long Acre, London WC2E 9LP.

For general mapping of South America with excellent topographical detail, it's hard to beat the sectional maps published by International Travel Map Productions (Canada). Coverage of Brazil is provided in *South America – South* (1987), *South America – North East* (1989), *South America – North West* (1987) and *Amazon Basin* (1991).

Within Brazil, the mapping used by most Brazilian and foreign travellers is produced by Quatro Rodas, which also publishes the essential *Quatro Rodas: Guia Brasil*, an annually updated travel guide in Portuguese. This guide is complemented by *Guia Rodoviário*, a compact book of maps in a handy plastic case, which covers individual states and provides useful distance charts.

The city maps provided in *Quatro Rodas: Guia Brasil* help with orientation. It's very much a question of pot luck if you hunt for maps from tourist offices. If you're after detailed street layout, take a look at the phone books. The telephone companies in many states include excellent city maps either in the Lista Telefônica (White Pages) or in the Páginas Amarelas (Yellow Pages); and the same companies are also starting to distribute 'shopping maps' which are equally useful.

MEDIA

Brazil's media industry is concentrated in the hands of a few organisations. The companies that own the two major TV stations, O Globo and Manchete, also control several of the nation's leading newspapers and magazines.

Newspapers & Magazines

English In major Brazilian cities you will find two daily newspapers in English. The best by far is the Latin American edition of the *Miami Herald*. This paper isn't cheap, but it's fairly comprehensive. Its strong points are coverage of Latin America and the American sports scene.

The *International Herald Tribune* has articles from the *New York Times* and the *Washington Post*, but it's a pretty thin paper, and more expensive than the other two newspapers.

Time and *Newsweek* magazines are available throughout Brazil. What can one say about these icons? Their coverage is weakest where the *Miami Herald* is strongest: Latin America and sports. The *Economist* is sold in Rio and São Paulo, but it costs about US$4. In the big cities you can find all sorts of imported newspapers and magazines at some newsstands, but they are very expensive.

Portuguese The *Folha de São Paulo* is Brazil's finest newspaper. It has excellent coverage of national and international events and has a good guide to entertainment in São Paulo. The Turismo section in the Thursday edition always has a table showing costs of internal flights. It's available in Rio and other major cities. The *Jornal do Brasil* and *O Globo* are Rio's main daily papers. Both have entertainment listings. *Balcão* is a Rio weekly with only classified advertisements, a good source for buying anything. *O Nacional* is a weekly paper that has some excellent critical columnists. *O Povo* is a popular daily with lots of gory photographs.

Among weekly magazines, *Veja*, the Brazilian *Time* clone, is the country's best-selling magazine. It's easy reading if you want to practise your Portuguese. *Isto É* has the best political and economic analysis, and reproduces international articles from the British *Economist*, but it's not light reading. It also provides good coverage of current events.

Environmental and ecological issues (both national and international) are covered in the glossy monthly magazine, *Terra*. It seems genuine about environmental concerns as well as having some great photos.

Sources of information and literature about Brazilian Indians are given in the Population & People section of the Facts about the Country chapter, and in the Books & Maps section of this chapter.

TV

English If you are having second thoughts about visiting Brazil because you don't want to miss the Superbowl, Wimbledon or, perhaps, The Miss Teen America Pageant, relax and go ahead and make those reservations. Thanks to the parabolic antenna, cable TV and the hospitality of the Sheraton, the InterContinental or any of several other big hotels, all the major American TV events are shown in Rio and São Paulo.

Portuguese Many of the worst American movies and TV shows are dubbed into Portuguese and shown on Brazilian TV. Brazil's most famous TV hosts, who have to be seen to be believed, are Xuxa, the queen of kiddy titillation, and Faustão. Both are strong statements on the evil of TV. Both are on the tube for countless hours.

Xuxa has coquettishly danced and sung her way into the hearts of tiny Brazilians everywhere. She is living proof that Freud had it right about children's sexuality. Faustão hosts *Domingão de Faustão*, a seemingly endless bump'n'grind variety show on Sunday afternoon.

What is worth watching? On Sunday night, starting at 9 or 10 pm, you can see the highlights of soccer matches played that day. And there's a good comedy show that starts daily at 5.30 pm called *Escolinha do Professor Raimundo*.

The most popular programmes on Brazil-ian TV are the *novelas* (soap operas), which are followed religiously by many Brazilians. These are actually quite good, and easy to understand if you speak some Portuguese. They often feature some of Brazil's best actors, and pioneer new techniques in the genre; several have had successful runs on European and Australian TV. The novelas go on the air at various times from 7 to 9 pm.

The news is on several times a night, but broadcast times vary from place to place. *O Globo* and *Manchete*, the two principal national networks, both have rather pedestrian national news shows. *Aqui Agora* (Here Now) is a sensational news show on SBT that is worth a look, even if you don't understand Portuguese.

Cable TV is a recent addition to broadcasting with ESPN (the sports network), CNN (Cable News Network), RAI (Radio Televisione Italia), and of course, MTV (music television) available to those few who can afford them.

FILM & PHOTOGRAPHY

Cameras are expensive and cumbersome objects. They will certainly suffer on the road and they may get broken, lost or stolen. But there are so many good shots out there that you'll kick yourself if you don't bring one along.

Your choice of camera will depend on your photographic requirements. Automatic 35-mm rangefinders will suffice for standard portraits and landscapes. But if you want to take general wildlife shots, a 200-mm or 300-mm zoom lens is essential. A 400-mm or 500-mm telephoto with a fixed focal length lens is preferred by photographers who are after close-up shots of wildlife.

If you want to get the right exposure, photography in the rainforest will require careful consideration of the lack of light. You'll have to experiment with a combination of fast film (400 ASA and upwards), a tripod, flash unit, and cable release. When exposed to the humid conditions of the forest for an extended period of time, your cameras and lenses may have their functioning impaired by fungus growth. The standard preventative measure is to keep your photographic gear sealed in bags together with silica-gel packs. Unseal only for use and reseal everything immediately after each photo session.

If you're shooting on beaches, remember to adjust for the glare from water or sand, and keep sand and salt water away from your equipment.

Useful accessories would include a small flash, a cable release, a polarising filter, a lens-cleaning kit (fluid, tissue and aerosol), plenty of silica-gel packs, and a bean bag or clamp ormonopod. Don't carry a flashy camera bag – use something less likely to attract the attention of thieves; and make sure your equipment is insured.

Photographic equipment and accessories are expensive in Brazil and you'd be well advised to buy your film and equipment before arrival. However, Kodak and Fuji print film is sold and processed almost everywhere. You can only get Ektachrome or Kodachrome slide film developed in the big cities and it's expensive to buy. If you're shooting slides it's best to bring film with you and have it processed back home. Heat and humidity can ruin film, so remember to keep it in the coolest, driest place available. Use a lead film bag to protect film from airport X-ray machines. This is especially important for the sensitive high-ASA films.

If you must get your film processed in Brazil, have it done either at a large lab in São Paulo or in Rio at Kronokroma Foto (☎ 285-1993) at Rua Russel 344, Loja E, near Praia do Flamengo's Hotel Glória. Bring in exposed film in the morning, when the chemical baths are fresh. In Rio the Fomar Photo Store (☎ 221-2332) at Rua São José 90, off Avenida Rio Branco, sells some camera accessories. Their friendly staff do quick camera cleaning. If your Nikon is on the blink, speak to Louis (☎ 220-1127) at Franklin Roosevelt 39 on the 6th floor near the US Consulate.

It's foolish to bring a camera to a beach unless it will be closely guarded – for more advice on camera security see the Dangers & Annoyances section in this chapter. Some Candomblé temples do not permit photography. Respect the wishes of the locals and ask permission before taking a photo of them.

HEALTH

Travel health depends on predeparture preparations, day-to-day attention to health-related matters and the manner of handling medical emergencies if they do arise. The following health section may seem like a who's who of dreadfully unpleasant diseases, but your chances of contracting a serious illness in Brazil are slight. You will, however, be exposed to environmental factors, foods and sanitation standards that are probably quite different from what you're used to. However, if you take the recommended jabs, faithfully pop your antimalarials and use common sense, there shouldn't be any problems.

While there's no worry of any strange tropical diseases in Rio and points further south, Amazonas, Pará, Mato Grosso, Amapá, Rondônia, Goiás, Espírito Santo and the Northeast all have some combination of malaria, yellow fever, dengue fever, leprosy, and leishmaniasis. Health officials periodically announce high rates of tuberculosis, polio, sexually transmitted diseases, hepatitis and other endemic diseases.

The following rundown of health risks includes some preventative measures, symptom descriptions and suggestions about what to do if there is a problem. It isn't meant to replace professional diagnosis or prescription, and visitors to the developing world should discuss with their physician the most up-to-date methods used to prevent and treat the threats to health which may be encountered.

Travel Health Guides

There are a number of books on travel health. *Staying Healthy in Asia, Africa & Latin America* (Moon Publications, 1993) by Dirk Schroeder, is probably the best all-round guide to carry. It's compact but very detailed and well organised.

Travellers' Health, (Oxford University Press) by Dr Richard Dawood, is comprehensive, easy to read, authoritative and also highly recommended, although it's rather large to lug around.

Where There is No Doctor, (Macmillan, 1994) by David Werner, is a very detailed guide intended for someone, like a Peace Corps worker, going to work in an underdeveloped country, rather than for the average traveller.

Travel with Children, (Lonely Planet Publications, 1995) by Maureen Wheeler, includes basic advice on travel health for younger children and for pregnant women.

Predeparture Planning

Health Insurance A travel insurance policy to cover theft, loss and medical problems is a wise idea. There is a wide variety of policies available and your travel agent will have recommendations. The international student travel policies handled by STA Travel or other student travel organisations are usually good value. Some policies offer lower and higher medical-expense options but the higher one is chiefly for countries like the USA which have extremely high medical costs. Check the small print:

1. Some policies specifically exclude 'dangerous activities' which can include scuba diving, motorcycling and even trekking. If such activities are on your agenda you won't want that sort of policy.

A locally acquired motor-cycle licence may not be valid under your policy.

2. You may prefer a policy which pays doctors or hospitals direct rather than you having to pay on the spot and claim later. If you have to claim later make sure you keep all documentation. Some policies ask you to call back (reverse charges) to a centre in your home country where an immediate assessment of your problem is made.

3. Check if the policy covers ambulances or an emergency flight home. If you have to stretch out you will need two seats and somebody has to pay for them!

Travel Health Information In the USA you can contact the Overseas Citizens Emergency Center and request a health and safety information bulletin on Brazil by writing to the Bureau of Consular Affairs Office, State Department, Washington, DC 20520. This office also has a special telephone number for emergencies while abroad: ☎ (202) 632-5525.

Read the Center for Disease Control's *Health Information for International Travel* supplement of *Morbidity & Mortality Weekly Report* or the World Health Organisation's *Vaccination Certificate Requirements for International Travel & Health Advice to Travellers*. Both of these sources (CDC and WHO) are superior to the Travel Information Manual published by the International Air Transport Association.

The International Association for Medical Assistance to Travelers (IAMAT) at 417 Center St, Lewiston, New York, NY 14092 can provide you with a list of English-speaking physicians in Brazil.

In the UK, contact Medical Advisory Services for Travellers Abroad (MASTA) (☎ (0171) 631-4408), Keppel St, London WC1E 7HT. MASTA provides a wide range of services, including a choice of concise or comprehensive 'Health Briefs' and a range of medical supplies. Another source of medical information and supplies is the British Airways Travel Clinic (☎ (0171) 831-5333).

In Australia you could contact the Traveller's Medical & Vaccination Centre in Sydney (☎ (02) 221-7133) or Melbourne (☎ (03) 9650-7600) for general health information pertaining to Brazil.

In Brazil, the Rio Health Collective (☎ 325-9300 ext 44) can put you in touch with an English-speaking doctor. They have a 24-hour answering service.

Public Health in Brazil

Life expectancy, like infant mortality, is a gross index of health care and development. In the southern states of Santa Catarina and Rio Grande do Sul the figures approach those of the USA and Western Europe; cancer and circulatory diseases are the biggest threats. In the North and Northeast, where infectious and parasitic diseases exact a very high toll, the average life expectancy is less than 50 years. Pockets of poverty in the Northeast, like the border region between Pernambuco and Paraíba, have average life expectancies as low as 39 years – rivalling the worst war-torn Third World nations in Africa and Asia.

The infant-mortality rate is about 90 per 1000 in Northeastern Brazil, but poor health is not confined to the North and the Northeast. The urban slums of the large southern cities are just as miserable. In Nova Iguaçu, a poor and dangerous suburb of Rio de Janeiro, 150 out of every 1000 babies die before the end of their first year. These figures are shocking in comparison to wealthier Brazilian community rates of 10 per 1000.

These statistics are attributable to diarrhoea and other infectious diseases caused by lack of sanitation, inadequate access to medical care and poor nutrition. According to government statistics, nearly one-third of Brazil's population is undernourished. The huge discrepancy in longevity and the quality of health are indicators of the vast difference between the wealthy and poor in Brazil.

According to transmissible-disease reports, there are 160,000 new cases of malaria per year. In 1986 there were 430,000 cases of malaria and 600,000 by 1991. In 1986 there were said to be some six million sufferers of Chagas' disease, between six and eight million people with schistosomiasis, 220,000 with leprosy (there are even some cases in the South), 72,000 with measles, 56,000 with tuberculosis, 4200 with typhoid fever, 300 with bubonic plague (there was an outbreak in Paraíba) and 156 victims of polio.

Hospitals & Pharmacies It's not necessary to take with you every remedy for every illness you might conceivably contract during your trip. Pharmacies stock all kinds of drugs and sell them much more cheaply than in the West. There are few restricted medications, so practically everything is sold over the counter. In the past, foreign pharmaceutical industries sold drugs which had exceeded their shelf life to South American firms, but fortunately this practice is not as widespread as it was previously. Nearly all drugs are manufactured by firms in São Paulo under foreign licence. However, when buying drugs anywhere in South America, be sure to check expiry dates and storage conditions. Some drugs available there may no longer be recommended, or may even be banned, in other countries.

In addition, travellers should be aware of any drug allergies they may have and avoid using such drugs or their derivatives while travelling in Brazil. Since common names of prescription medicines in South America are likely to be different from the ones you're used to, ask a pharmacist before taking anything you're not sure about.

Pharmacies in Brazil are known as *farmácias* and medicines are called *remédios*. The word for doctor is *doutor* or *médico*, and medicine tablets are known as *comprimidos*.

Some pharmacists will give injections (with or without prescriptions). This is true of the Drogaleve pharmacy chain. Sometimes hygiene is questionable, so always purchase fresh needles, and make sure other health professionals take similar precautions.

Some private medical facilities in Rio de Janeiro and São Paulo are on a par with US hospitals, but be wary of public hospitals in the interior. They are notorious for reusing syringes after quick dips in alcohol baths, for lack of soap, and other unsanitary practices. University hospitals are likely to have English-speaking physicians. UK and US consulates have lists of English-speaking physicians.

Brazilian blood banks don't always screen carefully. Hepatitis B is rampant, so if you should require a blood transfusion, do as the Brazilians do: have your friends blood-typed and choose your blood donor in advance.

Medical Kit It's a good idea to carry a small, straightforward medical kit, which may include:

- Aspirin or paracetamol (acetominophen in North America) – for pain or fever
- Antihistamine (such as Benadryl) – useful as a

decongestant for colds and allergies, to ease itching from insect bites, or to prevent motion sickness
• Antibiotics – useful if you're travelling off the beaten track. Most antibiotics are prescription medicines
• Kaolin and pectin preparation such as Pepto – Bismol for stomach upsets and Imodium or Lomotil to bung things up in case of diarrhoeal emergencies during long-distance travel
• Rehydration mixture – for treatment of severe diarrhoea. This is particularly important when travelling with children.
• Antiseptic liquid or cream and antibiotic powder for minor injuries
• Calamine lotion – to ease irritation from bites and stings
• Bandages and bandaids
• Scissors, tweezers and a thermometer – but remember that you cannot transport mercury thermometers on airlines
• Insect repellent, sunblock (15+), suntan lotion, chap stick and water purification tablets (or iodine)
• Sterile syringes are recommended for travel in Amazônia, particularly Brazil, due to the AIDS risk. Be sure you have at least one large enough for a blood test – those normally used for injections are too small. For sources of requisite medical supplies, refer to the Travel Health Information section.

Ideally, antibiotics should be administered only under medical supervision and should never be taken indiscriminately. Overuse of antibiotics can weaken your immune system and can reduce the drug's efficacy in the future. Take only the recommended dosage at the prescribed intervals and continue using the antibiotic for the prescribed period, even if you're feeling better sooner. Antibiotics are quite specific to the infections they will react with, so if you're in doubt about a drug's effects or suffer any unexpected reactions, discontinue use immediately.

Health Preparations Make sure you're healthy before embarking on a long journey, have your teeth checked and if you wear glasses or contact lenses, bring a spare pair and a copy of your optical prescription. Losing your glasses may be a real problem in remoter areas, but in larger Brazilian cities you can have a new pair made with little fuss.

At least one pair of good-quality sunglasses is essential, as the glare is strong and dust and sand can get blown into the corners of your eyes. A hat, sunscreen lotion and lip protection are also essential.

Particular medications may not be available locally. Take the prescription with the generic rather than brand name so it will be universally recognisable. It's also wise to carry a copy of the prescription to prove you're using the medication legally. Customs and immigration officers may get excited at the sight of syringes or mysterious powdery preparations. The organisations listed in the Travel Health Information section can provide medical supplies such as syringes, together with multilingual customs documentation.

Immunisations Vaccinations provide protection against diseases you may encounter along the way. A yellow-fever vaccination and related documentation is strongly recommended for every traveller in Brazil. In addition, Brazilian authorities will not grant entrance, especially in Amazônia, without it. The vaccination certificate remains effective for 10 years. Other commonly recommended jabs for travel to South America are typhoid, tetanus DPT, polio and meningitis vaccines as well as Havrix as protection against hepatitis A. Some physicians will also recommend a cholera vaccine but its effectiveness is minimal.

Tetanus DPT Boosters are necessary at least every 10 years and are highly recommended as a matter of course.

Polio Polio is endemic in Brazil. Recent outbreaks have been reported in the southern states of Paraná, Santa Catarina and Rio Grande do Sul. A complete immunisation series should be boosted if more than 10 years have elapsed since the last course.

Typhoid Protection lasts for three years and is useful if you are travelling for longer periods in rural tropical areas. The most common side effects from this vaccine are pain at the injection site, fever, headache and a general unwell feeling.

Hepatitis A This is the most common travel-acquired illness which can be prevented by vaccination. Protection can be provided in two ways – either with the antibody gamma globulin or with a new vaccine called Havrix.

Havrix provides long term immunity (possibly

more than 10 years) after an initial course of two injections and a booster at one year. It may be more expensive than gamma globulin but certainly has many advantages, including length of protection and ease of administration. It is important to know that being a vaccine it will take about three weeks to provide satisfactory protection – hence the need for careful planning prior to travel.

Gamma globulin is not a vaccination but a ready-made antibody which has proven very successful in reducing the chances of hepatitis infection. Because it may interfere with the development of immunity, it should not be given until at least 10 days after administration of the last vaccine needed. It should also be given as close as possible to departure because it is at its most effective in the first few weeks after administration and the effectiveness tapers off gradually between three and six months.

Yellow Fever Protection lasts for 10 years and is recommended for all travel to South America. You usually need to visit a special yellow-fever vaccination centre. Vaccination isn't recommended during pregnancy, but if you must travel to a high-risk area, it is still probably better to take the vaccine. Once you've taken the jabs, keep the yellow WHO certificate in your passport to avoid problems when passing through Acre, Amapá, Amazonas, Maranhão, Mato Grosso and Mato Grosso do Sul, Tocantins, Pará, Rondônia and Roraima.

Basic Rules

Food Care in what you eat and drink is the most important of all health rules; stomach upsets are the most common travel health problem but the majority of these upsets will be minor. Do not be paranoid about sampling the local foods on offer – this is all part of the travel experience and should not be missed.

Water The number-one rule is *don't drink the water*, and that includes ice. If you don't know for certain that the water is safe always assume the worst. Reputable brands of bottled water or soft drinks are generally fine, although in some places refilling bottles with tap water is not unknown. Only use water from containers with a serrated seal – not tops or corks. Take care with fruit juice, particularly if water may have been added. Milk should be treated with suspicion, as it is often unpasteurised. Boiled milk is fine if it is kept hygienically and yoghurt is always good. Tea or coffee should also be OK, since the water should have been boiled.

Water Purification The simplest way of purifying water is to boil it thoroughly. Vigorously boiling for five minutes should be satisfactory, however, at high altitudes water boils at a lower temperature, so germs are less likely to be killed.

Simple filtering will not remove all dangerous organisms, so if you cannot boil water it should be treated chemically. Chlorine tablets (Puritabs, Steritabs or other brand names) will kill many but not all pathogens, including giardia and amoebic cysts. Iodine is very effective in purifying water and is available in tablet form (such as Potable Aqua), but follow the directions carefully and remember that too much iodine can be harmful.

If you can't find tablets, tincture of iodine (2%) or iodine crystals can be used. Four drops of tincture of iodine per litre or quart of clear water is the recommended dosage; the treated water should be left to stand for 20 to 30 minutes before drinking. Iodine crystals can also be used to purify water but this is a more complicated process, as you have to first prepare a saturated iodine solution. Iodine loses its effectiveness if exposed to air or damp so keep it in a tightly sealed container. Flavoured powder will disguise the taste of treated water and is a good idea if you are travelling with children.

Food There is an old colonial adage which says: 'If you can cook it, boil it or peel it you can eat it – otherwise forget it'. Salads and fruit should be washed with purified water or peeled where possible. Ice cream is usually OK if it is a reputable brand name, but beware of Third World street vendors and of ice cream that has melted and been refrozen. Thoroughly cooked food is safest but not if it has been left to cool or if it has been reheated. Shellfish such as mussels, oysters and clams should be avoided as well as undercooked meat, particularly in the form of mince. Steaming does not make shellfish safe for eating.

If a place looks clean and well-run, and if the vendor also looks clean and healthy, then the food is probably safe. In general, places that are packed with travellers or locals will be fine, while empty restaurants are questionable. The food in busy restaurants is cooked and eaten quite quickly with little standing around and is probably not reheated.

Nutrition If your food is poor or limited in availability, if you're travelling hard and fast and therefore missing meals, or if you simply lose your appetite, you can soon start to lose weight and place your health at risk.

Make sure your diet is well balanced. Eggs, tofu, beans, lentils and nuts are all safe ways to get protein. Fruit you can peel (bananas, oranges or mandarins for example) is always safe and a good source of vitamins. Try to eat plenty of grains (rice) and bread. Remember that although food is generally safer if it is cooked well, over-cooked food loses much of its nutritional value. If your diet isn't well balanced or if your food intake is insufficient, it's a good idea to take vitamin and iron pills.

In hot climates make sure you drink enough – don't rely on feeling thirsty to indicate when you should drink. Not needing to urinate or very dark yellow urine is a danger sign. Always carry a water bottle with you on long trips. Excessive sweating can lead to loss of salt and therefore muscle cramping. Salt tablets are not a good idea as a preventative, but in places where salt is not used much adding salt to food can help.

Everyday Health Normal body temperature is 98.6°F or 37°C; more than 2°C higher indicates a high fever. The normal adult pulse rate is 60 to 80 per minute (children 80 to 100, babies 100 to 140). You should know how to take a temperature and a pulse rate. As a general rule the pulse increases about 20 beats per minute for each °C rise in fever. Respiration (breathing) rate is also an indicator of illness. Count the number of breaths

per minute: between 12 and 20 is normal for adults and older children (up to 30 for younger children and 40 for babies). People with a high fever or serious respiratory illness (like pneumonia) breathe more quickly than normal. More than 40 shallow breaths a minute usually means pneumonia.

In Western countries with safe water and excellent human waste disposal systems we often take good health for granted. In years gone by, when public health facilities were not as good as they are today, certain rules attached to eating and drinking were observed, eg washing your hands before a meal. It is important for people travelling in areas of poor sanitation to be aware of this and adjust their own personal hygiene habits.

Clean your teeth with purified water rather than straight from the tap. Avoid climatic extremes: keep out of the sun when it's hot and dress warmly when it's cold. Avoid potential diseases by dressing sensibly. You can get worm infections by walking barefoot or dangerous coral cuts by walking over coral without shoes. You can avoid insect bites by covering bare skin when insects are around, by screening windows or beds and by using insect repellents. Seek local advice: if you're told the water is unsafe due to jellyfish, crocodiles or bilharzia, don't go in. In situations where there is no information, discretion is the better part of valour.

Medical Problems & Treatment
Potential medical problems can be broken down into several areas. Firstly there are the problems caused by extremes of temperature, altitude or motion. Then there are diseases and illnesses caused through poor environmental sanitation, insect bites or stings, and animal or human contact. Simple cuts, bites and scratches can also cause problems.

Self-diagnosis and treatment can be risky, so wherever possible seek qualified help. Although we do give drug dosages in this section, they are for emergency use only. Medical advice should be sought where possible before administering any drugs.

An embassy or consulate can usually recommend a good place to go for such advice. So can five-star hotels, although they often recommend doctors with five-star prices. (This is when that medical insurance really comes in useful!) In some places standards of medical attention are so low that for some ailments the best advice is to get on a plane and go somewhere else.

Climatic & Geographical Considerations

Sunburn Most of Brazil lies in the humid tropics, where the sun's rays are more direct and concentrated than in temperate zones. Even in cooler highland areas, everyone – particularly fair-skinned people – will be susceptible to hazardous UV rays. The use of a strong sunscreen is essential because serious burns can occur even after brief exposure. Don't neglect to apply it to any area of exposed skin, especially if you're near water.

To be safe, choose the highest rated sunscreen available. In addition, a hat will serve to shade your face and protect your scalp. Sunglasses will prevent eye irritation (especially if you wear contact lenses).

Prickly Heat Prickly heat is an itchy rash caused by excessive perspiration trapped under the skin. It usually strikes people who have just arrived in a hot climate and whose pores have not yet opened sufficiently to cope with greater sweating. Keeping cool but bathing often, using a mild talcum powder or even resorting to air-conditioning may help until you acclimatise.

Heat Exhaustion In the humid lowlands of Brazil and on the beach, heat combined with humidity and exposure to the sun can be oppressive and leave you feeling lethargic, irritable and dazed. A cool swim or lazy afternoon in the shade will do wonders to improve your mood. You'll also need to drink lots of liquids and eat salty foods in order to replenish your supply of these products lost during sweating.

Dehydration or salt deficiency can cause heat exhaustion. Take time to acclimatise to high temperatures and make sure you get sufficient liquids. Wear loose clothing and a broad-brimmed hat. Do not do anything too physically demanding.

Salt deficiency is characterised by fatigue, lethargy, headaches, giddiness and muscle cramps, and in this case salt tablets may help. Vomiting or diarrhoea can deplete your liquid and salt levels. Anhydrotic heat exhaustion, caused by an inability to sweat, is quite rare. Unlike the other forms of heat exhaustion it is likely to strike people who have been in a hot climate for some time, rather than newcomers.

Heatstroke This serious, sometimes fatal, condition can occur if the body's thermostat breaks down and body temperature rises to dangerous levels. Continuous exposure to high temperatures can leave you vulnerable to heatstroke. Alcohol intake and strenuous activity can increase chances of heatstroke, especially in those who've recently arrived in a hot climate.

Symptoms include minimal sweating, a high body temperature (39 to 40°C), and a general feeling of unwellness. The skin may become flushed and red. Severe throbbing headaches, decreased co-ordination, and aggressive or confused behaviour may be signs of heatstroke. Eventually, the victim will become delirious and go into convulsions. Get the victim out of the sun, if possible, remove clothing, cover with a wet towel and fan continually. Seek medical help as soon as possible.

Fungal Infections Fungal infections, which occur with greater frequency in hot weather, are most likely to occur on the scalp, between the toes or fingers (athlete's foot), in the groin (jock itch or crotch rot) and on the body (ringworm). You get ringworm (which is a fungal infection, not a worm) from infected animals or by walking on damp areas, like shower floors.

To prevent fungal infections wear loose, comfortable clothes, avoid artificial fibres, wash frequently and dry carefully. If you do get an infection, wash the infected area daily with a disinfectant or medicated soap and water, and rinse and dry well. Apply an anti-fungal powder like the widely available Tinaderm. Try to expose the infected area to air or sunlight as much as possible and wash all towels and underwear in hot water as well as changing them often.

Motion Sickness If you're susceptible to motion sickness, then come prepared because the roads in Brazil aren't always straight and smooth. Eating lightly before and during a trip will reduce the chances of motion sickness. If you are prone to motion sickness try to find a place that minimises disturbance – near the wing on aircraft, close to midships on boats, near the centre on buses. Fresh air usually helps; reading and cigarette smoke don't. Commercial motion-sickness preparations, which can cause drowsiness, have to be taken before the trip commences; when you're feeling sick it's too late. Ginger is a natural preventative and is available in capsule form.

Jet Lag Jet lag is experienced when a person travels by air across more than three time zones (each time zone usually represents a one-hour time difference). It occurs because many of the functions of the human body (such as temperature, pulse rate and emptying of the bladder and bowels) are regulated by internal 24-hour cycles called circadian rhythms. When we travel long distances rapidly, our bodies take time to adjust to the 'new time' of our destination, and we may experience fatigue, disorientation, insomnia, anxiety, impaired concentration and loss of appetite. These effects will usually be gone within three days of arrival, but there are ways of minimising the impact of jet lag:

- Rest for a couple of days prior to departure; try to avoid late nights and last-minute dashes for travellers' cheques, passport etc.
- Try to select flight schedules that minimise sleep deprivation; arriving late in the day means you can go to sleep soon after you arrive. For very long flights, try to organise a stopover.
- Avoid excessive eating (which bloats the stomach) and alcohol (which causes dehydration) during the flight. Instead, drink plenty of non-carbonated, non-alcoholic drinks such as fruit juice or water.
- Avoid smoking, as this reduces the amount of oxygen in the aeroplane cabin even further and causes greater fatigue.
- Make yourself comfortable by wearing loose-fitting clothes and perhaps bringing an eye mask and ear plugs to help you sleep.

Infectious Diseases
Diarrhoea A change of water, food or climate can all cause the runs; diarrhoea caused by contaminated food or water is more serious. Despite all your precautions you may still have a mild bout of travellers' diarrhoea but a few rushed toilet trips with no other symptoms is not indicative of a serious problem. Moderate diarrhoea, involving half-a-dozen loose movements in a day, is more of a nuisance. Dehydration is the main danger with any diarrhoea, particularly for children where dehydration can occur quite quickly. Fluid replacement remains the mainstay of management. Weak black tea with a little sugar, soda water, or soft drinks allowed to go flat and diluted 50% with water are all good. With severe diarrhoea a rehydrating solution is necessary to replace minerals and salts. Commercially available ORS (oral rehydration salts) are very useful; add the contents of one sachet to a litre of boiled or bottled water. In an emergency you can make up a solution of eight teaspoons of sugar to a litre of boiled water and provide salted cracker biscuits at the same time. You should stick to a bland diet as you recover.

Lomotil or Imodium can be used to bring relief from the symptoms, although they do not actually cure the problem. Only use these drugs if absolutely necessary – eg if you *must* travel. For children Imodium is preferable, but under all circumstances fluid replacement is the most important thing to remember. Do not use these drugs if the person has a high fever or is severely dehydrated.

In certain situations antibiotics may be indicated:

- Watery diarrhoea with blood and mucous. (Gutparalysing drugs like Imodium or Lomotil should be avoided in this situation.)

• Watery diarrhoea with fever and lethargy.
• Persistent diarrhoea for more than five days.
• Severe diarrhoea, if it is logistically difficult to stay in one place.

The recommended drugs (for adults only) would be either norfloxacin 400 mg twice daily for three days or ciprofloxacin 500 mg twice daily for three days.

The drug bismuth subsalicylate has also been used successfully. It is not available in Australia. The dosage for adults is two tablets or 30 ml and for children it is one tablet or 10 ml. This dose can be repeated every 30 minutes to one hour, with no more than eight doses in a 24-hour period.

The drug of choice for children would be co-trimoxazole (Bactrim, Septrin or Resprim) with dosage dependent on weight. A three-day course is also given. Ampicillin has been recommended in the past and may still be an alternative.

It's interesting that, in addition to the initial 'shakedown', most people experience upon arriving in South America, they experience it again upon arriving home. One therefore suspects that South Americans may have similar discomforts when they visit other countries (the Yankee Quickstep or the Wallaby Hops?) thanks to unfamiliar diet and bacteria.

Giardiasis This is prevalent in South America. The parasite causing this intestinal disorder is present in contaminated water. The symptoms are stomach cramps, nausea, a bloated stomach, watery foul-smelling diarrhoea and frequent gas. Giardiasis can appear several weeks after you have been exposed to the parasite. The symptoms may disappear for a few days and then return; this can go on for several weeks. Tinidazole, known as Fasigyn, or metronidazole (Flagyl) are the recommended drugs for treatment. Either can be used in a single treatment dose. Antibiotics are of no use.

Dysentery This is a serious illness that is caused by contaminated food or water and is characterised by severe diarrhoea, often with blood or mucus in the stool. There are two kinds of dysentery. Bacillary dysentery is characterised by a high fever and rapid onset; headache, vomiting and stomach pains are also symptoms. It generally does not last longer than a week, but it is highly contagious.

Amoebic dysentery is often more gradual in the onset of symptoms, with cramping abdominal pain and vomiting less likely; fever may not be present. It is not a self-limiting disease. It will persist until treated and can recur and cause long-term health problems.

A stool test is necessary to diagnose which kind of dysentery you have, so you should seek medical help urgently. In case of an emergency, the drugs norfloxacin or ciprofloxacin can be used as presumptive treatment for bacillary dysentery, and metronidazole (Flagyl) for amoebic dysentery. For bacillary dysentery, norfloxacin 400 mg twice daily for seven days or ciprofloxacin 500 mg twice daily for seven days are the recommended dosages.

If you're unable to find either of these drugs then a useful alternative is co-trimoxazole 160/800 mg (Bactrim, Septrin or Resprim) twice daily for seven days. This is a sulpha drug and must not be used by people with a known sulpha allergy.

In the case of children the drug co-trimoxazole is a reasonable first-line treatment. For amoebic dysentery, the recommended adult dosage of metronidazole (Flagyl) is one 750-mg to 800-mg capsule three times daily for five days. Children aged between eight and 12 years should have half the adult dose, and the dosage for younger children is one-third the adult dose.

An alternative to Flagyl is Fasigyn, taken as a two-gram-daily dose for three days. Alcohol must be avoided during treatment and for 48 hours afterwards.

Cholera The cholera vaccine is between 20 to 50% effective according to most authorities, and can have some side effects. Vaccination is not usually recommended,

A	B
C	D
E	F

A: Aerobics on a Rio beach
B: Beach futvolei
C: Train surfer

D: Waterfall slide
E: Capoeira
F: Fitness station on Copacabana beach

ALL PHOTOS BY JOHN MAIER, JR

The Rio Carnival

nor is it legally required by Brazilian authorities. If you are travelling further afield, and want to avoid unplanned-for jabs, it may be worth getting a shot before you leave.

During 1991, a major epidemic of the disease was reported in South America, particularly in Peru and the upper reaches of the Brazilian Amazon; be particularly wary of shellfish or other seafood. Keep up to date with information about this and other diseases by contacting travellers' clinics or vaccination centres, and avoid areas where there are outbreaks.

Cholera is characterised by a sudden onset of acute diarrhoea with 'rice water' stools, vomiting, muscular cramps and extreme weakness. You need medical attention, but your first concern should be rehydration. Drink as much water as you can – if it refuses to stay down, keep drinking anyway. If there is likely to be an appreciable delay in reaching medical treatment, begin a course of tetracycline – which, incidentally, should not be administered to children or pregnant women. Be sure to check the expiry date since old tetracycline can become toxic. An alternative drug is Ampicillin. Remember that while antibiotics might kill the bacteria, it is a toxin produced by the bacteria which causes the massive fluid loss. Fluid replacement is by far the most important aspect of treatment.

Viral Gastroenteritis This is not caused by bacteria but, as the name implies, a virus. It is characterised by stomach cramps, diarrhoea, vomiting and slight fever. All you can do is rest and keep drinking as much water as possible.

Hepatitis Hepatitis is a general term for inflammation of the liver. There are many causes of this condition: drugs, alcohol and infections are but a few.

The discovery of new strains has led to a virtual alphabet soup, with hepatitis A, B, C, D, E and a rumoured G. These letters identify specific agents that cause viral hepatitis. Viral hepatitis is an infection of the liver, which can lead to jaundice (yellow skin),

fever, lethargy and digestive problems. It can have no symptoms at all, with the infected person not knowing that they have the disease. Travellers shouldn't be too paranoid about this apparent proliferation of hepatitis strains; hep C, D, E and G are fairly rare (so far) and following the same precautions as for A and B should be all that's necessary to avoid them.

Viral hepatitis can be divided into two groups on the basis of how it is spread. The first route of transmission is via contaminated food and water (hepatitis A and E), and the second route is via blood and bodily fluids (hepatitis B, C and D).

Hepatitis A This is a very common disease in most countries, especially those with poor standards of sanitation. Most people in developing countries are infected as children; they often don't develop symptoms, but do develop life-long immunity. The disease poses a real threat to the traveller, as people are unlikely to have been exposed to hepatitis A in developed countries.

The symptoms are fever, chills, headache, fatigue, feelings of weakness and aches and pains, followed by loss of appetite, nausea, vomiting, abdominal pain, dark urine, light coloured faeces, jaundiced skin and the whites of the eyes may turn yellow. You should seek medical advice, but in general there is not much you can do apart from resting, drinking lots of fluids, eating lightly and avoiding fatty foods. People who have had hepatitis must forego alcohol for six months after the illness, as hepatitis attacks the liver and it needs that amount of time to recover.

The routes of transmission are via contaminated water, shellfish contaminated by sewerage, or foodstuffs sold by food handlers with poor standards of hygiene.

Taking care with what you eat and drink can go a long way towards preventing this disease. But this is a very infectious virus, so if there is any risk of exposure, additional cover is highly recommended. This cover comes in two forms: gamma globulin and Havrix. Gamma globulin is an injection where you are given the antibodies for hepatitis A, which provide immunity for a limited time. Havrix is a vaccine, where you develop your own antibodies, which gives lasting immunity. The best preventative measure available is the Havrix vaccine. The vaccine involves three shots, the first two a month apart, which you should arrange before you leave home, and a third shot a year later. After the third shot you'll be covered for ten years. The alternative is a gamma globulin jab before departure from home and booster shots every three or four months thereafter while you're away (beware of unsanitary needles!). Gamma globulin only offers three months effective coverage and if you're likely to forget to have the booster shots, go for the Havrix vaccine.

Hepatitis E This is a very recently discovered virus, of which little is yet known. It appears to be rather common in developing countries, generally causing mild hepatitis, although it can be very serious in pregnant women.

Care with water supplies is the only current prevention, as there are no specific vaccines for this type of hepatitis. At present it doesn't appear to be too great a risk for travellers.

Hepatitis B This is also a very common disease, with almost 300 million chronic carriers in the world. Hepatitis B, which used to be called serum hepatitis, is spread through contact with infected blood, blood products or bodily fluids, for example through sexual contact, unsterilised needles or blood transfusions. Other risk situations include having a shave or tattoo in a local shop, or having your ears pierced. The symptoms of type B are much the same as type A except that they are more severe and may lead to irreparable liver damage or even liver cancer. Although there is no treatment for hepatitis B, a cheap and effective vaccine is available; the only problem is that for long-lasting cover you need a six-month course. The immunisation schedule requires two injections at least a month apart followed by a third dose five months after the second. Persons who should receive a hepatitis B vaccination include anyone who anticipates contact with blood or other bodily secretions, either as a health-care worker or through sexual contact with the local population, particularly those who intend to stay in the country for a long period of time.

Hepatitis C This is another of the recently defined viruses. It is a concern because it seems to lead to liver disease more rapidly than hepatitis B.

The virus is spread by contact with blood – usually via contaminated transfusions or shared needles. Avoiding these is the only means of prevention, as there is no available vaccine.

Hepatitis D Often referred to as the 'Delta' virus, this infection only occurs in chronic carriers of hepatitis B. It is transmitted by blood and bodily fluids. Again there is no vaccine for this virus, so avoidance is the best prevention. The risk to travellers is certainly limited.

Typhoid Typhoid fever is another gut infection that travels the faecal-oral route – ie contaminated water and food are responsible. Vaccination against typhoid is not totally effective and it is one of the most dangerous infections, so medical help must be sought. In its early stages typhoid resembles many other illnesses: sufferers may feel like they have a bad cold or flu on the way. Early symptoms are a headache, a sore throat, and a fever which rises a little each day until it is around 40°C or more. The victim's pulse is often slow relative to the degree of fever present and gets slower as the fever rises – unlike a normal fever where the pulse increases. There may also be vomiting, diarrhoea or constipation.

In the second week the high fever and slow pulse continue and a few pink spots may appear on the body; trembling, delirium, weakness, weight loss and dehydration are other symptoms. If there are no further complications, the fever and other symptoms will slowly diminish during the third week. However you must get medical help before this because pneumonia (acute infection of the lungs) or peritonitis (perforated bowel) are common complications, and because typhoid is very infectious.

The fever should be treated by keeping the victim cool and dehydration should also be watched for.

The drug of choice is ciprofloxacin at a dose of one gram daily for 14 days. It is quite expensive and may not be available. The alternative, chloramphenicol, has been the mainstay of treatment for many years. In many countries it is still the recommended antibiotic but there are fewer side affects with Ampicillin. The adult dosage is two 250-mg capsules, four times a day. Children aged between eight and 12 years should have half the adult dose, and younger children should have one-third the adult dose.

People who are allergic to penicillin should not be given Ampicillin.

Tuberculosis (TB) Although this disease is widespread in many developing countries, it is not a serious risk to travellers. Young children are more susceptible than adults and vaccination is a sensible precaution for children under 12 travelling in endemic areas. TB is commonly spread by coughing or by unpasteurised dairy products from infected cows. Milk that has been boiled is safe to drink; the souring of milk to make yoghurt or cheese also kills the bacilli.

Bilharzia Bilharzia is carried in water by minute worms. The larvae infect certain varieties of freshwater snails found in rivers, streams, lakes and particularly behind dams. The worms multiply and are eventually discharged into the water surrounding the snails.

They attach themselves to your intestines or bladder where they produce large numbers of eggs. The worm enters through the skin, and the first symptom may be a tingling and sometimes a light rash around the area where it entered. Weeks later, when the worm is busy producing eggs, a high fever may develop. A general feeling of being unwell may be the first symptom, and once the disease is established abdominal pain and blood in the urine are other signs.

Avoiding swimming or bathing in fresh water where bilharzia is present is the main method of preventing the disease. Even deep water can be infected. If you do get wet, dry off quickly and dry your clothes as well. Seek medical attention if you have been exposed to the disease and tell the doctor your suspicions, as bilharzia in the early stages can be confused with malaria or typhoid. If you cannot get medical help immediately, praziquantel (Biltricide) is the recommended treatment. The recommended dosage is 40 mg/kg in divided doses over one day. Niridazole is an alternative drug.

Diphtheria Diphtheria can be a skin infection or a more dangerous throat infection. It is spread by contaminated dust contacting the skin or by the inhalation of infected cough or sneeze droplets. Frequent washing and keeping the skin dry will help prevent skin infection. A vaccination is available to prevent the throat infection.

Malaria This serious disease is spread by mosquito bites and is endemic in many parts of Brazil.

If you are travelling in endemic areas it is extremely important to take malarial prophylactics. Symptoms include headaches, fever, chills and sweating which may subside and recur. Without treatment malaria can develop more serious, potentially fatal effects.

Antimalarial drugs do not prevent you from being infected but kill the parasites during a stage in their development.

There are a number of different types of malaria. The one of most concern is falciparum malaria. This is responsible for the very serious cerebral malaria. Falciparum is the predominant form in many malaria-prone areas of the world, including Africa, South-East Asia and Papua New Guinea, and has been reported in Brazil.

Contrary to popular belief cerebral malaria is not a new strain.

The problem in recent years has been the emergence of increasing resistance to commonly used antimalarials like chloroquine, maloprim and proguanil. Newer drugs such as mefloquine (Lariam) and doxycycline (Vibramycin and Doryx) are often recommended for chloroquine and multidrug-resistant areas. Expert advice should be sought, as there are many factors to consider when deciding on the type of antimalarial medication, including the area to be visited, the risk of exposure to malaria-carrying mosquitoes, your current medical condition and your age and pregnancy status. It is also important to discuss the side-effect profile of the medication, so you can work out some level of risk-versus-benefit ratio. It is also important to be sure of the correct dosage of the medication prescribed to you. Some people have inadvertently taken weekly medication (chloroquine) on a daily basis, with disastrous effects. While discussing dosages for prevention of malaria, it is often advisable to include the dosages required for treatment, especially if your trip is through a high-risk area that would isolate you from medical care. The main messages are:

1. Primary prevention must always be in the form of mosquito-avoidance measures. The mosquitoes that transmit malaria bite from dusk to dawn and during this period travellers are advised to:
   - wear light-coloured clothing
   - wear long pants and long-sleeved shirts
   - use mosquito repellents containing the compound DEET on exposed areas (overuse of DEET may be harmful, especially to children, but its use is considered preferable to being bitten by disease-transmitting mosquitoes)
   - avoid highly scented perfumes or aftershave
   - use a mosquito net – it may be worth taking your own
2. While no antimalarial is 100% effective, taking the most appropriate drug significantly reduces the risk of contracting the disease.
3. No one should ever die from malaria. It can be diagnosed by a simple blood test. Symptoms range from fever, chills and sweating, headache and abdominal pains to a vague feeling of ill-health, so seek examination immediately if there is any suggestion of malaria.

Contrary to popular belief, once a traveller contracts malaria he or she does not then have it for life. One of the parasites may lie dormant in the liver but this can also be eradicated using a specific medication. Malaria is curable, as long as the traveller seeks medical help when symptoms occur.

Dengue Fever There is no prophylactic available for this mosquito-spread disease; the main preventative measure is to avoid mosquito bites. A sudden onset of fever, headaches and severe joint and muscle pains are the first signs before a rash starts on the trunk of the body and spreads to the limbs and face. After a further few days, the fever will subside and recovery will begin. Serious complications are not common but full recovery can take up to a month or more.

Chagas' Disease There is a very small possibility of contracting this disease. It is caused by a parasite which lives in the faeces of the reduvid beetle which, in turn, lives in the thatching of dirty huts in the lowland, Northeast and Chaco regions of Bolivia, Argentina, Paraguay and Brazil.

The disease, transmitted through the bite of this beetle (more colourfully called the assassin bug), causes progressive constriction and hardening of blood vessels, which places increasing strain on the heart. At present there is no cure and Chagas' is always fatal over a period of years. Researchers in developed countries seem to be largely unaware of this serious disease. The best prevention is to use a mosquito net if you'll be sleeping in thatched buildings. If you are bitten, wash the affected area well and don't scratch the bite, otherwise the faeces and consequently the parasite may be rubbed into the wound.

Haemorrhagic Fever Incidences of this illness have been reported in low-lying rainforest areas, especially in the Amazon Basin. It is transmitted by mosquitoes and can be prevented by using the same mosquito protection recommended against malaria.

The most salient symptom is an odd pinprick-type rash which is caused by capillary haemorrhaging. Accompanying symptoms include chills, fever, fatigue, congestion and other influenza-like symptoms. It can be very dangerous and professional attention, preferably in a hospital, should be immediately sought.

Worms The majority of people living in rural Brazil have worms. If you adopt the diet and lifestyle of the interior, you are also likely to acquire a worm load. The most common form you're likely to contract are hookworms. They are usually caught by walking barefoot on infected soil. They bore through the skin, attach themselves to the inner wall of the intestine and proceed to suck the blood. Abdominal pain and sometimes anaemia are the result.

Threadworms, or *strongyloidiasis*, are also found in low-lying areas and operate very much like hookworms, but symptoms are more visible and can include diarrhoea and vomiting. If you stay long and travel rough you can become home for a tribe of cattle and pig tapeworms, Ascaris, hookworm or trichura. Schistosomiasis is endemic to Brazil and thus freshwater bathing (rivers, streams, ponds, irrigations ditches, etc) can be dangerous.

Prevent exposure to parasitic worms (and other faecal-oral diseases) by drinking and brushing teeth with boiled, bottled or filtered water only. Wash produce in the same kind of clean water and make sure all foods, particularly meat, fish, molluscs and pork, are well cooked – they harbour flukes and tapeworms. Don't walk around barefoot, always wash your hands before preparing meals and after using the toilet, and keep your nails short and clean.

A stool test when you return home isn't a bad idea if you think you may have contracted worms. Infestations may not be obvious for some time and although they are generally not serious, they can cause further health problems if left untreated. Worms may be treated with thiabendazole or mabendazole taken orally twice daily for three or four days. As usual, however,

medical advice is best because the symptoms of worms so closely resemble those of other, more serious conditions.

Myiasis This very unpleasant affliction is caused by the larvae of some tropical flies which lay their eggs on damp or sweaty clothing. The eggs hatch and the larvae burrow into the skin, producing an ugly boil as the parasite develops. To kill the invader, place drops of hydrogen peroxide, alcohol or oil over the boil to cut off its air supply, and then squeeze the boil to remove the bug. However revolting the process, at this stage the problem is solved.

Yellow Fever Yellow fever is endemic in much of South America, including the Amazon Basin. This viral disease, which is transmitted to humans by mosquitoes, first manifests itself as fever, headache, abdominal pain and vomiting. There may appear to be a brief recovery before it progresses into its more severe stages, when liver failure becomes a possibility. There is no treatment apart from keeping the fever as low as possible and avoiding dehydration. The yellow-fever vaccination, which is highly recommended for every traveller in South America, offers good protection for 10 years.

Typhus Typhus is spread by ticks, mites or lice and begins as a severe cold followed by a fever, chills, headache, muscle pains, and rash. There is often a large and painful sore at the site of the bite and nearby lymph nodes become swollen and painful.

Trekkers may be at risk from cattle ticks or wild-game ticks. Seek local advice on areas where ticks are present and check yourself carefully after walking in those areas. A strong insect repellent can help and regular bushwalkers should consider treating boots and trousers with benzyl benzoate and dibutylphthalate.

Tetanus This potentially fatal disease is found in underdeveloped tropical areas and is difficult to treat, but is easily prevented by vaccination. Tetanus occurs when a wound becomes infected by a bacterium which lives in human or animal faeces. Clean all cuts, punctures and bites. Tetanus is also known as lockjaw and the first symptom may be difficulty in swallowing, followed by a stiffening of the jaw and neck, and then by painful convulsions of the jaw and whole body.

Rabies Throughout Brazil, but especially in low-lying humid areas, rodents and bats carry the rabies virus and pass it on to larger animals and humans. Avoid any animal that appears to be foaming at the mouth or acting strangely. Bats, especially vampire bats, are common in the Amazon Basin and are notorious carriers of rabies. Be sure to cover all parts of your body at night, especially your feet and scalp. Dogs are also particularly notable carriers. Any bite, scratch or even lick from a mammal should be cleaned immediately and thoroughly. Scrub with soap and running water and then clean with an alcohol solution. If there is any possibility that the animal is infected, help should be sought. Even if the animal isn't rabid, all bites should be treated seriously as they can become infected or result in tetanus. A rabies vaccination is now available and should be considered if you spend a lot of time around animals.

If you do get bitten, try to capture or kill the offending animal so that it may be tested. If that's impossible, then you must assume the animal is rabid. The rabies virus incubates slowly in its victim, so while medical attention isn't urgent, it shouldn't be delayed.

Meningococcal Meningitis The disease is spread by close contact with people who carry it in their throats and noses. They probably aren't aware they are carriers and pass it around through coughs and sneezes. This very serious disease attacks the brain and can be fatal. A scattered blotchy rash, fever, severe headache, sensitivity to light and stiffness in the neck preventing nodding of the head are the first symptoms. Death can occur within a few hours, so immediate treatment

with large doses of penicillin is vital. If intravenous administration is impossible, it should be given intramuscularly. Vaccination offers reasonable protection for over a year, but you should check for reports of recent outbreaks and try to avoid affected areas.

Diphtheria Diphtheria can appear as a skin infection or a more serious throat infection. It is spread by contaminated dust coming in contact with the skin or being inhaled. About the only way to prevent the skin infection is to keep clean and dry – not always easy in South America. The throat infection is prevented by vaccination.

Gonorrhoea & Syphilis Sexual contact with an infected partner spreads a number of unpleasant diseases. While abstinence is 100% effective, use of a condom will lessen your risk considerably. The most common of these diseases are gonorrhoea and syphilis which in men first appear as sores, blisters or rashes around the genitals and pain or discharge when urinating. Symptoms may be less marked or not evident at all in women. The symptoms of syphilis eventually disappear completely but the disease continues and may cause severe problems in later years. Antibiotics are used to treat both syphilis and gonorrhoea.

HIV/AIDS HIV, the Human Immunodeficiency Virus, may develop into AIDS, Acquired Immune Deficiency Syndrome. It is a very serious problem in Brazil and should be a major concern to all visitors. Any exposure to blood, blood products or bodily fluids may put the individual at risk. In South America, transmission is predominantly through heterosexual sexual activity. This is quite different from industrialised countries where transmission is mostly through contact between homosexual or bisexual males, or via contaminated needles shared by intravenous drug users. Apart from abstinence, the most effective preventative is always to practise safe sex using condoms. It is impossible to detect the HIV-positive status of an otherwise healthy-looking person without a blood test.

HIV/AIDS can also be spread through infected blood transfusions; most developing countries cannot afford to screen blood for transfusions. It can also be spread by dirty needles – vaccinations, acupuncture, tattooing and ear or nose piercing can potentially be as dangerous as intravenous drug use if the equipment is not clean. If you do need an injection, ask to see the syringe unwrapped in front of you, or better still, take a needle and syringe pack with you overseas – it is a cheap insurance package against infection with HIV.

Fear of HIV infection should never preclude treatment for serious medical conditions. Although there may be a risk of infection, it is very small indeed.

Cuts, Bites & Stings

Cuts & Scratches The warm, moist conditions of the tropical lowlands invite and promote the growth of 'wee beasties' that would be thwarted in more temperate climates. Because of this, even a small cut or scratch can become painfully infected and lead to more serious problems.

Since bacterial immunity to certain antibiotics can build up, it's not wise to take these medicines indiscriminately or as a preventative measure. The best treatment for cuts is to cleanse the affected area frequently with soap and water and apply Mercurochrome or an antiseptic cream. Where possible, avoid using bandages, which keep wounds moist and encourage the growth of bacteria. If, despite this, the wound becomes tender and inflamed, then use of a mild, broad-spectrum antibiotic may be warranted.

Bichos de Pé These small parasites live on Bahian beaches and sandy soil. They burrow into the thick skin of the foot at the heel, toes and under the toenails and appear as dark boils. They must be incised and removed completely. Do it yourself with a sterilised needle and blade. To avoid *bichos de pé* wear footwear on beaches and dirt trails, especially where animals are present.

Snakebites Although threat of snakebite is minimal in Brazil, those walking around the forested northern areas may wish to take precautions. The most dangerous snakes native to Brazil are the bushmaster and the fer-de-lance (*jararacussu* or *jararaca*) – the latter is responsible for the highest number of reported snakebites in Brazil. To minimise chances of being bitten, wear boots, socks and long trousers when walking through undergrowth. A good pair of canvas gaiters will further protect your legs. Don't put your hands into holes and crevices, and be careful when collecting firewood. Check shoes, clothing and sleeping bags before use.

Snakebites do not cause instantaneous death and antivenenes are usually available, but it is vital that you make a positive identification of the snake in question or, at very least, have a detailed description of it.

If someone is bitten by a snake, keep the victim calm and still, wrap the bitten limb as you would for a sprain and then attach a splint to immobilise it. Tourniquets and suction on the wound are now comprehensively discredited. Seek medical help immediately and, if possible, bring the dead snake along for identification (but don't attempt to catch it if there is a chance of being bitten again). Bushwalkers should carry a field guide with photos and detailed descriptions of the possible perpetrators.

Insects Ants, gnats, mosquitoes, bees and flies will be just as annoying in Brazil as they are at home. Brazilian mosquitoes are not like their North American brethren: they are smaller, quicker, and are less detectable during the big drill. Their bites are vicious, their appetites insatiable and they're harder to smack. Cover yourself well with clothing and use insect repellent on exposed skin. Burning incense and sleeping under mosquito nets in air-conditioned rooms or under fans also lowers the risk of being bitten. Protect yourself especially from dusk to dawn, when mosquitoes, including the malaria-transmitting *Anopheles*, like to feed. Also nasty are the bites of the pium flies.

If you're going walking in humid or

densely foliated areas, wear light cotton trousers and shoes, not shorts and sandals or thongs. Regardless of temperature, never wear shorts or thongs in the forest and remember to carry an effective insect repellent. Bee and wasp stings are usually more painful than dangerous. Calamine lotion offers some relief and ice packs will reduce pain and swelling.

Body lice and scabies mites are also common in South America, so a number of shampoos and creams are available to eliminate them. In addition to hair and skin, clothing and bedding should be washed thoroughly to prevent further infestation.

Women's Health
Gynaecological Problems Poor diet, lowered resistance due to use of antibiotics, and even contraceptive pills can lead to vaginal infections when travelling in hot climates. To prevent the worst of it, keep the genital area clean, wear cotton underwear, and skirts or loose-fitting trousers.

Yeast infections, characterised by a rash, itch and discharge, can be treated with a vinegar or lemon juice douche or with yoghurt. Nystatin suppositories are the usual medical prescription. Trichomonas is a more serious infection which causes a discharge and a burning sensation when urinating. Male sexual partners must also be treated, and if a vinegar and water douche is not effective, medical attention should be sought. Flagyl is the most frequently prescribed drug.

Pregnancy Most miscarriages occur during the first three months of pregnancy, so this is the most risky time to travel as far as your own health is concerned. Miscarriage is not uncommon, and can occasionally lead to severe bleeding. The last three months should also be spent within reasonable distance of good medical care. A baby born as early as 24 weeks stands a chance of survival, but only in a good modern hospital. Pregnant women should avoid all unnecessary medication, but vaccinations and malarial prophylactics should still be taken

where possible. Additional care should be taken to prevent illness and particular attention should be paid to diet and nutrition. Alcohol and nicotine, for example, should be avoided.

Women travellers often find that their periods become irregular or even cease while they're on the road. Remember that a missed period in these circumstances doesn't necessarily indicate pregnancy. There are health posts or Family Planning clinics in many urban centres in developing countries, where you can seek advice and have a urine test to determine whether or not you are pregnant.

Back Home
Be aware of illness after you return. Take note of odd or persistent symptoms of any kind, get a check-up and remember to give your physician a complete travel history. Most doctors in temperate climes will not suspect unusual tropical diseases. If you have been travelling in malarial areas, have yourself tested for the disease.

WOMEN TRAVELLERS
Depending on where they travel in Brazil, lone women will be greeted with a range of responses. In São Paulo, for example, where there are many people of European ancestry, foreign women without travelling companions will scarcely be given a sideways glance. In the more traditional rural areas of the Northeast, where a large percentage of the population is of mixed European, African and Indian origin, blonde-haired and light-skinned women – especially those without male escorts – will certainly arouse curiosity.

Although *machismo* is an undeniable element in the Brazilian social structure, it is manifested less overtly than in Spanish-speaking Latin America. Perhaps because attitudes toward sex and pornography are quite liberal in Brazil, males feel little need to assert their masculinity or prove their prowess in the eyes of peers. Flirtation – often exaggerated – is a prominent element in Brazilian male/female relations. It goes both ways and is nearly always regarded as amusingly innocent banter; no sense of insult, exploitation – or intent to carry things further – should be derived from it. If unwelcome attention is forthcoming, you should be able to stop it by merely expressing disgust or displeasure.

Once you've spent an hour in Copacabana or Ipanema, where some women run their errands wearing fio dental, the famous Brazilian skimpy bikini, you'll be aware that dress restrictions – at least in some parts of Brazil – aren't as strict as they could be. It seems largely a matter of personal taste, but it's still best to synchronise your dress to local standards. What works in Rio will not necessarily be appropriate in a Northeastern city or a Piauí backwater.

Although most of the country is nearly as safe for women as for men, there are a few caveats which are also likely to apply at home. It's a good idea to keep a low profile in the cities at night and avoid going alone to bars and nightclubs if you'd rather not chance this being misinterpreted. Similarly, women should not hitch either alone or in groups; and even men or couples should exercise discretion when hitching. Most important, some of the more rough-and-ready areas of the north and west, where there are lots of men but few local women, should be considered off limits to lone female travellers.

DANGERS & ANNOYANCES
Security
Brazil gets a lot of bad international press about its violence and high crime rate. Not surprisingly, a recent official survey of foreign visitors to Brazil reported that concern about safety and security was one of the major reasons for feeling apprehensive about travelling to Brazil. During this research trip, all authors felt that Brazil's reputation as a violent nation, especially regarding travellers, is a bit exaggerated. But since many readers may not have previously experienced the type and extent of crime evident in Brazil (or other Latin American country), this section has been written in detail to heighten awareness. However, it is neither necessary nor helpful to become

paranoid. By using a common-sense approach, there are many things travellers can do to reduce the risks.

Predeparture Precautions
If you work on the elements of vulnerability, you can significantly reduce the risks. For starters, you should take with you only those items which you are prepared to lose or replace. Travel insurance is essential for replacement of valuables and the cost of a good policy is a worthwhile price to pay for minimum disturbance or even abrupt termination of your travel plans. Loss through petty theft or violence is an emotional and stressful experience which can be reduced if you think ahead. The less you have, the less you can lose.

Don't bring any jewellery, chains, or expensive watches, and if you have to wear a watch, then use a cheapie worth a few dollars. Even better, buy your cheapie watch in Brazil and keep it in your pocket, not on your wrist.

Be prepared for the worst – make copies of your important records: a photocopy of your passport (page with passport number, name, photograph, location where issued and expiration date, and all visas), tourist card (issued on entry to Brazil), travellers'-cheque numbers, credit-card numbers, airline tickets and essential contact addresses. Keep one copy on your person, one copy with your belongings and exchange one with a travelling companion.

By law you must carry a passport with you at all times, but many travellers opt to carry a photocopy (preferably certified) whilst they amble about town, and leave the passport locked up somewhere safe. A passport is worth several thousand dollars to some people, so keep a close eye on it. If you do lose it, a photocopy of the lost passport and a copy of your birth certificate can usually speed up the issuing of a new passport at embassies and consulates.

Credit cards are useful in emergencies, for cash advances and for regular purchases. Make sure you know the number to call if you lose your credit card and be quick to cancel it if lost or stolen. New-style credit card coupons do not have carbon paper inserts and offer more protection against misuse. If you sign an old-style coupon, be sure to ask for the carbon inserts and destroy them after use. Similarly, destroy any coupons which have been filled out incorrectly. These are worthwhile precautions against unwanted duplication of your credit card details.

Cabling money is difficult, time-consuming and expensive. You must know the name and address of both the bank sending (record this and keep this with your documents) and the bank receiving your money. In Rio, Casa Piano on Avenida Rio Branco is the most experienced with overseas transactions. The Brazilian American Cultural Center (BACC), which has offices in the USA and Brazil, provides a special remittance service for members – for details and main address of BACC, refer to the Useful Organisations section in this chapter.

Security Accessories Make sure that your backpack is fitted with double zippers which can be locked using small combination locks. Padlocks are also good, but are easier to pick. A thick backpack cover or modified canvas sack improves protection against pilfering, planting of drugs, and general wear and tear. Double zippers on your daypack can be secured with safety pins, which reduce the ease of access favoured by petty thieves. A medium-size combination lock or padlock is useful to replace the padlock on your hotel door. Rubber wedges are handy to prevent access to doors or windows. To deter thieves operating with razors, you can line the inside of your daypack (and even your backpack) with lightweight wire mesh.

Don't keep all your valuables together: distribute them about your person and baggage to avoid the risk of losing everything in one fell swoop. Various types of money belt are available to be worn around the waist, neck or shoulder; and leather or cotton material is more comfortable than synthetics. Such belts are only useful if worn *under* clothing – pouches worn outside clothing are easy prey and attract attention. Determined thieves are wise to conventional money belts, and some travellers now also use cloth pouches sewn into trousers or attached inside with safety pins. Other methods include belts with a concealed zipper compartment; and bandages or pouches worn around the leg. Or you could follow what locals do: wear a leather or vinyl pouch over a shoulder or on the side of the hip. Wear it like a local – 'with attitude', and stay alert.

If you wear glasses, secure them with an elastic strap to deter petty theft.

Finally, the extra pair of eyes provided by a travelling companion are an obvious asset.

Security Precautions in Brazil
There are certain key things you can do to reduce attention from criminals. Your style of dress should be casual and preferably something that blends in – inexpensive clothes bought in Brazil would be an obvious choice.

Most travellers carry a daypack. Whether you're in a bus station, restaurant, shop or elsewhere, whenever you have to put your daypack down, *always* put your foot through the strap. It makes things more difficult for furtive fingers or bag-slashers.

If you have a camera with you, never wander around with it dangling over your shoulder or around your neck – keep it out of sight as much as possible. It's also unwise to keep it in a swanky camera bag, which is an obvious target. We sometimes carried a camera in a sturdy plastic bag from a local supermarket.

Get used to keeping small change and a few banknotes in a shirt pocket so that you can pay bus tickets and small expenses without extracting large amounts of money which could quickly attract attention. This easily accessible money is also useful to rapidly appease a mugger. If you carry a wallet, keep it in your front pocket, and don't use it on public transport or in crowded places where it might attract unwelcome attention.

Before arriving in a new place, make sure you have a map or at least a rough idea of the area's orientation. Try to plan your schedule so you don't arrive at night, and do use a taxi if this seems the appropriate way to avoid walking through high-risk areas. A travelling companion is useful, since solo travellers are more easily distracted. Be observant and learn to look like a street-smart local.

Favourite Scams Distraction is a common tactic employed by street thieves. The 'cream technique' is now very common throughout South America, and Brazil is no exception. The trick commences when you're walking down the street or standing in a public place, and someone surreptitiously sprays a substance on your shoulder, your daypack or anything else connected with you. The substance can be anything from mustard to chocolate or even dog muck. An assistant (young or old, male or female) then taps you on the shoulder and amicably offers to clean off the mess...if you'll just put down your bag for a second. The moment you do this, someone makes off with it in a flash. The golden rule is to ignore any such attempt or offer, and simply endure your mucky state until you can find a safe place, such as your hotel, where you can wash. Just a couple of hours after arriving in Rio, we experienced an unsuccessful attempt of this kind.

Another distraction technique involves one or more people working to divert you or literally throw you off balance. This trick usually happens when you're standing in the street or somewhere busy like a bus station. One or more characters suddenly ask you a question, bump into you or stage an angry discussion or fight around you, and whilst you are off balance or diverted, there'll be an attempt to pick your pockets or grab your gear.

Never change money on the street; always ignore the itinerant moneychangers who whisper favourable rates into your ear as you pass; and never follow any of these types into a sidestreet for such a transaction. No exceptions – never means never.

There have also been some reportings of druggings. Exercise caution when you are offered cigarettes, beer, sweets, etc. If the circumstances make you suspicious or uneasy, the offer can be tactfully refused by claiming stomach or other medical problems.

These scams are continuously being developed, and imported or exported across borders. Keep abreast of new scams by talking to other travellers. In our experience, theft and security are sources of endless fascination and stories; some are true, some are incredible, and some are taller than Corcovado! If you think this section is useful and would like to forewarn other travellers about new developments, we'd appreciate your feedback. You might even derive consolation from letting off steam, and satisfaction by steering other travellers out of the clutches of criminals.

Credit Card Scam
About six weeks after getting back to Australia we received a nasty surprise on the monthly Visa statement. Someone in Brazil had used our card at a lumberyard in Cabo Frio to the tune of around US$1000. The transaction took place on the 20th of March, and we had left Brazil on the 3rd! This kind of thing is, according to our bank, quite common. Typically, your number will only be used once or twice. Thankfully, we weren't liable for the money they spent. It seems that somebody had taken the number from a coupon. We only used it a few times, so the suspects are a car rental firm in São Paulo, a restaurant in Rio de Janeiro and a hotel in Mato Grosso. Our money is on the restaurant in Rio. One of the waiters probably took down the number and sold it to his cousin who happens to be building a house near Cabo Frio.

Andrew Draffen

On the Beach Don't bring anything to city beaches apart from just enough money for lunch and drinks. No camera, no bag and no jewellery. Wear your bathing suit and bring a towel. That's it. If you want to photograph the beach, that's OK, but go with a friend, then return the camera to your room before staying on the beach. Don't hang out on deserted city beaches at night.

The favourite beach rip-off scam (apart from the fast snatch and grab) is where the thieves wait for you to be alone on the beach guarding you and your friend's gear (because you decided to take it in turns to go in the water). One thief will then approach from one side and ask you for a light or the time. While you're distracted, the thief's partner grabs your gear from the other side. It's a tried and tested trick, and usually works.

In the Northeast, male travellers have reported that 'good-time' ladies at beach bars make friendly advances over drinks which are drugged. The semi-comatose traveller is then accompanied back to his hotel, where the woman explains that she needs the key to help her 'drunken friend' to his room – where she cleans out all his valuables and then makes a quick exit.

Here's a typical beach mugging as experienced by one traveller in Rio:

I didn't look like a tourist; I wasn't carrying a camera or wearing flashy jewellery, just a cheap digital watch. I had the equivalent of US$50 in Brazilian currency, plus another US$100 in travellers' cheques. I knew better than to go to Copacabana beach with a lot of money, but then I thought nothing bad could happen to me.

Lulled by the beauty of Copacabana and the sound of the surf, I felt safe. I stripped down to my bathing suit, held my jeans, T-shirt and sandals in my hands like weights, and started running along the shoreline. There were no bathers or people lying on the sand, but there were plenty of joggers running in pairs and lots of soccer games going on. A man jogging alone on the hard-packed sand called for the time; a minute later he turned back, pointed to his bare wrist and shouted hoarsely. He said something about the watch which I couldn't understand, but I shouted back the time anyway: 'It's 4.30'. The sun wouldn't set for an hour and a half.

Ducking my head under the lines of some surfcasters, I slowed down to wade in the water and cool off, holding my things above the water. I turned around in the foot-deep surf and a crazed man with an eight-inch blade raised over his head was yelling at me in Portuguese, 'Give me everything you have. Give me your money'. I pulled the wallet out of my jeans and handed it to him.

'And the clothes!', he said. His head and neck were cocked to the side, trembling. Two surfcasters were only 20 feet away and they didn't do a damn thing. I could see people in the distance, but the incline of beach at the water's edge seemed like a wall of sand. I didn't shout, so as not to alarm the thief.

'The watch too!'

I fumbled with the watch band.

'Come on hurry up! The watch.'

He came towards me. I circled backwards in the water, afraid to trip, afraid he would lose his patience and kill me for the watch. I gave it to him.

The thief sprinted 100 yards down the beach and dropped to the ground with the bundle. He left my clothes and my travellers' cheques on the sand.

A soccer player left his game and approached me. 'It's a good thing you gave him the money because that guy was working with a group. They were standing right there, five men, two with pistols. The bandits, they don't bother us. We have an understanding with them.'

Maybe he was telling the truth or just covering up for not helping me. But I felt a lot better about just handing over my money. You hear stories about how dangerous Copacabana is, yet it's so beautiful, so wide-open that it puts you off guard. The beach doesn't fit your conception of what a dangerous place should look like. And yet it may well be the most likely place to get robbed in Brazil.

William Herzberg, USA

Streets, Buses & Taxis Thieves watch for people leaving hotels, car-rental agencies, American Express offices, tourist sights – places with lots of foreigners. Then they follow their targets. If you notice you are being followed or closely observed, it helps to pause and look straight at the person(s) involved or, if you're not alone, simply point out the person(s) to your companion. This makes it clear that the element of surprise favoured by petty criminals has been lost.

Don't advertise the fact that you're a foreigner by flashing big bills or wearing jewellery. Keep your watch out of sight in your pocket. Don't carry much money in the streets and even less on the municipal buses. Carry just enough money on your person for the evening's entertainment and transport, and keep it discreetly stashed away in a money belt, money sock, secret pocket or shoe.

Always have enough money on hand to appease a mugger (about US$2 to US$5). We've heard of Israeli tourists (fresh from military training) foiling attempted muggers, disarming them and breaking all their fingers, but we do not recommend resistance. There have been other reports of tourists shot dead whilst pursuing muggers – an absurd price to pay for the loss of valuables. Don't carry weapons because in many cases this could make matters much worse. In any case, if you've prepared for your trip along the lines mentioned earlier in this section, you'll probably feel happier just letting the unpleasant event pass.

If you ride on the buses, have your change ready before boarding. You are less of a target once you have passed the turnstile. Avoid the super-crowded buses. If you talk out loud, it's easier for thieves to identify you. If you have valuables, take taxis rather than buses.

Long-distance bus travel is usually well organised. If you hand over luggage to be placed in the baggage compartment, make sure you receive and keep your receipt. Two or more items can be padlocked together. We always try to take our pack inside and put it on the overhead luggage racks. If you have to place baggage on the roof, secure it with a padlock.

Although taxi drivers and their tricks with taxi fares can be irritating (see the Getting Around chapter for more details), taxis currently pose minimal problems with outright theft.

When entering or leaving a taxi, it's advisable (particularly for solo travellers) to keep a passenger door open during the loading or unloading of luggage – particularly if this is being done by someone other than the driver. This reduces the ease with which a taxi can drive off with your luggage, leaving you behind! A neater solution for those who travel light is to fit luggage inside the taxi rather than in the boot.

Also, when entering or leaving a taxi, always remember to watch your luggage (slip your foot or your arm through a strap). Opportunistic thieves are quick to make off with items whilst you are distracted by price-haggling or baggage arrangement. If you're travelling as a pair (or larger group), it's a good general precaution to always have at least one person remain close to the open passenger door or inside the taxi whenever luggage is still in the taxi.

Before starting, immediately question the presence of any shady characters accompanying the driver, and don't hesitate to take another taxi if you feel uneasy. If there are mechanical or orientation problems en route, do not allow yourself to be separated from your luggage. When you arrive at your destination, *never* hand over your luggage to a person who tries to help you out of the car and offers to carry something, unless you are quite positive about their identity. Otherwise, you may see your luggage disappearing down the street.

Hotels If you consider your hotel to be reliable, place valuables in its safe and get a receipt. Make sure you package your valuables in a small, double-zippered bag which can be padlocked, or use a large envelope with a signed seal which will easily show any tampering. Count your money and travellers' cheques before and after retrieving them from the safe – this should quickly identify any attempts to extract single bills or cheques which might otherwise go unnoticed.

Check the door, doorframe, and windows of your room for signs of forced entry or unsecured access. If your hotel provides a padlock, it's recommended to use your own combination lock (or padlock) instead. A hotel padlock obviously increases the number of people with access to your room; and there have been reports of criminals holding up hotel receptionists at gunpoint whilst an accomplice takes the keys and cleans out the rooms. Don't leave your valuables strewn around the room. It's too much of a temptation to cleaners and other hotel staff.

Boats Passengers on local boats, particularly in northern Brazil, are the target of thieves who take advantage of crowded conditions, long journeys and unsecured baggage – particularly at night. Before boarding, beware of entrusting your baggage to someone wearing an official uniform who requests to see your ticket and even issues a receipt. We met a German traveller who had done this in Belém, only to return several hours later to find that the official had been bogus, the padlock for the boat's 'storage room' had belonged to the impostor, and the German's backpack had disappeared.

On board, make sure you keep all valuables on your person, never flash your money around, and keep your camera out of sight as much as possible. Double zippers on your baggage should be padlocked and a bicycle padlock or chain is useful to secure your baggage to a fixture on the boat. Some travellers use a large eyelet hook and a rope to suspend baggage from the ceiling next to their hammock. Do not assume cabins have secure access.

It is important that any baggage you are not carrying on your person is secured to the boat. Thieves prefer to rifle through unsecured and unobserved baggage, extract valuables and then simply dump large evidence (the baggage) overboard. This happened to one of the authors when a daypack was stolen and dumped overboard during a long Amazon trip. The loss of money was sustainable (and replaceable), but the biggest blow was the loss of dozens of rolls of film (for another book) and personal effects.

The Police

If something is stolen from you, you can report it to the police. No big investigation is going to occur but you will get a police form to give to your insurance company. However, the police aren't to be trusted either. Brazilian police are known to plant drugs and sting gringos for bribes. The bribes are like pyramids: the more people are involved, the bigger the bribe becomes.

Drugs

Marijuana and cocaine are plentiful in Brazil, and very illegal. The military regime had a rather pathological aversion to drugs and enacted stiff penalties, which are still in force. Nevertheless, marijuana and cocaine are widely used, and, like many things in Brazil, everyone except the military and the police has a rather tolerant attitude towards them. Bahia seems to have the most open climate. But because of the laws against possession, you won't bump into much unless you know someone or go to an 'in' vacation spot with the young and hip like Arraial d'Ajuda, Morro de São Paulo or Canoa Quebrada.

There are some wild hallucinogenic substances in the Amazon. The best known is *Banisteriopsis caapi*, better known as yagé or ayahuasca, which comes from a jungle vine and has ritual uses amongst certain tribes and cults. For more details about the cults refer to the Other Cults section under Religion in the Facts about the Country chapter. For further reading on the topic of drugs, refer to the Amazon & Indians section under Books & Maps in this chapter.

Drugs provide a perfect excuse for the police to get a fair amount of money from you, and Brazilian prisons are brutal places. Police checkpoints along the highways stop cars and buses at random. Police along the coastal drive from Rio to São Paulo are notorious for hassling young people and foreigners. Border areas are also very dangerous. A large amount of cocaine is smuggled out of Bolivia and Peru through Brazil. Be very careful with drugs. Don't buy from strangers and don't carry anything around with you.

If you're coming from one of the Andean countries and have been chewing coca leaves, be especially careful to clean out your pack before arriving in Brazil. Here's what happened to a traveller who didn't:

I got out of jail after four days with the help of the consul, and was supposed to stay in Rio for 14 days waiting for trial, but my lawyer found out that the judge wanted to send me to jail so he suggested I leave immediately. The consul gave me a passport and I flew south to Porto Alegre and crossed the border into Uruguay without difficulty before flying home.

My parents were very happy of course, but it cost them a lot of money to get me out. A lady from the consulate in Rio wrote and told me that I'd been sentenced to four years in jail, and it was only 17.7 grams of coca leaves!

I'm glad to be home, safe and in one piece, and I don't have to fight with those disgusting cockroaches! Just think of it – four years in a Brazilian jail! I can't even imagine it but it was so close.

Name withheld for obvious reasons

This woman was one of the lucky ones. Don't forget to clean out that pack!

Beggars

A disconcerting aspect of travel in Brazil, particularly in the cities of the Northeast, is the constant presence of beggars. With no social-welfare system to sustain them, the elderly, blind, crippled, mentally ill and jobless take to the streets and try to arouse sympathy in any way they can.

Since giving even a pittance to every beggar encountered will be financially impossible for most visitors, everyone has to formulate their own idea about what constitutes an appropriately humanitarian response. Some travellers choose to give to only the most pathetic cases or to those enterprising individuals who provide some value for the money, such as by singing or playing a musical instrument. Others simply feel that contributions only serve to fuel the machine that creates beggars and ignore them.

All we can offer on this issue is a couple of guidelines, the rest must be left to your conscience. The physically impaired are always underemployed, and frequently have to fall back on selling lottery tickets and telephone tokens, but they do manage to earn something. The mentally indigent or the elderly, who would appear to have no other possible means of support, may be especially good candidates. Keep in mind, however, that many families simply set their older members on the pavement with a tin bowl hoping to generate a little extra income. For those who go begging for bones, scraps and leftovers, or others who are truly trying to

change their situations, a bowl of soup or a nutritious hot meal will go a long way.

Regarding the numerous children who beg, it's probably best not to give money since it will lead to their exploitation by unscrupulous adults and will give the impression that something can be had for nothing. For a child who appears truly hungry, a piece of fruit or other healthy snack will be greatly appreciated. If such gifts are refused and money is demanded, it should be fairly obvious what's really going on.

Plumbing

Much of the plumbing in Brazil is jerry-built or poorly installed and can pose problems to the uninitiated. Therefore, some explanation and instruction for use may be helpful.

First of all, bathtubs are rare outside of expensive tourist hotels, as are hot and cold running water. It is possible however, to have hot, or tepid, showers thanks to a frightening and deadly-looking device that attaches to the shower head and electrically heats the water as it passes through. Bare wires dangle from the ceiling or run into the shower head.

The dangling variety indicates that you're not going to get a hot shower because the device is broken, as many are. Don't bother getting undressed until you've verified that it's working.

On the wall, you will find a lever that looks suspiciously like an old-time electrocutioner's switch. You have to flip the switch after the water is running (yes really), so it's best to leave your shoes or flip-flops on and not get wet until this is done.

When the heater is activated, it will begin to emit an electrical humming sound and the lights in the room will dim or go out altogether. This is because the heater requires a great deal of electricity to operate effectively.

The temperature of the water can then be adjusted by increasing or decreasing the flow. A larger volume of water cannot be adequately heated in the time it takes to pass through the shower head, so a shower of a bearable temperature often becomes nothing but a pressureless drip.

When it's time to turn the water off, don't

touch the controls until you've dried off and have your footwear on. This may be tricky, especially if the shower stall is small. Before turning the water off, flip the switch on the wall and then turn off the water.

WORK

Travellers on tourist visas aren't supposed to work in Brazil. The only viable paid work is teaching English in one of the big cities, but you need to be able to speak a bit of Portuguese and allow enough time to get some pupils. I taught English in São Paulo for five months a few years ago and found that I was able to earn between US$5 and US$10 per hour. Teaching company executives during their lunch hour and taking private pupils at home were my most lucrative classes, but both these take some time to set up.

To find work, look in the classifieds under 'Professor de Ingles', or ask around at the English schools.

Volunteer work with welfare organisations is quite easy to find if you're prepared to do some door-knocking. One traveller we met walked up to the front door of a Catholic home for abandoned children in Recife and asked if there was anything he could do. The priests in charge gave him a place to sleep and he spent the next two months helping to cook, getting the children out of jail, telling them stories and breaking up knife fights. He said it was the highlight of his trip.

ACTIVITIES
Windsurfing

Windsurfing is catching on. In Rio you can rent equipment down at Barra da Tijuca. I saw lots of windsurfing at Ilhabela in São Paulo, Porto Seguro and Belém, among other places.

Hang-Gliding

It's easy to fly *duplo* in Rio. Go to Pepino beach, where you'll see the gliders landing, and for US$80 someone will take you up (straight up) Pedra Bonita and fly down with you on a glider built for two (see the Rio de Janeiro chapter for more information).

Surfing

Today surfing is popular all along the coast and there are some excellent waves to be had, especially in the south. Santa Catarina has the best surfing beaches and holds the Brazilian championships at Joaquina beach near Florianópolis. In Rio state, Saquarema has the best surf. Búzios and Itacoatiara beach in Niterói are also popular breaks. There's also plenty of surf close to the city of Rio – see the Rio de Janeiro chapter for details. The waves are best in the Brazilian winter (from June to August).

Surfing Vocabulary Despite their reputation for aggressiveness in the water, once on land Brazilian surfers become very interested in foreign surfers and their travels. They also are reasonably willing to lend their boards if you ask politely.

surfer	*surfista*
wave	*onda*
surfboard	*prancha*
to break	*quebrar*
wind	*vento*

Are there any waves?
  Tem ondas?
Could I borrow your board please?
  Pode me emprestar sua prancha por favor?
Let's go surfing.
  Vamos pegar ondas.

Other Water Sports

As you would expect in a place with such a long coastline and so many beach lovers, all water sports are popular. And as you would expect in a place with such a large gap between rich and poor, they're restricted to those who can afford them. What this means to the traveller is that in order to rent the equipment needed to practise any of the above activities you need to go to established resorts.

Sailing is big in Búzios in Rio state and the larger resorts along the coast. Diving doesn't match the Caribbean, but it is worthwhile if you're keen. Angra dos Reis is the best place in Rio state, and Porto Seguro in Bahia has been recommended.

Fishing in the interior of Brazil is fantastic. The Rio Araguaia in Goiâs and Tocantins is known as a fishing paradise, with a large variety of fish including the pintado, dourado and tucunaré. In the Pantanal, licensed fishing is allowed on the Taquari, Coxim, Aquidauana, Cuiabá and Paraguay rivers. Fishing for piranha is not undertaken by serious anglers, though it's good fun.

Hiking & Climbing

Hiking and climbing in Brazil are best during the cooler months of the year – April to October. During the summer, the tropical sun heats the rock up to oven temperatures and turns the jungles into steamy saunas. Climbing during the summer is still pursued, although usually in the early morning or late afternoon when the sun's rays are not so harsh.

The best thing about rock climbing in Brazil is that one hour you can be on the beach, and the next on a world-class rock climb 300 metres above a city. Brazil has lots of fantastic rock climbs, ranging from the beginner level to routes still unconquered. In Rio de Janeiro, the centre of rock climbing in Brazil, there are 350 documented climbs that can all be reached within 40 minutes from the city centre.

There are lots of great places to hike in Brazil, both in the national and state parks and along the coastline. Lots of good hikes are mentioned in the appropriate chapters. It's also a good idea to contact some of the climbing clubs (see the Rio city chapter for addresses), who have details of trekking options.

Climbing Vocabulary Although most Brazilians in the clubs know a little English, not everyone does. It helps to know a little Portuguese to smooth the way.

equipment	*equipamento*
bolt	*grampo*
rope	*corda*
carabiner	*mosquetão*
harness	*baudrie*
backpack	*mochila*
webbing	*fita*
chalk powder	*pó de magnésio*
rock	*rocha*
summit	*topo/cume*
crack	*fenda*
route	*via/rota*
a fall	*queda*
to be secured	*estar preso*
a hold	*uma agarra*
to belay	*dar segurança*
to make a stupid mistake and fall	*tomar uma vaca*

HIGHLIGHTS

Brazil offers much more than Carnival and Amazon River trips. The following are suggestions for you to explore and enjoy the country.

Historical Cities & Architecture

Salvador and Pelourinho; Olinda; Alcântara and São Luís; Lençóis; Cachoeira; Goiás Velho; Ouro Prêto and other historical cities in Minas Gerais; Parati.

Museums

Museu Emílio Goeldi (Belém); Museu Histórico (Alcântara); Museu do Homem do Nordeste (Recife); Museu da Borracha (Rio Branco); Museu Dom Bosco (Campo Grande); Museu Folclorico Edson Carneiro and Museu da República (Rio de Janeiro);

Museu Biológico de Professor Melo Leitão (Santa Teresa).

Beaches

Prainha (Natal, Rio Grande do Norte); Tambaba (Paraíba); Prejuiças (Lençóis Maranhenses, Maranhão); Morro de São Paulo (Bahia); Jericoacoara (Ceará); Pepino and Barra (Rio de Janeiro); Parati (Rio state); Joaquina (Florianópolis); Ilha do Mel (Paraná).

Festivals

Boa Morte (Cachoeira); Bumba Meu Boi (São Luís); Carnival (Olinda); Círio de Nazaré (Belém); Cavalhadas (Pirenópolis); Semana Santa (Goiás Velho); New Year's Eve on Copacabana beach (Rio de Janeiro).

Food & Drinks

Baiana cuisine; exotic forest fruits and juices; Mineiro cuisine; fresh fruit *batidas*; a well-made *caipirinha*. (See the Food section for details.)

Restaurants

Miako (Japanese, Belém); Casa do Benin (African, Salvador); Pousalegre (Baiana and Chinese, Lençóis); Raizes (Northeastern specialities, Natal); Cervantes (meat and pineapple sandwiches, Rio de Janeiro); Tio Flor (gaúcho cuisine, Porto Alegre); Colombo (coffee, cakes and atmosphere, Rio de Janeiro).

Accommodation

Canto das Águas (Lençóis); Pousada dos Quatro Cantos (Olinda); Hotel Rio Branco

---

Doing It Yourself
One of our readers offers his comments on climbing in Brazil:

If you're a climber travelling to Brazil, don't hesitate to bring a bit of gear and do some routes. You don't need much – a pair of boots, a chalk bag, harness, 10-mm rope, 10 quick-draws and a couple of long slings are enough. You can sell used gear very quickly and easily in Rio – just contact the clubs for interested members. Practically all routes are bolted; most bolts are really solid, though those around the sea-cliff areas can be rusty and a bit dubious.

Hanging belays are very common – they usually consist of a single bolt. It can be very unnerving when you're 200 metres off the ground, leading off a single anchor with 20 metres to the next piece of protection.

The routes are usually long and interesting, if a little run-out. Cracks aren't very abundant and where they do exist they usually peter out fairly quickly. The rock is old and weathered, and generally very solid. Friction is excellent – but the small, sharp edges (especially on the crags around Rio) can be pretty severe on boots. You tend to lose quite a bit of rubber. However, it's easy and cheap to get boots resoled in Rio. I had an old pair of Rocksters resoled for US$15, and it was a very neat and professional job. Just call Eduardo Cabral (☎ 239-2773), or contact Club Excursionista Carioca. You can also stay at the club for US$3 a night. It has a fridge, bathroom and toilet, and is only a block from Copacabana beach.

Most of the climbing in Brazil is centred around the southern states as far north as Rio. Some interesting areas include:

Pedra do Bau This is a 300-metre rock pinnacle near Campos do Jordáio in the Serra da Mantiqueira. The valley itself is popular for hang-gliding and para-gliding. Two peaks provide various free and artificial routes: Pedra do Bauzinho, the smaller of the two, has some easy climbs but is mainly used as a descent route (via two abseils) to a knife-edge ridge which provides access to Pedra do Baú – a striking, isolated pinnacle of rock. Several climbs of moderate grades ascend the pinnacle, and all are provided with bolts.

Três Picos This is an amazing place near Nova Friburgo in Rio state. From Nova Friburgo, ask

(Rio Branco); Pousada do Mordomo Régio (Alcântara); Nhundiaquara (Morretes); Pouso Chico Rei (Ouro Prêto); Pousada do Ypê (Goiás Velho).

Music & Dance
Sunday night in Pelourinho (Salvador); forro on Ilha do Mel (Paraná); forró at the Estudantina club (Rio de Janeiro); Samba do Enredo at the Rio Carnival.

Wildlife Viewing
Pantanal Matogrossense; Tefé (Amazonas).

National Parks & Natural Attractions
Parque Nacional de Aparados da Serra (Itaimbezinho canyon); Iguaçu Falls; Parque Nacional da Chapada dos Guimarães; Parque Nacional de Caparaó; Parque Nacio-nal da Chapada Diamantina; Parque Nacio-nal dos Lençóis Maranhenses; Parque Nacional Marinho de Fernando de Noronha; Parque Nacional da Serra da Capivara.

Religious Experiences
Candomblé (Bahia); Colônia Cinco Mil (Rio Branco); Vale de Amanhecer (Brasília).

Sports
Capoeira (Bahia); football (Rio); *futvolei* (foot volleyball) (Rio).

Offbeat Attractions & Activities
Olaria de Brennand (Recife); train ride from Cuiabá to Paranaguá (Paraná); dune-buggy rides (Natal); Ribeirão do Meio water slides (Lençóis); catamaran excursions from São Luís to Alcântara; nudist beach at Tambaba

---

for directions to the bus stop for the No 620 bus to São Lourenço. The 1½-hour trip to Três Picos traverses mostly dirt roads – ask to be let off at the Três Picos turn-off. Walk up this dirt road for about six km (all uphill) and head for the three granite domes which dominate the valley. If you're unsure of the way, ask for directions to Renaldo's fazenda – his farm is the last in the valley, at the base of the cliffs. Renaldo has two huts which he allows climbers to use, and one has electric light. It's customary to give him 50 cents per person per night for the use of the huts, though he won't ask for it. The last bus leaves Nova Friburgo for São Lourenço at 6.50 pm.

This is one of the best climbing areas in Brazil. The rock is small-crystal granite, with great friction. Routes vary in size from 400 to 700 metres, on three separate granite domes: Capacete (400 metres), Pico Maior (700 metres) and Pico Médio (500 to 600 metres). The grades vary from 5.9 to 5.12 and above (Australian grade 18 and beyond). From the summit, views are spectacular – to the south lies Serra dos Órgãos (Dedo de Deus, etc); to the east lies Rio (visible on a clear day); and north and west lie rolling, mountainous valleys. The potential for new routes is enormous and you could spend a long time here. It's wise to take up a few days' food, as the round trip to the nearest shop, on foot, is about 14 km. Drinkable spring water is provided at the huts.

Rio Pão de Açúcar (Sugar Loaf) is the stereotypical, 'must-do' climbing area close to the city. The easy solo route described in the Rio chapter of this book is worthwhile. It's more bushwalking than climbing, though one exposed section requires caution. I've clambered up this route dozens of times and have yet to tire of it. If you start the walk at about 3 pm you'll get to the top in time to see the sun set over Rio – a worthwhile experience. It's not necessary to pay the cost of the cable-car ride back down – just hop on.

On Saturday, the Carioca Climbing Club opens up the artificial climbing wall built into the side of the topmost cable-car station. Anybody is welcome to join in – just bring boots, a harness and chalk-bag. The wall has several routes, all bolted, with a tendon-grinding roof and overhung section.

The more serious routes on Pão de Açúcar start from the base of the cliff under the cable car. The routes include: Cavallo Louco (a classic), Italiano, Cisco Kid, Babylonia and Acid Wall. It's also possible to climb some routes at night, under the floodlights set up for the tourist lookout.

Greg Caire

(João Pessoa); pororoca tidal bore (Amapá); Salão Internacional de Humor do Piauí (International Humour Festival of Piauí, Teresina); steam train from São João del Rei to Tiradentes (Minas Gerais); hot spa at the Parque das Aguas (Caxambu); double hang-gliding (Rio); tubing down the Rio Nhundiaquara (Morretes); piranha fishing (Pantanal); Butantan snake farm (São Paulo).

SUGGESTED ITINERARIES

The following is a list of possible itineraries:

One Week Why only a week? Brazil deserves much more! Pick a city and stay put. Either Rio de Janeiro, the *cidade maravilhosa* or vibrant, exciting Salvador. Going anywhere else, unless you've got friends, business or an adventure destination in mind, is a waste of time. Rio would be our first pick because you have the classic postcard views and the Cariocas, a lively, happy-go-lucky people. In both cities there's lots of music, something you should see and hear as much as possible during your week. Both cities offer short, interesting side trips. In Rio state, there are four national parks within a few hours of the city for great hiking in the lush Atlantic rainforest, fantastic diving and beaches along the south coast toward the colonial gem, Parati, and Búzios, the beach resort for Rio's beautiful people, a couple of hours to the north.

Close to Salvador there's the island of Itaparica, the largest island in the Baía de Todos os Santos, and there are some great beaches close to the city. The Recôncavo region, with its colonial towns, is close by.

Two to Three Weeks Better than one week but still not enough! An extra couple of weeks means you can move a little more. A Brazil Airpass allows you five flights in 21 days, and you can add on extra flights for US$100. If you don't mind moving around a bit, travel light and have some fun. In 14 – 21 days, your route may include:

Belo Horizonte Belo Horizonte isn't much of a city and the airport is miles from the centre, but it's a good base from which to explore the colonial towns with their rich baroque churches. Ouro Prêto is the most beautiful, but there are others close by, like Mariana and Tiradentes. Renting a car for a couple of days is a good idea here.

Brasília Brasília is such a curious place and it is the capital after all. It's good for two days at a maximum, and rent a car – the city was built for driving not walking.

Cuiabá Capital of the western state of Mato Grosso, Cuiabá is the place to fly into for a three or four-day Pantanal trip. Make sure you also visit Chapada dos Guimarães.

Florianópolis Florianópolis is the capital of the southern state of Santa Catarina, located on the island of Santa Catarina. It's a good place to rent a car for a couple of days and explore a lovely island with some great beaches.

Fortaleza Fortaleza is a good base for seeing the northern beaches. Buy a hammock and go to the beach, or take a bus and spend a couple of days in the amazing Jericoacoara dunes

Foz do Iguaçu These falls should be included on any itinerary for a minimum of two days. A sight not to miss.

Manaus Manaus is the capital of the northern state of Amazonas. Three or four days here may include a jungle trip. The city itself has some historical attractions like the opera house and market.

Recife There are good beaches here and the colonial town of Olinda is next-door. You could easily spend two days here.

Rio de Janeiro Rio is a good starting and finishing point for any trip. You could easily spend 14 – 21 days in Rio state and never be bored. Instead of buying an airpass, you could rent a car and tour the state. There's lots of variety, from beaches to mountains.

Salvador Try to spend at least a week in Salvador. It is truly the black Rome. There is so much African heritage here, and yet it's so Brazilian too. A must for music lovers.

There are lots of other cities or town that you could visit. We once included Tabatinga, a small town on the border with Peru and Colombia. It was an interesting experience, as well as a good way to head back into Peru.

Ninety Days or More Now you have a reasonable amount of time. Ninety days is the maximum visa length before you need to leave the country or get an extension (if you need a visa that is). You'll be able to move much slower and get a good feel for the variety that Brazil offers. Many travellers with this much time will be including Brazil in their itinerary for a tour around South America. We advise you to spend the last part of your tour in Brazil, because once you get here, you won't want to leave!

The classic travel route around Brazil is entering through Paraguay or Bolivia at Corumbá, spending some time exploring the Pantanal, then moving east through São Paulo to Rio, checking out Rio city and state and then moving north into Bahia, lying on the beach at one of the hip resorts like Arraial d'Ajuda, Trancoso or Morro de São Paulo. The city of Salvador is on the route and it's definitely worth some time. Most travellers then move through the Northeast region, with its multitude of beaches, before arriving in Belém and moving up the Amazon River, and onto Peru or Colombia.

It's surprising how many travellers choose to end their trip with a 21-day airpass. It's a good way to take in some of the out-of-the-way places you may have missed.

If you have six months, spend one month in Rio (from the start of February until Carnival would be ideal). Spend December or January at a hip beach in the Northeast – you'll meet lots of Brazilians on holiday (then you can go and visit them later!). Spend two weeks in the city of Salvador, three weeks in the Pantanal, two weeks in the Amazon, three days at Foz do Iguaçu and two weeks in Minas Gerais. Travel through the Northeast for a month or so. Of course, you may want to stop and stay put for a while. That's the best thing about travelling for long periods. You'll have a great time.

ACCOMMODATION

We have managed to tackle the problem of inflation reasonably well by quoting all prices in US dollars, but it is impossible to counteract the weird price changes caused when the government freezes prices, unfreezes them and then freezes them again. And when they introduce a currency that's actually stronger than the US dollar, it's too much for our brains to handle. Most of the prices listed will be reasonably accurate, but once in a while there is bound to be a shocker. For advice about security and accommodation, refer to the Dangers & Annoyances section in this chapter.

Camping

Camping is becoming increasingly popular in Brazil and is a viable alternative for travellers on limited budgets or those who want to explore some of the country's national or state parks. For detailed information on camping grounds it's a good idea to buy the *Guia Quatro Rodas Camping Guide* from any newsstand. You may also want to contact the Camping Club of Brazil, Rua Senador Dantas 75, 25th floor, Rio de Janeiro. The club has 52 sites in 14 states.

Minimum-Impact Camping The following guidelines are recommended for those camping in wilderness or other fragile areas of Brazil:

- Select a well-drained campsite and, especially if it's raining, use a plastic or other type of waterproof groundsheet to prevent having to dig trenches.
- Along popular routes, set up camp in established sites.
- Biodegradable items may be buried but anything

with food residue should be carried out – including cigarette butts – lest it be dug up and scattered by animals.

- Use established toilet facilities if they are available. Otherwise, select a site at least 50 metres from water sources and bury wastes in a cat-hole at least several inches deep. If possible, burn the used toilet paper or bury it well.
- Use only biodegradable soap products (you'll probably have to carry them from home) and to avoid thermal pollution, use natural-temperature water where possible. When washing up dishes with hot water, either let it cool to outdoor temperature before pouring it out or dump it in a gravelly, non-vegetated place away from natural water sources.
- Wash dishes and brush your teeth well away from watercourses.
- When building a fire, try to select an established site and keep fires as small as possible. Use only fallen dead wood and when you're finished, make sure ashes are cool and buried before leaving. Again, carry out cigarette butts.

Youth Hostels

Youth hostels in Brazil are called *albergues de juventude*, and in the last few years the Brazilian organisers have been getting their act together. There are now more than 90 hostels and more are planned. Most state capitals and popular tourist areas have at least one. Although quality varies widely, the cost is very reasonable and is regulated by the federation in Brazil. A night in a hostel will cost between US$6 to US$8 per person, depending on inflation. It's not always necessary to be a member to stay in one, but it'll cost you more if you're not. Hostelling International cards are accepted, but if you arrive in Brazil without one you can buy guest membership cards for about US$20 from the head office in each state. Booklets listing the hostels and describing how to get there (in Portuguese) are available at these offices and most travel agents.

The head office of the Federação Brasileira dos Albergues de Juventude (FBAJ) (☎ (021) 2524829) is at Rua da Assembléia 10, sala 1211, Centro, Rio de Janeiro, CEP 20011, RJ. The FBAJ publishes a useful directory of Brazilian hostels, and it's available from most newsstands for US$6.

Dormitórios

A *dormitório* is dorm-style sleeping with several beds to a room. These are usually the cheapest places in town, often costing as little as US$3 or US$4 a head per night.

Pousadas

Most budget travellers stay at a *pousada* (small guesthouse) where a room without a bathroom can go for as little as US$5 or US$7 per person. These rooms with communal bathrooms down the hall are called *quartos*. Similar rooms with a private bathroom are called *apartamentos*, and cost a couple of dollars more. Not all pousadas are cheap; there are some five-star ones.

Hotels

If you want to travel in style, Brazil has modern luxury hotels all over the place. Decent hotels can cost as little as US$15 to US$20 a double per night and, at the other end of the scale, as much as US$100 to US$250 per night in Rio and São Paulo. Often a 10% tax is added to the bill.

Aparthotels, available in the larger cities, provide the comforts of a good hotel without some of the glitter. They are also a bit cheaper. A good, medium-priced aparthotel should cost somewhere from US$50 per night for a double room.

Most hotels in Brazil are regulated by Embratur, the federal tourism authority. They also rate the quality of hotels from one to five stars. Regulated hotels must have a price list with an Embratur label which is usually posted on the wall in every room and behind the reception desk. Even so, it still pays to bargain.

It's a good idea to look at a room before deciding to take it. Check the shower for hot water, check the bed, check the lock on the door. Three big sleep killers in Brazil are mosquitoes, heat and, in rural areas, roosters! Fans do wonders for stopping the first two, but you can't do much about the third – visualising yourself with your hands around the rooster's neck doesn't help, unfortunately!

Many medium-priced and expensive

hotels have safes which are safe to use so long as you get a receipt.

In the off season many hotels have promotional rates. Ask about them. Sometimes good hotels have a few quartos or cheaper rooms which are not advertised. It pays to enquire about these, as they allow you to use all the facilities of the hotel while paying considerably less than the other guests.

For more details about bargaining, refer to Bargaining under the Money section in this chapter.

There are a few games played by hotel clerks to get you into a more expensive room. If you want a single room there are only doubles; if you want a quarto, there are only apartamentos. Don't say yes too quickly – if you feign a desire to look for alternative lodging, they will often remember that there is a cheaper room after all. In reality, some hotels don't have singles. It is generally much cheaper to travel with someone, as rooms for two are nowhere near twice as expensive as rooms for one.

Reservations If you're staying in middle to high-class hotels, reservations are a good idea in touristed centres (especially in Rio) during vacations (July and December to February) and in any vacation mecca (eg Búzios) during weekends. We try to list hotel phone numbers for this purpose, but you can also get them from travel agents and tourist information offices. Be wary of taxi drivers, particularly in Rio, who know just the hotel for you. You may find yourself being taken to an expensive hotel which pays the cabby a commission.

Another good reason for making a reservation in this class of hotel is that the price may be up to 30% cheaper than the 'rack-rate' you'd get if you just walked in off the street. If your language skills aren't up to it, get a travel agent to do it for you.

To avoid summer crowds, it is not a bad idea to travel during the week and stay put, usually in a city, during the weekends, when the locals are making their pilgrimages away from the cities. This minimises your contact with crowded buses and hotels and gets you into the city for the weekend music and festivities.

Motels

Motels are a Brazilian institution and should never be confused with hotels. They have names like Alibi, Ilha do Capri, Motel Sinless, L'Amour and Wet Dreams. Rented by the hour, for short stays only, the motel is the Brazilian solution to the lack of privacy caused by overcrowded living conditions. Used by adults who still live with their parents, kids who want to get away from their parents and couples who want to get away from their kids, they are an integral part of the nation's social fabric, a bedrock of Brazilian morality, and are treated by Brazilians with what most outsiders consider to be incredible nonchalance.

The quality of motels varies, reflecting their popularity with all social classes. Most are out of the city centre, with walled-in garages for anonymity. A personal favourite is the Asturia in São Paulo. In a three-storey apartment, it has a hot tub on the top floor with skylights that open. On the 2nd floor is a sauna and bathroom. The suites have circular vibra-beds with mirrors overhead, a video recorder with adult movies piped over loudspeakers, and room service with a menu full of foods and sex toys (with instructions).

Most travellers don't spend much time in motels, but they can be quite useful, and a lot of fun if you're travelling as a couple. If you're having trouble finding accommodation, they're not too expensive.

Accommodation in Remote Areas

If you're travelling where there are no hotels – the Amazon or the Northeast – a hammock and a mosquito net are essential. With these basics, and friendly locals, you can get a good night's rest anywhere.

Most fishing villages along the coast have seen an outsider or two and will put you up for the night. If they've seen a few more outsiders, they'll probably charge you a couple of dollars.

FOOD

Vou matar quem 'tá me matando.
I'm going to kill what's killing me.
(A popular saying when sitting down to eat)

The hub of the Brazilian diet revolves around *arroz* (white rice), *feijão* (black beans) and *farofel* (manioc flour). It's possible to eat these every day in Brazil and in some regions it's hard not to. The tasty black beans are typically cooked in bacon. The white rice is often very starchy. Farofel, the staple of the Indians, slaves and Portuguese for hundreds of years, is a hardy root that grows everywhere. It seems to be an acquired taste for foreign palates.

From the rice-bean-farofel group, meals go in one of three directions: *carne* (steak), *galinha* (chicken) and *peixe* (fish). This makes up the typical Brazilian meal and is called *prato feito* (set meal) or *prato do dia* (plate of day) in *lanchonetes* from Xique Xique to Bananal. They are typically enormous meals and incredibly cheap, but after a while they can become a trifle monotonous. If quantity is your thing, you can live like a king.

What is done with the meat, chicken or fish? It's cooked, and that's about it. Don't

get me wrong, it's generally very good meat, but Brazilians don't do much with it. Steak is the national passion. They like it big and rare. The best cuts are *filet* and *churrasco*. Chicken is usually grilled, sometimes fried. Fish is generally fried.

But that's not the end of the story. In the cities you can get many of the dishes that you like back home. There's also fine dining. For US$7 to US$12 you can have a superb Italian, Japanese or Indian dinner in Rio or São Paulo. *Churrascarias* and *rodízios* bring you all the meat you can eat and a variety of other goodies for a fixed price (around US$5 in Rio). They must be tried – vegetarians have no problem filling up at the salad bar either, if they don't mind seeing all that meat. Rodízios are especially good in the South.

Lanchonetes are stand-up fast-food bars where you can order sandwiches and *pasteis* (crumbed hors d'oeuvres). *Restaurantes* have more proper sit-down meals. Never order *um almoço* (a lunch) unless you have a big appetite or care to share with a friend – the portions are immense.

For a long time in Brazil, the standard fare for budget travellers has been the *prato feito* (made plate), a large helping of rice, beans, salad and beef, chicken or fish. Now, many restaurants and lanchonetes also offer self-serve, *por kilo* buffets. After you put what you want on the plate, they weigh it, and you pay according to the weight. Most people will only eat around half a kilo, so if you see a sign saying 'self-serve comida por kilo – $R6', you'll pay around $R3 for a meal.

Regional Cuisine

Despite much sameness there are regional differences. The cooking in the Northern interior (*comida do sertão*) has a heavy Indian influence, using many unique, traditional tubers and fruits. On the Northeastern coast the cuisine (*comida baiana*) has a distinct African flavour using peppers, spices and the delicious oil of the *dendê* palm tree. The slaves also introduced greater variety in the preparation of meat and fish, and dishes like *vatapá* and *caruru*.

Minas Gerais is the home of *comida*

mineiro, a heavy but tasty cuisine based on pork, vegetables like *couve* (spinach-like leaf) and *quiabo* (bean-like vegetable); and *tutú*, a kind of refried bean-paste. In the South, *comida gaúcha* from Rio Grande do Sul revolves around meat, meat and more meat. This cuisine has the most extensive vocabulary for different cuts of meat that you're ever likely to hear.

Breakfast

Breakfast is called *café da manhã*; it's often shortened to *café*, which is also the word for coffee. Served at most hotels (with the possible exception of the very cheapest places), for no extra charge, café includes coffee, steamed milk, fruit, biscuits or bread, maybe cheese and meat, and rarely eggs. If you tire of this, or don't like it in the first place, go into any *padaria* (bakery) or market and buy a good *iogurte* (yoghurt), then get some fruit which is always abundant and delicious.

Lunch

Lunch is the main meal for Brazilians. Lanchonetes, as mentioned earlier, are everywhere. Portions are almost always big enough for two. Most cities now have vegetarian restaurants which serve salads, casseroles, brown rice, etc. With any luck the food might be healthy, but it's rarely tasty. A better choice may be a *suco* (juice) bar for a natural fruit juice and sandwich. Many places have a self-serve, por kilo, lunch buffet.

Dinner

Dinner doesn't vary much from lunch, unless you go to a better restaurant. Most dishes can be divided between two people (if you can't eat it all ask for a doggie bag (*embalagem*) and give it to someone on the street).

In the cities, Brazilians dine late. Restaurants don't get busy in Rio and São Paulo until 10 pm on weekends. A 10% tip is generally included in the bill. If not it's customary to leave at least 10%. Most places in Rio will bring you a *couvert*, whether you ask or not. This is optional, so you are per-

fectly within your rights to send it back. The typical couvert is a ridiculously overpriced and tedious basket of bread, crackers, pheasant eggs and a couple of carrot and celery sticks. Most restaurants will still bring bread with your soup at no extra charge.

Standard operating procedure in most Rio restaurants is to overcharge the customer. Some places don't even itemise their bills. Don't hesitate to look at the bill and ask the waiter: *pode discriminar?* (can you itemise?). Also, take your time and count your change – short-changing is very common in Brazil. It's all part of the game. They good-naturedly overcharge and you can good-naturedly hassle them until the bill is fixed. They are used to it.

Brazilian Dishes

The following are some common Brazilian dishes:

acarajé – this is what the Baianas, Bahian women in flowing white dresses, traditionally sell on street corners throughout Bahia. The Baianas are an unforgettable sight but you're likely to smell their cooking before you see it. It's the wonderful-smelling dendê oil. Acarajé is made from peeled brown beans, mashed in salt and onions, and then fried in dendê oil. Inside these delicious fried balls is *vatapá* (see this list), dried shrimp, pepper and tomato sauce. Dendê oil is strong stuff. Many stomachs can't handle it.

angú – a cake made with very thin cornflour, called *fubá*, and mixed with water and salt.

bobó de camarão – manioc paste cooked and flavoured with dried shrimp, coconut milk and cashew nuts.

camarão á paulista – unshelled fresh shrimp fried in olive oil with lots of garlic and salt.

canja – a big soup made with chicken broth. More often than not a meal in itself.

caranguejada – a kind of crab cooked whole and seasoned.

carne de sol – a tasty, salted meat, grilled and served with beans, rice and vegetables.

caruru – one of the most popular Brazilian dishes brought from Africa, this is made with okra or other vegetables cooked in water. The water is then drained, and onions, salt, shrimps and malagueta peppers are added, mixed and grated together with the okra paste and dendê oil. Traditionally, a sea fish such as garoupa is then added.

casquinha de carangueijo or *siri* – stuffed crab. The meat is prepared with manioc flour.

cozido – any kind of stew, usually with more vegetables than other stew-like Brazilian dishes (eg potatoes, sweet potatoes, carrots and manioc).

dourado – found in freshwater throughout Brazil; a scrumptious fish.

feijoada – the national dish of Brazil, feijoada is a meat stew served with rice and a bowl of beans. It's served throughout the country and there are many different variations, depending on what animal happens to be walking through the kitchen while the chefs are at work. All kinds of meats go into feijoada. Orange peel, peppers and farinha accompany the stew.

frango ao molho pardo – chicken pieces stewed with vegetables and then covered with a seasoned sauce made from the blood of the bird.

moqueca – a kind of sauce or stew and a style of cooking from Bahia. There are many kinds of moqueca: fish, shrimp, oyster, crab or a combination. The moqueca sauce is defined by its heavy use of dendê oil and coconut milk, often with peppers and onions. A moqueca must be cooked in a covered clay pot.

moqueca capixaba – a moqueca from Espírito Santo uses lighter *urucum* oil from the Indians instead of dendê oil.

pato no tucupi – roast duck flavoured with garlic and cooked in the *tucupi* sauce made from the juice of the manioc plant and *jambu*, a local vegetable. A very popular dish in Pará.

peixada – fish cooked in broth with vegetables and eggs.

peixe a delícia – broiled or grilled fish usually made with bananas and coconut milk. Delicious in Fortaleza.

prato de verão – this dish, which translates literally as summer plate, is served at many suco stands in Rio. Basically, it's a fruit salad.

pirarucu ao forno – pirarucu is the most famous fish from the rivers of Amazônia. It's oven-cooked with lemon and other seasonings.

tacacá – an Indian dish of dried shrimp cooked with pepper, jambu, manioc and much more.

tutu á mineira – a bean paste with toasted bacon and manioc flour, often served with cooked cabbage. A typical dish of Minas Gerais.

vatapá – a seafood dish with a thick sauce made from manioc paste, coconut and dendê oil. Perhaps the most famous Brazilian dish of African origin.

xinxim de galinha – pieces of chicken flavoured with garlic, salt and lemon. Shrimp and dendê oil are often added.

Fruit

Expand your experience of fruit juices and ice creams beyond pineapple and orange; in Brazil you can play blind man's buff with your taste buds. From the savoury nirvana of *graviola* to the confusingly clinical taste of *cupuaçú*, fruits and juices are a major Brazilian highlight. For more details about styles of juices, refer to Fruit Juices under Drinks in the following section.

To get you started, we have included here a partial list of Brazilian fruits, particularly those found in Rio. Many of the fruits of the Northeast and Amazon have no English equivalent, so there's no sense in attempting to translate their names: you'll just have to try the exotic tastes of *ingá, abiu, mari-mari, pitanga, taperebá, sorva, pitamba, uxí, pupunha, seriguela, bacuri* and *jambo*. The following taste descriptions are unashamedly subjective: be bold with your choices and enjoy!

abacate – avocado
abacaxí – pineapple
açaí – gritty, forest-berry taste and deep

purple colour. This fruit of the açaí palm tree is also used in wines and syrups.

acerola – wonderful cherry flavour. A megasource of vitamin C.

ameixa – plum, prune

bacaba – Amazonian fruit used in wines and syrups.

betarraba – beetroot

biribá – Amazonian fruit eaten plain.

burití – a palm-tree fruit with a mealy flavour and a hint of peach followed by an odd aftertaste. Also used in ice cream and for wine.

cacau – pulp from cocoa pod; tastes wonderfully sweet and creamy. It's nothing like cocoa, which is extracted from the bean.

caja – pear-like taste

cajú – fruit of cashew (the nut is enclosed in an appendage of the fruit). It has a tart taste, like a cross between lemon and pear.

carambola – starfruit. It has a tangy, citrus flavour.

cenoura – carrot

cupuaçú – cool taste, strangely clinical. It's best with milk and sugar.

fruto-do-conde – green, sugar-apple fruit, very popular.

gengibre – ginger. Commonly drunk as *atchim* (a mixture of lemon and ginger).

genipapo – tastes like curdled cow piss – not everyone's favourite! Better as a liqueur.

goiaba – guava

graviola – custard apple. Aromatic and exquisite taste.

jaca – large fruit of the jackfruit tree.

laranja – orange

limão – lemon

mamão – papaya (pawpaw)

manga – mango

mangaba – tart flavour, similar to pear.

maracujá – passion fruit

melancia – watermelon

melão – honeydew melon

morango – strawberry

murici – mealy fruit with vague caramel taste

pera – pear

pêssego – peach

pupunha – a fatty, vitamin-rich Amazonian fruit taken with coffee.

sapotí – gritty, semi-sweet Worcestershire-sauce taste. Brits may even recognise a hint of Marmite. Rather confusing for a fruit!

tamarindo – pleasantly acidic, plum-like

tangerina – mandarin orange, tangerine

tapereba – gritty texture, the flavour resembles cross between acerola and sweet potato.

uva – grape

DRINKS
Fruit Juice

Sucos in Brazil are divine. They vary by region and season (the Amazon has fruits you won't believe). Request them *sem açúcar e gelo* or *natural* if you don't want sugar and ice. Often you'll get some water mixed into a suco; if you're worried about getting sick ask for a *vitamina*, which is juice with milk. Banana and avocado are great with milk.

Another way to avoid water is to drink orange juice, which is rarely adulterated and it mixes well with papaya, carrot, and several other fruits. An orange, beet and carrot juice combo is popular in Rio. There is an incredible variety of fruits and combinations. Spend some time experimenting.

Caldo de cana is a tasty juice extracted directly from lengths of sugar cane, usually while you wait. The machine that does the crushing is a noisy, multi-cogged affair that has to be cranked up every time someone wants a drink. Caldo and pasteis are a favourite combination amongst Brazilians.

Coffee

Brazilians take their coffee as strong as the devil, as hot as hell, and as sweet as love. They call it *cafezinho* and drink it as an espresso-sized coffee without milk and cut with plenty of sugar. The cafezinho is taken often and at all times. It's sold in stand-up bars and dispensed in offices to keep the workers perky. We've known Brazilians to take one to bed with them to go to sleep. If you don't like the sugar, hunt around for a coffee stand that has espresso. They're easy to find in cities and large towns. *Café com leite* is coffee with hot milk, usually drunk for breakfast.

Chá or tea is not nearly as important a drink as coffee, except in the state of Rio Grande do Sul, where the gaúchos drink *maté*, a strong tea drunk through a silver straw from a hollow gourd.

Soft Drinks

Soft drinks *(refrigerantes)* are found everywhere and are cheaper than bottled water. Coke is number one, Guaraná is number two. Made from the berry of an Amazonian plant, Guaraná has a delicious, distinctive taste.

Alcohol

Para que nossas mulheres não fiquem viúva.
May our wives never be widows (A drinking toast).

Cachaça is found everywhere – even in the most miserable frontier shantytowns. Bottled beer usually follows the introduction of electricity to a region. At the pinnacle of Brazilian civilisation is *chopp* (see below), which is only found in large and prosperous economic centres with paved roads and electricity.

Beer Brazilians, like most civilised people, enjoy their beer served icy cold *(bem gelada)*. A *cerveja* is a 600-ml bottled beer. Of the common brands, Antártica is the best followed by Brahma (although some Brazilians argue that Brahma is better in Rio), Skol, Kaiser and Malt 90. The best beers are the regional ones, like Bohemia from Petrópolis, Cerpa and Original from Pará, Cerma from Maranhão and the tasty Serramalte from Rio Grande do Sul. Bavaria is a tasty beer which only comes in 300-ml bottles and is found in the more up-market bars. Caracu is a stout-like beer, also only available in 300-ml bottles. Very popular now is Xingu, a sweet black beer from Santa Catarina. Hunt around for it – you won't be sorry. Imported beer is all the rage amongst Brazilians, but we believe that when in Rome (or Rio)....

Brazilians gesture for a tall one by horizontally placing the Boy Scout sign (three fingers together) a foot above their drinking tables. A *cervejinha* is 300-ml of bottled or canned beer. Cans are more expensive than bottles. Some experts argue that it tastes better from the can – this is a debatable subject and one on which you'll have to form your own opinion after researching the matter. If you're buying beer to take away, you'll be charged a hefty deposit for the bottles unless you trade in empties.

Chopp (pronounced 'shoppee') is a pale blonde pilsener draft, lighter and far superior to canned or bottled beer. In big cities you may even find *chopp escuro*, a kind of light stout. Usage: *Moço, mais um chopp!* (Waiter, one more 'shoppee'!).

Wine Jorge Amado wrote a satire about nationalist generals running Brazil who drink Brazilian wine in public and avoid the stuff like the plague in private. Well, Brazilian wine is improving but it's not great. Forrestier is at the top of a very low heap of vintages. The whites are better than the reds and the Argentine wines are much better than both.

Cachaça *Cachaça, pinga* or *aguardente* is a high-proof, dirt cheap, sugar-cane alcohol produced and drunk throughout the country. Cachaça literally means 'booze'. Pinga (which literally means 'drop') is considered more polite, but by any name it's cheaper than spit and far more toxic. The production of cachaça is as old as slavery in Brazil. The distilleries grew up with the sugar plantations, first to supply local consumption and then to export to Africa to exchange for slaves.

There are well over 100 brands of cachaça, with differences in taste and quality. A cheap cachaça can cut a hole in the strongest stomach lining. Velho Barreiro, Ypioca, Pitú, Carangueijo, and São Francisco are some of the better labels. Many distilleries will allow you to take a tour and watch the process from raw sugar to rot gut and then sample some of the goodies. The smaller distilleries usually make a much smoother cachaça than the commercial brands.

Other Alcoholic Drinks *Caipirinha* is the Brazilian national drink. The ingredients are simple: cachaça, lime, sugar and crushed ice, but a well-made caipirinha is a work of art. *Caipirosca* is a caipirinha with vodka replacing cachaça. *Caipirissima* is still another variation, with Bacardi rum instead of cachaça. *Batidas* are wonderful mixes of cachaça, sugar and fruit juice.

ENTERTAINMENT
Movies
English Most movies in the cinemas are screened in their original language with Portuguese subtitles; consequently there are plenty of films in English. Brazil gets most of the hits from the USA, including many of the violent Rambo-type films. Brazilians also adore comedians like Woody Allen and the Marx Brothers. I must admit I don't completely understand why. When I saw *Hannah & Her Sisters* in Rio I was the only person in the theatre laughing; in the scene where Woody becomes a Catholic and tries to explain his existential crisis to his father, a New York Jew, I realised that the Brazilians didn't have a clue as to why it was so funny.

The Marx Brothers films are dubbed, which raises problems with the puns. When Groucho tells Chico that the loot is out near the viaduct and Chico responds, in his thick accent, 'Vi-a-duck, Vi not a chicken', there is no way this exchange can be duplicated in Portuguese.

Portuguese From the romanticism of *Black Orpheus* to the realism of *Cinema Novo* and Glauber Rocha, Brazil has produced a number of excellent films. Since the end of the dictatorship there has been a film renaissance. *Pixote*, Hector Babenco's compelling film about young street urchins, won the best film award at Cannes. Many recent Brazilian films are historical, providing special insight into the country.

Rio has many film aficionados and special events. The Cineclub Botafogo is always a good venue. There are special events like the annual film festival in September, and cinema on the beach at Copacabana in the summer.

Spectator Sports
Football Soccer was introduced to Brazil after a young student from São Paulo, Charles Miller, returned from his studies in England with two footballs and a rule book and began to organise the first league. It quickly became the national passion, and Brazil has since won three World Cups. Brazilians are crazy about the game.

The government is prepared to spend whatever it takes to win the World Cup, but becomes worried because of the financial drain when no one goes to work on game days. When the team lost to arch-rivals Argentina in the 1990 World Cup, millions cried on the streets and a mass depression gripped the country for weeks.

Fans worship their heroes. Matches are played on Sunday and Wednesday. Announcers have the ability to stretch the word 'goal' for at least 20 seconds (GOOOOOOOOOOOOOOOOOOOOOL!). Brazilians play the world's most creative and artistic style of football. You'll see tiny kids playing skilled, rough matches in the streets, on the beaches, just about anywhere.

Go to a game. It's an intense spectacle, and one of the most colourful pageants I've ever seen. The fans are insane but they know their football. Each good play is rewarded with superlatives. A fancy dribble past an opponent receives a Spanish bullfight *olé*; a goal results in delirium.

Volleyball Surprisingly volleyball is Brazil's second sport. A natural on the beach, it's also a popular spectator sport on TV. A local variation you'll see on Rio's beaches is volleyball played without the hands (footvolei). It's quite fun to watch but it's bloody hard to play.

Motor Racing Brazilians love speed. Taxi drivers may give you a hint of it, and since the early '70s Brazilians have won more Formula One Grand Prix world championships than any other nationality. Emerson

Pelé

On 23 October 1940, Édson Arantes do Nascimento was born in Três Corações, Mines Gerais. He became the greatest soccer player in the world, known to everyone as Pelé. Although he retired long ago, Pelé's presence is everywhere in Brazil – on TV advertising a department store, in the newspapers receiving an award for community service, on billboards promoting shoes and in the hearts and minds of every Brazilian. If he ran for president he'd be a sure thing. But Pelé is above politics – he is king of Brazil.

His public image is impeccable. He's never smoked, never been photographed with a drink in hand and NEVER been involved with drugs. Even when an illegitimate daughter surfaced after 25 years, his name remained untarnished. Of course he did the right thing by including her in his will.

In his 22-year career, the teams in which he played gained 53 titles; three World Cup titles (Sweden in 1958, Chile in 1962 and Mexico in 1970), dual world club championships (with Santos in 1962 and 1963), two South American championships, 11 Paulista state championships and four Rio-São Paulo tournaments.

In 1971, Pelé retired from the Brazilian team and in 1974 he retired from Santos. In 1975 the New York Cosmos coaxed him north to the USA. He played there until 1977, when they won the American championship. He finally retired at the end of that year, after a game between the Cosmos and Santos, in which he played the first half for the Cosmos and the second half with Santos.

In 1363 games (112 for the Brazilian team), he scored 1282 goals. When he scored his 1000th goal in 1969 he dedicated it 'to the children of Brazil'. Pelé called getting the goal 'one of the greatest blessings a man could ever expect to receive from God'.

In 1981 he received the title 'Athlete of the Century' from the French magazine *L'Ecluipe*. In Brazil he is known simply as O Rie (The King).

In 1985 Pelé was included in Brazil's new government. He was given the title of *Ministro Extraordinário dos Esportes* – the Extraordinary Minister of Sport. ■

Fittipaldi was world champion twice in the '70s, Nelson Piquet won his third world championship in 1987, and Ayrton Senna took it out three times. The Brazilian Grand Prix traditionally kicks off the Formula One season in Rio around March each year.

THINGS TO BUY

A smart souvenir hunter can do well in Brazil, provided they know a little about Brazilian culture. Most people find the best souvenirs to be music, local crafts and artwork.

Brazilian music (discussed in the Facts about the Country chapter) is sure to evoke your most precious travel memories. The best record stores in the country are in the big shopping malls of São Paulo.

Although nearly everything can be found in Rio and São Paulo, there is a premium for moving craft and art pieces from the hinterland into the fancy stores of the big cities. The inexpensive exceptions include the weekly hippie fair at Ipanema (see the Rio de Janeiro city chapter), the ubiquitous FUNAI stores and museum gift shops.

Most of the Indian crafts sold in FUNAI stores are inexpensive, but the quality generally matches the price. Museum gift shops, on the other hand, stock some very worthwhile souvenirs. They are particularly good for prints of local art. The Carmen Miranda museum in Rio de Janeiro sells good T-shirts of the great lady herself complete with her fruit headdress.

Outside the big cities, your best bet for

craftwork are artisan fairs, co-operative stores and government-run shops. The Northeast has a rich assortment of artistic items from which to choose. Salvador and nearby Cachoeira are notable for their rough-hewn wood sculpture. Artisans in Fortaleza and the southern coast of Ceará specialise in fine lace cloths. The interior of Pernambuco, in particular Caruaru, is famous for the wildly imaginative ceramic figurines and the traditional leather hats worn by the sertanejos. Functional and decorative hammocks are available in cities throughout the Amazon. These string, mesh or cloth slings are fixtures in most Brazilian homes. They are indispensable for travellers and make fine, portable gifts.

The state of Minas Gerais is most famous for its gemstones. However, if you're in the market for fine jewellery and precious stones, wait until you return to the big cities to make your purchases. Buy from a large and reputable dealer like Amsterdam-Sauer, Roditi or H Stern. Stern is an international dealership based in Ipanema and its reputation for quality and honesty is beyond reproach. It isn't a discount store, but its jewellery is less expensive in Brazil than in its outlets in other parts of the world.

Brazilian leather goods are moderately priced, but the leather isn't particularly supple. The better Brazilian shoes, belts, wallets, purses and luggage are sold in the up-market shops of Ipanema and Copacabana. Brazilian shoes are extremely good value, but much of the best is reserved for

A Dead King

Ayrton Senna da Silva, 34, was the third-highest paid athlete in the world in 1993, earning US$18.5 million. To Brazilians he was a living legend – their triple-champion; living proof that Brazilians could take on the world, and win. Then, on 1st May 1994, during the Italian Grand Prix at the Imola circuit in San Marino, tragedy struck.

Three things worried Senna before the San Marino race: the poor performance of his car, the risks created by the prohibition of electronic equipment (such as active suspension) in Formula One racing and the safety of the track. On the first day of training, the 29th of April, Rubens Barichello lost control of his Jordan and rolled it twice. He escaped with a few scratches. The next day, Austrian Roland Ratzemberger came off the track at the Villeneuve curve and hit the wall. He died hours later.

The race itself began badly: Pedro Lamy in a Lotus and JJ Lehto of Benetton collided at the start and two of Lamy's tyres hit four spectators. In the pits, one of the tyres from the Minardi driven by Michele Alboreto flew off and injured six people.

Then, at 9.13 am Brazilian time, Senna's Williams left the track on Tamburello curve at 300 km/h and smashed against the wall. It was transmitted live on TV and the scene traumatised the whole of Brazil. The champion was dead.

Senna was awarded a state funeral with full honours. His Brazilian fans turned out in huge numbers to pay their respects. When the plane carrying his body arrived in São Paulo, 250,000 fans waited in sorrow. The service was attended by 110,000 mourners, and 250,000 followed their idol to Morumbi cemetery.

In Brazil, Ayrton Senna is now worshipped as a sporting god. ■

export and larger sizes are difficult to find. High-quality, cheap, durable, leather soccer balls with hand-stitched panels are sold all over Brazil in sporting-goods stores. Inflated soccer balls should not be put in the cargo hold of a plane.

In an effort to draw industry to the Amazon, the Brazilian government lifted many tax and tariff restrictions in Manaus. The advantage to tourists in this free-trade zone is minimal unless you are particularly interested in picking up electrical equipment which has been assembled in Brazil.

Finally, here are a few more ideas for the avid souvenir hunter. Coffee-table picture books on Brazil, videotapes of Carnival and of highlights of the Brazilian national team

and Pelé in various World Cup matches are hawked in the streets of Copacabana. Guaraná powder, a stimulant (said to be an aphrodisiac), is sold in health-food stores and chemists around the country. Mounted reprints of old Rio lithographs are sold in Rio's Cinelândia district on the steps of the opera house. The smallest of Brazil's bikinis are sold at Bum-Bum or Kanga shops. Candomblé stores are a good source of curios, ranging from magical incense guaranteed to bring good fortune and increase sexual allure, wisdom and health, to amulets and ceramic figurines of Afro-Brazilian gods. If you are travelling in Brazil during Carnival make sure you pick up a copy of the Carnival edition of *Manchete* magazine.

ALL PHOTOS BY JOHN MAIER, JR

Impressions of Rio city

Top: View from Pão de Açúcar
Middle: Cable-car ride to Pão de Açúcar
Bottom: View of Pão de Açúcar

Getting There & Away

Most travellers start their Brazilian odyssey by flying down to Rio, but this is only one of many ways to arrive. Other gateway airports include Recife, popular with German package tourists on their way to one of the many beach resorts catering to their needs, Fortaleza, Salvador and Manaus, capital of the state of Amazonas, and Belém, capital of the state of Pará. Manaus and Belém are both halfway between Rio and Miami.

Brazil also has land borders with every other country in South America, with the exception of Chile and Ecuador, so while some travellers may be bussing in from Uruguay in the south, others may be arriving via the *trem da morte* (death train) from Bolivia. By river, many travellers take a slow boat down the Amazon from Iquitos in Peru or into the Pantanal via the Rio Paraguai from Asunçíon.

However you're travelling, it's worth taking out travel insurance. Work out what you need – you may not want to insure that grotty old army surplus backpack, but everyone should be covered for the worst possible case: an accident, for example, that will require hospital treatment and a flight home. It's a good idea to make a copy of your policy, in case the original is lost. If you are planning to travel for a long time, the insurance may seem very expensive – but if you can't afford it, you certainly won't be able to afford to deal with a medical emergency overseas.

AIR

Cheap deals on air travel are volatile. With some legwork you can usually save a couple of hundred dollars. Check newspapers and discount or Latin American specialist travel agents for good deals.

Varig, Brazil's international airline, flies to many major cities in the world. From the USA the basic carriers which serve Brazil are Varig, American Airlines, United Airlines and Japan Airlines (JAL) (from the west coast); from the UK, British Airways and Varig; and from Australia, Qantas, and Aerolineas Argentinas.

Discount tickets have restrictions. The most pernicious is the limit on the amount of time you can spend in Brazil. Charter flights often restrict a stay to as little as three weeks. Most other tickets have a 90-day limit. There's usually a premium for tickets valid over 180 days. Although the Brazil Airpass is no longer the bargain it once was, it's worth mentioning here that you *must* purchase it outside Brazil. (See the Getting Around chapter for more information.)

If you are planning to stay in Brazil for more than 90 days, cheap airline tickets are a big problem. You are required to buy a return ticket before you will be issued with a visa in the USA, but it's not hard to get around this (see the Visa section in the Facts for the Visitor chapter). Unfortunately, the cost of a one-way ticket is more than half the price of a return economy fare. For example, from Los Angeles to Rio return costs about US$900 if you buy from the airlines, but you may be able to obtain a discount ticket for as little as US$700 from a specialist travel agent. The fare for a one-way ticket is US$850, and for a round trip valid for over three months the fare is doubled. Absurd! This means it may be cheaper to buy a discounted return ticket with a 90-day limit, bury the return portion ticket and then buy a ticket in Brazil when you are ready to go home.

If you plan to stay more than six months in Brazil you also have to consider leaving the country to get a new visa. Ask about package deals. We were able to get a round-trip Aerolineas Argentinas ticket from New York to Buenos Aires with an unlimited stopover in Rio. This gave us a free ride to Buenos Aires to get new visas after several months in Brazil – but check if this is still available.

To/From the USA

The *New York Times*, the *LA Times*, the *Chicago Tribune* and the *San Francisco Examiner* all produce weekly travel sections in which you'll find any number of travel agents' ads. Council Travel and STA Travel have offices in major cities nationwide. The Brazilian American Cultural Center (BACC) (☎ (1-800) 222-2746) offers its members low-priced flights to Brazil (for more details about BACC, see the section on Useful Organisations in the Facts for the Visitor chapter).

Also highly recommended is the newsletter *Travel Unlimited* (PO Box 1058, Allston, MA 02134) which publishes details of the cheapest airfares and courier possibilities for destinations all over the world from the USA.

From the USA the gateway cities for major carriers are New York, Los Angeles and Miami. All have basically the same fare structure. Economy fares often have to be purchased two weeks in advance and restrictions commonly require a minimum stay of two weeks and a maximum of three months. Varig offers this type of return ticket to Rio costing US$726 (ex Miami), US$787 (ex New York) and US$886 (ex Los Angeles). A popular choice for budget travellers is the cheap Miami-Asunción-São Paulo flight operated by Lineas Aereas Paraguayas (LAP) that costs around US$540. This LAP ticket requires a two-week advance purchase and is for a minimum stay of two weeks and a maximum of three months.

Air Bolivia has a Miami-Manaus service and a return ticket, with a two-week advance purchase and a two-week to one-month stay, costs US$798.

Some of the cheapest flights from Brazil to the USA are charters from Manaus to Miami (the Disneyworld express!). Manaus, which lies halfway between Rio and Miami, is a useful gateway city if you plan to make a long circuit around Brazil.

To/From Canada

Travel CUTS has offices in all major cities. The *Toronto Globe & Mail* carries travel agents' ads, and the magazine *Great Expeditions* (PO Box 8000-411, Abbotsford BC V2S 6H1) is useful. Travellers interested in booking flights with Canadian courier companies should obtain a copy of the newsletter published by Travel Unlimited (see the USA section for details).

To/From the UK

Look for travel agents' ads in the Sunday papers, the travel magazine *Complete Traveller* and listings magazines such as *Time Out*. Also look out for the free magazines widely available in London – start by looking outside the main train stations.

To initiate your price comparisons, you could contact travel agents such as: Journey Latin America (JLA) (☎ (0181) 747-3108) which publishes a very useful *Flights Bulletin*; Travel Bug (☎ (0161) 721-4000); Trailfinders (☎ (0171) 938-3444); STA (☎ (0171) 937-9962); and South American Experience (☎ (0171) 379-0344). For courier-flight details, contact Polo Express (☎ (0181) 759-5383) or Courier Travel Service (☎ (0171) 351-0300).

The Globetrotters Club (BCM Roving, London WC1N 3XX) publishes *Globe*, a newsletter for members which covers obscure destinations and can help find travelling companions.

Prices for discounted flights between London and Rio start around £300 one way or £550 return – bargain hunters should have little trouble finding even lower prices.

To/From Europe

The newsletter *Farang* (La Rue 8 á 4261, Braives, Belgium) deals with exotic destinations, as does the magazine *Aventure au Bout du Monde* (116 Rue de Javel, 75015 Paris). One reader from Germany quoted us these prices to Brazil, flying with British Airways US$1000; Varig/Luftansa US$1200; United US$1100, with stops in New York and/or Washington.

To/From Australia & New Zealand

Aerolineas Argentinas flies to Brazil over the South Pole once a week (twice during peak periods) via Sydney, Auckland and Buenos Aires to Rio de Janeiro. This ticket is valid for six months. If you shop around, you should be able to pick up a fare for approximately A$1950 from Sydney, a bit more from Melbourne or Brisbane. Aerolineas has some other interesting fares: a Circle Americas fare to South and North America for A$2969; Circle Pacific fares via South America for A$3455; a Two-Continents fare that includes Africa and South America for A$3500; and a Round-the-World fare via South America for A$3199 that's valid for one year. They also have some winter specials you should watch for, like A$1650 fare to Brazil for up to 45 days.

Qantas flies Sydney-Rio de Janeiro via Los Angeles for A$4200. The Los Angeles-Rio leg is on Varig, and a maximum of two stopovers are allowed in the Pacific in places like Honolulu and Tahiti. A Qantas/Varig Round-the-World ticket costs A$3700. United Airlines flies Sydney-Auckland-Los Angeles-New York-Rio for A$2749. South African Airways have a flight to Rio via Johannesburg for A$1329 one way and A$2149 return. The return fares allow for a free side-trip within South Africa.

To/From Asia

Hong Kong is the discount plane ticket capital of the region. Its bucket shops, however, are at least as unreliable as those of other cities. Ask the advice of other travellers before buying a ticket.

STA, which is reliable, has branches in Hong Kong, Tokyo, Singapore, Bangkok and Kuala Lumpur.

From the Orient, the hot tickets are with JAL and Singapore Airlines. JAL flies Tokyo-Los Angeles-Rio de Janeiro-São Paulo, and they often have the best fares to Rio from the west coast of the USA.

Round-the-World Tickets & Circle Pacific Fares

Round-the-World (RTW) tickets which include a South American leg have become very popular in the last few years. These tickets are often real bargains, and can work

out no more expensive or even cheaper than an ordinary return ticket. From the UK, a RTW ticket including Rio starts at around UK£1300. From the USA, a RTW ticket including Rio starts at around US$2500.

Official airline RTW tickets are usually made available by co-operation between two airlines which permit you to fly anywhere you want on their route systems, as long as you don't backtrack. Other restrictions are that you (usually) must book the first sector in advance and cancellation penalties then apply. There may be restrictions on how many stops you are permitted and usually the tickets are valid from 90 days up to a year. An alternative type of RTW ticket is one put together by a travel agent using a combination of discounted tickets.

Circle Pacific tickets use a combination of airlines to circle the Pacific – combining Australia, New Zealand, South America, North America and Asia. As with RTW tickets there are advance-purchase restrictions and limits to how many stopovers you can take.

Arriving in Brazil by Air

Information regarding arriving in Brazil by air can be found in the Getting Around sections for individual cities.

Leaving Brazil by Air

To buy a ticket out of Brazil, non-resident foreigners have to change at a bank the equivalent in US dollars of the price of the ticket. After presenting the receipt given by the bank to the travel agent or airline company, the ticket can be issued. Another option is to use an international credit card, which is then debited by calculating the real at the turismo rate.

In the past, the official dollar rate was much less than the parallel rate. This meant that travellers, who required a bank receipt to purchase tickets out, effectively had to pay more for flights than locals, who could change dollars at the parallel rate.

At the time of writing, the official dollar rates and the parallel rates were very close and it appeared that these discrepancies would end. Unfortunately that hasn't happened. Here's why.

Travel agents now offer a number of discounted tickets, but to buy one a foreigner has to go to the bank and change the US dollar equivalent of a full-price ticket. With the receipt, the ticket can be issued at the discount price, but it leaves the buyer with a couple of hundred dollars worth of reais. The alternatives are to spend them or to buy US dollars from a casa de câmbio.

It should be stressed that this situation could change at any time, so find out about any restrictions well before you plan on buying a ticket.

To the USA, a Manaus-Miami flight costs US$750 one way. A Recife-Miami flight is around US$700 one way, and from Rio add another US$100.

To Europe, the cheapest tickets are Recife-Madrid or Recife-Lisbon. The cost is US$1300 one way. From Rio it costs about US$100 more.

To Australia the cheapest flights are the transpolar Aerolineas Argentina flights, which cost around US$2000 one way. Note

---

Air Travel Glossary

Apex Apex, or 'Advance Purchase Excursion', is a discounted ticket which must be paid for in advance. There are penalties if you wish to change it.

Baggage Allowance This will be written on your ticket: usually one 20-kg item to go in the hold, plus one item of hand luggage.

Bucket Shop An unbonded travel agency specialising in discounted airline tickets.

Bumped Just because you have a confirmed seat doesn't mean you're going to get on the plane (see Overbooking).

Cancellation Penalties If you have to cancel or change an Apex ticket there are often heavy penalties involved. Insurance can sometimes be taken out against these penalties. Some airlines impose penalties on regular tickets as well, particularly against 'no-show' passengers (see No-Shows).

Check In Airlines ask you to check in a certain time ahead of the flight departure (usually 1½ hours on international flights). If you fail to check in on time, and if the flight is overbooked, the airline can cancel your booking and give your seat to somebody else.

Confirmation Having a ticket written out with the flight and date you want doesn't mean you have a seat until the agent has checked with the airline that your status is confirmed. Meanwhile you could just be 'on request'.

Discounted Tickets There are two types of discounted fares – officially discounted (see Promotional Fares) and unofficially discounted. The lowest prices often impose drawbacks like flying with unpopular airlines, inconvenient schedules or unpleasant routes and connections. A discounted ticket can save you other things than money – you may be able to pay Apex prices without the associated Apex advance booking and other requirements. Discounted tickets only exist where there is fierce competition.

Full Fares Airlines traditionally offer first-class (coded F), business-class (coded J) and economy-class (coded Y) tickets. These days there are so many promotional and discounted fares available from the regular economy class that few passengers pay full economy fare.

Lost Tickets If you lose your airline ticket an airline will usually treat it like a travellers' cheque and, after inquiries, issue you with another one. Legally, however, an airline is entitled to treat it like cash – that is, if you lose it then it's gone forever. So take good care of your tickets.

No-Shows No-shows are passengers who fail to show up for their flight, sometimes due to unexpected delays or disasters, sometimes due to simply forgetting and sometimes because they made more than one booking and didn't bother to cancel the one they didn't want. Full-fare passengers who fail to turn up are sometimes entitled to travel on a later flight. The rest are penalised (see Cancellation Penalties).

On Request An unconfirmed booking for a flight (see Confirmation).

Open Jaws A return ticket where you fly out to one place but return from another. If available, this can save you backtracking to your arrival point.

that all these are full-price fares. Discounts are available and worth hunting around for, even if you do have to go through the paper shuffling described above.

At the time of writing, the airport tax for domestic flights was about US$7, and for international flights, around US$18. The appropriate tax is usually added to the price of your ticket.

Buying a Plane Ticket

Your plane ticket will probably be the single most expensive item in your budget, and buying it can be an intimidating business. There is likely to be a multitude of airlines and travel agents hoping to separate you from your money, and it is always worth putting aside a few hours to research the current state of the market. Start early: some of the cheapest tickets have to be bought months in advance, and some popular flights sell out early. Talk to other recent travellers – they may be able to stop you making some of the same old mistakes. Look at the ads in newspapers and magazines (not forgetting the South American press if you have access

---

Overbooking Airlines hate to fly with empty seats and since every flight has some passengers who fail to show up (see No-shows) airlines often book more passengers than they have seats. Usually the excess passengers balance those who fail to show up but occasionally somebody gets bumped. If this happens guess who it is most likely to happen to? The passengers who check in late.

Promotional Fares Officially discounted fares like Apex fares which are available from travel agents or direct from the airline.

Reconfirmation At least 72 hours prior to departure time of an onward or return flight you must contact the airline and 'reconfirm' that you intend to be on the flight. If you don't do this the airline can delete your name from the passenger list and you could lose your seat. You don't have to reconfirm the first flight on your itinerary or if your stopover is less than 72 hours. It doesn't hurt to reconfirm more than once.

Restrictions Discounted tickets often have various restrictions on them – advance purchase is the most usual one (see Apex). Others are restrictions on the minimum and maximum period you must be away, such as a minimum of 14 days or a maximum of one year (see Cancellation Penalties).

Standby A discounted ticket where you only fly if there is a seat free at the last moment. Standby fares are usually only available on domestic routes.

Tickets Out An entry requirement for many countries is that you have an onward or return ticket, in other words, a ticket out of the country. If you're not sure what you intend to do next, the easiest solution is to buy the cheapest onward ticket to a neighbouring country, or a ticket from a reliable airline which can later be refunded if you do not use it.

Transferred Tickets Airline tickets cannot be transferred from one person to another. Travellers sometimes try to sell the return half of their ticket, but officials can ask you to prove that you are the person named on the ticket. This is unlikely to happen on domestic flights, but on an international flight tickets may be compared with passports.

Travel Agencies Travel agencies vary widely and you should ensure that you use one that suits your needs. Some simply handle tours while full-service agencies handle everything from tours and tickets to car rental and hotel bookings. A good one will do all these things and can save you a lot of money. But if all you want is a ticket at the lowest possible price, then you really need an agency specialising in discounted tickets. A discounted ticket agency, however, may not be useful for other things, like hotel bookings.

Travel Periods Some officially discounted fares, Apex fares in particular, vary with the time of year. There is often a low (off-peak) season and a high (peak) season. Sometimes there's an intermediate or shoulder season as well. At peak times, when everyone wants to fly, not only will the officially discounted fares be higher but so will unofficially discounted fares, or there may simply be no discounted tickets available. Usually the fare depends on your outward flight – if you depart in the high season and return in the low season, you pay the high-season fare. ■

to it). Consult reference books and watch for special offers, and then phone around travel agents for bargains. (Airlines can supply information on routes and timetables; however, except at times of inter-airline war they do not supply the cheapest tickets.) Find out the fare, the route, the duration of the journey and any restrictions on the ticket. (See Restrictions in the Air Travel Glossary.) Then sit back and decide which is best for you.

You may discover that those impossibly cheap flights are 'fully booked, but we have another one that costs a bit more...' Or the flight is on an airline notorious for its poor safety standards and leaves you in the world's least favourite airport mid-journey for 14 hours. Or they claim only to have the last two seats available for Brazil for the whole of July, which they will hold for you for a maximum of two hours. Don't panic – keep ringing around.

Use the fares quoted in this book as a guide only. They are approximate and based on the rates advertised by travel agents at the time of going to press. Quoted airfares do not necessarily constitute a recommendation for the carrier.

If you are travelling from the UK or the USA, you will probably find that the cheapest flights are being advertised by obscure bucket shops whose names haven't yet reached the telephone directory. Many such firms are honest and solvent, but there are a few rogues who will take your money and disappear, to reopen elsewhere a month or two later under a new name. If you feel suspicious about a firm, don't give them all the money at once – leave a deposit of 20% or so and pay the balance when you get the ticket. If they insist on cash in advance, go somewhere else. And once you have the ticket, ring the airline to confirm that you are actually booked on the flight.

You may decide to pay more than the rock-bottom fare by opting for the safety of a better-known travel agent. Firms such as STA, who have offices worldwide, Council Travel in the USA or Travel CUTS in Canada are not going to disappear overnight, leaving you clutching a receipt for a non-existent ticket, and they do offer good prices to most destinations.

Once you have your ticket, write its number down, together with the flight number and other details, and keep the information somewhere separate. If the ticket is lost or stolen, this will help you get a replacement.

It's sensible to buy travel insurance as early as possible. If you buy it the week before you fly, you may find, for example, that you're not covered for delays to your flight caused by industrial action.

Air Travellers with Special Needs

If you have special needs of any sort – you've broken a leg, you're vegetarian, travelling in a wheelchair, taking the baby, terrified of flying – you should let the airline know as soon as possible so that they can make arrangements accordingly. You should remind them when you reconfirm your booking (at least 72 hours before departure) and again when you check in at the airport. It may also be worth ringing around the airlines before you make your booking to find out how they can handle your particular needs.

Airports and airlines can be surprisingly helpful, but they do need advance warning. Most international airports will provide escorts from the check-in desk to the plane where needed, and there should be ramps, lifts, accessible toilets and reachable phones. Aircraft toilets, on the other hand, are likely to present a problem; travellers should discuss this with the airline at an early stage and, if necessary, with their doctor.

Guide dogs for the blind will often have to travel in a specially pressurised baggage compartment with other animals, away from their owner, though smaller guide dogs may be admitted to the cabin. All guide dogs will be subject to the same quarantine laws (six months in isolation, etc) as any other animal when entering or returning to countries currently free of rabies such as the UK or Australia.

Deaf travellers can ask for airport and

in-flight announcements to be written down for them.

Children under two travel for 10% of the standard fare (or free, on some airlines), as long as they don't occupy a seat. They don't get a baggage allowance either. 'Skycots' should be provided by the airline if requested in advance; these will take a child weighing up to about 10 kg. Children between two and 12 can usually occupy a seat for half to two-thirds of the full fare, and they do get a baggage allowance. Push chairs can often be taken as hand luggage.

LAND
To/From Argentina
Coming from or going to Argentina, most travellers pass through Foz do Iguaçu (see the Foz do Iguaçu section in the Paraná chapter for more information).

To/From Bolivia
Corumbá Corumbá, opposite the Bolivian border town of Quijarro, is the busiest port of entry along the Bolivia-Brazil border. It has both rail and bus connections from São Paulo, Rio de Janeiro, Cuiabá and southern Brazil.

Between Quijarro and Santa Cruz, there's a daily train during the dry season, but during the wet you may have to wait for several days. Taxis are available between the rail-head at Quijarro and the frontier. For further information, see under Corumbá in the Mato Grosso chapter.

Cáceres From Cáceres, north of Cuiabá, you can cross to San Matías in Bolivia. There are daily buses which do the 4½-hour trip for US$10. Bolivia's Transportes Aereos Militares (TAM) operates flights each way between San Matías and Santa Cruz, Bolivia (via Roboré) on Saturday. During the dry season, there's also a daily bus between the border town of San Matías and San Ignacio de Velasco (in Bolivia's Jesuit missions), where you'll find flights and bus connections to Santa Cruz.

Coming from Bolivia, there are daily *micro* buses (again, only during the dry season) from San Ignacio de Velasco to the border at San Matías, from where you'll find onward transport to Cáceres and Cuiabá.

Guajará-Mirim Another popular crossing is between Guajará-Mirim in Brazil and Guayaramerín, Bolivia, via motorboat ferry across the Rio Mamoré. Guayaramerín is connected with Riberalta by a road which should be extended to Cobija/Brasiléia in the near future. At present, there's a dirt track to Cobija which is impassable in the wet season – in the dry, there's a bus once a week. Another long dusty route strikes southward toward Rurrenabaque and La Paz with a spur to Trinidad, the capital of the Bolivian Amazon. The Madeira to Mamoré railway from Guajará-Mirim to Porto Velho has long since been abandoned, but there are eight bus connections twice daily (during the dry season) between Porto Velho and Guajará-Mirim – a 5½-hour bus ride on the new road.

It's possible to take a six-day river trip up the Mamoré to Trinidad, and from there on to Puerto Villarroel near Cochabamba. When the water is high enough to accommodate cargo transport, it's also possible to travel up the Rio Beni from Riberalta at least as far as Rurrenabaque, which is 15 hours by bus from La Paz. Conditions are basic, so be prepared. Alternatively, AeroSur has daily flights from both Guayaramerín and Riberalta, Lloyd Aero Boliviano (LAB) has three flights per week from both Guayaramerín and Riberalta. For further information see under Guajará-Mirim and Guayaramerín in the Rondônia & Acre chapter.

Brasiléia In Acre state, in the far west of Brazil, there's a border crossing between Brasiléia and Cobija in Bolivia. You can either take a rowboat ferry across the Rio Acre or a taxi across the international bridge over the Rio Abunã. For more details, see under Brasiléia and Cobija in the Amazonas & Roraima chapter.

To/From Colombia
Leticia The Colombian border crossing is at

Leticia/Tabatinga. For further information on the Triple Frontier region, refer to Benjamin Constant, Tabatinga and Leticia in the Amazonas & Roraima chapter.

To/From French Guiana

Both Brazilians and foreigners may enter French Guiana from Oiapoque by motorised dugout, but it is reportedly not possible for non-Brazilian passport holders to enter Brazil overland from French Guiana. The obvious corollary is that you shouldn't enter French Guiana at St Georges (the French Guianese town opposite Oiapoque) unless you intend to fly from Cayenne or to re-enter Brazil elsewhere. This route will be feasible during the dry season only. Those who require a French visa should pick it up in Belém. For further information see under Macapá in the Amapá chapter.

To/From Guyana

The border crossing is at Bonfim in Roraima state and is reached via Boa Vista. You may want to save yourself the trouble of a difficult overland passage by flying directly to Georgetown on one of the two weekly Varig/Cruzeiro flights from Boa Vista. See under Boa Vista for more details.

To/From Paraguay

Foz do Iguaçu/Ciudad del Este and Ponta Porã/Pedro Juan Caballero are the two major border crossings. See the Foz do Iguaçu section in the Paraná chapter and the Ponta Porã section in the Mato Grosso chapter for details.

To/From Peru

Islandia & Santa Rosa The main route between Brazil and Peru is along the Amazon from Tabatinga (Brazil) to Iquitos. Some boats leave from Islandia (the Peruvian port village on an island at the junction of the Rio Yauari and the Amazon) and from Santa Rosa a few km further upstream in Peru. For further information on the Triple Frontier region, refer to Benjamin Constant, Tabatinga and Leticia in the Amazonas and Roraima chapter.

Iñapari There is another border crossing into Peru at Assis Brasil. From Brasiléia, take a bus 110 km west to Assis Brasil where you'll get an exit stamp. Across the Rio Acre from Assis Brasil is the muddy little Peruvian settlement of Iñapari where you must officially check into Peru with the police. For more details, see sections on Brasiléia and Assis Brasil.

To/From Suriname

It isn't possible to enter Suriname overland from Brazil without first passing through either French Guiana or Guyana.

To/From Uruguay

Coming from Uruguay, travellers usually pass through the border town of Chuy/Chuí: Chuy is the Uruguayan town on one side of the main street and Chuí is the Brazilian town on the other side. See the Rio Grande do Sul chapter for details.

There are four other border crossings: at Aceguá; from Rivera to Santana do Livramento; from Artigas to Quaraí; and at Barra do Quaraí near the border with Argentina.

If you're driving from Brazil, you'll need to stop at the Brazilian checkpoint to get an exit stamp and the Uruguayan checkpoint for the Uruguayans to check that you have a Brazilian exit stamp and a Uruguayan visa (if you need one). Buses will stop at the checkpoints.

To/From Venezuela

Santa Elena From Boa Vista (Roraima state) you can cross into Venezuela via the border town of Santa Elena. There's a Venezuelan Consulate in Boa Vista, open Monday to Friday, 8 am to noon. Everyone requires a visa to enter Venezuela overland. You'll need a photo, an onward ticket, sufficient funds, and probably a letter from your embassy, bank and/or employer guaranteeing that you're gainfully employed or financially sound. Further information is included under Boa Vista and Santa Elena in the Amazonas and Roraima chapter.

Road

Drivers of cars and riders of motorbikes entering Brazil will need the vehicle's registration papers, and an international driver's permit in addition to their domestic licence. You should also carry liability insurance. You may also need a *carnet de passage en douane*, which is effectively a passport for the vehicle, and acts as a temporary waiver of import duty. The carnet may need to have listed any more expensive spares that you're planning to carry with you, such as a gearbox. This is necessary when travelling in many countries, including those in South America, and is designed to prevent car-import rackets.

Another document used in South America is the *libreta de pasos por aduana*, a booklet of customs passes. It supposedly takes the place of the carnet, but since the refundable bond for the libreta is only US$100, it doesn't seem much of a deterrent to selling a vehicle.

Some travellers recently reported that the only documents they required were the title of the vehicle and a customs form issued on arrival which must be presented upon departure. Contact your local automobile association for details about all documentation. Remember that it's always better to carry as much documentation as you can.

Anyone planning to take their own vehicle with them needs to check in advance what spares and petrol are likely to be available. Lead-free is not on sale worldwide, and neither is every little part for your car. Brazil has plenty of Volkswagen spares.

You don't see many long-distance cyclists in Brazil. Crazy drivers who only respect vehicles larger than themselves, lots of trucks on the main roads spewing out unfiltered exhaust fumes, roads without shoulder room and the constant threat of theft are just some of the reasons for this. We wouldn't recommend long-distance cycling in Brazil. It seems a downright dangerous thing to do.

If you're still determined to tackle Brazil by bike, before you leave home, go over your bike with a fine-toothed comb and fill your repair kit with every imaginable spare. As with cars and motorbikes, you won't necessarily be able to buy that crucial gismo for your machine when it breaks down somewhere in the back of beyond as the sun sets.

Bicycles can travel by air. You can take them to pieces and put them in a bike bag or box, but it's much easier simply to wheel your bike to the check-in desk, where it should be treated as a piece of baggage. You may have to remove the pedals and turn the handlebars sideways so that it takes up less space in the aircraft's hold; check all this with the airline well in advance, preferably before you pay for your ticket.

RIVER

One novel way to enter Brazil from Paraguay is to sail up the Rio Paraguai on either the *Presidente Carlos Antônio López* or the *Bahía Negra*, from Asunción to Corumbá, in the Brazilian state of Mato Grosso do Sul.

These boat services are supposed to leave twice monthly, but sailings depend on favourable river conditions. The journey is via Concepción (310 km and 26 hours from Asunción) continuing to Corumbá, a further 830 km (72 hours). Boats depart on Friday at 8 am from Asunción, and the fare is US$35 tourist class, or US$25 for deck space only. For further information, contact the Flota Mercantil del Estado (☎ 448-544) at Estrella 672, Asunción.

TOURS

The following list of organisations and tour agencies provides a sample of the tour options available for independent travellers with special interests.

Brazil

Expeditours (☎ (021) 287-9697; fax (021) 521-4388) is one of the largest ecological tour operators in Brazil. They specialise in the Amazon and Pantanal, but run many other programs for the special-interest traveller. They are highly recommended.

Tatu Tours (☎ (071) 245-9322), Avenida Centenário 2883, Edifício Victoria Centre, sala 105, Barra, Salvador, CEP 40147-900,

BA specialises in natural and cultural-history tours around Bahia.

Focus Tours (☎ (031) 223-0358), Rua Alagoas 1460/s503, 30130, Belo Horizonte, MG (speak to Edina in English or Portuguese), runs a variety of tours with a strong emphasis on the environment and ecology; see also the section on the USA for their American office.

UK

The boom in ecotourism worldwide has prompted the creation of groups and organisations in the UK and elsewhere to monitor the effects of tourism and provide assessments and recommendations for those involved. For more information on ecotours, try contacting: the Centre for the Advancement of Responsible Travel (☎ (0732) 35-2757); Tourism Concern (☎ (0181) 878-9053); and Green Flag International (☎ (0223) 89-3587).

USA

Assessments and information about ecological and other types of tours can be obtained from the North American Coordinating Center for Responsible Tourism, 2 Kensington Rd, San Anselmo, CA 94960; One World Family Travel Network, PO Box 4317, Berkeley, CA 94703; and Travel Links, Co-op America, 2100 M St NW, Suite 310, Washington DC 20036.

Focus Tours (☎ & fax (612) 892-7830), 14821 Hillside Lane, Burnsville, MN 55306, is rated highly for its dedication to conservation and use of naturalists as guides. Tour members are given the use of telescopes and bird-identification books, and guides also use professional recording equipment to call out otherwise shy animals. Tour destinations include the Pantanal (and Chapada das Guimarães), Minas Gerais, Amazon, Parque Nacional do Itatiaia and Serra da Canastra. Doug Trent, from Michigan, has been

running ecological tours to Brazil since before the word 'ecotourism' was coined, and what he doesn't know about birds isn't worth knowing. Although he has a number of tour agendas, Doug is very flexible, and would be happy to include destinations of special interest to his clients. Doug tells us that on 40% of his tours they spot a jaguar. We haven't met any other tour guides who can claim a figure that high!

Brazilian Views (☎ (212) 472-9539), 201 E 66th St, Suite 21G, New York, NY 10021, is a small agency offering a wide range of special-interest tours based on topics such as horticulture, weaving, birdwatching, arts and crafts, gems and minerals, etc. Victor Emanuel Nature Tours (☎ (1-800) 328-8368), Box 33008, Austin, TX 78764, specialises in birdwatching trips. Earthwatch (☎ (617) 926-8200), 680 Mt Auburn St (PO Box 403), Watertown MA 02272, organises trips for volunteers to work overseas on scientific and cultural projects with a strong emphasis on protection and preservation of ecology and environment. Other organisations which provide tours with a similar emphasis include Conservation International (☎ (202) 429-5660), 1015 18th St, NW, Suite 1000, Washington DC 20036 and The Nature Conservancy (☎ 703-8415300), 1815 N Lynn St, Arlington VA 22209.

For more addresses, see the Environment & Ecology section in the Facts about the Country chapter.

Australia

Inca Tours (☎ (043) 512-133; fax (043) 512-526; toll-free 1800-024-955) specialise in travel to South America. Lew Pullbrook, who runs it, has been visiting the continent for years and really knows his way around. Lew organises trips for small or larger groups and he's happy for backpackers to call for a bit of advice. His office is at 5 Alison Road, Wyong, NSW 2259.

Getting Around

AIR

Flying in Brazil is not cheap, but with the seemingly endless expanses of sertão, Amazon and Pantanal between many destinations, the occasional flight can be an absolute necessity. And even if you don't use it, having extra money for flights can add flexibility to your travel plans.

Brazil has three major national carriers and several smaller regional airlines. The biggies are Varig/Cruzeiro, VASP and Transbrasil. Together they cover an extensive network of cities; they don't all go to the same places, but at least one of them goes to every major city. As this edition was being researched, there was a price war between these three airlines. Among the offers to attract customers were a 30% discount on flights booked seven days in advance, 30% discount on night flights and even a 50% discount given to couples going on their honeymoon! If you plan on doing a bit of flying, check whatever special discounts are available.

If you use a credit card to purchase domestic flights with Varig, make sure you check which rate of exchange is used. Unlike the other Brazilian airlines, Varig has been known to charge for domestic flights in dollars at the official rate of exchange – most unfavourable for the credit-card holder.

Strange routes, bizarre connections, long lay-overs and frequent stops are always a danger on domestic flights. Planes flying along the coast often stop at every city, so if you're going from Rio to Fortaleza it's possible that the plane will stop at Salvador, Maceió, Recife and João Pessoa on the way. Sometimes these outrageously indirect flights are unavoidable, but not always. Some travellers use these flights as an alternative to the airpass. Transbrasil has a flight like this from Belém to Rio, for around US$350, with unlimited stopovers, valid for 6 or 12 months. If you are only travelling the coastal regions, it seems a much better deal.

The smaller domestic airlines include Nordeste, Rio Sul, TABA, Votec and Tam. They mostly use the Bandeirante, a small Brazilian-built prop-plane (which some claim is not too safe) and fly to smaller cities where the major carriers don't go. We used Nordeste to fly to Ilhéus once when we couldn't get a seat on a plane directly to Salvador.

There are also many air-taxi companies, which mostly fly in the Amazon region. These flights are expensive, although the price usually drops if there are more passengers – and sometimes you can bargain.

Aeronautica, the military transport planes, has been known to give free flights when they have extra space, but you might have to wait a while. First the officers get a seat, then the soldiers, then the civilians. Go to the desk marked 'CAN' in the airport and ask about the next military flight, then show up again two days before scheduled departure time and sign up. It helps to have a letter of introduction from a consulate. Some air bases (eg Santarém) restrict flights to Brazilian nationals, but it's not as rigid as it often appears. The whole process is hit and miss but it's worth a try, particularly in the North in cities like Boa Vista, Macapá, Porto Velho, Manaus, Santarém, Rio Branco, Belém and São Luís.

Airpass

The Brazil Airpass is no longer the great deal that it once was. It now costs US$440 and buys you five flight coupons for five flights. It's possible to pay US$100 each for an additional four flight coupons, adding up to US$840 for nine flights. All travel must be completed within 21 days.

Before buying an air pass, you should sit down and work out whether it is really a good investment for your purposes. There are often delays flying in Brazil and it's rare that you don't waste a day in transit. Unless you're intent on a whistle-stop tour of the

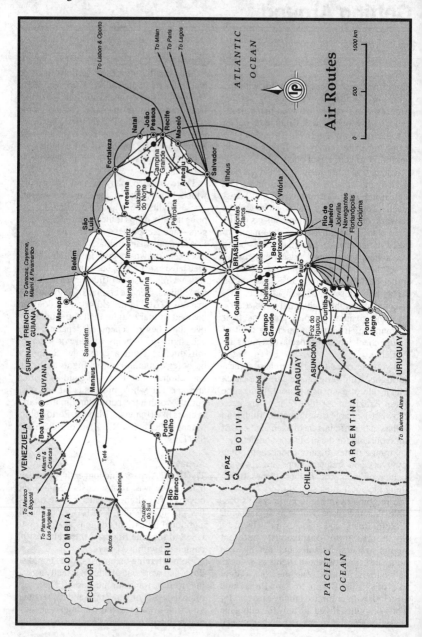

country, there are only so many flights that you will want to take in two or three weeks.

The pass must be purchased outside Brazil, where you'll get an MCO (miscellaneous charges order) in your name with 'Brazil Air Pass' stamped on it, which you exchange for an air pass from one of the three airlines in Brazil. All three airlines offer the same deal, and all three fly to most major cities, although Varig/Cruzeiro flies to more cities than the other two. If you are buying an air pass and have specific plans to go to a smaller city, you may want to check with a travel agent to see which airline goes there (for example, only VASP flies to Corumbá, the port of entry to the southern Pantanal).

Air-pass holders who get bumped from a flight for any reason should reconfirm all their other flight reservations. We were bumped from a Manaus-Foz do Iguaçu flight once and then found that because we weren't on that particular flight, all our other air-pass reservations had been scrubbed from the computer. This experience has also been reported by other travellers.

The air pass cannot be used to fly on the Rio-São Paulo shuttle which lands at the downtown airports of both cities, but it can be used to fly between the international airports of both cities. The MCO is refundable if you don't use it in Brazil.

Airport Tax

At the time of writing, the airport tax for domestic flights was about US$7. The exact figure for the appropriate tax can vary slightly, but is usually added to the price of your ticket. If you have an airpass, you'll have to pay it at each airport. Yes, it is a real ripoff.

Reservations

Air reservations can appear and disappear mysteriously. If you have a reservation it's often necessary to both confirm it and reconfirm it, even if you've already bought the ticket. If you have been told a flight is full, keep trying to make the reservation and perhaps alter your tactics by going directly to the airline's central ticket office or the airport.

Because flying is expensive, it's rarely difficult getting on a flight, with the exception of the vacation periods from December up to Carnival and July. Make reservations as early as possible for Carnival time! However, if you get caught short, don't assume all is lost. Several times travel agents were unable to get us reservations, assuring us that there wasn't a ticket to Salvador within two months of Carnival, and we got the reservation simply by going to the airline counter at the airport.

BUS

Onde fica essa cidade? Lá onde o vento faz a volta.
Where is that city? There where the wind turns around.
(Popular saying about distances in Brazil.)

Except in the Amazon Basin, buses are the primary form of long-distance transportation for the vast majority of Brazilians. Bus services are generally excellent. Departure times are usually strictly adhered to, and the buses are clean, comfortable and well-serviced Mercedes, Volvos and Scanias. The drivers are generally good, and a governor limits their wilder urges to 80 km per hour.

Bus travel throughout Brazil is very cheap (fares work out to less than US$2 per hour): for example, the six-hour trip from Rio to São Paulo costs US$11, and the 22-hour trip from Rio to Foz do Iguaçu is US$37.

All major cities are linked by frequent buses – one leaves every 15 minutes from Rio to São Paulo during peak hours – and there is a surprising number of scheduled

long-distance buses. It's rare that you will have to change buses between two major cities, no matter what the distance. For tips on security and bus travel, see the Dangers & Annoyances section in the Facts for the Visitor chapter.

'Progress is roads' goes the saying in Brazil. And wherever there is a road in Brazil, no matter what condition it's in, there is a bus that travels it. We will never forget the bus that rescued us on an almost deserted peninsula out near Ponta do Mutá – a place where few people go, and no one seems to have heard of. How we got there is hard to explain, how the bus got there is impossible to explain. The 'road' was more like a wide trail, impassable by normal car and apparently unknown to Brazilian cartographers. But the bus came and eventually delivered us to a humble fishing village of no more than a hundred people.

Like everything in Brazil, bus service varies by region. The South has the most and the best roads. The coastal highways are usually good, at least until São Luís. The Amazon and the sertão are another story. It's no surprise that roads in the sertão are bad. It's the way in which they are bad that's so strange. In several areas the road alternates every few hundred metres between dirt (which is better) and pothole-infested paved road (which is much worse). This pattern is without logic, it conforms to no obvious geographical or human design, and it forces constant speeding up and slowing down.

There has been a tremendous increase in road construction in previously unsettled regions in Brazil. This applies particularly to the Transamazônica highway and the Amazon region where roads have become the cornerstone of government strategies for economic development and military schemes to defend Brazilian borders. But many of these roads are precarious at best. Most are unpaved and are constantly being washed out during the rainy season when buses get stuck and are always being delayed. In the dry season buses are usually scorching hot, dusty and stuffed with people. As countless books have documented, bus transportation in the Amazon is always an adventure, teaching a healthy respect for the power and the size of the forest.

Bus Types
There are two types, or classes, of long-distance buses. The ordinary or *comum* is the most common. It's quite comfortable and usually has a toilet on board. The *leito* or *executivo* is Brazil's version of the couchette. Although they usually take as long to reach their destination as a comum and cost twice as much, leitos, which often depart late at night, are exceptionally comfortable. They have air-con, spacious, fully reclining seats, blankets and pillows, and more often than not a steward serving sandwiches, coffee, soda and água mineral. If you don't mind missing the scenery, a leito bus can get you there in comfort and save you the cost of a hotel room.

With or without bathrooms, buses generally make pit-stops every three or four hours. These stops are great places to meet other bus passengers, buy bizarre memorabilia and wish you were back home eating a healthy vegetarian quiche.

Bus Terminals (Rodoviárias)
In every big city, and most small ones, there is a central bus terminal (*rodoviária*). The rodoviárias are most frequently on the outskirts of the city. Some are modern, comfortable stations. All have restaurants, newsstands and toilets, and some even have post offices and long-distance telephone facilities. Most importantly, all the long-distance bus companies operate out of the same place, making it easy to find your bus.

Inside the rodoviária you'll find ticket offices for the various bus companies. They usually post bus destinations and schedules in their windows; occasionally they are printed on leaflets; sometimes you just have to get in line and ask the teller for information. This can be difficult if you don't speak much Portuguese and the teller is in a highly agitated state after the 23rd cafezinho or speaks with an accent from the interior of Ceará. The best strategy is probably to have a pen and paper handy and ask the teller to write down what you need to know.

When you find a bus company that goes to your destination, don't assume it's the only one; there are often two or more and the quality may vary.

Ticket Purchase & Reservation

Usually you can go down to the rodoviária and buy a ticket for the next bus out. Where this is difficult, for example in Ouro Prêto, we try to let you know. In general though it's a good idea to buy a ticket at least a few hours in advance, or if it's convenient, the day before departure. On weekends, holidays and from December to February this is always a good idea.

Aside from getting you on the bus, buying a ticket early has a few other advantages. First, it gets you an assigned seat – many common buses fill the aisles with standing passengers. Second, you can ask for a front row seat, with extra leg space, or a window seat with a view (ask for a *janela* or an odd-numbered seat).

You don't always have to go to the rodoviária to buy your bus ticket. Selected travel agents in the major cities sell tickets for long-distance buses. This is a great service which can save you a long trip out to an often chaotic rodoviária. The price is the same and the travel agents are more likely to speak some English and are usually less rushed.

TRAIN

There are very few railway passenger services in Brazil, despite the fact that there is over 30,000 km of track. Most trains only carry cargo. Of the passenger services that do exist, many have been scaled down or even discontinued in the last few years, as the national railway company becomes more and more debt-ridden. Enthusiasts should not despair, however, as there are still some great train rides. The Curitiba-Paranaguá train that descends the coastal mountain range offers some unforgettable views, as does the steam train that runs from São Paulo to Santos every weekend. Speaking of steam

trains, affectionately known in Brazil as Maria Fumaças (Smoking Marys), the 13-km run from São João del Rei to Tiradentes in Minas Gerais, is great fun. Other pleasant short trips are those from Joinville to the island of São Francisco do Sul, in Santa Catarina, and the ride through the mountains from Campos do Jordão to Santo Antônio do Pinhal, in São Paulo, the highest stretch of track in the country.

Probably the train of most interest to travellers is the route from São Paulo to Corumbá, on the Bolivian border. It's no longer possible to take a train for the whole journey. The Bauru (SP) to Campo Grande leg must be done by bus. (See the São Paulo chapter for details.)

TAXI

Taxi rides are reasonably priced, if not cheap, but you should be aware of various tricks used by some drivers to increase the charges. We encountered some superb, friendly, honest and knowledgeable taxi drivers. However, we also met plenty of rogue cabbies with unsavoury characteristics.

Taxis in the large cities usually have meters with prices which are subject to frequent updates using a *tabela* (price sheet) to convert the price on the meter to a new price. This is OK as long as the meter works and the tabela is legal and current (don't accept photocopies). Unless you are certain about a standard price for a standard trip (and have verified this with the driver) or you have purchased a ticket from a taxi ticket office (described later in this section), you must insist that drivers turn on their meters (no excuses) at the beginning of the ride and show you a valid tabela at the end.

What you see is what you pay – no extras if you've only loaded a couple of pieces of baggage per person or the driver thinks the trip to the town centre has required 'extra' fuel. If the meter doesn't work or the driver won't engage it for whatever reason, then negotiate a fare before getting on board, or find another cab. If you want to get a rough idea about the going rate prior to taking a taxi ride into town, ask a newsagent or an official at the rodoviária, train station or the airport.

As a general rule, Tarifa I (standard tariff) applies from approximately 6 am to 10 pm (Monday to Saturday); Tarifa II (higher tariff) applies outside these hours, on holidays and outside city limits. Sometimes there is a standard charge, typically for the trip between the airport and the city centre. Many airports and rodoviárias now have a system for you to purchase a taxi ticket from a *bilheteria* (ticket office). However, in a few places, the ticket office applies a much higher rate than if you flag a taxi down outside the rodoviária or airport – we've indicated where this is the case.

The same general advice applies to taxis without meters. You must agree on the price beforehand, and make sure there is no doubt about it. Learn the numbers in Portuguese. If the driver hesitates for a long time or starts using fingers instead of talking to you about numbers, you may find the price has been grasped from imagination rather than being the normal rate. You don't want to have an argument at the end of the ride – it's not worth it, even if you win.

If the driver claims to have no change, hold firm and see if this is just a ploy to extract more from you. We often found that change mysteriously appeared out of the driver's pocket when we said we'd be happy to wait in the taxi until change could be found. You can avoid this scenario by carrying change. (More tips can be found under the heading called Small Change in the Money section of the Facts for the Visitor chapter.)

If possible, orient yourself before taking a taxi, and keep a map handy in case you find yourself being taken on a wild detour – even following the route on the map during the ride isn't a bad idea, and it's an effective way of orienting yourself. Never use taxi touts – an almost certain ripoff. Deal directly with the taxi driver at the taxi rank, or with the taxi company. The worst place to get a cab is wherever the tourists are. Don't get a cab near one of the expensive hotels. In Rio, for example, walk a block away from the beach

at Copacabana to flag down a cab. Many airports have special airport taxis which are about 50% more expensive than a regular taxi which is probably waiting just around the corner. If you are carrying valuables, however, the special airport taxi, or a radio-taxi can be a worthwhile investment. These are probably the safest taxis on the road.

For more tips on security and taxi travel see the Dangers & Annoyances section in the Facts for the Visitor chapter.

CAR & MOTORBIKE

The number of fatalities caused by motor vehicles in Brazil is estimated at 80,000 per year. The roads can be very dangerous, especially the busy highways like the Rio to São Paulo corridor. Most of the problems stem from the Brazilian drivers. If you thought the Italians were wild drivers, just wait. This isn't true everywhere, but in general the car owner is king of the road and shows it. Other motorists are treated as unwelcome guests at a private party. Pedestrians are shown no mercy, and certainly no courtesy.

Especially in Rio, the anarchic side of the Brazilian personality emerges from behind the driver's wheel as lane dividers, one-way streets and even footpaths are disregarded and violated. Driving is unpoliced, traffic violations unheard of. One of the most bizarre examples of this we encountered was while being given a lift by police on a highway north of Salvador – after waiting for several hours while every other car barrelled past without a thought of stopping. The police car, running at its top speed of about 140 km, was passed by several other cars at speeds of over 150 km. As each car passed, the police simply shook their heads and sighed, *Não respeito* (No respect).

Despite all appearances to the contrary, Brazil does hold to the convention that a red light means 'stop'. In practice, this old-fashioned, but often useful, concept has been modified to mean 'maybe we'll stop, maybe we'll slow down – but if it's night we'll probably do neither'.

Drivers use their horns incessantly, and buses, which have no horns, rev their engines instead. One of the craziest habits is driving at night without headlights. This is done, as far as we can tell, so that the headlights can be flashed to warn approaching vehicles.

Many drivers are racing fans and tend to drive under the influence, pretending they are Formula One drivers. The worst are the Rio bus drivers, or maybe the São Paulo commuters, or maybe the Amazonian truck drivers, or maybe...we could go on and on.

Driving in Brazil

I decided to do this research trip by car accompanied by a mate from Australia, Peter Bolgarow. We looked at buying one for between US$3000 and US$4000, but the only car you can buy for that price is a 1979 Volkswagon Brasília. They're reliable enough, but don't have any power, something that really helps on Brazilian highways when you get stuck behind slow-moving trucks. Instead we opted to rent a car for three months. The cost of renting a car by the month works out at about half the daily-rental rate per day, so it worked out that we'd spend about the same amount of money, and we wouldn't have to worry about the car all the time. We also wouldn't have the problem of reselling a car at the end of a long trip.

The car we rented was a late-model Volkswagon Gol (Golf) 1000. In Brazil it's known as the people's car, because it's the cheapest car around. A new one costs US$8000 – a government-fixed price that aims to let poorer people access new cars, but in reality merely creates a black market for the cars. To get one at the fixed price takes several months.

The Gol's 1000 cc motor went really well for the whole 10,000 km. At first, it lacked a bit of power, and top speed was 120 km/h, but after running it in with a solid month's driving, it would get to 140 km/h no problem.

Road conditions varied from excellent to pretty bad, and we ended up with 10 flat tyres for the trip. Flat tyres are very common in Brazil, and, luckily, there are *borracheiros* (tyre repairers) at frequent intervals along the roads.

The most serious thing that happened was a slight collision that broke a headlight and put a scratch in the rear passenger door of the other car. Since we didn't want to pay for the damage, we went to get a police statement the next day in Cuiaba. On our first attempt the sergeant in charge wouldn't let us in the station with short pants on, but since we had all of our luggage in the car, this wasn't too inconvenient. We eventually got the statement after a couple of hours sitting around waiting. But we still got screwed by the rental car company when we returned the car. They had a clause in very fine print which said that the renter had to pay 70% of the daily rental rate for each day that the car was off the road getting fixed!

Driving in Brazil was an interesting experience, but it took a while to get used to. It's no surprise that Brazil has the highest road toll in the world – some drivers are just plain crazy. You have to be on the lookout as you go around a blind corner, because there's probably a Brazilian coming the other way who's decided to overtake a truck. Car wrecks are piled up at the police checkpoints that dot the highways. We saw some horrible wrecks.

The police we met on the roads were a mixed bunch. At the checkpoint on the São Paulo-Paraná border, a cop pulled us over to look at our papers. He found some bogus problem and told us that there would be a fine. Then he said that we'd have to leave the car there as well. Five minutes later and US$60 poorer, we were on our way. On the other side of the coin, we got stopped for speeding – doing 120 km/h in an 80 km/h zone. But the cop was very friendly. He asked us a bit about Australia and then let us go. He said he didn't want to give Australians the impression that Brazilian police officers were bastards. Only some of them are it seems.

Peter rides a motorcycle in Australia. Here are his comments about riding a bike in Brazil:

A road/trail bike would be ideal because of it's versatility. The biggest one I saw in Brazil was the XT600. These popular bikes are light, reliable and have ample power. Smaller bikes are OK for the cities, but on the Brazilian highways, with heavy truck traffic and pollution, it's wise to have a larger one.

Unless you're a competent rider, it's not a good idea to motorcycle around Brazil. There are road laws but no one obeys them, so anything goes. If you do decide to do it, then go for it. Brazil is a beautiful country, but try to keep your eyes on the road.

Andrew Draffen

This cult of speed, a close cousin to the cult of machismo, is insatiable; its only positive aspect is that, unlike grandma driving to church on Sunday, these drivers tend to be very alert and rarely fall asleep at the wheel.

Driving at night is hazardous, at least in the Northeast and the interior, where roads are often poor and unreliable. Like malaria, potholes are endemic and poorly banked turns are the norm. It's always a good idea to slow down when you enter a town, since many have speed bumps, variously known as *quebra-molas*, *lombadas*, *ondulações* or *sonorizadores*, which you never see until it's too late. Another big danger is the farm trucks with inexperienced drivers carrying workers and cargo to town.

On the bright side, many trucks and buses in the Northeast help you pass at night with their indicators. A flashing right indicator means it's clear to go, a flashing left means that a vehicle is approaching from the opposite direction. Everything happens more slowly in the Northeast, and this holds true for driving too.

Car Rental

Renting a car is expensive with prices similar to those in the USA and Europe. But if you can share the expense with friends it's a great way to explore some of the many remote beaches, fishing villages and back roads of Brazil. Several familiar multinationals dominate the car-rental business in Brazil and getting a car is safe and easy if you have a driver's licence, a credit card and a passport. You should also carry an international driver's licence.

There is little competition between the major rental companies. Prices are usually about the same, although there are occasional promotional deals (the only ones we encountered were during off-season weekends in non-tourist towns). Fiat Unos are the cheapest cars to rent, followed by the Volkswagen Golf and Chevette (which has a good reputation). Sometimes the rental companies will claim to be out of these cheaper models; if this is the case, don't hesitate to shop around. Also, when you get prices quoted on the phone, make sure they include insurance, which is required. When looking at the contract, pay close attention to any theft clause which appears to load a large percentage of any loss onto the hirer. Another tricky clause we found was that if you have an accident and get a police statement, you don't have to pay for the damage. But you do have to pay 70% of the daily hire for the number of days it takes the rental company to fix the car!

The big companies have offices in most cities; they are always out at the airport and often in the centre of town as well. In the phone book, look under *autolocadoras* or *locadoras de automóveis*. There are usually discounts for weekly and monthly rentals, and no drop-off charges.

Motorcycles

Renting a bike is as expensive as renting a car. If you want to buy a bike, Brazil manufactures its own, but they are expensive. The most powerful we saw was 600 cc.

Motorcycles are popular in Brazil, especially in and around the cities. Theft is a big problem; you can't even insure a bike because theft is so common. Most people who ride keep their bike in a guarded place, at least overnight. For the traveller this can be difficult to organise, but if you can manoeuvre around the practical problems, Brazil is a great place to have a motorcycle.

BICYCLE

You don't see many long-distance cyclists in Brazil. We wouldn't recommend cycling there, as conditions are very dangerous. See the Road section in the Getting There & Away chapter for more details.

HITCHING

Hitching is never entirely safe in any country in the world, and we don't recommend it. Travellers who decide to hitch should understand that they are taking a small but potentially serious risk. People who do choose to hitch will be safer if they travel in pairs and let someone know where they are planning to go.

Hitching in Brazil, with the possible

exception of the Amazon and Pantanal, is difficult. The phrase for hitching in Portuguese is *carona*, so ask '*pode dar carona*' ('can you give me/us a lift'). The best way to hitch – practically the only way if you want a ride – is to wait at a petrol station or a truck stop and talk to the drivers. But even this can be difficult. A few years back there were several assaults by hitchhikers and the government began to discourage giving rides in public service announcements.

BOAT

Although river travel in Brazil has decreased rapidly due to the construction of a comprehensive road network, it is still possible to travel by boat between some of the river cities of the Rio São Francisco. See the River Travel section in the Bahia chapter, and the São Francisco River Trip heading under Belo Horizonte in the Minas Gerais chapter for more details.

For information on river travel in the Amazon region, see the North chapters.

LOCAL TRANSPORT
Local Bus

Local bus services tend to be pretty good in Brazil. Since most Brazilians take the bus to work every day, municipal buses are usually frequent and their network of routes is comprehensive. They are always cheap and crowded.

In most city buses, you get on at the back and exit from the front. Usually there's a money collector sitting at a turnstile at the rear of the bus, with the price displayed nearby. If you're unsure if it's the right bus, it's easy to hop on the back and ask the money collector if the bus is going to your destination – *você vai para...?* If it's the wrong bus no one will mind if you hop off, even if the bus has gone a stop or two.

Crime can be a problem on buses. Rather than remain at the rear of the bus, it's safer to pay the fare and go through the turnstile. Try to avoid carrying valuables if you can. If you must take valuables with you then keep them well hidden. For more tips about security and travel on local buses, see the Dangers & Annoyances section in the Facts for the Visitor chapter.

Jumping on a local bus is one of the best ways to get to know a city. With a map and a few dollars you can tour the town and maybe meet some of the locals.

The Southeast

JOHN MAIER, JR

The Southeast

The Southeast region, known in Brazil as the Sudeste, comprises almost 11% of the country's land area and is home to a whopping 44% of Brasileiros – 90% of whom live in cities. The region is made up of the states of Rio de Janeiro, Espirito Santo, São Paulo and Minas Gerais.

Geographically, the Southeast contains the most mountainous areas of the Planalto Atlântico: the serras da Mantiqueira, do Mar and do Espinaço, making it popular with hikers and climbers.

Most of the region was once covered by the lush Mata Atlântica, but this has been devastated since the arrival of the Portuguese. Inland, Minas Gerais also contains areas of cerrado and caatinga. Two great rivers begin in the mountains of the Southeast; the Paraná, formed by the Paraíba and Grande rivers, and the São Francisco, which begins in the Serra da Canastra in Minas.

The Southeast is the economic powerhouse of Brazil and contains 60% of the country's industry. This wealth attracts migrants from all over Brazil, who flock to the three largest cities of Brazil – São Paulo, Rio de Janeiro and Belo Horizonte – in search of something better.

Attractions of the Southeast include the *cidade maravilhosa* Rio de Janeiro; historic colonial towns (Parati, Ouro Prêto and many others in Minas); national parks (Serra dos Órgãos, Itatiaia and Caparaó); and the people themselves – the hard-working Paulistas (from São Paulo), the fun-loving Cariocas (from Rio), the strong-willed Capixabas (from Espirito Santo) and the spiritual Mineiros (from Minas Gerais).

Highlights

* Double hang-gliding in Rio de Janeiro
* Hiking and diving on Ilha Grande (Rio state)
* A Flamengo-Fluminense football game at Maracanã stadium (Rio de Janeiro)
* Colonial village of Parati (Rio de Janeiro)
* Trekking the old gold route from São Jose Barreiro to Parati (you actually cross the São Paulo-Rio border during this trek)
* Trekking through the Parque Nacional Serra dos Orgãos from Teresópolis to Petrópolis (Rio de Janeiro)
* Cycling from Leblon to Flamengo in Rio on Tuesday evenings with hundreds of other bikers (Rio de Janeiro)
* Brazilian baroque churches in the colonial towns of Minas Gerais
* Hiking in the Parque Nacional de Caparaó on crisp, clear winter days (Minas Gerais)
* Steam train ride from São João del Rei to Tiradentes (Minas Gerais)

Rio de Janeiro City

Rio is the cidade maravilhosa (marvellous city). Jammed into the world's most beautiful city setting – between ocean and escarpment – are more than seven million Cariocas, as the inhabitants are called. This makes Rio one of the most densely populated places on earth. This thick brew of Cariocas pursues pleasure like no other people: beaches and the body beautiful; samba and cerveja; football and cachaça.

Rio has its problems, and they are enormous. A third of the people live in the favelas that blanket many of the hillsides. The poor have no schools, no doctors and no jobs. Drug abuse and violence are endemic. Police corruption and brutality are commonplace. The breakdown in law and order recently forced the state government to ask the President to send federal troops into the favelas, in an attempt to curb drug trafficking. Nevertheless, in Rio everything ends with samba – football games, weddings, work, political demonstrations and, of course, a day at the beach. There's a lust for life, and a love of romance, music, dance and talk that seem to distinguish the Cariocas from everyone else. For anyone coming from the efficiency and rationality of the developed, capitalist world this is potent stuff. The sensuality of Carnival is the best known expression of this Dionysian spirit, but there are plenty more.

Rio has its glitzy side – its international tourist crowd and the lives of its rich and famous. But happily it's also a good city for the budget traveller. There are plenty of cheap restaurants and hotels. The beaches are free and democratic. There's lots to explore in the city centre and in several other neighbourhoods with their parks and museums. Mass transportation is fast and easy. And if you can meet some locals – not nearly so hard as in New York, London or Sydney – well, then you're on easy street.

History
Gaspar de Lemos set sail from Portugal for Brazil in May 1501 and entered a huge bay in January 1502. Mistaking the bay for a river, he named it Rio de Janeiro. It was the French, however, who first settled along the great bay. Like the Portuguese, the French had been harvesting brazil wood along the Brazilian coast, but unlike the Portuguese they hadn't attempted any permanent settlements until Rio de Janeiro.

As the Portuguese colonisation of Brazil began to take hold, the French became concerned that they'd be pushed out of the colony. Three ships of French settlers reached the Baía de Guanabara in 1555. They settled on a small island in the bay and called it Antarctic France. Almost from the start, the town seemed doomed to failure. It was torn by religious divisions, isolated by harsh treatment of the Indians and demoralised by the puritanical rule of the French leader, Nicolas de Villegagnon. Antarctic France was weak and disheartened when the Portuguese attacked and drove the French from their fortress in 1560.

A greater threat to the Portuguese were the powerful Tamoio Indians, who had allied with the French. A series of battles occurred, but the Portuguese were better armed and better supplied than the French, whom they finally expelled. They drove the Tamoio from the region in a series of bloody battles.

The Portuguese set up a fortified town on the Morro Castelo in 1567 to maximise protection from European invasion by sea and Indian attack by land. They named it São Sebastião do Rio de Janeiro, after King Sebastião of Portugal. The founding 500 Cariocas built a typical Brazilian town: poorly planned, with irregular streets in medieval Portuguese style. By the end of the century the small settlement was, if not exactly prosperous, surviving on the export of brazil wood and sugar cane, and from fishing in the Baía de Guanabara.

In 1660 the city had a population made up of 3000 Indians, 750 Portuguese and 100

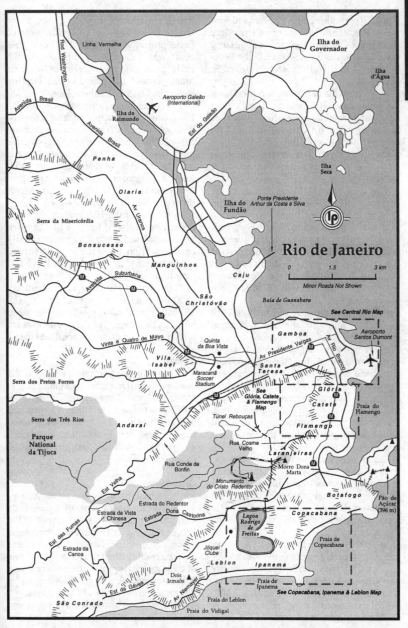

blacks. It grew along the waterfront and what is now Praça 15 de Novembro (often referred to as Praça Quinze). Religious orders came – the Jesuits, the Franciscans and the Benedictines – and built austere, closed-in churches.

With its excellent harbour and good lands for sugar cane, Rio became Brazil's third most important settlement (after Salvador de Bahia and Recife-Olinda) in the 17th century. Slaves were imported and sugar plantations thrived. The owners of the sugar estates lived in the protection and comfort of the fortified city.

The gold rush in Minas Gerais at the beginning of the 18th century changed Rio forever. In 1704 the Caminho Novo, a new road to the Minas gold fields, was opened. Until the gold began to run out, half a century later, a golden road went through the ports of Rio. Much of the gold that didn't end up in England, and many of the Portuguese immigrants didn't return to Minas, but stayed on in Rio.

Rio was now the prize of Brazil. In 1710 the French, who were at war with Portugal and raiding its colonies, attacked the city. The French were defeated, but a second expedition succeeded and the entire population abandoned the city in the dark of night. The occupying French threatened to level the city unless a sizeable ransom in gold, sugar and cattle was paid. The Portuguese obliged. During the return voyage to an expected heroes' welcome in France, the victors lost two ships and most of the gold.

Rio quickly recovered from the setback. Its fortifications were improved, many richly decorated churches were built and by 1763 its population had reached 50,000. With international sugar prices slumping, Rio replaced Salvador de Bahia as the colonial capital in 1763.

In 1808 the entire Portuguese monarchy and court – barely escaping the invasion by Napoleon's armies – arrived in Rio. The city thus came to house the court of the Portuguese Empire – or at least what was left of it. With the court came an influx of money and skills that helped build some of the city's

lasting monuments, like the palace at the Quinta da Boa Vista and the Jardim Botânico (a pet project of the king). The Portuguese court was followed by talented French exiles, such as the architect Jean de Montigny and the painters Jean Baptiste Debret and Nicolas Antoine Taunay.

The coffee boom in the mountains of São Paulo and Rio revitalised Brazil's economy. Rio took on a new importance as a port and commercial centre, and coffee commerce modernised the city. A telegraph system and gas street lights were installed in 1854. Regular passenger ships began sailing to London in 1845, and to Paris in 1851. A ferry service to Niteroí began in 1862.

At the end of the 19th century the city's population exploded because of European immigration and internal migration (mostly ex-slaves from the declining coffee and sugar regions). In 1872 Rio had 275,000 inhabitants; by 1890 there were about 522,000, a quarter of them foreign-born. By 1900 the population had reached 800,000. The city spread rapidly between the steep hills, bay and ocean. The rich started to move further out, in a pattern that continues today.

Climate

You can expect some rain in Rio. In the summer, from December to March, it gets hot and humid. Temperatures in the high 30°Cs are common and there's more rain than at other times, but it rarely lasts for too long. In the winter, temperatures range from the 20°Cs to low 30°Cs, with plenty of good days for the beach.

Orientation

Rio is divided into a *zona norte* (north zone) and a *zona sul* (south zone) by the Serra da Carioca, steep mountains that are part of the Parque Nacional da Tijuca. These mountains descend to the edge of the city centre, where the zonas norte and sul meet. Corcovado, one of these mountain peaks, offers the best way to become familiar with the city's geography – from it you have views of both zones.

Rio is a tale of two cities. The upper and middle classes reside in the zona sul, the lower class, except for the favela dwellers, in the zona norte. Favelas cover steep hillsides on both sides of town – Rocinha, Brazil's largest favela with somewhere between 150,000 and 300,000 residents, is in Gávea, one of Rio's richest neighbourhoods. Most industry is in the zona norte, as is most of the pollution. The ocean beaches are in the zona sul.

Unless they work in the zona norte, residents of the zona sul rarely go to the other side of the city. The same holds true for travellers, unless they head north to the Maracanã football stadium or the Quinta da Boa Vista, with the national museum, or the international airport which is on the Ilha do Governador.

Centro Rio's centre is all business and bustle during the day and absolutely deserted at night and on weekends. It's a working city – the centre of finance and commerce. The numerous high-rise office buildings are filled with workers who pour onto the daytime streets to eat at the many restaurants and shop at the small stores. Lots of essential services for the traveller are in the centre. The main airline offices are here, as are foreign consulates, Brazilian government agencies, money exchange houses, banks and travel agencies.

The centre is the site of the original settlement of Rio. Most of the city's important museums and colonial buildings are here. Small enough to explore on foot, the city centre is lively and interesting, and occasionally beautiful (despite the many modern, Bauhaus-inspired buildings).

Two wide avenues cross the centre: Avenida Rio Branco, where buses leave for the zona sul, and Avenida Presidente Vargas, which heads out to the *sambódromo* and the zona norte. Rio's modern subway follows these two avenues as it burrows under the city. Most banks and airline offices have their headquarters on Avenida Rio Branco.

We found sightseeing was safer here during the week, because there are lots of people around. On weekends, you stand out much more.

Cinelândia At the southern edge of the business district, Cinelândia's shops, bars, restaurants and movie theatres are popular day and night. There are also several decent hotels here that are reasonably priced. The bars and restaurants get crowded at lunch and after work, when there's often samba in the streets. There's a greater mix of Cariocas here than in any other section of the city. Several gay and mixed bars stay open here until late.

Lapa By the old aqueduct that connects the Santa Teresa trolley and the city centre is Lapa, the scene of many a Brazilian novel. This is where boys used to become men and men became infected. Prostitution still exists here but there are also several music clubs, like the Circo Voador and Asa Branca, and some very cheap hotels. Lapa goes to sleep very late on Friday and Saturday.

Santa Teresa This is one of Rio's most unusual and charming neighbourhoods. Situated along the ridge of the hill that rises from the city centre, Santa Teresa has many of Rio's finest colonial homes. In the 1800s Rio's upper crust lived here and rode the *bonde* (tram) to work in the city. The bonde is still there but the rich moved out long ago.

During the '60s and '70s many artists and hippies moved into Santa Teresa's mansions. Just a few metres below them the favelas grew on the hillsides. Santa Teresa was considered very dangerous for many years and is now heavily policed. It's still necessary to be cautious here, especially at night.

Catete & Flamengo Moving south along the bay, you'll come to Catete and Flamengo, two areas which have the bulk of inexpensive hotels in Rio. Flamengo was once Rio's finest residential district and the Palácio do Catete housed Brazil's president until 1954, but with the new tunnel to Copacabana the upper classes began moving out in the 1940s. Flamengo is still mostly residential. The apartments are often big and graceful, although a few high-rise offices have recently been built amongst them. With the

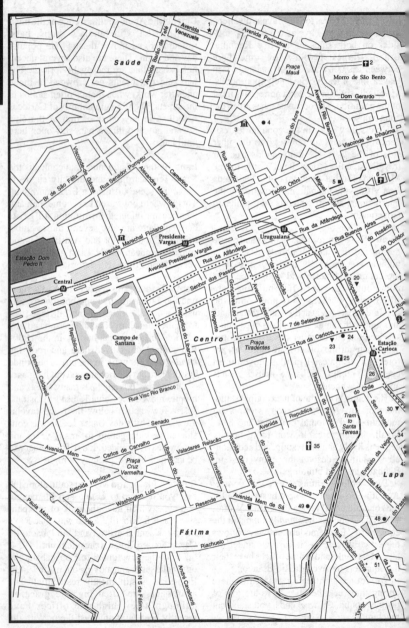

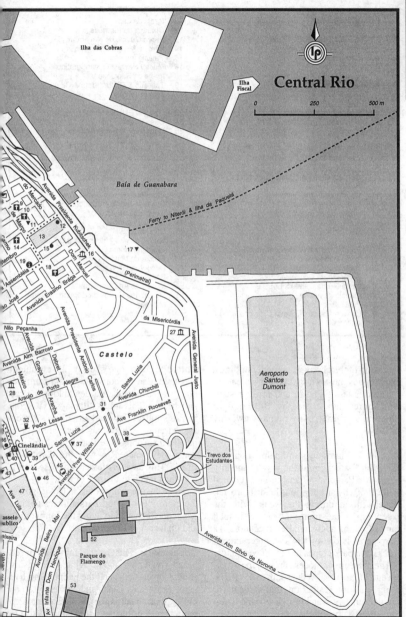

Ilha das Cobras

Ilha
Fiscal

Central Rio

0   250   500 m

Baía de Guanabara

Ferry to Niterói & Ilha da Paquetá

17 ▼

(Perimetral)

da Misericórdia

27 🏛

Castelo

Aeroporto
Santos
Dumont

Santa Luzia

Avenida Churchill

Avenida Presidente Kubitschek

Avenida Presidente António Carlos

Avenida General Justo

Mercado

de Março

Camp...

9
10
11
12
13
14
15
16
18
19

Dom Manuel

Avenida Erasmo Braga

Nilo Peçanha

Avenida Alm Barroso

México

Araujo de Porto Alegre

Debret

Graça

Araínha

31

Avenida Franklin Roosevelt

38

28

32 Pedro Lessa

Santa Luzia

37 ▼

Cinelândia

39
40
43 44
46
45

Avenida Pres Wilson

47

Ave Luís

asseio
úblico

eixeira

Avenida Beira Mar

Avenida Dom Henrique

Av Infante Dom Henrique

52

Parque do
Flamengo

53

Avenida Alm Silvio de Noronha

Trevo dos
Estudantes

São José

Assembléia

tembro

Nilo José

PLACES TO STAY

5	Guanabara Palace Hotel
38	Aeroporto Othon Hotel
40	Itajuba Hotel
41	Nelba Hotel

PLACES TO EAT

11	English Bar
17	Restaurante Alba Mar
20	Confeitaria Colombo
23	Bar Luis
29	Café do Teatro
30	Suco (Juice) Bars
33	Cheio de Vida
34	Macrobióteca
36	Outdoor Cafés & Political Debating
37	Hotel Ambassador
42	Churrascolândia Restaurante
43	Lanchonete Bariloche
51	Restaurante Ernesto

OTHER

1	Polícia Federal (Visa Extensions)
2	Igreja São Bento
3	Palácio da Conceicao
4	Fortaleza da Conceicao
6	Igreja NS da Candelaria
7	Palácio Itamaraty
8	Post Office
9	Igreja e Museu da Santa Cruz dos Militares
10	Igreja da Lapa
12	Chafariz da Piramide
13	Praça Quinze de Novembro
14	Igreja e Museu do Carmo
15	Palácio Imperial
16	Museu Naval e Oceanográfico
18	Igreja de São José
19	TurisRio & Riotur (State & City) Tourist Offices
21	Riotur Booth
22	Hospital Estadual Souza Aguiar
24	Casa Oliveira
25	Convento de Santo Antônio
26	Crafts Market
27	Museu Histórico Nacional
28	Museu Nacional de Belas Artes
29	Teatro Municipal
31	Praça Ana Amélia
32	Suburban Dreams
35	Catedral de San Sebastiãn
39	Buses to Southern Suburbs: Flamengo, Copacabana etc
44	Praça Floriano
45	US Consulate
46	Varig/Cruzeiro Airlines Main Office
47	Praça Mahátma Gandhi
48	Escola da Música
49	Circo Voador
50	Bar Brasil
52	Museu de Arte Moderna
53	Museu dos Mortos da Segunda Guerra Mundial

exception of the classy waterfront buildings, Flamengo is mostly a middle-class area.

There is less nightlife and fewer restaurants here than in nearby Botafogo or Cinelândia, which are five minutes' away by subway.

Parque do Flamengo Stretching along the bay from Flamengo all the way to the city centre, the Parque do Flamengo was created in the 1950s by an enormous landfill project. Under-utilised during the week, with the exception of the round-the-clock football games (joining a few hundred spectators at a 3 am game is one of Rio's stranger experiences), the park comes to life on weekends.

The museum of modern art is at the northern end of the park. At the south end is Rio's, a big outdoor restaurant that's ideal for people and bay watching. The park is not considered safe at night.

Botafogo Botafogo's early development was spurred by the construction of a tram that ran up to the botanical garden linking the bay and the lake. This artery still plays a vital role in Rio's traffic flow and Botafogo's streets are extremely congested. There are several palatial mansions here that housed foreign consulates when Rio was the capital of Brazil. This area has fewer high-rise buildings than much of the rest of Rio.

There are not many hotels in Botafogo but there are lots of good bars and restaurants where the locals go to avoid the tourist glitz and high cost of Copacabana.

Copacabana This is the famous curved beach you know about. What's surprising about Copacabana is all the people who live there. Fronted by beach and backed by steep hills, Copacabana is for the greater part no more than four blocks wide. Crammed into this narrow strip of land are 25,000 people per sq km, one of the highest population densities in the world. Any understanding of the Rio way of life and leisure has to start with the fact that so many people live so close together and so near to the beach.

Only three parallel streets traverse the length of Copacabana. Avenida Atlântica runs along the ocean. Avenida NS de Copacabana, two blocks inland, is one way, running in the direction of the business district. One block further inland, Rua Barata Ribeiro is also one way, in the direction of Ipanema and Leblon. These streets change their names when they reach Ipanema.

Copacabana is the capital of Brazilian tourism. It's possible to spend an entire Brazilian vacation without leaving it, and some people do just that. The majority of Rio's medium and expensive hotels are here and they are accompanied by plenty of restaurants, shops and bars. For pure city excitement, Copacabana is Rio's liveliest theatre. It is also the heart of Rio's recreational sex industry. There are many *boîtes* (bars with strip shows) and prostitutes; anything and everyone is for sale.

From Christmas to Carnival there are so many foreign tourists in Copacabana that Brazilians who can't afford to travel abroad have been known to go down to Avenida Atlântica along the beach and pretend they are in Paris, Buenos Aires or New York. As always when there are lots of tourists, there are problems. Prices are exorbitant, hotels are full and restaurants get overcrowded. The streets are noisy and hot.

Ipanema & Leblon These are two of Rio's most desirable districts. They face the same stretch of beach and are separated by the Jardim de Alah, a canal and adjacent park. They are residential, mostly upper class and becoming more so as rents continue to rise. Most of Rio's better restaurants, bars and nightclubs are in Ipanema and Leblon; there are only a few hotels, although there are a couple of good aparthotels.

Barra da Tijuca Barra is the fashionable suburb with Rio's rich and famous. The beach is beautiful, and apartments in the closed condominiums are expensive. Like fungi in a rainforest, hundreds of buildings have sprung up wherever there happens to be an open space. Whether condo, restaurant, shopping centre or disco, these big, modern structures are, without exception, monstrosities.

Information

Tourist Offices Riotur (☎ 541-7522) has a tourist information hotline. Call them from 9 am to 5 pm, Monday to Friday, with any questions. The receptionists speak English and more often than not they'll be able to help you.

Riotur (☎ 297-7177; fax 531-1872) is the Rio city tourism agency. The main office is at Rua da Assembléia 10, 8th floor, Centro,

---

Igreja da Penha

From Rio's international airport you can spot a church perched on a huge boulder in the suburban area called Penha.

The site for the church was chosen by a wealthy man after he and his family were having a picnic there. A snake appeared, threatening to attack them. Afraid, he went down on his knees and prayed for NS da Penha to help him. As if by a miracle, a lizard appeared and scared away the snake. Impressed by the event, he promised to build a church on the top of the hill as thanks for the divine help he received.

The hill now has a stairway with 365 steps to the church, representing the 365 days of the year. Every year during the October festivities of NS da Penha, followers climb the steps on their knees to pay their respects. ■

but the special 'tourist room' is in Copacabana at Avenida Princesa Isabel 183. There, you'll find free brochures (in Portuguese and English) which include maps. It's open Monday to Saturday from 9 am to 6 pm You can also get the brochures at their information booths at the main rodoviária (open daily from 6 am to 11 pm), Pão de Açúcar (daily, from 8 am to 7 pm), the international airport at Galeão (daily, from 5 am to 11 pm), Cosme Velho at the Corcovado railway station (daily, from 7 am to 7 pm), the Instituto Brasileiro da Pâtrimonio Cultural at Avenida Rio Branco 44 (daily, from 10 am to 5 pm), and sometimes in your hotel. When arriving in Rio by bus, the Riotur booth at the rodoviária can save you a lot of time by calling around town to find a vacant hotel and making a reservation. The staff only have lists of the mid-range to top-end hotels, but if you give them the phone number of a cheaper one they will be happy to call it. Riotur is also in charge of Carnival and puts out a special programme during this time.

TurisRio (☎ 531-1922; fax 531-2506) is the Rio state tourism agency. Its office is in the same building as Riotur's (metro stop Carioca), on the 7th floor. Embratur (☎ 273-2212; fax 273-9290) is Brazil's national tourism agency. The main office is in Brasília, but there's a branch at Rua Mariz e Barros 13 near Praça da Bandeira on the north side of town. For the average traveller, neither of these agencies is worth a special trip.

Money Changing money in Rio at the parallel rate is easy, especially if you have cash. Have a look at the *dólar paralelo* (*comprar*) exchange rates posted on the front page of *O Globo* or *Jornal do Brasil*. The exchange houses should give you the listed rate for cash and a few points less for travellers' cheques.

In the centre of the city, there are several travel agencies/casas de câmbio on Avenida Rio Branco, a couple of blocks before and after the intersection with Avenida Presidente Vargas (be cautious carrying money in the city centre). The Casa Piano office at

Avenida Rio Branco 88 is one of the best places to change. There's also an office in Ipanema at Visconde de Pirajá 365. Cambitur has several offices: Rua Visconde de Pirajá 414, Ipanema; Avenida NS de Copacabana 1093, Copacabana; and Avenida Rio Branco 31, Centro. Another is Exprinter at Avenida NS de Copacabana 371, Copacabana, and Avenida Rio Branco 128 and 57, Centro.

Most of the banks in the city also have currency-exchange facilities, but they change at the turismo rate, which is a bit less than the parallel.

You can get Visa cash advances at any Banco do Brasil.

At the international airport, there are three exchange houses: Imperial, which only changes cash and is open daily from 6 am to midnight, Cambitur, which changes travellers' cheques but closes at 2 pm on the weekend and Escobar, which also changes travellers' cheques and is open daily from 6 am to 10 pm. All change at the turismo rate. Porters and cleaners at the airport will also offer to change money. They don't change travellers' cheques, but change cash at the 'gringo ripoff' rate.

Post & Telephone Any mail addressed to Posta Restante, Rio de Janeiro, Brazil, ends up at the post office at Rua Primeiro de Março 64, in the city. They hold mail for 30 days and are reasonably efficient.

Faxes and telexes can be sent from any large post office. Post offices usually open from 8 am to 6 pm weekdays and until noon on Saturday. The branch at the International Airport is open 24 hours a day.

Telephone International phone calls can be made from the following locations in Rio:

Aeroporto Santos Dumont – 6 am to 11 pm
Centro – Praça Tiradentes 41, open 24 hours
Copacabana – Avenida NS de Copacabana 540
(upstairs), open 24 hours
Ipanema – Rua Visconde de Pirajá 111, 6 am to 11 pm
Rodoviária Novo Rio – open 24 hours
Méier – Dias da Cruz 182, 6.30 am to 11 pm

There are certain emergency phone numbers for which you don't need fichas to call from public phones: police 190, ambulance 192 and fire 193. There is a special police department for tourists called Rio Tourist Police (☎ 511-5112), open 24 hours a day at Avenida Afrânio de Mello Franco, Leblon, across the street from Scala.

American Express The American Express agent in Rio is Kontik-Franstur SA (☎ 235-1396). The address is Avenida Atlântica 2316-A, Copacabana CEP 20040, Copacabana, Rio de Janeiro, Brazil. They do a pretty good job of getting and holding onto mail. Beware of robbers when leaving their office. There's another office at Praia de Botafogo 228, bloco A, 5th floor, sala 514, that's open weekdays from 9 am to 6 pm.

Foreign Consulates The following countries have consulates in Rio:

Argentina
    Praia de Botafogo 228, 2nd floor, Botafogo (☎ 551-5198; fax 552-4191); open Monday to Friday, noon to 5 pm
Bolivia
    Avenida Rui Barbosa 664, No 101, Botafogo (☎ 551-1796; fax 551-3047); open Monday to Friday, 8.30 am to 1 pm
Canada
    Rua Lauro Muller 116, 1104 Botafogo (☎ 275-2137; fax 541-3898); open Monday to Friday, 9 am to 1 pm
Chile
    Praia do Flamengo 344, 7th floor, Flamengo (☎ 552-5349); open Monday to Friday, 8.30 am to 12.30 pm
Colombia
    Praia do Flamengo 284, No 101, Flamengo (☎ 552-6248; fax 552-5449); open Monday to Friday, 9 am to 1 pm
Ecuador
    Avenida NS de Copacabana 788, 8th floor, Copacabana (☎ 235-6695; fax 255-2245); open Monday to Friday, 8.30 am to 1 pm
France
    Avenida Presidente Antônio Carlos 58, 8th floor, Centro (☎ 210-1272; fax 220-4779); open Monday to Friday, 9 am to 12.30 pm
Germany
    Rua Presidente Carlos de Campos 417, Laranjeiras (☎ 553-6777; fax 553-0814); open Monday to Friday, 8.30 to 11.20 am

Israel
    Avenida NS de Copacabana 680, Copacabana, (☎ 255-5432; fax 235-6048); open Monday to Friday, 9 am to 4 pm
Japan
    Praia do Flamengo 200, 10th floor, Flamengo (☎ 265-5252; fax 205-7135); open Monday to Friday 9 am to 5 pm (closed for lunch)
Netherlands
    Praia de Botafogo 242, 7th floor, Botafogo (☎ 552-9028; fax 552-8294); open Monday to Friday, 9 am to noon.
Paraguay
    Avenida NS de Copacabana 538, No 404, Copacabana (☎ 255-7572; fax 255-7532); open Monday to Friday, 9 am to 1 pm
Peru
    Avenida Rui Barbosa 314, 2nd floor, Botafogo (☎ 551-6296; fax 551-9796); open 9 am to 1 pm
Sweden
    Praia do Flamengo 344, 9th floor, Flamengo (☎ 552-2422; fax 551-9091); open Monday to Friday, 9 am to noon.
Switzerland
    Rua Candido Mendes 157, 11th floor, Glória (☎ 242-8035; fax 263-1523); open Monday to Friday, 9 am to noon
Uruguay
    Rua Arthur Bernardes 30, Catete (☎ 225-0089); open 8 am to 1 pm
UK
    Praia do Flamengo 284, 2nd floor, Flamengo (☎ 552-1422; fax 552-5796); open Monday to Thursday, 9 to 11.30 am and 1.30 to 3.30 pm (on Friday, open in the morning only)
USA
    Avenida Presidente Wilson 147, Centro (☎ 292-7117; fax 220-0439); open Monday to Friday, 8 am to 4.30 pm

Visa Extensions If you need to renew your visa for another three months, go to the Polícia Marítima building (☎ 203-2142, ext 37) at Avenida Venezuela 2, Centro (near the far end of Avenida Rio Branco). It's open from 8 am to 4 pm for visa extensions. Bring a passport, money and airline ticket (if you have one). The fee is around US$12.

Travel Agencies Rio has no shortage of tourist agents eager to give advice, book bus and plane tickets and organise tours. They can also save you unnecessary trips to the rodoviária by selling bus tickets in advance. Many agents are brusque and unhelpful but

THE SOUTHEAST

some are quite the opposite, so it's usually worth walking out on type one to find type two.

In Copacabana, try **Extra Brazil Touren** (☎ 267-3741) at Rua Julio de Castilho 63/402. **Le Monde Passagems, Viagems e Turismo** (☎ 287-4042) in the shopping centre at Rua Visconde de Pirajá 260, Ipanema, is useful (speak to Mark or Carlos). Just around the corner at Vinícius de Moraes 120 is **Brazilclub Tours** (☎ 267-5093), which doesn't sell bus tickets but, unlike Le Monde, is open Saturday morning. Talk to Victor, who speaks English and French. **Dantur Passagems e Turismo** (☎ 205-1144) at Largo do Machado 29, shop 41, is useful if you're staying in the Catete/Botafogo/Flamengo area.

Guidebooks There are several guidebooks to Rio. *Guia Rio* by Quatro Rodas has the most comprehensive list of restaurants, hotels, bars and activities. It's well worth buying if you understand Portuguese and are going to be in Rio a long time. It's sold at newsstands. However, it covers only the upper end of the price spectrum. *Rio – The Guide* by Christopher Pickard covers a lot of ground, has excellent descriptions of Rio's fine restaurants and is in English, but it too is not oriented to the budget traveller (you can find it in hotel souvenir shops).

If you're a student of colonial architecture and plan on seeing the remains of old Rio, the Riotur office at Assembléia sells a book in Portuguese entitled *Guia do Patrimônio Cultural Carioca Bens Tomados*. It's filled with detailed maps and descriptions of the city's historic buildings. Also in Portuguese, the Michelin guide to Rio is excellent. Museum buffs may want to get hold of a copy of the museum guidebook by AGIR, in both Portuguese and English.

Available at newsstands, the *Guia Gay* is a small booklet with a lot of useful information.

During Carnival, *The Rio Carnaval Guide*, by Felipe Ferreira, in both Portuguese and English, is a detailed and often humorous read. Speaking of humour, buy a copy of Priscilla Ann Goslin's *How to be a Carioca – The Alternative Guide for the Tourist in Rio*. As well as containing a lot of laughs, her insights into the Carioca lifestyle are right on the mark.

Bookshops Finding good English books is difficult outside Rio and São Paulo, so stock up before heading into the interior. **Nova Livraria Leonardo da Vinci** is Rio's best bookshop; it's at Avenida Rio Branco 185 (it's one floor down on the *sobreloja* level). It has a lot of books in French also. **Edifício Marques do Herval** (☎ 224-1329) is a serious bookstore, with Rio's largest collection of foreign books and knowledgeable staff who, for a tidy sum, will order just about any book you want. It's open 9 am to 7 pm Monday to Friday and 9 am until noon on Saturday.

Livraria Dazibão at Rua Visconde de Pirajá 571-B in Ipanema stocks many Penguin paperbacks. **Livraria Kosmos**, next to the Copacabana Palace Hotel, has many foreign-language books. Each of the **Livraria Siciliana** chain has a collection of paperbacks in English. They are at Visconde de Pirajá 511, Ipanema, and Avenida NS de Copacabana 830, Copacabana.

Stúdio Livros at Rua Visconde de Pirajá 462 has current magazines and paperbacks in English. At the Leblon end of Ipanema, at Rua Visconde de Pirajá 640, there's a small used-book store that has old, funky and cheap books in English.

The newsstands on Avenida Rio Branco in the Centro have large selections of foreign newspapers and magazines.

Libraries **Instituto Brasil-Estados Unidos** (IBEU) (☎ 255-8939) has an English library with a large fiction collection, many books about Brazil in English and a good selection of current magazines from the USA. To borrow books you have to take classes there or buy a membership, but it's cheap. The library is at Avenida NS de Copacabana 690, 3rd floor.

With an American passport you can get into the American Consulate, which has a fantastic periodical room. It's on the corner of Avenida Presidente Wilson and Rua México; open 8 am to 4 pm, Monday to Friday.

Health The Rio Health Collective (☎ 325-9300 ext 44) offers a free telephone referral service. The staff speak English and can hook you up with an English-speaking doctor or specialist, in any part of the city.

24-Hour Pharmacies These include Farmácia Piauí at Avenida Ataulfo de Paiva 1283, Leblon (☎ 274-8448); at Rua Barata Ribeiro 646, Copacabana (☎ 255-6249); at Rua Ministro Viveiros de Castro 32, Leme (☎ 275-3847); and at Praia do Flamengo 224, Flamengo (☎ 284-1548).

Laundry There are laundromats in Copacabana at Rua Miguel Lemos 56 and Avenida NS de Copacabana 1226. In Flamengo, there's one at Rua Marquês de Abrantes 82. All are open Monday to Saturday from 8 am to 10 pm.

Art Supplies Casa Matos is the big chain. There's a store in Copacabana at Avenida NS de Copacabana 690. The small Arte Técnica shop is in Flamengo, at Rua do Catete 228, *loja* (shop) 119. It has better-quality supplies and also sells poster tubes which can carry home some of Rio's best gifts – art prints, giant photos and posters.

Walking Tour

There's more to Rio than beaches. Don't miss exploring some of the city's museums, colonial buildings, churches (of course) and traditional meeting places – restaurants, bars, shops and street corners. The centre of Rio, now a pot pourri of the new and old, still has character and life. Here's our suggested walking tour. Many of the places mentioned are described in more detail in the appropriate sections.

Take a bus or the metro to **Cinelândia** and find the main square along Avenida Rio Branco, called **Praça Floriano**; it's the heart of Rio today. Towards the bay is the Praça Mahatma Gandhi. The monument was a gift from India in 1964. Behind the praça and across the road, the large aeroplane hangar is the **Museu de Arte Moderna**.

Praça Floriano comes to life at lunch time and after work when the outdoor cafés are filled with beer drinkers, samba musicians and political debate. The square is Rio's political marketplace. There's daily speech making, literature sales and street theatre. Most city marches and rallies culminate here on the steps of the old **Câmara Municipal**.

Across Avenida Rio Branco is the **Biblioteca Nacional**. Built in 1910 in neo-classic style, it's open to visitors and usually has exhibitions. The most impressive building on the square is the **Teatro Municipal**, home of Rio's opera, orchestra and gargoyles. The theatre was built in 1905 and remodelled in 1934 and shows the influence of the Paris Opéra. The front doors are rarely open, but you can visit the ostentatious Assyrian Room Restaurant & Bar downstairs (entrance on Avenida Rio Branco). Built in the '30s, it's completely covered in tiles, with beautiful mosaics. In Avenida Rio Branco you'll also find the **Museu Nacional de Belas Artes**, housing some of Brazil's best paintings.

Now do an about-face and head back to the other side of the Teatro Municipal and walk down the pedestrian-only Avenida 13 de Maio (on your left are some of Rio's best suco bars). Cross a street and you're in the Largo da Carioca. Up on the hill is the recently restored **Convento de Santo Antônio**. The original church here was started in 1608, making it Rio's oldest. The church's Santo Antônio is an object of great devotion to many Cariocas in search of husbands. The church's sacristy, which dates from 1745, has some beautiful jacaranda-wood carving and Portuguese blue tiles.

Gazing at the skyline from the convent, you'll notice the Rubik's-cube-like **Petrobras building**. Behind it is the ultra-modern **Catedral Metropolitana** (the inside is cavernous with huge stained-glass windows). If you have time for a side trip, consider heading over to the nearby bonde (tram) that goes up to **Santa Teresa.**

Next find the shops along 19th-century Rua da Carioca. The old wine and cheese shop has some of Brazil's best cheese from the Canastra mountains in Minas Gerais. They also have bargains in Portuguese and Spanish wines. Two shops sell fine Brazilian-made instruments, including all the Carnival rhythm-makers, which make great gifts. There are several good jewellery stores off Rua da Carioca, on Rua Ramalho Ortigão.

Whenever we're near Rua da Carioca 39 we stop at the **Bar Luis** for a draft beer and lunch or snack. Rio's longest running restaurant, it was opened in 1887 and named Bar Adolf until WW II. For decades, many of Rio's intellectuals have chewed the fat while eating Rio's best German food here.

At the end of the block you'll pass the **Cinema Iris**, which used to be Rio's most elegant theatre (sadly, it's now a porno movie and strip joint), and emerge into the hustle of Praça Tiradentes. It's easy to see that this was once a fabulous part of the city. On opposite sides of the square are the **Teatro João Caetano** and the **Teatro Carlos Gomez**, which show plays and dance performances. The narrow streets in this part of town house many old, mostly dilapidated, small buildings. It's well worth exploring along Rua Buenos Aires as far as **Campo de Santana** and then returning along Rua da Alfândega. Campo de Santana is a pleasant park, once the scene – re-enacted in every Brazilian classroom – of Emperor Dom Pedro I, King of Portugal, proclaiming Brazil's independence from Portugal. Have a wander in the park and try to spot some of the agoutis that run wild there.

Back near Avenida Rio Branco, at Rua Gonçalves Dias 30, hit the **Confeitaria Colombo** for coffee and turn-of-the-century Vienna. Offering succour to shopping-weary matrons since 1894, the Colombo is best for coffee (very strong) and desserts.

From here, cross Avenida Rio Branco, go down Rua da Assembléia, stop at Riotur and TurisRio if you want tourist information,

then continue on to **Praça Quinze de Novembro**. In the square is the **Pyramid Fountain**, built in 1789, and a **crafts market**. Facing the bay, on your right is the **Palácio Imperial**, which was the royal palace and the seat of government. With independence it was ingloriously relegated to the Department of Telegraphs but has recently been restored.

On the opposite side of the square is the historic **Arco de Teles**, running between two buildings. Walking through the arch you'll see, immediately on your left, the elegant and very British **English Bar** – a good place for a quiet, expensive lunch or drink. The stores along the stone streets here have a waterfront character. There are several seafood restaurants, fishing supply stores and a couple of simple colonial churches. It's a colourful area.

Back at Praça Quinze de Novembro, take the overpass to the **waterfront**, where ferries leave to **Niterói** and **Ilha da Paquetá**. The ferry to Niterói takes only 15 minutes and you never have to wait long. Consider crossing the bay and walking around central Niterói if you have some time (the feel is different from Rio – much more like the rest of Brazil). Even if you return immediately the trip is worth it just for the view.

When you're facing the bay, the **Alba Mar** restaurant is a few hundred metres to your right. It's in a green gazebo overlooking the bay. The food is good and the atmosphere just right. On Saturday the building is surrounded by the tents of the **Feira de Antiguidades**, a strange and fun hotch potch of antiques, clothes, foods and other odds and ends.

If you want to extend your walking tour, go back through Arco de Teles and follow the street around toward Rua Primeiro de Março. Walk up along the right-hand side and you'll come to the **Centro Cultural do Banco do Brasil (CCBB)**. Go in and have a look at the building and any of the current exhibitions. Most are free. Then have a look behind the CCBB at the **Casa França-Brasil**. From there, you'll be able to see the **Igreja NS de Candelária**. Have a look inside and then keep going up Rua Primeiro de Março, through the naval area, to Rua Dom Geraldo, the last street before the hill. **Mosteiro de São Bento** is on top of the hill. To get there, go to Rua Dom Geraldo 40 and take the lift to the 5th floor. From Rua Dom Geraldo, head back toward Avenida Rio Branco, and try to imagine that in 1910 it was a tree-lined boulevard, with sidewalk cafés – the Champs Elysées of Rio.

Beaches

The beach, a ritual and way of life for the Carioca, is Rio's common denominator. People of all walks of life, in all shapes and sizes congregate on the sand. To the casual observer one stretch of sand is the same as any other. Not so. The beach is complex. Different times bring different people. Different places attract different crowds. Before and after work, exercise is the name of the game. Tanning is heaviest before 2 pm. On prime beach days, the fashionable pass the morning out at Barra and the afternoon back at their spot in Ipanema.

Every 20 metres of coastline is populated by a different group of regulars. For example, Arpoador has more surfers and people from the zona norte. In front of the luxury hotels you'll always find tourists and a security force watching over them.

Swimming isn't recommended at any of the bay beaches because of the sewage and industrial waste that pollutes the water. Work on the long-awaited treatment plants is just beginning.

Flamengo This popular beach is a thin strip of sand on the bay, with a great view. The park and beach were a landfill project. It's within an easy walk of most of the budget hotels in Catete/Flamengo. There's a different class of Carioca here than on the luxurious beaches to the south, and it's fun to watch them play.

Botafogo This small beach is on a calm bay inlet looking out at Pão de Açúcar. The Rio Yacht Club and Bâteau Mouche are next door.

Copacabana/Leme One of the world's most famous beaches runs 4.5 km in front of one of the world's most densely populated residential areas. From the scalloped beach you can see the granite slabs that surround the entrance to the bay – a magnificent meeting of land and sea. The last km to the east, from Avenida Princesa Isabel to the Leme hill, is called Praia do Leme. When you go to Copacabana, which you must, do as the locals do: take only the essentials with you. The area is now heavily policed, so it's OK to walk around during the evening. Avenida NS de Copacabana is more dangerous; watch out at weekends when the shops are closed and there are few locals around.

There is always something happening on the beach during the day and along the footpaths at night: drinking, singing, eating and all kinds of people checking out the scene; tourists watching Brazilians, Brazilians watching tourists; the poor, from nearby favelas, eyeing the rich, the rich avoiding the poor; prostitutes looking for tricks and johns looking for treats.

Arpoador This small beach is wedged between Copacabana and Ipanema. There's good surfing here, even at night when the beach is lit, and there's a giant rock that juts out into the ocean with a great view.

Ipanema/Leblon These two beaches are really one, although the beach narrows on the Leblon side, separated by the canal at Jardim de Alah. Ipanema, like the suburb, is Rio's richest and most chic beach. There isn't quite the frenzy of Copacabana, and the beach is a bit safer and cleaner. There are only two sidewalk cafés facing the ocean in Ipanema – Barril 1800 and Albericos – and one in Leblon – Canecão.

Ipanema is an Indian word for 'dangerous, bad waters'. The waves can get big and the undertow is often strong. Be careful, and swim only where the locals are swimming.

Different parts of the beach attract different crowds. Posto nine is Garota de Ipanema beach, right off Rua Vinícius de Morais. Today it's also known as the Cemetério dos

Elefantes because of the old leftists, hippies and artists who hang out there, but it's also popular with the young and beautiful who like go down there around sunset and smoke a joint. The Farme de Armoedo at Rua de Armoedo, also called Land of Marlboro, is the gay beach.

Vidigal Under the Sheraton Hotel and the Morro Dois Irmãos, this beach is a mix of the hotel and favela dwellers who were pushed further up the hill to make way for the Sheraton.

Pepino/São Conrado After the Sheraton there is no beach along the coast for a few km until Pepino beach in São Conrado. You can also take Avenida Niemeyer to the tunnel leading to Barra da Tijuca.

Pepino is a beautiful beach, less crowded than Ipanema. It's where the hang-gliders hang out when they're not hanging up there. Along the beach are two big resort hotels, the Hotel InterContinental and Hotel Nacional. Behind them, nestled into the hillside, is Brazil's biggest favela, Rocinha.

Bus No 546, 547 or 557 goes to Pepino. Don't take valuables, as these buses are frequent targets of robbers. There is also an executive bus (No 2016 'São Conrado') that goes along Copacabana and Ipanema beaches to Pepino.

Praia Barra da Tijuca The next beach out is Barra. It's 12 km long, with clean, green water. The first few km are filled with bars and seafood restaurants (Peixe Frito is recommended). Further out there are only *barracas* (food and drink stalls) on the beach. It's calm on weekdays, and crazy on hot summer weekends.

Barra's population has doubled in the last 10 years and it's currently the most fashionable place to live in Rio. There are more than a hundred closed condominiums, and the area is now known as the California Carioca.

Further Out The beaches further south – Prainha, Grumari, Marambaia – are very beautiful and worth exploring but not easily accessible by public transport. They only get busy on weekends when bus lines swell. All have barracas. Prainha, the next beach past Barra, is one of the best surfing beaches in Rio. Grumari is arguably the prettiest beach near the city, and there is a restaurant on the beach where the crabs are good.

To reach these beaches by car you can turn off the Rio-Santos road, BR-101, at Barra and follow the beach road. If it's a busy weekend, go a few km further and turn left at Estrada Bemvindo Novais, at Recreio dos Bandeirantes or Estrada Vereador.

Maracanã

This stadium, Brazil's temple of soccer and a colossus among colosseums, easily accommodates over 100,000 people and on occasion – the World Cup Game of 1950 or Pelé's last game – has squeezed in close to 200,000 crazed fans (although it's difficult to see how). If you like sports, if you want to understand Brazil, or if you just want an intense, quasi-psychedelic experience, then by all means go see a game of *futebol*, preferably a championship game or one between rivals Flamengo (Fla) and Fluminense (Flu).

Brazilian soccer is perhaps the most imaginative and exciting in the world. Complementing the action on the field, the stands are filled with fanatical fans who cheer their team on in all sorts of ways: chanting, singing and shouting; waving banners and streamers in team colours; pounding huge samba drums; exploding firecrackers, Roman candles and smoke bombs (in team colours); launching incendiary balloons; throwing toilet paper, beer and even dead chickens – possibly Macumba inspired. The scene, in short, is sheer lunacy.

Obviously, you have to be very careful if you go to Maracanã. Don't wear a watch or jewellery. Don't bring more money than you need for tickets, transport and refreshments. The big question is how to get to and from the game safely.

The big games are held on Sunday at 5 pm year-round. Tourist buses leave from major hotels at 2.30 pm (they often run a bit late) for 5 pm Sunday games. They cost about US$25, which is a ripoff, but it's the safest and easiest way to get to the game. They drop you off and pick you up right in front of the gate and escort you to lower-level seats. Unfortunately this is not the best perspective for watching the game, but it is the safest because of the overhead covering which protects you from descending objects (like cups full of bodily fluids).

However you get to the stadium, it's a good idea to buy these lower-level seats, called *cadeira*, instead of the upper-level bleachers, called *arquibancada*. The price is US$8, unless it's a championship game, when it's more.

The metro is closed on Sunday, and taking a bus or cab can be a hassle. Getting to the stadium isn't too difficult: catch a bus marked 'Maracanã' (from the zona sul, No 434, 464 or 455; from Centro, No 238 or 239) and leave a couple of hours before game time. Returning to your hotel by bus is often a drag. The buses are flooded with passengers and thieves set to work on the trapped passengers. Taking a cab is a possible alternative, but they can be hard to flag down; the best strategy is to walk away from the stadium a bit.

Surprisingly, driving a car to the stadium is pretty easy. You should leave a couple of hours before kick-off and, for easy departure, park away from the stadium. The traffic isn't all that bad and if you arrive early you can watch the preliminary games.

Pão de Açúcar (Sugar Loaf)
Sugar Loaf, God's gift to the picture-postcard industry, is dazzling. Two cable cars lift you 1300 metres above Rio and the Baía de Guanabara. From here, Rio is undoubtedly the most beautiful city in the world. There are many good times to make the ascent, but sunset on a clear day is the most spectacular. As day becomes night and the city lights start to sparkle down below, the sensation is delightful.

Everyone must go to Sugar Loaf, but if you can, avoid going from about 10 to 11 am and 2 to 3 pm when most tourist buses are arriving.

The two-stage cable cars (☎ 295-8244)

leave about every 30 minutes from Praça General Tibúrcio at Praia Vermelha in Urca. They operate daily from 8 am to 10 pm and cost US$8. On top of the lower hill there's a restaurant/theatre. The Beija Flor samba school puts on a show on Monday from 9 pm to 1 am. Less touristy shows are the Friday and Saturday Carioca nights. They have some excellent musicians; check the local papers for listings.

To get to Sugar Loaf take a bus marked 'Urca' from Centro and Flamengo (No 107); from the zona sul, take No 500, 511 or 512. The open-air bus that runs along the Ipanema and Copacabana beaches also goes to Sugar Loaf.

Corcovado & Cristo Redentor
Corcovado (Hunchback) is the mountain and *Cristo Redentor* (Christ the Redeemer) is the statue. The mountain rises straight up from the city to 709 metres. The statue, with its welcoming outstretched arms, stands another 30 metres high and weighs over 1000 tonnes (a popular song talks about how the Cristo should have his arms closed against his chest because for most who come to Rio the city is harsh and unwelcoming).

The statue was originally conceived as a national monument to celebrate Brazil's 100 years of independence from Portugal. The 100 years came and went in 1922 without the money to start construction, but in 1931 the statue was completed by French sculptor Paul Landowski, thanks to some financial assistance from the Vatican.

Corcovado lies within the Parque Nacional da Tijuca. You can get there by car or by taxi, but the best way is to go up in the cog train – sit on the right-hand side going up for the view. The round trip costs US$11 and leaves from Rua Cosme Velho 513 (Cosme Velho). You can get a taxi there or a bus marked 'Rua Cosme Velho' – a No 184 or 180 bus from Centro, a No 583 from Largo Machado, Copacabana and Ipanema, or a No 584 from Leblon.

During the high season, the trains, which only leave every 30 minutes, can be slow going. Corcovado, and the train, are open from 8 am to 6.30 pm. Needless to say, the view from up top is spectacular.

Santa Teresa Bondinho

The *bondinho* (little tram) goes over the old aqueduct to Santa Teresa from Avenida República do Chile and Senador Dantas in Centro. Santa Teresa is a beautiful neighbourhood of cobbled streets, hills and old homes. Favelas down the hillsides have made this a high-crime area. Young thieves jump on and off the tram very quickly. Go, but don't take valuables. Public transport stops at midnight, so you'll need a car if you are going anywhere after that time.

There's a small Museu do Bonde at the central tram station with a history of Rio's tramways since 1865 for bonde buffs. You may wonder why people choose to hang onto the side of the tram even when there are spare seats. It's because they don't have to pay.

The Museu Chácara do Céu (☎ 224-8991), Rua Murtinho Nobre, 345 Santa Teresa, has a good collection of art and antiques.

Parks & Gardens

Parque Nacional da Tijuca Tijuca is all that's left of the tropical jungle that once surrounded Rio de Janeiro. In 15 minutes

you can go from the concrete jungle of Copacabana to the 120-sq-km tropical jungle of Parque Nacional da Tijuca. A more rapid and drastic contrast is hard to imagine. The forest is exuberant green, with beautiful trees, creeks and waterfalls, mountainous terrain and high peaks. Candomblistas leave offerings by the roadside, families have picnics, and serious hikers climb the summit of Pico da Tijuca (1012 metres).

The heart of the forest is the Alto da Boa Vista with several waterfalls (including the 35-metre Cascatinha Taunay), peaks and restaurants. It's a beautiful spot. You can get maps at the entrance.

The entire park closes at sunset and is rather heavily policed. Kids have been known to wander off and get lost in the forest – it's that big. It's best to go by car, but if you can't, catch a No 221, 233 or 234 bus.

The best route by car is to take Rua Jardim Botânico two blocks past the botanical garden (heading away from Gávea). Turn left on Rua Lopes Quintas and then follow the Tijuca or Corcovado signs for two quick left turns until you reach the back of the botanical garden, where you go right. Then follow the signs for a quick ascent into the forest and past the Vista Chinesa (get out for a view) and the Mesa do Imperador. Go right when you seem to come out of the forest on the main road and you'll see the stone columns to the entrance of Alto da Boa Vista on your left in a couple of km.

You can also drive up to Alto da Boa Vista by heading out to São Conrado and turning right up the hill at the Parque Nacional da Tijuca signs.

Jardim Botânico Open daily from 8.30 am to 5.30 pm, the garden was first planted by order of the prince regent Dom João in 1808. There are over 5000 varieties of plants on 141 hectares. Quiet and serene on weekdays, the botanical garden blossoms with families and music on weekends. The row of palms, planted when the garden first opened, and the Amazonas section with the lake containing the huge Vitória Regia water lilies, are some of the highlights. It's not a bad idea to take insect repellent.

The garden is on Rua Jardim Botânico 920. To get there take a 'Jardim Botânico' bus: from Centro, No 170; from the zona sul, No 571, 572, or 594.

After the garden walk, go a few blocks down Rua Jardim Botânico, away from the beach, to Alfaces at Rua Visconde da Graça 51 for an excellent light lunch with an assortment of salads and good desserts at outdoor tables.

Parque Lage Just a few blocks down from the Jardim Botânico at Rua Jardim Botânico 414, this is a beautiful park at the base of Parque Nacional da Tijuca. There are gardens, little lakes and a mansion which now houses the Instituto de Belas Artes – there are often art shows and sometimes performances there. It's a tranquil place, with no sports allowed and a favourite of families with small children. It's open from 8 am to 5.30 pm. Take a 'Jardim Botânico' bus.

Parque do Flamengo Flamengo is a park with loads of fields and a bay for activities and sports. There are three museums – Museu Carmen Miranda, Museu dos Mortos da Segunda Guerra Mundial and Museu de Arte Moderna. Inside the park, along the bay, the Barracuda Rio restaurant (☎ 265-4641) is a great spot for bay and people watching. There's a deck and tables outside where you can drink or eat, and inside you can get a more substantial meal. It's also open for dinner.

To get there take buses marked 'Via Parque do Flamengo': from Centro, No 125 or 132, and from the zona sul, No 413 or 455.

Parque da Catacumba With high-rise buildings on both sides, Catacumba is on the Morro dos Cabritos, which rises from the Lagoa Rodrigo de Freitas. It was the site of a favela which was destroyed to make the park. A shaded park for walkers only, it's a good place to escape the heat and see some excellent outdoor sculptures. At the top of the hill there is a great view. Catacumba also has free Sunday afternoon concerts during the summer in its outdoor amphitheatre featuring some of Rio's best musicians. Check the Sunday newspaper for details.

Parque da Cidade Up in the hills of Gávea, this park is also calm and cool, and popular with families. Open daily from 8 am to 5.30 pm, the Museu da Cidade is in the park grounds.

Parque do Catete The grounds of the old presidential palace are now the Parque do Catete, a quiet refuge from the city; the park has monkeys hanging from the giant trees.

Quinta da Boa Vista Rio's main park and museum of natural history makes a great Sunday outing, and if you want to make a day out of it, the zoo, Nordeste Fair (see Things to Buy) and Maracanã soccer stadium are all nearby. The park is open daily from 8 am to 7 pm.

Museums

Museu Nacional This museum and its grand imperial entrance are still stately and imposing, and the view from the balcony to the royal palms is majestic. However, the graffitied buildings and unkempt grounds have suffered since the fall of the monarchy. The park is large and busy, and, because it's on the north side of the city, you'll see a good cross-section of Cariocas.

The museum is open Tuesday to Sunday from 10 am to 5 pm, and admission is about US$1 (free on Thursday). There are many interesting exhibits: dinosaur fossils, sabre-toothed tiger skeletons, beautiful pieces of pre-Columbian ceramics from the littoral and planalto of Peru, a huge meteorite, hundreds of stuffed birds, mammals and fish, gory displays of tropical diseases and exhibits on the peoples of Brazil.

The last of these are the most interesting. Rubber-gatherers and Indians of the Amazon, lace workers and *jangadeiro* fisherfolk of the Northeast, candomblistas of Bahia, gaúchos of Rio Grande do Sul and *vaqueiros* (cowboys) of the sertão are all given their due. What's interesting about these exhibits is that, with a little bit of effort and a lot of travelling, you can see all of these peoples in the flesh. The Indian exhibit is particularly good – better than that of the FUNAI Museu do Índio.

The museum is at the Quinta da Boa Vista. To get there from Centro take the metro to São Cristóvão or bus No 472 or 474; from the zona sul take bus No 472 or 474 as well.

Museu Nacional de Belas Artes At Avenida Rio Branco 199 is Rio's premier fine-art museum (☎ 240-0160). There are over 800 original paintings and sculptures in the collection. The most important gallery is the Galeria de Arte Brasileira, with 20th-century classics such as Cândido Portinari's *Café*. There are also galleries with foreign art (not terribly good) and contemporary exhibits.

The museum is open Tuesday to Friday from 10 am to 5.30 pm; and Saturday, Sunday and holidays from 3 to 6 pm. Photography is prohibited. Take any of the city-bound buses and get off near Avenida Rio Branco, or take the metro to Carioca station.

Museu Histórico Nacional Restored in 1985, this former colonial arsenal (☎ 220-5829) is filled with historic relics and interesting displays, one of the best being the re-creation of a colonial pharmacy. The building is near the bay at Praça Marechal Âncora.

Museu Folclorico Edson Carneiro The small Edson Carneiro museum should not be missed – especially if you're staying nearby in the Catete/Flamengo area. It has excellent displays of folk art – probably Brazil's richest artistic tradition – a folklore library, and a small crafts store with some wonderful crafts, books and folk records at very cheap prices.

The museum is next to the grounds of the Palácio do Catete. The address is Rua do Catete 181, Catete, and it's open Tuesday to Friday from 11 am to 6 pm, and Saturday, Sunday and holidays from 3 to 6 pm.

Museu da República & Palácio do Catete The Museu da República and the Palácio do Catete have been wonderfully restored. Built between 1858 and 1866 and easily distinguished by the bronze eagles on the eaves, the palace was occupied by the president of Brazil from 1896 until 1954, when Getúlio Vargas killed himself here. His bedroom, where it took place, is on display. The museum, which occupies the palace, has a good collection of art and artefacts from the republican period. It's open Tuesday to Friday from noon to 5 pm. Admission costs US$0.50.

Museu do Índio At Rua das Palmeiras 55, Botafogo, the Museu do Índio (☎ 286-8799) has a good library with over 25,000 titles, a map and photo collection and a quiet garden. The Indian exhibits in the Museu Nacional at the Quinta da Boa Vista are better.

Museu H Stern The headquarters of the famous jeweller H Stern, at Rua Visconde de Pirajá 490, contains a museum. You may find the 12-minute guided jewellery tour interesting if you're in the neighbourhood. With a coupon you can get a free cab ride to and from the store and anywhere in the zona sul.

Museu Carmen Miranda The small Carmen Miranda Museum in Parque do Flamengo is across the street from Avenida Rui Barbosa 560 and is open Tuesday to Friday from 11 am to 5 pm, and Saturday and Sunday from 1 to 5 pm. Carmen, of course, was Hollywood's Brazilian bombshell, although she was actually born in Portugal. She made it to Hollywood in the 1940s and has become a cult figure in Rio. During Carnival hundreds of men dress up as Carmen Miranda lookalikes. The museum is filled with Carmen memorabilia and paraphernalia, including costumes, T-shirts, posters, postcards, records and a small exhibit.

Museu Villa-Lobos This museum is in a

century-old building and is dedicated to the memory of Heitor Villa-Lobos. This great Brazilian composer, regarded as the father of modern Brazilian music, was the first to combine folkloric themes with classic forms. As well as personal items, there's also an extensive sound archive. At Rua Sorocaba 200 in Botafogo, it's open from Monday to Friday from 10 am to 5.30 pm.

Museu de Arte Moderna At the northern end of Parque do Flamengo, looking a bit like an airport hangar, is the Modern Art Museum. Construction began in 1954, but for much of the past few years all that one has been able to see of the museum are its grounds, designed by Brazil's most famous landscape architect, Burle Marx (who land-scaped Brasília).

The museum was devastated by a fire in 1978 which consumed 90% of its collection. The museum has worked hard to rebuild its collection, and today it's the most important centre of contemporary art in Rio, with a permanent display of over 4000 works by Brazilian artists.

Museu Naval e Oceanográfico This museum chronicles the history of the Brazilian navy from the 16th century to the present. It's close to Praça 15 de Novembro and is open every day from noon to 4.45 pm.

Museu Naval In Bauru, behind the Modern Art Museum, the Naval Museum is open Tuesday to Friday from 11.30 am to 5.30 pm, Saturday and Sunday from 9 am to 5.30 pm. It documents the Brazilian navy's role in WW II and has ship models.

Museu Histórico e Diplomático Housed in the restored Itamaraty Palace, which was home to Brazil's presidents from 1889 until 1897, the museum has an impressive collection of art and antiques. Located at Rua Marechal Floriano 196 (a short walk from Presidente Vargas metro station), the museum has guided tours on Monday, Wednesday and Friday from 1 to 4 pm. To guarantee a tour in English or French, call the palace on (☎ 253-7961).

Sambódromo & Museu do Carnaval Designed by Oscar Neimeyer and completed in 1984, the Sambadrome also houses the Museu do Carnival. It contains lots of material relating to the history of Rio's samba schools. It's open Tuesday to Sunday from 11 am to 5 pm. Enter through Rua Frei Caneca. Empty sambadromes are like empty stadiums – there's not a lot happening.

Museu Chácara do Céu Located at Rua Murtinho Nobre 93, Santa Teresa, this is a delightful museum that occupies part of the old mansion of wealthy industrialist and arts patron Raymundo Ottoni de Castro Maya. It contains art and antiques from his private collection, which he bequeathed to the nation, including works by Monet, Vlaminck, Portinari and Picasso to name a few. The house is surrounded by beautiful gardens and has a great view of Guanabara Bay.

It's open from Wednesday to Saturday from noon to 5 pm and on Sunday and holidays from 1 to 5 pm. Entry is US$4, free on Sunday. To get there, take the No 206 or 214 bus from the Menezes Cortes bus terminal in the Centro to the 'Curvelo' stop. You can take the tram, but don't carry valuables.

Museu Histórico do Exército e Forte de Copacabana Built in 1914, the fort preserves its original characteristics, with walls up to 12 metres thick and fortified with Krupp cannons. The museum displays weapons, but one of the best reasons to visit is the fantastic view of Copacabana. The fort is open from Tuesday to Sunday between 10 am and 4 pm. Entry is free.

Museu Casa do Pontal Owned by French-man Jaques Van de Beuque, this impressive collection of over 4,500 pieces is one of the best folk-art exhibitions in Brazil. Works are grouped according to themes, including music, carnival, religion and folklore.

The museum is located just past Barra at

the Estrada do Pontal 3295. It's open on weekends from 2 to 5.30 pm

Ilha da Paquetá

This island in the Baía de Guanabara was once a very popular tourist spot and is now frequented mostly by families from the zona norte. There are no cars on the island, so transport is by foot, bicycle (there are literally hundreds for rent) and horse-drawn carts. There's a certain dirty decadent charm to the colonial buildings, unassuming beaches and businesses catering to local tourism. Sadly, the bay is too polluted to safely swim in and the place gets very crowded.

Go to Paquetá for the boat ride through the bay and to see Cariocas at play – especially during the Festa de São Roque, which is celebrated over five days in August. Boats leave from near the Praça 15 de Novembro in Centro. The regular ferry takes one hour and costs US$0.50. The hydrofoil is worth taking, at least one way. It gets to the island in 25 minutes and costs US$7. The ferry service (☎ 231-0396) goes from 5.30 am to 10.30 pm, leaving every two to three hours. The hydrofoil leaves every hour on the hour from Rio (8 am to 5 pm) and returns every hour from Paquetá (8 am to 5.30 pm).

Jóquei Clube

There's lots to see at the race track. The stadium, which seats 35,000, is on the Gávea side of the Lagoa Rodrigo de Freitas at Praça Santos Dumont 31 (take any of the buses that go to Jardim Botânico). It's a beautiful horse-racing track with a great view of the mountains and Corcovado, and it costs only a few cents to enter. It's rarely crowded and the fans are great to watch – it's a different slice of Rio life. Racing usually takes place every Saturday and Sunday afternoon, and Monday and Thursday night.

City Sunset

Sunset is a nice time to be around the central plaza in the city. The sky can be beautiful and floodlights illuminate the big buildings like the municipal theatre and national library.

Ballooning

The most popular flight is the one between the Autódromo de Jacarepaguá and Barra da Tijuca. The flights, in balloons which can hold four people, last about 30 minutes and climb between 150 to 1500 metres. Children must be over five. For details call (☎ 221-8441).

Cycling

Cycling is popular with Cariocas. There is a bike path around Lagoa das Freitas, one in Barra da Tijuca, and one on the oceanfront from Ipanema to Leme. The *ciclóvia* (bike path) is currently being extended into the city to Praça 15. If you have a bit of road sense and don't mind mixing it with the traffic, a bike is a fun way to get around the zona sul. On Tuesday nights Riobikers take to the streets. Riobikers started out as a group of cyclists who enjoyed riding in a group. The idea caught on and now every Tuesday night, thousands of bikers take to the road from Leblon to the Museu de Arte Moderna in Aterro do Flamengo. The streets are closed to other traffic after 9 pm and the bikers move off at around 9.30 pm from Leblon.

Stop Bike (☎ 275-7345), in the small arcade at Rua Barata Ribeiro 181, has a few mountain bikes to rent for US$15 a day, and they give good deals if you rent for longer. The woman who runs the store speaks English. If you just want to cruise the beachfront at Copacabana and Ipanema, bikes can be rented on Sunday and holidays on Avenida Atlântica in front of Rua República do Peru. They cost US$3 per hour.

Clube Kraft Point (☎ 205-6155), organises groups who want to do some night riding during the week. On weekends they organise group trail-riding in the Tijuca forest. As long as you have a bike, you can join in.

Golf

Rio has two 18-hole golf courses close to the city: Gávea Golf Club (☎ 322-4141) at Estrada da Gávea 800, and Itanhangá Golf Club (☎ 429-2507) at Estrada da Barra 2005. The clubs welcome visitors from 7 am to sunset, but the Gávea Golf Club only accepts visitors from the major hotels like the Inter-Continental (which is next door) and the Rio Sheraton.

Green fees are about US$70 a round, plus club hire of US$15. On weekends, you need to be invited by a member.

A cheaper option is Golden Green (☎ 433-3950), which has six tricky par-three holes. It's open daily from 7 am to 6 pm. Cost is US$18 for six holes and US$28 for 12 holes. Club and cart rental are an extra US$10. It's near Barra beach at Posto 7.

Helicopter Flights

Joy flights over the city can be arranged by Helisight (☎ 511-2141; 259-6995 on weekends). They have three helipads at strategic, scenic locations: Mirante Dona Marta, just below Cristo Redentor, at Lagoa Rodrigo de Freitas and from Morro da Urca, the first cable-car stop as you go up to the Sugarloaf. Helisight has 10 different flights to choose from. Five-minute flights cost US$30 and a 30-minute flight costs US$500 for four people. These flights are a definite 'video opportunity'.

Surfing

In Rio city, surfing is very popular, with the locals ripping the fast, hollow beach breaks. When the surf is good, it gets crowded. Arpoador, between Copacabana and Ipanema, is where most surfers congregate, though there are some fun beach breaks further out in Barra, Grumari, Joá and Prainha. Boards can be rented in Rio, but they're so cheap that you'd be crazy not to buy one, especially if you've planned a surfing expedition down the coast. A brand-new board is a steal at US$150 to US$200, and we saw some decent second-hand ones for as little as US$50. Galeria River (pronounced 'heever'), at Rua Francisco Otaviano 67 in Arpoador, is an arcade full of surf shops. Loja three of Ocean has a reasonable selection.

Sailing

Out in Barra, you can get into sailing Hobie Cat 16s. Bix Sportsmix (☎ & fax 439-4552) at Avenida Sernambetiba 3500, Bloco B, Apt 302, rents these catamarans for US$40 for two hours, not including preparation time. It does include pick-up and drop-off at your hotel. A 10-hour course is US$175. The instructors are highly experienced, and speak several languages, like English, Dutch, German and French.

Hang-Gliding, Para-Gliding and Ultra-Leve

If you weigh less than 80 kg (about 180 lb) and have US$80 you can do the fantastic – hang-glide off the 510 metre Pedra Bonita on to Pepino beach in São Conrado. This is one of the giant granite slabs that towers above Rio. No experience is necessary. To arrange a double flight (voo duplo) go out to Pepino and the pilots will be waiting on the beach. We're told that the winds are very safe here and the pilots know what they are doing. Guest riders get their bodies put in a kind of pouch that is secured to the kite.

Flight Information Most tandem pilots can mount a camera with flash, wide-angle lens, motor drive and a long cable release on a wing tip to take pictures of you in flight. If you want to take pictures yourself you must realise that take-off and landing pictures are impossible since you can't be encumbered with equipment. Your camera must fit into the velcro pouch in the front of your flight suit. It's a good idea to have the camera strapped around your neck and a lens cover strapped to the lens or you will risk losing the equipment and beaning a Carioca on the head. Flights are usually extremely smooth so it's possible to take stable shots. Hang-gliders themselves are dramatic shots, especially when taken from above.

Know your exact weight in kg in advance. Ideally your pilot should be heavier than you. If you're heavier than the pilot, he or she will have to use a weight belt and switch to a larger glider. If you're over 80 kg you're out of luck. You don't need any experience or special training – anyone from seven to 70 years can do it.

Cautious flights depend on atmospheric conditions. You can usually fly on all but three or four days per month, and conditions during winter are even better. For the experience of a lifetime, it's not that expensive: US$80 for anywhere from 10 to 25 minutes of extreme pleasure. The price includes being picked up and dropped off at your hotel. If you fly early in the day, you have more flexibility with delays.

The best way to arrange a flight is to go right to the far end of Pepino beach on Avenida Prefeito Mendes de Morais, where the fly-boys hang out at the Voo Livre club.

One of the recommended flyers is Alonso Cunha, who can be reached on his beeper (☎ 266-4545, code 8LB). Ruy Marra is another excellent tandem-glider pilot and widely regarded as one of the best pilots in Rio. He runs Super Fly Agency (☎ 322-2286) in Lagoa at Avenida Epitácio Pessoa 3624, room 201. (Ruy is also the person to see if you're interested in para-gliding.) Also recommended is Rejane Reis (☎ 322-6872). For more information call the Associação Brasileiro de Voo Livre (☎ 322-0266), which also offers classes.

Ultra-leve (ultralight) flights, are more

Hang-Gliding over Rio

The climb up to the take-off point was awesome. Pedra Bonita looms over São Conrado's Pepino beach. The road winds up through the lush green Tijuca forest. We were waved on through the private entrance to the hang-gliding area and the engine whined as we climbed the extremely steep hill.

When we reached the top, our pilot assembled the glider, untangled the cables, tightened the wing nuts and slipped elastic bands over the wing struts. Up close the glider looked flimsy. We put on our flight suits and practised a few take-off sprints near the platform, literally a five-metre-long runway of wooden boards inclined 15° downhill. We were 550 metres above sea level and a few km inland from the beach. If I were a rock and Rio were a vacuum, it would take me over 10 seconds to kiss the dirt.

I wore old sneakers for traction and two good-luck charms to amuse the ambulance crew that I anticipated would be piecing through the tangled ball of crumpled metal, torn nylon and mangled flesh down below.

With the glider resting at the top of the runway, we clipped ourselves onto it and checked the balance of the craft as we hung side by side. The pilot adjusted his weight belt, all the straps, the velcro leg cuffs and helmet and gave me very brief instructions: hold on to the cuff of his shorts, keep my hands to myself, resist the temptation to hold the control bar or cables (this can throw the glider, so don't touch), and when he gave the count 'um, dois, tres, ja!', go very fast.

We checked the windsocks on either side of the platform, the surface of the sea and the rippling of the leaves to ascertain the direction, speed and flow of the wind. A smooth wind coming inland from a flat sea is best. 'Um, dois, tres, ja!' Four bounding steps and we were flying. It's not the free-fall sinking feeling you get from elevators, but a perfect calm. I closed my eyes and felt as if I was still – the only movement, a soft wind caressing my face. Miraculously, it seemed I was suspended between earth and sky. To our left was Rocinha, the most famous of the zona sul's favelas, to the right Pedra Bonita, and below us the fabulous homes of Rio's rich and famous. We floated over skyscrapers and Pepino beach, made a few lazy circles over the water and before I knew it, it was time for the descent. Upon landing we stood upright, pointed the nose up, the glider stalled and we touched down on the sand gentle as a feather.

In an emergency, like a sudden change in weather, a hang-glider pilot can fly down to the beach in less than 90 seconds. Pilots also carry a parachute which is designed to support the weight of two passengers and the glider itself, which is supposed to fall first and cushion the blow.

Andrew Draffen

comfortable than hang-gliders, but you have to listen to the motor. The trips last around 30 minutes and leave from the Aeroclube do Jacarepaguá. The Clube Esportivo de Ultra-Leve (☎ 342-8025) has some long-range ultralights that can stay up for over two hours. Flights cost around US$20.

Hiking & Climbing

Excellent hiking is possible surprisingly close to the city. There are three national parks with trail systems in Rio state: Parque Nacional da Tijuca (see entry later this chapter), Parque Nacional da Serra dos Órgãos and Parque Nacional do Itatiaia (see the Rio de Janeiro State chapter for information on these latter two parks).

Clubs For anyone interested in climbing and hiking, Rio's clubs are the best source of information as well as the best meeting place for like-minded people. The clubs meet regularly and welcome visitors. All of the following clubs are well organised and have bulletin boards listing excursions on the weekends:

Centro Excursionista Brasileiro
  Avenida Almirante Barroso 2-8 Andar, Centro, Rio de Janeiro, RJ CEP 20031. CEB has a membership of 900, meets on Wednesday and Friday evenings and is geared toward trekking and day hikes. CEB also runs a small restaurant which is open from 6 pm, Monday to Friday, where people meet informally to plan excursions.
Centro Excursionista Rio de Janeiro
  Avenida Rio Branco 277/805, Centro, Rio de Janeiro, RJ CEP 20040. CERJ, with an active membership of 50, meets on Tuesday and Thursday evenings. CERJ offers the greatest diversity of activities ranging from hikes to technical climbing.
Clube Excursionista Carioca
  Rua Hilário de Gouveia 71/206, Copacabana, Rio de Janeiro, RJ CEP 22040 (Marcelo Ramos ☎ (021) 227-8398). Meeting on Wednesday and Friday evenings at 10.30 pm, this club specialises in difficult technical climbing.

Tijuca The Parque Nacional da Tijuca is a 120-sq-km park with an excellent trail system. It is also home to different species of birds and animals including iguanas and monkeys. The Alto da Boa Vista section of Tijuca forest, which is part of the national park, has several good day hikes. Maps of the forest are obtained at the small artisan shop just inside the park entrance, which is open from 7 am to 9 pm daily. To get there take bus No 221 from Praça 15 in the centre to Praça Afonso Viseu in Alto da Boa Vista.

Pão de Açúcar On Pão de Açúcar (396 metres), Rio's Sugar Loaf, there are 32 established climbing routes. Climbers are often seen scaling the western face below the cable cars. One of the best hikes is up the back side of Pão de Açúcar. Besides the breathtaking view of the ocean below, one is also compensated by not having to pay for the cable-car ride. The hike takes 1½ hours and doesn't require equipment or a lot of climbing experience, but does have two 10 to 15-metre exposed parts that require agility and common sense.

The hike begins on the left-hand side of Praça General Tibúrcio (the same praça where the cable cars are boarded), where a paved jogging track runs for 1200 metres along the base of Morro de Tijuca and Pão de Açúcar. At the end of the track pick up the trail on the other side of the cement tank in the tall grass. Follow this trail (always taking the uphill forks) for 100 metres. At the old foundations, some 30 metres above the water, the trail ascends steeply for 60 metres until levelling off on a narrow ridge. From the ridge, the broad eastern flank of Pão de Açúcar is seen. The trail to follow is up the far left-hand side ridge.

At the base of the rock the trail deviates slightly to the right for the next 40 metres until coming to two iron bolts on the smooth exposed rock. This is the first exposed area, which, while crossed easily without ropes, requires agility and alertness. There is nothing to break a fall except the rocks in the ocean, 120 metres below.

From the second bolt stay next to the rock slab for the following six metres. In the gap between the first rock slab and the next slab it is safer to step up on to the second rock slab rather than continuing along the exposed face. Another 20 metres higher up there is a third iron bolt, which is a good place to take in the view before tackling the crux of the climb – above the clearly defined path. At the fourth bolt, the hike becomes a climb for the next 10 metres. This section is best climbed by finding the holds behind the rock slabs and pulling yourself up. After the sixth and final bolt, the climbing is over. Follow the well-defined path up 200 metres to the small children's park at the top.

Corcovado Corcovado (710 metres) offers technically difficult climbs with fantastic views of Pão de Açúcar and Lagoa Rodrigo. Private guides and the clubs are the best means for unravelling its many diverse routes. Well-equipped and experienced climbers can easily climb its eastern face on the route K-2 (rated 5.9).

The climb begins 200 metres below the summit. To get to the base of the climb, take the train to the top and instead of ascending the stairs to the left, follow the road out of the parking lot for 15 minutes. After the first rocky outcrop on the northern side, descend two more turns in the road. At the second turn there is a cement railing, behind which is a poorly maintained trail.

Follow this trail as it hugs the base of the rock for 200 metres around to the eastern face of the mountain. Don't get discouraged by the tall grass which obstructs the trail; just keep to the base of the rock. On the eastern face the start of the climb is at the 20-metre crack in the whitened rock. From there the climb is clearly marked with well-placed bolts to the top, just underneath the statue of Christ.

Tai Chi Chuan
Enthusiasts might like to join in one of the daily sessions held at Praça NS da Paz in Ipanema. There are sessions at sunrise and at 5 pm.

Tennis
The climate's not ideal for tennis, but if you fancy a game, you can book a court at the InterContinental (☎ 322-2200) or Sheraton

(☎ 274-1122). Courts are available to non-guests. Lob Tênis (☎ 205-9997) at Rua Stefan Zweig 290 in Laranjeiras, rents courts for US$25 an hour and opens until midnight. In Barra, there are many tennis centres, including Akxe Sportside Club (☎ 325-3232) at Avenida Professor Dulcídio Cardoso 100, Clube Canaveral (☎ 399-2192) at Avenida das Américas 487 and Rio Sport Center (☎ 325-6644) at Avenida Ayrton Senna 2541.

Walking & Jogging
There are some good walking and jogging paths in the zona sul. If you're staying in the Flamengo-Catete area, Flamengo Park has plenty of space and lots of workout stations. Around Lagoa Rodrigo de Freitas is 9.5 km of cycling, jogging and walking track. At the Parque do Cantalago there, you can rent bicycles, tricycles or quadricycles. Along the seaside, from Leme to Barra da Tijuca, there's a bike and footpath. On Sunday the road itself is closed to traffic and is full of cyclists, joggers, rollerbladers and prams.

Closed to bikes but not to walkers and joggers is the Pista Cládio Coutinho, between the mountains and the sea at Praia Vermelha in Urca. It's open daily from 7 am to 6 pm and is very secure because the army maintains guard posts. People in bathing suits aren't allowed in (unless they're running). It's a nice place to be around sunset.

Language Courses
The Instituto Brasil-Estados Unidos (IBEU) (☎ 255-8332) has a variety of Portuguese-language classes that start every month or two. The cost for a four-week course that meets three times a week is about US$150. For information stop by Avenida NS de Copacabana 690, on the 5th floor.

Next door to IBEU is a Casa Matos store which sells the language books for the IBEU courses. It's a good place to pick up a book or dictionaries to study Portuguese on your own. Other places that offer courses include Britannia (☎ 511-0143), with branches in Botafogo, Leblon and Barra; Berlitz (☎ 240-

6606) in the Centro and Ipanema; and Feedback (☎ 221-1863), in the Centro, Copacabana, Ipanema, Botafogo and Barra.

Organised Tours

City Tours Most of the larger tour companies operate sightseeing tours of Rio. They include Gray Line (☎ 294-1444; fax 259-5847), Expeditours (☎ 287-9697; fax 521-4388) and Kontik-Franstur (☎ 255-2442). Their brochures are sitting on the reception desks of many hotels. Tours cover the usual tourist destinations and their prices are quite reasonable. A four-hour tour to Corcovado and Tijuca costs around US$25.

For a more personalised tour, Rio Custom Tours (☎ 274-3217), run by Maria Lúcia Yolen, is recommended. Maria Lúcia is an excellent guide who likes to show that Rio is not all samba, beaches and Corcovado. Some of her tours include the Sunday mass at São Bento, complete with Gregorian chants, a trip to the Casa do Pontal and its excellent folk-art collection, and a tour through Santa Teresa. She will pick you up and drop you off at your hotel.

Historic Rio Tour Run by art historian Professor Carlos Roquette (☎ 322-4872), who speaks English and French as well as Portuguese, these tours bring old Rio to life. Itineraries include a night at the Teatro Municipal, colonial Rio, baroque Rio, imperial Rio and a walking tour of the Centro. Professor Roquette really knows his Rio, and if you have an obscure question, I'm sure he would welcome it.

Favela Tour If you want to visit a favela you'd be crazy to do it on your own. Since large amounts of cocaine are trafficked through them each week, there are lots of young, heavily-armed characters around. Don't get the idea though, that favelas are complete slums. The ones I've seen reminded me more of some poor country village. But unless you go with a local, there will be a lot of suspicious eyes on you. The safest alternative is to take one of the favela tours that now operate in Rio. Marcelo Armstrong (☎ 322-2727, mobile 989-0074)

is the pioneer of favela tourism. He takes individuals and small groups to visit Rocinha, the largest favela in Rio, and Vila Canoas near São Conrado. The tour takes in a school, medical centre and private houses, and you come away with a good idea how a favela operates. Some of the climbs are steep, so you need to be reasonably fit. You can take a camera, but ask permission before taking anybody's picture and don't take photos of suspicious or armed characters. Avoid going after heavy rain, because mudslides are common.

Villa Riso Colonial Tour Villa Riso in São Conrado, next to the Gávea Golf Club, recreates a colonial fazenda (farm), complete with employees wearing colonial gear. The house and gardens actually date from the early 18th century. A three-hour tour includes a buffet lunch (normally a feijoada or churrasco) and a medley of Brazilian theatrical music. You must make reservations (☎ 322-1444; fax 322-5196). The cost is US$40 and this includes picking you up and returning you to your hotel.

Bâteau Mouche On New Year's Eve 1988, 55 people out of the 59 on board drowned when an overloaded Bâteau Mouche bay cruiser capsized in Baía de Guanabara. This private company still runs cruises, and they're much more careful with the number of passengers they let on board. Their modern boats cruise the bay and go out into the Atlantic. They usually have a morning and afternoon cruise that costs from US$25 to US$35. The scene is too slick-touristy for our taste but the voyage out into the ocean is undeniably beautiful. Don't take their bay cruise, because for a 50th of the price you can take a ferry or hydrofoil to Paquetá island and cover much of the same ground while travelling with the locals.

Ferry to Niterói This is the poor person's Bâteau Mouche. It costs about US$0.30 and the views are great, particularly returning to Rio around sunset. Over at Niterói you can walk around a bit to see Rio's poor relation or catch a local bus to Niterói's beaches. Leaving from Praça 15 de Novembro (in Centro), the ferry goes every 20 minutes and is always full of commuters. Buses to Praça 15 de Novembro include: from Flamengo, No 119; from Copacabana, No 119, 413, 415, 154, 455 or 474; and from Ipanema, No 474 or 154.

Carnival

Carnival is a pagan holiday originating perhaps as Roman bacchanalia celebrating Saturn or in the ancient Egyptian festival of Isis. Carnival was a wild party during the Middle Ages until tamed in Europe by Christianity, but the sober Church of the Inquisition could not squelch Carnival in the Portuguese colony, where it came to acquire African rhythms and Indian costumes.

People speculate that the word Carnival derives from *caro-vale*, meaning 'goodbye meat'. The reasoning goes something like this: for the 40 days of Lent, nominally Catholic Brazilians give up liver or flank steaks. To compensate for the big sacrifices ahead, they rack up sins in a delirious carnal blowout in honour of King Momo, the king of Carnival.

Carnival is celebrated everywhere in Brazil and each region has a particular way of celebrating. In Bahia, Carnival is celebrated in the streets under the blasting loudspeakers of the trio elétrico trucks; in Recife and Olinda merry-makers dance the frevo. These are more authentic Carnivals than Rio's glitzy celebration, which has become the big draw for the tourism industry. More than anywhere else in Brazil, Carnival in Rio is a spectator event, but it's a fantastic spectacle nonetheless.

Every year wealthy and spaced-out foreigners descend on Rio en masse, get drunk, get high, bag some sunrays and exchange exotic diseases. Everyone gets a bit unglued at this time of year and there are lots of car accidents and murders. Some of the leaner and meaner Cariocas can get a little ugly with all the sex, booze and flash of money. Apartment rates and taxi fares triple and quadruple and some thieves keep to the spirit of the season by robbing in costume.

The excitement of Carnival builds all year and the pre-Lenten revelry begins well before the official dates of Carnival. A month before Carnival starts, rehearsals at the *escolas de samba* (samba clubs) are open to visitors on Saturday. The rehearsals are usually in the favelas. They're fun to watch, but, for your safety, go with a Carioca. Tourist Carnival shows are held all year round at Scala, Plataforma 1 and up top at Pão de Açúcar.

The escolas de samba are actually predated by the *bandas* (nonprofessional equivalents of the escolas de samba), which are now returning to the Carnival scene as part of the movement to return Rio's Carnival to the streets. Last year there was a Banda da Ipanema, a Banda do Leblon, a Banda da Boca Maldita and a Banda Carmen Miranda, among others. The bandas are great fun, a good place to loosen up your hip joints for samba, and there are excellent photo opportunities; transvestites always keep the festivities entertaining.

Riotur has information on the scheduled bandas, or you could just show up in

The Carnival of Bate-Bola Boys

The general rule during Carnival is to dance and enjoy yourself as much as you can handle. The *bate-bola* boys (ball-beating boys) of the suburbs, start fooling around a week or two beforehand. The boys dress in a metal mesh, cloth horror mask and a clown-like costume, choosing the pattern and colours in secret in order to maintain their disguise. They roam the suburbs scaring the other kids by beating their air-filled, bull's-bladder ball on the ground. The tradition has lost popularity since *ladrões* (robbers) started using the costume. ■

Ipanema (most of them are in Ipanema), at Praça General Osório or Praça Paz around 5 pm or so, a couple of weekends before official Carnival. Other street festivities are held in Centro on Avenida Rio Branco. Riotur has all the information in a special Carnival guide.

Carnival Balls Carnival balls are surreal and erotic events. In one ball at Scala we saw a woman (transsexual?) bare her breasts and offer passers-by a suck while rickety old ladies were bopping away in skimpy lingerie. A young and geeky rich guy was dancing on tables with prostitutes past their prime, young models and lithe young nymphets, all in various stages of undress. Breasts were painted, stickered with adhesive tattoos, covered with fish-net brassieres or left bare. Bottoms were spandexed, G-stringed or mini-skirted.

More action took place on the stages. One stage had a samba band, the other was crushed with young women. They didn't dance, but ground their hips and licked their lips to the incessant, hypnotic music and the epileptic flashing of the floor lights. Throngs of sweaty photographers and video crews mashed up to the stage. Everyone played up for the camera, vying for space and the attention of the photographers. The Vegas headdresses, the pasty-faced bouncers and the rich men in private boxes overlooking the dance floor lent a Mafiosi feel to the place.

Carnival is the holiday of the poor. Not that you could tell from the price of the tickets to the balls. Some of them cost more than the minimum monthly wage. There are snooty affairs like the ones at the Copacabana Palace (☎ 255-7070, US$80), Hotel InterContinental (☎ 322-2200, US$150) or the new venue in Barra, the Metropolitan (☎ 385-0515, US$80 plus a stiff cab fare). Raunchier parties are held in Leblon at Scala (☎ 239-4448, US$40), Canecão (☎ 295-3055, US$40) in Botafogo and Help Disco in Copacabana,(US$20). Tickets go on sale about two weeks before Carnival starts and the balls are held nightly for the week preceding Carnival and through Carnival. Buy a copy of the *Veja* magazine with the Veja Rio insert. It has details of all the balls and bandas.

There are three rules of thumb: beautiful, flirtatious and apparently unescorted women are either escorted by huge, jealous cachaça-crazed men wielding machetes, or else they are really men dressed up as women; everything costs several times more within the club than outside; and, finally, don't bring more money than you're willing to lose – the club bouncers are big, but not that effective.

Street Carnival What do Cariocas do in the afternoon and early evening during Carnival? They dance in the streets behind *bandas* (marching bands with brass and percussion instruments), which pump out the banda theme song and other Carnival marching favourites while they move along. To join in the fun, all you need to do is jump in when you see the banda pass. They are one of the most traditional aspects of Carnival in Rio. There are many bandas and including Banda de Ipanema, one of our favourites. This is a traditional banda that parades two Saturdays before Carnival from Praça General Osório in Ipanema. It's full of drag queens and party animals. It starts around 5 pm and goes until around 9 pm. The banda also parades again on Carnival Saturday.

Banda Carmen Miranda, with its famous gay icon, is also lot of fun, not only for gays but everyone. It parades through Ipanema around 4 pm on the Sunday before Carnival. There are lots of bandas in Copacabana before and during Carnival too.

The street parades in Avenida Rio Branco in the Centro and Boulevard 28 de Setembro in Vila Isabel, both on Carnival Saturday, are really worth checking out, but you won't see many other tourists there. Just carry a few dollars in your pocket for beers and a snack, and you'll have nothing to worry about.

The Sambódromo Parades In the Sambódromo, a tiered street designed for samba parades, the Brazilians harness sweat, noise and confusion and turn it into art. The 16 top-level samba schools prepare all year for an hour of glory in the sambódromo. The best escola is chosen by a hand-picked set of judges on the basis of many components including percussion, the *samba do enredo* (theme song), harmony between percussion, song and dance, choreography, costume, storyline, floats and decorations and others. The championship is hotly contested; the winner becomes the pride of Rio and Brazil.

The parades begin with moderate mayhem, then work themselves up to a higher plane of frenzy. The announcers introduce the escola, the group's colours and the number of wings. Far away the lone voice of the *puxador* starts the samba. Thousands more voices join him, and then the drummers kick in, 600 to 800 per school. The booming drums drive the parade. This samba do enredo is the loudest music you're ever likely to hear in your life. The samba tapes flood the airwaves for weeks prior to the beginning of Carnival. From afar the parade looks alive. It's a throbbing beast slowly coming closer – a pulsing, Liberace-glittered, Japanese-movie-monster slimemould threatening to engulf all of Rio in samba and vibrant, vibrating mulattas.

The parades begin with a special opening wing or *abrealas*,which always displays the name of the school and the theme of the escola. The whole shebang has some unifying message, some social commentary, economic criticism or political message, but it's usually lost in the glitter. The abrealas is then followed by the *commissão de frente*, who greet the crowds. The escola thus honours its elderly men for work done over the years.

Next follow the main wings of the escola, the big allegorical floats, the children's wing, the drummers, the celebrities and the bell-shaped Baianas twirling in their elegant hoop skirts. The Baianas honour the history of the parade itself, which was brought to Rio from Salvador de Bahia in 1877. The *mestre-sala* (dance master) and *porta-bandeira* (standard bearer) waltz and whirl. Celebrities, dancers and tambourine players strut their stuff. The

costumes are fabulously lavish: 1.5-metre-tall feathered headdresses, flowing sequin capes and rhinestone-studded G-strings.

The floats gush neo-baroque silver foil and gold tinsel. Sparkling models sway to the samba, dancing in their private Carnivals. All the while the puxador leads in song, repeating the samba do enredo for the duration of the parade. Over an hour after it began, the escola makes it past the arch and the judges' stand. There is a few minutes' pause. Globo and Manchete TV cranes stop bobbing up and down over the Pepsi caps and bibs of the foreign-press corps. Now garbage trucks parade down the runway clearing the way for the next escola. Sanitation workers in orange jump suits shimmy, dance and sweep, gracefully catching rubbish thrown from the stands and then taking their bows. It's their Carnival too. The parade continues on through the night and into the morning, eight more samba schools parade the following day, and the week after, the top eight schools parade once more in the parade of champions.

Getting tickets at the legitimate prices can be tough. Many tickets are sold 10 days in advance of the event; check with Riotur on where you can get them, as the outlet varies from year to year. People queue up for hours and travel agents and scalpers snap up the best seats. Riotur reserves seats in private boxes for tourists for US$200.

If you do happen to buy a ticket from a scalper (don't worry about finding them – they'll find you), make sure you get both the plastic ticket with the magnetic strip and the ticket showing the seat number. Different days have different coloured tickets, so check the date as well.

Don't fret if you don't get a ticket. It's possible to see the show without paying an arm and a leg. The parades last eight to 10 hours each and no one can or wants to sit through them that long. Unless you're an aficionado of an escola that starts early, don't show up at the sambódromo until midnight, three or four hours into the show. Then you can get tickets at the grandstand for about US$10. And if you can't make it during Carnival, there's always

The Malhação do Judas

Holy Week is the time to see films and plays about of the crucifixion of Jesus Christ and attend church services. For some kids in Rio, apart from receiving Easter eggs, it's time to organise the Malhação de Judas.

They make a manikin out of old clothes and then hang it up in the street on a post and call it Judas, the traitor of Jesus. On the morning after good Friday, Sabado de Alleluia, they act out the Malhação do Judas (beating of Judas). They beat the figure with wooden bats and stone it until it falls off the post. Then it is cut into quarters and burnt. Often they stick a tag on the Judas, with names of unpopular people or politicians from the locality. ■

the cheaper (but less exciting) parade of champions the following week.

If you can avoid it, don't take the bus to or from the sambódromo; it's safer to take the metro, which is open 24 hours a day during Carnival. It's also fun to check out the paraders in their costumes on the train.

By the way, there's nothing to stop you taking part in the parade. Most samba schools are happy to have foreigners join one of the *alas* (wings). All you need is between US$200 and US$300 for your costume and you're in. It helps to arrive in Rio a week or two in advance to get this organised. Ask at the hotel how to go about it. It usually takes just a few phone calls.

Carnival Dates Dates for the Carnival parade in coming years are:

1996	18 & 19 February
1997	9 & 10 February
1998	22 & 23 February
1999	14 & 15 February
2000	5 & 6 March

Places to Stay

Rio has a star system. Hotels are ranked from one star for the cheapest to five for the most luxurious. Rio has 12 five-star hotels to choose from, 22 four-star hotels, 40 three-star hotels, 16 two-star hotels, three one-star hotels, 23 aparthotels, 36 motels (see Entertainment) and 47 hotels unclassified by Embratur (our speciality), but still regulated.

So what do these stars mean? Well, a five-star hotel has a pool or two, at least two very good restaurants, a nightclub and bar,

gym, sauna and a beauty salon. A four-star hotel has a good restaurant, a sauna and a bar. A three-star hotel may have everything a four-star hotel has, but there's something that downgrades it; the furnishings may be a bit beat-up, cheaper, or a bit sparser. There's a big gap between three-stars and two-stars. A two-star hotel is usually clean and comfortable, but that's about all. By the way, all hotels with a star rating have air-con in the rooms, though some of the older models sound like you're in a B-52 bomber! All rated hotels also have a small frigobar (refrigerator) in the rooms; sometimes empty or full of nibbles costing triple what they would in the nearby supermarket. Bathrooms have bidets, a sign of the continental influence.

Below one and two-stars there are still plenty of decent places to stay if you're travelling on a tight budget and need a safe place to sleep. Air-con is usually optional (if available), but mostly the rooms have fans. Hotels which are not regulated by Embratur may try to slip in additional charges and other assorted petty crimes against the tourist. Threaten to call Sunab price regulation if this happens, discuss a price before accepting a room and also ask if a 10% service charge is included.

Breakfast is usually included in the room rate. It ranges from sumptuous buffets at the top-end to coffee and a bread roll at the bottom. In between there should be fresh juice, good coffee, fresh rolls with a slice of ham and cheese and a couple of pieces of fruit.

Reservations are a good idea in Rio, espe-

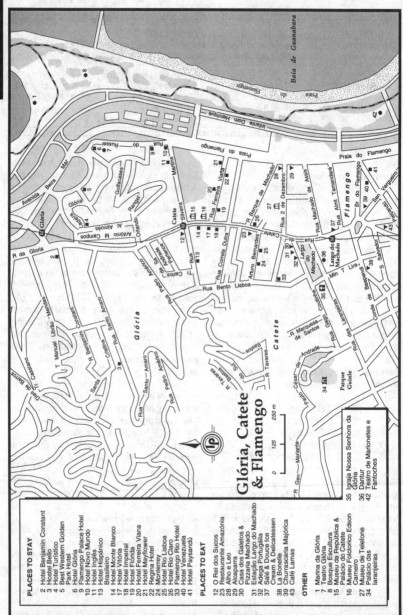

Glória, Catete
& Flamengo

0   125   250 m

PLACES TO STAY

2   Hotel Benjamin Constant
3   Hostel Bello
4   Hotel Turístico
5   Best Western Golden
    Park Hotel
6   Hotel Glória
9   Flamengo Palace Hotel
10 Hotel Novo Mundo
11 Hotel Inglês
13 Hotel Hispânico
    Brasileiro
14 Hotel Monte Blanco
17 Hotel Vitória
18 Hotel Imperial
19 Hotel Florida
20 Hotel Ferreira Viana
21 Regina Hotel
22 Mayflower
24 Monterrey
25 Hotel Rio Lisboa
26 Hotel Rio Claro
33 Flamengo Rio Hotel
40 Hotel Venezuela
41 Hotel Paysandú

PLACES TO EAT

12 O Rei dos Sucos
23 Restaurante Amazônia
28 Alho e Leo
29 Alcaparra
30 Casa dos Galetos &
    Pizzaria Machado
31 Estação Largo do Machado
32 Adega Portugália
37 Salé & Douce Ice
    Cream & Delicatessen
38 La Bonelle
39 Churrascaria Majórica
43 Café Lamas

OTHER

1   Marina da Glória
7   Teatro Glória
8   Bosque Escultura
15 Museu da República &
    Palácio do Catete
16 Museu Folclórico Edson
    Carneiro
27 Museu de Telefone
34 Palácio das
    laranjeiras
35 Igraja Nossa Senhora da
    Glória
36 Dantur
42 Teatro de Marionetes e
    Fantoches

cially if you plan to stay in a mid-range or top-end hotel. Aside from the fact that a reservation ensures you a room, you can save up to 30% on the room rate just by booking in advance. If you want to make sure you have an ocean view, request it when you make your reservation. It will cost around 20% more than other rooms. At Carnival time hotel prices go up and everyone gives dire warnings of there being no places to stay. It's not a good time to arrive without a reservation, even the bottom-end places get full.

Prices we've quoted here in the mid-range and top-end hotels are the rate for a standard room if you walk-in off the street, so you should be able to get the price down a bit by reserving in advance.

Places to Stay – bottom end

The best area for budget hotels is around Glória, Catete and Flamengo. This used to be a desirable part of the city and is still quite nice. Many of the places used to be better hotels, so you can get some pleasant rooms at very reasonable prices. These hotels are often full from December to February, so reservations are not a bad idea.

From Glória to Lapa, near the aqueduct, on the edge of the business district, there are several more budget hotels. Generally, these are hardly any cheaper than the hotels further from the city in Catete, yet they are run-down and the area is less safe at night. If, however, everything else is booked up you'll see several hotels if you walk along Rua Joaquim Silva (near the Passeio Público), then over to Avenida Mem de Sá, turn up Avenida Gomes Freire and then turn right in to Praça Tiradentes. The *Hotel Marajó* at Avenida Joaquim Silva 99 is recommended.

Glória The *Hotel Turístico* (☎ 225-9388), Ladeira da Glória 30, is one of Rio's most popular budget hotels, even though their prices are getting a bit high. There are always plenty of gringos staying here. It's across from the Glória metro station, 30 metres up the street that emerges between two sidewalk restaurants. The rooms are clean and safe,

with small balconies. The hotel is often full but they do take reservations. Singles/doubles start at US$15/25 for quartos and US$20/30 for apartamentos.

Right near the Glória metro station, the *Hotel Benjamin Constant*, at Rua Benjamin Constant 10, is one of the cheapest places around. The rooms are small and dingy, but the cost is only US$4.50 per person.

Catete & Flamengo The *Hotel Ferreira Viana* (☎ 205-7396) at Rua Ferreira Viana 58 has cramped, cheap rooms at US$8/12 for singles/doubles (US$15 with air-con) and a hot shower down the hall.

On busy Rua do Catete are three budget hotels worthy of note. The *Hotel Monte Blanco* (☎ 225-0121), at Rua do Catete 160, a few steps from the Catete metro stop, is very clean, has air-con, and singles/doubles for US$14/16. Ask for a quiet room in the back; they have round beds and sparkling wall paint. Up the stairs at Rua do Catete 172, the *Hotel Vitória* (☎ 205-5397) has clean apartamentos for US$11/16 for singles/doubles.

The *Hotel Imperial* (☎ 205-0212), at Rua do Catete 186, is a funky hotel with car parking. The quality and prices of the rooms vary, starting at US$25/35 for singles/doubles with bathrooms. Some of the rooms have air-con. The *Hotel Rio Claro* (☎ 225-5180), a few blocks down at Rua do Catete 233, has musty singles for US$12 and doubles with air-con, TV and hot shower for US$16.

The *Hotel Hispánico Brasileiro* (☎ 225-7537), at Rua Silveira Martins 135, has big, clean apartamentos. Singles are US$14 and doubles US$16.

Turn down the quiet Rua Arturo Bernardes for a couple more budget hotels: the *Monterrey* (☎ 265-9899) and *Hotel Rio Lisboa* (☎ 265-9599) are at Nos 39 and 29 respectively. The first is cheaper and friendlier. Single/double quartos go for US$7/10 and apartamentos cost US$15. At the Rio Lisboa, single quartos cost US$7 and apartamentos are US$9/15 for singles/

doubles. These two are the cheapest places in Catete.

Botafogo Rio has a couple of quite good youth hostels. *Chave do Rio de Janeiro* (☎ 286-0303; fax 246-5553), in Botafogo, is a model youth hostel. You'll meet lots of young Brazilians here from all over the country. It gets busy, so you need to make reservations during peak holiday times. The only problem with this place is its location, but if you get the hang of the buses quickly, it shouldn't hamper you too much. From the rodoviária, catch a No 170, 171 or 172 bus

and get off after the Largo dos Leões. Go up Rua Voluntários da Pátria until Rua General Dionísio, then turn left. The hostel is at number 63.

Copacabana A good place for budget travellers to stay in Copacabana is the *Copacabana Praia* youth hostel (☎ 236-6472), at Rua Tenente Marones de Gusmão 85. Although it's a few blocks from the beach it's still excellent value. A relaxed and friendly place, it costs US$8 for members, US$10 for non-members and US$25 for double apartments with a stove and a refrig-

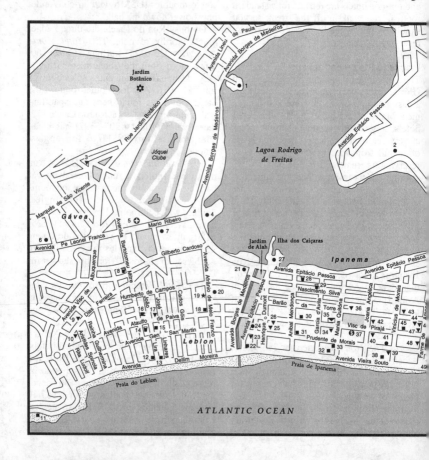

erator. They will also rent you sheets if you don't have any.

Camping

In Barra, the Camping Clube do Brasil has a campground *CCB-9* (☎ 493-0628) at Avenida Sernambetiba 3200. It has good facilities and is opposite the beach. The cost is US$8 per person. The club also has another site, *CCB-10* (☎ 437-8400), further out at Recreio dos Bandeirantes, also opposite the beach. The price is the same. There are two other campgrounds in Recreio. *Novo Rio* (☎ 437-8213) at Avenida das Américas,

km 18, has a grassy area with plenty of shade. It charges US$12 per person. *Ostal* (☎ 437-8213), at Avenida Sernambetiba 18790, is opposite the beach. It costs US$8 per person and they also rent small chalets for US$12 a head.

Places to Stay – middle

If you want to be near the beach, there are several reasonably priced hotels in Copacabana, a couple in Ipanema and even some in Leblon. They all get busy in the high season, so it might pay to book ahead. For the same price you can get a cheerier room in

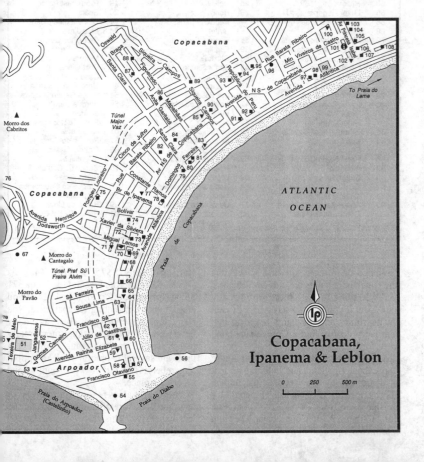

Copacabana, Ipanema & Leblon

ATLANTIC OCEAN

0   250   500 m

PLACES TO STAY		97	Ouro Verde	94	Churrascaria Jardim
		98	Lancaster	100	Cervantes
11	Sheraton Hotel	103	Merlin Copacabana	102	Mab's
12	Marina Palace	104	Rio Copacabana		
13	Marina Rio		Hotels	**OTHER**	
15	Hotel Carlton	105	Continental		
18	Leblon Palace Hotel	106	Acapulco Copacabana	1	Clube Naval Ilha
22	Praia Ipanema	107	Meridien Hotel		Piraqué
30	Hotel São Marco	108	Leme Palace	2	Parque Carlos
31	Marlpanema				Lacerda
32	Caesar Park	**PLACES TO EAT**		4	Estácio de Remo
33	Everest Rio Hotel			5	Hospital Miguel Couto
38	Sol Ipanema	3	Guimas	6	Planetário
45	Hotel Vermont	9	Celeiro	7	Clube de Regatas
55	Arpoador Inn	10	Restaurante Bozó		do Flamengo
57	Rio Palace	16	Café Leblon	8	People's (Nightclub)
58	Copacabana Praia	17	Sabor Saúde	14	Un Deux Trois
	(Youth Hostel)	23	Chez Michou		(Nightclub)
60	Riviera	25	Delicats	19	Rio Tourist Police
65	Luxor Regente	26	Boni's	20	Scala
66	Hotel Martinique	34	Kabuki Japanese	21	Clube Monte Líbano
68	Debret		Buffet	24	Lord Jim's
72	Biarritz Hotel	36	Banana Café	27	Clube dos Caiçaras
73	Rio Othon Palace	39	Esquina	28	Chiko's Bar
74	Hotel Copa Linda	40	Chaika's	29	Mistura (Nightclub)
75	Copacabana Chalé	42	Sabor Saúde	35	Post Office
	(Youth Hostel)	43	Porcão	37	Casa de Câmbio
78	Rio Atlântica	44	Natural	41	Garota da Ipanema
79	Califórnia Othon	46	Bar Bofetada	51	Praça General Osório
80	Luxor Copacabana	47	Sindicato do Chopp	54	Parque Garota
81	Hotel Toledo	48	Via Farme		de Ipanema
82	Hotel Angrense	49	Alberico's	56	Forte de Copacabana
84	Grande Hotel Canada	50	Le Bon Jus	61	Jazzmania
86	Copa d'Or	52	Il Veronese	67	Parque do Cantagalo
87	Copacabana Praia	53	Barril 1800	69	Galeria Alaska
88	Hotel Santa Clara	59	The Americana		(Nightclub)
89	Atlântico		Restaurant	70	Casas de Câmbio &
90	Castro Alves	62	Lope's Confeiteria		Post Office No 1061
92	Copacabana Palace	64	Restaurante Lucas	76	Parque de Catacumba
93	Apa Hotel	71	Macro Nature	96	Stop Bike
95	Copacabana Hotel	77	Confeitaria Colombo	99	Praça do Lido
	Residência	83	Arataca	101	Riotur Tourist Office
		85	Adega Perola		

Flamengo or in the centre near Cinelândia (the Cinelândia hotels are also convenient if you're heading to the airport or rodoviária soon). But if you want to stay where the sun always shines and the lights never go out, you can probably find a Copacabana hotel room for US$20 to US$25.

Another relatively inexpensive option in Copacabana, Ipanema and Leblon is to rent an apartment by the week or the month. There are loads of agencies. You could try Brasleme Imóveis (☎ 542-1347), at Rua Barata Ribeiro 92-A, Copacabana. They rent apartments for a minimum of three days

starting from US$75. Apartur Imóveis (☎ 287-5757), at Rua Visconde de Pirajá 371 S/204, Ipanema, offers similar deals. If you are interested in renting an apartment, you could look under *temporada* in any daily newspaper. Renting an apartment really makes sense if you're staying a while or if there are several people in your group, but remember it's a bit of work finding and securing a place.

There are also residential hotels or aparthotels that are often more spacious and less expensive. This has been the fastest-growing sector in the hotel industry in the last few years, so there are lots of small, modern apartments available. They seem to be popular with business travellers in town for a couple of months. Prices vary from the mid-range to top-end, and during the low season, discounts of 30% are not unusual.

Cinelândia The *Nelba Hotel* (☎ 210-3235), at Rua Senador Dantas 46, is in a good central location in the heart of Cinelândia. A two-room, three-bed suite with air-con, a high-pressure hot shower, phone and TV is US$18/28 for singles/doubles. The *Itajuba Hotel* (☎ 210-3163; fax 240-7461), at Rua Álvaro Alvim 23, has better rooms (with refrigerators) than the Nelba Hotel and is quieter. Singles/doubles are US$22/30.

Santa Teresa The *Hotel Santa Teresa* (☎ 242-0007) is attractive and has a small pool, car parking and rates that include three meals. Singles/doubles with a bath are US$20/25; without a bath, US$14/20. Santa Teresa is a beautiful neighbourhood, but somewhat dangerous and after midnight there is no public transport. The hotel is at Rua Almirante Alexandrino 660. Take a taxi to get there if you're carrying valuables. If not, take the bondinho to Vista Alegre and then follow the tracks downhill to the old mission-style building.

Catete & Flamengo The *Hotel Flórida* (☎ 285-5242; fax 285-5777), one of Rio's best budget hotels, is at Rua Ferreira Viana 81, near the Catete metro station. Popular with package tour groups, The Flórida has only three faults: it's not in Ipanema, it always seems to be booked up, and it's jacked up its prices since a recent renovation. Rooms have private baths with good, hot showers and polished parquet floors. Singles/doubles cost US$50/73 (air-con is available). There's a cheap little restaurant and a safe deposit for valuables. Make your reservations well in advance for stays during the high season.

Down the block at Rua Ferreira Viana 29, the *Regina Hotel* (☎ 225-7280; fax 285-2999) is a respectable mid-range hotel with a snazzy lobby, clean rooms and hot showers. Singles/doubles start at US$24/29.

At Rua Silveira Martins 20 is the *Hotel Inglês* (☎ 265-9052), a good two-star hotel where singles/doubles cost US$22/29.

Further into Flamengo, near the Largo do Machado metro station, the elegant palm-tree-lined Rua Paiçandú has two excellent mid-range hotels. The *Hotel Venezuela* (☎ 205-2098), at No 34, is clean and cosy. All the rooms have double beds, air-con, TV and hot water. It costs US$25 a double. The *Hotel Paysandú* (☎ 225-7270), at No 23, is a two-star Embratur hotel with singles and doubles for US$24/32. Both are good value for money.

Leme The *Acapulco* (☎ 275-0022), at Rua Gustavo Sampaio 854, is a three-star Embratur hotel costing US$40/50 for singles/doubles with bath. It's one block from the beach, behind the Meridien Hotel.

Copacabana Near the youth hostel, at Rua Décio Vilares 316, is a delightful mid-range option, the *Hotel Santa Clara* (☎ 256-2650) with singles/doubles starting at US$22/25.

As far as budget hotels go, the *Hotel Angrense* (☎ 255-3875) is one of Copacabana's cheapest. They have clean and dreary singles/doubles for US$17/25 with a bath and US$14/19 without. It's at Travessa Angrense 25. The road isn't on most maps but it intersects Avenida NS de Copacabana just past Rua Santa Clara. A few blocks away, the *Hotel Copa Linda* (☎ 267-3399) is almost as cheap. The small and basic rooms cost US$19 a single and US$26 a double. It's at Avenida NS de Copacabana 956 on the 2nd floor.

There are several hotels that offer more for the money than the two just mentioned. Right nearby, the *Grande Hotel Canada* (☎ 257-1864; fax 255-3705), at Avenida NS de Copacabana 687, has singles for US$27 and doubles for US$35 (there is no elevator for the cheapest rooms). The rooms are modern, with air-con and TV. It's two blocks from the beach in a busy area.

The *Hotel Martinique* (☎ 521-4552; fax

287-7640) combines a perfect location with good rooms at a moderate cost. It's on the quiet Rua Sá Ferreira at No 30, one block from the beach at the far end of Copacabana. Clean, comfortable rooms with air-con start as low as US$28/40 for singles/doubles, and they have a few tiny singles for US$19. It's a friendly place.

Also one block from the beach, the *Hotel Toledo* (☎ 257-1990; fax 287-7640) is at Rua Domingos Ferreira 71. The rooms are as fine as many higher priced hotels. Good value singles/doubles start at US$35/43 and they also have some tiny singles for US$20. The *Biarritz Hotel* (☎ 521-6542; fax 287-7640) is a small place at Rua Aires Saldanha 54, close to the beach behind the Rio Othon Palace. Singles/doubles start at US$22/35 and all rooms have air-con and TV. Also try the *Apa Hotel* (☎ 255-8112; fax 256-3628), three blocks from the beach at Rua República do Peru 305. Singles/doubles are US$37/46.

If you want to spend more money and stay on the beachfront, the *Hotel Trocadero* (☎ & fax 257-1834), at Avenida Atlântica 2064, has three-star singles/doubles at US$70/80. Their restaurant, *Moenda*, serves very good Brazilian food. The old *Excelsior* (☎ 257-1950; fax 256-2037), at Avenida Atlântica 1800 near the Copacabana Palace, is being refurbished. Spacious singles/doubles are US$65/70. The *Riviera* (☎ 247-6060; fax 247-0242), at Avenida Atlântica 4122, has basic singles/doubles for US$60/65. It's the cheapest place on the beachfront.

Ipanema & Leblon There are two relatively inexpensive hotels in Ipanema. The *Hotel São Marco* (☎ 239-5032; 259-3147) is a couple of blocks from the beach at Rua Visconde de Pirajá 524. Rooms are small but with air-con, TV and refrigerator. Singles/doubles start at US$45/48. The *Hotel Vermont* (☎ 521-0057; fax 267-7046), at Rua Visconde de Pirajá 254, also has very simple rooms at US$35/40. Call for reservations at both these hotels.

You can get an oceanside apartment at the *Arpoador Inn* (☎ 247-6090; fax 511-5094),

on Rua Francisco Otaviano. This six-floor hotel is the only hotel in Ipanema or Copacabana that doesn't have a busy street between your room and the beach. The musty beachfront rooms are more expensive than those facing the street but the view and the roar of the surf makes it all worthwhile. Singles cost from US$38 to US$65 and doubles from US$40 to US$70. The *Hotel Carlton* (☎ 259-1932), at Rua João Lira 68, is on a very quiet street, one block from the beach in Leblon. It's a small, friendly hotel, away from the tourist scene. Singles/doubles are US$40/45.

Places to Stay – top end
The *Rio Flat Service* (☎ 274-7222; fax 239-8792) has three residential hotels that are more like apartments. All apartments have a living room and a kitchen. Without the frills of fancy hotels, they still have a swimming pool, breakfast and room service. Apartments start at US$50. The *Copacabana Hotel Residência* (☎ 256-2610), at Rua Barata Riveiro 222, is similar to Rio Flat Service.

The *Everest Rio Hotel* (☎ 287-8282; fax 521-3198) is a decent five-star place, a block from the beach at Rua Prudente de Morais 1117. Popular with business travellers, their corporate rate is US$70 a double.

Of the many top hotels in Rio, the old-style *Copacabana Palace* (☎ 255-7070; fax 235-7330), at Avenida Atlântica 1702, is the one favoured by royalty and rock stars. It recently had a massive facelift, and is a true luxury hotel. It has a great pool. Standard apartments cost US$140/160 a single/double, or you might like to try the Presidential Suite for only US$1500 a night. In Ipanema, the *Caesar Park* (☎ 287-3122; fax 521-6000), at Avenida Vieira Souto 460, is favoured by ex-dictators, and business people with large expense accounts. Singles/doubles begin at US$260/290. The Imperial Suite is a steal at US$3000 a night.

Places to Eat
As in most of Brazil, restaurants in Rio are abundant and cheap. The plates at the many

lanchonetes are big enough to feed two and the price is only US$3 to US$4. For something lighter, and probably healthier, you can eat at a suco bar. Most have sandwiches and fruit salads. Make a habit of asking for an embalagem (doggie bag) when you don't finish your food. Wrap it and hand it to a street person.

Centro *Bar Luis*, at Rua da Carioca 39, is a Rio institution that opened in 1887. The city's oldest *cervejaria* (public house), on Rio's oldest street, is a bar-less old dining room serving good German food and dark draft beer at moderate prices. It's open Monday to Saturday for lunch and dinner, until midnight.

Hotel Ambassador, at Rua Santa Luzia 651, off Avenida Graça Aranha, has a business lunch buffet which is a good way to fill your belly. For US$6 it's all you can eat, with plenty of fruit and desserts included.

Café do Teatro (☎ 262-6164), at Avenida Epitácio Pessoa 1244, under the Teatro Municipal is a place to recall the good old days. Entering the dark, dramatic Assyrian Room, with its elaborate tilework and ornate columns, is like walking into a Cecil B De Mille film. The 70-year-old restaurant is where Rio's upper crust used to dine and drink after the theatre; it must be seen to be believed. They serve lunch only and close on Saturday and Sunday. It's somewhat expensive and semi-formal, but don't be deterred – you can have a drink and light snack by the bar, listen to piano music, and breathe in the Assyrian atmosphere.

Confeiteria Colombo is at Rua Gonçalves Dias 34, one block from and parallel to Rio Branco. It's a big Viennese coffee house/restaurant where you can sit down for a meal, or stand if you're just having a dessert or cake. The Colombo is best for coffee and cake or a snack. Another old-style coffee house is *Casa Cavé* on the corner of Rua 7 de Setembro and Uruguiana. It has good ice cream.

The *English Bar* (☎ 224-2539), at Travessa do Comércio 11, Arco do Teles, is open 11.30 am to 4 pm Monday to Friday.

It's a quiet and classy English pub that serves a good lunch. Steaks go for US$8 to US$10, fish for a bit less. It's off the Praça 15 de Novembro, right through the Arco do Teles.

The green gazebo structure near the Niterói ferry is *Alba Mar* (☎ 240-8378) at Praça Marechal Âncora 184. It looks out on the Baía de Guanabara and Niterói. Go for the view and the seafood. It stays open from 11.30 am to 10 pm Monday to Saturday. Dishes start at US$8 and the peixe brasileira is recommended.

Cheio de Vida is a reasonably priced place in the centre at Avenida 13 de Maio 33, 403. It's not the easiest place to find, but it's worth the effort. Their food has a 'natural' touch. Try the zucchini pizza. *Simples Delírio do Nectar*, at Avenida General Justo 365A, has top salad plates for US$3 and main-course dishes like pork and potatoes, or shrimp with mandioca, for around US$4.

Cinelândia *Macrobiótica* (☎ 220-7585) is one floor up at Rua Embaixador Regis de Oliveira 7. Macrobiotics is pretty popular in Brazil's cities and the food here is inexpensive and simple. Try the soup and rice dishes. They are open Monday to Friday from 11 am to 5.45 pm.

Lanchonete Bariloche is at Rua Alcindo Guanabara 24-D, across from Rua Senador Dantas. This cheap little counter joint has wood-grilled steaks for US$5 and is open until 2 am. *Churrascolândia Restaurante* (☎ 220-9534), at Rua Senador Dantas 31, is a steakhouse which also has tasty steaks cooked on a wood grill for US$6.

Lapa & Santa Teresa *Restaurante Ernesto* on the corner of Rua da Lapa and Rua Teotônio Regatas, is close to the arch of the viaduct that the trolley crosses to head up to Santa Teresa. It's a good place to eat if you're going to a show in the city. In Santa Teresa at Rua Almirante Alexandrino 316-B, *Bar do Arnaudo* has excellent carne do sol. It's closed Monday.

Catete & Largo do Machado Area There are lots of options in the Largo do Machado area. Some Cariocas feel that this is the best part of Rio for food fans. On Largo do Machado, *Estação Largo do Machado* has good fish, while *Casa dos Galetos*, on Rua Catete, is good for chicken and steak, and has reasonable salad. Also on Catete, *Pizzaria Machado* has a pasta rodízio for lunch on weekdays. *Adega Portugália*, at Largo do Machado 30-A, is an Iberian-style bar and restaurant, with garlic and meat hanging from the ceiling and wine bulging off the shelves. It serves various fish and meat dishes that vary from the usual Rio fare. Try the bolinhos de bacalhau (cod-fish balls) for US$0.50 each with a Portuguese wine. For a feast try the roast cabrito (kid – the four-legged kind with little horns growing out of its head) for US$7. *O Cortiço* has a good lunch buffet for US$3.

Salé & Douce Ice Cream & Delicatessen is at Rua do Catete 311, next to the São Luís cinema and across from the Largo do Machado subway entrance. In addition to Babushka's ice cream they have healthy sandwiches for about US$3. *Restaurant Amazónia* (☎ 225-4622), at Rua do Catete 234, has good steak and a tasty broiled chicken with creamed-corn sauce, both for about US$6.

La Bonelle, at Rua Conde de Baependi 62, has high-quality food, and just around the corner, *Luigis* at Senador Correa 10, has a good reputation. A couple of up-market places in the area are *Alho e Óleo*, at Rua Barque de Machado 13, and *Alcaparra*, at Praia do Flamengo 150.

For an early morning (or late afternoon) juice in Catete, you can't go past *O Rei dos Sucos* (The King of Juices) on the corner of Rua Catete and Rua Silveira Martins. It has a top range of fruits which they juice, including a lot of Amazonian ones with hard-to-pronounce names.

Botafogo & Flamengo David, the owner of *Rajmahal* (☎ 541-6999) at General Polidoro 29, Botafogo, is British, but the food is all Indian and quite good. Meals cost about US$10 and the place is a bit off the beaten path. The restaurant is spacious and refresh-ingly calm for Rio. It's open in the evenings from Tuesday to Sunday.

At Avenida Repórter Nestor Moreira 11, *Sol e Mar* (☎ 295-1896), is somewhat pricey and stuffy, and comes complete with sere-nading violinists. It's one of the few places in the city that's right on the bay and the outdoor tables provide a spectacular view. Seafood dominates the menu. The restaurant is next to the Bâteau Mouche at Botafogo beach and is open daily from 11 am to 3 am. A favourite with wealthy tourists.

The popular *Churrascaria Majórica* (☎ 245-8947), at Rua Senador Vergueiro 11/15, Flamengo, has good meat, reasonable prices and an interior done in gaúcho kitsch. It's open for lunch and dinner.

Café Lamas (☎ 205-0198) has been oper-ating at Rua Marques de Abrantes 18-A in Flamengo, since 1874 and is one of Rio's most renowned eateries. It has a lively and loyal clientele and is open for lunch and dinner with a typical meaty menu and stan-dard prices; try the grilled linguiça, or filet mignon.

Leme *Mário's* (☎ 542-2393), at Avenida Atlântica 290, Leme, has an all-you-can-eat deal for US$8. Many people think this is Rio's best churrascaria and they may be right. Be prepared to wait during prime time as they get a big tourist crowd. It's open from 11.30 to 1.30 am.

Restaurante Shirley, at Rua Gustavo Sampaio 610-A, has delicious seafood plates from US$7 to US$12. Try the mussel vinai-grette appetiser or the octopus and squid in ink for US$10.

Copacabana *Lope's Confeiteria*, at Avenida NS de Copacabana 1334, off Júlio de Castilhos, is an excellent lanchonete with big portions and little prices for typical Brazilian food.

The *Americana Restaurant*, on Avenida Rainha Elizabete off Avenida NS de Copacabana, has lunches and dinners which are hearty and reasonably priced. The steak with potatoes or vegies is excellent for US$6.

Restaurante Lucas, at Avenida Atlântica

3744, is across from Rua Sousa Lima and has reasonably priced German dishes starting at US$6.

Churrascaria Jardim, at República do Peru 225, has a rodízio, a-la-carte and self-serve, por-kilo options. At Siqueira Campos 138, *Adega Perola* has quite a few items not usually found in Rio. Try their chicken in red wine.

Arataca, at Rua Domingues Ferreira 41, (near the American Express office) is one of several Arataca restaurants in Rio which feature the exotic cuisine of the Amazon. This place is actually a counter-lunch stand and deli, around the corner from one of their regular restaurants, with the same food as at the restaurants but for only half the price. In addition to the regional dishes such as vatapá for US$4 and pato (duck) for US$5, they serve real guaraná juice (try it) and delicious sorbets made from Amazonas fruits.

Mab's, on Avenida Atlântica (the Copacabana side of Princesa Isabel, across from the Meridien), has excellent seafood soup in a crock, chock-full of piping hot creepy-crawlies for US$6.

Cervantes, on Avenida Prado Junior, is Rio's best sandwich joint and is also a late-night hang-out for a strange and colourful crew. It's on the infamous Avenida Prado Junior, where everyone and everything goes at night. Meat sandwiches come with pineapple (US$3). The steaks and fries are excellent too.

Macro Nature, down the Travessa Cristiano Lacorte, is the best vegetarian restaurant and health-food store in Copacabana. The menu is brief and very organic; the soups excellent. They have sucos, sandwiches, yoghurt and health foods to go and everything is cheap. The 'ponto de encontro de pessoas saudáveis' (the meeting point for healthy people) as they call themselves is open Monday to Friday from 9 am to 10.30 pm, Saturday and Sunday from 9 am to 6 pm.

Ipanema If you can't afford to stay at the *Caesar Park* hotel, go down there one Wednesday or Saturday from noon to 4 pm and sample their famous Brazilian feijoada.

Ex-President Collor considers it the best around, and for US$15 it's excellent value for money.

Via Farme (☎ 227-0743), at Rua Farme de Amoedo 47, offers a good plate of pasta at a reasonable price, something which is usually hard to find. The four-cheese pasta and the seafood pasta dishes are excellent and portions are large enough for two to share. Most dishes are less than US$8. They are open from noon to 2 am.

Barril, at both 1800 Avenida Vieira Souto and Avenida Rainha Elizabete at the beach, is open late into the night. This trendy beach café, below Jazzmania (see Entertainment), is for people-meeting and watching. After a day at Ipanema beach, you can stroll over to the *Shell Station*, across the street from Barril 1800, for Babushka's terrific ice cream.

Boni's, at Rua Visconde de Pirajá 595, is a favourite for fast food. Excellent pastries and fresh coffee that's strong enough to turn Bambi into Godzilla. *Chaika's*, at Rua Visconde de Pirajá 321, is open from 8 am to 2 pm. This is where the girl from Ipanema really eats. There's a stand-up fast-food bar, and a restaurant in the back with delicious hamburgers, the sweetest pastries and good cappuccinos (a rarity in Rio). Chaika's stays busy late into the night.

Il Veronese, at Rua Visconde de Pirajá 29A, is off Gomes Carneiro. For an inexpensive meal, Veronese has takeaway Italian pastas (the best in Rio according to local sources), pizzas and pastries.

Porcão (☎ 521-0999), at Rua Barão da Torre 218, has steadily been moving up in the churrasco ratings. Again, it's all you can eat for about US$8 a person. They open at 11 am and close at 2 am.

Bar Lagoa on the lake, is Rio's oldest bar/restaurant. It doesn't open till 7.30 pm but only closes at 3 am. There's always a good crowd and you can just drink beer, or you can eat a full meal for US$7 to US$10. The food is excellent, the menu typically Brazilian, and the atmosphere great.

Natural (☎ 267-7799), at Rua Barão da Torre 171, is a very natural health-food restaurant which has an inexpensive lunch special with soup, rice, vegies and beans, for less than US$4. Other good dishes are pancakes with chicken or vegetables.

Esquina, a 24-hour bar and restaurant at the corner of Vinícius de Morais and Prudente de Morais, has a splendid mural, good atmosphere and huge lunch portions for around US$4 – very cheap by Ipanema standards.

Delicats, on Avenida Henrique Dumont near Rua Visconde de Pirajá, is Rio's only deli and has lots of homemade food. They make the best potato knish (dumplings) south of New York. They also have pastrami, herring, rye bread and other treasures from the old country, but sadly no bagels.

Le Bon Jus, at the corner of Teixeira de Meio and Visconde de Pirajá, is a good juice and sandwich bar, as is *Lino's*, one block west at the corner of Farme de Amoedo and Visconde de Pirajá. Readers recommend the 'heavenly' sucos.

Banana Café, at Rua Barão da Torre 368, is a trendy (but overpriced) bar and restaurant. They have 19 different types of pizza and eight types of sandwich. If you're drinking, try a 'black velvet' (dark chopp with champagne). It's open till 6 am.

Chez Michou, at Rua Paul Redfern 44, is a popular creperie with a young crowd. They stay open till 4 am, but are closed on Tuesday.

Fans of Japanese food should try the *Kabuki Japanese Buffet*, at Rua Visconde de Pirajá 365. It's reasonably priced and open Monday to Saturday from 10 am to 7 pm.

Leblon *Sabor Saúde*, at Avenida Ataulfo de Paiva 630, is Rio's best health-food emporium and is open daily from 8.30 am to 10.30 pm. They have two natural-food restaurants: downstairs has good meals for US$3 while upstairs is more expensive (they have great buffet feasts for US$6). There's also a small grocery store and takeaway-food counter.

Celeiro, at Rua Dias Ferreira 199, has a fantastic salad bar. It's open from 11.30 am to 5 pm every day except Sunday. Don't let the silly name put you off at *Restaurante Bozó* (☎ 274-0147), at Rua Dias Ferreira 50

– the staff are very serious about their food. Try the scrumptious and filling medallions of filet mignon wrapped in bacon and smothered in pepper sauce.

Most Cariocas have a favourite churrascaria. The serious carnivores have a current favourite because last month's favourite has slipped a bit. Prices don't vary much between churrascarias: it's usually all you can eat for about US$8-10. *Plataforma* (☎ 274-4052), at Rua Adalberto Ferreira 32, is one of the best. It's always busy late at night and is a big hang-out for actors and musicians. Tom Jobim was a big fan of its chopp. The restaurant is open from 11 am to 2 am daily.

Café Leblon specialises in sandwiches. The turkey with plum chutney for US$3 is great. The decor is interesting too, with marble tables and photos of old Rio. It's at Avenida Bartolomeu Mitre 297 and stays open late.

Gávea *Guimas* (☎ 259-7996), at José Roberto Macedo Soares 5, is one of our favourite restaurants. It's not cheap, but the prices (US$20 to US$30 per person) are fair for the outstanding cuisine you're served.

Guimas offers what most restaurants in Rio lack: creative cooking. Try the pernil de carneiro (lamb with onions) or the Oriental shrimp curry and a Rio salad. The small, but comfortable open-air restaurant opens at 8 pm and gets very crowded later in the evening. If you order one of their boa lembrança specials, you'll receive an attractive ceramic plate. They don't accept credit cards.

Parque Nacional da Tijuca *Os Esquilos* is a beautiful colonial restaurant in Alto da Boa Vista. It has a typical Brazilian menu which isn't expensive. It is open Tuesday to Sunday from noon to 7 pm.

Ice Cream *Babushka's* and *Alex* are the two best ice-cream chains in town.

Fine Dining Rio is loaded with fancy restaurants which are not that expensive for the visitor. In most you can spend less than US$15 – especially if you decline the couvert, which is always a ripoff – and the most expensive are often less than US$30. Here's a list of some of the best:

Chinese
  Mr Zee, Rua General San Martin 1219, Leblon (☎ 294-0591)
French
  Laurent, Rua D Mariana 209, Botafogo (☎ 266-3131)
  Club Gourmet, Rua General Polidoro 186, Botafogo (☎ 295-1097)
  Ouro Verde, Avenida Atlântica 1456, Copacabana (☎ 542-1887)
Italian
  Quadrifoglio, Rua Maria Angélica 43, Jardim Botânico (☎ 226-1799)
Polish
  A Polonese, Rua Hilário de Gouveia 116, Copacabana (☎ 237-7378)
Portuguese
  Antiquarius, Rua Aristides Espinola 19, Leblon (☎ 294-1049)
Swiss
  Casa da Suiça, Rua Cândido Mendes 157, Glória (☎ 252-2406)

Entertainment

To find out what's going on at night, pick up the *Jornal do Brasil* at any newsstand and turn to the entertainment section. On Friday they insert an entertainment magazine called *Programa* which lists the week's events.

Nightlife varies widely by the neighbourhood. Leblon and Ipanema have up-market, trendy clubs with excellent jazz. Botafogo has cheaper, popular clubs with more dancing and samba. Cinelândia and Lapa in the centre have a lot of samba and pagode and are also the heart of gay Rio. Try some of the bars around Sala Cecília Mendez. Copacabana is a mixed bag, with some good local hang-outs but also a strong tourist influence with a lot of sex for sale.

Entertainment is less organised and more spontaneous in Rio than you'd expect. Much of Rio's nightlife happens on the streets, in front of bars, in restaurants and anywhere outside with room to drink and sing. Most bars stay open until 4 am on busy weekend nights and to around 2 am other nights.

Centro & Lapa Getting a taxi late at night in Lapa or Cinelândia isn't a problem; there is also limited bus service all night long. You can catch buses to the zona sul along the Praça Mahatma Gandhi on Avenida Luis de Vasconcelos.

Suburban Dreams, at Pedro Lessa 41, Centro, behind the Biblioteca Nacional, is a bar, open until very late, and right in the centre. It's the only thing open on the block. The suburbs referred to here are the poorer areas on the outskirts of the city. The bar is frequented by many gays, blacks and zona norte people. It's a good change from the zona sul club scene but don't bring too much money to this part of town late at night. There's no cover charge.

Café Bohemia is a vegetarian restaurant by day and has wild transvestite shows on Friday, Saturday and Sunday nights. For a couple of dollars you get dancing and a very funny show if you can get by in Portuguese. It's on Avenida Santa Luzia; turn right off Avenida Rio Branco. The show starts about 1 or 2 am.

Bar Brasil in Lapa is an old bohemian hang-out and is always lively. Some Cariocas who live in the zona sul only come into the centre to go to Bar Brasil. Lapa is generally an interesting area to explore at night.

Botafogo Cochrane, off Rua Voluntários da Pátria, is one of Rio's more popular gay bars. Vaticano, Rua da Matriz 62, is a hip bar, popular with the arty Rio set.

Copacabana Galeria Alaska, on Avenida NS de Copacabana, has a transvestite show and dancing and is a centre of gay Rio.

Ipanema & Leblon Jazzmania (☎ 287-0085), on Rua Rainha Elizabeth, is Rio's most serious jazz venue. They have more international stars than any other club, but also the best of Brazilian jazz. The club is expensive at around US$10 cover on the weekend and a little less on weekdays. The music starts about 11 pm and goes late.

People's (☎ 294-0547), at Avenida Bartolomeu Mitre 370 in Leblon, is a posh club with some of the best names in jazz. To hear the great music you have to pay a US$8 cover charge and endure the incessant smoking and talking from the snobby crowd. When it gets crowded the Yves St Laurent types seems to get in and seated, while the Lonely Planet crowd gets left at the door.

There are several other expensive restaurants/clubs in Ipanema and Leblon which have good jazz but look like a scene right out of Los Angeles or New York. Chiko's Bar, at Avenida Epitácio Pessoa 560 on the lake, goes late and has no cover charge. Mistura Up, at Rua Garcia d'Avila 15, and Un Deux Trois (☎ 239-0198), at Rua Bartolomeu Mitre 123, are also popular.

Lord Jim's British pub is the place to go if you want to play darts. It's at Rua Paul Redfern 63 in Ipanema. The Garota de Ipanema is at Rua Vinícius de Morais 49 and has lively, open-air dining. There are always a few foreigners checking out the place where Tom Jobim and Vinícius de Moraes were sitting when they wrote *The Girl from Ipanema*. A recent Brazilian Playboy survey rated its chopp as the best in Rio – a bold claim indeed, but who can resist a sample? The *petiscos* are delicious.

The Zeppelin Bar, behind the Sheraton Hotel on Avenida Niemeyer, is a quaint bar and restaurant overlooking the ocean. It's medium-priced with great live folk and pop music from Thursday to Sunday night. It has a very relaxed atmosphere.

Our favourite bar is also Rio's oldest. In a town that's losing its traditions rapidly to modern Western schlock, Bar Lagoa has changed little. They tried to close it down to build a high-rise, high-tech, condo complex, but opposition was too strong. It's open from about 7.30 pm to 3 or 4 am with food, drink and a loud Carioca crowd.

Brazilian Dancing The following clubs have popular Brazilian music like samba and forró and Rio's popular dance classes. You're unlikely to find any tourists, or middle-class Brazilians there. If you want to learn about Brazil and dance, or just watch Brazilians dancing, these are the places.

Pagode da Passarela has samba and pagode on Friday and Saturday nights. It's very crowded because it's affordable to almost everyone: US$0.50 for women and US$1 for men. It's in the centre near Praça 11. Bola Preta (☎ 240-8049) is a big dance house with different types of popular music each night. They have *serestas*, *roda de samba* and pagode. The club's right in the centre, on Avenida 13 de Maio. Another good place to samba, but out in the suburbs, is Pagode Domingo Maior (☎ 288-7297), at Rua Gonzaga Bastos 268, Vila Isabel. It's probably a good idea to go with a Brazilian if you don't speak Portuguese.

If you'd rather not go into town, Clube do Samba (☎ 399-0892) is out in Barra at Estrada da Barra 65. They have samba and pagode Friday and Saturday nights. On Sunday you can get a feijoada there. This is a middle-class club, with admission costing about US$8.

Forró is the popular dance music of Brazil's Northeast and there are plenty of Northeasterners in Rio going out dancing every weekend. We actually like the accordion-laced forró more than most of the current samba, and the dancing is a blast. A good club for forró is Estudantina (☎ 232-1149) at Praça Tiradentes 79, Centro. They go Thursday, Friday and Saturday nights until about 4 am. The cover charge is US$3.

Samba Schools As early as October or November the samba schools begin holding rehearsals and dances, typically on Saturday night. These are generally open to the public for watching and joining in the samba. Almost all the escolas da samba are on the north side of town and, of course, things get going late, so you need a car or a taxi. Check with Riotur or the newspaper to get the schedules and locations. Each school has a *quadra* (club/arena) but they also hold rehearsals around town. The major schools' addresses are:

Portela
   Rua Clara Nunes 81, Oswaldo Cruz
   (☎ 390-0471)

Mocidade Independente de Padre Miguel
Rua Coronel Tamarindo 38, Padre Miguel (☎ 332-5823)
São Clemente
Rua Assunção 63, Botafogo
Império Serrano
Avenida Ministro Edgard Romero 114, Madureira (☎ 450-1285)
Mangueira
Rua Visconde de Niterói 1072, Mangueira (☎ 234-4129)
Beija Flor
Rua Pracinha Wallace Paes Leme 1025, Nilópolis (791-2866)
Império da Tijuca
Rua Conde de Bonfim 1226, Usina da Tijuca
Salgueiro
Rua Silva Teles – Andaraí

Big Shows Circo Voador under the Arcos da Lapa is a big tent with reggae, samba and trio elétrico music. The crowd is mostly from the north side. It's one of my favourites and is very reasonably priced. They get many of the best bands from Bahia and São Paulo. Their Sunday night dance gets really crowded. It starts at 11 pm and goes till late. Cover charge is US$3.

Down the block is Asa Branca (☎ 252-0966). They have samba and pagode shows that aren't especially for tourists, though they are staged shows. Scala, Plataforma I and Oba Oba have expensive Vegas-style shows with naked samba. Scala II has many top musicians like Gilberto Gil playing there these days. It's a show house, flashy and artificial, but I'd go anywhere to see a Gil show.

Pão de Açúcar has a regular performance of the samba school Beija Flor on Monday from 9 pm to 1 am. It's expensive and touristy, but it's samba. Carioca nights are held Friday and Saturday from 10 pm to 4 am. Mostly rock, but not always, the shows are not terribly expensive and are under the small pavilion on Morro da Urca – the first stop to Sugar Loaf. It's a spectacular view.

Canecão also gets the big stars of music. It's right next to the giant Rio Sul shopping mall at the entrance to the Copacabana tunnel.

Maracanãzinho is the smaller stadium

next to Maracanã in S[...] biggest shows, like Milt[...] there.

Parque Catacumba, [...] has free outdoor concerts o[...] Check the newspaper.

Discos There are many discos with bright lights and loud music in the big city, but the hip venues change regularly – check out a copy of *Programa*. Interestingly, many of the discos have stiff dress codes and admission charges, designed in part to deter the many prostitutes who come to meet tourists. Some are even called private clubs and require you to pay US$20 through a concierge at your five-star hotel in order to enter.

Help calls itself the biggest disco in Latin America and no one seems to doubt it. It's at Avenida Atlântica 3432 in Copacabana. Lots of drunken gringos seem to get robbed just outside. Calígola in Ipanema is where the rich and famous hang out. The current favourite is Resumo da Ópera; it's in Lagoa at Avenida Borges de Medeiros 1426.

Things to Buy

Most stores are open Monday to Friday from 9 am to 7 pm (some stay open even later). Saturday has half-day shopping, from 9 am to 1 pm. The malls usually open from 10 am to 10 pm, Monday to Friday, and 10 am to 8 pm on weekends.

Pé de Boi This store sells the traditional artisan handicrafts of Brazil's Northeast and Minas Gerais, and it's all fine work. There's lots of wood, lace, pottery and prints. It's not an inexpensive store; you have to buy closer to the source to get a better price, but if you have some extra dollars – US$10 to US$20 at a minimum – these pieces are the best gifts to bring home from Brazil: imaginative and very Brazilian.

The small store is worth a visit just to look around. Ana Maria Chindler, the owner, knows what she's selling and is happy to tell you about it. Pé de Boi (Bull's Foot) (☎ 285-4395) is in Botafogo on Rua Ipiranga 53. It en Monday to Friday until 7 pm and on urday from 10 am to 1 pm.

FUNAI Brazil's Indian agency has a tiny craft shop at Avenida Presidente Wilson 16-A (it's actually around the corner from the main entrance). Open Monday to Friday from 9 am to noon and 1 to 6 pm, the store has woven papoose (baby) slings for US$5, jewellery from US$0.50 to US$5 and musical instruments.

Casa Oliveira This beautiful music store (☎ 222-3539) is at Rua da Carioca 70 in Centro – Rio's oldest street. It sells a wide variety of instruments, including all the noise makers that fuel the Carnival *baterias* (rhythm sections), a variety of small mandolin-like string instruments, accordions and electric guitars. These make great presents and it's a fun place to play even if you don't buy.

Malls Brazilians, like Americans, seem to measure progress by shopping malls. They love to shop at these monsters. Rio Sul was the first mall to maul Rio. There are all kinds of stores. The C&A department store has a good range of clothes and is inexpensive. Rio Sul is right before you enter the Copacabana tunnel in Botafogo. There are free buses from Copacabana. Barra Shopping, in Barra da Tijuca, is newer and bigger. It's at Avenida das Américas, on the right as you drive south into Barra. It's hard to miss! They're about to build a tribute to Ayrton Senna out the front – a giant racing helmet.

Bum Bum Since your bathing suit has too much fabric attached to the seams, resign yourself to buying a new one. Bum Bum is the trendsetter of the bikini world, and it knows it. It's not cheap, but you're paying for style not fabric. It's in Ipanema at Rua Visconde de Pirajá 437. If you're on a budget, there are plenty of other boutiques that sell bikinis for less money but with just as little fabric. Ki-Tanga is a good example.

Hippie Fair This is an arts and crafts fair, with many booths selling jewellery, leather goods, paintings, samba instruments and clothes. There is some awful stuff here and some that's OK. Prices go way up during the peak tourist season and the air rings with the sounds of New Yorkers hunting down good buys.

The fair takes place every Sunday at the Praça General Osório in Ipanema. But you can find the same items at Praça 15 de Novembro in Centro or at the northern end of Copacabana beach. If you're just beginning to travel in Brazil, skip it.

Nordeste or São Cristóvão Fair The Nordeste Fair is held at the Pavilhão de São Cristóvão on the north side of town every Sunday, starting early and going until about 3 pm. The fair is very Northeastern in character. There are lots of *barracas* (stalls) selling meat, beer and cachaça; bands of accordions, guitars and tambourines playing the forró; comedy, capoeira battles and people selling magic potions. It's a great scene.

Of course there's plenty to buy. Besides food, they have lots of cheap clothes, some good deals on hammocks and a few good nordeste gifts like leather vaqueiro (cowboy) hats. If you're ready for adventure and have a car, it's best to arrive the night before the market. This is set-up time and also party time. At about 9 or 10 pm the barracas open for dinner and beer. Some vendors are busy setting up, others are already finished. Music and dance starts, and doesn't stop until sunrise. It's great fun so long as you're careful.

Getting There & Away

Air From Rio flights go to all of Brazil and Latin America. Shuttle flights to São Paulo leave from the conveniently located Aeroporto Santos Dumont, in the city centre along the bay. Almost all other flights – domestic and national – leave from Aeroporto Galeão.

Incoming visitors at Galeão pass through customs and then continue into a large lobby where there's a tourist-information counter run by a private company called RDE which can arrange hotel and taxi reservations. The staff also try to palm off a 'travellers passport' for the outrageous sum of US$25, and attempt to pressure befuddled travellers with the argument that government regulations require purchase of this junk package. This is a load of nonsense and a blatant ripoff attempt.

All three major Brazilian airlines have their main offices in the centre (metro stop Cinelândia). You can also walk over to Aeroporto Santos Dumont where they have ticket counters and make reservations from there.

Varig/Cruzeiro (☎ 292-6600 for reservations or 292-5220 for information) has its main office in Centro at Avenida Rio Branco 277 (☎ 220-3821). There are also offices at Rua Rodolfo Dantas 16 in Copacabana (☎ 541-6343), and Rua Visconde de Pirajá 351, Ipanema (☎ 287-9040). The city office is much more reliable and knowledgeable than the other Varig offices.

VASP (☎ 292-2080) has a city office at Rua Santa Luzia 735. They also have offices at Aeroporto Santos Dumont (☎ 292-2112), at Avenida NS de Copacabana 262 (☎ 292-2112) in Copacabana, and at Rua Visconde de Pirajá 444 (☎ 292-2112) in Ipanema.

Transbrasil (☎ 297-4422) is in the centre at Avenida Calógeras 30. The other office is at Avenida Atlântica 1998 (☎ 236-7475) in Copacabana.

Nordeste Linhas Aéreas (☎ 220-4366) is at Aeroporto Santos Dumont. It goes to Porto Seguro, Ilhéus and other smaller cities in the Northeast. Rio Sul (☎ 262-6911) does the same for the south and is also at Aeroporto Santos Dumont.

International airlines with offices in Rio include:

Aerolineas Argentinas
    Rua da Assembléia 100, 29th floor,
    Centro (☎ 292-4131; fax 224-4931)
Aero Peru
    Praça Mahatma Gandhi 2, Centro
    (☎ 210-3124)

Air France
    Avenida Presidente Antônio Carlos 58, 9th floor,
    Centro (☎ 212-6226; fax 532-1284)
Alitalia
    Avenida Presidente Wilson 165, 5th floor, Centro
    (☎ 240-7822; fax 240-7493)
Avianca
    Avenida Presidente Wilson 165, No 801
    (☎ 220-7697; fax 220-9848)
British Airways
    Avenida Rio Branco 108, 21st floor, Centro
    (☎ 221-0922; fax 242-2889)
Continental
    Rua da Assembléia 2316, 10th floor, Centro
    (☎ 531-1761; fax 531-1984)
Iberia
    Avenida Presidente Antônio Carlos 51, 8th floor,
    Centro (☎ 282-1336; fax 240-9842)
Japan Air Lines
    Avenida Rio Branco 156, No 2014, Centro
    (☎ 220-6414; fax 220-6091)
KLM
    Avenida Rio Branco 311A, Centro
    (☎ 292-7747; fax 240-1595)
Lan Chile
    Avenida Nilo Peçanha 50, 13th floor, Centro
    (☎ 220-9722; fax 532-1420)
LAP-Lineas Aereas Paraguayas
    Avenida Rio Branco 245, 7th floor, Centro
    (☎ 220-4148; fax 240-9577)
Lloyd Aero Boliviano
    Avenida Calógeras 30, Centro
    (☎ 220-9548; fax 533-2835)
Lufthansa
    Avenida Rio Branco 156 D, Centro
    (☎ 282-1253; fax 262-8845)
Qantas
    Avenida Ataulfo de Paiva 226, 5th floor
    (☎ 511-0045; fax 239-8349)
SAS
    Avenida Presidente Wilson 231, 6th floor, Centro
    (☎ 210-1222; fax 220-9494)
United Airlines
    Avenida Presidente Antônio Carlos, Centro
    (☎ 240-5068; fax 220-9946)

Bus From Rio there are buses to everywhere. They all leave from the loud Novo Rio Rodoviária (☎ 291-5151 for information), Avenida Francisco Bicalho in São Cristóvão, about 20 minutes north of the centre. At the rodoviária you can get information on transport and lodging if you ask at the Riotur desk on the ground floor.

Excellent buses leave every 15 minutes or so for São Paulo (six hours). Most major destinations have leito (executive) buses leaving late at night. These are very comfortable. Many travel agents in the city sell bus tickets. It's a good idea to buy a ticket a couple days in advance if you can.

National Bus Destinations & Times

Angra dos Reis	2¾ hours
Belém	60 hours
Belo Horizonte	7 hours
Brasília	18 hours
Cabo Frio	3 hours
Curitiba	11 hours
Florianópolis	20 hours
Foz do Iguaçu	22 hours
Goiânia	18 hours
Ouro Prêto	7 hours
Parati	4 hours
Petrópolis	1½ hours
Porto Alegre	27 hours
Recife	38 hours
Salvador	28 hours
São João del Rei	5½ hours
Vitória	8 hours

International Bus Destinations & Times

Asunción, Paraguay	25 hours
Buenos Aires, Argentina	46 hours
Montevideo, Uruguay	39 hours
Santiago, Chile	74 hours

Getting Around

To/From the Airport All international and nearly all domestic flights use Galeão international airport, 15 km north of the city centre on Ilha do Governador.

Aeroporto Santos Dumont is in the heart of the city on the bay. It's used for the São Paulo shuttle and some flights to a variety of other destinations like Porto Seguro or Belo Horizonte. You can take the same bus as for Galeão airport or get to the city and take a taxi, or simply walk to the airport from Centro.

Bus – air-con There are two air-con airport bus routes operating from 5.20 to 12.10 am, every 40 minutes to one hour (about US$4). One route goes to the centre and to Santos Dumont airport, the other route goes to the city centre and along the beaches of Copacabana, Ipanema, Leblon, Vidigal, and São Conrado. The driver will stop wherever you ask along the route. On both routes, you can stop at the rodoviária if you want to catch a bus out of Rio immediately. If you want to catch the metro, ask the driver to let you off right outside the entrance to Carioca metro station.

You can catch the bus on the 2nd floor (arrivals) of the main terminal, at the Galeão sign. The tourist desk inside the airport has schedule and price information. If you're heading to the airport you can get the bus in front of the major hotels along the beach, but you have to look alive and flag them down. The bus company is Empresa Real. Galeão should be written on the direction sign.

It is safer to catch one of these buses or take a taxi rather than a local bus if you have many valuables.

Bus – local On the far corner, to your right as you leave the main terminal at Galeão, there is a small terminal for local buses on Rua Ecuador. There are bus numbers and routes posted, so it's pretty easy to get oriented.

For Copacabana, the best is bus No 126, 127 or 128. The best bus to Ipanema and Leblon is No 128, but you can also take No 126 or 127 to Copacabana and then catch another bus to Ipanema and Leblon.

For the budget hotels in Catete and Glória, take bus No 170 ('Gávea – via Jóquei'), which goes down Rua do Catete and then turns up Rua Pedro Americo and along Rua Bento Lisboa. If you want the Catete budget hotels, get off at the stop near the corner of Bento Lisboa and Rua Silveira Martins and walk a block down to Rua Catete.

An alternative is to take any bus that goes to the centre on Avenida Rio Branco. Get off near the end of Avenida Rio Branco and hop on the metro. Get off the metro at Catete station, which is in the heart of the budget hotel area.

Taxi Many taxis from the airport will try to rip you off. The safe course is to take a radio-taxi, where you pay a set fare at the airport. This is also the most expensive way to go. A yellow-and-blue comum (common) taxi is about 20% cheaper if the meter is working and if you pay what is on the fare schedule. A sample fare from the airport to Copacabana is US$18 in a yellow-and-blue taxi versus US$24 in a radio-taxi. If you're entering Brazil for the first time, on a budget, a good compromise is to take a bus to somewhere near your destination and then take a short taxi ride to your hotel.

Sharing a taxi from the airport is a good idea. Taxis will take up to four people. To ensure a little bit of security, before entering the taxi at the airport you can usually get a receipt with the licence plate of your taxi and a phone number to register losses or complaints. If you're headed to Leblon or Ipanema, the Tunnel Reboucas is more direct than the beach route.

Bus The buses are a real mixture of the good, the bad and the ugly. The good: Rio's buses are fast, frequent, cheap and, because Rio is long and narrow, it's easy to get the right bus and usually no big deal if you're on the wrong one. The bad: Rio's buses are often crowded, slowed down by traffic and driven by raving maniacs who drive the buses as if they were motorbikes. The ugly: Rio's buses are the scene of many of the city's robberies.

Don't carry any valuables on the buses. Don't advertise being a foreigner, and do have your money ready when you enter the bus. Be particularly cautious if you're boarding a bus in a tourist area. If you feel paranoid about something on the bus, get off and catch another.

In addition to their number, buses have their destinations, including the areas they go through, written on the side. Nine out of 10 buses going south from the centre will go to Copacabana and vice versa. All buses have the price displayed above the head of the money collector. The buses you need to catch for specific destinations are listed under individual sights.

There are also special air-conditioned buses (see To/From the Airport). The Castelo-Hotel Nacional and Castelo-São Conrado buses are good to take for Pepino beach. From the Castelo station there are buses to Petrópolis and Terosópolis, which saves a trip out to the rodoviária. There is an open-air tourist bus that goes along the beaches and then over to Pão de Açúcar.

If you're staying in the Catete/Flamengo area and want to get to the beaches by bus, you can either walk to the main roadway along Parque do Flamengo and take any bus marked 'Copacabana' or you can walk to Largo do Machado and take the No 570 bus.

Train The train station, Estação Dom Pedro II, is at Praça Cristiano Ottoni on Avenida Presidente Vargas. To get there take the metro to Central station.

Metro Rio's excellent subway system is limited to points north of Botafogo and is open from 6 am to 11 pm daily, except Sunday. The two air-con lines are cleaner, faster and cheaper than buses (discounts are offered with multiple tickets). The main line from Botafogo to Saens Pena has 15 stops, of which the first 12 are: Botafogo, Flamengo, Largo do Machado, Catete, Glória, Cinelândia, Carioca, Uruguiana, Presidente Vargas, Central, Cidade Nova and Estácio, which is common to both lines. At Estácio the lines split: the main line continues west towards the neighbourhood of Andarai, making stops at Afonso Pena, Engenho Velho and Tijuca, and the secondary line goes north towards Maracanã stadium and beyond. The main stops for Centro are Cinelândia and Carioca.

Taxi Rio's taxis are quite reasonably priced, if you're dividing the fare with a friend or two. Taxis are particularly useful late at night and when carrying valuables, but they are not a completely safe and hassle-free ride. First, there have been a few rare cases of people being assaulted and robbed by taxi drivers. Second, and much more common, the drivers have a tendency to exaggerate fares.

Here's how the taxi is supposed to operate: there should be a meter and it should work; there should be a current tabela to determine the fare; upon reaching your destination, check the meter and look that up on the tabela, usually posted on the passenger window, which is used to determine the fare.

Now, what to watch out for: most importantly, make sure the meter works. If it doesn't, ask to be let out of the cab. The meters have a flag that switches the meter rate; this should be in the number one position (20% less expensive), except on Sunday, holidays, evenings between 10 pm and 6 am, and when driving outside the zona sul (some taxis will switch to the high rate near the airport, which is legal). Make sure meters are cleared before you start (find out the current starting number). Make sure the tabela is original, not a photocopy. The taxi drivers that hang out near the hotels are sharks. It's worth walking a block to avoid them. Most people don't tip taxi drivers, although it's common to round off the fare to the higher number.

The meters are weighted towards distance not time. This gives the drivers an incentive to drive quickly (for a head rush tell your driver that you are in a bit of a hurry) and travel by roundabout routes. Taxis don't always run during thunderstorms because alcohol-powered cars stall easily in the wet, but buses usually plough on ahead. It's

illegal for cabs to take more than four passengers. This is, of course, irrelevant except for the fact that most cabs won't do it because of conventions of the trade.

The white radio-taxis (☎ 260-2022) are 30% more expensive than the comums, but they will come to you and they are safer.

Car Car rental agencies can be found at the airport or clustered together on Avenida Princesa Isabel in Copacabana. There doesn't seem to be much price competition between the companies. Prices are not cheap, at about US$70 a day, but they go down a bit in the off season. When they give prices on the phone the agencies usually leave out the cost of insurance, which is mandatory. Most agencies will let you drop off their cars in another city without an extra charge.

Motorcycle Mar e Moto (☎ 2744398) rents motorcycles but it is cheaper to rent a car. It's in Leblon at Avenida Bartolomeu Mitre 1008.

Walking For God's sake be careful! Drivers run red lights, run up on footpaths and stop for no one and nothing.

Rio de Janeiro State

The small state of Rio de Janeiro offers the traveller much more than just the cidade maravilhosa. Within four hours of travel from any point in the state, and often much less, are beaches, mountains and forests that equal any in Brazil. Many of these places offer more intimate settings in which to meet Cariocas who have known about the natural wonders surrounding the city for years. You won't find virgin sites, as you will in the Northeast – tourism here is fairly developed and prices are higher than in most of Brazil. But if you have only a couple of weeks in Brazil and think that you'll be returning some day, an itinerary that covers the entire state of Rio would be one of the best possible. For those with all the time in the world, it's easy to pass a month or two here.

Rio de Janeiro state, which lies just above the Tropic of Capricorn, has an area of 44,268 sq km – about the size of Switzerland – and a population of more than 14 million. The littoral is backed by steep mountains, which descend into the sea around the border with São Paulo and gradually rise slightly further inland in the north. This forms a thin strip of land nestled between the lush green mountains and the emerald sea, with beaches that are the most visually spectacular in Brazil.

Divided by the city of Rio and the giant Baía de Guanabara, which has 131 km of coast and 113 islands, there are two coastal regions, each with somewhat different natural characteristics: the Costa Verde (to the west) and the Costa do Sol (to the east).

Along the Costa Verde, where the mountains kiss the sea, there are hundreds of islands, including Ilha Grande and the Restinga de Marambaia, which make for easy swimming and boating. The calm waters and the natural ports and coves allowed safe passage to the Portuguese ships that came to Parati to transport sugar cane, and later gold, to Europe. They also protected pirates, who found a safe haven on Ilha Grande.

Beaches wait to be explored, particularly further away from Rio city, where the coastal road stays close to the ocean and the views are spectacular. The most famous spots are Angra dos Reis, Parati and Ilha Grande.

To the east, the mountains begin to rise further inland. The littoral is filled with lagoons and swamp land. Stretching away from the coast are *campos* (plains) which extend about 30 km to the mountains. Búzios and Cabo Frio, famous for their beauty and luxury, are only two hours from Rio by car. Saquarema, one of Brazil's best surfing beaches, is even closer.

Driving due north from Rio city, you pass through the city's industrial and motel sections and soon reach a wall of jungled mountains. After the climb, you're in the cool Serra dos Órgãos. The resort cities of Petrópolis and Teresópolis are nearby, and many smaller villages offer Cariocas an escape from the tropical summer heat. The fantastic peaks of the Parque Nacional da Serra dos Órgãos, outside Teresópolis, provide superb hiking and climbing opportunities.

The other mountain region where Cariocas play is the Itatiaia area, in the corner of the state that borders São Paulo and Minas Gerais. Getting there takes only four hours, the route passing near the steel city of Volta Redonda.

Indian Names

Many place names in Rio state are derived from Indian words. Among them are:

Araruama – place where the macaw eats
Baré – in the middle of many fish
Cunhambebe – women who speak too much
Grataú – ghost's den
Grumari – a kind of tree
Guanabara – arm of the sea
Guaratiba – place with much sun or place with many holes
Ipanema – place that gives bad luck or place of dangerous sea
Itacuruçá – stone's cross
Itaipu – stone that the sea hits
Itaipuaçu – little Itaipu
Jabaquara – crack in the earth

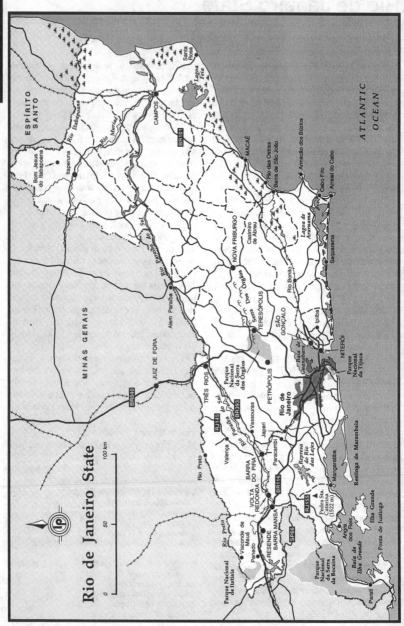

Rio de Janeiro State

Jeribá – a kind of coconut palm
Mangaratiba – banana orchard
Maricá – belly
Parati – a kind of fish
Paratininga – dry fish
Sapeca – burned
Saquarema – lagoon without shells
Tijuca – putrid-smelling swamp

West of Rio de Janeiro

ILHA GRANDE

Ilha Grande is what Hawaii must have been like before the arrival of the British. It's all tropical beach and jungle, with only three towns on the island. Freguesia de Santana is a small hamlet with no regular accommodation. Parnaioca has a few homes by a lovely strip of beach near the old prison. Abraão has plenty of pousadas and camping grounds, and ferry connections to Mangaratiba and Angra dos Reis.

If you really want to get away from it all, Ilha Grande may well be the place to go. The options are pretty attractive. You can rent a boat in Abraão for US$8 per hour and buzz around to Freguesia or Parnaioca. There are trails through the lush, steamy jungle to various beaches around the island. For instance, it is a 2½-hour trek to Praia Lopes Mendes, claimed by some to be Brazil's most beautiful beach. Praia de Parnaioca also ranks up there. And these are just two of the island's 102 beaches!

Vila do Abraão

Abraão could be a movie set for *Papillon*. It has a gorgeous, palm-studded beachfront of pale, faded homes, and a tidy white church. Not far away are the ruins of an old prison that will still give you the creeps if you go inside.

As a base on Ilha Grande, you can not go past Abraão, and not many do. It's a popular

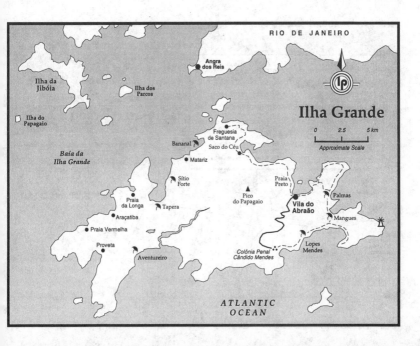

weekend destination for young Cariocas, so things get pretty busy then, but during the week it's very peaceful. It's OK to rouse the dogs sleeping on the dirt and cobblestone streets. They're friendly, and seem to enjoy tramping around the island to the abandoned penitentiary, the beaches, the forest, the hills and the waterfalls.

Orientation

To the left of the dock (when you're facing the ocean) in Abraão are the ferry ticket office, a guesthouse for military police, the road to Praia Preta and the trail to the ruined old prison. To the right of the dock is the cobblestoned Rua da Igreja, and at the far end of the beach, a clockwise trail leads around the island to Praia Lopes Mendes and the other beaches of Ilha Grande.

Information

Tourist Office There's a tourist information booth close to the dock that opens when the ferries arrive. Staff speak only Portuguese, but have useful information on available accommodation and island activities. The tourist office in Angra dos Reis also has information about Ilha Grande.

Money Change money before you get to Ilha Grande. The top-end hotels, tourist stores and the Banco do Brasil branch will usually change cash dollars, but for anything else, you'll need to go back to the mainland.

Places to Stay

Cheap lodging on Ilha Grande is not difficult to find. There are expensive hotels and cheap to mid-range pousadas on the island, and a few campgrounds in Abraão.

The cheapest option is to camp. *Camping Renato*, up a small path beside Dona Penha's, has well-drained, secure sites and basic facilities, as well as an on-site café and

PLACES TO STAY

6 Hotel Mar da Tranquilidade
12 Camping das Palmeiras
13 Dona Penha's
14 Hotel Alpino
15 Pousada Tropicana
17 Cerca Viva
20 Youth Hostel

PLACES TO EAT

1 Casa da Mulata
5 Bar do Carlinhos

7 Bar Casarão da Ilha
10 Restaurante da Janeth
11 Pizzaria Juan Lorenzo

OTHER

2 Post Office
3 Ferry Dock
4 Tourist Information Booth
8 Igreja de São Sebastião
9 Telephones
16 Dive Gear Rental
18 Mercado
19 Assembléia de Deus

Vila do Abraão

Ferry To Angra
Ferry To Mangaratiba

To Palmas & Lopes Mendes

0   50   100 m

Approximate Scale

Praia do Canto

Rua Getúlio Vargas

To Praia Preto, Cachoeira & Aqueduto

To Colonia Penal

bar. They charge US$2 per person. Other campgrounds include *Das Palmeiras*, which is also close to Dona Penha's, and *Cerca Viva* (☎ 551-2336), a campground and pousada combined. In a secure spot at Rua Getúlio Vargas 351, they rent small on-site tents for US$18/24 for two days. Quartos are US$32 a double for two days and apartamentos cost US$43 for two days. Prices go down if you stay longer.

The youth hostel, *Ilha Grande* (☎ (021) 264-6147), at Getúlio Vargas 13, is a good option here. It's well located, with friendly staff, and costs US$7/10 for members/non-members. Reservations are a good idea, especially on weekends and holidays.

Most of the pousadas in Abraão cost between US$30 and US$40 a double. A good option is the *Tropicana* (☎ 335-4572), at Rua da Praia 28. It's a very nice place, run by a French/Brazilian couple, and has singles/doubles for US$30/40.

At right angles to the beachfront, Rua da Igreja is the second-most important street on the island. It features a white church, a few bars and the *Hotel Mar da Tranquilidade* (☎ 288-4162, or for reservations from Rio (021) 392-8475). The hotel has charming but expensive doubles with hot showers for US$60, including breakfast and lunch. Singles are US$30. Around the corner, in Rua Getúlio Vargas, the *Hotel Alpino* (☎ (011) 229-1190) is in a beautiful garden setting. Doubles are US$30 outside the tourist season.

Just before the Alpino is *Penhas*, the house of Dona Penha. Look for the yellow gate on the right-hand side. Dona Penha has gone up-market in the last few years, with singles/doubles going for US$20/25. Ilha Grande's most expensive hotel is the *Paraiso do Sol* (☎ (021) 263-6126), minutes away by boat or two hours away on foot from Abraão, at Praia das Palmas, on the trail to Praia Lopes Mendes. Doubles with full board are US$200.

Places to Eat

Restaurante de Janeth is a decent place which serves prato feitos with abundant por-tions of fresh fish (US$4). It's just around the corner from the church. *Casa da Mulata*, on the way to the old prison, also has good prato feitos (US$3). There are also lots of places along the beachfront.

Getting There & Away

Catch a Conerj ferry from either Manga-ratiba or Angra dos Reis. If you take the 5.30 am bus from Rio to Mangaratiba, you can catch the ferry that runs daily at 8.30 am from Mangaratiba to Abraão. There are five buses a day from Rio to Mangaratiba: at 6 and 9 am, and 12.30, 3 and 7 pm. Outgoing bus schedules are similarly staggered, but they begin half an hour earlier.

The boat returns from Abraão to Manga-ratiba at 4.30 pm on Monday, Wednesday and Friday, on Tuesday and Thursday at 11 am and on Saturday and Sunday at 4 pm. Mangaratiba is nothing more than a poor little fishing town. If you're stuck there, you can stay at the *Hotel Rio Branco*, a small and dumpy place near the main square, which offers US$12 doubles (US$18 with private bath).

The ferry from Angra dos Reis to Abraão leaves at 4 pm on Monday, Wednesday and Friday, returning from Abraão at 10.15 am on the same days. It's a 1½-hour, US$5 ride. If you miss the ferry, you can hire a fishing boat to the island (about US$30) from either Mangaratiba or Angra.

ANGRA DOS REIS

Angra dos Reis is a base for nearby islands and beaches, not a tourist attraction in itself. The savage beauty of the tropical, fjord-like coastline along this stretch of BR-101 has been badly blemished by industrialisation. Supertankers dock in Angra's port, a rail line connects Angra to the steel town of Volta Redonda, there's a Petrobras oil refinery, and, thanks to the military government and the International Monetary Fund (IMF), a controversial nuclear power plant has been built nearby.

The closest beaches to Angra are at Praia Grande and Vila Velha. Take the 'Vila Velha' municipal bus.

Information

Tourist Office The Centro de Informações Turísticas is in Largo da Lapa, right across from the bus station. Staff have information about places to stay on Ilha Grande. There's another tourist information booth close to the waterfront, with the same information.

Money Cambisul câmbio, in Travessa Santa Luzia, changes cash. The Banco do Brasil changes travellers' cheques.

Post & Telephone The post office is just behind the tourist office, in Praça Lopes Trovão. Long-distance telephone calls can be made from Avenida Raul Pompéia 97, right next to the Hotel Londres.

Places to Stay

There are no real cheapies here. The best budget bet is the central *Porto Rico* (☎ 65-0992), at Rua Colonel Carvalho 54. Small apartamentos with fan but without breakfast go for US$12/16 a single/double. The *Cherry Hotel*, at Rua Peroia Peixoto 64, is in the heart of Angra, off Rua Coronel Carvalho. It charges US$35 per person without breakfast. The *Pousada Praia Grande* (☎ 65-0605), at Estrada do Contorno 1890, Praia Grande, Angra dos Reis, is on the right-hand side, 200 metres before the Angra Inn. Take the 'Vila Velha' bus from the rodoviária. The hotel has a nice courtyard, and classy doubles for US$30.

The *Palace Hotel* (☎ 65-0032), at Rua Coronel Carvalho 275, is a clean, three-star Embratur hotel with TV, air-con, telephone and hot water. Doubles cost US$50.

Places to Eat

A couple of good seafood places are *Taberna 33* and *Costa Verde*, almost next door to one another near the corner of Rua Coronel Carvalho and Rua Raul Pompéia. If your budget doesn't run to seafood, there's *Pastelaria Verolme* on the corner of Travessa Santa Luzia near the waterfront. Their fresh pasteis washed down with caldo da cana (sugar-cane juice) are excellent.

Getting There & Away

Angra dos Reis is almost three hours (150 km) from Rio de Janeiro's Novo Rio bus station. Buses to Rio leave Angra every hour from 4.30 am to 9 pm (US$7). To Parati, there are six buses a day, the first leaving at 6 am (US$5, two hours).

PARATI

Oh! Deus, se na terra houvesse um paraíso, não seria muito longe daqui!
(Oh! God, if there were a paradise on earth, it wouldn't be very far from here!)
Amerigo Vespucci

Amerigo was referring to steep, jungled mountains that seem to leap into the sea, a scrambled shoreline with hundreds of islands and jutting peninsulas, and the clear, warm waters of the Baía da Ilha Grande, as calm as an empty aquarium. All this still exists, if no longer in a pristine state, along with one of Brazil's most enchanting towns – the colonial village of Parati, which Amerigo did not get to enjoy.

Parati is both a great colonial relic, well preserved and architecturally unique, and a launching pad for a dazzling section of the Brazilian coastline. The buildings are marked by simple lines that draw the eye to the general rather than the specific, and earthy colours and textures that magnify, through contrast, the natural beauty that envelops the town. So while the individual buildings in Parati may well be beautiful, the town when viewed as a whole is truly a work of art.

Dozens of secluded beaches are within a couple of hours of Parati by boat or bus. There are good swimming beaches close to town, but the best are along the coast toward São Paulo, and out on the bay islands.

One of the most popular spots between Rio and São Paulo, Parati is crowded and lively throughout the summer holidays, brimming with Brazilian and Argentine holiday-makers, and good music. That the town is all tourism there is no doubt; there are so many boutiques and so few cheap places to eat and sleep. But if you get around these obstacles, Parati is a delight, and there are plenty of beaches to accommodate all visitors.

History

Parati was inhabited by the Guianas Indians when Portuguese from the capitania of São Vicente settled here in the early part of the 16th century. With the discovery of gold in Minas Gerais at the end of the 17th century, Parati became an obligatory stopover for those coming from Rio de Janeiro, as it was the only point where the escarpment of the Serra do Mar could be scaled. The precarious

road was an old Guianas Indian trail that cut past the Serra do Facão (nowadays Cunha, São Paulo) to the valley of Paraíba and from there to Pindamonhangaba, Guaratinguetá and then the mines.

Parati became a busy, important port as miners and supplies disembarked for the gold mines and gold was shipped to Europe. The small town prospered and, as always, the wealthy built churches to prove it. There was so much wealth in Parati that in 1711, Captain Francisco do Amaral Gurgel sailed from Parati to save Rio de Janeiro from a threatened French siege by handing over a

PLACES TO STAY
1 Pousada Familiar
4 Pousada Marendaz
6 Hotel Coxixo
9 Pousada do Seu Walter
12 Pousada da Matriz
15 Hotel Solar dos Gerânios
25 Hotel Estalagem
27 Hotel/Restaurante
   Santa Rita
29 Pousada Pardeiro
34 Pousada do Ouro

PLACES TO EAT
18 Hiltinho
19 Pizza Bucaneiros
22 Vagalume
24 Café Paraty
26 Version Française

32 Chez Regine
33 Txai Café

OTHER
2 Rodoviária
3 Banco do Brasil
5 Mercado
7 Centro de Informações
   Turísticas
8 Parati Tours
10 Post Office
11 Capela do Propósito
13 Matriz NS dos Remédios
14 Praça Matriz
16 Bar da Terra

17 Taberna Pub
20 Igreja NS do Rosário
21 Telephones
23 Banco do Brasil
28 Igreja Santa Rita
30 Secretária de Turismo
31 Mercado
35 Capela de NS das Dores
36 Forte Defensor Perpétuo

BAÍA
DE
PARATI

Parati

0   50   100 m

ransom of 1000 crates of sugar, 200 head of cattle and 610,000 gold cruzados.

Parati's glory days didn't last long. After the 1720s, a new road from Rio to Minas Gerais via the Serra dos Órgãos cut 15 days off the route from Parati and the town started to decline. In the 19th century, the local economy revived with the coffee boom, and now, with the recent construction of the road from Rio, the town's coffers are once again being filled. Parati is also renowned for its excellent cachaça.

The town is easy to look around: just walk on the *pes-de-moleque* (street urchins' feet), the local name for the irregular cobblestone streets, washed clean by the rains and high tides. It's a couple of km off the Rio to Santos highway, at the south-west corner of Rio de Janeiro state. Until 1954 the only access to Parati was by sea. In that year a road was built through the steep Serra do Mar, passing the town of Cunha, 47 km inland. In 1960 the coastal road from Rio, 253 km away, was extended to Parati, and beyond to São Paulo, 330 km away.

Climate

Like Rio, Parati gets hot and muggy in the summer. The rains are most frequent in November, January and May. Be ready for plenty of nasty mosquitoes.

Orientation

Parati is small and easy to find your way around, but one thing that becomes confusing is street names and house numbers. Many streets have more than one name, which has the locals, as well as the tourists, thoroughly perplexed. The house-numbering system seems totally random.

Information

Tourist Office The Centro de Informações Turísticas (☎ 71-1266, ext 20), on Avenida Roberto Silveira, is open daily from 7 am to 7 pm. The Secretária de Turismo e Cultura (☎ 71-1256), in the Antigo Quartel do Forte, near the port, is open daily from 8 am to 6 pm.

Parati Tours (☎ & fax 71-1327) is located at Avenida Roberto Silveira 11, just before you hit the colonial part of town. It's also useful for information. Their five-hour schooner cruises are US$18 (US$30 with lunch). They also rent bicycles (US$2.50 an hour, or US$10 per day).

Money The Banco do Brasil is on Avenida Roberto Silveira, and changes cash and travellers' cheques between 11 am and 2.30 pm. Don't get in line; go straight to the manager's desk.

Post & Telephone The post office is on the corner of Rua da Cadeia and Beco do Propósito. The Telerj stations are in front of the Centro de Informações Turísticas and at Rua Dr Samuel Costa 29.

Churches

Parati's 18th-century prosperity is reflected in its beautiful old homes and churches. Three main churches were used to separate the races – NS do Rosário for slaves, Santa Rita for freed mulattos and NS das Dores for the white élite.

The Igreja NS do Rosário e São Benedito dos Homens Pretos (1725), on Rua Dr Samuel Costa, was built by and for slaves. Renovated in 1857, the church has gilded wooden altars dedicated to Our Lady of the Rosary, St Benedict and St John. The pineapple crystals are for prosperity and good luck.

Igreja Santa Rita dos Pardos Libertos (1722), on Praça Santa Rita, has a tiny museum of sacred art, and some fine woodwork on the doorways and altars. Capela de NS das Dores (1800), Rua Dr Pereira, was renovated in 1901. The cemetery is fashioned after the catacombs.

Matriz NS dos Remédios (1787), on Praça Mons Hélio Pires, was built on the site of two 17th-century churches. Inside there is art from past and contemporary local artists. According to legend, construction of the church was financed by a pirate treasure hidden on Praia da Trindade.

ANDREW DRAFFEN

GREG CAIRE

JOHN MAIER, JR

Top: A view of Niterói
Middle: Wading near Trinidade
Bottom: Low tide at Parati

GREG CAIRE

JOHN MAIER, JR

ANDREW DRAFFEN

JOHN MAIER, JR

Top Left:	Caverna do Santana
Top Right:	Sunbathing in downtown São Paulo
Bottom Left:	Serro, Minas Gerais
Bottom Right:	Vaqueiros, São Paulo state

Forte Defensor Perpétuo

The Forte Defensor Perpétuo was built in 1703 to defend from pirate attacks the gold being exported from Minas Gerais. The fort was rebuilt in 1822, the year of Brazil's independence, and was named after Emperor Dom Pedro I. It's on the Morro da Vila Velha, the hill just past Praia do Pontal, a 20-minute walk north of town. The fort houses the Casa de Artista e Centro de Artes e Tradições Populares de Parati.

Beaches & Islands

The closest fine beaches on the coast – Vermelha, Lulas and Saco – are about an hour away by boat (camping is allowed on the beaches). The best island beaches nearby are probably Araújo and Sapeca, but many of the islands have rocky shores and are private. The mainland beaches tend to be better. These beaches are all small and idyllic; most have a barraca (serving beer and fish) and, at most, a handful of beachgoers.

Parati has 65 islands and 300 beaches in its vicinity. Whatever the count, there are enough. Following this is a list of the most accessible beaches north of town. Don't limit yourself to this list, as there are plenty more to be found. If you do come across any really special beaches and you can bear to share your secret, we'd love to know about them. See the Getting Around section for information on how to get to the less accessible beaches.

Praia do Pontal On the other side of the canal, 10 minutes away on foot, is Parati's city beach. There are several barracas and a lively crowd, but the beach itself is not attractive and the water gets dirty.

Praia do Forte On the side of the hill, hidden by the rocks, Praia do Forte is the cleanest beach within a quick walk of the city. It is relatively secluded and frequented by a youngish crowd.

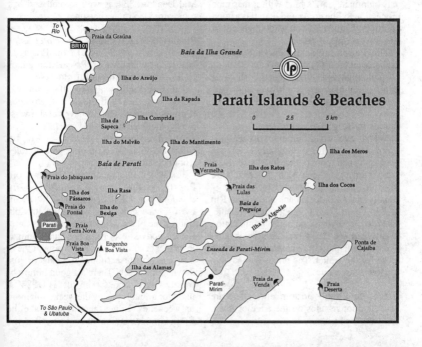

THE SOUTHEAST

Praia do Jabaquara Continue on the dirt road north past Praia do Pontal, over the hill, for two km to Praia do Jabaquara, a big, spacious beach with great views in all directions. There is a small restaurant, and a campground that's better than those in town. The sea is very shallow, so it's possible to wade way out into the bay.

Festivals

Parati is known for its colourful and distinctive festivals. The two most important are the Festa do Divino Espírito Santo, which begins nine days before Pentecostal Sunday, and the NS dos Remédios, on 8 September. The former is planned throughout the year and features all sorts of merrymaking, revolving around the *fólios*, musical groups that go from door to door singing and joking.

The Festas Juninas, held during the month of June, are filled with dances, including the *xiba* (a circle clog dance) and the *ciranda* (a xiba with guitar accompaniment). The festivals culminate on 29 June with a maritime procession to Ilha do Araújo. Parati is a good option for Carnival if you want to get out of Rio for a couple of days.

The Parati region produces excellent cachaça, and in 1984 the town council, in its wisdom, inaugurated the annual Festival da Pinga. The pinga party is held over an August weekend.

Places to Stay

Parati has two very different tourist seasons. From about October to February hotels get booked up and room prices double, so reservations are a good idea. Many places require the full amount to be paid in advance – usually placed in their bank account in Rio or São Paulo. This is often nonrefundable. The rest of the year, finding accommodation is easy and not expensive, the town is quiet and some of the boutiques and restaurants close for the winter. The prices quoted here are low-season rates.

Places to Stay – bottom end There are several campgrounds on the edge of town, just over the bridge.

The *Pousada Familiar* (☎ 71-1475), at Rua José Vieira Ramos 262, is close to the bus station and charges US$9 per person, including a good breakfast. It's a friendly place, run by Lúcia, a Brazilian, and her Belgian husband, Joseph. Joseph speaks English, French, German, Spanish and, of course, Flemish, and is very helpful. The pousada also has clothes-washing facilities.

Another recommended place is the *Pousada Marendaz* (☎ 71-1369), at Rua Dr Derly Ellena 9. Run by Rachel and her four sisters, it's more of a family home than a hotel. They charge US$10 per person. Another cheapie is the *Pousada do Seu Walter* (☎ 712-341), at Rua Marechal Deodoro 489. Simple apartamentos without breakfast are US$8 per head.

The *Hotel Estalagem* (☎ 71-1626), on Rua da Matriz, charges US$20/30 a single/double. Ask for the room upstairs – it has a great view. They also have kayaks for rent. The *Pousada da Matriz* (☎ 71-1610), at Rua Mal Deodoro 334, is well located and has rooms for US$15 per person.

Places to Stay – middle The *Hotel Solar dos Gerânios* (☎ 71-1550), on Praça da Matriz (also known as Praça Monsenhor Hélio Pires), is a beautiful old hotel with wood and ceramic sculptures, flat brick and stone, rustic heavy furniture and *azulejos* (Portuguese tiles). Rooms have hot showers. Singles/doubles start as low as US$15/25.

The *Bela Vista* (☎ 71-1429), at Rua do Comércio 46, is a good choice, with doubles from US$35 to US$40.

Located in the mountains, 16 km from Parati, is the *Hotel Fazenda le Gite d'Indaiatiba* (☎ 71-1218; fax 71-2188). Run by a French guy (if you have any trouble finding the place, ask for the French's hotel – everybody knows it), it has small bungalows in a beautiful setting with a great view. You can go horse riding, trekking or just down to the beach. There's a good library of mostly French books. The cost is US$40 a night for a double during the week, a bit more on weekends. To get there by bus, take the Barra Grande via Grauna and get off at the last stop in Grauna. By car, head toward Rio for 12 km, then turn off at the Fazenda Grauna road and follow it for four km.

Places to Stay – top end There are three splendid, four-star colonial pousadas in Parati. Owned by a famous Brazilian actor, the *Pousada Pardeiro* (☎ 71-1370; fax 71-1139), at Rua do Comércio 74, has a tranquil garden setting, refined service and impeccable decor. This is one of the best pousadas in Brazil, with single/double rooms going for US$80/100.

The *Hotel Coxixo* (☎ 71-1460; fax 71-1568), at Rua do Comércio 362, is just a notch below the Pousada Pardeiro, but they have some standard rooms that are a good deal at US$40. The pousada is cosy and colonial, with beautiful gardens and a pool, and the rooms are simple but comfortable and pretty. To get the US$40 doubles, make reservations early; most doubles go for US$70.

The *Pousada do Ouro* (☎ 71-2033; fax 71-1311), at Rua da Praia 145, is the kind of place you can imagine bumping into Mick Jagger, Sonia Braga, Tom Cruise or Marcello Mastroianni, especially when you enter the hotel lobby and see photos of them posing in front of the pousada. The hotel has everything – bar, pool and a good restaurant. Doubles cost US$85 to US$105.

Places to Eat
Parati has many pretty restaurants, and all seem to charge too much. To beat the inflated prices in the old part of town, try the sandwiches at the lanchonete on Praça da Matriz.

The best restaurants in the old town include the *Galeria do Engenho*, at Rua da Lapa, which serves large and juicy steaks for US$10, and *Vagalume*, at Rua da Ferraria. *Hiltinho*, Rua da Cadeia, at the edge of the Praça da Matriz, is more expensive, but there's a good menu and it serves ample portions. Another recommended restaurant is *Pizzaria Bucaneiros*, on Rua Dr Samuel Costa. They have tasty pizzas.

Entertainment
Café Parati, a popular hang-out on the corner of Rua do Comércio and Rua da Lapa, has become very up-market. Bar Dinho, at the corner of Rua da Matriz and Praça da Matriz, has a young, hip crowd and a good atmosphere. They have a cover charge of around US$5 for the music (it just appears on your bill). Bar da Terra, over the bridge, gets pretty lively, and the Taberna Pub, near the Hiltinho restaurant, is the place to hear some jazz. Or just wander the streets and you'll hear some music, outside at the restaurants by the canal or inside one of the bars.

Getting There & Away
The rodoviária (☎ 71-1186) is on the main road into town, Rua Roberto Silveira, half a km up from the old town.

There are six daily buses from Parati to Rio; it's a four-hour trip, with the first bus leaving at 3.30 am and the last at 8 pm. Buses leave Rio for Parati at 6 and 9 am, and 12.30, 3, 6.20 and 8 pm. It's a US$10 trip.

Eighteen buses a day go from Parati to Angra dos Reis, the first leaving at 5 am and the last at 7.20 pm (US$3, two hours). There are two daily buses (at 11 am and 11.30 pm) for São Paulo (six hours). Three daily buses go to Ubatuba (at 7 am, noon and 7 pm), and three more go to Cunha.

Getting Around
To visit the less-accessible beaches, many tourists take one of the schooners from the docks. Departure times vary with the season, but the information is easy to get hold of. Tickets cost US$18 per person, with lunch served on board for an additional US$12. The boats make three beach stops of about 45 minutes each.

An alternative is to rent one of the many small motorboats at the port. For US$10 per hour (more in the summer), the skipper will take you where you want to go. Bargaining is difficult, but you can lower the cost by finding travelling companions and renting bigger boats – they hold six to 12 passengers.

If you figure on a one-hour boat ride and an hour at the beach, you need to rent a boat for a minimum of three hours. Of course, there are even more beautiful beaches further away.

The strategy of the boat skippers, since they usually can't return to port for another boatload, is to keep you out as long as possible. So don't be surprised if the first beach you go to is out of beer, or the next beach would be much more pleasant because of its cleaner water. These can be very compelling reasons not to return as scheduled, but paradise has a price.

AROUND PARATI
Praia Barra Grande

About 20 km up the Rio to Santos highway, Barra Grande is an easy-to-reach alternative to the beaches in Baía de Parati. There are 11 municipal buses a day leaving from Parati, the first at 7.10 am.

Praia de Parati-Mirim

For accessibility, cost and beauty, this beach is hard to beat. Parati-Mirim is a small town 27 km from Parati. The beach has barracas and houses to rent. From Parati, it's a couple of hours by boat. If you're on a budget, catch a municipal bus, which makes the 40-minute trip for only US$0.50. Get the 'Parati Mirim' bus from the rodoviária at 6.50 am, or 1 or 4.40 pm.

Praia do Sono

They don't get much prettier than this beach. Past Ponta Negra on the coast going south, about 40 km from Parati, Praia do Sono can have rough water and is sometimes difficult to land on. It's a four to five-hour boat ride. The much cheaper alternative is to take the Laranjeiras bus from Parati, then get directions in Laranjeiras for the 1½-hour walk to Sono. Buses leave Parati at 5.15 am, and 12.30 and 6.40 pm. There's food but no formal lodging at the beach.

Praia da Trindade

About five km before Sono, this is another beautiful beach. It has lots of simple pousadas, so you can stay here for a night or two. The beach is accessible by boat, as well

as by the same bus as for Praia do Sono. Ask the driver to let you off at the entrance to Trindade. From the bus stop, it's a four-km downhill walk.

Inland

The old gold route, now the road to Cunha (six km), is a magnificent jungle ride up the escarpment. The steep, dirt part of the road gets treacherous in the rain. Catch the 'Cunha' bus.

Take the 'Ponte Branca' bus from Parati to the Igrejinha da Penha, a small, triple-turreted hillside church. You'll find a 750-metre jungle trail to a beautiful waterfall and water slide. Buses charge US$0.25 for the round trip, and leave at 5.45, 9 and 11.30 am, and 2 and 6 pm.

Fazenda Bananal-Engenho de Murycana is four km off the Parati to Cunha road, 10 km from town. It's a touristy spot with an old sugar mill, a restaurant, a zoo, and free samples of cachaça and batidas.

Parque Nacional da Serra da Bocaina

On the border between Rio and São Paulo, where the mountains of the Serra do Mar meet the sea, is the Parque Nacional da Serra da Bocaina. Rising from sea level to the 2132-metre Pico da Boa Vista, the park contains a mixture of vegetation, from Mata Atlântica in the lower altitudes to Mata Araucária (pine forests) and windswept grassy plateaus in the higher altitudes.

Wildlife is plentiful and includes a large population of the rare spider monkey, as well as other monkeys such as the howler and ringtailed. Other animal species include the tree porcupine, sloth, deer, tapir, giant anteater and the otter. Birds found in the park include the harpy and black-hawk eagles and the black-beaked toucan.

Places to Stay The park possesses no tourist infrastructure, but there is an expensive hotel near the park: the *Pousada Vale dos Veados* (☎ (0125) 77-1192), which charges US$80 a double. Reservations are necessary.

Getting There & Away Travellers going

from Parati to Cunha actually pass through the southern end of the park. If you have a car and are driving in from the coast, take the Cunha-Campos Novo road to the park. If you're coming from the Rio-São Paulo Dutra (multilane highway), turn off at Queluz and drive for 37 km, passing through the town of Areias and continuing on to São José dos Barreiros, the closest town to the park. In São José, contact M W Trekking (☎ (0125) 77-1178), on the main square. It's run by José Milton, an enthusiastic guy who speaks English. He has lots of different programmes into the Serra da Bocaina, including the three-day trek down the old *trilha de ouro* (gold route) to the coast. Call for details and to make reservations. The three-day trek costs US$130, all inclusive.

The Mountains

PETRÓPOLIS

Petrópolis is a lovely mountain retreat with a decidedly European flavour. It's only 60 km from Rio de Janeiro, making it an ideal day trip. Petrópolis is where the imperial court spent the summer when Rio got too muggy, and it's still the home of the heir to the throne, Princess Isabel's grandson, 78-year-old Dom Pedro de Orleans e Bragança. He runs a real-estate business, and can often be seen riding his horse around town.

Wander around, visiting Petrópolis' attractions, or ride by horse and carriage through the city's squares and parks, past bridges, canals and old-fashioned lamps.

Information

From any newsstand or souvenir shop, you can pick up a copy of the *Guia de Petrópolis*, in Portuguese and English, for US$6. It's even sold at newsstands in Rio.

Walking Tour

This tour is around four km and takes about two hours, including time spent at the attractions. Start at the **Catedral São Pedro de Alcântara**, which houses the tombs of Dom Pedro II, Dona Teresa and Princesa Isabel.

As you leave the cathedral, turn right down Rua 13 de Maio and walk a couple of hundred metres past some crummy shops, until you reach the river. Cross over and turn left for the **Palácio Cristal**, an iron-and-glass structure built in France, then imported in 1879 to serve as an orchid hothouse. Continue down Rua Alfredo Pachá. You'll see the Bohemia beer brewery on your right. Sorry, no free samples.

Turn left again into Avenida Rui Silvera and go down to Praça Rui Barbosa. Cut across the park to the right, and up towards the pink university building with the floral clock in front. Next door, perched up high, is the **Casa de Santos Dumont**, the interesting summer home of Brazil's father of aviation. It's open Tuesday to Sunday from 9 am to 5 pm. Go in and have a look.

As you leave, turn right and start walking uphill, then turn right at the first street on your right. There's a sign advertising the Hotel Margaridas. Keep walking uphill, always taking the right fork, until you reach the **Trono de Fátima**, a 3.5-metre sculpture of NS de Fátima Madonna, imported from Italy. From here you have a great view of the town and surrounding hills.

Head back down the hill, past the university and through Praça Rui Barbosa (you may want to grab a drink in the park), then along Avenida Koeller, where you'll pass some fine mansions. Turn right at Avenida Tiradentes and make your way up to Petrópolis' main attraction, the **Museu Imperial**, housed in the perfectly preserved and impeccably appointed palace of Dom Pedro II. One interesting exhibit is the 1720-gram imperial crown, with its 639 diamonds and 77 pearls. The museum is open Tuesday to Sunday from noon to 5.30 pm; it costs US$0.30 to get in.

Places to Stay

The *Hotel Comércio* (☎ 42-3500), at Rua Dr Porciúncula 56, is directly across from the rodoviária. Quartos are clean and cheap, at

US$5/7 for singles/doubles. Apartamentos cost US$14/18 a single/double.

If you want to spend a bit more money, both the *Hotel York* (☎ 43-2662), at Rua do Imperador 78, and the *Casablanca Palace* (☎ 42-0162), at Rua 16 de Março 123, have singles/doubles for US$25/30. The York is closer to the rodoviária.

The *Hotel Casablanca* (☎ 42-6662) is almost right next to the Museu Imperial, at Avenida 7 de Setembro 286, and has singles/doubles for US$40/45. Yes, the two Casablanca hotels are run by the same people.

There are some beautiful top-end hotels around Petrópolis. Elected the most charming in Brazil by the Guia Brasil 4 Rodas in 1995, the *Pousada Alcobaça* (☎ (0242) 21-1240) is at Rua Agostinho Goulão 298, in the suburb of Corrêas. With beautiful gardens crossed by a small river, it has a pool, a sauna and a tennis court. Doubles go for US$100. The excellent restaurant, which is open to the public, offers main courses for around US$15.

Places to Eat

A good place for a healthy vegetarian buffet lunch is *Naturalmente*, upstairs in the shopping centre at Rua do Imperador 288. Pay US$5 for all you can eat.

Rua 16 de Março has lots of eateries, such as *Kafta*, the Arab restaurant at No 52, *Maurício's* seafood place (at No 154) and the *Midas Steak House* (at No 170).

Entertainment

For a drink in elegant surroundings, try Casa d'Angelo, on the corner of Rua do Imperador and Rua da Imperatriz. In the suburb of Itaipava, there are lots of nightspots along the Estrada Bernardo Coutinho. Try Bar Nucrepe, at No 12,701.

Getting There & Away

From Rio, buses to Petrópolis leave every

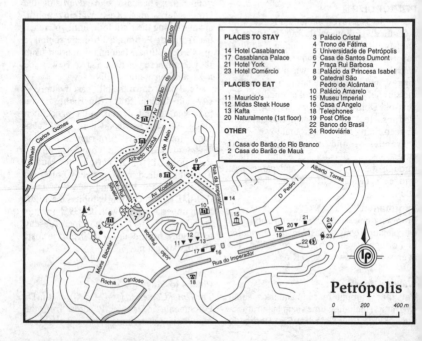

PLACES TO STAY

14 Hotel Casablanca
17 Casablanca Palace
21 Hotel York
23 Hotel Comércio

PLACES TO EAT

11 Maurício's
12 Midas Steak House
13 Kafta
20 Naturalmente (1st floor)

OTHER

1 Casa do Barão do Rio Branco
2 Casa do Barão de Mauá
3 Palácio Cristal
4 Trono de Fátima
5 Universidade de Petrópolis
6 Casa de Santos Dumont
7 Praça Rui Barbosa
8 Palácio da Princesa Isabel
9 Catedral São
    Pedro de Alcântara
10 Palácio Amarelo
15 Museu Imperial
16 Casa d'Angelo
18 Telephones
19 Post Office
22 Banco do Brasil
24 Rodoviária

Petrópolis

0   200   400 m

half-hour from 5 am onwards. The trip takes 1½ hours and costs US$2.50.

AROUND PETRÓPOLIS

If you have the use of a car, take a ride out on the Estrada Industrial. It's 70 km to the little church of São José de Rio Preto. You'll pass a few good restaurants on the way: *Tarrafa's* and *Boi na Brasa* (for steak) and, in Corrêas, the expensive French restaurant *One for the Road*.

In Itapaiva, visit the Recanto porcelain factory. In Pedra do Rio, find the hiking trail to the Rocinha waterfalls in the Secretaria neighbourhood, then visit the farms and ranches of Posse.

VASSOURAS

Vassouras, a quiet resort 118 km north of Rio, was the most important city in the Paraíba valley in the first half of the 19th century. Surrounded by the huge fazendas of the 19th-century coffee barons, the town still wears the money they poured into it. They were literally barons, for 18 of them were given titles of nobility by the Portuguese crown. With the abolition of slavery in 1888 and the resulting decline in coffee production, Vassouras' importance diminished, and this preserved the town.

Museu Chácara da Hera

Vassouras' favourite grande dame is the noble heiress Eufrásia, a woman who claimed devotion to Vassouras despite palaces in London, Brussels and Paris. Her home, the Museu Chácara da Hera, is on Rua Fernandes Junior, and is open Wednesday to Sunday from 11 am to 5 pm.

Fazendas

There are a few old churches in the centre, as well as old buildings of the schools of medicine, philosophy and engineering, but the real attractions of Vassouras are the coffee fazendas. Unfortunately, if you don't have a car, you're in for some long hikes. Although the fazendas are protected by the historical preservation institutes, permission must be obtained from the owners before

touring the grounds. For more information, ask at the Casa de Cultura, next to the cinema on Praça Barão do Campo Belo.

Nine km from town is the Fazenda Santa Eufrásia, one of the oldest in the area, dating from the end of the 18th century. If you have a car, take the road to the small town of Barão de Vassouras, five km away. Pass through the town, and after three km you'll see the impressive Fazenda Santa Mônica, situated on the banks of the Rio Paraiba. The Fazenda Paraiso and the Fazenda Oriente are further out on the same road.

Places to Stay & Eat

The *Pensão Tia Maria*, just up from the bus station, at Rua Domingos de Almeida 134, charges US$10 per person. They don't have any double beds. Other accommodation is expensive. The *Mara Palace* (☎ 71-1993), at Rua Chanceler Dr Raul Fernandes 121, charges between US$35 and US$55 for a deluxe double. At Avenida Rui Barbosa 526, the *Hotel Parque Santa Amália* (☎ 71-1346) charges US$50 for doubles.

The *Pensão Tia Maria* and a few other places nearby have reasonable comida caseira. But for top restaurants, you are a hundred years too late.

Getting There & Away

The bus station is on Praça Juiz Machado Jr. Frequent buses make the 2½-hour trip to Rio (US$6). The first leaves at 6.45 am, with others leaving every 1½ hours after that.

TERESÓPOLIS

Do as Empress Teresina did and escape the steamy summer heat of Rio in the cool mountain retreat of Teresópolis (910 metres), the highest city in the state, nestled in the strange, organ-pipe mountains of the Serra dos Órgãos. The road to Teresópolis first passes the sinuous curves of a padded green jungle, then winds and climbs past bald peaks which have poked through the jungle cover to touch the clouds.

The city itself is modern, prosperous and dull. The principal attraction is the landscape and its natural treasures – in particular the

Teresópolis

0   0.5   1 km

1	Tourist Stand	7	Várzea Palace
2	O Tigre do Papel		Hotel
3	Post Office	8	Center Hotel
4	Tudo em Cima	9	Cheiro de Mato
5	Hotel Avenida	10	Rodoviária
6	Igreja Matriz		

strangely shaped peaks of Pedra do Sino (2263 metres), Pedra do Açu (2230 metres), Agulha do Diabo (2020 metres), Nariz do Frade (1919 metres), Dedo de Deus (1651 metres), Pedra da Ermitage (1485 metres) and Dedo de Nossa Senhora (1320 metres). With so many peaks, it's no wonder that Teresópolis is the mountain climbing, rock climbing and trekking centre of Brazil.

There are extensive hiking trails in the region, and it's possible to trek over the mountains and through the jungle to Petrópolis. Unfortunately the trails are unmarked and off the maps, but it's easy and inexpensive to hire a guide at the national

park, or go with a group organised by one of the hiking and mountaineering clubs in Rio.

Teresópolis is not simply for alpinists: it's a centre for sports lovers of all kinds. The city has facilities for motocross, volleyball and equestrian activities – many of Brazil's finest thoroughbreds are raised here – not to mention soccer. The city bears the distinction of hosting Brazil's World Cup soccer team; the national team is selected and trained here.

Orientation
Teresópolis is built up along one main street, which changes names every few blocks. Starting from the highway to Rio in the Soberbo part of town and continuing north along the Avenida Rotariana (with access to the national park), the road is renamed Avenida Oliveira Botelho, Avenida Alberto Torres, Feliciano Sodré and then Avenida Lúcio Meira. Most of the sites are west of the main drag and up in the hills. The cheap hotels are found in the neighbourhood of the Igreja Matriz de Santa Tereza, Praça Baltazar da Silveira.

Information
Tourist Office The Terminal Turístico tourist office is in Soberbo, at the intersection with the road to Rio. It's open daily from 8 am to 11 pm, and the view of Rio from the office is great. If you're travelling by bus, however, it's a hassle to get to; you can pick up the same maps at the tourist stand on Avenida Lúcio Meira, which is open Monday to Friday from 8 am to 5 pm.

Post & Telephone The post office is on Avenida Lúcio Meira. The rodoviária has a Telerj station for long-distance telephone calls.

Parque Nacional da Serra dos Órgãos
The main entrance to the national park is open daily from 8 am to 5 pm (admission US$0.25). The 3.5-km walking trail, waterfalls, swimming pools, tended lawns and gardens make this a very pretty park for a picnic. There are some chalets for rent at the

park substation, 12 km towards Rio. There are also campsites.

Other Attractions

The **Mulher de Pedra** (Rock Woman) rock formation, 12 km out towards Nova Friburgo, really does look like a reclining woman.

Colina dos Mirantes is a good place to view the Serra dos Órgãos range and the city. On clear days you can see as far as the Baía de Guanabara. To get there, take Avenida Feliciano Sodré. The Quebra Frascos, the royal family of the Second Empire, lived in this neighbourhood. The best spot for viewing the **Dedo de Deus peak** is from Soberbo.

Places to Stay – bottom end

The *Várzea Palace Hotel* (☎ 742-0878) is at Rua Prefeito Sebastião Teixeira 41/55, behind the Igreja Matriz. This grand old white building with red trim has been a Teresópolis institution since 1916. Can it be a budget hotel? Cheap and classy singles/doubles without bath are US$15/19 (US$18/28 with bath).

Other relatively cheap hotels are nearby, including the *Center Hotel* (☎ 742-5890), at Sebastião Teixeira 245, which has singles/doubles for US$17/23. The *Hotel Avenida* (☎ 742-2751) is in front of the Igreja Matriz, at Rua Delfim Moreira 439. Singles/doubles here cost US$20/28.

Places to Stay – top end

The more expensive hotels are out of town. The *Hotel Alpina* (☎ 742-5252) is three km on the road to Petrópolis and has singles/doubles for US$45/60. There's a golf club across the road.

Along the Teresópolis to Nova Friburgo road are two hotels. Run by the Hari Krishnas, the *Pousada Vrajabhumi* (☎ 742-3011), is at Km 6, in the middle of a forest reserve. There are chalets and natural swimming pools, and rates start at US$60 a double (including all meals, which are vegetarian). The hotel restaurant is open to the public for lunch and dinner. At Km 27, the *Hotel Rosa*

dos Ventos (☎ 742-8833) is the only Brazilian hotel in the international Relais & Chateaux chain. It has everything except youth – no one under the age of 16 is permitted to stay here. Daily rates, breakfast and lunch included, are US$110 to US$250.

Places to Eat

Restaurante Irene (☎ 742-2901), at Rua Yeda 730 (parallel to Rua Sebastião Teixeira), basks in its reputation for Teresópolis' best *haute cuisine*. It's expensive, and reservations are required.

Cheiro de Mato, at Rua Delfim Moreira 140, is a decent vegetarian restaurant. *Bar Gota da Água*, at Praça Baltazar da Silveira 16, is also known as *Bar do Ivam*. It's a comfy little place, serving trout with a choice of sauces for US$7. Try it with alcaparra (a bitter, pea-like vegetable) or almond sauce. For dessert, have some apple strudel and Viennese coffee a few doors down, at *Lanches Mickey*. *Tudo em Cima*, at Rua Delfim Moreira 409, serves an admirable soufflé of bacalhau (US$6). *O Tigre do Papel* is a good Chinese restaurant in the centre, at the end of Rua Francisco Sá.

Getting There & Away

The rodoviária is on Rua 1 do Maio, off Avenida Tenente Luiz. Buses to Rio depart every half-hour from 5 am to 10 pm (US$4, 1½ hours, 95 km). There are seven buses to Petrópolis (from 6 am to 9 pm), and plenty to Novo Friburgo.

Getting Around

To get to the park from the city centre, take the hourly 'Albequerque Soberbo' bus (US$0.50). Its last stop is the Terminal Turístico in Soberbo.

NOVA FRIBURGO

During the Napoleonic Wars, Dom João II encouraged immigration to Brazil. At the time, people were starving in Switzerland, so in 1818, 300 families from the Swiss canton of Friburg packed up and headed for Brazil. The passage to Brazil was horrible; many died, but enough families survived to settle in the mountains and establish a small village in the New World.

Like Teresópolis and Petrópolis, Nova Friburgo has good hotels and restaurants, as well as many lovely natural attractions: waterfalls, woods, trails, sunny mountain mornings and cool evenings. (It's chilly and rainy during the winter months, from June to August.) The Cónego neighbourhood is interesting for its Germanic architecture and its apparently perpetually blooming flowers.

Information

Tourist Office The tourist office on Praça Dr Demervel B Moreira is open daily from 8 am to 8 pm. As well as maps, they have a complete list of hotels, including the cheapest, with updated prices.

Post & Telephone Both the post office and the telephone office are on Praça Getúlio Vargas. There's also a branch of the post office at the bus station.

Things to See & Do

Most of the sights are a few km out of town. Scout out the surrounding area from **Morro da Cruz** (1800 metres). The cable-car station

Nova Friburgo

0   250   500 m

PLACES TO STAY

8 Avenida Hotel
9 Sanjaya Hotel
10 Hotel Montanus
12 Fabris Hotel

PLACES TO EAT

3 Churrascaría Majórica
7 Walislau Center
11 Oberland

OTHER

1 Cable-Car Station
2 Local Buses
4 Post Office
5 Tourist Office
6 Telephones
13 Rodoviária

is in the centre, at Praça do Suspiro. Cable cars to Morro da Cruz run from 10 am to 6 pm on weekends and holidays. **Pico da Caledônia** (2310 metres) offers fantastic views, and launching sites for hang-gliders. It's a six-km uphill hike, but the view is worth it.

You can hike to **Pedra do Cão Sentado**, explore the **Furnas do Catete** rock formations, or visit the mountain towns of **Bom Jardim** (23 km north on BR-492) or **Lumiar** (25 km from Mury and a little bit before the entrance to Friburgo). Hippies, cheap pensions, waterfalls, walking trails and white-water canoe trips abound in Lumiar.

Places to Stay

The *Fabris Hotel* (☎ 22-2852), at Avenida Alberto Braune 148, costs US$12/14 for its clean singles/doubles. The *Hotel Montanus* (☎ 22-1235), at Rua Fernando Bizzotto 26, has simple singles/doubles for the same price, but you can bargain them down. The *Avenida Hotel* (☎ 22-1664), at Rua Dante Laginestra 89, is a bit cheaper, with quartos for US$10/14 a single/double.

A good mid-range place in the centre is the *Sanjaya Hotel* (☎ 22-6052), at Avenida Alberto Braune 58. They charge US$30/35 a single/double.

In Lumiar, try the *Pousada dos Gnomos* (☎ (021) 256-3926 in Rio), close to a nice waterfall. Rooms for US$35 a double with a good breakfast.

Rates at the top hotels are all for double occupancy and include full board. In town, *Sans Souci* (☎ 22-7752), at Rua Itajai, charges US$110. The *Hotel Garlipp* (☎ 42-1330) is in Mury, 10 km out on the road to Niterói, and charges US$110.

Places to Eat

If you want to eat very well, try one of the two Swiss/German delicatessens on Rua Fernando Bizzotto for a hefty cold-cut sandwich on black bread with dark mustard. One of the two delis, the *Oberland* (☎ 22-9838), at No 12, doubles as a restaurant, with a very cosy wood-panelled room. The menu is short but the food is great. Try the weisswurst (veal sausage) with sauerkraut (US$4), and the chocolate cakes for dessert.

The *Churrascaría Majórica*, in the centre, at Praça Getúlio Vargas 74, serves a decent cut of filet mignon (US$15) – it's enough for two. The *Walislau Center*, a small shopping complex on the other side of Praça Getúlio Vargas, has a few bars and cafés on the 1st floor. It gets crowded in the evenings.

Entertainment

The place to go is Baixo Friburgo, Rua Francisco Sobrinho, opposite the Friburguense Football Clube. There are four bars in a row – Ancoradouro, Campestre, Deixo Saudade and Frago Legal. On Friday and Saturday nights, it's packed.

Things to Buy

Cinderela Artesanato works with semiprecious stones and sells heraldic family shields. Praça Getúlio Vargas has shops where home-made liqueurs and jams are sold. Nova Friburgo bills itself as the lingerie capital of Brazil, and there are lots of factory outlets around town.

Getting There & Away

Nova Friburgo is a little over two hours (US$6) by bus from Rio via Niterói on 1001 Lines. The ride is along a picturesque, winding, misty jungle road. From Novo Friburgo, buses to Rio leave every half-hour to an hour from 5.40 am. To Teresópolis there are four daily buses, at 7 and 11 am, and 3 and 6 pm (US$4, two hours). If you're heading to the coast, an adventurous trip is to catch a bus to Lumiar and from there catch another to Macaé.

Getting Around

The local bus terminal is behind Praça Getúlio Vargas. Local buses go to just about all the tourist attractions. Ask for details at the tourist office.

The Itatiaia Region

The Itatiaia region, a curious mix of Old World charm and New World jungle, is comprised of Itatiaia, Penedo and Visconde de Mauá. This idyllic corner of Rio de Janeiro state was settled by Europeans – Penedo by Finns, Itatiaia and Visconde de Mauá by Germans and Swiss – but it is now popular among Brazilians of all ethnic groups. Resende is the main centre for the area.

The climate is alpine temperate and the chalets are Swiss, but the vegetation is tropical and the warm smiles are purely Brazilian. There are neatly tended little farms with horses and goats, and small homes with clipped lawns and flower boxes, side by side with large tracts of dense jungle untouched by the machete. This is a wonderful place to tramp around green hills, ride ponies up purple mountains, splash in waterfalls and blaze jungle trails without straying too far from the comforts of civilisation – a sauna, a fireplace, a soft bed, a little wine and a well-grilled trout! Budget travellers beware: the region is frequented by wealthy Cariocas and Paulistas, so food and accommodation tend to be expensive.

The region lies in the Serra da Mantiqueira's Itatiaia massif, in the northwest corner of Rio de Janeiro, and borders the states of São Paulo and Minas Gerais. The Parque Nacional do Itatiaia is due north of the Serra de Bocaina. Itatiaia Turismo (☎ 511-1147), at Rua Visconde de Pirajá 540 in Rio, arranges weekend bus tours from Rio to Penedo, Visconde de Mauá and Itatiaia.

RESENDE

Resende, the largest city in the area, is the transport hub for Penedo and Visconde de Mauá. Resende has no tourist attractions, but it is the home of Brazil's military academy (Academia Militar das Agulhas Negras) and a university.

Places to Stay

The military presence and the university may account for the presence of very cheap hotels in the Campos Elízio part of the city. The best is the *Hotel Presidente* (☎ 54-5464), at Rua Luis Pistarni 43, with simple but clean single/double quartos for US$6/9. Double apartamentos are US$12. Lodging doesn't come much cheaper in this part of Brazil. Unless you are camping, you are likely to pay at least twice as much in Penedo, Mauá or the national park, but it's worth the extra to stay in those places rather than commute from Resende.

Getting There & Away

Buses from Rio de Janeiro and São Paulo go to and from Resende several times a day. From Resende it's reasonably easy to hitch, or catch a taxi or bus to your final destination. Cidade de Aço lines runs 11 buses a day to Resende from Rio, the first leaving at 7 am and the last at 9 pm (US$6, 2½ hours).

PENEDO

Finnish immigrants, led by Toivo Uuskallio, settled Penedo in 1929. If the beautiful Scandinavian woodwork doesn't convince you of this, the number of saunas will. The Finns planted citrus groves along the banks of the Rio das Pedras, but when this enterprise failed, they turned to preparing Finnish jams and jellies, home-made liqueurs and sauces.

Apart from jungle and waterfalls, Penedo has few attractions. The Museu Kahvila, at Travessa da Fazenda 45, is a lanchonete which also displays Finnish clothing, books and photographs.

Things to See & Do

There are three waterfalls worth visiting: **Três Cachoeiras** (near Tião), the very pretty **Cachoeira do Roman** (which is on private grounds, 10 minutes' walk uphill from the Pousada Challenge) and **Cachoeira do Diabo** (right near the Pousada Challenge).

About 40 minutes of uphill hiking from Hans Camping takes you into very dense jungle, although there are trails inside. Hopefully you will run into the large bands of big monkeys and steer clear of the wildcats. At the point where Penedo's main asphalt road turns to dirt, you can hire horses (US$3 per hour) or a horse and carriage (US$6 per hour).

Dances There is now only a sprinkling of Finns among the assortment of Brazilian people, but they all get together for polkas, mazurkas, and *letkiss* and *jenkiss* dances every Saturday night at the Clube Finlandê. From 9 pm to 2 am, the Finnish dancers put on Old World togs and do traditional dances. Admission is US$3.

Saunas Next door and across the street from the Clube Finlandia are the Sauna Bar and Sauna Finlandesa. These sweat shops are open to the public from early afternoon until 10 pm (later if enough people are interested). Admission is US$3.

Places to Stay & Eat

Penedo is expensive, due to the number of weekend tourists who come up from Rio, but the accommodation is well above average, the food is good and daily rates usually include breakfast and lunch. *Hans Camping*, several km up from the last bus stop, charges US$4 per person for campsites. It has a

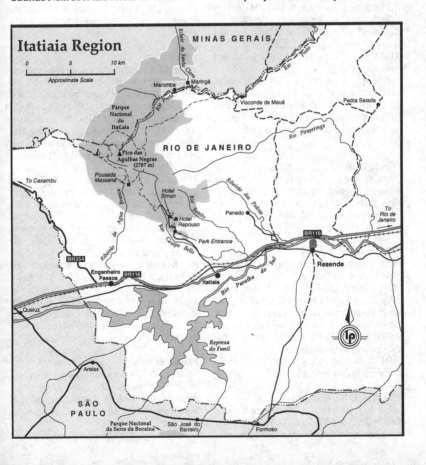

Itatiaia Region

sauna, a natural swimming pool, a bar and a nearby waterfall.

The *Pousada Casa Grande* (☎ 51-1383) is close to the bus stop, at Praça Finlândia 10. This 200 year-old farmhouse where colonisation of the region began is a bit dilapidated, but the rooms are large and clean. Doubles are US$18.

The *Pousada Challenge* (☎ 51-1389), about a km up from Tião on the Estrada da Fazendinha, has very clean prefabricated chalets which sleep three. Doubles cost US$40, including breakfast, lunch and use of the pool and sauna.

The *Hotel Baianinha* (☎ 51-1204), next to Tião on the Cachoeiras, asks US$12/15 for its simple singles/doubles. The Baianinha kitchen specialises in fish and Bahian dishes (US$5 to US$12). The food is good and portions are huge.

Palhoça, at Avenida das Mangueiras 2510, has a good prato feito (US$3). *Casa do Chocolate*, at Avenida Casa das Pedras 10, has sandwiches, 50 different ice-cream flavours if it's hot, and hot chocolate if it's cold.

Things to Buy

Penedo's many small craft shops specialise in jellies, honey, chutneys and preserves, chocolates, cakes and candles. Casa Encabulada, on Avenida das Mangueiras, is an artists' co-operative.

Getting There & Away

From Resende, it's much easier to get to Penedo and Itatiaia than to Visconde de Mauá. There are 22 Penedo-bound buses daily, from 6 am to 11 pm. The bus services the three-km main street and continues past the end of the paved road to Tião, which is the final stop. The Hotel Baianinha is the second-last stop. Pousada Challenge is a brisk half-hour walk from Tião; Hans Camping is 20 minutes further up.

VISCONDE DE MAUÁ

Mauá is prettier and a little more tranquil than Penedo, and harder to reach. It's a lovely place, with streams, tinkling goat bells, cosy

chalets and country lanes graced with wild-flowers. There are horses for hire by the footbridge (US$2.50 per hour), but some of them are pretty small.

Orientation

Mauá is actually made up of three small villages a few km apart. The bus stops first at Vila Mauá, the largest village. Vila Maringá, on the other side of the Rio Preto, is actually in Minas Gerais, and has lots of restaurants and places to stay. At the end of the bus route is Vila Maromba, which has restaurants and pousadas, but not as many as Maringá. Most travellers stay in Maringá or Maromba. Hitching around here is fairly easy.

Information

There are two places for tourist information. One is a cabana at the entrance to Vila Mauá, where you'll find information about activities and a list of places to stay, though not the cheapest ones. It's open Tuesday to Sunday from 8 am to 8 pm (closed for lunch). The Casa do Turista has similar information. It's one km further along the road to Maromba.

Things to See & Do

The **Santa Clara Cachoeira**, the nicest waterfall in the area, is a 40-minute walk from Vila Maromba in Maringá. For a jungle experience, climb up through the bamboo groves on either side of the falls.

The young and the restless can follow the trail from Maromba to the **Cachoeira Veu de Noiva** in the Parque Nacional do Itatiaia, a full day's hike each way. It's possible to kayak the rapids of the Rio Preto, if you are so inclined. The Rio Preto, which divides Minas Gerais from Rio, also has small river beaches and natural pools to explore.

Places to Stay

Most pousadas offer full board with lodging; small signposts at each intersection make them easy to find. If you don't want full board, you can bargain the price down quite a bit.

In Maringá, the cheapest place to stay is

the *Casarão* (☎ 54-3030). It's a youth hostel, campground and regular pousada rolled into one. Small, simple apartamentos with verandah and hammock are US$28 a double. Campsites are US$2 per person. The youth hostel costs US$8, plus US$2 for breakfast. They also organise treks. The bus stops right outside.

The *Hotel Casa Alpininha* (☎ 87-1292) is in Maringá, on the other side of the river. Doubles cost US$30, including breakfast and lunch. Lots of places in Maringá charge around US$40 a double.

Maromba has a few cheap pousadas, next to the bus stop. The *Pousada Sonhador*, on the right-hand side of the church, charges US$10/15 a single/double, including breakfast. It also serves a good prato feito. About three km up from Maromba is the *Pousada Tiatiaim*, which is in a great location and charges US$40 a double.

Places to Eat
Natural and vegetarian food is served at *Pureza* in Maringá. People here like brown rice, granola with tropical fruits and yoghurt mixed in, and caipirinhas with natural honey. The food is good but expensive.

Renascer, also in Maringá, serves trout for US$4. *Casarão* serves comida caseira. The US$8 plate is plenty for two people.

Things to Buy
The Companhia Visconde de Mauá is a hippie store selling T-shirts, embroidered blouses, natural perfumes and soaps.

Getting There & Away
The daily bus from Resende to Visconde de Mauá (US$3, about 2½ hours on a winding dirt road) leaves at 4 pm Monday to Saturday; to make it, you must hitch, catch the 1 pm bus from Rio, or pay for a taxi (US$35). The bus leaves for Resende at 8.30 am every day, except Sunday, when it leaves at 5 pm.

Getting Around
If you get sick of walking, Bike Montanha, in Maringá, rents mountain bikes for US$2 an hour.

PARQUE NACIONAL DO ITATIAIA
This national park, established in 1937 to protect 120 sq km of ruggedly beautiful land, contains over 400 species of native birds, as well as jaguars, monkeys and sloths. It features lakes, rivers, waterfalls, alpine meadows and primary and secondary Atlantic rainforests. Don't let the tropical house plants fool you: temperatures drop below freezing in June, and some years, Itatiaia even has a few snowy days!

Sloth

Museum

The park headquarters, the museum and Lago Azul (Blue Lake) are 10 km in from the Via Dutra highway. The museum, open Tuesday to Sunday from 8 am to 4 pm, has glass cases full of stuffed and mounted animals, pinned moths and snakes in jars.

Activities

Mountain-climbing, rock-climbing and trekking enthusiasts will want to pit themselves against the local peaks, cliffs and trails.

Every two weeks, a group scales the Agulhas Negras peak. At 2787 metres, it's the highest in the area. For more information, contact the Grupo Excursionista de Agulhas Negras (☎ 54-2587), and refer to the section on Hiking & Climbing in the Facts for the Visitor chapter.

A walk to the Abroucas refuge, at the base of Agulhas Negras, is a 26-km, eight-hour jungle trek from the park entrance. The mountain refuge can sleep 24 people and is accessible by car from the Engenheiro Passos to São Lourenço road (near the Minas Gerais and Rio de Janeiro border). Reservations are required. Call IBAMA in Resende (☎ (0243) 52-1461) and get maps and advice from the park IBAMA office before setting off.

Simpler hikes include the walk between Hotel Simon and Hotel Repouso (where the painter Guignard lived, worked and left a few of his paintings), and the 20-minute walk from the Sítio Jangada to the Poronga waterfalls.

Places to Stay

Camping is the cheapest option inside the park. There's the campground *Aporaoca*, four km from the main entrance to the park. (When you get to the Gula & Artes store and the ice-cream shop, there's a signpost; the campground is 200 metres up behind these places.) Sites are US$3 per person.

There is a youth hostel: *Ipê Amarelo* (☎ 52-1232), at Rua João Mauricio de Macedo Costa 352, in Campo Alegre, a suburb of Itatiaia. They have bicycles for rent.

The *Pousada do Elefante*, close to the

Hotel Simon, is the cheapest hotel in the park. It's basic but well located. They charge US$30/50 for singles/doubles with board. Other hotels are expensive, three-star Embratur affairs with saunas and swimming pools, such as the *Hotel Simon* (☎ 52-1122), which charges US$90 for a double with full board. The *Hotel do Ypê* (☎ 52-1453) charges US$80 a double or US$100 to stay in a chalet. Not far from the park entrance, the *Hotel Aldéia da Serra* (☎ 52-1152) is reasonably priced, with chalets for US$45/60 a single/double, all inclusive.

Getting There & Away

Every 20 minutes on weekdays and every 40 minutes on weekends (from 7 am to 11.20 pm), there is a bus from Resende to the town of Itatiaia. From Praça São José in Itatiaia, take the kombi with the 'Hotel Simon' sign up to the park. It leaves at 8 and 10 am, noon, and 2, 5 and 7 pm. The ride costs US$2, and you'll also have to pay the park entry fee (US$1) as you go through the main gate. A taxi costs US$15.

East of Rio de Janeiro

SAQUAREMA

After the famous beaches of Rio and Baía de Guanabara, with their high-rise hotels and bars spilling onto the sands, the quiet, clean beaches east of Rio are a welcome change.

Saquarema, 100 km from Rio de Janeiro, sits between long stretches of open beach, lagoons and jungled mountains. The town takes unusual pride in the natural beauty of its setting. Polluting industries are forbidden in the municipality, so it's still possible to find sloths and bands of monkeys in the jungles. Motorboats aren't allowed to muck up the lakes and lagoons, which means the water is still pure and the fish and shrimps are abundant. The long shoreline of fine, white sand and clean water attracts surfers, sports fishers and sun worshippers.

Saquarema is a horse-breeding and fruit-growing centre; you can visit the orchards and pick fruit, or hire horses and take to the hills. Adventurers who tramp the jungle trails in search of the elusive mico-leão marmoset are sure to discover beautiful waterfalls, if not the primates. All in all, there are plenty of things to do away from the beach.

Ah, but the beaches...Bambui, Ponta Negra and Jaconé, south of town, are long, and empty save for a couple of fishing villages. The waves are big, particularly off Ponta Negra, and three km north of Saquarema in Praia Itaúna, where an annual surfing contest is held during the last two weeks of May.

History
On 17 March 1531, Martim Afonso de Sousa founded a Portuguese settlement here and met with the Tamoio Indian chief Sapuguaçu. Nonplussed by de Sousa's five ships and 400 sailors, Sapuguaçu chose to ally the Tamoios with the French. In 1575 Antônio Salema, then Governor of Rio de Janeiro, decided to break the Tamoio-French alliance, and with an army of over 1000 men, massacred the Indians and their French military advisers.

The next big event in Saquarema's history was the slave revolt of Ipitangas, in which 400 slaves took over the plantation mansion and kicked out their master. For a few days, the slaves held the town, and fought against the cavalry which rode out from Niterói. The town pillory, Bandeque's Post (named after the leader of the slave revolt), was in use as recently as the end of last century.

Information
Tourist Office The Secretaria de Turismo at the Prefeitura is quite useless. The best place to go for information, especially about places to stay, is Saquatur Toulouse Lagos Turismo (☎ & fax 51-2161), at Avenida Oceânica 165 in Itauna. The manager, Conceição, is very helpful. As well as being a travel agent, she has a complete listing of hotels and is happy to call around to see if there are any vacancies.

Money There's a Banco do Brasil in town. If

they aren't changing money, ask Conceição, at her travel agency.

Post & Telephone The post office is close to the bus stop in Praça Oscar de Macedo Soares. The posto telefônico is in Rua Barão da Saquarema.

Festival
Saquarema hosts the NS de Nazaré mass on 7 and 8 September. It attracts around 150,000 pilgrims, second only to the Nazaré celebrations of Belém.

Places to Stay – bottom end
The youth hostel, *Ilhas Gregas* (☎ 51-1008), is excellent. Only 100 metres from the beach, at Rua do Prado 671 in Itaúna, they have bicycles, a swimming pool, a sauna and a bar/restaurant. It's easy to catch a taxi here from the bus station in Saquarema, but if you feel like a hike, get off the bus at the petrol station 'Sudoeste' and walk for half an hour along Avenida Oceânica, until you get to the centre of Itaúna (where there are lots of beachfront bars and kiosks). Go along Avenida NS de Nazareth and take the second street on the left (Rua das Caravelas), then the first street on your right (Rua do Prado).

The *Pousada da Mansão* (☎ (021) 259-2100 in Rio), at Avenida Oceanica 353, has rooms in the old mansion for US$10/20 a single/double, and there's camping there too. Sonia, who runs the place, speaks English and French. The *Hotel Saquarema* (☎ 51-2275), right at the bus stop, charges US$15 per person, but stay there only as a last resort. It's OK, but there are better places for the same price.

The *Pousada da Titia* (☎ 51-2058), at Avenida Salgado Filho 774, is a good alternative, with quartos for US$14 a double and apartamentos for US$20. The *Barra Bel* (☎ 51-2322), at Avenida Oceânica 1028 in Itaúna, is also recommended.

Places to Stay – top end
There are stacks of places charging around US$40 a double. (If you're thinking of staying in one of these places, go and see

Conceição at Saquatur. She has brochures and all the latest information. It will save you quite a lot of legwork.) Some of the popular ones are the *Maasai Hotel Club* (☎ 51-1092), near Itaúna beach, the *Pousada dos Socos*, at Rua dos Socos 592, and the *Pousada Pratagi* (☎ 51-2161), at Avenida Salgado Filho 4484.

The *Hotel Fazenda Serra da Castelhana* (☎ 719-0412) charges US$75 a double with full board and has very good food. It's in the suburb of Palmital.

Places to Eat
For prato feito, *Pensão Tia Tiana* is a favourite with locals. There are lots of lanchonetes at Itaúna. *Pinho's*, at Rua das Pitangas 145, is a cheap, family-run place that's highly recommended by hungry surfers. Ilhas Gregas also has a decent restaurant. You might also like to try *Berro da Agua*, at Avenida Oceânica 165, and the restaurant at the *Barra Bel*.

Getting There & Away
From Rio to Saquarema, there are seven buses a day from 6.30 am to 6.30 pm (until 8.30 pm Friday to Sunday). The same number go the other way from 5.30 am to 5.50 pm (7.50 pm Friday to Sunday). The two-hour trip costs US$4. To get to Cabo Frio, take a local bus to Bacaxá. From there, buses to Cabo leave every half-hour.

ARRAIAL DO CABO
Arraial do Cabo sits on a square corner of land, with Cabo Frio 10 km due north and Praia Grande stretching due west 40 km (continuous with Praia Maçambaba). The village of Arraial do Cabo spreads out from the edges of four bays and has beaches that compare with the finest in Búzios, but unlike Búzios, Arraial is a place where people live and work. The saltworks of the Companhia Nacional de Alcalis, north of town, extract table salt and *barrília*, a type of phosphate tied to the salt.

Information
There's no tourist office in Arraial, but you don't really need one, as the layout is fairly straightforward and the attractions are the beaches. The post office is in Praça Castelo Branco and the Telerj office is next to the Hotel Praia Grande.

Beaches
'Discovered' many years ago by Amerigo Vespucci, **Praia dos Anjos** has beautiful turquoise water, but a little too much boat traffic for comfortable swimming. The favourite beaches in town are **Praia do Forno**, **Praia Brava** and **Praia Grande**.

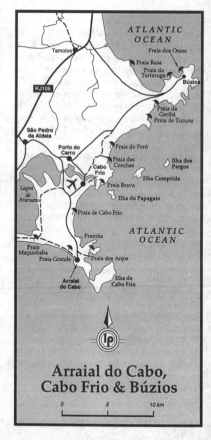

Arraial do Cabo, Cabo Frio & Búzios

Stretching along a pretty piece of road to Cabo Frio, Praia do Forte has bleached-white sand and a backdrop of low scrub, cacti and grasses. The Museu Oceanográfico on Praia dos Anjos is open Tuesday to Sunday from 9 am to 4.30 pm.

To get to the **Gruta Azul** (Blue Cavern) on the far side of Ilha de Cabo Frio, ask fisherfolk at Praia dos Anjos for a tour – it should cost about US$20. Be alert to the tides: the entrance to the underwater cavern isn't always open.

To see the wild orchids between Cabo Frio and Arraial do Cabo, ask the bus driver to let you off at the access road, and then hike inland.

Places to Stay

Camping Praia Grande, at Avenida Getúlio Vargas 103, is a walled-in grassy area reasonably close to the beach. Sites cost US$4 per person. The *Hotel Praia Grande* (☎ 22-1369), at Rua Dom Pedro 41, is a good cheapie in the centre of town, with US$14/20 singles/doubles.

At Praia dos Anjos, the *Porto dos Anjos* (☎ 22-1629), at Avenida Luis Correa 8, is a house that's been converted into a pousada. Their double rooms (US$20) have sea views. The *Pousada Restaurante dos Navegantes* (☎ 22-1611), on Praia Grande, is a very pretty resort hotel with a courtyard pool. Singles/doubles cost US$40/60.

Places to Eat

Garrafa de Nansen Restaurante is a classy seafood place where you can eat very well for about US$10 per person. Cheaper eats are available at *Meu Cantinho*, in the Centro at Rua Dom Pedro I, No 18. Their US$7 fish dinners will easily feed two. At Praia Grande, the *Canoa Quebrada* restaurant is a good choice, especially if you're in the mood for seafood moqueca. It's located at Rua Epitácio Pessoa 26.

Getting There & Away

Take the municipal bus from Cabo Frio (US$0.40), which loops around Arraial and returns to Cabo Frio every 20 minutes.

CABO FRIO

The Cabo Frio district formerly comprised Cabo Frio (the most populous town), Búzios (the wealthy, sophisticated resort) and Arraial do Cabo (which has since become independent, politically and economically, because of its salt industry).

History

According to Márcio Verneck, a local historian, Cabo Frio was inhabited at least 5500 years ago. Before the Portuguese arrived, the warring Tamoio and Goitacazes tribes lived here. In 1503 the Portuguese armada, under the command of Amerigo Vespucci, landed at Praia dos Anjos in Arraial do Cabo. Twenty-four men were left behind to start a settlement, one of the first in the Americas. Fantastic reports about this community were the model for Thomas More's *Utopia*.

The economy of the Portuguese settlement was based on the coastal brazil wood, which was felled and shipped back to Europe. Portuguese vessels were at the mercy of Dutch and French corsairs until 1615, when the Portuguese defeated their European foes, founded Santa Helena de Cabo Frio, and took the French-built fort of São Mateus to protect their trade. In time, the Franciscans joined the settlement and built the NS dos Anjos convent. They were followed by the Jesuits at Fazenda Campo Novo. By the 1800s, with the brazil-wood stands completely destroyed, the economy was geared toward fishing and, more recently, tourism, saltworks and chemical industries.

Orientation & Information

Canal do Itajuru links the Lagoa de Araruama to the Atlantic Ocean. Cabo Frio lies to one side of this canal. The town is a two-km hike along Avenida Júlia Kubitschek from the bus station. There's a map of Cabo Frio on the wall of the bus station.

The tourist booth at Avenida do Contorno, Praia do Forte, has hotel information, but no English is spoken. There's a Banco do Brasil at Praça Porto Rocha 44. The post office is at Largo de Santo Antônio 55, in the centre, and the Telerj office is in Praça Porto Rocha.

Forte São Mateus

This stone fortress, a stronghold against pirates, was built in 1616, and is open from 10 am to 4 pm Tuesday to Sunday. It's at the end of Praia do Forte.

Dunes

There are three sand-dune spots in and about Cabo Frio. The dunes of Praia do Peró, a super beach for surfing and surf-casting, are six km north in the direction of Búzios, near Ogivas and after Praia Brava and Praia das Conchas. The Dama Branca (White Lady) sand dunes are on the road to Arraial do Cabo. The Pontal dunes of Praia do Forte town beach stretch from the fort to Miranda hill.

The dunes can be dangerous because of robberies, so get advice from the locals before heading out to the beaches and dunes.

Places to Stay

Cabo Frio is a bit too built-up, and it's hard to understand why anyone would want to stay here rather than at Arraial do Cabo or Búzios. If you do enjoy staying in crummy beach cities, *Camping das Palmeiras* (☎ 45-3863), at Rua Diniz, Quadra B, Área A, Praia do Siqueira, has campsites for US$2 per person. They also rent decent apartamentos with ceiling fan for US$20 a double.

There are a couple of youth hostels very close to the bus station, both of which charge US$7 a night. The *Pousada Suzy* (☎ 43-1742) is about 100 metres to the right as you leave the bus station, at Avenida Júlia Kubitschek 22. The owners are very friendly. Much nicer is the *Albergue Muxarabi*, directly behind Pousada Suzy, in Rua R. The nicest youth hostel is the *Praia das Palmeiras* (☎ 43-2866), at Rua Praia das Palmeiras 1. They have a minibus that does trips to Búzios. To get there on foot from the bus station, go up Rua Geraldo de Abreu. After 100 metres, turn left on Avenida Excelcior (by the canal) and follow it to the shore of the lagoon. The hostel is 50 metres to the left. In total, the distance is 1.2 km.

The cheapest hotels in the Centro are located on Rua José Bonifácio. Try the *Atlântico* (☎ 43-0996), at No 31, where basic apartamentos with fan are US$22/30 a single/double.

There are lots of top-end hotels along the waterfront, but for the money, you'll have a better time in Búzios.

Places to Eat

There are some good eateries around Praça Porto Rocha, in the Centro. *Bacalhauzinho*, at No 27, has excellent bacalhau and a nice atmosphere. *Junior* is close by, at No 26, with sidewalk tables and US$3 prato feito. For dessert, try *Confeitaria Branca*, at No 15.

Getting There & Away

The old coastal road takes longer than BR-101 but provides a beautiful, level route winding around foggy green mounds. There are regular buses from Rio de Janeiro and Niterói (US$6, three hours).

Getting Around

To get to Arraial do Cabo from Cabo Frio, catch a local bus from the bus stop just up to the right as you leave the bus station. To get to Búzios, cross the road and catch a bus from the stop on your left. Local buses cost US$0.50.

BÚZIOS

Búzios, a lovely beach resort, is on a peninsula (scalloped by 17 beaches) which juts into the Atlantic. A simple fishing village until the early sixties, when it was 'discovered' by Brigitte Bardot and her Brazilian boyfriend, the village is now littered with boutiques, fine restaurants, fancy villas, bars and posh pousadas. During the holiday season, prices here are twice those in the rest of Brazil.

Búzios is not a single town but, rather, three settlements on the peninsula – Ossos, Manguinhos and Armação – and one further north on the mainland, called Rasa. Ossos

(Bones), at the northernmost tip of the peninsula, is the oldest and most attractive. It has a pretty harbour and yacht club, a few hotels and bars, and a tourist stand. Manguinhos, at the isthmus, is the most commercial; it even has a 24-hour medical clinic. Armação, in between, has the best restaurants, along with city necessities such as international telephones, a bank, a petrol station, the post office and a pharmacy. North-west along the coast is Rasa and the island of Rasa, where Brazil's political dignitaries and the rich relax.

Information

Tourist Office The Secretaria de Turismo (☎ 23-1143), at Praça Santos Dumont 111 in Armação, is not worth a special trip – any travel agent can give you the same information. The Ekoda Tourist Agency (☎ 23-1490), at Rua das Pedras 13 in Armação, is open seven days a week from 10 am to 8 pm. Staff change money, represent American Express, and arrange accommodation (not the cheaper places) and tours.

From any newsstand, pick up a copy of *Guia Verão Buzios* (US$3). It has information in English as well as in Portuguese, including a list of places to stay (but not prices).

Money Fairtour, close to Bradesco on Travessa Turíbio de Farias, runs a câmbio.

Boat Trips

The schooner *Queen Lory* makes daily trips out to Ilha Feia, Tartaruga and João Fernandinho. There is a 2½-hour trip which costs US$15 and a four-hour trip for US$20. These trips are good value, especially since caipirinhas, soft drinks, fruit salad and snorkelling gear are included in the price. To make a reservation, ask at your pousada or visit Queen Lory Tours, Rua Angela Diniz 35.

Beaches

In general, the southern beaches are trickier to get to, but they're prettier and have better surf. The northern beaches are more sheltered and are closer to the towns.

Working anticlockwise from south of Maguinhos, the first beaches are **Geribá** and **Ferradurinha** (Little Horseshoe). These are beautiful beaches with good surf, but the Búzios Beach Club has built condos here.

Next on the coast is **Ferradura**, which is large enough for windsurfing, and **Lagoinha**, a rocky beach with rough water. **Praia da Foca** and **Praia do Forno** have colder water than the other beaches. **Praia Olho de Boi** (Bull's Eye) was named after Brazil's first postage stamp. It's a pocket-size beach reached by a little trail from the long, clean beach of **Praia Brava**.

João Fernandinho and **João Fernandes** are both good for snorkelling, as are the topless beaches of **Azedinha** and **Azeda**. **Praia dos Ossos, Praia da Armação, Praia do Caboclo** and **Praia dos Amores** are pretty to look at, but not for lounging around. **Praia da Tartaruga** is quiet and pretty. **Praia do Gaucho** and **Manguinhos** are town beaches further along.

Places to Stay

If you want to camp, *Geribá* (☎ 23-2020), at Rua da Âncora 1, Praia da Geribá, is a good spot. It's 150 metres from the beach and charges US$9 per person. They also rent basic quartos for US$16 per person.

Lodging is somewhat on the expensive side, especially in summer, so consider looking for accommodation in Saquarema or Cabo Frio, or rent a house and stay a while. In the low season, however, you should be able to find a room as cheap as those in Cabo Frio or Arraial. Most places charge the same price for singles as they do for doubles. Búzios is a romantic place and solo travellers are unusual. In general, rooms to let are cheaper than pousadas. All accommodation listed has showers and prices include a light breakfast. The high season is December to March and again in July.

The *Zen-Do* (☎ 23-1542), at Rua João Fernandes 60, is a private home with rooms to let. Yesha Vanicore runs a progressive household and has doubles for US$30 in the low season. Yesha, a friendly lady, speaks English and is an excellent vegetarian cook. The *Pousada Mediterrânea* (☎ 23-2353), at Rua João Fernandes 58, is a whitewashed and tiled little hotel. Low-season doubles with a lovely inland view are US$30. The *Pousada la Chimere* (☎ & fax 23-1460), at Praça Eugênio Harold 36, is an excellent splurge: it has a lovely courtyard, and large, well-appointed rooms with a view over the square. Doubles are US$45 in low season, US$60 in high season. Close to the bus station, the *Don Quixote* (☎ & fax 23-1487), at Estrada da Usina Velha 300, is good value, charging US$30 a double in low season.

In Armação, try the *Pousada do Arco Iris* (☎ 23-1256; fax 23-2148), at Rua Manoel Turibe de Farias 182. Its double rooms go for US$20 in low season, and US$40 in high season.

Places to Eat
For good, cheap food, eat grilled fish right on the beaches. Brava, Ferradura and João Fernandes beaches have little thatched-roof fish and beer restaurants.

Most of the better restaurants are in or near Armação. *Restaurante David*, on Rua Manoel Turibe de Farias, is good value – an ample US$6 prato feito usually includes shark fillet (cassão) with rice, beans and salad. *Gostinho Natural* is very popular and their servings are huge.

For fancier fare, try *Le Streghe* (The Witch), on Rua das Pedras, has great pasta and northern Italian dishes, and obsequious service. *Au Cheval Blanc*, a few doors down, has a reputation for fine French food. Both have main courses starting at US$12.

Chez Michou Crêperie, also on Rua das Pedras, is a popular hang-out because of their incredible crepes – any kind you want. The outdoor bar has delicious pinha coladas (US$3).

On Avenida Beira Mar between Ossos and Armação are *Satíricon* (with overpriced Italian seafood) and the *Orient Express* (a flash Japanese sushi bar and steakhouse).

Entertainment
The centre of action in Búzios is the Rua das Pedras in Armação. And it all starts late – don't even think of getting here before midnight. There are some good bars, restaurants and nightclubs (on weekends and in season), but mostly, it seems that everybody just likes walking up and down the street looking at everybody else.

Getting There & Away
From Cabo Frio to Búzios (Ossos), take the municipal bus (a 50-minute, 20-km, bone-crunching cobblestone run). There are four direct buses daily to Rio, leaving from the bus stop on the Estrada da Usina Velha. The three-hour trip costs US$7, with the first bus leaving at 7 am and the last at 6 pm (8.45 pm on Sunday).

Getting Around
Rent A Bike, at Avenida José Bento Ribeiro Dantas 843, and Casa Central Bicicleta, at Rua Lúcio Quintanilha 152, both in Armação, rent bicycles for around US$20 a day.

BARRA DE SÃO JOÃO
Barra de São João, not to be confused with São João da Barra (which is further north up the coast), is an easy-going place set on a narrow spit of land between a small river and the Atlantic. Old, well-preserved colonial homes with azulejos give the town a warm, Portuguese feel, and the village architecture is protected by law. The long, quiet beach is good for surf-casting.

Places to Stay
Don't get the idea that accommodation will be any cheaper here than in Búzios. All the 'simple' pousadas in town charge at least US$25 a double. They include *Pousada Moraes*, at Avenida Amaral Peixoto 388, and the *Hotel Brasil*, 100 metres away and on the opposite side of the road.

Getting There & Away
Barra de São João, 35 km from Macaé and

57 km from Cabo Frio, is serviced by 10 buses a day.

MACAÉ

Once a calm fishing village, Macaé is now a fast-growing petroleum-refinery city with Petrobras oil rigs 100 km offshore. A few years ago the place was swarming with American technicians working on the gas pipeline now being built to Rio. Due to helicopter traffic to and from the oil rigs, Macaé has perhaps the third-busiest airport in Brazil, after Rio and São Paulo. The best beach in town, Praia Cavalheras, is not polluted...yet.

Places to Stay & Eat

The *Pousada Del Rey* (☎ 62-6650) is at Rua Vereador Manuel Braga 192, only a block from the bus station. It's clean, and a good deal, with US$8/12 singles/doubles. The owner, Daniel, a Spaniard from Salamanca, recommends the *Cantinho do Bobo* for family-style food.

Getting There & Away

If you're heading to Minas Gerais, there's a daily bus to Belo Horizonte, at 7 pm (US$25, nine hours). To Vitória, there's a bus at 2 pm (US$8.50, five hours). Three buses a day go to Salvador, at 10.20 am, and 5.20 and 8.10 pm (US$37, 22 hours).

RESERVA BIOLÓGICA DO POÇO DAS ANTAS

A few km off BR-101, between Casmiro de Abreu and Silva Jardim, the Poço das Antas reserve was created to protect the endangered mico-leão (Golden Lion Tamarin monkey) and its natural habitat, coastal jungle. Fifty mico-leãoes were sent from a breeding programme in the USA. The small monkeys, with their golden, lion-like manes, are hard to spot. More monkey business is conducted in nearby Cachoeiras de Macaco,

in the Instituto de Estúdos de Simiologia (Simian Studies Institute).

MACAÉ TO CAMPOS

The stretch from Macaé to Campos is rolling ranch land. Here and there are remnants of tropical forest, palms and scraggly undergrowth in uncleared ravines and hill clefts. A dark mountain range runs along the coast 50 km inland. Most of the land between the Atlantic and the mountains is planted with sugar cane.

BARRA DA ITABAPOANA

At the extreme north-east corner of Rio de Janeiro state is Barra da Itabapoana, which borders the Atlantic Ocean and Espírito Santo on the far side of the Rio Itabapoana. There's not much to the town: a dilapidated church, a few riverboats, two or three street lights, a Telerj station, a fish market and a menagerie of pigs, chickens, horses and dogs. The beach is two km from the church (turn left at the cemetery).

Places to Stay & Eat

Dona Sede runs a pension near the church, charging US$9 per person. She can prepare your meals, but the best bet is *Restaurante São Remo*, by the fish market, which proves that it's possible to get good food in the middle of nowhere: their pasteis de camarão are superb, and US$3 buys a plate of fried fish with shrimp sauce plus rice, beans and salad.

Getting There & Away

There is one daily bus (at 6 am) that crosses into Cachoeiro do Itapemirim, Espírito Santo. From here the choice is to either head directly to Vitória or take the slower, more picturesque coastal route.

Two buses a day make the three-hour, 76-km trip on the dirt road from Barra da Itabapoana to Campos. One bus leaves at 3 pm, the other at 6 pm.

Espírito Santo

If Brazil were to conduct a contest for the least appealing state, Sergipe would be a contender but Espírito Santo would win the prize. Perhaps Espírito Santo suffers from the glory of neighbouring Minas Gerais, Rio de Janeiro and Bahia states. In any case, it's a small state without much to interest the traveller.

Colonised in the 16th century, Espírito Santo became an armed region to prevent

Espírito Santo

```
0        50       100 km
```

gold from being smuggled out of Minas. In the 1800s, Germans and Italians settled in the hills of the interior. Until the 1960s, coffee plantations were the prime source of income, but coffee has been superseded by heavy industry.

The coastline away from Vitória is clean but not particularly pretty. The turbulent surf kicks up sand, giving the water a muddy-brown hue rather than the aquamarine found in Bahia or Rio.

In all fairness, Espírito Santo does have some attractions, humble as they may be. Some of the fishing villages and beaches on the southern coast are attractive, however, they have no provisions for tourists. To the north, Conceição da Barra and the nearby sand dunes at Itaúnas are worth a visit. Excellent seafood is available in Espírito Santo; especially noteworthy is the moqueca capixaba, which is made without dendê oil.

VITÓRIA

Vitória, capital of the state of Espírito Santo, is 521 km from Rio de Janeiro and 602 km from Porto Seguro, making it a convenient place to break the journey between Rio and the state of Bahia. Founded in 1551, Vitória has remarkably little to show of its colonial past. It's a port city, connected by rail with Minas Gerais. Large amounts of export coffee and timber pass through here, and the port at nearby Tubarão is the outlet for millions of tonnes of iron ore.

Orientation

The rodoviária is a km from the centre of town. There are two strips of beach: Praia do Camburí, a 10-minute bus ride north-east of the city, and Praia da Costa, 12 km south of town, at Vila Velha.

Information

Tourist Office Cetur (☎ 223-9090), the state tourism authority, has the tough job of promoting tourism in Espírito Santo. Their main office is in the centre, at Avenida Princesa Isobel 629 (on the 1st floor of the Vitória Center building), open on weekdays from 9 am to 6 pm. They also maintain a booth at the rodoviária; it's supposed to be open daily from 8 am to 7 pm, but don't bet on this. They have lots of coloured brochures of the various points of interest in the state, but no decent maps of the city.

The Cetur advisers also have hotel information (but not prices) for the mid and top-end range.

The best map of the city and its surrounds can be found in the middle pages of the local telephone directory (unless you happen to look in the copy we used).

Money The quickest and easiest way to change cash is to go to the Escal souvenir shop just off Avenida Marechal Mascarenhas and round the corner from the Banco do Brasil, in Avenida Governador Bley. You'll have to go there or to the nearby BEMGE (State Bank of Minas Gerais) to change travellers' cheques.

Post & Telephone The main post office is in the city centre, on Avenida Jerônimo Monteiro, and there's a branch at the rodoviária. There are three posto telefônicos: at the rodoviária, at the airport and on Rua do Rosário, in the centre. They all open at 6.30 am and close between 10.30 and 11 pm.

Praia do Camburí

This five-km stretch of beach is where you'll find lots of restaurants, nightspots and mid-range hotels. It's not good for swimming, as its proximity to the port at Tubarão means there's usually some oil or chemicals in the water.

Vila Velha

This was the first place in Espírito Santo to be colonised. The most interesting thing to do in Vila Velha is climb up to the Convento

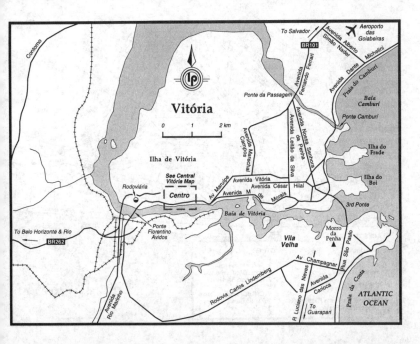

da Penha, set atop a 154-metre granite outcrop. In the week after Easter, thousands of devotees come to this major pilgrimage centre to pay homage to the image of NS de Penha, some even making the climb on their knees. Even if you don't usually visit convents, the panoramic view of Vitória makes the climb worth it.

Praia da Costa, the main Vila Velha beach, is close to the convent. It has fewer hotels and restaurants than Camburí, but is better for swimming.

Other Attractions

The pink **Anchieta Palace**, on Praça João Climaco, is a 16th-century former Jesuit college and church. It's now the seat of state government, and the only part you can enter is the tomb of Padre Anchieta, co-founder of São Paulo. Close by is the **Catedral Metropolitana**, with its neogothic exterior and interesting stained-glass windows.

Teatro Carlos Gomes, on Praça Costa Pereira, is a replica of La Scala in Milan. The **Parque Moscoso** is where Capixabas (as natives of the state are called) go for a break.

Places to Stay

There is a row of 'crash-pad' hotels across from the bus station, the best of which is the *Spala*, at US$8 per person. The centre is easy to get to, however, and it's worth making the effort to get away from the bus station and its uninspiring surroundings.

In the centre are lots of cheap hotels. The *Hotel Restaurante Europa*, at the start of Rua 7 de Setembro next to Praça Costa Pereira, is a good deal: clean quartos for US$5 a head and big apartamentos for US$7 a head. The food in their restaurant is cheap, with large servings. The *Hotel Catedral* (☎ 223-4173) is, you guessed it, near the cathedral, at Rua Pedro Palácios 213. The receptionist here reads the Bible in his spare moments – it's

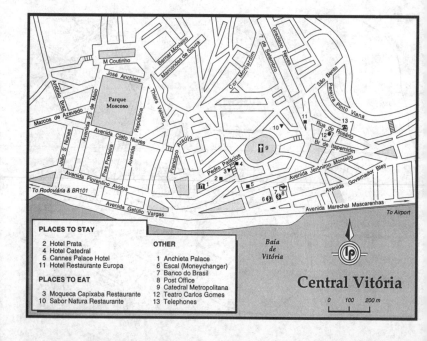

PLACES TO STAY

2 Hotel Prata
4 Hotel Catedral
5 Cannes Palace Hotel
11 Hotel Restaurante Europa

PLACES TO EAT

3 Moqueca Capixaba Restaurante
10 Sabor Natura Restaurante

OTHER

1 Anchieta Palace
6 Escal (Moneychanger)
7 Banco do Brasil
8 Post Office
9 Catedral Metropolitana
12 Teatro Carlos Gomes
13 Telephones

Baía de Vitória

Central Vitória

0   100   200 m

that kind of place. Quartos cost US$7/9 a single/double and apartamentos are US$9/12; it's cheap, clean and honest.

The *Hotel Prata* (☎ 222-4311) is right next to the Anchieta Palace, at Rua Nestor Gomes 201. They charge US$13/18 for musty singles/doubles; you have to be out by 10 am. The breakfast is good, though. The *Cannes Palace Hotel* (☎ 222-1522; fax 222-8061), at Avenida Jerônimo Monteiro 111, is a more expensive option, at US$35/45 for singles/doubles – but if you're going to spend that sort of money, you may as well be on the beach.

Out at Camburí, the cheapest beachfront place is the *Hotel Praia* (☎ 227-8777), at Avenida Dante Michelini 207, with singles/doubles for US$25/35. The *Camburi Praia* (☎ 227-1322), Dante Michelini 1007, costs a few dollars more.

If you want to stay at Praia da Costa, the youth hostel *Praia da Costa* (☎ 329-3227) is two blocks from the beach, at Avenida São Paulo 1163.

The *Hostess* (☎ 329-2111), at Avenida Antônio Gil Velloso 442, is a three-star hotel with singles/doubles for US$35/45. The *Hotel Senac* (☎ 325-0111; fax 325-0115), Ilha do Boi, is Vitória's five-star hotel. Rooms start at US$90 a double.

Places to Eat

Restaurante Piratas, at Avenida Dante Michelini 747, Praia do Camburí, has a good squid vinaigrette for US$7. Ask for the couvert. *Churrascaria Canoas*, at Avenida Dante Michelini 47, has a US$8 rodízio.

In the city centre, the *Sabor Natura Restaurante* (for vegetarians) is near Praça Costa Pereira, at Rua 13 de Maio 90. It's open from 8 am to 6.30 pm daily, but the US$3 set lunch is served only from 11 am to 3 pm. Another good lunch buffet in the centre is the US$7, all-you-can-eat session at the *Cannes Palace Hotel*, at Avenida Jerônimo Monteiro 111. The *Moqueca Capixaba Restaurante* is a good place to eat the dish of the same name. The restaurant is on the steps leading down from the park in front of the cathedral; it's closed on Sunday.

Getting There & Away

It's all too easy to get to Vitória – the trick is to get away. The bus station on Ilha do Príncipe has connections to all major cities. There are nine buses a day to Belo Horizonte (US$12, eight hours). To Ouro Prêto, there's a direct bus at 10.45 pm. To Porto Seguro, there's one daily bus, at 9 am. The 11-hour trip costs US$16. Eleven buses a day make the eight-hour journey to Rio de Janeiro (US$11).

Getting Around

To/From the Airport The airport is 10 km from the city centre; take the local bus marked 'Aeroporto' from the bus station (US$0.50).

Bus All local buses run from the various stops outside the main rodoviária. As in Rio de Janeiro, the route is written on the side of the bus. To get to the centre, catch any bus that goes along Avenida Vitória. When you pass the pink palace on the left-hand side, get out at the next stop. It's only a three-minute ride.

For Praia do Camburí, catch any bus that goes along Avenida Dante Michelini. To Vila Velha, catch an all-yellow or all-blue bus. To get to Praia da Costa, you'll have to catch a bus from the Vila Velha terminal.

Ferry An alternative, more scenic way to get to Vila Velha from the centre is to catch a ferry from the Terminal Aquaviário, on Avenida Beira Mar. They run on weekdays, every hour from 6 am to 7 pm.

GUARAPARI

Guarapari is Espírito Santo's most prominent resort town. It's too big a city to be a proper beach town, but there are 23 beaches in the municipality, each with a lovely mountain backdrop. The best beach is Praia do Morro; unlike the others, it doesn't have too many stones, and it does have the healing monazitic radioactive sands touted in Espírito's brochures.

Guarapari was an excellent base for a family holiday. We enjoyed being off the beaten tourist track in a genuine Brazilian holiday resort – albeit out of season. From Praia do Morro there is an excellent walk around the headland through brushland where birds abound, to lovely unspoiled coves. There are superb views back towards Guarapari and Muquicaba with the backdrop of the dramatic coastal range of mountains. To the south of Guarapari, at the tiny resort of Meaipe, there is a magnificent beach. At lunchtime, stroll off the sand into the Cantina de Curuca for excellent lobster and prawns.

M K Barritt (UK)

Places to Stay

The youth hostel and campground, *Guaracamping* (☎ 261-0475), at Avenida F, QD 40, isn't far from the bus station and is well signposted.

From the bus station, it's a 10-minute walk to the centre. There are two central budget places on Rua Dr Silva Melo, only a block from Praia do Meio and Praia da Areia Branca. At No 98, the *Hotel Maryland* (☎ & fax 261-0553) has single/double apartamentos for US$18/30. Almost next door is the *Areia Preta* (☎ 261-2717), which has singles/doubles for US$15/24, as well as a reasonable Chinese restaurant. A bit more up-market and in the same vicinity are the *Solar da Ruth* (☎ 261-1836), at Rua Dr Silva Melo 215, a very friendly one-star hotel close to the beach (singles/doubles for US$22/34), and the *Coronado* (☎ 361-0144; fax 261-1444), a three-star place right on the beach (US$38/45).

The best place close to the bus station is the *Star* (☎ 261-2439), popular with overnight travellers who don't want to carry bags into town. It's a couple of blocks from Prainha beach, at Rua Santo Antônio 287, and costs US$14/21 a single/double. The *Best Western Porto do Sol* (☎ 361-1111; fax 261-2929), at Avenida Beira Mar 1, by Muquiçaba beach, is Guarapari's four-star hotel. Singles/doubles cost US$90/110.

Places to Eat

Pizzaria do Angelo, on the corner of Rua Dr Silva Melo and Rua Joaquim Silva Lima, is a good, cheap place in a pleasant, green setting. *Cabana Ali Babá e os 40 Quibes*, an interestingly named restaurant at Avenida Beira Mar 382, serves good Middle Eastern food. For seafood, *Peixada do Irmão*, at Rua Jacinto de Almeida 72, is highly recommended.

Getting There & Away

Buses run from Vitória to Guarapari every hour from 6 am to 9 pm (US$2, 1¼ hours). To Vitória, buses run hourly from 6 am to 9.30 pm. Frequent buses make the 28-km trip to Anchieta.

ANCHIETA

Anchieta is 88 km south of Vitória. Its attractions are the 16th-century church of NS de Assunção and, alongside, the Museu Padre Anchieta. The church walls are original; they were built by Padre Anchieta and the local Indians. The museum is no big deal, although it contains the chair of Padre Anchieta, and other relics. It's closed on Monday.

Places to Stay

There aren't any real cheapies in Anchieta. The *Hotel Porto Velho* (☎ 536-1181), right above the bus stop, has singles/doubles with TV and refrigerator for US$30/38. A bit cheaper is the *Anchieta* (☎ 536-1258), 100 metres further down the road, which combines a pleasant, colonial style with some wild floral wallpaper and curtains. Singles/doubles cost US$22/28.

Places to Eat

Popular with locals is the *Varandão*, in the centre, at Rua Costa Pereira 204, which serves good moqueca for US$7. The *Restaurante Peixada do Garcia*, on Praia Ubu, 10 km north towards Guarapari, is reputedly excellent.

Getting There & Away

To Guarapari, buses run every 20 to 30 minutes from 6 am to 6.50 pm. To Piúma, 12 km away, they run every 30 to 40 minutes from 6 am to 7.20 pm.

PIÚMA

Known as the City of Shells, Piúma is a small village 100 km south of Vitória. The rarest shell in the world, *Oliva Zelindea*, is occasionally found here. There are some nice beaches around Piúma, and some nearby offshore islands which are worth a look.

The coastline is dominated by the 300-metre-high, cone-shaped Monte Aghá, which is a good place for hang-gliding and climbing.

Islands

Ilha do Gamba is connected to the mainland by a thin isthmus, and is home to lots of seabirds. Ilha dos Cabritos, 15 minutes away by boat, has a good seafood restaurant. Ilha do Meio preserves wild orchids and native trees, and a large variety of lobsters, sea horses and starfish are found in the surrounding waters. To get a boat to the islands, ask the locals with boats on the beach.

Beaches

Praia Boca da Barra and Praia Maria Nenen are surf beaches, while Praia Acaiaca has calm water.

Places to Stay

The cheapest place in town is a dormitorio close to the bus station, on the corner of the town square. You can sleep here for US$5. At Rua Feliciano Lopes 23, the *Vila Rica* (☎ 520-1753), charges US$15 per head for small, clean apartamentos with fan. Vila Rica also has a campground. Rooms with a sea view are available at the *Pousada Itaputanga* (☎ 520-1348), on Rua Franklin Ferreira de Souza, for US$40 a double.

Another nice place is the *Solar de Brasilia* (☎ 520-1521), 50 metres from the beach, at Avenida Eduardo Rodrigues 15. Singles/doubles are US$38/50. The breakfast is excellent, and the hotel has a swimming pool.

The three-star *Monte Aghá* (☎ 520-1622; fax 520-1677), at Avenida Minas Gerais 20, is the most expensive hotel in Piúma, with singles/doubles for US$45/60.

Places to Eat

Most of Piúma's restaurants are located along the beachfront, on Avenida Beira Mar. *Belabatok* has great seafood and carne do sol. *d'Angelus*, right alongside Belabatok, is also very popular, offering a cheap, self-serve lunch for US$5 a kilo.

Getting There & Away

There are frequent buses that go to Anchieta and Marataízes. Only four buses a day go to Vitória.

MARATAÍZES

The town of Marataízes caters to the working-class Mineiro holiday crowd during high summer season, and lives off its small fishing industry the rest of the year. Every morning the town beach throbs with fisherfolk, who pull lines in teams, haul in and sort their catch, fix nets and push tiny boats into the foamy sea. It is possible to hire a boat from Marataízes or Itapaiva beach to the islands of Francês, Ovos or Itaputera.

Places to Stay

Marataízes has lots of cheap places and a few more expensive ones. The *Xodó* (☎ 532-1291) is a well-located youth hostel and camping ground at Avenida Atlântica 1930. Another cheapie (and further from the bus station) is the *Pousada Cantinha do Valdir* (☎ 532-2604), at Avenida Costa e Silva 132. Valdir himself is quite a character, and he loves the sound of his own voice. He charges US$8 per person, and US$15 for two-person apartments with a kitchen, so you can cook the local fish any way you want. It's pretty basic, but it's cheap. The *Pensão Santa Izabel* (☎ 532-1439), at Rua Soares 80, is clean and cheap at US$10 a head (US$18 if you want meals as well). The *Hotel Atlântico* (☎ 532-1427) has apartamentos for US$12 per person. Close to the Praia Hotel, at Rua Alegre 83, it's only a block from the beach.

Across the road from the bus station, the *Hotel Marataízes* (☎ 532-1383) charges US$12 per person. From here, it's a three-minute walk to the main beach.

Of the expensive hotels, the *Praia Hotel*

(☎ 532-2144; fax 532-3515), at Avenida Atlântica 99, is the pick of the bunch; it faces the beach. Singles/doubles are US$38/55, but there's a 20% discount in the low season.

Places to Eat
The strip along Avenida Atlântica is full of bars and restaurants. *Gaivota*, at No 712, has all the seafood dishes. There's also a reasonable café at the *Xodó*. The restaurant in the *Praia Hotel* is a bit more expensive, but highly recommended. Near the bus station is *Bar Restaurante Pic Tot*, a friendly place with huge servings.

Getting There & Away
Three buses a day go to Vitória, at 6 and 6.15 am and 3.10 pm. There's also a bus to Rio de Janeiro, which leaves at 10.30 pm.

AROUND MARATAÍZES
Praia Marape is a lovely beach adjacent to a poor little fishing village about 30 km south of Marataízes. There is no formal accommodation here, but hardy travellers can make do. Praia das Neves, Praia Moroba and Praia Lagoa Boa Vista are reasonable beaches further to the north.

DOMINGOS MARTINS
Domingos Martins, also known as Campinho, is a small village settled by Germans in 1847. The pride of the town is the musical water clock decorated with figures of the 12 apostles; it's in the Restaurante Vista Linda, seven km below the town proper. In town, Recanto dos Colibris, at the far end of Avenida Presidente Vargas, is a pretty gathering spot.

The town is a good base for exploring the streams and forests of the mountains. Fifty km further into the mountains, at Aracê, are some fancier resort hotels with horses for hire.

Places to Stay & Eat
The cheapest hotel is the *Campinho*, close to the bus stop. Singles/doubles here are US$12/17. The *Hotel e Restaurante Imper-*

ador (☎ 268-1115), at Rua Duque de Caxias 275, has a sauna. Doubles cost US$30.

Out of town, the *Vista Linda* offers diners a great view of the valley and of the musical clock. The restaurant in the *Imperador* is also worth a try.

Getting There & Away
Nine buses a day make the 41-km trip from Vitória to Domingos Martins (US$2, one hour).

SANTA TERESA
Santa Teresa is a small town settled by Italian immigrants. It has a pretty, flowered plaza, and a cool, mountain climate suitable for vineyards. Nearby trips include the valley of Canaã and the Reserva Biológica Nova Lombardia.

Museu Biológico de Professor Melo Leitão
The town's main attraction, this museum represents the life's work of Augusto Ruschi, a staunch environmentalist and world-renowned hummingbird expert, who died in 1986 after being poisoned by a frog. The museum also has a small zoo, a butterfly garden, a snake farm, and a large number of orchids and other flora. It's open only on weekends, from noon to 5 pm. Time your visit to Santa Teresa accordingly, as the museum is very interesting.

Places to Stay & Eat
At Avenida Getúlio Vargas 115, the *Hotel Pierazzo* (☎ 259-1233), has very nice some single/double rooms for US$18/23. The cheaper alternative is the *Globo*, at Rua Jerônimo Vervloet 190, which charges US$8 per person.

A few doors down from the Pierazzo is the *Restaurante Zitus*, which does good pasta. Go upstairs from the lanchonete.

Getting There & Away
Santa Teresa is 76 km from Vitória, and seven buses a day make the journey (US$3, two hours).

CONCEIÇÃO DA BARRA

Situated in the north of the state, 254 km from Vitória, the small town of Conceição da Barra lies between the mouths of the Itaúnas and Cricaré rivers.

There are some quiet beaches in the area, such as Praia da Barra, Bugia and Guaxindiba, but the main attractions are the Dunas de Itaúnas: 20 to 30-metre-high dunes of fine sand that engulfed the small village of Vila de Itaunas. Only the church tower is still visible. From the top of the dunes, it's possible to see the sea, the Rio Itaúnas and the surrounding Atlantic rainforest. The dunes are 23 km from Conceição da Barra.

Places to Stay & Eat

There are plenty of places to stay in town. Budget travellers should think seriously about slinging a hammock in a fisher hut at Bugia, or camping out near the dunes.

The *Dunas de Itaúnas* (☎ 762-1302) has single/double apartamentos for US$9/14. It's in the centre, on Rua Mendes de Oliveira.

Also central is *Rustico's Hotel* (☎ 762-1193), at Rua Muniz Freire 299, with single/double apartamentos for US$12/20.

The top-end place to stay in town is the three-star *Barramar Praia Hotel* (☎ 762-1311), at Praia de Guaxindiba. It charges US$37/45 a single/double.

The best places to eat are the barracas on the beaches, which serve the local speciality: puã de caranguejo, a tasty crab stew. These shacks also serve coconut milk, fried fish and, of course, killer batidas.

Getting There & Away

There is only one daily direct bus from Vitória, leaving at 10 am and arriving in Conceição at 2 pm (US$10). You could catch a bus to São Mateus, and then one of the frequent buses that make the 35-km trip from there to Conceição da Barra. Alternatively, take any bus going to Bahia along BR-101, get off at the turn-off to Conceição, and hitch or walk the 15 km to town.

Minas Gerais

The state of Minas Gerais is as large as France, part of a vast plateau that crosses Brazil's interior. Rising along the state's southern border with Rio and São Paulo is the Serra da Mantiqueira, with some of Brazil's highest peaks. These mountains stalled the development of Minas Gerais until the gold boom at the beginning of the 18th century. Running south to north, from São João del Rei through Ouro Prêto and past Diamantina, is the Serra do Espinhaço, Brazil's oldest geological formation. This range separates Minas' two principal river systems: the great São Francisco to the west and the Rio Doce to the east.

Minas has good roads but travel is usually a sinuous affair. Much of the terrain is characterised by hills, deep valleys and plateaus running off the larger mountains. Because of the plentiful rains, the south, east and much of the centre were once thickly forested, but the land has been cleared for mining and agriculture and, today, there is little forest left. In the rainy season the land is still green, but forests are pretty much limited to Minas' several large parks and reserves. The northern extension of the state is sertão and less populated than the rest of Minas. It's an arid land, with shrub-like trees that look dead during the dry season but quickly regain their foliage when it rains. The most common tree is the pepper tree (*aroeira*).

For the traveller, Minas presents a welcome contrast to the rest of Brazil. Nestled in the Serra do Espinhaço are the *cidades históricas* – historic colonial cities which grew up with the great gold boom. The foothills and streams of these mountains were scoured for gold throughout the 18th century. Minas' exquisite colonial towns are seemingly frozen in another epoch. Their baroque churches and sacred art – mostly sculptures from one of the world's great artists, Aleijadinho – represent over half of Brazil's national monuments.

Minas also has several hydromineral spas in the mountainous south-west corner and a number of prehistoric caves close to the capital, Belo Horizonte. Founded as recently as 1897, Belo Horizonte is Brazil's third largest city. While residents often speak well of this sprawling place, there is little beauty, natural or otherwise, to stimulate the visitor.

The major historical cities are clustered in three spots along the Serra do Espinhaço range: São João del Rei, with Tiradentes and Prados nearby, is 200 km south of Belo Horizonte; Ouro Prêto and Mariana are 100 km south-east of Belo Horizonte; and Diamantina, with Serro further down the road, is 290 km north of Belo Horizonte.

Ouro Prêto, declared a World Cultural Heritage Site by UNESCO, has more of everything than any city in Brazil – more homogeneous baroque architecture, more churches, more Aleijadinho, more museums and more fame. It also has more tourists, more traffic, more boutiques, more locals hawking things to visitors and more expensive hotels and restaurants. If you go to Ouro Prêto and don't have time to visit the other clusters of historic cities, be sure to visit nearby Mariana, which remains less affected by tourism.

It's hard to tell anyone to bypass Ouro Prêto, and if you really like colonial or baroque art and architecture, or the sculpture of Aleijadinho and churches, then you definitely should go there. But if your time is limited and your visit is during the peak tourist season, it's worth considering spending more time at some of the other historic cities and less time at Ouro Prêto.

Diamantina has the fewest tourists and is the most tranquil of the region's historic cities. Its many buildings form a beautiful display of colonial architecture. São João and Tiradentes are a good combination to visit: the former has several churches and works of Aleijadinho in a small lively city with little tourism, and the latter is a tiny

A: German-style architecture in Blumenau
B: Windmill, Blumenau
C: Waterfall in Rio Grande do Sul
D: Fisherman, Ilha de Santa Catarina
E: The mighty Iguaçu Falls

ALL PHOTOS BY ANDREW DRAFFEN

A	B
	C
D	

A: Presidential guard
B: *Os Candangos*, Brasília
C: Catedral Brasília
D: Interior of Catedral Brasília

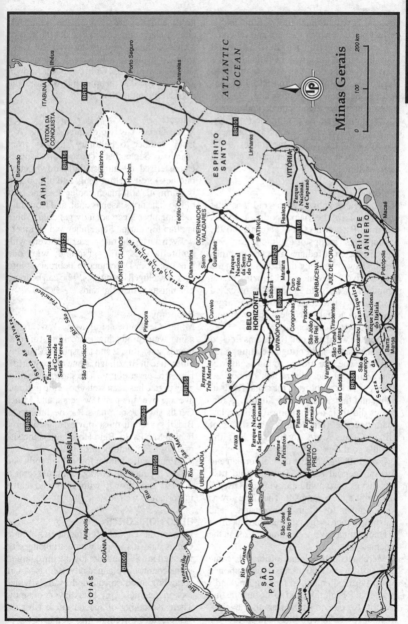

Minas Gerais

0   100   200 km

ATLANTIC OCEAN

BAHIA

Ilhéus
ITABUNA
VITÓRIA DA CONQUISTA
BR101
BR116
Brumado
Geralzinho
Itaobim
BR122
Porto Seguro
Caravelas
BR101
ESPÍRITO SANTO
Linhares
BR101
VITÓRIA
Parque Nacional de Caparaó
RIO DE JANEIRO
Macaé
Teófilo Otoni
GOVERNADOR VALADARES
IPATINGA
Realeza
BR116
MONTES CLAROS
Diamantina
Serro
Guanhães
Parque Nacional da Serra do Cipó
BR262
Mariana
Ouro Preto
BARBACENA
JUIZ DE FORA
Petrópolis
Serra do Espinhaço
Curvelo
Sabará
BELO HORIZONTE
BR040
Congonhas
São João del Rei
Prados
Tiradentes
São Tomé das Letras
Cacambu
Parque Nacional do Itatiaia
Mantiqueira
Barra Mansa
Pirapora
Rio São Francisco
Parque Nacional Grande Sertão Veredas
São Francisco
São Gotardo
Represa Três Marias
DIVINÓPOLIS
São Lourenço
Varginha
BR381
Poços de Caldas
Serra da
BR365
Araxá
Parque Nacional da Serra da Canastra
Passos
Represa de Furnas
RIBEIRÃO PRETO
BR040
Serra de Caiapó
BRASÍLIA
BR050
UBERLÂNDIA
Rio São Marcos
Rio Corumbá
Represa de Peixotos
Rio Grande
UBERABA
São José do Rio Preto
SÃO PAULO
Anápolis
GOIÂNIA
BR050
GOIÁS
BR020
Rio Paranaíba
Araçatuba

colonial town untouched by time and a perfect place in which to relax and reflect.

The mystery card when shuffling around your itinerary is the town of Congonhas. It's a couple of hours' bus ride from Belo Horizonte, São João or Ouro Prêto. Bus connections between Congonhas and São João or Ouro Prêto are inconvenient, and there is one, and only one, attraction: the *Prophets*, the masterpiece of Aleijadinho. You need just a few hours to view the statues at the *basílica*, but it's an inspirational sight and well worth the trouble.

History

No one really knows when gold was first discovered in the backwoods of Minas Gerais. But sometime around 1695, bandeirantes (groups of explorers from São Paulo in search of Indian slaves and precious metals) saw gold along the banks and in the beds of rivers flowing from Brazil's oldest mountains. The gold deposits were called *faisqueiras* (sparkles) because the larger pieces were actually visible – all the miners had to do was pick them up.

Soon the word was out. Brazilians flocked to Minas Gerais and Portuguese immigrated to Brazil. The two groups soon fought over land claims in the Guerra dos Emboabas. Slaves were brought from the sugar fields of Bahia and the savannahs of Angola, as few whites did their own mining. Until the last quarter of the 18th century, the slaves of Minas Gerais were digging up half the world's gold.

Over 100 years before the Californian and Australian gold rushes, Brazil's gold rush was just as crazy, wild and violent. Disease and famine were rampant. The mine towns were known for their licentiousness, and prostitutes such as the famous Chica da Silva in Diamantina have been immortalised in the cinema.

Merchants and colonial officials became rich, as did a few gold miners. Gold siphoned off to Portugal ended up feeding England's Industrial Revolution, and so the only lasting benefits to come to Brazil were the development of Rio de Janeiro (the main port for the gold) and the creation of the beautiful, church-clad mining cities that dot the hills of Minas Gerais. Ouro Prêto was the most splendid of these. Vila Rica de Ouro Prêto (Rich Town of Black Gold), as it was known, grew to 100,000 people and became the richest city in the New World.

Climate

Minas Gerais has two distinct seasons: wet from October to February and dry from March to September. The rainy season is characterised by almost daily downpours, but they rarely last for long, and although it is warm, it's still much cooler than the heat of Rio. The dry season is cool, and from July to September it can actually get cold. There is often fog during September and October.

Even during the rainy season, travel – with umbrella – is quite practical, with one proviso: from December to February, Ouro Prêto is deluged by tourists, who can be more of a nuisance than the rain.

Economy

Minas Gerais (General Mines) wears its name well, producing more iron, tin, diamonds, zinc, quartz and phosphates than any other state in Brazil. It has one of the world's largest reserves of iron. The state's industrial growth rate has been well above the national average over the past few years, and Minas Gerais should soon pass Rio de Janeiro as Brazil's second-most powerful economy, behind São Paulo. Belo Horizonte is the site of a large Fiat automobile plant.

Minas is also known for its high milk and cheese production. The agricultural sector is diverse and strong, with fruit and cattle important as well.

BELO HORIZONTE

Belo is the capital of mineral-rich Minas Gerais state. It's a rapidly industrialising city, founded in 1897 and already the third largest in the country. A planned city, Belo is a giant sprawling affair surrounded by hills which lock in the thick, grey-black layers of smog. There is nothing of special interest for the visitor; most travellers who stop here are on their way to Ouro Prêto or Diamantina, with perhaps the occasional soul heading to Brasília.

Most travellers, as soon as they hit the historical cities, regret having spent any time at all in Belo Horizonte. But if you find yourself here with time to spare, there are a couple of museums worth a visit.

Information
Tourist Office Belotur (☎ 222-5500), the municipal tourist organisation, puts out an excellent monthly guide in Portuguese, English and French. It's very comprehensive, listing not only the main tourist attractions but also how to get there using local buses. It includes flight times, detailed long-distance bus schedules and everything else you wanted to know about Belo Horizonte but didn't know how to ask.

Belotur has booths at Confins airport (open daily from 8 am to 6 pm), in front of the Parque Municipal (open on weekdays from 8 am to 8 pm and on weekends from 8 am to 4 pm) and at the rodoviária (open the same hours as the park booth). Staff speak a bit of English and can also supply you with state tourist information.

Money Change money at the Banco do Brasil, Rua Rio de Janeiro 750, close to Praça Sete. It opens at 10 am and stays open during lunch. There are lots of other banks and câmbios in the city centre – try Nascente Turismo, at Rua Rio de Janeiro 1101. Câmbios usually open at 11 am.

Post & Telephone The main post office is at Avenida Afonso Pena 1270, but there's one at the rodoviária, too. Telemig has telephone posts at Rua dos Tamoios 311, at the rodoviária and at Confins airport.

Museu de Mineralogía
There are 5000 specimens here in a curious gothic building at Rua da Bahia 1149. The displays include replicas of all the world's largest diamonds, meteorites and rough diamonds, and some of the largest crystals

you'll ever see. It's open daily from 8.30 am to 5.30 pm.

Museu Histórico Abílio Barreto
In an old colonial farmhouse, this museum is all that remains of the town of Curral del Rey, on which Belo Horizonte was built. It contains a fascinating archive of old photographs, as well as other assorted historical bric-a-brac. The museum is at Rua Bernardo Mascarenhas, in Cidade Jardim, and is open Tuesday to Sunday from 10 am to 5 pm. To get there, take a No 8902 bus marked 'Luxemburgo/Sagrada Familia' from the stop on Avenida Amazonas between Rua dos Tupinambás and Avenida Afonso Pena.

Pampulha
Fans of architect Oscar Niemeyer won't want to miss his creations in the suburb of Pampulha, in the north of the city, around a large lake, but others may be disappointed. The area has an unkempt feel about it. There's the Igreja de São Francisco de Assis, built in the 1940s, and the Museu de Arte de Belo Horizonte, among others. To get there, take the No 2004 'Bandeirantes/Olhos/d'Agua' bus. Be prepared to do a bit of walking once you arrive.

Gruta de Maquiné
An interesting and popular day trip from Belo Horizonte is to the Gruta de Maquiné, the most famous of Minas' many caves. Its seven huge chambers are well lit to allow guided tours to pass through. A bus to the caves departs from the rodoviária every day at 9.15 am and returns at 3 pm, which gives you ample viewing time. The trip costs US$4. There are cafés at the cave: *Chero's* is recommended; their comida mineira is quite cheap.

Rio São Francisco River Trip
Trips can be arranged in Belo Horizonte for passage on the paddle-steamer *Benjamin Guimaraes*, which still travels on the river between Pirapora (around 320 km north of Belo Horizonte) and the small town of São Francisco.

The *Benjamin Guimaraes* has 12 cabins and a bar/restaurant on board. The five-day tourist trip begins every Sunday and costs US$500 per person, which includes the bus fare from Belo Horizonte to Pirapora. For more details and to confirm the schedule, call ☎ (031) 201-7144 in Belo Horizonte. For information on the history of the 'River of National Unity', see the Rio São Francisco section in the Bahia chapter.

Places to Stay – bottom end
Youth Hostels There are two youth hostels in town. They're your cheapest option,

though both are a bit of a hike from the bus station. The *Pousada Beagá* (☎ 337-1845; fax 275-3592), at Rua Santa Catarina 597, is in the suburb of Lourdes. (From the rodoviária, follow Avenida Paraná up to Rua Santa Catarina.) It's open from 7 am to 11 pm. The *Pousadinha Mineira* (☎ 446-2911; fax 442-4448) is at Rua Araxá 514. From the rodoviária, follow Avenida Santos Dumont up to Rua Rio de Janeiro, then turn left and go up a couple of blocks to Avenida do Contorno. Cross the avenue and, going straight ahead, follow Rua Varginha up a few blocks to Rua Araxá.

Central Belo Horizonte

Hotels You'll see lots of hotels right next to the rodoviária, but most are pretty dingy, and the area is a sleazy, red-light district after dark. If that doesn't bother you, try the *Hotel Madrid* (☎ 201-1088), just in front of the bus station, at Rua dos Guaranis 12. Quartos here are US$10/16 a single/double; apartamentos cost US$13/18. One block further on down Rua dos Guaranis, at No 124, the *Hotel Magnata* (☎ 201-5368) has simple, well-kept apartamentos for US$12/18 a single/double. Both these hotels are strictly *familiar*, meaning they don't rent rooms by the hour.

Places to Stay – middle & top end

The *BH Centro* (☎ 222-3390; fax 222-3146), at Rua Espírito Santo 284, has

single/double rooms without bath for US$12/18 and double rooms with bath for US$25. At Avenida Paraná 241 in the city centre, a couple of blocks from the west side of Avenida Afonso Pena, is the *Hotel Continental* (☎ 201-7944). It's clean, friendly and not too noisy, and some rooms have little balconies. Fifties-style apartamentos are a good deal at US$17/24.

The *Hotel Esplanada* (☎ 273-5311), a two-star Embratur hotel at Avenida Santos Dumont 304, charges US$18/26 for singles/doubles without bath, and US$26/38 with bath.

The *Hotel Amazonas* (☎ 201-4644), at Avenida Amazonas 120, is a classy, three-star Embratur place. They charge US$65 for doubles with TV, air-con and balcony. In the centre, across from the park, the *Othon Palace* (☎ 273-3844; fax 212-2318) is Belo Horizonte's five-star hotel. It has singles/doubles for US$120/140.

Places to Eat

There are lots of lanchonetes and fast-food places clustered around Praça Sete – such as *Bang Bang Burguer* (try saying that in Portuguese), where the waiters all wear cowboy hats, at Rua São Paulo 679. Wander around and see what you feel like.

For lunch, *Vida Campestre Natural*, Rua Afonso Pena 774, has good, cheap, natural food. The *Dragon Centre* is a reasonable Chinese restaurant close to Praça Sete, at Afonso Pena 549. *Torino*, at Rua dos Guajajaras 460, is a small place with a wood-fired oven, a varied menu and a self-serve, por-kilo lunch.

One of our French readers highly recommends *O Gaulês*, a French restaurant at Rua Major Lopes 500, in the suburb of São Pedro, for its excellent service and refined cooking. The chef is French, of course.

Most of the other really flash restaurants are in the suburb of Savassí; the Belotur monthly guide has a listing.

Entertainment

The Belotur monthly guide has a good listing of discos. Right near the central hotels on

---

PLACES TO STAY

2	Hotel Madrid
4	Hotel Magnata
5	Hotel Esplanada
6	Hotel Magalhes
7	BH Centro
8	Hotel Bragança
9	Hotel Gontijo
10	Hotel Continental
17	Brazil Palace Hotel
24	Othon Palace

PLACES TO EAT

11	Dragon Centre Restaurant
14	Torino
16	Bang Bang Burguer
19	Vida Campestre Natural

OTHER

1	Rodoviária
3	Praça da Rodoviária
12	Buses to Pampulha
13	Restaurante Praça Sete
15	Praça Sete
18	Tourist Information Booth
20	Telephones
21	Banco do Brasil
22	Shopping Cidade
23	Mercado Central
25	Câmbio
26	Post Office
27	Museu de Mineralogía

Praça Sete is the Restaurante Praça Sete. It has a beer-hall atmosphere, with good local music from 10 pm to 3 am. If you can stand the horrible sound system, it's fun.

Things to Buy

The Centro de Artesanato Mineiro (☎ 222-2765), Avenida Afonso Pena 1537, Palácio das Artes (at the edge of the Parque Municipal), is a government store with a varied assortment of mineiro crafts: ceramics, jewellery, tapestries, rugs, quilts and soapstone sculptures. It's open on Saturday from 9 am to 8.45 pm and on Sunday from 9 am to 1.45 pm.

The Gem Center is not far from the municipal park, at Avenida Alvares Cabral 45. Around 20 reputable gem dealers have small shops in the building.

A huge Feira de Arte e Artesano is held on Sunday from 9 am to 1 pm on Avenida Afonso Pena between Rua da Bahia and Rua dos Guajajaras, with good food and local crafts. If you're around, check it out.

Getting There & Away

Air Belo Horizonte is connected to reach Rio and São Paulo by frequent one-hour VASP/Cruzeiro/Transbrasil *ponte aerea* (air-bridge) flights. There are daily flights from Belo to just about anywhere in Brazil.

Transbrasil is at Rua dos Tamoios 86 (☎ 226-3433) and at Confins airport (☎ 689-2475). Varig/Cruzeiro is at Rua Espírito Santo 643 (☎ 273-6060) and at Confins airport (☎ 689-2244). VASP has offices at Avenida Olegário Maciel 2221, Lourdes (☎ (0800) 99-8277 toll free) and at Confins airport (☎ 689-2411).

Bus Buses take seven hours to Rio (US$7), 9½ hours to São Paulo (US$15), 12 hours to Brasília (US$20) and around 22 hours to Salvador (US$35). Buses leave every hour for Ouro Prêto, the first at 7 am and the last at 8.15 pm. The trip takes 1¾ hours and costs US$4.

There are eight buses a day to Mariana, from 6 am to 11 pm. The two-hour trip costs US$4.50. Six daily go to Diamantina

(US$10, 5½ hours), the first at 5.30 am and the last at midnight. Seven daily go to São João del Rei, the first at 6.15 am and the last at 7 pm. From 5 am to midnight, buses run to Sabará every 15 minutes; catch them downstairs at the local bus section of the rodoviária.

If you're heading to the mineral spring resorts, there are four buses a day to Poços das Caldas (US$24), two to Caxambu (US$7), at 7.30 am and 11 pm, and three to São Lourenço (US$8), at 12.30 am, and 3 and 9.30 pm.

Getting Around

To/From the Airport Belo Horiztonte has two airports. Most planes use the new international Aeroporto Confins (also known as Aeroporto Tancredo Neves), which is 40 km from the city. The closer, sleepy Aeroporto da Pampulha handles some of the Rio and São Paulo shuttle flights.

The best way to get to the airport is by bus from the rodoviária. There's a conventional bus that leaves every half-hour to an hour (depending on the time), between 4.45 am and 10.45 pm; the trip costs US$1.50. Even though it's not advertised, this bus will stop at Aeroporto da Pampulha on the way to Aeroporto Confins – but make sure the driver knows your destination.

There is also an air-con executivo bus (US$4). It leaves from the executivo terminal at Praça Raoul Soares every 45 minutes to an hour between 5.15 am and 9.45 pm.

Historical Towns

SABARÁ

Sabará stands on the muddy banks of the Rio das Velhas (Old Ladies' River). It was the first major gold-mining centre in the state, and during its peak was one of the world's wealthiest towns. This is reflected in its houses, mansions, churches, statues, fountains and sacred art. Sabará is now a poor town dominated by a Belgian metalworks. In the boom years of the early 1700s, when the

Rio das Velhas was 15 times wider, slave boats would sail all the way down the Rio São Francisco from Bahia. Sabará produced more gold in one week than the rest of Brazil produced in a year. You can still pan the riverbed for gold flakes, but the nuggets are long since gone.

Orientation & Information

Since it's only 25 km and half an hour by bus from Belo Horizonte, Sabará makes an easy and interesting day trip. There's an information booth at the entrance to town, but it's useless. The major sights are signposted from Praça Santa Rita anyway.

Churches

Most of the churches have small entry fees.

Matriz de NS de Conceição The Portuguese Jesuits, cultural ambassadors of the far-flung Portuguese Empire, were among the first Westerners to make contact with the orient. As a result, the Matriz de NS de Conceição (1720) is a fascinating blend of Oriental arts and Portuguese baroque – overwhelming with its gold leaf and red Chinese scrolls.

Restationed in Brazil, the Jesuits brought the Oriental arts to Sabará, as is evident in the pagodas on some of the church door panels by the sanctuary. There are several other interesting little details in the church. Floorboards cover the graves of early church members, the gold and silver nuggets nailed on these tablets indicating whether the deceased was rich or poor.

On the ceiling of the church is the patron saint of confessors, John Nepomuceno of 14th-century Czechoslovakia, who is shown holding his tongue. King Wenceslau ordered St Nepumeco's tongue cut out because the saint refused to reveal whether or not the Moldavian queen was faithful. Nepumeco died of his wound, but became very popular posthumously in Czechoslovakian cult circles and, inexplicably, in Minas Gerais during the gold era. Note the little angel at his side shushing churchgoers with a finger to his lips. The church is open from 8 am to

noon and 2 to 6 pm daily. It's on Praça Getúlio Vargas.

Igreja de NS do Ó After surviving an attack by his own troops in 1720, Captain Lucas Ribeiro de Almeida built a chapel in thanks to the Virgin Mary. Like NS de Conceição, the chapel has Oriental details, and it's just as popular with pregnant women (and those who pray for fertility). It's plain on the outside but gilded on the inside. The chapel gives no clues as to the meaning of its name, Our Lady of O. It's open from 8 am to noon and 2 to 6 pm.

Igreja de NS do Rosário This half-built church on Praça Melo Viana was started and financed by slaves but was never finished. It now stands as a memorial to the abolition of slavery in 1888. The church is open daily from 8 am to noon and 2 to 6 pm.

Igreja NS do Carmo Aleijadinho had a lot to do with the decoration of this church on Rua de Carmo. His touch is everywhere, especially in the faces of the statues of São Simão and São João da Cruz.

O Teatro Imperial

Sabará has an elegant old opera house, O Teatro Imperial (1770). The crystal lamps and three tiers of seats in carved wood and bamboo cane are testimony to the wealth of days gone by. On Rua Dom Pedro II, it's open Tuesday to Sunday from 8 am to 5 pm.

Museu do Ouro

Housed in an old gold foundry (1730), the gold museum, on Rua da Intendência, contains art and artefacts of Sabará's glory years, mostly related to the gold-mining industry. The museum is open Tuesday to Sunday from 8 am to 5 pm.

Places to Stay

There's not much choice here. *Solar dos Sepúlveda* (☎ 671-2705), at Rua Intendência 371, next to the gold museum, is your only option. In a two-storey colonial house with a pool, it costs US$35 a double.

Places to Eat

This is a good opportunity to try a feijão mineiro with couve at *Restaurante 314*, at Rua Commandante Viana 314. *Quinto do Ouro*, at Rua Borba Gato 45, does a good frango com quiabo.

Getting There & Away

Viação Cisne buses shuttle the 25 km to Belo Horizonte, leaving every 15 minutes from the bus stop on Avenida Victor Fantini; you can also catch one on the road out of town.

CONGONHAS

Little is left of Congonhas' colonial past except the extraordinary *Prophets* of Aleijadinho at the Basílica do Bom Jesus de Matosinhos. While the town is commonplace, these dramatic statues are exceptional. They are Aleijadinho's masterpiece and Brazil's most famed work of art. It's worth taking the trouble to get to Congonhas just to see them.

Set in a broad valley, Congonhas is 72 km south of Belo Horizonte, three km off BR-040. The city grew up with the search for gold in the nearby Rio Maranhão, and the economy today is dominated by iron mining in the surrounding countryside.

The 12 Prophets

Already an old man, sick and crippled, Aleijadinho sculpted the *Prophets* from 1800 to 1805. Symmetrically placed in front of the Basílica do Bom Jesus de Matosinhos, each of the prophets from the Old Testament was carved out of one or two blocks of soapstone. Each carries a message: six of them are good, six bad, and all are in Latin.

Much has been written about these sculptures – their dynamic quality, the sense of movement (many talk of the appearance they give of a Hindu dance or a ballet), how they complement each other and how their arrangement in front of the church prevents them from being seen in isolation. The poet Carlos Drummond de Andrade wrote that the dramatic faces and gestures are 'magnificent, terrible, grave and tender' and commented on 'the way the statues, of human size, appear to be larger than life as they look down upon the viewer with the sky behind them'.

Before working on the *Prophets*, Aleijadinho carved or supervised his assistants in carving the wooden statues which were placed in the six little chapels that represent the Passion of Christ: The Last Supper, Calvary, Imprisonment, Flagellation and Coronation, Carrying of the Cross and the Crucifixion.

Some of the figures, such as the Roman soldiers, are very crude and clearly done by assistants, while others are finely chiselled. The statues were restored in 1957 by the painter Edson Mota, and the gardens were designed by Burle Marx.

Festivals

Held from 7 to 14 September, the Jubileu do Senhor Bom Jesus do Matosinhos is one of the great religious festivals in Minas Gerais. Each year, approximately 600,000 pilgrims arrive at the church to make promises and do penance, receive blessings and give and receive alms. The Holy Week processions in Congonhas are also famous, especially the dramatisations on Good Friday.

Places to Stay & Eat

The *Colonial Hotel* (☎ (031) 731-1834) is antique and basic, but it has a pool and it's right across the street from the *Prophets*. Single rooms cost US$8/12 without/with bath, and doubles are US$10/20. There is a good restaurant, the *Cova do Daniel*, downstairs. Across the road, *360 Graus* is a decent churrascaria/pizzeria.

Do yourself a favour and don't stay in this town – there's nothing to keep you here after you've seen the *Prophets*.

Getting There & Away

If you get an early start, you can avoid spending a night in Congonhas. We've included detailed bus schedules to enable you to make quick connections.

There are six daily buses from Belo Horizonte to Congonhas (US$4, 1¾ hours). The last return bus to Belo Horizonte leaves

Congonhas at 8.20 pm. Buses leave every hour for Conselheiro Lafaiete, where you can get a midnight bus to Rio.

To get from Congonhas to Ouro Prêto, you can either go to Belo Horizonte or make a connection in Conselheiro Lafaiete. The latter route can be faster if you make a good connection. The drive from Lafaiete to Ouro Prêto is almost all dirt road; it's very slow and often crowded, but quite scenic, with a view of several large mining projects. Try to get to Lafaiete a bit early to make sure you get a bus; if you do miss the last bus, there are a couple of hotels across from the rodoviária.

From Lafaiete to Ouro Prêto (US$4, 2½ hours), buses run Monday to Friday at 7.05 and 9 am, noon, and 3 and 6 pm; on Saturday at 7.05 am, noon, and 3 and 6 pm; and on Sunday at 6 am, and 3 and 6 pm.

From Ouro Prêto to Lafaiete, buses leave Monday to Saturday at 5 am (except Saturday) and 9 am, noon, and 2.50 and 6 pm; on Sunday they leave at 6 am, noon, and 2.40 and 6 pm.

To get from Congonhas to São João del Rei, catch one of the Belo Horizonte to São João del Rei buses that stops off at Congonhas. There are seven a day, the first at 7.30 am and the last at 8.20 pm.

Getting Around

From the Congonhas rodoviária, the 'Basílica' bus leaves every half-hour and costs US$0.30. It's a 15-minute ride up the hill to the basilica and the *Prophets*. Get off the bus just after it passes the church (as it begins to go downhill) for the best approach and first view of the statues. The same bus returns you to the rodoviária.

OURO PRÊTO

Ouro Prêto is in the remote Serra do Espinhaço range, and the odd-shaped peak of Itacolomy (1752 metres), 18 km out of town, is the first clue that you're approaching Ouro Prêto. The first bandeirantes to penetrate the region used it as a reference point.

History

According to the Jesuit Antonil, a mulatto servant in the Antônio Rodrigues Arzão expedition went to the rivulet Tripui to quench his thirst and pocketed a few grains of an odd black metal he found in the stream bed. The little nuggets were reported to the governor of Rio and turned out to be gold. The exact location of the river was forgotten during the long expedition; only the strange shape of the peaks of Itacolomy were remembered.

On 24 June 1698, Antônio Dias de Oliveira rediscovered the area, convinced he had found the promised El Dorado. The mines were the largest deposits of gold in the western hemisphere, and the news and gold fever spread fast. Stories tell of men who acquired fabulous wealth from one day to the next, and others who died of hunger with their pockets full of gold.

Back in Portugal, King Dom João V was quick to claim a royal fifth in tax, and a chain of posts was established to ensure that the crown was getting its cut. In theory, all the gold was brought to these *casas de intendéncias* to be weighed and turned into bars, and the royal fifth set aside. Tax shirkers were cast into dungeons or exiled to Africa. One common technique used to avoid the tax was to hide gold powder in hollow images of the saints. Bitter over the tax, the Paulista miners rebelled unsuccessfully against the Portuguese. Two years later, in 1711, Vila Rica de Ouro Prêto, the present town's predecessor, was founded.

The finest goods from India and England were made available to the simple mining town. The gold bought the services of baroque artisans, who turned the city into an architectural gem. At the height of the gold boom in the mid-18th century, there were 110,000 people in Ouro Prêto (the vast majority of whom were slaves) versus 50,000 in New York and about 20,000 in Rio de Janeiro. The royal fifth, estimated at 100 tonnes of gold in the 18th century, quickly passed through the hands of the Portuguese court, built up Lisbon and then financed the British Industrial Revolution.

The greed of the Portuguese led to sedition on the part of the inhabitants of Vila Rica

PLACES TO STAY

18 Pousada do Mondego
20 Pouso Chico Rei
25 Albergue Ouro Prêto
26 Pousada Ciclo do Ouro
28 Pousada Ouro Prêto

OTHER

1 Rodoviária
2 Hospital & First Aid
3 Capela do Padre Faria
4 Igreja de Santa Efigênia dos Prêtos
5 Mina do Chico Rei
6 Escola de Minas
7 Igreja das Mercês e Misericórdia
8 Igreja SF de Paula
9 Igreja do Rosário
10 Igreja de São José
11 Casa dos Contos & Ponto do Leilão
12 Telephone Office
13 Praça Tiradentes/Tourist Office
14 Casa de Tomás Antônio Gonzaga
15 Largo do Dirceu & Igreja NS da Conceição
16 Oratorio Vira-Saia
17 Largo do Coimbra Art Market
19 Museu da Inconfidência
21 Teatro Municipal
22 Post Office
23 Igreja NS do Carmo
24 Igreja de São Francisco de Assis & Museum
27 Igreja de NS das Mercês e Perdões (de Baixo)
29 Matriz de NS do Pilar
30 Train Station

Ouro Prêto

(1720). As the boom tapered off, the miners found it increasingly difficult to pay ever-larger gold taxes. In 1789, poets Claudio da Costa and Tomás Antônio Gonzaga, Joaquim José da Silva Xavier (nicknamed Tiradentes, meaning tooth-puller after his dentistry skills) and others whose heads were full of the French revolutionary philosophies hatched the Inconfidência Mineira. This attempt to overthrow the Portuguese was crushed in its early stages by agents of the crown. Gonzaga was exiled to Mozambique, and Costa did time in prison. Tiradentes, the only man not to deny his role in the conspiracy, was abandoned by his friends, jailed for three years without defence, then drawn and quartered.

By decree of Emperor Dom Pedro I, Vila Rica, capital of Minas Gerais since 1721, became the Imperial City of Ouro Prêto. In 1897, the state capital was shifted from Ouro Prêto to Belo Horizonte. This was the decisive move that preserved Ouro Prêto's colonial flavour. The former capital assumes the symbolic role of state capital once a year, on 24 June. The city was declared a Brazilian national monument in 1933, and in 1981 UNESCO proclaimed Ouro Prêto a World Cultural Heritage Site.

Climate
The city is one km above sea level, and temperatures vary from 2°C to 28°C. Winters are pretty cold. It can be rainy and foggy all year round, but you can expect daily showers in December and January. The best time to visit Minas is between March and August.

Orientation
Praça Tiradentes, a few blocks down from the rodoviária on the main road, is the town centre. Ouro Prêto is divided into two parishes. If you stand in Praça Tiradentes facing the Museu da Inconfidência, the parish of Pilar is to the right, the parish of Antônio Dias to the left.

All of Ouro Prêto's streets have at least two names: the official one and the one used by the locals because the other one is too much of a mouthful. Rua Conde Bobadella, the street leading off to the right from Praça Tiradentes as you're facing the Museu da Inconfidência, is commonly known as Rua Direita. Similarly, Rua Conselheiro Quintiliano is known as Rua das Lajes and Rua Senador Rocha Lagoa as Rua das Flores. To add to the confusion, the names are rarely posted.

The town is very hilly and the rain-slicked, cobblestone streets are extremely steep. Bring comfortable walking shoes with good tread.

If you plan to spend only one day in Ouro Prêto, make sure it's not a Monday, as almost all the museums and churches are closed then.

Information

Tourist Office The tourist office, at Praça Tiradentes 41, is open from 8 am to 6 pm during the week and from 8 am to 5 pm on weekends. English is spoken, and staff give out a leaflet which indicates the opening times of the museums and churches; they also sell good maps (US$2) and copies of the *Guia de Ouro Prêto*, by Manuel Bandeira, in Portuguese (US$10). *Passeio a Ouro Prêto*, by Lucia Machado de Almeida, has sections in English, French and Portuguese and costs US$22. By the same author is the *Minas Gerais Roteiro Turístico-Cultural das Cidades Historicas* (Embratur-AGGS). I'd like to thank Embratur for permission to use this material when discussing the myths and legends of Ouro Prêto.

If you want to pack in a lot of sightseeing with little effort, hire an official guide (US$30 for a full-day tour) at the tourist office. Cássio is a great guide and speaks excellent English. He really knows his baroque. Other guides include João Bosco, who speaks English and Italian, Herculiano, who speaks good English, and Affonso, who speaks Spanish. Beware of unofficial guides: there are some nasty characters hanging around.

The tourist office also organises treks into the surrounding hills and horseback rides to Itacolomy. The cost is around US$40 for the day. Speak to João or Renaldo a day before you go, to give them enough time to get the horses ready.

Money The Banco do Brasil câmbio is at Rua São José 195, and most of the jewellery stores in town will change cash dollars.

Post & Telephone The post office is in Rua Direita, close to Praça Tiradentes. The telefônica for long-distance calls is on the steep Rua das Flores, on the left as you walk down from the praça.

Things to See

Apart from Niemeyer's **Grande Hotel Ouro Prêto** and two other modern monstrosities, no 20th-century buildings defile this stunningly beautiful colonial city. Spend a day walking on the cobblestone roads around the dark rock walls of the village admiring its carved fountains, statues and crumbling orange-tiled roofs. Gaze through the mist at a skyline of bare green hills, church steeples and grey skies.

The following sightseeing itinerary was made keeping the quirky visiting hours in mind. The schedule is crowded for one day, but if you hustle it's possible to see most of the sights in the **Antônio Dias parish** in the morning, lunch in or about **Praça Tiradentes**, and spend the afternoon visiting the **Pilar parish** and the **mineral museum** and the **Inconfidência museum**. Bear in mind that you need at least two days to see the town properly, and more if you intend to visit some of the nearby historical towns.

Most churches charge around US$1.25 per person admission, so travellers on a tight budget might have to pick and choose. Our favourites are, in rough order: **Igreja de São Francisco de Assis** (if you only visit one, make sure it's this one), **Igreja de Santa Efigênia dos Prêtos**, **Matriz de NS do Pilar** and **Capela do Padre Faria**.

Start at about 7.30 am from Praça Tiradentes and walk along Rua das Lajes, the road to Mariana, for a panoramic view of town.

If, after all this, you're enthusiastic for more, the tourist office can sell you some fine guidebooks – there's plenty to see. Those after something strenuous can hike to the peak of Itacolomy; it takes three hours to walk the 18 km from Praça Tiradentes. **Parque Itacolomy** (the easiest approach is from Mariana) is a pleasant excursion – the park has some good walking trails, waterfalls and orchids, and the colonial town of **Mariana** is only 12 km away. Buses leave every half-hour.

Capela do Padre Faria Work your way downhill off the road to this chapel. Padre Faria was one of the original bandeirantes, and the chapel (built between 1701 and 1704) is Ouro Prêto's oldest house of worship. The chapel is set behind a triple-branched papal cross (1756), the three branches representing the temporal, spiritual and material powers of the Pope. It's the richest chapel in terms of gold and artwork, but unfortunately, due to poor documentation, the artists are anonymous. In 1750 the church bell rang for Tiradentes (when his body was taken to Rio); later, it rang once again, for the inauguration of Brasília. Note that the angel on the right-hand side of the high altar has butterfly wings. The church is open from 8 am to noon.

Igreja de Santa Efigênia dos Prêtos Descending the Ladeira do Padre Faria back towards town, you'll come to the Igreja de Santa Efigênia dos Prêtos. The church was built between 1742 and 1749 by and for the black slave community. Santa Efigênia, patron saint of the church, was the Queen of Nubia, and the featured saints, Santo Antônio do Nolo and São Benedito, are black. The slaves prayed to these images that they wouldn't be crushed in the mines.

The church is Ouro Prêto's poorest in terms of gold and its richest in terms of artwork. The altar is by Aleijadinho's master, Francisco Javier do Briton. Many of the interior panels are by Manuel Rabelo de Souza (see if you can find the painting of Robinson Crusoe), and the exterior image of NS do Rosário is by Aleijadinho himself. The church was financed by gold extracted from Chico-Rei's gold mine, Encardadeira. Slaves contributed to the church coffer by washing their gold-flaked hair in baptismal fonts. Others managed to smuggle gold powder under fingernails and inside tooth cavities. The church is open from 8 am to noon.

Oratorio Vira-Saia At the beginning of the 18th century, there was a rash of ghost incidents in the city. Phantoms would spring from the walls near Santa Efigênia church and wing through town, spooking the townspeople. The simple village folk would faint and drop their bags of gold powder, which the bandit-like ghosts would snatch. The terrorised people asked the bishop for permission to build oratories, and the bishop complied. Designed to keep evil spirits at bay, the oratories (glass-encased niches containing images of saints) were built on many

---

Chico-Rei

The first abolitionist in Brazil was Chico-Rei, an African tribal king. Amidst the frenzy of the gold rush, an entire tribe, king and all, was captured in Africa, placed in chains, sent to Brazil and sold to a mine owner in Ouro Prêto. Chico-Rei worked as the foreman of the slave-miners. Working Sundays and holidays, he finally bought his freedom from the slave master, then freed his son Osmar. Together father and son liberated the entire tribe. This collective then bought the fabulously wealthy Encardadeira gold mine, and Chico-Rei assumed his royal functions once again holding court in Vila Rica and celebrated African holidays in traditional costume. News of this reached the Portuguese king, who immediately prohibited slaves from purchasing their own freedom. Chico-Rei is now a folk hero among Brazilian blacks. ∎

street corners. Not many oratories remain, but there's one on Rua dos Paulistas (also called Bernardo Vasconcelos) and another on Rua Antônio Dias; the most famous one of all is the Oratorio Vira-Saia. Nowadays these few remaining oratories are used to scare off evil spirits during Holy Week.

The small oratory of Vira-Saia is at the bottom of the Ladeira de Santa Efigênia (also known as Vira-Saia), on the corner with Rua Barão do Ouro Branco. 'Vira-saia' has two possible meanings: it either originates from the Portuguese *virar* (turn) and *sair* (depart) or is the direct translation of vira-saia, which means turncoat or traitor.

In the latter part of the 18th century, gold caravans destined for the Portuguese crown were robbed on a regular basis, despite measures to cloak shipments by altering dates and routes. It didn't take long to surmise that it was an inside job. Someone working in the Casa de Fundição was leaking information.

Who would suspect that Antônio Francisco Alves, a pillar of the community, upstanding citizen, mild-mannered businessman and gentle father, was in reality the brains behind the Vira-Saia bandits – the very same outfit which looted the government's gold caravans? After a caravan's route was planned, Alves would steal out to the oratory and turn the image of NS das Almas within the sanctuary to face the direction of the gold traffic.

A reward was posted for the identity of the criminal. Finally a member of Alves' own band, Luis Gibut, turned him in. Gibut was a French Jesuit who fell in love with a beautiful woman, abandoned the order, and became a highway bandit and, eventually, the turncoat's turncoat. This same Luis Gibut was responsible for teaching Aleijadinho the misspelled Latin phrases which the artist incorporated into many of his works.

Alves, his wife and his daughters were dragged off into the jungle to meet their fate. Sra Duruta, a good neighbour, came to the rescue and saved Alves, but it was too late for his wife and kids. Alves was one step ahead of the long arm of the law, but he didn't get off scot free. Shortly afterwards, he was plugged by another unnamed Vira-Saia. The criminal gang continued to do successful robberies without its first chief. Luis Gibut, ex-Jesuit, traitor and poor speller, is probably still doing time in purgatory.

Largo do Dirceu Largo do Dirceu is next, just before you get to the Igreja Matriz NS da Conceição de Antônio Dias. This used to be a popular hang-out of the poet Tomás Antônio Gonzaga and his girlfriend and muse, Marília. It figures prominently in *Marília de Dirceu*, the most celebrated poem in the Portuguese language.

Matriz NS da Conceição de Antônio Dias & Around The cathedral of the Antônio Dias parish, Matriz NS da Conceição de Antônio Dias was designed by Aleijadinho's father, Manuel Francisco Lisboa, and built between the years 1727 and 1770. Note the painting of the eagle: its head points downwards, symbolising the domination of the Moors by the Christians. Aleijadinho is buried by the altar of Boa Morte. The cathedral is open from 8 to 11.30 am and 1 to 5 pm.

The Museu do Aleijadinho adjoins the church and has the same hours. Nearby is Encardideira, the abandoned mine of Chico-Rei (ask around for directions). It's dangerous, full of crumbling secret passageways and rumoured to be haunted.

Casa de Tomás Antônio Gonzaga Rua do Ouvidor 9 is the address of Tomás Antônio Gonzaga's house, now the seat of the municipal government. Back in 1789, the gold tax and antimonarchist sentiment in Minas were rising concurrently. This is where Gonzaga, his poet friend Claudio da Costa (author of *Vila Rica*), Tiradentes and others conspired unsuccessfully to overthrow the Portuguese monarchy. The sad little event came to be known as the Inconfidência Mineira.

Igreja de São Francisco de Assis Across the street from Gonzaga's house is the Igreja de São Francisco de Assis. After the *Prophets* in Congonhas, Aleijadinho's masterwork, this is the single most important piece of

Brazilian colonial art, and it was lovingly restored in 1992. The entire exterior, a radical departure from the military baroque style, was carved by Aleijadinho alone, from the soapstone medallion to the cannon water-spouts and the military (two-bar) cross. The interior was painted by Aleijadinho's long-term partner, Manuel da Costa Ataíde.

The sacristy is said to be haunted by the spirit of an 18th-century woman. In the dead of night, her head dissolves into a skull and she screams, 'I'm dying, call Father Carlos'. The church and adjoining Aleijadinho museum are open from 8.20 to 11.45 am and 1.30 to 4.45 pm.

Praça Tiradentes Praça Tiradentes is the centre of town. It's a good place to have lunch, catch your breath by the statue of Tiradentes, or take in some museums before the churches of the Pilar parish open in the afternoon.

The Museu da Inconfidência, formerly the old municipal building and jail, is an attractive civic building built between 1784 and 1854. Used as a prison from 1907 until 1937, the museum contains the Tiradentes tomb, documents of the Inconfidência Mineira, torture instruments and important works by Ataíde and Aleijadinho. The museum is open from noon to 5.30 pm.

Igreja NS do Carmo The Igreja NS do Carmo was a group effort by the most important artists of the area. Begun in 1766 and completed in 1772, the church features a facade by Aleijadinho. It's open from 8 to 11.30 am and 1 to 5.30 pm.

Casa de Tiradentes The home of Joaquim José da Silva Xavier (Tiradentes) is nearby. After his failed rebellion against the Portuguese, and his execution in Rio, Tiradentes' head was paraded around town. His house was demolished, and its grounds were salted so that nothing would grow there.

Aleijadinho

The church of São Francisco de Assis, the Carmo church facade, the *Prophets* of Congonhas do Campos and innumerable relics in Mariana, Sabará, Tiradentes and São João del Rei were all carved by Aleijadinho (Antônio Francisco Lisboa). Brazil's Michelangelo lost the use of his hands and legs at the age of 30 but, with a hammer and chisel strapped to his arms, he advanced art in Brazil from the excesses of the baroque to a finer, more graceful rococo. The Mineiros have reason to be proud of Aleijadinho – he is a figure of international prominence in the history of art. Aleijadinho's angels have his stylistic signature: wavy hair, wide-open eyes and big, round cheeks.

The son of a Portuguese architect and a black slave, Aleijadinho lived from 1730 to 1814 and was buried in the Matriz NS da Conceirção, within 50 paces of his birth site. By federal decree he was declared patron of Brazilian arts in 1973. For many years Manuel da Costa Ataíde, from nearby Mariana, successfully collaborated with Aleijadinho on many churches. Aleijadinho would sculpt the exterior and a few interior pieces, and Ataíde would paint the interior panels. With his secretly-concocted vegetable dyes, Ataíde fleshed out much of Aleijadinho's work. ■

Escola de Minas The Escola de Minas in the old governor's palace in Praça Tiradentes has a very fine museum of mineralogy. It's open from noon to 5 pm Monday to Friday.

Casa dos Contos The Casa dos Contos (Counting House) is now a public library and art gallery. Claudio da Costa was imprisoned here after participating in the Inconfidência Mineira. It is open from 12.30 to 5 pm. Next door is the old Ponto do Leilão, where slaves were taken to be tortured.

Matriz de NS do Pilar The Matriz de NS do Pilar is the second-most opulent church in Brazil (after Salvador's São Francisco) in terms of gold, with 434 kg of gold and silver and one of Brazil's finest showcases of artwork. Note the wild-bird chandelier holders, the laminated beaten gold, the scrolled church doors, 15 panels of Old and New Testament scenes by Pedro Gomes Chaes, and the hair on Jesus (the real stuff, donated by a penitent worshipper).

Legend has it that the Pilar and Antônio Dias parishes vied for the image of NS dos Passos. In order to settle the argument, the image was loaded onto a horse standing in Praça Tiradentes and rockets were fired to scare the horse; the idea was that the image would belong to the parish to which the horse bolted. Since the horse knew only one path, it galloped straight to the Matriz do Pilar. The church is open from noon to 5 pm.

Teatro Municipal Built in 1769 by João de Souza Lisboa, the Teatro Municipal is the oldest theatre in Minas Gerais and perhaps in all of Brazil. The theatre is open to visitors from 1 to 5.30 pm.

Festivals
Ouro Prêto's Semana Santa (Holy Week) procession, held on the Thursday before Palm Sunday and sporadically until Easter Sunday, is quite a spectacle. The Congado is to Minas what Candomblé is to Bahia and Umbanda is to Rio: the local expression of Afro-Christian syncretism. The major Congado celebrations are for NS do Rosário

(on 23 to 25 October, at the Capela do Padre Faria), for the New Year and for 13 May (the anniversary of abolition).

The Cavalhada held in Amarantina (near Ouro Prêto) during the Festa de São Gonçalo, from 17 to 23 September, isn't as grand as the one in Pirenópolis, but is impressive nonetheless. The Cavalhada is a re-enactment of the battles between Christians and Moors in Iberia.

Carnival in Ouro Prêto is popular, too, a special feature being the *janela erótica* (erotic window), where people dance naked behind a thin curtain.

Places to Stay – bottom end
Ouro Prêto is a university town, with schools of pharmacy and biochemistry, mineralogy, geology and engineering. No less than 20% of the homes in Ouro Prêto are devoted to student lodging known as *repúblicas*. Although they are the cheapest places to stay in town, most of the repúblicas are closed from Christmas to Carnival. Another problem with repúblicas is their lack of security, as they put strangers together in the same room; for this reason, we wouldn't recommend staying in one. For an extra couple of dollars, you're better off in a pousada.

The tourist office has a complete list of places to stay, including the cheapest, and they'll ring around to find a vacancy for you. On weekends, holidays and during exam periods, the town gets crowded, but finding a room shouldn't be a problem.

The youth hostel *Albergue Ouro Prêto* (☎ 551-3201) is in a good, central location, at Rua das Mercês 136.

The pousada next to the Igreja de São Francisco de Assis (on your right as you face the church) is one of the cheapest around. A bed in a basic but clean four-bed room is US$7 per person. *Hospedaria Casarão* (☎ 551-2056), at Rua Direita 94-B, is a family home above a store. They have eight rooms and charge US$8 per person.

An excellent pousada is the *Pousada Ouro Prêto* (☎ 551-3081; fax 551-4314), at Largo Musicista José das Anjos Costa (also called das Mercês) 72, right in front of Igreja NS das Mercês. It's a friendly place, and Gerson, who runs it, speaks English. It has a fantastic view, and all the comforts that delight the traveller. The charge is US$15/25 for single/double apartamentos. Gerson also runs another pousada nearby, and charges a bit less for rooms there.

Places to Stay – middle

There are a number of mid-range hotels close to the centre of town. The *Hotel Pilão* (☎ 551-3066), at Praça Tiradentes 57, has quartos for US$15/20 a single/double and apartamentos for US$20/35. The *Hotel Colonial* (☎ 551-3133), at Travessa Camilo Veloso 26, has single/double apartamentos for US$35/45. The *Pousada Nella Nuno* (☎ 551-3375), at Rua Camilo de Brito 59, has nice double quartos for US$20 and apartamentos for US$27 a double. There's lots of art here, and the owner is an artist herself.

Places to Stay – top end

The *Pouso Chico Rei* (☎ 551-1274), at Rua Brigideiro Mosqueira 90, has wonderful doubles completely furnished in antiques (US$35/55 without/with bath). There's one single room (US$17) but you would have to be lucky and reserve it way in advance. The *Pousada do Mondego* (☎ 551-2040; fax 551-3094), at Largo do Coimbra 38, is close to Igreja São Francisco; it's in an 18th-century colonial mansion. Singles/doubles are US$80/100, but you'll pay a bit more if you want the view. This is an excellent top-end choice. The recently opened five-star *Solar NS do Rosário* (☎ 551-4200; fax 551-4288), at Rua Getúlio Vargas 270, even boasts its own mine. Classy singles/doubles go for US$85/135.

Places to Eat

Most of the restaurants are clustered along two streets: Rua Direita and Rua São José. It's really just a matter of deciding what you want to eat. Ouro Prêto is a good place to try some regional cooking. One typical Minas dish is tutu a mineira, a black-bean feijoada with couve (a type of kale). *Restaurante*

Casa Do Ouvidor, on Rua Direita, is the place to try it. If the mineiro food is a bit heavy for you, *Café e Cia*, at Rua São José 187, has good sandwiches and a great view of the town. They also have a self-serve, por-kilo lunch.

Entertainment

The kids hang out in Praça Tiradentes, before thronging to Club Ouro Prêto for some slow and steamy dancing. It's open on Saturday and Sunday nights from 8 to 11 pm. During the rest of the week, there's a lot of spontaneous music in the bars along Rua Direita. The Scotch Bar, on Rua Direita, on your left about halfway down the hill, has a young, hip crowd.

Things to Buy

A soapstone quarry in Santa Rita de Ouro Prêto, 28 km away, provides endless supplies for attractive, Henry Moore-style carvings, and imitations of Aleijadinho. Woodcarvings, basketwork and unglazed ceramics are sold in the souvenir shops of Praça Tiradentes. Wilson Prolin, a fine local painter, has a studio in town.

Imperial topaz is found only in this area of Brazil, and there are lots of gem shops around Praça Tiradentes. Casa das Pedras and Grupiara Pedras both sell topaz with a certificate of guarantee.

Getting There & Away

There are 11 buses a day running from Belo Horizonte to Ouro Prêto, the first leaving at 6.45 am and the last at 10.15 pm (1¾ hours, 98 km). During the peak tourist period, try to buy your bus tickets at least a day in advance or you may find yourself without a ride. One bus a day makes the seven-hour trip to Rio (US$13).

AROUND OURO PRÊTO
Minas de Passagem

We got a kick out of Minas de Passagem. It is probably the best gold mine to visit in the Ouro Prêto region. There's an immense system of tunnels that goes down very deep and then spreads horizontally. Only a fraction of the mine is open to the public, but for most terrestrials, it's enough. The descent into the mine is made in an antique, steam-powered cable car (though the guide is quick to assure you that the cable itself is new), giving you a very good idea of just how dangerous and claustrophobic mining can be.

The mine was opened in 1719. Until the abolition of slavery, it was worked by black slaves, many of whom died (not from the cable-car ride, as you might think after taking it, but from dynamiting into the rock). Our guide, who worked in the mine as recently as 1985 and was then earning the minimum wage of US$35 a month, told us that the life of the 'free' miner was little better than that of the slave.

The mandatory guided tour, led by former miners, is short and quite informative, especially if someone in the group asks the right questions. The mine is open from 9 am to 6 pm daily and the entry fee is US$12.

The mine is between Ouro Prêto and Mariana. Take any local bus that runs between the two and ask the driver to let you off at Minas de Passagem.

MARIANA

Founded in 1696, Mariana is a pleasant old mining town with a character unlike its busy neighbour, Ouro Prêto. Only 12 km by paved road from Ouro Prêto, Mariana is touristed but not overrun, retaining the high-altitude tranquillity of many of the mining towns. Relax and unwind here. It's also a good place to stay if you want to avoid Ouro Prêto by night.

Information

The tourist terminal, where the bus from Ouro Prêto will stop, contains an information office which sells maps (US$2) and Portuguese-language guidebooks. This is the place to arrange a guide if you want one. Some French is spoken.

Things to See

Mariana has plenty of interesting sights. The 18th-century churches of São Pedro dos Clérigos, NS da Assunção and São Francisco, and the Catedral Basílica da Sé, with its fantastic German organ dating from 1701, are all worthwhile. The museum at Casa Capitular is also worth a look. While walking through the old part of town, you'll come across painters and wood sculptors at work in their studios.

Places to Stay

The *Hotel Providência* (☎ 557-1444), at Rua Dom Silveiro 233, is an interesting cheapie. Originally the living quarters for nuns, who still run a school next door, it has a chapel (if you're feeling pious), and an excellent swimming pool with individual changing boxes. You have to go through the school to get to it, so don't walk around in your swimming gear or the nuns might have heart attacks. Quartos are US$10 per person and apartamentos are US$13/22 a single/double. Just around the corner, at Rua Con Rego 149, the *Pousada do Chafariz* (☎ 557-1492) has modern rooms with TV and frigobar for US$18/30 a single/double.

The *Hotel Central* (☎ 557-1630), at Rua Frei Durão 8, is a real budget hotel, with quartos for US$10/18 a single/double. The *Hotel Faisca* (☎ 557-1206), at Rua Antônio Olinto 48, is similarly priced.

The best hotel in town is the *Pouso da Typographia* (☎ 557-1577; fax 557-1311), at Praça Gomes Freire 220. It's worth going in just to look at the two antique printing presses in the foyer. Singles/doubles cost US$44/71, but you can bargain the price down during the week.

Places to Eat

Portão da Praça, at Praça Gomes Freire 108, serves excellent regional dishes. *Papinna Della Nonna*, at Rua Dom Viçoso 27, is Mariana's Italian restaurant, and a good one at that; it's very close to Praça Gomes Freire, at Rua Dom Viçoso 27. *Restaurante Tambaú*, near the town square, also has good regional food at reasonable prices.

Getting There & Away

A bus leaves Ouro Prêto for Mariana every

half-hour from the far side of the Escola de Minas. The trip takes 35 to 40 minutes. There are direct buses from Mariana to Belo Horizonte, 113 km away.

SÃO JOÃO DEL REI

One of Minas Gerais' original gold towns, São João del Rei is a thriving small city, whose old, central section features several of Brazil's finest churches. With hotels and sights all within walking range in the old city centre, there's little cause to see the more modern part of town; nevertheless, it's evident that the city hasn't been frozen in time, unlike most of the other historic cities of Minas Gerais.

The old section is protected by Brazil's Landmarks Commission, and police guard the churches at night. The city is bisected by Rio Lenheiro, which is traversed by two 18th-century stone bridges. In addition to the Aleijadinho-inspired churches, there are several fine colonial mansions – one of which belonged to the late and still-popular ex-president Tancredo Neves – a good museum, and a surprising variety of other sites and activities.

The city sits between the Serra de São José and the Serra do Lenheiro, near the southern end of the Serra do Espinhaço. It's hilly country near the Rio das Mortes (River of the Dead), where many prospectors were killed during the gold-rush days. The most famous incident took place in 1708, when a band of Emboadas, recent Portuguese immigrants, surrounded about 50 Paulistas or bandeirantes, São Paulo natives of mixed Portuguese and Indian blood. The Paulistas were massacred after laying down their arms in surrender. This was the bloodiest atrocity in the near civil war that these two groups fought over control of the mines; the place where it happened is called the Capão da Traição (Copse of Treason).

Orientation

São João del Rei is sandwiched between two hills, both of which provide excellent views, particularly at sunset. The *Cristo Redentor* monument, overlooking the city, stands on one hill and the Capelinha do Senhor do Bonfim on the other. Both hilltops are the last stop for the local city bus 'Sr dos Montes', which leaves from in front of the train station.

Information

Tourist Office The tourist information office is in the Terminal Turístico, in Praça Antônio Vargas, a block from Avenida Presidente Tancredo Neves. It's open from 6 am to 6 pm. The Secretária Municipal de Turismo, close to the Igreja São Francisco, is also useful. Bosco Tavares, who works there, speaks English and is very helpful. It's open from 8 am to 5 pm.

Money There's a Banco do Brasil on Avenida Ermilia Alves, and the BEMGE state bank has a câmbio close to the Hotel Lenheiro Palace.

Post & Telephone The post office is on Avenida Tiradentes. There are telephone posts on Rua Ministro Gabriel Passos and at the rodoviária, for long-distance calls.

Churches

Be sure to take a walk at night, when floodlights illuminate the churches and give them a fantastic appearance.

Igreja de São Francisco de Assis This exquisite baroque church, full of curves and carvings, looks out on a palm-lined, lyre-shaped plaza. Begun in 1774, the church was Aleijadinho's first complete project, but much of his plan was not realised. Still, the exterior, with an Aleijadinho sculpture of the *Immaculate Virgin* and several angels, is one of the finest in Minas. There is some uncertainty about what work Aleijadinho did and did not do on the interior. He probably did the main altar, but his work was completely altered. In the second altar to the left, there is an image of *São João Evangelista* which is the work of Aleijadinho, as is the *Santo Antônio*. Notice the fine woodwork, particularly in the rear of the church.

Tancredo Neves, the man who led Brazil

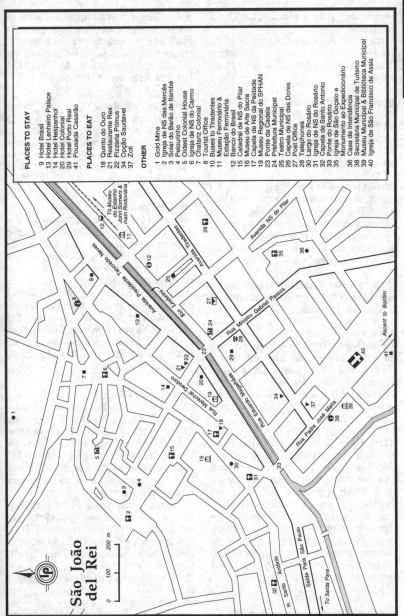

São João del Rei

0   100   200 m

PLACES TO STAY
9   Hotel Brasil
13 Hotel Lenheiro Palace
14 Hotel Hespanhol
20 Hotel Colonial
29 Hotel Porto Real
41 Pousada Casarão

PLACES TO EAT
18 Quinto do Ouro
21 Restaurante Rex
22 Pizzeria Primus
34 Opção Saudavel
37 Zoti

OTHER
1   Gold Mine
2   Igreja do NS das Mercês
3   Solar do Barão de Itambé
4   Pelourinho
5   Oldest Colonial House
6   Igreja de NS do Carmo
7   Chafariz Colonial
8   Tourist Office
10 Buses to Tiradentes
11 Museu Ferroviário &
     Estação Ferroviária
12 Banco do Brasil
15 Catedral de NS do Pilar
16 Museu de Arte Sacra
17 Capela de NS da Piedade
19 Museu Regional do SPHAN
23 Ponte da Cadeia
24 Teatro Municipal
25 Prefeitura Municipal
26 Capela de NS das Dores
27 Post Office
28 Telephones
30 Largo do Rosário
31 Igreja de NS do Rosário
32 Capela de Santo Antonio
33 Ponte do Rosário
35 Igreja de São Gonçalo e
     Monumento ao Expedicionário
36 Casa da Intendência
38 Secretária Municipal de Turismo
39 Museu Municipal & Biblioteca Municipal
40 Igreja de São Francisco de Assis

To Museu do Estanho & John Somers & main Rodoviária

Avenida Presidente Tancredo Neves

Avenida Tiradentes

Rua Leitão

Avenida NS do Pilar

Rua Ministro Gabriel Passos

Rua Marechal Deodoro

Rua Eduardo Magalhães

Rua Padre José Maria

Ascent to Bonfim

R Santo Antônio

São Paulo

Saida Para

To Saida Para

from military rule, is buried in the church graveyard.

The church is open from 8 am to noon. On Sunday, the local Coalhada (all-white) orchestra and choir perform at the 9.15 am mass.

Igreja de NS do Carmo Begun in 1732, this church was designed by Aleijadinho. He also did the frontispiece and sculpture around the door. In the second sacristy is a famous unfinished sculpture of Christ. The church is open from 8 to 11 am and 4 to 7 pm.

Catedral de NS do Pilar Begun in 1721, this church has exuberant gold altars. There are also fine Portuguese tiles. The mulatta Rapadura orchestra and choir accompany the 7 pm mass here on Wednesday. On Thursday and Friday, the Coalhada takes their place. The church is open from 8 to 11 am.

Igreja de NS do Rosário This simple church was built in 1719 to honour the protector of the slaves. It's open from 8 to 10 am.

Museums
Museu Regional do SPHAN One of the best museums in Minas Gerais, this well-restored 1859 colonial mansion has good sacred art on the first two floors, and an industrial section on the 3rd floor, with tools and instruments. It's open Tuesday to Sunday from noon to 5 pm.

Museu Ferroviário Train freaks take heart: you are at one with the Mineiros, who also love their trains. The expertly renovated railway museum, housed in the train station, has a wealth of artefacts and information about the train days of the late 19th century. Don't forget to walk down the track to the large rotunda that looks like a colosseum: it houses the trains and is the best part of the museum. The museum is open Tuesday to Sunday from 8 am to 5 pm (closed for lunch between 11 am and 1 pm). Admission costs US$0.50.

Museu do Estanho John Somers This is a

pewter factory with a display and store for visitors, owned by an Englishman (there is a small English community in São João). The museum is down the river towards the rodoviária, at Avenida Leite de Castro 1150. It is open daily from 9 am to 5 pm.

Museu de Arte Sacra Open daily (except Monday) from 9 am to 5 pm, the museum has a small but impressive collection of art from the city's churches. Look closely at the figure of Christ mourned by Mary Magdalene and you'll see that the drops of blood are rubies.

Mina de Ouro-Tancredo Neves
This former gold mine is a thin wedge that descends 53 metres through solid rock. Apart from the adrenalin rush of going into the mine, you'll get an interesting demonstration of the regional mining techniques. It's all very impressive, and free.

If you don't mind walking through a pretty depressing favela to get there, put on some decent walking shoes and follow the signs from town till you reach a steep hill. Walk up the hill into the favela and turn left along the footpath. The mine is right there, behind the 'Exportak' sign.

Maria Fumaça Train
Chugging along at 25 km/h on the steam-powered Maria Fumaça along a picturesque 13-km stretch of track from São João to Tiradentes makes a great half-hour train ride. The line has operated nonstop since 1881 with the same Baldwin locomotives, and since being restored, the 76-cm-gauge track is in perfect condition.

The train runs only on Friday, Saturday, Sunday and holidays, leaving São João at 10 am and 2.15 pm and returning from Tiradentes at 1 and 5 pm. This schedule often changes, so it's best to check. The train costs US$3 and gets crowded; be there early. Going to Tiradentes, sit on the left side for a better view.

Don't forget that if you're only going to Tiradentes for the day and need more time than the return train allows, you can easily take a later bus back to São João.

Festivals

São João has a very lively Carnival – locals claim it's the best in Minas Gerais. With all the music in town (there's a school of music, and several bands and orchestras), this is a credible boast. The Semana da Inconfidência, from 15 to 21 April, celebrates Brazil's first independence movement and the hometown boys who led it. (This festival is also held in Tiradentes.)

Another important festival is the Inverno Cultural, during July, with lots of theatre, concerts and dances. The list of festivals just goes on and on – 15 religious and 10 secular on one calendar – so stop by the tourist office for a schedule of events; someone is probably celebrating something in São João.

Places to Stay – bottom end

There is a good stock of inexpensive hotels in the old section of the city, right where you want to be. The *Hotel Brasil* (☎ 371-2804), just around the corner from the Terminal Turístico, at Avenida Presidente Tancredo Neves 395, facing the river, is a former grand hotel. It's a real bargain at US$3 a single.

The historic *Hotel Colonial* (☎ 371-1792) is clean and very colonial. Rooms without bath go for US$8 a person, and most have a view of the river. The *Aparecida Hotel* (☎ 371-1548), right next to the Terminal Turístico, has singles for US$10; it's not bad if the other hotels are full. The *Hotel Hespanhol* (☎ 371-4677), at Rua Marechal Deodoro 131, has quartos for US$15 a single and apartamentos for US$20/25. All rooms are clean and relatively spacious.

Places to Stay – top end

The *Hotel Lenheiro Palace* (☎ & fax 371-3914), facing the river, at Avenida Presidente Tancredo Neves 257, has charm and style for US$42/50 a single/double. Up the hill behind the Igreja de São Francisco is the *Pousada Casarão* (☎ 371-1224), at Rua Ribeiro Bastos 94. Like many of Minas' elegant mansions turned pousadas, this place

is exquisite, and it has a small swimming pool. The rooms cost US$28/35 for singles/doubles.

The *Hotel Porto Real* (☎ & fax 371-1201) is São João's modern hotel, and the biggest eyesore on the riverfront. It has singles/doubles for US$50/60.

Places to Eat

Pizzeria Primus has good pizza – try the primus special. It's open late, at Rua Arthur Bernardes 97. The *Cantina do Italo*, on Rua Ministro Gabriel Passos, has a good reputation for pasta. For regional cooking, try *Restaurante Rex*, at Rua Arthur Bernardes 137, *Quinto do Ouro*, at Praça Severiano de Resende 4, or *Gruta Mineira*, on Rua Marechal Deodoro.

For a vegetarian lunch and a good juice, *Opção Saudavel*, Avenida Tiradentes 792, has a set menu, but you need to drop in at least an hour beforehand to tell them you're coming, because they bring the food from home. On the same street, *Zoti* is a lively late-night place for beer and light meals.

Entertainment

The music of Minas is extremely good and different from anything else you've ever heard. Try the Teatro Municipal for weekend concerts. The restaurant Cabana da Espanhola has live music Thursday to Sunday. It's at Avenida 31 de Março. Another central place to try is Feitiço Mineiro, near the Catedral do Pilar; it has live music on Friday and Saturday nights.

Getting There & Away

Bus The long and winding road from Rio to São João traverses the Serra da Mantiqueira. The roads and scenery are good on this $5\frac{1}{2}$-hour bus ride. São João is 190 km south of Belo Horizonte, $3\frac{1}{2}$ hours away by bus.

Direct buses for São João leave Rio daily at 9 am, and 4 and 11 pm. The return bus from São João to Rio leaves at 8.30 am, 1.30 and 4 pm and midnight Monday to Saturday, and at 4, 10 and 11.30 pm on Sunday. The fare is US$9. There are also frequent buses to Juiz de Fora, where you can transfer to a São João or Rio bus.

From São João to Belo Horizonte (via Lagoa Dourada), there are seven buses a day. From Monday to Friday, the first bus leaves at 6 am and the last at 6.30 pm. There are extra buses on Sunday night, until 10 pm. The trip takes 3½ hours and costs US$6. This is also the bus to Congonhas, two hours and US$4 down the road. You won't be able to buy a ticket directly to Congonhas, but ask for a ticket there anyway. Let the driver know you are going to Congonhas and you'll be dropped off at the Congonhas turn-off. You can wait there for a local bus, or cross the road where you see a statue and walk 500 metres down to the rodoviária on the right-hand side to catch a 'Basilica' local bus.

For the quickest route to Ouro Prêto, catch a bus to Conselheiro Lafaiete; from there take the bus to Ouro Prêto (for schedules, see the Congonhas section).

To Tiradentes, catch the local bus from in front of the train station.

Train For details of the picturesque train ride to Tiradentes, see the earlier section on the Maria Fumaça Train.

Getting Around
The yellow local buses will get you to the rodoviária in 10 minutes. They leave from the small bus stop in front of the train station. You can also take a taxi (US$5). To get to the Terminal Turístico from the rodoviária, catch any yellow bus from the bus stop to your left as you walk out, not from the more obvious one directly in front. All the buses stop at the Terminal Turístico.

TIRADENTES
They don't make towns any prettier than Tiradentes. Ten km down the valley from São João del Rei, its gold-era rival, colonial Tiradentes sits on a hill below a mountain. With few signs of change over the last two centuries, the town has that magic quality of another age – and for some odd reason, that's a very good feeling.

Originally called Arrail da Ponta do Morro (Hamlet on a Hilltop), Tiradentes was renamed to honour the martyred hero of the Inconfidência, who was born at a nearby farm. The town's colonial buildings run up a hillside, where they culminate in the beautiful Igreja Matriz de Santo Antônio. If you stand between the church's Aleijadinho-carved frontispiece and famous sundial, there is a colourful view of the terracotta-tiled colonial houses, the green valley, and the towering wall of stone formed by the Serra de São José.

Information
Tourist Office The Secretária de Turismo is at Rua Resende Costa 71, the only three-storey building in town. The staff have maps and other useful information. Luiz Cruz speaks good English and is very helpful – ask about guides and walks into the surrounding mountains. The post office is in the same building.

Igreja Matriz de Santo Antônio
Named after the town's patron saint, this church is built on the site of a former church. Commenced in 1710 and restored in 1983, it is one of Brazil's most beautiful. There are two bell towers, and a frontispiece by Aleijadinho, one of the last that he completed. Leandro Gonçalves Chaves made the sundial in front of the church, in 1785.

The all-gold interior is rich in symbols from the Old Testament. There is a painting by João Batista showing the miracle of Santo Antônio making a donkey kneel before the Pope. There is also a polychrome organ, built in Portugal and brought to Tiradentes by donkey in 1798. Ask about performances. The church is open from 8 am to 5 pm, but usually closes for lunch from noon to 1 pm.

Museu do Padre Toledo
This museum is dedicated to another hero of the Inconfidência, Padre Toledo, who lived in this 18-room house where the Inconfidêntes first met. The museum features regional antiques and documents from the 18th century.

Igreja da Santissima Trindade

After a short walk on Rua da Santissima Trindade, you arrive at this simple pilgrimage church. Dating from 1810, it was built on the site of a small chapel where Tiradentes chose the triangle (symbolising the holy trinity) as the flag for the new nation.

Solar da Ponte

This colonial mansion, now an expensive hotel impeccably restored and decorated, is well worth walking through. The first building on the other side of the little stone bridge, it's marked by a small sign.

Chafariz de São José

Constructed in 1749 by the town council, this beautiful fountain has three sections: one for drinking, one for washing clothes and one for watering horses. The water comes from Mãe d'Agua via an old stone pipeline.

Serra de São José

This area is one of Minas' remaining untouched segments of Atlantic rainforest. Mãe d'Agua is at the base of these mountains. Lush with moss and plants, the waters are clear and fresh. A 25-minute walk from Tiradentes, Mãe d'Agua can also be reached by car. Other walks include: A Calçada, a stretch of the old road that linked Ouro Prêto with Rio de Janeiro; Cachoeiras do Mangue, the falls where you can see an old gold mine on the road made by slaves; and Cachoeira do Bom Despacho, a waterfall on the Tiradentes-Santa Cruz road. Each of these takes about four or five hours. A seven-hour walk will allow you to cross the range. For guides and information about walks into the mountains, ask at the tourist office.

Places to Stay

Tiradentes has lots of good but expensive pousadas and only a few cheap places. If you

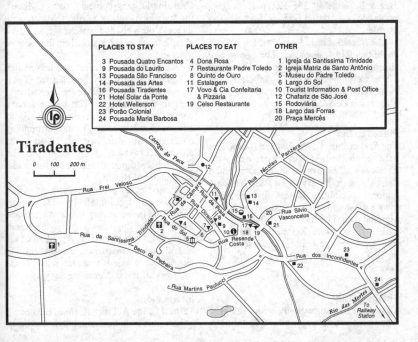

PLACES TO STAY	PLACES TO EAT	OTHER
3 Pousada Quatro Encantos	4 Dona Rosa	1 Igreja da Santissima Trinidade
9 Pousada do Laurito	7 Restaurante Padre Toledo	2 Igreja Matriz de Santo Antônio
13 Pousada São Francisco	8 Quinto de Ouro	5 Museu do Padre Toledo
14 Pousada das Artes	11 Estalagem	6 Largo do Sol
16 Pousada Tiradentes	17 Vovo & Cia Confeitaria	10 Tourist Information & Post Office
21 Hotel Solar da Ponte	& Pizzaria	12 Chafariz de São José
22 Hotel Wellerson	19 Celso Restaurante	15 Rodoviária
23 Porão Colonial		18 Largo das Forras
24 Pousada Maria Barbosa		20 Praça Mercês

Tiradentes

0   100   200 m

can't find anything within your budget, ask around for homes to stay in, or commute from São João del Rei. Try to avoid staying here on the weekend, as it gets crowded and the prices quoted below can double.

The *Pousada do Laurito* is the best cheapie in town, with a good central location and singles/doubles for US$11/22. Next to the bus station, the *Pousada Tiradentes* (☎ 355-1232) has some charm and costs US$10/20 a single/double. The *Hotel Wellerson* (☎ 355-1226) also has singles/doubles for US$10/20. With a great little garden, the *Pousada Quatro Encantos*, near the Santo Antônio church, charges US$30 a double.

If you want to stay in a nice place further out of town, with a bit of space, try the *Pousada da Terra*, 800 metres from the train station along a dirt road. They charge US$12 per person.

Near the train station are both the *Porão Colonial* (☎ 355-1251) and the *Pousada Maria Barbosa* (☎ 355-1227). Both have pools and cost around US$14/28 for singles/doubles.

The *Hotel Solar da Ponte* (☎ 355-1255) is an old colonial mansion. The rooms are simple, small and beautifully decorated. There's a salon and sauna, and afternoon tea is included in the US$110 a double price. Singles are US$75.

Places to Eat

The *Restaurante Padre Toledo* has excellent bife acebolada (beef with onions). *Estalagem* does a mean feijão com lombo (beans with pork). Try *Dona Rosa* for some regional specialities. *Quinto do Ouro* is the town's most up-market restaurant, with both regional and international dishes. On the main square, *Celso Restaurante* has good food at reasonable prices. For dessert, stroll up to *Confeitaria da Vovó* for coffee and cake.

Things to Buy

Tiradentes has surprisingly good antiques, woodwork and silver jewellery. The antique stores sell furniture, clocks, china and even chandeliers.

Getting There & Away

Tiradentes is about 20 minutes from São João del Rei. The best approach is the wonderful railroad trip from São João del Rei (see the section on that city for details).

Buses come and go between São João and Tiradentes every 40 minutes (slightly less frequently on weekend afternoons). From São João, the first and last buses leave for Tiradentes at 5.50 am and 5.45 pm on weekdays, 7 am and 5.45 pm on Saturday and 8.15 am and 10 pm on Sunday. From Tiradentes, the last bus back to São João del Rei leaves at 6.20 pm from Monday to Saturday and at 8.30 pm on Sunday. There is no direct bus service to other places from Tiradentes.

DIAMANTINA

Diamantina is a 5½-hour drive north from Belo Horizonte. After passing the town of Curvelo (the geographical centre of Minas), the stark landscape of northern Minas, with its rocky outcrops and barren highlands, is a sharp contrast to the lush hills in the south of the state.

One of Brazil's prettiest and less-visited colonial gems, the city boomed when diamonds were discovered in the 1720s, after the gold finds in Minas. The diamonds have petered out, but the fine colonial mansions and the excellent hiking in the surrounding mountains still draw visitors. Diamantina also happens to be the birthplace of Juscelino Kubitschek, former Brazilian president and the founder of Brasília.

Because of its isolation, Diamantina is a well-preserved colonial city. The centre, apart from the relatively new cathedral and a couple of incongruous traffic lights, hasn't changed for hundreds of years. Most of the churches and historical houses remain closed, but it doesn't matter much – the exteriors are more interesting anyway.

Information

Tourist Office At Praça Antônio Eulálio 57, a short walk from the cathedral, is the tourist office, where you'll find a *roteiro turístico* (tourist guide) in Portuguese which includes a map. The staff also have access to the keys to most of the tourist attractions, many of which seem to be undergoing restoration indefinitely.

Money The Banco do Brasil is in a beautiful colonial building in the main praça. Unfortunately, they don't change travellers' cheques. Try at the BEMGE branch nearby.

Post & Telephone There are two post offices: at Rua Quintanda 31 and at Praça Dr

Prado 71. Long-distance telephone calls can be made from the telephone post opposite the Hotel Dália.

Igreja de NS do Carmo

Constructed between 1760 and 1765, this church has its tower built at the rear because Chica da Silva disliked being awakened by bells. The church is the most opulent in Diamantina, and it's worth having a look inside. It has an organ made in Diamantina and wrought in gold, as well as rich, golden carvings.

PLACES TO STAY
1 Pousada do Garimpo
7 Hotel Nosson
7 Hotel Tijuco
9 Hotel Dália
17 Hotel Carvalho

PLACES TO EAT
13 Varanda's Restaurante
16 Cantinha do Marinho
17 Restaurante Confiança
20 Restaurante Grupiara

OTHER
2 Rodoviára
4 Casa de Juscelino Kubitschek
5 Casa da Glória
6 Carpet Factory
8 Igreja de São Francisco de Assis
10 Museu do Diamante
11 Telephones

12 Banco do Brasil
14 Catedral de Santo Antônio
15 BEMGE
18 Post Office
21 Igreja de NS do Bonfim
22 Tourist Office
23 Casa da Chica da Silva
24 Igreja de NS do Carmo
25 Old Mercado Municipal
26 Igreja de NS de Amparo
27 Igreja de NS do Rosário dod Pretos

Diamantina

0   100   200 m

Igreja de NS do Rosário dod Pretos

This is the oldest church in town, dating from 1731. Very interesting here is the tree that grew up through a wooden cross. You can see the pieces of the cross in the tree.

Museu do Diamante

The house of Padre Rolim, one of the Inconfidêntes, is now a museum, with furniture, coins, instruments of torture and other relics of the diamond days. It's open from noon to 5.30 pm Tuesday to Sunday.

Casa da Chica da Silva

This colonial mansion, on Praça Lobo de Mesquita, was the home of diamond contractor João Fernandes de Oliveira and his mistress and former slave, Chica da Silva. It's empty at the moment, but from the outside it's possible to get an idea of the lifestyle of the extravagant mulatta. The huge colonial door leads to her private chapel.

Mercado Municipal

Built by the army in 1835, the market, in Praça Barão Guaicuí, was in use until only a couple of years ago. Its wooden arches inspired Niemeyer's design for the presidential palace in Brasília.

Casa da Glória

Consisting of two houses on opposite sides of Rua da Glória connected by an enclosed, 2nd-storey passageway, Casa da Glória was originally the residence of the diamond supervisors and the first bishop of Diamantina. Today it's the Institute of Geology.

Casa de Juscelino Kubitschek

This small house, at Rua São Francisco 241, reflects the simple upbringing of the former president, whose grandparents were poor Czech immigrants. Kubitschek himself believed that his early life in Diamantina influenced him greatly.

Walks

While you are here, walk a couple of km down the Caminho dos Escravos (built by slaves) to the Serra da Jacuba. Then walk eight km on the road to São Goncalo to see the *furnas* (caverns).

Places to Stay

The *Hotel Nosson* (☎ 531-1565), opposite the bus terminal, is friendly and cheap at US$6 per person. The only problem with staying there is that every time you go into the centre, it's a long uphill walk back. For the same price, you can stay at the more central *Hotel Carvalho* (☎ 531-1526), at Rua Quintanda 20, but it's pretty basic. For a bit extra, the *Hotel Dália* (☎ 531-1477), at Praça Juscelino Kubitschek 25, is much better. It's in a nice old building in a good location, almost next door to the Museu do Diamante. It has single/double quartos that cost US$10/16 and apartamentos that go for US$20/30.

The top-end hotels in town are the *Hotel Tijuco* (☎ 581-1022), at Rua Macáu do Meio 211, another Niemeyer erection (US$25/35 for singles/doubles, more if you want a room with a view), and the *Pousada do Garimpo* (☎ 531-2523), a tasteful place a little further out of town, at Avenida da Saudade 265 (US$40/54).

Places to Eat

Popular pick is the *Cantinha do Marinho*, at Beco do Motta 27, which has good mineiro dishes. Try their lombo com tropeiro. They also have a cheap self-serve lunch. *Restaurant Confiança*, at Rua da Quitanda 39, next to the post office, has good regional food but is a bit expensive. Try their frango com quiabo. The *Restaurante Grupiara*, at Rua Campos Carvalho 12, is also recommended.

Getting There & Away

Buses leave Belo Horizonte for Diamantina daily at 5.30, 9 and 11.30 am, 2.30 and 6.30 pm and midnight. The trip costs US$10. Buses return to Belo Horizonte Monday to Friday at 6 and 10.45 am, noon, and 3.30 and 6 pm; on Saturday at 6 and 10.45 am, noon, and 3.30 and 6 pm; and on Sunday at 6 am, noon, and 3.30 and 6 pm.

SERRO

Dominated by the Igreja de Santa Rita, Serro is a tranquil *cidade histórica* 90 km from Diamantina. It's a cold, windy place surrounded by granite hills, which in the past provided refuge for runaway slaves. The city is rich in folkloric traditions and is the home of the famous *queijo serrano* (one of Brazil's finest cheeses).

Colonial Buildings

As well as the Igreja Santa Rita, Serro contains such historic churches as the Igreja NS do Carmo (1781), in Praça João Pinheiro, and the Igreja Senhor Bom Jesus de Matosinhos, in Praça Cristiano Otoni.

Other colonial buildings worth a look are the Casa do Barão de Diamantina – now used as the town hall – with 40 rooms which were to have held Dom Pedro II and his entourage during a visit that never happened, and the Chácara do Barão do Serro, across the valley, which has a small museum.

Festival

The Festa do Rosário, which takes place on the first Sunday in July, features folkloric characters – *catopês*, *caboclinhos* and *marujos* – who dance and stage mock fights in the streets.

Places to Stay & Eat

The *Pousada Vila do Principe* (☎ 941-1485), at Rua Antônio Honório Pires 38, has apartamentos for US$10/15 a single/double.

The hotel/restaurant *Itacolomi*, in Praça João Pinheiro, is a good place to stay. Single/double apartamentos cost US$8/11.

Another popular place to stay is the small town of Milho Verde, about halfway between Diamantina and Serro. It's a liberal place (ie there are no cops in town), with a few simple pousadas.

Getting There & Away

From Diamantina, there is only one daily bus to Serro. It leaves at 3.45 pm (3.25 pm on weekends) and takes two hours. From Serro to Belo Horizonte, there is one bus at 1 pm

(US$12, six hours). To Diamantina, there's a daily 8.30 am bus.

Mineral Spa Towns

The southern mineral spa towns of Minas are well-developed health resorts whose excellent mineral springs have various therapeutic applications. Of the 13 spa towns, Caxambu, with its century-old Parque das Aguas, and São Lourenço, surrounded by the green hills of the Serra da Mantiqueira, are of most interest to the traveller. Been travelling hard and fast? Recovering from a tropical disease? Sick of seemingly idyllic beaches? Overdosing on baroque? If the answer is yes to one or all of these questions, the spa towns await you.

CAXAMBU

Brazilians debate the origin of the name Caxambu. Some claim it is a combination of two African words: *cacha* (drum) and *mambu* (music). A *cacha-mambu* or *caxambu* is a conically shaped drum from the Congo which the founders of the city likened to the knolls of the area. Others believe it came from the Indian *catá-mbu* (water that bubbles), in reference to the medicinal fountains. Most couldn't care less where the name came from.

It wasn't until 1870 that the springs were first tapped. Realising the curative properties of the waters, medical practitioners flocked to the town. In 1886 Dr Policarpo Viotti founded the Caxambu water company (nationalised in 1905).

The water of Caxambu was celebrated on the international water circuit, winning gold medals long before Perrier hit Manhattan singles bars. Caxambu took the gold medal in Rome's Victor Emmanuel III Exposition of 1903, and another gold medal in the St Louis International Fair of 1904, then the Diploma of Honour in the University of Brussels Exposition of 1910.

These water Olympics were discontinued during WW I, and Caxambu's history was uneventful until 1981, when Supergasbras and Superagua, private firms, took over the government concession. Caxambu is sold throughout Brazil, and in Miami, Florida, where the US Food & Drug Administration has approved it. Caxambu is the only Brazilian mineral water thus honoured.

Caxambu is a tranquil resort for the elderly and the middle class, who come here to escape the heat of Rio and the madness of Carnival. Some couples have been coming here every summer for 30 years or more.

Information

Tourist Office Obtain maps and other information from the tourist office in Praça 16 de Setembro, open from 8 to 11 am and noon to 6 pm.

Money For some unknown reason, the Banco do Brasil branch here won't change money – try the larger hotels. Forget travellers' cheques.

Post & Telephone The post office is on Avenida Camilo Soares, right next to the Hotel Gloria. Telephone calls can be made from Rua Major Penha 265.

Parque das Aguas

The Parque das Aguas is like a Disneyland for the rheumatic. Given the proper temperament and surroundings, nursing your ailments can be fun. People come to take the mineral waters, smell the sulphur, compare liver spots, watch the geyser spout every couple of hours, rest in the shade by the canal and walk in the lovely gardens.

The park is not only good, it's good for you. Liver problems? Go to the Dona Leopoldina magnesium fountain. Skin disorders? Take the sulphur baths of Tereza Cristina. Anaemic? The Conde d'Eu e Dona

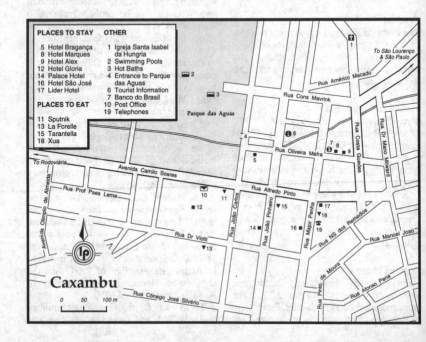

PLACES TO STAY
5 Hotel Bragança
8 Hotel Marques
9 Hotel Alex
12 Hotel Gloria
14 Palace Hotel
16 Hotel São José
17 Lider Hotel

PLACES TO EAT
11 Sputnik
13 La Forelle
15 Tarantella
18 Xua

OTHER
1 Igreja Santa Isabel da Hungria
2 Swimming Pools
3 Hot Baths
4 Entrance to Parque das Aguas
6 Tourist Information
7 Banco do Brasil
10 Post Office
19 Telephones

Parque das Aguas

To São Lourenço & São Paulo

Rua Américo Macado
Rua Cons Mavrink
Rua Costa Guedes
Rua Dr Mario Milward
Rua Oliveira Mafra
To Rodoviária
Avenida Camilo Soares
Rua Prof Paes Leme
Avenida Olímpio de Almeida
Rua Alfredo Pinto
Rua João Carlos
Rua João Pinheiro
Rua Major Penha
Rua NS dos Remedios
Rua Manoel Joao
Rua Dr Viotti
Rua Cônego José Silvério
Rua Pinto de Moura
Rua Afonso Pena

Caxambu

0   50   100 m

Isabel fountains are rich in iron. VD? The Duque de Saxe fountain helps calm the bacteria that cause syphilis. For stomach troubles, drink the naturally carbonated waters of Dom Pedro (there's a water-bottling plant on the premises). The alkaline waters of the Venancio and Viotti fountains are good for dissolving kidney stones, while the Beleza waters soothe the intestines. The multipurpose water of the Mayrink fountains 1, 2 and 3 is good for gargling, eye irritations and table water (without the bubbles).

The park is open daily from 7 am to 6 pm, and admission to the grounds is US$1. Separate fees are required for paddleboats, the rifle range, hydrotherapeutic massages at the bath house, the jacuzzi, sauna, clay tennis courts, swimming pool, skating rink and chairlift to the top of Morro Cristo.

Other Attractions

The eight-metre-high **Morro Cristo** hill has an image of Jesus. On Rua Princesa Isabela is the **Igreja de Santa Isabel da Hungria**, built by the princess once she conceived due to the miraculous waters of Caxambu.

Take a **horse-and-buggy tour** into the countryside; a 1½-hour ride from the park entrance will only set you back US$15 for two. The standard tour includes a mini-zoo, the Fabrica de Doce and the Chacarra Rosallan. The **mini-zoo** at the Hotel Campestre has caged monkeys, a wilting peacock, and a siriema bird which looks like an eccentric European aristocrat disgraced and in exile. The **Fabrica de Doce** has locally-produced honey (US$3), liqueurs (US$0.50) and preserves (US$2). The last stop is **Chacara Rosallan's**, an old farm with a flower orchard and fruit grove. Rosallan is famous for two of her fruit liqueurs: jaboticaba and bottled tangerine. Empty bottles are passed over the tiny tangerines and strapped to the tree; the tangerine grows within the bottle and, weeks later, is made into a liqueur.

Places to Stay

Unlike São Lourenço, Caxambu lacks really cheap places to stay, but if you're here

outside peak holiday times, you can get some good deals. Most hotel prices include all meals.

The *Hotel São José* (☎ 341-1094), at Rua Major Penha 264, is an apartment hotel with TVs, big double beds, and hot showers. Apartamentos are US$20 per person (with breakfast only). The *Hotel Marques* (☎ 341-1013), at Rua Oliveira Mafra 223, has singles/doubles for US$18/28, or US$23/46 with full board. Next door, the *Hotel Alex* (☎ 341-1331) is similarly priced.

The four-star *Hotel Gloria* (☎ 341-1233), at Avenida Camilo Soares 590, is a very posh resort complex with a range of activities for the leisure set. Doubles with TV, bath, bar, telephone and three meals a day are US$110 for two. Facilities include a big gym with indoor basketball court, tennis (clay courts in the park), a physical rehabilitation centre and a sauna.

The *Hotel Bragança* (☎ 341-1117), directly in front of the Parque das Aguas entrance, is not quite as fancy but is more than adequate. Singles/doubles are US$40/60, including full board.

An excellent top-end deal can be had at the impressive *Palace Hotel* (☎ 341-1044). With full board the prices are US$70/85 for singles/doubles, but with breakfast only, the cost drops to US$30/38. Their food must be pretty good!

Places to Eat

La Forelle, an interesting Danish restaurant at Rua Dr Viotti 190, has excellent fondue, and also specialises in salmon and trout dishes. *Tarantella*, near the park entrance, at Rua João Pinheiro 326, has the best pasta and pizza in town. *Sputnik*, on Avenida Camilo Soares, close to the park, is a good lanchonete for a snack. *Xua*, at Rua Major Penha 225, is the place to go for mineiro food.

Getting There & Away

Seven daily buses make the 49-km trip between Caxambu and São Lourenço on a winding, wooded road. There are four buses a day to São Paulo (US$9, 6½ hours), and two to Rio (US$8, 5½ hours), at 8 am and midnight, via Cruzeiro and Resende.

SÃO LOURENÇO

São Lourenço is another pleasant city of mineral waters. Just south of Caxambu, it's 275 km from Rio de Janeiro, 296 km from São Paulo and 401 km from Belo Horizonte. The principal attraction is the Parque das Aguas, featuring waters with a variety of healing properties, a sauna and a lake with paddle boats. It's open daily from 8 am to 5.20 pm. Other diversions include goat-cart rides for children and horse-and-buggy rides for adults.

Information

Tourist Office In front of the Parque das Aguas, the tourist office is open every day from 8 to 11 am and 1 to 6 pm. Staff have a list of hotels and a map of the attractions.

Money The Banco do Brasil is on Avenida Dom Pedro II, at No 266.

Post & Telephone The post office is on Rua Dr Olavo Gomes Pinto. The telefônica is at Rua Coronel José Justino 647.

Circuito das Aguas

Volkswagen Kombi half-day tours of the Circuito das Aguas (Water Circuit) can be arranged for US$20 per person. If possible, organise it the day before. The vans will take up to eight people, and normally visit Caxambu, Baependi, Cambuquira, Lambari and Passo Quatro, but you can also talk (bribe?) the driver into taking you to the mysterious stone village of São Tomé das Letras (80 km away). Taxis and vans congregate at Avenida Getúlio Vargas.

You could also visit Poços das Caldas, a city built on the crater of an extinct volcano; this mineral spring town was settled by crystal-glass blowers of the island of Murano, near Venice. There are full-day tours to Poços das Caldas that cost US$35 and leave at 7 am.

Templo da Euboise

Members of the Brazilian Society of Euboise believe that a new civilisation will arise in the seven magic cities of the region: São Tomé das Letras, Aiuruoca, Conceição do Rio Verde, Itanhandu, Pouso Alto, Carmo de Minas and Maria da Fe. You can visit their temple on weekends from 2 to 4 pm, but you won't be allowed in if you're wearing shorts or sandals.

Places to Stay

The *Pensão Casa Grande* (☎ 331-3178), at Rua Barão do Rio Branco 195, up from the bus station, is the cheapest place in town. The rooms are basic; they cost US$7 per person. Nearby, at No 611 Avenida Dom Pedro II, the *Hotel Colombo* (☎ 331-1577) has clean, carpeted rooms. Apartamentos are US$10/16 a single/double. If you can be bothered walking a bit further, the *Hotel Estância* (☎ 331-3369), at Rua Dr Olavo Gomes Pinto 195, is nicer, with singles/doubles for US$16/20.

The *Hotel Metropole* (☎ 331-1290), Rua Wenceslau Brás 70, has quartos ranging from US$12 to US$20 with breakfast, US$24 to US$40 with full board. Apartamentos cost US$4 more than quartos. They also have a pool. The *Hotel Miranda* (☎ 331-1033), at No 545 Rua Dom Pedro II, is not a bad deal, with quartos at US$20/24 a single/double with full board. On the same street, at No 587, the *Hotel Imperial* (☎ 331-1762) has apartamentos at US$28/40 with full board.

The four-star *Hotel Brasil* (☎ 331-1422), at Rua João Lage 87, across from the park, is the top-of-the-line hotel in São Lourenço. Doubles with full board start at US$120 (less 30% in low season).

Places to Eat

The restaurants in town can't compete with the food served in the hotels. *Restaurante Namaste*, just across from the park entrance, is a good place for lunch. It's open from 9.30 am to 4 pm every day except Tuesday. There's also a good health-food restaurant in the park itself.

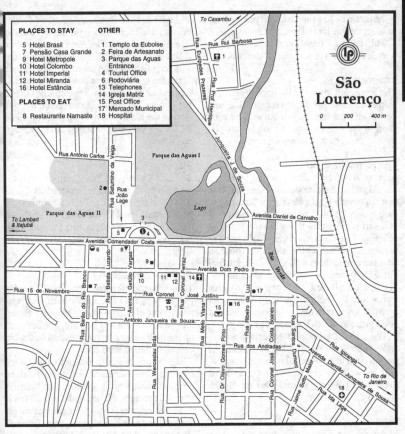

São
Lourenço

0   200   400 m

PLACES TO STAY
5 Hotel Brasil
7 Pensão Casa Grande
9 Hotel Metropole
10 Hotel Colombo
11 Hotel Imperial
12 Hotel Miranda
16 Hotel Estância

PLACES TO EAT
8 Restaurante Namaste

OTHER
1 Templo da Euboise
2 Feira de Artesanato
3 Parque das Aguas Entrance
4 Tourist Office
6 Rodoviária
13 Telephones
14 Igreja Matriz
15 Post Office
17 Mercado Municipal
18 Hospital

Entertainment

São Lourenço's nightlife is pretty tame. In the evenings, teenagers and young adults dress up and hang out on the fence and around the entrance of the Hotel Metropole. The club there has dances, a bar and music video on a large screen. If that's not your scene, there's a cinema on Avenida Dom Pedro II.

Getting There & Away

There are six buses daily to Rio de Janeiro (US$7, five hours), six daily to São Paulo (US$8, six hours) and 11 daily to Caxambu (US$0.75, 45 minutes).

SÃO TOMÉ DAS LETRAS

In southern Minas, 310 km from Belo Horizonte, São Tomé das Letras is a stone village at an altitude of 1450 metres. The name refers to the inscriptions on some of the many caverns in the region. If you're into mysticism or superstition, this is the place to go. Considered by local mystics to be one of the seven sacred cities of the world, the town is filled with hippies, strange stories of flying saucers, visits of extraterrestrials, a cave that is the entrance to a subterranean passageway to Macchu Picchu in Peru, and more.

This is also a beautiful mountain region, with great walks and several waterfalls.

Information

The Prefeitura Municipal is opposite the bus stop in the main square, but can provide only verbal information in Portuguese. There's a shop in the main square, to the left as you look at the church, that sells maps.

Things to See & Do

Most of the town's churches and buildings are old and made from slabs of quartzite. One that isn't is the **Igreja Matriz de São Tomé**, dating from 1740, in the main square. It contains some excellent frescoes by the artist Joaquim José da Natividade. Right next to the church is the **Gruta de São Tomé**, a small cave which, as well as its shrine to São Tomé, has some of the strange inscriptions. The **Igreja de Pedra**, made of stone, is worth a photograph. The lookout, only 500 metres up from town, provides great views and is a good place to watch the sunset or sunrise.

The caves **Carimbado** (three km away) and **Chico Taquara** (3.5 km) both contain the puzzling inscriptions. The popular waterfalls to walk to are **Euboise** (three km), **Prefeitura** (seven km) and **Véu de Noiva** (12 km).

Festival

In August, the Festas de Agosto attract lots of pilgrims.

Places to Stay

There's a youth hostel, the *Pousada Mahã-Mantra* (☎ 989-5563), 20 metres up behind the stone church to the right, and camping at Gruta do Leão, which supposedly has enchanted water.

São Tomé has grown a lot in the last few years, so there are lots of pousadas. There are no five-star hotels yet, but the way things are going, it's only a matter of time. All pousadas charge between US$8 and US$20 per person, but not all provide breakfast.

Spotlessly clean is the *Pensão Dona Célia*

(☎ (101) 244), at Rua Joaquim José Mendes Peixoto 11. There's no sign, but it's easy to find. Ask anybody. The *Pousada Arco Iris*, at Rua Armando Duplessis Vilela, is popular with travellers. Just up the road, the *Pousada Serra Branca* is one that does provide breakfast and lunch or dinner. They charge US$18 per person for apartamentos. Near the bus stop in the main square is the *Pousada Por do Sul*. It's very simple and one of the cheapest in town.

Places to Eat

Bar das Letras, at Rua Camilo Rios 15, serves a good prato feito, and *Bar do Gê*, at Rua Gabriel Luiz Alves 28, is a surprisingly good restaurant. The bar *All Days of Peace and Music Woodstock*, in Rua Camilo Rios, is a good place to meet people who've seen UFOs.

Getting There & Away

The town is best reached from Três Corações (which happens to be Pelé's birthplace and has a statue of him), 38 km to the west. Buses leave daily at 6 am and 3.30 pm. The dirt road up the mountains is precarious and buses are cancelled during hard rains.

Hitching is possible, but not easy. To try hitching from Três Corações, cross the river next to the bus station and turn into the first street on the right, the one with the train track down the middle. About 50 metres down on the left-hand side, there's a bus stop. Take the 'B Ventura' bus to its final destination. It'll save you a long uphill walk through town.

São Tomé das Letras can also be reached from Caxambu, 60 km to the south, but not by local bus.

National Parks

PARQUE NACIONAL DE CAPARAÓ

This park is popular with climbers and hikers from all over Brazil. The panoramic views are superb, taking in the Caparaó valley that divides Minas Gerais and Espírito Santo. Caparaó contains the highest mountains in southern Brazil, including the third-highest peak in the country: the Pico da Bandeira, at 2890 metres. Other peaks include Cristal (2798 metres) and Calçado (2766 metres). All three can be reached via a good network of trails that exist within the park. Climbing gear isn't necessary.

Despite being ravaged by fire in 1988 and by human interference for the last 300 years, the park has a few lush remnants of Mata Atlântica, mostly in Vale Verde, a small valley split by the Rio Caparaó.

Wildlife in the park is not exactly plentiful, but there are still some opossums, agoutis and spider monkeys to be seen. Birdlife includes various eagle, parrot and hummingbird species.

Between November and January, there's lots of rain and it's too cloudy for good views. The best time to visit the park is between June and August – although these are the coldest months, the days are clear. Bring warm clothes!

The park is open daily from 7 am to 5 pm and costs US$0.50 to enter. Make sure you pick up a map.

Places to Stay

It's possible to camp inside the park. There are two official campsites: *Tronqueira*, eight km from the park entrance, and *Terreirão*, a further 4.5 km away, halfway to the summit of Pico da Bandeira.

Camping costs US$2 a night, but it's a good idea to reserve a site about a week before you arrive by ringing IBAMA (☎ (031) 275-4266 in Belo Horizonte).

If you don't have a tent, the nearest place to stay is the *Caparaó Park Hotel* (☎ 741-2559), a short walk from the park entrance. It's a pleasant, friendly place, but a bit on the expensive side, with singles/doubles for US$30/35. If that's too steep, ask around for a room to rent in Alto do Caparaó, the village closest to the park.

Getting There & Away

Caparaó can be reached via Belo Horizonte, or from Vitória, in Espírito Santo. You'll need to catch a bus to the town of Manhumirim, and then another local bus to Alto do Caparaó, a further 25 km away.

Unfortunately, the bus timetables work against the budget traveller. There are two buses a day to Manhumirim from both Belo Horizonte and Vitória. From Belo, they leave at 10 am and 5 pm, from Vitória at 9.30 am and 3.30 pm. The trip from either takes around five hours. The problem is that there are only two local buses a day to Alto do Caparaó: at 8 am and noon. To avoid staying in Manhumirim, catch one of the many buses going to Presidente Soares and ask to be dropped off at the Caparaó turn-off, then hitch the rest of the way. Alternatively, if you can afford it, take a taxi from Manhumirim to Alto do Caparaó (US$15 to US$25, depending on the mood of the driver and your own bargaining ability).

PARQUE NACIONAL DA SERRA DO CIPÓ

Formed by mountains, rivers, waterfalls and open grasslands, the Parque Nacional da Serra do Cipó is one of Minas' most beautiful. Its highlands, together with an arm of the Serra do Espinhaço, divide the water basins of the São Francisco and Doce rivers. The park contains no infrastructure for tourism.

Most of the park's vegetation is cerrado and grassy highlands, but the small river valleys are lush and ferny, and contain a number of unique orchids. Animal species include the maned wolf, tamarin monkey, banded anteater, tree hedgehog, otter, jaguar and there are large numbers of bats. Birdlife includes woodpeckers, blackbirds and hummingbirds. The park is also home to a small, brightly coloured frog which secretes deadly toxins from its skin. Brazilians call it *sapo-de-pijama* (the pyjama-frog).

Other attractions of the park include the 70-metre waterfall Cachoeira da Farofa, and the Canyon das Bandeirantes, named after the early adventurers from São Paulo, who used the area as a natural road to the north in their search for riches.

A recent traveller to Parque Nacional de Serra do Cipó writes:

It was a great experience. I would call the lack of infrastructure an advantage. Some people stay near the Rio do Cipó, but few actually go into the park itself. To camp in the park, stay on the bus for about 20 km past the hotel near the Rio do Cipó. There are two small stone bridges just 100 metres from each other. Ask the driver to let you off at the 4WD road to the right, just past those bridges. Follow the track (all quartz and quartzite) for about five km until it becomes a footpath through the bushes. Don't lose the track because the vegetation is dense. After three to four km more you get to a small, very dry plateau where you'll be completely alone and have a superb view over the canyons to both sides. Just pitch your tent for a few days and take day trips down into the canyons or wander over the mountains higher up. There are waterfalls and pools down in the river which are very nice to swim in. There is marvellous vegetation and nasty beasties, including snakes, giant spiders and scorpions. When you return to Belo Horizonte, make sure you make a short stop just past the Rio do Cipó. There's a great pub opposite the hotel, about 50 metres to the right. It's actually an old watermill, the mood is great and the owner speaks English. It's worth a visit!

Geert Van de Wiele (Belgium)

Getting There & Away

Located about 100 km north-east of Belo Horizonte, the park is reached by catching a bus to Lagoa Santa, then another bus to Conceição do Mato Dentro. The road passes next to the park and Cardeal Mota, the nearest town.

PARQUE NACIONAL DA SERRA DA CANASTRA

In the south-east of Minas Gerais, the Parque Nacional da Serra da Canastra is the birth-place of the Rio São Francisco – the river of national unity. With altitudes varying between 900 and 1500 metres, the vegetation is cerrado with grassy tablelands. Although the fauna has been devastated by hunting and bushfires over the years, the park is a reasonable place to see animals, especially early in the morning. Deer, armadillos, banded ant-eaters, jaguars and maned wolves may be spotted, as well as eagles, vultures and owls. Another big attraction is the 200-metre-high Casca d'Anta waterfall. The best time to visit the park is between April and October.

Places to Stay

The park contains a campsite, but no hotels. The closest town, São Roque de Minas, has basic hotels.

Getting There & Away

It's about 350 km from Belo Horizonte to São Roque de Minas. From São Roque, it's a further 40 km to Casca d'Anta.

São Paulo State

São Paulo is South America's richest state – the industrial engine that powers the Brazilian economy: 30 of Brazil's 50 largest companies are in São Paulo, as is 50% of the nation's industry. The state contains South America's largest city, São Paulo, a megalopolis with 17 million inhabitants in its metropolitan area. One in every nine Brazilians lives here in São Paulo city.

São Paulo City

The city of São Paulo is Brazil's most cosmopolitan and modern. It is a city of immigrants and ethnic neighbourhoods. Millions of Italians came here at the end of the 19th century, millions of Japanese arrived this century, and millions of Brazilians from the countryside and from the Northeast are still pouring in. This diversity and industrial development has produced Brazil's largest, most-cultured and best-educated middle class. These Paulistanos (inhabitants of the city; inhabitants of the state are called Paulistas) are lively and make well-informed companions. They call their city Sampa and, despite constantly complaining about street violence, traffic problems and pollution, they wouldn't dream of living anywhere else.

São Paulo is on a high plateau: cold in the Brazilian winter and smoggy-hot in the summer. It can be an intimidating place, but if you know someone who can show you around or if you just like big cities, it's worth a visit. At its best it offers the excitement and nightlife of one of the world's great cities.

History

Founded in 1554 when a group of Jesuit priests led by Manoel de Nóbrega and José de Anchieta arrived at the Piratinanga plateau, São Paulo remained an unimportant backwater for many years. By the beginning of the 17th century, it had a few churches and a small village. The growing Indian slave trade saw the town become a headquarters for the bandeirantes, the slave-trading pioneers who, in their treks into the Brazilian interior, explored much unknown territory. For them, the Treaty of Tordesillas, which divided South America between Spain and Portugal, was nothing more than a line on a map, and they were largely responsible for expanding the boundaries of Portuguese territory.

By the 18th century, the bandeirantes had turned their attention to mineral exploration, and had discovered gold mines in Minas Gerais, Goiás and Matto Grosso. São Paulo was used as a stopover by the increasing number of pioneers, explorers and fortune-hunters heading for the interior, as well as by sugar dealers taking their shipments to the port of Santos.

During the early part of the 19th century, two events significantly changed São Paulo. The first was the declaration of Brazilian independence, which led to the city becoming a provincial capital. The second occurred a few years later with the founding of the Law Faculty, which attracted a new, transient population of students and intellectuals. As a political and intellectual centre, São Paulo became a leader both in the campaign to abolish slavery and in the founding of the republic.

The last decades of the 19th century brought dramatic change. The rapid expansion of coffee cultivation in the state, the construction of railroads and the influx of millions of European immigrants caused the city to grow rapidly. São Paulo's industrial base began to form, and the import restrictions caused by WW I meant rapid industrial expansion and population growth, which continued after the war. The population reached 580,000 by 1920, 1.2 million by 1940, two million by 1950, 3.1 million by 1960 and 5.2 million by 1970. By the year

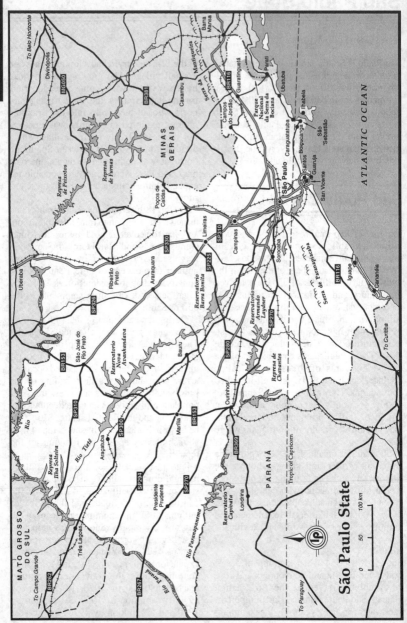

São Paulo State

2005, the population is expected to top 25 million.

Orientation

Getting around São Paulo can be difficult even if you speak Portuguese, have a car, time and money, and you know the streets and traffic patterns. For the traveller, it takes much longer to get a feel for the layout of São Paulo than for just about any city in the world. Why? First, it's a big, sprawling city. Second, there is no plan or pattern to the arteries. Third, there are few natural or artificial landmarks by which to orient oneself. There is no ocean or river (of importance), and either few dominating boulevards or so many, depending on how you look at it, that they are of little use to the visitor. Visibility is limited by buildings everywhere. Even maps reflect the difficulty of bringing the city down to comprehensible dimensions. At first glance, they are of practically no use. The solution is to go underground. The metro, São Paulo's subway system, is one of the best in the world. And it's cheap, too.

Parks, museums, art galleries, zoos, you name it – all are spread throughout the metropolitan area. It's best to pick up *Veja* at a newsstand or go to a tourism booth for a good list.

As a city of immigrants, certain suburbs of São Paulo are associated with the nationalities that settled there. Liberdade, just south of Praça da Sé, is the Oriental area. Bela Vista and nearby Bixiga are Italian. Bom Retiro, near Estação da Luz train station (the metro also runs through here), is the old Jewish quarter. The large Arab community is based around Rua 25 de Março, to the north of Praça da Sé. In all these areas, you'll find restaurants to match the tastes of their inhabitants.

Avenida Paulista, to the south-west of the centre, is an avenue of skyscrapers, and the adjoining suburb of Cerqueira César contains the city's highest concentration of good restaurants, cafés and nightclubs. When people refer to São Paulo as the 'New York of the Tropics', this is the area they have in mind. Adjoining Cerqueira César is the stylish Jardims district, home to many of the city's middle and upper-class residents.

Information

Tourist Office The city's many tourist information booths have excellent city and state maps. They are also good for bus and metro information. English is spoken.

The information booth on Praça da República (along Avenida Ipiranga) is helpful, and staff speak English, French Italian and Spanish. It's open daily from 9 am to 6 pm. There's a post office attached to this booth.

Other tourist offices are found at: Avenida Paulista, near MASP (open from 9 am to 6 pm); Avenida São Luís, on the corner of Praça Dom José Gaspar (open from 9 am to 6 pm daily); and Aeroporto de Congonhas (open 24 hours a day). There is also an information booth out the front of the shopping centre Iguatemi. Contact the main tourism office on ☎ 267-2122, ext 627, or 640 on weekends.

The state tourist office is located in the beautiful, deco Banco de São Paulo building, at Praça Antônio Prado 9, and is worth a visit if you plan on staying for a while.

Paulistanos would not dream of driving in the city without one of several large city street directories. If you are staying in the city for a while, the *Guia São Paulo* by Quatro Rodas has street maps and hotel and restaurant listings. *O Guia* has the clearest presentation of any street guide, and it also lists tourist points. Probably the best street guide to check out is the *Guia Caroplan*, as it has an extensive English-language section.

Also at newsstands, for US$1 (free at large hotels), is *São Paulo this Month* – a monthly entertainment guide with an English-language section.

Money Changing money is easy in São Paulo, and you'll get top rates. The only time you're likely to have a problem is on weekends. There are several travel agencies and casas de câmbio across from the airline offices on Avenida São Luís, close to Praça da República, which are a good bet. Most

THE SOUTHEAST

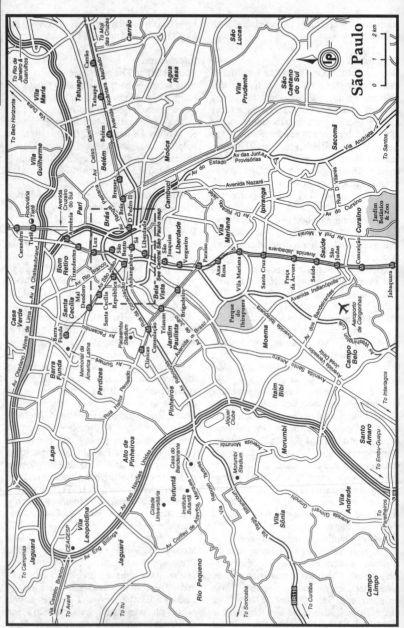

São Paulo

banks in this area have foreign-exchange counters.

American Express/Kontik-Franstur (☎ 259-4211) is on the 1st floor at Rua Marconi. (From the Praça da República, on the Avenida Ipiranga side, go down Barão de Itapetininga and turn left after two blocks.) They close for mail pick-up from noon to 2 pm. This is also the place to come to if you need to purchase travellers' cheques with your American Express card. There is another branch inside the Sheraton, near Avenida Paulista.

Post & Telephone The main post office is in the Praça do Correio, right where Avenida São João meets Anhangabaú. The posta restante service, downstairs, will hold mail for 30 days. Fax services are available in the same building.

The Telesp long-distance telephone office is close to Praça da República on the Ipiranga side. It's 200 metres down Rua 7 de Abril, on the right as you walk away from the praça.

Foreign Consulates The following countries have consulates in São Paulo:

Argentina
    Avenida Paulista 1106, 9th floor (☎ 284-1355); open from 9 am to 1 pm
Australia
    Rua Tenente Negrão 140, 12th floor (☎ 829-6281); open Monday, Wednesday and Friday from 9 am to noon
Bolivia
    Rua da Consolação 37, 3rd floor (☎ 255-3555); open from 9 am to 1 pm
Canada
    Avenida Paulista 1106, 1st floor (☎ 287-2122); open from 8 am to 5 pm
Chile
    Avenida Paulista 1009, 10th floor (☎ 284-2044); open from 8.30 am to 1.30 pm
France
    Avenida Paulista 1842, 14th floor (☎ 287-9522); open from 8.30 am to noon
Germany
    Avenida Brigadeiro Faria Lima 1383, 12th floor (☎ 814-6614); open from 8.30 to 11.30 am
Israel
    Avenida Brigadeiro Faria Lima 1766, 13th floor (☎ 815-7788); open from 9 am to noon

Paraguay
    Avenida São Luís 50, 9th floor (☎ 255-7818); open from 8.30 am to 4 pm
Peru
    Rua Laplace 739 (☎ 531-0943); open from 9 am to 1 pm
UK
    Avenida Paulista 1938, 17th floor (☎ 287-7722); open from 9 am to noon and 2 to 4 pm
USA
    Rua Padre João Manoel 933 (☎ 881-6511); open from 8 am to 5 pm

Visas For visa extensions, the Polícia Federal office is at Avenida Prestes Maia 700. It's open from 10 am to 4 pm. Go up to the 1st floor.

Bookshops There's a good selection of English books at the Book Centre, Rua Gabus Mendes 29, near the Praça da República. Livraria Cultura, at Avenida Paulista 2073, has quite a wide variety of titles. Livraria Francesa, at Rua Barão de Itapetininga 275, deals exclusively with books in French.

Health If you have a serious health problem, Einstein Hospital (☎ 845-1233) is one of the best in Latin America.

Tourist Police Deatur is the tourist-police service and has english-speaking staff. It has two offices in the city: at Avenida São Luís 115 (☎ 214-0209), open from 8 am to 8 pm, and at Rua 15 de Novembro (☎ 607-8332), open from 8 am to 7 pm. Both offices are closed on weekends.

Walking Tour

The triangle formed by Praça da Sé, Estação da Luz metro station and Praça da República contains the old centre of São Paulo, and it's certainly worth having a look round this area. A good place to start is the **Mercado Municipal**, at Rua da Cantareira 306. Dating from 1933, this lively market used to be the city's wholesale market, until the CEAGESP (a huge new market) was built. Check out the German-made, stained-glass windows with their agricultural themes.

Not far from the market is the geographical centre of the city, Praça da Sé, and the **Catedral**, completed in 1954. There's a lot of busking here, but don't bring any valuables, as there are lots of pickpockets and bag snatchers. Close by is the **Patío do Colégio**, where the city was founded in 1554 by the Jesuits José de Anchieta and Manoel da Nóbrega. The church and college have been reconstructed in colonial style.

A couple of blocks from Praça da Sé, in the Largo São Francisco, is the traditional **Law Faculty** of the University of São Paulo. The surrounding bars are local student handouts, especially **Bar & Restaurante Itamaraty**.

Up Rua Libero Badaró and across the **Viaduto do Chá** (the bridge that crosses the Vale do Anhangabaú) is the **Teatro Municipal**, the pride of the city. It's built in baroque style with art-nouveau elements. The area between here and Avenida Ipiranga is for pedestrians only, and gets really busy during the day. There are plenty of clothing and footwear shops, bookshops, travel agencies, record stores, one-hour photo places and lunch counters.

Up on Avenida Ipiranga, on the corner with Avenida São Luís, is the tallest building in town, the 41-storey **Edifício Itália**. There's a restaurant and piano bar at the top, as well as a viewing terrace. Strictly speaking, you're supposed to be a customer to go there; if you're not, act like one. The best time to go up is right on sunset. This is the only time you'll ever get to see the horizon, and, as the sun goes down over the nearby hills and the city lights start to sparkle, you could almost convince yourself that São Paulo is beautiful.

Next to the Itália is another one of the city's landmarks, **Edifício Copan**, with its famous curve – yet another Niemeyer project. Along Avenida Ipiranga, just past Praça da República, is the intersection with Avenida São João. When people get nostalgic about the city (yes, some do), this is the place they write songs about. **Bar Brahma**, on the corner, is a classic bar where you may want to go and try to compose yourself.

The area between here and the Estação da Luz gradually deteriorates. Rua Santa Efigênia is where Paulistanos go for cheap electronic goods, and the area between here and the station is known as *boca do lixo* (mouth of trash) – it's a red-light area with striptease shows, and desperate characters hang out here after dark.

Museu de Arte de São Paulo (MASP)

This museum has Latin America's best collection of Western art, including the work of many French impressionists. There are also a few great Brazilian paintings: the Candido Portinaris alone are worth the trip. There are also temporary exhibits, and a pleasant cafeteria in the basement. Outside the museum, there is the Feria de Antiquidades do MASP, held on Sunday from 9 am to 5 pm. The fair is full of old odds and ends, big and small – including furniture, books and toys.

The museum is open Tuesday to Sunday from 11 am to 6 pm (on Thursday, there is no entry fee). Go early, as the light can be very bad late in the day. The MASP is at Avenida Paulista 1578. To get there, take the metro to Paraiso station, then change for Trianon.

For a bit of relaxation after the museum, visit the small park – a tropical oasis amidst the mountains of concrete – across Avenida Paulista.

Parque do Ibirapuera

There's lots to do in this park, and many people doing it on weekends. The best way to get here is to take the metro to Santa Cruz station and then catch the No 775-C 'Jardim Maria Sampião' bus. The large edifice across the street from the park is the São Paulo state legislature. Just outside the park, at the end of Avenida Brasil, is Victor Brecheret's huge monument *Bandeiras*, built in memory of the pioneers of the city.

Inside the park is a planetarium, a lake, monuments, a Japanese pavilion and several museums.

Museu de Arte Contemporânea

This museum has many of the big names in modern art and a good collection of modern

Brazilian artists. It's housed, at least part of it, in the Bienal building, which also has a couple of enormous exhibition halls. The rest of the collection is at the Cidade Universitária, which is open Tuesday to Sunday from 1 to 6 pm.

The Bienal is also worth a mention. It's the largest art exhibition in Brazil, and if you happen to be in town when it's on, don't miss it. It takes place every odd year.

Museu de Arte Moderna

This is the oldest museum of modern art in the country. It's opening hours are Tuesday to Friday from 1 to 7 pm, and from 11 am to 7 pm on weekends.

Museu de Folclore & Museu Aeronautica

These two museums are in the dome-shaped building. The former includes an Afro-Brazilian cult altar and folkloric costumes from all over Brazil. The latter features the flying machines of Santos Dumont, considered the father of Brazilian aviation. Both museums are open Tuesday to Sunday from 2 to 5 pm.

Museu de Arte Sacra & Jardim da Luz

The best of Brazil's many sacred-art museums is at Avenida Tiradentes 676. Take the metro to Tiradentes. The museum is open Tuesday to Sunday from 1 to 5 pm. After your visit you can walk two blocks down Avenida Tiradentes to the park, Jardim da Luz, and the old British-built metro station, Estação da Luz.

Museu Lasar Segall

Lasar Segall was a great Lithuanian expressionist artist who made Brazil his home and became leader of the modern movement in the country in the 1920s. In addition to displaying his work, the museum (☎ 572-8211) gets some very good exhibitions. Unfortunately, it's a long way from town, at Afonso Celso 362, Vila Mariana. Take the metro to Santa Cruz. The museum is open Tuesday to Sunday from 2.30 to 6.30 pm.

Fundação Maria Luisa e Oscar Americano

Also a long way from the centre, at Avenida Morumbi 3700 in the posh suburb of Morumbi, this modern Brazilian home in beautifully landscaped surroundings contains lots of imperial antiques, and eight oils by the Dutch artist Frans Post, which were painted in Olinda. It's open Tuesday to Sunday from 10 am to 5 pm and is a great place to come for afternoon tea. To get there, take a No 7241 'Jardim Colombo' bus from Praça Republica.

The Butantã Snake Farm & Museum

One of the most popular tourist sights in town, the Instituto Butantã is also an important research centre. It has many snakes that are milked for their poison to make serum, but unfortunately they no longer let you watch. Open Tuesday to Sunday from 9 am to 4.45 pm, the farm and museum are at Avenida Vital Brasil 1500, at the edge of the Cidade Universitária. Take the No 702-U bus marked 'Butantã-USP' from in front of the tourist booth at Praça da República.

Casa do Bandeirante

Not far from the snake farm, this typical pioneer's abode, with a sugar mill, ox cart and farm implements, is interesting if you're in the area. It's in Praça Monteiro Lobato, and is open Tuesday to Sunday between 9 am and 5 pm.

Memorial da Américo Latina

Close to Barra Funda metro station, at Rua Mario de Andrade 664, this group of buildings is another Niemeyer creation. Outside is a seven-metre cement hand. Inside are the Centre of Latin American studies, an auditorium with free concerts, and various handicraft exhibits. Portinari's painting *Tiradentes* hangs in the Salão de Atos, and huge panels by Carybé and Poty represent the people of South America.

Organised Tours

There used to be cheap, government-sponsored, multilingual bus tours on Sunday.

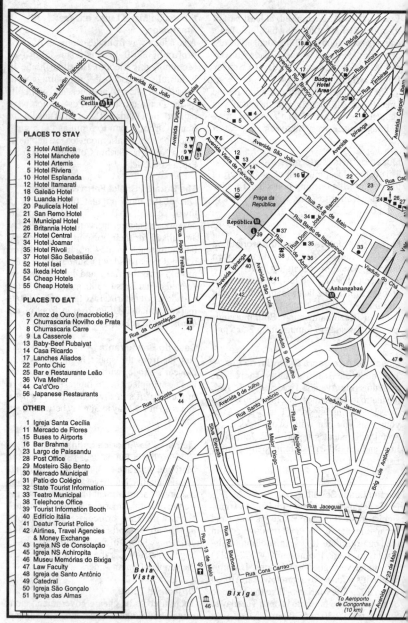

PLACES TO STAY

2 Hotel Atlântica
3 Hotel Manchete
4 Hotel Artemis
5 Hotel Riviera
10 Hotel Esplanada
12 Hotel Itamarati
18 Galeão Hotel
19 Luanda Hotel
20 Pauliceía Hotel
21 San Remo Hotel
24 Municipal Hotel
26 Britannia Hotel
27 Hotel Central
34 Hotel Joamar
35 Hotel Rivoli
37 Hotel São Sebastião
52 Hotel Isei
53 Ikeda Hotel
54 Cheap Hotels
55 Cheap Hotels

PLACES TO EAT

6 Arroz de Ouro (macrobiotic)
7 Churrascaria Novilho de Prata
8 Churrascaria Carre
9 La Casserole
13 Baby-Beef Rubaiyat
14 Casa Ricardo
17 Lanches Aliados
22 Ponto Chic
25 Bar e Restaurante Leão
36 Viva Melhor
44 Ca'd'Oro
56 Japanese Restaurants

OTHER

1 Igreja Santa Cecília
11 Mercado de Flores
15 Buses to Airports
16 Bar Brahma
23 Largo de Paissandu
28 Post Office
29 Mosteiro São Bento
30 Mercado Municipal
31 Patío do Colégio
32 State Tourist Information
33 Teatro Municipal
38 Telephone Office
39 Tourist Information Booth
40 Edifício Itália
41 Deatur Tourist Police
42 Airlines, Travel Agencies
   & Money Exchange
43 Igreja NS de Consolação
45 Igreja NS Achiropita
46 Museu Memórias do Bixiga
47 Law Faculty
48 Igreja de Santo Antônio
49 Catedral
50 Igreja São Gonçalo
51 Igreja das Almas

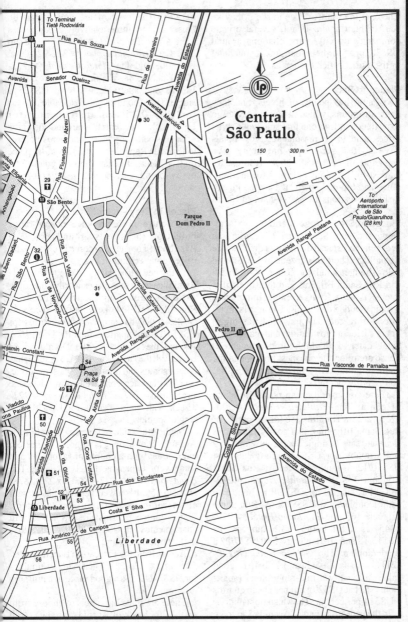

Check at the tourist office to see if they've started them again. If not, several private companies do city tours, charging around US$30 for a four-hour tour. Ask at your hotel or the tourist office for details.

Places to Stay

São Paulo has plenty of hotels, and they come in groups, which makes it easy to go to a street and find one that suits your style. Prices tend to be reasonable. Most hotels have a 10% surcharge, but many give weekend discounts of 20%. Rooms are hardest to find midweek, and for the mid-range and top-end hotels, it's a good idea to make reservations a week or so in advance.

Places to Stay – bottom end

Down and out in São Paulo is done in an area between the Estação da Luz and the Praça da República. There are dozens of budget and below-budget hotels on Rua dos Andradas and Rua Santa Efigênia and the streets that intersect them from Avenida Ipiranga to Avenida Duque de Caxias. The area is pretty safe during the day but seedy at night. There's a lot of prostitution, and many of the hotels cater to this high-turnover clientele. These are often the cheapest hotels, and the management will usually indicate that you're not welcome.

There are several cheap places on Santa Efigênia. The *Pauliceía Hotel* (☎ 220-9733), at Rua Timbiras 216 (on the corner of Rua Santa Efigênia), is a good deal, and is clean and safe. A single quarto goes for US$9 and a double for US$10. Apartments cost US$10/12 a single/double. At Rua Santa Efigênia 348, the *Luanda Hotel* (☎ 222-2441) has singles for US$5/9 without/with bath. Doubles cost US$8/12. At Rua Santa Efigênia 163, the *San Remo Hotel* (☎ 229-6845) is a bit better, with quartos for US$13/18 and apartamentos for US$17/22 a single/double. The *Galeão Hotel* (☎ 220-8211), at Rua dos Gusmões 394, is good value. It's really a mid-range hotel (apartments start at US$20), but has cheap quartos – US$14 per person. They also do laundry.

In the pedestrian part of Avenida São João,

between the post office and Largo de Paissandu, are three relatively cheap places – the *Municipal Hotel* (☎ 228-7833), at No 354, the *Britannia Hotel* (☎ 222-9244), at No 300, and the *Hotel Central* (☎ 222-3044), at No 288. The first has quartos from US$18 and apartamentos from US$23 a single. The second has single/double quartos for US$10/15 and apartamentos for US$13/18. The Central is around the same price. It's better to stay around here or closer to Praça da República than in a similar place on Rua Santa Efigênia, unless of course you enjoy being surrounded by electronics stores.

Places to Stay – middle

City Centre There are loads of mid-range hotels on the streets around Praça da República. They tend to come in clusters, by price, along certain streets.

In the pedestrian streets close to Praça da República are a few places worth a mention. A stone's throw from the tourist booth, at Rua 7 de Abril 364, the *Hotel São Sebastião* (☎ 257-4988) has single/double quartos for US$14/17 and apartamentos for US$19/22. Around the corner, at Rua Dom José de Barros 28, the *Hotel Rivoli* (☎ 231-5633) has apartamentos and quartos for the same price. A nice little place a bit further down the same street, at No 187, is *Hotel Joamar* (☎ 221-3611), with apartamentos for US$20/25 a single/double.

On the other side of Praça da República is Avenida Vieira de Carvalho, a dignified, quiet street with a couple of favourites and some very expensive hotels as well. The *Hotel Itamarati* (☎ 222-4133; fax 222-1878) is at No 150. It's a well-kept old place, with clean rooms and helpful management. Single/double quartos are US$21/29 and apartamentos are US$26/34. It's very close to the airport bus stop.

Across from the Estação da Luz, the *Hotel Florida* (☎ 220-2811) has singles/doubles for US$34/49. It's a good place in a crummy location.

There are three big hotels to choose from on the 700 block of Avenida Ipiranga, with rooms starting in the same price range: *Plaza Maraba Hotel* (☎ 220-7811), with singles/doubles for US$30/38; the *Terminus* (☎ 222-2266), with singles/doubles for US$39/45; and the *Excelsior* (☎ 222-7377), the best and most expensive of the three, with singles/doubles for US$50/59.

Liberdade An alternative to staying in a hotel in the central district is to head over to Liberdade, the Japanese, Chinese and Korean district. The metro stops very close to the hotels, and it's quieter, safer and more interesting at night. You can also pig out on cheap Japanese food. There are several less expensive hotels as you walk downhill from the metro station at Praça da Liberdade (there's an information booth here that can give directions). The *Ikeda Hotel* (☎ 278-5853), at Rua dos Estudantes 134, has singles starting at US$10 and doubles for US$18. The *Hotel Isei* (☎ 278-6646), at Rua de Glória 290, has singles/doubles for US$16/26.

More expensive places in Liberdade include the *Banri* (☎ 270-8877), at Rua Galvão Bueno 209, where singles/doubles start at US$35/45. The *Osaka Plaza* (☎ 270-1311; fax 270-1788), right across the street from the metro, has all the modern amenities, with doubles starting at US$68. Reservations are often needed about a week in advance for these two hotels.

Around Avenida Paulista Close to Avenida Paulista, there are no real bargains, but the two-star *Pamplona Palace* (☎ 285-5301), at Rua Pamplona 851, is the closest you'll get. Singles/doubles go for US$27/35. The *Hospedaria Mantovani* (☎ 889-8624), at Rua Eliseu Guilherme 269, is a large house that's been converted into a small hotel. It's very clean and well kept, with double apartamentos for US$35.

Places to Stay – top end
As in Rio, the residential hotels all offer excellent deals. The *Trianon Residence* (☎ 283-0066; fax 283-0181), near Avenida Paulista, at Alameda Casa Branca 363,

Cerqueira César, features an excellent location, close to the centre but not in it. It has comfortable doubles for US$88. The *Augusta Park Residence* (☎ 255-5722; fax 256-2381), at Rua Augusta 922, Consolação, is a bit cheaper, charging US$58/68 for singles/doubles.

In the centre there is the *Othon Palace* (☎ 239-3277), at Rua Libero Badaró 190, with singles/doubles starting at US$75/83.

Over on Avenida Casper Libero, a quiet street for the centre of town, there are some good hotels. The *Marian Palace* (☎ 228-8433) has singles/doubles starting at US$70/80. Down the block, the *Planalto* (☎ 227-7311) also offers all the amenities. It's a bargain: singles/doubles start at US$40/50. The same applies to the *Delphos* (☎ 228-6411), next door, where singles/doubles cost US$45/54. The *Best Western São Paulo Centre* (☎ 228-6033; fax 229-0959), at Largo Santa Efigênia 40, is an old, elegant beauty. Singles/doubles start at US$92/100.

Among São Paulo's luxury hotels are the *Maksoud Plaza* (☎ 253-4411; fax 253-4544), with single/double rooms for US$245/250, the *Grand Hotel Ca'd'Oro* (☎ 256-8011; fax 231-0359) and the *São Paulo Hilton* (☎ 256-0033; fax 257-3137), with singles/doubles going for US$190/220. The *Sheraton Mofarrej* (☎ 284-5544), at Alameda Santos 1437, is the most expensive place in town, charging US$310/340 for singles/doubles.

Places to Eat
The best reason to visit São Paulo is to eat. Because of the city's ethnic diversity, you can find every kind of cuisine at reasonable prices. There is also a million cheap lanchonetes, great pizzerias and churrascarias, and some of the best Italian and Japanese food that you'll find outside those countries.

Paulistanos love to go out to dinner, and they go out late. Although restaurants open earlier, most don't fill up until 9 or 10 pm on weekdays, later on weekends. Many stay open on weekends until 2 or 3 am.

The places mentioned in this section are

the more traditional ones. That they've been around for a long time is a recommendation in itself, as Paulistanos are very particular diners. The selection given is limited to areas easily reached by public transport. If you have a car or don't mind grabbing a taxi, there are hundreds of other eateries to choose from. The best place to get a listing of good restaurants is in the São Paulo lift-out section of the weekly *Veja* magazine. The bilingual *São Paulo this Month* also has a decent listing, with prices included, and mentions restaurants where English is spoken. If you're really keen, Guia Quatro Rodas publishes a small guide to the best restaurants in São Paulo and Rio. It's available from any newsstand.

City Centre If you're staying here, there are a few inexpensive places that are close by and several notches above the rest. *Ponto Chic* is a friendly, informal restaurant, but the best reason to go is the famous Brazilian sandwich, the bauru, which Ponto Chic invented many moons ago. The bauru consists of beef, tomato, pickle and a mix of melted cheeses, served on French bread. The price is US$5. Not only is it popular in urban and backland Brazil, it is also served in Paris.

Ponto Chic is only a few blocks from the Praça da República, at Largo Paissandu 27, and is open until 4 am.

Another winner is the *Lanches Aliados*, at the corner of Avenida Rio Branco and Rua Vitória. It's a cheap lunch spot with excellent food. The *Casa Ricardo* features 20 different sandwiches and is reasonably priced. Open until 7 pm, it's at Avenida Vieira de Carvalho 48.

For vegetarians, *Viva Melhor* is pretty fair. It's open Monday to Friday for lunches only, closing at 3 pm. It's at Rua 7 de Abril 264 (Centro). The *Mel*, at Rua Araújo 75, has some excellent natural and vegetarian lunches. The curried mushroom and tofu pancake is particularly tasty. The Mel is open from 11 am to 4 pm Monday to Friday.

If it's lean meat you seek, *Baby-Beef Rubaiyat* has three churrascarias: the one in the centre (☎ 222-8333) is at Avenida Vieira de Carvalho 116. Also in Avenida Vieira de Carvalho, *Carlino* (☎ 223-1603), at No 154, is a reasonably cheap Italian restaurant that's been there for over a century. Further up on Largo do Arouche are lots of restaurants, including *Arroz de Ouro* a macrobiotic lunch spot.

The *Bar e Restaurante Leão*, at Avenida São João 320, has all-you-can-eat Italian meals and a salad bar, at reasonable prices.

Ca'd'Oro (☎ 256-8011), in the hotel of the same name, Rua Augusta 129, is considered one of the best. It's very expensive; a jacket and reservations are recommended.

Bela Vista & Bixiga Loaded with Italian restaurants and bars, these districts offer some of the best places in the city at night. On Rua Avanhandava, in Bela Vista, there are two very good and very Italian restaurants. *Gigetto* and *Famiglia Mancini* have large selections of pasta and wine, stay crowded until very late with the after-theatre crowd. They are both moderately priced – US$4 buys a large plate of pasta. Gigetto is supposed to be an actors' hang-out.

In Bixiga, Rua 13 de Maio has stacks of Italian restaurants. *Cantina e Pizzeria Lazzarella* (☎ 288-1995), at Rua 13 de Maio

589, is full of Brazil kitsch. The live, if dated, music features a multilingual sing-along. It's festive, the food is good and large plates of pasta cost just US$6. *Speranza* (☎ 288-8502), at Rua 13 de Maio 1004, is one of the best pizzerias in town.

Cerqueira César There are lots of restaurants and bars in the area bounded by Avenida Paulista, Rua da Consolação, Rua Estados Unidas and Alameda Ministro Rocha Azevedo. Most are fairly expensive, but there are quite a few reasonable ones. A good sandwich place is the very traditional *Frevo*, at Rua Oscar Freire 603. If you want to be really Paulistano, order one of their beirute á modas and a chopp. Waiters calling for a chopp yell for a rabo de peixe (fish tail). *Baguette*, another sandwich and beer place, is at Rua da Consolação 2426, in front of the cinema. It's open 24 hours a day and is packed at 3 am.

Almanara (☎ 853-6916), at Rua Oscar Freire 523, is a traditional place that serves good Arab food. The churrascarias *Wessel Grill* (☎ 280-9107), at Rua Bela Cintra 1855, *Rodeio* (☎ 883-2322), at Rua Haddock Lobo 1498, and *Esplanada Grill* (☎ 881-3199), at Rua Haddock Lobo 1682, are all excellent but expensive.

An interesting place with a great view is *Jinro* (☎ 283-2543), a Korean restaurant on the 25th floor at Avenida Paulista 807. The food is good and the prices reasonable.

There are a few French restaurants in the area, but nothing cheap. If bucks aren't a worry, try *Marcel* (☎ 881-7557), at Alameda Lorena 1852. The soufflés are famous.

There are several fine and reasonably priced Italian restaurants. *L'Osteria do Piero* (☎ 853-1082), at Alameda Franca 1509, features roast kid with broccoli and agnollotti. It is closed on Monday. *Babbo Giovanni* (☎ 853-2678), at Rua Bela Cintra 2305, has good, inexpensive pizza.

For a big splurge, many think *Massimo* (☎ 248-0311), at Alameda Santos 1826, is the city's best Italian restaurant. *Z Deli*, at Alameda Santos 1518, is a Jewish deli that's a popular lunch spot with Paulistanos. Veg-

etarians won't feel left out in this area. *Associação Macrobiótica*, at Rua Bela Cintra 1235, has a healthy fixed menu, and *Sattva*, at Rua da Consolação 3140, has some imaginative vegetarian dishes.

Liberdade Liberdade has lots of inexpensive Oriental restaurants, and good food at the Sunday street fair. There are several good Japanese restaurants to choose from on Rua Tomás Gonzaga. *Gombe*, at No 22, is always full. They have great sushis and sashimis and excellent kushi-yaki. Other favourites include *Takão*, at Rua Barão de Iguapé 324, which has a delightful karaoke, and the *Diego*, at Praça Almeda Junior 25, with its strong, Okinawan dishes. The *Sushi-Yassu*, at Rua Tomás Gonzaga 110-A, is the most famous, and the most expensive – about US$10 a meal. It's closed on Monday.

Entertainment

This city swings at night. Everyone is out playing until the wee hours, and you feel it – where else can you get stuck in a traffic snarl at 3 am? São Paulo's nightlife approaches the excitement, diversity and intensity of New York's. To enjoy it, all you need is money (plenty) and transportation.

The best list of events is probably found in the weekly *Veja* magazine, which has a special São Paulo edition. It also lists restaurants, bars, museums, fairs, etc. Another good source is the *Illustrada* section of the *Folha de São Paulo*.

Rua 13 de Maio in Bixiga hums at night. There are several clubs, many restaurants and even a revival movie theatre. It attracts a young crowd, so prices are reasonable. You can go there, look around and plan out a full evening in one neighbourhood. The biggest club is the Café Piu-Piu, at No 134. It has music every night except Monday: jazz, rock, and a sequin-shirted, 20-gallon-hatted band that plays American country music. Café do Bixiga, at No 76, is a traditional bar that stays open late. Try the *pinga com mel*.

Bela Vista is another good area for nightlife. There's lots happening and it's central, though the clubs are not as close together as those in Bixiga. Spazio Pirandello, at Rua Augusta 311, is always lively – the crowd includes both gay and straight clientele. There's art on the walls and a bookshop downstairs.

The Bar Brahma is the city's oldest drinking establishment. It's at the corner of Rua São João and Avenida Ipiranga, in the heart of the central hotel district. From 7 pm to midnight, the antique surroundings host equally dated live music. The best tables are upstairs. The bar is friendly and relaxing, and is a popular after-work hang-out for many Paulistano professionals.

Another time-capsule bar is the Riviera Restaurant & Bar, at the corner of Rua Consolacão and Avenida Paulista. This bar takes you back to the seedy 1940s. It's inexpensive and unassuming – a good place to go with a friend to talk and unwind. If you want to speak some English, try Finnegan's Pub, at Alameda Itú 1541 in Cerqueira César. Paulistanos know it as a gringo bar, and it gets lively. The Paris Café is a hang-out by the university.

São Paulo has a lively gay scene. A popular club is Corintho, Alameda dos Imarés 64, with live shows starting at 11 pm Wednesday to Sunday. Homo Sapiens, at Rua Marques de Itú, and Nostro Mondo, at Rua da Consolação 2556, are a couple of others.

If you're looking for the best and money is no object, try one of the following places:

Dance Clubs
Cha Cha Cha – plays house/garage music, at Rua Tabapuã 1236, Itaim, on Saturday night
Allure – plays FM-radio hits, at Rua Frei Galvão 135, Jardins
Massivo – plays disco music, at Alameda Itu 1548, Cerqueira César, on Thursday night
Mistura Brasileira – plays samba, at Rua Alfreres de Magalhães 103, Santana, every night
Samantha Santa – plays techno music, at Frei Caneca 916, Cerquiera César

Music Venues
Bourbon Street – plays live music, at Chanés 127, Moema
Santana Samba – plays rap and other black music, at Avenida Cruzeiro do Sul 3454, Santana

Things to Buy

Shopping is almost as important to Paulistanos as eating out. Those who can afford it like to shop in one of the many large malls that dot the city. For the traveller, these malls don't hold much interest – prices tend to be higher than those in the centre of town. However, if you're a big fan of malls, you'll find a list of addresses in the *São Paulo this Month* guide.

More interesting are the many markets and fairs that take place around town, especially on weekends. One of the most popular is held in the Praça da República on Sunday from 8 am to 2 pm. It's a great place for people-watching. Items on sale include Brazilian precious stones, leather gear, woodcarvings, handmade laces and paintings. Some of the painters, especially the native artists, are excellent. My favourite is Tavares, from the interior of the state, whose themes include football games and trips to the dentist.

Liberdade, the Oriental district, has a big street fair all day on Sunday and is only five minutes from the centre by metro. The fair surrounds the metro station.

A couple of markets worth a look are the Mercado Municipal (see Walking Tour) and the CEAGESP market (on Avenida Doutor Gastão Vidigal, in the suburb of Jaguaré). The huge CEAGESP market is the centre of food distribution for the whole city, and is quite a sight. The best time to go is Tuesday to Friday from 7 am to noon, when there's a flower market as well. On other days, it just has lots and lots of produce.

Another excellent market takes place every weekend in Embu, 28 km from São Paulo. It's renowned for its rustic furniture, ceramics, paintings and leather items, and you'll find things here from all over Brazil. If you can't make it to the fair on the weekend, it's still worth coming during the week, as most of the artists have permanent shops and there are stacks of handicrafts stores. While you're in Embu, have a look at the old Jesuit church in the main square; it contains a small sacred-art museum, and the first organ made in Brazil.

Getting There & Away

Air From São Paulo, there are flights to everywhere in Brazil and to many of the world's major cities. Before buying your ticket, be sure to check which airport the flight departs from and how many stops it makes (flights to coastal cities often make several stops along the way).

The São Paulo to Rio shuttle flies every half-hour (or less) from Congonhas airport into Santos Dumont, in central Rio. The flight takes less than an hour, and you can usually go to the airport, buy a ticket (US$300) and be on a plane within the hour. Most of the major airlines have offices on Avenida São Luís, near the Praça da República (☎ 530-3922) is at Rua da Consolação 362, Transbrasil (☎ 228-2022) is at Avenida São Luís 250 and VASP (☎ 220-3622) is at Avenida São Luís 91. Aerolineas Argentinas (☎ 214-4233) is at Rua Araújo 216, on the 6th floor.

Bus The Terminal Tietê rodoviária is easy to reach – just get off at the Tietê metro station, which is adjacent to and connected with it. It's an enormous building, but easily navigated. The information desk (in the middle of the main concourse on the 1st floor) is of limited value. Only Portuguese is spoken.

Bus tickets are sold on the 1st floor, except for the Rio shuttle, which has its ticket offices on the ground floor at the rear of the building. Buses leave for destinations throughout Brazil, and there are also buses to major cities in Argentina, Paraguay, Chile and Uruguay.

All the following buses leave from the Terminal Tietê. Frequent buses traverse the 429 km of the Via Dutra highway to Rio, taking six hours. The cost is US$11 for the regular bus and US$18 for the leito. There are also buses travelling to Brasília (US$28, 14 hours), Belo Horizonte (US$15, 9½ hours), Foz do Iguaçu (US$26, 15 hours), Cuiabá (US$35, 24 hours), Campo Grande (US$21, 14 hours), Salvador (US$45, 33½ hours), Curitiba (US$10, six hours) and Florianópolis (US$20, 12 hours).

Buses to Santos, Guarujá and São Vicente

leave every five minutes from a separate bus station at the end of the southern metro line (Jabaquara station). It's a one-hour trip.

If you're staying outside the city centre, find out whether there's a local bus station nearby at which buses stop on their way out of town. For example, several south-bound buses stop at Itapemirim Turismo (☎ 212-5402), Avenida Valdemira Feirrara 130, near the Cidade Universitária, on their way to Florianópolis, Curitiba, etc. If you catch the bus here, it saves an hour's drive into the city and an hour's ride back.

Train The Estação da Luz metro station also services what's left of the long-distance train routes to Bauru (from where you can get a bus to Campo Grande – see below). Long-distance routes have been severely cut back in recent times, so it'll pay to check the following information. The information booth (☎ 227-3299, 991-3062) at Luz station has all the details.

You can't get a direct train to Campo Grande or Corumbá from São Paulo – you have to take the train or bus from São Paulo to Bauru, catch a bus to Campo Grande and then get another train to Corumbá. Trains go to Bauru every day at 8 am, noon, and 4 and 11 pm. Buses from Bauru to Campo Grande leave at 4.30 pm. For connections from Campo Grande to Corumbá and Bolivia, see the Campo Grande Getting There & Away section in the Mato Grosso chapter.

Getting Around

To/From the Airport São Paulo has three airports. Congonhas serves Rio and other local destinations. It is the closest airport – 14 km south of the city centre. Avoid the radio-taxis at the front of the terminal and ask for the comums (regular taxis); there's a small sign marking the place. The ride into town costs about US$10.

To catch a bus into the city, walk out of the terminal and then to your right, where you'll see a busy street with a pedestrian overpass. Head to the overpass but don't cross: you should see a crowd of people waiting for the buses along the street, or ask for the bus marked 'Banderas'. The trip takes about an hour, and the last bus leaves at around 1 am.

The Aeroporto Viracopos is 97 km from the city, near Campinas. Avoid this airport if possible. A taxi from here into town will cost about US$60.

Aeroporto de Cumbica, São Paulo's international airport, is at Guarulhos, 30 km east of the city. There's a bus that goes to Praça da República, Terminal Tietê rodoviária and Congonhas airport. It costs US$6. Another bus (also US$6) does a circuit of 11 four and five-star hotels in the Jardims area and the centre. From the airport to the centre, a comum taxi will cost US$20 and a radio-taxi US$30.

Metro If you're on a limited budget, a combination of metro and walking is the best way to see the city. The metro is new, cheap, safe and fast. It's open from 5 am to midnight. You can buy all sorts of tickets, but if you're going to be around for a few days, the most useful is the *multiplo 10*, which gives you 10 rides for US$3.50. A single ride costs US$0.60.

There are currently three metro lines, two of which intersect at Praça da Sé. The third, newer line gives access to Avenida Paulista and begins at Paraiso station. Liberdade is one stop away from Praça da Sé, the budget hotel area is served by the Luz and República stations, while the rodoviária, Terminal Tietê, is four stops north of Luz – get off at Tietê station.

Bus Buses are slow, crowded during rush hours and not too safe. Unlike Rio, you can wait quite a while for the bus you want, and trying to figure out which one that is can be difficult. The tourist information booths are excellent sources of information about buses.

Taxi Both the comum and radio-taxi services are metered. Radio-taxis (☎ 251-1733) cost 50% more than the comum and will pick you up anywhere in the city.

The Paulista Coast

UBATUBA

The Ubatuba litoral is a stunning stretch of beach along the northern São Paulo coast. The pre-eminent beach resort for the well-to-do of São Paulo, it has many elegant beach homes and hotels, especially south of the town of Ubatuba. To the north of town, all the way to Parati, the beaches are wilder, cleaner and often deserted. There are few hotels, but plenty of campsites.

Most travellers don't go to Ubatuba, unless they are spending some time in São Paulo and want to escape for the weekend, or are driving along the Rio-Santos coastal road. Although the beaches are top-notch, they're rather expensive, get crowded in summer and retain little of the old fishing culture that animates so many Brazilian coastal towns.

Information

You'll find a tourist office shack in Ubatuba, where Rua Professor Thomaz Galhardo hits the bay. It's open from 8 am to 6 pm, with helpful staff and a useful map.

There's a Banco do Brasil branch on the corner of Rua Dona Maria Alves and Rua Carvalho. The post office is on Rua Dona Maria Alves, while the posto telefônico is at Rua Professor Thomaz Galhardo 81.

Beaches

Within the district of Ubatuba, there are some 74 beaches and 15 islands. If you're staying in the city and don't have wheels, there's a fine beach a couple of km south of town, with barracas and some surfing. Other recommended beaches south of Ubatuba include **Toninhas** and **Enseada** (eight km away), **Flamengo** (12 km), **Lazaro** and **Domingas Dias** (14 km).

North of town, the beaches are hidden away down the steep hillside. They are harder to find, but well worth the effort. The best beaches are **Vermelha** (nine km away),

Itamambuca (11 km), **Promirim** (22 km) and **Ubatumirim** (32 km).

Port

The port is at Praia de Saco de Rebeiro, 12 km south of Ubatuba. Mykonos Turismo (☎ 41-1388), with offices at the port, offers daily cruises into the Baía da Enseada and out to the Ilha Anchieta. The four-hour cruise costs US$20.

Festival

On 29 June, Ubatuba celebrates the Festa de São Pedro Pescador with a big maritime procession.

Places to Stay

If you don't have a car, Ubatuba is the most convenient place to stay, because you can catch local buses to some of the beaches. Hotels within a couple of blocks of the bus station include the *Hotel Xareu* (☎ 32-1525), at Rua Jordão Homem da Costa 413, the *Hotel São Nicolau* (☎ & fax 32-3310), at Rua Conceição 213, and the *Parque Atlântico* (☎ 32-1336), next door, at Rua Conceição 185. None of these hotels are cheap – all charge around US$30/40 a single/double.

If you're on a budget, your best bet is to go over to Praia do Perequê, a 10-minute walk away, and check in at the *Jangadeiro Hotel* (☎ 32-1365), at Avenida Abreu Sodré 111. Singles/doubles cost US$10/15. There's also a campground nearby, at Avenida Leovegildo dias Viera 1854, Itaguá.

At the *Ubatuba Palace* (☎ 32-1500), the city's finest hotel, singles/doubles cost US$60/70.

Places to Eat

A good fish restaurant is *Ladis*, on the waterfront, at Avenida Leovegildo dias Viera 196. Also on the waterfront, but a bit closer to the centre, *Cantina Perequim* is an Italian restaurant that's popular with locals. It's at Rua Guarani 385. *Gauchão* is the best churrascaria in town, at Rua Guarani 378. *Kilo & Cia* is in the centro, at Rua Dona Maria Alves 393; it has a good self-serve, por-kilo lunch.

Gaivota, at Avenida Leovegildo dias Viera 240, offers a varied menu and is popular with locals.

Getting There & Away

Bus There are two bus stations in Ubatuba, less than two blocks apart. The main rodoviária is on Rua Professor Thomaz Galhardo, between Rua Hans Staden and Rua Cunhambebe. The Reunidas bus company, which also runs buses to Rio and São Paulo, has a ticket office in a lanchonete on the corner of Rua Professor Thomaz Galhardo and Rua Coronel Domiciano.

To São Paulo (US$7, four hours), there are eight daily buses, the first leaving at 12.30 pm and the last at 6.30 pm. Buses to Parati leave at 9.40 am, and 5 and 9.40 pm. For Rio (US$9, five hours), buses leave at 12.45 pm and 9.45 am.

Car Ubatuba is 72 km south-west of Parati on the paved coastal road – a 1½-hour drive at a reasonable speed. Rio is 310 km (five hours) away. Heading south along the coast from Ubatuba, you reach Caraguatatuba (54 km away), São Sebastião and Ilhabela (75 km), and Santos (205 km). After Caraguatatuba, the road begins to deteriorate and an unending procession of speed bumps rear their ugly heads.

São Paulo is 240 km from Ubatuba. By far the fastest route is to turn off the coastal road onto SP-099 at Caraguatatuba, then climb the escarpment until you meet the Rio-São Paulo highway, BR-116, at São José dos Campos. This is a beautiful, rapid ascent, and the road is in good condition.

CARAGUATATUBA

The coastal town of Caraguatatuba, 55 km from Ubatuba and 25 km from São Sebastião, is not very attractive, and the beaches around the city are below the regional standard.

Places to Stay & Eat

If you do get stuck here, there are a few cheap hotels – ask around for the *Hotel Central*, *Hotel Atlântico* or *Hotel Binoca* – and plenty of restaurants. There are also several hotels at Praia Massaguaçu, 10 km north of town.

Getting There & Away
From the rodoviária, at Avenida Brasília 50, buses leave for points north and south along the coast, and for São Paulo and Rio.

SÃO SEBASTIÃO
The coastal town of São Sebastião faces the Ilha de São Sebastião (popularly known as Ilhabela), which is a 15-minute ferry trip across the channel. Huge oil tankers anchor in the calm canal between the island and mainland, waiting to unload at São Sebastião. The town itself is unassuming. There's not much here, but at least São Sebastião has avoided the tourist-industry blight, thanks to its poor beaches. Most visitors stay here either because they can't find lodging at Ilhabela or to enjoy the canal's excellent windsurfing conditions.

Information
English is spoken at the very helpful tourist office on the waterfront, at Avenida Dr Altino Arantes 174. It doesn't have information on Ilhabela, just on the coastal towns towards Guarujá. The office is open from 8 am to 6 pm Monday to Friday and from 8 am to 10 pm on weekends.

Places to Stay
The *Porto Grande* (☎ 52-1101), on the coast road just north of town, right on the beach, is the best hotel around, and the owner changes dollars at close to the parallel rate. Basic singles/doubles are US$56/70, while more luxurious singles/doubles cost US$80/95. The hotel serves a good dinner, and has a maritime museum.

For something cheaper right in the centre of town, try the *Hotel Roma* (☎ 52-1016), at Praça Major João Fernandes 174. Doubles start at US$15. Also good value is the *Pousada da Sesmaria* (☎ 52-2437), at Rua São Gonçalo 190, close to the centre. Singles/doubles start at US$12/20.

Places to Eat
Along the waterfront, you'll find several good fish restaurants, including *Super Flipper*. Eat the fish, not the shrimp.

Getting There & Away
The rodoviária, at Praça da Amizade 10, has a regular service to São Paulo, Rio, Santos and Caraguatatuba.

The Rio-Santos highway is slow going between São Sebastião and Santos. A much quicker route to São Paulo (200 km) is through Caraguatatuba, despite a zillion speed bumps along the coastal road.

ILHABELA
With an area of 340 sq km, Ilhabela is the biggest island along the Brazilian coast. The island's volcanic origin is evident in its steeply rising peaks, which are covered by dense, tropical jungle. There are 360 waterfalls, and the flatlands are filled with sugar-cane plantations. The island is known for its excellent jungle hiking and its fine cachaça.

Although Ilhabela is a beautiful place, visiting it can be a bit of a drag. During summer, the island is besieged by Paulistas, and the normal population of 13,000 swells to over 100,000. Besides the threat this poses to the environment, the crowds create all sorts of logistical difficulties: many hotels fill up, waits of two to three hours for the car ferry are common, and prices soar. To add to all that, the bugs are murder, especially the little bloodsuckers known as *borrachudos*. Use plenty of insect repellent at all times.

The time to go to Ilhabela is on weekdays in the low season. Once you arrive, the name of the game is to get away from the west coast, which faces the mainland and where almost all human activity is concentrated. To get to the other side of the island requires either a car, a boat trip or a strong pair of hiking legs.

Information
The Secretária de Turismo de Ilhabela is at the old airstrip, Campo de Aviação. They have a complete list of hotels, pousadas,

chalets and campgrounds. The post office and the ticket office for buses to São Paulo are in the same street.

There's a tourist information post at the roundabout 200 metres from the ferry dock, in the suburb of Barra Velha. It's open every day from 9 am to noon and 2 to 6 pm. Staff have information about hotels (including prices) and sightseeing trips, and a serviceable map of the island.

Colonial Buildings
Vila Ilhabela has quite a few well-preserved colonial buildings, including the slave-built Igreja NS da Ajuda (dating from 1532), the Fazenda Engenho d'Agua in Itaquanduba (constructed in 1582) and the Fazenda Santa Carmen (at Feiticeira beach).

Beaches
There are more than 50 beaches on the island, but most of them are hard to reach and are accessible only by boat or on foot.

Of the sheltered beaches on the island's north side, **Praia Pedra do Sino** and **Praia Jabaquara** are recommended. On the east side, where the surf is stronger, try **Praia dos Castelhanos** (good camping and surf), **Praia do Gato** and **Praia da Figueira**.

Waterfalls
Two km inland from Perequê beach, **Cachoeira das Tocas** is made up of various small waterfalls with accompanying deep pools and water slides. It costs US$1 to get in, which includes all the insect repellent you need. It's a great place to go if you're sick of the beach. **Cachoeira de Água Branca**, in the middle of the jungle, is another waterfall to check out. Access is from Veloso beach.

Pico São Sebastião
If you're feeling energetic, the 1379-metre peak of São Sebastião, in the suburb of Barra Velha, provides a great view.

Activities
Paulistas on holiday like their toys; as a consequence, you can rent almost anything here: powerboats, yachts, kayaks, jet-skis, windsurfers, motorbikes, dune buggies, bicycles, tennis courts, diving gear and helicopters are just some of the alternatives.

Places to Stay
There's a lack of cheap lodging on Ilhabela, which is why many people choose to stay in São Sebastião, where the hotels are cheaper.

Near the beach, the *Pousada dos Hibiscos* (☎ 72-1375), at Avenida Pedro Paula de Morais 714, has doubles for US$60. It's 800 metres from town. Also close to town is the *Costa Azul* (☎ 72-1365), at Rua Francisco Gomes da Silva Prado 71. Its prices are similar to those at the Hibiscos.

If you plan on staying for a few days, self-contained chalets are a reasonably priced option. *Chalé Praia Grande* (☎ 72-1017), in the southern part of the island, is the cheapest, at US$12 per day. There are lots of campgrounds near Barra Velha, where the ferry stops, and just a bit further south, at Praia do Curral.

There is certainly no lack of top-end hotels on the island. The five-star *Itapemar* (☎ 72-1329) is close to town, in Saco da Capela, and costs US$105 a double. Other top-end recommendations include the *Porto Pousada Saco da Capela* (☎ 72-2255) and the *Ilhabela Turismo Ltda* (☎ 72-1083), both in Saco da Capela, and the *Petit Village* (☎ 72-1393), on Rua Morro da Cruz in Itaguassú. Reservations are a good idea, especially on weekends.

Places to Eat
New restaurants open all the time on Ilhabela. In Vila Ilhabela itself, there are a few good, cheap lanchonetes: two in the pedestrian mall and a couple on Rua da Padroeira. *Cheiro Verde*, at Rua da Padroeira 109, has a good prato feito for US$3, while *Convés*, at No 139, has tasty sandwiches. Right on the pier, at *Pier Pizza*, you can have a tasty chopp and watch the fisherfolk pull in a few swordfish.

A bit further from Vila is *Deck*, at Avenida Almirante Tamandaré 805, a popular seafood restaurant. *Recanto da Samba*, on the waterfront, is a great place to have a beer and stare at the mainland.

Getting There & Away

The ferry between São Sebastião and Ilhabela runs frequently from 5.30 am to midnight (often till much later in summer). Cars cost US$4, pedestrians travel free. The trip takes 15 minutes.

BOIÇUCANGA

A popular weekend spot for Paulistas, Boiçucanga is well serviced by simple hotels and decent restaurants. While the beach here is not as good as those at nearby Maresias and Camburi, there are some good walks into the Mata Atlântica (Atlantic rainforest).

Information

A good source of information here is José Mauro B Pinto y Silva, who runs a tourist information service/câmbio/video-rental place called Amart (☎ 65-1276), at Avenida Walkir Vergani 319. An experienced budget traveller who speaks good English, José is a friendly guy who can help you out with just about anything, including cheap places to stay. He's a good person to see about treks into the forest.

Beaches

There are some great beaches along this stretch of coastline, and if you have a car, you'll be able to explore them easily. If you're relying on buses it's a bit harder, but still possible.

Both **Maresias** and **Camburi** are good surf beaches. **Barra do Sahy** is a beach with calmer water, and some nearby offshore islands which you can visit. Kayaks can be rented on the beach for US$5 an hour.

Places to Stay & Eat

There are campgrounds at all the beaches, and they are a good, cheap option. Maresias' youth hostel (☎ 65-1561) is one km from the beach, at Rua da Sudelpa 111. They rent bicycles for US$2 a day, and a kombi for short sightseeing trips.

Cheaper hotels in Boiçucanga include the

Dani (☎ 65-1299), at Avenida Walkir Vergani 455, with singles/doubles for US$15/20, and *Pousada Boiçucanga*, at No 522, with rooms for US$15. The *Big Pão* padaria (bakery), on the corner nearby, has good snacks and *Le Moussier*, at Rua Luziana 226, has an excellent chicken pie, as well as coffee and cakes. In the evenings, the *Bali Bar* gets lively, especially on weekends.

At Camburi, just off the main road, an enjoyable top-end place to stay is the *Pousada das Praias*, on the old SP-55 road (Antiga SP-55), at No 22. During the week, doubles go for US$40, but on weekends the price goes up to US$60.

Getting There & Away

Regular buses run along the coast – José has a timetable posted in his shop window.

GUARUJÁ

The closest beach to the city of São Paulo, 87 km away, Guarujá is the biggest and most important beach resort in the state. If you enjoy beach cities, it has plenty of hotels, restaurants, boutiques, etc.

Places to Stay & Eat

If you do end up here, your best budget bet is the *Hotel Rio* (☎ 86-6081), a block from Praia das Pitangueiras at Rua Rio de Janeiro 131. It's a small place and quite popular, with singles/doubles for US$15/25. Further along the same street, at No 193, the *Pensão Europa* (☎ 86-6879) has simple rooms (without breakfast) from US$20 per person. There are many other, more expensive places.

You'll find stacks of restaurants and bars along the waterfront.

Getting There & Away

The rodoviária is just outside town, at Avenida Santos Dumont 840. From there, catch a local bus into the city. Buses to São Paulo leave every half-hour, the US$3 trip taking just over an hour. On the way, you'll pass through Cubatão, once one of the most polluted places in the world. It still looks bad, but it used to look a lot worse.

SANTOS

The largest and busiest port in Latin America, Santos was founded in 1535 by Brás Cubas. The city has seen better days, and as a destination for travellers, it holds little interest. Only the facades remain of many of the grand 19th-century houses built by wealthy coffee merchants, and the water at local beaches is definitely suspect.

Information

There are tourist information booths at Praça das Bandeiras, Praia do Gonzaga and the rodoviária. If you need to change money, try Casa Branco, in the centre, at Praça da República 29.

Places to Stay & Eat

On the waterfront, at Avenida Presidente Wilson 36, the *Hotel Gonzaga* (☎ 4-1411) is quite a decent cheapie, with single/double quartos for US$18/28. There are lots of other seafront hotels. The *Praia Paulista* (☎ 34-4700), at No 134, has reasonable double apartamentos from US$22, and the *Maracanã Santos* (☎ 37-4030), at No 172, is good value at US$26 a double. This area is also where most of the restaurants are located.

Getting There & Away

The bus station is right in the centre, at Praça dos Andradas 45. Frequent buses go to São Paulo, 72 km away.

IGUAPE

Iguape was founded in 1538, making it one of the oldest towns in Brazil.

Information

Tourist information is available from the pre-ifeitura, Rua 15 de Novembro 272. It's open on weekdays from 8 to 11 am and 1 to 5 pm.

Things to See

The attractions of the town are the **Museu de Arte Sacra** (in the limestone Igreja do Rosário) and the **Mirante do Morro do Espia** (a lookout with a good view of the port and surrounding area). The most popular beaches in the area are Varela, Prelado, Rio Verde, Una and Juréia. Five minutes by ferry from Iguape is **Ilha Comprida**, with a 74-km stretch of beach.

Places to Stay

In the centre of town, the *Solar Colonial* (☎ 41-1591) has good doubles for US$18. *De Martis* (☎ 41-1325), at Rua Major Rebello 258, is a bit cheaper, with singles/doubles for US$6/10. On Ilha Comprida, the *Alpha* (☎ 42-1270), at Rua São Lourenço 14, and *Vila das Palmeiras* (☎ 42-1349), at Rua Júlio de Almeida, cost US$15 a double. At Juréia beach, the *De Ville* (☎ 42-1238) charges US$15 a double.

Eating in Iguape means seafood, seafood and more seafood. Try *Gaivota* and *Arrastão*, both on the seafront at Ilha Comprida.

Getting There & Away

Four buses a day, the first at 6 am and the last at 8 pm, make the trip from Iguape to São Paulo. To get to Cananéia, take a bus to Pariquero and switch from there. An alternative is to hitch along the beach on Ilha Comprida.

CANANÉIA

Founded in 1531, Cananéia is considered the oldest city in Brazil, and was the first port of call of Martim Afonso de Sousa's fleet of Portuguese settlers.

Beaches

The town doesn't have its own beach, but **Ilha Comprida** is only 10 minutes away by boat. To the south are the popular beaches of **Prainha** and **Ipanema** (with its waterfall) and, a two-hour boat ride away, **Ilha do Cardoso**, an ecological reserve with some nice, deserted places.

Other Attractions

In Cananéia itself, there's not a lot to do, and the colonial buildings are in poor shape. There's a marine museum at Rua Professor Besnard 133, if you're hard up, or you could walk up Morro de São João for a good view of the surrounding islands.

Places to Stay
The *Recanto do Sol* (☎ 51-1162), on Rua Pedro Lobo, has reasonable singles/doubles for US$16/20. A cheaper alternative is the *Beira-Mar* (☎ 51-1115), at Avenida Beira-Mar 219. The *Hotel Coqueiro* (☎ 51-1255), on Avenida Independência, has doubles for US$30, and a swimming pool.

Places to Eat
Cananéia is renowned for its oysters. The town also has a couple of excellent Japanese restaurants; on Rua 33, the *Naguissa*, at No 25, is open for lunch and dinner from Tuesday to Sunday. The *Bom Abrigo*, on Avenida Luís Wilson Barbosa, is open for dinner only (closed on Tuesday).

Getting There & Away
A direct bus leaves Cananéia for São Paulo at 4.30 pm.

CAMPOS DO JORDÃO
Three hours by bus from São Paulo, Campos do Jordão, in the Serra da Mantiqueira, is a popular weekend mountain getaway for Paulistas, who like to feel cold and eat *pinhão* (large pine nuts). At an altitude of 1700 metres, Campos is a good place from which to check out some of the last remaining virgin *araucária* (Parana pine) forests, and to hike to the top of some high peaks, with their spectacular views of the Paraíba valley and of the coastal mountain range, the Serra do Mar. The railway line which connects Campos with Santo Antônio do Pinhal is the highest in Brazil.

Orientation
Campos is made up of three main suburbs: Abernéssia (the oldest), Jaguaribe (where the rodoviária is located) and Capivari (the tourist centre, with a large concentration of restaurants, chocolate shops and three-star hotels). Capivari is the best base for visitors. The three suburbs are connected by a tram line.

Information
Tourist Office If you're driving, there's a tourist information office at the gateway to the valley, just before Abernéssia. There's another office in Capivari, close to the tram stop in the old train station. Normally, the offices are open from 8 to 11.30 am and 1.30 to 6 pm on weekdays, but during the July peak period, they open from 8 am to 6 pm every day. Staff speak no English, but are reasonably helpful, offering hand-outs with average maps and a complete list of hotels.

Money There's a Banco do Brasil in Abernéssia, but you should be able to change cash dollars at some of the boutiques in Capivari.

Post & Telephone Telesp has a posto telefônico in Abernéssia, in front of the tram stop. The post office is also in Abernéssia, on Avenida Dr Januário Miraglia.

Things to See & Do
The state park, better known as **Horto Florestal**, is 14 km from Capivari. It contains the largest araucária reserve in the state, and there are some fine walks. Staff at the reception desk (near the trout farm) hand out maps.

The **Gruta dos Crioulos** (Creoles' Cave) was used as a hiding place by slaves escaping from the surrounding fazendas. The cave is seven km from Jaguaribé on the road to Pedra do Baú, which is a huge, rectangular granite block, 1950 metres high. To get to the top of the block, you have to walk two km and climb 600 steps carved into the rock. It's 25 km from Campos.

Another spot that deserves a visit is the **Pico do Itapeva**, 15 km away. From an altitude of 2030 metres, it's possible to see almost all of the Paraíba valley, with its industrial cities and the Rio Paraíba.

Close to Capivari is a chairlift to the top of the 1800-metre-high **Morro do Elefante**, which has a good view of the town. The **Palácio Boa Vista**, 3.5 km from Abernéssia, is the state governor's summer residence, and contains many antiques. It's open on

Wednesday, and on weekends and holidays from 10 am to noon and 2 to 5 pm.

The train ride from Campos to Santo Antônio do Pinhal is a three-hour round trip, including the 40 minutes spent in Santo Antônio. The train makes the 19-km journey from Campos at 9.40 am on weekdays, and at 9.40 and 10.20 am and 1.25 pm on weekends and holidays. For the best views, sit on the right-hand side when leaving Campos.

Places to Stay

There's a *youth hostel* (☎ 35-3077) a few km out of town, at Recanto Feliz. To get there, take the 'Recanto Feliz' local bus to its final destination. The hostel itself is OK, but the surroundings are crummy. They accept non-members only if accompanied by members.

July is peak tourist period in Campos, and hotel prices double or even triple then. The *Pousada Emilio Ribas* (☎ 63-2711), close to the tourist office, on Avenida Emilio Ribas, is worth a try. Their rates – US$12 a head, without breakfast – are as low as any in the centre.

Close to the centre, the *Hotel Saint Moritz* (☎ 63-1450), at Rua Marcondes Machado 119, costs US$20 a head, including breakfast. The *Nevada Hotel* (☎ 63-1422) includes all meals in its price of US$60 a double. The oldest and most stylish place to stay is the *Toriba* (☎ 62-1566), on Avenida Ernesto Diedericksen, four km from Abernéssia. Its single/double rooms go for US$100/150.

Places to Eat

There are lots of restaurants in Capivari. *Esquina do Pastel*, at Avenida Macedo Soares 203, has excellent pasteis. *Baden-Baden*, at Rua Djalma Forjaz 93, serves German food. The *Matterhorn*, in the mock-Tudor Boulevard Geneve, is a fashionable delicatessen. Don't forget to eat the tasty pine nuts – try some fried in butter or mixed with rice.

Getting There & Away

Bus From São Paulo to Campos, there are seven daily buses, the first at 6 am and the last at 6.15 pm. In the other direction, from Campos to São Paulo, there are also seven buses a day, from 6 am to 6.20 pm. The trip costs US$7.

Train For details of the train ride to Santo Antônio do Pinhal, see the Things to See & Do section.

Getting Around

The tram that connects the suburbs of Campos is itself a tourist attraction. It runs every half-hour between 6.30 am and 8 pm, and gets very crowded.

Local buses run out to the state park. Take the 'Horto Florestal' to its final stop.

Bicycles, including mountain bikes, can be rented in Capivari from Verde Vital, in Cadij shopping centre, if you feel like a bit of a pedal. If you want to horse around, rent one near the chairlift, or 10 km out on the road to the park, where the trails are better.

The South

ANDREW DRAFFEN

The South

The Southern region, known in Brazil as Região Sul, includes the states of Paraná, Santa Catarina and Rio Grande do Sul. It covers almost 7% of the country's land area and contains 23 million inhabitants – just over 15% of Brazil's population. Most of these people are descendants of the German, Italian, Swiss and Eastern European immigrants who settled the region in the latter half of the 19th century. They have kept alive their customs, language and architecture, so you'll see painted wooden houses with steep roofs and onion-spire churches, and find small towns where Portuguese is still the second language.

Geographically, Paraná, Santa Catarina and the northern part of Rio Grande do Sul are dominated by planaltos (tablelands): near the coast is the Planalto Atlântico, formed of granite, and in the interior is the Planalto Meridional, formed of volcanic basalt, with rich, red soil known as *terra roxa*. In the southern interior of Rio Grande do Sul are the *pampas* – the grassy plains while on the coast there are three large salt-water lagoons: Patos, Mirim and Mangueira.

With the exception of the north of Paraná, the climate is subtropical, and the vegetation varies from Mata Atlântica remnants on the Paraná and Santa Catarina coast to the almost-extinct Mata Araucária and pine forests of the Planalto Meridional. Snow is not uncommon on the Planalto Meridional during winter.

The economy of the region has changed dramatically in the last 30 years. The pampas, where once roamed huge herds of cattle driven by gaúcho cowboys, is now dominated by endless fields of soya beans – much of which goes to feed European cattle. Heavy industry, encouraged by cheap electricity from the Itaipu Dam, has transformed the South into Brazil's second-most developed region.

Highlights

* Iguaçu Falls – one of the natural wonders of the world (Paraná)
* Spectacular train ride from Curitiba to Paranaguá, through mountains covered in Atlantic rainforest (Paraná)
* Riding tyre tubes down the Rio Nhundiaquara near Morretes (Paraná)
* Saturday night forro on Ilha do Mel (Paraná)
* The beaches and surf of Ilha da Santa Catarina (Santa Catarina)
* The colourful, meat-loving gaúchos of Rio Grande do Sul
* The sound and light show at the ruins of the São Miguel mission (Rio Grande do Sul)
* Itaimbézinho Canyon at the Parque Nacional de Aparados da Serra (Rio Grande do Sul)
* The region's primeval araucária tree

Proud of their differences from other Brazilians, Sulistas (Southerners) – especially the gaúchos from Rio Grande do Sul – are growing increasingly dissatisfied with the central government in Brasília. Talk of separatism is rife, and a recent poll in the three southern states showed that 40% of respondents favoured independence.

Paraná

CURITIBA

Curitiba, the capital of Paraná, is one of Brazil's urban success stories. As in many of Brazil's cities, thousands began to flood into Curitiba in the 1940s. With only 140,000 residents in 1940, the city has grown tenfold, to more than 1½ million people today. Yet, with the assistance of a vibrant local and state economy, Curitiba has managed to modernise in a sane manner – historic buildings have been preserved, a handful of streets have been closed to cars and there are many parks, gardens and wide boulevards.

Surprisingly, a progressive mayor instituted several incentives, including lower bus prices, to get people out of their cars – and the strategy worked. Traffic congestion was reduced, and today it's easy to get around in Curitiba. Drivers go slowly and stop at red lights, few horns honk, pedestrians cross streets without blood-type identification bracelets, and although I haven't researched it, I bet Curitiba's divorce, heart attack, murder and dog-abandonment rates are all down.

The local Curitibanos are mostly descended from Italian, German and Polish immigrants. There is a large university population, which gives the city a young feel, and a good music scene as well.

At 900 metres above sea level, Curitiba is atop the great escarpment along the route from Rio Grande do Sul to São Paulo. Due to this location, it flourished briefly as a pit stop for gaúchos and their cattle until a better road was built on an alternative route.

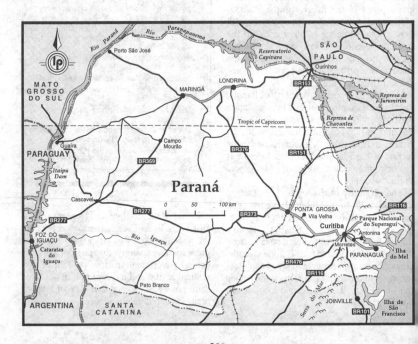

Curitiba quickly went back to sleep. It wasn't until the tremendous growth of the coffee plantations in northern Paraná, at the beginning of the 20th century, that the modern city of Curitiba began to take shape.

Like the gaúchos of old, most visitors are just passing through Curitiba. The highway from São Paulo (400 km away) to Florianópolis (300 km) and Porto Alegre (710 km) intersects Curitiba, and it's the turn-off for the train ride to Paranaguá and the bus to the Iguaçu Falls.

There's not much in Curitiba for the out-of-towner, but it's still possible to pass a pleasant day in a park, museum or older neighbourhood waiting for your bus or train to leave. This is an easy city to walk around, and if you have errands to do or clothes to buy, Curitiba is a good place for it.

Information

Tourist Office The Departmento de Turismo (☎ 223-3535; fax 252-3266), on the 5th floor at Rua Ébano Pereira 187, has a useful map, and some brochures about the city's attractions. English and French are spoken.

Money Many travel agencies double as câmbios. ABC is at Rua Buenos Aires 178, Brementur is at Rua Candido Lopes 352, Diplomatur is at Rua Presidente Faria 143, and Jade and Esatur are on Rua 15 de Novembro, at No 477 and No 384 respectively.

Post & Telephone There are good post offices at Rua 15 de Novembro 700 and Rua Marechal Deodoro 298. Telepar, the phone company, is at Rua Visconde de Nácar 1415.

Foreign Consulates The following South American countries have consulates in Curitiba:

Bolivia
    Rua Bruno Filgueira 1662 (☎ 232-5698)
Chile
    Rua Marechal Deodoro 235, 1st floor
    (☎ 222-4484)

Paraguay
    Rua Voluntários da Pátria 400, 5th floor
    (☎ 222-9226)
Peru
    Rua Alameda Doutor Murici 926, 2nd floor
    (☎ 233-4711)
Uruguay
    Rua Saldanha Marinho 961 (☎ 232-0436)

Many other countries also have consulates in Curitiba. They include:

Austria
    Avenida Marechal Floriano Peixoto 228, 17th
    floor (☎ 224-6795)
France
    Avenida Paraná 968 (☎ 253-4208)
Germany
    Avenida João Gualberto 1237 (☎ 252-4244)
Italy
    Rua Marechal Deodoro 630, 21st floor
    (☎ 222-6066)
Japan
    Rua Marechal Deodoro 630, 18th floor
    (☎ 224-3861)
Switzerland
    Rua Marechal Floriano Peixoto 228, 11th floor
    (☎ 223-7553)
UK
    Rua Presidente Faria 51 (☎ 322-1202)

Bookshops English books are available at Livraria-Curitiba, Rua Voluntários da Pátria 205 (Praça Santos Andrade), Rua Marechal Deodoro 275 and Rua 15 de Novembro; and at the Livraria Ghignone, at Rua 15 de Novembro 409.

Passeio Público
Take a stroll in the Passeio Público, where Curitibanos have relaxed since 1886. Because it's right in the centre of town, on Avenida Presidente Carlos Cavalcanti, the park is always busy. There's a lake and a small zoo. The park closes on Monday.

Rua 15 de Novembro
Known by locals as Rua das Flores since 1720, when it was already the main commercial boulevard, it's good for walking, shopping and people-watching. It was the first pedestrian mall in Brazil, created in 1972.

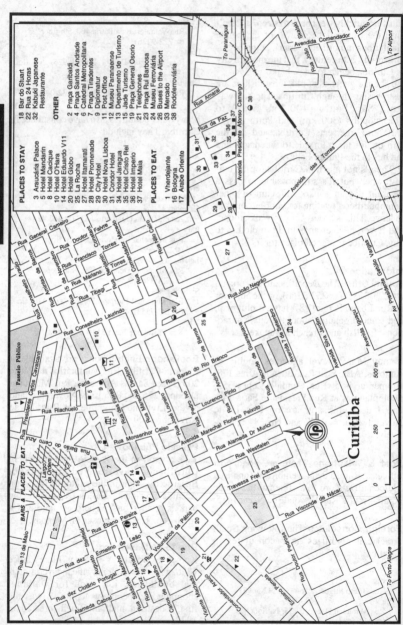

PLACES TO STAY

3 Araucária Palace
5 Hotel Mandarin
8 Hotel Cacique
10 Hotel O'Hara
14 Hotel Eduardo V11
20 Hotel Globo
25 La Rocha
27 Hotel Itamarati
28 Hotel Promenade
29 City Hotel
30 Hotel Nova Lisboa
31 Condor Hotel
34 Hotel Jaragua
35 Hotel Cristo Rei
36 Hotel Imperio
37 Hotel Maia

PLACES TO EAT

1 Vherdejante
16 Bologna
17 Arabe Oriente

18 Bar do Stuart
22 Rua 24 Horas
32 Kabuki Japanese
     Restaurante

OTHER

2 Praça Garibaldi
4 Praça Santos Andrade
6 Catedral Metropolitana
7 Praça Tiradentes
9 Diplomatur
11 Post Office
12 Museu Paranaense
13 Departmento de Turismo
15 Jade Turismo
19 Praça General Osorio
21 Telephones
23 Praça Rui Barbosa
24 Museu Ferroviária
26 Buses to the Airport
33 Mercado
38 Rodoferroviária

Curitiba

Setor Histórico

Over by Praça Tiradentes and the Catedral Metropolitana, take the pedestrian tunnel and you'll be in the cobblestoned historic quarter, the Largo da Ordem. They've done a very good job of restoring some of the city's historic edifices, and there are several restaurants, bars and art galleries. It's also a good place for a drink and some music at night.

Santa Felicidade

The old Italian quarter, about eight km from the centre, is widely touted for its bars and restaurants, many of which are monuments of kitsch. There's really not much to see here, and there are good Italian restaurants in the centre of town. If you really want to come here, catch a 'Santa Felicidade' bus from Travessa Nestor de Castro, just behind the cathedral. It's a 20-minute ride.

Rua 24 Horas

This is a covered arcade about 100 metres long, with gift shops, restaurants and bars that open – you guessed it – 24 hours a day. It's a popular addition to the city, and very crowded around 3 am.

Museu Paranaense

The Museu Paranaense, at Praça Generoso Marques, is in an art-nouveau building that used to house the municipal government. It's worth a visit just to check out the building itself. Chronicling the history of the state of Paraná, the museum has a hotch potch of objects and a collection of artefacts from the Guarani and Caigangues Indians. It's open Monday to Friday from 10 am to 6 pm and on weekends from 1 to 6 pm. Entry is free.

Museu da Habitação do Imigrante

Located in the Parque João Paulo II, this museum is a tribute to Paraná's Polish colonists. It consists of a few log cabins containing objects used by the pioneers, and is open every day from 9 am to 5 pm. The park itself is a pleasant one in which to wander. To get there, catch an 'Abranches' bus from Praça Tiradentes. The entrance to

the park is not well marked, so keep your eyes peeled. It's on the right-hand side, about three km from town.

Other Museums

Among other museums that are worth a look is the Museu Ferroviária, in the old train station on Avenida 7 de Setembro. It's open Tuesday to Friday from 10 am to noon and 1 to 6 pm and on weekends from 1 to 6 pm. Also try the Museu de Arte Sacra in the Igreja da Ordem (Largo da Ordem). It's open Tuesday to Friday from 10 am to noon and 1.30 to 6.30 pm. On weekends, it's open from 9 am to 1 pm.

Train Ride to Paranaguá

Completed in 1880, the railroad from Curitiba to the port of Paranaguá is the most exciting in Brazil. Leaving from Curitiba at an altitude of 900 metres, the train descends a steep mountainside to the coastal lowlands. The 110-km track goes through 13 tunnels and crosses 67 bridges. The view below is sublime and, depending on the cloud formations and tone of the sunlight, often surreal: threatening mountain canyons, tropical lowlands and the vast, blue Atlantic.

When you arrive in Paranaguá three hours later, you will have seen the world change rapidly and radically: the climate is hot and muggy, and often rainy in the winter; the land is flat and low until it hits the wall of mountain; the vegetation is short, lush and uniform; and the people are sturdy, with strong Indian features and faces defined by years by the sea.

The bad news is that, due to government cutbacks, trains run daily only during the peak Brazilian tourist periods: January, February and July. Otherwise, they run only on weekends.

When they are actually running, there is a regular train (*trem*) and a tourist train (*litorina*) that both run from Curitiba to Paranaguá and then back to Curitiba. The trem runs every day in January and February. From March to September (excluding July) it runs on weekends. In July, and from October to December, it runs on Wednesday,

Friday and weekends. But the trip on Wednesday and Friday is one way to Morrettes.

The trem departs at 7.30 am and leaves Paranaguá for the return trip at 4.30 pm, stopping at every station along the way. Tickets cost US$5.

The air-con litorina runs to almost the same timetable. The difference is that in July and from October to December, it runs one way to Morrettes on Tuesday and Thursday. The litorina leaves Curitiba at 9 am and starts back at 3.30 pm. Tickets cost US$10. It's full of tourists, and has a recorded description of the sights in Portuguese, English, Spanish and French. It makes photo stops, but doesn't stop at the stations.

Both trains take about three hours each way. For the best view on the way down to the coast, sit on the left-hand side.

Getting tickets can be tricky. They can be bought up to two days in advance. This means that if you arrive in Curitiba late and want to take the train the next day, you should go to the station at about 6 am so that if there are no seats left for the litorina, you can get on the trem. Even if tickets for both trains are sold out, don't take the bus yet. Some of the local travel agencies seem to buy a few extra tickets for the litorina in case they get customers for a tour; if they don't, they come to the train station to sell the extra tickets. So hang about and ask around – you may get lucky.

Tickets are sold at the train station behind the rodoviária. For information, contact the ticket office in Curitiba (☎ 234-8441).

Places to Stay – bottom end

There is a youth hostel at Rua Padre Agostinho 645, in the suburb of Mercês. Catch the 'Campina do Siqueira – Capão do Imbui' bus, which heads to Campina do Siqueira from outside the bus station. Get out at Praça 29 de Março and walk two blocks along Rua Desembargador Molta, to the crossroads with Rua Padre Agostinho.

Across from the rodoferroviária are some of Curitiba's inexpensive hotels. On Avenida Presidente Afonso Camargo there are three hotels in a row. The *Hotel Maia* (☎ 264-1684) has single/double quartos for US$10/15. Next door, at No 367, is the *Hotel Imperio* (☎ 264-3373). It's very clean and friendly, and charges US$9/17 for single/double quartos. Right alongside is the *Hotel Cristo Rei*, the cheapest of the bunch, with singles/doubles for US$6/10. The staff has a sense of humour there: when I asked the manager whether they had apartamentos, he just laughed and said they only had apertamentos (apertar is Portuguese for pinch or squeeze).

Another good one to head for is the *Hotel Itamarati* (☎ 222-9063), at Rua Tibagi 950. In a quieter street, it's excellent value, with singles/doubles for US$11/17. Across from the market, the *Hotel Nova Lisboa* (☎ 264-1944), on Avenida 7 de Setembro, has singles/doubles for US$12/20.

If you want something closer to the centre, take Avenida Presidente Afonso Camargo to Avenida 7 de Setembro and then turn right on Rua João Negrão. About halfway between the rodoferroviária and the centre of town is *La Rocha* (☎ 233-6479), at Rua João Negrão 532. Basic singles/doubles cost US$5/12 without breakfast.

In the centre itself are a couple of decent places. The *Mandarin* (☎ 233-6915), at Travessa Tobias de Macedo 120, close to the Museu Paranaense, has apartamentos for US$17/22 a single/double. The *Hotel Cacique* (☎ 233-8122), at No 26, right on Praça Tiradentes, is quite a bit cheaper, at US$12/20 a single/double.

Places to Stay – middle

A bit more expensive, but popular with travellers, is the *Condor Hotel* (☎ 262-0322), a few doors up from the Nova Lisboa on Avenida 7 de Setembro. Single/double rooms with bath cost US$23/30.

An excellent mid-range alternative in the centre is the *Hotel O'Hara* (☎ 232-6044), in a colonial building at Rua 15 de Novembro 770, opposite Praça Santos Andrade. At US$25/30 for singles/doubles, it's good value for this price range. Also centrally located is the *Hotel Globo* (☎ 234-7013). It's at Rua Senador Alencar Guimarães 72, very close to Praça General Osorio. Singles/doubles are US$27/33.

Places to Stay – top end

The top-end hotels across from the rodoferroviária are the *Hotel Jaragua* (☎ 264-4322; fax 264-7763), at Avenida Presidente Afonso Camargo 279, which charges US$40/50 for singles/doubles, and the *Hotel Promenade* (☎ 224-3022), at Rua Mariano Torres 976, with singles/doubles for US$60/70.

In the centre, close to Praça Tiradentes, at Rua Cândido de Leão 15, the *Hotel Eduardo VII* (☎ 232-0433) has singles/doubles for US$33/50. The *Araucária Palace* (☎ 224-2822) is opposite the performing-arts centre, at Rua Amintas de Barros 73. Singles/doubles cost US$75/90.

Places to Eat

Rua das Flores has some classic confeitarias. *Schaffer*, at No 424, was founded in 1918 and is famous for its coffee and cakes. *Confeitaria das Famílias*, at No 374, is well known for its afternoon tea.

In Rua 24 Horas, there are several places: *Le Lasagne* serves five types of lasagne in individual portions for US$3, while *Le Mignon* serves a varied menu, with cheap 'chef's suggestions'.

The *Bologna* (☎ 223-7102) has the city's best Italian food – the tortellini has a city-wide reputation. Moderately priced, it's at Rua Carlos de Carvalho 150, and is open for lunch and dinner daily (except Tuesday). Also in the city centre is the *Arabe Oriente*, on the 1st floor at Rua Ébano Pereira 26. Open daily for lunch and dinner, it has big portions and good food. The *Kabuki Japanese Restaurante*, at Avenida 7 de Setembro 1927, has inexpensive Japanese meals. It's open for lunch and dinner daily (except Monday).

There are several very pleasant, medium-priced restaurants in the Largo da Ordem area – walk around, look at menus and see what looks best. Readers have recommended *No Kafe Fest* (for its excellent café colonial)

and *Schwarzwald* (for its roast duck). The latter is also a good place for a chopp in the evening.

The *Vherdejante* vegetarian restaurant has chicken and fish dishes and excellent self-serve, fixed-price lunches. It's at Rua Presidente Faria 481, in front of the Passeio Público, and is open Monday to Saturday.

The *Bar do Stuart*, Praça General Osorio 427, has great small meals and a classy ambience. It's open daily until midnight (except Sunday, when it closes at 2 pm). In Santa Felicidade, *Família Fandanelli*, at Rua Manoel Ribas 5667, is handy for travellers because the 'Santa Felicidade' bus stops in front. They serve a dish that has to be tasted to be believed – a combination of white grapes, almonds, pasta and a thick, white cheese sauce. É uma delícia.

Entertainment

Up in Largo da Ordem, there are several bars featuring rock music. There's also the Casa Nilo Samba, at Rua Mateus Leme 65, which has samba and choro. Up the hill, John Edwards Bar is at Rua Jaime Reis 212. It's a bit pricey, but has good jazz, blues and bossa nova from Wednesday to Sunday nights. John Edwards, the owner, is an American from San Francisco.

The London Pub in Lagoa da Ordem is a small place with great local jazz. It's informal, cheap and always crowded with a mix of mostly arty and university types. The music starts late and goes late.

Things to Buy

The Feira de Arte e Artisano, held in Praça Garibaldi on Sunday from 10 am to 2 pm, offers an excellent variety of arts & crafts.

Getting There & Away

Air There are flights from Curitiba to all major cities in Brazil.

Bus The rodoferroviária (☎ 234-8441) is clean and well organised. The entrance is on Avenida Presidente Afonso Camargo. Bus schedules are posted and easy to understand,

and some companies even have printed schedules that they hand out.

There are many daily buses to São Paulo (US$12, six hours) and Rio (US$20, 11 hours), and to all major cities to the south. There are 12 buses a day to Foz do Iguaçu: the first leaves at 6.45 am and the last two (both leitos) at 9.15 and 11.40 pm. The price is US$19 for a regular bus and US$37 for a leito.

From Curitiba you can also get direct buses to Asunción (US$23), Buenos Aires (US$71) and Santiago (US$90).

If you miss the train, or there just isn't one, there are plenty of buses to Morretes, Antonina and Paranaguá. Try to get a bus that goes along the Estrada da Graciosa, the old pioneer road completed around 1873. The trip isn't as stunning as the train ride but it's still pretty. It takes just over 1½ hours to get to Paranaguá.

Train See the Train Ride to Paranaguá information earlier in this section for details of this scenic train trip. If you can time it, there are steam-train rides from Curitiba to Lapa, an historic city 70 km away, on the first Sunday of each month, and from Morrettes to Antonina on the third Sunday of each month.

Getting Around
To/From the Airport Alfonso Pena Airport is a 20 to 30-minute drive from the city (about US$20 by taxi). Cheap public buses marked 'Aeroporto' leave every hour from the bus terminal on Rua João Negão.

Bus You can walk to most places of interest, as the city is fairly compact, but if you're footsore, there's an excellent local-bus network. Destinations are well marked and fares are US$0.20. The main bus terminals are on Praça Tiradentes, Praça General Osorio and Praça Rui Barbosa.

Particularly useful is the white 'Circular Centro' minibus. It does regular circuits of the city, stopping at the Passeio Público, Praça Tiradentes, Praça Santos Andrade near the university, and outside the rodoviária.

Look for the bus stop with the white acrylic top.

Another useful bus is the 'Linha Turismo', which does a two-hour tour of the city's main attractions, including some you wouldn't see just walking around the centre. It departs from Praça Tiradentes, in front of the cathedral, every hour between 9 am and 5 pm, Tuesday to Sunday. You can get off the bus at any of the attractions and hop on the next white 'Linha Turismo' bus that passes. At each stop there is a timetable posted. It costs US$3.50 for four tickets (allowing you to get on and off at four stops).

Also handy is the green 'Pro-Parque' bus, which takes Curitibanos to one of their city's many parks. It operates on Sunday and public holidays. The one to the zoo leaves from the Passeio Público almost every hour from 8 am to 6.30 pm.

AROUND CURITIBA
Vila Velha
An interesting day trip is a visit to the 'stone city' of Vila Velha, 93 km from Curitiba on the road to Foz do Iguaçu. Here you'll find an interesting collection of sandstone pillars created by millions of years of erosion. There's also a place to swim and an elevator ride into a crater lake.

To get there, catch a semi-direito bus to Ponta Grossa from the rodoferroviária and ask to be let out at the entrance to the state park. Unless you camp, there's nowhere to stay in the park, but there are always plenty of buses back to Curitiba. If you're going on to Foz, catch a bus or hitch into Ponta Grossa, 22 km away.

MORRETES
Founded in 1721 on the banks of the Rio Nhundiaquara, Morretes is a tranquil little colonial town in the midst of the lush coastal vegetation zone. It's a good place to relax, swim in the river and take some walks in the nearby state park.

Several buses and the train stop at Morretes on the way to Antonina and Paranaguá. If you like the feel of the place, just hop off – the spectacular part of the train ride is over anyway. The town itself is very small, and it's easy to find your way around.

Marumbi State Park

The park offers some great hikes, and is very popular with Curitibanos, who get off the train at one of its many stops and hike down the old pioneer trails that were the only connections between the coast and the Paranaense highland in the 17th and 18th centuries. The best two to walk on are the Graciosa trail, which passes close to the Estrada da Graciosa, and the Itupava trail. Views from both are fantastic.

To get to the park from Morretes, catch a bus to São João de Graciosa. It's a couple of km from there to the park entrance, where you can pick up a trail map. Don't forget to take some insect repellent!

Rio Nhundiaquara

This river served as the first connection between the coast and the highlands. Now, one of the best things to do on it is hire a truck inner tube from the guy who runs the service station and go 'tubing' (in Portuguese *bóia*, or *cross*). The guy who rents the tubes will also take you upriver and drop you off. It takes about four hours to float back down. See Dona Gloria at the Hotel Nhundiaquara for more details.

Cascatinha

Five km from Morretes on the Rio Marumbi is Cascatinha, a large lake which is good for swimming. It's a fine place to camp. There's a cachaça factory nearby.

Places to Stay

There are three hotels in Morretes. The *Hotel Nhundiaquara* (☎ 462-1228) is the best place to stay. It's on the river, at Rua General Carreiro 13. The owner, Dona Gloria, is really helpful. She charges US$9/16 for singles/doubles with bath, US$7/10 without. Being next to a fast-flowing river, it's also free from mosquitoes!

The *Hotel Bom Jesus* (☎ 462-1282), on Rua 15 de Novembro, is a bit dearer, with quartos for US$8. The most expensive hotel

in town is the *Porto Real Palace* (☎ 462-1344), with singles/doubles for US$20/30. It's just up from the train station, on Rua Visconde de Branco.

Places to Eat

The speciality of the region is a filling dish called barreado, a mixture of meats and spices cooked in a sealed clay pot for 24 hours. Originally it was cooked during Carnival, to give the revellers a huge protein fix, but today it's considered the state dish. There are a few places around town that serve it, but the best place to try it is in the restaurant of the *Hotel Nhundiaquara*. Eat it for lunch – not dinner!

ANTONINA

Antonina is 14 km east of Morretes and 75 km east of Curitiba on the Baía de Paranaguá. Direct buses link Antonina, Curitiba and Paranaguá. Similar to Morretes, Antonina is old and peaceful. Its first settlers panned for gold in the river. There's a fine church in the centre, the Igreja de NS do Pilar, that was begun in 1715 and rebuilt in 1927. Its festival is held on 15 August.

The beaches along the bay are not very good, but Antonina is an easy place to kick back and take in the great view of the Baía de Paranaguá.

Places to Stay

There are five hotels in town, but none of them could be considered a real bargain. The *Christina Hotel* (☎ 432-1533), on Rua 15 de Novembro, and the *Monte Castelo* (☎ 432-1163), on Travessa Ildefonso, both have quartos that cost around US$15/20 a single/double. They also have apartamentos for a couple of dollars more.

The cheapest place is the *Tokio*, close to the train station, at Rua Consuelo Alves de Araújo 287, but it's a long way from the waterfront. Singles/doubles cost US$4/6. The *Hotel Luz* (☎ 432-1625), at Rua Comendador Araújo 189, is good value, costing US$8/15 for singles/doubles, but again, it's a bit of a walk to the water.

The most expensive hotel in Antonina is

the *Regency Capela Antonina* (☎ 432-1357), at US$47/53 a single/double – more if you want a view of the bay. It's at,Praça Coronel Macedo 208.

Places to Eat

The *Bahia Bonita*, on Travessa 7 de Setembro, serves seafood and other dishes, as well as making some of the tastiest fruit batidas around. There's a great view of the bay. The restaurant is closed on Monday. Along the waterfront, *Tia Rosinha*, at Rua Antônio Prado 54, serves good seafood and barreado.

PARANAGUÁ

The train ride from Curitiba isn't the only reason to go to Paranaguá. It's a colourful city, with an old section near the waterfront that has a feeling of tropical decadence. There are several churches, a very good museum and other colonial buildings that are worth a look. Although there has been some renovation, you still feel surrounded by decay. Fortunately, there aren't enough tourists to destroy this air of authenticity. Paranaguá is also the place from which you leave for Ilha do Mel and the mediocre beaches of Paraná.

One of Brazil's major ports, Paranaguá is 30 km from the sea, on the Baía de Paraná. Goods from a vast inland area, encompassing the state of Paraná and parts of São Paulo, Santa Catarina, Mato Grosso do Sul and Rio Grande do Sul, are shipped from here.

The primary exports have been gold, mate, Madeira and coffee, and are now corn, soy, cotton and vegetable oils.

Paranaguá's old section is small enough to wander around without a set itinerary. Without much effort, you can see most of Paranaguá's colonial buildings, churches, waterfront bars and various markets in a couple of hours.

Information

There's a tourist information office inside the train station. Staff are helpful, friendly and often have maps as well as a list of hotels (with prices). If you need to change money,

try Tassi Turismo or Maritur Turismo, both on Faria Sobrinho. For travellers' cheques, the Banco do Brasil is at Largo Conselheiro Alcindino 103.

Museu de Arqueológico Etnologia

Don't miss it! Many Brazilian museums are disappointing; this one is not. Housed in a beautifully restored Jesuit school that was built from 1736 to 1755 (the Jesuits didn't get to use the school for long, as they were expelled from Brazil in 1759), the museum has many Indian artefacts, primitive and folk art, and some fascinating old tools and wooden machines – an enormous basket weaver, for instance.

At the front desk are notebooks with descriptions of the exhibits in English. The museum is at Rua 15 de Novembro 567 (near the waterfront). It's open Tuesday to Sunday from noon to 5 pm.

Churches

The city's churches are simple, unlike baroque churches. The Igreja de NS do Rosário is the city's oldest. Also worth visiting are the Igreja São Francisco das Chagas (1741), Igreja de São Benedito (1784) and Igreja de NS do Rocio (1813).

Waterfront

Down by the waterfront, you'll find the new and old municipal markets, and depending on the time and day, both can be quite lively. Nearby is a bridge that leads to the Ilha dos Valadares. There are 8000 people on the island, mostly fisherfolk and mostly poor. During festivals, they dance the Paraná fandango: a hybrid dance that combines the Spanish fandango and the dances of the Carijó Indians.

There are no regular boat trips to Ilha do Mel, except during the summer, but there is a tourist boat that explores the river. The boats leave daily at 10.30 am, noon, and 2 and 4 pm from the end of Avenida Arthur de Abreu, and the trip lasts 1½ hours.

Places to Stay

The cheapest places are along the waterfront,

on Rua General Carneiro. The street has character, but it's dark and almost deserted at night, so you need to be careful. The *Pensão Bela Vista* (☎ 422-5737) and the *Hotel Santiago*, a couple of doors away, both have basic rooms for US$3 per person.

The *Hotel Litoral* (☎ 422-0491), at Rua Correia de Freitas 65, is the best deal in town. Rooms are large and open onto a sunny courtyard; single/double quartos go for US$6/8 and apartamentos for US$8/15.

Just round the corner, on Rua Dr Leocádio, the *Hotel Palácio* (☎ 422-5655) has apartamentos for US$12/19 a single/double. In the same area, but more up-market, is the *Monte Libano* (☎ 422-2933), with singles/doubles for US$24/40. It's at Rua Julia da Costa 152.

The best hotel in town is the *Dantas Palace* (☎ 422-1555), at Rua Visconde de Nácar 740, where singles/doubles start at US$40/50.

Place to Eat

The *Café Itibere*, on the main praça, has super coffee, and there is a good suco stand nearby, in front of the train station. The *Pensão Bela Vista*, on Rua General Carneiro,

PLACES TO STAY	PLACES TO EAT	OTHER	
4 Monte Libano	10 Restaurante Bobby	1 Igreja de NS do Rocio	14 Igreja de São Benedito
5 Hotel Litoral	11 Vegetariano Natural	2 Post Office	15 Tassi Turismo
6 Hotel Palácio	12 Café Itibere	3 Local Bus Station	16 Maritur Turismo
18 Dantas Palace	22 Mercado Municipal	7 Telephones	17 Palácio Visconde de Nácar
19 Hotel Karibe	do Café	8 Train Station	20 Câmbio
26 Hotel Santiago	28 Restaurante	9 Tourist Office	21 Igreja São Francisco das Chagas
27 Pensão Bela Vista	Danúbio Azul	13 Igreja NS do Rosário	23 Museu de Arqueológico e Etnologia
	Panorâmico		24 Rodoviária
			25 Handicraft Market

serves a big meal for US$3, and you can eat outside along the waterfront, enjoying the bela vista.

The *Restaurante Bobby*, at Rua Faria Sobrinho 750, is the best place in town for seafood. They have a traditional dining room and serve good-sized portions of fish, shrimp and meat. Most meals cost US$4 to US$7, but you can easily spend less by ordering one meal for two people. The seafood moqueca is excellent. The restaurant is open daily for lunch and dinner, except for lunch on Monday.

Restaurante Danúbio Azul Panorâmico has seafood upstairs, beer and pizza downstairs. Meals are US$4 to US$8, and this place is open daily for lunch and dinner, except Sunday dinner. It's down at Rua 15 de Novembro 95, with an excellent view of the waterfront. A few blocks away, at the end of Avenida Coronel José Lobo, *Palhano's* is recommended for open-air drinks on the waterfront.

The *Mercado Municipal do Café* is a good place to have lunch. It's been restored, and contains five small restaurants, all serving cheap seafood.

Getting There & Away
Bus All out-of-town buses leave from the rodoviária on the waterfront. The first of many buses to Curitiba leaves at 6 am, the last at 11 pm. The trip costs US$3 and takes an hour and 40 minutes. There are many buses to both Antonina (1½ hours) and Morretes, if you want to stop off on the way to Curitiba.

If you're going south, eight buses go to Guaratuba daily, where you can get another bus to Joinville (the last one leaves Guaratuba at 5.30 pm). The first bus to Guaratuba leaves Curitiba at 6.30 am and the last at 11 pm. You can also return to Curitiba for buses south.

To go to the beaches, catch a 'Praia de Leste' or a 'Pontal do Sul' bus at the rodoviária. There are 13 daily buses that drive the 30 km to the coast at Praia de Leste, then go north along the coast, past Ipanema, Shangri-lá and finally Pontal do Sul (for Ilha

do Mel). The first bus leaves at 5.50 am and the last returns from Pontal do Sul at 8.15 pm. It's 1½ hours and US$1 to Pontal do Sul. In the low season, there are still plenty of buses, but you may have to change at Praia de Leste.

Train The train, when it's running, returns to Curitiba at 3.30 and 4.30 pm (see the Train Ride to Paranaguá section).

PARQUE NACIONAL DO SUPERAGUÍ
Comprising the Superaguí and Peças islands in the Baía de Paranaguá, this marine park was created in 1989. It is renowned for its mangroves and salt-marshes and also contains a great variety of orchids, dolphins, jaguars and parrots, threatened with extinction as the Mata Atlântica shrinks.

The principal island of the park, the Ilha do Superaguí, is the most visited. Boats disembark at Vila Superaguí, a fishing settlement with a population of about 200. There is a small pousada (*Pousada Superaguí*, charging US$10 per person), a basic restaurant and some small general stores. Some of the families rent rooms in their simple, wooden houses. There is no electricity.

To maintain the environment and to make sure the local culture remains relatively undisturbed, all visitors must report to the IBAMA checkpoint, about two km from the village.

Beaches away from Vila are deserted. The longest is Praia a Deserta, a 20-km-long strip of fine, white sand. The water is calm, but swimmers need to watch out for the stinging jellyfish which appear when the water gets warm.

The trip, apart from Guaraqueçaba, is interesting, as the boat passes through mangroves and provides a great view of one of the world's best-preserved salt-water lagoons. It takes about 2½ hours, depending on sea conditions, and is made in small fishing boats. The cost is around US$30 for the round trip, made on the same day, or US$10 if you go on the larger boat, which leaves on weekends at 6 am and returns at around 3 pm. This boat anchors in front of the old municipal market. For reservations, phone 482-1275.

The closest town to the Parque Nacional do Superaguí is Guaraqueçaba, which is a bit of a dump. It's accessible by bus from Curitiba or Paranaguá.

An alternative route to Superaguí is via Paranaguá, but you need a bit of patience and a lot of luck. The diesel depot for boats in Paranaguá is on Rua General Carneiro, near the old Mercado do Café, and it's possible to meet men from the island refuelling their boats for the return voyage. You can identify their boats by the words 'S.AGUI' painted on the bow or stern. How much they charge you for the ride depends on how plentiful the fish were and the price of diesel.

PARANÁ BEACHES

Descending the Serra do Mar from Curitiba, you get a good view of the Paraná coast. The broad beach runs uninterrupted from Pontal do Sul to Caiobá. With the notable exception of Ilha do Mel, these are unspectacular beaches, hot and humid in the summer and too cold in the winter. There's plenty of camping and numerous seafood barracas, and each town has a few hotels. Unfortunately, the condominium blight is spreading.

Praia de Leste

This small, unattractive town has a couple of hotels, and the closest beach to Paranaguá, a bit more than half an hour away. The beach is open and windy, and there are some beach breaks for surfing. You can check your luggage in at the rodoviária (US$0.50), if you want to go for a swim.

This is the place to catch buses south to Guaratuba. These get very crowded on summer weekends, so get there early.

Pontal do Sul

The end of the line, this is where you get off for the Ilha do Mel. The bus stops three km from the canal where boats leave for Ilha do Mel. In between are summer homes and lots of open, unused beaches.

ILHA DO MEL

The Ilha do Mel, an oddly-shaped island at the mouth of the Baía de Paranaguá, wasn't discovered by the Portuguese until the 18th century. In 1767, to secure the bay and its safe harbours from French and Spanish incursions, King Dom José I ordered a fort built. Since then, not too much has happened. The few people on the island were ordered out during WW II, in the name of national defence. Most significantly, the island is now part of the Patrimônio Nacional, which has prevented it from being turned into more cheesecake for the rich.

The island is popular in the summer because of its excellent beaches, scenic walks and relative isolation. Its undoing might be that it is becoming too popular. However, it is administered by the Instituto de Terras e Cartografia Florestal (ITCF), which intends to preserve the island more or less as it is.

Unfortunately, they can't stop the sea from making changes. By the time you read this, erosion will have opened a channel at Nova Brasília, cutting the island in two. You'll see lots of houses crumbling into the sea as you walk from Nova Brasília to the fort.

From January to Carnival, and during Easter, the island is very popular with a young crowd, but there is still a lot of beach, and always room for an extra hammock. If you're travelling up or down the coast, it's crazy not to visit the island at least for a day. Many people end up staying much longer.

Orientation

The island has two parts, connected by the beach at Nova Brasília, where most of the locals live. The bigger part is an ecological station, thick with vegetation and little visited, except for Praia da Fortaleza. On the ocean side are the best beaches – Praia de Fora, Praia do Miguel and Praia Grande. All are reached by a trail that traverses the beaches and coves, and the steep hills that divide them. The bay side is muddy and covered with vegetation.

Boats from Pontal do Sul go to either Nova Brasília or Praia dos Encantadas.

Brasília, the larger settlement, provides access to the most comfortable, expensive pousadas. Encantadas, on the south-west side of the island, is a bit smaller, with only eight pousadas. During the summer, Encantadas is the most popular and crowded, while Brasília and nearby Praia do Farol are the surfers' favourite hang-outs, because they're close to Praia Grande. Out of season, Ilha do Mel is a very tranquil place.

The entire island can be walked around in eight hours, but by far the best walking is along the ocean side (east) from the southern tip of the island up to Praia da Fortaleza.

Bichos de pé are prevalent on the island, so keep something on your feet when you're off the beach.

Beaches

The best beaches face the ocean toward the east. **Praia Grande** is a 20-minute walk from Nova Brasília and a two-hour walk from Praia dos Encantadas. According to local surfers, it has the best waves in Paraná, and on winter weekends, boatloads of surfers come across. The walking is excellent along this stretch, too. **Praia da Fora**, close to Praia dos Encantadas, also has good waves.

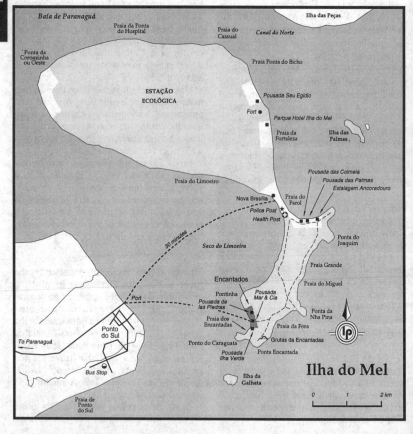

Other Attractions

Points of interest include the **Grutas das Encantadas**, small caves at the southern tip (Ponta Encantada) where, legend has it, beautiful mermaids enchant all who come near them. The fort, **Fortaleza de NS dos Prazeres**, was built in 1769 to guard the bay at Praia da Fortaleza. From inside the fort, a trail leads up to the WW II gun emplacements and a magnificent view of the whole area. The **Farol das Conchas lighthouse**, built in 1872 on the orders of Dom Pedro II, stands at the island's easterly point, at Praia do Farol. The fisherfolk on the island regularly catch hammerhead sharks, which they call 'Formula Ones'.

Festival

Ilha do Mel goes crazy at Carnival. Last year's attendance was estimated at 20,000.

Places to Stay

If you happen to arrive on the island on a holiday weekend or at another peak time, rooms will be hard to find, but it's easy to rent some space to sling a hammock. There are 10 designated camping areas on the island: seven in Praia dos Encantadas, two in Nova Brasília and one at Praia Farol das Conchas. All have electricity and water and cost US$2 per person. You're not supposed to camp outside these areas. Watch out for the tides if you decide to crash out on the beach.

There are pousadas at Nova Brasília, Praia da Fortaleza, Praia Farol das Conchas and Praia dos Encantadas. Prices range from US$8 per person in the simple places up to US$40 a double. During high season, they go up 20% to 50%.

The biggest concentration of places is at Praia Farol das Conchas, to the right as you reach Nova Brasília. The *Pousadinha* (☎ 978-3662), well signposted from Nova Brasília, is highly recommended. Staff speak French, English and Italian. Low-season prices are US$20 for a double quarto and US$25 for a double apartamento. The place also has its own generator, a plus on an island where the main generator is turned off from

midnight to 10 am. Another popular place at Farol is the *Estalagem do Pirata*, which costs US$10 per person, which includes a good breakfast. The *Estalagem Ancoradouro* (☎ 252-1559), run by Arnaldo, out towards the lighthouse, charges US$8 per person. Other good pousadas in the area are *Pousada das Colmeia* and *Pousada das Palmas*.

At Praia da Fortaleza, 200 metres past the fort, there are a couple of places. Try the *Pousada Seu Egidio*. Just before the fort is the island's only hotel, the aptly-named *Parque Hotel Ilha do Mel* (☎ (041) 223-2585; fax 232-5723), with rooms for US$40 a double.

At Praia dos Encantadas, there are two beachfront places. The *Pousada Mar & Cia* (☎ 335-2611) has single/double quartos for US$7/18 and apartamentos for US$13/30. Next door is the *Ilha Verde* (☎ 978-2829). It's well signposted, and the owner, Christina, raves about the beautiful sunsets on the doorstep. Prices range from US$10 for a dorm bed to US$30 or US$40 for an apartamento. Also worth a mention is the *Pousada de las Piedras*, run by a Colombian/Brazilian Christian couple. As you get off the boat, walk up the beach to your left, past the beachfront restaurants, until you get to a trail leading inland. From there it's best to ask for directions, but the place is not too hard to find. They charge US$8 per person, including a good breakfast. The two rooms up the top are best.

Places to Eat

There are barracas with food and drinks at Nova Brasília, Praia dos Encantadas and Praia da Fortaleza. On Friday and Saturday nights, you'll find music and forró, and when the beer is gone it's time for pinga, the local cachaça. At Brasília, the *Davi* restaurant, just past the health post, has a good prato feito for US$2. Nearby, *Toca do Abutre* serves excellent fish for US$3.

At Praia dos Encantadas, there are three good beachfront cafés in a row: *Delírios*, *Zorro* and *Ilha do Mel*. All serve much the same thing – seafood. You'd be crazy to eat anything else on Ilha do Mel anyway.

Getting There & Away

Take the 'Ponto do Sul' bus from Paranaguá, or if you are coming from Guaratuba, transfer at Praia de Leste for the same bus. The bus stops three km from the canal where the boats leave for Ilha do Mel. There's usually a taxi, which charges monopoly prices: US$5 for the five-minute ride. Look for someone to split the cost with, or you can walk or hitch.

If you decide to walk when you get off the bus, return 20 metres to the paved main road and turn right. Follow this road for a little more than a km, until it veers right and approaches the sea. Then turn left on a sandy but well-travelled road for about two km, until the end, where you'll find several barracas and a few boats. That's it.

The boats cost US$2, and from December to March they make the half-hour voyage to the island every hour or so, usually from 8 am to 5 pm. The rest of the year, they aren't as frequent, but you should have no problems finding one.

Getting Around

If there are a few of you or if you have lots of luggage, it might be worth hiring a small cart to transport your stuff to a pousada. Look for them when you get off the boat. Taxis cost US$8 to Praia do Farol, US$10 to the fort and US$14 to Praia Grande. If you get sick of walking, mountain bikes can be rented at Praia do Farol (US$4 an hour).

OTHER BAÍA DE PARANAGUÁ ISLANDS

There are several other islands in the Baía de Paranaguá that can be visited, but you'll have to do some scraping around to get there, as there are no regular boat services.

The Ilha dos Currais is known for its birdlife and the Ilha da Cotinga for its mysterious inscriptions and ruins. The Ilha das Peças and the Ilha do Superaguí make up the Parque Nacional do Superaguí.

FOZ DO IGUAÇU

Arising in the coastal mountains of Paraná and Santa Catarina (the Serra do Mar) at the modest elevation of 1300 metres, the Rio Iguaçu snakes west for 600 km, pausing behind the Foz do Areia Cruz Machado and Salto Santiago dams and picking up a few dozen tributaries along the way. It widens majestically and sweeps around a magnificent forest stage before plunging and crashing in tiered falls. The 275 falls are over three km wide and 80 metres high, which makes them wider than Victoria, higher than Niagara and more beautiful than either. Neither words nor photographs do them justice: they must be seen and heard. They're what the Romantic poets had in mind when they spoke of the awesome and sublime.

Thousands of years before they were 'discovered' by whites, the falls were a holy burial place for the Tupi-Guaraní and Paraguas tribes. Spaniard Don Alvar Nuñes, also known as Cabeza de Vaca (presumably because of his stubbornness), happened upon the falls in 1541 in the course of his journey from Santa Catarina, on the coast, to Asunción. He named the falls the Saltos de Santa Maria, but this name fell into disuse and the Indian name of Iguaçu, meaning Great Waters in Tupi-Guaraní, was readopted. No agreement has been made on spelling – in Brazil it's Iguaçu, in Argentina Iguazú and in Paraguay Iguassu. In 1986 the international commission of UNESCO declared the region (along with the Pantanal) a World Heritage site.

With a population increase from 35,000 to 190,000 as a result of the Itaipu dam construction, the Brazilian border town of Foz do Iguaçu is a frenzied place which can be dangerous, particularly at night. Ciudad del Este (in Paraguay) is a real pit, while Puerto Iguazú (in Argentina) is much more mellow.

Orientation

The falls are roughly 20 km east of the junction of the Paraná and Iguaçu rivers, which form the tripartite Paraguayan, Brazilian and Argentine border (marked by obelisks).

The Ponte Presidente Tancredo Neves bridges the Rio Iguaçu and connects Brazil to Argentina. The Rio Paraná, which forms the Brazilian-Paraguayan border, is spanned by the Ponte da Amizade; 15 km upstream is Itaipu, the world's largest hydroelectric project.

The falls are unequally divided between Brazil and Argentina, with Argentina taking the larger portion. To see them properly you must visit both sides – the Brazilian park for the grand overview and the Argentine park for a closer look. Travellers should allow at least two full days to see the falls. Even more time is required if you want to do it at a leisurely pace or visit Ciudad del Este or the Itaipu dam.

The best time of the year to see the falls is between August and November. If you come during the May to July flood season, you may not be able to approach the swollen waters on the catwalks. It's always wet at the falls. The area gets over two metres of rain annually, and the falls create a lot of moisture. Lighting for photography is best in the morning on the Brazilian side and in the late afternoon on the Argentine side.

Information

Tourist Office Foztur maintains six information booths, all with the same information: maps, lists of hotels with a one-star and up rating, and tourist newspapers with English-language descriptions of the attractions. All the staff are very helpful and most speak English. Some also speak Italian, Spanish and German. There are booths at Rua Barão do Rio Branco, in the city (open from 6.30 am to 10 pm), at the rodoviária (6 am to 6 pm), at the airport (9 am until the last plane), at Ponte Presidente Tancredo Neves, on the Argentinian border (8 am to 6 pm), just before the Ponte da Amizade, on the Paraguayan border (8 am to 8 pm), and at the entrance to the city, on highway BR-27 (7 am to 6 pm).

Teletur (☎ 1516) maintains a 24-hour information service with English-speaking operators.

Money Recently the câmbios have been giving more favourable rates in Foz do Iguaçu than anywhere else in Brazil - try

Câmbio Dick (near the old bus station, at Avenida Brasil 40) or Frontur (at Avenida Brasil 75). There are plenty of others, but these two change both cash and travellers' cheques.

Post & Telephone The post office is on Praça Getúlio Vargas. International telephone calls can be made from Rua Rui Barbosa 475 or from Rua Marechal Floriano Peixoto 1222.

Visas Visitors who spend the day outside Brazil will not require visas, but those who intend to stay longer must go through all the formalities. In Foz do Iguaçu, the Argentine Consulate (☎ (045) 574-2969) is at Travessa Eduardo Branchi 26. It's open Monday to Friday from 9 am to 2 pm. The Paraguayan Consulate (☎ (045) 523-2898), at Rua Bartolomeu de Gusmão 738, is open on weekdays from 8.30 am to 1 pm and 3 to 6 pm. Brazil has a consulate in Puerto Iguazú (☎ 57-2061), at Avenida Victoria Aguirre 77, open on weekdays from 8 am to noon. In Paraguay, the Brazilian Consulate (☎ 616-2308) is at Rua Pay Perez 337, on the corner with Pampliega. It's open from 8 am to noon.

The Falls – Brazilian side

Although the Brazilian side has a smaller chunk of the falls, the Brazilians have the Grand View across the churning lower Rio Iguaçu to the raging falls. The Brazilian park is larger, with 1550 sq km of rainforest, but the Argentine forest is in better shape.

Walk to the observation tower by the Floriano falls, then over to Santa Maria falls. There's also a new walkway that gives an even better view of the Garganta do Diablo (Devil's Throat).

If you can spare the cash, treat yourself to an outrageously beautiful helicopter ride over the waterfalls. For US$50, you get seven minutes of intense pleasure in the air. The choppers will take up to three passengers, but it's best to sit by the edge of the bubble. You can extend the ride to see Itaipu dam too. Helisul Taxi Aereo (☎ 523-1190) operates from Hotel das Cataratas, right at the waterfalls on the Brazilian side, from April to October between 9 am and 5 pm and from November to March between 9 am and 7 pm. Travellers flying into Foz or Puerto Iguazú with accommodating weather and pilots can see the falls from the air.

You can catch a boat to the Garganta do Diablo from near the observation tower. Sometimes the boat operators have an odd sense of humour – they'll cut the engine and float to the edge of the falls.

The Falls – Argentine side

The Argentine side is noted for its close-up views of the falls and the forest. The entrance to the Argentine park is 18 km from Puerto Iguazú. There are three separate walks on the Argentine side: the Passeios Inferiores, the Passeios Superiores and the Garganta do Diablo, which should be saved until last for dramatic effect.

The Passeios Inferiores is a view of the falls from below on a 1.5-km circuit. Take the boat to Isla San Martin (the boat service operates from 8 am to 5.30 pm, and is free) for spectacular close-up views of the falls.

The Passeios Superiores' concrete catwalks behind the waterfalls used to go as far

Foz do Iguaçu

as Garganta do Diablo, until floods a few years back swept them over the edge. The path goes only as far as the Salto Adán y Eva.

There's a dirt road running a few km from the park entrance to Puerto Canoas. (There used to be a shuttle bus, but when we were there, the service had been suspended indefinitely – check to see.) From here you can take a hair-raising boat ride out to Garganta do Diablo, where 13,000 cubic metres of water per second plunge 90 metres in 14 falls, arranged around a tight little pocket.

The view at the precipice is hypnotising. Visitors will be treated to a multisensory

THE SOUTH

Iguaçu Falls

PLACES TO STAY

2	Hotel Del Rey
3	Hotel Tarobá
4	Vale Verde
6	Imperial Hotel
8	Minas Foz Hotel
11	Hotel Senhor do Bonfim
12	Pousada da Laura
14	Hotel Internacional Foz
16	Hotel Diplomata
21	Hotel Luz
26	Ilha do Capri
32	Rouver Hotel

PLACES TO EAT

7	Rafain Centro Gastronômico
9	Churrascaria Búfalo Branco
10	Restaurante Calamares
15	Maria & Maria's Confeitaria #1
18	4 Sorelle
19	Restaurante Du Cheff
20	Restaurante Pei-kin
22	Bebs
23	Barbarela
25	Ver o Verde
29	Maria & Maria's Confeitaria #2
31	Bier Garten Chopparia

OTHER

1	Urban Bus Terminal (Buses to Iguaçu Falls, Argentina & Paraguay)
5	Câmbio Dick
13	Telephones
17	Paraguayan Consulate
21	Varig/Cruzeiro
24	Coart Artists' Co-operative
27	Teletur Tourist Information
28	Post Office
30	Telephones
33	Argentine Consulate

experience: roaring falls, huge rainbow arcs, drenching mist and, in the distance, parrots and hawks cruising over deep, green forest. Watch for the swifts, which drop like rocks into the misty abyss, catch insects in midair, shoot back up, and dart behind the falls to perch on the cliffs.

The Itaipu Dam

How did Brazil ever manage to run up such a huge foreign debt? Part of the answer is by engaging in mammoth projects like Itaipu, the world's largest hydroelectric works. The US$18 billion joint Brazilian-Paraguayan venture has the capacity to generate 12.6 million kilowatts – enough electricity to supply the energy needs of Paraguay and southern Brazil. The concrete used in this dam could have paved a two-lane highway from Moscow to Lisbon.

Fortunately the dam will not affect the flow of water in Iguaçu, as the Paraná and Iguaçu rivers meet downstream of the falls. The Itaipu dam has, however, destroyed Sete Quedas (the world's largest waterfall, with 30 times the water spilled by Iguaçu) and created a 1400-sq-km lake. Local weather, and plant and animal populations have been altered, and the complete environmental repercussions of these changes will not be felt for decades. Guided tours of the Itaipu dam are given six times a day: at 8, 9 and 10 am, and 2, 3 and 4 pm. The hour-long tours are free of charge. The Itaipu dam is 19 km from Foz.

Ciudad del Este (Paraguay)

Across the Ponte da Amizade, at Ciudad del Este, you can play roulette or baccarat at the Casino de Leste, or purchase up to US$250 of duty-free imported goods (no great deals) or some nifty Paraguayan lacework and leather goods.

Forest Tour (Argentina)

There's more to the 550-sq-km Argentine park than just waterfalls. If you intend to do a forest tour, do it on the Argentine side; they do a better job of protecting their parklands than do the Brazilians, and there are guides at the visitors' centre in the park. If you can, arrange the tour the evening before, and pick up a wildlife list and study it. Try to arrive at the park before 7 am (when the entrance fee of about US$1 is waived) or in the late afternoon, the best times to spot birds and wildlife.

Go in a small, nature-loving group and bring binoculars and a tape recorder (to record the sounds of the forest). You'll see fantastic butterflies (they congregate about pools of urine and on sweaty handrails to sip salts), parrots, parakeets, woodpeckers, hummingbirds, lizards, three-cm-long ants, beautifully coloured spiders and all sorts of orchids, lianas and vines.

We saw two species of toucan, but there are four species in the park. Our guide explained that their long beaks are deceptive, being actually so light and spongy that the birds are back-heavy and therefore clumsy flyers. The toucans eat fruit, eggs, chicks and leaves of the amba (*Cecropia adenopus*) tree. Amba leaves are used to make a medicinal tea which is good for coughs.

Other creatures in the park include monkeys, deer, sloth, anteaters, raccoons, jaguar, tapir, caiman and armadillo, but as in other tropical rainforests, large animals are not very abundant and tend to be nocturnal. You can see them on display at the natural history museum at the Argentine park headquarters.

The foliage is lush and lovely: 2000 species of plants stacked in six different layers, from forest-floor grasses, ferns and bushes to low, middle and high tree canopies. The forest cover, in addition to harbouring a wide variety of animals and insects, protects the soil from erosion, maintains humidity and moderates temperatures. Tarzan vines, lianas and epiphytes connect and blur the distinction between the forest levels.

Festival

The Pesca ao Dourado (Dorado Fishing Contest) takes place in the last week of October.

Bus No 7

Ciudad del Este is mostly an unattractive jumble of high-pressure shops using US dollars. But if you have an hour or two to spare, you can quickly reach 'real Paraguay' on one of the colourful, comfortable and inexpensive local buses that leave from just beyond the main crossroads at the far (west) end of the main street. Just stay on the bus to the end of the journey, then come back!

We caught a No 7 and soon reached dirt roads. Small-holdings had new thatched roofs, outdoor ovens, horse carts and cows in the front garden. There wasn't another white face to be seen – it felt much more 'third world' than the sophistication of southern Brazil. We felt we had reached the 'real' Latin America at last. Of course, this is tame for those who are heading for Bolivia, but it was a highlight of our more conventional visit to Brazil.

Jill & David Wright – UK

Places to Stay – bottom end

Camping *Camping Club do Brasil* (☎ 574-1310) is the closest campground to the falls. Just before the entrance to the park, there's a dirt road to the left. The campground is 600 metres along this track. Camping costs US$9 per person, and there's a restaurant and a swimming pool. Closer to the city of Foz, *Internacional* (☎ 574-2184) is in a well-treed area with a swimming hole. Camping costs US$4 per person, and they also rent apartamentos (US$25) that can hold up to six people. The Internacional is on the right-hand side, a couple of km out of Foz on the road to the falls, and is well signposted.

Hotels Foztur keeps a complete list of rated (one-star and up) hotels, but they don't have information about the real cheapies.

Around the old bus station are lots of cheap hotels, but the area is pretty seedy in the evenings. Popular with travellers is the *Hotel Senhor do Bonfim* (☎ 572-1849), in a small dead-end street just off Rua Almirante Barroso. It charges US$5 per person and have fans in every room – absolutely essential when it's hot in Foz.

Nearby, at Rua Rebouças 641, the *Minas Foz Hotel* (☎ 574-5208) has apartamentos for US$8 per person, not incuding breakfast.

At Rua Rebouças 335 is the *Vale Verde* (☎ 574-2925), which used to be the youth hostel. We've received a few complaints from readers about the paper-thin walls and lack of privacy, but the lady who runs the place is helpful. She charges US$6 per person without breakfast, but for an extra US$1 you can have breakfast in the café out the front.

The best place for budget travellers is the *Pousada da Laura* (☎ 574-3628), at Rua Naipi 629 (the sign is quite small, so look carefully). Laura speaks English, French and Spanish and her pousada is clean, safe and friendly. You can even watch TV (from the USA via satellite) with the family in the living room. It's in a quieter, tree-lined street close to the local bus station, and it costs US$7 per person.

Places to Stay – middle

Our favourite is the *Ilha do Capri* (☎ 523-2300), at Rua Barão do Rio Branco 409. Singles/doubles go for US$20/30. It's handy for buses, close to a few eateries, and has a pool and a good breakfast. A bit cheaper is the *Consul* (☎ 574-5712), at Rua Rui Barbosa 1343. They rent small, air-con apartamentos for US$10/15 a single/double, without breakfast.

The *Imperial Hotel* (☎ 523-1299), at Avenida Brasil 168, is reasonable, with

Green Toucan

apartamentos for US$14/19 a single/double. The rooms in front get a bit noisy. The *Hotel Diplomata* (☎ 523-1615), at Avenida Brasil 678, has a pool. They charge US$30/40 for singles/doubles, but if you ask nicely, they might let you use the pool anyway.

The *Hotel Del Rey* (☎ 523-2027) and the *Hotel Tarobá* (☎ 574-3890) are next door to one another on Rua Tarobá, near the intersection with Avenida República Argentina. Both charge US$30 a double. The Del Rey has a pool and larger rooms. Both are well located for catching buses.

Places to Stay – top end

At the top end, the classiest place to stay is the *Hotel das Cataratas* (☎ 74-2666), right at the waterfalls. Singles/doubles cost US$90/100, but Brazil Airpass holders can get a 15% discount. Back in the city itself, the five-star *Hotel Internacional Foz* (☎ 74-4855), at Rua Almirante Barroso 345, charges US$100/120 a single/double.

Places to Eat

The best buffet deal in town is at the *Restaurante Calamares*, at Rua Rebouças 476. At US$3 for all you can eat, it's a good energy boost after a hard day at the falls. Along Rua Almirante Barroso between Rua Jorge Sanways and Rua Xavier da Silva are lots of good places. For Italian food, *4 Sorelle* is at No 650. For seafood, try *Restaurante Du Cheff*, at No 683 – it's expensive but excellent.

Readers have recommended *Maria & Maria's Confeitaria* for good cakes, sandwiches and hot chocolate. They have two locations, at No 495 and No 1285 Avenida Brasil. *Pastel Mel*, in the third lane off Avenida Juscelino Kubitscek, at No 26, has 30 different types of pancakes (US$3 each) and 20 types of pasteis (US$1 each).

A good churrascaria is *Búfalo Branco*, at Rua Rebouças 530. *Restaurante Pei-kin*, at Rua Jorge Samways 765, serves fair Chinese food. Vegetarians can lunch at *Ver o Verde*, at Rua Edmundo do Barros 111, between 11 am and 3 pm. It has a cheap, self-serve buffet for US$4. *Bebs*, at Avenida Juscelino

Kubitschek 198, is a popular student hangout that gets pretty lively. The *Bier Garten*, on the corner of Avenida Jorge Schimmelpfeng and Rua Marechal Deodoro da Fonseca, serves a good variety of pizza, steaks and chopp. It's in a good setting, and gets crowded at night.

Getting There & Away

Air There are frequent flights from Foz do Iguaçu to Asunción, Buenos Aires, Rio and São Paulo. VASP (☎ 523-2212) is at Avenida Brasil 845, Transbrasil (☎ 574-1734) is at Avenida Brasil 1225 and Varig/Cruzeiro (☎ 523-2111) is at Avenida Brasil 821.

In Puerto Iguazu, Aerolineas Argentinas (☎ 20168) is at Aguirre 295, and offers services to Buenos Aires' Aeroparque for US$184. Dinar (☎ 20566) at Cordoba 236, flies to Aeroparque Thursday and Sunday afternoons for US$130. Lapa (☎ 20214) at Bonpland 110, Local 7, has a similar schedule, but only charges US$99.

Aerolineas Argentinas (☎ 572-0194 in Argentina) and Austral (☎ 572-0144) have daily flights to Buenos Aires.

Bus The trip from Foz do Iguaçu to Curitiba is 635 km, takes 12 hours and costs US$16. There are seven daily buses on the BR-277. To São Paulo, eight buses make the 15-hour trip (US$26). To Rio there are six buses per day (US$36, 22 hours).

There are several buses a day from Ciudad del Este to Asunción (US$8, seven hours, 320 km).

Three buses a day run from Puerto Iguazú to Buenos Aires (US$55, 20 hours).

Getting Around

To/From the Airport Catch a 'P Nacional' bus. They run every 22 minutes from 5.30 am to 7 pm and then every hour until 12.40 pm. The bus ride takes half an hour and costs US$0.50. A taxi to the airport costs US$20.

To/From the Rodoviária All long-distance buses arrive at and depart from the new international bus station, six km from the centre of town on Avenida Costa e Silva. To get to the centre, walk down the hill to the local bus stop and catch an 'Anel Viaria' bus – it says 'Centro' in nice, big letters. They start at 5.30 am and run every 15 minutes until 1.15 am.

Bus All local buses leave from the urban bus terminal on Avenida Juscelino Kubitschek.

To/From the Brazilian Falls Catch a 'Cataratas' bus (US$0.80) to get to the Brazilian side of the falls. On weekdays, buses run every two hours, the first bus leaving the terminal at 8 am and the last at 6 pm. The last bus leaves the falls at 7 pm. On weekends and public holidays, the first bus leaves the terminal at 8 am and the second at 10 am; thereafter buses leave every 40 minutes until 6 pm. The last bus leaves the falls at 7 pm.

At the entrance to the park, you'll have to get out and pay the US$3 entry fee. The bus will wait while you do this.

To/From the Argentine Falls In Foz, catch a 'Puerto Iguazú' bus to get to the Argentine side of the falls. Buses start running at 7 am and leave every 13 minutes (on Sunday, every 50 minutes) until 8.50 pm. The fare is US$1.20. In Puerto Iguazú, transfer to an 'El Pratico' bus.

At the bus station in Puerto Iguazú, you can pay for everything in one go: the bus fares to and from the park, the bus to and

from Puerto Canoas, entry to the park and the boat ride to Isla San Martin. The entrance fee for the park can be paid in Argentine pesos or in US dollars. If you have only reais, the ticket seller at the bus station will change into pesos the amount required for the park entrance fee; this can then be paid on arrival at the park. All up, the bus costs US$4, plus US$3 for park entry and US$4 for the boat at Puerto Canoa out to the Garganta do Diablo.

The bus leaves every hour from 6.40 am to 8.15 pm, but not at 1 pm (which is siesta time).

To/From Itaipu From the local bus stop opposite the urban terminal in Foz, take a 'Conjunto C' bus heading to Itaipu. There's one every 20 minutes from 5.30 am to 11 pm, but keep in mind that Itaipu closes for visits after 4 pm. The buses run north along Avenida JK. Their last stop is at the Ecomuseu (worth a look), about 400 metres from the Itaipu visitors' centre.

To/From Ciudad del Este From the urban terminal in Foz, buses for Ciudad del Este begin running at 7 am and leave every 10 minutes. They run north along Rua Almirante Barroso, turn left into Avenida República Argentina and then turn right into Avenida Presidente Tancredo Neves.

THE SOUTH

Santa Catarina

The Germans and Italians who settled in Santa Catarina in the 19th century, unlike most immigrants in the rest of Brazil, owned their small, family-run farms. This European model of land-use has produced a far more egalitarian distribution of wealth than in most of Brazil – 83% of the farmland is owned by farmers with less than 1000 hectares.

Many of the state's four million people still own their rich farmland, which, combined with some healthy small-scale industry, has created one of Brazil's most prosperous states. This relative affluence, the very visible German presence and the efficient services give the state the feel of Europe rather than of Brazil – at least in the highlands, which are green and pastoral. If Santa Catarina reminds one of Switzerland, it's less because of geography and more because of the sedate middle-class consumerism. Most travellers don't come to Santa Catarina to visit a foreign culture – they come for the beaches.

There's no doubt that the beaches are beautiful: they're wide and open, with Caribbean-like coves and bays, clear, clean emerald-blue water, and views of offshore islands. The water is very warm during the summer months, and there are plenty of calm, protected beaches for swimming. Santa Catarina also has some of Brazil's better surfing spots. The currents can be very dangerous in places, so be careful.

While there are still fishing villages along the coast, you don't really find the kind of primitive fishing villages that predominate in the Northeast. The setting is less exotic and less tropical, the villagers less secluded and less friendly, and the escape from Western civilisation less complete.

Many of Santa Catarina's beaches have become fashionable vacation spots for well-to-do Paulistas, Curitibanos and Argentines, so during the January-February holiday season, the beaches and hotels are jammed. Several little Copacabanas have sprouted up in beach towns such as Camboriú, and this

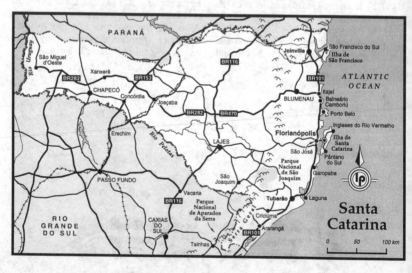

growth is changing the coastline at an unbelievable pace.

Santa Catarina's climate is nice and hot during the Brazilian summer. In the winter, the wind along the coast picks up considerably, although it never gets too cold. The best months to go, unless you like the crowds, are March, April, November and December.

Compared with other parts of Brazil, this is a polite and proper place, where children are subdued and well mannered. You may be excluded from a restaurant because your jeans are worn and you will probably be excluded from a bar if you're not wearing a shirt. You must wear either bermuda-length shorts or long trousers on intercity buses – no swim suits. What's so unusual about this Brazilian state is not that it has these rules but that they are respected and enforced.

JOINVILLE

Imagine a city where blondes stroll through town on clean, well-lit, heavily policed streets, perusing Bavarian-facaded, neon-named shops full of modern Western appliances, with well-manicured lawns, flower festivals, and a central park in which children play at night. A city that is polite, efficient and pleasant. Now here's the hard part: imagine that this city is in Brazil.

Santa Catarina's second largest city, Joinville (pronounced joyvilee) is described in its own tourist brochure as 'an industrial city'. The industry, however, is outside the pleasant inner city, which is quite habitable and seems like the kind of place to raise a family. For the traveller, Joinville is relaxed and pleasant, if unexciting.

Joinville is on the BR-101, 180 km north of Florianópolis and 123 km south of Curitiba. The road is good and the views are beautiful around the town, particularly where the highway traverses the lush coastal mountains. The drive down to Guaratuba (on the coast to the north) is stunning.

Orientation

The city centre is small, with most stores and services concentrated on and around Rua 15 de Novembro and Rua Princesa Isabel.

Information

Tourist Office

There is a tourist office in front of the Colón Palace Hotel, open Monday to Sunday from 8 am to 6 pm. It offers mediocre maps and silly brochures, and the staff speak German and a little English. There is a travel agency behind the office.

Post & Telephone

The post office is on Rua Princesa Isabel. Make phone calls from the telefônica next to the tourist information office.

Museu Nacional da Imigração

Housed in the old palace (built in 1870) at Rua Rio Branco 229, the Museu Nacional da Imigração is full of objects used by the pioneers of the state. It's open Tuesday to Friday from 9 am to 6 pm.

Alameda das Palmeiras

In front of the Museu Nacional is an impressive, palm-lined walkway. These Imperial palms are over a century old. Don't miss the rare 'dual' palm. It's the second palm on the right as you face away from the museum.

Museu Arqueológico do Sambaqui

At Rua Dona Francisca 600 is the Museu Arqueológico do Sambaqui, an exposition of the Sambaqui Indian lifestyle. It's worth a visit on a rainy day. The museum is open Tuesday to Friday from 9 am to noon and 2 to 6 pm.

Museu de Arte de Joinville

This is quite an interesting one. It houses works by local artists, and contains a small restaurant. It's at Rua 15 de Novembro 1400, and is open Tuesday to Sunday from 9 am to 9 pm.

Mirante

A high tower on top of the Morro da Boa Vista, the Mirante is a good place to get your bearings. It also provides a 360° view of Joinville, and you can see the Baía da Babitonga and São Francisco do Sul.

Festivals

For the last 53 years, Joinville has hosted a Festival of Flowers each November. The orchids are the main attraction. During July, the city also hosts the largest dance festival in Latin America.

Places to Stay – bottom end

The centrally located *Hotel Ideal* (☎ 22-3660), on Rua Jerônimo Coelho, has singles/doubles from US$6/12. A bit more expensive, but much nicer, the *Hotel Príncipe* (☎ 22-8555) is just up the road, at

No 27. It's clean, with very friendly staff, and tends to fill up early. Singles/doubles start at US$14/24. A bit further away, at Rua 15 de Novembro 811, the *Hotel Mattes* (☎ 22-3582) has rooms from US$8/14.

Places to Stay – top end

The *Colón Palace Hotel* (☎ 33-6188; fax 33-2969), facing Praça Nereu Ramos, has a pool and great breakfast (try the chocolate milk). Singles/doubles cost around US$35/45. For the same price, the *Anthurium Palace* (☎ & fax 33-6299), at Rua São

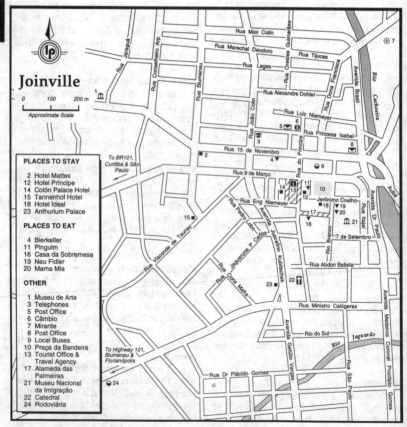

Joinville

0   100   200 m
Approximate Scale

PLACES TO STAY
2 Hotel Mattes
12 Hotel Príncipe
14 Colón Palace Hotel
15 Tannenhof Hotel
18 Hotel Ideal
23 Anthurium Palace

PLACES TO EAT
4 Bierkeller
11 Pinguim
16 Casa da Sobremesa
19 Neu Fidler
20 Mama Mia

OTHER
1 Museu de Arte
3 Telephones
5 Post Office
6 Câmbio
7 Mirante
8 Post Office
9 Local Buses
10 Praça da Bandeira
13 Tourist Office & Travel Agency
17 Alameda das Palmeiras
21 Museu Nacional da Imigração
22 Catedral
24 Rodoviária

José 226, has colonial charm and a sauna, but no pool. The *Tannenhof* (☎ & fax 33-8011), at Rua Visconde de Taunay 340, is Joinville's best and most expensive hotel. Single/double rooms start at US$60/70.

Places to Eat

Joinville boasts good German food and is a major chocolate producer. The *Bierkeller*, at Rua 15 de Novembro 497, has the city's best value in German food, lots of pork, and a feijoada for lunch on Saturday. Prices are reasonable – about US$4 to US$7 a meal.

For quieter dining, the restaurant at the *Colón Palace Hotel* is a good change of pace; it's reasonably priced and has good meat dishes. *Mama Mia*, at Rua Rio Branco 193, is recommended. They offer Italian dinners for under US$6. Next door, on the corner of Rua Jerônimo Coelho and Rua Rio Branco, *Neu Fidler* is an excellent steak restaurant/choparria. It's possible to make a complete hog of yourself for around US$7. At Rua Rio Branco 299, *Pinheiro* is more expensive, but has the city's best fish.

For dessert, you can't go past the *Casa da Sobremesa*, in the Alameda das Palmeiras. It offers around 50 exotic ice-cream flavours; two scoops for US$1.

Things to Buy

If you're in town on the second Saturday of the month, check out the artisan fair in Praça Nereu Ramos.

Getting There & Away

Air There are regular flights from Joinville to Curitiba, Florianópolis, Rio and São Paulo.

Bus Buses make the 2½-hour trip from Joinville to Curitiba 24 hours a day, every one to two hours. For São Paulo, a bus leaves at 9.30 pm (US$16, nine hours). There's a 6.45 pm bus direct to Rio (US$28, 15 hours).

If you're going south, the BR-101 runs along the coast, and many buses service this route. Most stop at any or all of the small beach towns, so it's easy to hop on a bus and get off at whichever beach looks good. If you're going to a set destination, such as Florianópolis, the express buses do not stop on the way and are much faster.

Florianópolis is a three-hour bus ride away; the express costs US$7. The first bus leaves Joinville at 6.30 am and the last at 11.45 pm. Semi-direitos, which run via Itajaí and Balneário Camboriú, leave every two to three hours, 24 hours a day.

Buses to Porto Alegre leave at 11.15 am and 9 pm, take nine hours and cost US$15. There's also a leito, which leaves at 9.35 pm.

There are frequent services to Blumenau (1½ hours). Two daily buses go to Foz do Iguaçu (at 5.10 and 9.30 pm), taking 10 hours and costing US$20.

The closest beaches are due east, on Ilha de São Francisco. Many buses make the 1¼-hour, US$2 trek, especially on weekends, when many Joinvilleians head to these beaches. The first bus leaves at 6.30 am and the last at 8.20 pm.

To get to the coast of Paraná and the city of Paranaguá, you have to catch the bus to Guaratuba. Buses leave at 7 and 10.45 am, noon, and 1.45 and 5.30 pm. The trip takes 1½ hours. Two buses go directly to Paranaguá, at 4 and 7.30 pm.

Train There is a daily 8 am train to São Francisco do Sul. It returns at noon.

Getting Around

The airport is 12 km from the city, and the rodoviária is two km out. From a bus stop at the side of the airport terminal, city buses leave every 20 minutes or so for the Praça da Bandeira, in the centre.

JOINVILLE TO FLORIANÓPOLIS

This stretch of coast has many beautiful beaches, but it's being developed rapidly and without controls. In general, the more famous a beach, the more developed and ugly it is. Balneário Camboriú, the area's best-known beach town, is an excellent example.

São Francisco do Sul

This historic city's island setting was

'discovered' way back in 1504 by the Frenchman Binot Paulmier de Goneville, but the city itself wasn't settled until the middle of the next century. It became the port of entry for the German immigrants who settled the land around Joinville.

Beaches The beaches on the **Ilha de São Francisco** are good, but their proximity to Joinville (and even Curitiba) makes them some of the most crowded. On the positive side, there are several cheap hotels in the city, and a variety of beaches accessible by local buses. There is also a lot of surfing.

Both **Prainha** and **Praia Grande** (to the south) have big waves and are popular surfing beaches. Swimming is not safe. Closer to the city, **Praia de Ubatuba** and **Praia de Enseada** are pretty, and safe for swimming, but they're developed and often crowded. For another option, ask in town about boats leaving from Capitania dos Portos to the **Ilha da Paz**.

Places to Stay Praia de Enseada has several hotels, and you can catch a bus from there directly to Joinville. The *Enseada* (☎ & fax 42-2122), at Avenida Atlântica 1074, on the beach, is reasonably priced at US$20 a double. The *Turismar* (☎ 42-2060), at Avenida Atlântica 1923, is a bit cheaper, with singles/doubles for US$10/16. In town, the *Kontiki* (☎ 44-0232), at Rua Camacho 33, across from the waterfront, is reasonable; it charges US$11 per person.

Barra Velha
If driving south from Joinville on the BR-101, this is the first point where the road meets the sea. Four km to the south of town, Praia do Grant is popular with the younger set. The surf beaches are Praia do Tabuleiro (two km from town) and Itajuba (five km away).

Places to Stay & Eat *Camping Simone* (☎ 46-0226) is at Rua Lauro Ramos 69. The *Mirante* (☎ 46-0343), at Rua Governador Celso Ramos 106, has decent quartos for US$14/22 a single/double. They also serve a

cheap buffet lunch. For a fine fish dinner, try *Agua Viva*, at Avenida Santa Catarina 248.

Piçarras
Piçarras, 14 km south of Barra Velha, has a good, big beach, and several small islands which can be visited. The town is lively in summer, but the campgrounds often fill up.

Places to Stay & Eat Apart from the three campgrounds, there are barracas and several hotels, including the cheaper *Real* (☎ 45-0706), at Avenida Nereu Ramos 607, and the *July* (☎ 45-0644), at Avenida Getúlio Vargas 44. Ask about houses to rent. There are lots of seafood restaurants. Try *Maneco*, at Avenida Nereu Ramos 299.

Penha
Penha is a big fishing town, so it's not completely overrun by tourism. Only six km from Piçarras, the ocean is calm at the city beaches, Praia da Armação and Prainha. There are simple hotels at these beaches. The beaches south of these two are less crowded. From Praia da Armação, boats leave every half-hour or so to the nearby islands of Itacolomi and Feia.

Places to Stay & Eat There are lots of campgrounds near the main beaches, and several very good beachside seafood restaurants as well. A cheap hotel on the beach, at Praia da Armação, is the *Itapocoroí* (☎ 45-0015), which has apartamentos for US$10/16 a single/double.

Itajaí
At the turn-off to Blumenau, Itajaí is an important port for the Itajaí valley. However, there's not much here to interest the tourist and the best beaches are out of town. There are a couple of hotels across from the rodoviária and several more on the main road going out of town to Camboriú. Plenty of buses come and go from Itajaí.

Balneário Camboriú
This little Copacabana, with its sharp hills dropping into the sea, nightclubs with 'pro-

fessional mulattos' and an ocean boulevard named Avenida Atlântica, is clearly out of control. In summer, the population increases tenfold.

Balneário Camboriú is Santa Catarina's most expensive town. Here you can meet well-heeled Argentines, Paraguayans and Paulistas who spend their summers in the ugliest beach-hugging high-rise buildings you can imagine. The spoiling of this beachfront is surely a crime against nature.

Outside the city, there is a Museu Arqueológico e Oceanográfico that's worth visiting (six km south on BR-101, open daily from 9 am to 6 pm), and a nude beach (a rarity in Brazil) at Praia do Pinho, 13 km south of the city.

Porto Belo

The beaches around Porto Belo are the last good continental beaches before Ilha de Santa Catarina. Praia de Bombas (three km away) and Praia Bombinhas (seven km from town by dirt road) are the prettiest beaches around. For a great walk, head out to Ponta do Lobo, 12 km from Praia Bombinhas. From Rua Manoel Felipe da Silva in Porto Belo, you can catch a boat to the islands of Arvorerdo and João da Cunha. Both have fine beaches.

Places to Stay Both Praia de Bombas and Praia Bombinhas have barracas and camp-grounds and are relatively uncrowded. The *Hotel Bomar* (☎ 69-4136), which has singles/doubles for US$9/15, is at Praia de Bombas. There are many campgrounds along the beaches.

Places to Eat On Avenida Governador Celso Ramos in Porto Belo, *La Ponte*, at No 1988, and *Petiscão*, at No 2170, both have tasty seafood.

BLUMENAU

Blumenau is 60 km inland from Itajaí, 139 km from Florianópolis and 130 km from Joinville. Nestled in the Vale do Itajaí on the Rio Itajaí, Blumenau and its environs were settled largely by German immigrants in the

second half of the 19th century. The area is serene, but the city itself wears its German culture way too loud. Everything is Germanicised with the commercial, but not creative, flair of Walt Disney. The city attracts tourists (mostly from not too far away), but isn't particularly special.

Information

Tourist Office There is an information post in the centre, on the corner of Rua Nereu Ramos and Rua 15 de Novembro. Staff speak German, and have useful maps and information about Blumenau and other towns in the Itajaí, including Pomerode.

Post & Telephone

The post office is on Rua Pe Jacobs. The telephone company is on Rua Uruguai, near the bridge.

Festival

Blumenau hosts an increasingly popular Oktoberfest, beginning on the first Friday in October.

Places to Stay

Hotels in Blumenau are very clean and efficiently run. The *Hotel Herman* (☎ 22-4370), at Rua Floriano Peixoto 213, has cheap singles/doubles from US$7.50/13, with breakfast. The manager is very friendly and loves to practise his German. Close by is the *City Hotel* (☎ 22-2205), at Rua Ângelo Dias 263. They have singles/doubles starting at US$5/9.

Moving up the price scale, the well-located *Hotel Gloria* (☎ 22-1988), at Rua 7 de Setembro 954, has singles/doubles from US$35/55. On the same street, at No 640, the *Hotel Rex* (☎ 22-5877) has all the amenities, with singles/doubles for US$40/60. Nearby, the *Hotel Plaza Hering* (☎ 22-1277, or (011) 800-8618 toll free from São Paulo), Blumenau's fanciest sleepery, charges US$70/90 for singles/doubles.

Places to Eat

Unfortunately, the cheaper hotels in town don't provide any breakfast, so the best place

THE SOUTH

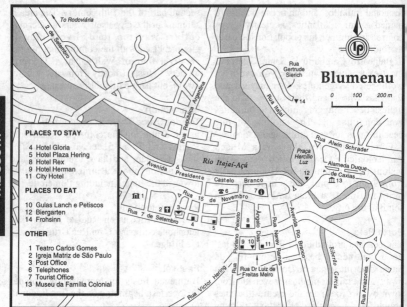

To Rodoviária

Rua
Gertrude
Sierich

Blumenau

0   100   200 m

Rua Itajaí

Rua República Argentina

2 de Setembro

▼14

Rua Alwin Schrader

Rio Itajaí-Açú

Praça
Hercílio
Luz

Avenida Presidente Castelo Branco

Alameda Duque
de Caxias
▥13
12▼

Rua 15 de Novembro

☎6   7🛈

🏛1

Rua 7 de Setembro

2🛈
3

Ângelo Dias

Rua Nerey Ramos

Avenida Rio Branco

Ribeirão Garcia

Rua Amazonas

Floriano Peixoto

8▪

9 10
▼▪ ▪11

Rua Floriano Hering

Rua Dr Luiz de
Freitas Melro

Rua Victor Hering

PLACES TO STAY

4 Hotel Gloria
5 Hotel Plaza Hering
8 Hotel Rex
9 Hotel Herman
11 City Hotel

PLACES TO EAT

10 Gulas Lanch e Petiscos
12 Biergarten
14 Frohsinn

OTHER

1 Teatro Carlos Gomes
2 Igreja Matriz de São Paulo
3 Post Office
6 Telephones
7 Tourist Office
13 Museu da Família Colonial

to head is the *Cafehaus Gloria*, in the Hotel
Gloria. Their US$5 café colonial is excellent.
It starts at 7 am. You could do a lot worse
than eat lunch or dinner there, too.

For average German food and a good
view, try *Frohsinn*, up the hill on Rua Itajaí.
They're open for lunch and dinner every day
except Sunday. The *Gruta Azul*, at Rua
Rudolfo Freygang 8, has also been recommended. You could try snacking at one of the
chopperias near the Rua República Argentina bridge. They're good places to go for a
beer in the evening, as is the *Biergarten*, in
Praça Hercílio Luz.

Getting There & Away

There are plenty of buses travelling to
Florianópolis from Blumenau. The direct
buses take 2½ hours and leave at 8 am, noon,
and 3 and 5 pm. Semi-direitos stop at Itajaí
and at Balneário Camboriú, and they arrive
in Florianópolis three hours after leaving
Blumenau.

Getting Around

The rodoviária is at Rua 2 de Setembro 1222;
take the 'Rodoviária' or 'Fortaleza' bus from
the city. A taxi costs US$7.

FLORIANÓPOLIS

Florianópolis, the state capital, fans out in
both directions from the spot where the coast
and the large Ilha de Santa Catarina almost
connect. The central section is on the island,
facing the Baía Sul. Over the hill, on the
north shore, is a long row of luxury high-
rises (none of which looks more than a
couple of years old), and modern restaurants
to feed their occupants. The mainland part of
the city has the industry. Much of the city's
shoreline appears barren due to undeveloped
landfill.

The city is modern, with some large structures such as the new rodoviária and many
works in progress. The island side of the city,
where you'll probably spend your time, has
a small-city feel. It's easy to get around on

foot, and there are regular public buses to the island's beautiful beaches.

Information

Tourist Office The main office of Setur (☎ 244-5822), the Florianópolis tourist bureau, is on the mainland side of the city, just before the bridge, at Rua Max de Sousa 236. They also have information posts at Praça 15 de Novembro, at the bus station and next to the old customs house. All provide maps and have hotel information. Staff will also help make reservations for hotels on the island. English and Spanish are spoken.

Lots of touts wait at the bus station for tourists, mostly Argentine or Uruguayan, to arrive. They have information about places to stay (they get their commission of course), and can be useful. Elcio is one who is helpful and speaks Spanish.

Money There's a very active street black market for cash dollars in the pedestrian mall on Rua Felipe Schmidt. These guys, mostly Spanish-speaking and armed with calculators and bulging money belts, change at the top rate, and the Argentine and Uruguayan tourists have no qualms about changing right there on the street. It's all done very openly. If the situation has altered, change your money at a travel agency, many of which have câmbios. For travellers' cheques, go to the Banco do Brasil at Praça 15 de Novembro, No 20.

Post & Telephone The post office faces Praça 15 de Novembro. The telephone company is two blocks up the hill from the praça. It's open from 8 am to 11 pm Monday to Friday and closes an hour earlier on Saturday, Sunday and holidays.

Praça 15 de Novembro & Around

While you'll probably want to get out to the beaches as soon as possible, it's definitely worth wandering around the city for a look at some of the colonial buildings.

From Praça 15 de Novembro and its 100-year-old fig tree, you can cross the road and go into the pink Palácio Cruz e Souza. It's the state museum, but the most interesting things to see are the ornate parquetry floors and the outrageous 19th-century ceilings. Entry is US$0.50. It's open Tuesday to Sunday from 10 am to 6 pm.

On the high point of the praça is the Catedral Metropolitana; it was remodelled this century, so not much from the colonial era remains. The least-remodelled colonial church is the Igreja de NS do Rosário, further up from the cathedral.

Waterfront

Back down on the old waterfront are the Alfândega (Customs House) and the Mercado Municipal, both colonial buildings that have been well preserved. The market is a good place to have a chopp and watch passers-by in the late afternoon.

Places to Stay

Hotels in Florianópolis are fairly expensive and fill up during the summer. Most of them, especially the budget places, are in the central district. Out on the island's beaches, there are few budget hotels, although it's possible to economise by renting a house or apartment with a group of people. There's lots of camping, which is the cheapest way to go.

Places to Stay – bottom end There's a good youth hostel (☎ 222-3781) at Rua Duarte Schutel, a 10-minute walk from the rodoviária. It charges US$7/8 for members/nonmembers.

All the bottom-end hotels are in the centre of town. There are a lot of cheapies close together on Rua Conselheiro Mafra. At No 399, the *Hotel Colonial* is seedy but friendly, with good-sized rooms. Quartos cost US$8/15 a single/double.

Across the road, at No 324, the *Hotel Cruzeiro* is a good deal at US$6 a head. On the next parallel street, Rua Felipe Schmidt, you'll find the *Hotel Cacique* (☎ 222-5359), at No 423, popular with travellers and touts alike; it's quite good but often full. They have quartos for US$10/18 a single/double (if you bargain), and a few apartamentos.

THE SOUTH

THE SOUTH

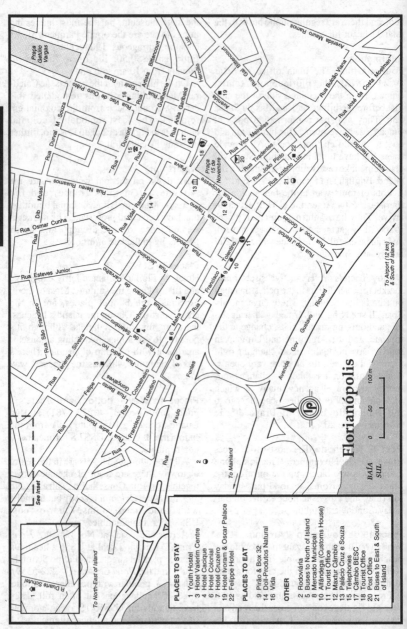

Florianópolis

BAÍA
SUL

To Airport (12 km)
& South of Island

To Mainland

0   50   100 m

PLACES TO STAY
1   Youth Hostel
3   Hotel Valerim Centre
4   Hotel Cacique
6   Hotel Colonial
7   Hotel Cruzeiro
19 Hotel Ivoram & Oscar Palace
22 Felippe Hotel

PLACES TO EAT
9   Pirão & Box 32
14 Doli-Produtos Natural
16 Vida

OTHER
2   Rodoviária
5   Buses to North of Island
8   Mercado Municipal
10 Alfândega (Customs House)
11 Tourist Office
12 Maxtur Câmbio
13 Palácio Cruz e Souza
15 Telephones
17 Câmbio BESC
18 Tourist Office
20 Post Office
21 Buses to East & South
    of Island

Another good place is the *Felippe Hotel* (☎ 222-4122), a couple of blocks past Praça 15 de Novembro, at Rua João Pinto 26. They charge US$8 per person, with breakfast. The receptionist, Luciano, speaks English and is a big Elvis fan.

Places to Stay – middle What this city lacks is a decent US$15 to US$25 hotel in the centre of town. If you find one, please let us know. A 15-minute walk (or a three-minute taxi ride) from Praça 15 de Novembro will get you to the *Veleiros Hotel* (☎ 223-6622), near the yacht club, at Rua Silva Jardim 254. Like most other hotels, they have a promotional offer during the low season – US$15/25 a single/double. The hotel has a great view of the bay.

The *Hotel Valerim Centre* (☎ 22-3280), at Rua Felipe Schmidt 74, has rip-off quartos for US$20 a single. Apartamentos go for US$30/40 a single/double.

Places to Stay – top end On Avenida Hercílio Luz, you'll find two places that are reasonable value. At No 66, the *Hotel Ivoram* (☎ 224-5388; fax 224-5890) has singles/doubles for US$40/50. The *Oscar Palace* (☎ 222-0099; fax 222-0978), at No 90, offers similar accommodation for a few dollars more.

The *Florianópolis Palace* (☎ 222-9633; fax 223-0300), Rua Artista Bittencourt 2, Centro, is Florianópolis' five-star hotel, and its singles/doubles cost US$90/110. It has everything you'd expect, as well as a private beach out at Canasvieiras.

Also central and luxurious is the *Faial Palace* (☎ 223-2766; fax 222-9435), at Rua Felipe Schmidt 87. It's a bit less expensive, with singles/doubles starting at US$60/70.

Places to Eat
The *Macarronada Italiana* is a great splurge, for some of Brazil's best pasta and formal service. It's open daily for lunch and dinner, and there's live dinner music Monday to Wednesday. It's on the Baía Norte, at Avenida Rubens de Arruda Ramos 196. Somewhat pricey are the *Lindacap* (☎ 224-

0558), at Rua Felipe Schmidt 178, Centro, and *Martim-Pescador*, at Beco do Surfista, about 20 km from the city; both are open for lunch and dinner. Martim-Pescador serves seafood, including the island's excellent shrimp.

Out at Lagoa, 14 km from the centre, *Nunes*, behind the post office, has large seafood dishes for about US$6. *Mar Massas*, also in Lagoa, at Rua Rita Louranço Silveira 97, is a popular pasta place. Another interesting restaurant to try is *Pirão*, upstairs in the old market. Also in the market, *Box 32* has some great seafood snacks. It gets crowded at night.

There are plenty of cheap lanchonetes in town, many of which are health-food oriented – try *Doll-Produtos Natural*. Vegetarians can get a healthy lunch at *Vida*, on Rua Visconde de Ouro Prêto, next door to the blue Alliance Française building.

Getting There & Away
Air There are daily direct flights from Florianópolis to São Paulo and Porto Alegre, as well as connections to most other cities. Flights to Rio make at least one stop. Watch out for multiple-stop flights, which may involve multiple plane changes.

Airlines in town include Aerolineas Argentinas (☎ 224-7835), Varig/Cruzeiro (☎ 236-1121), Transbrasil (☎ 236-1229), at Praça Pereira Oliveira 16, and VASP (☎ 224-1122).

Bus Long-distance buses link Florianópolis with Porto Alegre (US$10, 7½ hours), Curitiba (US$8, five hours), São Paulo (US$20, 12 hours), Rio (US$30, 20 hours), Foz do Iguaçu (US$24, 16 hours), Buenos Aires (US$60, 27 hours) and Montevideo (US$43, 21 hours).

There are frequent buses up and down the coast, as well as inland to Blumenau, Brusque and Lajes. Travel along BR-101, the coastal highway, is considerably quicker by direct bus. Local indirect buses can be easily flagged down along the highway.

THE SOUTH

Getting Around

To/From the Airport The airport is 12 km south of the city (US$9 by taxi). Buses marked 'Aeroporto' go regularly to the airport until 10 pm, leaving from the first platform at the central rodoviária. It's a half-hour ride by bus.

ILHA DE SANTA CATARINA

The island's east-coast beaches are the most beautiful, with the biggest waves and the greatest expanses of empty sand. They are also the most popular for day trips, and most do not have hotels. The north-coast beaches have calm, bay-like water, and resorts with many apartment-hotels and restaurants. The west coast, facing the mainland, has great views, a quiet, Mediterranean feel and small, unspectacular beaches.

East Coast

The following beaches are listed from north to south. Praia dos Ingleses, 34 km from Florianópolis, is becoming quite developed, and although the beach is a good one, the surroundings aren't very attractive. There are lots of hotels and restaurants catering to the Brazilian, Argentine and Uruguayan tourists, but nothing's cheap. *Sol & Mar* (☎ 269-1271) has doubles for US$40.

Praia do Santinho has a few beach houses and barracas and one of the island's most beautiful beaches. The island's longest beach, Praia do Moçambique (or Praia Grande), is 14 km long and undeveloped. It's hidden by a pine forest from the dirt road that runs a couple of km inland from it. The camping here is good.

Barra da Lagoa, a big, curved beach at the end of Praia do Moçambique, is a short bus trip (No 403, 'Barra da Lagoa') from Florianópolis. It is still home to many indigenous fisherfolk, descended from the original Azorean colonists. Although there are more hotels and restaurants here than anywhere else on the east coast, except Praia dos Ingleses, there are still not many of them, and they are not modern eyesores. The barracas are excellent, and it seems every second house is for rent. A good place to stay

is the *Gaivota* (☎ 232-3208), run by a very friendly family. Try to get a front room for the great view. Singles/doubles cost US$15/20 (without café, but you can get a good one round the corner for US$3.50). This is the best beach to head for if you want to stay a few days.

Praia Mole is a beautiful stretch of beach, with one hotel, the four-star *Cabanas da Praia Mole* (☎ 232-0231; fax 232-0482). The beach is hip in summer. A good bar there is *Mole Blues*. Paulo, the manager, is a Carioca who lived a long time in Los Angeles. He speaks excellent English and is a fun guy.

Praia da Joaquina hosts the Brazilian surfing championship in January and the Hang Loose championship in September. It has a couple of hotels. At the *Joaquina Beach* (☎ 232-0059; fax 232-1180), right on the beach, doubles cost US$35 (twice that in the high season). The *Hotel Cris* (☎ 232-0380; fax 232-0075) is the same price. A bit cheaper is the *Pousada Felicidade da Ilha*, run by Dona França, on the approach road to Joaquina. She has apartamentos for US$10 per person.

There are a few restaurants, and this is the busiest beach on the island. The crowd is young and hip and the surf pumps. Surfboards can be hired from the Surf Punks surf shop, right next to the Barra da Lagoa turn-off. Giba, the guy who runs the surf shop, also has a comfortable pousada, a short walk from Joaquina for an early morning surf. Dune-surfing is also popular on the Joaquina dunes, and you can hire a board right there.

The three main beaches to the south are the most remote, and quite spectacular. Praia do Campeche has a few barracas, and the beach is long enough for everyone to find a private patch of sand. Praia da Armação is similar. As at Campeche, the current is often strong.

Pântano do Sul, at the end of the paved road, is a small fishing village with a couple of restaurants. The mountains here close in on the sea, which is calm and protected. The *Pousada Sol de Costa* (☎ & fax 222-5071) is a tranquil place that charges US$15 per

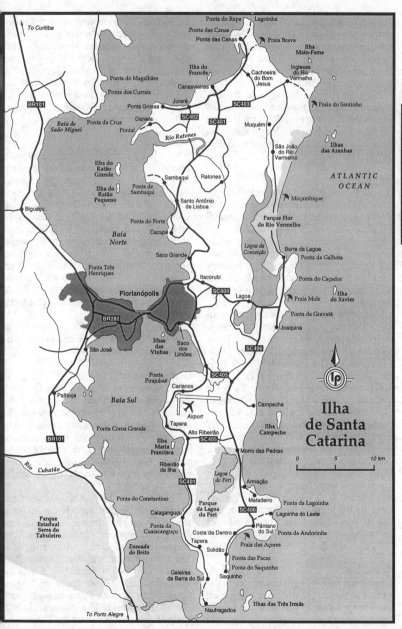

Ilha
de Santa
Catarina

0   5   10 km

person. To get there, turn right just before entering the village of Pântano do Sul, then continue past the newly developed Praia das Açores until you reach Costa de Dentro. There you'll find the pousada. The owner, Valdir, speaks English.

We must mention here one of the best places on the island for observing birds and other wildlife. It's very undeveloped. To get there, you have to walk along a hilly trail from either Armação or Pântano do Sul. Don't miss it.

North Coast

The north coast is the most developed coast on the island, and the beaches are narrow; however, the sea here is warm, calm, incredibly clean, and perfect for swimming.

Canasvieiras, in particular, has many apartments, families with holiday homes, and nightlife (during the summer). In many ways it is the least attractive beach town on the island, and plenty more construction is planned.

Most of the north coast's many apartment-hotels are pricey, but a few are affordable if you have at least three or four people. There are no real budget hotels, so if you're alone, it's expensive. The least expensive place is the *Ivoram Praia* (☎ 266-1041), a five-minute walk from the beach on the 'Camping Canasvieiras' road. They have one-bedroom apartments with big kitchens, and will add another bed so as to accommodate up to four people. It's tight, but for US$30, it's a good deal for the area. Another possibility is the *Canasvieiras Praia* (☎ 266-0310; fax 266-0310), with doubles for US$40.

A few km west, Jurerê is similar to Canasvieiras but a bit quieter. Out at Praia do Forte are the ruins of the Fortaleza de São José da Ponta Grossa, built in 1750. Jurerê has two top-end hotels, including the *Jurerê Praia Hotel* (☎ 282-1108; fax 282-1644).

West Coast

If you want to explore the west coast, the town of Sambaqui is charming and peaceful. There are a handful of barracas, and some beachgoers on weekends. After the town and the barracas, keep walking on the dirt road a few hundred metres for a more private beach, or continue another km to reach an even more secluded area. Both beaches are tiny and cosy, with good views. The road is blockaded soon after this second beach.

On the south-west coast, the old colonial town of Ribeirão da Ilha has an impressive little church, the Igreja NS da Lapa.

The Interior

It's not just the beaches: the entire island is beautiful. Lagoa da Conceição is the most famous region in the interior. The views of the lagoon, surrounding peaks and sand dunes make for great walks or boat rides. Lots of boats are for hire right next to the bridge. Typical costs are US$20 for two hours, but the boats can take up to 10 people, so try to get a group together. This town also has some simple hotels (which are overpriced, but so is everything outside Florianópolis). The *Andrinus* (☎ 232-0153) has quartos for two at US$25 and apartamentos for two at US$35.

If you're down south, the turn-off to Lagoa do Peri is at Morro das Pedras. The lake is fun to explore.

Getting Around

Local buses serve all of the island's beach towns, but the schedule changes with the season, so it's best to get the times at the tourist office or at the central rodoviária in Florianópolis. During the tourist season, additional microbuses leave from the centre and go directly to the beaches. These microbuses take surfboards; regular buses don't.

The buses for the east and south of the island (including Lagoa and Joaquina) leave from the local bus terminal in front of Rua João Pinto. Buses for the north leave from the local bus terminal close to the rodoviária. The buses, marked with their destinations, include services for Sambaqui, Lagoa da Conceição, Campeche, Barra da Lagoa, Canasvieiras (Jurerê), Ponta Grossa, Barra do Sul, Ribeirão da Ilha, Pântano do Sul, Ingleses-Aranhas and Ponta das Canas.

The island is one of those places where a one-day car rental is a good idea, though fairly expensive (US$60 to US$80). With a car, you can see most of the island and pick a beach to settle on. Alternatively, try one of the bus tours offered by the travel agencies. Ponto Sul (☎ 235-1399) is a good one, charging US$15 for an eight-hour tour.

Another excursion is with Scuna-Sul (☎ 224-1806). A three-hour Baía Norte cruise on a big sailboat costs US$15. The boats leave from near the steel suspension bridge – Brazil's longest.

SOUTH OF FLORIANÓPOLIS
Garopaba

The first beach town south of Florianópolis, Garopaba is 95 km from Florianópolis, including a 15-km drive from the main BR-101 highway. A lot of surfers settled here in the '70s, but the little town has not been overrun by tourism. The beaches are good, and you can still see the fisherfolk and their way of life. Garopaba is now the base for Mormaii Surfwear, who sponsor a big surfing contest in August.

Praia do Garopaba is one km from the town. Praia do Silveira, three km away, is good for surf, while Siriú, 11 km away, has some large sand dunes. Avoid the next town, Imbituba: it's polluted by a chemical plant.

Places to Stay For a cheap sleep, there are lots of campgrounds on Garopaba beach. Or ask about rooms in houses – you'll find plenty for rent. The *Hotel Garopaba* (☎ 54-3126), close to the town square, is a new place, with double apartamentos for US$30. One block away from the sea is the *Lobo Hotel* (☎ 54-3129), on Rua Marques Guimarães, with doubles for US$22.

Places to Eat Try the hilltop *Unter Deck*, on Rua Nereu Ramos, for good food with a nice view. It's open every day for lunch and dinner. Also recommended is the *Rancho da Vovó*, at Rua João Orestes Araújo 510. *Viva Mar*, next to the church on the main square, serves good seafood.

Laguna

Laguna has an active fishing industry and is the centre of tourism for the southern coast. Situated on the southern point of the line that divided the Americas between Spain and Portugal in the Treaty of Tordesillas in 1494, it's a historic city, settled by Paulistas in the 1670s. Laguna was occupied by the farrapos soldiers and declared a republic in 1839 in the Guerra dos Farrapos, which was fought between republicans and monarchists.

Museums If it's a rainy day, have a look at **Museu Anita Garibaldi**, on Praça República Juliana, which honours the Brazilian wife of the leader of Italian unification. The museum is open from 8 am to 6 pm. The **Casa de Anita Garibaldi**, on Praça Vidal Ramos, contains some of Anita's personal possessions. It's open daily from 8 am to 6 pm (closing for lunch between noon and 2 pm).

Beaches The best beaches in the area are out on the **Cabo de Santa Marta**, 16 km from the city plus a 10-minute ferry ride. The ferry operates from 7 am to 10.30 pm. There are beautiful dunes here, and it is possible to camp or to stay in barracas. Rooms can be also be rented in houses.

For something closer to town, try the **Praia do Gi**, five km north of Laguna. There are hotels and restaurants along the beach.

From Mar Grosso, the city beach, you can take a one-hour boat ride to **Ilha dos Lobos**, a rather unspoilt ecological reserve.

Places to Stay Accommodation in Laguna is not cheap. Your best bet is the *Farol Palace* (☎ 44-0596), on the waterfront, opposite the market. Singles/doubles here are US$8/12. The *Ondão* (☎ 44-0940), on Avenida Rio Grande do Sul, is the cheapest place at Mar Grosso, with singles/doubles for US$12/20.

Places to Eat Seafood is the order of the day here. In Mar Grosso, try *Arrastão*, at Avenida Senador Galotti 629, or *Baleia Branca*, next to the beach, on Avenida Rio Grande do Sul.

Laguna's eateries, like its hotels, tend to be expensive.

Further South

Further south are the coal-mining towns of Tubarão and Criciúma. Unless you want to go to the mineral baths, there's no reason to stay in either. Both have a handful of hotels, and are serviced by regular buses along the coastal route. From Tubarão you can get to several mineral baths, including Termas do Gravatal (20 km), Termas da Gurada (12 km) and baths on the Rio do Pouso (19 km).

The Termas do Gravatal are very popular and have many facilities. The radioactive waters are said to heal rheumatism, ulcers and a variety of other ailments. Unfortunately, none of the four-star hotels in the park grounds is inexpensive. There is camping, however, and you can easily come up from Tubarão for the day.

SÃO JOAQUIM

Not many overseas travellers come to Brazil to see snow, but if they did, this is where they'd come. The mountains are scenic in winter. São Joaquim is Brazil's highest city, at 1355 metres.

Bom Jardim da Serra

Bom Jardim da Serra, in the middle of the Serra do Rio do Rastro, is a hair-raising but beautiful 45-km drive from São Joaquim. There you'll find access to the Parque Nacional de São Joaquim. The park is completely undeveloped, so if you want to explore, ask the locals about hiring a guide.

Places to Stay

There aren't many places to stay in town. The cheapest is the *Maristela* (☎ 33-0007), at Rua Manoel Joaquim 220, where singles/doubles cost US\$9/12. Close by, at No 213, the *Nevada* (☎ 33-0259) has singles/doubles for US\$11/17. The *Minuano* (☎ 33-0656) has chalets for US\$20. It's at Rua Uribici 230, next to the Parque da Maçá.

An interesting alternative is the *Fazenda Santa Rita* (☎ 33-2170, (0482) 22-8304). It's close to the national park, at Km 31 on the São Joaquim to Bom Jardim da Serra road. At this working dairy farm, visitors can ride horses, swim in the river, walk on nearby nature trails or help herd the cows. They charge US\$30 per person, everything included. The fazenda's restaurant serves Italian food, and typical regional dishes such as churrasco de cordeiro mamão.

Places to Eat

For a good churrasco lunch, try the restaurant at the *Minuano* hotel. *Água na Boca*, at Rua Marcos Batista 907, serves a decent pizza.

Getting There & Away

Buses run between São Joaquim and Florianópolis. There aren't too many of them, so check the schedules before heading out.

Rio Grande do Sul

PORTO ALEGRE

Porto Alegre, gaúcho capital and Brazil's sixth-biggest city, lies on the eastern bank of the Rio Guaíba at the point where its waters empty into the huge Lagoa dos Patos. This modern city makes a living mostly from its freshwater port and from commerce. Originally settled by the Portuguese in 1755 to keep the Spanish out, Porto Alegre was never a centre of colonial Brazil; it's mainly a product of the 20th century, which is when many of the German and Italian immigrants arrived here.

Although most travellers just pass through Porto Alegre, it's an easy place in which to spend a few days. There are some interesting museums and impressive neoclassical buildings, as well as friendly gaúchos (and their barbecued meat – the city abounds in churrascarias).

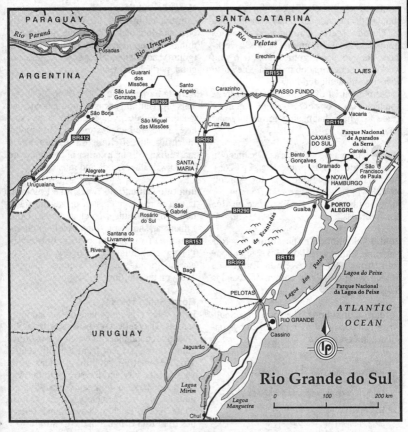

Rio Grande do Sul

Information

Don't forget that Porto Alegre has distinct seasonal weather changes: it gets very hot in summer (above 40°C) and you need a good jacket in winter. City beaches are too polluted for swimming.

Tourist Office Epatur (☎ 227-1383), the tourist information agency for the city, has a post in the Usina do Gasômetro, the old thermoelectric power station, at Avenida Presidente João Goulart 551. It has an excellent map of the city, with descriptions of the main attractions in Spanish and English. It's open from 9 am to 6 pm.

CRTur (☎ 221-7147) has information about both city and state. They're in the Casa de Cultura Marío Quintana, at Rua dos Andradas 736, on the ground floor. On weekdays, they're open from 9 am to 6 pm; weekend hours are noon to 6 pm. They also have a booth at the rodoviária.

From a tourist office, newsstand or large hotel, pick up a copy of *Programa*, a monthly guide to what's happening in the city and state.

Money There are lots of casas de câmbio in Porto Alegre. Try Exprinter (☎ 221-8266), Avenida Salgado Filho 247, or Aerotur (☎ 228-8144), on the ground floor in the same building as the CRTur office on Rua dos Andradas.

Post & Telephone The post office is at Rua Siqueira Campos 1100. Make telephone calls from CRT, at Avenida Borges de Medeiros 512, on the corner of Avenida Salgado Filho.

Foreign Consulates The following South American countries are represented by consulates in Port Alegre:

Argentina
Rua Prof Annes Dias 112, 1st floor (☎ 224-6810)
Paraguay
Quintino Bocaiuva 554, sala 302 (☎ 346-1314)
Uruguay
Rua Siqueira Campos 1171, 6th floor
(☎ 224-3499)

Museu Histórico Júlio de Castilhos

Near the cathedral, at Rua Duque de Caixas 1231, this interesting museum contains diverse objects concerning the history of the state: things such as special moustache cups, a pair of giant's shoes and a very intricate wooden chair. It's open from 9 am to 5 pm Tuesday to Friday and from noon to 5 pm on weekends.

Museu de Arte do Rio Grande do Sul

In the Praça da Alfândega, this one has a good collection of works by gaúcho artists. Hours are 10 am to 7 pm Tuesday to Sunday.

Mercado Público

Constructed in 1869, the market is a lively one, and lots of stalls sell the unique tea-drinking equipment of the gaúchos: the *cuia* (gourd) and *bomba* (silver straw). These are good, portable souvenirs.

Parque Farroupilha

This big, central park is a good place to see gaúchos at play. If you're due for some exercise, there are bicycles to rent. On Sunday morning, the Brique da Redenção, a market/fair, fills up a corner of the park with antiques, leather goods and music.

Instituto Gaúcho de Tradição e Folclore

If you're really interested in gaúcho traditions, this institute's chief archivist, Dona Lilian, can show you some excellent photographs. You can also buy books (in Portuguese) relating to every aspect of gaúcho life. It's at Rua Siqueira Campos 1184, on the 5th floor.

Morro Santa Teresa

Porto Alegre is renowned for its stunning sunsets. They reflect on the waters of the Rio Guaíba. A good place to watch one is Morro Santa Teresa, six km from the city centre. This 131-metre-high hill provides good views of the city and the river. On the way up there, have a look at Porto Alegre's unusual, high-rise cemetery. To get to Morro Santa Teresa, catch a 'Nova Santa Teresa' bus from Rua Uruguai in the Centro.

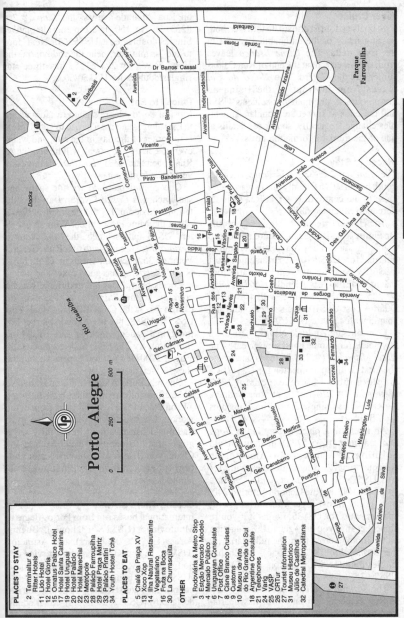

Porto Alegre

0   250   500 m

PLACES TO STAY

2 Terminaltur &
  Ritter Hotels
11 João Hotel
12 Hotel Glória
15 Ornatus Palace Hotel
17 Hotel Santa Catarina
19 Hotel Uruguai
20 Hotel Paládio
22 Hotel Marechal
23 Metrópole
28 Palácio Farroupilha
29 Hotel Praça Matriz
33 Paládio Piratini
34 Youth Hostel Tchê

PLACES TO EAT

5 Chalé da Praça XV
13 Xoco Xop
14 Ilha Natural Restaurante
  Vegetariano
16 Fruta na Boca
30 La Churrasquita

OTHER

1 Rodoviária & Metro Stop
3 Estação Mercado Modelo
4 Mercado Público
6 Uruguayan Consulate
7 Post Office
8 Cisne Branco Cruises
9 Customs
10 Museu de Arte
  do Rio Grande do Sul
18 Argentine Consulate
21 Telephones
24 Varig
25 VASP
26 CRTur
27 Tourist Information
31 Museu Histórico
32 Júlio de Castilhos
32 Catedral Metropolitana

River Cruise

Two boats do tourist cruises on the river, both passing many of the uninhabited islands in the river delta. The *Cisne Branco* leaves from the waterfront at the end of Rua Caldas Júnior, in the Centro. The *Noiva do Caí* leaves from in front of the Usina do Gasômetro. A one-hour cruise costs US$4 and the ones at sunset are popular. Timetables change frequently, so ask for details at one of the tourist information posts.

Places to Stay

The *Tchê* (☎ 225-3581) is Porto Alegre's youth hostel. It's a friendly place, reasonably close to the centre of town, at Rua Coronel Fernando Machado 681.

The *Hotel Uruguai* (☎ 228-7864), at Rua Dr Flores 371, is a clean, secure and cheap place to stay. They have single/double quartos for US$5/10. Apartamentos cost US$6/12. Nearby, at Avenida Vigarió José Inácio 644, the very friendly *Hotel Palácio* (☎ 225-3467) is popular with travellers. Quartos cost US$10/15 a single/double and apartamentos go for US$15/23.

Over on Rua Andrade Neves, there are a few hotels (and some good spots to eat). The *Hotel Marechal* (☎ 228-3076) is one of the cheapest, with apartamentos for US$9/12 a single/double. More expensive, the *Metrópole* (☎ 226-1800), at Rua Andrade Neves 59, has single/double apartamentos for US$15/25.

An interesting place to stay is the *Hotel Praça Matriz* (☎ 25-5772), in an ornate old building at Largo João Amorim de Albequerque 72. Singles/doubles with TV cost US$18/30. The *Hotel Santa Catarina* (☎ 224-9044), at Rua General Vitorino 240, is a good mid-range alternative, with apartamentos for US$35. Forget it if you're alone, because you only get a 10% reduction on the room. Across from the rodoviária, try the *Terminaltur* (☎ 227-1656), which has singles/doubles with air-con and TV for US$20/35.

The *Ornatus Palace Hotel* (☎ 221-4555), at Rua General Vitorino 146, has apartamentos for US$59/66 a single/double. Back on Rua Andrade Neves, the *Lido* (☎ 26-8233), at No 150, is a top-end alternative. Singles/doubles cost US$55/70. Next door to the Terminaltur, near the rodoviária, the *Hotel Ritter* (☎ 221-8155) has three-star singles/doubles for US$50/60.

Places to Eat

Most of Porto Alegre's good restaurants are in the suburbs and are a hassle to get to. Meat is the order of the day in the city, and wherever you are, a juicy steak will be nearby. At Rua Riachuelo 1331, *La Churrasquita* is a vegetarian's nightmare.

One central place to try for sucos and sandwiches is *Caseiro Natural*, in the subterraneo Malcom. Try the ice cream at *Banca 40*, at the Mercado Público. With an excellent US$3 buffet lunch, the *Ilha Natural Restaurante Vegetariano*, at Rua General Votorino 35, packs the locals in. Close by, at No 98, *Xoco Xop* has good cakes and juices.

Locals brag about the traditional gaúcho cooking at the *Pulperia*, at Trevessa do Carmo 76, at the Cidade Baixa. Meals cost US$5 to US$8, but it's a good splurge. For traditional gaúcho cooking and a folkloric floorshow, try *Tio Flor*, at Avenida Getúlio Vargas 1700. It's not too expensive and the show is well done.

One real Porto Alegre tradition is to have a late afternoon chopp at the *Chalé da Praça XV*, on Praça 15 de Novembro, in front of the market. Constructed in 1885, it's the most traditional bar/restaurant in the city, and a great place to people-watch. Around the Chalé, you'll see old-fashioned street photographers, known in Portuguese as lambe-lambes.

Getting There & Away

International buses run from Porto Alegre to Montevideo (US$27, 13 hours), Buenos Aires (US$52, 24 hours) and Asunción (US$36, 16 hours). Other buses service Foz do Iguaçu (US$25, 18 hours), Florianópolis (US$12, 7½ hours), Curitiba (US$17, 11 hours), São Paulo (US$27, 18 hours) and Rio de Janeiro (US$37, 27 hours). Road conditions in the state are generally excellent.

Getting Around

Porto Alegre has a one-line metro that the locals call Trensurb. It has 15 stations, but the only ones of any use to the visitor are the central station by the port (called Estação Mercado Modelo), the rodoviária (which is the next stop) and the airport (three stops further on). The metro runs from 5 am to 11 pm. A ride costs US$0.25.

LITORAL GAÚCHO

The Litoral Gaúcho is a 500-km strip along the state of Rio Grande do Sul – from Torres (in the north) to Chuí (at the Uruguayan border). Of all Brazil's coast, this stretch is the least distinguished, the least varied. The beaches are really one long beach uninterrupted by geographical variations, wide open, with little vegetation and occasional dunes. The sea here is choppier and the water less translucent than in Santa Catarina.

In winter, currents from the Antarctic bring cold, hard winds to the coast. Bathing suits disappear, as do most people. Most hotels shut down in March, and the summer beach season doesn't return until November at the earliest, with the arrival of the northern winds.

The three big resort towns on the north coast are Torres, Capão da Canoa and Tramandaí. Torres, the furthest from Porto Alegre, is only three hours away by car. All three have medium-sized airports, luxury hotels and up-market nightlife, and they all fill up in summer with Porto Alegrenses, Uruguayans and Argentines. This is not a place to get away from it all. There are many campgrounds and cheaper hotels in the towns, but the flavour is much more that of well-to-do weekend resorts than of fishing villages.

Torres

Torres is 205 km from Porto Alegre. It is well known for its fine beaches and the beautiful, basalt-rock formations along the coast. This is good country in which to walk and explore, and if you can get here early or late in the season, when the crowds have thinned

out, it's especially worthwhile. There is also an ecological reserve, on the Ilha dos Lobos.

Information There's a really good tourist office on the corner of Avenida Barão do Rio Branco and Rua General Osório. It publishes a list of hotels, including the cheapest ones. There are a few câmbios in town. Try Brasiltur, at Rua Corte Real 950. For travellers' cheques, there is a Banco do Brasil branch.

Festival A big drawcard over the last few years has been the ballooning festival, held in the middle of April.

Places to Stay Torres has plenty of campgrounds and is full of hotels, a surprising number of which are simple and reasonably priced. If you're there in the low season, make sure you get a low-season discount – you should pay considerably less than the summer rate.

The cheapest hotel in Torres is the *Hotel Medusa* (☎ 664-2378), at Rua Benjamin Constant 828. Singles/doubles are US$5/9. At Avenida Barão do Rio Branco 148, the *Hotel Mar del Plata* (☎ 664-1665) is a good place, with doubles for US$20. The town's best hotel is the four-star *Continental Torres* (☎ 664-1811), at Rua Plínio Kroeff 405, next to the Rio Mampituba.

Places to Eat At last count there were more than 35 restaurants in Torres. For seafood, *Mariscão*, at Avenida Beira Mar 145, is recommended. For churrasco, *Bom Gosto*, at Barão do Rio Branco 242, is excellent. A tasty pizza is served by *Ravena*, at No 117.

Capão da Canoa

This smaller resort, 140 km from Porto Alegre, lacks the glamour and glitz of Torres. Its best-known beach is Praia de Atlântida, three km from town. The beach is big and broad, and there's an active windsurfing scene on the lagoons.

Places to Stay As in Torres, there are several campgrounds here. For less expensive lodging, try the *Dalpiaz*, at Avenida Arariboia 787, with basic but clean quartos for US$3 per person. The *City*, in an old building at Rua Pindorama 513, has double apartamentos for US$20, without breakfast. At Atlântida beach, three km away, the *Atlântida* (☎ 665-2032) is the most expensive hotel in Capão, with doubles for US$85.

Places to Eat Lots of the restaurants here close down over winter. In summer, try the *Taberna Don Ciccilo*, at Rua Guaracy 1826. *Espetinho Gaúcho*, at Rua Tupinambá 583, has a cheap buffet (US$3).

Tramandaí

Only 120 km from Porto Alegre, Tramandaí's permanent population of some 15,000 swells to half a million in January. On summer weekends, the beaches are the busiest in the state; they're good, though not as nice as those around Torres.

Festival There is a good festival here in late June, the Festa de São Pedro, with a procession of boats on the sea.

Places to Stay Tramandaí has a lot of camping and several less-expensive hotels, but reservations are still in order during January and February. There's a good youth hostel (☎ 226-5380) on Rua Belém.

In the centre, the *Centenário* (☎ 661-1788), at Travesa Pellegrini 42, has small, clean apartamentos for US$16 a double. Close to the beach, at Avenida Fernando Amarel 1202, the *Siri* (☎ 661-1460) rents well-maintained apartamentos for US$22 a double.

Places to Eat Most of the town's restaurants are on Avenida Emancipação. At No 265, *Palato* is good for seafood, as is *Taverna do Willy*, at No 315. *Yellows*, at No 323, has a more varied menu.

Chuí

The small border town of Chuí is about 225 km south of Rio Grande on a good paved road. One side of the main street, Avenida Brasil, is Brazilian; the other side is the Uruguayan town of Chuy. The Brazilian side is full of Uruguayans doing their monthly grocery shopping, buying car parts and taking care of their clothing needs for the next six months. The Uruguayan side is a good place to change money, buy cheap, duty-free Scotch whisky and post letters.

Visas It's much better to get your Uruguayan visa in Porto Alegre than at the border at Chuí, but it can be done here. You won't need a medical examination, but you do have to wait overnight. The Uruguayan Consulate (☎ 65-1151), at Rua Venezuela 311, is open from 9 am to 3 pm. Visas cost US$20.

Places to Stay & Eat Hopefully, you've had the good sense to organise your visas well before arriving in Chuí and are on a direct bus to your destination. If you haven't, you're in travellers' purgatory: a dusty, dirty border town waiting overnight for your visa.

There are a few simple hotels. Try the *Hotel e Restaurante São Francisco* (☎ 65-1096), at Rua Colombia 741. It charges US$6 per person. Across the road, *Hospedagem Bianca* and *Hospedagem Roberto* are a bit cheaper. In Uruguay, the *Plaza Hotel*, at Rua General Artigas 553, has singles/doubles for US$20/30.

The restaurant in the São Francisco is as good as any around town. Fast food is readily available in both countries.

Getting There & Away The rodoviária is at Rua Venezuela 247, and buses leave constantly for most cities in southern Brazil.

You can buy tickets to Montevideo on the Uruguayan side of Avenida Brasil. Seven buses leave daily for Punta del Este and Montevideo, the first at 4 am and the last at midnight.

All buses crossing the border into Uruguay stop at the Polícia Federal post on Avenida Argentina, a couple of km from town. You must get off the bus here to get your Brazilian exit stamp. In Uruguay, the bus will stop again for the Uruguayan officials to check your Brazilian exit stamp.

PELOTAS

If they gave out awards for the most outrageous-looking bus station in Brazil, Pelotas would be a major contender in the 'Imaginative Uses of Concrete' category.

Pelotas, 251 km south of Porto Alegre, was a major port in the 19th century for the export of dried beef, and home to a sizeable British community. The wealth generated is still reflected in the grand, neoclassical mansions around the main square, Praça General Osório. Today the town is an important industrial centre, and much of its canned vegetables, fruits and sweets is exported.

There's really no reason to stay in Pelotas, but if you're waiting at the rodoviária for a bus connection and you have some time to spare, it's worth going into the centre for a look.

Places to Stay

If you do get stuck here, *The Rex* (☎ 22-1163), at Praça Coronel Osório 205, has quartos for US$8/12 and apartamentos for US$10/15. The *Palace* (☎ 22-2223), at Rua 7 de Setembro 354, is a bit cheaper.

Places to Eat

The *Shangay*, at Rua 7 de Setembro 301, has reasonable Chinese food. On the same street, at No 306, the *Bavaria* serves German food. Pelotas is renowned for its sweets, which can be sampled from the many stalls on Rua 7 de Setembro, or at *Otto Especialidades*, next to the Bavaria restaurant.

RIO GRANDE

Once an important cattle centre, Rio Grande lies near the mouth of the Lagoa dos Patos, Brazil's biggest lagoon. To the north, the coast along the lagoa is lightly inhabited. There's a poor dirt road along this stretch, which is connected with Rio Grande by a small ferry. While not a great drawcard, this active port city is more interesting than Pelotas if you want to break your journey in this area.

Information

There's a tourist office at Rua Riachuelo 355,

but it's rarely open in the low season. The only tourist brochure in town is available from any travel agency or big hotel, such as the Charrua. A good place to change money is at the Turisbel, a bar and gemstone shop at Rua Luíz Loreá 407. Its English-speaking Greek owner will even change Australian dollars. For travellers' cheques, there is a Banco do Brasil branch. The post office is at Rua General Netto 115.

Catedral de São Pedro

The oldest church in the state, this cathedral was erected by the Portuguese colonists. In baroque style, it's classified as part of the Patrimônio Histórico. Even if you don't usually look at churches, this is an interesting one.

Museu Oceanográphico

This interesting museum on Avenida Perimetra, two km from the centre, is the most complete of its type in Latin America. It has a large shell collection, and skeletons of whales and dolphins. It's open daily from 9 to 11 am and 2 to 5 pm.

Other Museums

The Museu da Cidade is in the old customs house which Dom Pedro II ordered built on Rua Richuelo. It's open on weekdays from 9.30 to 11.30 am and 2.30 to 5 pm and on Sunday from 2.30 to 5 pm. Across the road is the Museu do Departamento Estadual de Portos, Rios e Canais (DEPREC), which houses the machinery used during the construction of the large breakwater. It's open on weekdays from 8 to 11.30 am and 1.30 to 5.30 pm.

São José do Norte

Boats leave from the terminal at the waterfront every 40 minutes and make the trip across the mouth of the Lagoa dos Patos to the fishing village of São José do Norte. This is a nice trip to do around sunset. The last boat back to Rio Grande leaves at 7 pm. The round trip costs US$2.

Places to Stay

There are a few cheap hotels in Rio Grande, but the one to head for is the *Paris* (☎ 32-8944), in a 19th-century building at Rua Marechal Floriano 112. It's seen better days, but is still impressive, and its courtyard is an excellent place in which to sit and contemplate the glory days of the city. Single/double quartos cost US$7/11, apartamentos US$10/14. Don't miss this one, even though getting there is a bit of a hike.

Moving up in price (but not in character), there is the *Europa* (☎ 32-8133; fax 32-1751), opposite Praça Tamandaré, at Rua General Netto 165. Singles/doubles cost US$23/32. The top hotel in town is the *Charrua Hotel* (☎ & fax 32-8033), on Rua Duque de Caixas, opposite Praça Xavier Ferreira. It usually costs US$40 a double, but in the low season, they'll cut this to US$30.

Places to Eat

For seafood, try the *Pescal*, at Rua Marechal Andrea 269. They're closed on Sunday. *Marcos*, Avenida Silva Paes 400, has a varied menu and a nice ambience. For coffee and a sandwich, *Restaurante Nova Gruta Baiana*, on Rua Marechal Floriano, opposite Praça Xavier Ferreira, is good. For a buffet lunch, the *Charrua Hotel* puts on a good spread.

Getting There & Away

The rodoviária is about six blocks from the centre, at Rua Vice Admiral Abreu 737. Buses connect Rio Grande with Uruguay and with all major cities in southern Brazil.

AROUND RIO GRANDE
Cassino

Twenty-five km south of Rio Grande, reached by local bus from Praça Tamandaré, Cassino is a D-grade beach resort popular in summer with Uruguayans and Argentines. If you like littered, windswept beaches, brown sea water and cars zipping up and down the beach, this is the place for you.

SERRA GAÚCHA

North of Porto Alegre, you quickly begin to climb into the Serra Gaúcha. The ride is beautiful, as are the mountain towns of Gramado and Canela, 140 km from Porto Alegre. First settled by Germans (in 1824) and later by Italians (in the 1870s), the region is as close to the Alps as Brazil gets. It's known as the Região das Hortênsias (Hydrangea Region). Both Gramado and Canela are popular resorts and are crowded with Porto Alegrenses in all seasons, but particularly when it's hottest in the big city. There are plenty of hotels and restaurants, especially in Gramado, and many have a German influence. Prices are high by Brazilian standards.

Hikers abound in the mountains here. In winter there are occasional snowfalls and in spring the hills are blanketed with flowers. The best spot is the Parque Estadual do Caracol, reached by local bus from Canela, eight km away.

Gramado

This popular mountain resort is a favourite with well-to-do Argentines, Uruguayans, Paulistas and gaúchos. It has lots of cosy restaurants, well-manicured gardens and expensive, Swiss-style chalet/hotels.

Information There's a useful Centro de Informações in the centre of town, on Praça Major Nicoletti, which has maps, and information on most hotels and restaurants. It's open from 9 am to 9 pm.

Parks Well-kept parks close to town include the Lago Negro, at Rua 25 de Julho 175, and the Parque Knorr, at the end of Rua Bela Vista. The Lago Negro park has pine trees and a small lake, while the Parque Knorr has lots of flowers and a good view of the spectacular Vale do Quilombo. There's also the Lago Joaquina Rita Bier, a lake surrounded by hydrangeas, at Rua Leopoldo Rosenfeldt.

Festival Each June, Gramado hosts the Brazilian Film Festival. It's a big event, and attracts the jet set.

Places to Stay There is no really cheap accommodation in Gramado. The *Dinda*

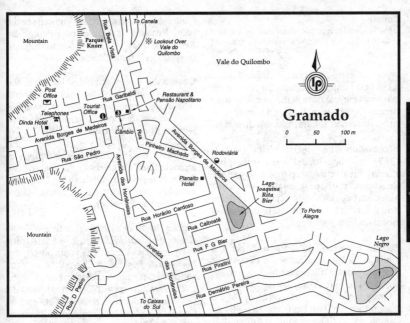

Hotel (☎ & fax 286-2810), at Rua Augusto Zatti 160, has apartamentos for US$20/30 a single/double, in the middle of town. Another recommended hotel is the *Planalto* (☎ 286-1210), across from the rodoviária, at Avenida Borges de Medeiros 2001. It's pleasant and clean, with plenty of hot water and a balcony for each room. It's better than some more expensive places, with single/double apartamentos for US$25/35. Close to the centre, at Borges de Medeiros 2512, the *Restaurant & Pensão Napolitano* (☎ 286-1847) is a good deal – its double rooms go for US$22.

There's no shortage of top-end places. The best ones are out on the road between Gramado and Canela. The *Villa Bella Gramado* (☎ 286-2688; fax 286-2812) has doubles from US$60.

Places to Eat Every second place in Gramado seems to be a restaurant, especially along Avenida das Hortênsias. A good churrascaria is *Recanto Gaúcho*, at No 5532. They have a rodízio (US$7) and live music. Fondue lovers should try *Le Chalet de la Fondue*, at No 1297. For vegetarians, *Natural*, at No 1370, has a good variety of dishes for US$5.

In the centre, try the *Napolitano* (for pasta), or *Tio Muller*, at Avenida Borges de Medeiros 4029 (with a rodízio of German food for US$6).

Getting There & Away The rodoviária is close to the centre, at Avenida Borges de Mendeiros 2100. There are frequent buses to Porto Alegre (US$4, two hours). Local buses from the rodoviária make the 15-minute trip to Canela.

Getting Around Bicycles are a good way to move around here. They can be rented at Rua Garibaldi 144 for US$10 a day.

Canela

If you're scared of leopards, hate mosquitos, but want to do some ecological tourism, come to Canela.
Canela tourist brochure

While not as up-market as Gramado, Canela is the best jumping-off point for some great hikes and bicycle rides in the area. There are cheaper hotels here than in Gramado, so budget travellers should make this their base.

Information The tourist office (☎ 282-1287) in Praça João Correa is helpful, offering a reasonable map that shows all the attractions. Staff speak English, will assist with hotel bookings and can put you in touch with the outfits that arrange rafting trips and mountain-bike adventures.

Parque Estadual do Caracol Eight km from Canela, the major attraction of this park is a spectacular 130-metre-high waterfall. You don't have to do any hiking to see it, as it's very close to the park entrance. On the road to the park, two km from the centre of Canela, is a 700-year-old, 42-metre-tall araucária pine.

The park is open daily from 7.30 am to 6 pm. Entry is US$0.40. A public bus to the park, marked 'Caracol Circular', leaves the rodoviária at 8.15 am, noon and 5.30 pm.

Ferradura A seven-km hike from just outside the park entrance brings you to Ferradura, a stunning 400-metre-deep horse-shoe canyon formed by the Rio Santa Cruz. You can camp in here, but you have to bring everything with you.

Parque das Sequoias This park at Rua Godofredo Raimundo 1747 was created in the 1940s by Curt Menz, a botanist who cultivated more than 70 different tree species with seeds from all over the world. This plantation occupies 10 hectares, and the rest of the park (25 hectares) is native forest. The park has lots of trails and a pousada.

Morros Pelado, Queimado & Dedão These hills provide great views of the Vale do Quilombo, and on clear days you can see the coast. Reached via the road to the Parque das Sequoias, they're five, 5.5 and 6.5 km (respectively) from Canela.

Castelinho One of the oldest houses in the area, Castelinho, is on the road to the park. Now a pioneer museum, a German restaurant and a chocolate shop, Castelinho was built without using metal nails.

Festival From 26 to 28 May, 80,000 pilgrims arrive in Canela to celebrate the Festa de NS de Caravaggio. A highlight of the festival is a six-km procession from the Igreja Matrix to the Parque do Saiqui.

Places to Stay Camping is available at *Camping Club do Brasil*, eight km from town on the park road. The youth hostel, the *Pousada do Viajante* (☎ 282-2017), is clean, and close to the centre, at Rua Ernesto Urban.

The *Hotel Turis* (☎ 282-2136), at Avenida Osvaldo Aranha 223, is the best cheapie in Canela. It's clean and friendly, and reasonable value (US$9 per person, including a bit of breakfast). The *Hotel Bela Vista* (☎ 282-1327), at Rua Osvaldo Aranha 160, has rooms and separate cabanas for US$21/30 a single/double.

The *Vila Vecchia* (☎ 232-1051), at Rua Melvin Jones 137, has apartamentos starting at US$28 a double. The *Pousada das Sequoias*, in the park of the same name, is two km from the centre. They have small chalets in picturesque surroundings for US$40.

The best top-end place to stay is the *Laje de Pedra* (☎ 282-1530; fax 282-2276), three km from the centre, near the airport. It has a great view of the Vale do Quilombo, as well as all the amenities you'd expect from a five-star hotel.

Places to Eat Highly recommended is *Cantina de Nono*, at Avenida Osvaldo Aranha 161. A plate of their comida caseira costs US$5. Big meat eaters will enjoy *Bifão & Cia*, at Avenida Osvaldo Aranha 301. *Casa Della Nonna*, at Avenida Júlio de

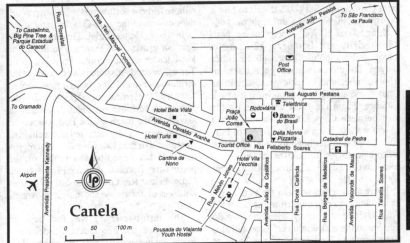

Canela

To Castelinho,
Big Pine Tree &
Parque Estadual
do Caracol

To Gramado

Airport

Rua Floresta

Rua Ten Manoel Correa

To São Francisco
de Paula

Avenida João Pessoa

Post Office

Rua Augusto Pestana

Hotel Bela Vista

Avenida Osvaldo Aranha

Hotel Turis

Praça João Correa

Rodoviária

Telefônica

Banco do Brasil

Della Nonna Pizzaria

Tourist Office   Rua Felisberto Soares

Catedral de Pedra

Cantina de Nono

Hotel Vila Vecchia

Avenida Presidente Kennedy

Rua Melvin Jones

Avenida Julio de Castilhos

Rua Dona Carlinda

Rua Borges do Medeiros

Avenida Visconde de Mauá

Rua Teixeira Soares

0   50   100 m

Pousada do Viajante
Youth Hostel

THE SOUTH

Castilhos 509, serves good pizzas. For lunch, the restaurant in the *Parque do Caracol* has a varied menu, with prato feitos for US$5.

Getting There & Away The rodoviária is in the centre of town. There are frequent buses from Canela to Porto Alegre, all travelling via Gramado.

Getting Around Ask at the tourist office about bicycle rental.

PARQUE NACIONAL DE APARADOS DA SERRA
One of Brazil's natural wonders, this national park is Rio Grande do Sul's most magnificent area. It is 70 km north of São Francisco de Paula and 18 km from the town of Cambará do Sul.

Things to See
The park preserves one of the country's last araucária forests, but the main attraction is the **Canyon do Itaimbézinho**, a fantastic narrow canyon with sheer 600 to 720-metre parallel escarpments. Two waterfalls drop into this deep incision in the earth, which was formed by the Rio Perdiz's rush to the sea.

Another of the park's attractions is the **Canyon da Fortaleza**, a 30-km stretch of escarpment with 900-metre drops. You can see the coast from here. Nearby, on one of the walls of the canyon, is the **Pedra do Segredo**, a five-metre monolith with a very small base. It's 23 km from Cambará, but unfortunately in a different direction from Itaimbézinho.

Places to Stay
Camping is a good option in this area, and there are good spots near the old Paradouro Hotel in the park and near the Fortaleza canyon.

Cambará do Sul has two hotels: the *Pousada Fortaleza*, 300 metres to the left as you face the city square from the bus station, and the *Hotel São Jorge*, 50 metres to the right. Go to the Pousada Fortaleza first; it's friendlier and not as dilapidated. They charge US$6 per person for decent apartamentos. If there's no one there when you arrive, the owner lives in the house on the left-hand side.

Getting There & Away
If you can't afford the four-hour taxi ride

from Cambará do Sul (US$45), or to hire a car (or aeroplane) for a day, put on your walking shoes if you expect to see both Itaimbézinho and Fortaleza. Hitching is lousy, and no public buses go to either canyon. The closest you can get is three km from Itaimbézinho, by taking the bus to Praia Grande and asking to be dropped at the park entrance. From the other entrance, on the road between Cambará and Tainhas, it's a 15-km walk to Itaimbézinho. To get to Fortaleza, you'll either have to walk 23 km or make a deal with Borges, the taxi driver, to take you there and back (around US$25, but it's worth it).

There are various ways to get to the park itself. One is to come up from the coast via Praia Grande and get off the 'Cambará do Sul' bus at the park entrance. You could also come up from Torres and change buses at Tainhas, but if you miss the connection, there's nowhere to stay in Tainhas. Both these roads from the coast are spectacular. Another route is to come up from São Francisco de Paula and get off at the other entrance to the park.

It's also possible to hike 20 km from Praia Grande into the canyon itself, but this is dangerous without a guide. People have been trapped in the canyon by flash flooding.

If you're driving, follow the 'Faixinal do Sul' signs from Praia Grande.

JESUIT MISSIONS

Soon after the discovery of the New World, the Portuguese and Spanish kings authorised Catholic orders to create missions to convert the natives into Catholic subjects of the crown and the state. The most successful of these orders were the Jesuits, who established a series of missions in a region which spanned parts of Paraguay, Brazil and Argentina. In effect, it was a nation within the colonies, a nation which, at its height in the 1720s, claimed 30 mission villages inhabited by over 150,000 Guaraní Indians. Buenos Aires was merely a village at this time.

Unlike those established elsewhere, these missions succeeded in introducing Western culture without destroying the Indian people, their culture or the Tupi-Guaraní language.

In 1608, Hernandarias, Governor of the Spanish province of Paraguay, ordered the local leader of the Jesuits, Fray Diego de Torres, to send missionaries to convert the infidels, and so in 1609, the first mission was founded. Preferring indoctrination by the Jesuits to serfdom on Spanish estates or slavery at the hands of the Portuguese, the Indians were rapidly recruited into a chain of missions. The missions covered a vast region of land that encompassed much of the present-day Brazilian states of Paraná, Santa Catarina and Rio Grande do Sul as well as portions of Paraguay and northern Argentina.

The Jesuit territory was too large to defend, and the Portuguese bandeirantes found the missionary settlements easy pickings for slave raids. Thousands of Indians were captured, reducing the 13 missions of Guayra (Brazilian territory) to two. Fear of the bandeirante slavers caused these two missions to be abandoned, and the Indians

Statue at the São Miguel das Missões ruins

and Jesuits marched westward and founded San Ignacio Miní (1632), having lost many people in the rapids of the Paraná. The missions north of Iguaçu were decimated by attacks from hostile Indian tribes and were forced to relocate south.

Between 1631 and 1638, activity was concentrated in 30 missions which the mission Indians were able to defend. In one of the bloodiest fights, the battle of Mbororé, the Indians beat back the slavers and secured their lands north of San Javier.

The missions, under administration based in Candelaria, grew crops, raised cattle and prospered. They were miniature cities built around a central church, and included libraries, baptisteries, cemeteries and dormitories for the Indian converts and the priests. The missions became centres of culture and intellect as well as of religion. An odd mix of European baroque and native Guaraní arts, music and painting developed. Indian scholars created a written form of Tupi-Guaraní and, from 1704, published several works in Tupi-Guaraní, using one of the earliest printing presses in South America.

As the missions grew, the Jesuit nation became more independent of Rome and relations with the Vatican became strained. The nation within a nation became an embarrassment to the Iberian kings and, finally, in 1777, the Portuguese minister Marques de Pombal convinced Carlos III to expel the Jesuit priests from Spanish lands. Thus ended, in the opinion of many historians, a grand 160-year experiment in socialism, where wealth was equally divided and religion, intellect and the arts flourished – a utopian island of progress in an age of monarchies and institutionalised slavery. Administration of the mission villages passed into the hands of the colonial government. The communities continued until the early 1800s, when they were destroyed by revolutionary wars of independence, then abandoned.

Today, there are 30 ruined Jesuit missions: seven lie in Brazil (in the western part of Rio Grande do Sul), eight are in the southern region of Itapuá, Paraguay, and the remaining 15 are in Argentina. Of these 15 Argentine missions, 11 lie in the province of Missiones, which hooks like a thumb between Paraguay and the Rio Paraná, and Brazil and the Uruguay and Iguaçu rivers.

Brazilian Missions

São Miguel das Missões This mission, 58 km from Santo Angelo, is the most interesting of the Brazilian ones. Every evening at 8 pm, there's a sound and light show. Also nearby are the missions of São João Batista (on the way to São Miguel) and São Lourenço das Missões (10 km from São João Batista by dirt road).

Paraguayan Missions

The missions of Paraguay, long since abandoned, are only now being restored. The most important mission to see is Trinidad, 25 km from Encarnación. The red-stone ruins are fascinating. If you have the time, see the missions of Santa Rosa, Santiago and Jesus.

Argentine Missions

In Argentina, don't miss San Ignacio Miní, 60 km from Posadas on Ruta Nacional 12. Of lesser stature is mission Santa Maria la Mayor, 111 km away from Posadas on Ruta 110, and mission Candelaria (now a national penitentiary), 25 km from Posadas on Ruta 12. It's possible to cut across the province of Missiones to San Javier (Ruta 4), crossing by ferry to Brazil at Puerto Xavier, or further south at Santo Tome, and taking a ferry across the Rio Uruguay to São Borja, Brazil.

The border at Uruguaiana, 180 km south of São Borja, is more commonly used. Uruguaiana is 180 km from São Borja and 635 km from Porto Alegre. Buses operate to Buenos Aires, Santiago do Chile and Montevideo. The Argentine Consulate (☎ (055) 412-1925) is at Rua Santana 2496, 2nd floor, while the Uruguayan Consulate (☎ (055) 412-1514) is at Rua Duque de Caixas 1606.

Places to Stay & Eat

In Brazil, Santo Angelo has several modest

but proper hotels, but it's great to stay out at São Miguel to see the sound and light show and the sunrise. The missions were always placed on high points in the countryside, so there's a great view. The *Hotel Barichello* is the only place to stay. It's very clean and run by a friendly family. Singles cost US$6 and doubles with a shower are US$12. It's a good place to eat, too.

In Paraguay, Encarnación has a couple of cheap, modest hotels and Chinese restaurants.

Across the Rio Paraná from Encarnación is the capital of the Argentine province of Posadas. A ferry operates from 8 am to noon and from 2 pm until sundown. Everything is more expensive, but the food is better and the lodging (there are 10 hotels to choose from) is fancier.

Getting There & Away

Use Encarnación as a base for visiting the missions of Paraguay. Riza buses leave daily from Ciudad del Este for Encarnación, 320 km south; from Asunción, they depart daily for the 370-km journey to Encarnación on Ruta 1. Either way, it's a pleasant ride through fertile rolling hills, a region where the locals (mostly of German descent) drink a variation of maté called *tereré*.

Getting Around

This is the sort of travelling that's best done by car, but unfortunately, car-rental fees are high and driving a rental car over borders is difficult. It's possible to hire a taxi from any of the three base cities: Posadas, Encarnación and Santo Angelo.

The Central West

ANDREW DRAFFEN

The Central West

Known to Brazilians as the Centro-Oeste, this region includes almost 19% of the country's land area. It's the most sparsely populated region in Brazil, containing only 6% of the total population.

Made up of the states of Mato Grosso, Mato Grosso do Sul, Goiás and the Distrito Federal of Brasília, this massive terrain was until the 1940s the last great unexplored area on earth.

Here, the Planalto Brasileiro has been greatly eroded to form the Guimarães, Parecis and Veadeiros *chapadões* (table-lands) between the river basins. In the south-west of Mato Grosso and the west of Matto Grosso do Sul is the wildlife paradise called the Pantanal Matogrossense. It's a unique geographical depression formed by a huge inland sea which dried up millions of years ago. Large portions become covered by water during the rainy season.

As well as the Pantanal, which is the drawcard of the region, the Central West contains many other natural attractions: national parks in two of the abovementioned tablelands (Chapada dos Guimarães and Chapada dos Veadeiros); the Parque Nacional das Emas; and the Rio Araguaia which extends into the northern state of Tocantins.

There are also interesting colonial towns (Goiás Velho and Pirenópolis) and large, planned cities (Goiânia and Brasília) that are worth a look.

Highlights

- Driving around Brasília looking at its unique architecture and town planning (Distrito Federal)
- The weird and wonderful religious sects around Brasília (Distrito Federal)
- The colonial towns of Goiás Velho and Pirenópolis (Goiás)
- Wildlife spotting in the Pantanal (Mato Grosso and Mato Grosso do Sul)
- The train ride from Corumbá to Campo Grande across the Pantanal (Mato Grosso and Mato Grosso do Sul)
- Piranha fishing in the Pantanal (Mato Grosso do Sul)
- Parque Nacional da Chapada dos Guimarães (Mato Grosso)

Distrito Federal

BRASÍLIA

I sought the curved and sensual line. The curve that I see in the Brazilian hills, in the body of a loved one, in the clouds in the sky and in the ocean waves.
Brasília architect Oscar Niemeyer

Brasília is a utopian horror. It should be a symbol of power, but instead it's a museum of architectural ideas.
Art critic Robert Hughes

The impression I have is that I'm arriving on a different planet.
Cosmonaut Yuri Gagarin

Brasília must have looked good on paper, and still looks good in photos. In 1987 it was added to the UNESCO list of World Heritage Sites, being considered one of the major examples of this century's modern movement in architecture and urban planning. But in the flesh, forget it. The world's great planned city of the 20th century is built for automobiles and air-conditioners, not people. Distances are enormous and no one walks. The sun blazes, with no trees for shelter.

It's a lousy place to visit and no one wanted to live there. Bureaucrats and politicians, who live in the model 'pilot plan' part of the city, were lured to Brasília by 100% salary hikes and big apartments. Still, as soon as the weekend comes, they get out of the city as fast as possible – to Rio, to São Paulo, to their private clubs in the country – anywhere that's less sterile, less organised, less vapid. Brasília is also one of the most expensive cities in Brazil.

The poor have to get out – they have no choice. Mostly from the Northeast, these *candangos* (pioneers) work in the construction and service industries. They live in favelas, which they call 'anti-Brasílias', as far as 30 km from the centre. This physical gulf between haves and have-nots is reminiscent of South Africa's township system.

All this is the doing of three famous Brazilians: an urban planner (Lucio Costa), an architect (Oscar Niemeyer) and a landscape architect (Burle Marx), each the leading figure in his field. They were commissioned by President Juscelino Kubitschek to plan a new inland capital, a city that would catalyse the economic development of Brazil's vast interior. With millions of dirt-poor peasants from the Northeast working around the clock, Brasília was built in an incredible three years – it wasn't exactly finished but it was ready to be the capital (Niemeyer today admits that it was all done too quickly). On 21 April 1960, Brazil's capital was moved from Rio to Brasília and thousands of public servants fell into a deep depression.

The old Brazilian dream of an inland capital had always been dismissed as expensive folly. What possessed Kubitschek to actually do it? Politics. He made the building of Brasília a symbol of the country's determination and ability to become a great economic power. Kubitschek successfully appealed to all Brazilians to put aside their differences and rally to the cause. In doing so, he distracted attention from the country's social and economic problems, gained enormous personal popularity and borrowed heavily from the international banks. His legacy to the country was rampant inflation.

Orientation

Seen from above, Brasília looks like an aeroplane (symbolising the fastest way out of town) or a bow and arrow (signifying the penetration of the interior and the destruction of the indigenous people). The planned city, the *plano piloto*, faces the giant artificial Lago do Paranoá. In the plane's fuselage (or the arrow) are all the government buildings and monuments. The plaza of three powers – the Palácio do Planalto, the Palácio do Congresso and the Palácio da Justiça – is in the cockpit. Out on the wings (*asas*) are block after block of apartment buildings (known as Superquadras or Quadras) but little else.

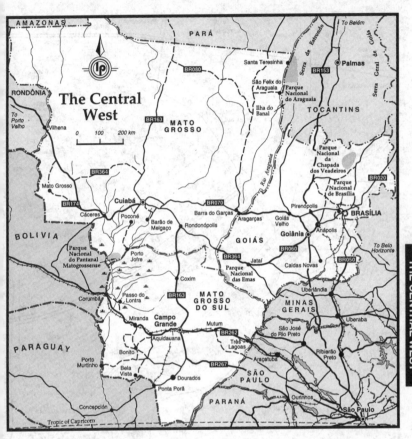

You can rent a car, take a tourist tour or combine a city bus (circular buses leave from the city rodoviária) with some long walks to see the bulk of Brasília's edifices. Remember that many buildings are closed on weekends and at night.

Information
Tourist Office Setur is the government tourist information service. Its office, inconveniently located on the 3rd floor of the Centro de Convenções, is open Monday to Friday from 1 to 6 pm. Setur also operates a tourist desk at the airport, which is open from 8 am to 1 pm and 2 to 6 pm Monday to Friday (from 10 am to 1 pm and 4.30 to 7.30 pm on weekends). If all you need is a map or a list of attractions, simply pick up a brochure from any one of the big hotels or travel agencies. The best map that we found was in the telephone book *Achei! (Found it!) O Guia de Brasília*. It also has lots of tourist information in Portuguese.

Money There are plenty of banks with moneychanging facilities in the Setor Bancário Sul (SBS – Banking Sector South) and Setor Bancário Norte (SBN – Banking

THE CENTRAL WEST

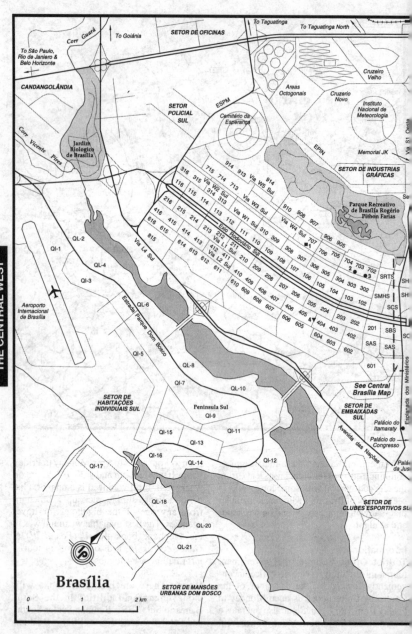

Brasília

0   1   2 km

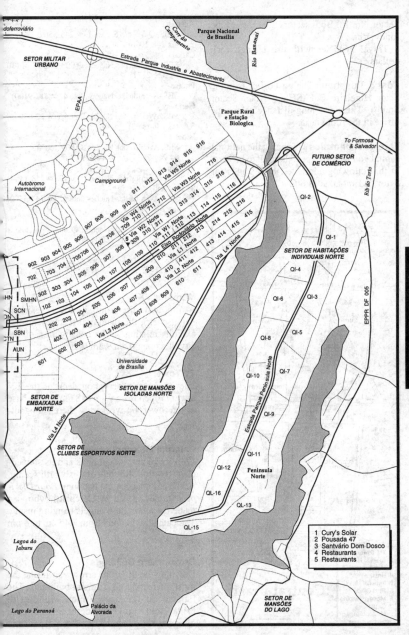

1 Cury's Solar
2 Pousada 47
3 Santvário Dom Dosco
4 Restaurants
5 Restaurants

Sector North). Both sectors are close to the rodoviária.

Travel agencies will also change cash dollars.

Post & Telephone The post office is in the Setor Hoteleiro Sul (SHS – Hotel Sector South). There's a long-distance telephone office in the rodoviária.

Foreign Embassies This being the national capital you would expect them all to be here. In the following addresses, SES stands for Setor de Embaixadas Sul.

Australia
SHIS, Q I-9, cj 16, casa 1 (☎ 248-5569; fax 248-1066)
Canada
SES, Avenida das Nações, Q 803, lote 16, sl 130 (☎ 321-2171)
France
SES, Avenida das Nações, lote 4 (☎ 312-9100)
Germany
SES, Avenida das Nações, lote 25 (☎ 224-7273; fax 244-6063)
Israel
SES, Avenida das Nações, Q 809, lote 38 (☎ 244-7675; fax 244-6129)
Sweden
SES, Avenida das Nações, lote 29 (☎ 243-1444)
Switzerland
SES, Avenida das Nações, lote 41 (☎ 244-5500; fax 244-5711)
UK
SES, Avenida das Nações, Q 801, cj K lote 8 (☎ 225-2710; fax 225-1777)
USA
SES, Avenida das Nações, Q 801, lote 3 (☎ 321-7272; fax 225-9136)

Memorial JK

Along with the tomb of JK (President Kubitschek), the memorial features several exhibits relating to the construction of the city. It's open from 9 am to 6 pm.

TV Tower

The 75-metre observation deck of the TV tower is open from 9 am to 8 pm. At the base of the tower, on weekends, there's a handicrafts fair.

Catedral Metropolitana

With its 16 curved columns and its stained-glass interior, the cathedral is worth seeing. At the entrance are the haunting *Four Disciples* statues carved by Ceschiatti, who also made the aluminium angels hanging inside. The cathedral is open from 7.45 am to 6 pm daily.

Government Buildings

Down by the tip of the arrow you'll find the most interesting government buildings. The Palácio do Itamaraty (open Monday to Friday until 4 pm) is one of the best – a series of arches surrounded by a reflecting pool and

THE CENTRAL WEST

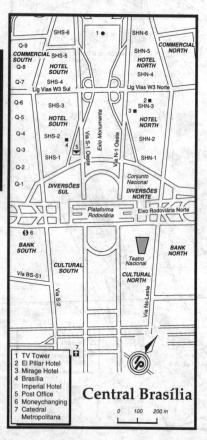

1	TV Tower
2	El Pillar Hotel
3	Mirage Hotel
4	Brasília Imperial Hotel
5	Post Office
6	Moneychanging
7	Catedral Metropolitana

Central Brasília

0   100   200 m

landscaped by Burle Marx. There's also the Palácio da Justiça, the Supreme Court (open Monday to Friday from noon to 6 pm), with water cascading between its arches, and the Palácio do Congresso (open Tuesday to Friday from 10 am to noon and 2 to 5 pm), with the 'dishes' and twin towers. The presidential Palácio da Alvorada is not open to visitors.

Santuário Dom Bosco

As impressive as the cathedral, or perhaps even more so, the Santuário Dom Bosco (Dom Bosco's Shrine) is made of concrete columns, with blue stained-glass windows. Located at Quadra 702 Sul, it's open daily from 8 am to 6 pm.

Parks

The **Parque Nacional de Brasília** ecological reserve is a good place to relax if you're stuck in the city. This park is open Tuesday to Sunday from 9 am to 5 pm, and is very popular on weekends. Apart from the attraction of its natural swimming pools, it is home to a number of endangered animals, including deer, banded anteaters, giant armadillos and maned wolves. The 'Agua Mineral' bus from the city rodoviária goes past the front gate.

Another good park is the city park, **Parque Recreativo de Brasília Rogério Pithon Farias**, where you'll find a swimming pool, and small lunch places at which to grab a snack.

Organised Tours

If you want to save your feet, guided tours of the city cost around US$18. The Hotel Garvey-Park is the travel-agency capital of Brasília, and most companies there offer sightseeing tours. You can also book bus tours at the airport or the rodoviária.

Places to Stay – bottom end

Camping is possible not far from the city, in the Setor de Garagens Oficiais. To get there, take the No 109 or No 143 'Buriti' bus from the rodoviária. Campsites cost US$3.

There are no cheap hotels in Brasília, but there are a few cheap pensions, mostly located on W3 Sul (to get there from the rodoviária, catch any bus going along W3 Sul). Many of them are used by people getting treatment at nearby hospitals, so they're often full. *Pousada 47* (☎ 224-4894) is a clean, well-kept place that charges US$10 per person. It's at Quadra 703, Bloco A, Casa 41/47. Next door, at Casa 54, *Pousada da Nilza* (☎ 226-5786) also charges US$10 a head, but it's much more dilapidated. *Getúlio Valente* (☎ 226-8507) runs two pousadas in the area; one is mostly for hospital patients and the other, much nicer one is for travellers. Reception is at Quadra 703, Bloco I, Casa 73. Valente charges US$15 per person.

Cury's Solar (☎ 243-6252) is popular with travellers. Neusa Batista runs a friendly place in which guests are encouraged to make themselves at home. Prices vary with room size: singles cost US$10 to US$15 and doubles are US$14 to US$24. Get off at the stop between Quadras 707 and 708. The house is in the third row from the street in 707. The address is Quadra 707 Sul, Bloco I, Casa 15. There's no sign, but it's easy to find.

Places to Stay – middle

The cheapest hotels fall into the mid-range, two-star category. A good one is the *Mirage Hotel* (☎ 225-7150), in the Setor Hoteleiro Norte (SHN, Q 02, Bloco N). They charge US$22/27 for singles/doubles. The restaurant there is good and the service very friendly. The *El Pillar Hotel* (☎ 224-5915) is also in the Setor Hoteleiro Norte (SHN, Q 03, Bloco F), with rooms for the same price as the Mirage. On the other side of the Eixo Monumental, in Setor Hoteleiro Sul, the *Brasília Imperial Hotel* (☎ 321-8747) has singles/doubles for US$25/30.

Keep in mind that whenever there's a special event in Brasília, all these hotels will be full. Many hotels in the hotel sectors give discounts of up to 40% on the weekends.

There are cheaper hotels out of town towards Taguatinga, in a sector called the SIA, but you'll save only a few dollars and

Brasília – Capital of the Third Millennium

In 1883 an Italian priest, João Bosco, prophesied that a new civilisation would arise between parallels 15 and 20 and that its capital would be built between parallels 15 and 16, on the edge of an artificial lake. Brasília is considered by many people to be that city, and a number of cults have sprung up in the area.

About 45 km from Brasília you'll find the Vale do Amanhecer (Valley of the Dawn), founded in 1959 by a clairvoyant, Tia Neiva. The valley is actually a small town, where you can see (or take part in) Egyptian, Greek, Aztec, Indian, Gypsy, Inca, Trojan and Afro-Brazilian rituals. They take place daily at 12.30, 2.30 and 6.30 pm. The 2000 mediums who live there follow the 'Doctrine of the Dawn'. They believe that a new civilisation will come with the third millennium. The main temple was inspired by the spiritual advice received by Tia Neiva. In the centre is an enormous Star of David, which forms a lake, pierced by an arrow.

About 80 km from the valley, near Santo Antônio do Descoberto, is the Cidade Ecléctica (Eclectic City), founded in 1956 by Yokanam, an ex-airline pilot. The main aim of its 3000 believers is the unification of all religions on the planet, and the values of fraternity and equality are expounded. Their ceremonies take place on Wednesday and Friday at 8 pm and on Sunday at 3 pm. There are strict dress regulations, but if you're not dressed suitably, they will give you a special tunic to wear.

In Brasília itself, the Granja do Ipê (Ipê Estate), on the southern exit from the city, is the site of the City of Peace & Holistic University. This institution aims to form a new generation with a mentality suited to the needs of the third millennium. The Templo da Boa Vontade (Temple of Goodwill) is at 915 Sul. It incorporates seven pyramids, joined to form a cone that is topped with the biggest raw crystal you will ever see.

Some people also believe that, in certain regions around Brasília, extraterrestrial contacts are more likely – on Km 69 of the BR-351 highway, for instance, or on the plateau that exists in the satellite city of Brasilândia. Believe it or not! ∎

spend a lot of time on buses. Since you only need to stay in Brasília for one or two days to see everything, do yourself a favour and spend the extra money.

Places to Stay – top end

The *Hotel Nacional Brasília* (☎ 321-7575; fax 223-9213) and the *Hotel Carlton* (☎ 224-8819; fax 226-8109) are two popular five-star lodgings. The former has an adjoining shopping mall and the latter is often the choice of delegations from the USA. Both have doubles starting at US$100. There are lots of three and four, as well as a few other five-star hotels in the hotel sectors. The Setur desk at the airport has a complete list, with prices.

Places to Eat

Both the shopping complexes near the rodoviária have lots of places to eat, with many offering lunch specials. The one on the north side (Conjunto Nacional) has the best selection.

Restaurants are located along the main avenues or in between the quadras. A couple of places with a good selection of restaurants and bars are the spaces between Quadras 405 and 404 Sul and between Quadras 308 and 309 Norte.

In the following addresses, SCL means Setor Comércio Local, which is the space provided in the quadras for shops, restaurants, etc. N or S means Norte (North) or Sul (South), followed by the quadra number, the block number and the store number.

There are good restaurants scattered around, too. A popular place is the *Bar Academia*, at SCLN 308, Bloco D, loja 11/19.

For nordestino cuisine, the *Xique-Xique* has carne de sol and feijão verde with manteiga da terra. It's at SCLS 107, Bloco A, loja 1. *Tiragostas* is one of the city's oldest bar/restaurants. It's a famous meeting point for artists and musicians, and has outdoor tables under trees. The prices are reasonable. It's at SCLS 109, Bloco A, loja 2/4.

Vegetarians needn't feel left out. For some good, natural food, there's *Cheiro Verde*, SCLN 313, Bloco C, loja 20. It's open Monday to Friday from 8 am to 8 pm. *Coisas da Terra*, at SCLN 703, Bloco D, loja 41, is open from 11.30 am to 2.30 pm and 5.30 to 8 pm on weekdays; weekend hours are noon to 6 pm.

Getting There & Away

Air With so many domestic flights making a stopover in Brasília, it's easy to catch a plane out of the city at almost any time. Almost all Brazilian cities are served, and there are also Varig flights to Miami. Flying time to Rio is 1½ hours. To São Paulo, it's 80 minutes.

Major airlines with offices in Brasília include Transbrasil (☎ 243-6133), TAM (☎ 223-5179), Varig/Cruzeiro (☎ 365-1550) and VASP (☎ 321-3636).

Bus From the giant rodoferroviária (☎ 233-7200), due west of the city centre, there are buses to places you've never heard of. Destinations include Goiânia (US$6, three hours), Anápolis (US$5, 2½ hours), Belém (US$56, 36 hours), Belo Horizonte (US$20, 11 hours), Rio (US$32, 18 hours), São Paulo (US$28, 14 hours) and Salvador (US$37, 25 hours). To Pirenópolis, there are five buses a day. There are also buses to Cuiabá (US$30, 20 hours), where you can make bus connections to Porto Velho and Manaus.

Getting Around

To/From the Airport The international airport (☎ 365-1224) is 12 km south of the centre. There are two buses marked 'Aeroporto' that go from the city rodoviária to the airport every 15 minutes. The fare is US$0.80 and the trip takes 35 minutes. A taxi between the airport and the city centre costs US$17.

Bus To get from the city rodoviária to the rodoferroviária (for long-distance buses), take the local No 131 bus (you can also flag it down along the main drag).

Car There are car-rental agencies at the airport, at the Hotel Nacional Brasília and at the Hotel Garvey-Park.

AROUND BRASÍLIA
Estância de Agua de Itiquira

Itiquira is a Tupi-Guaraní Indian word meaning 'water that falls'. From the viewpoint at this 170-metre free-fall waterfall, you can see the valley of the Paranãs to the south. There's forest, several crystal-clear streams with natural pools for a swim, and the requisite restaurants and bars.

Itiquira is 110 km from Brasília; you need a car. Leave through the satellite cities of Sobradinho and Planaltina and the town of Formosa. The road is dirt for the next 35 km.

Cachoeira Saia Velha

This is a pleasant swimming hang-out not too far from the city. Take the road to Belo Horizonte for about 20 km. When you reach the *Monumento do Candango*, a ridiculous statue made by a Frenchman for the people who built Brasília, there's a sign to the waterfall. The road is to the left of the monument.

For US$8 per car, you can sample the live music on Saturdays, including food and beer. There are also several natural swimming pools. There are camping areas but no hotel.

Cachoeira Topázio

This is a pretty fazenda with a waterfall, camping facilities, food and drink. To get there, take the road to Belo Horizonte to the Km 93 marker. Turn right, taking the road out to the cachoeira. Admission is US$8 per car.

THE CENTRAL WEST

Goiás

GOIÂNIA

The capital of the state of Goiás, Goiânia is 200 km south-west of Brasília and 900 km from both Cuiabá and São Paulo. Planned by urbanist Armando de Godói and founded in 1933, it's a fairly pleasant place, with lots of open spaces laid out around circular streets in the centre. There are three main zones – housing is in the south, administration is in the centre, and industry and commerce are in the north. Goiânia's economy is based on the commercialisation of the region's cattle.

Information

Tourist Office Goiastur, the state tourist body, is located on the 3rd floor of the Serra Dourada stadium, in the suburb of Jardim Goiás. The effort to get there is not worth it. Everything you ever wanted to know about Goiânia, and lots of things you didn't, can be found in the *Nova Guia Turístico de Goiânia*, a book available for US$5 at most newsstands. It includes a map of the city and details of local bus routes.

Turisplan Turismo (☎ 224-1941) is at No 388 Rua 8. This central travel agency sells aeroplane and bus tickets.

Money You'll find the Banco do Brasil at Avenida Goiás 980. The Banco do Estado de Goiás (BEG!) is at Praça do Bandeirante 546, on the corner of Avenida Goiás and Avenida Anhanguera.

If you're going to Goiás Velho or Pirenópolis, change money here.

Post & Telephone The post office is right in the centre of town, at Praça Cívica 11. Long-distance telephone calls can be made from the Setor Norte Rodoviária, from the airport and from the corner of Rua 3 and Rua 7.

Things to See & Do

There's not much for the visitor in Goiânia.

Our advice is to get out to one of the nearby colonial towns as quickly as you can. But if you have some time to kill, try the **Parque Educativo**, on Avenida Anhanguera in Setor Oeste. It has a zoo, a zoological museum and an anthropology museum. It's open from 8 am to 6 pm.

Excursions within a 200-km radius of Goiânia include the **Caldas Novas** hot springs, **Lake Pirapitinga**, **Pousada do Rio Quente** and the interesting rock formations of **Parauna**.

Places to Stay

There are a couple of cheap places near the rodoviária. The *Star Hotel*, at No 537 Rua 68, is run by a friendly family. Some strange characters live there but it's OK for a night. Very basic quartos go for US$5 per person. The centre of town is so close, however, that it's worth staying there instead.

The *Hotel Del Rey* (☎ 225-6306) is centrally located, in the Rua 8 pedestrian mall, at No 321. Apartamentos cost US$12/18 a single/double. Another cheapie is the *Hotel Paissandú* (☎ 224-4925), at Avenida Goiás 1290, with quartos for US$10/18 a single/double and apartamentos for US$13/25. All of the rooms have fans. The *Goiânia Palace* (☎ 225-0671) charges the same prices as the Paissandú, but doesn't have fans. The *Principe Hotel* (☎ 224-0085), at Avenida Anhanguera 2936, costs a couple of dollars more but is better value.

In the mid-range, the *Vila Rica Hotel* (☎ 223-2733), at Avenida Anhanguera 3456, and the *Cabiúna Palace* (☎ 224-4355), at Avenida Paranaiba 698, each charge US$35 a double. Both are two-star Embratur hotels.

There are plenty of top-end alternatives. A couple of centrally located ones are the *Hotel Karajás* (☎ 224-9666; fax 229-1153), at No 860 Rua 3, which charges US$40/50 a single/double, and the *Hotel Bandeirantes* (☎ 224-0066), near the corner of Avenida

Anhanguera and Avenida Goiás, which charges US$55/65.

Places to Eat

Since they are surrounded by cattle, the locals eat lots of meat. They also like to munch on pamonha, a very tasty green-corn concoction sold at pamonharia stands all over town. Try it.

If you want to taste some typical Goiânian dishes, such as arroz com pequi, arroz com guariroba or peixe na telha, then head for the *Centro de Tradições Goiánas*, at No 515 on Rua 4, above the Parthenon Centre, or *Dona Beija*, on Avenida Tocantins between Rua 4 and Avenida Anhanguera. Our favourite dish is the empadão de Goiás, a tasty meat pie.

Praça Tamandare, a short bus ride or a long walk from the centre, has quite a several restaurants and bars surrounding it; try *Churrascaria e Chouparia do Gaúcho* for meat, beer and live music or *Modiglianni* for a good pizza. Wander around and see what takes your fancy.

The *Restaurante Macrobiótica Arroz Integral*, at No 326 Rua 93, in Setor Sul, is Goiânia's antichurrascaria. It's open from 11 am to 2 pm and 6 to 9 pm. Other natural food

PLACES TO STAY

1 Hotel Paissandú
2 Cabiúna Palace
3 Príncipe Hotel
6 Hotel Bandeirantes
7 Vila Rica Hotel
8 Goiânia Palace
9 Hotel Del Rey
10 Hotel Karajás

PLACES TO EAT

11 Reserva Natural

OTHER

4 Mercado
5 Banco do Brasil
12 Parthenon Centre
13 Telephone Centre
14 Post & Telegraph Office
15 Catedral Metropolitana
16 Palácio do Governo

Goiânia

0   250   500 m

THE CENTRAL WEST

is available in the centre at *Reserva Natural*, No 475 Rua 7, close to the Parthenon Centre. It's open for lunch Monday to Friday from 11 am to 2.30 pm.

Getting There & Away
Air In addition to the regular domestic carriers, there are several air-taxi companies which go anywhere and everywhere in the Mato Grosso and Amazon, but they are expensive. One company quoted me US$1500 for a return trip to Parque Nacional das Emas, in a plane that would hold four people.

Major airlines include Varig/Cruzeiro (☎ 224-5049) and VASP (☎ 223-4266).

If you're interested in hiring an air-taxi, call Sete Taxi Aereo (☎ 207-1519) or União (☎ 207-1600).

Bus The huge, relatively new rodoviária (☎ 224-8466), No 399 Rua 44, still holds the award for the most TV sets on poles (14 – down from 22 on the last research trip) in a rodoviária. There are buses to Brasília (US$6, three hours), Cuiabá (US$26, 16 hours) and Caldas Novas (US$7, three hours). Buses to Goiás Velho (US$6, 2½ hours) leave every hour from 5 am to 8 pm. For Pirenópolis (US$6, two hours), there's a 5 pm bus.

Distances from Goiânia to major cities are immense – it's 2000 km to Belém, 900 km to Belo Horizonte, 2620 km to Fortaleza, 3289 km to Manaus, 2414 km to Recife, 1340 km to Rio, 1730 km to Salvador and 900 km to São Paulo.

Getting Around
Aeroporto Santo Genoveva (☎ 207-1288) is six km from the city centre – US$10 by taxi.

You can walk from the rodoviária into town – it's 15 minutes to the corner of Avenida Anhanguera and Avenida Goiás. Alternatively, catch a local bus at the bus stop 50 metres from the main terminal as you walk towards town. A couple to look for are the No 163 'Vila União – Centro' and the No 404 'Rodoviária – Centro'. Both go down Avenida Goiás. To get to Praça Tamandare, catch the 'Vila União' bus.

GOIÁS VELHO
The historic colonial city of Goiás Velho was formerly known as Vila Boa. Once the state capital, it is 144 km from Goiânia and is linked to Cuiabá by dirt road. The city and its baroque churches shine during Semana Santa (Holy Week).

History
On the heels of the gold discoveries in Minas Gerais, bandeirantes pushed further into the interior in search of more precious stones and, as always, Indian slaves. In 1682, a bandeira headed by the old Paulista Bartolomeu Bueno da Silva visited the area. The Goyaz Indians gave him the nickname *anhanguera* (old devil) when, after burning some cachaça (which the Indians believed to be water) on a plate, he threatened to set fire to all the rivers if they didn't show him where their gold mines were. Three years later, having been given up for dead, the old devil and a few survivors returned to São Paulo with gold and Indian slaves from Goiás.

In 1722, his son, who had been on the first trip, organised another bandeira. The gold rush was on. It followed a pattern similar to that in Minas Gerais. First came the Paulistas, then the Portuguese Emboadas and soon the black slaves. With everything imported from so far away, prices were even higher than in Minas Gerais, and many suffered and died, particularly the slaves. The boom ended quickly.

Information
Serra Dourada Turismo (☎ 371-1528), next to the river, at Avenida Sebastião Fleury Curado 2, is a new outfit that organises treks, mountain-bike rides, horse rides and ox-cart rides into the surrounding hills. Prices are reasonable: US$5 for a six-hour tour. They're also happy to give out information (in Portuguese) about the area. The office is open from 8 am to 6 pm daily.

Things to See

Walking through Goiás Velho, the former state capital, you quickly notice the main legacies of the gold rush: 18th-century colonial architecture, and a large mulatto and mestizo population. The streets are narrow, with low houses, and there are seven churches. The most impressive is the oldest, the **Igreja de Paula** (1761), at Praça Zaqueu Alves de Castro.

The **Museu das Bandeiras** is well worth a visit. It's in the old town council building (1766), at Praça Brasil Caiado. Other interesting museums are the **Museu de Arte**

Sacra (in the old Igreja da Boa Morte (1779), on Praça Castelo Branco), with lots of 19th-century works by local Goiânian Viega Vale, and the **Palácio Conde dos Arcos** (the old governor's residence). All museums are open from 8 am to 5 pm Tuesday to Saturday and from 8 am to noon on Sunday.

Festival

The big occasion in Goiás Velho is Semana Santa (Holy Week). The main streets of town are lit by hundreds of torches, carried by the townsfolk and dozens of hooded figures in a

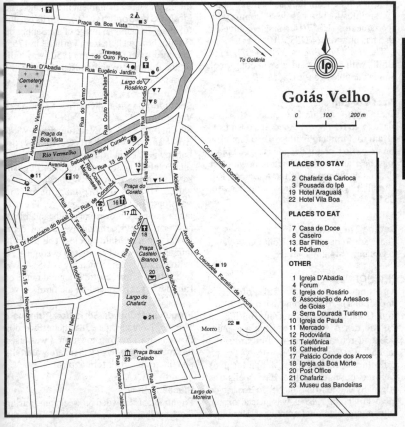

Goiás Velho

0   100   200 m

PLACES TO STAY

2   Chafariz da Carioca
3   Pousada do Ipê
19 Hotel Araguaiá
22 Hotel Vila Boa

PLACES TO EAT

7   Casa de Doce
8   Caseiro
13 Bar Filhos
14 Pódium

OTHER

1   Igreja D'Abadia
4   Forum
5   Igreja do Rosário
6   Associação de Artesãos de Goias
9   Serra Dourada Turismo
10 Igreja de Paula
11 Mercado
12 Rodoviária
15 Telefônica
16 Cathedral
17 Palácio Conde dos Arcos
18 Igreja da Boa Morte
20 Post Office
21 Chafariz
23 Museu das Bandeiras

THE CENTRAL WEST

procession which re-enacts the removal of Christ from the cross and his burial.

Places to Stay

You can camp in town at the *Chafariz da Carioca*, just behind the Pousada do Ipê.

The best low-budget place is the *Pousada do Ipê* (☎ 371-2065), a colonial house on Praça da Boa Vista. It offers a good breakfast and nice views, and the owners organise treks and horse rides. Quartos are US$12/17 a single/double and apartamentos are US$15/20. Cheaper, but not nearly as pleasant, is the *Hotel Araguaiá* (☎ 371-1462), at Avenida Dr Deusdete Ferreira de Moura. It's a bit of a hike from the bus station – about 15 minutes – but has very comfortable apartamentos (US$7/14 a single/double). It also has quartos for US$6/10.

The *Hotel Vila Boa* (☎ 371-1000) is up on a hill, with a view and a swimming pool. Singles/doubles go for US$60/90.

Places to Eat

The *Caseiro*, at Rua D Candido 31, is the place to go for regional food. It's open from 11 am to 3 pm and 6.30 to 10.30 pm. Near the Praça do Coreto, *Pôdium* is a good place for a beer and a snack. The run-down place upstairs at the corner of the praça and Rua Moretti Foggia serves great empadãos for US$3.

Getting There & Away

There are frequent buses from Goiás Velho to Goiânia, 144 km away.

PIRENÓPOLIS

Another historic colonial gold city, Pirenópolis is 70 km from Anápolis, 128 km from Goiânia and 165 km from Brasília, on the Rio das Almas. It's become a popular weekend retreat for the well-off from the capital.

Founded in 1727 by a bandeira of Paulistas in search of gold, Pirenópolis was originally called Minas da NS do Rosário da Meia Ponte. In 1989 it was placed on the Patrimonio Nacional (National Heritage)

register. The city's colonial buildings sit on striking red earth under big skies.

Information

Cerrado Ecoturismo (☎ 331-1374), at Rua Santana 13, organises treks, mountain-bike rides and tours at reasonable prices. Their historic tour leaves from the Igreja NS do Rosário Matriz every day at 9.30 am and 2.30 pm. They also do daily treks up the Morro do Frota, starting at 7.30 am from the Pousada das Siriemas.

Churches

The **Igreja NS do Rosário Matriz** (1732) is the oldest sacred monument in the state. The **Igreja NS de Bonfim** (1750), with its beautiful altars, contains an image of the Senhor de Bonfim brought here from Portugal in 1755. The **Igreja NS do Carmo** (1750) was built by the Portuguese and is used today as the Museu das Artes Sacras.

Santuário de Vida Silvestre – Fazenda Vagafogo

Six km from town, the Vagafogo Farm Wildlife Sanctuary is well worth a visit. Landowners Evandro Engel Ayer and Catarina Schiffer, both of whom speak English, have set aside 23 hectares of cerrado and gallery forests on the margins of the Vagafogo river as a nature reserve. The rich fauna includes brown capuchin and black howler monkeys, armadillos, pampas deer, agouti and many bird species. The forest is impressive, with a canopy top averaging 25 metres. Entry to the sanctuary is US$4. For sale at the visitors' centre is a good range of fruit preserves produced on the farm.

Parque Estadual da Serra dos Pireneus

The park contains the 1385-metre Pico dos Pirineus, 18 km from town on a well-used dirt road. Along the way there are waterfalls and interesting rock formations.

Places to Stay

Pirenópolis is crowded on weekends, during the Cavalhadas and at Carnival time, and prices then are almost double those quoted here. All pousadas fill up during the Cavalhadas festival, so most visitors camp out near the Rio das Almas or rent a room from a local.

There are lots of pousadas in town. The simple *Pousada Dona Geny*, on Rua dos Pirineus, charges US$8 a head. The *Hotel Rex* (☎ 331-1121), at Praça da Matriz 15, is pretty basic, with quartos going for US$10 per person. The *Pousada das Cavalhadas* (☎ 331-1261), Praça da Matriz 1, has double apartamentos for US$30.

In the mid-range, the pink-and-white *Pousada Matutina Meiapontense* (☎ 331-1101) is a friendly, comfortable place with a swimming pool. Apartamentos go for US$40/48 a single/double.

A couple of expensive, top-end places have sprung up in the last few years: the *Hotel Fazenda Quinta da Santa Barbara* (☎ 331-1304), at Rua do Bonfim 1, and the *Pousada dos Pirineus* (☎ 331-1028; fax 331-1462), at Alto de Carmo, just past the bridge.

Places to Eat

The *Restaurante As Flor*, on Avenida São Jayme, serves good regional cuisine. Don't fill up on your main course – there is an assortment of 18 different desserts, each sweeter than the last. The *Restaurante Aravinda*, in Rua do Rosário, is also recommended. *Nena*, at Rua Aurora 4, has an excellent buffet lunch of regional dishes for US$5.

Things to Buy

At Piretur, Avenida Comandante Joaquim Alves, you'll find a good selection of local crafts in ceramic, leather, wood, straw and soapstone. Pirenópolis is also considered to be the national silver capital, with more than 80 studios scattered around town.

THE CENTRAL WEST

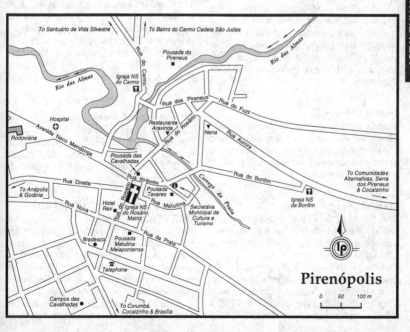

Pirenópolis

0   50   100 m

Festa do Divino Espírito Santo

Pirenópolis is famous for the acting out, 45 days after Easter, of the story Festa do Divino Espírito Santo, a tradition begun in 1819. If you're in the neighbourhood, make a point of seeing this stunning and curious spectacle, one of the most fascinating in Brazil.

For three days, the town looks like a scene from the Middle Ages. *Cavalhadas, congadas, mascardos, tapirios* and *pastorinhos* perform a series of medieval tournaments, dances and festivities, including a mock battle between Moors and Christians in distant Iberia. Riding richly decorated horses, the combatants wear bright costumes and bull-headed masks. In the end, proving that heresy doesn't pay, the Moors are defeated on the battlefield and convert to Christianity.

The festival is a happy one, and more folkloric than religious. The town's population swells several-fold during the festival. ■

Getting There & Away

There are bus services from Anápolis and Goiânia, as well as from Brasília.

CALDAS NOVAS

Caldas Novas, 167 km from Goiânia and 393 km from Brasília, has more than 30 hot springs, with average temperatures of 42°C (107°F). Now a very popular resort, the region has dozens of hotels at all levels of price and luxury. Studies have shown that the healing waters are particularly beneficial for people suffering from high blood-pressure, poor digestion, weak endocrine glands or impotency.

Tourist Office

There's a tourist information booth in Praça Mestre Orlando, open from 8 am to noon and 1 to 6 pm. It has lots of information about the various springs you can dip into, most of which are out of town.

Places to Stay

One km from the city is *Real Camping*, at Rua do Balneário, which has a canteen and two thermal swimming pools. The cost is US$6 a head.

A couple of relatively cheap places in the centre are *Serra Dourada* (☎ 453-1300) at Rua Orozimbo Correia Neto 200, with simple apartamentos costing US$15 a double, and *Santa Clara* (☎ 453-1764) at Rua America 109 which charges US$25 a double.

The best place to stay is the *Pousada do Rio Quente* (☎ 421-2255), 28 km from town, on the banks of the Rio Quente. They charge US$90 a double, including lunch.

Places to Eat

The *Comida Caseira e Natural*, at Rua José Borges 550, is a self-serve health-food place, open from noon to 3 pm and 6 to 9 pm. It's closed on Wednesday. Meat-eaters will prefer the rodízio at *Choupana*, on the corner of Rua Rui Barbosa and Avenida Orcalino Santos. It's open from 11.30 am to 4 pm and 7 to 10.30 pm.

Getting There & Away

The rodoviária is at the end of Rua Antônio Coelho de Godoy. Frequent buses go to Brasília (US$15, six hours) and Goiânia (US$7, three hours), as well as to Rio de Janeiro and São Paulo.

PARQUE NACIONAL DA CHAPADA DOS VEADEIROS

Just over 200 km north of Brasília, this scenic park is located in the highest area of the Central West. With high waterfalls, natural swimming pools and oasis-like stands of wine palms, it has become a popular destination for ecotourists.

Animal life includes the maned wolf, banded anteater, giant armadillo, capybara and tapir. Birds include rheas, toucans and vultures. The best time to visit the park is between May and October. Admission is US$1.

Places to Stay
Camping is the best option here – it costs about US$1 a night. Basic accommodation can be found in the small nearby town of São Jorge.

Getting There & Away
From Brasília, take a bus to Alto Paraiso de Goiás, from where you can either catch a local bus to São Jorge, or walk to the park, a couple of hours away.

If you have a car, take the road to Alto Paraiso and turn left 50 metres before entering the town. Take the dirt road to Colinas for 30 km, then follow the sign to the park entrance, five km away. São Jorge is a bit further on.

PARQUE NACIONAL DAS EMAS
Emas is a relatively small (1300 sq km) park in the corner of the state of Goiás, where it meets the states of Mato Grosso and Mato Grosso do Sul. The park lies along the Brazilian great divide, between the Amazon and Paraná river basins, at the headwaters of the Araguaia, Formoso and Taquari rivers.

The three rivers take divergent paths to the Atlantic. The Araguaia courses north to the equator via the Tocantins and the mighty Amazon. The Rio Taquari travels westward to flood the Pantanal, then flows south via the Paraguai. The Rio Formoso changes name midstream to Corrientes, and flows into the Parnaiba and then the Paraná. The Paraguai and the Paraná flow on either side of Paraguay, meet at Argentina, and enter the Atlantic a few hundred km east of Buenos Aires and some 35° latitude south of the mouth of the Amazon.

Surrounded by rapidly encroaching farmlands, the Parque Nacional das Emas is on a high plateau covered by grassy plains and open woodlands. There is little foliage to obstruct the sighting of wildlife, which includes anteaters, deer, capybara, foxes,

tapir, peccaries, armadillos, and blue and yellow macaws. It is the home of endangered wolves, and is the exclusive sanctuary of the jacamari and other rare species. Another interesting spectacle in the park is the large number of termite mounds, which at certain times of the year 'glow' in the dark (the result of fluorescence produced by the termite larvae).

During the dry season (July to October),

Blue Macaw

THE CENTRAL WEST

the area is dry enough for spontaneous fires. In 1988, a fire raged for five days, burning 65% of the park area. Be careful with sparks!

Places to Stay

Basic accommodation inside the park costs about US$5 per person per night. You'll need to take your own food, but there is a kitchen and a cook available. It's also possible to camp in the park, and this costs around US$2 per person per night.

Getting There & Away

Access to the park is tough: even though it's surrounded by farmland, there are no paved roads or regular bus routes. Visitors must arrange with private companies for 4WD or air-taxis from as far away as Cuiabá, Goiânia and Campo Grande.

Adventurous types may consider taking BR-364 to Alto do Araguaia/Santa Rita do Araguaia (531 km from Goiânia, 423 km from Cuiabá), then hitching 63 km to Plaça dos Mineiros, and 40 to 60 km further along dirt roads to the park.

RIO ARAGUAIA

For information on this park, refer to the section on the Rio Araguaia in the Pará, Amapá & Tocantins chapter.

Mato Grosso & Mato Grosso do Sul

Mato Gross and Mato Gross do Sul are separate states, although until the late '70s this region was all Mato Grosso state. The vast wetlands of the Pantanal extend across parts of both states. This chapter contains a separate section on the Pantanal, but see also the sections on Cuiabá and Corumbá for more information on the Pantanal.

Mato Grosso

There's a well-known story about a naturalist in the Mato Grosso. Disoriented by the sameness of the forest, the naturalist asked his Indian guide – who had killed a bird, put it in a tree and, incredibly, knew where to return for it at the end of the day – how he knew where the tree was. 'It was in the same place' the Indian replied.

To begin to appreciate the Mato Grosso's inaccessibility and vastness, read the classic *Brazilian Adventure*, by Peter Fleming. It also happens to be one of the funniest travel books ever written. Fleming tells the story of his quest to find the famous British explorer Colonel Fawcett, who disappeared in the Mato Grosso in 1925 while searching for the hidden city of gold. For a more scientific report on the region, see *Mato Grosso: Last Virgin Land*, by Anthony Smith.

Mato Grosso means bundu, bush, savannah, outback; an undeveloped thick scrub. Part of the highland plain that runs through Brazil's interior, the Mato Grosso is a dusty land of rolling hills and some of the best fishing rivers in the world, such as the Araguaia.

This is also the land where many of Brazil's remaining Indians live. They are being threatened by rapid agricultural development (which is bringing in poor peasants from the south and Northeast who are desperate for land) and by a government which is less than fully committed to guaranteeing them their rights. In 1967, an entire government agency, the Indian Protective Service, was dissolved. No less than 134 of its 700 employees were charged with crimes and 200 were fired. In two years, the director had committed 42 separate crimes against Indians, including collusion in murder, torture and the illegal sale of land.

There's a saying in Brazil that 'progress is roads'. Key routes such as the Belém to Brasília and the Cuiabá to Santarém roads have catalysed the opening of vast stretches of the Mato Grosso to cattle, rice, cotton, soybean, corn and manioc, as well as to mining. Goiás, where wealthy ranchers fly from one end of their huge tracts of land to the other in private planes, is one of the fastest-growing agricultural belts in the country.

Cuiabá is a frontier boom town. New roads have opened the lands of the Mato Grosso and southern Amazon, bringing to the area peasants desperate for land, and increasing exports of agricultural products. Since the 1950s, Cuiabá's population has been growing at 14% annually, a national record. It is *the* boom town in the country of boom towns. In 1969 Cuiabá got its first TV channel, the litmus test of progress in Brazil. It was named the *boca de sertão* (mouth of the backlands).

This is Brazil's frontier, the Wild West, where an often-desperate struggle for land between peasants, Indians, miners, rich landowners and hired guns leads to frequent killings and illegal land expropriation.

CUIABÁ

Founded in 1719 by gold and slave-seeking bandeirantes, Cuiabá has little historic or cultural heritage to interest travellers. However, it's a lively place and a good base for excursions into the Pantanal and Chapada dos Guimarães, as well as a rest stop on the way to the Amazon and expeditions to

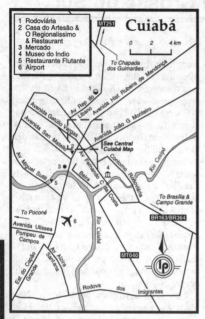

1 Rodoviária
2 Casa do Artesão &
  O Regionalissimo
  & Restaurant
3 Mercado
4 Museo do Indio
5 Restaurante Flutante
6 Airport

Cuiabá

0   2   4 km

To Chapada
dos Guimarães

See Central
Cuiabá Map

To Brasília &
Campo Grande

To Poconé

BR163/BR364

tions often failed. With the end of the gold boom and the decay of the mines, Cuiabá would have disappeared, except that the gold was never completely exhausted (garimpeiros still seek their fortunes today); also, the soil along the Rio Cuiabá allowed subsistence agriculture, while the river itself provided fish.

As in many mining towns, there was tension here between Paulistas and recent Portuguese immigrants. In 1834, the small town was torn apart by the Rusga (Brawl), in which a nativist movement of Paulistas, inspired by wild rumours following Brazilian independence, slaughtered many Portuguese on the pretext that the victims wanted to return Brazil to Portuguese rule.

Information

Tourist Office Funcetur (☎ 322-5363), the Mato Grosso tourist authority, is in the city centre, in Praça da República. The staff are helpful, speak English, and have information on hotels and pousadas in the Pantanal. The office is open Monday to Friday from 8 am to 6 pm.

Parque Nacional das Emas and the Rio Araguaia.

The city is actually two sister cities separated by the Rio Cuiabá: old Cuiabá and Várzea Grande (where the airport is located, by the Rio Cuiabá). We found the people here incredibly friendly and gracious.

History

A Paulista, Pascoal Moreira Cabral, was hunting Indians along the Rio Cuiabá when he found gold in 1719. A gold rush followed, but many gold-seekers never reached Cuiabá. Travelling over 3000 km from São Paulo by river took five months; along the way there was little food, many mosquitoes, rapids, portages, disease and incredible heat.

There was usually one flotilla of canoes each year, bringing supplies, slaves and miners and returning with gold. Although there were several hundred people in a flotilla, including many soldiers to protect the canoes against Indian attacks, the expedi-

Money Bemat, the state bank, has an exchange on the corner of Rua Joaquim Murtinho and Avenida Getúlio Vargas which changes cash and travellers' cheques; it's open from 10 am to 3 pm Monday to Friday. The Banco do Brasil, a bit further up Avenida Getúlio Vargas, also exchanges money.

Post & Telephone The post office is in Praça da República, next to Turimat. The posto telefônico is on Rua Barão de Melgaço, near the corner with Avenida Isaac Póvoas.

Health Remember to start taking your antimalarial tablets prior to visiting the Pantanal. Cuiabá's municipal hospital (☎ 321-7418) is on Avenida General Valle. Hospital Modelo (☎ 322-5599), a private clinic at Rua Comandante Costa 1262, is within walking distance of the Hotel Mato Grosso. Hospital Universidade (Jaime Muller), on Avenida CPA, is open only during business hours.

Museu do Indio

Cuiabá's tourist brochures make much noise about satellite-tracking antennas, but the antennas are no big deal. The Museu do Indio (Rondon) is, however, played down. The museum has exhibits of the Xavantes, Bororos and Karajas tribes and is worth a visit. It is at the university, on Avenida Fernando Correia da Costa, and is open Monday to Friday from 8 to 11.30 am and 1.30 to 5.30 pm. The university also contains a small zoo. To get there, catch a No 133 bus, or any other 'Universidade' bus, on Avenida Tenente Coronel Duarte.

Market

The market by the bridge that crosses the Rio Cuiabá is a good one, at least before and after the heat of the day. It's interesting not so much for buying as for looking at the people and their products. Try the waterfront bars for a drink afterwards.

Santo Antônio de Leverger

Santo Antônio de Leverger, Mato Grosso's *cidade morena*, is where Cuiabanos go for river-beaching from June to October. It's on the Rio Cuiabá, 28 km south of Cuiabá in the direction of Barão de Melgaço.

Organised Tours

Travel agencies in town arrange reservations, guides and transport for photo-safaris into the Pantanal or weekend trips to Chapada dos Guimarães, and can help with the logistics of more ambitious trips to the Parque Nacional das Emas. Ametur (☎ 624-1000), Rua Joaquim Murtinho 242, close to Turimat, has been recommended. The tours are expensive (around US$75 a day), but well organised.

An alternative and relatively cheap excursion is with Joel Souza, a very enthusiastic guide who speaks fluent English, German and Italian. His office (☎ 624-1386) is at Avenida Getúlio Vargas 155A, but he often meets incoming flights. Joel's two-day trips into the Pantanal cost around US$120, including food, accommodation, transport and the boat ride – you won't find anything cheaper than this in Cuiabá or Poconé.

Festival

The Festa de São Benedito takes place during the first week of July, at the Igreja NS

THE CENTRAL WEST

The Indians of Mato Grosso

To reach Cuiabá, the Portuguese had to cross the lands of several groups of Indians, many of whom were formidable warriors. They included the Caiapó (who even attacked the settlement at Goiás), the Bororo of the Pantanal, the Parecis (who were enslaved to mine the gold), the Paiaguá (who defeated several large Portuguese flotillas and caused periodic panic in Cuiabá itself) and the Guaicuru (skilled riders and warriors with many years' experience in fighting the Europeans).

As a result of being nomadic people in a region without abundant food, the Guaicuru women performed self-abortions, refusing to have children until they were near menopause. On longer journeys, when the women stayed behind, the Guaicuru men took male transvestites with them as sexual partners. Both women and men could divorce easily, and often did, several times a year.

Despite important victories, many Indians had been killed or enslaved by the time the gold boom began to fade, in the mid-1700s. Today, however, several tribes remain in northern Mato Grosso, living as they have for centuries. The Erikbatsa, noted for their fine featherwork, live near Fontanilles and Juima, the Nhambikuraa are near Padroal and the Cayabi live near Juara. There are also the Indians of Aripuana park and, of course, the tribes under the care of FUNAI at Xingu park. The only tribe left in the Pantanal to still subsist by hunting and fishing is the Bororo.

You probably won't be able to overcome FUNAI's obstacles to visiting the Indians, but if you want to visit FUNAI, the office (☎321-2325) is at Rua São Joaquim 1047. The condition of the building speaks volumes about the government's lack of concern about Indian affairs. ■

do Rosário and the Capela de São Benedito. The holiday has a more Umbanda than Catholic flavour; it's celebrated with traditional foods such as bola de queijo and bola de arroz, and regional dances such as O Cururu, O Siriri, Danças do Congo and dos Mascarados.

Places to Stay

There are some cheap hotels across from the rodoviária, but with the centre only a short bus ride away, there's little point in staying there. In town, one of the popular cheapies is the *Hotel Samara* (☎ 322-6001), at Rua Joaquim Murtinho 270, with basic singles/doubles costing US$8/12. The *Hotel Presidente* (☎ 321-6162), at Avenida Getúlio Vargas 345, has single/double quartos for US$15/22 and apartamentos for US$9/11. It's a bit noisy, but very close to the Praça da República and the bus stop to/from the rodoviária. If you like the action around the waterfront market, you could stay in the *Hotel Rio* (☎ 321-4554), right on the Praça do Porto. Basic apartamentos cost US$12 a head.

A travellers' favourite is the *Hotel Mato Grosso* (☎ 321-9121), at Rua Comandante

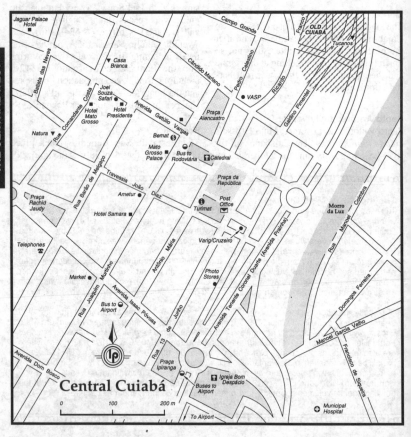

Central Cuiabá

0   100   200 m

Costa 2522. It has US$25/30 apartamentos, and a good breakfast as well. The *Jaguar Palace Hotel* (☎ 322-9044; fax 322-6698), at Avenida Getúlio Vargas 600, is a three-star hotel with a pool. Singles/doubles go for US$55/67, but if you take a Pantanal trip with Joel Souza, he can arrange a 50% discount here.

At the top end, the *Best Western Mato Grosso Palace* (☎ 322-9304; fax 321-2386), on Rua Joaquim Murtinho, is a four-star job offering singles/doubles from US$80/100.

Places to Eat
Cuibá offers some great fish dishes, including pacu assado com farofa de couve, piraputanga assado and pirão de Bagre – try one at the floating restaurant *Flutuante*, next to Ponte Nova bridge. Six km from the centre, it's complicated to reach by public bus. From the waterfront market, though, it's a 20-minute walk. The restaurant is open daily from 11 am to 11 pm.

On Rua 13 de Junho, next to the Casa do Artesão, *O Regionalissimo* serves excellent regional food. The cost is US$4 for buffet-style meals – lots of fish and the sweetest of sweets. It's open daily for lunch and dinner (closed on Mondays).

In the centre, a cheap, wholesome lunch spot with comida por kilo is *Casa Branca*, at Rua Comandante Costa 565. Vegetarians can lunch at *Naturama*, on Rua Comandante Costa, near the Hotel Mato Grosso. In the evening, *Choppão*, on Praça 8 de Abril, is always packed with locals, who come to drink the excellent chopp and to dine from the varied menu. Likewise, *Tucanos Restaurante e Chopparia*, Avenida CPA 674, has a good pizza and gets pretty lively, even during the week.

Entertainment
When the sun sets and temperatures drop a bit, the city comes to life. A great place to go, especially if you spend only one night in Cuiabá, is Ninho's Bar, at Rua Laranjeiras 701. It has a spectacular view of the city, good chopp, and live music almost every night. There's a popular disco, Operalight, a stone's throw away, if you want a change of pace.

Things to Buy
The Casa do Artesão, on Rua 13 de Junho, has lots of local handicrafts, including ceramics, woodcarvings, straw baskets, paintings and hammocks. The FUNAI Artindia store, at Rua Barão de Melgaço 3944, is open from 8 to 11.30 am and 1.30 to 6 pm on weekdays. It has Indian baskets, bows and arrows, jewellery and headdresses for sale. Guaraná Maués, at Avenida Isaac Póvoas 611, has lots of guaraná products.

Getting There & Away
Air There are flights between Cuiabá and the rest of Brazil with Transbrasil (☎ 682-3597), VASP (☎ 682-3737) and Varig/Cruzeiro (☎ 682-1140). Make reservations well in advance if you're travelling in July, when many Brazilians are on holiday.

Bus Cuiabá's rodoviária (☎ 321-4803) is on Avenida Marechal Rondon, on the highway towards Chapada dos Guimarães. To get there, catch a municipal bus from the city, near the Praça da República. Six buses a day make the two-hour trip to Poconé (US$5); the first leaves at 6 am. To Barão de Melgaço (US$11, three hours), there are two daily buses, at 7.30 am and 3 pm. For Chapada dos Guimarães (US$3.50, 1½ hours), there are six daily buses, but take the 8 am bus if you've only got a day to spend there.

Six buses a day go to Cáceres (US$11, three hours). Porto Velho is a hard 21-hour (US$35) ride. There are three buses daily, at 8 am, and 3 and 5 pm. To Goiânia (US$25, 16 hours), there are five buses daily. Rondonópolis, Coxim and Campo Grande are serviced by the same bus; there are six daily. The buses take three hours to Rondonópolis, seven hours to Coxim and 10 hours to Campo Grande. To Alta Floresta (US$30, 14 hours), there are four buses a day, the first leaving at 7.30 am and the last at 9.30 pm.

Getting Around

To/From the Airport Marechal Rondon airport (☎ 381-2211) is in Varzea Grande. As you leave the airport, the city is seven km to your right. To catch the local bus to town, cross the road, and walk to the left until you reach the Las Velas hotel. The bus stop is opposite the hotel entrance. Catch a 'Jardim Primavera', 'Cohabcanela' or 'Costa Verde' bus to the city centre.

Bus In Cuiabá, you enter local buses through the front door. From the rodoviária, take the No 202 'Rodoviária' bus to its final stop in the city. You'll be on the corner of Rua Joaquim Murtinho and Avenida Getúlio Vargas. Other buses go via the rodoviária (destinations are written on the side of the bus), but if you're about to catch one, make sure it's going to the centre, because all local buses enter the rodoviária facing the same direction.

Car All the car-rental places have branches in the centre and in or near the airport. There are often promotional rates, so shop around. The best cars for the Pantanal are the Volkswagen Golf and the Fiat Uno. Note that the Porto Jofre station has only gas and diesel; Poconé and Pousada Pixaim (55 km from Poconé, 85 km from Porto Jofre) have álcool.

On average, a rental car will cost around US$70 a day.

CHAPADA DOS GUIMARÃES

After the Pantanal, Chapada dos Guimarães is the region's leading attraction. This rocky plateau is 800 metres higher than and 64 km north-east of Cuiabá, in a beautiful region reminiscent of the American south-west. Surprisingly different from the typical Mato Grosso terrain, this place is not to be missed. We spent two days here but would have loved to spend a week.

Véu de Noiva & the Mirante Lookout

The two exceptional sights in the Chapadas are the 60-metre Véu de Noiva (Bridal Veil) falls, and the Mirante lookout, the geo-graphic centre of South America. Both are quite easy to find. Six km beyond Salgadeira, you'll see the turn-off for Véu de Noiva, on your right. It's well signposted.

Alta Mira is eight km from the town of Chapada. Take the last road in Chapada on your right and go eight km; you'll see a dirt road with a sign saying 'Centro Geodésico'. Turn right and drive the couple of hundred metres to the rim of the canyon. The view is stupendous; off to your right you can see the Cuiabá skyline.

Start walking downhill over the bluff, slightly to your right. A small trail leads to a magical look-out, perched on top of rocks with the canyon below. This is Chapada's most dazzling place.

On your way back to town, stop off at Alambique Jamacá, a small distillery which produces some fine local cachaça. There's a sign, so you can't miss it. They produce one with a special root that is renowned as an aphrodisiac. José, who makes it, is living proof of its efficacy – he and his wife have seven kids.

Other Attractions

Driving to Chapada, you pass **Rio dos Peixes**, **Rio Mutaca** and **Rio Claro**, which are all popular weekend bathing spots for Cuiabanos. The sheer, 80-metre drop called **Portão do Inferno** (Hell's Gate) is also unforgettable.

Take a waterfall shower at **Cachoeirinha** and peek into the chapel of **NS de Santãna**, a strange mixture of Portuguese and French baroque. A hike to the top of Chapada's highest point, **Morro do São Jerônimo**, is well worthwhile.

A bit further out of town is the 1100-metre-long **Aroe Jari** cavern and, in another cave, the **Lagoa Azul** (Blue Lake).

Organised Tours

If you don't have a car, your best bet is to take an excursion with Jorge Mattos, who runs Ecoturismo (☎ & fax 791-1393), on Praça Dom Wunibaldo in the town of Chapada. Jorge, an excellent, English-speaking guide who really knows his way around Chapada, meets the 8 am bus from Cuiabá every day, when it arrives at 9.30 am. He runs three excursions: to the national park (which contains the most spectacular waterfalls), to the Blue Lake and the Aroe Jari cavern, and to the stone city. To the park and the stone city, it costs around US$15; to the lake and cavern it's US$30 – much cheaper than if you organised something similar in Cuiabá.

Unfortunately, if Jorge doesn't find at least five people, the price goes up. All tours take between four and six hours, depending on the enthusiasm of the group. If you want to spend just a day there, he can have you on the last bus back to Cuiabá (at 6 pm).

An alternative is to hire a car and explore the area on your own, stopping at different rock formations, waterfalls and bathing pools at your leisure. If you do have the use of a car, drop by the Secretária de Turismo (on the left-hand side as you drive into town, just before the square), open from 8 to 11 am and 1 to 4 pm on weekdays. A useful map is available – you'll need it!

Places to Stay
There is good camping at Salgadeira, just before the climb into Chapada, but if you want to rough it, you can basically camp anywhere.

Lodging in the area ranges from the very basic but friendly *Hotel São José* (☎ 791-1152), at Rua Vereador José de Souza 50, which charges US$3 per person, to the *Hotel Pousada da Chapada* (☎ 791-1171), a couple of km from town on the road to Cuiabá, charging US$50 a double (book at Selva Turismo in Cuiabá).

In between are a couple of good alternatives. The very popular *Turismo Hotel* (☎ 791-1176; fax 791-1383) is at Rua Fernando Correo Costa 1065, and is run by a German family. Single/double apartamentos here cost US$18/25. The *Hotel Quincó* (☎ 791-1404), at Praça Dom Wunibaldo 464 (next to Ecoturismo), has singles/doubles for US$9.50/19.

All of these places, with the exception of the Pousada da Chapada, are close to the rodoviária.

Places to Eat
On the main praça, the *Nivios* has excellent regional food – all you can eat for US$8. Also popular is *O Mestrinho*, at Rua Quincó Caldas 119. The *Turismo Hotel* has a restaurant.

Getting There & Away
Buses leave Cuiabá's rodoviária for Chapada dos Guimarães every 1½ hours from 8 am to 6 pm. In the other direction, the first bus leaves Chapada dos Guimarães at 6 am and the last at 6 pm. The cost is US$3.50.

CÁCERES
The city of Cáceres, founded in 1778 on the left bank of the Rio Paraguai, is an access point for a number of Pantanal lodges and for San Mathias (in Bolivia). Cáceres is 215 km from Cuiabá on BR-070, close to the Ilha de Taiamã ecological reserve.

Lots of travellers arrive with the misunderstanding that they'll be able to get a cement barge to Corumbá. You'd have to be very lucky, and unless you have unlimited time to hang around, forget it. Even the port captain has no idea when the boats are likely to arrive.

If you're going to Bolivia, get a Brazilian exit stamp from the Polícia Federal office at Rua Antônio João 160.

Places to Stay
Cáceres has a number of modest hotels and restaurants for visitors. The best cheapie near the bus station is the *Capri Hotel* (☎ 223-1771), at Rua Antônio Vargas 99. It has spacious, clean, air-conditioned rooms and friendly staff. Singles/doubles cost US$11/16. The *Hotel Avenida* (☎ 221-1553) is just around the corner, in Avenida 7 de Setembro. It charges US$5 a head for basic quartos. Closer to the river, the *Rio Hotel* (☎ 221-1387), on Praça Major João Carlos, is a good option. Its apartamentos with fans cost US$12/18 a single/double. You could also try the *Hotel Comodoro* (☎ 221-1525),

on Praça Duque de Caixas, with aparta-mentos for US$16/25 a single/double.

The *Hotel Barranquinho* (☎ 221-2641, ext 3, or (011) 285-3022 in São Paulo), at the confluence of the Jauru and Paraguai rivers and 18 km from the Pirapitanga waterfalls, is 72 km and 2½ hours from Cáceres by boat. *Frontier Fishing Safari* (☎ 011) 227-0920 in São Paulo) is 115 km by boat from Cáceres.

Places to Eat
A good fish restaurant, the *Corimba* is near the river, at the corner of Rua 6 de Outubro and Rua 15 de Novembro. The *Pilão*, in Praça Barão do Rio Branco, is a decent churrascaria.

Getting There & Away
Regular buses make the journey between Cuiabá and Cáceres (US$11, three hours). To San Matías (in Bolivia), there is a daily bus, at 4 pm (US$10, 4½ hours). For more details, see To/From Bolivia in the Land section of the Getting There & Away chapter.

BARÃO DE MELGAÇO
Along with Cáceres and Poconé, Barão de Melgaço, 35 km south-east of Cuiabá, is a northern entrance into the Pantanal. Nearby, there are ruined fortresses from the Paraguayan wars, and Sia Mariana and Chacororé, two huge bays full of fish.

Places to Stay
The *NS de Carmo Hotel* (☎ 713-1141), at Avenida A Leverger 33, is 600 metres from the bus station. Double apartamentos are US$20. The top-end place is the *Barão Tur Hotel* (☎ 713-1166, or 322-1568 in Cuiabá), which charges US$70 a double.

Getting There & Away
There are two buses a day that make the three-hour, US$11 trip from Cuiabá, leaving at 7.30 am and 3 pm.

POCONÉ
The northern entry point to the Pantanal from Cuiabá, Poconé marks the beginning of the Transpantaneira 'highway'. In May, the pink city of Poconé celebrates the week-long Semana do Fazendeiro e do Cavalo Panteiro with a cattle fair and rodeos. Most of the locals are descendants of Indians and blacks. Many have hunted the *onça* (jaguar) and have amazing stories to tell. They also wear some excellent straw hats!

Orientation
When you arrive at the rodoviária, you are two km from the start of the dirt road which becomes the Transpantaneira; the centre of town is about halfway. To get there, turn left as you leave the bus station, walk the couple of blocks down to Rua Antônio João, then turn right and walk up six blocks – you'll be in the town square (more like a rectangle). The Hotel Skala is 100 metres to your right. On your left, behind the church, is the road that leads to the beginning of the Trans-pantaneira. There are a few pousadas here.

Places to Stay & Eat
The *Dormitório Poconé*, on Avenida Anibol de Toledo, near the rodoviária, has basic, run-down rooms with fan for US$6. The nearby *Bar e Restaurante 4 Rodas* is better; good, cheap rooms with fan cost US$8, including breakfast. They also serve over a dozen cheap, hearty dishes – all you can eat. In the middle of town is the *Skala* (☎ 721-1407), Rua Bem Rondon 64. Rooms with fan start at US$15/22. There are some rooms with bath, for the same prices.

The best places to stay, especially if you intend to hitch on the Transpantaneira, are out of town, near the beginning of that road. The first one you'll pass is the *Pousada Centro-Oeste* (☎ 721-1220), on the right-hand side, which charges US$15 a double (though they will bargain). The rooms with fan are a bit on the dingy side, but it's a friendly place, and serves a decent prato feito. Just up the road, on the same side, is the *Hotel Santa Cruz* (☎ 721-1439), where apartamentos cost US$25 a double. A further 400 metres up, on the left-hand side, the *Hotel Restaurante Aurora do Pantanal* (☎ 721-1339) has spacious apartamentos with fan for US$15/25 a single/double. They also serve prato feito.

Getting There & Away

There are six buses a day from Cuiabá to Poconé, from 6 am to 7 pm, and six in the opposite direction, from 6 am to 7.30 pm. The 100-km, two-hour ride costs US$5. The bus is often packed, so get a seat early if you want to appreciate the vegetation typical of the Pantanal's outskirts: *pequís, piúvas, babaçus, ipês* and *buritis*. The bus passes the airport at Varzea Grande.

The Pantanal

The Amazon may have all the fame and glory, but the Pantanal is a far better place to see wildlife. In the Amazon, the animals hide in the dense foliage, but in the open spaces of the Pantanal, wildlife is visible to the most casual observer. It's not easy to get to, and almost impossible to do on the cheap, but if you like to see animals in their natural state, the Pantanal – with the greatest concentration of fauna in the New World – should not be missed.

A vast wetlands in the centre of South America, the Pantanal is about half the size of France – some 230,000 sq km. Something less than 100,000 sq km of this is in Bolivia and Paraguay; the rest is in Brazil, split between the states of Mato Grosso and Mato Grosso do Sul.

The Pantanal (Terra de Ninguem, or Nobody's Land) has few people and no towns. Distances are so great and ground transport so poor that people get around in small aeroplanes or motorboats; 4WD travel is restricted by the seasons. The only road that plunges deep into the Pantanal is the Transpantaneira. This raised dirt road sectioned by 89 small, wooden bridges ends 145 km from Poconé, at Porto Jofre. Only a third of the intended route from Poconé to Corumbá has been completed, because of lack of funds and ecological concerns.

The road and a strip of land on either side of it comprise the Transpantanal national park. Although IBAMA is trying to expand its jurisdiction to protect the entire Pantanal region, it administers only one other park in the Mato Grosso portion of the Pantanal: the Parque Nacional do Pantanal Mato-grossense, which encompasses the old Cará-Cará biological reserve. The rest of the Pantanal (around 90%) is privately owned.

Geography & Climate

Although *pantano* means 'swamp' in both Spanish and Portuguese, the Pantanal is not a swamp but, rather, a vast alluvial plain. In geological terms, it is a sedimentary basin of quaternary origin, the drying remains of an ancient inland sea called the Xaraés, which began to dry out, along with the Amazon Sea, 65 million years ago.

First sea, then immense lake and now a periodically flooded plain, the Pantanal – 2000 km from the Atlantic Ocean yet just 100 to 200 metres above sea level – is bounded by higher lands: the mountains of the Serra de Maracaju to the east, the Serra da Bodoquena to the south, the Paraguayan and Bolivian Chaco to the west and the Serra dos Parecis and Serra do Roncador to the north. From these highlands, the rains flow into the Pantanal, forming the Rio Paraguai and its tributaries (which flow south and then east, draining into the Atlantic Ocean between Argentina and Uruguay).

During the rainy season (October to March), the rivers flood their banks, inundating much of the low-lying Pantanal and creating cordilheiras (patches of dry land where the animals cluster together). The waters reach their high mark – up to three metres – in January or February, then start to recede in March. This seasonal flooding has made systematic farming impossible and has severely limited human incursions into the area. However, it does provide an enormously rich feeding ground for wildlife.

The floodwaters replenish the soil's nutrients, which would otherwise be very poor, due to the excessive drainage. The waters teem with fish, and the ponds provide excellent ecological niches for many animals and

THE CENTRAL WEST

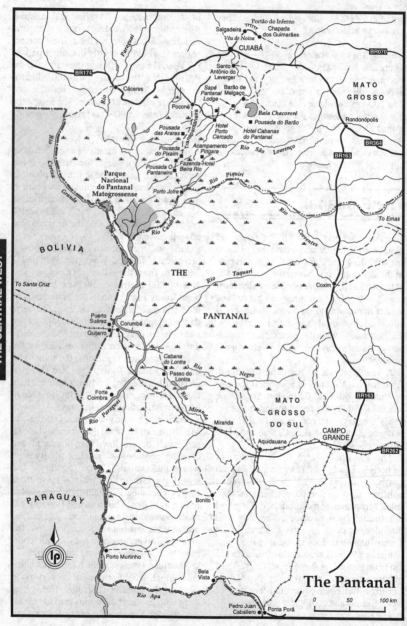

The Pantanal

plants. Enormous flocks of wading birds gather in rookeries several sq km in area.

Later in the dry season, the water recedes, the lagoons and marshes dry out, and fresh grasses emerge on the savannah (the Pantanal's vegetation includes savannah, forest and meadows, which blend together, often with no clear divisions). The hawks and jacaré compete for fish in the remaining ponds. As the ponds shrink and dry up, the jacarés crawl around for water, sweating it out until the rains return.

Flora & Fauna
For details, see the Flora & Fauna section in the Facts about the Country chapter.

Ecology & Environment
The fragile equilibrium of the Pantanal is under threat from poaching and pollution. For more information, refer to the Ecology & Environment section in the Facts about the Country chapter.

When to Go
If possible, go during the dry season (from April to September/October). The best time to go birding is during the latter part of the dry season (July to September), when the birds are at their rookeries in great numbers, the waters have receded and the bright-green grasses pop up from the muck. Temperatures are comfortable in the dry season – hot by day and cool by night – with plenty of rain.

Flooding, incessant rains and heat make travel difficult during the rainy season (November to March), though not without some special rewards: this is when the cattle and exotic wildlife of the Pantanal clump together on the small islands. The heat peaks in November and December, when temperatures over 40°C are common, roads turn to breakfast cereal, and the mosquitoes are fierce and out in force. Many hotels close at this time.

The heaviest rains fall in February and March. Every decade or so, the flooding is disastrous, destroying both humans and animals. In 1988, the southern Pantanal was devastated: fazendas were destroyed, cattle and wild animals drowned and starved, and the city of Corumbá was submerged for weeks.

Fishing is best during the first part of the dry season (April-May), when the flooded rivers settle back into their channels, but locals have been known to lasso 80-kg fish throughout the dry season and well into December. This is some of the best fishing in the world. There are about 20 species of piranha, many vegetarian and all good eating, as well as the tasty dourado, a feisty 10 to 20-pounder. Other excellent catches include pacu, suribim, bagre, giripoca, piraputanga, piapara, cachara, pintado, pirancajuva and pintado, to name but a few.

Although hunting is not allowed, fishing – with the required permits – is encouraged. Fishing permits are available from the IBAMA offices in Cuiabá (☎ 644-1511) and Campo Grande (☎ 382-1802). Enthusiasts can study their quarry at Cuiabá's fish market, located in the market near the bridge.

What to Bring
You can't buy anything in the Pantanal, so come prepared. The dry season is also the cooler season. Bring attire suitable for hot (but not brutal) days, cool nights, rain and mosquitoes. You'll need sunscreen, sunglasses, a hat and cool clothes, sneakers or boots, light raingear, and something for the cool evenings. Mosquito relief means long pants and long-sleeved shirts, vitamin B12 and insect repellent. Autan is the Brazilian brand recommended by eight out of 10 Pantaneiros, but some travellers claim that the mosquitoes have become so used to it that they've even started to like it!

Binoculars are your best friend in the Pantanal. Bring an alarm clock (to get up before sunrise) and a strong flashlight (to go hunting for owls and anacondas after dark). Don't forget plenty of film, a camera, a tripod and a long lens (300 mm is about right for wildlife).

Guides
If you want to enhance your Pantanal experience and money isn't a problem, a good

THE CENTRAL WEST

guide can identify animal and bird species, explain the diverse Pantanal ecology, and take care of any hassles along the way. But you don't need a guide – there's only one road to follow and the wildlife is hard to miss.

If language or time is a problem and money isn't, write to Douglas Trent of Focus Tours (☎ (612) 892-7830), 14821 Hillside Lane, Burnsville, MN 55306, USA; in Brazil, contact Focus (☎ (031) 373-3734), Belo Horizonte, MG. Focus specialises in nature tours and Doug is active in trying to preserve the Pantanal. He has all the bird calls on tape, and plays them over a loud-speaker to attract the real thing. For more about Focus, see the Tours section in the Getting There & Away chapter. For more information on Pantanal tours, see Corumbá in the Mato Grosso do Sul section of this chapter.

Places to Stay

Pantanal accommodation is divided into four general categories: fazendas, pousadas, pesqueiros and botels. Fazendas are ranch-style hotels which usually have horses and often boats for hire. Pousadas range from simple accommodation to top-end standard. Pesqueiros are hang-outs for fisherfolk, and boats and fishing gear can usually be rented from them. A botel (a contraction of boat and hotel) is a floating lodge.

Reservations are needed for all accommodation, especially in July, when lots of Brazilian tourists holiday here.

Unfortunately, nearly all accommodation is expensive. Rates usually include transport by plane, boat or 4WD from Corumbá or Cuiabá, good food and modest lodging. More often than not, reservations are handled by a travel agent and must be paid for in advance. It's also a good idea to call ahead for weather conditions – the rainy and dry seasons are never exact, and proper conditions can make or break a trip.

Transpantaneira Accommodation on the Transpantaneira, the elevated dirt road that

begins just outside Poconé and extends 145 km to Porto Jofre, is plentiful.

At Km 27, the *Pousada São Sebastião do Pantanal* (☎ (065) 322-0178) has a restaurant, boats and horses. Full board and lodging costs US$30 per person. This would be a good option in the wet season, when the Transpantaneira becomes impassable. Just up the road, at Km 30, the *Pousada das Araras* (☎ (065) 381-4959) has a pool, as well as boats and horses. This place is used by many tour companies as part of their package. Four days for two people costs US$400.

Moving on down the road to the Rio Pixaim, at Km 65, you'll find two places; our advice is to check both before deciding where to stay, as their prices are similar. The *Pousada do Pixaim* (☎ (065) 322-8961) is the more rustic of the two – a classic Pantanal building (wooden, on stilts). It has air-con, tasty meals (included in the accommodation price), clean rooms with electric showers, and the last álcool and gas pump until you return to Poconé – so fill up! This hotel used to be the budget travellers' favourite, but prices have risen since the installation of air-con. We preferred the old overhead fans, but you can't please everybody. Prices are US$37/43 a single/double. Across the bridge, the much more modern *Fazenda-Hotel Beira Rio* (☎ (065) 321-9445) is just a little more expensive: US$50/57 a single/double. It's popular with package tourists from São Paulo. Boats can be rented for US$20 an hour and horses for US$12 an hour. Boats can also be rented at the Pousada do Pixaim, for about the same price.

Forty km further down the road is the newest and cheapest pousada on the Transpantaneira: the *Pousada O Pantaneiro* (☎ (065) 721-1545), run by Lerinho and his son Eduardo. It's a simple place, charging US$25 per person for room and board.

Porto Jofre is where the Transpantaneira meets its end, at the Rio Cuiabá. It's a one-hotel town – in fact, it's not even a town. Campers can stay at Sr Nicolino's fishing camp, near the river, for US$4 per person. He provides clean bathrooms and cooking

ANDREW DRAFFEN

JOHN MAIER, JR

JOHN MAIER, JR

JOHN MAIER, JR

Top Left: Curiosity shop, Goiás Velho
Top right: Pantanal sunset
ottom Left: Charcoal worker in Mato Grosso do Sul
tom Right: Wading in the Pantanal

Top: Women near Campo Grande, Mato Grosso do Sul
Bottom: A farmer keeping a piranha at arm's length

facilities, and also rents boats. Alternatively, take the turn-off (it's the only one) a couple of km to the *Hotel Santa Rosa Pantanal* (☎ 322-0948). For US$100/130 a single/double, the Santa Rosa will put you up in a bungalow that sleeps four and feed you three fish meals a day. It's nothing fancy, but you get hot showers plus decent food (a choice of fried fish, grilled fish, stewed fish or salted fish).

The Santa Rosa has a swimming pool and a foosball (table-top soccer) table. Boats (very expensive), horses (expensive) and beer cost extra. Reservations are a good idea – the next hotel is probably in Bolivia. Lots of budget travellers get a shock when they arrive and find out the price. Perhaps you could persuade the manager to let you hang your hammock in the workers' apartments (at the edge of the hotel grounds), but don't count on it.

Mato Grosso Several fazendas in the northern Pantanal are off the Transpantaneira. Easily accessible by car is the *Hotel Porto Cercado* (☎ (065) 322-0178 in Cuiabá), along the Rio Cuiabá, 42 km from Poconé. Singles/doubles cost US$60/80, meals included. At the expensive *Hotel Cabanas do Pantanal* (☎ (065) 321-4142 in Cuiabá); 52 km from Poconé, a three-day package costs US$300.

The *Acampamento Pirigara* (☎ (065) 322-8961), on the banks of the Rio São Lourenço and the Rio Cuiabá, is 45 minutes by plane from Poconé and about six hours by boat from Porto Cercado. To stay in the hotel costs only US$30 per person, all-inclusive, but the plane ride costs US$200. The boat is cheaper, but operates only during the dry season.

One of the newer lodges is *Sapé Pantanal Lodge* (☎ (065) 322-3426), on the margins of the Rio Cuiabá, one hour by boat from the Porto Cercado. Four-day packages with full board cost US$480. This one has been highly recommended by several readers, so if money is no object, check it out.

Mato Grosso do Sul Southern gateways to the Pantanal are the cities of Corumbá, Aquidauana and Miranda. Most travellers head to Corumbá, while Aquidauana and Miranda are popular with Brazilian anglers.

Around Aquidauana are a number of mid-range to expensive hotel-fazendas. *Aguapé Pousada* (☎ (067) 241-2889; fax 241-2987), 57 km from Aquidauana, charges US$90 a day, but you can camp there for US$8 a day and buy meals at the restaurant. The *Hotel-Fazenda Salobra* is 90 km from Aquidauana and costs US$60 a day. *Pousada Mimosa* (170 km away) is for those who like a bit of adventure. It charges US$40 a day. The *Fazenda Rio Negro* is the old Rondon homestead where the soap opera *Pantanal* was filmed. Forty minutes by plane from Aquidauana, it costs US$120 a day. For more information about these places, go to the Panbratour office in Aquidauana.

One of the cheapest places to stay in the Pantanal is the *Pesqueiro Clube do Pantanal* (☎ (067) 242-1464 in Miranda). They charge about US$25 per person (with full board), and fishing trips by boat can be arranged. Also in the vicinity of Miranda is the *Miranda Pesca Clube* (☎ (067) 242-1323 in Miranda), five km from town, and the *Hotel Beira Rio* (☎ (067) 242-1262 in Miranda) eight km from town. The latter has air-con and hot showers and is rigged out like a pesqueiro. Full board costs US$40 per person. There is cheap accommodation and boat hire where the Campo Grande to Corumba road crosses the Rio Miranda (15 km from Miranda going toward Corumbá), but these places are geared to fishers, not sightseers.

The top-end place in the southern Pantanal is the *Refúgio Ecológico Caiman* (☎ (067) 725-5267 in Campo Grande, (067) 242-1102 in Corumbá, (011) 246-9934 in São Paulo), 36 km from Miranda. Begun six years ago with the building of the Pousada Caiman, the complex today boasts four pousadas in different areas of a 53,000-hectare fazenda. Guests can stay in one of the pousadas, or participate in an itinerant package – moving from one pousada to another. Caiman offers 25 different programmes that can be done on

THE CENTRAL WEST

foot, on horseback or by truck. All are led by one of the multilingual guides who live on the fazenda. This is real ecological tourism – it isn't cheap (four-day packages start at US$500), but it's highly recommended.

There are a few places located downstream of the Rio Miranda and a bit deeper into the Pantanal, at Passo do Lontra, 120 km and two hours (dry season) from Corumbá; to get there, take the dirt road leading off the road to Campo Grande. Alternatively, you can take the train to Campo Grande and arrange for the lodge transport to pick you up from the Carandazal station. The *Cabana do Lontra* (☎ (067) 383-4532 in Campo Grande) is an excellent place, another classic Pantanal wood-on-stilt structure, with lots of wildlife around. They charge US$40 per person, including full board, but are quite willing to bargain, especially out of season. It's highly recommended.

Sixteen km from Passo da Lontra, the *Fazenda Santa Clara* (☎ (067) 231-5797) is popular with travellers for a couple of reasons. The first is that you can do it on your own, without waiting around for a group to form. The second is that they're well organised, with an office in Corumbá (Rua Frei Mariano 502), and take people out to the fazenda every day. Rates are US$85/110/130 for two/three/four days, full board included. Use of boats, horses and fishing gear costs extra.

Serious fishing enthusiasts should consider the *Pesqueiro Taruma* (☎ (067) 231-4197 in Corumbá), on the Rio Paraguai 70 km from Corumbá. It's small, but well equipped, with air-con, hot shower, fridge and boats, and costs US$80 a day, including meals. The Taruma closes from November to January. The *Paraiso dos Dourados* (☎ (067) 231-5223 in Corumbá), at Fazenda Morrinhos, 72 km from Corumbá, offers its guests hot water, air-con, fridge, boats and good fishing.

Botels defy any permanent address. Most of them operate out of Corumbá and are used for fishing trips, which usually last a minimum of five days. Arara Pantaneira (☎ (067) 231-4851) rents the boats *Albatroz*

and *Arara Pantaneiro*. The daily cost is US$200 per person, including food, bait, and small boats to zip around in. *Pantanal Tour* (☎ (067) 231-4683) runs both the *Cabexi I* and the *Cabexi II*, which cost US$1600 a day for eight people.

Getting There & Away

There are two main approach routes to the Pantanal: via Cuiabá in the north and via Corumbá in the south. From Cuiabá, the capital of Mato Grosso, there are three 'gateways' to the Pantanal – Cáceres, Barão de Melgaço and Poconé – all of which lead to Porto Jofre, on the Transpantaneira. Corumbá is best accessed by bus from Campo Grande, capital of Mato Grosso do Sul; the route runs via Aquidauana and Miranda.

Coxim, a small town on BR-163, east of the Pantanal and accessible by bus or air-taxi from either Campo Grande or Cuiabá, is a third point of entry to the Pantanal. However, it has a very limited tourist infrastructure.

Getting Around

Since the lodges are the only places to sleep, drink and eat, and public transport doesn't exist, independent travel is difficult in the Pantanal. The cement boat that makes the run from Corumbá to Cáceres is very infrequent. You can always try to hitch a ride on a plane with one of the local fazendeiros. Driving is less expensive, but not easy. Only a few roads reach into the periphery of the Pantanal; they are frequently closed by rains, and reconstructed yearly. Only the Transpantaneira highway goes deep into the region. See the boxed aside.

Car Rental Hitching may be the cheapest way to go, but it doesn't allow you to stop whenever you want to observe wildlife. In Cuiabá, there are several car-rental agencies just outside the airport grounds to your right, and they're often cheaper than the agencies inside the airport. There is some competition, so shop around and ask about

Driving down the Transpantaneira

It is, of course, impossible to know everything about travel in the Pantanal, but based on several trips and conversations with literally dozens of Pantanal experts, we think the best way to visit the Pantanal, if you're in it for the wildlife and your budget is limited, is driving down the Transpantaneira, preferably all the way to Porto Jofre.

Why the Transpantaneira? First, it's the best place to see wildlife – especially in the meadows near the end of the road, at Porto Jofre. Second, renting a car in Cuiabá and driving down the Transpantaneira is less expensive than most Pantanal excursions, which require flying, boating, or hiring a guide with a 4WD. And third, if you're on a very tight budget, you can take a bus to Poconé and hitch from there (it's pretty easy), if necessary returning to Poconé for cheap accommodation.

The Transpantaneira is the best place we've seen in South America for observing wildlife, which is drawn to the roadway at all times of the year. During the wet season, the roadway is an island, and during the dry season, the ditches on either side of the road serve as artificial ponds, drawing birds and game towards the tourist.

Thousands of birds appear to rush out from all sides, ocelots and capybara seem frozen by the headlights, and roadside pools are filled with hundreds of dark silhouettes and gleaming, red jacaré eyes. It's very easy to approach the wildlife; you can walk within spitting range of the jacaré, and if you're crazy enough to go cheek to cheek with one, you can spot the fleas which live off the lacrimal fluid of their eyeballs.

If you are driving from Cuiabá, get going early. Leave at 4 am to reach the Transpantaneira by sunrise, when the animals come to life, and have a full day's light in which to drive to Porto Jofre.

The approach road to the Transpantaneira begins in Poconé (two hours from Cuiabá), by the Texaco station. Follow the road in the direction of the Hotel Aurora. The official Transpantaneira Highway Park starts 17 km south of Poconé. There's a sign and a guard station (where you pay a small entry fee) at the entrance, but we've seen herds of ema, many birds and jacaré well before the park entrance. Thirty km down the road, stop off at Bar Figeira and meet Zico, the 'pet' jacaré.

Stopping to see wildlife and slowing down for 118 rickety little wooden bridges, it's easy to pass the whole day driving the Transpantaneira – arriving at the expensive Hotel Santa Rosa in time for dinner, soon after sunset. Weekdays are best if you're driving, as there's less traffic kicking up dust.

Hitching down the Transpantaneira is easy enough – it's hitching back that's difficult. There aren't a lot of cars or trucks, but many stop to give rides. The best time to hitch is on weekends, when the locals drive down the Transpantaneira for a day's fishing. Make sure you get on the road early. We've done the entire route from Porto Jofre to Poconé several times with all sorts of folk: a rancher and his family, two American birders, an IBAMA park ranger, a photo-safari guide, some Italian tourists, an ex-poacher and a photojournalist doing an article on jacaré poaching.

Wildlife is abundant along the length of the Transpantaneira, but reaches a climax in the meadows about 10 to 20 km before Porto Jofre. The flora here is less arid, less scrubby. The birds, jacaré and families of capybara scurry into the ponds along the road. On our last trip, we saw several toucans, flocks of luminescent-green parrots and six blue hyacinth macaws in the big trees that divide the great meadows. There are enormous flocks of birds and individual representatives of seemingly every species. For details, see the Flora & Fauna section in the Facts about the Country chapter. ■

promotional rates. No matter what anyone tells you, you don't need a 4WD to drive the Transpantaneira. The best car is a VW Gol (Golf) or a Fiat Uno. The Brazilian Gurgel looks like a 4WD but doesn't act like one. Stick with the Gol in the Pantanal. Flat tyres can be a problem, so make sure you have a spare.

If you are planning to drive the Transpantaneira, you should try to protect yourself by reserving a Gol a few weeks in advance – it costs nothing, and you can always shop around for a better deal once you have arrived there. Do not forget to fill up your fuel tank at Poconé and at the Pousada do Pixaim.

Mato Grosso do Sul

CAMPO GRANDE

Founded around 1875 as the village of Santo Antônio de Campo Grande, Campo Grande really began to grow when the railway came through, in 1914. The city became the capital of Mato Grosso do Sul in 1977 by decree of military president Ernesto Giesel, when the new state splintered off from Mato Grosso. It is known as the Cidade Morena because of its red earth. Manganese, rice, soy and cattle are the sources of its wealth. Campo Grande lies 716 km south of Cuiabá and 403 km south-east of Corumbá.

There are no tourist attractions in Campo Grande, but because it's a transport hub, most travellers end up staying here overnight before heading out. Like all big cities, Campo Grande has plenty of hotels and restaurants, and gets lively on weekends when the gaúchos come to town.

Information

Tourist Office Semcetur runs a small information booth in the pedestrian mall on Rua Barão do Rio Branco, between Rua 14 de Julho and Rua 13 de Maio. It's supposed to be open Monday to Saturday from 7.30 am to 7.30 pm, but don't count on it.

Money The Banco do Brasil has a câmbio at Avenida Afonso Pena 2202. There's also a câmbio at Rua Dom Aquino 1682.

Post & Telephone The post office is on the corner of Rua Dom Aquino and Avenida Calógeras. The telefônica is near the corner of Rua Rui Barbosa and Rua Dom Aquino.

Museu Dom Bosco

The Museu Dom Bosco, Rua Barão do Rio Branco 1843, is the only museum in town that's worth a look. It has an excellent collection of over 10,000 insects, including 7000 butterflies. There are lots of stuffed animals, and interesting exhibits about the Bororo, Moro, Carajá and Xavante Indians. Reasonably priced handicrafts are also available. The museum is open daily from 7 to 11 am and 1 to 5 pm.

Places to Stay – bottom end

If you're a light sleeper, bear in mind that hotels near the railyards are pretty noisy, though not as much as they used to be. The *Hotel Copacabana*, a stone's throw from the train station, at Rua Dr Temistocles 83, and the *Hotel Esperança*, next door, are two flophouses where the gaúchos and outlaws crash out. Both charge US$5 a head, but they're only for those on the tightest of tight budgets. Of the two, the Esperança is the friendlier. Just across from the train station, the *Hotel Gaspar* (☎ 383-5121) is good value for money. Singles/doubles start at US$12/22. Down the road, at Avenida Calógeras 2828, the *Hotel União* (☎ 382-4213) is a bit cheaper, with singles/doubles for US$9/16.

The pick of the budget places, though, is the *Hotel Continental* (☎ 382-3072), at Rua Maracajú 229. It's very clean, and there's a washing machine for getting that red dust out. Quartos with fan are US$6/12, and apartamentos go for US$9/14. If the Continental is full, try the *Hotel Americano* (☎ 721-1454), at Rua 14 de Julho 2311. It has single/double quartos for US$8/14 and apartamentos for US$13/16. Near the bus station, the *Novo Hotel* (☎ 721-0505), Rua Joaquim Nabuco 185, is very clean and charges US$9 per person.

Places to Stay – middle & top end

More expensive places include the *Palace Hotel* (☎ 384-4741), an excellent place right in the centre, and not too noisy either. Singles/doubles cost US$15/22, and breakfast is good, too. The Palace is often full. Also centrally located is the *Fenícia* (☎ 383-2001), at Avenida Calogeras 2262. Singles/doubles go for US$35/47. At the top end, the *Exceler Plaza* (☎ 382-0102; fax 382-0141), at Avenida Afonso Pena 444, on the road to the airport, has doubles for US$130.

Places to Eat

The *Restaurante Hong Kong* is an excellent Chinese restaurant close to the cheap hotels. We can highly recommend their curry and tofu dishes. *Seriema*, at Avenida Afonso Pena 1919, is a popular churrasco and pasta place with a nice atmosphere and live music.

For a self-serve, por kilo vegetarian lunch, *NutriBem*, at Rua Pedro Celestino 1696, is good. It's open from 11 am to 2.30 pm every day except Saturday. *Viva a Vida* is another natural-food place that's good for lunch. It's at Rua Dom Aquino 1354, right next to the Bolivian Consulate.

The bars along the pedestrian mall on Rua Barão do Rio Branco have standard menus. This mall is also a good place to come for a chopp or three.

Getting There & Away

Air There are daily connections to all major cities. For the major airlines, call Varig (☎ 383-4070, or 763-1213 at the airport) or VASP (☎ 382-4070, or 763-2389 at the airport).

Antônio João airport (☎ 763-2444) is seven km from town; to get there, take the 'Vila Popular' bus from near the rodoviária.

THE CENTRAL WEST

Campo Grande

0   0.5   1 km

PLACES TO STAY	17 Fenícia Hotel	21 Bar
1 Hotel Esperança	26 Novo Hotel	22 Coisas da Terra
2 Hotel Copacabana		23 Seriema
3 Hotel Estação	**PLACES TO EAT**	
4 Hotel Gaspar	9 Restaurante	**OTHER**
5 Hotel União	Hong Kong	11 Telephones
6 Hotel Priape	10 Nutribem	14 Museu Dom Bosco
7 Hotel Tupi	16 Viva a Vida	15 Semcetur
8 Hotel Continental	19 Churrascaria	18 Post Office
12 Palace Hotel	Campo Grande	24 Casa de Artesão
13 Hotel Americano	20 Bar	25 Rodoviária

There are several air-taxis available for trips into remote areas of the Pantanal.

Bus The rodoviária, at Rua Joaquim Nabuco 200, is a huge one, with lots of bars, barbers and a porno movie theatre. The visiting gaúchos need never leave the bus station!

To Corumbá, there are seven buses a day; the first leaves at 6.30 am and the last at midnight. The trip takes seven hours (four hours less than the train) and costs US$16. Eight buses a day make the 10-hour trip to Cuiabá. To Ponta Porã, there are 10 buses a day. The 8.30 am executivo bus will get you there by 1 pm. This is the fastest – the others are milk runs that stop for everyone. The cost is US$17.50 for the executivo and US$11 for the ordinary bus. There are also daily buses to Brasília (US$34, 23 hours), Belo Horizonte (US$34, 23 hours), São Paulo (US$27, 14 hours) and Foz do Iguaçu (US$20, 13 hours).

Train The train station is on Avenida Calógeras, close to the centre of town. Trains are cheaper than buses, except when you travel in cabins, but if you do decide to go by rail, take mosquito repellent. To check rail information, call (067) 383-2762 in Campo Grande.

To Corumbá, there are trains on Wednesday and Saturday, leaving at 7.03 am. The ticket office opens at 5 am, but you can purchase tickets up to 10 days in advance. Double cabins cost US$30; 1st/2nd class is US$12/8. There is a daily train travelling to Ponta Porã, at 9.20 am, and it takes about nine hours to get there. The train to Bauru has been discontinued.

CORUMBÁ

This port city on the Rio Paraguai and the Bolivian border is the southern gateway to the Pantanal. Corumbá, or Cidade Branca (White City), was founded and named in 1776, by Captain Luis de Albuquerque.

By 1840 it was the biggest river port in the world, boasting a dozen foreign consulates. Ships would enter the Rio de la Plata in the South Atlantic and sail up the Rio Paraná to its confluence with the Rio Paraguai, then continue up to Corumbá. The crumbling but impressive buildings along the waterfront reflect the wealth that passed through the town during the 19th century. With the coming of the railway, Corumbá lost its importance as a port and went into decline.

The city is 403 km north-west of Campo Grande by road or rail. Due to its strategic location near the Paraguayan and Bolivian borders (Puerto Suarez is only 19 km away), Corumbá has a reputation for poaching, drug-trafficking and gun-running. Be cautious if you come here.

Orientation

The train station and bus station are near each other, six blocks from the centre of town. The waterfront is three blocks from the centre in the opposite direction.

Information

Tourist Office Not much is available here in the way of government tourist information, but there are lots of travel agencies in town, most of them promoting the same things. Some good ones are Pantanal Safari (☎ 231-2112), at Rua Antônio Maria Coelho 330, and Pantur (☎ 231-4343), at Rua América 969. Colibri Pantanal Safari (☎ & fax 231-3934), run by Swiss Claudine Roth out of the Pousada Pantaneira, Rua Frei Mariano 1335, organises Pantanal tours lasting two to 10 days. They don't come much cheaper – a three/four-day tour costs US$60/70.

Money The Banco do Brasil, at Rua 13 de Junho 914, has a câmbio on the 2nd floor. When we were there, they were actually giving a better rate for travellers' cheques than for cash dollars. There's also an active black market for cash dollars in Corumbá – you'll find lots of ladies with handbags full of money on the corner of Rua Mario Coelho and Rua Delamare.

Post & Telephone The post office is in Rua Delamare, across from the Praça da República. Telems has a telefônica on Rua Dom Aquino.

Foreign Consulates The Bolivian Consulate (☎ 231-5605) is at Rua Antônio Maria Coelho 881, near the intersection of Rua América. It's open from 8.30 am to 1.30 pm Monday to Friday. Oddly, intending visitors to Bolivia may have to check out of Brazil before applying for a visa here.

The Paraguayan Consulate (☎ 231-1691) is at Rua Firmo de Matos 508. On the Bolivian side, the nearest Brazilian Consulate is in Santa Cruz.

Visas For a Brazilian entry/exit stamp, go to the Polícia Federal office located at the rodoviária. It's open from 8 to 11.30 am and 2 to 5 pm daily.

Things to See & Do
Corumbá's star attraction is the Pantanal, and you can get a preview of it from **Morro Urucum** (1100 metres). Tourists looking for something different might consider a two-day excursion to **Forte Coimbra**, which is a seven-hour boat trip south on the Rio Paraguai. In days gone by, the fort was a key to the defence of the Brazilian west, and you still need permission from the Brigada Mista (at Avenida General Rondon 1735) to visit it.

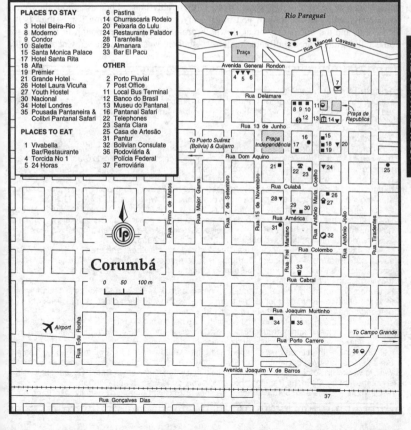

THE CENTRAL WEST

PLACES TO STAY
3 Hotel Beira-Rio
8 Moderno
9 Condor
10 Salette
15 Santa Monica Palace
17 Hotel Santa Rita
18 Alfa
19 Premier
21 Grande Hotel
26 Hotel Laura Vicuña
27 Youth Hostel
30 Nacional
34 Hotel Londres
35 Pousada Pantaneira &
   Colibri Pantanal Safari

PLACES TO EAT
1 Vivabella
   Bar/Restaurante
4 Torcida No 1
5 24 Horas
6 Pastina
14 Churrascaria Rodeio
20 Peixaria do Lulu
24 Restaurante Palador
28 Tarantella
29 Almaara
33 Bar El Pacu

OTHER
2 Porto Fluvial
7 Post Office
11 Local Bus Terminal
12 Banco do Brasil
13 Museu do Pantanal
16 Pantanal Safari
22 Telephones
23 Santa Clara
25 Casa de Artesão
31 Pantur
32 Bolivian Consulate
36 Rodoviária &
   Polícia Federal
37 Ferroviária

Rio Paraguai
Rua Manoel Cavassa
Praça
Avenida General Rondon
Rua Delamare
Praça de Republica
Rua 13 de Junho
To Puerto Suárez (Bolivia) & Quijarro
Praça Independência
Rua Dom Aquino
Rua Cuiabá
Rua Firmo de Matos
Rua Major Gama
Rua 7 de Setembro
Rua 15 de Novembro
Rua Antônio Maria Coelho
Rua América
Rua Frei Mariano
Rua Antônio João
Rua Tiradentes
Rua Colombo
Rua Cabral
Corumbá
0 50 100 m
Airport
Rua Edu Rocha
Rua Joaquim Murtinho
Rua Porto Carrero
To Campo Grande
Avenida Joaquim V de Barros
Rua Gonçalves Dias

· Daily **boat tours** of the Corumbá environs are available through all travel agencies. An all-day trip on the boat *Pérola do Pantanal* will set you back US$25, including lunch. See Pantanal Safari for more details. Other packages include sightseeing trips to Bolivia and day trips by road.

Pantanal Tours

Many budget travellers are choosing to go on cheap three to four-day tours into the Pantanal. These trips, generally costing around US$20 a day, can be very rough-and-ready affairs – try to imagine boy scouts on cachaça. Accommodation is in hammocks, under thatch or in somebody's shack. Food is generally pretty good, though you must take water, and the trucks may break down. Some of the 'guides' are ex-alligator hunters,

so their attitude towards animals leaves a lot to be desired. You'll see lots of birds and plenty of alligators, but the mammals are understandably a bit shy, especially when being chased by a truck at 80 km/h.

If you want something well organised, and riding around in the back of a pick-up truck doesn't grab you, pay a bit more and stay at a hotel-fazenda for a few days. If you're prepared to take it as it comes, you might have a good time.

Before signing on with one of these trips, and certainly before parting with any cash, there are a few things you should check out. Firstly, find out how far into the Pantanal you will be going – it should be at least 200 km, preferably more. Then ask about the itinerary, and get it in writing if possible. Is the programme flexible enough to account for sudden weather changes? Check out the

---

Tripping through the Pantanal
I ended up staying over a month in Corumbá, going out on four tours, so I sort of got an overview of the whole scene – and a lot of stories (good and bad) from other backpackers.

The Guides
You don't have to find a guide, they'll find you. They meet the buses and trains at the stations, they come to hotels, they approach you in restaurants or outside the Banco do Brasil (a *very* trying place to be on the last Friday of the month!). The sales pitch is pretty standard: albums of photos taken on their tours, letters of recommendation from satisfied tourists, and often a bit of badmouthing the other guides thrown in for good measure. Sometimes this last technique includes showing you 'letters' from tourists waxing lyrically about how terrible Guide A or Guide B was. These left me pondering a) why anyone would write a letter of complaint not to the guide but to someone completely different, and b) that someone whose publicity consists of telling you not how good they are, but how bad everyone else is, lacks imagination, talent and ethics. All offer three or four-day tours, including bottled water, tents and/or hammocks.

All the guides know the Pantanal well, they're predominantly born and bred in the area. Most speak only Portuguese, although Corumbá is a border town so quite a few are familiar with Spanish too. Some of them know the names of some of the wildlife in English or Hebrew that they've picked up from tourists.

Generally a tour is made up of a guide, a driver, a cook and five to ten tourists. These guys tend to freelance, alternately forming a team or competing with each other. Some of the ones I met and/or heard about from others who did tours with them:

Katu – he's the elder statesman of the bunch, he's been a guide for over ten years. He doesn't leap off the truck and sprint around and catch armadillos and alligators with the same vigour as the younger ones, but he's got tons of experience and everyone likes him.

Murilo Reis – the second most experienced, he started working as a guide when he was a teenager. He has lived in Hamburg for a year, and in April 1993 returned from London where he went to work with some Brits and Kiwis that he'd met when they were in Brazil. So, although he's spent most of his life in the Pantanal, he speaks very good English and German.

Gil Tours – Gil is a smooth character, he speaks English but doesn't usually take tours but

truck. Does it look OK? Does it have a radio or carry a first-aid kit in case of emergency? A bite from the *boca da sapo* snake will kill in half an hour if left untreated.

Expect to spend at least one day simply travelling deep into the Pantanal, and one day returning. Then allow at least two days for seeing wildlife at close quarters. Definitely insist on doing this on foot – vehicles should be used only for access, *not* for pursuit. Your chances of enjoying the Pantanal and its wildlife are greatly increased if you go with a reputable guide who: forsakes the 'mechanical chase' approach; accompanies small groups (preferably less than five persons) on an extensive walking trip through the area for several days; camps out at night (away from drinking dens!); and takes you on walks at the optimum times to observe wildlife – before sunrise, at dusk and

during the night. A trip along these lines will require at least four days (preferably five).

Insist on meeting your guide (or make it clear in writing that you will go only with a designated guide), and avoid signing on through an intermediary. How many years has your guide been in the Pantanal? Remember that speaking English is less important than local knowledge. Someone who has spent their life in the Pantanal won't speak much English. Prior to departure, be sure to read the Pantanal section (especially the What to Bring part) earlier in this chapter.

There are a lot of shonky guides around. In Corumbá they're known as *guias piratas* (pirate guides). They're not registered with the Associação das Guias (Guides' Association), so if you have some complaint or want your money back, you have no course of action. On these shonky tours, there is a lot

himself; he hires guides (who don't speak English). He seems to have the habit of keeping people waiting about without telling them what's going on, but the tours themselves are fine.

Tucanturs – the star attraction is Pedro, who worked with Murilo for four years. He doesn't speak English but understands a bit, and speaks Spanish. Great guide.

Johnny Indiano – has spent his life in the Pantanal and is especially good at finding nests and newborn animals. There seem to be a lot of guides who've adopted the name Johnny.

The Tours

We spent the first day basically driving out there, and the last day driving back, which was good because we got a long way into the Pantanal. Sometimes they have trouble with the trucks. It's difficult terrain for any vehicle, but the drivers really knew what they were doing, and they were all capable mechanics who quickly and effectively fixed anything that needed repairing on the spot. They never chased animals with the truck, only on foot, to give us a closer look and then they released them.

The food was good, they provide for vegetarians like me, and there's plenty of bottled water. Round the campfire at night, sometimes caipirinhas were offered, but most of us stuck to hot tea or coffee. We slept in a big tent with a very good mosquito net, or in hammocks strung up in an outside (mosquito screened) room on a farm. Before we left the campsite, all the rubbish was burned, or put in bags to take back to Corumbá. We went on lots of lovely long walks early in the mornings, and again in the evenings. It's amazingly beautiful in the Pantanal, the landscape itself is so interesting even without all the incredible creatures that live there. The sunrises and sunsets are spectacular, and the night sky takes your breath away.

The main thing to take is effective insect repellent, and apply it liberally in the evenings. There are about one zillion mosquitoes, all extremely partial to tourists. They never seem to bother the guides – one of those intensely unfair little facts of nature!

Maryann Sewell – New Zealand

Please let us know about your Pantanal trip. Feedback from this area is very helpful, as it's such a popular backpacker destination, and things change so fast. ∎

of cachaça drinking, the theory being that since cachaça is cheaper than gasoline, it costs less to convince drunk tourists that they're having a good time. Then there's no need to drive as far as promised. Tales of woe with pirate guides include abandonment in the marshes, assorted drunken mayhem and even attempted rape.

Places to Stay

There's a youth hostel (☎ 231-2305) at Rua Antônio Maria Coelho 677.

Close to the bus and train stations, the *Hotel Londres* (☎ 231-6717) has apartamentos with fans for US$8/13 a single/double. The *Pousada Pantaneira* (☎ & fax 231-3934), at Rua Frei Mariano 1335, near the defunct Hotel Schabib, is cheaper, but pretty run-down. Claudine, the Swiss lady who runs the place, says she's going to make some improvements.

In the centre, there are a number of cheapies located on Rua Delamare between Rua Antônio Maria Coelho and Rua Frei Mariano. The *Salette* (☎ 231-3768) has rooms starting at US$8/10 a single/double. Next door, at the *Condor*, quartos with fan go for US$5 per person – good value, as the place is clean and friendly.

Moving up a bit in price, the *Hotel Santa Rita* (☎ 231-5453), at Rua Aquino Corrêa 860, has good, big apartamentos for US$10/18. The ones at the front have small balconies. The *Hotel Laura Vicuña* (☎ 231-5874) is new and very comfortable. Single/double apartamentos cost US$18/28.

An interesting place to stay, though a bit out of the way, is the *Hotel Beira-Rio* (☎ 231-2554), Rua Manoel Cavassa 109, on the waterfront. Popular with anglers, it charges US$15 per person in air-con rooms.

At Rua Antônio Maria Coelho 389 is the *Premier* (☎ 231-4937), where singles/doubles with air-con and TV cost US$16/25. The rooms are on the small side. Hard to miss is the drug-runners favourite, the two-star *Santa Monica Palace* (☎ 231-3001; fax 231-7880), at Rua Antônio Maria Coelho 345. It charges US$37/58 for singles/doubles with the lot, including a pool.

The *Nacional* (☎ 231-6868; fax 231-6202), at Rua América 936, is the most expensive hotel in town. Singles/doubles go for US$41/63.

Places to Eat

Bar El Pacu, on Rua Cabral, is a good, cheap restaurant with excellent fish. Try a delicious local speciality, peixe urucum (fish with cheese melted on top in a condensed milk sauce), for US$4. El Pacu is run by Herman the German, an interesting character who has spent a long time in the Pantanal.

Peixaria do Lulu, on Rua Antônio João, is another good fish restaurant. The *Churrascaria Rodeio*, at Rua 13 de Junho 760, features live music as well as tasty meat dishes. The *Restaurante Paladar*, on Rua Antônio Maria Coelho, has comida caseiro por kilo. For cheap Japanese food, try *Soba-Yá*, at Rua Delamare 1181. They have sashimi for US$2. The *Almanara*, next to the Hotel Nacional, is recommended for Lebanese food.

In the evening, there's lots of action on Avenida General Rondon. Three places in a row – *24 Horas*, *Pastina* and *Torcida No 1* – all get crowded. They have standard menus. The hippest little eatery in town is *Vidabella*, a small bar/restaurant tucked away near the corner of the park at the bottom of Rua 7 de Setembro. Run by Nilo, a friendly Italian who's lived in Corumbá for many years, it serves pizza, pasta, pasteis, etc. Main courses (around US$10) are enough for two. It's also OK to go there just for a drink and to check out the great view of the Pantanal.

Things to Buy

The Casa de Artesão, in the old prison at Rua Dom Aquino 405, has a good selection of Indian art and artefacts, as well as the best Pantanal T-shirts in Corumbá.

Getting There & Away

Like Campo Grande, Corumbá is a transit point for travel to/from Bolivia and Paraguay. The Crossing the Border discussion at the end of this section gives details on crossing the border between Corumbá and Quijarro, Bolivia.

Air The airport (☎ 231-3322) is three km from the town centre. VASP is the only major airline servicing Corumbá. They have offices at Rua 15 de Novembro 392 (☎ 231-4441) and at the airport (☎ 231-4308). VASP offers connections to Brazilian capitals, while air-taxis fly to remote points of the Pantanal.

For Bolivian air connections, contact Pantur (see the Information section under The Pantanal heading earlier in this chapter). Pantur is the agent for LAB (Lloyd Aereo Boliviano) and TAM (Transportes Aereos Militares).

There are LAB flights between Puerto Suarez and Santa Cruz on Monday, Wednesday and Saturday. The Pantur price for a one-way ticket is US$120, which includes transport between Corumbá and Puerto Suarez. If you arrange your own transport to Puerto Suarez, the price drops to US$100.

TAM has flights between Puerto Suarez and Santa Cruz on Tuesday and Saturday. Pantur charges US$100 for a one-way ticket, including transport between Corumbá and Puerto Suarez (US$85 if you arrange your own transport).

Bus From the rodoviária, buses run to Campo Grande six times a day, from 7 am to midnight. The trip costs US$12 and takes seven hours, much quicker than the train.

Train To Campo Grande, there are trains every Monday and Friday at 8 am (US$12/8 in 1st/2nd class). Train services are constantly being reduced, so if you want to use them, check out the timetables as soon as you arrive in town.

Once across the Bolivian border, most people will be heading towards Santa Cruz. The train servicing the rail line between Santa Cruz and Quijarro, the Bolivian border town opposite Corumbá, is known as the Death Train. However, the journey is a beautiful one, passing through lush jungle, Chaco scrub and oddly shaped mountains to the steamy, sticky Pantanal area near the frontier. The many cattle ranches, agricultural projects, logging operations and Mennonite colonies along the railway are all indicators of the current developmental thrust of the long-neglected Bolivian Oriente (East). Despite all the economic changes and growth in the area, there is still a diverse and abundant supply of wildlife and vegetation. Colourful flowers, birds and butterflies thrive in the warm, moist conditions, and larger species, though rarely seen, still exist in limited numbers.

Be sure to have plenty of insect repellent on hand, since there are often long, unexplained stops in low-lying, swampy areas and the zillions of mosquitoes get voraciously hungry in those parts.

Those taking the train should anticipate delays. Three classes of service are available – Pullman, 1st and 2nd – but it's difficult to distinguish between them. There's a distinctly bovine feeling that comes over anyone riding this train. The boxcars have their drawbacks, but they're still more comfortable than the overcrowded coaches!

From Quijarro to Santa Cruz, the Pullman service runs on Tuesday and Saturday and the Rápido service on Wednesday and Sunday. In the opposite direction, both Pullman and Rápido trains run on Monday and Friday. The trip takes anywhere from 20 to 25 hours. In either direction, fares are B$59/39/27 in Pullman/1st class/2nd class. You'll have the same problems getting tickets in Quijarro as in Santa Cruz, although Quijarro taxi drivers will sell tickets at inflated prices – B$45/35 for 1st/2nd class. Make sure they're not already punched and that they're for the correct day and train.

Ferrobus The ferrobus, a bus on bogies which is considerably faster than the train, goes from Quijarro to Santa Cruz on Wednesday and Sunday. From Santa Cruz to Quijarro, it leaves on Tuesday, Thursday and Saturday. The tickets cost B$85/68 for 1st/2nd class. Securing a ticket can be extremely difficult, but again, the taxi drivers in Quijarro may be able to help.

THE CENTRAL WEST

For real Bolivian-style luxury, there's the Expreso Especial Bracha, a rapidly deteriorating rail car offering air-con, videos and minimal food service. Westbound, it runs on Tuesday and Saturday, and eastbound on Monday and Friday. In Corumbá, tickets should be reserved three or four days in advance through Receptivo Pantanal at Rua Frei Mariano, 502. They cost US$40 per person.

Boat The Paraguayan company Flota Mercantil del Estado runs boat services between Asunción (Paraguay) and Corumbá. Boats leave every second Friday. The five-day trip costs US$50 for a cabin or US$40 for a hammock. It's much cooler to take the cheap class and sling your hammock on deck. Meals are not included in the ticket price, but acceptable food is available in the on-board restaurant. Some boats go south on the Paraguai as far as Buenos Aires. Boat transport up through the Pantanal is difficult and infrequent – enquire at the Porto Geral.

Crossing the Border Today, the Bolivian border town of Quijarro is not much more than a muddy little collection of shacks. Taxis operate between Quijarro station and the border, a distance of about two km. You may have to bargain over the unrealistic initial rates – the drivers are banking on foreigners not knowing the distance to be travelled and agreeing to pay whatever they ask. The going rate is currently US$2 per person.

Moneychangers at the frontier accept cash only and are more interested in dollars than cruzeiros. Have your requisite amount readily and discreetly available for a smooth transaction, unless you relish the attention of onlookers. Since it appears the new cruzeiro is following in the footsteps of its hyperinflationary predecessors, it's impossible to quote a reliable exchange rate here; your best bet is to ask travellers going in the opposite direction what a fair rate will be.

Some people report being charged US$0.50 for a Bolivian exit stamp. Others have paid US$2.50 to leave Bolivia at Quijarro. Some pay nothing. It depends on the officer on duty at the time.

Just over the bridge, on the Brazilian side, you may be subjected to a customs search, but Brazilian immigration is at the federal police post at the Corumbá rodoviária. Anyone entering or exiting Brazil must check in here and complete immigration formalities. For about US$0.30, a city bus will take you into Corumbá, five km from the border. If you're coming from Bolivia, you won't be allowed to enter Brazil without a yellow-fever vaccination certificate. There is a vaccination clinic in Corumbá, but it's open for just one hour per day Monday to Saturday.

Getting Around

A taxi from either the bus or the train station to the centre of Corumbá costs US$2. For a taxi from the centre to the Bolivian border, expect to pay US$6. The city bus between the centre and the Brazilian border runs about twice an hour and costs US$0.60. The Brazilian border post is open daily from 8 to 11 am and 2 to 5 pm.

AQUIDAUANA

Aquidauana and Anastácio are twin towns situated on the Rio Aquidauana, 138 km from Campo Grande. They represent the beginning of the Pantanal and there are a number of excellent hotel-fazendas in the area. In Aquidauana there's not much to interest the traveller, though it's a pleasant place in which to spend a night.

Information

Panbratour (☎ 241-2986), at Rua 7 de Setembro 459, is an Aquidauana-based travel agency that specialises in the Pantanal. It also sells excellent photos of the area. Staff can give you the latest information on the hotel-fazendas available. Buriti Viagens e Turismo (☎ 241-2718), at Rua Manoel Antônio Paes de Barros 720, is another helpful agency. If you need to change money, try these places.

Places to Stay

A couple of popular cheapies close to the train station are the *Hotel Fluminense* (☎ 241-2038), Rua Teodoro Rondon 365, and the *Hotel Lord*, a couple of blocks away. Both charge US$5 per person.

The *Portal Pantaneiro Hotel* (☎ 241-4328), at Rua Pandía Calógeras 1067, is a very reasonably priced mid to top-end place, with singles/doubles starting at US$18/28. This one is excellent value.

Places to Eat

The *Churrascaria Princesa do Sul*, at Rua Marechal Mallet 1047, is popular. It's closed on Sundays. The *Lanchonete Asa Branca*, on Rua Manoel da Costa, has a good prato feito. The *Panificadora Viana*, at Augusto Mascarenhas 165, is a popular hang-out in the evenings.

Getting There & Away

Aquidauana is four hours by train or 2½ hours by bus from Campo Grande. There are frequent buses. The train station is right in town but the bus station is a 15-minute walk from the centre. There is one daily bus to Bonito at 4.30 pm.

COXIM

Coxim is a small town about halfway between Cuiabá and Campo Grande, on the eastern border of the Pantanal. Its drawcard is the Piracema, when fish migrate up the Taquari and Coxim rivers, leaping through rapids to spawn. The Piracema usually takes place from September to December; if you're travelling this road during that period, it's worth stopping off to have a look. The fishing (pacú, pintado, curimbatá, piracema and dourado) is good from August to December. A fishing licence is required. There are also some pretty waterfalls in the area, notably the Palmeiras falls, on the Rio Coxim.

Places to Stay & Eat

There are a number of cheap hotels in town. If you arrive late at night, the *Hotel Neves* (☎ 291-1273) is convenient, close to the bus station. Clean quartos with fan cost US$8 per person, a bit more with air-con. The town is three km away, on the banks of the river.

A couple of reasonable hotels with river frontage are the *Rio* (☎ 291-1295), at Rua Filinto Muller 651, and *Preto 27* (☎ 291-1117), at No 238. Both have singles/doubles with fan for US$12/16. The Rio also has single quartos for US$8.

The *Piracema* (☎ 291-1610) is a good place by the river, but it's three km out of town. Instead of going into town from the bus station, head down the highway for another 500 metres. It's next to the bridge. Apartamentos with air-con and frigobar cost US$18, and there's a good restaurant, open daily from 11 am to 3 pm and 6 to 11 pm. The *Grande Hotel* (☎ 291-1133) is the most expensive place, with singles/doubles for US$25/30.

Getting There & Away

All buses between Campo Grande and Cuiabá stop at Coxim.

Getting Around

All the hotels can arrange boats, the going daily rate being around US$70. To get to the Palmeiras falls, 27 km away, a taxi will cost US$15 to US$30 for a return trip – ask a few different taxi drivers.

BONITO

Apart from the Pantanal, the small town of Bonito is one of the major tourist destinations in the state of Mato Grosso do Sul. The town itself has no attractions, but the natural resources of the area are impressive. There are many caves in the region, the main ones being Lago Azul (an underground lake that's 156 metres deep) and NS Aparecida. To visit the caves, you need a guide, because the caves are locked and the guides have the keys.

Another attraction of the area is the incredibly clear rivers, where it's possible for divers to see the fish eyeball to eyeball.

Tours

Hapakany Tur (☎ 255-1315), at Rua Pilad

Rebuá 626, is a well-organised outfit. Sergio da Gruta, who runs it, is a good guy and knows the area very well. He offers several different excursions, including a rubber-rafting day trip. Prices vary, but are mostly around the US$30 mark. See the Getting Around section below for more information about tours.

Places to Stay

Camping five km out of town on the banks of the Rio Formoso, at the *Balneário Municipal*, would be the best option. The cost is US$5, and you can buy full meals at the canteens there. In town, there are a few cheap hotels, notably the *Bonanza* (☎ 255-1162), at Pilad Rebuá 623, which charges US$14/20 a single/double. The *Hotel da Praça* (☎ 255-1369), on the square where the bus stops, serves a good breakfast, and charges US$10 for a basic double room.

At the top end is *Fazenda Mimosa* (☎ 255-1179). Close to the Gruta do Mimoso, 32 km from town, accommodation is in a large, rustic farmhouse. The fazenda has horses for rent, walking trails and, of course, the nearby cave. The cost is US$35, and this includes three meals a day cooked in their wood-fired oven. The local pinga is not a bad drop either. Reservations are a good idea here.

Places to Eat

On the main square, *Lanchonete Rincão* has a good prato feito for US$2. The *Tapera*, just around the corner, at Pilad Rebuá 480, has a reasonable (US$8) fish dinner for two. They also have a self-serve lunch (US$5).

Getting There & Away

Bonito is 248 km from Campo Grande. There's one bus a day, at 3 pm, via Aquidauana. The trip takes 6½ hours, because the roads are rough after Aquidauana. There is a daily bus to Ponta Porã, at 12.30 pm.

Getting Around

Unfortunately, most of Bonito's attractions are some distance from the centre and there's no public transport. Your best bet is to use one of the tour agencies around town. Average prices are US$10 for a boat trip on the Rio Formoso, US$7 for a trip to the Aquário Natural, US$20 for a diving trip to the Rio Sucuri, US$3 for a trip to the Gruta Azul and US$12 to the Baleário Municipal (US$12).

PONTA PORÃ

Ponta Porã is a border town divided from the Paraguayan town of Pedro Juan Caballero by Avenida Internacional. It was a centre for the yerba maté trade in the late 1800s, long before it started attracting Brazilians, who like to play in the Paraguayan casinos, shop for perfumes, electronics and musical condoms, and hang out in ritzy hotels.

Immigration

Getting exit/entry stamps involves a bit of legwork, so if you're in a hurry, grab a cab. For Brazilian entry/exit stamps, go to the Polícia Federal (☎ 431-1428), at Rua Marechal Floriano 1483. It's open on weekdays from 7.30 to 11.30 am and 2 to 5 pm. The Paraguayan immigration office (☎ 2962), where you need to go for entry/exit stamps, is seven blocks away, in Pedro Juan Caballero. It's inside Inmobiliaria Ycua Bolaños, a real-estate office 5½ blocks from the border, on Calle Curupayty. It's open from 7.30 to 11.30 am and 1 to 5 pm Monday to Saturday.

The Paraguayan Consulate (☎ 431-1913) is at Avenida Presidente Vargas 120 in Ponta Porã. It's open Monday to Friday from 8 am to noon. The Brazilian Consulate is on Avenida Dr Francia in Pedro Juan Caballero.

Places to Stay – bottom end & middle

There are plenty of cheap places in both countries. The ones on the Paraguayan side of the border don't include breakfast. In Brazil, the *Hotel Alvorada* (☎ 431-5866), at Avenida Brasil 2977, is such good value that it's almost always full. Quartos go for US$8/14 a single/double and apartamentos for US$10/16.

A few blocks away, at Rua Guia Lopes 57, the *Barcelona Hotel* (☎ 431-3061) is a reasonable alternative with apartamentos for US$10/15 a single/double, though their plumbing is a bit rough. Opposite, the *Hotel Guarujá* (☎ 431-1619) is more expensive, but better, with singles/doubles for US$15/28.

At Avenida Internacional 2604, the *Hotel Internacional* (☎ 431-1243) has single quartos for US$12 and apartamentos for US$16/24 a single/double. It's in a good location.

Over the border in Paraguay, there are a few hotels close to each other on Calle Mariscal López. A couple of good ones are the *Hotel Guavirá* (☎ 2743), at No 1327, and the *Hotel Peralta* (☎ 2346), at No 1257. Both of them charge around US$8/14 for a single/double.

Places to Stay – top end

At the top end, the best place in Brazil is the *Pousada do Bosque* (☎ 431-1181; fax 431-1741), Avenida Presidente Vargas 1151, charging US$50/60 for single/double rooms. In Paraguay, the *Hotel Casino Amambay* (☎ 2573) is the dictators' choice.

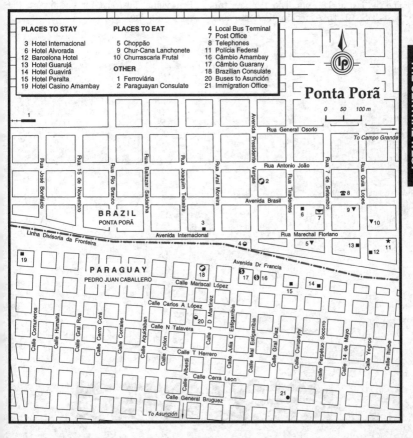

PLACES TO STAY
- 3 Hotel Internacional
- 6 Hotel Alvorada
- 12 Barcelona Hotel
- 13 Hotel Guarujá
- 14 Hotel Guavirá
- 15 Hotel Peralta
- 19 Hotel Casino Amambay

PLACES TO EAT
- 5 Choppão
- 9 Chur-Cana Lanchonete
- 10 Churrascaria Frutal

OTHER
- 1 Ferroviária
- 2 Paraguayan Consulate
- 4 Local Bus Terminal
- 7 Post Office
- 8 Telephones
- 11 Polícia Federal
- 16 Câmbio Amambay
- 17 Câmbio Guarany
- 18 Brazilian Consulate
- 20 Buses to Asunción
- 21 Immigration Office

Ponta Porã

THE CENTRAL WEST

Places to Eat

Choppão, at Rua Marechal Floriano 1877, is a good place to go for a beer and a snack, as is the *Chur-Cana Lanchonete*, on the corner of Avenida Brasil and Rua Guia Lopes. The *Churrascaria Frutal*, at Rua Guia Lopes 288, is a huge, flashy place that's just right for a splurge.

Getting There & Away

Air There are daily flights between Ponta Porã and São Paulo.

Bus To Campo Grande, 335 km away, there are nine buses a day; the first leaves at 1 am and the last at 9.30 pm. The 5½-hour trip costs US$10. To Asunción, there are constant buses leaving from the bus station on Calle Alberdi, three blocks from the border.

Train The train to Campo Grande leaves at 4.20 pm daily. It's a nine-hour trip that costs US$6/4 in 1st/2nd class.

Getting Around

The public transport on the Brazilian side of the border is excellent and simple. The local bus terminal is on Avenida Internacional, near the corner of Avenida Presidente Getúlio Vargas. To get to the long-distance rodoviária, take the bus marked 'São Domingos (Rod)'. For the train station, take the 'Ferroviária' bus, and for the airport, the 'Aeroporto' bus.

The Northeast

CHRIS McASEY

The Northeast

The Northeast region, known in Brazil as the Nordeste, covers more than 18% of the country's land area and contains 45 million inhabitants – nearly 30% of Brazil's population. The region is divided into nine states: Bahia, Sergipe, Alagoas, Pernambuco, Paraíba, Rio Grande do Norte, Ceará, Piauí and Maranhão. The archipelago of Fernando de Noronha lies over 500 km east of Recife and was placed under the political administration of Pernambuco state in 1988.

The many attractions of the Northeast include: historical cities (São Luís, Olinda and Salvador); colonial villages (Alcântara, Lençóis, etc); national parks (Lençóis Maranhenses, Chapada da Diamantina, Sete Cidades, etc); and the region's fascinating African heritage.

The geography of the Northeast is characterised by four divisions. The *zona da mata* (forest zone) covers the coastal area and extends up to 200 km inland. The forest, known as the Mata Atlântica, now exists only in tiny pockets – the rest was destroyed to make way for sugar-cane cultivation during the colonial period. With the exception of Teresina in Piauí state, all the major cities of the Northeast were established in this zone.

Further west, the *agreste* forms a transitional strip of semifertile lands which merges into the sertão.

The sertão (backlands) is characterised by a dry and temperate climate. Droughts, sometimes lasting for many years, have been the bane of this area for many centuries. The land is commonly referred to as caatingas because the landscape is dominated by vast tracts of caatinga (a scrubby shrub). The largest towns of the sertão are dotted along the Rio São Francisco, which provides irrigation. The bleak and brutal life of the Sertanejo (inhabitant of the sertão) has received literary coverage in *Os Sertões* (published in English as *Rebellion in the Backlands*), by Euclides da Cunha, and the novel *Vidas Secas* (Dry Lives), by Graciliano

Highlights

- African heritage and culture – music, dance, religion, cuisine and festivals (Bahia)
- Hikes and water slides in the Parque Nacional da Chapada Diamantina (Bahia)
- Candomblé ceremonies and festivals in Salvador and Cachoeira (Bahia)
- Pelourinho's Tuesday-night mini-Carnival in Salvador (Bahia)
- The *roda de capoeiras*: semicircles of musicians and dancer/fighters on the streets of Bahian towns
- Diving in the Parque Nacional Marinho de Fernando de Noronha (Pernambuco) and Parque Nacional Marinho dos Abrolhos (Bahia)
- Colonial river towns along the Rio São Francisco, particularly Penedo (Alagoas)
- Colonial cities of Olinda (Pernambuco) and São Luís (Maranhão)
- Dune-buggy rides on Natal's beaches (Rio Grande do Norte)
- Sand-dune surfing in the Parque Nacional dos Lençóis Maranhenses (Maranhão)
- Ceará's vast stretches of deserted coastline

Ramos. The Cinema Novo films of Glauber Rocha portray violence, religious fanaticism, official corruption and hunger in the sertão.

The state of Maranhão and the western

margin of Piauí state form the *meio norte*, a transitional zone between the arid sertão and the humid Amazon region.

The social problems of the Northeast include poverty, underemployment, housing shortages, a decaying educational system and an absence of basic sanitation. For example, in the state of Bahia, many towns and villages lack basic sanitation, infant mortality rates are high and half the population is illiterate. The number of unemployed in the state has been estimated at around 30% of the adult population.

Superintendência do Desen-Volvimento do Nordeste (SUDENE), the official government agency for development in the Northeast, has attempted to attract industry and boost the economy of the region, but these efforts have been hampered by the lack of energy sources, transport infrastructure, skilled labour and raw materials. Many

Nordestinos (inhabitants of the Northeast) have emigrated to the Southeast and Central West in search of a living wage or new land for cultivation.

The economy of the zona da mata depends on the cultivation of crops such as sugar and cacao, and on the petroleum industry which is based on the coast. The inhabitants of the agreste make their living from subsistence farming, small-scale agriculture (vegetables, fruit, cotton and coffee) and cattle ranching (beef and dairy). In the sertão, the economy is based on cattle ranching, cotton cultivation and subsistence farming, which puts the *carnaubeira*, a type of palm, to a multitude of uses. The meio norte is economically reliant on *babaçu*, another type of palm, which provides nuts and oil. The latter is converted into lubricating oil, soap, margarine and cosmetics. São Luís has become a major centre for the production of aluminium.

Bahia

Bahia is Brazil's most historic state, and has retained strong links with the African heritage of many of its inhabitants. Its capital, Salvador da Bahia, was also once the capital of colonial Brazil, from 1549 to 1763, and was the centre of the sugar industry which sustained the country's prosperity until the 18th-century decline in international sugar prices.

The state of Bahia divides into three quite distinct regions: the *recôncavo*, the *sertão* and the *litoral*.

The recôncavo is a band of hot and humid lands which surrounds the Baía de Todos os Santos. The principal cities are Cachoeira, Santo Amaro, Maragojipe and Nazaré, which were once sugar and tobacco centres and the source of wealth for Salvador.

The sertão is a vast and parched land on which a suffering people eke out a meagre

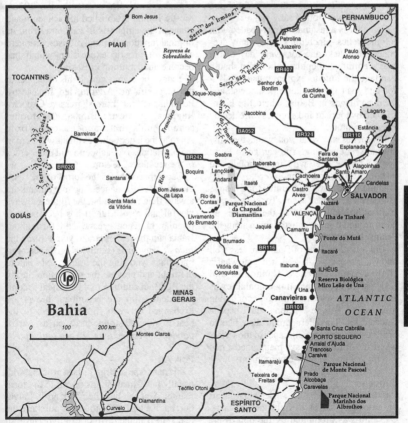

existence raising cattle and tilling the earth. Periodically, tremendous droughts, such as the great drought of 1877-79, sweep the land. Thousands of Sertanejos pile their belongings on their backs and migrate south or anywhere they can find jobs. But with the first hint of rain in the sertão, the Sertanejos return to renew their strong bond with this land.

The litoral south of Salvador, with beautiful, endless beaches, is a cacao-producing region, and there are important cities like Valença, Ilhéus and Itabuna. North of Salvador the coast is only sparsely populated with a few fishing villages. The southern beaches are calm, while the northern beaches are often windy with rough surf.

Salvador is a fascinating city loaded with colonial relics – including many richly decorated churches, one for every day of the year according to popular belief. You should also take the time to explore outside Salvador and visit the smaller cities, towns and fishing villages in Bahia, where life is unaffected by tourism and even less affected by the 20th century.

If beaches are what you want, the only difficulty is choosing. You can go to Porto Seguro for beaches with fancy hotels and restaurants or cross the river to Arraial d'Ajuda, Trancoso and Caraiva for a hipper, less developed beach scene. To really escape civilisation, you can go to the beaches up north around Conde, or to the south along the Peninsula do Maraú.

The inland regions of Bahia are less well known, but are worth a visit if you want a change from beaches. Cachoeira and Lençóis are both interesting colonial towns and Lençóis provides a handy base for hiking trips in the Parque Nacional da Chapada Diamantina. Travellers might also like to explore the bizarre moonscapes of the sertão, where the Sertanejos have maintained a rich culture despite the poor environment.

Capoeira

Capoeira originated as an African martial art developed by slaves to fight their masters. Capoeira was prohibited by the oppressors

and banished from the *senzalas* (slave barracks). The slaves were forced to practise clandestinely in the forest. Later, in an attempt to disguise this dance of defiance from the authorities, capoeira was developed into a kind of acrobatic dance. The clapping of hands and plucking of the *berimbau*, a stringed musical instrument that looks like a fishing rod, originally served to alert fighters to the approach of the boss and subsequently became incorporated into the dance to maintain the rhythm.

As recently as the 1920s, capoeira was still prohibited and Salvador's police chief organised a police cavalry squad to ban capoeira from the streets. In the 1930s, Mestre Bimba established his academy and changed the emphasis of capoeira, from its original function as a tool of insurrection, to a form of artistic expression which has become an institution in Bahia.

Today, there are two schools of capoeira: the Capoeira de Angola, led by Mestre Pastinha, and the more aggressive Capoeira Regional of Mestre Bimba. The former school holds that capoeira came from Angola; the latter believes that it was born in the plantations of Cachoeira and other cities of the recôncavo region.

Capoeira combines the forms of the fight, the game and the dance. The movements are always fluid and circular, the fighters always playful and respectful. It has become very popular in recent years, and throughout Bahia and the rest of Brazil you will see the *roda de capoeiras* (semicircles of spectator-musicians who sing the initial *chula* before the fight and provide the percussion during the fight). In addition to the musical accompaniment from the berimbau, blows are exchanged between fighter/dancers to the beat of other instruments, such as *caxixi*, *pandeiro*, *reco-reco*, *agogô* and *atabaque*.

Folk Art

Bahia has some of Brazil's best artisans, who usually have small shops or sell in the local market. You can buy their folk art in Salvador, but the best place to see or purchase the real stuff is in the town of origin because so

Capoeira

much of the production is regional and specialised.

The main materials used in Bahian folk art are leather, wood, earth, metal and fibre. Feira de Santana is known for its leatherwork: the best examples are in the city's Casa do Sertão folklore museum. Maragojipinho, Rio Real and Cachoeira produce earthenware. Caldas do Jorro, Caldas de Cipo and Itaparica specialise in straw crafts. Rio de Contas and Muritiba have metalwork. Ilha de Maré is famous for lacework. Jequié, Valença and Feira de Santana are woodworking centres. Santo Antônio de Jesus, Rio de Contas and Monte Santo manufacture goods made of leather and silver.

Religion
Much of Bahian life revolves around the Afro-Brazilian religious cults known as Candomblé. To the Christian observer, Candomblé provides a radically different view of the world. It combines African traditions of music, dance and language into a system of worship and enjoyment of life in peace and harmony.

Much of Candomblé is secret – it was prohibited in Bahia until 1970 – but the public ceremony, conducted in the original Yoruba tongue, takes place in a *terreiro*. In Salvador, the Casa Branca on Avenida Vasco da Gama 463, in the Engenho Velho neighbourhood, is a centre for Candomblé activities.

See the Religion section of the Facts about the Country chapter for more detail about Candomblé and the Jogo dos Búzios (Casting of Shells). For suggested reading on religion, see the Books & Maps section of the Facts about the Country chapter.

Salvador

Salvador da Bahia, often abbreviated to Bahia by Brazilians, is the capital of Bahia state and one of Brazil's cultural highlights. This city of 2.1 million people has managed to retain its African soul and develop the best of its colonial legacy into a unique, vibrant culture. Ornate churches still stand on cobblestone streets. Festivals are spontaneous, wild, popular and frequent. Candomblé services illuminate the hillsides. Capoeira and afoxé dance through the streets. The restoration of the historic centre of Salvador has revitalised areas that were previously considered dangerous and largely off limits to tourists.

However, despite the current boom in tourism, Salvador also suffers from social and economic problems, with a great number of citizens who are jobless, homeless, hungry, abandoned and sick.

History

According to tradition, on 1 November 1501, All Saints' Day, the Italian navigator Amerigo Vespucci sailed into the bay, which was accordingly named Baía de Todos os Santos. In 1549, Tomé de Souza came from Portugal bringing city plans, a statue, 400 soldiers and 400 settlers, including priests and prostitutes. He founded the city in a defensive location: on a clifftop facing the sea. After the first year, a city of mud and straw had been erected, and by 1550 the surrounding walls were in place to protect against attacks from hostile Indians. Salvador da Bahia became the capital of the new region, and remained Brazil's most important city for the next three centuries.

During its first century of existence, the city depended upon the export of sugar cane, but tobacco cultivation was later introduced and cattle ranching proved profitable in the sertão. The export of gold and diamonds mined in the interior of Bahia (Chapada Diamantina) provided Salvador with immense wealth. The opulent baroque architecture is a testament to the prosperity of this period.

Salvador remained the seat of government until 1763 when, with the decline of the sugar-cane industry, the capital was moved to Rio. Overlooking the mouth of Baía de Todos os Santos, which is surrounded by the recôncavo, Brazil's richest sugar and tobacco lands, Bahia was colonial Brazil's economic heartland. Sugar, tobacco, sugarcane brandy and, later, gold were shipped out, whilst slaves and European luxury goods were shipped in.

After Lisbon, Salvador was the second city in the Portuguese Empire: the glory of colonial Brazil, famed for its many gold-filled churches, beautiful colonial mansions and numerous festivals. It was also renowned, as early as the 17th century, for its bawdy public life, sensuality and decadence, so much so that it became known as the Bay of All Saints...and of nearly all sins!

The first black slaves were brought from Guinea in 1538, and in 1587 historian Gabriel Soares estimated that Salvador had 12,000 whites, 8000 converted Indians and 4000 black slaves. A black man was worth six times as much as a black woman in the slave market. The number of blacks eventually increased to constitute half of the population and the traditions of Africa took root so successfully that today Salvador is called the African soul of Brazil.

In Salvador, blacks preserved their African culture more than anywhere else in the New World. They maintained their religion and spirituality, within Catholicism. African food and music enriched the homes of both black and white, while capoeira developed among the slaves. *Quilombos*, runaway slave communities, terrified the landed aristocracy, and uprisings of blacks threatened the city several times.

In 1798, the city was the stage for the Conjuração dos Alfaiates (Conspiracy of the Tailors), which intended to proclaim a Bahian republic. Although this uprising was quickly quelled, the battles between those who longed for independence and those loyal to Portugal continued in the streets of

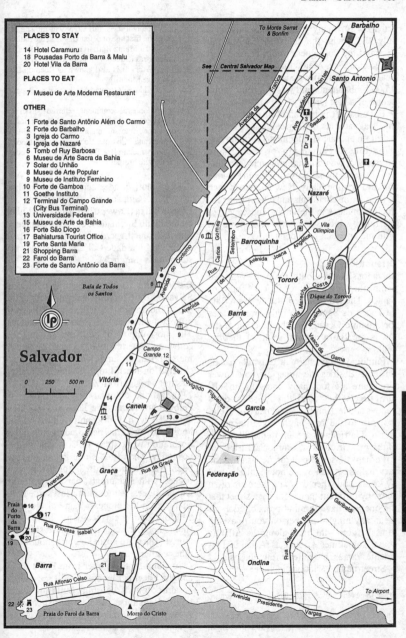

PLACES TO STAY

14 Hotel Caramuru
18 Pousadas Porto da Barra & Malu
20 Hotel Vila da Barra

PLACES TO EAT

7 Museu de Arte Moderna Restaurant

OTHER

1 Forte de Santo Antônio Além do Carmo
2 Forte do Barbalho
3 Igreja do Carmo
4 Igreja de Nazaré
5 Tomb of Ruy Barbosa
6 Museu de Arte Sacra da Bahia
7 Solar do Unhão
8 Museu de Arte Popular
9 Museu de Instituto Feminino
10 Forte de Gamboa
11 Goethe Instituto
12 Terminal do Campo Grande
   (City Bus Terminal)
13 Universidade Federal
15 Museu de Arte da Bahia
16 Forte São Diogo
17 Bahiatursa Tourist Office
19 Forte Santa Maria
21 Shopping Barra
22 Farol do Barra
23 Forte de Santo Antônio da Barra

Baía de Todos
os Santos

Salvador

0   250   500 m

THE NORTHEAST

Salvador for many years. It was only on 2 July 1823, with the defeat in Cabrito and Pirajá of the Portuguese troops commanded by Madeira de Melo, that the city found peace. At that time, Salvador numbered 45,000 inhabitants and was the commercial centre of a vast territory.

For most of the 19th and 20th centuries the city stagnated as the agricultural economy, based on archaic arrangements for land distribution, organisation of labour and production, went into uninterrupted decline.

Only recently has Salvador begun to move forward economically. New industries such as petroleum, chemicals and tourism are producing changes in the urban landscape, but the rapidly increasing population is faced with major social problems.

Orientation

Salvador sits at the southern tip of a V-shaped peninsula at the mouth of Baía de Todos os Santos. The left branch of the 'V' is on Baía de Todos os Santos; the right branch faces the Atlantic Ocean; and the junction of the 'V' is the Barra district, south of the city centre.

Finding your way around Salvador can be difficult. Besides the upper city and lower city, there are too many one-way, no-left-turn streets that wind through Salvador's valleys and lack any coherent pattern or relationship to the rest of the existing paved world. Traffic laws are left to the discretion of drivers. Gridlock is common at rush hour.

Perhaps most difficult for the visitor is the fact that street names are not regularly used by locals, and when they are, there are often so many different names for each street that the one you have in mind probably doesn't mean anything to the person you're asking to assist you – the road along the Atlantic coast, sometimes known as Avenida Presidente Vargas, has at least four aliases.

Street-name variations include:

Praça 15 de Novembro is popularly known as Terreiro de Jesus.
Rua Dr J J Seabra is popularly known as Bairro do Sapateiro (Shoemaker's Neighbourhood). In early colonial days, this street was the site of a moat, the first line of defence against the Indians.
Rua Francisco Muniz Barreto is also called Rua das Laranjeiras (Street of Orange Trees).
Rua Inácio Accioli is also known as Boca do Lixo (Garbage Mouth)!
Rua Leovigildo de Caravalho is known as Beco do Mota.
Rua Padre Nobrega is commonly referred to as Brega. The street was originally named after a priest. It developed into the main drag of the red-light district, and with time, Nobrega was shortened to Brega, which in Brazilian usage is now synonymous with brothel!

A steep bluff divides central Salvador into two parts: Cidade Alta (Upper City) and Cidade Baixa (Lower City). These are linked by the Plano Inclinado Gonçalves (funicular railway), the Lacerda Elevator, the Plano Inclinado Liberdade/Calçada and some very steep roads (*ladeiras*).

Cidade Alta This is the historic section of Salvador. Built on hilly, uneven ground, the site of the original settlement was chosen to protect the new capital from Indian attacks. The most important buildings – churches, convents, government offices and houses of merchants and landowners – were constructed on the hilltops. Rational planning was not a high priority.

Today, the colonial neighbourhoods of Pelourinho, Terreiro de Jesus and Anchieta are filled with 17th-century churches and houses. The area has been undergoing major restoration work since 1993, which continues today. The result is that Pelourinho has been transformed into a tourist mecca, packed with restaurants, bars, art galleries and boutiques. Although it's lost some of its character in the process (many of the street vendors and local residents have been shunted off), the area is now much safer and tourist police are posted on just about every other corner.

Just around the corner from Praça da Sé and the Lacerda Elevator, you'll see a large, cream-coloured colonial building which houses Bahiatursa, the state tourism agency. A few blocks further is Praça Castro Alves, a major hub for Carnival festivities.

From here, Avenida 7 de Setembro runs southwards (parallel to the bay) until it reaches the Atlantic Ocean and the Barra district, which has many of the city's top-end and mid-range hotels and bars.

Heading east from Barra district, the main road along the Atlantic coast, sometimes called Avenida Presidente Vargas (at least on the maps), snakes along the shore all the way to Itapoã. Along the way it passes the middle-class Atlantic suburbs and a chain of tropical beaches.

Cidade Baixa This is Bahia's commercial and financial centre, and port. Busy during working days, and filled with lunch places, the lower city is deserted and unsafe at night. Heading north, away from the ocean and along the bay, you pass the port and the ferry terminal for Ilha de Itaparica, and continue to the bay beaches of Boa Viagem and Ribeira (very lively on weekends). These are poor suburbs along the bay and the further you go from the centre, the greater the poverty. Watch for the incredible architecture of the *algados*, which are similar to favelas, but built on the bay.

CIA, the Centro Industrial de Aratu, is three times the size of Salvador and sprawls around the bay of Aratu, which empties into Baía de Todos os Santos. It's the first rationally planned industrial park in Brazil and over 100 firms operate there.

Information
Tourist Offices There is an ongoing feud between Emtursa, the tourist authority for the city of Salvador, and Bahiatursa, the state tourist organisation. As a result, neither authority is keen to tell travellers about information available from their counterpart.

Emtursa's main office (☎ 243-6555) is at Largo do Pelourinho 12, and there's a small information post inside the Museu da Cidade across the street, open Tuesday to Saturday from 10 am to 6 pm.

The main tourist office of Bahiatursa (☎ 241-4333) is in Palácio Rio Branco, Rua Chile 2. The office is open daily from 8 am to 6 pm. The staff are helpful and provide advice on accommodation, events, and where and when to see capoeira and Candomblé. The notice board inside the office has messages to help you find friends, rent houses and boats, buy guidebooks and even overseas airline tickets.

There are also Bahiatursa offices at: Rua Francisco Muniz Barreto 12, Pelourinho (☎ 321-2463), open daily from 8 am to 7 pm; Praça Azevedo Fernandes, Largo do Barra (☎ 247-3195), open Monday to Saturday from 8 am to 7 pm; Mercado Modelo (☎ 241-0242), open from 8 am to 6 pm Monday to Saturday; the rodoviária (☎ 358-0871), open daily from 9 am to 9 pm; and the airport (☎ 204-1244), open daily from 8. 30 am to 10 pm.

Bahiatursa operates an alternative accommodation service to locate rooms in private houses and the like during Carnival and summer holidays. This can be an excellent way to find cheap rooms. Information on travel throughout the state of Bahia is also available, but don't expect much detail.

For general tourist information or help, you can try dialling ☎ 131 for a service called Disque Turismo (Dial Tourism).

Gay & Lesbian Information is available from Centro Cultura (Triângulo Rosa; ☎ 243-4903), Rua do Sodré 45, which is close to the Museu de Arte Sacra da Bahia. The centre publishes an entertainment guide to Salvador's gay scene, *Guia para Gays*, which costs US$4. You can also contact the centre for information on HIV/AIDS.

Money The main branch of Banco do Brasil is at Avenida Estados Unidos 561, in Cidade Baixa. Other useful branches of this bank are on Terreiro de Jesus, Pelourinho; on Avenida Miguel Bournier, Barra; and at the airport. Banco Economico also has a handy branch at Rua Alfredo Brito 17, Pelourinho.

Currently, street moneychangers aren't the slightest bit interested in foreign currencies. This situation may change, but it's not advisable to change money on the street at any time.

THE NORTHEAST

THE NORTHEAST

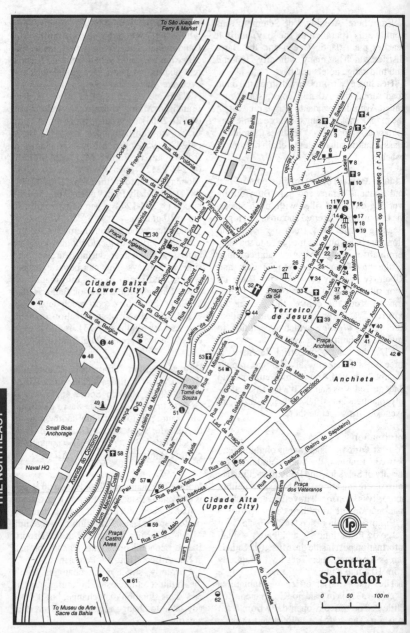

Central
Salvador

0   50   100 m

PLACES TO STAY

3	Albergue do Solar
6	Pousada do Passo
7	Albergue de Jurentude do Pelô
10	Hotel Solara
12	Hotel Pelourinho
41	Albergue de Jurentude das Laranjeiras
54	Hotel Themis
56	Palace Hotel
57	Hotel Chile
59	Hotel Pousada da Praça
61	Hotel Maridina

PLACES TO EAT

8	Casa do Benin
11	Banzo
16	Senac
18	Restaurante da Dinha
22	Micheluccio
23	Uauá
25	Dona Chika-ka
33	Cantinho da Sé
34	Salada das Frutas
37	Temporo da Dada
38	Yamoto
40	Bargaço

OTHER

1	Banco do Brasil
2	Igreja e do Santíssimo Sacramento Ida Rua do Pao
4	Igreja Convento de Ns do Carmo/Museu do Carmo
5	Igreja da Ordem Terceira do Carmo
9	Igreja NS do Rosário
13	Largo do Pelourinho
14	Fundaçáo Casa de Jorge Amado

15	Museu da Cidade
17	Olodum
19	Filhos do Ghandi
20	Bar do Reggae
21	Praça Quincas Berro D'gua (Praça Dois M)
24	Didá Music & Dance School
26	Antiga Faculdade de Medicina (Old Medical Faculty)
27	Museu Afro-Brasileiro/Museu de Arqueolgia e Etnología
28	Plano Inclinado Gonçalves (Funicular Railway)
29	VASP
30	Post Office
31	Police Post
32	Catedral Basílica
35	Igreja Sáo Pedro dos Clérigos
36	Largo de Tereza Batista
39	Igreja de Ordem Terceira de Sáo Domingus
42	Coraçáo de Mangue
43	Igreja Sáo Francisco
44	Praça da Sé Bus Station
45	Casa dos Azulejos
46	Mercado Modelo & Bahiatursa Tourist Office
47	Terminal Turístico Marítimo (Boat to Itaparica)
48	Small Boats to Itaparica
49	Bunda Statue
50	França Bus Terminal, Buses to São Joaquim, Ferry & Igreja NS do Bonfim
51	Palácio Rio Branco & Bahiatursa Tourist Office
52	Lacerda Elevator
53	Igreja da Misericórdia
55	Casa de Ruy Barbosa
58	Igreja NS de Conceicáo
60	Varig
62	Terminal da Barroquinha

There's an American Express/Kontik-Franstur SA office (☎ 242-0433) in the Cidade Baixa, at Rua da Argentina 1, which holds mail for travellers. It's open Monday to Friday from 8 am to 6 pm, but the mail office often closes for lunch.

Post & Telephone The central post office is in Cidade Baixa, on Praça da Inglaterra. There are also post offices at Rua Alfredo de Brito 43, Pelourinho; at the airport; and at the rodoviária. Watch out for price hikes and make sure items are franked.

Many hotels have an international phone

service, which is more convenient than running off to a telephone station. If you are not so lucky, some of the convenient Telebahia posts are:

Telebahia Mercado Modêlo
    Praça Visconte de Cairu, Comércio. Open
    Monday to Saturday from 8 am to 5 pm, and from
    8 am to noon on Sunday.
Telebahia Barra
    Avenida 7 de Setembro 533, Porto da Barra.
    Open daily from noon to 10 pm.
Telebahia Shopping Barra
    Avenida Centenário 2992, Barra. Open daily
    from 9 am to 10 pm, and from 9 am to 7 pm on
    Sunday.

Telebahia Rodoviária
 Open daily from 6 am to 10 pm.
Telebahia Aeroporto
 Aeroporto Internacional Dois de Julho. Open
 daily from 7 am to 10 pm.

There are also telephone stations in Iguatemi Shopping Centre, Campo da Pólvora and Centro de Convenções da Bahia.

Foreign Consulates The following countries maintain consulates in Salvador:

France
 Travessa Francisco Gonçalves 1, Comércio
 (☎ 241-0168). Open Monday, Tuesday and
 Thursday from 2.30 to 5 pm.
Germany
 Rua Lucaia 281, salas 204-6, Rio Vermelho
 (☎ 247-7106). Open Monday to Friday from 9
 am to noon.
UK
 Avenida Estados Unidos 4, salas 1109-1113,
 Comércio (☎ 243-9222). Open Monday to
 Thursday from 9 to 11 am and 2 to 4 pm, and
 Friday from 9 to 11 am.
USA
 Avenida Antônio Carlos Magalhães, Edifício
 Cidadela Center I, sala 410, Pituba (☎ 358-
 9166). Open Monday to Friday from 9 to 11 am
 and 2 to 4 pm.

Visa Extensions For visa extensions, the Polícia Federal (☎ 321-6363) is at Rua Oscar Pontes, Água de Meninos s/n (no number), Comércio. Take a 'Calcada' bus from the Avenida da França bus stop at the base of the Lacerda Elevator, and get off at the Mercado Popular. Walk back about 100 metres towards the city centre and turn right. You'll see the blue and grey Polícia Federal building at the end of the street, near the docks.

Travel Agencies Tatu Tours (☎ 245-9322) is at Avenida Centenário 2883, Edifício Victoria Centre, sala 105, Barra, Salvador, CEP 40147-900, BA. The company specialises in natural and cultural history tours around Bahia, including specialist topics such as Afro-Brazilian culture, and is happy to deal with groups or independent travellers.

 The following travel agencies sell bus tickets in addition to all the normal services.

They can save you a trip out to the rodoviária, but check first, as some agents do not sell tickets to all destinations:

Amaralina Viagens
 Barra (☎ 336-1099)
Itaparica Turismo
 Avenida Manoel Dias da Silva 1211, Pituba
 (☎ 248-3433)
Itapemirim
 Avenida 7 de Septembro 1420 (☎ 321-6633)
Itapoan Turismo
 Campo da Pólvora 21, Centro (☎ 321-0141)
Turbahia
 Avenida Estados Unidos 60, Cidade Baixa
 (☎ 243-8598)

Bookshop Livraria Brandão, at Rua Rui Barbosa 15B, is a huge second-hand bookstore with a large range of foreign-language books to buy or exchange.

Maps & Guidebooks Most newsagencies have maps on sale – *Planta Turística de Salvador* is useable, and Emtursa sells a handy small map, *Salvador – Mapa de Balso*. Bahiatursa has a free map and services guide to Pelourinho, and a monthly guide to cultural events, *Bahia Eventos & Serviços*. The Fundação Cultural puts out a similar, but more detailed guide with reviews, called *Agenda Cultural*, available at Bahiatursa offices. Bahiatursa also publishes a glossy, detailed guide once a year, *Guia Turístico Bahia*, which has useful listings. Most tourist offices and hotels have copies of *Itinerário*, a free monthly listing of cultural events in Salvador. The weekly magazine *Veja* also publishes a regular supplement containing excellent articles and listings for the latest cultural events in Bahia.

Business Hours In Salvador, shopkeepers often close for lunch from noon to 3 pm. Work has a different flavour: slow, relaxed and seemingly nonchalant.

 The slow pace often frustrates and irritates visitors, but if you can reset your internal clock and not get uptight or unsettled, you are likely to be rewarded with many kindnesses and surprises.

Dangers & Annoyances Salvador has a reputation for theft and muggings, and tourists clearly make easy targets. Paranoia is counterproductive, but you should be aware of the dangers and understand what you can do to minimise problems. See the Security information in the Dangers & Annoyances section of the Facts for the Visitor chapter.

The following are some general points to remember when visiting Salvador: dress down; take only enough money with you for your outing; carry only a photocopy of your passport; and don't carry a camera outside Pelourinho.

Look at a map for basic orientation before you set out to see the sights. Although tourist police maintain a highly visible presence in the centre of Salvador, particularly Pelourinho, this does not apply in other areas. The Lacerda Elevator is renowned for crime, especially at night around the base station, and pickpocketing is common on buses and in crowded places. Don't hesitate to use taxis during the day and especially after dusk.

On the beaches, keep a close eye on juvenile thieves, often referred to as *capitões d'areia* (captains of the sand), who are quick to make off with unguarded possessions.

During Carnival, tourist authorities highly recommend that tourists form small groups and avoid deserted places, especially narrow alleyways.

Emergency Useful numbers include: Disque Turismo (dial tourism) ☎ 131; Pronto Socorro (first aid) ☎ 192; and Polícia Civil (police) ☎ 197. There are several police posts in the city centre – for example, near the bus stop on Praça da Sé. In the same area, there are tourist police (identified by an armband) on patrol.

Things to See & Do

Historic Salvador is easy to see on foot, and you should plan on spending a couple of days wandering among the splendid 16th and 17th-century churches, homes and museums. One good approach is to ramble through the old city in the morning, head out to the beaches in the afternoon, and devote the evening to music, dance or Candomblé.

The most important sections of Salvador's colonial quarter extend from Praça Castro Alves along Ruas Chile and da Misericórdia to Praça da Sé and Terreiro de Jesus, and then continue down through Largo do Pelourinho and up the hill to Largo do Carmo.

Catedral Basílica Starting at the Praça da Sé, walk a block to the Terreiro de Jesus (Praça 15 de Novembro on many maps). The biggest church on the plaza is the Cathedral of Bahia, which served as a Jesuit centre until the Jesuits were expelled from Brazil in 1759. The cathedral was built between 1657 and 1672, and its walls are covered with Lioz marble which served as ballast for returning merchant ships. Many consider this the city's most beautiful church. The interior has many segmented areas and the emphasis is on verticality – raise your eyes to admire the superb ceiling. Entrance costs US$1. The cathedral is open from 8 to 11 am and 3 to 6 pm, Monday to Saturday, and from 5 to 6.30 pm on Sunday.

Museu Afro-Brasileiro The Antiga Faculdade de Medicina (Old Medical Faculty) houses the Afro-Brazilian Museum, with its small but excellent collection of orixás from both Africa and Bahia. There is a surprising amount of African art, ranging from pottery to woodwork, as well as superb ceremonial Candomblé apparel. Other highlights include wooden panels representing Oxum (an orixá revered as the goddess of beauty) which were carved by Carybé, a famous Argentine artist who has lived in Salvador for many years. Entrance costs US$0.50 and the museum (☎ 321-0383) is open Tuesday to Saturday from 9 am to 5 pm. For more information on orixás see the Candomblé information in the Religion section of the Facts about the Country chapter.

In the basement of the same building is the **Museu de Arqueologia e Etnologia** (Archaeology & Ethnology Museum), which is open Monday to Friday from 9 am to noon and 2 to 5 pm.

Igreja São Francisco Defying the teachings and vows of poverty of its namesake, this baroque church, east of Praça da Sé, is crammed with displays of wealth and splendour. Gold leaf is used like wallpaper. There's an 80-kg silver chandelier and imported azulejos (Portuguese ceramic tiles).

Forced to build their masters' church and yet prohibited from practising their own religion (Candomblé terreiros were hidden and kept far from town), the African slave artisans responded through their work: the faces of the cherubs are distorted, some angels are endowed with huge sex organs, some appear pregnant. Most of these creative acts were chastely covered by 20th-century sacristans. Traditionally blacks were seated in far corners of the church without a view of the altar.

Notice the polychrome figure of São Pedro da Alcântara by Manoel Inácio da Costa. The artist, like his subject, was suffering from tuberculosis. He made one side of the saint's face more ashen than the other so that São Pedro appears more ill as you walk past him. José Joaquim da Rocha painted the hallway ceiling using perspective technique, which was considered a novelty at the time.

The poor come to Igreja São Francisco on Tuesday to venerate Santo Antônio and receive bread. The Candomblistas respect this church's saints and come to pray both here and in Igreja NS do Bonfim.

Depending on restoration work, opening hours are Monday to Saturday from 7.30 to 11.30 am and 2 to 6 pm, and Sunday from 7 am to noon.

Igreja da Ordem Terceira de São Francisco Next door to the Igreja São Francisco is the 17th-century Church of the Third Order of São Francisco. Notice the frontispiece, in the Spanish baroque or plateresco style, which remained hidden until it was accidentally discovered in the 1930s when a workman hammered off some plaster to install wiring. Opening hours are Monday to Friday from 8 to 11.30 am and 2 to 5 pm.

Igreja São Pedro dos Clérigos The Igreja São Pedro dos Clérigos is on Terreiro de Jesus, next to Cantina da Lua. This rococo church, like many others built in the 18th century, was left with one of its towers missing in order to avoid a tax on finished churches. It opens only during mass (usually from 8 to 9.30 am on Sunday), and if you visit during this time, do not disturb the service.

Pelourinho To see the city's oldest architecture, turn down Rua Alfredo de Brito, the small street which descends into the Pelourinho district.

'Pelourinho' means 'whipping post', and this is where the slaves were tortured and sold (whipping of slaves was legal in Brazil until 1835). The old slave-auction site on Largo do Pelourinho (also known as Praça José de Alencar) has recently been renovated and converted into the **Fundacão Casa de Jorge Amado** (Jorge Amado Museum). According to a brass plaque across the street, Amado lived in the Hotel Pelourinho when it was a student house. The exhibition is disappointing, but you can watch a free video of *Dona Flor* or one of the other films based on Amado's books. The museum is open Monday to Friday from 9 am to 6 pm.

Next door is the **Museu da Cidade**. The Exhibitions on display include costumes of the orixás of Candomblé, and the personal effects of the Romantic poet Castro Alves, author of *Navio Negreiro*, and one of the first public figures to protest against slavery. The museum is open Tuesday to Saturday from 9 am to 6 pm.

Igreja NS do Rosário dos Pretos, across the Largo do Pelourinho, was built by and for the slaves. The 18th-century church has some lovely azulejos and is beautifully lit up at night. The church is open Monday to Friday from 8 am to 5.30 pm, and on Saturday and Sunday from 8 am to 2 pm.

Igreja do Santíssimo Sacramento da Rua do Paço From Pelourinho, go down the hill and then continue uphill along Ladeira do Carmo. You will reach a set of steps on the

A & B: Rio Itapicuru shores, Seribinha, Bahia
C: A view of Seribinha, Bahia
D: Lavagem do Bonfim festivities, Salvador, Bahia

GUY MOBERLY

GUY MOBERLY

GREG CAIRE

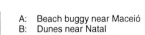

GREG CAIRE

A	
B	
C	D

A: Beach buggy near Maceió
B: Dunes near Natal
C: Old Portuguese building facade
D: Caju fruit, São Luís

left which lead up to the church in an approach reminiscent of the Spanish Steps of Rome. The first Brazilian film to win an award at the Cannes film festival, *O Pagador de Promessa*, was filmed here.

Igreja da Ordem Terceira do Carmo This church, at the top of the hill on Ladeiro do Carmo, was founded in 1636 and contains a baroque altar and an organ that dates from 1889.

Igreja e Convento de NS do Carmo & Museu do Carmo Next door, this religious complex is moderately interesting. Among the sacred and religious articles in the museum is a famous sculpture of Christ created by Francisco Chagas (also known as O Cabra). There's also a treaty declaring the expulsion of the Dutch from Salvador on 30 April 1625. The document was signed at the convent, which served as the general's quarters at the time. The museum is open Monday to Saturday from 8 to 11.30 am and from 2 to 5 pm.

For a glimpse of old Salvador, continue walking for a few blocks past dilapidated buildings which teem with life. Also notice an odd-looking public oratory, **Oratório da Cruz do Pascoal**, plunked in the middle of Rua Joaquim Távora.

Praça Tomé de Souza While not officially recognised or protected by the Brazilian historical architecture society SPHAN, this plaza in the centre has several beautiful and important sites. The **Palácio Rio Branco** was built in 1549 to house the offices of Tomé de Souza, the first governor general of Brazil. The palace has been rebuilt and refurbished over the years, and the large, cream-coloured, birthday-cake building is now headquarters for Bahiatursa.

Elevador Lacerda The Lacerda Elevator, inaugurated in 1868, was an iron structure with clanking steam elevators until these were replaced with a new system in 1928. Today, electric elevators truck up and down a set of 85-metre, vertical cement shafts in less than 15 seconds, and carry over 50,000 passengers daily.

Things weren't always so easy. At first, the Portuguese used slaves and mules to transport goods from the port in Cidade Baixa to Cidade Alta. By 1610, the Jesuits had installed the first elevator to negotiate the drop. A clever system of ropes and pulleys was manually operated to carry freight and a few brave souls.

You should watch out for petty crime around the elevator, particularly after dusk – see the Dangers & Annoyances section.

Cidade Baixa Descending into the lower city you'll be confronted by the **Mercado Modelo**. Filled with souvenir stalls and restaurants, it's Salvador's worst concession to tourism. If you've missed capoeira, there are displays for tourists outside the building – anyone contemplating taking photos is well advised to negotiate a sensible price beforehand or risk being suckered for an absurd fee. The modernist sculpture across the street is referred to as *bunda* (arse) by the locals – which gives it a much more appealing aspect. There are many cheap lanchonetes in Cidade Baixa and the area is worth exploring.

Mercado São Joaquim To see a typical market, take either the 'Ribeira' or the 'Bonfim' bus from the bus stop beside the elevator (base station). Get off after the Pirelli Pneus store on your left, after about three km. Mercado São Joaquim is a small city of waterfront barracas, open all day, every day except Sunday. It's not exactly clean (watch out for the green slime puddles) – and the meat neighbourhood can turn the unprepared into devout vegetarians. You are bound to come across spontaneous singing and dancing at barracas where cachaça is served.

Igreja NS do Bonfim Take the 'Bonfim' bus across the road from the market to the Igreja NS do Bonfim, further along the Itapagipe peninsula. Built in 1745, the shrine is famous for its miraculous power to effect cures. In the Sala dos Milagres you will see votive offerings: replicas of feet, arms, heads, hearts – parts of the body devotees claim were cured.

For Candomblistas, Bonfim is the church of Oxalá and thus their most important church. In January, the Lavagem do Bonfim, one of Bahia's most important festivals, takes place here and Candomblé priestesses (mães de santo) lead the festivities together with Catholic priests. See the Festivals section later in this chapter for more detail. There are also huge services at Bonfim on the first and last Friday of each month.

When you approach the church you'll undoubtedly be offered a *fita* (ribbon) to tie around your wrist. With the fita you can make three wishes that will come true by the time it falls off. This usually takes over two months and you must allow it to fall off from natural wear and tear. Cutting it off is said to bring bad luck.

The church is open from 6 am to noon and 2.30 to 6 pm Tuesday to Sunday.

The Bay From the church there is a very interesting half-hour walk to the bay, where you'll find the old **Monte Serrat lighthouse and church** (good crab at the barracas). Nearby is **Praia da Boa Viagem**, where one of Bahia's most popular and magnificent festivals, Procissão do Senhor Bom Jesus dos Navegantes, takes place on New Year's Eve. See the Festivals section later in this chapter for more details.

The beach is lined with barracas and is animated on weekends. It's a poorer part of town and quite interesting. From Boa Viagem, there are buses back to the bus stop beside the Lacerda Elevator (base station).

Museu de Arte Sacra da Bahia This museum is housed in a 17th-century convent which has been beautifully restored. The sacred art on display includes excellent and varied sculptures and images in wood, clay and soapstone – many were shipped to Salvador from Portugal. Opening hours are Monday to Friday from 9.30 to 11.30 am and 2 to 5.30 pm.

Museu de Arte Moderna On the bay, further down from the centre toward Campo Grande, is the Solar do Unhão, an old sugar estate that now houses the small Museu de Arte Moderna, a restaurant and a ceramic workshop. Legend has it that the place is haunted by the ghosts of tortured slaves. One look at the ancient pelourinho (whipping post) and torture devices on display makes the idea credible. However, it's a lovely spot; the art exhibits are often good and the restaurant has a tranquil atmosphere and a view.

This area has a reputation for crime (especially mugging of tourists), and buses don't pass close to it – it's better to take a taxi to and from the Solar do Unhão. Opening hours are Tuesday to Sunday from 1 to 5 pm.

Candomblé Before doing anything in Salvador, find out about the schedule for Candomblé ceremonies so you don't miss a night in a terreiro. The Federação Baiana Do Culto Afro-Brasileiro (☎ 321-0145), at Rua Alfredo do Brito 39, Pelourinho, is open Monday to Friday from 8 am to noon and provides information on Condomblé services. Pass through the clinic and speak to Ari in the back room. Bahiatursa has many Candomblistas on its staff who can provide the addresses of terreiros – the *Eventos & Serviços* guide available at Bahiatursa offices lists a monthly schedule with transport details. Activities usually start around 8 or 9 pm and can be held any day of the week. For details about Candomblé, refer to the religion section in the Facts about the Country chapter.

Capoeira School To visit a capoeira school, it's best to get the up-to-date schedule from

An Evening of Candomblé

A long evening of Candomblé in Casa Branca, Salvador's oldest terreiro, is quite an experience. The women dress in lace and hooped skirts, dance slowly, and chant in Yoruba. The men drum complex and powerful African rhythms. The terreiro is dominated by the women: only women dance, and only they enter a trance, the principal goal of the ceremony. Men play a supporting role.

The dance is very African, with graceful hand motions, swaying hips and light steps. When a dancer enters the trance, she shakes and writhes while assistants embrace and support her. Sometimes, even spectators go into trances, although this is discouraged.

The mãe de santo or pai de santo runs the service. The *mãe pequena* is entrusted with the training of priestesses; in this case, two *filhos de santo*: one a girl over seven years of age, the other a girl under seven. The initiates are called *abian*.

On a festival morning, the celebration commences with an animal sacrifice. Only initiates may attend this service. Later in the afternoon the *padê* ceremony is held to attract the attention of Exú, and this is followed by chanting for the orixás, which is accompanied by *alabés* (atabaque drummers).

The festival we attended was for Ormolú, the feared and respected orixá of plague and disease. He is worshipped only on Monday and his Christian syncretic counterpart is either St Lazuras or St Roque. His costume consists of a straw belt encrusted with seashells, straw mask and a cape and dress to cover his face and body, which have been disfigured by smallpox.

When the dancers had received the spirit of Omolú in their trance, some left the floor. They returned with a person dressed from head to toe in long straw-like strands to represent Omolú. The dancing resumed.

Although the congregants of Casa Branca are friendly and hospitable, they don't orient their practice to outsiders. Westerners may attend, and many white Brazilians are members. After the ceremony, guests are invited to the far end of the house for sweets and giant cakes – one cake decorated like the Brazilian flag. ∎

Bahiatursa, which has a complete listing of schools and some class schedules in its monthly *Eventos & Serviços* guide. The Associação de Capoeira Mestre Bimba is an excellent school. It's at Rua Francisco Muniz Barreto 1, 1st floor, Terreiro de Jesus, and operates Monday to Saturday, from 9 to 11 am and 4 to 7 pm.

Beaches The beaches of **Pituba**, **Armação**, **Piatã**, **Placaford** and **Itapoaã** may not be as famous as Ipanema and Copacabana, but they are more beautiful. Although these beaches are all within 45 minutes by bus from the centre, Pituba, Armação and Piatã are becoming increasingly polluted and are not recommended for swimming. The state government has made plans for a new central treatment plant which will pump outfall five km out to sea – in the meantime, it's advisable to head for **Placaford**, **Itapoã** or further north. For information on beaches north of Itapoã, see the North of Salvador section.

If you just want to experience Salvador's beach scene, **Barra** has the first beaches and is the liveliest – but swimming is not advisable on the Atlantic Ocean side, due to heavy pollution. Surprisingly, the water on the bay side at Barra certainly *looks* clear and inviting – locals love it, so you can make up your own mind. There are plenty of restaurants, barracas and bars along the waterfront, although it can get a bit sleazy at night. You can see Bahia's oldest fort, the polygonal **Santo Antônio da Barra**, which was built in 1598 and fell to the Dutch in 1624. The view from the fort of Itaparica is splendid.

See the Getting Around section for details about transport to these beaches.

Festivals

Salvador's Carnival receives greatest emphasis, but it is by no means the only festival worth attending. There are many others, particularly in January and February, which attract huge crowds. Since the 17th century, religious processions have remained an integral part of the city's cultural life. Combining elements of the sacred and profane, Candomblé and Catholicism, many of these festivals are as wild as Carnival and possibly more colourful.

Carnival Carnival in Salvador is justly world famous. For four nights and three days, the masses go to the streets and stay until they fall. There's nothing to buy, so all you have to do is follow your heart – or the nearest trio elétrico – and play.

Carnival, usually held in February or March, starts on a Thursday night and continues until the following Monday. Everything, but everything, goes during these four days. In recent years, Carnival has revolved around the trios elétricos. The trios play a distinctively upbeat music from the tops of trucks that slowly wind their way through the main Carnival areas (Praça Castro Alves, Campo Grande and Barra). Surrounding the trios is a sea of dancing, drinking revellers.

Carnival brings so many tourists and so much money to Salvador that there's been an inevitable tendency towards commercialisation, although this trend is still light years behind Rio. Fortunately, local residents have been very critical of this trend, and arts and community groups have now been given a greater say in the arrangements of Salvador's Carnival. A more authentic festival has resulted from this: events have been decentralised, and freer and more impromptu expression is encouraged. Let's hope the spontaneity continues.

Take a look at the newspaper or go to Emtursa or Bahiatursa for a list of events. Don't miss the afoxés (Afro blocos, large groups of Carnival revellers), such as Badauê, Ilê-Aiyê, Olodum, Timbalada, Muzenza and the most famous, Filhos de Gandhi (Sons of Gandhi). The best place to see them is in Liberdade, Salvador's largest black district.

Also, explore Carnival Caramuru in Rio Vermelho and the smaller happenings in Itapoã, the old fishing and whaling village which has a fascinating ocean procession on the last day of Carnival, when a whale is delivered to the sea.

The traditional gay parade is held on Monday at Praça Castro Alves. Many of Brazil's best musicians return to Salvador for Carnival, and the frequent rumours that so and so will be playing on the street are often true (for example, Gilberto Gil and Baby Consuelo have both taken part).

Many clubs have balls just before and during Carnival. If you're in the city before the festivities start, you can also see some of

Capoeira
One capoeira group in Salvador is notorious for extracting money from unsuspecting tourists. Unfortunately, the group is also one of the most spectacular to watch. I should have known better, but I stopped to watch them one afternoon and was immediately asked for money 'for the school'. I handed over what I considered a reasonable sum, and having done so, thought I might as well take a photo. After taking a quick snap of the action, the '*Mestre*', a man mountain with muscles on his muscles, pulled out of the circle and approached me. He asked me for money, and I explained that I'd already given. 'Yes', he said, peering down at me with a broad smile, 'but you need to pay more for the Mestre'. I refused, but as he became more persistent (and the crowd around grew more amused at the encounter), I reached into my pocket and dropped a bunch of coins into his massive palm. He looked from the coins to me, then threw the coins onto the ground in apparent disgust. Moving closer, he took my head gently into his hands and gave me a 'friendly' headbutt! ∎

the blocos practising. Just ask Emtursa or Bahiatursa.

Hotels do fill up during Carnival, so reservations are a good idea. Stay near the centre or in Barra. Violence can be a problem during Carnival, and some women travellers have reported violent approaches from locals. A common experience you may encounter at Carnival is when you are sucked into the crowd right behind a trio elétrico and have to dodge all the dancers with their flying elbows! See the Dangers & Annoyances section for more details on avoiding crime.

Procissão do Senhor Bom Jesus dos Navegantes This festival, which originated in Portugal in 1750, is one of Bahia's most popular celebrations. On New Year's Eve, the image of Senhor dos Navegantes is taken to Igreja NS da Conceição, close to Mercado Modelo in Cidade Baixa. On the morning of New Year's Day, a maritime procession, consisting of dozens of boats, transports the image along the bay and returns it to the beach at Boa Viagem, which is packed with onlookers eager to celebrate with music, food and drink.

Festas de Reis Also of Portuguese origin, this festival is held in Igreja da Lapinha on 5 and 6 January.

Lavagem do Bonfim This festival, which takes place on the second Thursday in January, is one of Salvador's most popular events and is attended by huge crowds. The festival culminates with the ritual *lavagem* (washing) of the church by mães and filhas de santo. Abundant flowers and lights provide impressive decoration, and the party atmosphere continues with the Filhos de Gandhi and trios elétricos providing musical accompaniment for dancers. If you want to do the nine-km walk to the church, it's best to leave early with the mães, before the trio elétricos blast into action.

Festa de São Lázaro This is a festival dedicated to the Candomblé orixá, Omulu, and culminates on the last Sunday in January with a mass, procession, festival and ritual cleansing of the church.

Festa de Iemanjá A grand maritime procession takes flowers and presents to Iemanjá, the Mãe e Rainha das Águas (Mother and Queen of the Waters). One of Candomblé's most important festivals, it's celebrated on 2 February in Rio Vermelho and accompanied by trios elétricos, afoxés and plenty of food and drink.

Lavagem da Igreja de Itapoã Celebrated in Itapoã, 15 days before Carnival, this warm-up for Carnival is all music and dance, with blocos and afoxés.

Festa São João This festival is celebrated on 23 and 24 June with pyrotechnics and many parties on the street where *genipapo*, a local liqueur, is consumed in very liberal quantities.

Santa Bárbara The festival of Santa Bárbara is the Candomblé festa of the markets. Probably the best spot to see the festivities from 4 to 6 December is in Rio Vermelho, at the Mercado do Peixe.

Festa de NS da Conceição This festival takes place on 8 December and features a procession in Cidade Baixa followed by Candomblé ceremonies in honour of Iemanjá.

Passagem do Ano Novo New Year's Eve is celebrated with all the zest of Carnival – especially on the beaches.

Places to Stay
Salvador has many hotels, but they can all fill up during the Carnival season, so reservations are a good idea. Bahiatursa can help you find lodging – just provide the staff with a general idea of your preferred price range and type of lodging. Bahiatursa also has lists of houses that take in tourists and these can be a source of excellent, cheap lodgings when hotels are full, especially during

summer holidays and Carnival. But beware, the tourist office makes selective referrals and it helps if you don't look too burnt-out or broke.

Camping On the outskirts of Itapoã, there are several campgrounds, such as *Camping Ecológico* (☎ 249-5900), Alameda da Praia s/n (no number), and *Camping Clube do Brasil* (☎ 242-0482) also at Alameda da Praia, s/n (no number). At Pituaçu, about 14 km from the centre, there's *Camping Pituaçu* (☎ 231-7413), on Avenida Pinto d'Aguiar.

Places to Stay – bottom end

Hostels – City Centre There are now a couple of excellent youth hostels close to the city centre, mostly clustered around Pelourinho. The *Albergue de Juventude das Laranjeiras* (☎ 321-1366) is a very flash new hostel located in the heart of Pelourinho, at Rua Inácio Acciolli 13. The *Albergue de Juventude do Pelô* (☎ 242-8061) is also popular and conveniently located, at Rua Ribeiro Santos 5. Close by is the *Albergue de Juventude Solar* (☎ 241-0055), at Rua Ribeiro Santos 45. The *Albergue de Juventude Dois de Julho* (☎ 243-9513), is at Rua Areal de Cima 44, which is just south of the city centre – very close to Praça Duque de Caxias.

Hostels – Beaches The following beach hostels are listed in sequence, from Barra district along the Atlantic coast towards Itapoã. The *Albergue de Juventude Senzala* (☎ 235-4177) is at Rua Greenfeld 128, Barra, Avenida, close to the lighthouse. Also in Barra district, just a couple of blocks west of Shopping Barra, you'll find the *Albergue de Juventude da Barra* (☎ 247-5678), at Rua Florianópolis 134, Jardim Brasil, Barra. Close to Ondina beach is the *Albergue de Juventude Solar* (☎ 235-2235), at Rua Macapá 461. Moving further down the coast, Amaralina beach is a couple of minutes on foot from the *Albergue de Juventude Lagash* (☎ 248-7399), at Rua Visconde de Itaboraí 514. Next to Pituba beach is the *Albergue de*

Juventude Casa Grande (☎ 248-0527) at Rua Minas Gerais 122.

Hotels The cheaper hotels in the old part of town are around Praça da Sé, Terreiro de Jesus, Praça Anchieta and Pelourinho. Prices have risen since the restoration of the area, and outside the youth hostels, good-value cheap accommodation is hard to find close to the historic centre.

The *Hotel Caramuru* (☎ 336-9951), at Avenida 7 de Setembro 2125, is away from the centre in a quiet location, but offers very good value. The hotel is in a large colonial mansion with a breezy, elevated eating area. Spacious and spotless double quartos cost US$18; double apartamentos cost US$22. The hotel also organises candomblé excursions, and trips to Itaparica and other destinations.

The *Hotel Pelourinho* (☎ 321-9022), at Rua Alfredo de Brito 20, right in the heart of Pelourinho, has long been a favourite with travellers, but is getting pricey. It's an older, converted mansion (reputedly the setting for Jorge Amado's novel *Suor*), and the management is security-conscious (there's a guard posted at the entrance to the building). Small apartamentos with fan cost US$20/28/36 for singles/doubles/triples. In the hotel courtyard there are handicraft shops and, right at the end, a restaurant-bar with views.

About 20 metres downhill from Largo do Pelourinho is the *Hotel Solara* (☎ 321-0202), which has apartamentos starting at US$12/16/20 for a single/double/triple. Breakfast is included in the price. Rooms are also used by locals for stays as short as two hours. Around the corner, at Rua Ribeiro dos Santos 3, the *Pousada do Passo* (☎ 321-3656) is in effect a youth hostel, with four and eight-bed rooms for US$10 per person (breakfast not included).

The *Hotel Themis* (☎ 243-1668), at Praça da Sé 57, Edifício Themis (7th floor), offers great views, but is run-down and in desperate need of work. A popular hang-out with French travellers, it has a bar and a restaurant. Apartamentos without a view cost US$12/16/20 for a single/double/triple;

apartamentos with a view cost US$14/20/24. The *Hotel Pousada da Praça* (☎ 321-0642), close to Praça Castro Alves at Rua Rui Barbosa 5, is centrally located and offers basic, but clean, quartos at US$12/15. Apartamentos cost US$16/20.

Just a short walk from Bahiatursa is the *Hotel Chile* (☎ 321-0245), at Rua Chile 7 (1st floor). It's a bit dark, but a good deal. Quartos start at US$9/12 for a single/double. Apartamentos cost US$20 for a double with air-con; and US$12/14 for singles/doubles without air-con. Close by is the *Hotel Maridina* (☎ 242-7176), at Avenida 7 de Setembro, Ladeira de São Bento, 6 (1st floor). This is a friendly, family-run hotel which offers good value for money. Apartamentos with fan cost US$12/18 for a single/double; or US$22/25 for a single/double with air-con.

Right on Praia da Barra at Avenida Sete de Setembro 3801, the *Pousada Malu* (☎ 237-4461) is a relaxed place offering clean quartos with fan for US$12/16; or double apartamentos for US$22. The *Pousada do Marcus* (☎ 235-5177), at Avenida Oceânica 281, functions as a youth hostel and is recommended by readers. Quartos cost around $US12 per person. The *Pousada Mana* (☎ 247-8438), at Rua Alfonso Celso, is about 300 metres from the beachfront and a bit quieter. Apartamentos cost US$16/22 for singles/doubles. There's a restaurant attached with some good-value, home-style cooking.

Along the beach, in the heart of Itapoã, the *Hotel Europa* (☎ 249-9344) has clean apartamento doubles for US$20. Across the street you have the beach, barracas for food and drink, and buses to the centre of Salvador. It's a 45-minute ride to the city centre, but the beaches are good, and it's close to the airport, which is convenient if you're flying out the next day.

Places to Stay – middle

The *Palace Hotel* (☎ 322-1155; fax 243-1109), at Rua Chile 20, is reasonable value and right in the centre of the city. Comfortable quartos with fan cost US$20/25.

Apartamentos with air-con start at around US$28/36.

If you'd rather stay opposite the beach in the Barra district, and within easy reach of the city centre, the *Hotel Villa Da Barra* (☎ 247-7908), at Avenida 7 de Setembro 3959, is a very good option. It's a colourful place with a breezy courtyard and café area. Two-level apartamentos with three beds and two bathrooms cost US$30/35. Close by at Avenida 7 de Setembro 3783, the *Hotel Porto da Barra* (☎ 247-7711) has single/double apartamentos with fan at US$28/32, and double apartamentos with air-con at US$35.

At Rio Vermelho, the *Hotel Catarina Paraguaçu* (☎ & fax 247-1488), at Rua João Gomes 128, is an old colonial building with comfortable apartamentos at $US35/40 for singles/doubles.

Places to Stay – top end

Facing the beach at Rio Vermelho is the *Meridien Bahia* (☎ 248-8011; fax 248-8902), which has singles/doubles for US$85/95. At Praia Ondina, closer to the city, are two top-class hotels: the *Bahia Othon Palace* (☎ 247-1044; fax 245-4877) which has singles/doubles for around US$80/95; and the *Salvador Praia* (☎ 245-5033; fax 245-5003), which has a private stretch of beach and charges US$90/100 for singles/doubles. The *Hotel Tropical da Bahia* (☎ 321-3699; fax 321-9725) is a five-star hotel between the city centre and Barra, at Praça 2 de Julho 2, Campo Grande. Room prices start at US$102/117, with a 20% discount for cash or credit card payment.

Places to Eat

Bahian cuisine is an intriguing blend of African and Brazilian cuisine based on characteristic ingredients such as coconut cream, ginger, hot peppers, coriander, shrimp and dendê oil. Dendê, an African palm oil with a terrific flavour, is used in many regional dishes (you'll also smell it everywhere). Since dendê has a reputation for stirring up trouble in travellers' bellies, you are advised to consume it in small quantities until you've become acclimatised. For names and short descriptions of typical Bahian dishes, refer to the food section in the Facts for the Visitor chapter.

The Pelourinho area is packed with restaurants, though many of them cater for tourists and are expensive. The best value for lunches are the popular comida-a-kilo restaurants, where you serve yourself and pay by weight. *Senzala*, at Rua João de Deus 9 (1st floor), is one of the best places.

A long-time favourite on Terreiro de Jesus, *Cantina da Lua* serves good-value refeicões and is a popular hang-out. Nearby, at Rua Alfredo Brito 5, *Salada das Frutas* is also popular with travellers for its cheap, healthy snacks, juices, refeicões and friendly atmosphere. *Micheluccio*, at Rua Alfredo Brito 33, is the place to head for excellent pizza.

Temporo da Dada, at Rua Frei Vicente 5, is a lively, casual restaurant with tasty seafood – the moqueca de caranguejo and moqueca de peixe are good. Two people can eat for around US$14. *Dona Chika Ka*, at Rua João Castro Rabello 10, continues to get rave reviews for its bobó de camarão (US$16).

If you're hanging out for some Japanese food, *Yamoto*, on Rua Frei Vicente, is an elegant Japanese restaurant with superb sushi – expect to pay around US$18 per person.

In the Largo do Pelourinho, there's a restaurant in the courtyard of the *Hotel Pelourinho*. The main attraction is the great view of the bay. The dishes are adequate but they tend to be overpriced, and the staff can be surly.

Next door to the hotel, *Banzo* is bright, animated and good value. There's a great selection of Bahian and European dishes plus all sorts of exotic drinks – expect to pay around US$10 for a main course plus a drink. When Grupo Olodum is giving one of its free Sunday evening concerts in Largo do Pelourinho, the Banzo balcony provides a good vantage point to view the gyrating crowds.

Across the street, at Largo do Pelourinho 5, *Restaurante da Dinha* is good for a cheap feed and to meet locals – the original *Dinha*, on Largo de Santana in Rio Vermelho, is widely known as having the best acarajé in Salvador. *Novo Tempo* is in the downstairs section of Olodum, on Largo do Pelourinho. It's a happening spot, with a lovely back courtyard, good music and seafood dishes from around US$12.

Also on Largo do Pelourinho is *Senac* (☎ 321-5502), a cooking school which offers a huge spread of 40 regional dishes in the form of a self-service buffet. It's not the best Bahian cooking, but for US$14 you can discover which Bahian dishes you like...and eat till you explode! Senac is open from 6 to 9 pm every day except Sunday. Folklore shows are presented on Thursday and Saturday from 8 to 9 pm – tickets cost US$5 per person.

At the crossroads downhill from Largo do Pelourinho is *Casa do Benin* (☎ 243-7629), a superb restaurant serving excellent African food in a small courtyard complete with palm trees, a pond and thatched hut. The main dishes start around US$10 – the moqueca de peixe and frango ao gengibre (ginger chicken) are close to culinary heaven! The restaurant is open daily, except Sunday, from 11 am to 6 pm. Another terrific restaurant for African-influenced cuisine is the colourful *Uauá*, at Rua Gregório de Matos 36.

Solar do Unhão (☎ 321-5551), which houses the Museu de Arte Moderna, also has a restaurant on the lower level in the old senzala (slave quarters). Ironically, the view from the restaurant is one of the best in the city, and as good a reason as any for a visit, but it's becoming a bit of a tourist trap. Dinner is usually accompanied by live music and a folklore show at 10 pm – expect to pay an extra US$12 cover charge. Crime is a problem in this area, so you should take a taxi.

Close to the rodoviária and adjacent to Hipermercado Paes Mendoça (☎ 244-0811), a restaurant serving fine steaks and ribs for about US$10. In Barra, *Cafe Cameroun* (☎ 247-2788), at Rua

Alfonso Celso 350, has been recommended by readers for its African food.

Excellent Bahian dishes at moderate prices are served at *Restaurante Iemanjá* (☎ 231-5570), on Avenida Otávio Mangabeira s/n (no number) on Armação beach, and *Agdá* (☎ 231-2851), at Rua Orlando Moscoso 1, Boca do Rio.

Last, best and hardest to find is *Bargaço* (☎ 231-5141), at Rua P, Quadra 43, Jardim Armação – it's on a small residential street near the Centro de Convenções (Convention Centre). National and international gourmets rate the seafood here as world class. The ensopada de camarão is divine, but you'll have to be prepared to splurge about US$15 – fame has set an upward trend for the prices. It's open daily from noon to midnight. There's also a new (and much easier to find) branch of *Bargaço*, in Pelourinho, on the corner of Rua Francisco M Barreto and Rua Inácio Accioli.

Entertainment

Salvador is justly renowned for its music. The blending of African and Brazilian traditions produces popular styles, such as trio elétrico (which dominates Carnival), tropicalismo, afoxé, caribé, reggae, lambada, jazz and Gilberto Gil.

Bars and clubs tend to come and go quickly in Salvador, so ask around and check the newspaper to confirm the following suggestions. If you want to plug into the arts, Fundação Cultural Estado da Bahia (☎ 321-0222) is at Praça Tome de Souza, Palácio Rio Branco, sala 31. The Fundação publishes a monthly guide, *Agenda Cultural*, which gives a comprehensive rundown of music events, theatre and dance performances, and art exhibitions. The weekly magazine *Veja* contains a supplement with tips on the hottest nightspots. Teatro Castro Alves (☎ 235-7616), on Praça Dois de Julho (Campo Grande), is the biggest music theatre in Salvador. The big acts play here, and they're often Brazil's best.

Pelourinho is now the nightlife capital of Salvador; its cobbled streets are lined with bars, and blocos practise almost every night.

Olodum play on Sunday nights in the Largo do Pelourinho and draw crowds of dancers into the streets. The famous Filhos de Gandhi have their centre close by, at Rua Gregório de Matos 53, and rehearse on Tuesday and Sunday nights. Didá, a music and dance school at Rua João de Deus 19, has a street practice on Friday night – a highlight is a 15-piece, all-female drum outfit.

During summer, the city sponsors a festival of music called *Ritos & Agitos*, with free live music at several outdoor venues, including Largo de Tereza Batista and Praça Quincas Berro d'Agua (known locally as Praça Dois M) in Pelourinho. Praça Dois M is also home to several hip bars – Habeus Copos and Kibe & CIA are two of the popular spots.

Other music venues around Pelourinho include Coração do Mangue, a small bar at Rua Francisco M Barreto 27 with a street stage and live music on Tuesday and Friday; and Bar do Reggae, at Rua Gregório de Matos 36, with dancers spilling out onto the street just about every night. Gueto, at Rua Alfredo de Brito 33, is the place to go for dance music.

Tuesday night is probably the biggest night in Pelourinho. Traditionally, important religious services known as 'Tuesday's Blessing' have been held every Tuesday at the Igreja São Francisco. The services have always drawn locals to Pelourinho, and since the restoration of the area, the weekly celebrations have turned into a mini-festival. Olodum play at the Teatro Miguel Santana, on Rua Gregório Matos, and other bands set up on Terreiro de Jesus, Largo do Pelourinho and anywhere else they can find space. Crowds pour into Pelourinho to eat, drink, dance and the party lasts until the early hours of the morning.

Ilê Aiyê, one of the most exciting Carnival blocos, gives free concerts every Saturday (at least during summer) in the Forte de Santo Antônio Além do Carmo, in Barbalho, from 9 pm. African culture is kept alive in Liberdade, which is a good place to see afoxé. It's best to go with someone who knows these areas.

Around the beaches, Rio Vermelho has some good nightspots, and many of the better hotels, such as the Salvador Praia, have fancy nightclubs. A few of the happening bars are Zona Franca, at Rua João Gomes 87; Intermezzo at Largo da Mariquita s/n (no number), with outside tables; and Extudo, at Rua Lidio Mesquita 4.

Barra is full of bars, discos and music. Some places are quite good, but it's more touristy and is starting to get a sleazy reputation. Habeas Copos, at Avenida Marquês de Leão 172, is an old favourite (and attracts an older crowd); Zimbabwe, at Rua Afonso Celso 473, has good music and specialises in *afrodisíacos* (aphrodisiac drinks)!

Pituba beach has several bars with music, such as Tocaia Grande, Rua Minas Gerais 784, which specialises in Arabian appetisers.

Those in search of *danceterias* (dance halls) could try Bell's Beach, a slick place at Avenida Octávio Mangabeira, Praia do Corsário, Boca do Rio; or head towards Amaralina to visit New Fred's (☎ 247-4399), at Rua Visconde de Itaboraí 125, which is a huge lambada mecca with room for 600 dancers.

Folklore shows, usually consisting of mini-displays of Candomblé, capoeira, samba, lambada, etc, are presented in the evening at: Senac in Pelourinho (see Places to Eat); Solar do Unhão, south of the city centre (see Places to Eat); and Moenda (☎ 231-7915), at Jardim Armação, next to the Centro de Convenções.

Things to Buy

For handicrafts, you can browse in Mercado Modelo, Praça da Sé, Terreiro de Jesus and numerous shops and galleries in Pelourinho – all places where articles and prices are geared to tourists. For a large, local market, try Mercado São Joaquim (also known as Feira São Joaquim), which is just north of the city centre. Dedicated shoppers should head for Shopping Iguatemi (Salvador's largest shopping centre) and Shopping Barra, both gigantic complexes with dozens of shops.

Getting There & Away

Air The big three domestic airlines all fly to Salvador, as does Nordeste, which goes to smaller cities in the region like Ilhéus and Porto Seguro. You can fly to most cities in Brazil from Salvador, but make sure you find out how many stops the plane makes: many flights in the Northeast operate as 'milk runs', stopping at every city along the Atlantic seaboard, which makes for a long ride. There are regular international flights between Salvador and: Miami; Frankfurt; Paris; Amsterdam; Lisbon; Madrid; Rome; New York; Buenos Aires; Tenerife; Montevideo; and, believe it or not, one weekly flight to Moscow!

Following is a list of Brazilian and foreign airlines with offices in Salvador:

Aerolineas Argentinas
  Rua Miguel Calmon 555, Edifício Citibank, sala 603, Comércio (☎ 242-1007)
Air France
  Rua Portugal 17, Edifício Regente Feijó, sala 606, Comércio (☎ 242-4955)
Lanchile
  Rua Miguel Calmon 555, Edifício Citibank, sala 609, Comércio (☎ 242-8144)
Lufthansa
  Rua Miguel Calmon 555, Edifício Citibank, sala 410, Comércio (☎ 241-5100)
Nordeste
  Avenida D João VI 259, Brotas (☎ 244-3355)
TAP (Air Portugal)
  Avenida Estados Unidos 10, sala 401, Comércio (☎ 243-6122)
Transbrasil
  Rua Portugal 3, Comércio (☎ 241-1044)
  Airport (249-2467)
Varig
  Rua Carlos Gomes 6, Centro (☎ 243-9311)
  Airport (☎ 204-1030)
VASP
  Rua Miguel Calmon 27, Comércio (☎ (0800) 99-8277)

Bus There are several departures daily to Rio (US$41, leito US$88, 26 hours). Buses leave three times daily for São Paulo (US$47, leito US$106, 32 hours) and Belo Horizonte (US$33, 24 hours).

There are seven departures daily to Aracaju (US$8) – buses travelling via the Linha Verde take around five hours. Some make a stop in Estância, others go direct to Aracaju. Four buses depart daily for Recife – the 13-hour trip costs US$22 (leito US$45). There are two daily departures to Fortaleza (US$32.50, 20 hours), and one daily departure to Belém (US$50, 34 hours).

There are three daily departures to Lençóis, at 7.30 am, noon and 10 pm (US$10.75, seven hours) – when the missing sections of the road are filled in, the trip time will improve. There are frequent departures daily to Valença (US$7, 4½ hours). Five buses depart daily for Ilhéus (US$16, seven hours), and there are two evening departures to Porto Seguro (US$22, 10 hours). There are frequent departures for Cachoeira (US$3.50, two hours) between 5.30 am and 7 pm. Take the bus marked 'São Felix'.

For access to beaches along the litoral north, four buses daily run to Conde (US$5, three hours). Some of these buses continue on to Sítio de Conde and Barra do Itiriri.

Boat Boats to points on Baía de Todos os Santos leave from the Terminal Turístico Marítimo (☎ 242-9411), on Avenida da França, one block towards the water from the Mercado Modelo. There are tours of the bay featuring Itaparica and Frade islands, and boats to Maragojipe. See the Baía de Todos os Santos and recôncavo sections for schedules. The small dock beside the Mercado Modelo has irregular motorboats to Mar Grande and Itaparica.

During summer (December to March), there are two daily boats to Morro de São Paulo from the Terminal Turístico Maritimo. The noon boat is a large launch which makes the trip in about 1½ hours – but it costs US$40. The second, smaller motorboat leaves at 2 pm, takes four hours and costs US$15.

Getting Around

Venice has its canals and gondolas; Salvador has its bluff, elevators, hills, valleys and one-way streets. The Lacerda Elevator runs daily from 5 am to midnight, linking the low and high cities. The Plano Inclinado Gonçalves, behind the cathedral near the Praça da Sé, makes the same link and is more fun (and less claustrophobic), but only operates Monday to Saturday from 5 am to 10 pm. The city's latest addition to the lift world is the Plano Inclinado Liberdade/Calçada, which links two poor neighbourhoods north of the city centre.

To/From the Airport Aeroporto Dois de Julho (☎ 204-1010) is over 30 km from the city centre, inland from Itapoã. The two taxi companies represented at the airport share a bilheteria (ticket office) and have the same prices. The table displayed in the office shows prices to several destinations in the city. A taxi ride from the airport to Praça da Sé costs US$27.50. The best way to reach the city centre is to take the Executivo bus marked 'Praça da Sé/Aeroporto'. The fare is US$0.90.

There are supposed to be buses leaving Praça da Sé for the airport every half-hour between 6 am and 7 pm, but the schedule is rather flexible, so leave yourself plenty of time. The bus starts at Praça da Sé (the stop is signposted), goes down Avenida 7 de Setembro to Barra, and continues all the way along the coast before heading inland to the airport. You can flag it down along the way. In light traffic, the ride to the airport takes about an hour; with traffic allow 1¾ hours.

A municipal 'Aeroporto' bus (fare US$0.50) follows the same route to the airport, but it gets very crowded, and isn't recommended if you're carrying a bag.

Bus The two most useful municipal bus stops in the city centre are Praça da Sé and Avenida da França.

Buses from Praça da Sé go to Campo Grande, Vitória and all the Atlantic coast beaches as far as Praia Flamengo, just past Praia Itapoã. Executive buses marked 'Praça da Sé/Aeroporto' also leave from here, and go along the beaches from Barra to Itapoã (US$0.90). Another way to go to the beaches is to take the Jardineira bus which departs hourly between 7.30 am and 7.30 pm from Praça da Sé and Itapoã. The 45-minute trip

(US$1.50) is on an open-deck bus along a scenic coastal route.

The Avenida da França stop is in Cidade Baixa beside the Lacerda Elevator. From here, take either the 'Ribeira' or the 'Bonfim' bus to the Itaparica ferry (get off after a couple of km, when you see the Pirelli Pneus store on your left); the Mercado São Joaquim (get off at the stop after Pirelli Pneus); or continue to Igreja NS do Bonfim and Ribeira.

To/From the Rodoviária The rodoviária (☎ 358-6633) is five km from the city centre, but it's a bit messy taking a bus there – many buses marked 'Rodoviária' drive all over the city – and can take up to an hour during rush hour. For a quicker trip, it's advisable to take a taxi, which costs US$4.50 from Praça da Sé. At the rodoviária, there's a bilheteria which sells fixed-price taxi tickets.

The most convenient way to go by bus to the rodoviária is to take the Iguatemi bus from Praça da Sé. From here, use the pedestrian footbridge to cross the highway to the rodoviária. The bus goes via Barra and Ondina and takes about 45 minutes. The fare is US$0.70. Alternatively, you can use the bus service between the rodoviária and Campo Grande and change there to a bus for the city centre.

The rodoviária is a self-contained complex with a Bahiatursa office, Telebahia office, supermarket, left luggage service, and a couple of inexpensive eateries. For more complex needs, you can pop across the pedestrian footbridge and visit Salvador's largest shopping centre – Shopping Iguatemi.

Around Salvador

ITAPARICA

Many Bahians love Itaparica, the largest island in Baía de Todos os Santos. They prefer to swim in the calm waters of the bay than in the rough and tumble of the ocean. It's quite a pretty island, but not really a must-see destination. Weekends here are crowded (especially in summer), transportation can be slow without a car, and the beaches aren't as pretty as the more accessible beaches north of the city.

The island is built up with many weekend homes, but has few budget hotels. Many of the beaches are dirty and the best part of the island is owned by Club Med. Yet there still are a few clean beaches where you can just lie on the sand beneath wind-swept palms and gaze across the bay at the city (try Barra Grande for example).

Orientation
Itaparica City At the northern tip of the island is the city of Itaparica and the São Lourenço Fort. Built by the Dutch invaders in the 17th century, the fortress figured prominently in Bahia's battle for independence in 1823. The Solar Tenente Botas (Mansion of Lieutenant Botas), on the square of the same name, the Igreja Matriz do Santíssimo Sacramento, on Rua Luis Gama, and the Fonte da Bica (mineral-water fountain) complete the city sights.

Along the Coast South along the coast, between Itaparica City and Bom Despacho, is Ponte da Areia, a thin strip of sand with barracas. The water is clear and shallow, and the sandy floor slopes gently into the bay.

South of Mar Grande (perhaps the most likeable town on the island), the beaches of Barra do Gil, Barra do Pote and Coroa all have excellent views of Salvador, while on the other side of Club Med is Barra Grande, Itaparica's finest open-to-the-public beach. The beaches further to the south up to and including Cacha Pregos are dirtier and generally less beautiful, although many Bahians consider Cacha Pregos the best beach on the island.

Tourist Office
There are two tourist information booths on the island: a tiny booth next to the rodoviária at Bom Despatcho, and another on Praça de São Bento in Mar Grande, both with irregular opening hours.

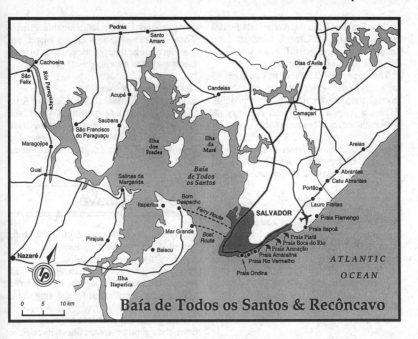

Baía de Todos os Santos & Recôncavo

Places to Stay & Eat

There's a pleasant youth hostel at Aratuba: the *Albergue de Juventude Enseada de Aratuba* (☎ 971-0060), at Quadra H, lotes 12/1, and some campgrounds at Praia de Berlinque, Praia de Barra Grande, and Praia de Cacha Pregos.

In Mar Grande, a good cheap option is the *Pousada Koisa Nossa* (☎ 833-1028), at Rua da Rodagam 173. As you exit the dock, walk across the square and follow the road for about 200 metres. It's a relaxed place, with a restaurant serving fresh, tasty refeições. Double quartos cost around US$18 with breakfast. If you want something more comfortable, have a look at the *Pousada Arco Iris* (☎ 833-1130), at Estrada da Gamboa 102. The pousada is in the restored mansion of an old fazenda set in spacious, shady gardens with a swimming pool and restaurant. Double quartos cost US$30; double apartamentos start at US$40. Discounts of up to 30% apply from April to November.

The best eating on the island is the seafood at the beach barracas. The *Timoneiro Restaurant*, 10 km from Cacha Pregos and three km from the Bom Despacho/Cacha Pregos junction, serves expensive but tasty shrimp dishes.

Getting There & Away

Boat There are two boats from Salvador to Itaparica. The first is a small boat that leaves from the Terminal Turístico Maritimo behind the Mercado Modelo and goes directly to Mar Grande. The trip costs US$0.90 and takes around 50 minutes. Boats depart daily every half-hour between 6.30 am and 7.30 pm. The last boat returns from Mar Grande at 5 pm. This schedule often changes. Other boats leave occasionally for Mar Grande from the small dock beside the Mercado Modelo.

The second boat is a giant car-and-passenger ferry that operates between São Joaquim and Bom Despacho. Take either the 'Ribeira' or 'Bonfim' bus from the Avenida da França bus stop (beside the Lacerda Elevator) for a couple of km and get off when you see a Pirelli Pneus store on your left.

The fare is US$0.70 and the ride takes 45 minutes. Ferries operate every 45 minutes from 5 am to midnight (summer schedule). Expect a long wait to get on the ferry on weekends, especially in summer.

Bus Frequent buses leave from the rodoviária at Bom Despacho travelling to Valença (US$3, two hours) and Camamu, on the mainland.

Getting Around
Bom Despacho is the island's transportation hub. Buses, VW Kombis and taxis meet the boats and will take you to any of the beaches. Bicycles are widely available to rent, and are a useful option if you want to explore under your own steam. Although the São Joaquim-Bom Despacho ferry operates until midnight, island transport becomes scarce after 8 pm.

OTHER BAÍA DE TODOS OS SANTOS ISLANDS
The easiest way to cruise the lesser islands and the bay itself is to get one of the tourist boats that leave from the Terminal Turístico Marítimo (☎ 242-9411), close to Mercado Modelo in Salvador. There are various tours; most take half a day, stopping at Ilha dos Frades, Ilha da Maré and Itaparica. The cost is about US$18.

Alternatively, hire a cheap, small boat from the small port next to the Mercado Modelo. Bahiatursa's bulletin board often has advertisements for boat trips.

Popular islands include Ilha Bom Jesus dos Passos, which has traditional fishing boats and artisans; Ilha dos Frades (named after two monks who were killed and cannibalised there by local Indians), which has attractive waterfalls and palm trees; and Ilha da Maré.

Ilha da Maré has the Igreja de NS das Neves, the quiet beaches of Itamoabo and Bacia das Neves, and one pousada, which

costs around US$15 for a double quarto. There are no restaurants on the island, but you can arrange through the pousada to have meals prepared by villagers.

Getting There & Away
Boats to Ilha da Maré (US$0.85) leave from São Tomé, about one hour by bus from the Avenida da França bus station. Take a 'Base Naval/São Tomé' bus and get off one stop before the end of the line (ask the conductor to let you know).

The Recôncavo

The recôncavo is the region of fertile lands spread around the Baía de Todos os Santos. Some of the earliest Brazilian encounters between Portuguese, Indian and African peoples occurred here, and the lands proved to be among Brazil's best for growing sugar and tobacco.

Along with the excellent growing conditions, the region prospered due to its relative proximity to Portuguese sugar markets, the favourable winds for sailing to Europe and the excellent harbours afforded by the Baía de Todos os Santos. By 1570 there were already 18 sugar mills *engenhos*, and by 1584 there were 40. The sugar-plantation system was firmly entrenched by the end of the 16th century and continued to grow from the sweat of African slaves for another 250 years.

Tobacco came a bit later to the recôncavo. Traded to African slave-hunters and kings, it was the key commodity in the triangle of the slave trade. Tobacco was a more sensitive crop to grow than sugar and the estates were much smaller. But big fortunes were made growing sugar, not tobacco. On the other hand, fewer slaves were needed – about four per tobacco farm – so many poorer Portuguese settlers went into tobacco and a less rigid social hierarchy developed. Many even did some of the work!

A second subsidiary industry in the recôncavo area was cattle ranching, which provided food for the plantation hands, and transport for the wood that fuelled the sugar engenhos and for delivery of the processed cane to market. Cattle breeding started in the recôncavo and spread inland, radiating west into the sertão and Minas Gerais, then north-west into Piauí.

If you have time for only one side trip from Salvador, visit Cachoeira and perhaps squeeze in Santo Amaro. A suggested itinerary is to take the weekday afternoon boat to Maragojipe and then the bus along the banks of the Rio Paraguaçu to Cachoeira. You can then visit Santo Amaro on the way back to Salvador. If you're in Cachoeira on Friday or Saturday nights, you may be able to attend a terreiro de Candomblé. From Cachoeira, there are frequent buses back to Salvador.

CACHOEIRA

Cachoeira, 121 km from Salvador and 40 km from Santo Amaro, is below a series of hills beside the Rio Paraguaçu. The river is spanned by Ponte Dom Pedro II, built by the British in 1885 as a link with its twin town, São Felix. Affectionately known as the jewel of the recôncavo, Cachoeira has a population of 32,000 and is at the centre of Brazil's best tobacco-growing region. Apart from tobacco, the main crops in the area are cashews and oranges.

The town is full of beautiful colonial architecture, uncompromised by the presence of modern buildings. As a result, it was pronounced a national monument in 1971 and the state of Bahia started paying for the restoration and preservation of historic buildings. However, these funds appear to have dried up and the municipal authorities in Cachoeira are continuing the work on their own dwindling budget.

Cachoeira is also a renowned centre of Candomblé and the home of many traditional artists and artisans. If you get an early start, Cachoeira can be visited in a day from Salvador, but it's less hectic if you plan to stay overnight.

Orientation

Cachoeira and São Felix are best seen on foot. There's nothing you really *have* to see, so it's best to just take it easy and explore.

History

Diego Álvares, the father of Cachoeira's founders, was the sole survivor of a ship bound for the West Indies that was wrecked in 1510 on a reef near Salvador. The Portuguese Robinson Crusoe was saved by the Tupinambá Indians of Rio Vermelho, who dubbed the strange white sea creature Caramuru or 'Fish-Man'. Diego Álvares lived 20 years with the Indians and married Catarina do Paraguaçu, the daughter of the most powerful Tupinambá chief. Their sons João Gaspar Aderno Álvares and Rodrigues Martins Alvares killed off the local Indians, set up the first sugar-cane fazendas and founded Cachoeira.

By the 18th century, tobacco from Cachoeira was considered the world's finest, sought by rulers in China and Africa, and was more profitable than sugar. Tobacco also became popular in Brazil. The holy herb, as it was called, was taken as snuff, smoked in a pipe or chewed.

THE NORTHEAST

The Resurrection of Cachoeira

The IBGE director has many dreams and plans to resurrect past splendours. Clearly delighted by our interest, he whisked us off on a tour of the town, which proved a bizarre experience. Everywhere he indicated renovated colonial edifices as being '*quasi feito*' or 'almost finished'. We followed the enthusiastic sweep of his arm and saw the opposite: gutted, roofless buildings with teetering facades and impromptu natural adornments from cacti or papaya trees perched on the remaining walls.

That is the appeal of Cachoeira, a town of surreal, faded grandeur, with friendly inhabitants who maintain enthusiasm and hope in the midst of economic decline. ■

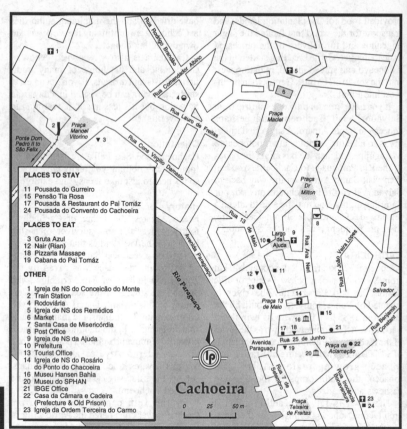

PLACES TO STAY

11 Pousada do Gurreiro
15 Pensão Tia Rosa
17 Pousada & Restaurant do Pai Tomáz
24 Pousada do Convento do Cachoeira

PLACES TO EAT

3 Gruta Azul
12 Nair (Rian)
18 Pizzaria Massape
19 Cabana do Pai Tomáz

OTHER

1 Igreja de NS do Conceicão do Monte
2 Train Station
4 Rodoviária
5 Igreja de NS dos Remédios
6 Market
7 Santa Casa de Misericórdia
8 Post Office
9 Igreja de NS da Ajuda
10 Prefeitura
13 Tourist Office
14 Igreja de NS do Rosário
   do Ponto do Chacoeira
16 Museu Hansen Bahia
20 Museu do SPHAN
21 IBGE Office
22 Casa da Câmara e Cadeira
   (Prefecture & Old Prison)
23 Igreja da Ordem Terceira do Carmo

Cachoeira

0   25   50 m

Early in the 19th century, Cachoeira achieved fame as a centre for military operations in Bahia to oust the Portuguese rulers. On 25 June 1822, the town became the first to recognise Dom Pedro I as the independent ruler of Brazil.

Information

The municipal tourist office, in a renovated building on Rua 13 de Maio, should be able to help with accommodation and general details about the town's sights. Another good place to get information is the Instituto Histórico e Geográfico Brasileiro (IBGE)

office on Praça da Aclamação. Some of the sights, especially churches, have experienced problems with theft and you may have to phone to arrange a visit.

Igreja da Ordem Terceira do Carmo

The Church of the Third Order of Carmelites, just south of Praça da Aclamação and alongside the Pousada do Convento, features a gallery of suffering polychrome Christs imported from the Portuguese colonies in Macau, and panelled ceilings. Christ's blood is made from bovine blood mixed with Chinese herbs and sparkling rubies. The church is now being promoted by the adjacent pousada as a convention centre. It's certainly a novel idea to seat delegates where there were once pews. Opening hours are Tuesday to Saturday from 2 to 5 pm and Sunday from 9 to 11.30 am.

Casa da Câmara e Cadeia

Nearby on the same square is the yellow-with-white-trim Casa da Câmara e Cadeia, the old prefecture and prison. Organised criminals ran the show upstairs and disorganised criminals were kept behind bars downstairs. The building dates back to 1698 and served as the seat of the Bahian government in 1822. The old marble pillory in the square was destroyed after abolition.

Museu do SPHAN

Across the square, a colonial mansion houses the humble SPHAN museum, with squeaky bats flapping over colonial furnishings. The museum is open daily, except Monday, from 9 am to noon and 2 to 5 pm.

Museu Hansen Bahia

The Hansen Bahia museum was set up in the home and birthplace of Brazilian heroine Ana Neri, who organised the nursing corps during the Paraguay War. Now the work of German (naturalised Brazilian) artist Hansen Bahia is displayed here. Among his powerful lithographs of human suffering is a series of illustrations of Castro Alves' poem *Návio Negreiro* (Slave Ship). The museum is open daily, except Tuesday and Sunday afternoons, from 8 am to noon and 2 to 5 pm. Prints are also on sale here.

Igreja de NS do Rosário do Porto do Cachoeira

The blue church with yellow trim, up from the Hansen Bahia museum, at the corner of Rua Ana Neri and Rua Lions Club, is the NS do Rosário do Porto do Cachoeira. The church has beautiful Portuguese tiles, and a ceiling painted by Teófilo de Jesus. Opening hours are erratic (although it's usually open in the mornings) – so it's best to phone ☎ 724-1294 and arrange a time with the custodian, who may also take you round the Museu das Alfaias, on the 1st floor. This museum contains remnants from the abandoned 17th-century Convento de São Francisco do Paraguaçu.

Igreja de NS da Ajuda

On Largo da Ajuda is Cachoeira's oldest church, the tiny NS da Ajuda, built in 1595 when Cachoeira was known as Arraial d'Ajuda. Phone ☎ 724-1396 to arrange a visit to the church and the Museu da Boa Morte – an interesting museum with displays of photos and ceremonial apparel of the exclusively female Boa Morte cult.

Santa Casa de Misericórdia

This is the municipality's oldest hospital. The complex contains a pretty chapel (founded in 1734) with a painted ceiling, gardens and an ossuary. It's open on weekdays from 2 to 5 pm.

Cachoeira's Churches

Cachoeira has dozens of churches of different denominations and competition for the soul is keen. Many of the churches are just simple halls on the 2nd floor of buildings. While searching for a particular candomblé terreio, we stumbled onto a street where several Friday night services were being held. After asking for directions to the terreio, we were greeted warmly and ushered upstairs into what we soon discovered was a Christian service. After managing to extract ourselves, we asked directions from another group of people, who tried to whisk us into their church. When we declined the offer and began to walk away, we were followed up the street by several people warning us not to mix with the 'bad people' at the terreio! ∎

THE NORTHEAST

Igreja de NS do Conceição do Monte

At the far end of town, near the bridge and the train station, is the Igreja de NS do Conceição do Monte. The climb to this 18th-century church is rewarded by a good view of Cachoeira and São Felix.

Praça Manoel Vitorino

Across from the ruined grand facade of the train station, the wide, empty and cobble-stoned Praça Manoel Vitorino feels like an Italian movie set. Try your Italian on the ice-cream seller or the pigeons, then move on to São Felix.

São Felix

When crossing the old Ponte Dom Pedro II, a narrow and dilapidated bridge where trains and cars must wait their turn, be careful where you step: loose planks have claimed the life of at least one person in recent years. When vehicles pass over the bridge it emits a wild cacophony of sounds – a bit like one of those urban/industrial/primitive percussion acts!

Apart from the view towards Cachoeira, São Felix has two other attractions: the **Casa da Cultura Américo Simas**, on Rua Celestino João Severino da Luz Neto (open Tuesday to Sunday from 8 am to 5 pm), and the **Centro Cultural Dannemann**, along the riverfront, at Avenida Salvador Pinto 29 (open Tuesday to Sunday from 8 am to 5 pm).

The Centro Cultural Dannemann has displays of old machinery and the techniques used for making *charutos* (cigars). The rich tobacco smells, the beautiful wooden working tables and the sight of workers hand-rolling monster cigars will take you back in time. The art space in the front of the building has exhibitions of sculpture, painting and photography. The handmade cigars sold here make good souvenirs or presents. Admission is free.

Candomblé

Try to see Candomblé in Cachoeira. This is one of the strongest and perhaps purest spiritual and religious centres for Candomblé. Long and mysterious Candomblé ceremo-nies are held in small homes and shacks up in the hills, usually on Friday and Saturday nights at 8 pm.

Visitors are not common here and the tourist office is sometimes reluctant to give out this sort of information, but if you show an interest in Candomblé, and respect for its traditions, you may inspire confidence.

Other Attractions

If you have a car or like long walks, you can visit the **Pimantel Cigar Factory**, 10 km out of town. **Suerdieck** is another cigar factory closer to the town.

There are also two old sugar mills near town: **Engenho da Cabonha**, eight km along the road to Santo Amaro, and **Engenho da Guaiba**, 12 km along the same road.

Festivals

Festa da NS de Boa Morte falls on the Friday closest to 15 August and lasts three days. This is one of the most fascinating Candomblé festivals and it's worth a special trip to see it. Organised by the Irmandade da Boa Morte (Sisterhood of the Good Death) – a secret, black, religious society – the festival is celebrated by the descendants of slaves, who praise their liberation with dance and prayer and a mix of themes from Candomblé and Catholicism.

The Festa de São João, celebrated from 22 to 24 June, is the big popular festival of Bahia's interior. It's a great celebration of folklore, with music, dancing, and plenty of food and drink. Don't miss it if you're in Bahia.

Other festivals include: NS do Rosário (second half of October), which includes games, music and food; NS da Ajuda (first half of November), which features ritual cleansing of the church and a street festival; and Santa Barbara or Iansã (4 December), a Candomblé ceremony held in São Felix at Fonte de Santa Bárbara (Fountain of Santa Bárbara).

Places to Stay – bottom end

The *Pousada do Pai Tomáz* (☎ 725-1288),

at Rua 25 de Junho 12, has comfortable single/double apartamentos for US$7/14. In São Felix, the *Pousada do Paraguaçu* (☎ 725-1550), at Avenida Salvador Pinto 1, is a relaxed place along the riverfront, with a verandah overlooking the water. Apartamentos with fan cost US$10/14 for a single/double, or US$17/23 with air-con. There's a restaurant attached.

The *Pensão Tia Rosa* (☎ 725-1792), opposite Museu Hansen Bahia, has basic single/double quartos for US$6/12, with a good breakfast included in the price. The *Pousada do Guerreiro* (no phone), at Rua 13 de Maio 14, has ragged but clean single/double quartos for US$8/15. Ask for an upstairs room.

Places to Stay – middle

The *Pousada do Convento de Cachoeira* (☎ 725-1716) is a lovely old hotel with a courtyard and swimming pool. The dark-wood rooms of the old convent now have air-con, frigobar and hot showers, and cost US$34/40 for a single/double – including a major spread for breakfast. An extra bed costs US$8, or you can splurge on the suite for US$50.

Places to Eat

The *Gruta Azul* (☎ 725-1295), at Praça Manoel Vitorino 2, is Cachoeira's best restaurant. The place has character: special recipes for seafood and batidas and a delightful shaded courtyard. Try the shrimp dishes for US$8 or maniçoba, the spicy local dish composed of manioc and various meats. If you're adventurous ask for the *boa morte* (good death) drink. Opening hours are 11 am to 3 pm and 7 to 9 pm daily, except Sunday, when the restaurant is closed in the evening.

On Rua 25 de Junho, there's more good food at *Cabana do Pai Thomáz* (the restaurant is across the road from the pousada) – check out the sensational scrap-yard roof decorations and the carved wooden panels and furniture. *Pizzaria Massapé* (open daily from 11 am to midnight) is close by.

Next to the tourist office is the *Nair* restaurant, named after the owner, but locals delight in turning things around and calling it Rian. The menu includes moqueca dishes and local specialities.

In São Felix, try the restaurant in the Pousada do Paraguaçu, which is open from 11 am to 11 pm.

Entertainment

Cruise the riverfront for beer drinking and forró dancing at the riverside bars. On Wednesday and Saturday, there's an open market on Praça Maciel – a good place to pick up handicrafts and observe local life.

Things to Buy

Cachoeira has a wealth of wood sculptors, some of whom do very fine work, and you will see plenty of studios as you walk through town. This is some of the best traditional art still available in Brazil. Two of the best sculptors are Doidão and Loucou, who carve beautiful, heavy pieces.

Getting There & Away

Bus There are frequent departures to Salvador between 5.30 am and 7 pm (US$3.50, two hours). The rodoviária (☎ 725-1214) is tiny and easy to miss – it's a small green building with white trim. Cachoeira also has regular buses that run to Maragojipe (US$0.80, half an hour).

Buses to and from Valença run via Santo Antônio. From Cachoeira, take one of the frequent buses to Santo Antônio and connect from there for Valença. Buses leave Santo Antônio for Cachoeira daily at 7 am, and 1 and 3 pm.

Train Salvador and Cachoeira are also connected by rail, but service is poor and may soon be suspended altogether.

Boat After Rio Paraguaçu was blocked by Pedra do Cavalo Barragem dam, Cachoeira no longer had the waterfalls for which it was named. The river has since silted up, making boat passage up from Maragojipe and Salvador difficult and irregular. You may want to check the latest information with the Vapor do Cachoeira boat service at the Companhia de Navegação Bahiano (Mercado Modelo docks, Salvador). Apparently, during the festival of São João there is an attempt at operating a regular boat service to Salvador.

Getting Around

Cachoeira is just the right size to cover on foot. If you want to cross the river to São Felix by canoe, rather than crossing the bridge on foot, they are available for hire at the waterfront.

IGREJA E CONVENTO DE SANTO ANTÔNIO DO PARAGUAÇU

Construction of this magnificent Franciscan church and convent was started in 1658 and completed in 1686. The convent functioned as a hospital and training centre for novices until 1855, when an imperial decree forbidding the admission of novices put a stop to its activities, and the buildings were gradually abandoned. In 1915, the contents of the convent and its walled grounds were sold. Despite some efforts at restoration, all that remains is the crumbling ruins, a powerful atmosphere and a sense of remote, faded glory, in this superb position beside the Rio Paraguaçu.

There are two pensões in São Francisco – ask for either Ednaide or José. José Gringa, who lives next to the telephone office, has the key to the convent, which is kept locked to prevent theft.

A bus departs daily at noon from the market in Cachoeira for the 44-km trip to the tiny village of São Francisco do Paraguaçu. The same bus returns to Cachoeira at 5.30 am the next day.

CANDEIAS

The Museu do Recôncavo (Vanderlei do Pinho) can be visited at the Engenho de Freguesia (sugar mill and plantation). In the restored colonial mansion and senzala (slave quarters), there are displays which graphically depict life on the plantations during the past centuries. The museum is open Tuesday to Sunday from 9 am to 3 pm. Candeias is about 45 km from Salvador, and the museum is a further seven km outside the town –

access is easiest if you have your own transport or take a taxi from Candeias.

SANTO AMARO

Santo Amaro is an old, run-down sugar town that sees very few tourists and has an unpretentious charm. If you're passing through on your way from Cachoeira, think about stopping for a few hours, especially if it's a market Saturday, when the town comes to life. If you decide to stay the night, there's often very good local music. Try *Pousada Amaro's* (☎ 241-1202), at Rua Conselhor Saraiva 27, for a good accommodation option.

In colonial days, Santo Amaro made its fortune from sugar. Today, the major industry is paper production; the paper mill is on the road to Cachoeira. The mill has spoiled the Rio Subaé and bamboo has replaced sugar cane on the hillsides.

Reminders of Santo Amaro's sugar legacy are the decrepit pastel mansions of the sugar barons, and the many churches. The plantation owners lived on Rua General Câmara, the old commercial street, and there is an effort being made to restore some of these buildings.

Many of the churches have been closed since a gang of thieves stole most of the holy images and exported them to France. The largest church, Santo Amaro da Purificação, is still open.

The Festa de Santo Amaro (24 January to 2 February) is celebrated by the ritual lavagem of the church steps. Santo Amaro is the birthplace of two of Brazil's most popular singers: Caetano Veloso and his sister Maria Betânia. During Carnival, they've been known to put in an appearance between trios elétricos.

Step out to the square across from the church for an evening's promenade. Despite active flirting, the sexes circle separately.

Getting There & Away

There are frequent bus services between Salvador and Santo Amaro (US$2.50, 70 minutes), and many of these continue the 32 km to Cachoeira/São Felix.

MARAGOJIPE

Circled by Baía de Todos os Santos and rich green fields patched with crops, Maragojipe is a pleasantly decaying tobacco-exporting port, 32 km from Nazaré and 24 km from Cachoeira. The port is surrounded by mangrove swamps, and locals push off from the pier in *saveiros* (home-made fishing boats) and dugout canoes.

For information, speak to Ronald at the Fundação Suerdieck Casa da Cultura, on Praça da Matriz. He will be delighted to tell you about local sights.

Things to See

The **Suerdieck & Company Cigar Factory** (established in 1920) is open for tours Monday to Friday from 8 am to 5 pm, and on Saturday morning.

On weekend nights head down to the dockside bars for local music. Swimming off the cement pier is popular.

Strolling through town, look out for the wrought-iron grill and sculpted facade of the pale-blue building on Rua D Macedo Costa.

Places to Stay & Eat

The *Oxumaré Hotel* (☎ 726-1104), at Rua Heretiano Jorge de Souza 3, has cramped single/double quartos which cost US$4/6.

Jumbo shrimp is the local delicacy. Otherwise, go for pizza at the port at *Pizzaria Recreio do Porto*, and *City Bar*, on Praça da Matriz, for sucos and snacks.

Getting There & Away

Bus Buses from Salvador to Maragojipe go via Santo Amaro and Cachoeira. There are six buses daily, the first departing at 7.10 am, the last at 4 pm. The trip takes three hours and costs US$4. There are no buses via Itaparica. We recommend going by boat.

Boat Boats leave from Salvador to Maragojipe (US$20, around 3½ hours) from Monday to Saturday at 2 pm from the Terminal Turístico Marítimo (☎ 242-9411), which is behind the Mercado Modelo. Stops are made at São Roque, Barra do Paraguaçu and

Enseada. The boat from Maragojipe to Salvador leaves Monday to Saturday at 5 am.

There are no boats from Maragojipe to Cachoeira since the Rio Paraguaçu silted up, but there are frequent buses.

NAZARÉ

Nazaré is an 18th-century city with some colonial buildings and churches, and a good market known for its *caxixis* (small ceramic figures).

The big festivals here are the folkloric NS de Nazaré (24 January to 2 February), and Feira dos Caxixis (Holy Week), which features a large market on Holy Thursday and Good Friday, followed by the holiday of Micareta.

For a place to stay, try the *Pousada da Fonte* (☎ 736-1287).

For transport between Nazaré and Salvador, you can either take the bus or the ferry boat.

North of Salvador

The coastal road north from Salvador is called the Rodovia do Côco (Coconut Highway). The excellent, paved road runs a few km from the ocean, as far as the entrance to Praia do Forte, 80 km north of Salvador. From Praia do Forte, the new Linha Verde (Green Line) road spans 142 km to Itanhi, on the border with Sergipe. The Linha Verde, constructed in 1993 and hailed as Brazil's first 'ecologically planned' road, runs between three and 12 km from the coast. The 'ecological planning' runs to a restriction on the construction of petrol stations and roadside restaurants and to the fact that the road doesn't hug the coast, as was originally planned.

There are access roads off the Linha Verde to several small towns and fishing villages, some of which are now becoming popular weekend destinations from Salvador. There are plans to develop tourist areas about every 10 km along the coast. Regular buses run

THE NORTHEAST

along the Linha Verde from Salvador to Conde, and enter a few coastal towns on the way. See the separate sections for each town for access details.

Municipal buses from Salvador go along the coast as far as Itapoã and then turn inland towards the airport. Buses to points further north along the Linha Verde – Praia do Forte and beyond – leave from the main rodoviária in Salvador.

The map 'Beaches of North Bahia, Sergipe & Alagoas' (in the Sergipe & Alagoas chapter) should be consulted in conjunction with the North of Salvador text.

AREMBEPE

Arembepe was one of Brazil's first hip beaches in the 1960s. Mick Jagger and Janis Joplin got the joint rolling and many local and foreign hippies followed. It is no longer a particularly attractive or popular retreat. Exclusive private homes and pollution from the giant Tibras chemical plant have tainted the rocky coast.

If you want to head to the sea for a day from Salvador, there are prettier beaches than Arembepe, and if you're getting out of Salvador, there are less spoiled fishing villages along the Bahian littoral.

Places to Stay

If you do end up in Arembepe, you can head for the campground, or try the *Pousada da Fazenda* (☎ 824-1030), which looks like one of the few leftovers from the hippie days. Doubles cost US$30. The *Praias de Arembepe Hotel* (☎ 824-1115), across from the praça, has single/double apartamentos for around US$20/25.

NORTH TO PRAIA DO FORTE
Guarajuba

A few km south of Praia do Forte, Guarajuba is a lovely beach accompanied by some tract housing which is clearly the beginning of major development. There are a couple of very expensive hotels in town. For cheaper accommodation, try *Pousada Colibri* (☎ 874-1091) on Rua Merluza, with double apartamentos for around $30.

Barra do Jacuípe

A more remote spot, Barra do Jacuípe sits at the mouth of a river only one km from the ocean. The beach is quite beautiful and, apart from a campground, there are no tourist facilities.

PRAIA DO FORTE

Praia do Forte, three km from the meeting point of the Rodovia do Côco and the Linha Verde, has fine beaches, a beautiful castle fortress, a sea-turtle reserve and, unfortunately, mostly expensive hotels. Until recently a fishing village, Praia do Forte is being developed as an ecologically-minded, up-market beach resort. The development has so far been held in check, but the beaches get very crowded on weekends and in summer.

Praia do Forte is the seat of one of the original 12 captaincies established by the Portuguese. The huge estate extended inland all the way to the present-day state of Piauí. Desperate to colonise as a means to contain his new territory, the King of Portugal set about granting lands to merchants, soldiers and aristocrats. For no apparent reason Garcia d'Ávila, a poor, 12-cow farmer, was endowed with this huge tract of land.

Garcia chose a prime piece of real estate – an aquamarine ocean-view plot studded with palm trees on Morro Tatuapaçu – and built his home, Castelo do Garcia d'Ávila, there. Today, the castle is in ruins and completely overgrown, but it still made a fine tropical setting for director Márcio Meyrelle's production of *Macbeth*.

The Banco do Brasil changes US dollars cash, but only Visa travellers' cheques.

TAMAR Turtle Reserve

The TAMAR (Tartaruga Marinha) turtle reserve is on the beach right next to the lighthouse and the overpriced Pousada Praia Forte. TAMAR is a jointly funded IBAMA and navy project started in 1982 to protect several species of marine turtles that are, or were, threatened. What you see is actually quite modest: several small feeding pools with anywhere from two to several dozen turtles, depending on the season. The TAMAR project gathers 50,000 turtle eggs a year along the coast, from which around 35,000 hatchlings are released. The eggs – moist, leathery, ping-pong-size balls – are buried in a fenced-off area in the sand to incubate. When the turtles hatch, they're immediately released to tackle the Atlantic.

There is a souvenir shop at the station, with nice turtle T-shirts (no ninjas here, although there's a teenage mutant turtle in one pool that was brought to the station after its growth had been stunted from being held in a pool too small for its size). Night tours to see the newly-hatched turtles being released into the ocean can be arranged through Odara Tourismo (☎ 876-1080).

TAMAR also has stations at Comboios, Espírito Santo (north of Vitória, near Lineares), to protect the leatherback and loggerhead turtles, and on Fernando de Noronha to preserve the green turtle.

Nowadays, commerce in endangered turtle species is illegal, but shells are still sold in Salvador's Mercado Modelo, and in Sergipe, turtle eggs are still popular hors d'oeuvres. Of the 60 km of beach under the jurisdiction of the TAMAR project in Bahia, 13 km of coastline are patrolled by the scientists alone; the remainder is protected by a cooperative effort in which fisherfolk – the very same who used to collect the eggs for food – are contracted to collect eggs for the scientists.

Places to Stay
The only cheap place to stay is at the campground, which is just 10 minutes on foot from the beach, has cold-water showers, shady, sandy sites, and basins for washing clothes. One of the cheaper hotels is the *João Sol* (☎ 876-1054), on Rua da Corvina. Prices for hotels may start to lower with increased competition. Some reasonable options are: the *Pousada Leyfradt* (no phone), on Rua Almeida do Sol near the main beach, with double apartamentos for US$38; the *Pousada Dos Coqueiros* (☎ 876-1037), with comfortable double apartamentos for

US$35; or the more up-market *Pousada dos Artistas* (☎ 876-1147), on Praça dos Artistas, with friendly management, and double apartamentos with refrigerator and hot water for US$50. There are discounts of up to 35% during low season.

Places to Eat
Brasa da Praia is an ambient seafood restaurant which sometimes has live music in the evenings. It's very expensive, but might be worth a splurge. The barracas along the beach serve local seafood and snack food.

Getting There & Away
Bus services to Praia do Forte run from just outside the rodoviária in Salvador. The trip takes two hours, and the service operates daily between 7.30 am and 6 pm. The last bus from Praia do Forte to Salvador leaves at 5 pm. More bus services are planned.

NORTH OF PRAIA DO FORTE
With the opening of the Linha Verde, access to the small towns and fishing communities along the Bahian north littoral is easier, at least as far as the Conde area. All through this region there are fenced-off tracts of land and small real-estate offices selling beachfront property.

North of Conde, there are only direct buses along the Linha Verde to Aracaju, with some making a stop in Estância (for access to Mangue Seco). You should be able to get off the bus at other points along the road, but local transport is scarce and you'll need to hitch or walk for access to beaches.

Imbassaí
Imbassaí is a quiet, pretty village 65 km from Salvador, a few km off the Linha Verde along a dirt road. The local authorities seem committed to riding the fine line between development and preserving the environment – the banning of buggies along the beach is a big plus. The surf can often be choppy and rough, but the small Rio Barroso runs parallel to the beach and is good for swimming.

Places to Stay & Eat Development of the beachfront has been kept to a minimum, with accommodation set back from the beach. Discounts of between 30% and 40% should apply outside the high season (December to March). The *Kioske de Alá*, in the village about 10 minutes' walk from most of the other pousadas, has fairly grimy double apartamentos for US$20. The *Pousada Brilho do Mar* (☎ 232-1876) is good value; small double chalets with balconies cost US$28, or US$36 with breakfast. The *Pousada Imbassaí* (☎ 971-6927), on the road into the village, has friendly management, and comfortable double apartamentos at US$35; or cabanas for four people are US$65. The *Pousada Caminho do Mar* (☎ 832-2499) has large luxury chalets with cooking facilities and refrigerator at US$49/52, with breakfast served on your private balcony.

Getting There & Away Four daily buses run from Imbassaí to Salvador, or you can walk to the Linha Verde to pick up more frequent buses from Conde.

Porto Suipé, Subaúma & Baixio

The beach towns of Porto Suipé, Subaúma and Baixio are five km, nine km and eight km respectively off the Linha Verde, with paved-road access to all of them. Porto Suipé is marked as the site for several large tourist projects, including a 'watery wonderland' theme park. The town itself is not very appealing, but there are some nice beaches to the south with calm water for swimming. Sabaúma is already quite developed, with lots of weekend beach homes, and land being bought up to construct more. There's a decent beach with strong surf, and a couple of hotels. Baixio is a pretty, clean town, but the beach is rocky and not great for swimming. There's one pousada in the town.

Conde

On the Rio Itapicuru, Conde is about three km off the Linha Verde and six km from the sea. It's the little big town of the area, and the jumping-off point for several beaches, the closest being Sítio. On Saturday, Conde hosts a large market where fisherfolk and artisans come to peddle their goods. In October, a series of rodeos take place, when cowboys from the inland regions hit town to strut their stuff.

Getting There & Away The town has regular bus services to Esplanada, Alagoinhas, Feira de Santana and Salvador, and local shuttle services to Sítio. There's plenty of river traffic on market days which makes it easy to get a ride down the river to the ocean. During summer, however, the river is often too low to make the passage.

Sítio

From Conde it's a six-km drive to Sítio (also known as Sítio do Conde), which has a decent beach, although it's often windy with choppy surf. From Sítio you can walk north or south along the coast to some beautiful, isolated beaches. Seribinha is a quiet fishing community about 14 km north of Sítio along a dirt road which passes through picturesque coconut-palm forest. The village is set on a thin strip of land between the Rio Itapicuru and the coast, close to where the river meets the ocean. Jangadas will take you across the river; from here it's about a half-hour walk to Cavalho Russo, a red-water lake. There's one pousada in Seribinha.

Places to Stay & Eat The cheapest options are the campgrounds. Ask for discounts during low season (April to November) at all the pousadas. One of the cheaper options is the *Pousada Casa Verde*, on the main square, which, during summer, is run by a friendly young couple from Rio who speak English and German. It has pleasant quartos that cost US$15/20 for singles/doubles, and apartamentos that go for US$20/25. Closer to the beach, the *Pousada Beira Mar* has single/double apartamentos for US$20/25. The *Pousada Laia* is a bit more up-market, but reasonably good value, with single/double apartamentos for US$25/35, including breakfast and dinner.

There are a couple of good restaurants in

town. *Zecas & Zecos*, on the main plaza, is the best place for seafood. *Sabor d'Italia* is run by an Italian and serves excellent pizzas and pastas. A note on the menu claims 'Não servimos katchup nem maionese' (we don't serve ketchup or mayonnaise). The *Restaurant Panela de Barro* serves tasty home-style cooking and has charmingly off-hand service.

Getting There & Away A couple of buses a day run from Salvador direct to Sítio via Conde. More buses from Salvador finish in Conde, where you can pick up buses to Sítio at 9.45 am, and 1.40, 6.45 and 7 pm.

Barra de Itariri

Barra is a 14-km drive along a dirt road south from Sítio. The road is never more than a few hundred metres from the sea, which is hidden behind a running dune spotted with coconut palms. Barra has become more popular since the construction of the Linha Verde, but it is still a charming spot, set along the banks of the Rio Itariri. The river can be waded or swum across, and the southern bank leads to an endless stretch of deserted beach. To the north are more deserted beaches; this stretch is known as 'Corre Nu' (run naked).

Barra has a couple of restaurants along the beachfront, and one pousada, with more in construction.

Getting There & Away Buses run from Sítio to Barra at 9 am and noon, and return from Barra to Sítio at 2 and 5 pm. Be prepared to push-start the bus, but don't get the position closest to the exhaust!

Mangue Seco

Mangue Seco is a remote and tiny town on the northern border of Bahia, at the tip of a peninsula formed by the Rio Real. The town was the setting for the Jorge Amado novel *Tieta do Agreste*, and a recent TV drama based on the novel, filmed in the village, captured the imagination of millions of Brazilians. Access to the town is still limited, but it is receiving more tourists since the opening of the Linha Verde. The lovely setting by the river is topped off by fine, white-sand ocean beaches 1.5 km away.

Places to Stay & Eat There is a campground by the river close to town. Cheap pousadas in town include the *Achonchego da Telma* and the *Grão de Areia* (☎ 224-7401), with quartos for around US$6/12. The *Pousada Mangue Seco* has more comfortable single/double apartamentos with fan and refrigerator for US$12/15, or tiny shacks by the swimming pool for US$6/10. The *Village Mangue Seco* (☎ 625-9130) is a more up-market place with a swimming pool, around one km from town along the road to the beaches. Single/double apartamentos cost US$30/40.

There are couple of good seafood restaurants in town with great riverfront locations – try *Bafo do Bode*, *Restaurant Frutas do Mar* or *Suruby*. *Restaurant Dunasmar* is the town action spot, with forró and dance music on weekends.

Getting There & Away The easiest access to Mangue Seco is from Pontal, in Sergipe. From Pontal there are frequent boats across the Rio Real to Mangue Seco (US$1 per person, 20 minutes) until around 6.30 pm. If you are coming from the north, a daily bus runs to Pontal from Estância at 4 pm. The bus runs via Indiaroba, near the border with Bahia, then doubles back to Pontal. If you are coming from Salvador, you can pick up the bus in Indiaroba at around 4.30 pm. The last 10 km or so to Pontal over a roller-coaster dirt road is entertaining, with locals egging on the driver to get airborne over the bumps! If the bus doesn't make the last boat, you'll have to bargain for a ride across – most boats want US$15 to make the crossing.

Road access is possible from Abadia, just off the Linha Verde, over a very poor road which weaves 35 km until it reaches Mangue Seco. There is no bus service on this road. The bus returns from Pontal to Estância via Indiaroba daily, at 5.30 pm.

Saco

Saco, actually across the border in the state

of Sergipe, gets weekender visitors from Estância, but is quiet during the week. It's a fine beach with good swimming. There is no accommodation, but bars and restaurants open on weekends.

Abaís

This is another weekend spot, but with a pousada. The beach, however, is not as good as the others in the area.

South of Salvador

VALENÇA

For most travellers, Valença is simply a stepping stone to the beaches of Morro de São Paulo, but it's also a small, friendly city worth a visit en route.

After routing the local Tupininquin Indians, the Portuguese settled here along the Rio Una in the 1560s, but were in turn expelled by the Aimores tribes. In 1799 the Portuguese returned to resettle and found Vila de Nova Valença do Santíssimo Coração de Jesus.

Today everything centres around the busy port and large market beside the Rio Una, where there are boats, historic buildings, and food and lodging facilities. The town is populated by a varied and interesting assortment of shipbuilders, vaqueiros (cowboys), textile manufacturing workers, artisans, fisherfolk and peasants.

Information

To obtain maps and information, visit the tourist office (☎ 741-3311, ext 1350), at Rua Comandante Madureira, close to the port. It's open from 8 am to 5 pm, Monday to Friday, and from 8 am to noon on Saturday. If you want to change money, there is a Banco do Brasil branch on Rua Governador Gonçalves.

Things to See & Do

In the centre of town, wander around the port, the central plaza and the market. At the far end of the port, the timbered ribbing of boat hulls resembles dinosaur skeletons. The saveiros (wooden sailboats) are used by the local fisherfolk, who pull out of port early in the morning and return by mid-afternoon with the catch of the day. The smell of sap and sawdust, old fish and sea salt mingles with the wonderful smell of nutmeg. Picked from nearby groves, the nutmeg are set on a cloth and left to dry in the sun.

For a good trek, follow the left bank of the Rio Una upstream towards the **Igreja NS de Amparo**, on the hill. At the base of the hill there's a trail straight up to the church which commands a beautiful view.

Cotton Factory

The large, white, fortress-like building houses a textile factory. Personal tours of the factory show the entire hot, noisy, smelly transformation of raw cotton into finished fabrics. This factory is typical of the old Brazilian economy, still prevalent in the Northeast. It's a good tour for those interested in economic development.

The factory is open to tourists on Saturday from 9 am to 5 pm, although you may be able to arrange a tour on other days. Authorisation is provided at the colonial building which stands to the left of the factory front.

Festivals

In addition to the traditional festivals of Bahia, Valença also celebrates Sagrado Coração de Jesus. A mass is held for the patron of the city, in June, and a festival in honour of the patron saint of workers, NS do Amparo, on 8 November.

Boi Estrela is a folklore festival where men and women dressed as cowhands accompany Catarina the Baiana while they play tambourines and chant. Zabiapunga, another folklore festival, features musical groups playing weird instruments and running through the city streets on New Year's Eve.

There's a good Carnival, with trios elétricos and the Carnival-like Micareta festival held 15 days after the end of Lent. Other festivals include Festa de Reis (6 January),

São João (23 June), NS do Rosário (24 September to 3 October), São Benedito, on Cairu Island (26 December to 6 January) and Iemanjá (February 2).

Places to Stay & Eat

The following prices are for high season – negotiate discounts of at least 25% in low season. The *Hotel Valença* (☎ 741-1807), at Rua Dr Heitor Guedes Melo 15, has single/double apartamentos for US$25/30. The *Hotel Guaibim* (☎ 741-1114), at Praça da Independência 74, is one block in from the port. Single/double/triple apartamentos cost US$17/28/41 – cheaper rooms are available without air-con or refrigerator. Next door, the *Pousada Rafa* has slightly cheaper apartamentos, but the price doesn't include breakfast.

The *Hotel Portal Rio Una* (☎ 741-2321; fax 741-2387), on Rua Maestro Barrinhão on the riverside, has more comforts and is accordingly more expensive – double apartamentos with air-con, refrigerator and TV start at around US$86.

There's a good comida a kilo restaurant, *Restaurante Carvalho*, at Rua Conselhor Cunha Lopes 33, near the Hotel Guaibim. *Restaurant Capixaba*, along the riverfront, at Rua Comandante Madureira 88, has a wide range of seafood dishes for around US$9 and is popular with locals. The

Recanto do Luís, in Cajaíba, is also recommended for seafood, and the Hotel Rio Una has its own restaurant, the *Panorama*.

Getting There & Away

There is a small airport just outside town serviced by air-taxi companies, but there are plans for a bigger airport at Praia Guaibim.

Bus The rodoviária is on Rua da Água, about 1.5 km from the port. If you are heading straight to Morro de São Paulo, the bus should be able to let you off at the port. There's a frequent bus service operating daily to Salvador (US$7, 4½ hours). Some buses go via Ilha de Itaparica (190 km) and drop you off at Bom Despacho for the 45-minute ferry ride to Salvador; others go all the way around Baía de Todos os Santos (290 km) into Salvador. There are also regular buses to Camamu (US$2.50, two hours).

Boat There are daily boat trips to Morro de São Paulo and Gamboa, on Ilha de Tinharé, the large island facing Valença. Although Salvador is only 110 km away by sea, the boat service is irregular.

AROUND VALENÇA

The best mainland beach in the vicinity is 16 km north of town, at Guaibim, which is rapidly developing into a popular resort. There are local buses, and the beach gets packed at weekends. The *Pousada São Paulo* and the *Santa Maria Praia*, both on Avenida Beira Mar, have single/double apartamentos for around US$15/20.

The islands of Boipeba and Cairu have colonial buildings and churches – their beaches aren't quite as good as Morro de São Paulo, but Boipeba in particular has started to attract travellers looking to escape the crowds of Morro. There are irregular boats to Boipeba from Valença, depending on passengers – ask around at the port.

VALENÇA TO ILHÉUS
Morro de São Paulo

Morro de São Paulo is an isolated fishing village that has recently been 'discovered' by

Brazilian and international tourists. Morro is on everyone's lips and has even made it on to the best-beach lists of several Brazilian magazines. The beaches are wonderful and the village is loaded with pousadas, restaurants and bars. Outside summer, it's still quite a relaxing place.

At the northern tip of Ilha de Tinharé, Morro de São Paulo has sandy streets where only beach bums, mules and horses tread – there are no roads and no cars. The clear waters around the island are ideal for scuba diving and for lobster, squid and fish. The settlement is comprised of three hills – Morro de Mangaba, Morro de Galeão and Morro de Farol. Climb up from the harbour through the 17th-century fortress gate and up to the lighthouse (1835). From the top you can survey the island and its beaches. The west side of the island – the river or Gamboa side – is mostly bordered by mangroves, while the east side is sandy.

There are four beaches in Morro de São Paulo: the rather dirty village beach, the barraca and camping beach (also less than clean in summer), the fazenda beach and the fourth beach. The fourth beach is by far the best – a long, lovely stretch of sand graced by tall, swaying palms which borders the eastern half of the island, and only one barraca in sight!

Garapua is a small settlement in the southwestern corner of the island with a couple of pousadas. The walk there along the beach takes about four hours, and is best done at low tide.

Information There's a small information booth as you come off the pier – opening hours are very erratic. The shop next door sells a map of the island, *Morro de São Paulo em perspectiva*, for US$3, which is cute but not very detailed. The character who runs the bookshop Livraria de São Paulo may be the best source of information – and he has a great range of books as well.

The Banco do Brasil on Caminho da Praia changes cash and travellers' cheques.

Boat Trip There are daily sailboat trips to

Boipeba, depending on the number of passengers, leaving at around 8 am and returning by 6 pm. The trip takes around two hours each way and costs US$12 per person. The boat operator sets up on Caminho da Praia most nights to recruit passengers; otherwise, ask at Forno a Lenha Pizzaria. There are a few pousadas on Boipeba, and it's a lot quieter and more primitive than Morro.

Places to Stay Without a doubt, the best deal for longer stays is to rent a house. Even in summer, it's possible to rent large, comfortable houses with cooking facilities and beds for seven or eight people for around US$60 per day. Ask the touts when you arrive at the port.

The food and accommodation scene is changing quickly and accommodation can be tight during the summer. There are nearly 70 pousadas in Morro de São Paulo – it's definitely worth hunting around before you commit yourself.

If you want to stay right amongst the action, the *Pousada Toucano* and the *Pousada Giras Sol*, on Caminho da Praia, are two good, cheap options, with quartos for around US$10 per person. If you want something a bit quieter in the wooded hills behind the village, head up Rua da Fonte (the street off Praça Aureliano Lima next to Pousada Casarão). The street splits three ways when you come to Fonte Grande, a lovely spot where locals do their washing. Off to the left you'll find the *Pousada Macondo*, a very friendly, relaxed place with clean quartos for US$10 per person, or US$13 with breakfast. The street running straight ahead (Caminho da Lagoa) leads to the *Pousada Bugainville*, a breezy, quiet place with double apartamentos with fan for US$30 (breakfast included). Take the right fork along Rua Porto de Cima for the *Hotel Porto de Cima* (☎ 783-1020), a more up-market place with double apartamentos for US$40.

Along the fazenda (or third) beach, the *Pousada Govinda* is a tiny, friendly pousada with a rustic beach bar out the front. Mini-quartos cost US$10 per person, or US$15 with breakfast. Near the far end of the beach, the *Pousada Fazenda Caeira* (☎ 783-1042) has spacious grounds and a resort look, but offers reasonable deals on a variety of accommodation. 'La Tartaruga', a house with two bedrooms and verandah, costs around US$50 per day.

Places to Eat The main street of Morro, Caminho da Praia, is a regular restaurant strip. *Ponte de Econtro* offers a wide range of excellent, tasty vegetarian food priced by the kilo. *Canto do Mar* and *Sabor da Terra* both have good-value seafood prato feito for around US$6. *La Strega* is a tiny restaurant with excellent pasta; across the road, at *Bella Donna*, you can eat spaghetti and watch the passing parade from the balcony. *Forno a Lenha Pizzaria* is the place to head for pizza – they're wood-fired and very good value.

Getting There & Away Take the *Brisa Biônica* (Bionic Breeze) or *Brisa Triônica* between Morro de São Paulo and Valença for a relaxed 1½-hour boat ride (US$2). You'll pass mangroves, yachts, double-masted square-rigged Brazilian 'junks', and palm-lined beaches that rival the Caribbean and South Pacific in beauty.

During the summer the schedule is as follows: seven boats per day depart Valença for Morro de São Paulo between 7.30 am and 5 pm. If you arrive later than this, you should still be able to find someone at the port in Valença to take you, but expect to pay double the price. Five boats daily depart from Morro to Valença between 6 am and 5 pm.

The rest of the year boats, are less frequent, except on weekends. The increasing popularity of Morro de São Paulo will undoubtedly cause frequent schedule changes – if you're coming from Salvador you can confirm these times at Bahiatursa.

During summer there are also direct boats daily to and from Salvador. One is a large launch which leaves Morro at 8 am, takes about 1½ hours and cost US$40. The other boat is a smaller motorboat which leaves Morro at 6 am, takes four hours and costs US$15.

Camamu

On the mainland, further down the coast towards Ilhéus, Camamu is a quiet, picturesque town which sits on a hill above a maze of mangrove-filled islets and narrow channels (no beaches). The town is the port of call for the many tiny fishing villages in the region, and has access by boat to stunning beaches along the Peninsula de Maraú. There's a lively dock-side morning market with fish, fruit and drying nutmeg.

Saveiro fishing boats are built and repaired right outside the port. The Açaraí waterfalls are five km away by bus or taxi and are worth a visit.

Places to Stay & Eat The *Pousada Green House* (☎ 255-2178), near the port at Rua Djalma Dutra 61, is friendly, family-run and great value, with spotless single/double quartos for US$6/12 and larger apartamentos for US$8/15 (breakfast included). The downstairs restaurant serves good seafood prato feito for US$3.50. *Rio Açaraí* (☎ 255-2312) is on Praça Dr Francisco Xavier Borges, in the cidade alta. It's a tough walk up the very steep road from the port, only to find a garish, modern hotel with single/double apartamentos from US$30/40.

Getting There & Away Buses depart for Valença and Salvador almost hourly, and five buses run daily to Ubaitaba on the BR-101 via Travessão (1½ hours; US$2). If you are coming from the south, buses run to Camamu via Ubaitaba and Travessão.

Peninsula de Maraú

If you want to get off the beaten path, this is the place. The peninsula that goes out to Ponta do Mutá and the village of Barra Grande has one long, dirt road (often impassable after rain), infrequent buses and a handful of very small fishing villages (you won't find any of them on a map). It's an unspoilt area with some breath-taking beaches, but they are hard to get to without a car. In most of the villages, you'll find beer, but little else, so you might have to work at finding food and lodging.

Barra Grande is a tranquil, slow-paced fishing village at the tip of the peninsula – a great place to stop for a while. The village is bordered by the calm beaches of Camamu Bay on one side and the surf beaches of the Atlantic Ocean on the other. It's the most easily accessible village on the peninsula, and has a handful of pousadas and a couple of restaurants.

Places to Stay & Eat – Barra Grande Out of high season you should be able to negotiate discounts of up to 30% on the prices quoted. For reservations, call the Telebahia office (☎ 258-2131).

There is a shady campground, *Lagosta Azul*, one km from the village on a small bay. There is a restaurant and bar attached. The *Pousada Entrada do Sol* is about a 10-minute walk from the village, with a lovely beachfront location. Comfortable apartamentos cost US$15/30 for singles/doubles. There's a small seafood restaurant next to the pousada.

In the village, the *Pousada Meu Sossego* (follow the signs) is a very friendly budget option, with bright single/double apartamentos with fan and mosquito nets for US$10/20. Another good budget option near the pier is the *Pousada Maria de Firmino*, with pretty gardens and apartamentos for US$15 per person (breakfast included). The *Pousada Tubarão* is a more up-market place, with attractive apartamentos for US$24 per person, and a restaurant attached.

Restaurant A Tapera is a tiny tropical-style restaurant with seafood refeições and pizzas.

Places to Stay & Eat – Beaches On Praia de Três Coqueiros, three km from Barra Grande, the *Tres Coqueiros Praia Hotel* has a wide variety of accommodation, from small cabanas at US$10 per person to large double apartamentos at US$60. It's not a particularly attractive area, and the beach is not a patch on most other beaches in the area.

Praia Bela is a gorgeous, wide beach around six km from Barra Grande. There are a couple of bars and restaurants; *Bar Frances*, run by a Frenchman, serves good seafood and very cold beer.

Praia de Saquaria has a couple of up-market pousadas with facilities and prices to match, including the *Pousada Bahia Boa* and the *Pousada Maraú*. Expect to pay around US$60 for a double apartamento. The *Pousada Saquaria* is a more inexpensive option.

Getting There & Away During summer, the motorboat *Sid Narref* makes two trips daily from Camamu to Barra Grande and back. This is a delightful two-hour voyage (US$2.50) weaving through several small, isolated islands, including Ilha Pedra Furada, Ilha Grande and Ilha de Campinhas. The boat leaves Camamu at 9 am and 6 pm, and returns from Barra Grande at 7 am and 3.30 pm. The rest of the year, the boat runs only on weekends, but there are often boats taking locals to market at Camamu – you should be able to organise a ride by asking around at the pier in Camamu.

There is an irregular bus service from Ubaitaba on BR-101 along 80 km of rough dirt road to Barra Grande. The road is impassable after rain.

Getting Around A variety of vehicles serves as 'taxis' in Barra Grande and can ferry you to beaches along the peninsula near Barra Grande – prices are negotiable.

Itacaré

Itacaré is a quiet colonial town at the mouth of the Rio de Contas. If movie moguls could find the town, they'd probably snap it up as a set to film *A Hundred Years of Solitude*. Distance and bad roads have so far shielded Itacaré from rapid growth of tourism, but don't expect this to last too long – there are already around 20 pousadas in the village and plans for a new coastal road. Ribeira, Concha, Tiririca and Resende beaches are recommended for a swim, and sometimes have good surf. There is no road along the coast, so you must return the way you came, unless you hike or hitch a ride on a fishing boat.

The one blemish on this tropical hideaway comes courtesy of Petrobras (the government oil company), which deposits little coin-sized spots of oil on many parts of the beach.

To get to the beaches north of Itacaré, cross the river by long dugout canoe. This contradictory scene – mangrove trees lining the riverbanks and Petrobras choppers thrashing overhead – looks like the opening of *Apocalypse Now*, just before the jungle goes up in napalm flames.

In Itacaré you can rent a canoe to visit O Pontal, a beautiful promontory just south of the bay. It's best to leave your camera behind, as the canoes are unstable. The *Pousada Iemanjá* has single/double quartos for US$10/14, with breakfast. *Pousada Litoral*, close to the bus stop, has more expensive apartamentos. *Reggae Bar e Restaurante* is the town nightspot and occasionally has live music.

Getting There & Away There is no coastal road southwards from Itacaré, so you must return to the main highway inland, unless you sail or walk along the coast. Buses depart for Ilhéus via Uruçuca at 6 am and 4 pm. From Ubaitaba, on BR-101, there are five daily buses to Itacaré (US$2, 2½ hours), the first at 6.30 am and the last at 4.30 pm.

Itacaré to Ilhéus

It's a four-hour trip by bus from Itacaré to Ilhéus. The journey is slow but stunning, one of the best in Brazil. The bus passes the occasional cacao plantation, stopping every few km to pick up another couple of locals whose features are an intriguing blend of black, Indian and white.

For the first two hours, the bus travels at a snail's pace from Itacaré to Uruçuca along a bad dirt road. Uruçuca is a tiny, secluded village surrounded by lush valleys of cacao trees, and worth exploring if you have the time.

From here the road heads down through groves of cacao, coconut and enormous bamboo, to reach the coast shortly before Ilhéus.

ILHÉUS

Ilhéus, the town that Jorge Amado (Brazil's best-known novelist) lived in and described with his novel *Gabriela, Cravo e Canela* (Gabriela, Clove and Cinnamon), retains some of the charm and lunacy that Amado fans know well. There's a half-hearted attempt to portray the city as an up-and-coming tourist mecca, but nobody believes it will happen, and Ilhéus remains largely unaffected by tourism. The colonial centre is small and distinctive, with its strange layout and odd buildings; the people are affable; the city beaches are broad and beautiful; and a short walk beyond these, there are even better beaches.

The best thing to do in Ilhéus is just wander. The centre is lively, with several old, gargoyled buildings such as the Prefeitura. If you walk up the hill to the Convento NS da Piedade, there's a good view of the city and littoral. Wherever you end up, it won't be more than a stone's throw from the beach. The Praia da Avenida, close to the city centre, is always active, but has reportedly been polluted by the port.

History

Ilhéus was a sleepy town until cacao was introduced into the region from Belém, in 1881. At the time, Brazil's many uncompetitive sugar estates, which had not followed the lead of other countries and introduced new production techniques to increase sugar output, were reeling from a drop in world sugar prices. Simultaneously, the slave system was finally coming to an end, with many slaves escaping and others being freed. With the sugar plantations in the doldrums, impoverished agricultural workers from the Northeast – black and white – flocked to the hills surrounding Ilhéus to farm the new boom crop: cacao, the *ouro branco* (white gold) of Brazil.

Sudden, lawless and violent, the scramble for the white cacao fruit displayed all the characteristics of a gold rush. When the dust settled, the land and power belonged to a few ruthless *coroneis* (rural landowners) and their hired guns. The landless were left to

THE NORTHEAST

work, and usually live, on the fazendas, where they were subjected to a harsh and paternalistic labour system. This history is graphically told by Amado, who grew up on a cacao plantation, in his book *Terras do Sem Fim* (published in English as *The Violent Land*).

Cacao still rules in Ilhéus. The lush tropical hills are covered with the skinny cacao trees with large, pod-shaped fruit dangling. If you take a drive you will still see cacao fazendas and rural workers like those Amado wrote about. You can also visit the small Regional Museu do Cacao, the port and, with a bit of effort and luck, a fazenda.

Orientation

The city is sandwiched between hills, beach and a small harbour at the mouth of the Rio Cachoeira. The airport and the road to the Olivença beaches are in the southern part of town, beyond the circular harbour.

Information

Tourist Office Tourist information and basic maps are provided by Ilhéustur (☎ 231-2861), on Praça Castro Alves. There is also an information booth at the rodoviária (☎ 231-4412), which has maps and can book hotels.

Money Banco do Brasil is at Rua Marques de Paranágua 112.

Travel Agency Grou Viagens (☎ 231-8741), at Avenida Soares Lopes 528, has reasonable prices and a flexible attitude to planning. Trips to Rio Almada and Rio Santana are worthwhile (for further information, see the Around Ilhéus section). Another recommended trip is to Primavera Fazenda, where you'll be taken through the process of cacao production.

Casa de Jorge Amado

The house at Rua Jorge Amado 21, where the

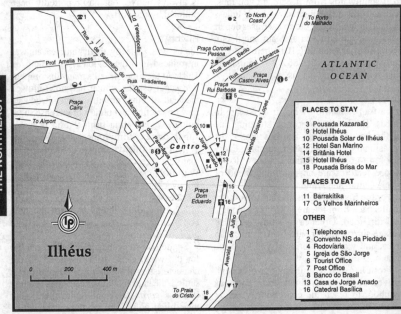

PLACES TO STAY

3 Pousada Kazarão
9 Hotel Ilhéus
10 Pousada Solar de Ilhéus
12 Hotel San Marino
14 Britânia Hotel
15 Hotel Ilhéus
18 Pousada Brisa do Mar

PLACES TO EAT

11 Barrakitika
17 Os Velhos Marinheiros

OTHER

1 Telephones
2 Convento NS da Piedade
4 Rodoviária
5 Igreja de São Jorge
6 Tourist Office
7 Post Office
8 Banco do Brasil
13 Casa de Jorge Amado
16 Catedral Basílica

Ilhéus

0   200   400 m

great writer lived with his parents while working on his first novel, *O Pais do Carnaval*, is in the process of being restored and turned into a museum. Not many writers can boast this sort of recognition while still alive!

Churches

The Igreja de São Jorge (1534), on Praça Rui Barbosa, is the city's oldest church and houses a small sacred-art museum. It's open Tuesday to Sunday from 8 to 11 am and 2 to 5.30 pm. The Catedral de São Sebastião (Basílica) is on Praça Dom Eduardo.

Museu Regional do Cacao

The recently restored and upgraded Museu Regional do Cacao displays cacao artefacts and modern painting by local artists. It's at Rua A L Lemos 126, and is open Tuesday to Friday from 2 to 6 pm and Saturday and Sunday from 3 to 6 pm. During the holiday season, from December to March, it's also open from 9 am to noon.

Festivals

As any knowledgeable Jorge Amado fan would guess, Ilhéus has highly spirited festivals. The best are: the Gincana da Pesca in early January; Festa de São Sebastião (much samba and capoeira) from 11 to 20 January; Festa de São Jorge (featuring Candomblé) on 23 April; Festa das Águas (Candomblé) in December; and, of course, Carnival with its full complement of trios elétricos.

Places to Stay – bottom end

The accommodation scene in Ilhéus has improved – there's now more of it, and some good budget options. Outside summer, discounts of around 25% apply on the prices quoted here. For campgrounds, see the Places to Stay information in the Olivença section.

The *Pousada Solar de Ilhéus* (☎ 231-5125), at Rua General Câmara 50, is a friendly, family-run place with good security. The manager speaks English and is interested in meeting travellers. It has spot-

Autosuggestion

The basílica, the city's most important building, is an enormous edifice with a striking facade and a grand entrance. After climbing its many steps and passing through the massive doors, I entered the church's spacious interior where I was suddenly confronted by the bizarre sight of a sporty, bright-red Ford Escort that was parked before the pews. The temporary use of the city's most famous House of the Lord to shelter an automobile was, it turned out, prompted by a raffle to fund a badly needed church restoration. ■

less single/double quartos with fan that cost US$15/22/30, with a superb breakfast included. Some of the rooms are better than others – make sure you get one with windows. There's a restaurant in the pousada serving lunch and dinner as well.

The *Hotel San Marino* (☎ 231-6511), at Rua Jorge Amado 29, is central and has four-bed quartos for US$10 per person – ask for a room at the front of the building. Double apartamentos start at US$30.

The *Pousada Kazarão* (☎ 231-5031), at Praça Coronel Pessoa 38, has single/double quartos for US$15/20 not including breakfast. The *Britânia Hotel* (☎ 231-1722), at Rua Jorge Amado 16, is a pleasant old-style hotel with quartos for US$15/25 a single/ double and apartamentos for US$20/30.

Places to Stay – middle

The *Pousada Brisa do Mar* (☎ 231-2644), on the beachfront at Avenida 2 de Julho 136, is a deco-style building with large, comfortable single/double apartamentos starting at US$30/40. The *Hotel Ilhéus* (☎ 231-4242), at Rua Eustáquio Bastos 44, in the centre, has a fading grandeur about it. Double apartamentos with fan cost US$30, and singles/doubles/triples cost US$44/55/65 with air-con.

Places to Stay – top end

The rather dingy *Ilhéus Praia Hotel* (☎ 231-2533; fax 231-2550) has single/double apartamentos starting at US$72/80. The *Hotel Jardim Atlântico* (☎ 231-4541; fax 231-5790), close to the airport, is excellent but very expensive.

If you're feeling like a total splurge, there is the *Transamérica Ilha de Comandatuba* (☎ 212-1122; fax 212-1114), which is on its own island (Ilha de Comandatuba) opposite the town of Una, 70 km south of Ilhéus. For US$180 per person per day, you have all meals included, the run of immense grounds, a private beach and every imaginable recreational facility.

Places to Eat

Behind the Catedral Basílica, along the beach, there are several reasonably priced seafood stands with outdoor tables. The centre is filled with cheap restaurants offering prato feito for a couple of dollars. *Barrakítika* is a popular hang-out with outdoor tables, seafood and pizza. There's good live music here on Thursday, Friday and Saturday. There's an excellent comida-a-kilo joint for lunch next to the Ilhéus Hotel on Rua Eustáquio Bastos, and another at Rua 2 de Julho 107.

For seafood with great views of the beach, try *Os Velhos Marinheiros*, on Avenida 2 de Julho, with dishes for around US$15 for two; or *O Céu é o Límite* (open daily from 11 am to 11 pm), four km west of town, on Avenida Itabuna. *Bar Vezúvio*, on Praça Dom Eduardo, has been described in Amado's books and is consequently a popular hang-

out for tourists. For Swiss and Bahian food, try *Ô-lá-lá*, at Avenida 2 de Julho 785; for Japanese food you should head for *Tokyo*, at Rua Barão de Rio Branco 23, Pontal.

Getting There & Away

Air There is a small airport which is serviced by Nordeste, VASP, Varig/Cruzeiro and air-taxis. You can fly to several major cities including Rio, Salvador, Recife and Belo Horizonte.

VASP (☎ 231-3185) is at Praça Antônio Muniz 22, Centro, and Varig (☎ 231-5904) is at Rua Coronel Paiva 56. If you're returning to Rio, the flight stops at Salvador but is still cheaper than flying directly from Salvador.

Bus Ilhéus is about 460 km south of Salvador and 315 km north of Porto Seguro. From highway BR-101 at Itabuna, it's a beautiful 30-km descent through cacao plantations to Ilhéus and the sea. For most major destinations, buses leave more frequently from Itabuna than Ilhéus, so it's usually quicker to go to Itabuna first, then shuttle down to Ilhéus.

The rodoviária (☎ 231-4570) in Ilhéus is a 15-minute bus ride from the centre. Buses to Salvador use two different approach routes. The regular route follows the long sweep around the recôncavo, and is recommended if you want to stop at Cachoeira on the way to Salvador. The other route runs via Nazaré and Ilha de Itaparica, where you change to the ferry for a stunning 45-minute ferry ride into Salvador.

Ilhéus has several buses daily to Salvador (US$16, seven hours); two a day to Valença at 6.30 am and 3.15 pm (US$7.50, five hours); three daily to Porto Seguro (US$8, five hours); and buses to Itacaré via Uruçuca at 7 am and 3.30 pm (US$3, four hours). Buses travelling to Canavieiras (US$4, two hours) leave every two hours from 6.30 am to 9.30 pm.

Getting Around

To/From the Airport The airport (☎ 231-

2323) is at Praia do Pontal, four km from the centre.

Bus The city bus station is on Praça Cairu, on the edge of the centre. From here, there are bus services to Itabuna, Olivença, the rodoviária and the airport.

AROUND ILHÉUS
Centro de Pesquisa do Cacao (CEPLAC)
You don't have to be a chocaholic to enjoy CEPLAC's model cacao plantation and research station at Itabuna. CEPLAC (☎ 214-3014), the government cacao agency, gives tours of the facility, demonstrating the cultivation and processing of the fruit. Opening hours are Monday to Friday from 8.30 to 11.30 am and 2.30 to 3.30 pm.

Buses for Itabuna leave around every half-hour from the city bus station in Ilhéus and also stop outside the rodoviária. Ask the bus driver to let you off at CEPLAC, eight km before Itabuna.

Olivença
There are good, clean beaches, many with barracas, all the way to Olivença, a spa town 16 km south of Ilhéus. You can also continue south of Olivença to yet more remote beaches. The beaches in Olivença are busy on weekends and there's some good surfing.

Places to Stay For campgrounds en route to Olivença, you can try *Camping Colónia da Stac* (☎ 231-7015) 13 km from Ilhéus, or *Camping Estância das Fontes* (☎ 212-2505), 18 km from Ilhéus.

In Olivença, the *Albergue Juventude Fazenda Tororomba* (☎ 269-1139), on Rua Eduardo Magalhães, is set on a large property with a swimming pool, bar and restaurant. Otherwise, try the *Repousada* (☎ 231-1362), at Rua Amor Perfeito 168, which is a bit out of town in a quiet location. Single/double apartamentos start at around US$25/30. The more expensive *Pousada Olivença* (☎ 269-1107) is on Praça Claudio Magalhães

Getting There & Away To get to Olivença

take one of the frequent Olivença buses from the central bus station in Ilhéus. The bus travels close to the beaches, so you can pick one to your liking and quickly hop off.

Reserva Biológica Mico Leão de Una
This small (50 sq km) biological reserve was established in 1980 to protect the *mico leão* (lion monkey) in its natural habitat of coastal forest and attempt to save the species from extinction – less than 100 remain in this reserve. It's not a park and it does not cater to visitors. Dr Saturnino Neto Souza, the director of the reserve, has been facing tourist pressure and consequent hostility from farmers and bureaucrats who are opposed to his conservation aims. At present, visits are discouraged.

If you are keen to visit, we suggest you make contact in advance with Dr Saturnino, either by phoning him at home in Una (☎ 236-2166 from 7 to 8 am or after 5.30 pm) or by writing to him at the following address: Rebio de Una, U5690, Una, Bahia. Alternatively, try calling IBAMA in Salvador (☎ 2231-2324) for information.

The monkeys (*Leontopithecus rosalia chrysomelas*) have the look and proud gaze of miniature lions: a blazing yellow, orange and brown striped coat, a Tina Turner mane and a long, scruffy tail. The mico leões are hard to spot in the wild, but behind the biologist's quarters there is one monkey in captivity and one monkey-boarder who comes in from the forest every evening for milk, cheese, bananas and some shut-eye. If you're lucky you'll also see tatu (armadillo),

Armadillo

paca (agouti), capybara and veado (deer) which are also native to the area.

Getting There & Away Getting to the reserve is a bit difficult without a car. Take a Canavieiras bus from the rodoviária in Ilhéus and travel 35 km south of Olivença along the coastal highway, until an IBAMA sign marks the turn-off to the reserve.

From here you have to hitch, which is difficult, or hike. Follow the turn-off for five km on a pitted dirt track over the Rio Mariu and past a fazenda. Turn right at the marker; the working station is three km further, within the park.

Canavieiras

Canavieiras is a small colonial town at the mouth of the Rio Pardo, in a cacao-producing region 118 km south of Ilhéus. There is some colonial architecture in the town, including the Igreja Matriz de São Boaventura (1718), and long stretches of semideserted beaches.

Places to Stay & Eat

The *Pousada Gabriela* (☎ 284-1155), at Rua Augusto Severo 1056, Centro, has small single/double apartamentos with fan for US$10/15. On Praia de Costa, try *Pousada Canto da Sereia*, which has a small restaurant attached, or the more comfortable *Pousada Farol da Ilha*.

Getting There & Away

Buses run to Canavieiras from the rodoviária in Ilhéus every two hours between 6.30 am and 9.30 pm. The trip takes about two hours and costs US$4. There is no road south along the coast from Canavieiras, but a daily boat makes the 2½-hour passage (US$3) to Belmonte, on the southern bank of the large Rio Jequitinhonha, where there are river beaches and a couple of pousadas. Sailing times vary with the tides – the tourist office in Ilhéus can give you the schedule; otherwise, call Loja O Girassol (☎ 284-1373) in Canavieiras or Posto Rio Mar (☎ 287-2112) in Belmonte. From Belmonte there are two buses daily, at 10.30 am and 1.30 pm to

Eunápolis (US$4.50, four hours) on BR-101. You might also find some transport from Belmonte going south along the coast to Santa Cruz Cabrália or Porto Seguro.

PORTO SEGURO

Porto Seguro, once a settlement of pioneers, is now a refuge for swarms of Brazilian and international tourists who come to party and take in some mesmerising beaches: tourism is the number-one industry in Porto Seguro. At last count this small city had nearly 120 hotels and pousadas – the place has exploded over the last five years. Other regional industries are lumber, fishing, beans, sugar cane, manioc and livestock.

History

After sighting land off Monte Pascoal in April 1500, Cabral and his men sailed three days up the coast to find a safe port. The Portuguese landed not at Porto Seguro (literally Safe Port), but 16 km further north, at Coroa Vermelha. The sailors celebrated their first mass in the New Land, stocked up on wood and fresh water, and set sail after only 10 days on shore. Three years later the Gonçalvo Coelho expedition arrived and planted a marker in what is now Porto Seguro's Cidade Alta (Upper Town). Jesuits on the same expedition built a church in Outeiro da Glória, to minister to the early colonists and convert the Tupiniquin Indians. The church is now in ruins. In 1526, a naval outpost was built in Cidade Alta, and once again, the men from the Companhia de Jesus built a chapel and convent, the Igreja da Misericórdia.

In 1534, when the colonies were divided into hereditary captaincies, Porto Seguro was given to Pero de Campos Tourinhos. In the following year Tourinhos founded a village at the falls of the Rio Buranhém, Porto Seguro, and seven other villages, each with a church. Despite the churches, Tourinhos was denounced to the Holy Inquisition as an atheist – apparently the captain didn't keep the holidays and, worse, he forced the colonists to work on Sunday, a blasphemy against God (and an abuse of

Porto Seguro

To Rodoviária

To Santa Cruz Cabrália

Airport

Rua Guava do Moço

Avenida Beira Mar

Praia do Rio da Vila

Praia do Cruzeiro

ATLANTIC

OCEAN

Avenida Dos Navegantes

Stadium

Avenida 22 de Abril

Rua da Vala

Rua Pero Vaz de Caminha

Avenida Getúlio Vargas

Rua 2 de Julho

Rua Cesar Oliveira

Rua Cabral

Avenida Portugal

Praça dos Pataxós

Ferry Route

Sea Wall

Rio Buranhém

To Arraial d'Ajuda, Trancoso & Caraíva

0   200   400 m

THE NORTHEAST

PLACES TO STAY

5 Camping da Gringa
8 Pousada Oasis de Pacatá
11 Pousada Jardim Paulista
12 Pousada Recanto de Campeão
19 Pousada do Cais
20 Pousada Naná
21 Pousada Aquarius
23 Pousada Inaiã

PLACES TO EAT

17 Bar-Restaurant Tres Vintens
18 La Tarrafa
22 Cafe Axé
28 Restaurante do Japonês

OTHER

1 Igreja NS da Pena
2 Igreja NS da Misericórida
3 Museu Antigo Paço Municipal
4 Igreja NS do Rosário dos Jesuitas
6 Reggae Night
7 VASP
9 Bar Escritório
10 Banco do Brasil
13 Fish Market
14 Delegacia de Polícia
15 Post Office
16 Igreja NS do Brasil
24 Buses to Santa Cruz Cabrália
25 Capitânia dos Portos
26 Nordeste
27 Telephones

cheap labour). Tourinhos was imprisoned, and shipped off to Portugal and the Inquisition. His son Fernando then inherited the captaincy.

Information recently unearthed at the Federal University of Bahia has revised some ideas about the history of the Indians during the colonial period. The Tupininquin, not the Pataxó, were the indigenous tribe when the Portuguese landed. They were rapidly conquered and enslaved by the colonists, but the Aimoré, Pataxó, Cataxó and other inland tribes resisted Portuguese colonisation and constantly threatened Porto Seguro. Military outposts along the coast, in Belmonte, Vila Viçosa, Prado and Alcobaça, were built to defend the Portuguese from European attacks by sea and Indian attacks by land.

The Indians still managed to take Porto Seguro on two occasions, and according to documents sent by colonial judges to the Portuguese crown, attacks reduced Porto Seguro to rubble in 1612 (thus undermining Porto Seguro's claims of having 16th-century buildings).

It is now believed that the Jesuit College in Cidade Alta was rebuilt after 1620. In 1759, the captaincy of Porto Seguro passed on to the crown and was incorporated into the province of Bahia.

Information & Orientation

Porto Seguro is connected by an asphalt road to BR-101 at Eunápolis, a little over 660 km south-west of Salvador. The town itself has no beaches, but it's the largest town in the area, with the most facilities for tourists, and there are plenty of beaches nearby. Porto Seguro's coastline is protected by reefs; the ocean is clear, shallow, and calm. Swimming is safe.

Tourist Office The Bahiatursa office in Porto Seguro has closed. There are small hotel information booths on Praça dos Pataxos and at the rodoviária.

Money Banco do Brasil is on Avenida 22 de

Abril, and is open Monday to Friday from 8 am to 1 pm.

Travel Agencies To arrange city tours or schooner trips to Trancoso, Coroa Alta, Recife da Fora or Monte Pascoal, contact BPS Agência de Viagem (☎ 288-1033), in BPS Shopping Centre, or Companhia do Mar Passeios de Escunas (☎ 288-2107), on Praça dos Pataxos. If you are in a group, these agencies can also arrange trips to Parque Nacional Marinho dos Abrolhos, but trips are much easier to organise in Caravelas. For more information see the Caravelas section.

Cidade Alta

If not the first, then among the first settlements in Brazil, Cidade Alta is marked with a stone (now fenced off and encased in glass) placed in 1503 by Gonçalvo Coelho. Walk north along Avenida 22 de Abril about one km. Once you've arrived at the roundabout, don't follow the sign that points left to the historic city, unless you're driving, but take the newly-built stairs up the hill. The attractions of this part of the city include superb views of the beaches and the opportunity to see very old buildings such as Igreja NS da Misericórdia (perhaps the oldest church in Brazil), the small Museu Antigo Paço Municipal (1772), Igreja NS da Pena (1535, rebuilt 1773), Igreja NS do Rosário dos Jesuitas (1549) and the old fort (1503).

Reserva Biológica do Pau Brasil

This 10-sq-km reserve, 15 km from town, was set aside principally to preserve the pau brasil (brazil wood tree), which was almost completely wiped out along the litoral during the early years of colonisation. For details about visiting this reserve, ask at the travel agencies.

Festivals

Porto Seguro's Carnival is acquiring a reputation throughout Brazil as a hell of a party, although it is not at all traditional. Locals fondly remember the Carnival in 1984 when the theme was the Adam and Eve story.

Costumes were pretty skimpy to start with, then everyone stripped off as if on cue. The police were called in the following year.

Many of Brazil's favourite musicians have beach homes nearby, and often perform during Carnival. On the Sunday before Carnival a beauty pageant is held at the Praia Hotel.

Municipal holidays celebrated include:

3 January until February
Bumba Meu Boi is celebrated with a musical parade (for details about this special event, see the São Luís section in the Maranhão chapter).

5 to 6 January
Terno de Reis is celebrated in the streets and at the churches. Women and children carrying lanterns and pandeiros (tambourines) sing O Reis and worship the Reis Magos (Three Wise Men).

20 January
Puxada de Mastro features a group of men who parade a mastro (symbolic figure) to the door of Igreja NS da Penha. Decorated with flowers, the mastro is hung in front of the church, with the flag and image of São Sebastião, and women then sing to the saint.

19 to 22 April
Discovery of Brazil is commemorated with an outdoor mass and Indian celebrations. This seems a rather baffling celebration, since the Indians were here first, and, later, fared badly at the hands of their 'discoverers'.

15 August
Festa de NS d'Ajuda is the culmination of a pilgrimage starting on 9 April. A mass procession, organised in homage to the miraculous saint, is followed by food, drink and live music.

8 September
Festa de NS da Pena is the same as Festa de NS d'Ajuda except for the additional enlivenment of fireworks.

25 to 27 December
Festa de São Benedito is held on 27 December at the door of the church of NS do Rosário. Boys and girls from Cidade Alta blacken their faces and perform African dances, such as congo da alma, ole or lalá, to the music of drums, cuica atabaque and xeque-xeque.

31 December
New Year's Eve is when everyone rushes around shouting 'Feliz ano novo Baiana!' (Happy New Year), strangers kiss and serious partying ensues.

Places to Stay – bottom end

Accommodation in Porto Seguro is generally more expensive and there is more of it

than further south at Arraial d'Ajuda. During the low season there must be at least 20 vacant rooms for every tourist, so bargain – it should be possible to negotiate at least a 25% discount. On the other hand, during the high season accommodation can be hard to find.

For campgrounds, you can try Mundaí Praia (☎ 288-2287) or Camping da Gringa (☎ 288-2076), both outside town on the road north to Santa Cruz da Cabrália.

The Pousada Naná (☎ 288-2265), at Avenida Portugal 450, has a switched-on young manager and clean apartamentos with fan for US$20 per person. Nearby, at No 524, the Pousada Inaia has standard apartamentos with refrigerator and fan at US$20 per person. The Pousada do Cais (☎ 288-2112), at No 382 is an arty, rustic place with individually decorated single/double rooms for US$22/44. The Pousada Aquarius (☎ 288-2738), at Rua P A Cabral 174, is a friendly, quiet place with single/double apartamentos for around US$35/40.

Places to Stay – middle

Many of the mid-range pousadas are charming hotels which reflect the character of their owners. Two pleasant options on Rua Marachel Deodoro are the Pousada Recanto de Campeão, and the Pousada Oasis de Pacatá, under Swedish management. Both these places are spacious and quiet, with double apartamentos for around US$50. The Pousada Jardim Paulista (☎ 288-2115), at Rua José Rodrigues 114, is a stylish pousada with double apartamentos with refrigerator and fan for US$50.

Places to Stay – top end

The poshest hotel in the area, the Porto Seguro Praia (☎ 288-2321; fax 288-2069), about four km north of town, is set back from the coastal road on Praia de Curuípe. The Hotel Phoenícia (☎ 288-2411), at Avenida 22 de Abril 400, is closer to town and near the beach. Both are big, expensive and impersonal.

THE NORTHEAST

Places to Eat

Restaurants in Porto Seguro are becoming expensive – in summer, many places have a minimum charge per table. The cheapest option is to eat at the stalls set up along Rua Portugal, where you can get a good chicken or meat, salad and farofa plate for US$2.

The *Bar-Restaurant Tres Vintens*, at Avenida Portugal 246, serves a delicious bobó de camarão for US$12. With a side dish, this is a meal for two. For good sushi, sashimi and hot shrimp dishes (US$10 to US$15), try *Restaurante do Japonês*, on Praça dos Pataxos. Readers have recommended *Cafe La Passarella*, on Avenida Portugal, for pasta.

La Tarrafa, at Avenida Portugal 360, is a rustic seafood bar with refeições for US$7.50 – wash it down with a cold brew. *Restaurant Havana*, at Praça dos Pataxos 202, has home-cooked meals for US$4. *Cafe Axé*, on Rua P A Cabral, is a good café for lunches and loud music.

Casa da Esquina, on Rua Assis Chateaubriand, has been recommended for seafood. It's open from 7 pm to 1 am. *Nativo*, on Avenida Getúlio Vargas, is the place to go for pastries and juices. Try cacao juice – it's not at all like chocolate, but it is very good. *Tia Seissa*, at Avenida Portugal 170, makes home-made liqueurs from tropical fruits and cachaça. Try pitanga (like cherry) and jenipapo at $1.50 a pop.

Entertainment

Porto Seguro is a hot spot for lambada enthusiasts. The lambada is an erotic and entertaining local dance which involves some agitated leg tangling and exaggerated hip wiggling whilst pressing belly buttons. The origins of the international hit *The Lambada* are disputed between Bolivians and Brazilians.

For live music and booze go to Rua Portugal or Passarela de Álcool (the equivalent of a 'booze alley'). The street is lined with bars and restaurants, and there's usually live music somewhere. Reggae Night, on Avenida Beira Mar, is a big club on the beach, with dance music and bands. Nearby,

Banana Reggae is another popular spot. If you want to try something different, Bar Escritorio, on Rua José Rodrigues, is a hole-in-the-wall bar with about 50 varieties of local cachaça – the top shelf features bottles with snake for extra bite!

Things to Buy

Pataxó Indians relocated from the interior of Brazil are nominally under the care of FUNAI. A few Pataxó are hanging on south of Caraiva and are trying to maintain some semblance of their traditional way of life. Those north of Porto Seguro sell trinkets (overpriced coloured feathers, pieces of coral, fibre wristbands with beads) to tourists at Coroa Vermelha. This make-believe village is simply a sad little collection of thatched-roof huts and dugout canoes by the beach. Porto Seguro also has souvenir shops that sell Pataxó jewellery, basketware and earthenware ceramics.

Please *don't* buy items made of turtle shell or consume turtles or their eggs! Most of the species of turtle found in Brazil are threatened with extinction. For more information about turtle conservation projects in Bahia, see the section on Praia do Forte and the TAMAR turtle reserve in this chapter.

Getting There & Away

Air Nordeste (☎ 288-1888) has a daily milk run to Porto Seguro, originating in São Paulo with stops in Rio (Santos Dumont airport), Brasília and Ipatinga (Minas Gerais). There are also daily services to Rio and Salvador, and flights on Saturday and Sunday to Belo Horizonte. VASP has weekend flights to Belo Horizonte, Rio, São Paulo, Brasília and Salvador.

Bus The rodoviária (☎ 288-2239) is two km outside town on the road to Eunápolis. São Geraldo runs a daily bus to São Paulo at 10.45 am (US$37, 24 hours) and Rio at 5.45 pm (US$27, 18 hours). Aguia Branca has four daily buses to Salvador (US$22; leito US$33, 11 hours). There are two daily departures for Vitória da Conquista (US$13, 11 hours) and three daily buses to Ilhéus (US$8, five hours) and Itabuna.

Between 5.20 am and 8 pm, buses depart almost hourly to Eunápolis (US$2, one hour) – some are direct buses, others make several stops along the way. Eunápolis is a large transport hub with more frequent bus departures than Porto Seguro. Buses to Santa Cruz Cabrália (40 minutes away) run about every hour between 6.20 am to 7 pm. You can also pick this bus up on Avenida Getúlio Vargas in the centre.

Getting Around

The ferry across the Rio Buranhém provides access to the road towards Arraial d'Ajuda, Trancoso and Caraiva. The pedestrian ferry charges US$0.50 and seems to operate every 15 minutes from dawn until late in the evening, but the car ferry charges US$3.50 per car (plus US$0.50 per passenger) and operates every half-hour between 7 am and 9 pm. The *Nova Lusitânia* and *Iracema*, both tired barges converted for use as ferries, make the 10-minute crossing past the rotting and listing hulks of beached fishing boats.

NORTH OF PORTO SEGURO

North of Porto Seguro, next to the paved coastal road, are several attractive beaches, such as Mundaí and Coroa Vermelha, and finally, at Km 25, the town of Santa Cruz Cabrália. These beaches are easily accessible by bus and, consequently, not as pristine as those to the south.

About five km north of town is the nicest of the northern beaches, Mundaí, with barracas at the mouth of the Rio Mundaí. North of Rio dos Mangues, at Ponta Grande, the highway cuts inland a bit. The beach is uncrowded, with tranquil waters – and hard to reach. Six km before Cabrália is Coroa Vermelha, with Pataxos craft stands, a monument to the discovery of Brazil and some fair beaches.

Santa Cruz Cabrália

There's not much to Cabrália, but its terracotta roofs and palm trees are pleasant enough. Climb up to the bluff for the view

overlooking the town and to visit Igreja NS da Imaculada Conçeição, the lonely, white church which was built by the Jesuits in 1630. The elderly caretaker will tell you the history of the region, as well as the inside story on Cabral's expedition. Fried shrimp and a batida de côco at the barracas by the church enhance the view of the offshore reef, the boats and the palm trees in and about the bay of Cabrália.

Places to Stay & Eat The *Pousada Xica da Silva* (☎ 282-1104), on Rua Frei Henrique de Coimbra (by the bus stop), has comfortable apartamentos with refrigerator at US$20 per person. Discounts are available in low season. The pousada also has a restaurant, bar and a swimming pool. There are also houses available to rent for longer stays. Across the street, at *Restaurante Vanda* you can get a good bobó de camarão for US$13. For lunches, try *Sabor da Terra*, at Rua Campos Tourinho 444, which has great sandwiches and juices.

Getting There & Away For access from Porto Seguro, see the Getting There & Away section for Porto Seguro. The last bus back to Porto Seguro leaves Cabrália at 4.30 pm, but sometimes as late as 5.10 pm.

SOUTH OF PORTO SEGURO

After taking the ferry across the Rio Buranhém, you rejoin the road, which continues along a long stretch of dreamlike beaches, with a bluff backdrop. Up on the bluff, a short walk from the beach, are the rapidly expanding villages of Arraial d'Ajuda (also known as NS da Ajuda) and Trancoso, which are 4.5 km and 26 km, respectively, from the ferry crossing. The rush to develop the region south of Porto Seguro is in full swing in Arraial d'Ajuda and Trancoso, which are being developed to match the facilities in Porto Seguro: paved roads, electricity, pousadas, chopp and, of course, bottled beer. South of Trancoso, a poor, unpaved road continues for 42 km to the small village of Caraiva.

Arraial d'Ajuda

Fifteen years ago, before the arrival of electricity or the road from Porto Seguro, Arraial was a poor fishing village removed from the world. Since then, the international tourist set has discovered Arraial and its desolate beaches, and a time-honoured way of life has all but vanished. The village has gone too hip too fast: along Arraial's maze of dirt streets, barefoot-poverty jet-set trippers eat the dust of trendy package tourists in dune buggies, and slick shopping galleries sit awkwardly alongside rustic reggae cafés. The increasingly littered main beach is lined with barracas and the beach-lounge set, while further south, hippies let it all hang out along the nude beach at Pitinga.

Yet, for some, Arraial d'Ajuda is the place to be. Younger and wilder than Porto Seguro, Arraial d'Ajuda is a wonderful place to tan and slough off excess brain cells. Newcomers soon fall into the routine: going crazy every evening, recovering the following morning and crawling back onto the beach for more surf, sun and samba.

Orientation Arraial d'Ajuda is built on a little hilltop by the sea. The main street running from the church to the cemetery is called Broadway. Many of the restaurants and bars, plus a couple of cheap pousadas, are here. Most of Arraial d'Ajuda's pousadas are tucked away on the ocean side of this hilltop, along the dirt streets. Mucugê is the name of the beach below the maze.

From the ferry landing, the dusty 4½-km road to Arraial d'Ajuda runs about 100 metres inland of Praia do Arraial and passes several pousadas. Heading south from Arraial d'Ajuda towards Trancoso, the road passes a series of beaches – Pitinga, Taipe, and Rio da Barra – before reaching Trancoso.

Travel Agency Arraial Tourismo, on Broadway, organises schooner trips to Trancoso and Caraiva. Three-day catamaran trips to Parque Nacional dos Abrolhos can be arranged (minimum four people) for US$300 per person, including food and lodging (bunks on board).

Warning There's now a police post in Arraial d'Ajuda and their attitude to drug-taking is less tolerant than in the past.

Beaches Praia Mucugê is good until 3 or 4 pm when the sun hides behind the hill. Many of the beach barracas are home to do-it-yourself samba and guitar music. The barraca facing the ocean on the far right has great music and a fantastic *batida de abacaxí* (vodka and pineapple). The barraca to the far left, Tia Cleuza, has good fried shrimp for a couple of dollars.

Praia Pitinga, the river beach closest to Arraial d'Ajuda, has red and green striped sandstone cliffs, sparkling water and large grained sand.

It's acceptable for women to go topless anywhere. Nude sunbathing is OK for both men and women on Pitinga beach and points further south.

Places to Stay Pousadas are popping up every day. Old pousadas change their names, management comes and goes, and owners trade property deeds like baseball cards. Prices also change very rapidly here. Out of season you should be able to negotiate heavy discounts on the prices quoted here, making some of the mid-range options quite good deals – try for discounts of 50% or more. Make sure your room has either a properly fitting mosquito net over the bed or preferably a fan.

For organised campgrounds, try *Camping do Gordo*, which has very basic facilities and is close to the ferry landing point; or *Camping Arraial d'Ajuda*, which is closer to town on the beach at Praia de Mucugê and has better facilities.

For cheap deals check out Rua Jotobá, which runs parallel to Broadway one block closer to the beach. At the end of the street, the *Pousada Mir a Mar* has clean single/double apartamentos with hammocks slung outside for US$15/20. Next door, the *Pousada Jatoba* is more basic, and has small apartamentos for US$15 per person. In a small lane running off Rua Jotobá, the *Pousada do Jasmin* is a friendly place with rustic apartamentos for US$10 per person. Just off the main square, on Broadway, the *Pousada Lua Cheia* (☎ 875-1059) is a shady, relaxed place with apartamentos at US$15 per person.

Along Rua Almeda Dos Flamboyants, the *Pousada do Brigette* (☎ 875-1085) is quiet and has pretty gardens. Double apartamentos cost US$35. The *Pousada Buganville* (☎ 875-1007), at Rua Almeda Dos Flamboyants 170, is a more up-market place under Brazilian/English management. Beautifully decorated, comfortable rooms cost US$25 per person.

Off Caminho do Mar (the street running to the beach), follow the signs to the *Pousada Vila do Beco*, with large, comfortable single/double apartamentos for US$25/40, and the *Pousada Le Grande Bleu* (☎ 875-1272), with similar prices and an attached restaurant serving crepes and pizzas.

Tucked away on Rua das Amandoeiras, the *Pousada Céu Azul* has a tropical flavour and lovely gardens. Small, clean single/double apartamentos cost US$25/30. Last but not least, the *Pousada O Sole Mio*, about one km from the balsa on the road to Arraial, has been recommended by readers for its spacious, shady gardens and good Italian food.

Places to Eat If you like to eat by the kilo, you'll do well in Arraial – comida a kilo is the latest trapping of the civilised world to hit Arraial. *Restaurant Nóna Madeira*, on Caminho do Mar, is the best by far. A doorway on Broadway near the church leads to *Restaurant São João*, which has good-value seafood prato feito for US$4.50, and an extensive menu of more expensive seafood dishes. It's a friendly, family-run place – you have to walk through the living room of the house to get in.

Behind the church on the edge of the bluff, *Josefina Grill Bar* is a colourful restaurant with smooth music and grilled seafood and salad dishes for US$10. Further along the road, *Restaurant Tubarão* is a breezy place with tasty, wood-fired pizzas. The barracas

down at the beach have excellent fried shrimp and other seafood.

Entertainment Arraial d'Ajuda is pretty lively in the evenings. Cruise Broadway for drinking and lambada or forró dancing – Chega Mais and Bali Bahia are two popular bars. The small shopping lanes off Caminho do Mar, A Galeria d'Ajuda and Beco dos Cores have some slick bars for more cashed-up travellers. Cine Bar is an open-air cinema with good movies every night for US$3. Cafe da Marta, about a 10-minute taxi ride from the village, has been recommended by readers as a hot spot for dancing. Arraial d'Ajuda's pousadas host open festas with musicians every evening. Once a month people gather on Praia de Mucugê to sing, dance and howl at the moon.

Getting There & Away For ferry details, see the Getting Around section for Porto Seguro. From the ferry landing there are four approaches to Arraial d'Ajuda: a lovely four-km hike along the beach, a taxi to town, a VW Kombi to Mucugê beach or a bus to town.

Getting Around VW Kombis congregate in front of the church on Broadway to ferry passengers to the beaches around Arraial. Bicycles can be hired at several shops on Broadway.

Trancoso

Trancoso lies on a grassy bluff overlooking the ocean and fantastic beaches. The central square, known as Quadrado, is lined with small, colourful colonial buildings and casual bars and restaurants nestling under shady trees. Horse riding is popular around the area, and there are some lovely walks in the surrounding rainforest.

Places to Stay & Eat Your best bet if you are planning a long stay is to rent a house on the beach. Negotiate sizeable reductions during the low season. Reservations can be made by telephoning the Telebahia office (☎ 867-1115). Next to the school on Rua

THE NORTHEAST

Itabela, the *Pousada Quarto Cresente*, is highly recommended. This is a quiet location, and the pousada has comfortable apartamentos, a well-stocked library and superb breakfast. Single/double quartos start at US$15/25, apartamentos at around US$20/35. Houses are also available for rent.

The colourful *Pousada Soloamanha*, on the Quadrado, is a rustic place with clean collective rooms for US$10 per person. The *Pousada Toca do Sabia* is a tranquil little pousada. It has single/double rooms with mosquito nets and hot water that cost US$20/30, with breakfast included. The *Pousada Gulab Mahal* is a slice of India: there are gardens and a rustic gym out the back. Single/double bungalow accommodation starts at US$20/30.

The *Pousada Hibisco* (☎ 868-1129) is more up-market, with large grounds and views over the forest and ocean. Double apartamentos start at US$50.

For good natural food and music, head for *Restaurant Ânima* or *Bar do Tio Estragio*. *Restaurant Amadoeira* has seafood and meat refeicões for US$5.

Entertainment Para-Raio is an ambient restaurant and dancing bar with outdoor tables under massive trees. Black White Danceteria is a large dance club open on weekends. Occasionally, raves are organised at secluded locations along the beach out of town, complete with bars, sophisticated sound and lighting systems and all-night dancing. The walking bridge across the river is missing several planks, so watch your step in the dark!

Getting There & Away Trancoso is 22 km from Arraial d'Ajuda on a poor and winding road or 13 km on foot along the beach. The bus from Arraial d'Ajuda to Trancoso leaves every two hours from 9 am until 5 pm. It originates from the ferry landing opposite Porto Seguro and stops at the bus depot in Arraial d'Ajuda, behind the main square. Buses are less frequent during the low season. The bus crosses the rickety bridge spanning the Rio Taipe and a 35° incline killer-hill just before town. When the bus reaches Trancoso, it stops at the beach first – if you are looking for accommodation, stay on the bus until it reaches the village.

The 13-km walk from Trancoso back to Arraial d'Ajuda along the beach is beautiful. Hikers must ford two rivers which, according to the tides and season, are either ankle or arm-pit deep.

There are also buses from Trancoso to Itabela on BR-101 – check the timetable at the bus ticket booth on the Quadrado in Trancoso.

Caraiva

Without electricity, cars or throngs of tourists, the hamlet of Caraiva is primitive and beautiful. The village is strung out along the east bank of the mangrove-lined Rio Caraiva. The bus stops on the far side of the river, where small dugout canoes ferry passengers across to the village for US$0.50. The beaches are long and deserted and dashed by churning surf. A warning: the black-sand streets of the village get incredibly hot – take footwear with you at all times.

Boat trips up the Rio Caraiva and to the Parque Nacional de Monte Pascoal are easily organised in the village. The tiny fishing village of Curuípe, nine km north, has no electricity or regular accommodation, but it's possible to stay with villagers – speak to Edivaldo. Corumbau, 12 km south, on the far side of the national park, is not as primitive, and has electricity and a couple of pousadas.

Places to Stay & Eat The prices quoted here are for summer – discounts should apply during low season. The *Pousada Canto da Duca* is a rustic establishment right on the beach, with a natural-food restaurant attached. Simple quartos and cabanas cost US$15 per person, with breakfast included. The *Pousada da Lagoa* is more comfortable and has a generator and a bar. Apartamentos cost US$20 per person.

Dendê is a sweet, simple restaurant serving typical Bahian food – the bobó de camarão and seafood moqeucas (US$6) are recommended.

Getting There & Away Buses leave Trancoso daily at 9 am and 4 pm for the 42-km trip along a rough dirt road to Caraiva. There are several precarious wooden bridges to cross – adopting a fatalistic attitude is recommended. Spontaneous cheering from passengers breaks out after each successful crossing! Buses return to Trancoso twice daily. There are also two buses daily, at 6 am and 3 pm, to Itabela, on BR-101, for connections north and south.

There is no road south along the coast from Caraiva – the options are to hire a boat or walk. It's a beautiful 40-km walk along the beach to Cumuruxatiba, passing through the Parque Nacional de Monte Pascoal and the village of Corumbau (12 km south), where there is accommodation. The walk is best done over two days, and it's only necessary to cut inland once.

For access to Corumbau, one bus leaves the large town of Itamaraju, on BR-101, daily at 2 pm.

PARQUE NACIONAL DE MONTE PASCOAL

On 22 April 1500 the Portuguese, sailing under the command of Pedro Álvares Cabral, sighted the broad, 536-metre hump of Monte Pascoal (Mt Easter), their first glimpse of the New World. They called the land Terra Vera Cruz (Land of the True Cross).

The park, 690 km from Salvador and 479 km from Vitória, contains a variety of ecosystems: Atlantic rainforest, secondary forests, swamplands and shallows, mangroves, beaches and reefs. The variety of the landscape is matched by the diversity in flora and fauna. There are several monkey species, including the endangered spider monkey, two types of sloths, anteaters, rare porcupines, capybaras (the world's largest rodent), deer, jaguar, cougar and numerous species of birds.

There are plans for a visitors' centre, marked trails, picnic tables, etc, but there is no infrastructure yet. Visitors can climb Monte Pascoal and roam through the forests at the western/BR-101 end of the park. The coastal side is accessible by boat or on foot from Caraiva in the north and Corombau to the south. The north-eastern corner of the park below Caraiva is home to a small number of Pataxó Indians – this section has been officially closed to tourism in the past, but the Pataxó don't discourage visitors.

According to recent reports, the Pataxó have succumbed to the lucrative offers of logging companies and allowed the park to be stripped of its valuable timber. The park currently covers only 12,000 hectares, a figure which represents half of its original size, and the shrinkage threatens to continue unchecked.

CUMURUXATIBA

Sandwiched between a bluff and the ocean, this two-street beach town is quiet and slow-paced. There's not much to it, apart from a long beach lined with amandoeira trees, a handful of pousadas and a surprising number of good restaurants.

Boat trips to Corumbau, Caraiva and Parque Nacional de Monte Pascoal can be arranged with Leo de Escuna on his schooner *Santa Cruz de Cabralia*. Contact him at Aquamar, a barraca along the beach.

THE NORTHEAST

Places to Stay & Eat

For camping, try *Camping Aldeia da Lua*, on Praia da Cumuruxatiba. For longer stays, houses for rent are advertised on the notice board at the Telebahia office on the main square, on Rua 13 de Maio. The *Albergue da Juventude Praia de Cumuruxatiba* is next to the beach on Avenida Beira Mar. The *Pousada Luana* (☎ 291-1204) is perched on the bluff overlooking the town and the ocean – it's worth the walk up the hill. Comfortable apartamentos with balconies and hammocks are good value at US$20/35 – discounts apply in low season.

La Naveva is under French management and serves delicious crepes. *Restaurant Santa Rita* is a rustic place with seafood refeições, and *Falesias* is a family-run pizza restaurant with a pleasant outdoor setting. Along the beachfront, there are some great barracas, such as *Estação do Cais*, which has good music and seafood.

Getting There & Away

Cumuruxatiba is 32 km north of Prado over a smooth dirt road. Buses run daily from the large town of Itamaraju on BR-101 to Cumuruxatiba via Prado at 6 am and 2.30 pm. Buses return to Prado daily at 5.30 am, 10 am and 4 pm.

PRADO & ALCOBAÇA

These little big towns on the coast south of Cumuruxatiba don't have much to offer travellers – their beaches are built up and not especially pretty. If you are heading to Cumuruxatiba to the north or Caravelas to the south, you'll have to either pass through or connect in one of them. Both towns have basic services and accommodation. Excursions to Parque Nacional Marinho dos Abrolhos are best organised in Caravelas.

On a dirt track 12 km north of Prado are the semideserted beaches of Paixão and Tororão. The dirt road continues 22 km to Cumuruxatiba. North of Cumuruxatiba, past the ocean border of Parque Nacional de Monte Pascoal, the village of Caraiva and all the way to Trancoso is a 60-km stretch of undeveloped coastline. Judging by the inter-est currently being shown by developers, it is unlikely to stay that way. Beyond Caraiva, there are only the miserable unpaved roads to Trancoso and Arraial d'Ajuda.

CARAVELAS

Caravelas, 74 km from Teixeira de Freitas on BR-101, is not only a gateway to Parque Nacional Marinho dos Abrolhos (see the next section for access details); it's also an interesting town in its own right, with a large fishing community and good beaches nearby.

Information

Visa card cash withdrawals can be made at the Banco do Brasil on Praça Dr Imbassahi. The IBAMA information office (☎ 297-1148), on Praça Dr Imbassahi, has colourful brochures in English, with useful information about the Parque Nacional dos Marinho Abrolhos. Abrolhos Tourismo (☎ 297-1149), also on Praça Dr Imbassahi, is a private travel agency, but it also acts as a kind of unofficial tourist office. English is spoken here. There is also a small tourist information office at the rodoviária.

A reader who spent four weeks in the area as a volunteer for a whale research project writes about Caravelas:

Caravelas is a small city with hardly any tourist facilities, which makes it a very quiet and original place. You can hardly buy a T-shirt there, and few people speak English. But the food in the Restaurant Jubarte (Humpback) is excellent. I recommend the shrimp with cheese. What also makes Caravelas special is that it lies in a delta area with mangroves and Atlantic jungle. Opposite the village is the big island of Caçumba (100 sq km), that is surrounded by the big 'arms' of the delta. Along the coast grows the mangrove and inland the forest. There are about 200 families living there, who cultivate the land for their own support. Some of their produce they sell on the mainland. There are three species of mangrove, red, black and white, and they all grow there. What makes the mangrove special is the extreme height of the trees (20 metres plus), probably the highest in the world. Enormous crabs take care of oxygen in the soil – the soil is clay and without crabs it would be too hard. In the jungle grows a variety of tropical fruits. There are lots of different species of birds and in the swamp near the shore, crocodiles live.

The second specialty of Caravelas is the harbour from where you can go to the protected marine National Park of the Abrolhos Archipelago. In wintertime (end of June to October) it is an area for Humpback whales who mate and give birth there. Their population is increasing and is estimated now at about 400 to 700. A nature protection organisation is doing research into their social behaviour and is making photos for identification.

Bettina van Elk, The Netherlands

Things to See & Do

To get a feel for the town's thriving fishing industry, check out the **Cooperativa Mista dos Pescadores** on Rua da Cooperativa opposite the hospital, or wander along the riverfront to **Praça dos Pescadores**, where the fisherfolk hang out after coming in from the day's catch. For beaches, head for **Praia Grauçá** (eight km north of town on a dirt track) and **Pontal do Sul** (across the Rio Caravelas). In addition, there are the island beaches of **Coroa da Barra** (half an hour by boat) and **Coroa Vermelha** (1½ hours by boat).

It's possible to go by boat along the mangrove-lined Rio Caravelas to the next beach town to the south, **Nova Viçosa**. Ask at the tourist office at the rodoviária, Abrolhos Tourismo or Abrolhos Embarcações. A snorkelling day trip to the island of Coroa Vermelho costs US$40 per person, with lunch included.

Places to Stay & Eat

There's an attractive campground, *Camping Coqueiral*, on Praia Grauçá. On the same beach, there are mostly expensive places to stay – for a budget option, try the *Pousada do Juquita*. In town, the *Pousada Shangri-Lá* (☎ 297-1059), at Rua 7 de Setembro 219, is a friendly, cheap place to stay. Collective rooms cost US$8 per person; apartamentos go for US$14 per person – breakfast is included in these prices. The *Pousada Tropical* (☎ 297-1078), at Rua 7 de Setembro 155, is also good value, with quartos for US$10 per person. The *Pousada da Ponte* (☎ 297-1150) has a nice riverfront location on Rua Anibal Benevolo, close to the pier. The management speaks English, German

and French, and scuba gear is available for hire. Apartamentos cost US$15 per person.

Across the river, on Ilha da Caçumba, the *Pousada da Ilha* is a real retreat, with a bar and a vegetarian restaurant. You can also get a massage here. Rooms cost around US$10 per person. To get there, go to Abrolhos Tourismo, on Praça Dr Imbassahi 8, in the centre and ask them to call the pousada by radio. The pousada will send someone across in a boat to pick you up from the pier.

Restaurant Jubarte, at Rua Barão Rio Branco 6, is a large, bright restaurant with seafood, meat and chicken refeições and a good range of salads. Seafood enthusiasts should head for *Museu da Baleia* and *Chalé Barra*, both on Praia Grauçá.

Getting There & Away

Air Pantanal Linhas Aéras flies to Caravelas from São Paulo.

Bus The rodoviária is in the centre of town, on Praça Teófilo Ofon. Expresso Brasileiro bus company runs six buses daily from Teixeira de Freitas on BR-101 to Caravelas via Alcobaça, the first at 7 am and the last at 6.20 pm. The trip takes about two hours and costs US$3.

Getting Around

Buses to Barra (for Praia Grauçá) leave hourly until 9 pm from the rodoviária.

PARQUE NACIONAL MARINHO DOS ABROLHOS

Abrolhos, Brazil's first marine park, covers part of an archipelago 80 km offshore from Caravelas. In 1832, Charles Darwin visited here whilst voyaging with HMS *Beagle*. The archipelago consists of five islands, but the only inhabited one is Santa Bárbara, which has a lighthouse, built in 1861, and a handful of buildings. Abrolhos is being preserved because of its coral reefs and crystal-clear waters. Underwater fishing within the park is prohibited. The only approach is by boat, and staying on the islands is prohibited. The Brazilian navy considers the area strategic,

THE NORTHEAST

therefore only underwater photography is permitted.

Unfortunately, the archipelago's coral reefs, home to at least eight different species of coral, have been badly affected by toxic chemicals routinely dumped by industry, especially a pulp and paper company in southern Bahia. Dynamite fishing has depleted the fish stocks and thereby caused rapid growth of seaweed (normally kept in check by herbivorous fish), which is destroying the coral reefs. Experts now maintain that the erosion caused by deforestation along the coastline is responsible for heavy levels of sediment in the ocean, which in turn prevents sufficient light reaching underwater organisms such as the coral.

Getting There & Away
Caravelas Caravelas is the most popular gateway to the park, with several operators offering a wide range of options, from day trips to five-day cruises. Abrolhos Tourismo (☎ 297-1149) runs a popular two-day schooner trip, with an overnight stay on board, for US$120 per person. The price includes park entrance fees, all meals, soft drinks and water. Snorkel hire costs an extra US$10. Abrolhos Embarcações (☎ 297-1172), at Avenida das Palmeiras 2, offers a similar two-day trip, or day trips by launch for US$95, including snacks and drinks.

Arraial d'Ajuda From Arraial d'Ajuda, Arraial Tourismo, on Broadway, organises three-day catamaran trips which cruise south along the Bahian coast, then on to Abrolhos. The fare of US$300 per person includes food, lodging (bunks on the boat), transport and visitor's licence from the Capitânia of Porto Seguro. A minimum of four passengers is needed.

West of Salvador

FEIRA DE SANTANA
At the crossroads of BR-101, BR-116 and BR-124, Feira de Santana is the main city of Bahia's interior, and a great cattle centre. There's not much to see here except the Feira de Gado, the big Monday cattle market (lots of tough leather), which is great fun, but don't expect to buy much, and the Mercado de Arte Popular (open daily except Sunday). The Casa do Sertão (folklore museum) and Museu Regional (Regional Museum) might also be worth a look.

Festivals
Two months after Carnival, Feira de Santana is the scene of the Micareta – a 60-year-old local version of Carnival which brings together the best trios elétricos of Salvador, with local blocos, samba schools and folklore groups.

The main action of the Micareta takes place on Avenida Getúlio Vargas, the city's main street, where 20 trios bop along for five days. The festivities begin on Thursday with

a boisterous dance and opening ceremony. The tennis and cajueiro clubs sponsor large dances like the traditional Uma Noite no Havaí (A Night in Hawaii). For those who missed out on Carnival in Salvador, the Micareta could be the next best thing.

Places to Stay

There are several cheap hotels near the rodoviária, such as the *Hotel Samburá* (☎ 221-8511), at Praça Dr Jackson do Amauri 132. In the top price range, there's the *Feira Palace* (☎ 221-5011), at Avenida Maria Quitéria 1572. It's a four-star affair with single/double apartamentos starting at US$45/50.

Getting There & Away

Frequent buses make the two-hour journey from Salvador for US$2. The rodoviária features an eye-catching mural painted by Lénio Braga in 1967.

SALVADOR TO LENÇÓIS

The seven-hour bus odyssey from Salvador to Lençóis first goes through Feira de Santana and then continues through typical sertão countryside: patches of low scrub and cactus where scrawny cattle graze and hawks circle above. In 1995, much of the road had been newly asphalted, but there were still odd sections where the asphalt drops out, as if someone hadn't done their sums properly.

The bus stops for lunch at Itaberaba where the rodoviária restaurant serves two typical sertão dishes: *carne de sol com pirão de leite* (dried salted beef with manioc and milk sauce to take the edge off the salt) and *sopa de feijão* (bean soup with floating UPO – Unidentified Pigs' Organs).

LENÇÓIS

Lençóis lies in a gorgeous, wooded mountain region – the Chapada Diamantina – an oasis of green in the dusty sertão. You'll find solitude, small towns steeped in the history and superstition of the garimpeiros (prospectors), and great hiking to peaks, waterfalls and rivers. If you want to see something different, and have time for only one excursion into the Northeastern interior, this is the one.

The natural beauty of the region and the tranquillity of the small, colonial towns has attracted a steady trickle of travellers for several years; some have never left. These new residents have spearheaded an active environmental movement that successfully lobbied the government to declare the region a national park.

History

The history of Lençóis epitomises the story of the diamond boom and bust. After earlier expeditions by bandeirantes proved fruitless, the first diamonds were found in Chapada Velha in 1822. After large strikes in the Rio Mucujê in 1844, prospectors, roughnecks and adventurers arrived from all over Brazil to seek their fortunes.

Garimpeiros began to work the mines, searching for diamonds in alluvial deposits. They settled in makeshift tents which, from the hills above, looked like sheets of laundry drying in the wind – hence the name of Lençóis (Portuguese for sheets). The tents of these diamond prospectors grew into cities: Vila Velha de Palmeiras, Andaraí, Piatã, Igatú and the most attractive of them all, the stone city of Lençóis. Exaggerated stories of endless riches in the Diamantina mines precipitated mass migrations, but the area was rich in dirty industrial stones, not display-quality gems.

At the height of the diamond boom, the French – who purchased diamonds and used them to drill the Panama Canal (1881-89), St Gothard Tunnel, and London Underground – built a vice consulate in Lençóis. French fashions and *bon mots* made their way into town, but with the depletion of diamonds, the fall-off in French demand (and subsequently the fall in diamond prices on the international market), the abolition of slavery, and the newly discovered South African mines, the boom went bust at the beginning of the 20th century.

The town's economy has long since turned to coffee and manioc cultivation, and to tourism. But diamonds are what the locals

THE NORTHEAST

still dream of. The last few garimpeiros are using powerful and destructive water pumps to wrench diamonds from the riverbeds.

Geology

According to geologists, the diamonds in Chapada Diamantina were formed millions of years ago near present-day Namibia. Interestingly, Bahia was contiguous to Africa before the continental drift. The diamonds were mixed with pebbles, swept into the depths of the sea – which covered what is now inland Brazil – and imprisoned when the conglomeration turned to stone. With the formation of Chapada Diamantina this layer of conglomerate stone was elevated, and the forces of erosion released the trapped diamonds which were then brought to rest in the riverbeds.

Information

The Secretária de Turismo Lençóis has a tourist office (☎ 334-1121) on Avenida Senor dos Passos. The office can help with accommodation and has photographs of the main attractions in the Chapada Diamantina.

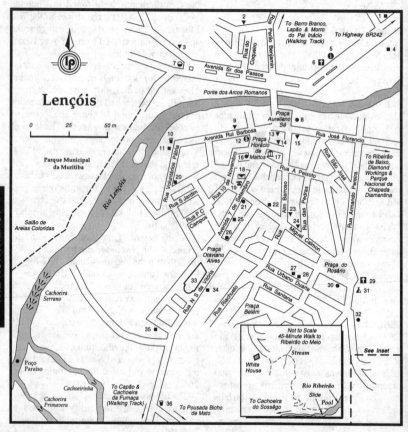

The enthusiastic young guides that hang around the tourist office can be useful for day trips – they charge about US$25 per day for groups of up to four people. Jaqueline Rocha Haj Lima in the office can recommend a guide who is familiar with the area you want to visit. For other suggested guides, see the following section on Parque Nacional da Chapada Diamantina.

The Prefeitura Municipal, at Praça Otaviano Alves 8, is a pretty building with B&W photos of old Lençóis, erratic opening hours and scant information. *Lampião*, a local newssheet, has some ecological information, plus the local football results and political scandals.

Money Banco do Brasil does not change money, but the tourist office can guide you to the town's moneychangers ($US cash only). A reader recently informed us that travellers' cheques may be changed at Casa de Helia, at Rua das Pedras 102.

Travel Agencies Lentur (334-11430), opposite Telebahia on Avenida 7 de Setembro, runs day trips by car to several destinations within the park for US$20 per person (a guide, admission fees and torches are included in the price). Protur (☎ 334-1126), at Rua da Baderna 35, Pousada Diangela and Pousada Bicho do Mato all offer similar deals.

Things to See
The city is pretty and easily seen on foot, although, unfortunately, most of the buildings are closed to the public. See the old **French vice consulate**, a beige 19th-century building where diamond commerce was negotiated, and **Casa de Afrânio Peixoto** (House & Museum of Afrânio Peixoto), with the personal effects and works of the writer Afrânio Peixoto. Also worth a visit is **Lanchonete Zacão**, run by local historian Mestre Oswaldo, which displays various mining relics and artefacts.

For details about hikes close to Lençóis and longer trips further afield in the park, see the Parque Nacional da Chapada Diamantina section.

Festivals
The principal holidays take place in January and September. Festa de Senhor dos Passos starts on 24 January, and culminates on 2 February with the Noite dos Garimpeiros (Prospectors' Night). Semana de Afrânio Peixoto, a week dedicated to the author, is held from 11 to 18 December and coincides with the municipality's emancipation from slavery. Lamentação das Almas is a mystic

---

PLACES TO STAY

1	Pousada Alcino
4	Pousada Canto das Águas
10	Bar Canto Verde
11	Pousada Sincora
20	Pousada Diangela
22	Pousada Diamantina
25	Pousada O Casaráo
27	Pousalegre
28	Pousada Re
31	Camping Lumiar
34	Hotel Colonial
35	Pousada de Lençóis

PLACES TO EAT

2	Lajedo Bar & Restaurant
3	Casa Redonda
9	Salon Mistura Fina
13	Restaurant Diamante Brito
14	Restaurant Ynave
15	Restaurant Amigo da Onça
23	Brilhante
24	Restaurant Os Artistas Damassa

OTHER

5	Tourist Information
6	Igreja Senhor dos Passos
7	Rodoviária
8	Mercado Municipal
12	Banco do Brasil
16	Old French Consulate
17	Museu doGarimpo & Lanchonete Zacáo (Restaurant)
18	Post Office
19	Telephone Office
21	Lemur Travel Agency
26	Prefeitura Municipal
29	Igreja Rosário
30	Casa de Afrânio Peixoto
32	Sr Dazim Horse Rental
33	Open Air Theatre & Football Pitch
36	Zion Bar

THE NORTHEAST

festival held during Lent. Lençóis is also noted for Jarê, the regional variation of Candomblé.

Places to Stay

Lençóis has plenty of places to stay, but you should still try to reserve at weekends – and definitely book in advance during the high season: January and February. Most of the cheaper places have collective rooms and charge on a per person basis. For longer stays, ask around about renting a house.

Places to Stay – bottom end *Camping Lumiar*, on Praça do Rosário, has shady campsites, passable bathrooms, a bar and a restaurant – but watch out for Pablito and his marauding chickens. The cost is US$2 per person.

The *Pousalegre* (☎ 334-1124) is a favourite with travellers. The rooms are certainly basic (there's a lack of windows and furniture) but the friendly staff, good breakfast (and other meals) more than compensate. Quartos cost US$8 per person. Close by, the *Pousada Re* (☎ 334-1127) is also a good option, and charges the same rates.

The *Pousada Sincora* (no phone) is housed in a large colonial building. It's a relaxed place with interesting art work on the walls. Collective rooms cost US$6 per person, or US$8 with breakfast. The *Pousada Diangela* (☎ 334-1192) is a large, bright building with a pleasant eating area and quartos for US$8 per person. Apartamentos cost US$12 per person.

The *Pousada Alcino* (☎ 334-1171) is in a beautifully converted colonial building. Rooms cost US$12 per person, including a highly recommended breakfast. The *Pousada Bicho de Mato* (no phone) is located in a quiet area a short walk from the centre, with views of the surrounding hills. Quartos cost US$10 per person, with breakfast included.

Places to Stay – middle The *Hotel Colonial* (☎ 334-1114) has pleasant single/double/triple apartamentos for US$20/26/38. Discounts of up to 20% apply outside summer season. The *Pousada O Casarão* (☎ 334-1198) has overpriced double quartos at US$24.

Places to Stay – top end The *Pousada Canto das Águas* (☎ 334-1154; fax 334-1188) has a great position, in a landscaped garden beside the river. Facilities include a restaurant, bar, and swimming pool. The apartamentos overlook the cascades which provide the pousada's background music – hence the name, which translates as Song of the Waters. Prices are around US$50/55/72 for singles/doubles/triples, including an enormous breakfast. Book well in advance during summer. At night, a dinner-plate-size toad squats guard at the gate!

At the top end of town is the attractive *Pousada de Lençóis* (☎ 334-1102; fax 334-1180), with gardens, swimming pool, restaurant and bar. Single/double/triple apartamentos with air-con start at US$50/55/70. Books about the region are sold at the reception desk.

Discounts of up to 30% apply at both of these hotels in low season.

Places to Eat

If you like breakfast, you'll never want to leave Lençóis, where it's included in the room price of numerous lodgings which seem to be competing for the coveted 'BBB' (Best Breakfast in Brazil) title. A local breakfast staple is *baje* (a warm, buttered manioc pancake with the consistency of a very chewy styrofoam polymer). After breakfast, you've only got a few hours until you're faced with equally magnificent culinary options for the other meals of the day!

Casa Redonda is a relaxed, friendly place with great-value, tasty cooking. The moqueca de peixe and stroganoff de frango (US$6) are highly recommended. *Brilhante* is a colourful natural food store and café with healthy sandwiches, snacks and juices. The *Pousalegre* and the *Pousada Diangela* both serve inexpensive meals, or try *Restaurant Diamente Brito* for the ubiquitous comida a kilo. *Restaurant Os Artistas Damassa* has good, cheap Italian food, and for a real taste of Europe, visit *Salon Mistura Fina*, where you can sip tea while listening to classical music. Other popular restaurants in town worth visiting are *Restaurant Ynave* and *Restaurant Amigo da Onça*.

Bar Canto Verde is an ambient outdoor bar with live music in the evenings. The *Lajedo Bar & Restaurant* (across the bridge, on the other side of town), *Arte Bar* and *Zion Bar* are evening hang-outs.

Things to Buy
There are night stalls on Praça Horácio de Mattos selling crochet, lacework, trinkets and bottles of coloured sand collected at nearby Salão de Areias Coloridas. Funkart Artesanato and the Mercado Municipal are other places to look for the work of local artisans.

Getting There & Away
Air There's a small airfield at Palmeiras, 65 km from Lençóis, but there are plans to build a runway in the Lençóis area capable of handling larger passenger aircraft.

Bus The rodoviária is on the edge of town, beside the river. Buses to Salvador leave daily at 9 am, and 4 and 10 pm. Buses to Lençóis leave Salvador at 7.30 am, noon and 10 pm. The trip currently takes seven hours – maybe less if the ditches get filled in – and the fare is US$10.75.

Car If you are using a car in Lençóis, there is a fuel station some 22 km east of town on BR-242, in Tanquinho. The nearest station to the west is around 30 km away. It's not a good idea to rely on the improvised fuel station in Lençóis, which may or may not be open, have fuel or want to sell it.

Getting Around
The town is easily covered on foot. For transport further afield, see the following section on Parque Nacional da Chapada Diamantina.

PARQUE NACIONAL DA CHAPADA DIAMANTINA
Many of the foreigners and Brazilians who

came to visit have settled permanently in Lençóis. They have been the backbone of a strong ecological movement which is in direct opposition to the extractive mentality of the garimpeiros and many of the locals. Riverbeds have been dug up, waters poisoned and game hunted for food and sport. Much of the land has been ravaged by forest fires. The hunting and depletion of habitat has thinned the animal population severely.

After six years of bureaucratic battles, biologist Roy Funch helped convince the government to create the Parque Nacional da Chapada Diamantina to protect the natural beauty of the area. Signed into law in 1985, the park roughly spans the quadrangle formed by the cities of Lençóis and Mucujê, Palmeiras and Andaraí. The park, 1520 sq km of the Sincora range of the Diamantina plateau, has several species of monkeys, beautiful views, clean waterfalls, rivers and streams, and an endless network of trails. Although bromelias, velosiaceas, philodendrons and strawflowers are protected by law, these plants have been uprooted nearly to extinction for the ornamental plant market.

The park is particularly interesting for rock hounds, who will appreciate the curious geomorphology of the region.

For information regarding minimising the impact of camping on fragile ecosystems, see the Minimum Impact Camping section under Accommodation in the Facts for the Visitor chapter.

Information
The park has little, if any, infrastructure for visitors. The map 'Parque Nacional da Chapada Diamantina' included in this book should give you a good idea of the great hiking opportunities.

Knowledgeable guides, such as Roy Funch and Luís Krug, can greatly enhance enjoyment of any trip into the park. Whether you take a guide or not, you should definitely not go alone. In the descriptions of park hikes that follow, we've indicated those trips which would be dangerous without a guide.

Funch, an ex-American from Arizona and now a naturalised citizen, came to Brazil 10

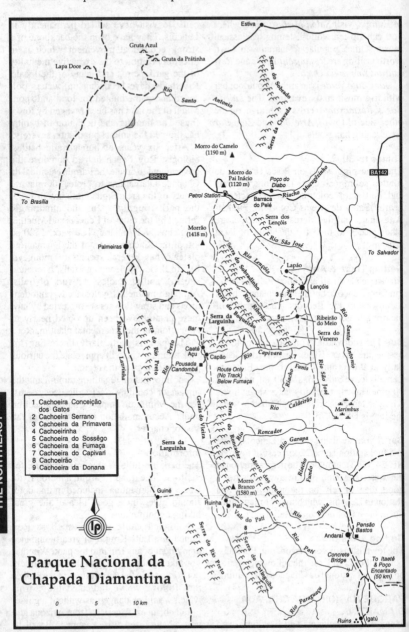

THE NORTHEAST

1 Cachoeira Conceição
   dos Gatos
2 Cachoeira Serrano
3 Cachoeira da Primavera
4 Cachoeirinha
5 Cachoeira do Sossêgo
6 Cachoeira da Fumaça
7 Cachoeira do Capivari
8 Cachoeirão
9 Cachoeira da Donana

Parque Nacional da
Chapada Diamantina

0   5   10 km

years ago with the Peace Corps. He pushed for the creation of the Parque Nacional da Chapada Diamantina and has a very detailed knowledge of the region. He is currently working on other projects, but can be contacted through the Fundação Chapada Diamantina (☎ 334-1188), at Rua Pé de Ladeira 212.

Luís Krug, from São Paulo, is a guide who knows the history, geography and biology of the area, as well as the trails. Contact Luís at Pousada Canto das Águas in Lençóis. In Palmeiras, Claude Samuel runs trips into the park from the Pousada Candombá (☎ 332-2176). Claude speaks English and French, and his donkey treks have been recommended by readers.

Day Trips Around the Park
For day trips around Lençóis, you can walk or hire a horse. For day trips further afield, you have the option of walking, hitching, using the bus, or taking one of the guided tours offered by the travel agencies and pousadas in Lençóis (see the Travel Agents section for details). The Grand Circuit, described later in this section, is best done on foot. For horse rental, contact Senhor Dazim (marked on the Lençóis map as 'Sr Dazim Horse Rental'), who has horses available. There's no sign on his house, so you may have to ask around – everyone in the neighbourhood knows him. You can choose from his list of horse rides and treks, which are all accompanied. Sample prices per person are: one hour ($3); half-day (US$20); whole day (US$26); three days (US$60). Negotiate discounts for groups of three or more.

Bus services are infrequent and scarce, particularly to the remote parts of the park.

Day Trips Around Lençóis
Rio Lençóis You can start a pleasant hike along the Rio Lençóis by following a trail south-west from the rodoviária (see the Lençóis map) and continuing through the Parque Municipal da Muritiba, upstream to Cachoeira Serrano (a series of rapids) and Salão de Areias Coloridas (literally Room of

Coloured Sands), where artisans gather their matéria prima for bottled sand paintings. If you continue up the river, you'll see Cachoeirinha waterfall on a tributary to your left, and after passing Poço Paraíso waterhole, you'll see Cachoeira da Primavera waterfall on another tributary on your left. From the rodoviária to here takes around 1½ hours on foot.

Ribeirão do Meio & Cachoeira do Sossêgo
This is another relaxing hike (45 minutes) that can be made to Ribeirão do Meio. Take the road uphill from Camping Lumiar, ignoring the left turning you'll see after about 100 metres, and continue until the road ends at a white house. After continuing for a short distance, take the left fork of a trail which descends and crosses a stream. Keep following the track until you reach a ridge overlooking Rio Ribeirão, a tributary of Rio São José.

At the foot of the ridge, you'll find Ribeirão do Meio, a series of swimming holes with a natural waterslide (bring old clothes or borrow a burlap sack). It is *very* important not to walk up the slide: several bathers who have done so have met with nasty accidents. Instead, swim across to the far side of the pool and climb the dry rocks at the side of the slide before launching off.

Upstream from Ribeirão do Meio, a trail leads to Cachoeira do Sossêgo waterfall. The hike involves a great deal of stone-hopping along the riverbed. On *no* account should you attempt this trail during high water or rain: the river stones are covered with lichen which becomes impossibly slippery. To walk there and back to Lençóis takes around five hours.

Gruta do Lapão
This is probably the largest sandstone cave in South America. Access is tricky and it's necessary to take a competent guide – ask at the tourist office. The walk takes around four hours.

Day Trips Further Afield
Lapa Doce, Gruta da Pratinha & Gruta Azul These three sights are best visited by

car – the guided day trips offered by travel agents and other operators in Lençóis usually take in all of these sights. Lapa Doce (70 km from Lençóis, then a 25-minute hike to the entrance) is a huge cave formed by a subterranean river. Access to the cave is via an immense sinkhole; inside there's an impressive assortment of cave decorations which prompt erotic comparisons. Admission costs US$0.50.

About 12 km from this cave are Gruta da Pratinha and Gruta Azul, two more caves of lesser interest which have been spoilt by pollution and vandalism.

Rio Mucugêzinho This river, 25 km from Lençóis, is a super day trip. Take the 8 am Palmeiras/Seabra bus, and ask the driver to let you off at Barraca do Pelé – the bus passes this place again at around 4 pm on its return trip to Lençóis. From Barraca do Pelé, pick your way about two km downstream to Poço do Diabo (Devil's Well), a swimming hole with a 30-metre waterfall. Further upstream, you'll find Rita and Marco, who have set up house in a cave, and run a snack bar outside.

Morro do Pai Inácio & Barro Branco Morro do Pai Inácio (1120 metres) is the most prominent peak in the immediate area. It's 27 km from Lençóis and easily accessible from the highway. An easy but steep trail takes you to the summit (200 metres above the highway) for a beautiful view.

Hikers may want to take the trail along Barro Branco between Lençóis and Morro do Pai Inácio – allow four or five hours one way for the hike.

Palmeiras, Capão & Cachoeira da Fumaça Palmeiras, 56 km from Lençóis, is a drowsy little town with a slow, slow pace and a scenic riverside position. The streets are lined with colourful houses. There is one pousada in the town and a couple of cheap pensãos.

The hamlet of Capão is 20 km from Palmeiras by road (see the Grand Circuit for a description of the hiking trail connecting Capão with Lençóis). From here, there's a six-km trail (two hours on foot) to the top of Cachoeira da Fumaça, also known as the Glass waterfall, after missionary George Glass, which plummets 420 metres – the longest waterfall in Brazil. Although marked on the map, the route to the bottom of the waterfall is very difficult, and isn't recommended.

The Grand Circuit
The grand circuit of the park covers around 100 km and is best done on foot in a clockwise direction. It takes about five days, but you should allow eight days if you include highly recommended side trips, such as Igatú and Cachoeira da Fumaça.

Lençóis to Andaraí For this section you should allow two days. On the first night, camp at a site near Rio Roncador. On the way, you pass Marimbus, a microregion with characteristics similar to the Pantanal. In Andaraí, either camp or stay at the basic *Pensão Bastos*.

Poço Encantado & Igatú These side trips are highly recommended. Poço Encantado, 56 km from Andaraí, is an underground lake which is clear blue and stunningly beautiful. You'll need a car to get there; hitching is difficult because there is very little traffic.

Igatú, 12 km from Andaraí, is a small community with an intriguing set of ruins (highly recommended). Either walk or drive to Igatú.

Andaraí to Vale do Patí & Ruinha This section takes a day, but you should allow an extra day to potter around the valley: for example, doing a side trip to Cachoeirão (a delightful waterfall) or enjoying the atmosphere in the tiny ghost settlement of Ruinha.

Vale do Patí to Capão This section, which crosses the beautiful plains region of Gerais do Vieira, is best covered in two comfortable days, although it's possible to do it in one very long day.

The tiny settlement of Capão serves as a base for the highly recommended hike to

Cachoeira da Fumaça (see the description in the Day Trips Further Afield section). In Capão, you can camp or stay at the *Pousada Candombá* for US$2.50 per person, with breakfast an additional US$1.50.

Capão to Lençóis You'll need a full day to hike this section. From Capão, follow the road through Caeté Açu, and when you reach the 'bar', take the track to the right. Follow the main track east, crossing the river several times, before veering off to reach Lençóis. There are a couple of campsites along the track on the section between the 'bar' and Lençóis.

RIO SÃO FRANCISCO

For the Brazilian, particularly the Nordestino, it's impossible to speak about the Rio São Francisco without a dose of pride and emotion. The third most important river in Brazil, after the Amazon and Rio Paraguai, there is no river that is anthropomorphised like the São Francisco. Those who live along its banks speak of it as a friend – hence the affectionate nickname *velho chico* or *chicão* (chico is short for Francisco).

The geographical situation of the São Francisco gave it a prominence in the colonial history of Brazil that surpassed the Amazon. Born in the Serra da Canastra, 1500 metres high in Minas Gerais, the Rio São Francisco descends from south to north, crossing the greater part of the Northeast sertão, and completing its 3160-km journey in the Atlantic Ocean after slicing through the states of Minas Gerais and Bahia, and delineating the borders of the states of Bahia, Pernambuco, Sergipe and Alagoas.

For three centuries the São Francisco, also called the 'river of national unity', represented the only connection between the small towns at the extremes of the sertão and the coast. 'Discovered' in the 17th century, the river was the best of the few routes available to penetrate the semi-arid Northeastern interior. Thus the frontier grew along the margins of the river. The economy of these settlements was based on cattle, to provide desperately needed food for the gold miners in Minas Gerais in the 18th century and, later, to feed workers in the cacao plantations in southern Bahia.

Although the inhabitants of the region were often separated by enormous distances, cattle ranching proved a common bond and produced a culture which can be seen today in the region's folklore, music and art.

The history of this area is legendary in Brazil: the tough vaqueiros who drove the cattle; the commerce in salt (to fatten the cows); the cultivation of rice; the rise in banditry; the battles between the big land-owners; and the religious fanaticism of Canudos. For more information, see the History section in the Facts about the Country chapter.

The slow waters of the São Francisco have been so vital to Brazil because in a region with devastating periodic droughts, the river provides one of the only guaranteed sources of water. The people who live there know this, and thus, over the centuries, they have created hundreds of stories, fairy tales and myths about the river.

One example is the *bicho da água* (beast of the water). It is part animal and part man that walks on the bottom of the river and snores. The crew on the riverboats throw tobacco to the bicho da água for protection.

The river's width varies from two hand-spans at its source in the Serra da Canastre, an empty, uninhabitable region where nothing grows, to 40 km at the Lagoa do Sobradinho, the biggest artificial lake in the world. As a result, Nordestinos believe that São Francisco is a gift of God to the people of the sertão to recompense all their suffering in the drought-plagued land.

River Travel

People have always travelled by the São Francisco. In the beginning there were sail-boats and rowboats, then came the motorboats, which became famous because of the personalities of the *barqueiros* who drove the boats and put *carrancas* on the front of them. Carrancas are wooden sculptures that represent an animal-like face – part

THE NORTHEAST

dog, part wolf – with big teeth and open mouth. These sculptures are now popular as folk art, and are sold in Salvador and at fairs along the river.

Today, with the river cities linked by roads, river traffic has decreased drastically, but it shouldn't prove too hard to find boats for short trips on local market days (usually Saturday). See the section on Penedo in the Alagoas chapter for details of trips on the lower Rio São Francisco.

Bom Jesus da Lapa, on the São Francisco in the interior of Bahia, is the site of one of the most important religious festivals and processions in the sertão. The festival is held on 6 August.

It may be possible to hire a local boat from Juazeiro, on the Pernambuco-Bahia border, to Xique-Xique, 200 km downstream in Bahia.

A reader wrote to us with the following assessment of river travel along the Rio São Francisco:

The river appears dead as a means of commercial travel, and only a small amount of transport by local narrow boat continues between the villages. The river has become sluggish as a result of construction of a hydroelectric plant on the seaward side of Lagoa do Sobradinho, and silting is so severe in some places that the shallow-draught local boats touch bottom.

Xique-Xique, at the southern end of Lagoa do Sobradinho, appears to have a mainly school-age population, most of whom are learning English and are keen to use it. A couple of islands close to the town have been declared a reserve for the protection of anteaters, which are said to be the only ones in the area.

Sergipe & Alagoas

Sergipe

Sergipe is Brazil's smallest state. It has all three zones typical of the Northeast: litoral, zona da mata and sertão. The coastal zone is wide and sectioned with valleys, with many towns dotted along the rivers.

What is there to see? There are a couple of interesting historical towns – Laranjeiras in particular is well worth a visit – and the towns along the Rio São Francisco have a unique, captivating culture – principally Propriá and Neópolis. The beaches, on the other hand, are not up to snuff, and the capital, Aracaju, is as memorable as last Monday's newspaper.

ESTÂNCIA

Estância, 68 km south of Aracaju, is one of the oldest towns in the state. The city has a certain amount of character, and a few historic buildings in the centre, but there's little reason to stop in Estância unless you want to head to the nearby beaches (see the Mangue Seco section in the Bahia chapter) or want to avoid spending the night in Aracaju.

Information

Estância has most basic services, including a large supermarket. The São João festivals in June are the big event.

Places to Stay & Eat

The town has a couple of hotels facing the main square, Praça Barão do Rio Branco. The *Hotel Turismo Estanciano* (☎ 522-1404) is spotless and comfortable, and has a restaurant attached. Quartos with fan cost US$8/15 for singles/doubles; apartamentos with fan go for US$10/18, or US$15/23 with air-con. Some of the cheaper rooms have high ceilings – so high the walls don't reach it! Try to get a room away from the restaurant. The *Hotel Bosco* (☎ 522-1887), 30

metres away, has quartos for US$4.50 per person and apartamentos for US$6 per person. The *Hotel Continenti*, behind the rodoviária, has reasonably clean quartos at US$3/6 for singles/doubles. *Pizzaria São Geraldo* does excellent pizzas.

Getting There & Away

The town is actually a bit off the BR-101, but most long-distance buses still stop in Estância. There are buses directly from Salvador, Aracaju, Propriá and Maceió to the north. If you are travelling south from Estância along the Linha Verde and want to visit the beach towns north of Salvador, the Bonfim bus company, which runs the Aracaju-Salvador route, makes you pay the full fare from Estância to Salvador (US$8.50) no matter where you get off along the way. There are four buses a day from Estância to Salvador, but two of them leave around 1 am and are impractical if you want to stop before Salvador. Daytime buses leave at 8.30 am and 1.45 pm. For access to Mangue Seco in Bahia, a bus leaves the rodoviária in Estância daily at 4 pm for Pontal, where there are frequent boats across the river to Mangue Seco until 6.30 pm. The 42-km trip to Pontal via Indiaroba takes about two hours.

SÃO CRISTÓVÃO

Founded in 1590, São Cristóvão is reputedly Brazil's fourth-oldest town, and was the capital of Sergipe until 1855. With the decline of the sugar industry, the town has long been in the economic doldrums and is trying to become a tourist attraction to bring in some cash.

Things to See

The old part of town, up a steep hill, has a surprising number of 17th and 18th-century colonial buildings along its narrow stone roads. Of particular distinction are: the **Igreja e Convento de São Francisco**,

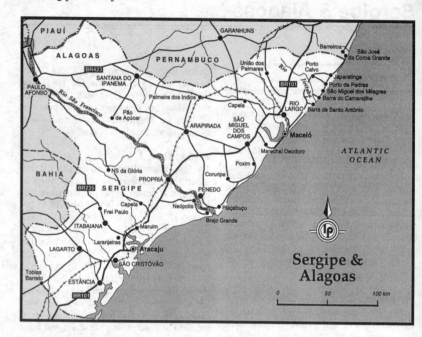

Sergipe &
Alagoas

which has a good sacred-art museum (at Praça São Francisco); the **Igreja de Senhor dos Passos** (Praça Senhor dos Passos); the **Antiga Assembléia Legislativa**; and the **Antigo Palácio do Governo**.

Festival

Every year the town comes alive for a weekend with the Festival de Arte de São Cristóvão. The festival has both fine and popular arts, with lots of music and dance. The festival is held during the last 15 days of October.

Places to Stay & Eat

There is no real accommodation in São Cristóvão, although there is a campground about two km from town. If you like sweets, São Cristóvão is renowned for its sweet makers, who produce a wide variety of doces caseiros (tempting homemade sweets and cakes).

Getting There & Away

Bus São Cristóvão is 25 km south of Aracaju on a good paved road, and seven km off the BR-101. The rodoviária is down the hill below the historic district, on Praça Dr Lauro de Freitas. Frequent buses running to São Cristóvão (US$0.85, 45 minutes) leave from the rodoviária velha (old bus terminal) in Aracaju. If you are travelling south to Estância, note that buses do not run there from São Cristóvão. You can take a bus back to the junction of BR-101 and try to flag down a bus to Estância, or return to the rodoviária nova in Aracaju and take one from there.

Train For details about the train trip from Aracaju to São Cristóvão, see the separate section under Aracaju.

LARANJEIRAS

Nestled between three lush, green, church-topped hills, Laranjeiras is the colonial gem of Sergipe. Filled with ruins of old sugar mills, terracotta roofs, colourful colonial facades and stone roads, the town is relatively unblemished by modern development. There are several churches and museums worth visiting and the surrounding hills offer picturesque walks with good views. It's a charming little town, easy to get to and well worth a few hours sightseeing or a day or two exploring the town, the nearby sugar mill and the countryside. The town centre has recently been renovated.

History
Laranjeiras was first settled in 1605. During the 18th and 19th centuries, it became the commercial centre for the rich sugar and cotton region along the zona mata west of Aracaju. At one point there were over 60 sugar mills in and around Laranjeiras. The processed sugar was sent down the Rio Cotinguiba about 20 km downstream to Aracaju and on to the ports of Europe. The large number of churches is a reminder of the past prosperity of the town.

Information
There is a city tourism office inside the Trapiche building in the Centro de Tradições, on Praça Samuel de Oliveira, where you can obtain brochures and information about guides for hire. It's open Tuesday to Sunday from 8 am to 5 pm.

Engenho
This old, partly-restored sugar mill a few km from town is in a lovely setting. It's now privately owned, and not generally open to the public, but it may be possible to arrange a visit if you ask at the tourist office. You can walk, or hire a guide and a car to take you there.

Igreja de Camandaroba
Out at the Engenho Boa Sorte, two km from town along the river, is the baroque Igreja de Camandaroba, the second building that the Jesuits constructed back in 1731.

Beaches of North Bahia, Sergipe & Alagoas

THE NORTHEAST

Igreja do Bonfim

This church is at the top of the hill called Alto do Bonfim and has recently been restored. If the door is closed, go around to the back and ask to be let in. The short walk is rewarded with a fine view, but keep an eye out for snakes.

Trapiche

The Trapiche houses the tourism office. It's a large, impressive structure that was built in the 19th century to house the cargo waiting to be shipped downriver.

Gruta da Pedra Furada

This is a one-km tunnel built by the Jesuits to escape their persecutors. The tunnel has been closed due to cave-ins, but there are plans to restore it. Ask at the tourist office to make sure it's open. The gruta is three km out of town on the road leading to the small village of Machado.

Museums

The small **Museu Afro-Brasileiro** is on Rua José do Prado Franco s/n (no number). Laranjeiras is considered to be the stronghold of African culture in Sergipe. It's open Tuesday to Sunday, from 8 am to 5 pm. Also recommended is the **Museu de Arte Sacra** (Sacred Art Museum) in Igreja NS da Conceição, Rua Dr Francisco Bragança s/n.

Festival

During the first week of January, the *Encontro Cultural* folklore festival is held in the town.

Places to Stay

The only pousada in town is the *Pousada Vale dos Outeiros* (☎ 281-1027), at Rua José do Prado Franco 124. There are good views of the surrounding hills from the back rooms. Quartos cost US$15/20 for singles/doubles; double apartamentos with air-con cost US$30.

Getting There & Away

Laranjeiras is 21 km from Aracaju and four km off the BR-101. Buses leave from and return to the rodoviária velha in Aracaju about every half-hour. It's a 35-minute ride (US$0.70) – the first bus leaves for Laranjeiras at 5 am and the last one returns at 9 pm. Any bus travelling the BR-101 can let you off at the turn-off for Laranjeiras. There's a conveniently-placed restaurant at the turn off, so you can have a drink and snack while you wait to flag down a bus from Aracaju. Otherwise, you can walk or hitch the four km to town.

ARACAJU

Aracaju just may be the Cleveland of the Northeast. The city has little to offer the visitor – there is no colonial inheritance – and it is visually quite unattractive. Even the beaches are below the prevailing high standard of the Brazilian Northeast.

Aracaju, 367 km north of Salvador and 307 km south of Maceió, was Brazil's first planned city. The modest requirements of the original plan called for a grid-pattern intersected by two perpendicular roads less than two km long. The city outgrew the plan in no time, and the Brazilian norm of sprawl and chaotic development returned to the fore.

History

Some of its lack of appeal stems from the fact that Aracaju was not the most important city in the state during the colonial era. In fact, when it was chosen as the new capital in 1855, Santo Antônio de Aracaju was a small settlement with nothing but a good deep harbour – badly needed at the time to handle the ships transporting sugar to Europe.

With residents of the old capital of São Cristóvão on the verge of armed revolt, the new capital was placed on a hill five km from the mouth of the Rio Sergipe. Within a year an epidemic broke out that decimated the city. All the residents of São Cristóvão naturally saw this as an omen that Aracaju was destined to be a poor capital.

Information

Tourist Office Emsetur, the state tourist organisation in Sergipe, is trying hard to grab a slice of the rich tourist cake that its adjacent states, Bahia and Alagoas, have been enjoying in recent years. The Centro do Tourismo in Aracaju was revamped in 1994, and houses the Emsetur tourist office (☎ 224-5168), which has loads of glossy brochures. It's open from 8 am to 10 pm daily. The complex also houses an artesanato market, 'Rua 24 Horas' (a shopping arcade), bars and cafés. There are other tourist information booths at the rodoviária and airport, both with erratic opening hours and limited information.

Money There is a branch of Banco do Brasil, at Praça General Valadão 341, in the centre.

Post Office The central post office is at Rua Laranjeiras 229.

Beaches

On the sandy barrier island of Santa Luzia, at the mouth of the Rio Sergipe, is **Praia Atalaia Nova** (*atalaia* is Portuguese for

watchtower), which is a popular weekend beach.

Praia das Artistas, **Atalaia Velha** and **Praia Aruana** are the closest beaches to the city. They are crowded (with traffic jams on weekends) and heavily developed with hotels and motels, restaurants, bars and barracas – the latter are a source of inexpensive seafood.

Further south on the road to Mosqueiro, **Praia Refúgio** is the prettiest and most secluded beach close to Aracaju. It's 15 km from the city. There are a few bars and one pousada.

Festivals

The maritime procession of Bom Jesus dos Navegantes, held on 1 January, is probably the best event. Festa de Iemanjá is celebrated on 8 December at Praia Atalaia Velha.

Train Trip

On weekends, a tourist train makes the trip

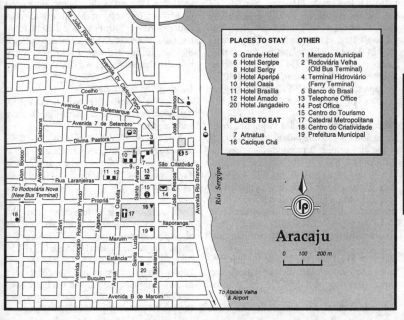

PLACES TO STAY
3 Grande Hotel
6 Hotel Sergipe
8 Hotel Serigy
9 Hotel Aperipé
10 Hotel Oasis
11 Hotel Brasília
12 Hotel Amado
20 Hotel Jangadeiro

PLACES TO EAT
7 Artnatus
16 Cacique Chá

OTHER
1 Mercado Municipal
2 Rodoviária Velha (Old Bus Terminal)
4 Terminal Hidroviário (Ferry Terminal)
5 Banco do Brasil
13 Telephone Office
14 Post Office
15 Centro do Tourismo
17 Catedral Metropolitana
18 Centro do Criatividade
19 Prefeitura Municipal

Aracaju

0   100   200 m

from Aracaju to São Cristóvão. The train leaves from the Estação do Bairro Siqueira Campos at 9 am. For more information, contact Emsetur in the Centro do Tourismo.

Places to Stay

Most of the hotels are in the centre or out at Praia Atalaia Velha on Avenida Atlântica. For a short stay, hotels in the centre are much more convenient and generally less expensive. It's worth asking for discounts at all the hotels, especially in low season (March to June, and August to November).

Places to Stay – bottom end For camping, try *Camping Clube do Brasil* (☎ 243-1413), on Atalaia Velha. The best budget option in town is the *Hotel Amado* (☎ 222-8932), although they seem to be aiming for the group-tour market. Clean apartamentos with fan cost US$12/18 for singles/doubles, or US$18/23 with air-con. For a rock-bottom choice in the centre of town, there's the *Hotel Sergipe* (☎ 222-7898). Apartamentos cost US$9/11 for singles/doubles. You should also be aware that this hotel is favoured by local clientele as a 'short time' joint. For much better value, try the *Hotel Oasis* (☎ 224-1181), which has bright apartamentos starting at US$17/23 for singles/doubles. The *Hotel Brasília* (☎ 222-8020) has apartamentos at US$19/29 for singles/doubles.

Places to Stay – middle A popular mid-range hotel is the *Jangadeiro* (☎ 211-1350), in the city centre. It provides clean apartamentos at US$26/30 for singles/ doubles. The *Serigy* (☎ 222-1088; fax 222-4194), at Rua Santo Amaro 269, has upgraded its apartamentos, which now cost US$32/40 for singles/doubles. Just round the corner is the *Hotel Aperipé* (☎ 211-1880), which offers apartamentos at US$34/40 for singles/ doubles. There's also the three-star *Grande Hotel* (☎ 211-1383; fax 222-2656) that provides good-value apartamentos with air-con and refrigerator at US$32/36 for singles/ doubles.

For mid-range accommodation on Praia Atalaia Velha, the *Pousada Do Sol* (☎ 243-1074; fax 243-2286), at Rua Atalaia 43, is recommended by locals.

Places to Stay – top end If you want a five-star hotel in Aracaju, the *Parque dos Coqueiros* (☎ 243-1511; fax 243-2186), out at Rua Francisco Rabelo Leite Neto 1075, Praia Atalaia Velha, is the place. Singles/ doubles cost US$88/96.

Places to Eat

Cacique Chá (closed on Sunday) is a garden restaurant on Praça Olímpio Campos, a central location which has made it a popular meeting place for the 'in' crowd. *Artnatus*, at Rua Santo Amaro 282, is a well-stocked health-food store which serves vegetarian lunch meals. The cafés in the Casa do Tourismo are good for a snack and drinks. Recommended seafood restaurants at Atalaia Velha include: *Taberna do Tropeiro* (with live music in the evening), at Avenida Oceânica 6; *Chapéu do Couro*, at Avenida Oceânica 128; and the highly recommended *O Miguel* (closed on Monday) at Rua Antônio Alves 340. For good Italian food, try *Villa Vietri*, at Avenida Francisco Porto 896, in Bairro Salgado Filho – midway between the centre and Atalaia Velha.

Getting There & Away

Air The major airlines fly to Rio, São Paulo, Salvador, Recife, Maceió, Brasília, Goiânia and Curitiba.

You will find a Varig office (☎ 211-1890) at Rua João Pessoa 71; VASP (☎ 224-1792) is at Avenida Barão de Maruim 67; and Transbrasil (☎ 211-1090) is at Rua São Cristóvão 14.

Bus Long-distance buses leave from the rodoviária nova (new bus terminal), which is about four km from the centre. There are nine buses a day to Salvador (US$8, or US$17.50 for a leito). Five of these buses take the new Linha Verde route along the coast (4½ hours), and the rest go inland via Entre Rios (six hours). There are four daily departures for the five-hour trip (US$7) to Maceió –

Top: Near Jericoacoara, Ceará
Middle: Fishing boats near Jericoacoara, Ceará
Bottom: Beach scene, Paracuru

Top: Fishermen at work, Ceará
Bottom: Preparing the fishing net, Ceará

some sections of the road are heavily pot-holed, so it can be slow going. Two daily departures to Recife take nearly nine hours and cost US$12. There's one direct bus daily to Penedo (US$3.50, three hours), and seven buses daily to Neópolis, where there is access to Penedo by a short ferry ride across the Rio São Francisco.

For transport details on São Cristóvão and Laranjeiras, see their respective Getting There & Away sections. Note that bus services for these two towns operate from the rodoviária velha (old bus terminal) – not from the rodoviária nova.

Getting Around
To/From the Airport The airport (☎ 243-2721) is 11 km south of town, just past Atalaia Velha. From the rodoviária velha, take the bus marked 'Aeroporto'.

Bus The rodoviária nova (new bus terminal, four km from the town centre) is connected with the rodoviária velha (old bus terminal, in the centre) by a frequent shuttle service (US$0.30, 25 minutes). The requisite bus stop is a separate entity – look for a large shelter with a series of triangular roofs about 100 metres to your right as you exit the rodoviária nova. A taxi from the rodoviária nova to the centre costs around US$4.

The rodoviária velha is in the centre of town on Avenida Divina Pastora. This is the bus terminal to use for local trips, including visits to São Cristóvão and Laranjeiras. To reach Atalaia Velha, take a bus marked 'Caroa Domeio/Santa Tereza' from the rodoviária velha.

Boat From the Terminal Hidroviário (Ferry Terminal), there are frequent ferries (US$0.40) to Barra dos Coqueiros on Ilha de Santa Luzia until 11 pm. The ferry terminal on Praia Atalaia Nova has begun to sink into the river, so the ferry now docks a short bus ride away from the main beach.

PROPRIÁ
Propriá is 81 km north of Aracaju, where BR-101 crosses the mighty Rio São Fran-

cisco. While the town is less interesting than the downriver cities of Penedo and Neópolis, it has the same combination of colonial charm and river culture. Thursday and Friday are the weekly market days in Propriá, when goods are traded from com-munities up and down the São Francisco.

Boat Trips
In recent years there has been a steady decline in long-distance boat travel on the Rio São Francisco. You should still be able to find boats going upriver as far as Pão de Açúcar, about a seven-hour ride by motor-boat, with stops at all the towns along the way. One scheduled boat departure is the *Oriente*, which leaves Propriá at 7 am on Saturday and returns from Pão de Açúcar on Monday. The *Vaza Baris* also makes occa-sional trips to Pão de Açúcar and Penedo.

There are also smaller boats which leave irregularly – for example, downstream to Penedo and Neópolis. You can bargain a ride on any of them, including the beautiful *avelas* with their long, curved masts and striking yellow or red sails. The trip downriver to Penedo takes about four or five hours by avela or rowboat and should cost around $4.

Festival
Bom Jesus dos Navegantes, on the last Sunday in January, is a colourful affair with a maritime procession and *reisado* – a dra-matic dance that celebrates the epiphany. It is highly recommended.

Places to Stay & Eat
Facing the main church, the *Hotel Imperial* (☎ 322-1294) has quartos starting around US$6/11 for singles/doubles, and nice doubles apartamentos (with fan) costing US$18. It's a very clean and friendly place with a pool table. The *Hotel Pan Americano* is a rock-bottom option along the riverfront in town, charging US$5 per person for basic quartos. At the other end of the scale, the *Hotel do Velho Chico* (☎ 322-1941) has a fine riverside position and comfortable

apartamentos starting at around US$35/42 for singles/doubles.

For a pleasant place to eat with a view of the river, we recommend *Beira Rio*, on Avenida Nelson Melo.

Getting There & Away

Propriá is about one km off BR-101. The rodoviária is about two km from town – a local bus meets most long-distance buses and will drop you in the centre. There are bus connections with Neópolis, Penedo, Aracaju and Maceió.

Alagoas

The small state of Alagoas is one of the pleasant surprises of the Northeast. The capital, Maceió, is a relaxed, modern city, and its beaches are enchanting, with calm, emerald waters. Penedo is the colonial masterpiece of the state, with a fascinating river culture on the Rio São Francisco.

Along the coast, there are many fishing villages with fabulous beaches shaded by rows of coconut trees. Buses run along the coastal roads to the north and south of Maceió connecting the villages which are beginning to be discovered by tourists and property developers.

History

The mighty republic of runaway slaves – Palmares – was in present-day Alagoas. During the invasion by the Dutch in 1630, many slaves escaped to the forest in the mountains between Garanhuns and Palmares. Today, where the towns of Viçosa, Capela, Atalaia, Porto Calvo and União dos Palmares stand, there were once virgin forests with thick growth and plenty of animals. Alagoas today has the highest population density in the Northeast.

MACEIÓ

Maceió, the capital of Alagoas, is 292 km north of Aracaju and 259 km south of Recife. A manageable place for the visitor, the city has a modern feeling, apart from a small historical area in the commercial centre, and offers endless sun and sea. Maceió has experienced a tourist boom over recent years, and the city beaches are being developed at a fast pace, particularly between Ponta Verde and Praia de Jatiúca.

Orientation

The rodoviária is about four km north of the city centre, which has inexpensive hotels and the bustle of commerce. On the east side of the city are Praia de Pajuçara and Praia dos Sete Coqueiros, which are three km and four km respectively from the centre.

Alagoas – It's a Long Way to the Top (and Back Again)

Alagoas has attracted much attention as the home state of former President Fernando Collor de Mello, who resigned the presidency, in December 1992, to avoid impeachment on corruption charges, and later became the first Brazilian president to face a criminal trial. Fernando Collor reached his position in a linear progression: from mayor of Maceió to governor of the state of Alagoas and thence to the presidency of Brazil. He suffered acute embarrassment when it was revealed that the Malta family, to which his wife belongs, had received lavish funds, dozens of cushy jobs and titles, and amazing deals for contracts. Hi wife Rosane was identified as a key figure in massive corruption perpetrated during her presidency of the nation's largest charity organisation. Brazilians joked that there was a massive *dinheiroduto* (money duct) running from Brasília to Alagoas!

Fernando Collor was eventually charged with involvement in a massive influence-peddling scheme in which he received about $US28 million in bribes and kickbacks. In December 1994, he was acquitted by the Supreme Court, in a five-three vote, which said there was insufficient evidence to implicate him in the scheme. ■

Information

Tourist Office Maceió has well-developed tourist information facilities. The head office of Ematur (☎ 221-9393), the state tourism organisation, is at Avenida Duque de Caxais 2014. Emturma (☎ 223-4016), the municipal tourism body, is at Rua Saldanha Da Gama 71. There are combined Emturma information booths/Telasa phone offices along the beachfront at Praia Pajuçara, Ponte Verde and Praia Jatiúca. These booths have loads of information on hotels, restaurants and transport tucked away in folders – including where to have your tarot read or your dog washed! There is also an information booth at the airport.

Money There's a branch of Banco do Brasil at Rua do Livramento 120. Aero Tourismo, in the Iguatemi shopping centre, also changes money at the same rate as the banks.

Post & Telephone There is a post office at Rua João Pessoa 5, in the city centre. Telasa, the state phone company, has offices in the centre at Rua Cons Lourenço de Albuquerque 369; along the beachfront at Praia Pajuçara, Ponta Verde and Praia Jatiúca; and at the airport and rodoviária.

French Consulate There is a French consulate (☎ 231-2555) at Lagoa da Anta 22, next to the Hotel Jatiúca.

Museums

In the centre, **Museu do Instituto Histórico** (open Monday to Friday from 8 am to noon and 2 to 5 pm) has exhibits about regional history. **Museu Theo Brandão** is in an attractive colonial building on the seafront, but is closed for 'renovations' – in fact, it seems to be being left to fall into decay.

Beaches

Just a short walk from the centre, the beaches of Praia do Sobral and Avenida are polluted. Praia Pajuçara (Ala) (three km from the centre) and Praia dos Sete Coqueiros (four km) are beginning to suffer from pollution as well. Your best bet is to head further north

for some of the best beaches in the Northeast. Protected by a coral reef, the ocean is calm and a deep-emerald colour. On shore there are loads of barracas, *jangadas* (local sailboats) and plenty of beach action.

The beaches to the north are **Ponta Verde** (five km), **Jatiúca** (six km), **Jacarecica** (nine km), **Guaxuma** (12 km), **Garça Torta** (14 km), **Riacho Doce** (16 km) and **Pratagi** (17 km).

You won't go wrong with any of these tropical paradises, but they do get busy on weekends and throughout the summer, when there are many local buses cruising the beaches. On Pajuçara, you'll find jangadas which will take you out about one km to the reef, where you can swim in the *piscina natural* (natural swimming pool), and observe the marine life (best done at low tide). The fare is US$4 per person.

Boat Trips

The schooner *Lady Elvira* departs daily from Pontal da Barra for a five-hour cruise to islands and beaches. The price per person is US$30 with lunch, or US$20 without lunch. For more information, contact Ematur (☎ 221-9393), at Avenida Duque de Caxais 2014. Small motorboats such as the *Turis Gomes* (☎ 221-0458) make similar cruises from Pontal da Barra for US$10 per person, or US$20 with lunch included.

Flora & Fauna

A reader writes the following:

If you are seriously interested in fauna and flora in Alagoas, the person to speak to is the biologist Gininho Britzky, Rua Augusta 251, in the city centre of Maceió (☎ 221-1987). With his long hair and beard he looks more like Jesus than the respected ecologist that he is. He has been fighting for years to protect the environment in Alagoas which is under constant attack, and he is well known locally. He speaks very little English, but will be happy to point you in the right direction, and may even be willing to go on trips with you to the few remaining pockets of forest and mangrove swamp. He won't ask for anything in return, but I think it would be polite to offer a donation to the environmental group that he heads: Brigada Ecológica de Alagoas, one of the environmental organisations mentioned in the excellent, but high priced ($35) environmental guide book: *Guia Do Meia Ambiente – Litoral De Alagoas*, which can be found in some Maceió bookshops and from the Instituto Brasileiro do Meio Ambiente (IBAMA) (☎ 241-1600).

W J (Bill) Hill, Northwich, Cheshire, England

Festivals
Maceió is reported to have a lively Carnival, which is still considerably calmer and safer than Rio's, and features active samba clubs. Locals reckon Barra de São Miguel has the best Carnival in the area. Festa do Mar takes place in December.

Places to Stay – bottom end
City Centre The *Hotel dos Palmares* (☎ 223-7024), on Praça dos Palmares 253, has quartos at US$10 per person (breakfast not included), or US$15/25/36 with breakfast. There's a nice elevated eating area which catches the breeze. Nearby, the *Hotel Maceió* (☎ 223-1883), at Rua Dr Pontas de Miranda 146, offers cell-like, but clean

apartamentos at US$10/20 for singles/doubles. The *Hotel Ney* (☎ 221-6500) is midway between the city centre and Praia de Pajuçara, at Avenida Duque de Caxais 910. Apartamentos with air-con start at US$21/27 for singles/doubles – try to get a room in the main building, preferably on the 2nd floor.

Although conveniently central, at Rua Dom Pedro Segundo 73, the *Hotel Parque* (☎ 221-9099) is rather institutional and drab, and doesn't merit its two stars. Apartamentos cost US$17/26 for singles/doubles.

Beaches Praia de Pajuçara is a good place to base – it's midway between the city centre and the better beaches, and has more budget accommodation than the beaches further north. For camping try *Camping Jatiúca* (☎ 235-1251), on Praia Cruz das Almas, around six km from the centre.

There are four youth hostels that are close to Maceió: the *Albergue de Juventude*

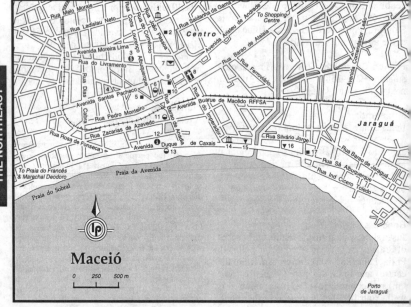

Maceió

0   250   500 m

Pajuçara (☎ 231-0631), at Rua Quintino Bocaiuva 63, Pajuçara, is safe, clean and friendly; the *Albergue de Juventude Nossa Casa* (☎ 231-2246), at Rua Prefeito Abdon Arroxelas 177, is on Praia de Ponta Verde; the *Albergue de Juventude Stella Maris* (☎ 325-2217) is at Avenida Engenheiro Paulo Brandão Nogueira 336, on Praia Jatiúca; and the *Albergue de Nosso Lar* (☎ 231-1582) is at Avenida Amélia Rosa 605, Praia Jatiúca.

The *Pousada Piscina do Mar* (231-6971) is a good budget option along the beachfront, at Avenida Dr Antônio Gouveia 123. Clean apartamentos cost US$12/20 for singles/doubles. The *Pousada da Praia* (☎ 231-6843), at Rua Jangadeiros Alagoanos 545, has changed management and has tried to move up-market. Basic quartos cost US$12/18 for singles/doubles. The *Pousada Saveiro* (☎ 231-9831), up the road at Rua Jangadeiros Alagoanos 905, is friendly and better value. Apartamentos (with fan) cost

US$6/12 for singles/doubles, or US$12/24 with air-con. The *Pousada Shangri-La* (231-3773), at Rua Jangadeiros Alagoanos 1089, is pretty dingy – quartos cost US$8 per person. Next door, the *Pousada Amazonia* is brighter and cleaner, and has similar prices.

Places to Stay – middle

City Centre If you want a good hotel in the centre, try the *Hotel Beiriz* (☎ 221-1080; fax 243-3455), at Rua João Pessoa 290. It's a large, three-star hotel with a pool and restaurant. Rooms with air-con, refrigerator and TV cost US$36/44 for singles/doubles.

Beaches The more reasonably-priced, mid-range options are the older hotels along Praia de Pajuçara. The newer hotels further north on Ponta Verde and Praia Jatiúca are generally more expensive.

The *Hotel Praia Bonita* (☎ 231-2565), at Avenida Antônio Gouveia 943, Praia de Pajuçara, has clean double apartamentos

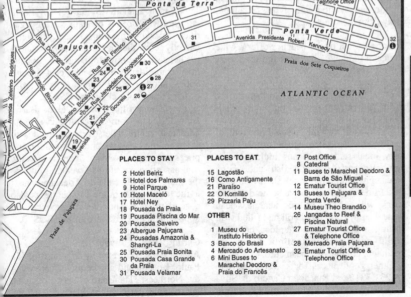

PLACES TO STAY

2 Hotel Beiriz
5 Hotel dos Palmares
9 Hotel Parque
10 Hotel Maceió
17 Hotel Ney
18 Pousada da Praia
19 Pousada Piscina do Mar
20 Pousada Saveiro
23 Albergue Pajuçara
24 Pousadas Amazonia & Shangri-La
25 Pousada Praia Bonita
30 Pousada Casa Grande da Praia
31 Pousada Velamar

PLACES TO EAT

15 Lagostão
16 Como Antigamente
21 Paraíso
22 O Komilão
29 Pizzaria Paju

OTHER

1 Museu do Instituto Histórico
3 Banco do Brasil
4 Mercado do Artesanato
6 Mini Buses to Marechal Deodoro & Praia do Francês

7 Post Office
8 Catedral
11 Buses to Marechel Deodoro & Barra de São Miguel
12 Ematur Tourist Office
13 Buses to Pajuçara & Ponta Verde
14 Museu Theo Brandão
26 Jangadas to Reef & Piscina Natural
27 Ematur Tourist Office & Telephone Office
28 Mercado Praia Pajuçara
32 Ematur Tourist Office & Telephone Office

THE NORTHEAST

with air-con for US$30. The *Pousada Casa Grande da Praia* (☎ 231-3332), at Rua Jangadeiros Alagoanos 1528, is a quiet place a few blocks back from the beachfront. Apartamentos with air-con and refrigerator cost US$24/30 for singles/doubles. The *Hotel Velamar* (☎ 231-5888), at Rua Antônio Gouveia 1359, is a cute little place dwarfed by the square block hotel next door. Apartamentos cost US$25/30 for singles/doubles.

The *Pousada Cavalo Marinho* (☎ 235-1247; fax 235-3265), about 15 km from the centre at Rua da Praia 55, Praia Riacho Doce, has been recommended by readers. Double rooms start at around US$25, with use of canoes, bicycles and bodyboards. The owner speaks English and German.

Places to Eat

City Centre If you want good seafood and feel like a splurge, visit *Lagostão* (☎ 221-6211), at Avenida Duque de Caxias 1384. A cheaper option, just one block to the east on the same road, is *Como Antigamente*, which does prato feito for US$5 and has seating in a courtyard at the back of the restaurant, away from the street noise.

Beaches Most of the beaches offer a wide choice of food, with barracas and snack bars serving seafood and local dishes along the beachfront.

Local seafood specialities worth trying are sururu (a small mussel) and maçunim (shellfish) cooked in coconut sauce, served as dishes on their own, or in a caldinho (cup of sauce) which can be eaten or drunk. Other tasty local seafood dishes include peixe agulha (deep-fried needle fish) and siri na casca com coral (crab in the shell with roe). Beachside food stalls serve some delicious snacks which should be tried: acarajé, a bean paste deep fried in dendê oil and filled with shrimp and potato; and tapioca pancakes filled with grated coconut or queijo coalhado, compressed bean curd.

Other good places for seafood are *Bem* (☎ 231-3316), at Rua João Canuto da Silva 21, Praia de Cruz das Almas, and *Restaurant*

Maré, on Avenida Alípio Barbosa, which is south-west of the centre, in Pontal da Barra. Both of these restaurants are medium-priced and open for lunch and dinner.

At Praia Pajuçara, *Paraíso* is a casual little café with a great range of juices and snack foods. *O Komilão* is a friendly place with reasonably priced seafood, meat and chicken refeições, and *Pizzaria Paju* is a breezy restaurant along the beachfront serving good pizza and pasta.

Entertainment

For reviews and listings of the latest bars, dance spots and cultural events in Maceió, pick up a copy of *Veja*, which includes an assortment of these places in its weekly supplement entitled *28 Graus*. A couple of places worth checking out are Trupi e Dance, at Rua Jangadeiros Alagoanos 1125, in Pajuçara, for loud and sweaty dance action, or Middo, at Avenida Robert Kennedy 2167, Praia dos Sete Coqueiros, which has pagode, forró and dance music.

Things to Buy

There is a artesanato market on Praia Pajuçara with dozens of stalls selling figurines, lacework, hammocks and jewellery. Directly across the road, Pajuçara Artesanato is a large shop selling similar goods. Beautifully embroidered hammocks cost around $60 – another good purchase is a *rede-cadeira* (hammock chair) for US$32.

The fishing village of Pontal da Barra, around 10 km from the centre, is also an artesanato centre. The streets are lined with shops selling lacework and embroidery, and prices are generally lower than in the city. You can often see women weaving outside the shops. The Mercado do Artesanato, next to the food market in the city centre, is also a good place to shop for hammocks – a double hammock goes for around $US20.

Getting There & Away

Air Maceió is connected by air with Rio, São Paulo, Brasília and all the major centres of the Northeast. There are plans to open an international terminal in Maceió – at the moment, there are charter services to Maceió from Rome, Madrid and Amsterdam.

The major airline offices are in the centre. Varig (☎ (0800) 99-7000; airport ☎ 322-1160) is at Rua Comendador Palmeira 129; VASP (☎ (0800) 99-8227; airport ☎ 322-1414) is at Rua do Comércio 56; and Transbrasil (☎ 221-8344; airport ☎ 322-1333) is at Rua Barão de Penedo 213.

Bus There are frequent daily departures to Recife (US$6.50, four hours) and Aracaju (US$7, five hours). Services operate five times daily to Salvador (US$15.50, 10 hours). Some buses to Salvador take the inland route; others go via the new Linha Verde road along the coast. If you want to make a 2256-km bus trip to Rio (US$52, 36 hours), there's a daily departure at 7 pm.

Buses leave for Penedo five times daily – the route via AL-101 along the coast is much quicker (US$5, around 2½ hours). São Domingus bus company services the coastal towns north of Maceió, with regular buses to Barra do Camarajibe, Barra de Santo Antônio, Japaratinga and Porto de Pedras.

Walking For details of walking from Recife to Maceió, see the Getting There & Away section for Recife (Pernambuco chapter).

Getting Around
To/From the Airport Aeroporto Dos Palmares (☎ 322-1300) is 20 km from the centre. Buses to the airport can be picked up at Praça Sinibu, on Rua Imperador. A taxi to the airport costs around US$15.

To/From the Rodoviária The rodoviária (☎ 223-4105) is about four km from the centre. To reach the centre, take the bus marked 'Ouro Prêto'. A taxi to the centre costs around US$4, and US$2 more to Pajuçara.

To/From the Beaches Buses marked 'Santuário', 'Jardim Vaticano' or 'Ponta Verde' run from the centre to Pajuçara. The 'Jatiúca' bus runs from the centre to Praia Jatiúca. If you want to travel further away

from the centre, the bus marked 'Jardineira' runs along the beaches north of town as far as Riacho Doce (recommended).

Buses run to Pontal da Barra from the bus stop on Rua Pedro Montero, near Praça dos Palamares.

SOUTH OF MACEIÓ
Praia do Francês
Only 22 km from Maceió, this is a popular weekend beach which is being rapidly developed and beginning to suffer from the ravages of tourism. The beach is lined with barracas and the ocean is lined with reefs. The water is calm and better for wading in than swimming. It's a very social beach on weekends, with plenty of drinking, seafood-scoffing, football and music.

There is a small Ematur information booth on the roadside as you come into town, which has some brochures and can give directions to accommodation.

Places to Stay & Eat There are now some cheap options in Praia do Francês. The *Pousada João* and *Pousada Nataly* are both pretty grungy, with quartos for US$6/12.

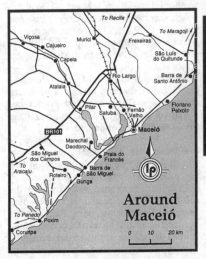

Around Maceió

Better value is the *Hotel Pousada do Pescador*, which has clean double apartamentos for US$20. Nicer still is the *Pousada Caravelas*, right on the beachfront, with double apartamentos at US$30. The *Pousada Bougainville* (☎ 231-1079) is also close to the beach, and recommended for a splurge. The French owner has virtually submerged the pousada in bougainvillea. Apartamentos cost US$32/38 for singles/doubles. The adjacent restaurant, *Chez Patrick*, is run by the same Frenchman and specialises in seafood. Main dishes are expensive, but you can also drop in for an appetiser and drink served in the restaurant's shady courtyard. Numerous barracas along the beach are a good source of cheap seafood, or you could try the *Restaurant do Pescador*.

Getting There & Away From Maceió, either take the bus from the stop opposite the ferroviária (hourly departure), or use the more frequent minibus service which departs about from 50 metres down the street. The same minibuses run between Praia do Francês and Marechal Deodoro.

Marechal Deodoro

Beside Lagoa Manguaba, a lagoon 21 km south-west of Maceió, is Marechal Deodoro, which was the capital of Alagoas between 1823 and 1839. Small and quiet, the town is worth a visit, perhaps combined with Praia do Francês as a day trip from Maceió.

Things to See Marechal Deodoro has several churches, the most famous of which are the **Igreja e Convento São Francisco**, which was begun in the 17th century, and the **Igreja de NS da Conceição**.

Inside Igreja e Convento São Francisco is the **Museu de Arte Sacra** (Museum of Sacred Art). It's open daily from 9 am to 1 pm, except on Sunday, when it's closed.

Brazilian history buffs may want to see the old governor's palace and the house where Marechal Deodoro was born. The latter has been turned into the **Museu Deodoro**, which is open daily from 9 am to 5 pm, except on Sunday, when it's closed. The exhibits give

a 'deodorised' view of Manuel Deodoro da Fonseca, emphasising his role as a military hero and the first president of Brazil, but omitting to mention that he achieved this position with a military putsch in 1889, and later proved to be a poor politician. The artesanato shop next door sells the lace and homemade sweets for which the town is renowned. The weekend market, held along the waterfront, is a lively, colourful event.

Place to Stay & Eat The *Hospedaria Deodorense* is a clean, basic place to stay – usually booked solid on weekends. Quartos

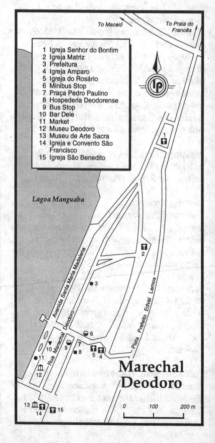

1 Igreja Senhor do Bonfim
2 Igreja Matriz
3 Prefeitura
4 Igreja Amparo
5 Igreja do Rosário
6 Minibus Stop
7 Praça Pedro Paulino
8 Hospedaria Deodorense
9 Bus Stop
10 Bar Dele
11 Market
12 Museu Deodoro
13 Museu de Arte Sacra
14 Igreja e Convento São Francisco
15 Igreja São Benedito

To Maceió
To Praia do Francês

Lagoa Manguaba

Avenida Sacria Maria Madalena

Rua Marechal Deodoro

Pista Prefeito Edval Lemos

Marechal Deodoro

0   100   200 m

cost US$12/18 for singles/doubles. Breakfast costs US$2. For other meals, speak to Dona Terezinho, in the house two doors up towards Praça Paulino. *Bar Dele* is a breezy bar along the waterfront.

Getting There & Away Buses to Marechal Deodoro depart hourly from the bus stop outside the old ferroviária in Maceió. It's quicker to go by one of the VW vans (US$1, half an hour) – they leave every 15 minutes or so from the BR petrol station on Praça dos Palmares. Yes, the VW van is definitely quicker: the demon drivers keep their accelerator foot down to the board, and your heart pressed to the roof of your mouth!

An alternative route from Maceió is to take the boat from Trapiche across Lagoa Manguaba.

Barra de São Miguel

Barra is 35 km south of Maceió, at the mouth of the Rio São Miguel. The fine beach is protected by a huge reef and there are kayaks for rent. Barra is not too crowded midweek, but it is being built up with summer homes for Maceió's wealthy. Praia do Gunga is a popular beach across the river with some expensive bars. You can rent jet-skis here, or go para sailing.

There are several options for boat trips up the river. The *Samadhi* is a large sailboat that makes a 4½-hour trip around the beaches, mangrove forests and islands for US$25 per person. The cost includes transport from Maceió, drinks and fruit on board, and a stop off for a swim at Praia do Francês on the return trip. For information and reservations, contact Raúl or Nidia (☎ 272-1523) who speak Spanish and English.

Places to Stay & Eat There are a couple of very expensive hotels in town. The *Pousada Mar e Sol* (☎ 272-1159), near the river, has apartamentos at US$28/32 for singles/doubles. It's overpriced but in an attractive position. If there is a group of you, better value are chalets for up to six people, with cooking facilities, for around $US60 per day. The *Condimínio Rio Mar* (☎ 272-1432) and

Recanto Barra Mar (☎ 272-1473) both offer chalet accommodation.

Bar do Tio has good shrimp and fish dishes for US$6 to US$10. Try the super mussels.

Getting There & Away Buses run four times daily to Barra, at 7.20 and 11.30 am, and 3.20 and 7.20 pm, from the bus stop at the Estação Ferroviária. The last bus leaves Barra for the return trip at 5.30 pm.

South of Barra de São Miguel

The recent upgrading of AL-101 along the Litoral Sul has made access to the beaches and villages south of Barra de São Miguel much easier. The road runs about one km from the coast, and regular buses run along it from Maceió to Penedo on the Rio São Francisco. Poxim is a small town with coconut-tree-lined beaches and several lagoons nearby.

Around 25 km south, Coruripe is a fishing village with a couple of restaurants and pousadas. South of Coruripe are stretches of deserted beaches until Pontal do Peba – but Praia do Peba is disappointing, well below the quality of those to the north. After Pontal do Peba, the road cuts inland to Piaçabuçu, on the north bank of the Rio São Francisco. There are a few hotels here, and boat trips can be organised upriver to Penedo or along the coast to Coruripe.

PENEDO

Penedo is best known as the *capital do baixo São Francisco* (capital of the lower São Francisco). The city has also been called *cidade dos sobrados* (city of two-storey homes) by the famous Brazilian sociologist Gilberto Freyre.

Among the attractions of the city, 42 km off the BR-101, are its many baroque churches and colonial buildings, and the opportunity to travel on the Rio São Francisco. Penedo bustles with people from the smaller villages up and down the river who come to buy and sell goods.

History

Penedo was founded in either 1535 or 1560 (opinions differ) by Duarte Coelho Pereira, who descended the Rio São Francisco in pursuit of Caete Indians responsible for the killing of bishop Pedro Fernandes Sardin-haeven. Penedo is claimed to be the river's first colonial settlement.

Information

There's a helpful tourist information office (open daily from 8 am to noon and 2 to 5 pm) and small city museum in the Casa da Apos-entadoria, just up from the fort on Praça Barão de Penedo.

Market

The street market is held daily in Penedo, but Friday and Saturday are the big days when the city is transformed into a busy port-of-call for farmers, fisherfolk and artisans. The waterfront becomes a pageant as families disembark – old people with finely carved features topped by strange hats, many grasping chickens by the neck in one hand and boisterous children by the neck in the other. On the river bank, traditional musicians play accordions. The market is filled with ceramics, baskets and shrimp traps made of reeds.

Churches

Penedo has a rich collection of 17th and 18th-century colonial buildings, including many churches. The **Convento de São Francisco e Igreja NS dos Anjos**, on Praça Rui Barbosa, is considered the finest church in the state. Even Dom Pedro II (Brazil's second and last emperor) paid a visit to this church. Construction was begun in 1660 and completed in 1759. The rococo altar is made of gold. The church is open Tuesday to Sunday from 8 to 11 am and 2 to 5 pm.

Igreja da Senhora das Correntes was completed in 1764. It has some fine work done with azulejos (glazed blue tiles), and a rococo altar. The church is open daily from 8 am to noon and 2 to 5 pm. You'll find it at Praça 12 de Abril.

The **Igreja NS do Rosário dos Pretos**, also known as the Catedral do Penedo, was built by slaves. It's on Praça Marechal Deodoro and is open every day from 8 am to 5 pm. **Igreja de São Gonçalo Garcia** was built at the end of the 18th century and has some of the city's finest sacred-art pieces. It's on Avenida Floriano Peixoto, but is currently closed for restoration.

Boat Trips

Saturday (the major market day) is the easiest day to find a boat up or down the São Francisco, but it's difficult now to find boats going upriver as far as Propriá.

The ferry between Penedo and Passagem, on the opposite side of the river, crosses every half an hour, but is only of interest if you're driving. From Passagem there's a road to Neópolis, which is linked by another road to BR-101. A better excursion is one of the motorboat crossings direct to Neópolis, a few km downriver. The 15-minute trip costs US$0.50 and boats depart every half an hour between 5.30 am and 10 pm. Neópolis is an old colonial town on a hill overlooking the river, with some interesting buildings and good crafts for sale. For other short boat excursions, take one of the frequent boats (operating between 6 am and 6 pm) to Carrapicho, a small town four km upriver noted for its ceramics.

A large motorboat for up to 30 people cruises to Carrapicho, Neópolis and river islands, with stops for swimming. The cost is US$30 per hour per boatload. A sailboat makes a similar trip, depending on the wind and tides, for US$20 per hour. Ask at the tourist office for departure times.

Festivals

The Festa do Senhor Bom Jesus dos Navegantes, held over four days from the second Sunday of January, features an elaborate procession of boats. Penedo also hosts a large annual Brazilian film festival.

Places to Stay

Penedo has some terrific hotels that are surprisingly cheap. Most are down by the waterfront, on or near Avenida Floriano Peixoto.

The *Pousada Colonial* (☎ 551-2677), on Praça 12 de Abril, is a romantic place to stay. It's a beautiful, converted colonial home on the waterfront with spacious apartamentos featuring stained-wood floors and antique furniture. Make sure you get one with a view of the river. Prices start at US$13/20 for single/double apartamentos.

The *Hotel São Francisco* (☎ 551-2273), on Avenida Floriano Peixoto, is clean, quiet and has comfortable apartamentos with balconies starting at US$19/28 for singles/doubles.

For a budget option, try the *Pousada Familiar*, at Rua Siqueira 77, with quartos at US$5/10 for singles/doubles.

Places to Eat

There are plenty of bars and lanchonetes where locals eat. We recommend *Forte da Rocheira*, which is open for lunch and dinner (until 11 pm) and serves abundant portions of seafood and meat for US$9 to US$12. The restaurant is in an old fort overlooking the river. Just follow the signs to get there. The restaurant in the *Pousada Colonial* also serves good fish and meat dishes.

Getting There & Away

Bus The rodoviária is on Avenida Duque de Caxias. There are six daily buses to Maceió (US$5). Buses leaving at 6 am and 5 pm take the coastal route along AL-101, which is much quicker than the inland route (around 2½ hours). There is one bus, at 6 am, to Propriá (US$2, two hours), which continues on to Aracaju (US$4, three hours). A quicker and more convenient way to get to Aracaju is to take the ferry across the river to Neópolis, where there are frequent buses to Aracaju.

Car If you are driving to Penedo, there is a 41-km paved road from BR-101 in Sergipe to Neópolis, on the Sergipe side of the river, and then a short drive from Neópolis to Passagem, where a ferry boat makes the 10-minute river crossing to Penedo every half an hour (US$0.75 for a car).

NORTH OF MACEIÓ

The Alagoas coast north of Maceió is ideal for independent travellers. The beaches are mostly undisturbed and tropically perfect, and the sea is calm and warm. There are several fishing villages with no tourism apart from a simple hotel or two – although the state government's 'Costa Dourada' (Golden Coast) development plans could bring about rapid changes.

The coastal road, which is unpaved and slow going along the most secluded stretches, runs within a few hundred metres of the ocean, a rare occurrence along the Brazilian litoral. If you want to follow it, head down to Barra de Santo Antônio. The road from here to Barra do Camarajibe is often in disarray and you have to cross some small rivers on local ferries, so check road conditions before departing.

Alternatively, from Maceió, AL-101 heads north and then divides outside Barra de Santo Antônio. The main road and most through-traffic heads inland on AL-413. It's a stunning drive (try to stop at Porto Calvo) through rolling hills covered in sugar cane, though there's the odd hill topped with virgin forest that escaped land clearing. A good road runs off AL-413 from the town of , hitting the coast at Barra de Camarajibe. From Barra do Camarajibe, the coast road is paved as far as Porto de Pedras, about 16 km before Japaratinga.

The AL-413 passes a large sugar-cane plant that processes the sugar-cane alcohol that fuels Brazil's cars. The Empresa de Santo Antônio employs about 800 workers in the factory and 4000 in the fields. Tours are possible and worthwhile, but hard to arrange.

A few buses from Maceió go all the way along the coast, but they are less frequent than those that run via AL-413. Ask for a bus that goes to Porto de Pedras or São Miguel dos Milagres.

Barra de Santo Antônio & Ilha da Croa

Barra is along the mouth of the Rio Jirituba, below a small bluff. This is relaxed fishing village only 40 km from Maceió and is now attracting tourists and people constructing beach homes – it can get busy on weekends and in summer.

The best beaches are out on the Ilha da Croa (narrow peninsula), on the other side of Rio Jirituba. You can catch a small boat across the river (US$0.50) and walk around two km across the peninsula to the beaches, or take a motorboat all the way (US$2). Balsas take cars across the river for US$3.

Tabuba beach is a quiet, pretty beach with a few bars three km south of Barra de Santo Antônio. There is a piscina natural off the beach – ask at the bars about a ride there by jangada.

Places to Stay & Eat The *Costa Verde Clube Hotel* (☎ 221-5581, 221-5308) is a fancy place, with a pool and horses, on the outskirts of town. Chalets cost around US$40 for two people. In town, the *Pousada Brisa E Sonhos* is a very friendly place on the river with quartos for US$6/10 with a good breakfast included. The Honeymoon Suite, a room featuring a huge double bed with built-in stereo and velvet bedspreads, costs US$12. The pousada also serves good meals. The *Pousada Tabuba* is a small pousada close to Tabuba beach, with apartamentos at around US$10/20 for singles/doubles.

The *Peixada da Rita*, along the river in Barra de Santo Antônio, serves sensational seafood.

Getting There & Away Direct buses and VW vans to Maceió (US$1, one hour) operate from 4.30 am to 10.30 pm. You can also walk for 20 minutes or hire a local cab to the main road, where you can flag down those buses which bypass the town.

Barra do Camarajibe

This idyllic fishing village, 33 km further up the coast, offers fish, beer and a beautiful beach. Tourism is just about to hit the village – the *Pousada Brisa Mar* and a large restaurant on the beachfront should both be in operation by the time this book is published. Buses run to Barra do Camarajibe from Maceió via São Luís do Quintude.

São Miguel dos Milagres

A bit bigger than its neighbours, São Miguel's soft beaches are protected by off-shore reefs and the sea is warm and shallow. There's one pousada and a petrol station in town.

Porto de Pedras

You've got to catch the local ferry to cross the river here. Porto de Pedras is a lively little fishing village with a road that connects to AL-413 at Porto Calvo. In the village there are bars, restaurants and the cheap and dingy *Hotel São Geraldo*.

Japaratinga

Japaratinga's shallow waters are protected by coral reefs and the beaches are backed by coconut trees and fishing huts. Under the moonlight you can walk a couple of km into the sea. The town has a petrol station and a telephone.

Places to Stay & Eat The *Hotel Sol Mar*, on the south side of town, has a campground and apartamentos at around US$12/18 for singles/doubles. The *Rei dos Peixes* is a small pousada with slightly lower prices. A more up-market place, the *Bitingui Praia Hotel*, about two km outside town, has been recommended by readers. Double rooms with air-con cost around US$40, and the hotel has a swimming pool and a restaurant. There's a large churrascaria and several seafood eateries in town.

Getting There & Away There are regular buses from Japaratinga to Maceió and Recife (137 km).

Maragoji

Slightly more developed, Maragoji has some weekend homes for Pernambucanos and a couple of cheap hotels – try the *Pousada da Gloria* or the *Pousada São Francisco*. The sea is protected by reefs and it's ideal for swimming.

Pernambuco

RECIFE

Recife is the country's fourth biggest city and the capital of Pernambuco. The 'Venice of Brazil' (a rather hopeful comparison), Recife is a city of water and bridges with *arrecifes* (reefs) offshore. Its sister city of Olinda was once the capital of Brazil and today is a beautiful enclave of colonial buildings filled with artists, students and bohemians.

Amidst all the recent development, Recife retains a rich traditional side, with some of Brazil's best folk art, including painting and sculpture, dance, music and festivals. It takes time to discover this side of the city, but it's well worth the effort.

Recife is the port of entry for many flights from Europe and has recently been trying to broaden its tourist appeal. The main beneficiary of these developments has been Boa Viagem, the Copacabana of Pernambuco. Site of the well-to-do nightclubs, restaurants and most of the mid-priced to expensive hotels, Boa Viagem has wide beaches which are essential for escaping Recife's muggy heat, although the water is not always very clean. Unless you want to be right on the beach, Olinda has more cheap accommodation and is a more interesting place to stay.

History

Recife developed in the 17th century as the port for the rich sugar plantations around Olinda. With several rivers and offshore reefs, Recife proved to be an excellent port and began to outgrow Olinda. By the 17th century, Recife and Olinda combined were the most prosperous cities in Brazil, with the possible exception of Salvador (Bahia). The neighbouring Indians had been subdued after brutal warfare, and the colonial aristocracy living in Olinda was raking in profits with its many sugar engenhos (mills). Naturally, all the work was done by slaves.

No European country had managed to grab a part of Brazil from the Portuguese until 1621, when the Dutch, who were active in the sugar trade and knew the lands of Brazil well, set up the Dutch West India Company to get their teeth into the Brazilian cake. A large fleet sailed in 1624 and captured Bahia, but a huge Spanish-Portuguese militia of 12,000 men recaptured the city the following year. Five years later the Dutch decided to try again, this time in Pernambuco. Recife was abandoned; the Dutch took the city and by 1640 they had control of a great chunk of the Northeast, from Maranhão to the Rio São Francisco.

The Dutch had hoped the sugar planters wouldn't resist their rule, but many Brazilian planters took up arms against the non-Catholic Dutch. In 1654, after a series of battles around Recife, the Dutch finally surrendered. This was the last European challenge to Portuguese Brazil.

Recife prospered after the Dutch were expelled, but in spite of the city's growing economic power, which had eclipsed that of Olinda, political power remained with the sugar planters in Olinda, and they refused to share it. In 1710 fighting began between the *filhos da terra* (the sugar planters of Olinda) and the *mascates* (the Portuguese merchants of Recife), the more recent immigrants. The Guerra dos Mascates (War of the Mascates), as it came to be known, was a bloody regional feud between different sections of the ruling class and native Brazilians and immigrants. In the end, with the help of the Portuguese crown and their superior economic resources, the mascates of Recife gained considerable political clout at the expense of Olinda, which began its long, slow decline.

More dependent on the sugar economy than Rio or São Paulo, Recife was eclipsed by these two centres as the sugar economy floundered throughout the 19th century.

Orientation

Recife is large, modern and more difficult to

negotiate than most cities in the Northeast. The city centre is a confusing mixture of high-rise offices, colonial churches and popular markets. During the day, traffic and tourists get lost in the maze of winding, one-way streets.

The heart of Recife, containing the old section of town, ranges along the waterfront in Boa Vista district, across the Rio Capibaribe to Santo Antônio district and then across to Ilha do Recife. All are connected by bridges.

Olinda is six km to the north over swamps and rivers, while Boa Viagem is six km to the south.

Information

Tourist Office The headquarters of Empetur (☎ 241-2111), the state tourism bureau, is in the monolithic Centro de Convenções (Complexo Rodoviária de Salgadinho), between the city centre and Olinda. To get there from the centre, take the 'Rio Doce/Conde da Boa Vista' bus. Smaller information booths are in the Casa da Cultura de Recife and the rodoviária (good, but with no literature). The information desk at the airport has maps and can book hotels.

Useful publications available from tourist offices include the *Pernambuco Tourist Guide*, which has a map of the beaches around Recife, *Itinerário* (a monthly mini-guide for Recife) and *Brazil Travel News – Pernambuco*, a glossy brochure about the state's main attractions. *Diário de Pernambuco*, one of the local newspapers, has cultural listings (museums, art galleries, cinemas, etc) in its daily Diversões (amusements) section.

Money There are convenient branches of Banco do Brasil at the airport; in the centre, at Avenida Dantas Barreto 541 (Santo Antônio); and in Boa Viagem, at Avenida Conselheiro Aguiar 3600.

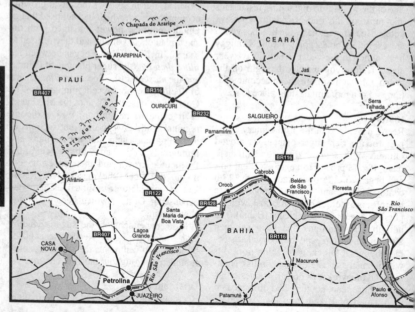

Post & Telephone The main post office is at Avenida Guararapes 250. The posta restante (Cep 50001-970) counter is in the basement. There are also convenient post offices at the airport and the TIP (Terminal Integrado de Passageiros – rodoviária).

TELPE (the state telephone company) has telephone stations with international service at TIP, at the airport, and in the centre, at Rua do Hospício 148.

Foreign Consulates The following countries have consulates in Recife:

France
    Avenida Conselheiro Aguiar 2333, 6th floor, Boa Viagem (☎ 465-3290)
Germany
    Avenida Dantas Barreto 191, 4th floor, Santo Antônio (☎ 424-3488)
UK
    Avenida Engenheiro Domingos Ferreira 2222, Boa Viagem (☎ 326-3733)

USA
    Rua Gonçalves Maia 163, Boa Vista (☎ 221-1412)

Visa Renewal If you need to renew a visa, go to the Polícia Federal building on Cais do Apolo (Ilha do Recife). Since it's best to phone first, ask the tourist office for the appropriate information.

Travel Agencies Andratur (☎ 326-4388), at Avenida Conselheiro Aguiar 3150, loja 7 (Boa Viagem), provides national and international tickets at discounted prices (for example, US$700 for a return flight from Recife to Miami with VASP). This company also sells packaged trips for Fernando de Noronha.

Mubatur (☎ 341-4519), at Rua Barão de Souza Leão 221, sala 23 (Boa Viagem), offers similar deals.

Bookshops There are several bookstalls

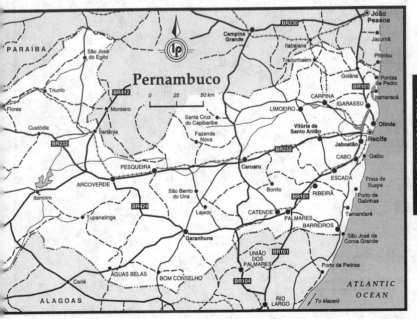

THE NORTHEAST

along Rua do Infante Dom Henrique. The airport bookshop and the Livro 7 de Setembro are the best bets if you're looking for foreign-language books.

Museums & Galleries

With such a long and important history, it's not surprising that Recife is loaded with churches and museums, but few of them are must-sees.

The best museum, **Museu do Homem do Nordeste** (Museum of the Northeast), is east of the city centre along Avenida 17 de Agosto. Catch the 'Dois Irmãos' bus from Parque 13 de Maio (in the city centre) and ask the driver to let you off at the right spot. The museum is divided into three sections: an anthropology section about the people of the Northeast; a popular-art section with some superb ceramic figurines; and a pharmacy exhibit about the region's herbal/indigenous medicine. Opening hours are 11 am to 5 pm on Tuesday, Wednesday and Friday, 8 am to 5 pm on Thursday, and 1 to 5 pm on Saturday, Sunday and public holidays.

The **Horto Zoobotânico**, with a zoo and botanical garden (both renovated in 1990), is

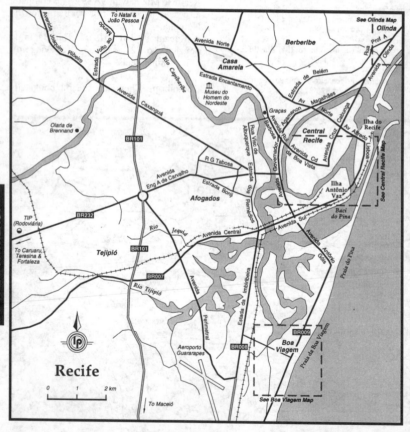

Recife
0   1   2 km

in the same neighbourhood. Opening hours are 8 am to 5 pm Tuesday to Sunday.

Train fetishists may like to visit the **Museu do Trem** (Train Museum), which is adjacent to Recife Metro Station – formerly known as Estação Central (Central Train Station).

For a look at some paintings by renowned artists of Pernambuco you can visit **Galeria de Arte Metropolitana**, at Rua da Aurora 265. It's open Tuesday to Saturday from noon to 6 pm.

Archaeology buffs will want to browse around in the **Museu Archeológico**, at Rua do Hospício, 130. It's open Tuesday and Wednesday from 2 to 6 pm.

Old City

To see the old city, start over at Praça da República, where you'll see the **Teatro Santa Isabel** (1850) and the **Palácio do Governo** (1841). Take a look at **Igreja de Santo Antônio** (1753) in Praça da Independência, and then visit **Catedral de São Pedro dos Clérigos**, on Pátio de São Pedro, an artists' hang-out. There are many intimate restaurants, shops and bars here, all with interesting local characters. On weekends there's often good music.

Walk down Rua Vidal de Negreiros to the **Forte das Cinco Pontas**, which was built by the Dutch in 1630, then rebuilt in 1677. Inside there's the **Museu da Cidade**, which displays maps and photos of the city. Opening hours are 10 am to 6 pm Tuesday to Friday and from 1 to 6 pm on Saturday and Sunday.

Nearby, at Praça Dom Vital, is the daily **Mercado do São José** (market) and the **Basílica de NS da Penha**. The market used to be a major centre for food and crafts from throughout Pernambuco, but now you'll find mostly manufactured goods here.

Casa da Cultura de Recife

The Casa da Cultura de Recife, across the street from Recife Metro Station, once served as a huge, colonial-style prison, but was decommissioned, renovated and redecorated in 1975. It's now home to many craft and souvenir shops. Good traditional music and dance shows are often performed outside the building, and the complex contains tourist information and telephone offices. It's open from Monday to Saturday 9 am to 7 pm and on Sunday from 2 to 7 pm.

Olaria de Brennand

The Olaria, a ceramics factory and exhibition hall, is set in thickly forested surroundings, a rare landscape for suburban Recife and an even rarer chance for travellers in the Northeast to see what the Mata Atlântica looked like several centuries ago. The buildings and exhibits in Olaria de Brennand are perhaps the most bizarre highlight of the Northeast – they are highly recommended.

History The Irish forbears of the present owner, Francisco Brennand, arrived in Brazil in 1823 to work as peasant farmers. The unmarried daughter of a sugar magnate took a liking to Brennand's father, who was employed by her father. She later inherited her father's property and, when she died, willed her entire estate and immense wealth to Brennand Senior.

The house in which Francisco Brennand was born, in 1927, was imported from England in prefabricated form. Brennand's father founded a brickworks in 1917 and continued this business until 1945. Francisco left for France, where he studied art and was influenced by Picasso, Miró, Léger and Gaudi. The property in Recife remained abandoned from 1945 until 1971, when Brennand returned from France and set about restoring the dilapidated buildings.

The Gallery/Museum This contains a permanent exhibition of around 2000 pieces which are *not* for sale (see the end of this section for address of the sales outlet in Boa Viagem).

Wander around sculptured collages of cubes, spheres and rectangles absorbed into animal shapes: worms with balaclava hats; blunt-headed lizards bursting out of parapets; cuboid geckos straddling paths; geese with flying helmets; birds of prey hatching

THE NORTHEAST

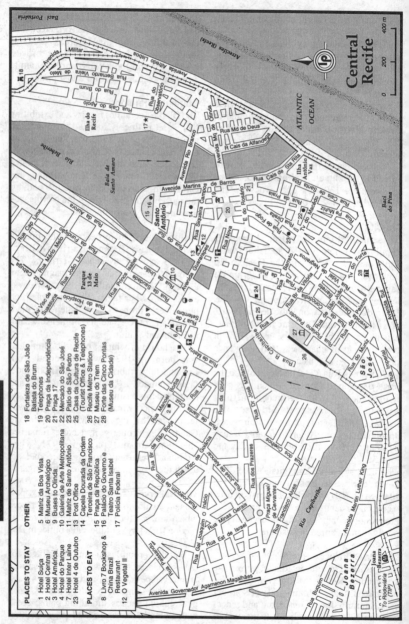

PLACES TO STAY

1 Hotel Suíça
2 Hotel Central
3 Hotel América
4 Hotel do Parque
7 Hotel Inter Laine
23 Hotel 4 de Outubro

PLACES TO EAT

8 Livro 7 Bookshop &
  China Brazil
  Restaurant
12 O Vegetal II

OTHER

5 Matriz da Boa Vista
6 Museu Archeológico
9 Buses to Olinda
10 Galeria de Arte Metropolitana
11 Matriz de Santo Antônio
13 Post Office
14 Capela Dourada da Ordem
  Terceira de São Francisco
15 Praça da República
16 Palácio do Governo e
  Teatro Santa Isabel
17 Policia Federal
18 Fortaleza de São João
  Batista do Brum
19 Telephones
20 Praça da Independência
21 Praça 17
22 Mercado do São José
23 Pátio de São Pedro
25 Casa da Cultura e Telephones
  (Tourist Office & Telephones)
26 Recife Metro Station
27 Museu do Trem
28 Forte das Cinco Pontas
  (Museu da Cidade)

Central Recife

from half-shells lodged in the walls; pigs formed from giant nails; and vistas of busts, buttocks, breasts, and phalluses...meanwhile, black swans glide over shoals of goldfish in ponds dotted with vulvas shaped like tortoises. Kooky, but fun!

The gallery/museum is open Monday to Thursday from 8 am to 5 pm, and from 8 am to 4 pm on Friday. For information, contact Oficina Ceramica Francisco Brennand (☎ 271-4814), s/a, Propriedade Santos Cosme e Damião s/n (no number), Varzea, CEP 50741 Recife – PE.

Olaria Brennand produces superb ceramics, which are sold in its shop (☎ 325-0025), at Avenida Conselheiro Aguiar 2966, loja 4, Galeria Vila Real, in Boa Viagem.

Getting There & Away From the centre of Recife, take the bus marked 'Caxangá' for the 11-km long ride to the Caxangá bus terminal. Continue walking about 100 metres away from the city and over the bridge. Then take the first road on the left – easily recognised by the roadside statue of Padre Cicero. Walk about two km, past a couple of stray hotels, until you reach a gaudy housing development. Take the road to the left at the T-junction and continue for about three km through dense forest to the office. Shady characters hang out in the area, so it's best if you are in a group. The walk takes about 1¼ hours.

Otherwise, you can take a taxi from the bus terminal or the bridge to the Olaria – and walk back after your visit. Tour companies and taxi companies will also do the trip from the centre of Recife or Olinda, but it's expensive unless you can form a small group to share the costs. For a recommended taxi company, see the Getting Around section for Olinda.

Festivals
The Recife-Olinda combination may be the best Carnival in Brazil, but even if you decide to carnival in Rio or Salvador, Recife starts celebrating so early that you can enjoy festivities there and then go somewhere else for Carnival proper. Two months before the start of Carnival, there are *bailes* (dances) in the clubs and Carnival blocos practising on the streets, with frevo dancing everywhere. Galo da Madrugada, Recife's largest bloco, has been known to bring 20,000 people in costume onto the beaches at Boa Viagem to dance.

There are supposedly 500 different Carnival blocos in the Recife area, and they come in all 'shakes' and colours. There are the traditional and well organised, the modern and anarchical. There are samba schools, there are afoxés, Indian tribes and *maracatus* (African processions accompanied by percussion musicians), but the main dance of Carnival in Pernambuco is the frenetic frevo. The Fundação da Cultura do Recife, which runs Carnival, has on occasion organised public frevo lessons for the uninitiated at the Pátio de São Pedro.

Along Boa Viagem beach, Carnival groups practise on weekends, and as Carnival approaches they add trios elétricos to the tomfoolery. The week before Carnival Sunday, the unofficial Carnival really starts. Several groups march through the city centre each day and at least one baile kicks off each evening – time to practise that frevo.

Big-time Carnival takes place from Saturday to Tuesday, nonstop. The big Carnival groups parade in wonderful costumes, singing and dancing. For the parade route and schedule, check the local papers or the tourism office. Along Avenida Guararapes there's a popular frevo dance that starts on Friday night and goes on and on.

Places to Stay – bottom end
Although we've included details here for accommodation in Recife, most budget travellers prefer staying in Olinda: it's cheap and beautiful, there's lots happening and you can walk everywhere. If you want the beach, head to Boa Viagem, where there is a youth hostel and a few reasonably priced pousadas.

City Centre There are a couple of decent places in central Recife near Parque 13 de Maio. The *Suiça* (☎ 222-3534), at Rua do Hospício 687, has quartos at US$3.50/5.50

for singles/doubles and apartamentos with fan for US$5.50/7.50. Down the road is the quaint but rather run-down *Hotel do Parque* (☎ 222-5427), at Rua do Hospício 51. It has quartos with fan that cost US$6/8; apartamentos cost US$11/13. The *Inter Laine Hotel* (☎ 224-9217), close by at Rua do Hospício 186, has clean apartamentos at US$15/20/25 for singles/doubles/triples. A block away, the *Hotel América* (☎ 221-1300), at Praça Maciel Pinheiro 48, has single/double apartamentos at US$11/13.50. It doesn't merit two stars; some rooms are dark and dingy – see the room first.

Boa Viagem The *Albergue de Juventude Maracatus do Recife* (☎ 326-1221), at Rua Dona Maria Carolina 185, is well located, clean, and has a good-sized swimming pool. Four-bed dorm rooms cost US$7 per person (breakfast not included).

Places to Stay – middle

City Centre The *Central* (☎ 221-1472), at Rua Manoel Borba 209, is a colonial mansion with a pleasant rambling design. Quartos are reasonable value at US$11.50/13, and apartamentos go for US$16/17.50 and up. You may be able to negotiate a discount on these prices for cash.

The *Hotel 4 de Outubro* (☎ 424-4477; fax 424-2598), at Rua Floriano Peixoto 141, is a modern, functional hotel near Recife Metro Station. Apartamentos start at around US$27.50/32.50 for singles/doubles.

Boa Viagem The moderately priced hotels here are often full during summer. As a general rule, prices drop the further you go back from the seafront. Discounts are easy to negotiate for longer stays in low season.

Three hotels are clustered close together along Rua Felix de Brito Melo. The *Hotel Pousada Aconchego* (☎ 326-2989; fax 326-8059), at No 382, features a swimming pool, a 24-hour restaurant and some interesting original art in the foyer and halls. Apartamentos go for US$27/31 for singles/doubles. The *Hotel Pedro do Mar* (☎ 325-5340) at No 604 is a friendly place and the manager

speaks English and German. Apartamentos cost US$26/30 for singles/doubles. The *Hotel Alameda Jasmins* (☎ & fax 325-1591), at No 370, also has a swimming pool but is looking a bit tired. Apartamentos go for US$25/30.

The *Rosa Hotel* (☎ 326-7893), a block away at Rua Mamanguape 584, is run by a friendly bunch of women and has a range of rooms available. The cheapest are six-bed dorm rooms for US$12 per person. The *Hotel Portal do Sol* (☎ 326-9740), at Avenida Conselheiro Aguiar 3217, is reasonably priced if you are staying in a trio; apartamentos go for US$22.50/25/31. The *Hotel 54* (☎ 325-0695), at Rua Professor José Brandão 54, has rooms at US$28/32.

Places to Stay – top end

Almost all the better hotels are in Boa Viagem. The *Hotel Tivoli* (☎ 326-5669), at Rua Tenente João Cicero 47, charges US$32/36 for singles/doubles.

If you want the best, or at least the most expensive, try the four-star *Hotel Savaroni* (☎ 465-4299; fax 326-4900), at Rua Boa Viagem 3772, which charges US$71/79 for singles/doubles, or move up a notch to the five-star *Recife Palace* (☎ 325-4044; fax 326-8895), at Avenida Boa Viagem 4070, where single/double rooms cost US$125/140. The Presidential Suite here is a steal at US$650.

Places to Eat

The city centre is loaded with lunch places, and at night it's easy to find something to your liking around the lively Pátio de São Pedro. The pátio offers a surprising variety of prices and styles. *Delírios e Delícias* (☎ 222-0671), perched right on the riverfront at Rua do Livramento 314 (Derby), has seafood and fondue – it's a splash-out option for the romantically inclined. Vegetarians should visit the self-service *O Vegetal II*, at Avenida Guararapes 210, on the 2nd floor, which is open from 11 am to 3 pm. It's closed on Saturday and Sunday.

Boa Viagem has the bulk of Recife's good restaurants. Avenida Boa Viagem, along the beach, is a regular restaurant row. Walk along here and you're bound to find something you like. *Chico's*, at Rua Mamanguape 157, is a self-serve place with stacks of different salads and cold cuts. The *Lobster* (☎ 268-5516), at Avenida Rui Barbosa 1649, is good if you want to splurge on lobster. It provides live music at dinner and opens daily from noon to midnight. *Maxime* (☎ 326-5314), at Avenida Boa Viagem 21, serves traditional seafood dishes; it's not cheap, but try the lobster (US$15) or one of the local fish, such as cavala (mackerel). Readers have recommended *Peixada do Lulas*, at Avenida

Boa Viagem 241, for its moderately priced seafood dishes.

Entertainment

For reviews and listings of the latest bars, dance spots, and cultural events in Recife, pick up a copy of *Veja*.

There is usually live music in the centre around Pátio de São Pedro in the evening on Thursday, Friday and Saturday.

The major nightlife centre for Recife is Graças district, which is a short taxi ride north-west of the city centre and is packed with bars and nightclubs. Some of the

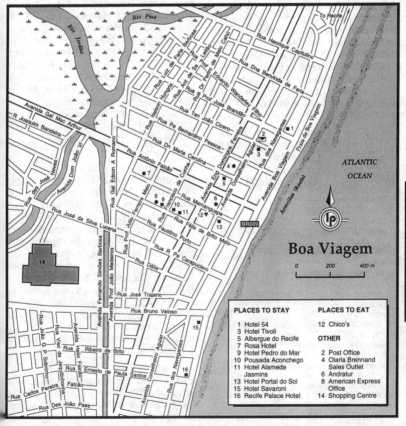

Boa Viagem

0   200   400 m

ATLANTIC OCEAN

PLACES TO STAY	PLACES TO EAT
1 Hotel 54	12 Chico's
3 Hotel Tivoli	
5 Albergue do Recife	**OTHER**
7 Rosa Hotel	
9 Hotel Pedro do Mar	2 Post Office
10 Pousada Aconchego	4 Olaria Brennand
11 Hotel Alameda	Sales Outlet
Jasmins	6 Andratur
13 Hotel Portal do Sol	8 American Express
15 Hotel Savaroni	Office
16 Recife Palace Hotel	14 Shopping Centre

THE NORTHEAST

options in Graças include Overpoint, at Rua Graças 261, a popular meeting place and dance club; Cravo e Canela, at Rua das Creoulas 260, a suave and relaxed bar; New Hits, at Rua Gervásio Fioravante 111, a very active dance club; Depois do Escuro, at Rua da Amizade 178, and Canto das Aguas, at Rua das Pernambucanas (at the end of the street, beside the river), which are divided into separate sections with enough space allotted for quiet drinkers and frenetic dancers.

Things to Buy

Recife is a good place to look for Pernambuco's traditional handicrafts, such as clay figurines, wood sculptures, leather goods and articles made from woven straw. Check out the shops and stalls in Casa da Cultura de Recife, Pátio de São Pedro, and markets such as Mercado do São José or the Feira de Arte e Artesanato, which is a market held in Boa Viagem during the late afternoon and evening on Saturday and Sunday.

Getting There & Away

Air There are flights to most major Brazilian cities, and also to Lisbon, Madrid, London, Paris, Miami and Amsterdam.

The following airlines have offices in Recife:

Air France
　　Rua Padre Carapuceiro 733, Boa Viagem (☎ 465-4416)
　　Aeroporto Guararapes (☎ 341-0333)
Nordeste
　　Aeroporto Guararapes (☎ 341-4222)
TAP
　　Avenida Guararapes 111, Santo Antônio (☎ 224-2700)
Transbrasil
　　Avenida Conde da Boa Vista 1546, Boa Vista (☎ 231-3244)
　　Aeroporto Guararapes (☎ 326-2081)
Varig-Cruzeiro
　　Avenida Guararapes 120, Santo Antônio (☎ 424-2155)
　　Aeroporto Guararapes (☎ 341-4411)
VASP
　　Avenida Guararapes 111, Santo Antônio (☎ 421-3611)
　　Rua Manoel Borba 488, Boa Vista (☎ 421-3088)
　　Aeroporto Guararapes (☎ 326-1699)

Bus The Terminal Integrado de Passageiros (TIP) (☎ 455-1999) is a combined Metro terminal and rodoviária, 14 km from the centre. The TIP now handles all interstate departures and many connections for local destinations. Buses to Igarassu and Ilha do Itamaracá now leave from the centre of Recife – you can also pick up buses to these destinations from the Mercado Santo Amaro between the city centre and Olinda.

There are frequent departures to Maceió (US$6.50, four hours), at least five daily departures to Salvador (US$21, 12 to 14 hours), and daily departures to Rio (US$58, or leito US$116, about 36 hours).

Heading north, it takes two hours to reach João Pessoa (US$3.50), five hours to Natal (US$7.50), 12 hours to Fortaleza (US$19.50, or leito US$30), 24 hours to São Luís (US$36) and 32 hours to Belém (US$47). There are frequent services to Caruaru (US$4.50, two hours), Garanhuns (US$7.50, 3½ hours), and Triunfo (US$12, eight hours).

Getting Around

To/From the Airport Aeroporto Guararapes (☎ 341-1888) is 10 km south of the city centre. Taxis cost about US$12 to the centre; catch a regular taxi – not a special airport taxi, which is about twice as expensive.

From the airport there are regular buses and micro buses (more expensive). The 'Aeroporto' bus runs to Avenida Dantas Barreto in the centre of Recife, stopping in Boa Viagem on the way. To Olinda, take the 'Aeroporto' bus to Avenida Nossa Senhora do Carmo in Recife and pick up a 'Casa Caiada' bus from there. Another option is to get off in Boa Viagem and take a 'Piedade/ Rio Doce' bus from there to Olinda.

Bus & Taxi Buses generally have signs which show the origin of the bus followed by its destination. To telephone a taxi, dial ☎ 224-5410.

Walking from Recife to Maceió

Two Swedish travellers wrote to tell us about their walk from Recife to Maceió:

We started from Olinda, where we left most of our luggage at our pousada. From the centre of Recife we took the train (hourly departures) to Cabo, and then walked to the beach at Gaibu. The reason we started outside Recife was because we had been warned about walking around in the suburbs.

Sun protection is a must. If you walk from Maceió to Recife, the sun is in your face the whole time. We're happy we did it the other way round because the sun can really burn. You should carry a portable stove and always have at least one litre of water per person. Many villages can provide water and food. A big knife is useful as it's easy to pick coconuts along the way. A tent isn't strictly necessary, but it's good to have the option. You don't really need a mosquito net either.

After three hours of walking from Gaibu, we reached a little village and the first river. Don't try to cross it. We made this mistake and found ourselves in the Complexo Portuário e Industrial de Suape, a large oil refinery, where we had a terrible time finding a way out. It's far better to wait for a bus to NS do Ó, and walk from there to Porto de Galinhas; continue past the beautiful Praia de Galinhas until you come to a small river which you can wade across (waist level) at low tide.

At Barra de Sirinhaém, boats take you across the river for free. Unfortunately there is a lot of garbage along the beaches; people throw many things in the river, and you can even find needles and other things from hospitals.

At Rio Formoso, boats cross the river, but you may have to wait a while before one arrives. We got a lift for free right away. After about four more km we came to Tamandaré, a village with shops, bars, hotels and boat-rental facilities.

At the next river, Rio Una, once again we got a ride across for free. Varza do Una is a very different village, and it can be difficult to find a place to stay, but ask around.

From here we had to hitchhike around a swamp to São José da Coroa Grande. From there we continued into Alagoas state where the highway AL-101 runs not further than 100 metres from the beach. This makes it easy to walk up to the road to get around rivers.

Maragoji is a big beach with many bars, boat-rental and other facilities. Japaratinga was the first place we slept at a pousada (*Rei dos Peixes*). Our next stop was at the Rio Manguaba, where we were taken across by boat for US$1. It's also possible to walk to the highway and take a ferry. On the other side is a small town, Porto de Pedras, which is a nice, colourful place with good, cheap restaurants and pousadas.

From here we started to follow the main road which was hot and boring until São Miguel dos Milagres (13 km from Porto de Pedras), where there is one pousada.

The following day we crossed the Rio Camarajibe by boat (fare 50c) and came to the nicest beach we found along this part of the coast. From there we walked three km to Barra de Santo Antônio.

Barra de Santo Antônio is nothing special. Ilha da Croa is a peninsula. Take a boat across the river, then walk along the beach to your right and cross to the other side of the peninsula. This only takes about 20 minutes.

This walk took us 11 days. We only walked in the morning and late afternoon, and we often stopped for hours and sometimes for days. We found enormous hospitality – fishing families were very generous and they adore the company of foreigners. People invited us to stay with them. It's easily possible to do this route in seven days, or even five days if you're in a hurry.

With blisters on our feet and red faces, we took a bus from here to Maceió – locals said the last 40 km to Maceió were nothing special. It was a great adventure and we loved every minute – almost!

Suzanne Gabrielsson & Leif Örnestrand

To/From Olinda From the city centre to Olinda, catch any bus marked 'Rio Doce'. The main bus stop in Olinda is Praça do Carmo. The 'Piedade/Rio Doce' bus runs between Olinda and Boa Viagem. Taxis from the centre of Recife to Olinda cost about US$6 and take 20 minutes. A taxi from the airport to Olinda will cost about US$15.

To/From Boa Viagem From the centre to Boa Viagem, take any bus marked 'CDU/Boa Viagem'. To return to the centre, take any bus marked 'Dantas Barreto'. A taxi from the centre to Boa Viagem costs around US$5.

To/From the TIP (Metro/Rodoviária) The shiny metro system is very useful for the 25-minute trip (US$0.50) between TIP and the metro terminus at the Recife Metro Station, in the centre. Travellers who want to go straight to Boa Viagem from TIP should get off at metro stop 'Joana Bezerra' and catch a bus from there to Boa Viagem. To Olinda, you can catch the metro into the centre, then take a 'Casa Caiada' bus from Avenida Dantas Barreto or a 'Rio Doce' bus from Avenida Guararapes. Alternatively, go to Boa Viagem and take a 'Piedade/Rio Doce' bus from there.

BEACHES SOUTH OF RECIFE

This is excellent beach territory protected by coral reefs. The sea is calm, the waters are crystal clear and the beaches are lined with coconut palms and white sand dunes. The coastal PE-060 road doesn't hug the ocean like the road in northern Alagoas, so you have to drive a dozen or so km on an access road to see what each beach is like. There are frequent bus services to all these beach towns from Recife. Many of the towns have one or two simple hotels and, away from Recife, all have excellent camping.

São José da Coroa Grande

The first beach town you reach after crossing into Pernambuco from Alagoas is São José da Coroa Grande. It's 120 km from Recife on the PE-060 coastal road. This fishing town is receiving attention from property developers, mostly for construction of weekend homes. There are a few restaurants and bars and two hotels: the *Hotel Valeiro*, on the beach, or the more comfortable *Hotel do Frances*, under French management, 200 metres back from the main beach.

Tamandaré

The next access road north of São José da Coroa Grande goes 10 km to the beach at Tamandaré. There is a small fishing village here with a few restaurants and a couple of cheap hotels. The beach is idyllic and you can see the old 17th-century Forte Santo Inácio.

Other Beaches

The road going north along the coast from Tamadaré will take you to the beaches of **Ponta dos Manguinhos**, **Guadalupe**, **Camela** and then heads to **Barra de Sirinhaém**, where there is a 10-km access road back to the main road.

The only lodging in these towns is with the local fisherfolk. During the week the beaches are practically deserted. Off the coast is the Ilha de Santo Aleixo.

Porto de Galinhas

Seventy km south of Recife is Porto de Galinhas (Port of Chickens). The name came as a result of the slave trade, which secretly continued after abolition. Upon hearing that the chickens from Angola had arrived, the masters of Recife knew to expect another load of slaves.

Porto de Galinhas has one of Pernambuco's most famous beaches, which curves along a pretty bay lined with coconut palms, mangroves and cashew trees. Unfortunately, there are some new housing estates creeping towards the town of Porto de Galinhas. Most of the beach, three km from town, is sheltered by a reef, but there are some waves for surfers. The water is warm and clear – you can see the colourful fish playing around your feet. There are plenty of jangadas for rent, but they're not cheap (US$3.50 per person per hour). Other boats can take you out to Ilha de Santo Alexio for US$15 per person.

Should you tire of Praia de Porto de Galinhas, head for Praia de Maracaípe, a more secluded beach three km away, which also has accommodation.

Places to Stay Many of the visitors here

either own homes (the celebrities and politicos of Pernambuco), rent for the season or camp (there's a campground at Praia de Maracaípe). If you want to stay a few days, several houses are available to rent. There are several cheap pousadas along Rua da Esperança, all within 100 metres of the beach, including *Pousada da Benedita*, *Pousada da Braz*, *Pousada Litoral* and *Pousada Meninão*. During low season, competition is keen and apartamentos go for around US$6/10 for singles/doubles, but expect to pay more than double these prices in high season (December to March). Chalets sleeping up to six people, with cooking facilities, are a good cheap option for groups – try *Chales Recanto Veraneio* (☎ 241-4199) or the more up-market *Chales Angra do Porto* (☎ 326-2533), both a short walk from town on the road to Praia Maracaípe.

Places to Eat Famed for its seafood, Porto de Galinhas has several eateries, but the town's most renowned is *Restaurant Braz*. Don't miss the lobster, cooked in coconut or tomato sauce or just plain grilled. Other fine restaurants in town include *Peixe na Telha*, on the beachfront, and *Brisa Maritima*. All these restaurants serve lobster, squid, shrimp and local fish cooked with coconut milk, pepper and cumin sauces. Try the barracas along the beach for fresh crabs. The locally made genipapo liqueur is worth tasting, too. *Bar Restaurante Itália* is recommended for Italian food.

Getting There & Away Five buses daily run to Porto de Galinhas (US$2, 1½ hours) from the Mercado São José on Avenida Dantas Barreto in Recife.

Getting Around Minibuses and VW vans serve local destinations. For a taxi, call ☎ 552-1107.

Gaibu & Cabo de Santo Agostinho

Although Gaibu is the larger town further up the coast, beach bums should head only as far as Cabo de Santo Agostinho, one of the state's finest beaches. There are facilities for snorkelling and spear-fishing. Take a walk to the ruins of the Forte Castelo do Mar, which is next to the church.

On a hill between Gaibu and Calhetas (you have to ask around for directions) there's a small, freshwater stream that's used for nude bathing.

Suape & Ilha do Paiva

Suape has been developed as an industrial port. Heading north again, Ilha do Paiva, nicknamed the island of lovers, is popular for its nude beaches. Take a boat from Barra dos Jangandas – it's worth a visit.

The mainland beaches here – Candeias, Venda Grande, Piedade – are semi-urban beaches with many barracas, hotels, and crowds on weekends. But they are still good beaches, with clean water and sometimes strong surf.

OLINDA

Beautiful Olinda, placed on a hill overlooking Recife and the Atlantic, is one of the largest and best-preserved colonial cities in Brazil. Although many of the buildings in Olinda were originally constructed in the 16th century, the Dutch burnt virtually everything in 1631. Consequently, most of what you now see has been reconstructed at a later date. For an account of Olinda's history, refer to the History section in the introduction to Recife.

While Recife plays the role of an administrative and economic centre, Olinda is recognised as its cultural counterpart: a living city with bohemian quarters, art galleries, museums, music in the streets and always some kind of celebration in the works.

Orientation

Olinda is six km north of Recife. The historical district, which constitutes about 10% of the city, is concentrated around the upper streets of the hill and is easily visited on foot. The beaches immediately adjacent to the city, Milagres for example, suffer from pollution and swimming is not recommended.

THE NORTHEAST

Olinda

0   50   100 m

THE NORTHEAST

Casa Caiada, the district at the foot of the hill, has several restaurants.

Throughout Olinda you'll no doubt hear the cry *guia* (guide). Olinda has more kids throwing their services at you than anywhere in Brazil. If you are driving with an out-of-state licence plate, wearing a backpack or dawdling in front of a church, you'll be approached. If you do take a guide, make sure the price is fixed *before* you start the tour.

Information
Tourist Office Whatever services you don't

find in Olinda you can secure in Recife (eg airline offices and car-rental agencies). The main tourist office (☎ 429 1039), at Rua do Sol 127 (in the grounds of the Hotel Pousada São Francisco), has maps, walking-tour brochures and information about art exhibitions and music performances. The office is open from 8 am to 1.30 pm Monday to Friday.

Money The Banco do Brasil is on Avenida Getúlio Vargas. Take a bus marked 'Ouro Prêto' from Praça do Carmo to the Bank Itau stop, then walk about 100 metres further north.

PLACES TO STAY

15	Pousada dos Quatro Cantos
21	Pousada Saude
22	Pousada d'Olinda
23	Albergue Pousada do Bonfim
24	Pousada Flor da Manhã
25	Albergue de Olinda
26	Hotel São Francisco Pousada & Tourist Office
41	Albergue do Sol

PLACES TO EAT

4	Oficina do Sabor
12	Restaurant Cantinho da Sé
16	Restaurant L'Atelier
29	John's Café
31	Donana
34	Mourisco
35	Creperie
37	Viva Zapata
38	Ponto 274
40	Pizzaria Leque Moleque

OTHER

1	Farol de Olinda (Lighthouse)
2	Recolhimento das Imãs
	Doretéias/Igreja NS da Conceicão
3	Igreja NS do Amparo
5	Igreja da Misericórdia
6	Observatorio Astronômico
7	Museu de Arte Sacra de Pernambuco
8	Seminário de Olinda/Igreja NS da Graça
9	Praça Dantas Barrêto
10	Convento São Francisco
11	Igreja da Sé
13	Igreja NS do Bonfim
14	Museu do Mamulenco
17	Mercado da Ribeira
18	Senado Ruins
19	Igreja da Boa Hora
20	Museu de Arte Comtemporânea
26	Tourist Office
27	Telephone Office
28	Praça do Carmo & Buses to Recife
30	Post Office
32	Atlântico
33	Igreja NS do Carmo
36	Igreja São Pedro
39	Palácio dos Governadores
42	Mosteiro de São Bento
43	Mercado Popular (Market)

Post & Telephone The main post office, on Praça do Carmo, offers a posta restante service (Cep 53001-970). International telephone calls can be made at the TELPE office nearby.

Walking Tour

Starting at Praça do Carmo, visit **Igreja NS do Carmo** (1580), which reopened recently after restoration. Then follow Rua de São Francisco to **Convento São Francisco** (1585), which is a large structure containing three elements: the convent, the **Capela de São Roque** (chapel) and the **Igreja de NS das Neves** (church) – approximate daily opening hours for these are 8 to 11.30 am and 2 to 4.30 pm.

At the end of the street, turn left onto Rua Frei Afonso Maria and you'll see the **Seminário de Olinda** and **Igreja NS da Graça** (1549) on the hill above. Daily visiting hours are from 8 to 11.30 am and from 3 to 5 pm.

Continue up the street and then onto Rua Bispo Coutinho. Climb up to **Alto da Sé**, ('Cathedral Heights'), which is a good spot to enjoy the superb views of Olinda and Recife. There are outdoor restaurants, and a small craft market with woodcarvings, figurines and jewellery. The imposing **Igreja da Sé** (1537) is open from 8 am to noon on Saturday and Sunday.

Continue a short distance along Rua Bispo Coutinho until you see the **Museu de Arte Sacra de Pernambuco** (MASPE) on your right. MASPE is housed in a building, constructed in 1696, that once functioned as Olinda's Episcopal Palace & Camara (Government Council). The museum contains a good collection of sacred art and a photographic homage to the city. It's open Tuesday to Saturday from 8 am to 2 pm.

About 75 metres further down the street, turn right into a pátio to visit **Igreja NS da Conceição** (1585).

Retrace your steps and continue down the street, now named Ladeira da Misericórdia, to **Igreja da Misericórdia** (1540), which has fine azulejos and gilded carvings inside. It's open daily from 8 to 11.30 am and 2 to 5 pm.

From here, turn right onto Rua Saldanha Marinho to see **Igreja NS do Amparo** (1613), which is currently under renovation.

Descend Rua do Amparo until you see the **Museu do Mamulenco** on your right. The museum houses a colourful collection of antique wooden puppets which chart the history of puppetry in theatre and education in the Northeast. A few doors down, at Rua do Amparo 45, is the house of Silvio Botelho, the creator of the *Bonecos Gigantes de Olinda*, giant papier-mâché puppets which are used in Carnival festivities. You should be able to pop your head in to watch him at work.

Continue along Rua do Amparo to join Rua 13 de Maio to see the **Museu de Arte Contemporânea** (MAC). This museum of contemporary art is recommended for its permanent and temporary exhibits. The museum is housed in an 18th-century *ajube*, a jail used by the Catholic church during the Inquisition – with its new paint job it's hard to imagine its grim past. It's open Tuesday to Friday from 9 am to noon and 2 to 5 pm, and on Saturday and Sunday from 2 to 5 pm.

Rua 13 de Maio continues in a tight curve to a junction with Rua Bernardo Veira de Melo and Rua São Bento. If you turn left here up Rua Bernardo de Melo, you'll come to **Mercado da Ribeira**, an 18th-century structure that is now home to art galleries and souvenir shops. If you retrace your steps down to Rua São Bento, you'll reach the huge **Mosteiro de São Bento** (1582), which has some exceptional woodcarving in the chapel. Brazil's first law school was housed here for 24 years (it's difficult to say what lawyers actually did in colonial Brazil, but it had little to do with justice). The monastery is open daily from 8 to 11 am and 2 to 5 pm.

Beaches

The city beaches are polluted, and not recommended for swimming. However, there are many excellent beaches north of Olinda, which are described later in this chapter.

Festivals

Olinda's Carnival has been very popular with Brazilians and travellers for several years (see also the Carnival section in Recife). The historic setting combined with the fact that so many residents know each other provides an intimacy and security that you don't get in the big-city Carnivals. It's a participatory Carnival: costumed blocos parade through the city dancing to frevo music and everyone else follows.

In recent years, there have been complaints of commercialisation creeping into Olinda's Carnival. On the other hand, Recife's Carnival has been getting better reviews lately. Since the two cities are so close, you could try out both of them. Publications with full information on Carnival schedules and events are supplied by the tourist office in Olinda.

Carnival in Olinda lasts a full 11 days. There are organised Carnival events, including balls (of course), a night of samba and a night of afoxé, but everything else happens in impromptu fashion on the streets. The official opening events – with the pomp and ceremony of the Olympic games – commence with a bloco of more than 400 'virgins' (men in drag), and awards for the most beautiful, the most risque and for the biggest prude.

Everyone dresses for the Carnival, so you'll want some sort of costume. The Carnival groups of thousands dance the frevo through the narrow streets. It's playful and very lewd. Five separate areas have orchestras playing nonstop from 8 pm to 6 am nightly.

Apart from Carnival, we also highly recommend the festival known as Folclore Nordestino, held at the end of August, which features dance, music and folklore from many parts of the Northeast.

Places to Stay

The main choice to make regarding accommodation is whether you want to stay in the old city, which has fewer hotels, or north of town, near the beaches at Bairro Novo or Farol. If you want to stay in Olinda during

Carnival, reserve several months in advance and be prepared for massive price hikes. During summer, prices are up to 30% higher as well.

For long stays outside high season (mid-December to March), the transport company Viagens Sob O Sol (☎ 429-3303; mobile 971-8102), at Rua Prudente de Moraes 424 (opposite Pousada dos Quatro Cantos), lets a beach apartment (capacity of five people) for US$170 per week.

Places to Stay – bottom end At the low end there are several pousadas and albergues (hostels). There are a lots of quasi-official pousadas that crop up before Carnival, which can be good deals. Albergues have dorm-style sleeping, and sometimes a few quartos and apartamentos.

For camping within easy reach of the historical district, there's *Camping Olinda* (☎ 429-1365), at Rua do Bom Sucesso 262.

The *Pousada Flor da Manhã* (☎ 429-2266), at Rua de São Francisco 162, is an old villa, previously used as a radio station, now revamped as a hotel under German/Brazilian management. Individual apartamentos are assigned names of countries and decorated accordingly. They range from the spartan 'India' with bunk beds for US$6 per person, to the more comfortable 'France', 'Peru' and 'Alemanha Romántica' (Romantic Germany – a homesick aberration?) at US$13/20, and up to US$15/25 for the 'Princesa' room. Ask about discounts for stays longer than three days; during Carnival it may be possible to sling hammocks for a minimal fee.

If you don't mind dorm-style sleeping, the *Albergue do Sol* (☎ 439-1134) is perched right on the waterfront, at Avenida Manoel Borba 300. The rooms are boxy, but the deck overlooking the ocean and the small swimming pool might make up for it. Four-bed rooms go for US$7 per person. The *Albergue de Olinda* (☎ 429-1592), at Rua do Sol 233, has clean collective rooms that sleep six people for US$6 per person. Apartamentos are also available at US$10/14 for singles/doubles.

Similar hostel lodging is provided by the *Albergue de Juventude Cheiro do Mar* (☎ 429-0101), at Avenida Marcos Freire 95. The *Albergue Pousada do Bonfim* (☎ 429-1674), at Rua do Bonfim 115-B, offers collective rooms at US$6 per person. The *Pousada Saude*, at Rua Sete de Setembro 8, is not exactly plush, but it's run by a large, chirpy family and has quartos at US$8/16 for singles/doubles.

Places to Stay – middle In the medium-price range, the *Pousada dos Quatro Cantos* (☎ 429-0220; fax 429-1845), at Rua Prudente de Morais 441, is housed in a fine colonial building with a leafy courtyard. Quartos cost around US$22/26. Apartamentos start at US$29/34; the splurge option is the suite (with two rooms plus a verandah), which costs US$38/42 for single/double occupation.

The *Pousada d'Olinda* (☎ 439-1163), at Praça João Alfredo 178, is a new up-market place with a swimming pool and garden. Quartos go for US$20/24, and apartamentos start at US$28/32.

The *Hotel Pousada São Francisco* (☎ 429-2109; fax 429-4057), at Rua do Sol 127, is a modern hotel that mostly caters for groups. Apartamentos cost US$28/33 for singles/doubles.

Places to Stay – top end For luxury sleeping, *Hotel Sofitel Olinda* (☎ 431-2955; fax 431-0670) is Olinda's five-star affair. It's north of town, on a so-so beach, with facilities for almost everything, including baby-sitting and a free bus to Recife. Room prices start at around US$90/100 for singles/doubles.

Places to Eat
The old city has a variety of restaurants tucked away in its cobbled streets – some are pricey, but there are usually a few reasonably priced dishes on the menu.

Cantinho da Sé has a great view from Alto da Sé, but it's a bit of a trap. *Ponto 274*, at Rua São Bento 274, is a garden restaurant with tasty, home-cooked fish, chicken and beef dishes for US$7 to US$10. The service is comically disorganised (our waiter spilt three drinks during our meal, mixed up several orders and changed her outfit three times!) – so it helps if you're not in a hurry. In a more expensive range is *Mourisco*, one of Olinda's best fish restaurants – although the servings are large and enough for two. A few doors away, at Rua 27 de Janeiro 65, *Viva Zapata* is a stylish Mexican restaurant open Thursday to Sunday from 7 pm to midnight. *Oficina do Sabor*, at Rua do Amparo 329, is an elegant place with views – it could be worth a splurge. The *Pousada Flor de Manha* has great-value seafood and salad dishes for around US$6 – Luís has been known to cook up a storm.

For the flavours of France, there's a cute creperie at Rua 13 de Maio 3, and Olinda's fine-dining capital, *Restaurante L'Atelier* (☎ 429-3099), at Rua Bernando Veira de Melo 91.

Down on Praça do Carmo, *John's Café* is a friendly café serving home-made pies, pastries and delicious ice cream. Nearby, *Pizzaria Leque Moleque*, on Rua Manoel Ribeiro, has great-value pizzas in a nice outdoor setting – it's a pity about the woeful 'live' music at night.

Along the beachfront opposite the post office, try *Donana*, at Praça João Pessoa 55, for Bahian food.

Out in Barra Novo, *Restaurant Taipei*, at Avenida Marcos Freire 1161, has passable Chinese food.

Entertainment

There are several music bars and a live-music venue in the old town, near Pousada Quatro Cantos, that are busy on the weekends. Alto da Sé has bars/restaurants that open late with live music.

Closer to the beach, Atlântico, on Praça do Carmo has live frevo and samba music and dancing until daylight over the weekend, or there's Pub Poco Loco, at Rua do Sol 225, and Fruta Pão, at Rua do Sol 349. A nearby nightspot for music and dancing is Las Vegas, at Avenida Marcos Freire 1571.

On Friday and Saturday nights the beach restaurant/bars north of town come to life.

The Ciranda de Dona Duda, on Janga beach, is famous for its participatory ciranda (round dance). The market at Milagres beach has a folk-music show Tuesday night.

Getting Around

Viagens Sob O Sol (☎ 429-3303, mobile 971-8102), opposite Pousada dos Quatro Cantos, has a variety of vehicles for hire, with or without guide/driver. This is an interesting option if you can form a group of four or more. Trips can be arranged to Porto de Galinhas, Itamaracá, Caruaru, Fazenda Nova (Nova Jerusalém), Olaria Brennand and various art and handicraft showrooms. Sample prices for a minibus (maximum eight passengers) are US$15 per person (minimum four) for trips along the coast to Itamaracá or Porto de Galinhas. A good deal is offered for transport to the airport – US$15 for up to five people. The company is run by two affable 'ghostbuster' look-alikes, Mauro and Felipe, who are always keen to embark on 'night sorties', trips to remote beaches or any other wild schemes!

Pousada Flor de Manhã organises several day trips each week to Porto de Galinhas and other beaches.

To/From Recife The main bus stop in Olinda is on Praça do Carmo. Buses marked 'Rio Doce/Conde da Boa Vista' and 'Casa Caiada' go to the centre of Recife. Taxis cost about US$6. From Recife, take any 'Rio Doce', 'Casa Caiada' or 'Jardim Atlantico' bus to Olinda.

To/From Boa Viagem Buses marked 'Rio Doce/Piedade' go to Boa Viagem (US$0.80).

BEACHES NORTH OF OLINDA

You've got to get out of town for a fine, clean beach. Head north to Janga beach (eight km) or at least Rio Doce (six km), and beyond to Praia do Ó (12 km), Praia do Pau Amarelo (14 km), Praia da Conceição (17 km) and Praia da Maria Farinha (23 km). The road goes along close to the beach, but don't be deterred by the ugly development beside the road: the beaches are generally undisturbed

except for barracas and crowds on weekends. Enjoy the local siri (small crab) and caranguejo (big crab) at the barracas. There are local buses to these beaches from Praça do Carmo.

IGARASSU

One of the oldest cities in Brazil, Igarassu is 35 km north of Recife and 20 km shy of Ilha de Itamaracá. Igarassu is small, untouristed and full of colonial buildings.

History

On 27 September 1535, the day of Saints Cosme and Damião, it was a busy day for town hero Duarte Coelho and his men. They managed to fight off both the Potigar Indians at the mouth of the Rio Igarassu and the French pirates offshore. Later in the afternoon, after a big meal, Duarte Coelho

founded the village, naming it São Cosme e Damião in honour of the saints. It later came to be known as Igarassu.

Information

Igarassu's tourist office (☎ 543-0435), at Praça da Bandeira 42, has brochures and beautiful free posters. It's open daily from 9 am to 6 pm.

Historic Section

Walking up the hill to the historic section, you'll find **Igreja Dos Santos Cosme e Damião**, which dates back to the foundation of Igarassu and is the oldest church still standing in Pernambuco state. Next door, on Largo São Cosme e São Damião, the **Museu Histórico de Igarassu** (city museum) displays sacred art, weapons and furniture from noble families. It's open from 8 am to 2 pm Tuesday to Sunday.

The Convento de Santo Antônio (1588), on Avenida Hermes, contains the **Museu Pinacoteca** (art museum), which has paintings depicting folk tales and popular legends. The convent and museum have recently been superbly restored and are well worth a visit. Both are open Tuesday to Sunday from 8 am to 2 pm.

Festivals

On 27 September, the Festa dos Santos Cosme e Damião celebrates the founding of Igarassu and honours its patron saints with Bumba Meu Boi and the ciranda dance (which actually originated in Itamaracá). The Festa do Côco is held during the last week of November.

Places to Stay & Eat

The *Pousada Porto Canoas* (☎ 436-2220; fax 341-4382), at Estrada da Gavoa 230 (Nova Cruz), has large bungalows sleeping up to five people. For singles or doubles, the price is US$35 including breakfast; for five people the cost is US$40 (breakfast not included).

Near the pousada, *Colina 77* has a fairly expensive international menu. In the old town, try *Ubá Refeições*, on Praça de Bandeira, or *Caminho da Ilha*, at Pe 35, for regional food and seafood.

Getting There & Away

Buses leave every 15 minutes for the 45-minute trip to Recife. The buses also stop at the Mercado Santo Amaro, between Recife and Olinda, where you can grab a bus to Olinda.

AROUND IGARASSU
Engenho Mojope

The area surrounding the town also has a few treasures. The Engenho Mojope, an old sugar estate built in 1750, has ruins of a mill, casa grande (plantation owner's mansion), chapel and slave quarters. It's now a campground belonging to Camping Clube do Brasil, and worth a stop if you're going by

car: take BR-101 3.5 km south from the Igarassu turn-off and turn right at the 'Camping Club' sign. The former plantation is one km further down the road.

Itapissuma

About 10 km from Igarassu is the small town of Itapissuma, which is worth visiting to see the Igreja São Gonçalvo do Amarante (1795), on Rua Manoel Lourenço.

ITAMARACÁ

Only 50 km from Recife, Ilha do Itamaracá is a pleasant and popular weekend beach scene. During the week it's usually empty. There is a regular bus service to the island, but getting to its many beaches takes time if you don't have a car.

Beaches

Itamaracá has a long history and a lot of beach. The better beaches are north and south of Pilar, Itamaracá's town beach. Two km north of town is Jaguaribe, a white-sand beach with barracas and reclining chairs for weekend sun worshippers. For more isolated beaches, hike five km further north along the coast to Praia Lance dos Cações and Fortinho. Immediately south of town is Praia Baixa Verde, and every three km south are more beaches: Praia Rio Ambo, Praia Forno de Cal, Praia de São Paulo and finally Praia de Vila Velha, which also is a historic old port near Forte Orange.

Forte Orange

This fort was built in 1630 by the Dutch and served as a base in a series of battles against the Portuguese colonies in Recife and Olinda. It's an impressive bastion, right on the water. There's now a four-star hotel nearby and souvenir shops rearing their ugly little heads, but during the week it's still very quiet.

Other Attractions

Just past the island's agricultural penitentiary, **Penitenciária Agricola**, is **Engenho Amparo**, an 18th-century sugar plantation. Further from town is **Vila Velha** (1526), the

SE VOCÊ NÃO SE CUIDAR A AIDS VAI TE PEGAR.

A: Drawing water, Ceará
B: Cemetery at Tatajuba, Ceará
C: Vaqueiros on the beach, Jericoacoara
D: AIDS-awareness poster, Belém
E: Cidade Velha, Belém
F: Carimbô dance, Belém

Mercado Ver-o-Peso, Belém

first port in the Northeast, and its church, **NS da Conceição** (1526). Take a VW bus to get to these and other distant points from the town of Itamaracá.

Places to Stay
The good news is that there is now some inexpensive accommodation on the island. In Pilar, the *Pousada Santa Inês* is a friendly place with quartos for US$15, single or double. In Jaguaribe, the *Pousada Rancho Ecológico*, at Avenida Rios 355 (follow the sign to Pousada Jaguaribe), is a fairly rustic place also costing US$15, single or double. Back in Pilar, the *Hotel do Marujo* (☎ 544-1157), at Rua Padre Merchado 85, has comfortable apartamentos for US$20/23.

The *Hotel Pousada Itamaracá* (☎ 544-1152), at Rua Fernando Lopes 210 (near the centre of town), is a modern hotel with a swimming pool and apartamentos at US$35/50 for singles/doubles.

Things to Buy
At Engenho São João, about 10 km in the direction of Igarassu, inmates from the agricultural penitentiary sell their products, which include lithographs and carrancas (carved figureheads).

Getting There & Away
There are 12 buses a day to the centre of Recife, also stopping at the Mercado Santo Amaro between Recife and Olinda.

PONTAS DE PEDRA
Pontas de Pedra, the last beach in Pernambuco if you're heading north, does its state proud. The reef, two km offshore, provides for calm, shallow water which is good for bathing and snorkelling.

Goiâna, 22 km in from the coast, at the junction of BR-101 and PE-49, has a few restaurants and bars, but no regular lodging.

CARUARU
If you like folk art and you wake up in Recife on a Wednesday or Saturday feeling like a day trip, you're in luck. Caruaru, South America's capital for ceramic-figurine art, is only a couple of hours away.

Feira Livre
The Feira Livre (Grand Open Fair), held in the centre of Caruaru on Wednesday and Saturday, is a hot, noisy crush of Nordestinos: vendors, poets, singers, rural and town folk, tourists, artisans and musicians. Zabumba (drum) bands are accompanied by the music of *pífanos* (vertical flutes), and *sulanqueiros* (rag merchants) hawk their scraps of clothing.

The market has become a popular tourist attraction, and many items on sale are produced for tourists. Alongside pots, leather bags and straw baskets are representations of strange beasts and mythical monsters crafted by artists as famous as Caruaru's master, Mestre Vitalino. To see the artists at work, visit Alto do Moura (described later in this section). If you want to buy some figurines, wait until you see what is offered in Alto do Moura before buying at the market.

In addition to ceramic artwork, you can hear singers and poets perform the *literatura de cordel* (literally 'string literature'): poetry by and for the people, sold in little brochures which hang from the fair stands by string (hence the name). The poems tell of political events (the death of Tancredo Neves is likened to a mother giving birth to a nation and then expiring before she can suckle her infant), national figures (Getúlio Vargas, José Sarney and Fernando Collor), miracles and festivals, as well as traditional comedies and tragedies (for example, about a woman who lost her honour to Satan). Although its role in diffusing popular culture is threatened by TV, literatura de cordel is still written, sold and performed in public by Caruaru's poets.

In a separate section of the main fair, there's the Feira do Troca-troca (Barter Market), where junk and treasure are traded.

Feira de Artesanato
This handicraft market on Parque 18 de Maio is open daily from 6 am to 5 pm.

Feira da Sulanca

This textile and clothing market, the largest in the Northeast, is set up on Parque 18 de Maio on Tuesday and Thursday.

Casa da Cultura José Condé

This cultural centre on Parque 18 de Maio contains a couple of museums. The most interesting is Museu do Forró, containing exhibits about forró, including records and musical instruments. It's open Tuesday to Friday from 9 am to noon and 2 to 5 pm, and on Saturday from 9 am to 1 pm.

Museu do Barro

This museum, containing displays of pottery produced by famous local artists, is inside the Espaça Cultural Tancredo Neves, at Praça José Vasconcelos 100. It's open from 9 am to noon and 2 to 5 pm Monday to Friday, and from 9 am to 1 pm on Saturday.

Alto de Moura

Alto de Moura, six km from Caruaru, is a small community of potters which specialises in producing *figurinhas* (figurines). Many of the potters are descendants of Mestre Vitalino, the most famous artist, who brought fame to Alto de Moura. Other noted artists are Zé Caboclo, Manuel Eudocio and Cunhado de Zé Caboclo. Museu Mestre Vitalino (Master Vitalino Museum), housed in the simple home of the master, contains his tools and personal effects. It's open from 9 am to noon and from 2 to 5 pm Monday to Saturday.

You can wander the streets and browse through dozens of workshops and galleries. If you want to buy figurines, you're better off buying here than in Caruaru.

Places to Stay

Caruaru is an easy day trip from Recife, so there's no real need to stay here overnight. There are some inexpensive hotels in town, including the *Hotel Central* (☎ 721-5880), at Rua Vigário Freire 71, and *Hotel Centenário* (☎ 721-9011), at Rua 7 de Setembro 84. Single/double apartamentos start at around US$14/18.

Places to Eat

Fortunately, there's plenty of cachaça and sugar-cane broth to quench your thirst, and local foods like dobradinhas (tripe stew), chambaril and sarapatel (a bloody goulash of pork guts) to appease your appetite. Spartan, inexpensive places for this type of food are *Bar do Biu*, at Rua Sanharó 8, and *Bar da Linguiça*, at Rua Nunes Machado 278.

If the appeal of these local foods fades, try *Barrilândia*, at Rua Silva Jardim 71. It's a good pizzeria with the feel of a Wild West saloon. On the flip side, for excellent regional cuisine in a tasteful setting, pull into *Estação Central*, at Avenida Magalhães 398.

Getting There & Away

Caruaru is linked by shuttle buses to Recife every half-hour. The trip takes two hours and costs US$4.50.

There is a daily bus service (US$1, one hour) to Fazenda Nova.

TRACUNHAÉM

If you've missed the fair at Caruaru, the next best thing, some say better, is to be in Tracunhaém for the Sunday fair. The village of Tracunhaém, 40 km from Recife in the direction of Carpina, is Pernambuco's number-two craft centre. Look for the ceramic work of master artisans Zezinho de Tracunhaem, Severina Batista and Antônio Leão.

FAZENDA NOVA & NOVA JERUSALÉM

The small town of Fazenda Nova, 50 km from Caruaru, is famous for its theatre-city reconstruction of Jerusalem, known as Nova Jerusalém. Surrounded by a three-metre-high wall with seven gateways, 70 towers and 12 granite stages, the reconstruction occupies an area equivalent to a third of the walled city of Jerusalem as it stood in the time of Jesus.

The time to visit is during Semana Santa (Holy Week, held in March or April – dates vary), when several hundred of the inhabitants of Fazenda Nova perform the Paixão de Cristo (Passion Play).

Places to Stay

There's a campground, *Camping Fazenda Nova*, at Nova Jerusalém. In the centre of Fazenda Nova, you can stay at the *Grande Hotel* (☎ 732-1137), at Avenida Poeta Carlos Pena Filho, s/n (no number), which has apartamentos costing US$18/20 for singles/doubles.

Getting There & Away

During Holy Week, there are frequent bus services direct from Recife, and travel agencies sell package tours to see the spectacle. During the rest of the year, there are daily bus connections between Fazenda Nova and Caruaru.

GARANHUNS

Garanhuns, 100 km from Caruaru and 241 km from Recife, is popular as a holiday resort because of its relatively high altitude (900 metres). It's not exactly the 'Suiça Pernambucana' (Switzerland of Pernambuco) as touted in the tourist brochures, but it does have pleasant parks and gardens, and cool air – all of which are a respite from the oppressive heat of the interior of the state.

Places to Stay & Eat

There's a campground, *Camping 13*, at Km 105 on the BR-423. The *Hotel Petrópolis* (☎ 761-0125), at Praça da Bandeira 129, has apartamentos around US$16/18 for singles/doubles. A more expensive option is the *Hotel Village* (☎ 761-3624), at Avenida Santo Antônio 149.

For an inexpensive self-service buffet lunch, try *Jardim*, at Praça Jardim 22. Fondue-lovers prepared to pay a bit extra should visit *Chez Pascal*, at Avenida Rui Barbosa 891. For regional dishes, there's *La Biritta*, at Rua Dr José Mariano 152.

Getting There & Away

There are several bus departures daily to Recife (3 hours; US$7.50).

TRIUNFO

This small town 448 km west of Recife lies at an altitude of 1000 metres. The cool climate and abundant vegetation have earned it the nickname 'cidade jardim' (garden city).

Things to See & Do

The **Museu do Cangaço** (Bandit Museum) displays a collection of weaponry and assorted personal items used by cangaçeiros, or brigands, whose most famous and fearsome leader was Lampião (described in the History section in Facts about the Country). Opening hours are 8 to 11 am and 2 to 4 pm Monday to Friday.

The town also has some fine examples of architecture: **Cine Teatro Guarany** (1922), on Praça Carolina Campos, is a stunning neoclassical piece. It's open daily from 8 am to noon.

For excursions in the region around the town, you could visit: **Pico do Papagaio**, which is a peak (1230 metres) with a great view, 10 km from town; **Cachoeira do Grito**, with a waterfall and swimming hole six km from town on the road to Flores, then one km on foot; or the pictographs at **Sítio Santo Antônio**, three km from town.

Places to Stay & Eat

The *Pousada Baixa Verde* (☎ 846-1103), on Rua Manoel Paiva dos Santos 114, has single/double apartamentos for US$10/12. The *Pousada Brisa da Serra*, at Rua Manoel Pereira Lima 185, has similar accommodation. It's also possible to order meals here; or try *Bar Guarany*, at Rua Manoel Pereira Lima, s/n (no number).

Getting There & Away

There are daily bus departures for Recife (US$12, 8 hours).

Fernando de Noronha

The archipelago of Fernando de Noronha, with a population of 1500, lies 145 km from Atol das Rocas, 525 km from Recife and 350 km from Natal. The 21 islands of the archipelago cover a total area of only 26 sq km.

In 1989, Fernando de Noronha was incorporated into the state of Pernambuco.

With its crystal-clear water (average water temperature 24°C) and rich marine life, the archipelago is a heavenly retreat for underwater pleasures. The main island is sparsely populated and tourism has become the main source of income for locals. It's now easier for independent travellers to visit, but it is possible that organised tours will be made compulsory again if numbers of visitors prove detrimental to the environment of the archipelago. Although Fernando de Noronha is now protected as a national marine park, the effects of tourism on its fragile ecosystem need to be monitored carefully (see the following History section).

Before You Go

The rainy season is from February to July and the islands' time-zone is one hour ahead of eastern Brazil. Bring everything you'll need for your stay (eg suntan lotion, insect repellent, magazines and snorkelling gear), as prices are very high due to the cost of transporting goods from the mainland. Definitely take sufficient Brazilian money with you. Don't rely on changing money on Fernando de Noronha, where the exchange facilities are virtually nil and the exchange rates are low.

History

Several hundred km off the coast from Natal, the archipelago was discovered by the Spanish adventurer and cartographer Juan de la Cosa. The islands first appeared on the maps by the name of Quaresma (which means Lent). A Portuguese expedition under the command of Fernando de Noronha sighted the islands once again in 1504. He was awarded the islands by his friend King Dom Manoel. It was the first inherited captaincy of the Brazilian colonies.

The islands, with their strategic position between Europe and the New World, were

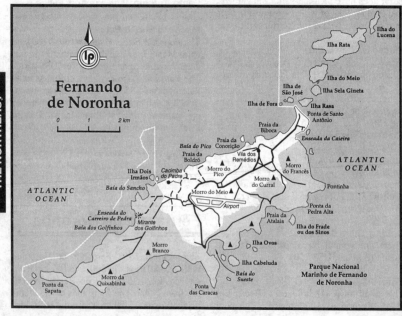

coveted by the English, the French and the Dutch who came to occupy the archipelago. But by 1557 the Portuguese managed to reclaim Fernando de Noronha and build a fortress. All that remains today of the European battles is the ruins of the fortress of NS dos Remédios and a few sunken shipwrecks.

Over the years, the islands were used as a military base by the USA during WW II, a prison, a weather station, an air base and, most recently, a tourist resort.

There has already been some misguided tampering with the island ecology. The *teju*, a black-and-white lizard, was introduced to eat the island rats which had come ashore with the Europeans in colonial days. Unfortunately, the teju prefers small birds and crab to rat.

A struggle between developers and environmentalists over the future of the island was resolved in 1988 when most of the archipelago was declared a Parque Nacional Marinho (Marine National Park) to protect the island's natural treasures. These include: 24 different species of marine birds; two species of marine tortoise – one, *tartaruga-de-pente* (*Eretmochelys imbricata*), that are in danger of extinction; sharks; stingrays; dolphins; whales; and a vast number of fish species.

Tourism has proved a blessing for the local economy and a bane for the ecosystem of the archipelago. Rapidly growing numbers of visitors have prompted locals to convert mangrove swamps into plots for the cultivation of more food, thereby depriving marine life of important breeding grounds and food sources. It has also been noted that fish have become accustomed to being fed by tourists and have taken to biting them.

Orientation

On the largest and only inhabited island, the population is concentrated in Vila dos Remédios. Although Pico hill, the highest point on the island, is only 321 metres above sea level, it is well over 4300 metres above the ocean floor, as the island is an extinct volcanic cone. The island-mountain is part of the mid-Atlantic ridge, an underwater mountain chain which is over 15,000 km long.

Information

Tourist Office Information is available from the Departamento de Meio Ambiente E Tourismo (☎ 619-1311), in the Palácio São Miguel in Vila dos Remédios. The PARNAMAR/IBAMA (☎ 619-1210) office is on Alameda do Boldró.

Money The island's one and only bank is Banco Real in Vila dos Remédios.

Post & Telephone The post office is in Vila dos Remédios. The TELPE office is in the Hotel Esmeralda do Atlântico, on Alameda do Boldró.

Emergency The Hospital São Lucas (☎ 619-1207), at Parque Flamboyant, looks after medical emergencies. The Polícia Civil (☎ 619-1432) has its headquarters at Vila do Trinta.

Travel Agencies Two of the island's better travel agencies are Dolphin Travel (☎ 619-1100), on Alameda do Boldró, and Mubatur (☎ 619-1266), also on Alameda do Boldró.

Island Rules Visitors are expected to obey the following rules:

- Don't dump rubbish or food on the ground, in the sea or on the beach.
- Don't take away or break off pieces of coral, shells or marine creatures.
- Don't use spearguns or traps.
- Don't bring any plants or animals to or from the archipelago.
- Respect areas set aside for ecological protection.
- Don't swim with the dolphins.
- Don't hunt under the water.

As mentioned in the introduction to this archipelago, tourism has already had some effect on the ecosystem, and it is hoped that observation of these rules will help redress this problem.

Beaches

Inside the boundaries of the park, IBAMA allows bathing at certain beaches, but restricts access to others to protect marine life.

The island beaches are clean, beautiful and almost deserted. The beaches of Caiera, Praia da Atalaia and Ponta das Caracas have rougher waters than Praia da Conceição. **Cacimba do Padre** beach is the only one with fresh water.

Baía dos Golfinhos (Dolphin Bay) is strictly off limits to swimmers, but access is permitted to **Mirante dos Golfinhos**, a viewpoint where you can watch hundreds of dolphins cavorting in the water every morning.

You can get to **Baía do Sancho** either by boat or by following a trail which leads through bramble and bush, past almond trees and over sharp rocks. Once at Baía do Sancho, you may be lucky enough to witness an odd meteorological phenomenon: without a cloud in sight, rain falls mysteriously on a spot of land 10 metres wide.

Diving

The Águas Claras company (☎ 619-1225) organises scuba-diving excursions with instructors (of variable quality) and will rent diving equipment. You can ask if diving is still permitted in Baía de Santo Antônio, where the *Paquistão* and *Ana Maria* wrecks lie seven metres under water. A Spanish corvette lies beneath 60 metres of water at Ponta da Sapata, the south-west tip of the island, but this area is now strictly out of bounds.

Places to Stay & Eat

The top hotel, the *Esmeralda do Atlântico* (☎ 619-1355; fax 619-1277), on Alameda do Boldró, is very expensive, and usually fully booked with package tours. There are over 40 pousadas and pensões, and many of the islanders let quartos in their private homes. Some of the recommended pousadas include: the *Canto da Sereia* (☎ 619-1200), in Vila dos Remédios; the *Pousada Da Rita* (☎ 619-1324), in Floresta Velha; the *Pousada Da Helena* (☎ 619-1223), in Vila

dos Remédios; and the *Pousada Monsieur Rocha* (☎ 619-1227), in Vila do Trinta. Rates for apartamentos start at around US$30/35 for singles/doubles, including breakfast, lunch and dinner. Quartos are about US$5 less per person.

Since accommodation prices usually include full board, restaurants are virtually nonexistent. There's a restaurant in Esmeralda do Atlântico hotel, or you could try *Restaurante e Bar Ilha Encantado*, at Conjunto Vacária. Bars on the island include: *O Mirante*, on Alameda do Boldró; *Bar do Meio*, on Praia do Meio; *Bar da Angélica* in Vila do Trinta; and *Bar da Vila*, in Vila dos Remédios.

Getting There & Away

Air Nordeste flies three times daily between Recife and Fernando de Noronha. The flight takes 1½ hours and a return ticket costs around US$290. Other options include flying from Recife to Fernando de Noronha, then on to Natal for around US$260. A return flight from Natal to Fernando de Noronha costs around US$230.

Nordeste (☎ 619-1144) is on Alameda do Boldró. The airport (☎ 619-1188) is a couple of km from the centre of Vila dos Remédios.

Tours Organised tours sold by travel agencies in Recife usually include airfare to and from Fernando de Noronha, lodging (apartamento, including full board) and guided tours of the island by land and sea. The prices per person for four/five/eight-day packages from Recife start at around US$630/710/869. Higher prices apply during high season and for apartamentos with air-con (which isn't really necessary).

Independent travellers can buy air tickets directly from Nordeste, and should have little difficulty negotiating lower prices for lodging and board on the island. This independent approach also allows travellers to pick and choose their accommodation. The accommodation included in most of the package tours is overpriced.

In Recife, Fernando de Noronha tours are packaged by Andratur and Mubatur – for phone numbers and address details, see the information section for Recife. In Rio, contact Quadratur (☎ 262-8011), and in São Paulo, contact Vista (☎ 255-7330).

Getting Around

Buggies, cars and small motorbikes are available from several operators, including Eduardo Galvão de Brito Lira (☎ 619-1355), at Esmeralda do Atlântico hotel, on Alameda do Boldró.

Boats are available from Associação Noronhense de Pescadores Anpesca (☎ 619-1449), at Vila Porto de Santo Antônio.

Paraíba & Rio Grande do Norte

Paraíba

JOÃO PESSOA
Founded in 1585, the coastal city of João Pessoa is the capital of Paraíba. It lies 120 km north of Recife, 688 km south of Fortaleza and 185 km south of Natal. While the city centre lacks flavour, Tambaú beach, seven km east, is a pleasant place to hang out for a few days.

The city is named after João Pessoa, the governor of Paraíba who formed an alliance with Getúlio Vargas to run for the presidency of Brazil in 1929. In response to advances from other political parties attempting to gain his support, João Pessoa uttered a pithy *'nego'* (I refuse), which is now given prominence in all Brazilian history books, and is emblazoned in bold letters on the state flag of Paraíba.

João Pessoa's aspirations to the vice presidency were short-lived: in July 1930 he was assassinated by João Dantas, an event which sparked a revolutionary backlash that eventually swept Getúlio Vargas to power (with considerable help from the military) in October 1930.

Orientation
The rodoviária is on the western edge of the city. The main hotel and shopping district, known as Praça, is further east; and close by is Parque Solon de Lucena, a large lake circled by trees, which locals simply call Lagoa. There are numerous bus stops here which are convenient for local transport (see the following Getting Around section), for example, to travel to the beach district of Tambaú or further up the coast to Cabo Branco.

Information
Tourist Offices PBTUR (☎ 226-7078), at Avenida Almirante Tamandaré 100, in Tambaú, provides maps and leaflets. It's inside the Centro Tourístico, diagonally opposite Tropical Hotel Tambaú. There are also tourist information stands at the rodoviária (which only opens irregularly) and at the airport.

Money Banco do Brasil is on Praça João Pessoa – a couple of doors down from Hotel Aurora. It's open from 10 am to 4 pm Monday to Friday. In Tambaú, the branch in the Centro Tourístico is open the same hours.

Post & Telephone The main post office in the centre of town is on Avenida Guedes Pereira. The main office of TELPA, the state telephone company, is at Rua Visconde de Pelotas 259.

Dangers & Annoyances João Pessoa has an odd variety of 'noisemobiles', vehicles converted to carry as many loudspeakers as possible. They cruise the streets deafening everyone with advertisements for underwear at amazing prices or airing political grievances.

Igreja São Francisco
The principal tourist attraction is the Igreja São Francisco, considered to be one of Brazil's finest churches. Construction was interrupted by successive battles with the Dutch and French, resulting in a beautiful but architecturally confused complex built over three centuries. The facade, church towers and monastery (of Santo Antônio) display a hotchpotch of styles. Portuguese tiled walls lead up to the church's carved jacaranda-wood doors. The church is open Tuesday to Saturday from 8 to 11 am and 2 to 5 pm, and on Sunday from 2 to 5 pm.

Museu Fotográfico Walfredo Rodrigues
The Walfredo Rodrigues Photographic Museum in the old Casa da Pólvora (Powder House), on Ladeira de São Francisco, has an

interesting collection of pictures of the old city. It's open daily from 7 am to noon and 1 to 5.30 pm.

Beaches

Aside from the rusty remains of battles against the French and Dutch, the beaches are clean. **Praia de Tambaú**, seven km directly east of the centre, is rather built-up, but nice. There are bars, restaurants, coconut palms and fig trees along Avenida João Maurício (north) and Avenida Almirante Tamandaré (south).

South of Tambaú is **Praia Cabo Branco**. From here it's a glorious 15-km walk along **Praia da Penha** – a beautiful stretch of sand, surf, palm groves and creeks – to **Ponta de Seixas**, the easternmost tip of South America. Clear water and coral make it a good spot for diving.

Immediately north of Tambaú, there are good urban beaches: **Manaíra**, **Praia do**

Bessa I, **Praia do Bessa II**, **Praia do Macaco** (a surf beach) and **Praia do Poço**.

Twenty km north of Tambaú are the **Forte Santa Catarina**, **Costinha** and **Camboinha** beaches.

In the past, Costinha was a centre for whale hunting, but this bloody practice should have ceased by now.

Praia Cabedelo has a couple of pousadas, restaurants and bars. Boats to **Ilha de Areia Vermelha**, an island of red sand which emerges from the Atlantic at low tide, also leave from here. In summer, dozens of boats park around the island and the party lasts until the tide comes in.

Boat Trips

Navegar Turismo (☎ 246-2191) operates excursions on a motor schooner to Areia Vermelha and Praia de Santa Catarina, and various sunset/moonlight cruises. The trips last between three and four hours.

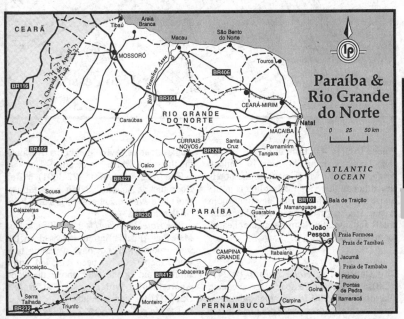

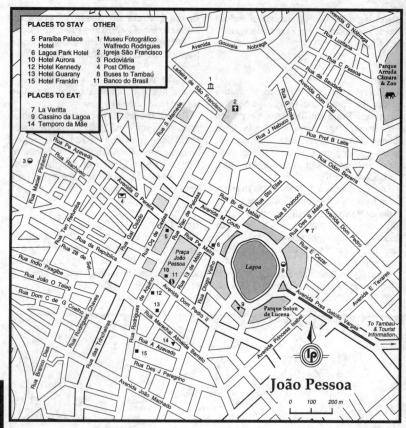

PLACES TO STAY
5 Paraíba Palace Hotel
6 Lagoa Park Hotel
10 Hotel Aurora
12 Hotel Kennedy
13 Hotel Guarany
15 Hotel Franklin

PLACES TO EAT
7 La Veritta
9 Cassino da Lagoa
14 Temporo da Mãe

OTHER
1 Museu Fotográfico Walfredo Rodrigues
2 Igreja São Francisco
3 Rodoviária
4 Post Office
8 Buses to Tambaú
11 Banco do Brasil

João Pessoa

0   100   200 m

Places to Stay – bottom end

João Pessoa's main attraction is Tambaú beach, and that's where many of the hotels are, although there are modest hotels in the centre as well. When enquiring about room prices, it's worth being persistent: some hotels will instantly claim that all the cheaper rooms are occupied.

City Centre The *Hotel Aurora* (☎ 241-3238), at Praça João Pessoa 51, has adequate quartos at US$6.50/10 for singles/doubles. Apartamentos with fan cost US$13/17.50 for

singles/doubles. Avoid the rooms overlooking the street, which can be noisy.

The *Hotel Franklin* (☎ 222-3001), at Rua Rodrigues de Aquino 293, is a basic, family-run place with quartos at US$6.50/11 for singles/doubles.

The *Hotel Guarany* (☎ 241-2308), at Rua Marechal Almeida Barreto 181, is clean, but some rooms with fan have a gaping hole where the air-con has been removed, and a similar void in the wall above the door. Apartamentos with fan start at around US$14/21 for singles/doubles.

The *Hotel Kennedy* (☎ 221-4924), at Rua

Rodrigues de Aquino 17, has apartamentos with air-con at US$14/17.50 for singles/doubles, with a sumptuous breakfast included; with fan and no breakfast, the price drops to US$6/9.

Tambaú The friendly hostel *Albergue de Juventude Tambaú* (π 226-5460) is at Rua Bezerra Reis 82. There's another hostel just south of Tambaú, at Cabo Branco: *Albergue de Juventude Cabo Branco* (π 226-3628), at Avenida Padre José Trigueiro 104.

The best deal in Tambaú is the *Hotel Pousada Mar Azul* (π 226-2660), at Avenida João Maurício 315. Huge apartamentos with a kitchen and refrigerator cost US$18, single or double. Breakfast is not included.

The *Hotel Gameleira* (π 226-1576), at Avenida João Maurício 157, has quartos (without fan) at US$14.50/15.50 for singles/doubles, and standard (with fan) apartamentos at US$15.50/20 for singles/doubles. If you want to upgrade, luxury rooms and suites are also available.

Praia de Seixas If you fancy camping at the easternmost tip of Brazil, there's a campground, *Camping-PB-01*, run by Camping Clube do Brasil at Praia de Seixas, which is about 16 km from the centre of João Pessoa.

Places to Stay – middle

City Centre The *Paraíba Palace Hotel* (π 221-3107; fax 241-2007), at Praça Vidal de Negreiros, s/n (no number), is quite an impressive colonial palace which includes a swimming pool and a restaurant. Although it is certainly a top-end hotel, its prices are currently a bargain in the middle range. The standard apartamentos start at US$35/45 for singles/doubles, and the luxury rooms cost US$50/60.

The *Hotel Lagoa Park* (π 241-1414; fax 241-1404), next to the Lagoa, at Parque Solon de Lucena 19, is a modern hotel with well-appointed rooms at US$32/42.50 for singles/doubles.

Tambaú The *Hotel dos Navegantes* (π 226-4018; fax 226-4592), at Avenida NS dos Navegantes 602, has apartamentos at US$40/44 for singles/doubles. It's close to the beach and has a swimming pool.

Places to Stay – top end

The five-star *Tropical Hotel Tambaú* (π 226-3660; fax 226-2390), at Avenida Almirante Tamandaré 229, on Praia de Tambaú, is the city's entry into the world of modern architecture. From a distance this immense edifice (part of the Varig hotel group) bears a close resemblance to a rocket launching pad. The hotel has standard singles/doubles for US$97/112, and luxury singles/doubles for US$136/156.

Places to Eat

City Centre *Cassino da Lagoa* has an open patio and a fine position beside the Lagoa. Seafood and chicken dishes are recommended. *La Veritta*, at Rua Desembargador Souto Maior 331, does good Italian food. *Temporo da Mãe*, at Rua Marechal Almeida Barreto 326, is a good bet for tasty regional dishes. *Sorveteria Tropical* is close to Hotel Guarany and serves ice cream in exotic flavours. Vegetarians can head for *O Natural*, at Rua Rodrigues de Aquino 177, but it serves lunch only.

On the 3rd floor of the *Paraíba Palace Hotel* is an excellent restaurant with an international menu. Prices here are high, but you can also simply order a beer with an appetiser or snack and enjoy the view of the weird moat and city life from the terrace.

Tambaú Rua Coração, a block back from the beachfront, near the Tropical Hotel Tambaú, is a compact restaurant strip with a variety of styles. *Adega do Alfredo*, at Rua Coração de Jesus 22, specialises in Portuguese dishes, but it's a bit of a tourist trap. *Nova China*, at Rua Coração de Jesus 100, is an inexpensive option for Chinese food. For seafood, there's *Meio Ambiente*, a cool bar and restaurant at Rua Coração de Jesus 144, or *Peixada do Duda*, at Rua Coração de Jesus 147. The ensopado de caranguejo (crab stew) here is superb.

Rosbife, opposite the Tropical Hotel

Tambaú on the corner of Avenida Olinda, is a good lunch spot with cold meats, salads and hot food priced by the kilo.

Entertainment

Nightlife in Tambaú centres around the beachfront along Rua João Maurício and Avenida Olinda, which runs off the beachfront near the Hotel Tambaú.

Bahamas, on Rua João Maurício next to the pier, is a popular meeting place and has live music on the weekend. For forró and lambada dancing in Tambaú, there's Opera Light, at Rua João Maurício 33, and Casa Blanca, at Praça Santo Antônio 22. Along Avenida Olinda, Colt, Estação and Forró Jazz are hip bars; there's usually some live music on weekends. On the corner of Avenida Almirante and Avenida Olinda, there's a small outdoor bar which caters for João Pessoa's alternative crowd – grunge types, surf rats, metal heads and punks all thrown together in the one place!

Things to Buy

Avenida Rui Carneiro, on Praia de Tambaú, has ceramic, wicker, straw and leather goods for sale. On weekends, craft stalls set up in front of Tropical Hotel Tambaú. In the city centre, Casa do Artesão Paraibano, at Rua Maciel Pinheiro 670, also has craft work for sale.

Getting There & Away

Air Aeroporto Presidente Castro Pinto (☎ 229-3200) is 11 km from the city centre. Flights operate to Rio, São Paulo and the major cities of the Northeast and the North.

The following are addresses for Brazilian airlines: Transbrasil (☎ 241-2822), at Rua General Osório 177, sala 1; Varig/Cruzeiro (☎ 221-1140), Avenida Getúlio Vargas 183; and VASP (☎ 221-3434), at Parque Solon de Lucena 530, Edifício Lago Center.

Bus The rodoviária (☎ 221-9611) is on Avenida Francisco Londres. There are frequent buses to Recife (US$3, two hours), Natal (US$4.50, 2½ hours) and Fortaleza (US$16, 10 hours). There are five daily departures running direct to Sousa (US$12.50, seven hours).

Getting Around

Bus Local buses can be boarded at the rodoviária; at the bus stop next to the main post office; and at the bus stops next to the Lagoa. Bus No 510 runs frequently to Tambaú (US$0.30, 25 minutes). Bus No 507 runs to Cabo Branco.

Taxi *Taxistas* on short hauls may try to charge tariff 2 (generally applicable at night and on Sunday) instead of tariff 1, which applies during the daytime. Take a careful look at the price table, and work out your position on the map and point out obvious 'detours'.

A taxi to the airport costs around US$18; from the rodoviária to the centre costs around US$2. To telephone a taxi, call Teletaxi (☎ 221-3187).

SOUTH OF JOÃO PESSOA
Jacumã & Praia do Sol

Thirty-five km south of João Pessoa, Praia Jacumã is a long, thin strip of beach featuring coloured sand bars, natural pools, mineral water springs and barracas.

The town's pousada, the *Valhall*, perched on a hill overlooking the ocean, is run by a group of young Swedes led by Leif, who has travelled widely in Brazil. Comfortable apartamentos cost US$15/18, with a huge Swedish/Brazilian breakfast included. In summer, there's live music in the attached bar/restaurant.

Halfway between Jacumã and João Pessoa is Praia do Sol, which is similar to Jacumã and an equally good place to relax – swaying in a hammock and sipping coconut milk in the shade.

The Buraquinho Forest Reserve, operated by IBAMA, is 10 km before João Pessoa on BR-230.

Getting There & Away There are direct buses to Jacumã from the rodoviária in João Pessoa. Travelling north from Pernambuco state on BR-101, ask to be dropped off at the

Conde/Jacumã turn-off, and take a local bus from there to Jacumã.

Tambaba

About 10 km south of Jacumã is Praia de Tambaba, the only official nudist beach in the Northeast. The beach, rated by Brazilians as among the top 10 in Brazil, is divided into two parts: one section is reserved exclusively for nudists, and the other is open to clothed bathers. To prevent problems, the nude section has public relations officers who explain the rules to bathers. There are two barracas along the beach. When the beach is crowded, men are not allowed in the nude section unless accompanied by a woman.

The Associação dos Amigos da Praia de Tambaba (Association of Friends of Tambaba) (☎ 290-1037, evenings only) can provide more information.

To Tambaba, Pousada Valhall may be able to arrange transport; otherwise it's a 1½-hour walk along the beach from Jacumã.

Pitimbu

Praia Pitimbu, 75 km south of João Pessoa, has a long, broad beach, a coconut grove, some thatched-roof houses, and a couple of bars frequented by sugar-cane farmers, fisherfolk and jangada sailmakers. There are no hotels, but if you look friendly and bring a hammock, someone will put you up for a nominal fee.

Travelling north on BR-101 from Pernambuco state into Paraíba state, there's a turn-off just after the border which leads 35 km down a rough road to Praia Pitimbu.

BAÍA DA TRAIÇÃO

Despite its peaceful, reef-sheltered waters, coconut palms and gentle breezes, Baía da Traição has a bloody past. Here in 1501, the first Portuguese exploratory expedition was slaughtered by the Tabajara Indians. In 1625 the Portuguese had it out with the Dutch, claimed victory and left some rusty cannons and the ruins of a fortress in their wake.

This fishing village, 85 km north of João Pessoa, has no regular lodging, but the beach is better than the one at Barra do Cunhaú,

which is further north along the coast, in the state of Rio Grande do Norte.

Getting There & Away

There's a partially paved turn-off to the beach on BR-101 at Mamanguape. The Rio Tinto bus company operates buses twice daily, at 5.30 am and 3 pm, from João Pessoa's rodoviária (US$2.50, two hours).

SOUSA

Sousa, 420 km west of João Pessoa, is known for an offbeat tourist attraction: dinosaur tracks. The tracks were discovered in 1920 by a geologist who was researching drought – a major preoccupation in the sertão. Later discoveries of tracks at over 13 different sites along the Rio do Peixe showed that the whole region had once been a Vale dos Dinossauros (Valley of Dinosaurs). There are at least three sites in the proximity of Sousa. The best is four km from town, at Passagem das Pedras da Fazenda Ilha, on the banks of the Rio do Peixe, where at least 50 prints have been left by dinosaurs which, judging by the depth and size of the imprints, weighed between three and four tonnes.

This site is subject to flooding during the rainy season and is best visited with a guide. Transport options are limited to either hiring a taxi at the rodoviária or asking the staff at the Hotel Gadelha Palace to arrange transport and a guide.

Travellers interested in handicrafts should make a side trip to the town of Aparecida, 14 km east of Sousa, which is famed as a centre for the production of superb hammocks, textiles, and goods made from leather and straw.

Places to Stay & Eat

The *Hotel Gadelha Palace* (☎ 521-1416), at Rua Presidente João Pessoa 2, has apartamentos for around US$18/22 for singles/doubles. There's a restaurant in the hotel, or if you hanker for pizza, try *Diagonal*, at Rua Getúlio Vargas 2.

Getting There & Away

There are six bus departures daily which run via Patos and Campina Grande to João

Pessoa (US$12.50, seven hours). Buses also depart four times daily to Juazeiro do Norte (described in the Ceará chapter).

Rio Grande do Norte

BAÍA FORMOSA

The fishing village of Baía Formosa has lovely beaches, a couple of cheap pousadas and little tourism.

Backed by dunes, Baía Formosa sweeps from the end of the village (on the southern part of the bay) to an isolated point to the north. Parts of the beach have dark volcanic rocks eroded into weird shapes by the surf. The beaches further south of town are spectacular and usually deserted. There's a couple of decent point breaks for surfers.

Places to Stay & Eat

Reservations can be made by calling the

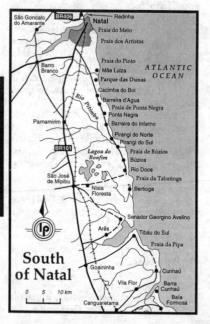

village telephone office (☎ 221-4343). The *Chalet Verde*, on Rua Jorge Gomes de Souza, is a quiet little place run by Rose, who speaks English. Rooms cost US$10/20 for singles/doubles. The *Pousada Dos Golfinhos*, at Rua Francisco Fernandes Freire 361, has a spectacular location overlooking the beach. A family of semi-tame sagú'i monkeys lives in a tree next to the small attached restaurant. Rustic quartos with fan are a bit overpriced at US$18/25 for singles/doubles. Bargaining could help here.

The *Pousada Sonho Meu*, at Rua Francisco de Melo 143, is a more up-market place, and perhaps a sign of things to come. Apartamentos with air-con and refrigerator cost US$35/40 for singles/doubles. The *Hotel Miramar*, at the end of the road by the port, is a friendly place, but the rooms are a bit dingy. Quartos cost around US$8 per person.

The *Pontinho da Vandete*, near Hotel Miramar at Praça da Conceição 137, has a 2nd-floor patio overlooking the water and serves good seafood dishes. *Pizzaria Baía dos Corais*, at Rua Manoel Francisco de Melo 195 (the main street), does excellent pizzas.

Getting There & Away

Seventeen km off BR-101 and 10 km from the Rio Grande do Norte-Paraíba border, Baía Formosa is serviced by two daily buses. The buses leave town for Natal at 5.30 am and 2.20 pm Monday to Saturday, and at 5 am and 4 pm on Sunday. Heading north, you should be able to meet the early bus at the junction of BR-101 at around 1 pm on its return to Baía Formosa. Otherwise, hitching is possible. Direct buses from Natal's rodoviária leave from Monday to Saturday at 11.30 am and 6 pm, and on Sunday at 7 am and 6 pm. The trip takes about two hours.

From the junction with BR-101, the road to Baía Formosa passes through miles of cane fields, which are often being burned off at some point. One of our authors had a close encounter with a fire in the tray of a small pickup, which nearly gave him a cropped head!

BARRA DO CUNHAÚ

Barra do Cunhaú, 10 km from Canguaretama on a dirt track, is a hybrid fishing village/resort town. You can camp in the coconut grove.

There are four buses a week, on Monday, Thursday, Friday and Saturday at 3.30 pm from Natal.

TIBAU DO SUL

The small and rocky beaches of Tibau do Sul – Praia da Madeira, Praia da Cancela and Praia da Pipa – are said to be among the finest in Rio Grande de Norte. From Goaininha, 75 km south of Natal on BR-101, there's a 20-km paved road to the coast.

Praia da Pipa

Pipa is the main attraction of Tibau do Sul and is developing into a small, laid-back resort with several pousadas, a hostel and some good restaurants and bars. The main beach is lovely, but it can get crowded on weekends. If you keep walking south of town, there are plenty more isolated beaches. Apart from beaches, there's the recently-established Sanctuário Ecológico, one km north of town, a flora and fauna reserve on 14 hectares which is trying to recreate the natural environment of the area.

Places to Stay & Eat Reservations can be made by calling the town telephone office (☎ 272-3800). The *Albergue Enseada Dos Golfinhos* is an excellent hostel just north of town. The bus can drop you there. The cheaper options in town are *My Place*, with clean apartamentos at US$9/12, and the *Pousada Tropical*. There are several midrange places (costing US$20/25 for singles/doubles), including the *Pousada da Barbara*, run by a German woman and located right on the main beach; *Gaivota*, *Oasis* and *Sito Verde* are others.

Casarão has great views overlooking the beach, and regional and seafood dishes. *Chico Mendes* is a friendly bar and restaurant with meat dishes, seafood and a wide range of salads.

Getting There & Away From the rodoviária nova in Natal, there are two daily buses to Pipa (US$2.50, two hours) from Monday to Saturday at 8 am and 3.15 pm. On Sunday, there's one bus, at 8 am. There's a daily bus from Goaininha to Pipa at 11 am. From Pipa, buses leave for Natal daily at 5 am and 4 pm. There's another bus that goes to Goaininha daily at 7.30 am.

It's possible to take a boat from Tibau across to Senador Georgino Averlino. Ask around at the port in Tibau.

SENADOR GEORGINO ALVINO TO BÚZIOS

This stretch of coast has some of the best beaches in Rio Grande do Norte, a state which has so many great beaches it's difficult to find one that's not worth raving about.

Búzios is a beach town 40 km south of Natal. The beach is nice, but the area is a bit dry and barren. A couple of hotels here cater to weekenders. The *Varandas de Búzios* (☎ 239-2121) has large chalets on the beach for US$35/50 for singles/doubles.

Resist the temptation to get off the bus at Búzios. After Búzios, the road crosses a stream and follows the coast – there's nothing here but small waves crashing against the beach, white dunes, coconut palms, uncut jungle and pretty little farms. The place is idyllic.

Getting There & Away

From Natal there are two buses a day, at 8.15 am and 4.30 pm, that go directly to Senador Georgino Alvino, but it's more fun to take a bus along the winding, cobbled coastal road. From Natal take a bus bound for Tabatinga to Búzios (one hour). Just to confuse you, weekday buses leave from the rodoviária nova at 6, 6.30 and 9.30 am, while other buses, at 10.15 am and 1.30 pm, leave from the rodoviária velha. On the weekend, all the buses leave from the rodoviária nova.

PIRANGI DO SUL & PIRANGI DO NORTE

Twelve km north of Búzios, the pretty twin beach towns of Pirangi do Sul and Pirangi do

Norte are split by a river which weaves through palm-crested dunes on its way to the ocean. It's a quiet area where wealthy folk from Natal have put up their beach bungalows. There are a few pousadas in the palm grove where the road crosses the river. The *Pousada Esquina do Sol* (☎ 238-2078) is a friendly place with apartamentos at US$15/28 for singles/doubles. Nearby is the world's largest cashew tree – its rambling sprawl of branches is over half a km in circumference, and still growing!

BARREIRA DO INFERNO

Twenty km from Natal is Barreira do Inferno (Hell's Gate), the Brazilian air force (FAB) rocket base. The base is open to visitors on Wednesday. The tour of the base includes a half-hour talk with slides and films. Intending visitors must call ☎ 222-1638, ext 202 (after 1.30 pm), at least one day in advance to reserve a place on the tour.

PONTA NEGRA

Ponta Negra is 14 km south of Natal. The beach is nearly three km in length and full of hotels, pousadas, restaurants, barracas and sailboats – at weekends the place really jumps. The water is calm towards the end of the bay and safe for weak swimmers. At the far end of the beach is a monstrous sand dune. Its face is inclined at 50° and drops straight into the sea. Bordered by jungle green, the slope is perfect for sand skiing, but there are moves to close it off to save the dune from ending up in the sea.

Evening activities consist of beer drinking and snacking at the barracas, and gazing for shooting stars and straying rockets.

Places to Stay

For camping, try *Camping Vale das Cascatas* (☎ 236-3229). There are also two hostels close together: the *Albergue de Juventude Lua Cheia* (☎ 236-3696), at Rua Estrela do Mar 2215, and the *Albergue de Juventude Verdes Mares* (☎ 236-2872), at Rua das Algas 2166.

There are dozens of pousadas and hotels. Some of the cheaper pousadas along the

beachfront include the *Pousada Bella Napoli Praia* (☎ 219-2667), at Avenida Beira Mar 3188, the *Pousada SOS Praia* (☎ 219-3330), at Rua Beira Mar 26, and *Londres Pousada* (☎ 236-2107), at Avenida Erivan Franca 11.

NATAL

Natal, the capital of Rio Grande do Norte, is a clean, bright city which is being developed at top speed into the beach capital of the Northeast. There is very little to see of cultural or historical interest: the main attractions are beaches, buggy rides and nightlife.

History

In 1535, a Portuguese armada left Recife for the falls of the Rio Ceará-Mirim (12 km north of present-day Natal) to drive out the French, who had set up trading posts in the area. Although the territory had been proclaimed by King João III of Portugal in 1534 as one of the 12 coastal captaincies, the Portuguese then abandoned the area for 60 years, until the French again began to use it as a base for attacks on the south. The Portuguese organised a huge flotilla from Paraíba and Pernambuco which met at the mouth of the Rio Potenji on Christmas Day 1597 to battle the French.

On 6 January, the day of Os Reis Magos (The Three Wise Kings), the Portuguese began to work on the fortress, which they used as their base in the war against the French. The Brazilian coastline was hotly contested, and in 1633 the fortress was taken by the Dutch, who rebuilt it in stone but retained the five-point star shape. First under Dutch and thereafter Portuguese occupation, Natal grew from the fortress, which was named the Forte dos Reis Magos.

With the construction of a railway and a port, Natal continued to develop as a small and relatively unimportant city until WW II. Recognising Natal's strategic location on the eastern bulge of Brazil, Getúlio Vargas and Franklin D Roosevelt decided to turn the sleepy city into the Allied military base for operations in North Africa.

Orientation

Natal is on a peninsula flanked to the north by the Rio Potenji and the south by Atlantic reefs and beaches. The peninsula tapers, ending at the Forte dos Reis Magos, the oldest part of the city. The city centre, Cidade Alta, was developed around the river port which was built in 1892.

Information

Tourist Office The Centro de Turismo (☎ 212-2267) in the Casa de Detenção (old prison) on Rua Aderbal Figueiredo is not very useful, though there's a fine view from the heights of this renovated prison.

The best source of information may be at the rodoviária nova (☎ 231-1170), which has a booth open daily from 8 am to 6 pm. It has maps and brochures and can book hotels. Francisco Assis de Oliveira, a hyperactive lawyer fighting part-time for truth and justice in Natal's tourist industry, is on duty there a couple of days a week. On other days his niece carries on the good work. Other sources of information are: SECTUR (☎ 221-5729), the municipal tourism authority, at Rua Trairi 563, Petrópolis (a district of

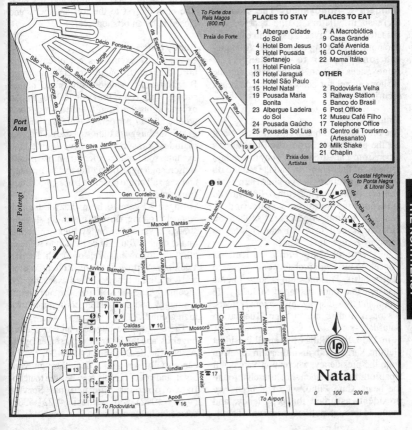

PLACES TO STAY	PLACES TO EAT
1 Albergue Cidade do Sol	7 A Macrobiótica
4 Hotel Bom Jesus	9 Casa Grande
8 Hotel Pousada Sertanejo	10 Café Avenida
11 Hotel Fenícia	16 O Crustáceo
13 Hotel Jaraguá	22 Mama Itália
14 Hotel São Paulo	
15 Hotel Natal	**OTHER**
19 Pousada Maria Bonita	2 Rodoviária Velha
23 Albergue Ladeira do Sol	3 Railway Station
24 Pousada Gaúcho	5 Banco do Brasil
25 Pousada Sol Lua	6 Post Office
	12 Museu Café Filho
	17 Telephone Office
	18 Centro de Turismo (Artesanato)
	20 Milk Shake
	21 Chaplin

Natal

0   100   200 m

THE NORTHEAST

Natal just east of the centre) – open from 9 am to noon and 2 to 6 pm, Monday to Friday, and EMPROTURN (☎ 219-3400), in the Convention Centre on Avenida Dinarte Mariz (Ponta Negra), open Monday to Friday from 9 am to 1 pm.

Money Banco do Brasil is at Avenida Rio Branco 510. It's open from 10 am to 4 pm Monday to Friday.

Post & Telephone The main post office is at Avenida Rio Branco 538. The telephone office is at the intersection of Avenida Prudente de Morais and Jundiai.

Dangers & Annoyances The dramatic increase in visitors to the beaches has attracted petty thieves. There's no cause for paranoia, but you should take the usual precautions – refer to the Dangers & Annoyances section in the Facts for the Visitor chapter for general advice on beach security.

Things to See

The principal non-beach attractions of Natal are the pentagonal **Forte dos Reis Magos** (open from 7 am to 5 pm Tuesday to Sunday) at the tip of the peninsula, and the **Museu da Câmara Cascudo**, at Avenida Hermes da Fonseca 1400. This museum of folklore and anthropology features a collection of Amazon Indian artefacts. It's open on Monday from 1 to 4 pm and Tuesday to Saturday from 8 am to 4 pm.

The **Museu Café Filho**, at Rua da Conceição 601, will probably only appeal to history buffs. This museum is housed in the mansion that once belonged to João Café Filho, and now displays his personal effects. It's open from 8 am to 5 pm Tuesday to Saturday.

In 1954, the military presented President Getúlio Vargas with an ultimatum to resign from the presidency, whereupon Vargas left a patriotic note and then shot himself through the heart. Café Filho, who had been vice president, assumed the presidency, and muddled through political crises until he suffered a major heart attack in 1955 and gave way to Carlos Luz. Although Café Filho recovered quickly and tried hard to be reinstated, he'd missed his turn on the political carousel and had to be content with his brief moment of fame as the first person from the state of Rio Grande do Norte to become a president.

Beaches

Natal's city beaches – **Praia do Meio**, **Praia dos Artistas**, **Praia da Areia Preta**, **Praia do Pinto** and **Praia Mãe Luiza** – stretch well over nine km, from the fort to the Farol de Mãe Luiza lighthouse. These are mostly city beaches, with bars, nightlife and big surf. The ones closest to the fort are rocky and closed in by an offshore reef.

Buggy Rides

Beach-buggy excursions are offered by a host of *bugeiros* (buggy drivers), mostly in Brazilian-built vehicles with brand names such as Bird, Baby, Praya or Malibuggy. An excursion lasting from 8 am to 4 pm costs around US$17 per person with four passengers in the buggy (a tight squeeze). The price includes transport and driver/guide, but excludes food and ferry fees (minimal). Take sunscreen, a tight-fitting hat and swimwear; and keep all photo gear in a bag as protection from sand.

Bugeiros seem to be a crazy bunch of wannabe racing drivers intent on demonstrating a variety of buggy tricks and spins on the dunes. You may be treated to some or all of the following: Wall-of-Death, Devil's Cauldron, Vertical Descent, Roller-Coaster, and something best described as Racing the Incoming Tide – if you lose, the surf claims the buggy and the passengers scramble for high ground.

There are pirate bugeiros and accredited bugeiros, and the latter are represented by the Associação de Bugeiros (☎ 225-2077). You can usually arrange a deal through your hotel, and youth hostels may be able to negotiate a discount. International Service (☎ 211-4092) and Affitasi (☎ 221-5385) seemed reliable outfits.

Although Brazilians and foreigners clearly have a fun time zooming around in buggies, the more remote beaches don't exactly benefit from the commotion and erosion. The coastline close to Natal has been claimed by bugeiros, but in years to come there may be a move to protect beaches further afield from their impact.

Places to Stay

Natal's hotel areas are around Cidade Alta (in the city centre) and along the city beaches. Ponta Negra, 14 km south of the city, also has some low-budget options. See the Places to Stay section in Ponta Negra.

City Centre There's a good central hostel, the *Albergue Cidade do Sol* (☎ 211-3233), near the rodoviária velha, at Avenida Duque de Caxias 190. They also have apartamentos for US$9 per person. Close by is the friendly and security-conscious *Hotel Bom Jesus* (☎ 212-2374), at Avenida Rio Branco 374. Clean quartos go for US$9.50/11.50 for singles/doubles, and apartamentos cost US$13/15 for singles/doubles.

The *Hotel Natal* (☎ 222-2792) has standard apartamentos at US$12/16 for singles/doubles, but better value are its apartamentos with air-con at US$14/18 for singles/doubles. Another budget option is the *Hotel Fenícia* (☎ 211-4378), at Avenida Rio Branco 586, although it's looking a bit the worse for wear. It's apartamentos cost US$15/20 for singles/doubles, but breakfast is not included. The *Hotel São Paulo* (☎ 211-4130), at Avenida Rio Branco 697, has apartamentos at US$10/15 for singles/doubles. Readers have recommended the *Pousada O Meu Canto*, at Rua Manoel Dantas 424, which is run by a friendly woman and functions like a hostel.

The *Hotel Pousada Sertanejo* (☎ 221-5396), at Rua Princesa Isabel, is stylish and moderately priced, with apartamentos with fan at US$15/22 for singles/doubles. The three-star *Hotel Jaraguá* (☎ 221-2355; fax 221-2351), at Rua Santo Antônio 665, has a sauna, swimming pool and panoramic view

from the 17th floor. Apartamentos cost US$46/53 for singles/doubles.

City Beaches There's a nifty hostel, the *Albergue de Juventude Ladeira do Sol* (☎ 221-5361), at Rua Valentim de Almeida, on Praia dos Artistas. Next door, the *Pousada Ondas do Mar* (☎ 211-3481) has adequate apartamentos at US$11/19 for singles/doubles. The *Pousada Gaúcho* (☎ 222-9904), at Avenida Governador Silvio Pedroza 136, has apartamentos at US$15/28 for singles/doubles, including breakfast and either lunch or dinner. The meals are home-cooked, wholesome and generous. A little further along the beachfront, the *Pousada Sol Lua* (☎ 212-2855), at Avenida Governador Silvio Pedrosa 146, is a friendly place with four-bed collective rooms for US$8 per person.

The *Pousada Maria Bonita* (☎ 222-3836; fax 211-2724), at Rua Feliciano Coelho 10, is a quiet place with comfortable apartamentos at US$22, single or double.

Places to Eat

For natural food, you can head for *A Macrobiótica*, on Rua Princesa Isabel, where the healthy atmosphere is exemplified by staff running around in white coats!

O Crustáceo, at Rua Apodi 414, specialises in seafood. The ambience is enhanced by a large tree poking through the roof in the centre of the restaurant. Coffee enthusiasts should get their caffeine fix at *Café Avenida*, on Avenida Deodoro. It also serves a delicious selection of pastries and cakes. The *Casa Grande*, at Rua Princesa Isabel 529, is a stylish place with regional food.

Mama Itália, at Rua Silvio Pedrosa 43, has a wide range of excellent pastas and pizzas. The spaghetti fruta do mar (US$10) is chock full of seafood and is delicious. The *Pousada Gaúcho* does great-value home-cooked meals.

Rio Grande do Norte boasts a few good brands of cachaça. Try a shot of Ohlo d'Água, Murim or Caranguejo with a bite of cashew fruit.

THE NORTHEAST

Entertainment

Chaplin is a pricey and popular bar on Praia dos Artistas. Across the road, Milk Shake may look like a McDonald's outlet, but there's good live music most nights and a lively dancefloor.

For folkloric shows and dancing, try Zás-Trás, at Rua Apodi 500, in the Tirol district. Inexpensive food is served in the restaurant section and the shows start at around 8 pm. After the show, the dancers will teach guests dances such as forró, *ciranda de roda* (round dancing) and something called *aeroreggae*. From 11 pm onwards, the dancefloor gets crowded and the action hots up.

Getting There & Away

Air There are flight connections to all major cities in the Northeast and the North, and to Rio and São Paulo.

Airline offices are in the Cidade Alta are: VASP (☎ 222-2290), at Avenida João Pessoa 220; Varig/Cruzeiro (☎ 221-1537), at Avenida João Pessoa 308; and Transbrasil (☎ 221-1805), at Avenida Deodoro 363. Nordeste (☎ 272-3131) has an office at the airport.

Bus There is one daily departure to Salvador at noon (US$27.50, 18 hours); six daily buses to Recife (US$7.50, 4½ hours); frequent departures to João Pessoa (US$4, 2½ hours); and three regular buses (US$17, eight hours) and one leito (US$26.50) departing daily to Fortaleza. A bus departs daily at noon for Rio (US$63, 44 hours). There are eight daily departures to Mossoró (US$6.50, 4½ hours); and one departure daily for Juazeiro do Norte (US$12.50, nine hours).

Getting Around

To/From the Airport Natal's Augusto Severo airport (☎ 272-2811) is 15 km south of town on BR-101. Bus 'A-Aeroporto' runs between the airport and the rodoviária velha (old bus station), in the city centre. The taxi fare to the city centre is around US$11.

To/From the Rodoviária The rodoviária nova (☎ 231-1170), the new bus station for long-distance buses, is about six km south of the city centre. Bus Nos 38 and 20 connect the rodoviária nova with the rodoviária velha (old bus terminal), which is on Praça Augusto Severo, in the city centre. The taxi fare to the centre is around US$3.50. Bus Nos 21 and 38 are useful for getting to Praia dos Artistas.

To/From the Beaches The rodoviária velha is the hub for bus services to: the airport (Bus 'A'); the rodoviária nova; city beaches, such as Praia dos Artistas; beaches further south, such as Ponta Negra (Nos 46 and 54) and Pirangi; and beaches in the north, as far as Genipabu.

A taxi from the centre to Praia dos Artistas costs around US$3, while to Ponta Negra it's about US$10.

NORTH OF NATAL

The beaches immediately north of Natal, where sand dunes plunge into the surf, are beautiful, but not quite as spectacular as the southern beaches.

Praia Redinha

Twenty-five km by road north of Natal, Praia Redinha features 40-metre-high dunes, a good view of Natal, lots of bars and *capongas* (freshwater lagoons).

Genipabu

Five km further north is Genipabu, where golden sand dunes, palm trees and dune buggies converge on a beach lined with numerous barracas, pousadas and restaurants. It's a popular, crowded place where you can swim, toboggan down the dunes, or take a half-hour jangada trip (US$3 per person).

Places to Stay Amongst the cheapest of the area's pousadas are the *Casa de Genipabu* (☎ 225-2141) and the *Pousada Marazul* (☎ 225-2065). The *Pousada Villa do Sol* (☎ 225-2132) is a more up-market place with a swimming pool, but they will discount heavily during the week.

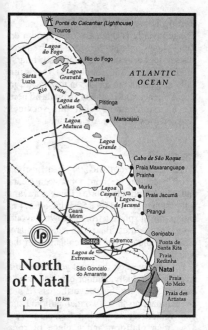

sumptuous lunchtime rodízio do mar (seafood buffet) for US$15 per person.

Marina's Jacumã, on Praia Jacumã, is under the same management and offers similar deals. Just inland from Praia Jacumã is Lagoa de Jacumã, a large lagoon where there is a small hut that serves superb lagosta na brasa (grilled lobster tails on a skewer) for US$3.

Getting There & Away Viação Rio Grandense buses from Natal's rodoviária nova service the area. Buses leave for Maxaranguape at 11 am, and 3.45 and 5.45 pm; to Jacumã at 3 pm; and Pitangui at 8 and 10 am, and 2 and 4.30 pm.

Touros
Eighty-three km north of Natal is Touros, a fishing village with several beaches, bars and a couple of cheap pousadas. It's a convenient base for exploring isolated beaches to the north, such as São Miguel do Gostoso and Praia do Cajueiro.

Places to Stay & Eat The *Hotel Atlântica* (☎ 263-2218), at Avenida Atlântica 4, has friendly management and apartamentos at $US14/28. The *Vila de Touros* (no phone), at Avenida Professor José Américano 51, offers similar accommodation. *O Castelo*, on Avenida Atlântica, serves local seafood.

Getting There & Away Buses leave from the rodoviária nova in Natal for Touros daily at 7 and 10 am and 4 pm.

AREIA BRANCA
The town of Areia Branca, 50 km from Mossoró and BR-304, is a small fishing port. It's possible to visit the super-modern salt docks 25 km away, but only with advance notice.

The hotel *Areia Branca Praia* (☎ 332-2344) is right on Upanema, the town beach. Apartamentos start at around US$12/18 for singles/doubles.

Getting There & Away Buses to Genipabu and Redinha leave Natal regularly from the rodoviária velha. Bear in mind the bus to Genipabu drops you about 1.5 km from the beach.

Praia Jacumã to Praia Maxaranguape
A coastal road is being built which will head north from Genipabu towards praias Jacumã, Muriú, Prainha and Maxaranguape. These are little, palm-graced bay beaches separated from one another by rivers and hills. The beaches are readily accessible, but off the beaten track. Muriú and Prainha (still undeveloped) are especially nice.

Places to Stay & Eat *Marina's Muriú* (☎ 228-2001, 221-1741), on Praia Muriú, has apartamentos at US$10/18 for singles/doubles. The owner will also rent out beach houses for longer stays. The pousada has a large restaurant outside which serves a

MOSSORÓ

To break the trip between Natal and Fortaleza, you might want to visit this town on the fringe of the sertão. About four km out of town there are hot springs at the *Hotel Termas de Mossoró*. The hotel is expensive, but you may be able to pay a small fee just to use the springs.

The Museu Histórico, at Praça Antônio Gomes 514, has all sorts of personal effects, weapons and documents connected with Lampião and his bandit colleagues, who attacked Mossoró in 1924. It's open from 8 am to 8 pm Tuesday to Friday; from 8 to 11 am and 1 to 5 pm on Saturday; and from 8 to 11 am on Sunday. For more details about Lampião, see the History section in the Facts about the Country chapter.

Money

The Banco do Brasil, on Praça Vigário Antônio Joaquim, changes money.

Places to Stay

For rock-bottom prices, try the *Hotel Zinelandia* (☎ 321-2949), at Praça São Merchado 89. The *Scala Hotel* (☎ 321-3034), at Rua Dionisio Figueira 222 (in the shopping arcade), has adequate apartamentos at US$11/14 for singles/doubles. The *Pousada Cooptur* (no phone), at Praça Antônio Joaquim 25, has apartamentos at US$15/25 for singles/doubles.

Getting There & Away

The rodoviária is three km out of town on Rua Felipe Camarão. Mossoró has frequent bus services to Natal (US$6.50, four hours) and Fortaleza (US$6, four hours). Buses run daily at 5 and 8 am and noon to Aracati, in Ceará (for access to Canoa Quebrada). There are also infrequent local bus services between Mossoró and Areia Branca.

TIBAÚ

Tibaú, 25 km from BR-304, is a bustling resort beach on the border between Ceará and Rio Grande do Norte. Truck caravans roll past the surf into Ceará, saving a few km and giving the place a frontier-town flavour. Locals sell bottles filled with sand in many different colours that they collect from the beach.

Four km west on the coast you come to a river and a friendly outdoor bar. The river's current is swift, but nevertheless it's a popular bathing spot. Two men pull you and your vehicle across on a low-tech car ferry – a wooden platform and a piece of rope pegged to both banks. Between ferry duty, the float serves as a diving platform for the bathers.

Follow the caravan of trucks. The coast from Tibaú (Rio Grande do Norte) to Ibicuitaba (Ceará) can be negotiated at low tide. From Ibicuitaba, the road is paved again.

Ceará, Piauí & Maranhão

Ceará

Ceará's pride and glory is its coastline – nearly 600 km of glorious beaches. The beach in this part of the Northeast engenders a special way of life. In nearly all of the small beach towns, the people of Ceará live out their folklore every day of the year. They make old-fashioned lacework and handicrafts, cook according to traditional recipes, sleep in hammocks, sail out on jangadas to catch fish and live in thatched-roof homes.

Should you stray inland into the sertão, you will see a rugged, drought-plagued land, a bleak landscape of dust and caatinga, peopled by vaqueiros (cowboys) who rely on their cattle for almost everything. The dried meat serves as food, tools are fashioned from the bones, and the hides provide clothing – nothing is wasted. For a complete contrast, visit the Serra de Baturité, a small chain of hills south-west of Fortaleza, which features an agreeable climate and coffee and banana plantations.

For all its size and wealth of culture, much of Ceará is poor and undeveloped. Poverty and disease are rampant and dengue and yellow fever are endemic.

FORTALEZA

Fortaleza is now a major fishing port and commercial centre in the Northeast. The tourist attractions of the city include a small historical section, a large selection of regional handicrafts, and a growing nightlife scene along Praia de Iracema and Praia do Meireles. Although the city beaches are not very clean, there are some super beaches 20 km beyond the city limits in either direction.

History

According to some revisionist Cearense historians, the Spanish navigator Vicente Yanez was supposed to have landed on Mucuripe beach on 2 February 1500, two months before Pedro Álvares Cabral sighted Monte Pascoal, in Bahia. Despite this early claim to fame, it was only in 1612 that the first colonisers sailed from the Azores to settle on the banks of the Rio Ceará.

The settlement at present-day Fortaleza was hotly contested: it was taken over by the Dutch in 1635, then, in turn, lost to the Tabajara Indians. In 1639, the Dutch under the command of Matias Beck landed once again, fought off the Indians and constructed a fortress. In 1654 the Portuguese captured the fortress and reclaimed the site. A town grew around the fortress, which was given the name of Fortaleza de NS da Assunção (Fortress of Our Lady of Assumption). Fierce battles with the local Indians continued to delay colonisation for many years.

Orientation

The city is laid out in a convenient grid pattern. The centre lies above the old historical section and includes the Mercado Central (Central Market), the sé (cathedral), and major shopping streets and government buildings.

East of the centre are the beaches of Praia de Iracema and Praia do Ideal; then continuing eastwards, Avenida President Kennedy (also known as Avenida Beira Mar) links Praia do Diário and Praia do Meireles, which are lined with high-rise hotels and restaurants. Beyond here are Porto do Mucuripe (the port) and the Farol Velha (Old Lighthouse). Praia do Futuro begins at the lighthouse and extends five km southwards along Avenida Dioguinho to the Clube Caça e Pesca (Hunting & Fishing Club).

Information

Tourist Office Coditur (☎ 253-1522), the state tourism organisation, has its head office in the Secretária De Industrio e Comércio (2nd floor, room 270), at Rua Castro e Silva 81. The branch office in the Centro de

Turismo (☎ 231-3566), at Rua Senador Pompeu 350 – inside a renovated prison – has stacks of information and can help with booking accommodation, tours to the beaches and details on bus transport. The Centro de Turismo is open every day from 7 am to 6 pm.

There are also Coditur booths at the airport (open 24 hours) and the rodoviária (open daily from 6 am to 10 pm).

Fortur (☎ 265-1177), the municipal tourism organisation, at Avenida Santos Dumont 5336 (Room 302), can give up-to-date information on local craft markets.

A tourist information telephone service, Disque Turismo (Dial Tourism), is also available – just dial ☎ 1516.

Money Banco do Brasil has a convenient branch in the city centre, on Rua Floriano Peixoto, open from 10 am to 3 pm Monday to Friday. In Meireles, there's a branch on Avenida Abolicão, open the same hours. The exchange counter in the Centro de Tourismo gives the same rate as the banks, and is open from 8 am to 5 pm Monday to Friday, and 8 am to noon on Saturday.

Ceará, Piauí & Maranhão

Post & Telephone The main post office in the centre is on Rua Floriano Peixoto. Teleceará, the state telephone company, has a convenient office in the city centre, at the intersection of Rua Floriano Peixoto and Rua Dr João Moreira. Other useful phone stations are at the airport (open 24 hours) and the rodoviária (open from 7 am to 10 pm).

Travel Agency Hoje Turismo (☎ 226-8293), at Rua Major Facundo 52, has friendly staff and competitive prices for national and international ticketing.

Dangers & Annoyances Travellers have reported pickpocketing in the city centre and petty theft on the beaches.

We also heard reports about solicitous females on Praia do Meireles who cuddle up to travellers, drug their drinks and relieve them of their valuables.

Museums

The **Centro de Turismo**, at Rua Senador Pompeu 350, is a restored prison which now contains a folk museum, tourist information office and shops selling artesanato. The **Museu de Arte e Cultura Popular** (folk museum) houses a variety of interesting displays of local handicrafts, art and sculpture. It's open from every day from 7 am to 6 pm.

The **Museu Histórico e Antropológico do Ceará**, a museum devoted to the history and anthropology of Ceará, is at Avenida Barão de Studart 410. A bizarre exhibit here is the crushed wreckage of a light plane, which is a reminder of the murky politics associated with military rule in Brazil during the '60s. In 1964, the Cearense Castello Branco, a hardcore right-winger from the military, organised a military coup to oust João Goulart, whom he accused of leftist politics, from the presidency, and then assumed the presidency himself. Disgusted democrats shed few tears when Castello Branco was killed in a plane crash outside Fortaleza in 1967 – hence the wreckage outside the museum.

The museum is open from 8 am to 5 pm Monday to Friday, and from 8 am to 2 pm on Saturday.

Car enthusiasts will want to visit the **Museu do Automóvel** (Veteran Car Museum), at Avenida Desembargador Manoel Sales de Andrade 70, in the Água Fria district on the southern edge of the city. The museum displays a variety of veteran cars including Buicks, Pontiacs, Cadillacs and Citroens. It's open Tuesday to Sunday from 8 am to 5 pm.

Teatro José de Alencar

The José Alencar Theatre (1910) is an impressive building; a pastel-coloured hybrid of classical and art-nouveau architecture which was constructed with cast-iron sections imported from Scotland. It is now used for cultural events.

Beaches

Fortaleza's city beaches are generally less than clean, with the exception of Praia do Futuro, but the locals don't seem to worry about it, so you can make up your own mind. There are clean beaches within 45 minutes of town (1½ hours or so by public transport), but the best beaches all lie further away from Fortaleza.

Near Ponte Metálica, the old port, **Praia de Iracema** was a source of inspiration to Luís Assunção and Milton Dias, Ceará's Bohemian poets of the '50s – some of this atmosphere lives on in a few bars and restaurants around Rua Dos Tabajaras. Ponte Metálica has been recently restored, and includes cafés, a space for art exhibitions and an outdoor music stage which has occasional free concerts. There's a lovely promenade along the waterfront and a capoeira school often practices here in the evenings. Unfortunately, the beach is now polluted and not recommended for swimming.

Praia do Meireles is also tainted with pollution and not safe for bathing, but it fronts Avenida President Kennedy, which is a hotel and restaurant strip and also a popular place to hang out in the evening.

Praia do Futuro is a clean length of sand that stretches five km towards the south along Avenida Dioguinho to the Clube Caça e Pesca. It is the best city beach. Like Rio de Janeiro's Barra de Tijuca, it is being built up at an alarming rate. There are barracas here which serve fried fish and shrimp. On Thursday night, there's live forró along the beach and comedy shows in some of the bars.

The beaches immediately north of Fortaleza, **Cumbuco** and **Iparana**, are both pleasantly tranquil. Harried travellers can relax, string up a hammock in the shade of the palm trees, sip coconut milk and rock themselves to sleep.

Parque Ecológico do Côco

This park, close to Shopping Center Iguatemi, was set up in 1991 after local ecological groups pressed for protection of the mangrove swamps from encroaching highways and the industrial zone. Entrances to the park, which is about seven km from the centre, are on Avenida Engenheiro Santana and Rua Vicente Leite. From the centre, take the bus marked 'Edison Quieroz' to Shopping Center Iguatemi, which is opposite the park.

Organised Tours

There are several tours available from Fortaleza, mostly to beach destinations such as Beach Park, Lagoinha, Jericoacoara, Canoa Quebrada, Morro Branco, Iguape and Prainha. Although there are regular bus services to all these places, the tours can be a good idea if you don't have time to arrange your own transport or don't want to stay overnight at the beach towns.

The tour prices include transportation only. Some sample per-person prices are: Beach Park, US$6; Morro Branco, US$10; Iguape, US$12; Lagoinha, US$18; and Canoa Quebrada, US$18.

Coditur can give up-to-date advice on reliable agencies. Recommended operators

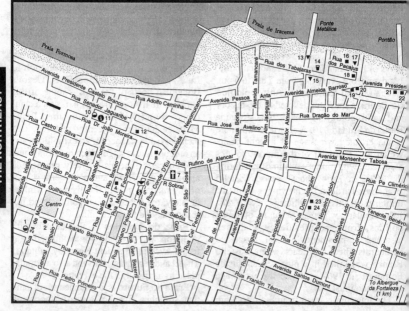

include: Ernanitur (☎ 244-9363), at Avenida Barão de Studart 1165; Valtur (☎ 231-9157), at Avenida Monsenhor Tabosa 1078 (Praia de Iracema); Egoturismo (☎ 221-6461), at Rua Barão de Aracati 644; and Petritur (☎ 261-8999), at Avenida Desembargador Moreira 2033.

Festivals

The Regata de Jangadas, a jangada regatta between Praia do Meireles and Praia Mucuripe, is held in the second half of July.

The Iemanjá festival is held on 15 August at Praia do Futuro. The Semana do Folclore, the town's folklore week, takes place from 22 to 29 August.

Places to Stay – bottom end

City Centre The *Albergue de Juventude da Fortaleza* (☎ 244-1850), at Rua Rocha Lima 1186, is good, but it's in Aldeota district, a long way from the centre and the beaches.

There are a few dives along Rua Senador Pompeu – the street is also home to many funeral parlours. Shop around for cleanliness not price, and check that you're not paying by the hour. The *Hotel Moreira* (☎ 252-4665) has quartos/dungeons at US$12/17 for singles/doubles. The *Hotel Passeio* (☎ 252-2104), at Rua Dr João Moreira 221, has reasonable apartamentos with fan at US$18/24 for singles/doubles.

A good budget option between the centre and the beaches is the friendly and clean *Pousada Do Tourista* (☎ 226-5662), at Rua Dom Joaquim 351, with quartos at US$10/20/24 for singles/doubles/triples. Nearby, the *Hotel Savoy* (☎ 226-8426), at Rua Dom Joaquim 321, has apartamentos (with fan) at US$18/25 for singles/doubles.

City Beaches Praia de Iracema is generally less expensive for accommodation than Praia do Meireles, and a more interesting

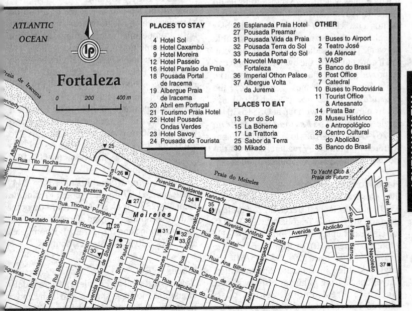

PLACES TO STAY		OTHER
4 Hotel Sol	26 Esplanada Praia Hotel	1 Buses to Airport
8 Hotel Caxambú	27 Pousada Preamar	2 Teatro José
9 Hotel Moreira	31 Pousada Vida da Praia	de Alencar
12 Hotel Passeio	32 Pousada Terra do Sol	3 VASP
16 Hotel Paraíso da Praia	33 Pousada Portal do Sol	5 Banco do Brasil
18 Pousada Portal	34 Novotel Magna	6 Post Office
de Iracema	Fortaleza	7 Catedral
19 Albergue Praia	36 Imperial Othon Palace	10 Buses to Rodoviária
de Iracema	37 Albergue Volta	11 Tourist Office
20 Abril em Portugal	da Jurema	& Artesanato
21 Tourismo Praia Hotel		14 Pirata Bar
22 Hotel Pousada	PLACES TO EAT	28 Museu Histórico
Ondas Verdes	13 Por do Sol	e Antropológico
23 Hotel Savoy	15 La Boheme	29 Centro Cultural
24 Pousada do Tourista	17 La Trattoria	do Abolicão
	25 Sabor da Terra	35 Banco do Brasil
	30 Mikado	

THE NORTHEAST

area to explore. The *Albergue de Juventude Praia de Iracema* (☎ 252-3267), at Avenida Almeida Barroso 998, on Praia de Iracema, is a convenient distance from the centre. The *Albergue de Juventude Volta da Jurema* (☎ 244-1254), at Rua Frei Mansueto 370, is less comfortable, but close to the glitz of Praia do Meireles.

The *Pousada Portal de Iracema* (☎ 261-5767), at Rua Dos Ararius 2, is a colourful place with freshly painted, clean quartos at US$10/17.50 for singles/doubles, and comfortable apartamentos with air-con and refrigerator for US$24/30. The *Abril em Portugal* (☎ 231-9508), at Avenida Almirante Barroso 1006, has apartamentos at US$11/14 for singles/doubles. Downstairs is a good restaurant. The *Hotel Pousada Ondas Verdes* (☎ 226-0871), at Avenida Beira Mar 934, has bright double apartamentos at US$20/30 (with sea view), or US$15/25 with refrigerator and fan (check that the room has all the windows it's supposed to).

The *Pousada Portal do Sol* (☎ 261-5767), at Rua Nunes Valente 275, close to Praia do Meireles, is recommended. Massive apartamentos cost US$25/30 for singles/doubles (check out the twin vanities and double shower). The pousada has a swimming pool, and if convenient for the owner, transport can be provided from the airport or rodoviária. Close by, at Rua Nunes Valente 245, the *Pousada Terra do Sol* (☎ 261-9509) has clean apartamentos with fan at US$15/30 for singles/doubles. The *Pousada Vida da Praia* (☎ 261-0444), at Rua José Vilar 252, has been recommended by readers, with apartamentos at US$20/25 for singles/doubles.

Places to Stay – middle

City Centre The *Hotel Caxambú* (☎ 231-0339), at Rua General Bezerril 22, has clean apartamentos (with frigobar) at US$25/35 for singles/doubles. The *Hotel Sol* (☎ 211-9166; fax 252-4610), at Rua Barão do Rio Branco 829, charges US$45/50 for singles/doubles in standard apartamentos. Travellers aspiring to higher office will take the Suite Presidencial, which costs US$135/150 for single/double occupancy.

City Beaches The *Hotel Paraíso da Praia* (☎ 231-3387; fax 226-1964), at Rua dos Pacajus 109, Praia de Iracema, has a swimming pool and good standard apartamentos at US$50/55 for singles/doubles. The *Turismo Praia Hotel* (☎ 231-6133), at Avenida Presidente Kennedy 894/814, Praia de Iracema, has apartamentos at US$30/40 for singles/doubles. Discounts are negotiable for cash payment.

The *Pousada Preamar* (☎ 224-6175), at Rua Silva Jatai 25, Praia do Meireles, has well-appointed, but musty, apartamentos with air-con and refrigerator at US$30/35 for singles/doubles.

Rodoviária The *Hotel Amuarama* (☎ 272-2111; fax 272-5625) is a surprisingly good three-star hotel next to the rodoviária. Apartamentos start at US$29/40 for singles/doubles. The hotel has a restaurant and a swimming pool.

Places to Stay – top end

Most of the top-end hotels are on Praia do Meireles, which has been heavily developed with competing hotels, many of which resemble multistorey carparks. There are two five-star hotels facing Meireles beach on Avenida Presidente Kennedy. The *Esplanada Praia Hotel* (☎ 244-8555; fax 224-8555), despite its star rating, has the outward appearance of a decaying tenement block. Room prices start at around US$105/130 for singles/doubles. At No 2500, the *Imperial Othon Palace* (☎ 244-9177; fax 224-7777), has rooms for US$104/116 a single/double.

The *Novotel Magna Fortaleza* (☎ 244-1122; fax 261-2793), at Avenida Presidente Kennedy 2380, is a very slick four-star hotel with a swimming pool and all mod-cons (TV, air-con, phone and refrigerator). Room rates start at US$80/95 for singles/doubles.

Places to Eat

You can eat well in Fortaleza. There's delicious crab, lobster, shrimp and fish, and a fantastic variety of tropical fruit, including cashews, coconut, mango, guava, sapoti, graviola, passionfruit, murici, cajá and more.

There are several local dishes worth tasting. Peixe a delícia is a highly recommended favourite. Try paçoca, a typical Cearense dish made of sun-dried meat, ground with a mortar and pestle, mixed with manioc and then roasted. The tortured meat is usually accompanied by baião de dois, which is a mixture of rice, cheese, beans and butter.

City Centre The centre has lots of eateries which offer snacks and prato feito at lunch; in the evening, you have a much wider choice at the city beaches. Vegetarians can chow down at *Restaurante Alivita*, at Avenida Barão do Rio Branco 1486, open for lunch only and closed on Sunday. In the courtyard inside the Centro de Turismo, there's *Xadrez*, a restaurant with tables outside in the shade. It's good for a cool beer and a snack.

City Beaches There are some excellent restaurants along Praia de Iracema, near the Ponte Metálica. On the pier, *Por do Sol* is a great place to sit, sip and snack while the waves crash below you. For Italian food, try *La Trattoria*, where the owner proudly claims 'cutting spaghetti is a crime, ketchup is forbidden; and no-one will be served beans and rice'! *La Boheme*, at Rua dos Tabajaras 380, is a sophisticated, arty restaurant with a gallery attached – even the chairs are individually painted works of art. If you are feeling like a major splurge, try the seafood dishes which are recommended.

For more earthy fare, *Abril em Portugal* is run by an affable Portuguese from Alentejo. Main dishes start at around US$4. The galinha de cabidela (chicken special) and arroz de mariscos (rice with shellfish) are delicious. It's closed on Monday.

Praia do Meireles is packed with restaurants. *Sabor da Terra* is a churrascaria on the beach, with tables set out in the open to catch the breeze. The Japanese restaurant *Mikado*, at Avenida Barão de Studart 600, specialises in teppanyaki.

At the aptly named *Restaurante Água Na Boca* (literally Water in the Mouth), Rua República do Líbano 1084 (Varjota district), we highly recommend the moqueca mixta, a combination of seafood cooked in coconut cream and dendê oil. This restaurant is closed on Monday, and open for lunch only on Sunday. In Mucuripe, *Restaurante Osmar*, at Rua São João 147, has been recommended for regional food and seafood. It's closed on Sunday.

Entertainment

London London, at Avenida Dom Luis 131, prides itself on being the most animated pub in Fortaleza. There's live music in the bar area and a pizzeria restaurant in another section of the pub.

Pirata Bar, at Rua dos Tabajaras 325, Praia de Iracema, is clearly the place to go, at least on Monday when it claims *a segunda feira mais louca do planeta* (the craziest Monday on the planet). The action includes live music for avid forró or lambada fans, who can dance until they drop. Admission costs US$5. Bar d'Italia is a lively bar right next to the Ponte Metálica. Oásis, at Avenida Santos Dumont 5779, is a gigantic dancehall with room for several thousand people. If you like sweaty action, there's boxing and freestyle wrestling for men and women on Wednesday. Admission costs US$4. It's open from 11 pm to 3 am Wednesday to Saturday.

During holiday season the hotel strip on Avenida Presidente Kennedy is full of outdoor bars, and merchants and artists hawking their goods. Oba Oba, at Avenida Washington Soares 3199 (Água Fria district), has shows, dancing and live music.

Clube de Vaqueiro (☎ 229-2799), at Anel Contôrno, between BR-116/CE-04, is a huge forró club, a long way from the centre and best reached by taxi. On Friday, there's a rodeo before 11 pm when the forró dancing kicks off.

Things to Buy

Fortaleza is one of the most important centres in the Northeast for crafts. Artisans

THE NORTHEAST

work with *carnaúba* palm fronds, bamboo, vines, leather and lace. Much of the production is geared to the tourist, but there are also goods for urban and Sertanejo customers. The markets and fairs are the places to look for clothing, hammocks, wood carvings, saddles, bridles, harnesses and images of saints.

Markets are held about town (usually from 4 pm onwards) from Tuesday to Sunday:

Tuesday
    Praça João Gentil, in Gentilândia (on the southern edge of the city)
Wednesday
    Praça Luiza Távora, in Aldeota district
Thursday
    Praça do Professor, on Avenida Aguanambi in front of Jornal O Povo (newspaper office)
Friday
    Praça Portugal, in Aldeota district
    Rua dos Tabajaras, at Praia de Iracema
    Praça Farias Brito, in Otávio Bonfim
    Praça da Igreja Redonda, in Parquelândia district
    Praça José Bonifácio
Saturday
    Praça Pio IX, on Avenida 13 de Maio
    Praça Presidente Roosevelt, in Jardim América district
    Praça da Aerolândia, on BR-116 close to the Aeroclube de Fortaleza (Fortaleza Flying Club)
Sunday
    Praça da Imprensa, in Aldeota district

You can purchase sand paintings on Calçadão da Avenida Beira Mar, watch the artists work and have them customise your design. This place is best visited in the evening.

Lacework, embroidery, raw leather goods, ceramics, and articles made of straw are also available from: the Central de Artesanato Luiza Távora (Handicrafts Centre), at Avenida Santos Dumont 1589, in Aldeota district; the Centro do Turismo, at Rua Senador Pompeu 350; the Mercado Central, on Rua General Bezerril; and tourist boutiques (clothing, jewellery, fashion) along Avenida Monsenhor Tabosa. Cashew nuts are also excellent value in Fortaleza.

Getting There & Away

Air Aeroporto Pinto Martins (☎ 272-6166) is six km south of the city centre. Flights operate to Rio, São Paulo and major cities in the Northeast and the North.

Following are addresses for Brazilian and foreign airlines:

Air France
    Rua Pedro Borges 33, sala 409 (☎ 221-3533)
British Airways
    Rua Castro e Silvo 121, sala 103 (☎ 221-5370)
Transbrasil
    Rua Oswaldo Cruz 1101, Aldeota (☎ 272-4669)
Varig
    Avenida Santos Dumont 2727, Aldeota (☎ 244-5101)
VASP
    Rua Barão do Rio Branco 959 (☎ 244-2244)

Bus The rodoviária (☎ 272-1566) is about six km south of the centre.

Bus services run daily to Salvador (US$32, 22 hours) and Rio de Janeiro (US$68, 48 hours); four times daily to Natal (US$12, eight hours), Teresina (US$14.50, ten hours) and São Luís (US$25, 16 hours); and thrice daily to Recife (US$19.50, 12 hours) and Belém (US$34.50, 22 hours).

The Redencão bus company runs buses at 9 am and 9 pm daily to Jericoacoara (US$10, 7½ hours) and 10 times daily to Quixada (US$5, 3½ hours). The Empresa São Benedito bus company runs three buses daily to Canoa Quebrada (US$4.50, 3½ hours). The Empresa Redentora bus company runs 10 buses a day to Baturité (US$3, 2½ hours). The Ipu Brasileira bus company runs services to Ubajara six times a day (US$9.50, six hours) and four times a day to Camocim via Sobral (US$10.50, 7½ hours). Four buses run daily to Juazeiro de Norte (US$16, nine hours).

Getting Around

To/From the Airport Aeroporto Pinto Martins is six km south of the centre and just a couple of km from the rodoviária. From the airport, there are buses to Praça José Alencar, in the centre. A taxi to the centre costs around US$8.

To/From the Rodoviária To reach the city centre, take any bus marked '13 de Maio' or 'Aguanambi'. A taxi to the centre costs around US$4.50.

To/From City Beaches From outside the Centro de Turismo, on Rua Dr João Moreira, take the bus marked 'Circular' along the beachfront to Praia de Iracema and Praia do Meireles. 'Meireles' buses also go to Praia do Meireles. A taxi from the centre to Praia de Iracema costs US$2.50.

From Avenida Castro E Silva (close to the Centro de Tourismo), 'Praia do Futuro' and 'Serviluz' buses run to Praia do Futoro.

To/From Beaches West of the City For beaches west of the city, such as Icaraí and Cumbuco, you can take a 'Cumbuco' bus from Praça Capistrano Abreu, on Avenida Tristão Gonçalves. You can also pick up the 'Cumbuco' bus along Avenida Presidente Kennedy.

BEACHES SOUTH-EAST OF FORTALEZA

The coastal road from Fortaleza south to Aracati, the CE-004, runs about 10 km inland. It's mostly a flat, dry landscape of shrubs, stunted trees and some lakes. The towns are small, with good beaches, jangadas and dunescapes.

Prainha

Thirty-three km south of Fortaleza via BR-116, and seven km from Aquiraz, is the beach town of Prainha (the name means Little Beach). Prainha is a great beach, but it gets packed on weekends. Local fisherfolk will give you rides on their jangadas.

Places to Stay & Eat There are two mid-range hotels in Prainha: the *Aquiraz Praia Hotel* (☎ 361-1177) and the *Prainha Solar Hotel* (☎ 361-1374). Apartamentos start at US$25/30 for singles/doubles. Both hotels are set back from the beach. A cheaper option is the *Pousada da Prainha* (☎ 361-1122), on Rua Berlin. *O Leôncio* is a good seafood restaurant.

Getting There & Away São Benedito buses to Prainha leave every hour until 8 pm from Praça da Escola Normal in Fortaleza.

Iguape

Iguape, five km south of Prainha, has a long stretch of white-sand beach with jangadas, a few lonely palm trees and sand dunes breaking the clean line of the horizon. The kids from town ski down the dunes on planks of wood.

In Iguape, women and children make wonderful lacework. Four or more wooden bobs are held in each hand and clicked rapidly and rhythmically. The bobs lay string around metal pins which are stuck in burlap cushions. Using this process, beautiful and intricate lace flowers are crafted.

Save your purchases for Centro das Rendeiras, six km inland, where the lacework is just as fine and cheaper. Also on sale are sweet cakes made from raw sugar-cane broth which is boiled into a thick mass, pressed and reboiled in vats.

Places to Stay & Eat There are two hotels in town, but you can easily rent rooms or houses. The *Pousada Dunas do Iguape* (☎ 370-1294) is close to the beach. Recommended restaurants are *Peixado do Iguape* and *João do Camarão*.

Getting There & Away São Benedito buses to Iguape leave every hour until 8 pm from Praça da Escola Normal in Fortaleza.

Praia do Morro Branco

Bounded on the coast by the Choro and Piranji rivers and inland by red cliffs, Morro Branco is four km south of the town of Beberibe. There are several brand-spanking new barracas along the beach for sipping and sunning. If you're feeling active, take a jangada ride to the caves, or hike to the cliffs of coloured sands and the natural springs at Praia das Fontes.

The big festival here, dedicated to São Francisco, is held on 3 and 4 September and features a grand procession.

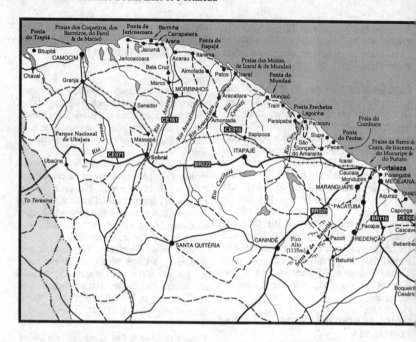

Places to Stay & Eat Along the beachfront, there's the *Pousada Sereia* (no phone), a friendly place with basic apartamentos at US$10/13 for singles/doubles, or the more up-market but fading *Pousada do Morro Branco* (☎ 330-1040), with apartamentos at US$25, single or double. In the village, the *Pousada Labrinito* (330-1121), at Rua Luiz Gama 120, has quartos at US$8/10 for singles/doubles.

Bar o Claudio is a relaxed little restaurant just off the beach, with a good range of local seafood dishes.

Getting There & Away Beberibe is 78 km south of Fortaleza on BR-116 and CE-004. There are five buses each day travelling to São Benedito running via Beberibe to Morro Branco from Fortaleza's rodoviária. The first of these leaves at 6.30 am and the last leaves at 7.20 pm (US$2.50, 2½ hours). There are also several buses running daily from Beberibe to Aracati.

Aracati

Aracati is a large town by the Rio Jaguaribe, a river that provided transport for sugar cane, and thus wealth, for Aracati in the 18th century.

Although the town is not in the best of shape architecturally, it's worth a few hours to look at some of the historical buildings. The Igreja Matriz de NS do Rosário, on Rua Dragão do Mar, dates from the late 18th century and is a fine example of colonial architecture. The attractive Sobrado do Barão de Aracati houses the Museu Jaguaribano, which contains sacred art and local handicrafts. For a look at more colonial houses, some of which have retained their azulejo facades, wander down Rua do Comércio (Rua Grande).

The town is also known for its handicrafts, and the best time to see them is at the Feira do Artesão (Artisan Market) held on Saturday.

The towns south of Aracati, poor little

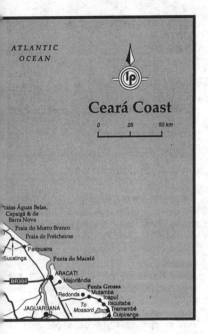

ATLANTIC
OCEAN

Ceará Coast

0   25   50 km

Praias Águas Belas,
Capaigá & de
Barra Nova
Praia do Morro Branco
Praia de Freicheiras
Paripueira
Sucatinga   Ponta do Maceió
BR304   ARACATI
Majorlândia
Ponta Grossa
Mutamba
Redonda   Icapuí
Ibicuitaba
To   Tremembé
JAGUARUANA   Mossoró   Cuipiranga

There are sharks waiting at Aracati's rodoviária to whisk you off to Canoa Quebrada in taxis – walk 700 metres down to Praça Mercado do Antigo and take a bus, passenger truck or jalopy instead. There are also regular buses from Aracati to Majorlândia and Beberibe.

Canoa Quebrada

Once a tiny fishing village cut off from the world by its huge, pink sand dunes, Canoa Quebrada, 13 km from Aracati, is still small and pretty, but it is no longer the Shangri-la of the past. There are lots of hip international types running about, and on weekends tourist buses roll in and dwarf the village. Other than the beach, the main attractions are watching the sunset from the dunes, riding horses bareback and dancing forró or reggae by the light of gas lanterns. If you still have energy remaining after a night of dancing, hire a horse (four hours for US$8 after bargaining) and ride out early in the morning.

Take care, bichos de pé (small parasites) are underfoot. Wear shoes all around town and wherever pigs and dogs roam freely.

villages often without electricity or running water, are set on stunningly beautiful, wide beaches. Developers have moved in to construct regular accommodation, but it's still easy to camp on barren beaches.

Places to Stay & Eat There are a few inexpensive hotels near the rodoviária. The *Pousada Litorânea* (☎ 421-1001), at Rua Cel Alexandrino 1251, is the best, with apartamentos costing US$8/10 for singles/doubles. There's also a restaurant downstairs. The *Brisa Rio* (☎ 421-0081), at Rua Cel Alexandrino 1179, and the *Pousada Canteiros* (☎ 421-1757), at Rua Alexandrino 1559, are the other good options. *Churrascaria Raimundo do Caranguejo*, at Rua Hilton Gondim Bandeira 505, serves good crab dishes.

Getting There & Away From Fortaleza's rodoviária, take one of seven daily buses to Aracati. The four-hour trip costs US$4.75.

Places to Stay The *Albergue Lua Estrela* (☎ 421-1401) is a youth hostel, but looks more like a resort hotel – there are great views from the attached restaurant. The *Pousada Alternativa* (☎ 421-1401) is a friendly place and good value. Some rooms have TV, refrigerator and air-con at US$8/10 for singles/doubles. Don't be put off by their saturation advertising. Other good options are the *Pousada Lua Morena*, at the end of the main, street towards the beach; *Duna's Pousada*, on the edge of the dunes behind the village, and the *Pousada Ma Alice* (☎ 421-1401), on the main street. *Tranquilandia* is a more up-market place with a grassy courtyard (a rare sight among the sandy streets of the village).

Getting There & Away There are three buses daily to Canoa Quebrada from Fortaleza's rodoviária at 8.30 am, and 1.40 and 2.40 pm (US$4.50, 4½ hours).

THE NORTHEAST

Majorlândia

Majorlândia, 14 km south of Aracati, has a wide, clean beach with many barracas and jangadas. It's not as hip as Canoa Quebrada, but the beach is lovely, and during the week, it's very quiet.

Places to Stay & Eat Inexpensive places to stay include: the *Hotel Sereia* (☎ 421-1748, ext 130), on Rua Raimundo Rodrigues; *Pousada Gaúcho* (☎ 421-1748, ext 195), on Rua do Jangodeira; *Apartamento Beira Mar* (☎ 421-1748, ext 134), on Avenida Praia; *Pousada Esquina das Flores* (☎ 421-1748, ext 188), on Rua Principal and the *Pousada Duna's Praia* (☎ 421-1846), on Avenida Praia.

Try *Restaurant Dengo da Bia* or the restaurant in the *Hotel Sereia* for seafood.

Quixaba

Five km further south of Majorlândia on a sandy track are the distinctive, chalky-white sandstone bluffs of Quixaba. From the bluffs, cut by gullies between cacti and palms, you can see the pink hills of Canoa Quebrada. You can rent a jangada and visit the neighbouring beaches.

Places to Stay The *Fillo* has clean and quiet rooms with electricity to let.

SOUTH TO RIO GRANDE DO NORTE

The 50 km south-east from Quixaba to the border with Rio Grande do Norte is just a series of primitive little beaches and towns mostly off the maps and definitely out of the guidebooks: Lagoa do Mato, Fontainha, Retirinho and Retiro Grande Mutamba, Ponta Grossa, Redonda and Retiro (a waterfall), Peroba, Picos, Barreiras and Barrinha, and, finally, Icapuí, which has a couple of pousadas.

Five buses a day go from Fortaleza to the village of Icapuí; it's a 4½-hour ride. A road continues to Ibicuitaba and Barra do Ceará beach. It's possible to drive from there to Tibaú, in Rio Grande do Norte, at low tide.

BEACHES NORTH-WEST OF FORTALEZA

Beach Park

This full-blown beach resort, 22 km up the coast from Fortaleza, is one of the most modern in Brazil, with facilities such as ultralights, surfboards, and buggies. It also has an Aqua Park, which features a huge swimming pool complex with the highest water-toboggan run in Brazil (24 metres, and speeds up to 80 km/h). It's quite expensive and would probably appeal more to travellers in search of structured fun.

Getting There & Away From Praça Tristão Gonçalvez in Fortaleza, take a 'Beach Park' bus to Beach Park. This bus also runs along Avenida Presidente Kennedy.

Paracuru

About 100 km from Fortaleza on BR-222 and CE-135, Paracuru is a Cearense version of Rio de Janeiro's Búzios. It's a clean, relaxed and fairly affluent town – there's even an up-market gym called Musculacão next to the bus station. Along the beach, coconut palms, natural freshwater springs and jangadas complete a tranquil beach picture. Although the beach attracts crowds from Fortaleza at weekends, it's quiet during the rest of the week. In recent years, Carnival in Paracuru has become a byword amongst Cearenses for hot beach action.

Places to Stay & Eat A good budget option is the *Pousada da Praça* (☎ 344-1271), on Praça da Matriz. Bright apartamentos cost US$10/12 for singles/doubles (breakfast not included). The *Pousada Villa Verde* (☎ 344-1181), on Rua Professora Maria Luiza, is set in lovely gardens with huge, shady trees. Basic quartos cost US$10/12 for singles/doubles (breakfast not included). The *Pousada da Gaviota* (☎ 344-1352), on Rua Coroneu Meireles, has apartamentos for US$15/21 for singles/doubles.

Restaurant Don Carlo, on Rua Saturnino de Carvalho, has a wide range of pastas, pizzas and seafood dishes.

Getting There & Away Eight buses run daily to Paracuru from Fortaleza's rodoviária (US$3, 2½ hours), the first at 5.45 am and the last at 7.00 pm.

Praia da Lagoinha

Praia da Lagoinha, a short distance up the coast from Paracuru, has lots of coconut palms, good camping and a small but deep lagoon near the sand dunes. The beach is considered by Ceareneses to be in the top three in the state, and its relative isolation has so far kept crowds down.

Places to Stay & Eat The *Pousada O Milton* (☎ 363-1232, ext 102) is right on the beachfront and has a popular restaurant – try the delicious fish stew. Other options are *Pousada Sol e Mar* (☎ 363-1232, ext 122) and *Pousada Ondas do Mar* (☎ 363-1232, ext 135).

Getting There & Away Three buses run daily to Lagoinha from Fortaleza's rodoviária at 7.30 am, and 1.30 and 3.30 pm (US$4, three hours).

Mundaú, Guajira & Fleixeiras

The beaches of Mundaú, Guajira and Fleixeiras, 155 km from Fortaleza via BR-222, are traditional fishing areas with wide, unspoiled sweeps of sand.

Places to Stay For budget accommodation in Fleixeiras, try the *Pousada da Célia* (☎ 351-1134, ext 105), on Praça da Igreja. On the beach, the mid-range *Solar das Fleixeiras* (☎ 344-1044, ext 136) has a restaurant and swimming pool. On Mundaú beach, there's the *Mundaú Dunas Hotel* (☎ 351-1210, ext 197), with a restaurant attached.

Getting There & Away Buses run from Fortaleza's rodoviária to Mundaú and Fleixeiras daily at 6 am and 4 pm (US$5.50, around four hours).

Itapipoca

The city of Itapipoca, about 120 km west of Fortaleza, can be used as a starting point for exploring the beaches of Baleia, Pracianos, Inferno and Marinheiros.

Places to Stay The *Hotel Municipal* (☎ 631-0197) is on Rua Anastácio Braga, in Itapipoca. Right on Praia Baleia is the *Pousada da Baleia*, which also has a churrascaria.

Jericoacoara

The latest remote 'in' beach to become popular among backpackers and hip Brazilians, Jericoacoara is a small fishing village where dozens of palms drowning in sand dunes face jangadas stuck on a broad grey beach. It's a long haul to get there, so you might as well stay a while – in fact, it may be harder to leave. Pigs, goats, horses, cows, bulls and dogs roam the sandy streets at will.

It's best to avoid bichos de pé and other parasites by not walking the streets barefoot. If you stay bicho-free, you can practise your steps at the forró held in an outdoor courtyard every Wednesday and Saturday – just follow the music. You can also climb the sand dunes (watching the sunset from the top is mandatory, but sand-surfing down is only for crazies), go for a ride on a jangada, or walk to Pedra Furada, a rock three km east along the beach. At low tide the beach route is easier than the hill route. You can also hire horses and gallop along the beach.

Organised Tours Tour operators in Fortaleza and up-market pousadas in Jericoacoara offer tour packages for Jericoacoara. The tours usually leave Fortaleza twice a week, at 7 pm on Tuesday and Friday; and return from Jericoacoara on Thursday and Sunday at 3 pm. See the Fortaleza section for details about tour operators.

Places to Stay There is plenty of cheap accommodation in Jericoacoara and also several up-market options – at a price. The cheap options aren't necessarily clean, and don't count on electricity or running water – just gas lanterns and running pigs. For longer stays, ask about renting a local house – you

THE NORTHEAST

should be able to get something for about US$3.50 per night. Words to the wise: bring a large cotton hammock or bed roll with sleeping sack.

Reservations can be made by calling the village telephone office (☎ 621-0544). An excellent inexpensive option is the *Pousada Casa do Turismo*, on Rua Das Dunas. The pousada also serves as the village post office and agent for the Fortaleza bus. Other good budget options are the *Pousada Islana*, on Rua Principal; *Pousada Calanda*, behind Pousada do Tourismo; and the *Pousada Acoara do Jerico*, along the beachfront.

More up-market lodgings include the *Pousada Capitão Tomás*, with a beach frontage; *Pousada do Avalon*, on Rua Principal; and the *Pousada Papagaio*. The *Pousada Hippopotamus* and the *Jericoacoara Praia Hotel*, both on Rua Forró, are the most expensive hotels in town. Package deals for these up-market pousadas typically include return transport from Fortaleza, two nights accommodation and one breakfast.

Places to Eat Food and drinks on the whole don't come cheap in Jericoacoara, although there are a couple of reasonable options. On Rua Principal, *Samambaia* is popular for its good-value prato feito; *Espaco Aberta* has a wide range of salads; *Senzala* and the *Pousada do Avalon* have good Italian food. *Jerizelba*, on Rua Forró, is popular for pre-forró pizza, and *Alexandre Bar* is the prime location along the beach for afternoon drinks, sunset-gazing and seafood dishes. Most of the budget places to stay also serve food.

Getting There & Away Two buses leave Fortaleza's rodoviária daily for Jericoacoara (US$9.75, around seven hours) at 9 am and 9 pm. In Gijoca, you are transferred to a passenger truck (included in the ticket price) for the 24-km rodeo ride to Jericoacoara. Of the two options, the night bus is quicker and cooler, but you arrive in Jericoacoara at around 3.30 am. Someone from one of the pousadas will meet the bus, and you can always move to another pousada later in the day.

If you have come by car, leave it parked in Gijoca, where some of the pousada owners can keep an eye on it. The ride over and around sweeping dunes, lagoons, bogs and flat scrub terrain is beautiful, but very hard on people and machines.

Transport leaves Jericoacoara for Fortaleza at 6 am and 10.30 pm.

To get to Jericoacoara from Sobral, a Vale do Acaraú bus runs from Sobral at noon over an abysmal road to Gijoca (US$5, three hours), and should connect with the Fortaleza bus there – if not, you should be able to collectively bargain a fare of about US$3 per person for a jeep. To get to Sobral, a bus leaves Gijoca at 2 am – take the 10.30 pm truck out of Jericoacoara and think up new and interesting ways to amuse yourself in Gijoca for three hours.

For details about access from Camocim, see Getting There & Away in the Camocim section.

Tatajuba

Tatajuba, about 30 km west of Jericoacoara, is a tiny, isolated fishing village perched on the mouth of a tidal river. The beach is broad and lonely, and there's a lagoon surrounded by extensive dunes about two km from the village. The only restaurant and pousada, the *Verde Folha*, is run by Marcus and Valéria, refugees from the 'big smoke' of Jericoacoara. They have a couple of rooms with beds and hammocks. Full board, including great home cooking, costs US$12 per person.

There is no regular transport to Tatajuba. The walk along the beach from Jericoacoara takes about five hours; leave early in the morning and take water. At Guriú, a little less than half way, there's a river to cross – canoes will take you over for about US$2. The river at Tatajuba can be waded at low tide. Don't try to cross it if the water is high, as the current is very strong.

Alternatively, you should be able to rent a boat in Jericoacoara to take you there; ask around at the beach.

Camocim

Camocim is a lively fishing port and market town at the mouth of the Rio Coreaú, in north-western Ceará, near the Piauí border. The town's economy revolves around the saltworks, lobster fishing and a busy everyday market. On Praia dos Barreiros and Praia do Farol, two and four km from town respectively, you can sip coconut milk while tanning.

Places to Stay & Eat The *Pousada Ponta Pora* and the colourful *Pousada Beira Mar* are both along the riverfront, on Avenida Beira Mar. The *Camocim Hotel*, at Rua Engenheiro Privat 174, has cheap quartos and apartamentos. Riverbank restaurants serve local seafood and typical Cearense dishes.

Getting There & Away Four buses run daily to Camocim via Sobral from Fortaleza's rodoviária (US$10.50, 7½ hours), the first at 7.30 am and the last at 6.30 pm.

From Camocim to Gijoca, a jeep leaves the central market at around 10.30 am daily, and if there are enough people, it will carry on to Jericoacoara. During high season there are boats sailing from Camocim to Jericoacoara – the trip takes four hours. Half the adventure is getting there.

SOBRAL

Sobral has two minor sights, faded glories from the past before all was changed by the construction of the BR-222. The Museu Diocesano Dom José (a museum of sacred art), on Avenida Dom José, houses an eclectic collection of images of saints. It's open Monday to Saturday from 2 to 5 pm. The Teatro Municipal São João, on Praça Dr Antônio Ibiapina, is an impressive neoclassical theatre (1880).

Places to Stay

Hotel Francinet's (☎ 611-1536), on Rua Coronel Joaquim Ribeiro, has apartamentos at US$10/20 for singles/doubles.

Getting There & Away

There are six buses a day to Camocim from Sobral. The earliest bus to make the 3½-hour trip leaves at 5.30 am, the last at 10 pm. One bus leaves Sobral daily, at noon, to Gijoca, for access to Jericoacoara.

MARANGUAPE

Thirty eight km from Fortaleza, on the way to the Serra de Baturité, is the town of Maranguape, famous for its Ypioca brand of cachaça. The Ypioca aguardente factory is six km from town; the turn-off is near the Shell station. There is no regular transportation to the cachaça plant, but it's not a bad hike and most of the traffic is headed in your direction.

At the gate, ask for a tour of the 138-year-old plant. Before you step within the grounds, a pungent sour-mash smell assaults the senses. Whirring, clanking, steam-spitting Industrial Revolution-era machinery crushes the cane to pulp and mush. The raw sugar-cane mash undergoes alcoholic fermentation, is distilled, then aged one to three years in huge wooden casks.

PACATUBA

Pacatuba is a cute little town in the shadow of the Serra de Baturité. The Balneário Bico das Andreas spring is smelly, dirty and not what it's cracked up to be.

The *Pousada das Andreas* (☎ 345-1252) charges US$18 for a four-room bungalow that sleeps eight and comes with kitchenette and refrigerator.

SERRA DE BATURITÉ

Ceará's interior is not limited to the harsh landscapes of the sertão. There are also ranges of hills which break up the monotony of the sun-scorched land. The Serra de Baturité is the range of hills closest to Fortaleza. A natural watershed, it is an oasis of green where coffee and bananas are cultivated around the cliffs and jagged spines of the hills. The climate is tempered by rain, the evenings are cool and morning fog obscures

Coffee Picker

Pico Alto (1115 metres), the highest point in the state.

Baturité

Founded in 1745, the town of Baturité (95 km west of Fortaleza) was once at the forefront of the fight against slavery, and is now the economic and commercial centre of the region. Most of the town's attractions are grouped around the Praça Matriz and include the *pelourinho* (whipping post), the baroque church of Matriz NS de Palma (1764), the Palácio Entre-Rios, and the Museu Comendador Ananias Arruda, which contains exhibits from the town's past (though surprisingly, little on the struggle to abolish slavery). There are also a few *termas* (resorts with mineral pools) clustered around the town. There are local handicrafts on sale in Baturité that include embroidery, tapestry and straw goods.

Places to Stay & Eat Apart from the accommodation in the nearby villages of Guaramiranga and Pacoti (see the next section), lodgings are also available in Baturité at the *Hotel Canuto*, on Praça Santo Luiza, and the *Balneário Itamaracá Club* (☎ 347-0113), at Sítio Itamaracá. *Eldorado*, at Avenida Dr João Paulino 1284 (near Praça Matriz), is a pizzeria and churrascaria with a pleasant outdoor setting.

Getting There & Away Ten buses leave Fortaleza's rodoviária daily for Baturité (US$3, 2½ hours).

Guaramiranga & Pacoti

Two of the prettiest villages on the heights of Serra de Baturité are Guaramiranga and Pacoti, 19 km and 26 km respectively from Baturité.

Places to Stay & Eat The *Hotel Escola de Guaramiranga* (☎ 381-1120, ext 148), a training centre for hotel staff, in Guaramiranga, has spotless apartamentos, a bar, a swimming pool and ping-pong tables. The singles/doubles rooms cost US$14/16. It's unmarked and tricky to find (no sign), but it's a great deal. The *Remanso Hotel da Serra* (☎ 227-7395, ext 195) is five km from Guaramiranga on the beautiful road to Pacoti. It has pleasant apartamentos at around US$20/25 for singles/doubles, a restaurant and a swimming pool. Slightly more expensive, and closer to Pacoti, is the *Estância Vale das Flores* (☎ 325-1233), at Sítio São Francisco. It's set in a park with a swimming pool, sports facilities, horse rental and mini-zoo.

Getting There & Away The Empresa Redentora bus company runs a daily bus direct to Guaramiranga from Fortaleza's rodoviária, at 3 pm (US$3, three hours). From Baturité, there's one bus, at 10 am, running to Guaramiranga and Pacoti, and another bus, at 5.30 pm, to Guaramiranga only.

CANINDÉ

Canindé, only 110 km inland from Fortaleza on the BR-020, is the site of one of the Northeast's great religious pilgrimages, O Santuário de São Francisco das Chagas. Since 1775 pilgrims have been coming to Canindé to offer promises to and ask favours of São Francisco de Assis. Nowadays around 250,000 fervent believers arrive each year, most from the sertão, almost all dirt poor. For Westerners the festival is both colourful and bizarre, and laced with superstition. You'll see many votive offerings and miracle cures. It's a scene right out of a Glauber Rocha film.

The festival begins on 2 September at 4 am and continues until 4 October. On 30 September, the climax of the festival begins with the celebration for the *lavradores* (farm workers), which is followed in turn by celebrations for the vaqueiros (cowboys) on 1 October, and for the *violeiros* (guitarists and luthiers) on 2 October.

The culmination of all the festivities begins at 3 am on 4 October, when the first of nine masses commences. These are followed by a 70,000-strong procession through the town.

PARQUE NACIONAL DE UBAJARA

The main attractions of the Parque Nacional de Ubajara, just a few km from the small town of Ubajara, are the cable-car ride down to the caves and the caves themselves.

Nine chambers with strange limestone formations extend over half a km into the side of a mountain. The main formations seen inside the caves are: Pedra do Sino (Bell Stone), Salas da Rosa (Rose Rooms), Sala do Cavalo (Horse Room) and Sala dos Retratos (Portrait Room).

The park, with its beautiful vistas, forest, waterfalls and three-km trail to the caves is well worth a visit. At 750 metres above sea level, temperatures in the surrounding area are kept cool and provide a welcome respite from the searing heat of the sertão.

In 1987 the lower station of the *teleférico*

(cable car) was wiped out by boulders which fell after winter rains. The station was jerked 18 metres off its foundation and pieces of the teleférico were flung 500 metres into the sertão. The cable-car system has been replaced, and now operates every day from 8.30 am to noon and 1 to 4 pm. The ride costs US$3. Guides accompany you on the one-hour tour through the caves.

Information

The IBAMA office, five km from Ubajara proper, at the entrance to the park, provides guides for the tour, but the information centre has been abandoned. If you fancy a strenuous hike, ask at the office if you can take the three-km *trilha* (trail) down to the cave. Allow at least half a day for the round trip. Start in the cool of the early morning, wear sturdy footwear and take enough to drink. Alternatively, you can walk down to the caves and take the cable car back up.

Places to Stay & Eat

The *Sítio do Alemão*, set on a shady coffee plantation about 1.5 km from the park entrance, is run by a German/Brazilian couple who can provide walking maps for the park and loads of information about local attractions. There are wonderful vistas over the sertão from the property. Day trips to Parque Nacional de Sete Cidades (140 km away on a good road) can also be arranged. Spotless chalets cost US$8 per person, with a generous breakfast.

There are two pousadas near the park entrance: the *Pousada da Neblina* (☎ 634-1297) has apartamentos at US$25/30 for singles/doubles and a swimming pool; and the *Pousada Gruta de Ubajaras* (634-1375) has apartamentos for US$10/16 for singles/doubles. Both of these pousadas also have restaurants.

The *Churrascaria Hotel Ubajara* (☎ 634-1261), at Rua Juvêncio Luís Pereira 370, in Ubajara, has single/double quartos that cost US$7/14.

Getting There & Away

Empresa Ipu-Brasília has six daily buses

THE NORTHEAST

from Fortaleza to Ubajara (US$9.50, six hours). The first bus leaves at 4 am, the last one at 9 pm. There are also bus connections to Teresina (US$8, six hours), the capital of Piauí state.

To reach the park entrance from the town of Ubajara, either walk the three km or take a taxi (US$5).

SERRA DA IBIAPABA

The Serra da Ibiapaba, a range of hills running along the undefined border with the state of Piauí, forms a rugged terrain of buttes, bluffs and cliffs, overlooking distant plains.

The town of Ipu lies 75 km south-east of Ubajara, in the Serra da Ibiapaba. The main attraction of Ipu (the name means Waterfall in the Tabajara Indian language) is the Bico do Ipu, a powerful waterfall that jets 100 metres downwards and fans out into sheets of mist and spray. A few km out of town are some strange stone stairs built by the Tabajara.

There is a sleazy restaurant under the falls, but no hotels in town. Ipu is worth a visit if it happens to be on your route, but it's not worth a special detour.

JUAZEIRO DO NORTE

Juazeiro do Norte, 528 km from Fortaleza, is a magnet for believers in Padre Cícero, who lived in this town and became a controversial figure of the sertão. Not only was he a curate, with several miracles to his credit, he also exercised a strong political influence. His astonishing rise to fame was started when an elderly woman received the host from him at mass and claimed that it had miraculously turned to blood. Soon he was being credited with all kinds of miracles, and later became drawn into a leading role in the social and political upheavals in the Northeast. Padre Cícero died in 1934, but despite attempts by the Catholic Church to deny his sainthood, the claims and adoration of his followers seem to be as strong as ever.

The best time to see this magnetic attraction and devotion is during the festivals and pilgrimages in honour of Padre Cícero. On 24 March, the Aniversário do Padre Cícero celebrates Padre Cícero in legend and song. The romaria (pilgrimage) to Juazeiro do Norte in honour of Padre Cícero takes place on 1 and 2 November and is known as the Dia do Romeiro e Festa do Padre Cícero.

The city of Padre Cícero is rich in wood and ceramic sculpture. Look for the work of Expedito Batista, Nino, Cizinho, José Celestino, Luís Quirino, Maria de Lourdes, Maria Cândida, Francisca, Daniel, José Ferreira and Maria das Dores.

Logradouro do Horto

On the hill above the town, accessible either by road or via a path laid out with the stations of the cross, is the colossal statue of Padre Cícero (25 metres), which was built in 1969 and now ranks as the fourth-tallest statue in the record books. Those taller are Cristo Rey (Cochabamba, Bolivia), Cristo Redentor on Corcovado (Rio) and the Statue of Liberty (New York). Nearby is a small chapel and a building filled with votive offerings which depict the afflictions and problems from which the worshippers have been freed: wooden or wax replicas of every conceivable body part, and graphic representations of survival from accidents.

Túmulo do Padre Cícero

Padre Cícero's tomb is beside the Capela NS do Perpétua Socorro, on Praça do Socorro.

Gráfica de Literatura de Cordel

If you are interested in literatura de cordel (literally string literature), visit this workshop on Rua Santa Luzia, where you can see the pamphlets being produced for sale on the premises. It's open from 7 to 11 am and 1 to 5 pm Monday to Friday. It's closed on Saturday afternoon.

Places to Stay

Since this town is a pilgrimage centre, there is no lack of accommodation, except during the main festivals. For inexpensive apartamentos, try the Juá Palace (☎ 511-0844), at Avenida Castelo Branco 2558, or the Viana Palace (☎ 511-2585), at Rua São Pedro 746.

Getting There & Away

There are four daily departures for Fortaleza (US$16, nine hours), and regular buses to all the major cities in the Northeast.

Piauí

Piauí, one of the largest states in the Northeast, is also one of the poorest states in Brazil, due to the oppressively hot and arid climate in its eastern and southern regions. The odd shape of the state – broad in the south, tapered at the coast – is due to a unique pattern of settlement which started from the sertão in the south and gradually moved towards the coast.

The climate on the Litoral Piauiense (Piauí coast) is kept cool(er) by sea breezes. If you're heading into the interior of the state, the best time for festivals and cool breezes is during July and August.The worst time, unless you want to be sunbaked to a frazzle, is between September and December.

Although Piauí is usually bypassed by travellers, it offers superb beaches along its short coast; interesting rock formations and hikes in the Parque Nacional de Sete Cidades; prehistoric sites and rock paintings in the Parque Nacional da Serra da Capivara, which ranks as one of the top prehistoric sites in South America; and the chance for rock hounds to visit Pedro Segundo, the only place in South America where opals are mined.

TERESINA

Teresina, the capital of Piauí, is famed as the hottest city in Brazil. Promotional literature stresses heat and yet more heat, with blurb bites such as 'Even the Wind Here Isn't Cool' or 'Teresina – As Hot As Its People'.

It's an interesting, quirky place which seems addicted to giving a Middle Eastern slant to the names of its streets, hotels and sights. The city itself is a Mesopotamia of sorts, sandwiched between the Rio Poty and Rio Parnaíba. Teresina is untouristed and unpretentious, and the inhabitants will stop you on the street to ask 'Where are *you* from?'. Like the British, residents of Teresina instantly warm to discussion of the weather, and especially of their favourite topic: *o calor* (the heat).

We recommend a visit if you yearn for attention or would like to feel famous for a day or so. And there's got to be something good going for a city that hosts an annual festival of humour!

Information

Tourist Offices PIEMTUR (☎ 223-4417), the state tourism organisation, at Rua Alvaro Mendes 1988, has helpful staff who happily dole out literature and advice. It's open from 9 am to 6 pm Monday to Friday.

The IBAMA office (☎ 232-1652), at Avenida Homero Castelo Branco 2240 (Jockey Club district), was one of the most active we encountered in Brazil. Leaflets about the national parks in Piauí are available here. It's open from 8 am to 5.45 pm Monday to Friday.

Travel Agencies For tours to sights in Piauí, contact Servitur Turismo (☎ 223-2065), at Rua Eliseu Martins 1136, or Espaço Turismo (☎ 223-3777), inside the shopping gallery of the Hotel Luxor.

Museu Histórico do Piauí

This state museum is divided into a series of exhibition rooms devoted to the history of the state; religious art; popular art; archaeology; fauna, flora and minerals; and an eclectic assortment of antique radios, projectors and other ancient wonders. Hidden in the corner of one room is a pathetic cabinet containing a flag, kerchief and some scribbled notes from *comunistas*, a flexible term used here to describe a group of independent thinkers, who were wiped out by the government in 1937.

Admission is free, and the museum is open Tuesday to Friday from 8 to 11 am and 3 to 6 pm, and on Saturday and Sunday from 8 am to noon.

Palácio de Karnak

This Greco-Roman structure once functioned as the governor's residence and contained valuable works of art and antiques. In the late '80s, the outgoing governor made a quick exit, together with many of the valuable contents.

Centro Artesanal

This centre for artesanato from all over Piauí and it is a pleasant spot to come browse among the shops which sell: leather articles; furniture; extremely intricate lacework; colourful hammocks; opals and soapstone (from Pedro Segundo); and liqueurs and confectionary made from genipapo, cajú and maracujá.

The Cooperativa de Rede Pedro Segundo, a producer of high-quality hammocks, sells beautiful linen hammocks at prices ranging from US$55 to US$130. Cotton hammocks start at around US$26.

Mercado Troca-Troca

In an attempt to perpetuate the old traditions of *troca troca* (barter), the government has made a permanent structure out of what was once an impromptu barter market. Unless you are curious to see the river, it's not worth a visit.

Potycabana

If you hanker after aquatic frolics and games as a respite from the searing heat, visit the Potycabana, an aquatic entertainment centre with water tobogganing and a surf pool, close to the Rio Poty.

Festivals

The main festivals, with typical dancing, music and cuisine of the Northeast, are held between June and August. The Salão Internacional de Humor do Piauí (Piauí Festival of Humour) is held during the second half of November and features comedy shows,

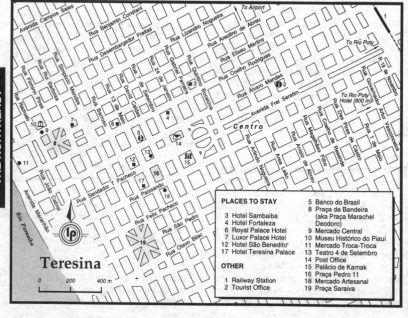

Teresina

0   200   400 m

PLACES TO STAY

3 Hotel Sambaiba
4 Hotel Fortaleza
6 Royal Palace Hotel
7 Luxor Palace Hotel
12 Hotel São Benedito'
17 Hotel Teresina Palace

OTHER

1 Railway Station
2 Tourist Office

5 Banco do Brasil
8 Praça da Bandeira
   (aka Praça Marachel
   Deodoro)
9 Mercado Central
10 Museu Histórico do Piauí
11 Mercado Troca-Troca
13 Teatro 4 de Setembro
14 Post Office
15 Palácio de Karnak
16 Praça Pedro 11
18 Mercado Artesanal
19 Praça Saraiva

exhibitions of cartoons, comedy routines and lots of live music.

Places to Stay – bottom end

The *Hotel São Benedito* (☎ 223-7382), at Rua Senador Teodoro Pachêco 1199, is a friendly place with quartos at US$7/12 for singles/doubles, and apartamentos at US$10/15. The *Hotel Fortaleza* (☎ 222-2984), at Rua Coelho Rodrigues 1476, is another good budget option with quartos (with fan) at US$7.50/13.50 for singles/doubles. Apartamentos with air-con cost US$9/18.

Camping *PIEMTUR Camping* (☎ 222-6202) is 12 km out of the city on Estrada da Socopo, the road running east towards União.

Places to Stay – middle

The two-star *Hotel Teresina Palace* (☎ 222-2770), at Rua Paissandu 1219, is fairly swish. It has a swimming pool, and provides apartamentos (with air-con) at US$31/36 for singles/doubles. The *Hotel Sambaiba* (☎ 222-6711), at Rua Gabriel Ferreira 230, gives a similar deal, with apartamentos at US$32/37 for singles/doubles. The *Royal Palace Hotel* (☎ 222-8707; fax 223-1521), at Rua 13 de Maio 233, has apartamentos (with air-con) starting at US$26/32 for singles/doubles.

Places to Stay – top end

Shaped like a pyramid, the five-star *Rio Poty Hotel* (☎ 223-1500; fax 222-6671), at Avenida Marechal Castelo Branco 555, is the poshest place in town. Rooms cost US$100/125 for singles/doubles.

Another luxury pad with very smooth service is the *Luxor Palace Hotel* (☎ 222-4911; fax 222-4171), at Praça Marechal Deodoro 310, which has rooms costing US$105/115 for singles/doubles – discounts of up to 30% are available for cash or credit-card payment.

Places to Eat

If you feel like seafood, try *Camarão do Elias*, at Avenida Pedro Almeida 457, or *O Pesqueirinho*, which is at Avenida Jorge Velho 6889, several km outside town on the riverside. It serves crab and shrimp stew. For a splurge, visit the *Forno e Fogão*, inside the Hotel Luxor which charges US$8 per person for a gigantic buffet lunch. There's also a good restaurant inside the Teresina Palace Hotel serving regional food. *Chez Matrinchan*, at Avenida NS de Fatima 671 (Jockey Club district), is divided into three elements: a restaurant serving French cuisine, a pizzeria and a nightclub. There's live music here on Friday and Saturday nights.

Getting There & Away

Air The airport is on Avenida Centenário, six km north of the centre. There are flights between Teresina and Rio, São Paulo, and the major cities in the Northeast and North.

Varig (☎ 223-4427) has an office at Rua Desembargador Freitas 1177, and VASP (☎ 223-3222) is at Rua Frei Serafim 1826.

Bus Teresina has regular bus connections with: Sobral (US$9.50, seven hours); Fortaleza (US$15, or US$23 for leito, ten hours); São Luís (US$10 for frequent daily service, seven hours); and Belém (US$19, 15 hours, five times a day).

To Parnaíba there are two executivo buses (US$10, four hours) and several standard buses (US$9, six hours) daily. There are bus connections twice daily to São Raimundo Nonato (US$14, 10 hours). To Piracuruca (US$7, 3½ hours), there are several departures daily, and buses run hourly between 5.45 am and 7 pm for Piripiri (US$4.50, three hours). There's one direct bus daily with the Empresa Barroso bus company to Pedro Segundo, at 4.15 pm, or you can take one of several connections daily from Piripiri.

Car If you're driving to São Luís, the *Pousada Buriti Corrente* (☎ 521-1668) (between Codó and Caxias) on BR-316 at Km 513, is a beautiful hotel with apartamentos at US$19/25 for singles/doubles, and a small zoo. It's 14 km from an alcohol factory. For tours, ask for Sérgio or Marcos.

Getting Around
To/From the Rodoviária The cheapest option is to take the bus from the stop outside the rodoviária – it's OK if you arrive at night, when it's cooler, but during the day it's a frying pan on wheels.

Although the rodoviária has a bilheteria with a mandatory price table posted on the window, the ticket price for a taxi ride to the city centre is calculated at US$9 – almost twice what you pay if you walk out to the road and hail one there. Clearly a scam.

LITORAL PIAUIENSE
Parnaíba
Parnaíba, once a major port at the mouth of the Rio Parnaíba, is a charming town which is being developed as a beach resort, along with the town of Luís Correia, which is 18 km away. It's well worth a trip from Teresina, and onward travel to Maranhão state is possible for adventurous travellers. Porto das Barcas, the old warehouse section along the riverfront, has been carefully restored, and contains a maritime museum, an artesanato centre, art galleries, bars and restaurants.

Information The Piemtur office (no phone) is in Porto das Barcas. They have some brochures, and can provide information about the boat trip around the Delta do Parnaíba and buses to local destinations.

The Banco do Brasil on Praça da Graça changes money.

The main post office is on Praça da Graça, next to the Banco do Brasil. The telephone office is at Avenida Presidente Vargas 390.

Beaches & Lagoons Praia Pedra do Sal, 15 km north-east of the centre, on Ilha Grande Santa Isabel, is a good beach divided by rocks into a calm section suitable for swimming, and a rough section preferred by surfers. Lagoa do Portinho is a lagoon surrounded by dunes about 14 km east of Parnaíba on the road to Luís Correia. It's a

popular spot for swimming, boating, sailing and fishing.

The prime beaches closer to Luís Correia are Praia do Coqueiro and Praia de Atalaia. The latter is very popular at weekends and has plenty of barracas selling drinks and seafood. The nearby lagoon, Lagoa do Sobradinho, is renowned for its shifting sands which bury surrounding trees.

Delta do Parnaíba The Delta do Parnaíba is a 2700-sq-km expanse of islands, beaches, lagoons, sand dunes and mangrove forest, with abundant wildlife, which straddles the border of Piauí and Maranhão. One photographer recently described the amount of wildlife as 'comparable to what I saw on good days in the Pantanal'. Sixty-five per cent of its area is in Maranhão state, but the easiest access is from Parnaíba. Day trips by boat around the delta run from Porto das Barcas on weekends, with a stop on Ilha do Caju – the cost is around US$30. Ilha do Caju has been owned for several generations by a family who are now trying to establish an ecological reserve there. There is one pousada on the island. For more details, contact the Piemtur office in Porto das Barcas.

Places to Stay The *Pousada Porto das Barcas* (no phone) is a friendly hostel in a restored warehouse right in Porto das Barcas. Dorm rooms cost US$3 per person, with a good breakfast included. There's a campground at Lagoa do Portinho, where the *Centro Recreativa Lagoa do Portinho* (☎ 322-1982) also provides apartamentos at $US10 per person and chalets at US$14 per person. The *Hotel Cívico* (☎ 322-2470; fax 322-2028), at Avenida Governor Chagas Rodrigues 474, in the centre of town, has a swimming pool and apartamentos starting at US$16/23 for singles/doubles.

At Luís Correira, there's the three-star *Rio Poty Hotel* (☎ & fax 367-1277), on the beach, or the *Hotel Central*, a cheaper, family-run place. On the beach at Pedra do Sol, the *Pousada do Sol* has been recommended by readers.

Places to Eat *Sabor e Arte*, on Rua Almirante Gervasio Sampaio, is a relaxed little place with cheap home-cooked meals and interesting original art on the walls. In Porto das Barcas, *Restaurant Portas das Barcas* has a great riverfront patio and local seafood dishes. Across the street, *Comilão* has good pizzas.

Getting There & Away For bus services between Parnaíba and Teresina, see the Getting There & Away section for Teresina. Agencia Empresa São Francisco runs two buses daily from Praça Santa Cruz to Tutóia (Maranhão state), at noon and 5 pm. The trip takes about four hours over a brain-rattling dirt road. From Tutóia there are trucks running to Barreirinhas, for access to the Parque Nacional dos Lençóis Maranhenses – see the Tutóia section in the Maranhão chapter for more details.

A small wooden boat plies a route daily through the Delta do Parnaíba to Tutóia (US$4, about six hours). This is a good way to check out some of the Delta do Parnaíba – if you have a hammock, you can sling it on the top deck, relax back and enjoy the voyage. The boat leaves from Porto Salgado, on the riverfront close to Porto das Barcas, between 10 am and noon – check at the port in the morning for departure times.

PARQUE NACIONAL DE SETE CIDADES

Sete Cidades is a small national park with interesting rock formations, estimated to be at least 190 million years old, which resemble *sete cidades* (seven cities). Various researchers have analysed nearby rock inscriptions and deduced that the formations are ruined cities from the past. The Austrian historian Ludwig Schwennhagen visited the area in 1928 and thought he'd found the ruins of a Phoenician city. The French researcher Jacques de Mabieu considered Sete Cidades as proof that the Vikings had found a more agreeable climate in South America. And Erich van Daniken, the Swiss ufologist, theorised that extraterrestrials were responsible for the cities which were ruined by a great fire some 15,000 years ago. There's clearly lots of scope here for imaginative theories. See what you think!

The road around the park's geological monuments starts one km further down from the Abrigo do IBAMA (IBAMA office and hostel). The loop is a leisurely couple of hours' stroll. It's best to start your hike early in the morning and bring water because it gets hot; watch out for the *cascavelas* – poisonous black-and-yellow rattlesnakes. The park is open from 6 am to 6 pm. Ask at the IBAMA office for information; guides are available at a small cost.

Sexta Cidade (Sixth City) and Pedra do Elefante, the first sites on the loop, are lumps of rock with strange scaly surfaces. The Pedra do Inscrição (Rock of Inscription) at Quinta Cidade (Fifth City) has red markings which some say are cryptic Indian runes. The highlight of Quarta Cidade (Fourth City) is the Mapa do Brasil (Map of Brazil), a negative image in a rock wall. The Biblioteca (Library), Arco de Triunfo (Triumphal Arch) and Cabeça do Cachorro (Dog's Head) are promontories with good views.

Places to Stay & Eat

Abrigo do IBAMA is a good-value hostel at the park entrance – rooms with fan cost US$6 per person. There's a restaurant attached to the hostel. Designated campsites are also available here.

The *Hotel Fazenda Sete Cidades* (☎ 276-2222), a two-star resort hotel six km from the park entrance, has attractive apartamentos for US$24/38 for singles/doubles. Even if you don't stay overnight, it's good for lunch and a quick dip in the pool.

Getting There & Away

The park is 180 km from Teresina and 141 km from Ubajara (Ceará state) on a fine paved road. Buses depart Teresina hourly between 5.45 am and 6 pm for Piripiri (US$4.50, three hours). There are several daily bus departures from Piripiri to Fortaleza (US$11, nine hours) and Parnaíba (US$4.50, three hours).

Getting Around

IBAMA courtesy bus transport for the 26-km trip to the park leaves from Piripiri daily at 7 am. There is usually some transport returning from Abrigo do IBAMA to Piripiri in the morning between 9 and 10 am, and a bus at 5 pm. A taxi from Piripiri costs around US$15. Hitchhiking is also effective. In the park itself, you can drive on the roads or follow the trails on foot.

PEDRO SEGUNDO

The town of Pedro Segundo lies in the hills of the Serra dos Matões, around 50 km south of Piripiri. Close to the town are several mines which are the only source of opals in South America.

The only accommodation in town is the *Hotel Rimo Pedro Segundo* (☎ 271-1543), on Avenida Itamaraty.

For bus services between Pedro Segundo and Teresina, see the Getting There & Away section for Teresina.

PARQUE NACIONAL SERRA DA CAPIVARA

The Parque Nacional Serra da Capivara, in the south-west of the state, was established in 1979 to protect the many prehistoric sites and examples of rock paintings in the region.

There are over 300 excavated sites which are opened to the public depending on the research schedule. If the staff have time, you may be lucky enough to receive a lift and be shown around. For details about access and archaeological sites, contact Doutora Niede Guidon at FUMDHAM (Fundação Museu do Homem Americano) (☎ 582-1612), at Rua Abdias Neves 551, São Raimundo Nonato. There are plans to open a museum and conduct guided tours of some of the sites.

Getting There & Away

For bus services between São Raimundo Nonato and Teresina, see the Getting There & Away section for Teresina.

Maranhão

Maranhão, with an area of 324,616 sq km and a population of five million, is the second largest state in the Northeast, after Bahia.

For many years after their discovery of Brazil, the Portuguese showed little interest in the area which now forms the state of Maranhão. In 1612, the French arrived to construct a fort at São Luís, which later became the capital of the state. See the section on São Luís for more details about the historical and economic development of Maranhão.

Although the southern and eastern areas of Maranhão are characterised by vast expanses of babaçu palms and typical sertão landscapes, the western and north-western regions merge into humid Amazon rainforests.

The rural economy of Maranhão is dependent on the babaçu palm, which serves an amazing multitude of purposes: the nuts can be eaten straight out of the fruit or crushed to produce vegetable oil (margarine) or industrial lubricating oils; the tips of the young palms can be eaten as 'palm hearts'; and the older trunks are used for construction of huts, with roofing material supplied by the leaves – which can also be used for the production of cellulose and paper. The residue from the crushed nuts provides excellent fertiliser and cattle feed; and the hulls of the fruits are used in the production of acetates, tar and methyl alcohol. Finally, the hulls are turned to charcoal for use in smelting. Things go better with babaçu!

The state's most recent impact on the country's political scene was made by Roseana Sarney, the daughter of former president José Sarney, who in November 1994 became the first woman in Brazil to be elected a state governor. Young and beautiful, 'Roseana', as she encouraged voters to call her, had her face splashed on just about every inch of available wall space during the campaign. She scraped into the job by the slimmest margin, with many residents claiming it was her family's connections and power that got her over the line. Meanwhile, her father recently established a $US12.5 million memorial to himself, complete with black-marble mortuary room, with part of the money paid by taxpayers.

SÃO LUÍS

São Luís, the capital of Maranhão, is a city with unpretentious colonial charm and a rich folkloric tradition – definitely a highlight for travellers in the Northeast. The population is a diverse mixture of Europeans, blacks and Indians. Apart from the attractions of the restored colonial architecture in the historical centre, São Luís offers passable beaches only half an hour from the centre (with better ones further afield), and the opportunity to cross Baía de São Marcos to visit Alcântara, an impressive historic town slipping regally into decay.

History

São Luís was the only city in Brazil founded and settled by the French. In 1612 three French ships sailed for Maranhão to try to cut off a chunk of Brazil. They were embraced by the local Indians, the Tupinambá, who hated the Portuguese. Once settled in São Luís, named after their King Louis XIII, the French enlisted the help of the Tupinambá to expand their precarious foothold by attacking tribes around the mouth of the Amazon.

But French support for the new colony was weak, and in 1614 the Portuguese set sail for Maranhão. A year later the French fled, and the Tupinambá were 'pacified' by the Portuguese.

Except for a brief Dutch occupation between 1641 and 1644, São Luís developed slowly as a port for the export of sugar, and later for cotton exports. As elsewhere, the plantation system was established with slaves and Indian labour, despite the relatively poor lands. When demand for these crops slackened in the 19th century, São Luís went into a long and slow decline.

In recent years the economy of São Luís has been stimulated by several mega-projects. A modern port complex has been built to export the mineral riches of the Serra dos Carajás, a range of hills in the Amazon which has the world's largest deposits of iron ore. In 1980s, Alcoa Aluminium built an enormous factory for aluminium processing – you'll see it along the highway south of the city. The US$1.5 billion price tag for this project was the largest private investment in Brazil's history. A missile station has been built near Alcântara, and oil has been found in the bay.

Orientation

Perched on a hill overlooking the Baía de

Bumba Meu Boi

São Luís is famous for its Bumba Meu Boi – a fascinating, wild folkloric festival with a Carnivalesque atmosphere in which participants dance, sing and tell the story of the death and resurrection of the bull – with plenty of room for improvisation. Parade groups spend the year in preparation, costumes are lavish and new songs and poetry are invented. There are three forms of Bumba Meu Boi in Maranhão: *bois de matraca*; *bois de zabumba*; and *bois de orquestra*.

The story and its portrayal differ throughout the Northeast, but the general plot is as follows:

Castrina, goddaughter of the local farm owner, is pregnant and feels a craving to eat the tongue of the best *boi* (bull) on the farm. She cajoles her husband, Chico, to kill the beast. Once the dead bull is discovered, several characters (caricatures drawn from all levels of society) do some detective work and finally track down the perpetrator of the crime. Chico is brought to trial, but the bull is resuscitated by various magic incantations and tunes. A pardon is granted and the story reaches its happy ending when Chico is reunited with Catrina.

The festivals start in the second half of June and continue into the second week of August. Give the tourist office a call to get the exact date. ■

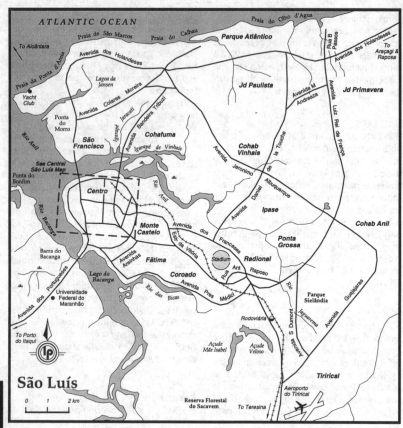

São Luís

0 1 2 km

São Marcos, São Luís is actually on an island of the same name. The historic core of São Luís, now known as Projeto Reviver (Project Renovation), lies below the hill. Going north from the old town, the Ponte José Sarney bridge will take you across to São Francisco, where there is the new and affluent district with several hotels, restaurants and trendy nightspots.

It's easy to get around on foot – despite the hills and confusing street layout – because everything is so close. In fact, as long as you're in the old part of town, a bus is rarely needed.

The most confusing thing about getting around São Luís is the existence of several different names for the same streets. There are the new official names that are on street signs and the historical names or nicknames that the locals use. No two city maps seem to be the same.

Alternative Street Names The following is a short list of streets with their common alternative names in brackets:

28 de Julho (Rua do Giz)
Rua da Estrêla (Rua Candido Mendes)

Rua Afonso Pena (Rua Formosa)
Rua do Sol (Rua Nina Rodrigues)
Rua do Egito (Rua Tarquinho Lopes)
Rua do Veado (Rua Celso Magalhães)
Rua dos Afogados (Rua José Bonifácio)
Rua de Nazaré (Rua de Nazaré e Odilo)
Rua das Barrocas (Beco dos Barqueiros; Rua Isaacs Martins)
Rua Jacinto Maia (Rua da Cascata)
Rua Portugal (Rua Trapiche)
Rua da Alfândega (Rua Marcelino de Almeida)
Praça Dom Pedro II (Avenida Dom Pedro II)

Information

Tourist Office São Luís has recently upgraded its tourist information facilities. Maratur, the state tourism organisation, has its head office just off Praça Dom Pedro II (see map). Other Maratur information booths are on Praça João Lisboa, next to the main post office; on Rua da Estrala, in the historic centre; at the rodoviária; and at the Centro de Artesanato (CEPRAMA), on Rua de São Panteleão 1232. Sebrae, a quasi-governmental industry organisation, has a high-tech tourist information booth on Praça Dom Pedro Segundo II. This is a good place to make contact with local guides, such as Simon Ramos (☎ 236-4069) or Senhor Obrito.

For details about national parks in the state, contact IBAMA (☎ 222-7288), at Avenida Jaime Tavares 25.

Money Banco do Brasil is at Avenida Gomes de Castro 46. Banco da Amazonia, at Avenida Pedro Segundo II 140, also changes money, and is more conveniently located if you are staying in the historical district.

Post & Telephone The main post office and TELMA, the state telephone company, are in the same building on Praça João Lisboa.

Foreign Consulates The following countries are represented in São Luís:

Denmark
    Rua do Sol 141 (☎ 222-4075)
France
    Rua Santo Antônio 259, Colégio Franco Maranhense (☎ 222-2732)
Germany
    Praça Gonçalves Dias 310 (☎ 221-2294)
Italy
    Avenida do Vale 9 (☎ 227-2387)

Travel Agencies In the shopping gallery at Rua do Sol 141, there are several travel agencies offering organised tours to Alcântara, Parque Nacional dos Lençóis Maranheses and other destinations in the state. The travel agencies also sell bus tickets at the same price as at the rodoviária. An efficient travel agency in the shopping gallery is Taguatur (☎ 232-0906) at loja 14. Riberão Tourismo, in the front of the shopping gallery facing the street, and Delmundo Tourismo (☎ 222-8719), close by, on Rua da Riberão, are also both reliable agencies.

You can obtain a guide at the travel agencies, or make contact with local guides at Sebrae, on Praça João Lisboa.

Catedral da Sé

Constructed by the Jesuits in 1726 as the Igreja NS da Boa Morte, this building became the official cathedral in 1762. Inside, there's a fine baroque altar and ceiling frescoes decorated with babaçu motifs.

Palácio dos Leões

Originally a French fortress built in 1612 by Daniel de la Touche, during the reign of Louis XIII, this is now the Palácio do Governo, the state governor's residence and office. The interior reflects the pomp of Versailles and French architectural tastes. Visiting hours are 3 to 6 pm on Monday, Wednesday and Friday.

Projeto Reviver

During the late 1980s, the state authorities finally agreed to restore the historical district, which had been neglected and decaying for many decades. The initial restoration project was completed in 1990, but the new governor, Roseana Sarney, has promised new funds for ongoing work.

Over 200 buildings have already been restored and the district has been turned into one of the architectural highlights of Brazil.

THE NORTHEAST

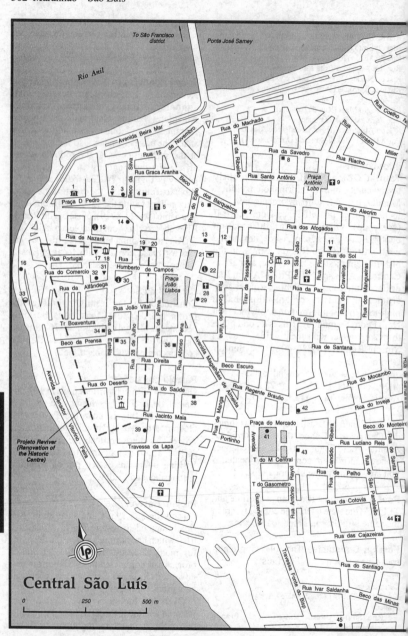

To São Francisco district

Ponte José Samey

Rio Anil

Avenida Beira Mar

Rua 15 de Novembro

Rua Graca Aranha

Rua da Silva

Beco

Rua do Machado

Rua da Ribeirão

Rua da Savedro

8

Rua Santo Antônio

Rua Riacho

Rua Jonsem

Rua Miller

Rua Coelho N

Praça Antônio Lobo

9

1

2 3

4

Praça D Pedro II

5

Rua do Egito

6

7

Rua dos Barqueiros

Rua do Alecrim

15

14

Rua dos Afogados

Rua de Nazaré

13   12

11

19 20

Rua Portugal

17 18

Rua Humberto de Campos

21

16

31

32 30

Rua do Comercio

Praça João Lisboa

22

Rua São João

23

24

Rua do Cruz

Rua da Paz

Rua da Passagem

Rua Flores

Rua do Sol

Rua dos Craveiros

Rua dos Mangueiras

33

Rua da Alfândega

28
29

Rua Godofredo Viana

Trav da Passagem

Tr Boaventura

Rua da Palma

Rua Grande

34

Beco da Prensa

35

Rua 28 de Julho

36

Rua João Vital

Rua Afonso Pena

Rua de Santana

Rua do Mocambo

Rua da Estrêla

Rua Direita

Rua do Deserto

Rua do Saúde

38

Beco Escuro

Rua Regente Braulio

Rua do Inveja

Avenida Magalhães de Almeida

42

Beco do Monteiro

37

Rua Jacinto Maia

Rua de Maria

Praça do Mercado

Ribeira

Rua Luciano Reis

Rua de Santa

39

Portinho

41

Rua Candido

Rua de São Pantaleão

Projeto Reviver (Renovation of the Historic Centre)

Travessa da Lapa

43

T do M Central

Rua de Pelho

Avenida

40

T do Gasometro

Rua Antônio Rayol

Rua da Cotovia

44

Guaxenduba

Rua das Cajazeiras

Rua do Santiago

Travessa Forta

Rua Ivar Saldanha

Beco das Minas

45

Avenida Senador Vitorino Feira

THE NORTHEAST

Central São Luís

0   250   500 m

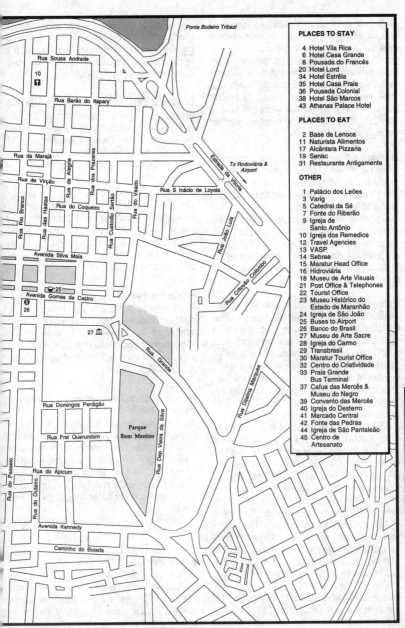

PLACES TO STAY

4 Hotel Vila Rica
6 Hotel Casa Grande
8 Pousada do Francês
20 Hotel Lord
34 Hotel Estrêla
35 Hotel Casa Praia
36 Pousada Colonial
38 Hotel São Marcos
43 Athenas Palace Hotel

PLACES TO EAT

2 Base da Lenoca
11 Naturista Alimentos
17 Alcântara Pizzaria
19 Senac
31 Restaurante Antigamente

OTHER

1 Palácio dos Leões
3 Varig
5 Catedral da Sé
7 Fonte do Riberão
9 Igreja de
Santo Antônio
10 Igreja dos Remedios
12 Travel Agencies
13 VASP
14 Sebrae
15 Maratur Head Office
16 Hidroviária
18 Museu de Arte Visuais
21 Post Office & Telephones
22 Tourist Office
23 Museu Histórico do
Estado de Maranhão
24 Igreja de São João
25 Buses to Airport
26 Banco do Brasil
27 Museu de Arte Sacre
28 Igreja do Carmo
29 Transbrasil
30 Maratur Tourist Office
32 Centro do Criatividade
33 Praia Grande
Bus Terminal
37 Cafua das Mercês &
Museu do Negro
39 Convento das Mercês
40 Igreja do Desterro
41 Mercado Central
42 Fonte das Pedras
44 Igreja de São Pantaleão
45 Centro de
Artesanato

THE NORTHEAST

To appreciate the superb colonial mansions and the many designs and colours of their azulejo facades, just wander around the district. Azulejos were first produced in Portugal and later became a popular product in France, Belgium and Germany. Since azulejos provided a durable means to protect outside walls from the humidity and heat in São Luís, their use became standard practice during colonial times.

Museu de Artes Visuais This museum has a fine collection of old azulejos, engravings, prints and paintings. It's open from 9 am to 5 pm Monday to Friday, and from 2 to 6 pm on Saturday and Sunday.

Opposite the museum is the old round market, where you can shop with the locals for dried salted shrimp (eaten with shell and all), cachaça, dried goods and basketwork, or visit the lunch counters for cheap local cooking.

Cafua das Mercês & Museu do Negro This museum is housed in the old slave market building where slaves were once kept after their arrival from Africa and until they were sold – notice the absence of windows. A small and striking series of displays documents the history of slavery in Maranhão. The museum is open from 1 to 5.30 pm Tuesday to Saturday, and from 2.30 to 5.30 pm on Sunday.

The African slaves brought to Maranhão were Bantus from Africa who were used primarily on the sugar plantations, and to a lesser extent for the cultivation of rice and cotton. They brought their own type of Candomblé, which is called Tambor de Mina in this part of Brazil. The museum director, Jorge Babalaou, is an expert on Candomblé and Bantu/Maranhense folklore. He may be able to indicate where you can visit a ceremony, but the major houses, the Casa das Minas, Casa de Nagô and Casa Fanti-Ashanti-Nagô, don't welcome visitors.

Museu do Centro de Cultura Popular This museum is at Rua 28 de Julho 221, just a few minutes on foot from the Cafua das Mercês.

The displays include a good collection of handicrafts from the state of Maranhão, and Bumba Meu Boi costumes and masks. It's open from 3 to 6 pm Monday to Friday, and from 10 am to 1 pm on Saturday and Sunday.

Centro do Criatividade This exhibition and performance space in the heart of Projeto Reviver is for culture vultures interested in the local art scene. There's a theatre for local plays and dance productions, an art gallery and a cinema showing arthouse films.

Igreja do Desterro

This church, notable for its facade, was built between 1618 and 1641 and is the only byzantine church in Brazil. There's a small adjoining museum, the Museu de Paramentos Eclesiásticos, with a display of ecclesiastical apparel.

Fonte das Pedras

This fountain, built by the Dutch during their brief occupation of São Luís, marks the spot where, on 31 October 1615, Jerônimo de Albuquerque and his troops camped before expelling the French. The fountain is located inside a small, shady park.

Museu Histórico e Artístico do Estado de Maranhão

This museum, housed in a restored mansion originally built in 1836, provides an idea of daily life in the 18th century, with an attractive display of artefacts from wealthy Maranhão families. There are furnishings, family photographs, religious articles, coins, sacred art – and President José Sarney's bassinet.

Opening hours are 10 am to 5 pm Tuesday to Saturday.

Fonte do Ribeirão

This is a delightful fountain, built in 1796, with spouting gargoyles. The three metal gates once provided access to subterranean tunnels which were reportedly linked to churches as a means to escape danger.

Beaches

The beaches are beyond São Francisco district and they are all busy on sunny weekends. You should beware of rough surf and tremendous tides in the area: ask for local advice about safe times and places to swim before you head for the beaches. For accommodation at the beaches, see the section on Places to Stay.

Ponta d'Areia is the closest beach to the city, only 3.5 km away, but the pollution has put a stop to bathing. It's a popular beach for those who want to make a quick exit from the city and visit the barracas and restaurants here for beach food.

The next beach, **Calhau**, is broad and beautiful and only 7.5 km from the city. The locals like to drive their cars onto Calhau (as well as the next beach, Olho d'Agua) park and lay out their towels alongside their machines. On weekends this causes congestion which spoils enjoyment of these good city beaches.

Olho d'Agua, 11.5 km from São Luís, has more beach barracas and football games. It's active and fun on weekends.

Praia do Araçagi, four km further, is the quietest and most peaceful of these beaches. There are only simple bars and a few weekend beach houses.

Tours

The tour agencies and tour guides described in the previous sections on Travel Agencies & Tour Guides provide city tours of São Luís and day trips to São José do Ribamar or Alcântara. Prices average US$35 per person per day and include transport and guide services only – you pay admission fees, meals, etc. Taguatur and Delmundo Tourismo both run tours to Parque Nacional de Lençóis Maranhenses. A three-day tour costs around $US175, including accommodation in Barreirinhas, bus and boat transport.

Festivals

São Luís has one of Brazil's richest folkloric traditions, which manifests itself during its many festivals. Carnival is supposedly a real hit. There are active samba clubs and distinctive local dances and music. Most Carnival activity is out on the streets and the tourist influence is minimal.

The Tambor de Mina festivals, held in July, are important events for followers of the Afro-Brazilian religions in São Luís, and São Luís' famous Bumba Meu Boi festival commences in the second half of June, continuing until the second week of August. The Festa do Divino, celebrated on Pentecost (between May and June), is especially spectacular in Alcântara.

Places to Stay – bottom end

City Centre The nicest budget option is the *Hotel Casa Grande* (☎ 232-2432), at Avenida das Barracas 98. Large, clean apartamentos cost US$10/12/15 for singles/doubles/triples, with a good breakfast included. Some of the rooms on the 3rd floor have views over the river. The *Hotel Estrêla* (☎ 222-7172), at Rua da Estrêla 370, is a popular cheapie in the heart of the historic district. Quartos (with fan) cost US$8/13 for singles/doubles. Don't leave valuables in your room. The *Hotel Praia Grande* close by, at Rua 14 de Julho 20, (☎ 221-4144) offers similar standard accommodation, with quartos at US$8/12 for singles/doubles and apartamentos at US$15, single or double.

There are several very cheap places along Rua da Palma and Rua Alfonso Pena which are right in the heart of town, but not too safe at night. The *Hotel São Marcos* (☎ 232-3763), at Rua do Saúde 178, has started to deteriorate and the management doesn't seem keen on cleaning it up. Apartamentos cost US$17/22 for singles/doubles. There's a swimming pool filled with murky water.

A much better deal is the *Hotel Lord* (☎ 222-5544), at Rua de Nazaré 258. It's a large, time-worn hotel with comfortable quartos at US$10/12 for singles/doubles; and apartamentos (with air-con) at US$14/17 for singles/doubles.

The *Athenas Palace Hotel* (☎ 221-4163), at Rua Antônio Rayol 431, just east of the Mercado Central, also offers good value. Apartamentos with fan cost US$12/14 for singles/doubles, or US$14/18 with air-con.

The area is not too safe at night (if you have a car, make sure the hotel staff let you use the locked parking lot behind the hotel).

Beaches The *Pousada Tia Maria* (☎ 227-1534) at QD 1, lote 12, on Ponta d'Areia beach, has apartamentos at US$18/25 for singles/doubles, but it's a bit out of the way.

Camping The nearest campground, *Unicamping* (☎ 222-2552), is close to Calhau beach – eight km out of town. For long-term accommodation (houses or rooms), call ☎ 222-2425.

Places to Stay – middle
City Centre The *Pousada do Francês* (☎ 221-4866; fax 223-0334), at Rua 7 de Setembro 121, is housed in a beautifully restored colonial building. Apartamentos with air-con, refrigerator and TV cost US$30/42 for singles/doubles, and some of the higher rooms have views. There's also a swish bar/restaurant in the hotel. The *Pousada Colonial* (☎ 232-2834), at Rua Afonso Pena 112, is in a restored colonial mansion and offers good value. Comfortable apartamentos cost US$24/28 for singles/doubles – discounts can be negotiated for cash payment.

Beaches At Araçagi beach there's one medium-priced hotel, the *Chalé da Lagoa* (☎ 226-4196), which is a relaxing place surrounded by gardens.

Places to Stay – top end
City Centre The five-star *Vila Rica* (☎ 232-3535; fax 222-1251) is very central, at Praça Dom Pedro II 299, with a view overlooking the bay. Singles/doubles cost a whopping US$196/208 – but 30% discounts for cash payment are available.

São Francisco There are several up-market hotels in the São Francisco district – north of town, on the other side of the Rio Anil. These are not recommended unless you have a car or prefer to stay outside the city centre.
The *Hotel São Francisco* (☎ 227-1155;

fax 235-2138), at Rua Luís Serson 77, has singles/doubles for US$50/60. The *Panorama Palace Hotel* (☎ 227-0067; fax 227-4736), at Rua dos Pinheiros Q-16, 15, has singles/doubles for US$45/55 or you could splurge US$85 for the Presidential Suite (600 sq metres!), which the management claims is the largest of its kind in Brazil.

Beaches The five-star *Sofitel Quatro Rodas* (☎ 227-0244; fax 227-4737) is at Calhau beach, a 15-minute drive from town. It has singles/doubles for US$85/95.

Places to Eat
The best maranhense food comes from the sea. In São Luís you'll find many of the familiar dishes of the Northeast, and regional specialities such as torta de sururu (mussel pie), casquinha de caranguejo (stuffed crab), caldeirada de camarão (shrimp stew) and the city's special rice dish – arroz de cuxá (rice with vinegar, local vegetables and shrimp).

City Centre There are plenty of lanchonetes serving cheap food. Across from the Fonte do Ribeirão, you'll find a couple of good snack bars with sucos.
The *Base da Lenoca*, on Praça Dom Pedro II, is a popular restaurant with a great position overlooking the Rio Anil – order a beer and a snack and enjoy the breeze. In the heart of the historic district, on Rua da Estrêla, there's the *Restaurante Antigamente*, which has tables on the street and seafood and meat dishes. Live music is offered here in the evening on weekends. *Senac*, at Rua de Nazaré 244, offers fine dining in a lovely colonial building. *Naturista Alimentos*, at Rua do Sol 517, has the best vegetarian food in the city. *Pizzaria Alcântara*, on Rua Portugal, has reasonable pizzas and refeicões.

São Francisco The main drag through São Francisco has many new restaurants, particularly pizzerias and bars. The *Oriental*, at Avenida Presidente Castelo Branco 47, has a nice view and serves Chinese food.

Further from the City Centre The seafood

is highly recommended at *Base do Germano* (☎ 222-3276), at Avenida Wenceslau Brás, in Camboa district. *Base do Edilson* (☎ 222-7210), at Rua Alencar Campos 31, in the Vila Bessa district, is a 10-minute drive from the city centre. The restaurant starts serving lunch at 11.30 am and dinner at 7 pm. The portions are not big for what you pay, but we'd suggest ensopado de camarão com molho pirão and peixada com pirão, for US$12.

Beaches At Ponte d'Areia, *Tia Maria* has good seafood, and it's also a fine place to watch the sunset over a cool drink. This is also the closest beach to the city with barracas serving food.

Entertainment

São Luís is currently the reggae centre of the Northeast, and many of the nightspots cater to *reggeiros* (reggae fans). The tourist office has a list of places to check out – some of them can be a bit dangerous, although this also seemed to be a prerequisite for a happening place! It's worth asking locals for recommendations. Espaco Aberto, at Rua Epitácio Cafeteria 117, São Francisco, is a good place to start.

For dancing, try Boate Génesis, at Avenida dos Holandeses Qd-28, 4, at Calhau beach; Boate Tucanos, at Avenida Jerônimo Albuquerque, Curva do 90, in the Vinhais district, north-east of the city centre; or Le Mason, at Rua Haroldo Paiva 110, São Crisóvão.

Things to Buy

São Luís is the place to look for the traditional handicrafts of Maranhão, such as woodcarving, basketry, lacework, ceramics, leatherwork, and woven goods made from linen, local plant fibres and straw. Also on sale are featherwork, and items made from woven straw or plant fibres (from baskets to bracelets) by the Urubus-Caapor Indians and the Guajajara Indians, both from the interior of Maranhão state.

CEPRAMA (Centro de Artesanato), at Rua de São Pantaleão 1232, is housed in a renovated factory and functions as an exhibition hall and sales outlet for handicrafts. It's open from 3 to 9 pm on Sunday and Monday, and from 9 am to 9 pm Tuesday to Saturday. Also worth visiting are the Centro Artesanal do Maranhão at Avenida Marechal Castelo Branco 605, and the Mercado Central. The Mercado Central is open from 7 am to 4 pm Monday to Saturday, and the Centro Artesanal do Maranhão is open from 8 am to 8 pm Monday to Friday and from 8 am to 1 pm on Saturday.

Getting There & Away

Air A new international airport is in the pipeline for São Luís, with construction due to start in 1995. Currently, domestic air services connect São Luís with Rio, São Paulo and the major cities in the Northeast and the North.

Following are the addresses for Brazilian and foreign airlines:

Air France
    Praça Gonçalves Dias 301 (☎ 221-2294)
Transbrasil
    Praça João Lisboa 432 (☎ 223-1414)
Varig/Cruzeiro
    Avenida Dom Pedro Segundo 268 (☎ 222-0332)
VASP
    Rua do Sol 43 (☎ 222-4655)

Bus The rodoviária is about eight km southeast of the city centre. Bus tickets can be booked and purchased in the city centre at several travel agencies listed under Information earlier in this section.

There are frequent daily buses to Teresina (US$10, seven hours); Belém (US$22, 12 hours, twice daily); Carolina (US$26, 12 hours, once daily via Imperatriz); Guimarães (US$24, ten hours, once daily); Fortaleza (US$25, 16 hours); and Recife (US$36, 24 hours, twice daily).

Boat The *hidroviária* (boat terminal) is on the quayside, just beyond the western end of Rua Portugal. From here, it's possible to take passage on boats sailing along the coast. Sailing times are always approximate and depend on the tides. The regular daily service to Alcântara is described in the Getting There & Away section for Alcântara. There are regular local services to Pinheiro, Porto de Itaúna and São Bento.

There are also departures at least once a week to Guimarães, a major centre for boat-building and fishing, and infrequent departures from there to destinations further along the western coast, such as Turiaçu, Luís Domingues and Carutapera (on the Pará border).

Getting Around

To/From the Airport The Aeroporto do Tirirical (☎ 245-1515) is 15 km south-east of the city. The bus marked 'São Cristóvâo' runs from the bus stop opposite the Banco do Brasil on Praça Deodoro to the airport in 35 minutes. There's a bilheteria system for taxis at the airport – a taxi to the centre costs US$13, but we were quoted as low as US$8 in the city centre for the same trip.

To/From the Rodoviária The rodoviária (☎ 223-0253) is about 10 km south-east of the city, on Avenida dos Franceses. Several buses go to the rodoviária from Praça Deodoro, and you can also pick one up at the Praia Grande bus terminal on Avenida Beira Mar. There's a bilheteria system for taxis – from the rodoviária to the city centre costs US$8.

To/From the Beaches Buses run to Ponta d'Areia and Calhau from Praça Deodoro and from the Praia Grande bus terminal on Avenida Beira Mar – take buses marked 'Ponta d'Areia' or 'Calhau'. For buses to Araçagi, Raposa and São José do Ribamar, there's a bus stop beside the Mercado Central. To get to Olho d'Agua, take a bus marked 'Olho d'Agua' from Praça Deodoro, or take a bus to Calhau and walk from there.

ILHA DE SÃO LUÍS
Praia da Raposa

Out at the tip of the Ilha de São Luís, 30 km from the city, is the interesting fishing centre of Raposa, also known for its lacework. It's a poor town, built on stilts above mangrove swamps, which gives it an unusual appearance. The bulk of the town's population is descended from Cearense immigrants. There are no tourist facilities but the ocean here is pretty and very shallow. There are lots of small fishing boats and it's not too hard to negotiate a ride. Bathing at the beach is dangerous due to extreme tidal variations. The water recedes up to one km at low tide.

Getting There & Away

There are frequent buses from São Luís – a convenient bus stop is the one beside the Mercado Central. The trip takes 45 minutes.

The São José do Ribamar Miracle

The origins of the town date back to the early 18th century when a Portuguese sailing ship went astray and started to flounder on the sandbanks of the Baia de São José. The desperate crew begged for mercy from São José das Botas and promised to procure the finest statue of the saint and construct a chapel for it if they were spared.

The ship and its crew were miraculously saved, and several years later, the promise was kept when a fine statue of the saint was installed in a chapel at the tip of the cape where the disaster was narrowly avoided. The settlement on this site later received the name São José do Ribamar: a fusion of the saint's name and the local Indian name for the rock formation at the cape.

According to local legend, the statue was moved away from its site beside the shore, but miraculously reappeared in its original position the next day – without any signs of human intervention. This miracle was repeated a couple more times, until the locals decided the statue should be left in its preferred place. During its trek, the statue left deep footprints along the rocky coastline which are now venerated by the townsfolk, who host the annual Festa do Pedroeiro (held in September) in honour of the saint. ■

São José do Ribamar

This fishing town is on the east coast of the island, 30 km from the city. There's a busy little waterfront with boats leaving for small towns along the coast. This is a good way to explore some of the untouristed villages on the island. On Sunday buses go from São José to nearby Ponta de Panaquatira, a popular weekend beach.

Places to Stay & Eat There are two hotels: the *Hotel Mar e Sol* and the *Hotel Tropical*. Both offer simple quartos for about US$8 per person, and both have restaurants. Beach camping is permitted at Panaquatira beach. The seven-metre tide is very fast, so don't camp close to the water.

Getting There & Away Frequent buses leave from São Luís (convenient bus stop beside the Mercado Central) for the 45-minute trip to São José do Ribamar. The last bus back to São Luís leaves at 10.30 pm.

AROUND SÃO LUÍS
Alumar

One of the world's largest aluminium processing plants is on the outskirts of São Luís. Alumar is a co-operative venture between the Brazilian government and a Shell Oil/Alcoa consortium. Bauxite ore is extracted from mines in Pará and brought by rail to the Alumar plant for processing. Tours are conducted on Saturday (☎ 216-1155). Call a few days in advance for reservations. A company bus leaves from Praça Teodoro in São Luís.

ALCÂNTARA

Across the Baía de São Marcos from São Luís is the old colonial town of Alcântara. Founded in the early 1600s with extensive slave labour, the town was the hub of the region's sugar and cotton economy. The beneficiaries of this wealth, Maranhão's rich landowners, preferred living in Alcântara to São Luís.

While the town has been in decline since the latter half of the 19th century, it is still considered an architectural treasure, and some experts claim that it is the most homogeneous group of colonial buildings and ruins from the 17th and 18th centuries in Brazil.

Construction of the Centro do Lançamento de Alcântara (CLA), a nearby rocket-launching facility, caused mutterings amongst residents, who disagreed with the forceful resettlement policy undertaken to clear the construction site. There couldn't be a greater contrast with this slumbering colonial town than a space-age launching pad!

Information

The tourist office in São Luís has brochures about Alcântara. Phone connections with Alcântara are effected through the TELMA office in Alcântara, where you can leave a message.

Things to See & Do

The town is very poor and decaying, but don't miss the following: the beautiful row of two-storey houses on **Rua Grande**; the **Igreja de NS do Carmo** (1665); and the best preserved **pelourinho** (whipping post) in Brazil, on Praça da Matriz.

The **Museu Histórico**, on the Praça da Matriz, displays a collection of sacred art, festival regalia and colonial furniture. Each room has its own guardian – a source of employment for the locals. Opening hours for the museum are 8 am to 2 pm Tuesday to Saturday, and 8 am to 1 pm on Sunday.

Once you've seen the main sights, you can walk to the beaches or take a boat trip out to nearby islands.

Festival

The Festa do Divino is held on the first Sunday after Ascension Day. Check the date for the festival (usually held in May) with the tourist office in São Luís.

This is considered one of the most colourful annual festivals in Maranhão, a fusion of African and Catholic elements with two children dressed as the emperor and empress paraded through the town and accompanied by musicians.

THE NORTHEAST

Places to Stay & Eat

Alcântara has simple campsites close to Praça da Matriz and near the *farol* (lighthouse). There are also several inexpensive hotels, such as the recommended *Pousada do Mordomo Régio* (☎ 101), the *Pousada do Imperador*, on Rua Grande, and the *Pousada Pelourinho*, beside Praça da Matriz (check out the Egyptian-styled dance space out the back). *Chale da Baronesa* is right on the beachfront, on Praia da Baronesa. It's a quiet, relaxing place to stay – simple chalets cost US$9/12 for singles/doubles, and there's a restaurant/bar as well.

All the hotels have restaurants, and there are two restaurants, *Restaurante Copos e Bocas* and *Restaurante da Josef*, close together on Rua Direito.

Getting There & Away

Boats from São Luís to Alcântara depart from the hidroviária (boat terminal) on the quayside, just beyond the western end of Rua Portugal. It's a good idea to buy your ticket the day before departure, and check the departure times, which vary according to the tide.

You have the choice of three types of boats

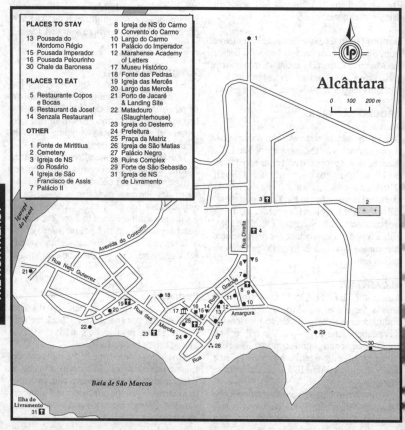

PLACES TO STAY
13 Pousada do Mordomo Régio
15 Pousada Imperador
16 Pousada Pelourinho
30 Chale da Baronesa

PLACES TO EAT
5 Restaurante Copos e Bocas
6 Restaurant da Josef
14 Senzala Restaurant

OTHER
1 Fonte de Miritítiua
2 Cemetery
3 Igreja de NS do Rosário
4 Igreja de São Francisco de Assis
7 Palácio II
8 Igreja de NS do Carmo
9 Convento do Carmo
10 Largo do Carmo
11 Palácio do Imperador
12 Marahense Academy of Letters
17 Museu Histórico
18 Fonte das Pedras
19 Igreja das Mercês
20 Largo das Mercês
21 Porto de Jacaré & Landing Site
22 Matadouro (Slaughterhouse)
23 Igreja do Desterro
24 Prefeitura
25 Praça da Matriz
26 Igreja de São Matias
27 Palácio Negro
28 Ruins Complex
29 Forte de São Sebasião
31 Igreja de NS de Livramento

Alcântara

0   100   200 m

THE NORTHEAST

for the trip to Alcântara. The *Batevento* is a large motorboat which leaves twice daily at 7 and 9.30 am. The trip takes about one hour. The boat returns from Alcântara at around 8 am and 4.30 pm. Early risers are rewarded with a significant discount – the early boats to and from Alcântara cost US$2, while the later boats cost US$4.50. As a result, the early boats are crowded – the best positions are the seats at the back of the boat or on the top deck.

For the more adventurous, there are two sailboats straight out of pirate tales – the *Newton Belle* and the *Mensageiro da Fé* – which also ply the route. Both leave from the hidroviária twice daily at around 7 am and 4 pm. Pandemonium reigns as the last passengers and cargo get stuffed below at sailing time. Try to avoid the crush by sitting outside at the front of the boat. The trip takes about 1½ hours. The early boats cost US$1 and the later boats US$2.

The third option is to go by catamaran. These boats are probably more suited to travellers able to cope with rough seas. Make sure you protect cameras etc, with plastic. The two catamarans making the trip are the *Teju* and the *Botinho*. They don't run to any particular schedule, so ask at the port for departure times.

PARQUE NACIONAL DOS LENÇÓIS MARANHENSES

The natural attractions of this national park include 1550 sq km of beaches, mangroves, lagoons, dunes and local fauna (turtles and migratory birds). The park's name refers to the immense dunes which look like *lençóis* (bedsheets) strewn across the landscape. Since 1981 this parcel of land has been set aside as a protected ecological zone, staving off the ruinous effects of land speculation.

The park has minimal tourist infrastructure, but it's currently possible to arrange a visit from the town of Barreirinhas (see the following section for details), which is two hours by boat from the dunes. The tiny fishing villages of Mandacaru and Ponta de Mangue, around 22 km north-east of Barreirinhas, are very hard to reach and have

no facilities for tourists, so take your own hammock.

Information

For more information, contact the tourist office in São Luís, or IBAMA (☎ 222-3006), at Avenida Jaime Tavares 25, also in São Luís.

Tours Several travel agencies in São Luís offer tours to the park. Taguatur (☎ 232-0906), at Rua do Sol 141, loja 14, and Delmundo Tourismo (☎ 222-8719), nearby on Rua da Riberão, both have three-day tours from around US$175, including transport, accommodation in Barreirinhas and a guide.

Barreirinhas

Barreirinhas, the jumping-off point for visiting the Parque Nacional dos Lençóis Maranhenses, is also a pretty little town on the banks of the Rio Preguiça. There is a river beach with sand dunes near the centre of town, and a couple of good pousadas and restaurants.

Pousada Lins organises tours of the park – the day trip by boat up the Rio Preguiça costs US$90 for up to five people. Otherwise, ask around for Edivaldo, a friendly and honest young guide, who can organise transport for day trips. If you don't want to do the full day trip, it's possible to hire boats along the riverfront to take you to the beginning of the park for a few dollars.

Places to Stay & Eat The *Pousada Lins* (☎ 349-1203), at Avenida Joaquim Soeiro de Cavalho 550, is the nicest place to stay. Quartos with fan cost US$6.50/13 for singles/doubles and spotless apartamentos with fan go for US$7.50/15. The *Pousada dos Viajante* (349-1106), on Rua Clarence Ramos, has basic quartos at US$3/6 for singles/doubles and apartamentos for US$6/12.

Restaurant Porta do Sol, at Avenida Joaquim Soeiro de Cavalho 583, is a friendly place serving local seafood and chicken dishes. *Restaurant Lins*, under the same

THE NORTHEAST

management as Pousada Lins, offers a similar menu.

Getting There & Away There's a daily bus service to Barreirinhas, leaving at 7 am from the rodoviária in São Luís (US$16, around eight hours). The trip is a bit of a shocker – the first half is along a road with major potholes, and the second half along a rutted dirt road – a bit like driving on corrugated iron. The return service from Barreirinhas departs daily at 6 am. The bus fills up quickly, so you should book tickets as far in advance as possible, at Taguatur on Rua Inaçio Lins.

To Tutóia, there's a couple of ruts through the sand passable only by 4WD vehicles. Transport may only go as far as the lost town of Rio Nove, about halfway to Tutóia, where there is one basic pousada. The 'road' passes by (and over) some superb dunescapes and very isolated, traditional fishing communities of straw huts. From Rio Nove, there should be another jeep to Tutóia, leaving daily at around noon.

Tutóia

Tutóia is a fishing port and beach town on the edge the Delta do Parnaíba, a 2700-sq-km expanse of rivers, dunes, beaches and mangrove forest which straddles the borders of Maranhão and Piauí.

On the beachfront, the *Pousada Cacão* is a beach shack with a bar decorated with shark's jaws and snake skins. Apartamentos cost US$8, single or double. The *Hotel Tres Irmões*, on Praça Igreja, in the centre, is run by a friendly family and has quartos with fan at US$3 per person.

Getting There & Away Two buses daily run over a rough dirt road to Parnaíba (Piauí). The trip takes about four hours. A small motorboat snakes through the delta daily to Parnaíba (US$4, about seven hours). To Rio Nove, there's a truck leaving daily at around 10 am, from Praça Getúlio Vargas. You can pick up another truck or jeep there to Barreirinhas – but you must be prepared to stay overnight.

THE NORTH COAST

The town of Guimarães is a centre for boat-building and fishing. Further north is Cururupu, a small town which is the gateway to the Lençóis de Cururupu – a huge expanse of coastal dunes similar to, but not to be confused with, those in the Parque Nacional dos Lençóis Maranhenses.

About 80 km offshore is Parcel de Manoel Luís, a coral reef named after the *Manoel Luís*, the first ship to be lost there. According to experts, this reef, extending over 288 sq km, is the largest in South America, and there are plans to turn it into a marine park. There are also plans to exploit it as one of the world's top attractions for divers, especially those with fat wallets tucked into their wetsuits.

RESERVA BIOLÓGICA DO GURUPI

This biological reserve in the Serra do Tiracambu, on the western border of the state, is not open to the public. This news does not seem to have reached the sawmill owners, loggers and assorted industrialists clustered on the fringe of the reserve, who are plundering it at top speed.

IMPERATRIZ

Imperatriz, 636 km from São Luís, is a rapidly expanding city on the border with Pará. The expansion is due to the rabid logging and mining of the surrounding region, which is turning the forests into ecological nightmares and attracting plenty of low-life characters to make a quick killing. The only possible reason to visit would be to change buses – otherwise, just keep going. The airports at Imperatriz and nearby Açailândia are frequently closed for days on end because of the huge clouds of smoke from forest fires.

CAROLINA

The town of Carolina, 242 km south of Imperatriz, lies beside the Rio Tocantins, and provides a handy base for visiting nearby natural attractions.

Pedra Caída, 35 km from town on the road towards Estreito, is a dramatic combination of rock canyons and waterfalls. Some of the other spectacular waterfalls in the region are: Cachoeira do Itapecuruzinho, 27 km from town on the road that goes toward Riachão; Cachoeira de São Simão, at Fazenda São Jorge, about 10 km from Carolina; and Cachoeira da Barra da Cabeceira. There are rock paintings and inscriptions at Morro das Figuras, close to Fazenda Recanto; and bat enthusiasts will want to visit the colony of bats in Passagem Funda, a large cave 70 km from Carolina.

Places to Stay
The town has several inexpensive hotels, including the *Santa Rita* (☎ 731-1224), the *Sansão* (☎ 731-1317) and the *Imperial* (☎ 731-1151).

The *Pousada do Lajes* (☎ 731-1348), three km outside town on the road towards Riachão, has chalets. The *Pousada Pedra Caída* is a tourist complex with chalets and sports facilities at the Pedra Caída waterfalls.

Getting There & Away
There's a daily bus service from São Luís (US$28, 12 hours); and four services daily from Imperatriz (four hours).

Getting Around
A frequent ferry service (15-minute ride) operates across the Rio Tocantins to the town of Filadélfia, which is in the state of Tocantins.

The North

ROBYN JONES

The North

The North of Brazil is made up of seven states: Pará, Amapá, Tocantins, Amazonas, Roraima, Rondônia and Acre.

In 1541, the Gonzalvo Pizarro expedition ran short of food supplies while searching for El Dorado, the mythical kingdom of gold. Captain Francisco de Orellana, who had joined the expedition earlier, offered to take a small group of soldiers and forage for supplies.

Orellana floated down the Rio Napo all the way to the Amazon, which received its name after the group reported attacks by female warriors (prompting comparisons in the West with the Amazons of Greek mythology). Although Orellana had disobeyed orders, his exploits found favour with the Spanish king, who sent him back on a second expedition, during which Orellana died from malaria.

Despite this foray into the region, the Spanish were not interested in claiming the territory, which had been assigned to the Portuguese under the terms of the Treaty of Tordesillas (signed in 1494).

The Amazon Basin, six million sq km of river and jungle, is the world's largest river basin in terms of volume and drainage area. Its flow is 12 times that of the Mississippi, with 12 billion litres of fresh water flowing down the river every minute – enough to supply New York City for 60 years! There are 80,000 km of navigable rivers in the Amazon system. Ocean-going vessels can sail deep into South America: from the mouth of the Amazon (300 km east of Belém) to the Solimões and Marañon rivers, and all the way to Iquitos in Peru.

Although the Amazon River dominates the record books, many of its tributaries are also enormous: the Rio Juruá is a 3280-km tributary of the Solimões, the Rio Madeira-Mamoré flows for 3240 km, the Rio Purus/Pauini is 3210 km in length (1667 km of which is navigable) and the Rio Tocantins is a respectable 2640 km long. The Rio

Highlights

- The village of Alter do Chão near Santarém with its clear water, beaches and the Centro da Preservação a Arte Indígena (Pará)
- The exotic range of fruit, vegetables, fish and medicinal herbs at Mercado Ver-o-Peso in Belém (Pará)
- Ilha do Marajó beaches, buffalo and birdlife (Pará)
- The white sands of Praia do Algodoal on a full-moon night (Pará)
- Fresh regional fish in the traditional restaurants of Belém (Amazonas) or Manaus (Pará)
- The remote Parque Nacional da Ilha do Bananal (Tocantins)
- A jungle trip outside Manaus, including canoeing through lakes, birdwatching and sighting fresh-water dolphins (Amazonas)
- The *pororoca*, the collision between the Atlantic tide and the Amazon River (Pará and Amapá)
- Colonial and Rubber Boom architecture of the Amazon such as the opera houses and palácios
- The Pedra Pintada near Boa Vista (Roraima)

Negro runs 1550 km (only the lower half is navigable and fully explored). For the people who live in the Amazon interior, the rivers are the only roads.

Things can get very wet, so bring along a

577

hooded poncho or windbreaker to keep yourself dry, and use ziplock plastic storage bags to compartmentalise tickets, travellers' cheques and other valuables (unless you prefer to entrust them to a hotel safe). You'll also need a hammock (fabric is preferable to net), a sheet, a blanket and some rope. To keep your possessions dry, the backpack should be waterproofed, wrapped in a groundcloth or a large plastic bag, then suspended above the floor of the boat.

Long-sleeved cotton shirts and light cotton trousers with elastic drawstrings at the ankles keep some of the bugs from nipping. Cloth or rubber thongs and sneakers are also comfortable boat/jungle gear. Bring a day pack containing toiletries, a torch, pocket knife, water bottle, a thick novel and plenty of insect repellent. Don't forget a camera, binoculars and a good birding guide. For suggested reading and reference material, see the Books & Maps section in the Facts for the Visitor chapter. Finally, antimalarials and pure drinking water should prevent most medical problems.

To see the wildlife of the Amazon – jacarés, monkeys, hawks, anacondas, toucans and botos (freshwater dolphins) – you must leave the major rivers and head for the *igarapés* (channels cutting through the jungle, so narrow that the forest brushes your face). If you opt for river travel with an independent operator, part of your agreement should include a canoe tour of the igarapés, since noisy motorboats only scare the wildlife away.

Remind your guide to bring fishing gear, straps and cords (to suspend packs), and of course cachaça, sugar and lemons for caipirinhas at the end of the day. Shop for food with your guide so that you can inflict your tastes on them, rather than vice versa.

Health Care in the Amazon

In the field of health care, there is hope for the poor of the Amazon. To most, little or no health care has been available, but the situation is changing, thanks to the efforts of Fundação Espernça (Hope Foundation), founded by the late Father Luke Tupper. Their primary health-care project is so successful that the United Nations is using it as a model for health projects in Africa.

The problems of providing health care in the Amazon are manifold. Homesteaders are widely scattered on minor tributaries, and other than river travel, there is no transportation network to reach them. The economic resources of these people are scanty.

During its first 10 years, Fundação Espernça's health-care programme was centred around a riverboat fitted with fancy medical equipment and staffed by interns and surgeons. The mobile hospital did not prove very effective: although 150,000 people were vaccinated, there was no continuity in health care, and after a while, the boat would visit communities only during election years.

In 1978 the World Health Organisation defined the task of cost-effective use of medicinal resources, emphasising the preventative medicine needs of women and children (formerly overlooked) and stressing community participation and education. In the following year, the Fundação Espernça began to mobilise rural communities in three areas: diet, sanitary practices and medical care.

Physicians and nurses sent into rural villages would not stay very long, despite their best intentions, as they were over qualified for the task and nearly all preferred to live in bigger cities. Therefore, the third and current approach to health care involves the transfer of information, control and prestige from health-care professionals to chosen villagers, who then receive a brief paramedical training in Santarém. These villagers lead their communities in digging wells and developing sanitation, teach fellow villagers a little hygiene and preventative medicine, treat some ailments and refer cases they can't handle to the urban medical centres.

Financial support for Fundação Espernça health projects comes from the Interamerican Bank of Development, the Companhia do Vale Doce hydroelectric plant and the Lion's Club. You can also help. If you wish to contact the organisation, the address is Fundação Espernça, Caixa Postal 222, CEP 68100 Santarém, Pará, Brazil. ∎

THE NORTH

Don't scrimp on water – carry at least two litres of bottled water per person per day. It's nice to have two styrofoam coolers on board, one to keep perishables from spoiling and the second to keep valuables dry when the weather becomes wet and wild. Last, but definitely not least, insist on life jackets.

Buses are a good way to cover lots of ground cheaply. Most of the river crossings throughout the back country are made on simple, motor-driven ferries that take one truck at a time. As it is a slow process, trucks are often lined up, especially at night, when the ferry isn't operating. The ferries break down frequently, and may take hours, even days, to repair.

Pará, Amapá & Tocantins

Brazil's territory in eastern Amazonia comprises the states of Pará, Amapá and Tocantins.

The state of Pará covers over one million sq km and includes a major stretch of the Amazon, and huge tributaries such as the Rio Trombetas, the Rio Tapajós and the Rio Xingu. Pará's attractions include the cities of Belém and Santarém, and Ilha de Marajó, one of the world's largest fluvial islands.

The state of Amapá straddles the equator in the north-eastern corner of Brazil. Most visitors to the state arrive or leave via the challenging route to or from French Guiana. Tocantins, Brazil's newest state, was carved out of Goiás state in 1989. The main attraction in Tocantins is the Parque Nacional do Araguaia on Ilha do Bananal, the largest fluvial island in the world.

Pará

The Tupi tribe who lived beside the Amazon estuary prior to colonisation used the term *'pa'ra'* (vast ocean) to describe its awesome size. In 1500, the Spanish navigator Vicente Yáñez Pinzón sailed past the estuary, noted the huge volume of fresh water issuing into the ocean, and turned back to investigate a short distance up the estuary. Concluding that navigation to the source of such a gigantic 'ocean river' was too risky, he headed back to Spain to report his discovery. For more about the history of Pará state, see the History in the Belém section.

The economic development of the state is concentrated on giant mining projects (such as Projeto Grande Carajás) and grandiose hydroelectric schemes (such as the Tucuruí dam). Much of the southern part of the state has been deforested, and there are serious ecological problems involved with land disputes, ranching and uncontrolled mining.

Pará state is divided into two time zones.

The delineation of these time zones seems to depend on local assessment, but as a general rule, the section of the state east of the Rio Xingu uses Brazilian standard time, while the section to the west of the river is one hour behind Brazilian standard time.

BELÉM

Belém is the economic centre of the North and the capital of the state of Pará. It's a city with a unique and fascinating culture derived from the peoples and ways of the forest, and animated by the exuberance of the port. Although Belém is clearly in a state of decay, the central area is pleasant, the sites of interest are close by and the people are friendly.

History

The Portuguese, sailing from Maranhão, landed at Belém in 1616, and promptly built the Forte do Castelo at an entrance to the Rio Mar (River Sea) to deter French, English, Spanish and Dutch boats from sailing up the Amazon and claiming territory. By 1626, the area encompassed by the present-day states of Pará and Maranhão was set up as a colony separate from the rest of Brazil. It had its own governor, who reported directly to the Portuguese king, and its own capital (in São Luís do Maranhão). This colony remained officially separate from the rest of Brazil until 1775.

Creating a separate administration for the territory stretching from Belém to São Luís made sense: prevailing winds and ocean currents along the coast of Brazil made it extremely difficult for ships to leave Belém and reach Salvador, and the inland route was long and perilous. The trip from Belém to Lisbon lasted just six weeks, whereas the journey to Salvador took considerably longer.

Belém's economy relied on *drogas do sertão* (the spices of the backlands). The white settlers (predominantly poor farmers who had emigrated from the islands of the

Belém

0   250   500 m

Baía do Guajará
(Río Amazonas)

To Main Airport
& Val de Cans

See Enlargement

Porto de Belém

Avenida Marechal Hermes

Avenida Pedro A Cabral

Rua da Municipalidade

Rua Senador Lemos

Avenida Serzedelo Correia

Trav Dom Pedro

Trav Dom Romualdo

Trav Dom Romualdo

Trav Almirante

Avenida Visconde de

Souza Franco

Rua Jerônimo Pimentel

Rua de Municipalidade

Rua Gaspar Viana

Rua 28 de Setembro

Trav Benjamin Constant

Rua Sen Mal Barata

Rua Ó de Almeida

Trav Quintino Bocaiúva

Trav Rui Barbosa

Rua Boaventura da Silva

Rua Aristides Lobo

Rua Tiradentes

Praça da
República

Rua O Cruz

Avenida Assis de Vasconcelos

Avenida Pres Vargas

Frei Gil de Vilanovo

Travessa 1 de Março

Rua S Antônio

Rua Gaspar Viana

Rua Castello França

Rua 15 de Novembro

Rua 7 de Setembro

Avenida Portugal

Rua Alfredo

Rua Malo

Rua Sen Manoel Barata

Rua dos Lobo

Padre Prudêncio

Trav Frutuosa Guimarães

Trav Campos Sales

Rua Carlos Gomes

Rua João Diogo

Rua do

Das

Travessa Padre
Eutíquio

Rua São
Pedro

Rua São
Francisco

Avenida 16 de Novembro

Avenida Tamandaré

Avenida Senador M Teodoro

Avenida Conselheiro Furtado

Rua Veiga Cabral

Rua Cezário Alvim

Rua do Triunviro

Rua de Óbidos

Trav Gurupá

Trav Alenquer

Rua Joaquim Tavares

Dr Malcher

Dr Assis

Siqueira Mendes

Praça
Dom
Pedro
II

Praça
Felipe
Patroni

Rocha

Trav São

Guilhon Aver

Guilhon Aver

Trav Benjamin Constant

Trav Dr Morais

Praça
Batista
Campos

Rua dos Tamoios

Rua dos Apinagés

Rua dos Tupinambás

Rua dos Mundurucus

Rua dos Pariquis

Avenida Roberto Camelier

Rua dos

1 ●
2 ▼
3 ●
4 ⌂
5 ▼
6 ●
7 ●
9 🏛
10 🏛
11 ■
12 ✦
13 ▼
14 ●
15 ■
16 ■
17 ▼
18 ▼
19 ●
20 ●
21 ▼

0   100   200 m

PLACES TO STAY

11 Hotel Plaza
15 Regente
16 Hotel Vanja
23 Manacá Hotel Residencia
24 Equatorial Palace
31 Hotel Ver-o-Peso
34 Hotel Canto do Rio
35 Transamazonas Hotel
36 Itaóca Hotel
40 Hotel Central
42 Hotels Fortaleza &
   Vitória Régia
44 Vidonho's Hotel
45 Hotel Milano
46 Excelsior Grão Pará
50 Hilton Hotel

PLACES TO EAT

2 Sabor da Terra
5 O Círculo Militar &
   Forte do Castelo
13 Lá Em Casa & O Outro
17 Cantina Italiana
18 Cosanostra Caffé, Degrau
   & Manga Café
21 Sorveteria Cairu
22 Au Bar
26 Spazzio Verde
27 Restaurante Avenida
38 Restaurante Vegetariano
   Mercado do Natural
39 Inter Restaurant

47 Casa dos Sucos
49 Bar do Parque
51 Miako

OTHER

1 Porto de Belém (Portão 17)
3 Paratur Park & Tourist Office
4 Escadinha Port
   (Boats to Camará)
6 Porto Rodomar
7 Porto Transarapari
8 Catedral Metropolitana
9 Palácio Lauro Sodré
   (Museu do Estado)
10 Palácio Antônio Lemos
   (Museu da Cidade)
12 Iguatemi Shopping Centre
14 Palacete Bolonha
19 French Consulate
20 Venezuelan Consulate
25 CENTUR
28 Basílica de NS de Nazaré &
   Museu do Círio
29 Museu Emílio Goeldi
30 Mercado Ver-o-Peso
32 ENASA Ferry Landing
   (Boats to Soure)
33 ENASA Office & Parque
   Dom Pedro Teixeira
37 Banco do Brasil
41 Casa do Cruzeiro Câmbio
43 Post Office
48 Teatro da Paz
52 Rodoviária

THE NORTH

Azores, off the coast of Portugal) were entirely dependent on the labour of the *filhos do mato* (sons of the forest), native Indians who knew the ways of the Amazon and who could find cacao, vanilla, cassia and cinnamon for export to Europe. These riches, and the enslavement and destruction of the Indians, made Belém a relatively prosperous settlement. For hundreds of years, the settlement survived by striking further and further into the Amazon, destroying tribes of Indians in one slaving expedition after another.

As elsewhere in Brazil, the Jesuits came to the Amazon to 'save' the Indians and to install them in *aldeias* (mission villages) throughout the region. Terrible epidemics killed many Indians, while Catholicism killed their culture. Indians who chose to escape this fate fled further into the Amazon, along smaller tributaries.

By the end of the 18th century, as its Indian labour force became depleted, the economy of Belém began to decline. In the 1820s, a split between the white ruling classes led to civil war. It quickly spread to the dominated Indians, mestizos, blacks and mulattos, and after years of fighting, developed into a popular revolutionary movement that swept through Pará like a wildfire. The Cabanagem rebellion was a guerrilla war fought by the wretched of the Amazon.

In 1835 the guerrilla fighters marched on Belém, taking the city after nine days of bloody fighting. They installed a popular government, which expropriated the wealth of the merchants, distributed food to all the people and declared Belém's independence. But the revolutionary experiment was immediately strangled by a British naval blockade, Britain being the principal beneficiary of trade with Brazil in the 1800s.

A year later, a large Brazilian force recaptured Belém. The vast majority of the city's population fled to the interior to resist again. Over the next four years, the military hunted down, fought and slaughtered two-thirds of the men in the state of Pará – they killed anyone who was black or brown – 40,000 out of a total population of some 100,000. The Cabanagem massacre was one of the bloodiest and most savage of many Brazilian military campaigns against its own people.

Decades later, the regional economy was revitalised by the rubber boom. A vast number of poor peasants fled the drought-plagued Northeast, particularly Ceará, to tap the Amazon's rubber trees. Most of the *seringuieros* (rubber gatherers) arrived and then died in debt.

By 1910 rubber constituted 39% of the nation's total exports. Belém's population grew from 40,000 in 1875 to over 100,000 in 1900. The town had electricity, telephones, streetcars and a distinctly European feel, in the midst of the tropical heat. The rubber boom provided the money for the city to erect a few beautiful monuments, such as the Teatro da Paz and the Palácio Antônio Lemos.

Climate

Belém is one of the rainiest cities in the world. There is no dry season – October has the least rain – but it rains more often and with greater abundance from December to June. This is not as bad as it sounds: the rain is often a brief, welcome relief from the heat. It is not unusual for the locals to arrange appointments according to daily rainfall time, saying: I will meet you tomorrow after the rain! The humidity is very high, but unlike Manaus, Belém gets breezes from the Atlantic Ocean, which makes its weather more bearable.

Orientation

As it approaches the Atlantic, the Amazon splinters into many branches and forms countless channels, numerous fluvial islands and, finally, two great estuaries. These estuaries separate the Ilha de Marajó, the 'island continent', from the mainland. The southern estuary is joined by the mighty Rio Tocantins and is known as the Baía de Marajó before it enters the Atlantic.

Belém is 120 km from the Atlantic, at the point where the Rio Guamá turns north and becomes the Baía do Guajará, which soon feeds into the massive Baía de Marajó. It's the biggest port on the Amazon, and from here, you can set sail for any navigable port of the Amazon and its tributaries. Distances are great, river travel is slow and often dull, and you may have to change ships along the way, but it is cheap.

The heart of town lies along Avenida Presidente Vargas, from the bay to the Teatro da Paz (in the Praça da República). Here, you'll find most of the best hotels and restaurants. Praça da República, a large central park, is a good place to relax and socialise in the early evening.

Just west of Avenida Presidente Vargas are several narrow shopping streets. Rua João Alfredo is good for cheap clothes and hammocks. Continue a few blocks to the Cidade Velho (Old Town), with its colonial architecture, or turn right to see the Mercado Ver-o-Peso and the waterfront.

Information

Tourist Office Paratur (☎ 224-7184; fax 223-6198), the state tourism agency, has its main office at the Feira de Artesanato do Estado, Praça Kennedy. The staff are helpful and provide free maps. It's open from 8 am to 6 pm Monday to Friday.

Money The main branch of the Banco do Brasil in Belém is at Avenida Presidente Vargas 248; there's another branch at the airport. The Banco Francês e Brasileiro (☎ 241-8723) is at Rua Boaventura da Silva 580. Other places for currency and travellers' cheque exchange are Casa do Cruzeiro Câmbio (☎ 241-5558), at Rua 28 de Setembro 62, Casa Francesa de Câmbio (☎ 241-2716), at Travessa Padre Prudencio 40, and Turvicam Turismo Viagens e Câmbio (☎ 241-5465), at Avenida Presidente Vargas 640, loja 3.

Post & Telephone The central post office is at Avenida Presidente Vargas 498. The head office of Telepará, the state telephone company, is nearby, at Avenida Presidente Vargas 620.

Foreign Consulates The following coun-

tries have diplomatic representation in Belém:

France
  Rua Presidente Pernambuco 269 (☎ 224-6818)
Germany
  Travessa Piedade 651, sala 201 (☎ 222-5634)
Holland
  Rua José Marcelina de Oliveira 304, Ananindeua (☎ 255-3339)
Japan
  Travessa Padre Eutíquio 2112 (☎ 222-1900)
Peru
  Honorary Consulate, Avenida José Bonifácio 2432 (☎ 229-7278)
UK
  Honorary Consulate, Rua Gaspar Viana 490 (224-4822)
USA
  Avenida Oswaldo Cruz 165 (☎ 223-0800)
Venezuela
  Avenida Presidente Pernambuco 270 (☎ 222-6396)

Travel Agencies Belém has a range of travel agencies offering city tours, river tours, and excursions to Ilha de Marajó, and it's worth comparing tour prices.

Amazon Star Turismo (☎ & fax 224-6244) is at Rua Carlos Gomes 14; Mururé Turismo (☎ 241-0891; fax 241-2082) is at Avenida Presidente Vargas 134; Carimbó Viagens e Turismo (☎ & fax 223-6464) is at Travessa Piedade 186; Neytour Turismo (☎ 241-0777; fax 241-5669) is at Rua Carlos Gomes 300; Ciatour (☎ 223-0787; fax 224-8352) is at Avenida Serzedelo Correia 163; Amazon Travel Service (☎ 241-1099; fax 241-4152) is at Rua dos Mundurucus 1826; and Lusotour (☎ 241-1011; fax 223-5222) is at Avenida Braz de Aguiar 471.

Bookshop For a reasonable selection of English-language books, go to Ponto e Virgula, with its two locations: at Avenida Conselheiro Furtado 1142, and in the Iguatemi Shopping Centre, Travessa Padre Eutíquio 1078.

Dangers & Annoyances Many readers have written to warn about the pickpockets who operate alone or in gangs at Mercado Ver-o-Peso. Don't take anything of value to this market, and also avoid evenings and Sunday afternoons. If you intend to travel by boat from Belém, watch your gear carefully – theft is becoming increasingly common. Theft at the rock-bottom hotels is also commonplace – see Places to Stay.

For more advice, see the Security section under Dangers & Annoyances in the Facts for the Visitor chapter. The same section contains a salutary tale about a bogus official at the boat dock in Belém.

Mercado Ver-o-Peso

Spanning several blocks along the waterfront, this big market operates all day, every day. Its name originated from the fact that the market was established as a checkpoint where the Portuguese would '*ver o peso*' (watch the weight) in order to impose taxes.

Many readers have commented unfavourably on the smell of putrefaction and the rampant crime in the market, but the display of fruits, vegetables, plants, animals and fish, not to mention the people, is fascinating. While this would be a photographer's paradise, don't wander around dreamily with your camera – you risk being accosted with a dirty big fish knife! It's best to get there early, when the boats are unloading their catches at the far end of the market. Watch for the *mura*, a human-size fish.

The most intriguing section is filled with medicinal herbs and roots, dead snakes, jacaré teeth, amulets with mysterious powers, and potions for every possible occasion. There are shops selling weird and wonderful religious objects used for Macumba ceremonies, such as incense to counter *mau olho* (evil eye), and *guias* (necklaces that, when blessed, are used to provide a connection with the spirit world). There are also restaurants and food stalls for good, cheap meals.

Teatro da Paz

Constructed in 1874 in neoclassical style, this theatre (☎ 224-7355) has hosted performances by numerous Brazilian stars and various international favourites, including Anna Pavlova, the Vienna Boys' Choir and the Cossacks. The architecture has all the sumptuous trappings of the era: columns, busts, crystal mirrors, and an interior decorated in Italian theatrical style. Opening hours are from 8 am to 6 pm Monday to Friday (weekend visits need to be booked in advance). Admission costs US$1.20. The theatre is in the centre of Praça da República.

Museu Emílio Goeldi

This museum (☎ 249-0163) was created in 1866 by the naturalist Domingos Soares Ferreira Pena. In 1894 the state governor, Lauro Sodré, contracted Dr Emílio Augusto Goeldi to direct and reorganise the museum. Presently, the museum is also a research institution for the study of the flora, fauna, peoples and physical environment of Amazonia.

The museum consists of three parts: a combined park and zoo, an aquarium, and a permanent exhibit. The zoo is one of the best in South America. It has *peixe-boi* (manatees) browsing on underwater foliage, sleek jungle cats, *ariranha* (giant river otters), monkeys and many strange Amazonian birds. There are even roving *pacas* (agoutis) scurrying free through the park.

The aquarium displays a small sample of the 1500 fish species identified in local waters (there are dozens of fish species still to be identified in the Amazon region), including hoover fish, window-cleaner fish, butterfly fish and leaf fish – the names are self-explanatory.

The permanent exhibit, called 'Amazonia: Man and the Environment', has a good display of minerals, artesanato of various Indian tribes, and an interesting collection of archaeological specimens, including intricately decorated ceramic burial urns from the Santarém and Ilha de Marajó pre-Columbian Indian civilisations.

At the time of writing, the museum shop had been crushed by a falling tree and was awaiting restoration. The shop sells posters, museum research publications, and booklets about Amazonian flora, fauna and culture.

The Museu Emílio Goeldi is open from 9 am to noon and from 2 to 5 pm Tuesday to

Thursday, from 9 am to noon on Friday and from 9 am to 5 pm on weekends. Admission to all three sections costs US$3.50. A gift shop sells a variety of T-shirts, minerals and Indian arts and crafts. The shop is closed for lunch from 12.45 to 2.45 pm.

The museum is at Avenida Governador Magalhães Barata 376. From the city centre, take the bus marked 'Aeroclube 20'. If you feel like walking from the centre, it takes about 35 minutes and you can include a couple of sights en route. Starting from the Teatro da Paz, walk down Avenida Nazaré, which becomes Avenida Governador Magalhães Barata, and continue past the Basílica de NS de Nazaré, which is close to the museum.

Basílica de NS de Nazaré

The basílica is visited annually by over one million worshippers during the Círio de Nazaré (see the boxed aside in this section.)

It was built in 1909, in Roman architectural style inspired by the Basilica of St Paul in Rome. Many of the materials and artisans were imported from Europe, and the interior is lined with fine marble. The elaborate altar piece frames a tiny statue of the Virgin, while the facade has a mural depicting the arrival of the Portuguese colonisers in Brazil. Included among Indians, soldiers and priests are a couple of men dressed in suits and ties! They are the figures of the wealthy patrons who sponsored the basílica's construction.

Downstairs is a sacred-art museum, Museu do Círio (☎ 224-9614) which is open from 8 am to 6 pm Tuesday to Friday and from 8 am to noon on weekends. Admission is free. Here you can buy the traditional *briquedos de abaetetuba* (toys made of balsa wood, which are sold in the streets during the Círio festival). The church is on Praça Justo Chermont – a short walk from the Museu Emílio Goeldi – and it's open daily from 6.30 to 11.30 am and 3 to 9 pm.

Our Lady of Nazaré

The origins of the image of Our Lady of Nazaré, the devotion to the Virgin and how she came to Belém are shrouded in myth and misunderstanding, but many people accept the following account to be the true version of events.

According to the Portuguese, the holy image was sculpted in Nazareth (in Galilee). The image of the Virgin made its way through many European monasteries before arriving at the monastery of Gauliana, in Spain. In 714, the forces of King Roderick, the last Visigoth king, were routed by the Moors at the battle of Gaudelette. Retreating to the only remaining patch of Christian soil in Iberia, at Asturias, the king took refuge at the monastery of Gauliana. Still pursued by the Moors, Roderick fled to Portugal with Abbot Romano, who had the presence of mind to bring the Virgin with him. Before his capture and execution, the abbot hid the Virgin from the iconoclastic Muslims, while King Roderick escaped unharmed.

Four hundred years later, shepherds in the mountains of Siano (now São Bartoloomeu) found the Virgin of Nazaré, and the statue became known as a source of protection. The first miracle occurred on 9 October 1182. Dom Fuas Roupinho was riding in pursuit of a stag when he was miraculously saved from falling off a cliff. According to local belief, his horse stopped so suddenly that bits of iron from the horseshoes were embedded in the stones underfoot. The miracle was attributed to the Virgin of Nazaré, upon whose help he had called in his moment of danger.

In the 17th century, Jesuits brought the cult and the image to north-eastern Brazil, and somehow the Virgin made her way to Vigia, in Pará, where she was worshipped. An attempt was made to bring the Virgin to Belém, but the image was lost in the jungle and forgotten. In October of 1700, Placido José de Souza, a humble rancher, led his cattle to drink from Murucutu Igarapé and rediscovered the Virgin. Placido placed the statue on a rough altar in his hut. News spread, and many of the faithful gathered from miles around. Before long, Placido's hut became the sanctuary of NS de Nazaré. In 1721 Bishop Dom Bartolomeu do Pilar confirmed that the image was the true Virgin of Nazaré. In 1793 Belém had its first Círio (see the section on Festivals later in this chapter), and the city has staged an annual celebration ever since. ■

Bosque Rodrigues Alves

This 16-hectare park at Avenida Almirante Barroso 1622 contains a lake, and a zoo with turtles and jacarés. Apart from the Museu Emílio Goeldi, this is the only large patch of greenery close to the city centre. Frequented by couples kissing in the grottos, it's a pleasant place to relax. Avoid it on Sunday, though, when little brats torment the turtles and jacarés by throwing plastic bags filled with water at their heads – one reader felt like feeding the perpetrators to the victims!

Opening hours are 7 am to 5 pm Tuesday to Sunday. From the city centre, take the bus marked 'Aeroclube 20'.

Cidade Velha

The old part of Belém is mostly run-down, but authentic. It's a good area in which to walk, drink and explore. There are colonial buildings notable for their fine azulejos (blue Portuguese tiles). A particularly striking example of the colonial style is Loja Paris N'America, on Rua Alfredo Santo Antônio.

Palácio Antônio Lemos (Art Museum)

This former palace (☎ 223-5664), which had almost been condemned and reportedly had animals roaming around inside, was renovated in 1993, and now houses the Belém Museum of Art (MABE) and the Municipal Government Headquarters.

It was built during the second half of the 19th century, when Belém was the largest city in the region and the main beneficiary of the rubber trade. At this time Belém was considered to be 'the tropical Paris', because its opulent architecture and customs were similar to those of the French capital. Built in the Brazilian imperial style, the symmetrical building has a grand central staircase made of Portuguese marble. Its vast rooms have a selection of opulent imported furniture, including a Louis XVI setting. The mayor's office is one of these grandiose rooms.

The Palácio Antônio Lemos (Palácio Azul), between Praça Dom Pedro II and Praça Felipe Patroni, is open for visits from 9 am to noon and 1 to 6 pm, Tuesday to Friday, and 9 am to noon on weekends. Admission is free.

Palácio Lauro Sodré (State Museum)

The former government house has recently been renovated and turned into the State Museum (☎ 225-2414). It was built during the 18th century to house the Portuguese crown's representatives in Belém. Early this century, in response to the French influence on Belém's bourgeois culture, the main rooms were redecorated, each in a different style. The service areas at the rear are just as interesting. There is a small chapel (stripped of its religious decoration during the time of the military government), stables and a slaves' dungeon. In 1835 the Cabanagem invaded the palace, killing the president on the front steps.

The Museu de Cidade is next door to the Palácio Antônio Lemos, facing Praça Dom Pedro II, and is open from 9 am to 1 pm Tuesday to Sunday. Guided tours are organised at museum reception. Admission costs US$2.50.

The Legend of Muiraquitã

Legend has it that in the Serra Yacy-taperé, there exists a lake that the Indians called 'Yacy-uaruá' (mirror of the moon). Annually, by the light of a full moon, the all-female Ikambiadas Indian tribe would celebrate the moon, and the mother Muyrakitan, who lived in the depths of the lake. The local men were invited to the party to have sexual relations with the Indian women. During the party, the women would dive into the lake to receive from mother Muyrakitan an amulet in the form of a small frog. These amulets were then presented to the lucky men participating in the party. ■

River Tours & Beach Excursions

The travel agencies mentioned in the Information section, earlier in this chapter, offer various river tours and excursions to nearby beaches. Prices range from US$25 per person for the standard river tour to US$35 per person for an excursion to the beach at Ilha do Mosqueiro. City tours and cultural tours can be good if you are short on time, as they give a quick overview of Belém. For information about excursions to Ilha de Marajó, see the requisite section later in this chapter.

The 'canned tours' of the Rio Guamá are heavily promoted, but not particularly exciting. In three hours you cruise the river, go down a channel, get out on an island, and walk down a path where many have travelled before to see the local flora (rubber, mahogany trees, açaí palms, *sumauma*, mangoes and cacao trees). This voyage into the known is recommended only if you have no time to really see the jungle and rivers. An interesting variation is the combined early bird half-day tour offered by Amazon Star. It starts 4 am, before sunrise, when you can see parrots and other birds leaving Parrot Island at the first light of day. This tour costs US$35, including breakfast.

Praia Funda, on Ilha de Cotijuba, 1½ hours by boat from Belém, has beaches, the ruins of an old prison and the Hotel Trilha Dourada. Boats depart from the Porto Rodomar, at Rua Siqueira Mendes, at noon on weekdays, returning at 5 pm. On weekends, the first boat departs at 8.30 am and the last returns at 3.20 pm. Tickets cost US$0.35 on weekdays and US$1.20 on weekends. An alternative is the two-day 'Sol e Mar' package offered by the Hotel Trilha Dourada – Lodge (☎ 241-5778; fax 226-3887), at Travessa Dom Pedro I, Alameda Francisco Ribeiro da Silva 65. The deal (US$24 per person) includes transport, and accommodation in cabanas (rustic huts), but no meals. The restaurant at the hotel serves meals for about US$12.

Festivals

Every year on the morning of the second Sunday of October, the city of Belém explodes with the sound of hymns, bells and fireworks. Started in 1793 as a tribute to the Virgin of Nazaré, the Círio de Nazaré is Brazil's biggest religious festival. People from all over Brazil flock to Belém, and even camp in the streets, to participate in the grand event. A crowd of 300,000 or so fills the streets to march from the Catedral Metropolitana (also known as the Igreja da Sé) to the Basílica de NS de Nazaré.

The image of the Virgin, centrepiece of the procession, is placed on a flower-bedecked carriage. While the faithful pray, sing hymns, give thanks or ask favours of the Virgin, the pious (often barefoot) bear heavy crosses and miniature wax houses, and thousands squirm and grope in the emotional frenzy of their efforts to get hold of the 300-metre cord for an opportunity to pull the carriage of the Virgin. Five hours and just 2.5 km later, the Virgin reaches the basílica, where she remains for the duration of the festivities.

After the parade, there is the traditional feast of *pato no tucupi* (duck cooked in manioc extract). Círio de Nazaré without this dish is akin to a US Thanksgiving without turkey. From the basílica, the multitudes head to the fairgrounds for mayhem of the more secular kind: food, drink, music and dancing. The party continues unabated for a fortnight. On the Monday 15 days after the first procession, the crowd reassembles for the Recírio parade, in which the Virgin is returned to her proper niche and the festivities are concluded.

Places to Stay

Despite the overall price increases in Brazil, Belém, with its abundance of two-star hotels, still has some of the best accommodation deals in the Amazon region. Several places with mid-range facilities charge reasonable rates. Consequently, even travellers on a tight budget may want to consider a minor splurge on the mid-range hotels described. Most of these hotels are central – along or close to Avenida Presidente Vargas (an ideal location). There are also cheap dives and opulent, old hotels. If you're just passing through, there are hotels in front of the rodoviária.

Places to Stay – bottom end There are still cheap places along the waterfront, on Avenida Castilho França, but you may have to compromise on security and cleanliness. The *Hotel Canto do Rio*, at Avenida Castilho França 548, appears to be caving in. Nevertheless, it rents singles/doubles with fan for US$7/12. The *Transamazonas Hotel*, on Travessa de Indústria, charges US$9/12 for singles/doubles. There have been consistent reports that the *Palácio das Musas* is prone to robberies by someone using double keys – avoid it.

However, for the same price or just a little more, there are much better options, with cleaner, safer and more comfortable rooms. The *Hotel Fortaleza* (☎ 241-5005), at Travessa Frutuoso Guimarães 276, provides good-value quartos – US$9/11 for singles/doubles – though we've had a few complaints about gringos being overcharged and hassled by the lady who runs the place.

The *Vitória Régia* (☎ 224-2833), at Travessa Frutuoso Guimarães 260, offers good deals, with standard single/double apartamentos at US$10/12 and special apartamentos (with air-con) at US$15/18, although the owner mentioned that there will soon be a 20% price rise.

The *Hotel Sete Sete* (☎ 222-7730), at Travessa Primeiro de Março 673, also offers good-value apartamentos: US$11/13 for singles/doubles. The *Hotel Central* (☎ 242-3011; fax 241-7177), at Avenida Presidente Vargas 290, is a large, old hotel that is popular with foreign travellers. It charges US$17/22 for single/double apartamentos with fan and US$25/32 for single/double apartamentos with air-con, but these prices may also be increased. You should watch your valuables carefully – several travellers have reported robberies in this hotel. When we enquired about the robberies, we were told that a past employee was the culprit, and that there had been no problems since he was sacked.

Places to Stay – middle *Vidonho's Hotel* (☎ 225-1444; fax 224-7499), at Rua Ó de Almeida 476, is a modern, spic-and-span place with all the amenities of an expensive hotel including colour TV and refrigerator-bar. Apartamentos cost US$22/31 for singles/doubles.

The *Hotel Milano* (☎ 224-7045) faces the Praça da República, at Avenida Presidente Vargas 640. The staff are very friendly, and the hotel has a reliable safe for depositing valuables. It offers standard apartamentos with air-con for US$27; luxury versions with a view cost US$30.

If you like the waterfront, the *Hotel Vero-Peso* (☎ 224-2267; fax 224-9764), across from the market, at Avenida Castilho França 208, offers standard single apartamentos for US$27 and more plush single/double versions for US$30/33. All rooms have air-con. The rooftop restaurant, now reopened, has good views of the river and the market. One reader wrote that his sleep was constantly interrupted by prostitutes knocking at the door.

The *Hotel Plaza* (☎ 224-2800), at Praça da Bandeira 130, is a 10-storey residential/commercial building converted into a hotel. The apartamentos each have a small kitchen and dining area. The simple versions (with air-con and refrigerator) cost US$23/26. The *Manacá Hotel Residencia* (☎ 223-3335; fax 241-3375), at Travessa Quintino Bocaiúva 1645, is pleasant, well located and secure. Double apartamentos with fan cost US$27. Optional extras include breakfast (US$6), TV (US$5), air-con (US$5) and refrigerator (US$5).

The *Excelsior Grão Pará* (☎ 222-3255; fax 224-974), at Avenida Presidente Vargas 718, is more up-market: single/double apartamentos are priced at US$65/75, while luxury rooms facing the square, with good views, cost US$76/83. The *Regente* (☎ 224-0755), at Avenida Governador José Malcher 485, has single/double apartamentos from US$49/55. The *Itaóca Hotel* (☎ 241-3434; fax 241-2082), at Avenida Presidente Vargas 132, offers apartamentos for US$71/79, with off-peak discounts of 30%.

Places to Stay – top end The *Hilton Hotel* (☎ 223-6500; fax 225-2942), at Avenida Presidente Vargas 882, reminded us of the fancy, sterile hotels where CIA operatives always stay in movies about the Third World. Standard singles/doubles cost US$193/217, but they will let you stay a night in the presidential suite for a mere US$850.

The *Equatorial Palace* (☎ 241-2000; fax 223-5222), at Avenida Brás de Aguiar 612, has lost its intimate atmosphere and become a bit dismal. Singles/doubles here cost US$110/122. The *Novotel* (☎ 229-8011; fax 229-8709), at Avenida Bernardo Sayão 4804, is inconveniently located about four km from the city centre. However, it is right on the river margin, and some tour agencies use this port for their river tours. Standard rooms cost US$120/140, but you can get discounts of up to 50%. Close to the airport is the *Hotel Vila Rica* (☎ & fax 233-4222), at Avenida Júlio César 1777. It has singles/doubles that cost around US$90/100.

Places to Eat

The food in Belém features a bewildering variety of fish and fruit, and (unlike much of Brazil) a distinct regional cuisine that includes several delicious dishes. Pato no tucupi is a lean duck cooked in tucupi sauce (a yellow liquid extract from manioc or cassava root, poisonous in its raw form). Try unhas de caranguejo (crab claws) and casquinha de caranguejo (stuffed crab). Maniçoba (a stew of maniva and meats) takes a week to prepare – shoots of maniva (a variety of manioc) are ground, cooked for at least four days, then combined with jerked beef, calves' hooves, bacon, pork and sausages. If you enjoy feijoada, Brazil's national dish, you will appreciate maniçoba.

Until quite recently, such endangered species as tartaruga (turtle) and peixe-boi (manatee) were regularly served in Belém's restaurants. This practice is now illegal.

Three of the best local fish are filhote, pescada amarela and dourada – great eating. And you are no doubt familiar with açai, acerola, uxi, murici, bacuri and sapoti, just a few of the luscious Amazonian fruits that are available.

For cheap victuals, snack bars throughout the city offer sandwiches and regional juices. Mercado Ver-o-Peso has a thousand and one food stands serving big lunches for small prices. It's also a good place to try the local fish. Another way to eat cheaply is buffet à kilo: choose what and how much you want, then pay according to the weight of your food. Get to these restaurants early for the best choice and the freshest food. The *Spazzio Verde*, at Avenida Brás de Aguiar 824, is recommended.

Vegetarians can try the *Restaurante Vegetariano Mercado do Natural*, at Rua Alfredo Santo Antônio, open only for lunch. For heavenly sucos made from one or more of the many Amazon fruits available in Pará, go to *Casa dos Sucos*, at Avenida Presidente Vargas 794, which also has a good-value self-service section upstairs. Close by is the *Bar do Parque*, an outside bar and popular meeting place where you can order a snack and a drink.

There is decent, good-value pasta at the *Cantina Italiana*, at Travessa Benjamin Constant 1401. For simple French dishes, look for Chez Jacques, at Rua Silva Santos 102 – this French expatriate runs *O Bistrô* in his front room. There's no sign outside the place. For typical Brazilian fare, try the *Inter Restaurant*, at Rua 28 de Setembro 304, which has meat, fish, and rice for about US$5.

Belém has several excellent restaurants where you can do some fine dining for US$11 to US$24. *Lá Em Casa* and *O Outro* (☎ 225-0320), two restaurants on the same site, at Avenida Governador José Malcher 247, serve all the best regional dishes. The *O Círculo Militar*, at the old Forte do Castelo, on Praça Caetano Brandão, has a great bay view and good regional cooking, but isn't cheap.

The *Miako*, behind the Hilton Hotel, is one of Brazil's best Japanese restaurants north of São Paulo. If you don't like Japanese food, typical Brazilian dishes are also available. The Miako is closed on the second and last Sunday of each month.

The *Restaurante Avenida*, at Avenida Nazaré 1086, on the opposite side of Praça da Basílica, has dishes for about US$10. *Casa Portuguesa*, at Rua Senador Manoel Barata 897, is also recommended.

Entertainment

Belém has many nightclubs, known in Brazilian as *boites* or *boates*. These popular nightspots offer music, shows and dance. For concerts and shows, check what's on at the Escápole (☎ 248-2217), at Rodovia Montenegro, Km 7, No 400; Vallery (☎ 225-2259), at Avenida Pedro Alvares Cabral 33; and Boite Olé-Olá (☎ 243-0129), at Avenida Tavares Bastos 1234. Lapinha (☎ 229-3290), at Travessa Padre Eutíquio 3901, also presents good shows.

The Cosanostra Caffé (☎ 241-1068), at Travessa Benjamim Constant 1499, is a hang-out for wealthier and intellectual types. It has a bar and restaurant with live instrumental music each night – jazz-latino, bossa nova, *chorinho* and blues. Happy hour is from 6 to 8 pm Monday to Friday. Also on Travessa Benjamim Constant, you will find Manga Café and Degrau, bars where you can sit outside and have beers and snacks. Au Bar (☎ 224-0777), at Travessa Benjamim Constant 1843, is an interesting restaurant, bar and pub, with live music. At the time of writing, it was a trendy spot among locals, and particularly good on Friday and Saturday after 10 pm.

Samba clubs include Rancho Não Posso me Amofiná (☎ 225-0918), at Travessa Honório José dos Santos 764, in the Jurunas district, and Quem São Eles (☎ 225-1133), at Avenida Almirante Wandenkolk 680, in the Umarizal district. This is the closest samba club to the city centre. The clubs operate on weekends all year round, but the best time to go is around Carnival.

The region has some great traditional music and dance which, unfortunately, is hard to find in Belém. Performances are occasionally arranged for tour groups, and while these may not be your cup of tea, it's worth doing anything to see and hear the old music and dance. Call the tourism office and tell them you want to see *carimbó*, which is a dance named after the kind of drum used for the performance, the Indian word for 'hollow wood sound'. Other dances include the *lundú*, the origin of which goes back to the Bantu slaves from Africa, and the *siriá*, the dance whose movements imitate the siri (a type of crab). Sabor da Terra (☎ 223-6820), at Avenida Visconde de Souza Franco 685, is a combined restaurant and club which presents an interesting carimbó dance show. The owner and presenter claims to be in the Guinness Book of Records for the highest number of folkloric show presentations. Sabor da Terra is open from 8.30 pm, Monday to Saturday.

If you have a cassette player, pick up a tape by local musician Pinduca, who is a carimbó maestro. Other popular local musicians and groups to look out for are Nilson Chaves, Marcos Monteiro, Grupo Oficina, Vital Nima and Banda Nova.

The Cultural Center Tancredo Neves (CENTUR), at Avenida Gentil Bittencourt 650, has an exhibition hall, a theatre, a cinema, and a library where you may find some English-language books or films.

Getting There & Away

Air Air services connect Belém with the major Brazilian cities. There are daily flights to Macapá (Amapá state), Santarém and Manaus. International destinations serviced from Belém include Cayenne (French Guiana), Paramaribo (Surinam), and Miami (USA). Both TABA and Surinam Airways fly to Cayenne. A one-way/return ticket costs about US$186/220.

The following national and international airlines have offices in Belém:

Air France
> General Agent at the airport (☎ 224-0844)

Alitalia
> Rua dos Mundurucus 1451 (☎ 241-7610)

American Airlines
> Travessa Piedade 551A, Reduto

British Airways
> Avenida Presidente Vargas 620, sala 204 (☎ 241-2805)

Japan Airlines
  Avenida Presidente Vargas 762, loja 7
  (☎ 223-6234)
Surinam Airways
  Rua Alfredo Santo Antônio 432, salas 1204-1206
  (☎ 212-7144)
TABA
  Avenida Governador José Malcher 883
  (☎ 223-6300)
TAP (Air Portugal)
  Rua Senador Manoel Barata 704, sala 1401
  (☎ 223-4385)
Transbrasil
  Avenida Presidente Vargas 780 (☎ 224-6977)
Varig/Cruzeiro
  Avenida Presidente Vargas 768 (☎ 225-4222)
VASP
  Avenida Presidente Vargas 620, loja B
  (☎ 224-5588)

Air-Taxi In Belém, air-taxis fly from Aeroporto Júlio César (☎ 233-3868), at Avenida Senador Lemos 4700. There are a few different carriers, such as Kovacs (☎ 233-1600), Bandeirantes (☎ 233-2868) and Dourado (☎ 226-2351).

Bus There are regular bus services to São Luís (US$22, 12 hours), Fortaleza (US$41, 25 hours), Recife (US$57, 34 hours) and Rio de Janeiro (US$94, 52 hours). There also direct buses from Belo Horizonte (US$82, 30 hours), São Paulo (US$87, 46 hours) and Brasília (US$63, 36 hours). At the time of writing, bus services to Santarém had been suspended.

Boat The government-operated Empresa de Navegação da Amazônia, or ENASA (☎ 223-3834), at Avenida Presidente Vargas 41, has significantly reduced its passenger-boat services. The private companies have improved the standard of their boats, and virtually superseded ENASA for passenger transportation.

Food is usually included in ticket prices, and includes lots of rice, beans and some meat. Downriver travel is considerably faster than up, but the upriver trip goes closer to the shore and is consequently more scenic.

To select a boat, go down to the docks and ask on board for information – most boats will take a day or two to load up before they depart. The best place to look is Portão 17 (Armazém 9), at the Porto de Belém. The entrance is where Avenida Visconde de Souza Franco meets Avenida Marechal Hermes. You can also get information from the boat-company agents at the praça (opposite the ENASA building) at the 'Escadinha Port'. Boats also depart from the Porto do Sal (in Cidade Velho) and the Porto das Lanchas (Avenida Castilho França, between Mercado Ver-o-Peso and the Forte do Castelo).

Beware of theft on boats – a very common complaint. Also, do not entrust baggage to a boat official or allow it to be stored in a locker unless you are quite certain about the identity of the official. Bogus officials and related locker thefts have been reported by readers. For more tips, see the security advice in the Dangers & Annoyances section of the Facts for the Visitor chapter.

To/From Santarém & Manaus ENASA operates the monthly Cruzeiro Pelo Rio Amazonas (Amazon Cruise) service to Manaus and back. This is not a good way to see the Amazon because the boat usually stays too far out in the middle of the wide river for passengers to see the forested riverbanks. It's expensive because you pay for 'love boat' distractions such as a swimming pool. The cruise from Belém to Manaus takes five days, with prices starting at US$430 per person for cabin accommodation. The boats (catamarans) depart from the dock on Avenida Castilho França, near Mercado Ver-o-Peso. For more information on ENASA services between Manaus and Belém, see the Getting There & Away section for Manaus.

Boats on the regular ENASA service leave Belém every Wednesday at 8 pm, arriving in Santarém by noon on Saturday and in Manaus on Tuesday morning, and stopping at several towns along the way. The fare to Santarém is US$61 and to Manaus it's US$87 *classe regional* with hammock accommodation and food included. The boat's capacity is 600 passengers, but several readers have advised that these regular ENASA services are very crowded, serve poor food and are prone to theft. Arrive early on the day of departure, and take your own snacks and water. Although the smaller operators may charge slightly more, the quality of their service is generally much better. The return service leaves Manaus on Thursday night at 8 pm, reaching Santarém on Saturday and Belém a couple of days later.

Agencia de Navegação a Serviço da Amazonia, or AGENASA (☎ 246-1085), previously known as EMNART, also represents other boat companies, and apparently is the largest agency servicing the passenger route Belém-Santarém-Manaus. AGENASA operates a booth at Belém's main bus terminal (rodoviária) for ticket sales, and a service to take passengers to the port. Boats to Santarém and Manaus depart on Monday, Tuesday, Wednesday and Friday. Tickets for Manaus cost US$90/141 per person in hammock space/four-person cabins; tickets for Santarém cost US$64/98. For information on other services to Manaus and Santarém, contact Numar Agency (☎ 223-8296), which has boats departing from Belém on Monday, Wednesday and Friday. Fares are similar to those charged by EMNART.

To/From Soure & Câmara The Arapari boat service to Câmara port (on Ilha de Marajó) takes three hours, and from Câmara you can catch a bus for the 30-km ride to Salvaterra. Soure is a short ferryboat ride across the Rio Paracauari. It sounds like a logistical hassle, but is quite an enjoyable trip. Boats to Câmara leave Escadinha port at 7 am Monday to Saturday. Tickets cost US$17.

The ENASA ferry to Soure departs on Friday at 8 pm and on Saturday at 2 pm. The return service leaves Soure on Sunday at 3 pm. The five-hour trip costs US$14/26 in economy/1st class (the only difference is a separate cabin in 1st class with more comfortable chairs).

To/From Macapá The Superintendência de Navegação do Amapá, or SENAVA (☎ 222-8710), at Rua Castilho França 234, has a service which leaves from Belém for Macapá (in Amapá state) on Friday at 10 am. The 24-hour journey costs US$17/90 in hammock space/cabin accommodation.

AGENASA (☎ 246-1085) and Numar Agency (☎ 223-8296) also operate boat services to Macapá. Tickets cost US$30.

Getting Around
To/From the Airports Belém's main airport, Aeroporto Internacional Val de Cans (☎ 233-4122), is on Avenida Júlio César. Airport facilities include a Paratur tourist-information booth, a branch of the Banco do Brasil, a newsagency, a post office and a restaurant.

Take the bus marked 'Perpétuo Socorro' from the city centre – it's quick (half an hour) and, of course, cheap. There's a bilheteria system for taxis; a trip from the airport to the city centre costs about US$15.

Remember, air-taxis leave from a different airport: Aeroporto Júlio César (☎ 233-3868), at Avenida Senador Lemos 4700.

To/From the Rodoviária The rodoviária (☎ 228-0500) is at the corner of Avenida Almirante Barroso and Avenida Ceará – about a 15-minute bus ride from the city. To reach the city centre from the rodoviária, take any bus marked 'Aeroclube 20', 'Cidade Nova 6' or 'Universidade (Presidente Vargas)'. All buses that are marked 'Cidade Nova 5' or 'Souza' run via Mercado Ver-o-Peso.

Bus The bus marked 'Aeroclube 20' is especially convenient because it runs from the city centre via the main city attractions: the Basílica de NS de Nazaré, the Museu Emílio Goeldi, the rodoviária and the Bosque Rodrigues Alves.

There are frequent buses to the beaches of Ilha do Mosqueiro. For details, see the Getting There & Away section for Ilha do Mosqueiro.

ILHA DO MOSQUEIRO
Mosqueiro is the weekend beach for Belenenses (inhabitants of Belém), who attempt to beat the heat by flocking to the

island's 19 freshwater beaches on the east side of the Baía de Marajó. It's close enough to Belém for plenty of weekend beach houses, and some well-to-do Belenenses even commute to the city. The island is particularly crowded between July and October. The beaches are not nearly as nice as those on Ilha de Marajó or the Atlantic coast, but if you want to get out of Belém for just a day, they're not bad.

Beaches
The best beaches are **Praia do Farol**, **Praia Chapéu Virado** and the more remote **Baía do Sol**.

Festivals
Mosqueiro's traditional folklore festival, held in June, features the dance and music of carimbó and *bois-bumbas*. In July, during the Festival de Verão, the island shows off some of its art and music. The Círio de NS do Ó, the principal religious event on the island, is celebrated on the second Sunday of December. Like Belém's Círio, this event is a very beautiful and joyous event, and well worth seeing if you're in Belém at the time.

Places to Stay & Eat
During the dry season, you can use the campsites on the island. There are also a handful of hotels. The *Ilha Bela* (☎ 771-1448), at Avenida 16 de Novembro 409-463, has aircon single/double apartamentos for around US$28/37, and a restaurant. The *Hotel Farol* (☎ 771-1219), at Praça Princesa Isabel 3295, on Praia do Farol, offers quartos for US$24 and apartamentos for US$30. There's a weekday discount of 10%, except during the July and January high seasons.

Maresias, on Praia Chapéu Virado, is recommended for seafood. If you can speak Portuguese, have a chat to Carlos, the owner, who used to be a local guide. On Praia do Murubira, the *Hotel e Restaurante Murubira* (☎ 771-1778) has single/double apartamentos for US$46/77, with discounts of up to 30% during the low season.

Getting There & Away
Ilha do Mosqueiro is a 1½-hour bus ride (84 km) from Belém. The island is linked to the mainland by good paved roads and a bridge. Buses to Ilha do Mosqueiro leave from the rodoviária in Belém every hour on weekdays and every half-hour on weekends. There are also boats to Ilha do Mosqueiro from the Porto Rodomar. They leave at 9 am and 6 pm Monday to Friday (returning at 3 pm), and at 9 am on weekends (returning at 6 pm). Tickets costs US$0.30 on weekdays and US$1.80 on weekends.

PRAIA DO ALGODOAL & MARUDÁ
Algodoal attracts younger Belenenses and a handful of foreign travellers. This beautiful spot, with its dune-swept beaches and sometimes turbulent sea, is very remote, with a small fishing village and simple hotels. But all this may change, hopefully not too radically, because Algodoal is in the process of being 'discovered'. The name Algodoal comes from the Portuguese word *algodão*, which means cotton (the sand dunes when viewed from a distance resemble hills of cotton). Ilha de Maiandeua, the Indian term for *mãe terra* (mother land), is the name of the island.

Marudá is a poor fishing village with a couple of cheap hotels and a respectable beach, so it's no problem if you're stuck there overnight. Cars cannot make the journey to Algodoal and will have to be left in Marudá.

Things to See & Do
Lagoa da Princesa is a freshwater lake about an hour's walk inland from Algodoal. The dark water of the lake is surrounded by white sand and native vegetation.

The tropical forest reserve of **Rio Centenário**, the largest igarapé on the island, has a forest of *miritizeiros* (the Amazonian royal palm) and other native species.

Ilha do Marco (Praia da Marieta) is about 10 km by boat from Algodoal, and has a petrified-tree cemetery, interesting rock formations and a natural swimming pool.

THE NORTH

There are no local tour operators or guides on the island. You could try contacting the Cabanas Hotel's manager, Lula, who enjoys showing the island to tourists.

Places to Stay

Prices in Praia do Algodoal double in the month of July, at Carnival time, during Holy week and on long weekends.

The *Cabanas Hotel* (☎ 223-5456), at Rua Magalhães Barata, has rustic single/double apartamentos with fan for US$18/30, which includes a good breakfast. The *Caldeirão*

(☎ 227-0984), on Avenida Beira Mar, has apartamentos with mosquito net for US$15/18 a single/double. The *Paraiso do Sol* (☎ 233-8470), at Passagen Vila Nova, Q 13, has chalets (with double beds and mosquito nets) for US$18. The *Hotel Bela Mar*, on Avenida Beira Mar, has apartamentos (with shower and mosquito net) for US$30.

Places to Eat

Both the *Hotel Bela Mar*, on Avenida Beira Mar, and the *Marcelina*, near the praça, have cheap set menus offering fish or meat. The

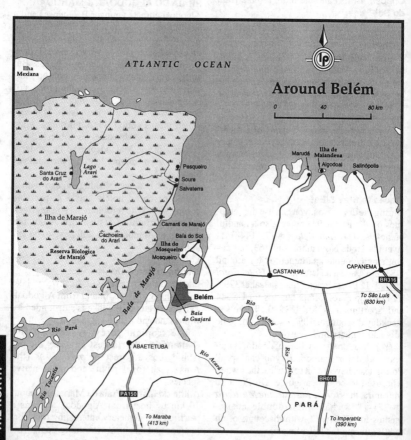

THE NORTH

The Legend of Praia da Princesa

Legend has it that long ago an enchanting green-eyed, blonde-haired princess lived on Praia da Princesa. Her home was a white sand-dune castle, and she appeared only on the night of a full moon.

At that time, turtles used to lay their eggs on the beaches and dolphins would come to play with the big fish around the island.

Wanting to teach men how to take care of the island, she appeared before a young fisherman. The fisherman, afraid of drowning in the lake of the big snakes which defended the castle, ran away. The princess cried, saying that if men did not stop destroying the island, she would have to go to another beach. Since that time, the turtles have stopped laying eggs on the beaches, and the dolphins and big fish have all gone away.

Several men have drowned at Praia da Princesa. It is said they were lured into the water by a green-eyed, blonde-haired woman. ∎

Restaurant Praia Mar, at Praia da Vila, has good views and a more varied menu. Also at Praia da Vila, *Lua Cheia* restaurant is the hang-out spot of the local youth. Bars for beers and peixe-frito (fried fish) can be found on Praia da Princesa; try *Bar do Gil*, *Julia* and *Porquinho*.

Dona Maria da Tapioca, on Rua Magalhães Barata, makes tapioca pancakes for breakfast. For cakes and sweets (afternoons only), there's *Dona Guiomar*, at Rua Bragantina.

Getting There & Away

Algodoal is north-east of Belém, on the tip of a cape jutting into the Atlantic Ocean. Getting there requires a four-hour, usually overcrowded stop-start bus ride from Belém to the town of Marudá (US$5), then a half-hour boat trip across the bay (US$2.50).

Buses leave the rodoviária in Belém daily at 6 and 9 am, and 12.30, 2.30 and 4.30 pm; on Friday, there is also a 7 pm bus. The last bus leaves Marudá for Belém at 3 pm (5 pm on Fridays). Extra buses sometimes run on weekends – check this at the rodoviária.

SALINÓPOLIS

Salinópolis is Pará's major Atlantic coastal resort, with good beaches (such as Praia da Atalaia) and some mineral spas. There are plenty of summer homes here, and during the July holiday month, Salinópolis is very crowded. If you want beautiful, deserted Brazilian beaches, this is not really the best place to go.

Places to Stay

For camping, there's *Amapá Camping* (☎ 823-1422), on Avenida Dr Miguel Santa Brigida. Hotel accommodation is generally expensive in Salinópolis. The *Hotel Salinas* (☎ 823-1173), at Passagem Guarani 190, offers apartamentos for around US$60.

Getting There & Away

There is a regular bus service from Belém to Salinópolis (US$5, three hours).

ILHA DE MARAJÓ

Ilha de Marajó, one of the largest fluvial islands in the world, lies at the mouths of the Amazon and Tocantins rivers. The island's 250,000 inhabitants live in 13 municipalities and in the many fazendas spread across the island. Although visiting the island is fairly straightforward for independent travellers, many travel agencies in Belém offer package tours to the main town (Soure) and remote fazendas. See the Soure section for details.

History

Researchers have discovered that the island was inhabited between 1000 BC and 1300 AD by successive Indian civilisations. The first of these, known as the Ananatuba civilisation, was followed by those of the Mangueiras, the Formiga Marajoara and,

THE NORTH

finally, the Aruã. The ceramics produced by these civilisations were ornamented with intricate designs in black, red and white. The best examples of these ceramics are displayed at the Museu Emílio Goeldi in Belém.

The resemblance of these designs to those found in Andean civilisations prompted the theory amongst some researchers that the inhabitants of Ilha de Marajó had originally floated down the Amazon from the Andes. In 1991, a team of international archaeologists reported the discovery of pottery fragments near Santarém which were estimated to be between 7000 and 8000 years old. These fragments predate what was previously considered the oldest pottery in the Americas.

Geography

Ilha de Marajó, slightly larger in size than Switzerland, has close to 50,000 sq km of land, which divides into two geographical regions of almost equal size. The eastern half of the island is called the *região dos campos*. This area is characterised by low-lying fields with savannah-type flora, and sectioned by strips of remaining forest. Various palm trees and dense mangrove forests line the coast. The island's western half, the *região da mata*, is primarily forest.

Climate

Marajó has two seasons: the very rainy, from January to June, and the dry (less rainy!), from July to December. During the rainy season, much of the island turns into swamp and the região dos campos becomes completely submerged under a metre or more of water. The island's few roads are elevated by three metres, but are nonetheless often impassable during the rainy season.

Fauna

The herds of buffalo which wander the fields provide Marajó's sustenance, being well adapted to the swampy terrain. There are many snakes, most notably large boas. The island is filled with birds, especially during the dry season, including the *guará*, a graceful flamingo with a long, curved beak. The sight of a flock of deep-pink guarás flying against Marajó's green backdrop is truly spectacular.

Soure

Soure (pronounced 'sorry'), the island's principal town, is on the Rio Paracauari, a few km from the Baía de Marajó. The tide along the city's shore oscillates a remarkable three metres. With regular boat services from Belém and easy access to several of the best beaches and fazendas, Soure is probably the best place to stay on the island, although since the introduction of the ferry to Câmara, Selvaterra is becoming more popular.

Like all the island's coastal towns, Soure is primarily a fishing village, but it's also the

---

Marajó Buffalo

Legend has it that a French ship was sailing to French Guiana with a load of buffalo that it had picked up in India. However, the boat sank off the shore of Ilha de Marajó and the buffalo swam to shore.

Today, Marajó is the only place in Brazil where buffalo roam in great numbers, and there are thousands of them. These are not the furry American bison of the American plains, but a tough-skinned, hairless buffalo that looks like a macho Indian Brahma bull.

There are four different uses for buffalo on Marajó: meat, dairy products, traction and breeding. Three qualities make buffalo better suited than cattle to Marajó's environment. First, they can survive the wet season when much of the land turns into swamps or lagoons, buffalo can walk on the soft ground with their wide hooves, and they can swim when the water gets deep. Second, their tough, three-layered hide is able to withstand the bites of the island's many snakes and parasites, and third, the buffalo can eat almost anything, and will even dive underwater to obtain food. ■

commercial centre for the island's buffalo business, and these animals rule the place like kings. The townsfolk work around the buffalo, or sometimes with or on them, but never obstruct their passage: right of way in town belongs indisputably to the buffalo!

Money There is no money-exchange service at the Banco do Brasil in Soure, but you can get cash advances on your Visa card.

Warning Bichos de pé (unpleasant jigger bugs that burrow into human feet) are found in and around the towns, and the island has many other nasty parasites. Keep your head on your shoulders and shoes on your feet.

Beaches The bay beaches near Soure are excellent and look more like ocean beaches. The beach is often covered with exotic seeds washed down from the Amazon forests. Praia Araruna, the most beautiful beach, is also the closest, just a 10-minute taxi ride from town. Ask the driver to pick you up at a set hour...and pay then. You can also walk the five km to the beach; ask for directions in town. The road passes through farmland where you might spot a flock of guarás, then follow two pedestrian bridges across the lagoons to the beach. The bay here, 30 km from the ocean, has both fresh and salt water. At low tide, you can walk about five km in either direction. The beach is deserted during the week, and could scarcely be called crowded on weekends.

Praia do Pesqueiro is 13 km from town (a 25-minute drive). Ask about buses at Soure. There are barracas serving great caranguejo (crab) and casquinha de caranguejo (stuffed crab), but lousy shrimp. When you're facing the sea, the best beach section lies to your right. Do not swim in the shallow lagoon between the barracas and the sea: it harbours prickly plants.

O Curtume If you head upriver about a 10-minute walk from town, you'll come to an old, simple tannery which sells sandals, belts and saddles made from buffalo. The merchandise on sale isn't very good, but it's illuminating to see the production line to the finished product. The tannery is located next door to the slaughterhouse.

Festivals On the second Sunday of November, Soure has its own Círio de Nazaré. The festival features a beautiful procession, and the town bursts with communal spirit. Everyone in the region comes to Soure for the festival, so accommodation can be difficult to find. The festival of São Pedro, on 29 June, is a very colourful celebration, and includes a maritime procession. If you're into buffalo culture, the Agro-Pecuária fair is held during the third week of September.

Places to Stay – Soure Although travel agencies in Belém are keen to promote their package tours to Ilha de Marajó, with accommodation booked in Soure, independent travel on the island is really no more difficult than anywhere else in the Amazon region. Providing you have a flexible schedule, it's easy to set out on your own.

The *Pousada Marajoara* (☎ 741-1287 in Soure; 223-8369 in Belém for reservations) does most of its business through package excursions. At the time we went there, business was very quiet, and the pousada appeared to be going downhill. The accommodation is fine, if a bit touristy. The local fish is the best dish, but there's also buffalo meat – and for dessert, don't miss the fantastic buffalo-milk flan. Independent travellers may be able to reserve rooms direct – apartamentos cost around US$42/54 for singles/doubles.

On the other side of town, the *Hotel Marajó* (☎ 741-1396), at Praça Inhangaíba 351, has a swimming pool and offers apartamentos with air-con for US$24/30. For cheaper lodging, try the *Soure Hotel* (☎ 741-1202), in the centre of town, which has apartamentos for US$15 with fan, or US$19 with air-con. It's simple, but a bit dowdy. The *Araruna Hotel* (☎ 229-3928), at Travessa 14, in between Avenidas 7 and 8, has simple rooms with air-con for US$18.

Places to Stay – Remote Fazendas The

fazendas where the buffalo roam are enormous estates occupying most of the island's eastern half. They are also beautiful, rustic refuges filled with birds and monkeys. Most of the fazendas have dormitories with an extra bunk or a place to hitch a hammock, but not all will welcome outsiders. The fazendas listed here have primitive dorms for tourists and will show you around by jeep or on foot.

The *Fazenda Bom Jardim* (☎ 231-3681 in Soure, 222-1380 in Belém for reservations) is a three-hour boat ride, or a slightly shorter taxi ride, from Soure. Air-taxis take half an hour from Belém. The fazendeiro, Eduardo Ribeiro, often comes to Soure, so if you want to stay at Bom Jardim, you may be able to track him down in town and organise transport out there with him.

The *Fazenda Jilva* (☎ 225-0432), 40 km from Soure, is reportedly one of the most beautiful. It has accommodation for about 10 people, and charges around US$100 per person per day. It's a 45-minute flight from Belém to the fazenda.

The *Fazenda Carmo Câmara* (☎ 223-5696) is well organised for tourist visits, and charges about US$100 per person per day.

For information about other fazendas, contact Paratur in Belém, or the travel agencies described under Tours in the Getting There & Away section. Another strategy would be to talk to the air-taxi companies at the Aeroclube Júlio César in Belém (☎ 233-3279). Some of the old pilots know the island very well.

Salvaterra

Salvaterra is separated from Soure by a short boat ride across the river. Shuttle boats leave every hour during the day and cost US$0.50. A 10-minute walk from town, Praia Grande de Salvaterra is a long, picturesque beach on the Baía de Marajó. It's popular on weekends, when the barracas open, but often windy. This is a good place to see the beautiful fenced corrals which dot Marajó's coastline (from the air, they appear as a string of heart shapes). The corrals are simple fences with netting that use the falling tide to capture fish.

Salvaterra has restaurants and accommodation along the Praia Grande beach. *Pousada Anastácia* has simple rooms (US$18) and a rustic restaurant. *Pousada Tropical*, on Avenida Beira Mar, next to the inlet Corrego da Praia Grande, has very basic rooms for US$9/12 a single/double. *Pousada dos Guarás* (☎ 241-0891 in Belém for reservations) has its own transport and guides to take you around to beaches and tourist spots. It charges US$64/71 for singles/doubles. The pousada also has two and three-day packages with tours included. If you're in a hurry or want someone else to take care of everything for you, it's a good deal, but there is no other reason to take the packaged option.

Around Ilha de Marajó

From Salvaterra, a dirt road goes to Câmara (24 km) and then continues to Cachoeira do Arari (51 km), a very pretty, rustic town which reportedly has a pousada.

To the north, accessible only by plane, is the town of **Santa Cruz do Arari**, on the immense Lagoa Arari. This town is completely submerged during the rainy season, and is famous for its fishing.

The western half of the island is less populated and less interesting for travellers. There are boat services to the city of **Breves**, which has a pousada. **Afuá**, on the northern shore, is built on water and also has a pousada. Both of these cities are linked to Belém by air-taxi.

Ilha Caviana, an island lying off the north coast of Ilha de Marajó, is an excellent base from which to observe the pororoca (the thunderous collision between the Atlantic tide and the Amazon). The best time to see this phenomenon is between January and April, at either full or new moon. Marcelo Morelio (☎ 223-4784) is a local pilot/guide who shuttles between Belém and Ilha de Marajó. He charges US$200 per person or US$1000 per group (a maximum of six people) for a flight to Ilha Caviana to see the pororoca.

Getting There & Away

Air Air-taxis fly regularly between Belém and Soure, and to other towns on the island. It's a beautiful 25-minute flight over the immense river and thick forests to Soure. The flights aren't as cheap as they used to be, but for a group with limited time, they may still be worthwhile. A five-seater from Belém to Soure costs US$360. Split five ways, that's US$72 a person. For details about air-taxi companies, see the Getting There & Away section under Belém.

Boat For details about boat services between Belém and Ilha de Marajó, see the Getting There & Away section for Belém.

From Macapá (Amapá state), there are boats to Afuá, on Ilha de Marajó. Local fishing boats sail the high seas, and it's possible to use them to get all the way around the island and to some of the fazendas.

Tours Excursions to Ilha de Marajó are offered by a number of agencies in Belém including Mururé Turismo (☎ 241-0891); Gran-Pará Turismo (☎ 224-3233), at Avenida Presidente Vargas 676; Carimbó Viagens e Turismo (☎ 223-6464), at Travessa Piedade 186; Vianney Turismo (☎ 241-5638), at Travessa Padre Eutíquio 2296; and Mundial Turismo (☎ 223-1981), at Avenida Presidente Vargas 780. Excursions include transport (by either boat or plane) and full board at a hotel in Soure or at one of the remote fazendas. As a rough rule of thumb, most of these package deals cost around US$150 per person per day if the trip is done by plane, or US$60 per person per day if the trip is done by boat.

PROJETO GRANDE CARAJÁS

If any project defies superlatives to describe its scale, it is the Projeto Grande Carajás. The multifocal project centres around the world's largest deposit of iron ore, but only US$4.5 billion of the project's US$60 billion budget will be directed towards the extraction of iron ore. The rest of the money is to be invested in the extraction of the area's other metals – manganese, copper, bauxite, nickel, potassium and gold, all found near the Serra Pelada – and in the development of an industrial zone whose size (400,000 sq km) rivals that of California.

In the tradition of previous Amazonian-scale enterprises, such as Henry Ford's Fordlândia and Daniel K Ludwig's Jari pulpwood project, the Carajás project started with American support. The venture began as a partnership between US Steel and Companhía Vale do Rio Doce (CVRD), a Brazilian company funded by both private and public capital. When iron prices dropped on the world market, US Steel pulled out of the collaboration.

The minerals are transported along the 900-km railroad from Carajás to the Atlantic coast at São Luis, Maranhão. There, at the Porto de Ponto da Madeira, large ships are loaded for export to Europe and Asia. In 1994, CVRD boasted a record year for iron-ore sales: 100 million tonnes. Eight million kilowatts of power for the project are already being generated by the Tucuruí dam (on the Rio Tocantins), and seven more dams are planned for the Tocantins and its tributaries. The environmental effects of clearing this much jungle, burning this much wood and flooding this much land will undoubtedly be stupendous. CVRD maintains that they have a responsible attitude towards preserving flora and fauna and limiting the project's impact on the environment.

Access to Carajás is by bus (via Marabá), or direct by plane.

SERRA PELADA

At its peak, in 1984, the Serra Pelada gold mines, near the Carajás project, west of Marabá, had 400,000 miners and hangers-on scraping away at the earth. With the digging done by hand, the site resembled a human anthill. It was not the whip but the promise of gold that drove prospectors to work like slaves. The mine area, a huge pit with criss-crossing claims, rivalled the pyramids in scale and epic sweep.

During the 1980s, the CVRD, which operates the nearby Projeto Grande Carajás, claimed the mineral rights to the area and

THE NORTH

attempted to wrest control of the mines from the prospectors. The enraged prospectors protested strongly, staging a march on Brasília and threatening to raid the Projeto Grande Carajás. In 1984 the government compromised by paying US$60 million to CVRD in compensation and then recognising the prospectors' claims.

In 1995 there were a mere 3000 or so miners endeavouring to scrape out a living or save enough money to leave. Without the resources to maintain and drain the open cut, mining has become too dangerous and unworkable to be very productive. It seems that CVRD is biding its time until the area is abandoned.

SANTARÉM

Santarém is a pleasant city with a mild climate (22°C to 36°C), Atlantic breezes, calm waters and beautiful forests. The region around Santarém was originally inhabited by the Tapuiçu Indians. In 1661, over three decades after Captain Pedro Teixeira's expedition first contacted the Tapuiçu, a Jesuit mission was established at the meeting of the Tapajós and Amazon rivers. In 1758 the village that grew around the mission was named Santarém, after the city of that name in Portugal.

In 1867, a group of 110 Confederates from the breakaway Southern states of the USA emigrated to Santarém, where they attempted to start new lives as farmers or artisans. Only a handful of these settlers managed to prosper; the rest drifted away from Santarém, were killed off by disease, or accepted the offer of a free return passage on an American boat to the USA.

Later developments in Santarém's history included the boom-and-bust cycle of the rubber plantations (for the story of the bust, see Henry Wickham – Executioner of Amazonas, in the History section of the Facts about the Country chapter), and a series of gold rushes which started in the 1950s and have continued to this day. The construction of the Transamazônica highway (in 1970) and the Santarém-Cuiabá highway (completed six years later) attracted hordes of immigrants from the Northeast, few of whom were able to establish more than a brief foothold before abandoning the region for the favelas of Manaus or Belém.

The economy is based on rubber, hard woods, brazil nuts, black pepper, mangoes, soybeans, jute and fish. The past 20 years has seen rapid development, with the discovery of gold and bauxite and the construction of the Curuá-Una hydroelectric dam. With the deterioration of the road links to Santarém, the area is suffering from its isolation from the rest of Pará. There is a popular movement to form a new state of Tapajòs, to guarantee that government funding reaches the area.

Orientation

Santarém lies 2½° south of the equator, at the junction of the Tapajós and Amazon rivers, about halfway between Manaus and Belém, and only 30 metres above sea level. Although it's the third largest city on the Amazon, Santarém is merely a sleepy backwater in comparison to Manaus and Belém.

The city layout is simple: the Cuiabá-Santarém highway runs directly to the Docas do Pará, dividing the city into old (eastern) and new (western) halves. East from the Docas do Pará, where the large boats dock, is Avenida Tapajós, which runs along the waterfront and leads to the marketplace and commercial district.

Information

Tourist Office There is no tourist office, but you can get information from the various tourist agencies listed below. Steve Alexander, an expatriate American, has written *Alexander's Guide to Santarém*, which is available from his agency, Amazon Tours (address given under Tour Agencies).

Money The Banco do Brasil branch in Santarém does not have an exchange service for cash or travellers' cheques, but you can get cash advances on Visa cards. Cash dollars can be exchanged at the Hotel Tropical, or try airline offices and chemists.

Post & Telephone The central post office is

at Avenida Rui Brabosa, adjacent to No 1189. There's a Posto Telefônico at Rua Fransisco Corrêa.

Tour Agencies The following agencies organise jungle tours and excursions around Santarém: Lago Verde Turismo (☎ 522-2118), at Rua Galdino Veloso 384; Amazônia Turismo (☎ 522-5820), at Rua Adriano Pimentel 44; Jatão Turismo (☎ 523-7766), at Avenida Rui Barbosa, opposite the Banco do Brasil; Santarém Tur (☎ 522-1533; fax 523-2037), at the Tropical Hotel; and Amazon Tours (☎ 522-2620; fax 522-1098), at Travessa Turiano Meira 1084 (advance booking necessary).

Waterfront
Walk along the waterfront of Avenida Tapajós from the Docas do Pará to Rua Adriano Pimentel. This is where drifters, loners and fisherfolk congregate. Include a stop at the Mercado de Peixes (Fish Market) and the floating market.

Centro Cultural João Fona
The Centro Cultural, at Praça Barão de Santarém, features a collection of pre-Columbian pottery.

River Beaches
Santarém's natural river beaches are magnificent. As elsewhere in the Amazon, the seasonal rise and fall of the waters uncovers lovely white river beaches, and sweeps them clean of debris at the end of the beach season.

Festivals
The Indian Festa do Sairé and the Christian ceremony of NS da Saúde have been celebrated on 23 June at Alter do Chão since 1880. The Sairé is a standard which is held aloft to lead a flower-bedecked procession. This is perhaps a re-enactment of the historic

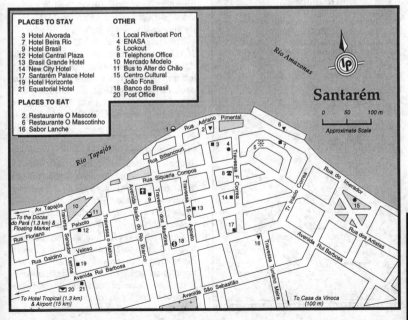

PLACES TO STAY
3 Hotel Alvorada
7 Hotel Beira Rio
9 Hotel Brasil
12 Hotel Central Plaza
13 Brasil Grande Hotel
14 New City Hotel
17 Santarém Palace Hotel
19 Hotel Horizonte
21 Equatorial Hotel

PLACES TO EAT
2 Restaurante O Mascote
6 Restaurante O Mascotinho
16 Sabor Lanche

OTHER
1 Local Riverboat Port
4 ENASA
5 Lookout
8 Telephone Office
10 Mercado Modelo
11 Bus to Alter do Chão
15 Centro Cultural João Fona
18 Banco do Brasil
20 Post Office

Santarém

meeting between the Tapuiçus and the Portuguese, or possibly a ritual which originated when the Jesuits introduced Christianity to the Indians. The patron saint of fisherfolk, São Pedro, is honoured with a river procession on 29 June, when boats decorated with flags and flowers sail before the city.

Fishing enthusiasts should note that October and November are the best months to fish for pirarucu and tucunaré in the Rio Itaqui and Lago Grande de Curuaí.

Places to Stay – bottom end

The *Hotel Beira Rio* (☎ 522-2519), at Rua Adriano Pimentel 90, on the waterfront, and the *Hotel Brasil* (☎ 522-4719), at Travessa dos Martires 30, in the commercial area, have singles/doubles for US$6/12. The *Hotel Alvorada* (☎ 522-5340) is opposite the Restaurante O Mascote. It charges US$7/12

The Legend of Santarém
Beware of walking the streets after the bells of Catedral NS da Conceicáo ring, for you may encounter a fire-breathing pig. Even if you avoid the pig, legend has it that at midnight a woman in white kneels down at the crossroads to pray; if you set eyes on her, you will die! ∎

for singles/doubles with fan, and US$11/18 for the air-con versions.

The *Hotel Central Plaza* (☎ 522-3814), at Rua Floriano Peixoto 887, near the market, has apartamentos with fan at US$14/16 for singles/doubles, and air-con versions for US$18/23. The *Equatorial Hotel* (☎ 522-1135), at Avenida Rui Barbosa 14, has single/double quartos for US$12/18 with fan, US$18/24 with air-con, and apartamentos for US$24/30 with fan, US$30/36 with air-con. The *Brasil Grande Hotel* (☎ 522-5660), at Travessa 15 de Agosto 213, has clean, good-value singles/doubles with fan for US$18/24. It also offers apartamentos with TV, air-con and refrigerator that cost US$30/38.

Places to Stay – middle & top end

The *Santarém Palace Hotel* (☎ 522-1285), at Avenida Rui Barbosa 726, has spacious (if a bit grungy) apartamentos for US$36/42. The *New City Hotel* (☎ & fax 523-2351), at Travessa Francisco Correia 200, offers free transport from the airport and organises tours. Standard apartamentos cost US$27/34 for singles/doubles.

The *Hotel Tropical* (☎ 522-1533; fax 522-2631), at Avenida Mendonça Furtado 4120, is the only luxury hotel in Santarém. Despite the amenities, such as air-con, swimming pool, restaurant and bar, it's definitely a bit frayed around the architectural edges. Room rates start at around US$90/104 for singles/doubles.

Places to Eat

Succulent species of local fish include curimatá, jaraqui, surubim, tucunaré and pirarucu. Local dishes use cassava: maniçoba is made from pork and cassava, while pato no tucupi is a duck and cassava-root concoction.

Restaurante O Mascote, at Praça do Pescador 10 (just off Rua Senador Lameira Bittencourt), has music in the evenings. Fish meals start at US$7; try the caldeirada de peixe and tucunaré recheado. *Restaurante Tapaiu*, in the lobby of the Hotel Tropical, also has a pleasing menu. Try *Peixaria Canta*

Galo, on Travessa Silva Jardim, for good fish dishes. *Restaurante Lumi*, on Avenida Cuiabá, not far from the Hotel Tropical, has Japanese-style food. *Casa da Vinoca*, on Travessa Turiano Meira, serves simple regional dishes from 4.30 to 9 pm.

Sabor Lanche, on the corner of Avenida Rui Barbosa and Travessa Turiano Meira, has good-value snacks and ice cream. *Mascotinho*, on Rua Adriano Pimentel, is an outdoor bar where you can enjoy a beer, pizza and snacks overlooking the Rio Tapajós.

Things to Buy

Artesanato Dica Frazão, a clothing and craft shop, is at Rua Floriano Peixoto 281. The proprietor, Senhora Dica, creates women's clothing from natural fibres, and patchwork decorated hammocks. Loja Regional Muiraquitã and Souvenir Artesanatos, both on Rua Senado Lameira Bittencourt, sell local handicrafts.

Getting There & Away

Air TABA services the small towns of the Amazon interior, while Varig/Cruzeiro and VASP provide connections to other major cities in Brazil (via Manaus and Belém). At the time of writing this book, Varig were offering Santarém as a free stop on their Brazil Airpass.

TABA (☎ 522-1939) is at Rua Floriano Peixoto 607, Varig/Cruzeiro (☎ 522-2084) is at Rua Siquiera Campos 277 and VASP (☎ 522-1680) is at Avenida Rui Barbosa 786.

Bus The rodoviária (☎ 522-1342) is five km from the Docas do Pará, on Avenida Cuiabá. There are regular bus services to Itaituba (370 km), and during the dry season, there are buses on the Transamazônica highway (BR-230) to Marabá (1087 km), from where you can continue to Belém (1369 km) via Imperatriz. Bus services to Cuiabá have been discontinued due to poor road conditions on the Santarém-Cuiabá highway (BR-163). Bus travel can be miserable and/or impossible during the wet season. Most travellers still rely on river transport.

Boat For details about boat services to Manaus, Santarém and Belém, see the respective Getting There & Away sections for Belém and Manaus. Anticipate three days to Manaus, three days to Belém and 12 hours to Itaituba. Cabins are normally already taken in Manaus or Belém. Docas do Pará, the deep-water pier, is where most of the boats to Belém and Manaus depart. The various private companies have booths in front of the main gate to the Docas, where you can check schedules and buy tickets. Ticket prices with Agencia Tarcisio Lopes (☎ 522-2034) are US$61/96 per person in hammock/cabin accommodation to Belém, US$45/84 to Manaus. The ENASA office (☎ 522-1934) is at the Eletrocenter shop, at Travessa Francisco Correa 34, and is open Monday to Friday from 7.30 to 11.30 am and 2 to 6 pm, and on Saturday from 8 am to noon.

The river trip between Santarém and Belém includes an interesting section downstream from Monte Alegre: the Narrows, where the boat passes closer to jungle. It's a breezy ride; the endless view of long, thin, green strips of forest and wider bands of river and sky is OK for the first day, but after a while, you'll start talking to your hammock and chewing on the life belts.

There is also a twice-weekly boat service (US$21/18 in 1st/2nd class, two days) between Santarém and Porto Santana, the major port, 20 km down the coast from Macapá (Amapá state) – see also the Getting There & Away section under Macapá.

Getting Around

To/From the Airport The airport is 15 km from the city centre; a bus service to the centre operates from 6 am to 7 pm. Alternatively, you may be able to use the courtesy shuttle bus which runs between the Hotel Tropical and the airport. The City Hotel also runs a free shuttle bus for their clients. The taxi fare is about US$15.

AROUND SANTARÉM

Alter do Chão

The village of Alter do Chão, a weekend

resort for the people of Santarém, is upstream on the Rio Tapajós. Alter do Chão has good fishing, a beautiful turquoise lagoon and white-sand beaches. It was once a sacred site for the Tapajós Indians. Due to improved access, many travellers are now finding it a more attractive option than Santarém.

Centro de Preservação da Arte Indígena Cultura e Ciências
This excellent and comprehensive exhibit of Indian art and artefacts, located on Rua Dom Macedo, far surpasses any such museums in Manaus or Belém. Established by an American expatriate and his Indian wife, the high-quality museum is quite a bizarre find in such a tiny village. Admission costs US$3.50. The museum has a shop, with a large variety of items for sale, though the items are generally more expensive than those in FUNAI shops elsewhere.

Beaches
Green Lake and Tapajós River have good beaches for swimming and walks.

Places to Stay & Eat
The *Pousada Alter-do-Chão* (☎ 522-3410), at Rua Lauro Sodré 74, has simple apartamentos with fan for US$24, and a great view of beach from the verandah. The *Tia Marilda*, at Travessa Antônio Agostinho 599, has double rooms with shower and fan that cost US$18. The *Pousada Tupaiulândia* (☎ 523-2157), on Travessa Pedro Teixeira, offers apartamentos for US$24 with fan, and US$36 with air-con.

For a good, simple fish or meat dish, try one of the restaurants on Praça 7 de Setembro, such as *Lago Verde*, *Toca da Jô* or *Mingote*.

Getting There & Away
Alter do Chão is three hours by boat, or 35 km by bus on a sealed road. You can take a local bus from the centre of Santarém, or you may be able to hitch a ride on a boat from the town docks. Buses leave Santarém at 8 and 10.30 am, returning at 6 pm.

Travel agencies such as Santarém-Tur (at the Hotel Tropical), Amazon Tours (☎ 522 1098) and Amazônia Turismo (☎ 522 5820)

organise day tours to Alter do Chão for around US$50 per person (depending on the size of the group).

Encontro das Águas
The meeting of the waters (*águas barrentas*), where the clear Tapajós and the light-brown Amazon merge, is worth a boat excursion, or at least a glimpse from Praça Mirante, near Restaurante O Mascote. The tourist agencies arrange trips from around US$25.

Floresta Nacional do Tapajós
This forest reserve covers an area of 650,000 hectares along the Rio Tapajós. The entrance to the reserve is about 83 km from Santarém on the Santarém-Cuiabá road. To visit, you must first seek permission from IBAMA in Santarém (☎ 522-2964), at Avenida Tapajo's 2267. You can then try to organise a visit, with their assistance or with Santarém-Tur (☎ 522-1533), at the Hotel Tropical.

Fordlândia & Belterra
Fordlândia and Belterra, Henry Ford's huge rubber plantations, date from the 1920s. Ford successfully managed to transplant an American town, but his Yankee ingenuity failed to cultivate rubber efficiently in the Amazon. Abandoned by Ford, the rubber groves are now operated as a research station by the Ministry of Agriculture.

During the dry season, one bus a day makes the trip from Santarém to Belterra, 67 km south of Santarém. The bus leaves Santarém at 11.30 am and returns at 2.30 pm. Getting to Fordlândia by boat takes about 16 hours from Santarém. Amazon Tours (see the Information section for Santarém) can arrange trips to Belterra and to Fordlândia. The cost is US$45 per person in groups of two, US$30 per person in groups of three to five.

Curuá-Una Hydroelectric Dam
The Curuá-Una Hydroelectric Dam is at Cachoeira de Palhão, 72 km from Santarém. It was built to meet the growing energy needs of the region, and is open to visitors.

PARQUE NACIONAL DA AMAZÔNIA

This national park lies close to the town of Itaituba, on the western boundary between the states of Pará and Amazonas. Most sources agree that at least 10% of the park's original one million hectares has been devastated as a result of *depredação* (predatory behaviour) by garimpeiros and prospective land-grabbers, who face an utterly absurd force of four IBAMA employees attempting to protect the park.

Information

To arrange a visit to the park, you must seek prior permission from Senhor Raimundo Nonato Russo (☎ 518-1530) at IBAMA, Posto do Fomento Estrada, 53 Bis, Km 02, Itaituba, 73 km from the park entrance. Once your visit has been approved, you may be given assistance with transport up the Rio Tapajós to the park station. The park administration operates on less than a shoestring, so don't expect too much.

The administrative station inside the park, at Uruá, has rudimentary facilities such as a campsite, but no special infrastructure for tourists. From this station, there are rough trails leading into the forest.

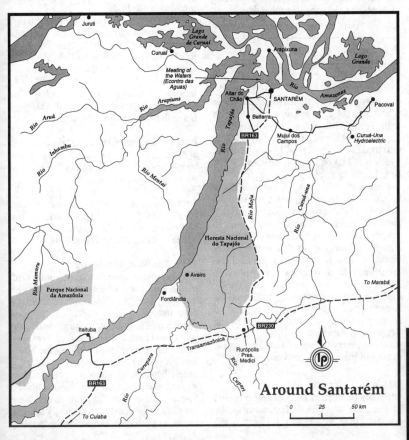

Around Santarém

0   25   50 km

THE NORTH

Getting There & Away

Air The easiest option is to take a TABA flight from Belém or Santarém to Itaituba. Flights leave Belém on Tuesday and Thursday at 7 am (US$248/493 one way/return). From Santarém, there are flights on Tuesday and Thursday at 8.30 am (US$114/222 one way/return).

Bus The bus service between Santarém and Itaituba takes about eight hours (assuming the road conditions are favourable) and costs around US$10. The bus service between Belém and Itaituba is unreliable and only recommended if you're prepared to spend up to three days slogging through delays.

Amapá

Three-quarters of the state's 289,000 inhabitants live in Macapá, leaving almost the whole state (142,358 sq km, extending north to the French Guiana border), to the remaining quarter of the population. Only 0.2% of the Brazilian population live in Amapá, which is the second least populated state of Brazil, after Roraima.

During the 18th century, the Portuguese built a fort at Macapá to protect access to the Amazon. The discovery of gold in the region prompted several attempts by the French to invade from French Guiana and claim Amapá. At the turn of this century, after international arbitration had snubbed the French and definitively awarded Amapá to Brazil, the area was promptly annexed by Pará. This annexation greatly displeased the Amapaenses, who relentlessly pursued autonomy until it was finally granted by the Brazilian government in 1943. Today, the state's economy is based on lumber and the mining of manganese, gold and tin ore.

MACAPÁ

Officially founded in 1815, Macapá, capital of the state of Amapá, lies close to the equator, in a strategic position on the Amazon estuary. Inhabited mostly by public servants, the town has few attractions.

The name Macapá comes from the native Indian word *macabas*, meaning the place of *bacabas*. Bacaba is a regional fruit which is used to make juices and ice cream.

Information

Tourist Office The DETUR/AP tourist information office (☎ 222-4135; fax 222-3071) is at Avenida Raimundo Alvares da Costa 18, Centro. DETUR also has a *posto de informaçoes* in the foyer of the municipal library, next to the telefônica on Rua São José; it's open from 8 am to noon and 2 to 6 pm Monday to Friday.

Travellers planning to continue north into French Guiana will require a visa. There are French consulates in Belém, Manaus, Recife, Salvador, Rio de Janeiro, São Paulo and Brasília, but *not* in the state of Amapá.

Money The Banco do Brasil branch on Rua Independência (near the fort) will exchange US dollars and travellers' cheques.

Post & Telephone The cental post office is at Avenida Coriolano Jucá 125, and there are telephones on the corner of Rua São José and Avenida General Gurião.

Tour Agencies Amapá Viagens e Turismo (☎ 223-2667; fax 222-2553) is at the Novotel hotel, while Martinica (☎ 222-3462) is at Rua Jovino Dinoá 2010.

Forte São José de Macapá

This grandiose stone fort was built in 1782 by the Portuguese to defend against French invasions from the Guianas. It is Macapá's most interesting sight and is still in good condition. The plan is a square with four pentagonal bastions at the corners. Protected inside the massive stone walls are the buildings which served as soldiers' quarters, a hospital, jail cells, gunpowder and rations stores, a chapel and the commandant's house. More than 800 labourers were involved in the construction, mostly Indians, blacks and caboclos, and during the building

ROBYN JONES

GUY MOBERLY

ROBYN JONES

ROBYN JONES

A: Ilha de Marajó
B: Santarém, Pará
C: Santarém beach market
D: Curiaú, Amapá

Top: Curiaú, Amapá
Bottom: Butcher shop in Careiro, Amazonas

of the foundations many died due to accidents in the wet and difficult conditions of building on the river bank. Many other workers died at the hands of the extremely repressive and violent administration. Attempts at escape were common and contributed to the appearance of African communities in the region.

Museu de Plantas Medicinais Waldemiro de Oliveira Gomes

The museum (☎ 223-1951), at Avenida Feliciano Coelho 1509, has a display of medicinal plants, a caboclo's house, Indian artefacts and a moth-eaten collection of stuffed birds and animals. It's open from 9 am to noon and 2 to 5 pm.

Casa do Artesão

The idea of this artists' workshop is to foster local arts and handicrafts, and to attract some tourist dollars, but most of the works for sale are unconvincing. It is located on Avenida Azarias Neto.

Marco Zero do Equador

If you absolutely *have* to have that picture of yourself astride the equator, you can catch a bus from the local bus terminal near the fort to the equator, via Porto Santana and Fazendinha, and then back to Macapá. At the equator, the bus driver pauses long enough

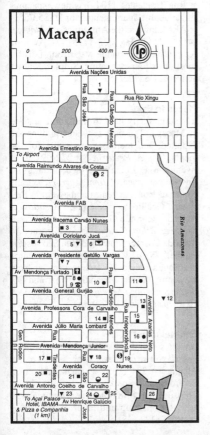

PLACES TO STAY

3	Amapaense Palace
4	HotelSanto Antonio
12	Kiosks
13	Novotel
14	Mercurio Hotel
15	Kamila Hotel
17	Frota Palace Hotel
20	Emmerick Hotel
21	Mara Hotel

PLACES TO EAT

1	A Peixaria
5	Sorveteria Macapá
7	Tom Marrom
18	Restaurante Kilão
23	Só Assados

OTHER

2	DETUR Office
6	Post Office
8	Biblioteca & DETUR Information Post
9	Telephones
10	Teatro das Bacabeiras
11	SENAVA
16	Casa do Artesão
19	Banco do Brasil
22	Onibus Urbano
24	Bus Stop (Santana, Fazendinha)
25	Mercado
26	Forte São José de Macapá

for travellers to race to the roof of the tourist restaurant, snap their pics and hop back onto the bus. Allow around three hours for the whole excursion.

Festivals

O Marabaixo is an Afro-Brazilian holiday celebrated 40 days after Semana Santa (Holy Week). The Festa de Joaquim, celebrated in the African village of Curiaú, is another Afro-Brazilian party held during month of August, with *ladainha* (praying), *batuque* (drumming) and *folia* (dancing in colourful costumes).

The Festa da Piedade Batuque is celebrated during the last week of June in Igarapé do Lago, a village 85 km from Macapá. The people from this village are strongly devoted to Nossa Senhora da Piedade, and celebrate their devotion through various religious rituals, including a river procession. The party's main performance is the batuque. Forty dancing women in costume depict the *bailantes escravas devotas* (devoted slave dancers). You can get festival programmes from the DETUR tourist office (for the address, see the Information section for Macapá).

Places to Stay

The *Emerick Hotel* (☎ 223-2819), at Avenida Coaraci Nunes 333, has a good atmosphere. Singles/doubles with fan are US$8/14, while single/double apartamentos cost US$14/19 with TV, and US$18/24 with air-con. The *Hotel Santo Antonio* (☎ 222-0226), at Rua Coriolando Jucá 485, opposite Cine Ouro, has single/double apartamentos for US$12/18 with fan, US$17/20 with air-con. It also has communal rooms, which cost US$7 per person. The *Kamila Hotel* (☎ 222-0250), at Júlio Maria Lombaerd 48, is a small hotel in a good position. Single/double apartamentos are US$10/11 with fan, US$14/18 with air-con.

The *Mercurio Hotel* (☎ 223-4061), at Rua Cândido Mendes 1300, has large singles/doubles for US$22/31. The *Mara Hotel* (☎ 222-0859), at Rua São José 2390, has single or double quartos with fan for US$19;

single/double quartos with air-con cost US$24/31. The *Muarama Hotel* (☎ 222-5495), at Rua Henrique Galucío 1623, offers apartamentos with air-con, TV and telephone for US$20/25 a single/double. The *Açai Palace Hotel* (☎ 223-4899), at Avenida Antônio Coelho de Carvalho 1399, offers single/double apartamentos for US$18/30 with fan, US$24/42 with air-con.

The two-star *Amapaense Palace* (☎ 222-3367; fax 222-0773), on Rua Tiradentes, has large apartamentos, with air-con, refrigerator and TV at US$34/47 a single/double, or US$28/39 without a window. The *Frota Palace Hotel* (☎ 223-3999; fax 222-4488), at Rua Tiradentes 1104, has new, spacious single/double apartamentos for US$53/65.

Also known as the Amazonas, the *Novotel* (☎ 223-1144; fax 223-1115), at Avenida Azarias Neto 17, on the waterfront, falls far short of its four-star rating. Singles/doubles here cost US$126/152.

Places to Eat

It is surprisingly hard to find good seafood in Macapá. The best saltwater prawns are exported, and therefore expensive for the locals. Try *A Peixaria* (☎ 222-0913), at Avenida Mãe Luzia 86. For comida-a-kilo (by weight) meals, *Tom Marrom*, on the corner of Rua Tiradentes and Rua Presidente Getúlio Vargas, and *Só Assados*, at Avenida Henrique Galúcio 290, are recommended. *Kilão Central*, on the corner of Avenida Coaraci Nunes and Rua São José, is another. *Pizza & Companhia*, at Avenida Henrique Galúcio 1634-A, is a bit far from the centre, but has a friendly owner and OK pizza. *Sorvetaria Macapá*, at Rua São José 1676, has the best ice cream.

Entertainment

Amapá's nightlife is virtually nonexistent, but if you're desperate for a dance, try Athenas (☎ 224-1165), which has a disco on Saturday and Sunday and live music on Thursday and Friday nights. Things generally don't heat up until after 11 pm. Entry costs US$12.

Getting There & Away

Air It's possible to fly with Air France from Paris to Cayenne, French Guiana, and then continue overland to Amapá; however, travellers who want to avoid overland hassles may prefer to fly from Cayenne to Macapá. TABA now has flights to Cayenne on Monday, Wednesday and Friday, departing from Macapá at 3.30 pm. The fare is US$146/172 one way/return.

TABA also flies to Oiapoque on Monday, Wednesday and Friday, departing from Macapá at 10.20 am. The fare for the 1¼-hour flight costs US$199 one way. There are also daily (except Sunday) TABA flights to Belém, for US$120.

TABA (☎ 223-1551) has an office at Alameda Francisco Serrano 34, and the Varig/Cruzeiro office (☎ 223-1743) is at Rua Candido Mendes 1039. Check the latest schedules and prices for flights to Oiapoque, Cayenne or Belém with these airlines.

Bus Macapá is linked by BR-156 to Oiapoque, the Brazilian border town beside the Rio Oiapoque, on the border with French Guiana. The first 170 km of the road, to just past Ferreira Gomes, is paved; the road then degenerates into an unpaved track. It's frequently washed out, and you should be prepared to hire vehicles or hitch on an impromptu basis. There are buses direct to Oiapoque, departing from Macapá on Monday, Wednesday and Friday. Tickets cost US$44 and the trip takes a minimum of 16 hours. If you have the time, it may be worth staging the trip: stopovers could include Ferreira Gomes, Tartarugalzinho, the township of Amapá, and Calçoene. You can pick up the bus timetables and buy tickets at Lanche no Ponto, at the local bus terminal. For details about crossing the border, see the relevant section in this chapter.

Boat For information about boat schedules and fares, contact SENAVA (☎ 222-3611), at Avenida Azarias Neto 20, or the Capitânia dos Portos office (☎ 223-4755), at Avenida FAB 427. SENAVA boats no longer go to Oiapoque. However, it may be possible to arrange a trip in a private boat, but there isn't a regular service and the trip is reportedly quite treacherous.

For details about boat services to Belém and Santarém, see the Getting There & Away sections for those cities. Note that boats to Santarém and Belém depart from Porto Santana, the main port, 20 km down the coast from Macapá. If you need to stay overnight in this archetypal Amazon port, a reader has suggested the Hotel Muller (☎ 632-6881), at Rua Filinto Muller 373, which charges US$5 per person for an apartamento with fan. There is a regular bus service between Porto Santana and Macapá.

Crossing the Border The Brazilian border town of Oiapoque, 560 km north of Macapá, is the main crossing point for overland travellers between Brazil and French Guiana.

The transport options available from Macapá to the border include a flight to Oiapoque, a privately arranged boat ride from the Macapá docks to Oiapoque, or a long and rugged bus trip to Oiapoque. For specific details, see the respective air, bus and boat descriptions in this Getting There & Away section.

Unless you have a great deal of time and patience or absolutely *must* do the trip overland, you may prefer to avoid all the hassles and hop on a plane. For more advice, see the French Guiana section in the discussion of land routes in the Getting There & Away chapter.

The clean, state-owned hotel in Calçoene is excellent value – US$5 for a double apartamento. The two hotels in Oiapoque charge US$5 for a double quarto and US$6 for a double apartamento.

Get your Brazilian exit stamp from the Polícia Federal in Oiapoque, and your French Guianese entry stamp at the *gendarmerie* in St Georges (French Guiana), reached by a 20-minute motorboat ride (US$2.50) from Oiapoque. There are also plans to construct a bridge over the river. If you need to change money, there's a casa de câmbio at the harbour in Oiapoque.

AROUND MACAPÁ
Curiaú

This African village eight km from Macapá was founded by escaped slaves. The name came from the Portuguese expression *criar búfalo*, which the African slaves pronounced 'criar-ú. They chose this area for its natural pastures, perfect for raising buffalo. The main street (lined with distinctive timber houses) and the flooding valley are very picturesque.

Parque Zoobotânico

This zoo was closed for renovation at the time of writing, but we were allowed into the park for a look. The zoo has tapirs, deer, monkeys, alligators, birds, and some jaguars which definitely fancied us for their next meal. You have to get off the bus on the way to Fazendinha.

Praia da Fazendinha

Buses run to Praia da Fazendinha, the local beach, 19 km from town. There are various bars and restaurants along the beach – *Bar du Bezerra* is recommended for good, cheap seafood.

Bonito and the Igarapé do Lago

Bonito and the Igarapé do Lago, 72 km and 85 km from Macapá, are good places for swimming, fishing and jungle walks.

Cachoeira de Santo Antônio

This is a waterfall in the municipality of Mazagão, an 18th-century Portuguese town which is accessible by ferry from Porto Santana.

Rio Araguari & The Pororoca

At the mouth of the Rio Araguari, about 100 km north of Macapá, you can observe (and hear!) the pororoca (thunderous collision between the Atlantic tide and the Amazon). The best time to see this phenomenon is between January and April, at either the full or new moon. Excursions by boat (15 hours) to see the pororoca are organised by the local tour agencies (for addresses, see the Information section for Macapá).

Serra do Navio

Serra do Navio, a mining town built in the 1950s to support the extraction of 40 million tonnes of manganese in the area, lies about 200 km north-west of Macapá. By 1990, the manganese reserves had started to run out, and the concession to explore the reserve finishes in 2003. The original mining consortium has handed over the town to national and international organisations which are interested in using Serra do Navio as a base for research into ecology, meteorology, hydrology and anthropology in the Amazon

Around Macapá

region. The University of São Paulo has already set up a small research station in the town.

To prevent Serra do Navio becoming a ghost town when mineral exploration ceases, the industrialisation of the area's forest products is being developed. The development of pharmaceutical products from medicinal plants, dyes for food and clothing, fruit products, natural insecticides, resins, essences and oils are among the projects. This is the starting point of a programme to set up 11 collection areas and processing bases around the Amazon forest. The objective of the programme is to raise the Amazonian per capita income (currently US$250 per annum, just 10% of the Brazilian average).

The Instituto de Estudos Amazônicas (IEA) runs a programme that offers young people of different nationalities work on IEA projects in return for free board and lodging for six months. One of their sites is in the Serra do Navio. For more information, contact IEA/ABIC, at Rua Espirito Santo 362, 90.010.370 Centro, Porto Alegre RS (☎ & fax 096-221-9075)

Getting There & Away Serra do Navio is connected to Porto Santana by a railway which crosses 200 km of savannah and native forest. The train, bought from a US wreckers' company 40 years ago, departs from Porto Santana on Friday and Sunday, taking five hours. Alternatively, you can drive to Serra do Navio (about four hours on BR-210), passing through beautiful forests. For more information, contact the mining consortium Indústria e Comércio de Minérios (☎ 281-1415).

RESERVA BIOLÓGICA DO LAGO PIRATUBA

The Piratuba biological reserve covers an area of almost 400,000 hectares in the northeast of Amapá state. The area has mangrove swamps along the coast, while the inland has dense tropical forest, rich in a variety of Amazonian palm trees such as açaí, andiroba and palmeiras. The local fauna includes some endangered species of alligator, as well

as turtles, flamingoes, sloths, river otters, monkeys and manatees.

Access to the biological reserve is by boat only, via the Rio Araguari, departing from the township of Cutias do Araguari, 130 km overland from Macapá.

ESTAÇÃO ECOLÓGICA DE MARACÁ-JIPIOCA

This ecological research station is north of the Piratuba biological reserve, on the northeast coast of Amapá state. Despite being an oceanic island, Ilha de Maracá doesn't have the waves and surf that are characteristic of most of the Brazilian coastal area. Instead the sea water enters an immense mangrove swamp which covers about one-third of the island's 72,000 hectares. The clay colour of the water indicates that the whole area is actually an extension of the Amazon, mixed with sea water. The area provides a habitat for large numbers of various species of aquatic birds.

Access to the island is by local boats from the township of Amapá, 308 km overland north of Macapá.

PARQUE NACIONAL DO CABO ORANGE

This national park is at the northernmost corner of Amapá state, covering an area of 619,000 hectares in the municipal districts of Calçoene and Oiapoque. Most of the park's area is within 10 km of the Atlantic coast, with the rivers Cassiporé and Utaçá crossing it to the ocean.

The native vegetation is influenced by sea water forming mangrove swamps and sandbanks. The fauna is rich and diverse, due to the variety of environments that provide habitats for a number of rare and endangered species. Manatees in the slow river waters, crab-eating raccoons, birds such as flamingoes and guarás in the mangrove swamps, endangered species of anteaters, armadillos and jaguars in the forest, and turtles laying eggs on the beaches.

Access to the park isn't easy – a rugged overland trip up to the town of Calçoene, 380 km from Macapá, then a boat ride out to sea and into the Rio Cassiporé, the extreme north of Amapá state. The park has an airport, accessible to small aircraft all year round.

The national parks, reserves and research stations in Amapá state are managed by IBAMA, and permission from them to visit these protected areas is required. For more information, contact IBAMA (☎ 223-2099), Superintendência Estadual, Rua Hamilton Silva 1570, Bairro Santa Rita, Macapá.

Tocantins

The new state of Tocantins encompasses what was previously the northern half of the state of Goiás. Until the Belém-Brasília highway was built, there was no road link between southern and northern Goiás. The new highway served mostly as an express-way from the north to the south of Brazil, and consequently, each region maintained a different cultural history.

Southern Goiás had mostly been colonised by people from the southern states of Brazil, who traditionally didn't mix with the native Indians or black slaves. Colonisation of the northern part of Goiás was mostly by people from the northern parts of Brazil, with strong miscegenation with native Indians and blacks, creating an new ethnic group with different physical characteristics and a distinctive culture. The separatist movements in what is now Tocantins started as far back as the early 19th century, with the most significant one, headed by Joquim Segurado, in 1821.

On 1 January 1989 a constitutional amendment creating the new state of Tocantins came into effect. The state was supposedly created to give the Indians of the region greater autonomy; however, they appear to have been conveniently shuffled aside to make way for grandiose Big Plans with lavish use of statistics and slogans, such as '20 anos em 2' (20 years of progress in two).

Siqueira Campos, a man who had pushed for the state's creation for 25 years, took part in a bitter tussle with rival politicians before emerging victorious as the new governor of the state. The political debate produced some strange claims. José Freire, one of Campos' toughest rivals, tried to prove that Campos was a murderer who had changed his name in the 1960s. Freire offered a substantial reward to anyone who could prove this theory by producing the relevant birth certificate and other pertinent papers. One curious flaw in Freire's argument was his inability to provide Campos' real name.

After ferocious politicking in three rival towns, the town of Palmas was officially declared the state capital. Campos, during his first term, launched into dozens of development projects, and the grandiose Palácio do Araguaia, seat of the state government, was the first building completed. He had a hard time keeping up with the pace of progress expected during the two years of his administration, and in the following elections, in 1991, he lost his post to Moisés Avelino. Avelino's administration aimed to set up the basic infrastructure for industrial development in the state, and the obsession with development continues: re-elected for a four-year term at the last state elections, in 1994, Siqueira Campos now uses the slogan '40 anos em 4' (40 years of progress in four).

Tocantins currently has over 1.2 million inhabitants in 123 municipalities assigned to 15 administrative regions over an area of 286,706 sq km. Technically, it belongs to the northern region of Brazil, with Pará and Mato Grosso states to the west, Maranhão and Bahia to the east and Goiás to the south.

Geographically, the state has three defined regions: north, with vegetation mostly influenced by the Amazon rainforests; median (Araguaia), an area of transition between forest and savannah; and central south-east, which is mostly savannah, with sections of deciduous forest on the borders with Bahia and Goiás. The state's climate is predominantly tropical: humid, with average temperatures between 25°C and 36°C.

PALMAS

The state capital is a planned city strategically placed in the centre of Tocantins. It is 973 km from Brasília and 1271 km from Belém. Unless you have a specific reason to visit, give it a miss.

In 1991, Palmas had 2000 inhabitants in the *plano piloto* (pilot plan), mostly public officials and construction workers. In 1995 its population was 25,000 in the town of Palmas and about 140,000 in its municipality. The original plan of organised growth seems to be getting out of hand, with migrants from other states arriving every day seeking new opportunities. Optimistic estimates envisage that the Palmas district will achieve a population target of half a million by the turn of the century.

At this stage, there is no official money-exchange facilities in Tocantins.

Things to See & Do

Apart from the grandiose **Palácio Araguaia**, and other government buildings, there isn't much to see in Palmas. The vast, sparse scale of the city is typical of the megalomania rampant in the state.

During the months of June, July and August, the beach of **Graciosa** (in the town of Canela, 12 km from Palmas) and the **Taquarassú** waterfalls (in Serra do Carmo, about 26 km from Palmas) are the places where locals go for relief from the heat.

Places to Stay

The accommodation in Palmas is generally expensive. You could try the *Hotel Casa Grande* (☎ 215-1713), on Avenida Antônio Segurado, or *Nivea's Plaza* (☎ 214-1917), at ACSUSO 50, conjunto 1, lote 9. The *Hotel Rio do Sono* (☎ 215-1733) and the *Pousada dos Girassois* (☎ 215-1187; fax 215-2321) are more up-market and expensive.

Getting There & Away

Air From Palmas airport (☎ 214-1805), accessed via Avenida Antoni Segurado, Km 2, there are flights leaving for Araguaína, Belém, Brasília, Redenção and Tucuruí with TAM (☎ 214-1969) and Air Taxi Nobre (☎ 214-1500).

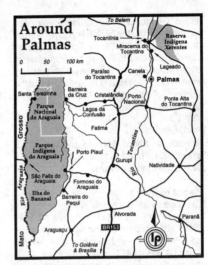

Around Palmas

Bus There are daily buses from the Palmas rodoviária (☎ 214-1603), Avenida Teotonio Segurado, to the interstate destinations of Belém, Brasília, Teresinha, Belo Horizonte, Rio and São Paulo. There are also regular buses to most towns in Tocantins.

GURUPI

One of the three largest towns in the state, with about 104,000 inhabitants, Gurupi is also one of Tocantins' most important agro-industrial areas. It is 712 km north of Brasília along the Belém-Brasília highway.

Information

Money There isn't an official money exchange in Tocantins, but you may exchange cash dollars at Urutur Turismo in Gurupi.

Travel Agency Urutur Viagens e Turismo (☎ 851-3398), Rua Antônio Lisboa da Cruz 1695, sala 5, is one the few travel agencies in Tocantins. It can provide information about places of interest around the state, including Ilha do Bananal.

To visit the Karajá and Javaés Indian reserves (on Ilha do Bananal) or the Xerente

Indian village (near Tocantínia), you need permission from the FUNAI office in Gurupi (☎ & fax 851-2708), at Rua Presidente Castelo Branco 1363. It takes a minimum of 10 days to get formal permission, so you may want to fax your request in advance (read the Visiting a Reservation section in Facts about the Country chapter).

Festivals
Festejos de Santo Antônio and the state's largest agricultural exhibition are both held during the month of June.

Places to Stay & Eat
There are two small hotels in front of the bus terminal – try the *Hotel Vila Rica* (☎ 851-2910) which is friendly and has clean quartos for US$8/12 a single/double. The *Veneza Plaza* (☎ 851-1441), at Avenida Pará 1823, charges around US$45 for apartamentos.

For a good-value self-service meal go to *Restaurante e Churrascaria Parolle*, at No 1373 Rua 05.

Getting There & Away
Air From Gurupi airport (☎ 851-2468), on Avenida Sergipe, there are flights to Santa Terezinha and São Félix do Araguaia on Monday, Wednesday, Friday and weekends. Tickets (around US$200) can be booked through Urutur Turismo (see the Information section for Gurupi).

Bus There are daily interstate buses from Gurupi to Belém, Brasília and Imperatriz, and at least twice-daily bus services to the main towns in the state. The bus terminal (☎ 851-1444) is on Rua 19.

FORMOSO DO ARAGUAIA
This small town is about 70 km west of Gurupi, towards Ilha do Bananal. It has about 19,000 inhabitants, mostly agricultural labourers, farmers and public servants.

Projeto Rio Formoso
If you are interested in agriculture you can visit the Projeto Formoso, a mega-sized rice plantation in an area claimed to be the largest continuous area of irrigated crop in the world! We saw wild deer and chameleons, as well as rheas and various other birds, living on the plantation.

Places to Stay & Eat
The town has two cheap hotels near the rodoviária: the *Grande Hotel* on Rua 2, and the *Hotel Bonanza* on Avenida Rio Branco. The latter has a restaurant, which serves good, simple meals.

Getting There & Away
There are buses twice daily from Gurupi to Formoso, and once a day from Goiânia.

MIRACEMA DO TOCANTINS
In the centre of Tocantins, this small town on the Rio Tocantins is a good place for a stopover if you are travelling through the state to or from Belém. It is 23 km off the BR-153, about 800 km from Belém and 1032 km from Brasília.

Beaches
During the dry months (July to September), the town's beaches, **Praia do Mirassol** and **Praia Ponte de Apoio** (just opposite the main street), are exposed. Huts for drinks and snacks are erected in the middle of the river. Access to Praia do Mirassol is via a suspended footbridge above the water. Other beaches include **Praia do Amor**, three km upriver from the town centre, and **Balneário do Lucena** (which reportedly has good infrastructure for visitors), 17 km upriver.

Places to Stay & Eat
The *Grande Hotel* (☎ 866-1851), at Rua Bela Vista 771, has clean, simple apartamentos and friendly service. Singles/doubles cost US$10/15. The *Miracema Palace* (☎ 866-1161) is a bit further out of town, as is the *Pousada Tocantins* (☎ 866-1161), on Avenida Tocantins on the way out to Miranorte, with apartamentos for around US$40. To get to these two, you may have to pay for taxi rides, which aren't cheap in Tocantins.

The *Restaurante Bom Paladar*, at Rua

Primero de Janeiro 318, Centro, has good, self-service meals. You could also try the *Restauant Palace*, at the Miracema Palace.

Getting There & Away
From the rodoviária (☎ 866-1281), at Avenida Tocantins 1376, there are daily buses to Belém, Brasília, Conceição do Araguaia, Goiânia, Imperatriz and Marabá, and at least two buses daily to Palmas and Porto Nacional.

AROUND MIRACEMA
Tocantínia
The town of Tocantínia is located on the opposite side of the Rio Tocantins to Miracema, a short crossing on the regular ferryboat. It is now compulsory to exit your vehicle, since a bus rolled off the ferry into the river! There are huts at both sides of the ferry port that sell inexpensive local Indian arts and handicrafts.

Tocantínia is 89 km from Palmas, on the edge of the Reserva Indígena Xerentes. One of the state government's development strategies is to build a highway linking Palmas to the Northeast. Misleading the Xerentes into believing that just a small bridge was going to be built over the Rio do Sono, they promptly began construction of a massive structure. In response, the Indians set up an *aldeia* (village) at the site to stop the work, recognising that a substantial highway was intended to cut straight through their reserve. The Xerente we spoke to said that if necessary, they would fight to the death to protect their land, because if the highway proceeded, their culture would be destroyed anyway. To visit an aldeia, you will need permission from FUNAI in Gurupi (see the Gurupi Information section).

Lageado
This very small town has a picturesque, rocky river beach and a waterfall. There are no hotels, but you can stay at Miracema (50 km away) or camp by the river.

PORTO NACIONAL
Founded in 1861, Porto Nacional (population over 43,000) is Tocantins' second-oldest town, after Natividade. It is 764 km from Goiânia and 70 km from Palmas.

Things to See & Do
The **Igreja de NS das Merçes** (1903) and, during the dry season, the river beaches are the town's main attractions. The beach of **Porto Real** is close to the town centre, **Carreira Comprida** is five km upriver and **Praia Rebojo** is two km downriver.

Woolly Monkey

Places to Stay & Eat

There are a couple of accommodation options including the *Shelton Hotel* (☎ 863-1686), at Rua Joaquim Aires 2262, and the *Hotel São Judas Tadeu* (☎ 863-1242), at Praça Belarmina Prado Aires 1563. The *Restaurante da Tia Júlia*, Praça Eugenio Jardim 27, is reported to be good for regional dishes.

Getting There & Away

Air The airport (☎ 863-1300) is at the end of Avenida Castelo Branco. There are regular flights from Porto Nacional to Brasília, Goiânia and São Paulo.

Bus The rodoviária (☎ 863-1224), on Avenida Luís Leite Ribeiro, has interstate buses daily to Brasília, Goiânia, Belo Horizonte, Teresinha, Rio and São Paulo, and more regular buses to Gurupi, Palmas, Miracema and Paraíso do Tocantins.

NATIVIDADE

The oldest town in Tocantins state (it's 258 years old), Natividade is 160 km from Porto Nacional. It has Portuguese and French-style architecture inherited from the colonial period.

The ruins of Igreja de NS do Rosário, which was built by black slaves during the last century, are the town's main attraction. Cachoeiras do Paraíso waterfalls (from December to June) are four km out of town, and there are beaches at the Rio Manoel Alves, 13 km out of town.

There are no hotels in Natividade, but it was reported that you can get a room from locals (ask around) or camp along the river's edge.

LAGOA DA CONFUSÃO

This small town, with just over 2000 inhabitants, is 87 km west of the Belém-Brasília highway and is one of the main tourist destinations in Tocantins. It has a lake about 4.5 km in diameter, with a protruding boulder in the middle. Its name, which means Lake of Confusion, comes from the disagreement over whether the rock moves around the lake!

Places to Stay

Praia do Rio Formoso has an isolated area for camping, 35 km out of town on the Estrada Lagoa-Ilha do Bananal. The *Hotel Lagoa da Ilha Praia Clube* (☎ 864-1110) is said to be the largest leisure and tourism complex in Tocantins state. The *Big Hotel* and the *Hotel Espora de Ouro* are both on Avenida Vitorino Panta.

Getting There & Away

There are daily buses to Lagoa da Confusão from Palmas and Porto Nacional.

AROUND LAGOA DA CONFUSÃO

Barreira da Cruz

Another gateway to the Parque Nacional da Ilha do Bananal, this fishing village is on the margin of Rio Javaés, 52 km from Lagoa da Confusão. There are buses between Lagoa da Confusão and Barreira da Cruz.

Lagoa dos Pássaros

Reportedly good for birdwatching from June to September, this lake is 45 km from Lagoa da Confusão via Rodovia Lagoa-Fazenda Conag.

RIO ARAGUAIA

The Rio Araguaia begins in the Serra dos Caiapós and flows 2600 km northwards, forming the borders of Mato Grosso, Goiás, Tocantins and Pará before joining the Rio Tocantins where the states of Tocantins, Maranhão and Pará meet, near Marabá. About 500 km from its source, the Araguaia bifurcates into the greater and lesser Araguaia rivers, which course west and east respectively and then rejoin, having formed the largest river island in the world, Ilha do Bananal.

The river is not easily accessible, so tours are a good idea. The best access from Mato Grosso is via Barra do Garças, about 500 km from Cuiabá. Barra do Garças has the Parque de Águas Quentes (hot springs). Camping facilities are open from May to October. It's a rapidly growing agricultural boom town of 30,000 people and there are four simple hotels.

The stretch of the Rio Araguaia from the town of Aruanã up to Ilha do Bananal is considered one of the best freshwater fishing areas in the world. The region is beginning to attract Brazilian holiday-makers during the dry season (June to September), when the receding waters uncover white beaches along the riverbank. Many Brazilians camp on the banks of the river. During the May to October fishing season, pintado, pirarucu, pacu, tucunaré, suribim and matrinchã are there for the taking.

Organised Tours

If you're serious about fishing and have the money, there are tours, arranged in Brasília and Goiânia (in Goiás state), where you meet a boat-hotel in Aruanã and sail around the island. If you want to explore the river without a tour, catch a boat in Aruanã or Barra do Garças (in Mato Grosso state); however, if you want to get as far north as Ilha do Bananal and don't have a lot of money, it's best to take a bus up to São Felix do Araguaia (in Mato Grosso state) and hire a boat from there.

ILHA DO BANANAL

Formed by the splitting of the Rio Araguaia, Ilha do Bananal is the world's largest river island, covering 20,000 sq km. The northern section is the Parque Nacional do Araguaia, but most of the island is an Indian reserve inhabited by Karajás and Javaés Indians. Farmers use the island's lush pastures for grazing their cattle. In September 1994 the federal government officially declared that all trespassers were to vacate the island. Since many of the 900 families have lived on the island for generations, this has caused a lot of ill feeling in the community. At the time of writing, compensation (in the form of relocation) was being arranged. The Indians were understandably becoming impatient with the bureaucracy, and threatening to take their own action.

Much of the island is covered with forest and there is plenty of wildlife, but only birds are visible in abundance. At sunset and sunrise you can reel in all sorts of fish, including dogfish with teeth so large that the Indians use them to shave with. There are tucunaré with colourful moustaches, ferocious tabarana, pirarucu (two-metre-long, 100-kg monsters) and several other slimy critters. The river also harbours botos (freshwater dolphins), jacaré, *soias* (rare, one-eyed fish) and *poraquê* (electric fish).

Peter Fleming describes an excursion in this region in his excellent travelogue entitled *Brazilian Adventure* (see the Books & Maps section in the Facts for the Visitor chapter). Fleming's route took him down the Araguaia to São Felix do Araguaia, where his group prepared for an expedition up the Rio Tapirapé in an attempt to discover what had happened to Colonel Fawcett, an English explorer who disappeared there in 1925.

Permission to visit the park can be obtained from IBAMA (the national parks service) in Brasília or Palmas (☎ 215-1873, 215-1865), or from the park director (☎ 224-2457, 224-4809), who lives in Goiânia (Goiás state). Of course, if you just show up, you may save a lot of time and hassle and get in just the same. There is simple accommodation available on the island, but no food other than what you bring.

Ilha do Bananal is also accessible from Formoso do Araguaia and Lagoa da Confusão, in the state of Tocantins.

Places to Stay & Eat

São Felix do Araguaia São Felix with a population of around 3000, is in Mato Grosso state, on the Rio das Mortes, and has a few simple hotels. On the river's edge, you'll find the very basic *Hotel Araguaia*. If you're tempted to take one of the rooms with air-con, don't. When the electricity is turned off, at 11 pm, those tomb-like rooms turn into ovens. Get a room that has a ceiling vent through to the hallway.

In town, you can arrange boat rides from fisherfolk and locals who hang out on the water's edge. The pizzeria and fish restaurant overhanging the water is recommended. In

July, the town may well be flooded with local tourists looking to catch some rays.

Santa Teresinha Another gateway to Ilha do Bananal is the small town of Santa Teresinha (in Mato Grosso state). A small hotel on the water's edge is popular with foreign naturalists, who use it as a base for visits to the Parque Nacional do Araguaia. Costs in this region, as in all of the Amazon, are higher than those in Rio or Salvador – so be prepared.

For other accommodation options, see also the Places to Stay sections for Lagoa da Confusão and Formoso do Araguaia (in Tocantins state).

Getting There & Away
To/From Barra do Garças The long, dry road to Ilha do Bananal begins 400 km west of Goiânia, at Barra do Garças (in Mato Grosso state). Buses leave early in Mato Grosso, in an unsuccessful attempt to beat the heat – the bus from Barra do Garças to São Felix do Araguaia leaves daily at 5 am.

If you don't want to take the bus, air-taxis cover the distance in one hour.

To/From Aruanã It's probably easier to reach the Araguaia from the state of Goiás (Goiânia in particular) than from Mato Grosso. For those without a 4WD at their disposal, the town of Aruanã, accessible by bus from both Goiânia (310 km) and Goiás town, is the gateway to the Araguaia. There is a campground at Aruanã. Hire a *voadeira* (a small aluminium motorboat) and a guide for a river trip to Ilha do Bananal.

To/From Barreira do Pequi and Porto Piauí There is a raft on the bank of the Rio Javaé which is used by farmers to access the village on Ilha do Bananal. At the time of writing, these farmers were in the process of being evicted from the Indian reserve.

Porto Piauí is on the opposite bank to the Javaés Indian village of São João do Javaés. There are daily buses to Barreira do Pequi (60 km) and Porto Piauí (36 km) from Formoso do Araguaia, but you will need permission from FUNAI in Gurupi to cross the river to Ilha do Bananal (see the Information section for Gurupi, earlier in this chapter).

To/From Barreira da Cruz It's possible to reach the Parque Nacional da Araguaia on Ilha do Bananal from this small fishing village on the margin of Rio Javaés, 52 km from Lagoa da Confusão, in Tocantins state. There are buses between Lagoa da Confusão and Barreira da Cruz.

Amazonas & Roraima

Amazonas

Amazonas, covering an area of over 1.5 million sq km, is Brazil's largest state. Approximately 75% of its two million inhabitants live in the metropolis of Manaus or in the much smaller cities of Manacapuru, Itacoatiara, Parintins and Coari.

For further coverage of the Amazon region, including Amazonas state, see the Facts about the Country chapter (Flora & Fauna; Ecology & Environment; National Parks). For information on getting around the Amazon region, see the introductory section of The North chapter.

Amazonas state is one hour behind Brazilian standard time.

MANAUS
Manaus lies beside the Rio Negro – 10 km upstream from the confluence of the Solimões and Negro rivers (which join to form the Amazon River). In 1669 the fortress of São José da Barra was built by Portuguese colonisers, who named Manaus after a tribe of Indians who inhabited the region. The village which grew from the fort was little more than a minor trading outpost populated by traders, black slaves, Indians and soldiers, until the rubber boom pumped up the town.

Although Manaus continues to be vaunted in countless glossy advertising brochures as an Amazon Wonderland, the city itself has few attractions. In addition, it is dirty, ugly and becoming increasingly crime-ridden, while the flora and fauna has been systematically despoiled for hundreds of km around the city. Many travellers now only use the city for the briefest of stopovers before making excursions far beyond Manaus, where it is still possible to experience the rainforest wonders that Manaus glibly promises but cannot deliver.

There is a new governor of Amazonas, Armando Amazonino Mendes, who replaced the long-standing Gilberto Mestrinho at the last state election, in November 1994. Mestrinho styled himself as 'the governor of men not animals and the forest', and maintained 'there are hardly any healthy trees in Amazônia and they should all be used before the woodworm gets to them'. Since Eco '92, comments such as these are no longer considered politically correct, but apparently the new governor has similar policies to the previous one, with promises of jobs and development, and such exploitation of the natural resources as is needed to satisfy business interests and win the popular vote. In the long term, this is clearly neither a recipe for sustainable use of the region's resources nor a viable option for producing jobs and development. Critical observers describe such a policy as 'smash, grab and run'.

Although hunting is widely practised, it is illegal. Hunting has already brought peixe-boi and many species of turtles close to extinction. Fishing, however, is acceptable anywhere, and is best from September to November. These are also the best months for swimming – rivers are low and beaches are exposed.

History
In 1839 Charles Goodyear developed the vulcanisation process which made natural rubber durable, and in 1888 John Dunlop patented pneumatic rubber tyres. Soon there was an unquenchable demand for rubber in the recently industrialised USA and Europe, and the price of rubber on international markets soared.

In 1884, the same year that Manaus abolished slavery, a feudal production system was established that locked the *seringueiros* (rubber tappers) into a cruel serfdom. Driven from the sertão by drought, and lured into the Amazon with the false promise of prosperity, they signed away their freedom to the *seringalistas* (owners of rubber plantations).

THE NORTH

Rua Emílio Moreira

Rua Major Gabriel

V Batel

Rua Ibiúna

Rua Igarapé de Manaus

Rua H de Figueiredo

Avenida Joaquim Nabuco

Rua Gettúlio Vargas

R L Cavalcante

Rua Costa Azevedo

Rua de Maio

Rua Rui Barbosa

Rua Barroso

Rua S Marinho

Rua José Clemente

Avenida Eduardo Ribeiro

Rua

Rua H Martins

Rua 10 de Julho

Rua Joaquim Sarmento

Rua Lobo D'Almada

Avenida Epaminondas

Rua Luiz Antony

Rua Mons Coutinho

Rua da Instalação

To Rodoviária (8.5 km) &
Aeroporto Internacional
Eduardo Gomes (14.5 km)

To Tourist Office
(500 m, See Inset)

Centro

Rua Cel Salgado

Inocentes

Rua H Antony

Rua Visc de Maué

Rua Tamandaré

Rua F José

Rua B Ramos

Rua Alexdre Amorim

Rua Xavier de Mendonça

Igarapé de São Raimundo

Rua Dr Arigó

Rua A Correia

Rua W de Matos

To Ponte de
São Raimundo

Avenida 7 de Setembro

Rua Marechal Deodoro

Rua Guilherme Moreira

Rua Dr Moreira

Rua Floriano Peixoto

Rua Marcílio Dias

Rua Mq de Santa Cruz

Porto
Flutuante

Museu
do Indio (200 m)

Candido Mariano

Rua Jonathas Pedroso

Rua Lima Bacuri

Rua José Paranaguá

Altmiro

Rua Izabel

Rua Dr

Rua Quintino Bocaiúva

Avenida Joaquim Nabuco

Rua dos Andradas

Rua Miranda Leão

Rua Miranda Leão

Rua Coelho

Rua 5 de Setembro

Rua Dr

Rua Br de S Domingos

Rua 10 de Santos

Rua dos
Bares

Educandos

Rua Marechal A de Miranda

Boulevard de Sá Peixoto

Rua Manuel Urbano

Igarapé

Rio Educandos

Mundurucus

To Pais de Andrade (Tarumã)

Rua Tapajós

Rua Ramos

Silva

Same Scale as Main Map

Rio Negro

Manaus

0   150   300 m

PLACES TO STAY

4	Hospedaria de Turismo 10 de Julho
6	Taj Mahal Continental Hotel
15	Hotel Krystal
27	Hotel Lord
32	Hotel Amazonas
33	Hotel Nacional
34	Hotel Rei Salomão
35	Hotel Central
38	Ana Cassia Palace Hotel
40	Hotel Continental
41	Pensão Sulista
43	Hotel Jangada & Hotel Ideal
45	Hotel Dona Joana
46	Hotel Rio Branco

PLACES TO EAT

8	Mandarim
9	Skina dos Sucos
10	Chapaty Restaurante Vegetariano
11	Restaurante La Veneza
12	Sorveteria Glacial
21	Restaurante Fiorentina
25	Mister Pizza
36	Churrascaria Búfalo
37	Bar São Marcos
42	Calçada do Rogério
47	Galo Carijó

OTHER

1	Emamtur Tourist Office
2	Porto de São Raimundo (Low-Water Port)
3	Bar do Armando
5	Teatro Amazonas (Opera House)
7	Colombian Consulate
13	Museu do Instituto Geográfico e Histórico do Amazonas
14	Biblioteca
16	Casa de Câmbio Cortez
17	Museu do Homem do Norte
18	Local Bus Terminus
19	Praça da Matriz & Catedral
20	Banco do Brasil
22	Praça Roosevelt (Praça da Policia)
23	Palácio Rio Negro
24	Hotel Tropical Bus Stop
26	Telephone Office
28	Post Office
29	Relógio Municipal (Town Clock)
30	Rodomar, Museu do Porto & Porto Flutuante (Floating Port) Boats to Tefé, Benjamin Constant/ Tabatinga, Santarém & Belém
31	British Customs House (Alfândega)
39	Mercado Municipal & Escadaria dos Remédios Port
44	Arts Centre Chaminé
48	Educandos Port Area

The seringalista sold goods to the seringueiro on credit – fishing line, knives, manioc flour, hammocks – and purchased the seringueiro's balls of latex. The illiteracy of the seringueiros, the brutality of *pistoleiros* (the hired guns of the seringalistas), deliberately rigged scales, and the monopoly of sales and purchases all combined to perpetuate the seringueiro's debt and misery. The seringueiros also had to contend with loneliness, jungle fevers, hostile Indian attacks and all manner of deprivation. Seringueiros who attempted to escape their serfdom were hunted down and tortured by the pistoleiros.

The plantation owners, the rubber traders and the bankers prospered, and built palaces with their wealth. Gentlemen had their shirts sent to London to be laundered, while ladies sported the latest French fashions. Manaus became Brazil's second city after Rio de Janeiro to get electricity, and an opera house was built in the heart of the jungle.

Despite Brazilian efforts to protect their world rubber monopoly, Henry Wickham managed to smuggle rubber seeds out of the Amazon. For details about this episode, see the History section in the Facts about the Country chapter. Botanists in Kew Gardens (London) grew the rubber-tree seedlings and exported them to the British colonies of Ceylon and Malaysia, where they were transplanted and cultivated in neat groves. The efficient Asian production was far superior to the haphazard Brazilian techniques, and the Brazilian rubber monopoly eroded. As more Asian rubber was produced, the price of latex on the world market plummeted. By the 1920s the boom was over, and Manaus declined in importance.

During WW II, when Malaysia was occupied by the Japanese, Allied demand created a new rubber boom. The seringueiros became known as the 'rubber soldiers', and 150,000 Nordestinos were once again recruited to gather rubber.

In many ways the international port of Manaus is still the capital of a land far removed from the rest of Brazil, and there has always been a fear of foreign domination of the Amazon. As a result, the government has made a determined attempt to consolidate Brazilian control of the Amazon by creating roads through the jungle and colonising the interior. It has also made Manaus an industrial city. In 1967 Brazil established a Zona Franca (Free-Trade Zone) in Manaus, and multinational industries, drawn to the area by tax and tariff benefits, have set up manufacturing plants. Although the Manaus free-trade zone has not spawned Brazilian industry – Brazilian entrepreneurs have not successfully competed with multinationals in the Amazon – the infusion of money has invigorated Manaus. Since the Brazilian government relaxed restrictions on imports, the Zona Franca has been less profitable.

Climate

Manaus is hot and humid. During the rainy season (January to June), count on a brief but hard shower nearly every day – the area gets over two metres of rainfall per year. During the rainy season, temperatures range from 23°C to 30°C. Dry-season weather (July to December) is usually between 26°C and 37°C. The city is 40.33 metres above sea level.

Orientation

The city of Manaus lies 3° south of the equator, on the northern bank of the Rio Negro, 10 km west of the confluence of the lesser Rio Negro and the greater Rio Solimões, which form the mighty Amazon River. Iquitos (Peru) and Leticia (Colombia) are 1900 km and 1500 km upriver, and Santarém and Belém are 700 km and 1500 km downriver.

The most interesting parts of Manaus as far as the traveller is concerned are close to the waterfront: Mercado Municipal, the customs house and the floating docks. The opera house is one of the most impressive reminders of Manaus' past opulence.

Information

Tourist Office Emamtur (☎ 633-2850; fax 233-9973), the state tourism organisation, has its headquarters at Avenida Paés de Andrade 379 (previously called Avenida Tarumã), open from 8 am to 1 pm Monday to Friday. It's a bit of a hike from the city centre, but worth a visit. You may also be able to get some information at the opera house.

For details about national parks in Amazonas, contact either IBAMA (☎ 237-3710), at Rua Ministro João Gonçalves de Souza, BR-319, Km 01, Distrito Industrial, or the Secretária Municipal de Desenvolvimento do Meio Ambiente (☎ 236 4122), at Rua Recife, Adrianópolis.

Money The main branch of Banco do Brasil, Rua Guilherme Moreira 315, is open for exchange from 9 am to 3 pm on weekdays. Casa de Câmbio Cortez, on Rua Guilherme Moreira and also at Avenida Sete de Setembro 1199, is a convenient option for quicker exchange. It's open from 9 am to 5.30 pm on weekdays and from 9 am to 12.30 pm on Saturday.

At the time of writing, the only bank in Manaus from which you could get cash advances from MasterCard was Banorte, at Avenida 7 de Setembro. For American Express cash advances, go to the Banco Economico (on Rua Saldanha Marinho) or to the Hotel Amazonas. Visa is the most accepted credit card in Manaus, as for most places around Brazil, and you can get cash advances from the Banco do Brasil.

Post & Telephone Manaus has 24 postal agencies spread around the central area and suburbs. The main post office, at Rua Marechal Deodoro, is open from 8 am to 6 pm Monday to Saturday and from 8 am to 2 pm on Sunday. The Brazilian postal system has apparently become more reliable.

There's a central office of Teleamazon, the state telephone company, on Rua Guilherme Moreira. It's open daily from 8 am to 11 pm.

Foreign Consulates The following is a list of countries represented in Manaus:

Bolivia
    Avenida Eduardo Ribeiro 520, sala 1410, Centro
    (☎ 234-6661)
Chile
    Rua Marques de Caravelas B15, casa 8, Parque
    das Laranjeiras (☎ 236-1621)
Colombia
    Rua Dona Libânia 262 (☎ 234-6777)
Ecuador
    Rua 6, casa 16, Jardim Belo Horizonte, Parque
    Dez (☎ 236-3698)
France
    Conjunto Jardin Espanha III, Q 02, 19 Parque
    Dez (☎ 236-3513)
Germany
    Rua Barroso 355, 1 Andar, sala A, Centro
    (☎ 232-0890)
Japan
    Rua Ferreira Pena 92, Centro (☎ 232-2000)
Peru
    Rua Ramos Ferreira 664, Centro (☎ 633-1954)
UK
    Rua Puraqué 240, Distrito Industrial
    (☎ 237-7038)
USA
    Rua Recife 1010, Adrianópolis (☎ 234-4546)
Venezuela
    Rua Ferreira Pena 179, Centro (☎ 23- 6004)

Dangers & Annoyances Theft at rock-bottom hotels is common – double keys are sometimes used to gain access to your room. When travelling by boat, watch your gear very carefully. Taxi drivers in Manaus have a poor reputation. Watch out for blatant rip-off attempts: spurious 'extra charges', slack use of meters and cosy 'deals' whereby hotel clerks are paid a fat commission by taxi drivers who are willing to pay for the privilege of being able to rip off foreign tourists.

For more tips, see the security advice in the Dangers & Annoyances section of the Facts for the Visitor chapter.

Escadaria dos Remédios Port

The Escadaria dos Remédios port, by the Mercado Municipal, is quite a scene, and well worth a visit. For a description, see the aside in this section.

Mercado Municipal

Looming above the Escadaria is the imposing cast-iron structure of the Mercado Municipal, designed in 1882 by Adolfo Lisboa after the Parisian Les Halles. Although the art-nouveau ironwork was imported from Europe, the place has acquired Amazonian character. In and around the market, you can purchase provisions for jungle trips: strange fruits, old vegetables, several varieties of biscuits, sacks of beans and rice, lanterns, rope, straw hats, perhaps some Umbanda figurines, powders and incense.

At the back end of the market, there's a grimy cafeteria where you can have lunch and contemplate Manaus' complete ignorance regarding sanitation. The water which keeps enormous fish and fly-covered meats cool, drains from the stalls, mingles with meat, fish and urine, flows underfoot, runs off into the river and mixes with discarded meats and produce and all the sewage of Manaus. Urubu vultures swarm around the refuse and roost in the rusty ironwork of the cafeteria. Take the tables at either end for the best view.

Escadaria dos Remédios Port

Most of the people you will observe at the Escadaria dos Remédios Port have Indian features, with straight, jet-black hair and tawny skin. These thin, stoop-shouldered stevedores lug barrels, casks and boxes between the trucks and riverboats. The curved decks of the riverboats are filled with cargo and people, and draped with hundreds of hammocks. Fisherfolk look on from the sidelines, while they smoke cigarettes and drink beer.

Men toss banana stalks from their dugout canoes onto the shore and from there onto the waiting trucks. A speaker blares nonstop love songs from warped tapes until the boats pull out, at 6 pm. The boats leave one by one: bells ring, horns blow and thin boys scurry about selling their last lengths of rope to tie up travellers' hammocks. ■

Arts Centre Chaminé

Located off Rua Isabel, facing the Igarapé dos Educandos, this old water-treatment plant has now been converted into an art gallery (☎ 234-7877) which often has some interesting exhibitions. It's open from 9 am to 6 pm.

Teatro Amazonas

Teatro Amazonas, the famous opera house of Manaus, was designed by Doménico de Angelis in eclectic neoclassical style at the height of the rubber boom, in 1896. The materials and artists were imported from Europe, and more than any other building associated with the administration of Mayor Eduardo Ribeiro, this opera house is symbolic of the opulence that was Manaus. Renovated in 1990, it's now open daily from 10 am to 5 pm. Admission costs US$4.00 and includes a compulsory guided tour. Opera and ballet performances are held here throughout the year. Ask the guide about the schedule or check the entertainment section in the local newspaper.

Palácio Rio Negro

The Palácio Rio Negro, built as a home for eccentric German rubber baron Waldemar Scholz, now serves as the seat of the state government. It's on Avenida 7 de Setembro, beside the first bridge over the Igarapé do Manaus.

British Customs House

The British Customs House (Alfândega) dates back to 1906. This sandy-coloured building with its neat, brown trim seems out of place in such a dilapidated city. Imported from the UK in prefabricated blocks, the building now serves as the Inspetoria da Receita Federal do Porto do Manaus.

Porto Flutuante

The Porto Flutuante (floating docks), also installed in 1906, were considered a technical marvel because of their ability to rise and fall as the water level of the river changes with the seasons. It's well worth a visit – you can watch the boats being loaded with produce, and the swarms of people using river transport.

Instituto Nacional de Pesquisa da Amazônia (INPA) & Bosque da Ciência

The National Amazon Research Institute (☎ 23-9400) receives most of its funding from the World Bank. One of the institute's central projects is a joint study with the Smithsonian Institute to determine the 'minimal critical size of ecosystems' – the smallest chunk of land that can support a self-sustaining jungle forest and all its attendant creatures. Various-sized parcels of jungle are studied, first in their virgin state, then later, after the surrounding land has been cleared to create islands of jungle. Changes in plant and animal populations are

---

Serpent Support for the Theatre

According to historian Daniel Fausto Bulcão, there was once a couple who lived in the interior, far from the city. The woman became pregnant, and in the course of her pregnancy, she had the misfortune to kill a cobra. When her nine months were up, she gave birth to two cobras, a male and a female, which she raised as her own children.

As the cobras began to grow, the mother was unable to control her unruly offspring, so she threw them into the river. The female cobra earned a reputation for being evil by tipping over riverboats, devouring children and drowning adults – killing simply for the pleasure of it. Her brother was of a milder temperament, and the two cobras fought continuously. One day, the male snake killed his sister, but not without suffering the loss of one eye. He is still alive and well, and has grown considerably over the years. Caboclos believe that he now lives beneath Manaus, his enormous head supporting the Teatro Amazonas and his body supporting the many river beaches of the Amazon. ■

carefully scrutinised. Initial results suggest that the complex interdependence of plants and animals and the heterogeneity of species pose a barrier to maintaining an isolated patch of jungle.

INPA scientists are also studying jacaré, fresh-water manatee, river otter and porpoises. These animals are on display in the botanical garden and zoo. Avoid feeding time at the jacaré enclosure if you don't want to see live mice sacrificed.

The grounds, located at Bairro Coroado, Alameda Cosme Ferreira 1756, Km 4, have recently been expanded to include raised walkways through the trees. The Casa da Ciência has a permanent exhibition of the institute's activities. Other projects include: the environmental impact of deforestation and of hydroelectric dams; mercury poisoning of the rivers by gold mining; kit housing for impoverished locals; stingless bees; and the study of medicinal orchids and bromelias. There is a giant leaf on display, measuring about two metres high.

The grounds are open from 8 am to noon and 2 to 6 pm Monday to Friday. Call ahead (☎ 642-3377) to find out the topic (and language) of Thursday's seminar series. To reach INPA, either take the bus marked 'São José' or use a taxi.

Museu do Homem do Norte

The Museum of Northern Man (☎ 232-5373), at Avenida 7 de Setembro 1385, is an ethnology and anthropology museum dedicated to the lifestyle of the river-dwelling Caboclos. It has an interesting display of Indian weapons, including the vicious *furador de olhos* (eye piercer). It's open from 9 am to noon and 1 to 5 pm Monday to Thursday and from 1 to 5 pm on Friday. Admission is US$1.20.

Museu do Indio

This Indian museum (☎ 234-1422) is on Avenida Duque de Caxias, near the intersection of Avenida 7 de Setembro. Displays include ceramics, featherwork, weaving, hunting and ritual objects of the tribes of the upper Rio Negro. Bad luck if you can't read Portuguese! The museum is open from 8.30 to 11.30 am and 2.30 to 5 pm on weekdays and from 8.30 to 11.30 am on Saturday. Admission is US$2.40.

Museu do Instituto Geográfico e Histórico do Amazonas

This historic museum (☎ 232-7077), at Rua Frei José dos Inocentes 117, has archaeological objects, fossils and stuffed animals from the region. It's open from 8 am to noon and 2.30 to 5 pm Monday to Friday.

Museu do Porto de Manaus

This museum of the Manaus docks (☎ 232-4250), at Travessa Vivaldo de Lima, has displays of maritime instruments, maps and projects of the Manaus docks from the beginning of the century. It's open from 8 to 11 am and 2 to 5 pm Monday to Friday and from 8 am to 1 pm on Saturday.

Museu de Ciencias Naturais da Amazonia

Run by the Associação Naturalista da Amazonia, this natural-science museum (☎ 644-2799), at Estrada Belém, Colônia Cachoeira Grande, has an comprehensive exhibit of fish, insects and butterflies from the Amazon region, with descriptions in English and Japanese. The aquarium has two-metre-long pirarucú fish. The museum shop sells Indian crafts. Open Tuesday to Sunday from 9 am to 5 pm, the museum is somewhat out of the way, but it's worth the trip. Take the 'São José' bus to INPA, then catch a taxi.

Parque Zoológico – CIGS

This military zoo makes you feel sorry for the animals cooped up in small cages. It claims to have more jaguars born in captivity than any other establishment in the world. The zoo is attached to the Centro de Instrução de Guerra na Selva (CIGS), a jungle-warfare training centre. The animals on display – tapir, monkeys, armadillos, snakes and birds – were collected by Brazilian soldiers on jungle manoeuvres and survival-training programmes. The zoo is on

Estrada da Ponta Negra, Km 12, near the beach and the Hotel Tropical. To get there, take a taxi, or a municipal bus marked 'Compensa' or 'São Jorge'. Zoo hours are 9.30 am to 4.30 pm Tuesday to Sunday. Admission is free.

Amazon Ecopark & Amazon Monkey Jungle

The Amazon Ecopark, a private nature reserve with a tourist centre, is located half an hour by boat from Manaus. The park runs survival courses in the tropical rainforest, with a local rainforest ranger. Next to the Ecopark is the Amazon Monkey Jungle, set up by the Living Rainforest Foundation for the rehabilitation of orphan animals. For information about tours, contact the Amazon Ecopark office (☎ 234-0939), Praça Auxiliadora 04, grupo 103, Centro, Manaus. Half-day tours cost about US$30.

Praia da Ponta Negra & Waterfalls Around Manaus

Praia da Ponta Negra is a popular river beach with a full range of amenities, including restaurants and bars. The best time to go is between September and November (and sometimes as early as July), when the waters recede, but it's a popular hang-out even when the high waters flood the sand and cleanse the beach for the following season. From the city centre, take the bus marked 'Praia da Ponta Negra'.

If you've missed the beach season, December to February is the best time to visit the waterfalls near Manaus: Cascatinha do Amor and Cachoeira do Tarumã. Further west from Manaus, near the opposite bank of the Rio Negro, is Cachoeira do Paricatuba.

São (Rabbi) Moyal

In Cemitério São João Batista, the general cemetery of Manaus (Praça Chile, Adrianópolis), is the tomb of Rabbi Moyal of Jerusalém. The rabbi came to the Amazon to minister to a small community of Jewish settlers, mostly merchants who had established a cacao, lumber and rubber-trading network. He died in 1910, and over the years his tomb has become a shrine for an odd Roman Catholic cult. This cult, complete with rosary beads, candles, coins and devoted followers, probably arose with the Jewish custom of placing pebbles on tombs when visiting grave sites. The people of Manaus, unfamiliar with Jewish customs (of Brazil's 120,000 Jews, less than 1000 live in Manaus), attribute the mysterious pebbles to the miraculous powers of the dead rabbi. Followers believe that the rabbi is a saint, and insist that he performs miracles for faithful supplicants.

Encontro das Águas

An interesting phenomenon is the Encontro das Águas (Meeting of the Waters), the point where the inky-black waters of the Rio Negro meet the clay-yellow waters of the Rio Solimões, though it's not absolutely necessary to take a tour – it can be seen just as well from the *balsa* (ferry) which shuttles between Careiro and the Porto Velho highway (BR-319). If you do include the meeting of the waters in your tour, you may lose time that could be better spent exploring the more interesting sights further along the river.

Jungle Tours

The top priority for most foreign visitors to Manaus is a jungle tour. Here, it's possible to arrange anything from standard day trips and overnight excursions to months of travel in the hinterland. It is common for travellers to be greeted at the airport by groups of tour-agency representatives keen to sign them up for trips. These representatives are a useful source of information, and may even offer transport into the city centre to a budget hotel, but you should hold off booking a tour until you've had time to shop around for the best deals.

There are now dozens of agencies vying for your custom, with trendy names ('Eco' and 'Green' have quickly become standard prefixes) and glossy brochures, touting all sorts of encounters with wildlife and Indians just a few km from the city.

What you *can* expect on day trips or tours

by boat lasting three or four days is a close-up experience of the jungle flora, with abundant birdlife and a few jacaré (more easily located at night by guides using powerful torches) and, if you're lucky, porpoises. It is also a chance to see what life is like for the caboclos in the vicinity of Manaus.

You *cannot* expect to meet remote Indian tribes or dozens of free-ranging beasts, because the former have sensibly fled from contact (after centuries of annihilation or forced assimilation) and the latter have been systematically hunted to the brink of extinction. In both cases, access has become synonymous with destruction.

This does not mean that the tours are not worthwhile, merely that prospective tour participants should ignore flowery propaganda and instead ask the tour operators for exact details. Does the tour include extended travel in small boats (without use of motor) along igarapés? How much time is spent getting to and from your destination? What is the cost breakdown (food, lodging, fuel and guides)? You may want to pay some of these expenses en route, thereby avoiding fanciful mark-ups, and should insist on paying only a portion of the costs at the beginning of the trip, settling the rest at the end. This payment schedule helps to maintain the interest of tour operators and guides in defining and abiding by a tour schedule. It also provides some leverage if promises are not kept.

If you are trying out jungle tours for the first time and intending to do extended trips in the Amazon region, it's useful to take a short trip from Manaus as a taster. This will allow you to assess the idea in practice and give you the confidence to do longer trips either from Manaus or from other parts of the Amazon. The latter option is becoming increasingly popular among travellers disenchanted with Manaus.

We have received a few enthusiastic letters from readers who thoroughly enjoyed their tours, and a whole heap of complaint letters from readers who felt the tours were a complete ripoff – see the section called Readers' Experiences later in this chapter.

For information about getting around the Amazon region by boat, see the Amazon by River and Things to Bring sections in the introduction to The North chapter.

Jungle Tours – big operators There are several reputable (but pricey) jungle-tour outfits. Organised tours cost US$100 to US$200 per person per day, and are far more expensive than tours you can arrange yourself. Organised tours usually use larger boats than those of the independent operators – too big to negotiate the narrow igarapés where the wildlife roams – though they may include canoe trips.

There are advantages to the organised tours; they are relatively hassle-free, there is nothing to arrange and English-speaking guides are often available. The larger firms are generally quite reputable. Amazon Explorers (☎ 633-3319; fax 234-5759), at Rua Nhamundá 21, Praça Auxiliadora, has English-speaking guides. Selvatur (☎ 622-2088; fax 622-2177), in the lobby of the Hotel Amazonas, on Praça Adalberto Valle, accommodates large tour groups on huge catamaran boats. It has a 'Meeting of the Waters' day tour (US$50), which includes en route igarapé sighting, a visit to Lago Januari, a jungle walk to see lily pads, a motorised canoe ride to Igapós and lunch.

The up-market packaged jungle tours based at jungle lodges are a good option for a comfortable and safe way to experience the Amazon jungle environment. Most trips include the standard jacaré spotting, piranha fishing, canoeing and visits to a caboclo's house. The following is a brief selection of the packages currently available.

The *Amazon Lodge* is a small-scale floating lodge on Lago Juma, about five hours by ferry, bus and boat from Manaus. A three-day package costs US$355. Make reservations through Nature Safaris (☎ 622-4144; fax 622-1420), at Rua Leonardo Malcher 734, Manaus. Also through Nature Safaris, you can book a three-day package (around US$250) at the *Amazon Village*, on the edge of Lago Puraquequara, about three hours by boat from Manaus.

THE NORTH

The Amazon Circuit

It seems odd that in the millions of sq km that make up the Amazon, everyone seems to congregate upon such a small spot during the pre-Carnival season, but Lago Janauário draws hordes of visitors at this time of year. One thing that cheapens the jungle experience here is the feeling of being pumped through a tourist circuit: everyone bangs on the flying buttresses of the same sambaiaba tree, cuts the same rubber tree for latex sap, then pulls over to an authentic jungle house where a monkey, a sloth, a snake and a jacaré are tied up to amuse visitors.

After a quick bite at a jungle restaurant, take the elevated walk to the Vitória Regia water lilies, beyond the make-believe Indian craft stalls (10 stores operated by one athletic Indian, who follows alongside the group and pushes feathered novelty-shop junk). At this point, one disregards the water lilies and the Kodak boxes floating alongside and compares notes with one's neighbour about respective tour costs, boat sizes and whether or not a flush toilet has been provided.

The water lilies, one-metre-wide floating rimmed dishes adorned with flowers above and protected by sharp spikes below, are lovely, despite it all. ∎

At the *Acajatuba Jungle Lodge*, on Lago Acajatuba, in the municipality of Iranduba (north-west of Manaus), a three-day package costs US$230. Reservations can be made through Ecotéis (☎ & fax 233-7642), at Rua Doutor Alminio 30, Manaus.

The *Tropical Lago de Salvador* is a small hotel on Igarapé dos Guedes, about 30 km from Manaus – a 35-minute boat trip from the Hotel Tropical. A three-day package costs US$328. Book through Fontur (☎ 656-2807; fax 656-2167), Estrada da Ponta Negra, at the Hotel Tropical in Manaus.

King's Island Lodge is 1600 km from Manaus, in São Gabriel da Cachoeira, close to the frontiers with Venezuela and Colombia. A six-day (minimum) package costs around US$900; the cost of the trip from Manaus (five to six days by boat or three hours by air) is not included. Reservations can be made through Nature Safaris.

The *Ariaú Jungle Tower* is on Lago do Ariaú, in the Arquipélago das Anavilhanas, three hours by boat from Manaus. This large complex has towers linked by raised platforms through the trees, leading to a 50-metre-high observatory. A three-day package costs US$340. Rio Amazonas Turismo (☎ 234-7308; fax 233-5615), at Rua Silva Ramos 41, Manaus, can arrange bookings.

The *Amazon Camp* is a small hotel on the Rio Urubu, about 200 km east of Manaus. A three-day package costs US$180. Reservations can be made through Anavilhanas Turismo (☎ 671-1411; 671-3888) at Rua Coração de Jesus 11, Bairro São Raimundo.

Another small hotel is the *Pousada dos Guanavenas*, on Ilha de Silves, an island 300 km east of Manaus (about five hours by car). A three-day package costs around US$235. Make reservations through Guanavenas Turismo (☎ 656 3656; fax 656-5027), at Rua Constantino Nery 2486.

The *Malocas Jungle Lodge* is on Rio Preto da Eva (a small tributary of the Amazon), 150 km from Manaus, a bus-plus-boat trip of about four hours. A three-day package costs US$210/120 on a bed/hammock. Bookings can be made through Iaratour (☎ & fax 633-2330), at Rua Mundurucus 90, sala 207, Manaus.

Jungle Tours – smaller operators If you speak Portuguese and don't mind travelling a bit rough, there are plenty of smaller operators offering tours. It is quite possible to end up feeling totally confused as you sift through the countless brochures. Often the choice simply comes down to luck! We met one group who had spent three whole days pondering which trip to take. On the carefully chosen tour, they spent a sleepless night in hammocks camped across an ant path, several ended up with mild food poisoning and the inebriated guide became a little too flirtatious. Try to meet the actual guide prior to committing to a trip.

It takes time to hammer out a deal, change money, arrange supplies and buy provisions – allow at least a day for this. When serious haggling is called for, ask the tour operator to itemise expenses. Disproportionately inflated estimates can work in your favour. If the food budget seems unreasonable, buy provisions in and about the Mercado Municipal. If the fuel budget seems too high, offer to pay at the floating gas stations. Subtract the items from your original quote. As a rough rule of thumb, expect prices to start at about US$45 per person per day, assuming two people on a two-day (one-night) trip, including boat transport, guide, food and hammock lodging. For more advice, see the

comments at the beginning of this section, and the Readers' Experiences section later in this chapter.

Amazonas Indian Turismo (☎ 233-3104), Rua dos Andrades 335, has been recommended. They take trips up the Rio Urubu, staying overnight in cabanas. A two-day (one-night) trip for two costs US$60 per person.

Moaçir Fortes of Amazon Expeditions (☎ 232-7492) speaks English, and operates his own boat from the Porto Flutuante. He runs a small, 1st-class operation, charging US$80 to US$100 per person per day, depending on the number of passengers on board (a maximum of 14, minimum of four). Everyone sleeps in a clean cabin that has hot showers. The boat is fitted out with canoes and a small outboard, and has a well-stocked

---

Amazon Tour Operators

Jungle tours are not that expensive. I had a three-day tour with Amazonas Indian Turismo and spent a wonderful time for US$100 (three days, everything included). During this trip I saw toucans, colibris, jacaré, Indians, mosquitoes and plenty more. A canoe trip at night in the swamps I'll never forget. Wow, how much I would like to go back there! The only problem was that the Indian guide didn't speak more than two words of English and I didn't speak any Portuguese.

We took a three-day (two nights) trip with Cristóvão Amazonas Turismo (☎233-3231). We paid US$200 each and felt we were cheated. It was a canoe trip staying with Indian families and included all food. Instead, we recommend contacting the boatmen's union direct. All the canoe guides have formed an association. The tour companies only pay the guides US$400 for a three-day trip with four people – and the guides do everything (arranging lodging, meals, etc). We had a guide called Raimundo and he was excellent. Take some money with you for the trip as Indian handicrafts can be purchased at a much cheaper price (than in Manaus). There really weren't any animals to be seen. Although we saw a few cows, cranes, and jacaré, and caught piranha, there wasn't any wildlife in the jungle during the day. Due to too many people touring the jungle, the animals probably come out at night – if at all.

You might warn travellers arriving in Manaus airport about the tourist-hunting girls who work freelance or for certain tour agencies. On my arrival, I felt insecure about finding a place to stay, so I was an easy victim. However, there was one good side to being caught: I got free transport to town and didn't have to worry about looking for a hotel – the girl put me into one that was good value. The bad side was the three-day boat trip she sold me. The experience of being on the Amazon is something I'll never forget – and I hope to get back there one day – but the trip as such was pure shit: a ridiculous 'guide' who had no interest in explaining anything, boring food (basically rice and noodles), 'mineral water' that tasted of gasoline, no visits to igarapés and not even a trip to Lago Janauário. The agency demanded US$70 per day.

We were told it's almost a must to go on a jungle tour if you go to Manaus. Unfortunately, we must say that it was very disappointing. We didn't see many animals on our two-day tour and it was also very expensive (US$85 per person), especially if you compare it, for example, to Ecuador where you can go on similar tours. We don't think the tours of the various tour agencies differ much. The one-day tour is not good: you spend 10 hours on the boat! ■

Around Manaus

THE NORTH

Labels on map:

To Amazon Camp
To Malo008 Jungle Lodge
Ponta Terra Nova
Ilha Terra Nova
Lago do Rei
Lago do Cambixi
Lago do Capitari
Amazon Lodge
Rio Amazonas
Ilha do Careiro
Lago do Mandu
Lago do Unico
Lago do Arroz
Paraná do Cambixi
Lago do Juma
Lago Jassiua
Ponta das Lajes
Lago do Joanico
Vila do Careiro
Paraná do Careiro
Ponta das Catalão
Balsa
Ilha Kiborema
Fazenda Santo Antônio
Lago Comprido
To Itacoatiara &
Coati Nacional de
Pesquisas da Seringueira
(National Rubber Research Institute)
Amazon Village
Aeroporto Internacional
Eduardo Gomes
Encontro das
Águas
Ilha Machantaria
Lago Manguari
Lago Alvores
BR319
To Boa Vista &
Venezuela
Cachoeira
do Tarumã
Manaus
Balsa
Lago
Jansuário
Lago do
Iranduba
Ilha
do Curari
Lago
Araça
To Porto Velho
Igarapé
Tarumã Açu
Cachoeira
das Almas
Cascatinha
do Amor
Praia da Ponta Negra
Hotel Tropical
Balsa
Vila do Iranduba
Tropical Lago
de Salvador
Colônia
Paricatuba
Ilha
Paciência
Lago
Grande
Lago
Jansatuca
Cachoeira
do Paricatuba
Colônia Lago
do Limão
Jutaí
Ariaú Jungle Tower
Lago do Limão
Manaquiri
Paraná
To Arawallanas Huts
Cachoeira
das Araras
Igarapé
Arara
Acajatuba
Jungle Lodge
Lago
Acajatuba
Rio Negro
Ilha
Sacada
Lago do
Matias
Colônia
Boa Vista
Rio Solimões
(Amazonas)
Ilha
do Barroso
Manaquiri
To Manacapuru
Lago
Santana

0   10   20 km

bar, a library full of wildlife guidebooks, binoculars and even a telescope on board.

Gerry Hardy is an English guide operating tours from Manacapuru together with a Brazilian guide, Elmo de Morais Lopes. Readers have generally liked the tours, but some have found the tone of the ecological explanations a bit patronising. Contact these guides through the Hotel Rio Branco (☎ 233-4019).

Suggested Excursions An overnight trip to Lago Janauário reserve (15 km from Manaus) – a standard excursion, often including the meeting of the waters – or a three-day (two-night) trip to Lago Mamori can both be recommended. The latter is especially good when the waters are high, when boats can float past the tree tops. A glimpse of life at the level of the jungle canopy is far richer than the view from the jungle floor.

A suggested longer tour takes you 100 km up the Rio Negro to the Arquipélago das Anavilhanas, near Nova Airão. This trip is best done between July and December. Whichever tour you choose, make sure to take a canoe ride on the igarapés: it's a Disneyland experience.

Amazon Tours What you get out of your trip depends on several factors: expectations, previous experience, the competence and breadth of knowledge of tour operators and guides, and the ability to accept life in the Amazon at face value – one enterprising tour operator advertises 'Selva sem Sofrimento' (the Jungle without Suffering!). Although the 'jungle' is often described in exaggerated terms as a 'Green Hell', it seems rather odd to want to turn a jungle tour into a luxury outing with all mod cons, thereby distancing yourself from the 'wild' characteristics that are the hallmark of such an experience.

See the boxed aside of various readers' comments about Amazon tours.

Festivals

A folklore festival held during the second half of June coincides with a number of saints' days and culminates in the Procissão Fluvial de São Pedro (São Pedro River Procession), when hundreds of regional boats parade on the river before Manaus to honour São Pedro, the patron saint of fisherfolk.

During the month of June, Manaus has a variety of regional folklore performances, including the party of the *bumbás* (stylised bulls), tribal dances and square dances. It represents a mixture of indigenous Amazonian culture with influences from the Northeastern and Portuguese cultures.

Places to Stay – bottom end

As with the rest of Brazil, since the introduction of the Plano Real, accommodation prices have increased. There's still plenty of cheap lodging in Manaus, however, ranging from grungy to decent. Most is located off Avenida Joaquim Nabuco.

The *Hotel Rio Branco* (☎ 233-4019), at Rua dos Andradas 484, is a popular budget place. Apartamentos with fan cost US$6/10 for singles/doubles, while apartamentos with air-con are US$12/13. The breakfast is very poor. At the *Hotel Ideal* (☎ 233-9423), at Rua dos Andradas 491, you'll pay US$7/11 for single/double apartamentos with fan (US$11/13 with air-con). The *Pensão Sulista* (☎ 234-5814) is at Avenida Joaquim Nabuco 347, near the junction with Rua Quintino Bocaiúva. Its clean quartos with fan cost US$7/10, while doubles with air-con are US$18. It gets hot, so make sure your room has a fan, and try to get a room without a tin roof. Breakfast (coffee and milk plus bread and butter) is served after 7 am, and there are clotheslines and washing tubs for your laundry.

The *Hotel Jangada* (☎ 232-2248), near the Hotel Ideal on Rua dos Andradas, offers dorm beds with fan for US$6 and double rooms for US$11. Prices include breakfast. Readers have warned that the *Hotel Paraíso* is notorious for theft and the use of double keys.

At the *Hotel Dona Joana* (☎ 233-7553), Rua dos Andradas 553, double apartamentos (with air-con) start at around US$12, and the suite costs US$18. The rooms at the top have good views across the river. Patrons of the rooftop restaurant are able to wander through the hotel, so don't expect much security.

The *Hotel Continental* (☎ 233-3342), at Rua Coronel Sergio Pessoa 198 (Praça dos Remédios), has apartamentos with air-con for US$18/23. The *Hotel Nacional* (☎ 233-7533), at Rua Dr Moreira 59, Zona Franca, has barely decent apartamentos for US$19/25.

The *Hospedaria De Turismo 10 De Julho* (☎ & fax 232-6280), at Rua 10 De Julho 679, is in a good location, near the opera house. It has secure, good-value single/double apartamentos with air-con for US$12/18, and fresh juice for breakfast.

Places to Stay – middle

There is a significant difference in quality between the top and mid-range hotels, many of which appear to cater to Brazilians making a flying visit to Manaus to shop like crazy for duty-free goods. Check your rooms for working air-con and showers before paying, and always check whether there is any discount. Most places have a 10% service charge. The mid-range hotels in the centre are mostly clustered along Rua Dr Moreira within the Zona Franca, where it is hectic during the day and dead at night.

The *Hotel Rei Salomão* (☎ 234-7344; fax 232-8479), at Rua Dr Moreira 119, is a spiffy three-star hotel. Single/double apartamentos cost US$43/53. The *Hotel Central* (☎ 622-2600; fax 622-2609), at Rua Dr Moreira 202, offers apartamentos for US$48/60. The *Ana Cassia Palace Hotel* (☎ 622-3637; fax 622-4812), at Rua dos Andradas 14, has apartamentos at US$66/83. Discounts are available for cash payment. Better located is the *Hotel Krystal* (☎ 233-7305; fax 633-3393), at Rua Barroso 54, opposite the library. It has new, clean apartamentos for US$46/58.

Places to Stay – top end

For details about jungle tours and package tours based on up-market jungle lodges, pousadas and safari camps, refer to the Jungle Tours – Big Operators section.

The 600-room *Tropical Hotel* (☎ 658-5000; fax 658-5026), Manaus' premier luxury hotel, is a self-contained resort 16 km out of Manaus, at Ponta Negra. Singles/doubles start at around US$175/200, and suites are available for a mere US$400. The hotel belongs to Varig's chain of Tropical hotels, so Varig passengers can get a 30% discount. A discount is also given if you arrive without a reservation and pay by cash or credit card.

Even if you don't stay here, you may want to visit this huge complex, which has a well-arranged mini-zoo (watch out for the bats at dusk – one of the authors was hit smack on the forehead!); a superb giant pool with waves, a sloping beach, palm trees and even Vitória Regia lilies; a coffee shop; and a staff of 1000 to keep guests happy.

The hotel also provides a shuttle service (US$5) to and from the centre of Manaus. Buses leave every few hours between 9 am and 7.30 pm. Pick up a timetable at the reception desk. The requisite bus stop in the centre of Manaus is on Rua Dr Moreira.

The *Hotel Amazonas* (☎ 622-2233; fax 622-2064), a four-star hotel on Praça Adalberto Valle, has singles/doubles starting at US$110/136. Readers have complained about poor soundproofing and noisy front rooms. The *Hotel Lord* (☎ 622-2844; fax 622-2576), at Rua Marcílio Dias 215, in the Zona Franca, offers standard single/double apartamentos for US$75/85. The bar of this hotel used to be a popular place for wealthy adventurer types to exchange old campaign stories. The *Taj Mahal Continental Hotel* (☎ 633-1010; fax 233-0068), at Avenida Getúlio Vargas 741, offers high-rise apartments at US$130/153 a single/double. The *Imperial Hotel* (☎ 622-3112; fax 622-1762), Avenida Getúlio Vargas 227, has apartamentos for US$123/157.

Places to Eat

Before taking a long riverboat ride or foray into the jungle, you should splurge on a few good meals in Manaus. The local fish specialities are tucunaré, tambaqui, dourada and pirarucu, served grilled (na brasa), pickled (escabeche) or stewed (caldeirada). Locals recommend the *Paramazom Restaurant* (233-6374), at Rua Santa Isabel 1176, Cachoeirinha, for good regional dishes.

Also recommended is *Galo Carijó*, opposite the Hotel Dona Joana on Rua dos Andradas. It features local fish and is favoured by locals, who drop in for 'uma cerveja estupidamente gelada' (an idiotically cold beer). Or try *Calçada do Rogério*, at Rua José Paranaguá 590.

For pizza and pasta dishes, there's the *Restaurante Fiorentina* (☎ 232-1295), at Praça Roosevelt 44, *Restaurante La Veneza*, at Avenida Getúlio Vargas 257, or *Mister Pizza*, at Rua José Paranaguá, opposite Praça da Policia. *Churrascaria Búfalo*, at Avenida Joaquim Nabuco 628, is a decidedly non-vegetarian place; in addition to serving massive steaks, it has an interesting buffet (à kilo) for meat-lovers. À kilo is a self-service system where you pay according to the weight of your meal. It has became popular in Brazil, and you will find various small restaurants offering a good-value buffet. It's worth a try! Vegetarians should head for *Chapaty Restaurante Vegetariano*, near the opera house, at Rua Costa Azevedo 105. Open from 11 am to 2.30 pm Sunday to Friday, it also has good nonvegetarian à kilo.

Mandarim, at Avenida Eduardo Ribeiro 650, serves inexpensive Chinese food. The *Taj Mahal Continental Hotel* has a disconcertingly squeaky revolving restaurant which overlooks the opera house.

Adventurous palates will venture to the street stalls and sample tacacá, a gummy soup made from lethal-if-not-well-boiled manioc root, lip-numbing jambu leaves and relatively innocuous dried shrimp. The best tacacá in town is on Avenida Getúlio Vargas, next to the Hotel Imperial. Tip: tacacá without goma (gum) is less offputting.

For dessert, there's always strange fruit to taste, including pupunha, bacaba and buriti. *Sorveteria Glacial* is the most popular ice-cream parlour in town. Since your body will be craving liquids, try *Skina dos Sucos*, which has great juices of those strange fruits. You should try guaraná, acerola, cupuaçú or graviola.

Along the road on the way to Tarumã, you can find various restaurants serving 'café regional', a local breakfast menu that includes fruit juices, manioc-derived dishes, corn cakes, bread and coffee. It is popular with nightclubbers to finish their evening.

Finally, one disgruntled reader wrote: 'Manaus is a pit – the restaurant at Hotel Amazonas is a bigger pit. I'm still not sure if I got the fish I ordered or some genuine Brazilian latex!'

Entertainment

Praça do Congresso (under renovation at the time of writing), at the inland end of Avenida Eduardo Ribeiro, is the centre of Manaus' nightlife. Bars and restaurants lie along Avenida Eduardo Ribeiro, Avenida 7 de Setembro and Avenida Getúlio Vargas. Bar do Armando, near the opera house, is a traditional rendezvous; it's open from noon to midnight. São Marcos, on Rua Floriano Peixoto, is another traditional bar, recommended for the best chopp and bolinhos de bacahau (fish balls) in town. It's open from 11 am to 9 pm.

The dancing establishments are all clustered in the Cachoeirinha district, north-east of the centre. Nostalgia (☎ 233-9460), at Avenida Ajuricaba 800, is a hot spot for forró. Popular dance spots include the Armazem (Avenida João Batista, near the Amazonas Shopping Centre) and the nightclub at the Hotel Tropical.

Things to Buy

Indian crafts of the Wai-wai and Tikuna tribes are sold at the Museu do Indio. The store is open from 8.30 to 11.30 am and 2.30 to 5 pm on weekdays and from 8.30 to 11.30 am on Saturday. Souvenir Vitoria Regia, at Rua Barroso 375, and Artezanato Da Amazonia, at Rua José Clemente 500, both near the opera house, sell a variety of Amazon arts and handicrafts. Casa das Redes, a couple of blocks inland from the Mercado Municipal in front of the Hotel Amazonas, has a good selection of hammocks at reasonable prices.

Manaus is a free-trade zone. This means

that locally manufactured products with foreign labels – particularly electronic goods – cost less here than elsewhere in Brazil. This doesn't result in significant savings to foreigners, but it does mean that everyone entering or leaving the city must theoretically go through customs. People entering by bus from the south pass through customs at the Careiro ferry landing. Customs is no problem with smaller riverboats, which are far less likely to attract the attention of officials. Travellers arriving via Manaus airport are supposed to declare foreign goods (eg cameras) to avoid a tariff upon departure, but nobody seems to worry about this rule any more.

Foreigners can purchase up to US$2000 worth of tariff-free goods. However, it's worth pointing out that this exceeds the value of goods which may be imported tax-free into the USA and elsewhere. The Zona Franca commercial district is bounded by Avenida Eduardo Ribeiro, Avenida 7 de Setembro and Avenida Floriano Peixoto.

Getting There & Away

Air The Aeroporto Internacional Eduardo Gomes (☎ 621-1212) is on Avenida Santos Dumont, 14 km from the city centre. A reader wrote that 'if you want to save some money the observation deck at the airport is a great place to lay out a sleeping bag and spend the night before an early morning flight'.

From Manaus, it's a five-hour flight to Miami with Lloyd Aereo Boliviano (LAB) or Varig/Cruzeiro, and a four-hour flight to Rio de Janeiro. There are international flights to Caracas (Venezuela), Iquitos (Peru), Georgetown (Guyana), Bogotá (Colombia) and La Paz (Bolivia). US-bound flights from Manaus are in flux. In general, it's cheaper to purchase the ticket abroad and have it sent to Brazil by registered mail.

VASP, Transbrasil and Varig/Cruzeiro serve all major cities in Brazil, and air-taxis and TABA fly to smaller Amazonian settlements. Varig flies to Tabatinga on Tuesdays and Fridays at 10.00 am (US$260).

Varig/Cruzeiro (☎ 622-3090) is at Rua Marcílio Dias 284; VASP (☎ 622 3470) is at Rua 7 de Setembro 993; TABA (☎ 633-3838) is at Avenida Eduardo Ribeiro 664; and Transbrasil (☎ 622-3738) is nearby, at Rua Guilherme Moreira 150.

The general agent for international airlines (☎ 622 2427, 233-9454) can be found at Avenida 7 de Setembro 1945. The general agent for Air France (☎ 233-4942) is at Rua Quintino 149.

Bus The rodoviária (☎ 236-2732 or 158) is six km from the town centre, at the junction of Rua Recife and Avenida Constantino Nery. Phone for information on road conditions. All road travel from Manaus involves ferry transport.

Overland travel southwards from Manaus to Porto Velho on BR-319 has been impossible since 1991. River travel along the Rio Madeira takes up the slack.

The 770-km road north from Manaus to Boa Vista (BR-174) has more unpaved sections, but is usually passable. It lies on either side of the equator, which means that travellers must contend with two rainy seasons. In addition, 100 km of this unpaved road cuts through the tribal lands of the Waimiris. Despite the FUNAI posts, there have been Indian attacks on this route.

The daily União Cascavel bus to Boa Vista takes about 18 hours, but delays are common and the trip can take a lot longer. A ticket costs US$40.

There are Aruaña bus services to the interior towns of Itacoatiara, 290 km east of Manaus (US$10), and Presidente Figueredo (US$6), while Transgil has buses to Manacapuru, 85 km south-west of Manaus (US$4.50).

Boat Three major ports in Manaus function according to high and low-water levels. Bairro Educandos is the port for sailing to Porto Velho. For sailing as far as Caracaraí, on the Rio Branco via the Rio Negro, the requisite high-water port is Ponte de São Raimundo; during low water, the port is Bairro de São Raimundo, about 2.5 km away. The Porto Flutuante serves mainstream Amazon destinations – Belém, Santarém,

Tefé and Benjamin Constant – and is the port used by ENASA.

For information, go to the Porto Flutuante entrance opposite the Praça da Matriz, where the various boat companies have booths that sell tickets and display destinations and fares. The ENASA ticket office (☎ 633-3280) is at Rua Marechal Deodoro 61. Another place with information about sailing times, fares, distances and ports of call is the Superintendência Nacional de Marinha Mercante, or SUNAMAM (☎ 633-1224), at the Merchant Marine Headquarters.

A more time-consuming method of locating a boat is to poke around Escadaria dos Remédios, the docks by the Mercado Municipal or the Porto Flutuante. Don't waste time with the Capitânia do Porto.

Ports of call are marked on the boats, and fares are pretty much standardised according to distance. If you are going on a long trip, it's advisable to get there in the morning of your departure day in order to secure a good spot. Some people even camp on the boat overnight. Remember that the waters drop roughly 10 to 14 metres during the dry season, and this restricts river traffic, particularly in the upper Amazon tributaries.

Although food and drink are included in the fare, it's a good idea to bring bottled water and snacks as a supplement. Unless you have cabin space, you will need a hammock, as well as rope to string it up. It can get windy and cool at night, so a sleeping bag is also recommended. Get there early and hang your hammock in the cooler upper deck, preferably towards the bow.

Beware of theft on boats – a very common complaint. For more advice, see the security section under Dangers & Annoyances in the Facts for the Visitor chapter.

To/From Santarém & Belém Heading downriver, the big boats go in the faster central currents several km from shore. Travelling upriver, they stay more in the slow currents by the riverbanks, though not as close as the smaller boats, which hug the shore. You won't miss much, as there's not much to be seen on the Amazon anyway. If viewing wildlife is a priority, this is not the way to go.

Apart from the ENASA (☎ 633-3280) services, there are now various companies operating passenger boats between Manaus, Santarém and Belém. Prices for hammock

River Town on the Amazon

space average at US$43 to Santarém and US$90 to Belém.

ENASA ferry-catamarans take two days to Santarém and four days downstream to Belém. Cabin accommodation for the five-day tourist cruise from Manaus to Belém starts at US$430 per person. ENASA also has a weekly boat to Belém, departing on Thursdays, which costs US$65. For details of regular ENASA services and other companies operating to Santarém and Belém, see the Getting There & Away sections for those.

To/From Benjamin Constant & Tabatinga

From Manaus, it's a seven-day trip (if all goes well) to Tabatinga on the *Almirante Monteiro*. On the *Avelino Leal* or the *Cidade de Terezina*, it's at least a week's journey to Tabatinga, with stops at Fonte Boa, Foz do Jutai, Vila Nova, Santo Antônio do Içá, Amaturé, São Paulo de Olivença and Benjamin Constant. Various boats make the trip, with ticket prices for passage averaging US$132/78 for cabin/hammock accommodation. Boats to Manaus leave from Tabatinga, spending a night in Benjamin Constant before continuing. The fare for the three to six-day trip is about US$200 in a shared cabin (US$110 if you hang your own hammock), including very basic meals. It is recommended that you take your own snacks and water.

To/From Leticia (Colombia) & Iquitos (Peru)

Travellers can cruise the river between Manaus and Iquitos, Peru. The return or outgoing leg can be flown with Varig/Cruzeiro (four flights a week) between Iquitos and Manaus via Tefé and Tabatinga. There is now an Expresso Loreto *rápido* (fast-boat) passenger service twice weekly from Tabatinga to Iquitos via Leticia. It takes 10 to 12 hours and costs US$50. Alternatively, cargo boats depart from Santa Rosa, Peru (which has replaced the old port, Ramon Castilha). The trip takes three days and costs US$25 to US$30.

For details about travelling to or from Peru on this route, see the overland section in the Getting There & Away chapter. Travellers coming downriver from Peru and Colombia should remember to get their passports stamped in Manaus, at the customs house beside the Porto Flutuante.

To/From Porto Velho

Another long river journey can be taken from Manaus up the Rio Madeira to Porto Velho. The one-week trip costs US$106/77 in cabin/hammock accommodation. For more details, see the Getting There & Away section for Porto Velho.

To/From Caracaraí

There is no longer a regular passenger boat to Caracaraí, but you may be able to find a cargo boat. A bus service operates between Boa Vista and Caracaraí, a trip of about four hours.

To/From São Gabriel da Cachoeira

It is possible to sail up the Rio Negro to São Gabriel da Cachoeira. It takes five or six days and costs US$70.

Getting Around

To/From the Airport

Aeroporto Internacional Eduardo Gomes (☎ 621-1212) is 14 km from the city centre, on Avenida Santos Dumont. The bus marked 'Aeroporto Internacional' runs between the local bus terminus and the airport from 6 am to midnight. The trip takes 40 minutes and costs US$0.50. There's a bilheteria system for taxis – from the airport to the centre costs US$15. When taking a taxi from the centre to the airport, taxistas may try to extract more money – see Dangers & Annoyances in the introduction to the Manaus section.

Bus The local bus terminus is on Praça da Matriz, near the cathedral and a few blocks from the Hotel Amazonas. Beware of child pickpockets here. From this terminus, you can catch buses to Ponta Negra and the sights in town (details provided under the individual sights). A more expensive (but quicker) option to reach Ponta Negra is the Tropical Hotel shuttle bus (details are provided in the Places to Stay – top end section for Manaus, under Tropical Hotel).

To/From the Rodoviária The rodoviária (☎ 236-2732 or 158) is six km from the centre of town. Buses marked 'Ileia', 'Santos Dumont' or 'Aeroporto Internacional' run from the centre via the rodoviária. A taxi to the centre costs around US$7.

MANACAPURU

It's possible to get an idea of the poverty of life in the interior without resorting to days of river travel. Manacapuru, 85 km south-west of Manaus and the Rio Negro, is a river town on the Rio Solimões. The river port and its traffic, the market, the homes and the people of Manacapuru all make for an interesting day trip.

A reader experienced life in Manacapuru first-hand:

I went to Manacapuru to visit my friend, a 33-year-old man who works in Manaus and on the rivers. Manacapuru's residential area is a collection of corrugated tin roof shacks. His home is a three room, eight by 24 foot building elevated less than two feet off the ground by stilts. 'It's ugly, but it's my house.' The house is tiny and spare, but tidy, and the floors are rough wood planks. Folded hammocks and tinted black and white prints of the matriarch, father and favourite daughter (now living in Porto Velho) adorn the walls.

My friend's extended family lives here: his wife (married since age 15), his mother, two of his six children, his brother, sister-in-law and their child (all three suffering with measles). The entire family is illiterate. There is no running water. Foot-wide canals are simply dug into the earth as an open sewerage system – not surprisingly, the water supply is contaminated. The poor sanitation is a direct cause of the high mortality rate from infectious diseases – of my friend's 14 brothers and sisters, only four have survived to adulthood.

Places to Stay

There are hotels in town, in case you miss the boat or the last bus back to Cacau Pirera. The *Hotel Coqueiro* (☎ 361-1505) is at Avenida Eduardo Ribeiro 725.

Getting There & Away

It's possible to take the ferry from São Raimundo to Cacau Pirera (half an hour) then the Transgil bus to Manacapuru (2½ hours) for US$4.50. There are daily boats to

Manaus from Manacapuru, six hours down the Rio Solimões, which cost US$11.

Take the 'São Raimundo' bus from the cathedral in Manaus to the ferry terminal of São Raimundo. There are nine ferries a day in each direction, from 5 am to 11 pm; passage is free. Ferry schedules coincide with buses between Cacau Pirera and Manacapuru.

MAUÉS

In late November or early December, the Festa do Guaraná is celebrated in the town of Maués (about 220 km east of Manaus), the largest cultivator of guaraná.

The first people to cultivate guaraná were the Saterê-Maûé Indians of the Amazon. Originally, the Saterê-Maûé lands encompassed the vast stretch of jungle between the Madeira and Tapajós rivers. Today the Maûé live in a small tribal reservation. They believe that their place of origin, Noçoquem, is on the left bank of the Tapajós, where the rocks talk, and their creation myth links them to guaraná.

Getting There & Away

There is a boat from Manaus downstream to Maués (US$24.50, 18 hours).

TEFÉ

The port of Tefé is about 600 km upstream from Manaus on the Rio Solimões (the Brazilian name for this stretch of the Amazon), and can be visited for jungle tours.

Joaquim de Jesus Lopes is a local who can tailor trips for biologists, ornithologists, botanists and curious travellers. These trips can last a minimum of three days, but Joaquim Lopes prefers to take full-week tours, and will do longer tours if advance notice is given. Only Portuguese is spoken. Travellers either take along their own tent and hammock or use jungle shelters. Tour costs include fuel, food, boat hire and guiding fee (discuss the price of each tour component individually) – expect to pay at least US$35 per day for a group of three people. Contact Joaquim Lopes at his home, at Rua Marechal Deodoro 801.

THE NORTH

The Origin of Guaraná

Long ago at Noçoquem, in the beginning of all things, lived two brothers and a sister, Ohiamuaçabe. Ohiamuaçabe, also known as Uniai, was so beautiful and wise that every animal desired her. Of all the animals, the snake was the first to express his desire and act upon it. With a magic perfume, the snake enchanted Uniai and made her pregnant.

Her brothers were none too pleased, and kicked Uniai out of Noçoquem. The child was born far from Noçoquem, but Uniai often told her son about Noçoquem and of the brazil-nut tree which grew there. Although the brothers had a parakeet and a macaw on guard at the brazil-nut tree, the child wanted to taste the delicious nuts, and as he grew stronger and more beautiful, his desire to taste the nuts also grew. Finally, he convinced his mother to accompany him to the tree.

The birds spotted the ashes of a fire in which mother and child had roasted the delicious brazil nuts. After the birds reported the incident, the brothers replaced the inept guard birds with a reliable monkey guard. Now that the boy knew the path to Noçoquem, he returned alone to the tree the following day. The monkey spied the boy, drew his bow and shot the child full of arrows.

Uniai found her dead child beneath the tree. As she buried him, she vowed: 'You will be great; the most powerful tree will grow from you; you will cure sickness, provide strength in war and in love'. From the boy's left eye grew the false guaraná *uaraná-hop*, while from his right eye grew the true guaraná *uaraná-cécé*. This is why the berries of the guaraná look like eyes.

Days later, a child was born from the guaraná tree and emerged from the earth. The child was Uniai's, and he was the first Maûé Indian.

To this day, the Maûé call themselves sons of guaraná, and because of this plant, their favourite decorative colours are red and green. The ritual drink of the Sateré-Maûé Indians is *çapo* of guaraná, which is prepared from the eye-like berries. The berries, collected before the fruit opens, are dried, washed in running water and cooked in earth ovens. Water is added, and the guaraná is moulded into black sticks, which are then dried in a smokehouse. The Maûé shave guaraná flakes from the black sticks, using either the raspy tongue of the pirarucu or a rough stone. The flakes are then mixed into water to make the çapo.

The Maûé drink çapo of guaraná on important occasions, to affirm the life force, to cure all illness, to bring strength in times of war and to bring fertility in times of peace.

Most Brazilians take their guaraná in the form of a tasty sweetened and carbonated soft drink. Coca Cola bottles one of the most popular brands of guaraná soda: Taí Guarana. Like Coke, guaraná is a mild stimulant, but unlike Coke, guaraná is said to have aphrodisiac powers. Brazilians take guaraná to keep themselves up for Carnival. Pharmacies and herbal medicine shops also sell guaraná, in the form of syrups, capsules and powders. ■

Places to Stay

The *Hotel Anilceis* is preferable to the *Hotel Cassandra*, which is cheaper, but less secure.

Getting There & Away

Air Varig/Cruzeiro serves Tefé from Manaus. They have an office in Tefé (☎ 743-2466), at Estrada do Aeroporto 269.

Boat The daily boat from the Porto Flutuante in Manaus leaves at 6 pm and arrives in Tefé about 36 hours later. Tickets cost US$45.

PRESIDENTE FIGUEIREDO

Located 128 km north of Manaus on the highway to Boa Vista, BR-174, is the munic-ipality of Presidente Figueiredo. It has various waterfalls, caves and grottos, including Refúgio Maroaga cave and Cachoeira da Iracema, which are reportedly worth visiting. The Santa Cláudia springs supply mineral water for Manaus.

Places to Stay

There are a few hotels including the *Hotel Maruaga* (☎ 324-1110), the *Hotel Vitoria-Regia* (☎ 312-1186) and the *Pousada Teu Chamego* (☎ 324-1228).

Getting There & Away

Aruanã buses run twice daily from Manaus

Top: Fish at Manaus market
Left: Favela, Manaus
Right: Loading bananas, Manaus

ROBYN JONES

GUY MOBERLY

GUY MOBERLY

Left: Scenery in Careiro, Amazonas
Right: Amazonas boy
Bottom: Amazon tributary

to Presidente Figueiredo, at 8 am and 3.30 pm (US$6).

PARINTINS

Parintins is 420 km east of Manaus, on the island of Tupinambarana, on the Rio Amazonas, near the border of Pará state.

The Parintins Folk Festival, the largest cultural festival of the northern region of Brazil, is held over three days during the last week of June. Dressed in outlandish costumes, the 10,000 or so participants in the parade fill the Bumbódromo (the stadium is shaped like a stylised bull!) and present the rival bulls, Bumbás Caprichoso (blue) and Garantido (red), dancing to the beat of drums and chanting.

The climax of the presentation is when the death of the bull is acted out. Legend has it that Pai Franciso kills his master's bull to satisfy the cravings of his pregnant wife for ox tongue. He is arrested by his master, with the help of some Indians, but is saved when the priest and the Indian witch doctor resuscitate the bull. With the bull arisen from the dead, the party resumes and builds to fever pitch.

Places to Stay

The town's few hotels are quickly booked before the festival. Alternatively, you could try a package tour with boat accommodation.

Getting There & Away

Air There are daily TABA flights from Manaus to Parintins, and during the festival air-taxis are available.

Boat Boats from Manaus take 26 hours and cost around US$28.

TABATINGA & BENJAMIN CONSTANT

These two Brazilian ports are on the border between Brazil, Colombia and Peru, known as the Triple Frontier. Neither is particularly attractive, and most travellers view them as transit points. If you have to wait a few days for a boat, the Colombian border town of Leticia is a much more salubrious place to hang out.

Getting There & Away

Air From Tabatinga, there are three flights weekly to Manaus (US$140) and two flights weekly to Iquitos (US$121 one way, US$156 return). Apart from these commercial passenger flights, cargo planes operate irregularly from Tabatinga to Manaus, and military planes from Ramón Castilla (Peru) to Iquitos (Peru).

Boat Boats down the Amazon to Manaus leave from Benjamin Constant, but usually go up to Tabatinga to load/unload. Regular boats depart from Tabatinga (theoretically) on Wednesday and Saturday mornings and from Benjamin Constant the same night, taking four days and costing US$85 in your own hammock or US$250 for a double cabin. Many other irregular cargo boats take passengers on deck, and some have cabins. Prices and journey times are similar. In the opposite direction, upstream from Manaus to Benjamin Constant, the trip takes between six and 10 days. Food is included but it is of poor quality.

There are frequent colectivos between the Leticia and Tabatinga ports (US$0.40); otherwise, it's a 20-minute walk. In Tabatinga, you must get an entry stamp in your passport from Brazilian officials (who like prospective foreign visitors to dress neatly). There is a ferry service, with two boats sailing daily between Tabatinga and Benjamin Constant (US$2.50, 1½ hours).

Upstream to Iquitos (Peru) from Leticia (Colombia), there is now an Expresso Loreto rápido (fast-boat) passenger service twice weekly. It takes 10 to 12 hours and costs US$50. Alternatively, there are irregular cargo boats departing from Santa Rosa (Peru), which has replaced the old port Ramón Castilla (across the river from Tabatinga), and from Islandia (Peru), on an island opposite Benjamin Constant. The journey takes about three days and costs US$40, food included. Travelling in the opposite direction, downstream from Iquitos to Santa Rosa, the trip takes about 36 hours. You can obtain your entry stamp from Peruvian officials in Puerto Alegría. For information on Islandia, see the requisite section later in this chapter.

LETICIA (COLOMBIA)

On the Amazon River where the borders of Colombia, Brazil and Peru meet, Leticia is the most popular place in Colombian Amazonia, mostly due to its well-developed tourist facilities and its good flight connections with the rest of the country. Leticia has become the leading tourist centre for Colombians thirsty to see primitive tribes and buy their handicrafts, and to get a taste of the real jungle. The influx has upset the natural balance, and today, the Indians work hard on their crafts to keep up with tourist demand. This has also caused prices to rise, so food, accommodation and (especially) the tours

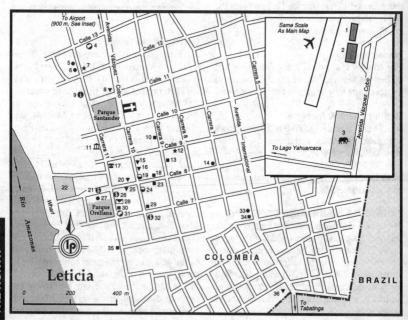

Leticia

offered by locals and travel agents are quite expensive.

For travellers, Leticia is interesting because it is linked via the Amazon to Manaus and Iquitos, and therefore offers reasonably easy travel between Brazil, Colombia and Peru. The best time to visit the region is in July or August, which are the only relatively dry months.

Information

Tourist Office The regional tourist office (☎ 27505) is at No 11-35 Carrera 11.

Money The Banco de Bogotá, at the corner of Carrera 10 and Calle 7, changes travellers' cheques for pesos (from 10.30 am to 1.30 pm). Banks in Leticia will not exchange cash dollars. There are several casas de câmbio near the corner of Calle 8 and Carrera 11 which convert to or from US dollars, Colombian pesos, Brazilian reais and Peruvian soles. There are also casas de câmbio in Tabatinga, Brazil, but they usually pay less than you can get in Leticia.

Post & Telephone The post office is located on Carrera II opposite the Parque Orellana. There are also telephones on Carrera II near the corner of Calle 9.

Immigration The DAS (security police) office on Calle 9 is open from 7 am to noon and 2 to 6 pm Monday to Saturday. This is where you get your passport stamped when leaving or entering Colombia.

Foreign Consulates The Brazilian Consulate is on Calle 13, and is open Monday to Friday from 8 am to 2 pm. The Peruvian Consulate, on Carrera 11, is open from 8.30 am to 2.30 pm Monday to Friday.

Things to See & Do

Leticia has become a tourist town not for what the town itself offers, but for the surrounding region. However, as all transport is by river and there are no regular passenger boats, it's difficult to get around cheaply on your own. All trips are monopolised by tourist agents and by locals with their own boats.

The one-day tour offered by the two major travel agencies, Turamazonas (in the Parador

---

PLACES TO STAY

10	Residencias Marina
13	Residencias Fernando
18	Residencias La Manigua
23	Residencias Primavera
29	Hotel Colonial
30	Hotel Anaconda
34	Residencias Internacional
35	Parador Ticuna

PLACES TO EAT

8	La Casa del Pan
15	Restaurante Buccaneer
16	Restaurante Sancho Panza
20	Cafetería La Barra
25	El Viejo Tolima
36	Restaurante Murallas de Cartagena

OTHER

1	Aerosucre Warehouse
2	Airport Terminal
3	Jardín Botánico Zoológico
4	Brazilian Consulate
5	Inderena
6	Satena
7	Police Station
9	Tourist Office
11	Museo Etnográfico
12	DAS (Tourist Police)
14	Gallera
17	Telephones
19	Colectivos to Tabatinga
21	Casas de Câmbio
22	Market, Três Fronteras & Expreso Amazonas
24	Taxi Stand
26	Banco Ganadero
27	Expreso Aéreo
28	Air Avianca & Post Office
31	Peruvian Consulate
32	Banco de Bogotá
33	Amazon Jungle Trips

THE NORTH

Ticuna) and Anaconda Tours (in the Hotel Anaconda), will cost you around US$30. These excursions are well-organised standard tours, and don't offer anything too adventurous.

It is better value to contract a local independent operator charging similar or higher prices than those offered by the agencies, then negotiate. Make sure you clearly delineate the conditions of the trip, the places you want to visit and the prices. Pay only part of the tour price on departure and the balance at the end. A three to five-day tour is the best idea.

A reader has recommended Antonio Cruz Pérez (☎ 27377), at Avenida International No 6-25, near the border. This guide is knowledgeable about the Indian way of life but does not want commercialisation to destroy it.

Among the places to visit, **Isla de los Micos**, 40 km up the Amazon from Leticia, is the number-one spot for the tour business. There are over 10,000 small, yellow-footed monkeys that live on the island. A footpath has been made through a part of the island and it allows you to see the lush jungle vegetation.

The **Parque Nacional Amacayacu** is a nature reserve which takes in a large area of jungle to the north of Puerto Nariño. A new and spacious visitors' centre has been built beside the Amazon. From the centre you can explore the park, but most places are accessible only by water.

The main Indian tribes living in the region are the Ticunas and Yaguas. The major settlement of the Ticunas is **Arara**, but the village is on the route taken by almost every tour, so it's become something of a theatre, with Indians as the actors. The Yaguas are more primitive, and ethnically different; they are noted for their *achiote*, a red paint used on the face.

Places to Stay

At a typical budget place in Leticia, you will pay around US$5/7 for singles/doubles – try the *Residencias La Manigua* (☎ 271210),

the *Apartamentos Jolamar* (☎ 27016) or the *Residencias Marina*. If those are full, try the *Residencias Internacional* (☎ 28066), on Avenida Internacional, near the border. The *Residencias Primavera* is across the street from La Manigua. It's not bad, but its bar with music at full volume can be quite irritating. At the pleasant *Residencias Fernando* (☎ 27362) you will pay US$8/12 for singles/doubles.

If you want something flashier, check out the *Parador Ticuna* (☎ 27241), with singles/doubles for US$40/55, or the *Hotel Anaconda* (☎ 27119), at the same price. The *Hotel Colonial* is in the same price range, but it is not as good.

Places to Eat

The food is not bad in Leticia, though it is fairly expensive. Obviously, the local speciality is fish; don't miss the delicious gamitana. Also try copoasú juice, known to Brazilians as cupuaçu, which is a local fruit somewhat similar in taste to guanábana. Fizzy drinks and beer are expensive.

The *Restaurante Sancho Panza*, on Carrera 10, it is one of Leticia's cheapest. It has a menu with set dishes for US$1.75. Next door, at the *Buccaneer*, or at *El Viejo Tolima*, on Calle 8, you can have tastier meals for slightly more. Opposite is *Cafetería La Barra*, a popular place for fruit juices. *La Casa del Pan*, in the Parque Santander, is a good place for breakfast. *Murallas de Cartagena*, next to the border, is open until late at night.

If you want to eat in a more up-market restaurant, try the *Hotel Anaconda* or the *Parador Ticuna*.

Getting There & Away

Air Air Avianca has three flights weekly to Bogotá (US$112). Aerosucre runs several cargo flights a week to Bogotá, and these sometimes take passengers (about US$75). Enquire at the airport. Satena flies to/from Bogotá on Sunday, in light planes (US$96). It is difficult to get on these flights unless you book in advance. Expreso Aéreo, a newly established local carrier, has flights from

Leticia to Iquitos on Wednesday and Sunday, in light planes (about US$102).

There are no international flights from Leticia to Brazil, but from Tabatinga, just across the border in Brazil, you can fly to Manaus or Iquitos – see the Getting There & Away section for Tabatinga.

Boat Boats down the Amazon to Manaus leave from Benjamin Constant. For details of these, and of connections between Leticia, Benjamin Constant and Tabatinga, see the Getting There & Away section for Tabatinga & Benjamin Constant.

Irregular cargo boats to Puerto Asís (Colombia), on the upper reaches of the Rio Putumayo, can take up to 20 days, and the price varies substantially – from US$60 to US$120, food usually included. From Puerto Asís, you can continue by road to Pasto, or head to Ecuador via San Miguel. It's much better to do this route in reverse, ie downstream, as it is faster and cheaper.

ISLANDIA (PERU)

Islandia is a grubby Peruvian river village on an island opposite Benjamin Constant. There's no accommodation available at Islandia, so boat passengers arriving from Iquitos must travel by motorised-canoe ferry to Benjamin Constant, where they can find a hotel and/or arrange river transport to Manaus.

The downstream trip from Iquitos to Islandia takes about 36 hours, with boats leaving every few days. The cost is around US$20, if you bargain. If you intend to exit Peru here, you'll either have to pick up a stamp at immigration in Iquitos or arrange with the boat captain to stop at Puerto Alegría, the riverside guard post in the border area. If entering Brazil, visit the Polícia Federal in either Benjamin Constant or Tabatinga. Alternatively, you can take the Expresso Loreto rápido from Iquitos to Tabatinga (US$50). It runs three times a week and the trip takes 10 to 12 hours. The boats call at Santa Rosa's immigration posts.

In Iquitos, there's a Brazilian Consulate at

Lores 363; the Colombian Consulate is on the Putumayo side of the Plaza de Armas.

Roraima

The remote and beautiful mountain region straddling the Venezuelan border to the north of Roraima is perhaps the ultimate Amazon frontier. Roraima is the least populated state in Brazil. This rugged land is home to the Yanomami, who represent about one-third of the remaining tribal Indians of the Amazon. Because the Indian lands are sitting on huge deposits of iron, cassiterite and gold, the Yanomami are threatened by the building of roads, and encroachment from garimpeiros and others seeking to expropriate these lands. Although the Brazilian government has declared the area a special Indian reserve, this declaration will be worthless unless the government is prepared to enforce it and eject trespassers from Yanomami lands.

For a description of the Yanomami, see the section on Indians under Population & People in the Facts about the Country chapter.

Roraima state is one hour behind Brazilian standard time.

BOA VISTA

A planned city on the banks of the Rio Branco, Boa Vista, the capital of Roraima, is the home of more than half the state's population. Most residents are public servants lured to the frontier by government incentives. Although there is now a sealed road between Boa Vista and Venezuela, and many locals take holidays to the Caribbean, the city feels very remote and isolated from the rest of Brazil. Boa Vista is growing at a bounding pace, but while lots of money has been pumped into the construction of an aquatic park, concert grounds and various sporting facilities, there is still much poverty. Most travellers consider this city 'the ultimate bore', 'one of the armpits of the universe', bereft of any interest, and nothing more than a transit point between Brazil and Venezuela. However, there are some intriguing sights in the vicinity of Boa Vista which are becoming increasingly accessible.

Orientation

The city is shaped like an archway, with the base of the arch on the Rio Branco and the arch itself formed by Avenida Major Williams and Avenida Terencio Lima. Avenues radiate from the top, dividing the outskirts into wedges. The city planners were clearly a race of giants: the scale of the place is totally unsuited to pedestrians, who could quite easily spend a whole day trying to do a couple of errands on foot.

The government buildings are located right in the centre, at the intersection of Avenida Ville Roy and Avenida Capitan Ene Garcez, while the commercial district runs from the centre of town along Avenida Jaime Brasil to Rua Floriano Peixoto, on the waterfront.

Information

Tourist Office The information booth at the rodoviária (☎ 224-0288) can supply you with a map and help with booking accommodation. The booth is open from 8 am to 5.30 pm Monday to Friday.

The office of CODETUR (☎ 224-0271; fax 224-4559), the state tourism administration, is at Rua Coronel Pinto 241. It has brochures containing general tourist information. Apparently, the state administration is interested in developing tourism, and advertises the state as an 'Ecological Sanctuary – a beautiful wilderness for the adventurer', but so far, there is very little tourist infrastructure in the region.

Money The Banco do Brasil (☎ 224-6606) is at Avenida Glaycon de Paiva 56, close to Praça do Centro Cívico. A useful moneychanger, with longer opening hours than the bank, is Casa de Câmbio Pedro José (☎ 224-9797), at Rua Araújo Filho 287. It's open to

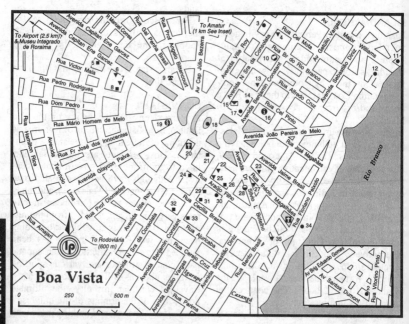

Boa Vista

the public from 8 am to noon Monday to Friday.

Post & Telephone The post office (☎ 224-0699) is on the north side of the Praça do Centro Cívico. The telephone office is on Avenida Capitan Epe Garcez 234.

Venezuelan Consulate The Venezuelan Consulate (☎ 224-2182) is on Avenida Benjamin Constant, and is open from 8 am to noon Monday to Friday. If you arrive early in the morning, you may be able to pick up your visa at noon. You will require one photo, a completed application form and an outbound ticket from Venezuela. Current visa fees are US$10 for British applicants and US$2 for US nationals (cash dollars only).

You'd be well advised to get your visa beforehand and avoid the delay in Boa Vista. More visa details for Venezuela can be found in the section called Visas for Adjoining Countries, in the Facts for the Visitor chapter.

Palácio da Cultura
At the Praça do Centro Cívico is the cultural centre, which has a auditorium for cultural events, a souvenir shop and a library. The library is open Monday to Friday from 8 am to 8 pm, and there you can find *Roraima, O Brasil do hemisfério Norte*. This interesting publication from AMBITEC Fundaçáo do Meio Ambiente e Tecnologia de Roraima describes the state's history, geography, economy and tourism, with a summary in English.

Parque Anauá
The park at Avenida Brigadeiro Eduardo Gomes is quite a hike from the centre, on the way to the airport. Within the vast grounds are gardens and a lake, a museum, an amphitheatre and various sporting facilities, including an aquatic park and a public swimming pool. The grand *forródromo* was recently completed, for forró concerts (typical music and dance enjoyed by immigrants from the Northeast).

Boa Vista Beaches
The main beach is **Praia Grande**, opposite Boa Vista on the Rio Branco. To get there, walk down from the city centre to the waterfront and look for Porto do Babá, at Avenida Major Williams. Cross on a small boat (US$2.50). Babá is a local who organises the Festa do Luau, a party on the beach under a

---

PLACES TO STAY

5	Uiramutan Palace
8	Hotel Euzebio's
21	Aipana Plaza
24	Hotel Ideal
26	Hotel Barrudada
29	Hotel Monte Libano
31	Hotel Brasil
32	Hotel Colonial
33	Hotel Imperial

PLACES TO EAT

4	Pik Nik
6	Pigalle
7	La Carreta
13	Coisas da Terra
22	La Gondola
23	Mister Kilo
25	Margô Pizzaria
27	Pigalle
35	Black & White

OTHER

1	Parque Anauá
2	Amatur
3	Rent-A-Car Lemans
9	Telephone Office
10	Venezuelan Consulate
11	Porto do Babá
12	Acquatour
14	Prefeitura
15	Post Office
16	CODETUR
17	Biblioteca e Palácio da Cultura
18	Palácio do Governo & Praça do Centro Cívico
19	Banco do Brasil
20	Catedral
28	Central Bus Terminal
30	Casa de Câmbio Pedro José
34	Centro do Artesanato

THE NORTH

full moon (*lua* in Portuguese), with an open fire, and drinks and fruits provided.

Other beaches include **Água Boa** (on the Rio Branco, 15 km from the city centre), and **Caçari**, **Curupira** and **Cauamé** (on the Rio Cauamé).

Organised Tours

Aquatour (☎ 224-6576) is at Rua Floriano Peixoto 505. Eliezer, a local artist and tour operator who speaks English, organises a variety of boat trips in the region, such as a day excursion to Fazenda São Marcos (a cattle ranch) and Forte São Joaquim (the ruins of a colonial fort), upstream on the Rio Branco, or trips to Serra Grande, beaches and creeks downriver. Day tours cost US40. A two-hour tour to Ponte dos Macuxí, Paraná do Surrão and Ilha da Praia Grande, including a walk through forest to an inland lake, costs US\$20. Overnight stays in the jungle (in hammocks) cost US\$60 per person, meals and drinks included. Eliezer also provides transport to the beach opposite Boa Vista (US\$3) and to campsites on the Rio Branco.

Amatur (☎ 224-0004; fax 224-0012) organises tours to Pedra Pintada archaeological site, Lago Caracaraña, waterfalls, Ilha de Maracá ecological station and along the Rio Branco, and 4WD ecological safaris can be organised if booked in advance.

Jean-Luc Félix (☎ 224-6536), Avenida NS da Consolata, is a Belgian who organises hikes to Serra Grande.

Places to Stay

The *Hotel Brasil* (☎ 224-9421), at Avenida Benjamin Constant 331, is definitely a rock-bottom cheapie, with quartos at US\$7/8 for singles/doubles. The *Hotel Colonial* (☎ 224-5190), at Rua Ajuricaba 532, has simple but comfortable rooms with air-con for US\$12 per person. At the *Hotel Ideal* (☎ 224-6296), Rua Araújo Filho 467, very basic singles/doubles cost US\$12/19. The *Hotel Monte Libano* (224-7232), at Avenida Benjamin Constant 319, has rooms with fan for US\$8/12, while the *Hotel Imperial* (☎ 224-5592), at Avenida Benjamin Constant 433,

has barely decent rooms for US\$10. The *Hotel Tres Nações* (☎ 224-3439) is near the bus terminal, at Avenida Ville Roy 188W, São Vicente. It charges US\$9/13/20 singles/doubles/doubles with air-con.

The *Hotel Barrudada* (☎ 224-9335; fax 224-5050), at Rua Araújo Filho 228, has recently been renovated. Clean apartamentos with air-con, TV and refrigerator cost US\$24/30 a single/double; the *Hotel Euzebio's* (☎ 224-0300; fax 224-8690), at Rua Cecília Brasil 1107, offers apartamentos for around US\$36/42.

Boa Vista's more up-market hotels include the *Uiramutan Palace* (☎ 224-9912; fax 224-9221), at Avenida Capitan Ene Garcez 427, which charges US\$50/72 for single/double rooms, and the *Aipana Plaza* (☎ 224-4800; fax 224-4116), at Praça do Centro Cívico, Joaquim Nabuco 53, with rooms at US\$75/96.

Places to Eat

Coisas da Terra, on Avenida Benjamin Constant, serves savoury snacks, quiche, pastries, cakes, and sucos. *Pigalle*, at Avenida Capitan Ene Garcez 153, does great pizza, and hosts live music at weekends. *Margô Pizzaria*, at Rua Benjamin Constant 193, is another place where you can get pizza and pasta.

Mister Kilo, at Rua Inácio Magalhães 346, has good-value self-service meals, and *La Gondola*, at Avenida Beijamim Constant 35W, is also a good place for inexpensive (prato feito) meals. *La Carreta*, at Rua Cecília Brasil 1107, next to Hotel Euzebio's, has a good-value meat buffet. For good local fish dishes, try *Black & White*, at Praça Barreto Leite 11.

Also worth a look are the hotel restaurants, such as those at the *Aipana Plaza* and the *Uiramutan Palace*.

Things to Buy

Centro de Artesanato, at Rua Floriano Peixoto 158, is open from 8 am to 6 pm Monday to Friday. Feira de Artesanato da Praça da Bandeira, open on Fridays, Saturday and Sunday from 5 to 11 pm, sells local and Indian arts and handicrafts.

Getting There & Away

Air Varig/Cruzeiro (☎ 224-2351), at Rua Araújo Filho 91, operates daily flights to and from Manaus. Meta Mesquita Taxi Aéreo (☎ 224-7300), at the Boa Vista international airport, flies to Manaus three times a week.

Bus From Boa Vista to Manaus, it's a 15-hour bus ride (road conditions and trip time are erratic), with one ferry crossing along the way. There's one departure daily (at 8 am) and the ticket costs US$40. Hitching can be difficult, as the traffic – mostly gravel trucks – is usually local.

If you're not limited by time, another option is to take the bus from Boa Vista to Caracaraí (US$5, two hours). From there, you may be able to catch a ride on a cargo boat to Manaus (a seven to 10-day trip).

For details of bus services to the Venezuelan and Guyanese borders, see the following Crossing the Border sections.

Crossing the Venezuelan Border The road linking Boa Vista to Santa Elena (Venezuela) has recently been paved, so the bus ride takes about 3½ hours in either direction. The bus departs daily at 8.30 am from the rodoviária in Boa Vista. Tickets (US$13) seem to sell out fast – buy yours the day before departure. For more details about the border crossing, see the Getting There & Away section for Santa Elena.

Crossing the Guyanese Border A bus from Boa Vista to Bonfim leaves on Mondays, Thursdays and Fridays at 4 pm. The 125-km trip takes four hours and costs US$8.50. Once in Bonfim, pick up your exit stamp from the Polícia Federal, then slog the five km to the border at the Rio Tacutu. There, you can hire a canoe across to Lethem (in Guyana), where there are places to stay. There is a road from Lethem to Georgetown, but it can become impassable in the wet. We met a couple of Canadians who had made the three-day trip overland from Georgetown to

Lethem on a truck, for US$10 each. For the return trip to Georgetown, they had decided to fly! Beware that Guyanese officials worry about illegal immigration from Brazil, and tend to scrutinise travellers fairly carefully here.

Guyana Airways flies to and from Georgetown and Lethem three times a week (US$55). Trans Air has daily flights, which groups can charter.

You may want to save yourself the trouble of a difficult overland passage by flying directly to Georgetown from Boa Vista – TABA has flights from Boa Vista to Georgetown for about US$130 return.

Getting Around

Whoever planned Boa Vista on such a vast scale clearly didn't think about pedestrians – getting around on foot is really difficult. Bicycles are a better option – to find out about renting one, ask Eliezer (at Aquatour), or at Porto do Babá.

The airport (☎ 224-3680) is four km from the city centre. To get there, take a bus marked 'Aeroporto' from the municipal bus terminal. The taxi fare from the airport to the centre is about US$10.

The rodoviária (☎ 224-0606) is some three km from the centre – about 40 minutes on foot! Take a bus marked '13 de Setembro' from the municipal bus terminal, and get off at the bus stop beside a supermarket (which is opposite the rodoviária). A taxi from the centre to the rodoviária costs about US$10.

AROUND BOA VISTA

Mt Roraima (2875 metres), one of Brazil's highest peaks, straddles the Brazilian/Venezuelan/Guyanese border. The easiest access for climbers is from the Venezuela side – for more details, see the section called Mt Roraima & the Gran Sábana, later in this chapter.

The archaeological site of **Pedra Pintada** (Painted Rock) is a large granite rock 140 km north of Boa Vista, next to the Rio Parimé. The mushroom-shaped boulder is about 60 metres across by 35 metres high, with painted inscriptions on its external face and

Around Boa Vista

Parque Nacional do Roraima Monte

0   50   100 km

Mont Roraima (2 875m)

To Cidade Bolívar & Caracas

VENEZUELA   Santa Elena

GUYANA

Santo Domingo

Pedra Pintada

Área Indígena Raposa Serra do Sol

Ilha de Maracá (Estação Ecológica de Maracá)

Área Indígena Aracá

Área Indígena São Marcos

Normandia

Lago Caracanã

To Georgetown

Lethem

Rio Uraricuera

BR174

Bonfim

Alto Alegre

Área Indígena Yanomami

Serra Grande

Mucajaí

Boa Vista

Área Indígena Manoá Pium

RORAIMA

BR210

Rio Grande

Caracaraí   To Manaus

---

caves at its base. There are no buses that go to the area, but tours can be organised by Amatur.

Lago Caracanã, a large lake 180 km from Boa Vista, is a popular weekend destination. A bus departs for the lake from the rodoviária in Boa Vista at 10 am on Saturday and returns at noon on Sunday. There's a campsite and a basic hotel at the lake.

The **Estação Ecológica da Ilha de Maracá** (an ecological reserve) is an island 120 km from Boa Vista, on the Rio Uraricoera. The reserve can only be visited with permission from IBAMA (☎ 224-4011) in Boa Vista.

The municipality of **Caracaraí** is 142 km south of Boa Vista, on the west margin of the Rio Branco. This region, considered the median part of the river, has a number of rock blocks forming river rapids and waterfalls, the most popular being the Bemquerer waterfall. The area also has primitive rock paintings.

SANTA ELENA (VENEZUELA)

Santa Elena is on the only land-border crossing between Venezuela and Brazil.

Information

Money Various shops, travel agencies and hotels will change US dollars (at rates 3% lower than the bank rate) and possibly travellers' cheques (but at rates up to 10% lower than the bank rate).

Immigration If you're heading for Brazil, pick up an exit stamp from the DIEX office, which is behind the Brazilian Consulate, on a hill near the bus terminal at the north-eastern edge of town. It's open from 8 am to noon and 2 to 5 pm Monday to Friday and from 8 to 10 am and 2 to 4 pm on weekends.

Places to Stay

There is no shortage of places to stay and eat in Santa Elena. Expect to pay at least US$7.50 for a standard room.

Getting There & Away

There are four buses daily between Santa Elena and San Francisco de Yuruaní, on the Cuidad Guayana to Santa Elena Highway. See also the Getting There & Away section for Mt Roraima & the Gran Sábana.

Crossing the Border A paved road runs through the Venezuelan towns of Ciudad Bolívar, Tumeremo and El Dorado to Santa Elena, then continues to Boa Vista, Brazil. Whether entering or leaving Venezuela at Santa Elena, you can count on numerous unpleasant encounters with the police and border patrols. They have a well-deserved reputation for 'confiscating' travellers' belongings.

Most people arrive in Santa Elena in the evening, but try to get there earlier if you hope to secure a hotel room. To avoid having to endure morning border mayhem, get your ticket, then your exit stamp at DIEX, the day before crossing.

When departing for Brazil, pick up your exit stamp from DIEX and board the bus for Boa Vista at the bus terminal near the immigration office. Be wary of fellow passengers and officials who board the bus. Theft is common, particularly during the periodic clumsy searches which punctuate the ride to the border.

Brazilians are strict about border control here, and carefully scrutinise travellers. If you've ever overstayed a Brazilian visa and found your way onto their records, you may want to try an alternative border crossing or simply fly in.

The road linking Santa Elena to Boa Vista has recently been paved; the bus trip now takes 3½ hours. The bus leaves Santa Elena at 8.30 am. The fare, payable in bolívares or Brazilian reais (Venezuela currency is abbreviated B$), is US$13 (B$750).

For details about the Venezuela Consulate and obtaining Venezuela visas in Boa Vista, refer to the Boa Vista section in this chapter.

MT RORAIMA & THE GRAN SÁBANA

From the Indian village of San Francisco de Yuruaní, 60 km north of Santa Elena, you can hire a guide to take you to the geographically spectacular and botanically unique area around Mt Roraima, which straddles the Brazilian/Venezuelan/Guyanese border.

From there, it's 22 km to Paray Tepui, a small Indian village and the entrance to the park. You may also hire a guide here. From Paray Tepui, the trail is easy to follow, although it quickly deteriorates after rain. There's the odd rattlesnake, but no other large wildlife.

Although you must bring food from Santa Elena, good water can be found in streams every four or five km along the way. The trail passes one of the world's highest waterfalls. The top of Roraima is a moonscape; it would be very easy to get lost, so don't wander far. You might consider spending an extra day on top of the mountain, but be prepared for cool drizzle and fog.

The return trip from Santa Elena will take five days, but some people allow up to two weeks in the area.

The following is a description by some readers who climbed the mountain:

In San Francisco de Yuruaní, the starting point for climbs up Roraima, you can hire a guide for US$15 to US$19 per day and for just a few dollars more, the guide will carry your gear. Guides are cheaper and easier to obtain in the Indian village of Paray Tepui. Hire a guide, because the dense cloud cover and strange landscape on top can get a person lost very quickly. Furthermore, guides know of two 'hotels' on the mountain, cliff overhangs under which you can camp and stay dry!

Jeeps to Paray Tepui charge a set rate of US$31 each way. If you choose not to hire a jeep, the hike between San Francisco and Paray Tepui is a full day. The best days for hitching between the two towns are on Sunday and Monday going to Paray Tepui, and on Friday returning to San Francisco, as the school teachers at Paray Tepui leave the town for the weekend. Mosquito repellent is absolutely essential.

Pack light but for wet weather. The trail runs under a waterfall when there is a lot of rain. If you want hot food on top, bring a stove, because there is absolutely no firewood there.

The Legend of Mt Roraima

In the past, there were no hills or mountains in this region. Various Indian tribes lived here, and game, fish and fruits were plentiful.

One day, an alien banana plant sprouted, and it grew vigorously. The witch doctors received a message prohibiting people from touching the plant because it was a sacred being. If those orders were disobeyed, game would disappear, fruit-bearing plants would shrivel and the region's geography would change. The banana plant produced various bunches of golden bananas, but the people dared not touch them. One morning, however, to the surprise of the local tribes, the plant and the golden bananas were found to have been cut down and taken away. Within moments, there was thunder and lightning. The game fled and the birds, singing mournfully, flew away. Then there was a downpour, and the ground started lifting spectacularly up into the clouds, forming Mt Roraima. ■

The trail from Paray Tepui runs over open savanna and crosses several small streams. You will cross one river which is about 10 metres wide and is called Quebrada de Piedras or Río de Atuc. The next large river is Cuquenan. It is 10 to 20 metres wide. Camp on the far side of Cuquenan.

The next day, you can make it all the way to the 'hotel' on top of Roraima, or you can camp at the base just before the trail enters the jungle. On the return trip, try to make it as far as the Quebrada de Piedras on the first night. If it is raining on Cuquenan, the levels of the rivers can rise very rapidly. You should cross them as quickly as possible – you may even need a rope.

Greg & Kevin Merrell, USA

The Gran Sábana has been described as 'beautiful open rolling grassland with pockets of cool jungle, all eerily deserted and silent'. It's best to visit the area in the dry season (December to March), but even then, you will still be wet much of the time.

Getting There & Away

You can travel by bus from Santa Elena to San Francisco de Yuruaní (60 km) and hike for six to eight hours to Paray Tepui, or hire a jeep in Santa Elena (at least US$80). If you'd rather hitch, the best chances of finding a lift will be at the petrol station at the north end of Santa Elena.

Getting around the Gran Sábana can be difficult if you want to rely on public transport – an organised tour from Santa Elena could be an option.

Rondônia & Acre

The states of Rondônia and Acre, previously undeveloped frontier regions, have undergone rapid development, mainly as a result of the construction of BR-364; the highway already runs from Cuiabá to Rio Branco, via Porto Velho, and it's projected to extend as far as Cruzeiro do Sul. The two states are of intense interest to environmentalists studying the effects of deforestation, which has left vast tracts of land looking like the aftermath of a holocaust. '

Many travellers will simply pass through these states en route to or from neighbouring Peru or Bolivia, but all should be aware that both states, especially Rondônia, are major distribution centres for the Peruvian and Bolivian cocaine trade. Travellers are generally left alone, providing they mind their own business.

Guajará-Mirim is an entry point for the 'Rota Formiguinha' (Ant Route), favoured by the small-scale smugglers – hence the reference to ants – who arrive from Bolivia with the white stuff hidden within their baggage or concealed in their vehicles. Large-scale smugglers use *aviãozinhos* (light aircraft) to pick up the cocaine in Bolivia and then fly it to the secret landing strips in Rondônia – for example, in the vicinity of Cacoal, Ji-Paraná and Rolim Moura. From there, the goods are distributed to Rio, São Paulo and fazendas in Mato Grosso state.

Another of the so-called 'Transcoca' highways runs is from San Joaquim (in Bolivia) to the Rio Guaporé, where the cocaine is ferried across to the Brazilian town of Costa Marques for distribution in Brazil.

Some of the cocaine is destined for domestic consumption, but most of it is ultimately exported to the USA and Europe. Recent reports have indicated that drug kingpins in both Rondônia and Acre have moved into the processing business. It is an open secret that various politicians in Rondônia are involved in drug-running.

Rondônia

In 1943 Getúlio Vargas created the Territory of Guaporé from chunks of Amazonas and Mato Grosso. In 1981 the Territory of Guaporé became the state of Rondônia, named in honour of Marechal Cândido Mariano da Silva Rondon, the soldier who 'tamed' the region. A legendary figure, Rondon was honoured by the Indians he helped subdue. He linked Cuiabá, Porto Velho and Rio Branco by telegraph to the rest of Brazil.

In recent years, roads and a gold rush displaced the Nordestinos from the desert into the jungles, and the few remaining Indians from the jungles into the cities. Rondônia's population is mostly made up the poor but hopeful migrants from the Northeast.

Rondônia state is one hour behind Brazilian standard time.

National Parks & Biological Reserves
In Porto Velho, contact IBAMA (☎ 223-3607), at Avenida Jorge Teixeira 3477, Bairro C E Silva, for details about national parks and ecological reserves in Rondônia. (Take the 'Aeroporto' bus from the centre and ask the conductor to tell you when to get off.) Only Portuguese is spoken, and the office is clearly overworked and restricted in its powers and facilities, but genuinely interested travellers who can travel rough may be helped with introductions to park staff and details about access options.

Reserva Biológica do Guaporé The main attractions in this reserve are flora and fauna similar to that found in the Pantanal – hence the reserve's nickname, 'Pantanal de Rondônia'. To reach the reserve, take a boat from Costa Marques to Pau d'Óleo (about six hours, 160 km). There is a government fazenda with accommodation (cabanas), and transport into the reserve. Prior to departure from Costa Marques, contact Senhor Amos (☎ 651-2239), who is in charge of the local IBAMA (Posto da Fiscalização) office, to check the latest information on access and facilities.

Reserva Biológica do Jarú At present there are two ways to visit this reserve, which is in the north-east corner of Rondônia. The long-distance option is to contact Senhor Erismar (☎ 421-4164), the regional director of IBAMA in the town of Ji-Paraná, 376 km from Porto Velho. The closest access to the park is provided by a private guide, Ubalde Almeida (☎ 521-2827). He arranges tours from Cachoeira Nazaré, where he also offers accommodation (cabanas).

Parque Nacional de Pacaás Novas As yet, there is no tourist access to this park, and no infrastructure. Those interested in a visit must seek permission from either Senhor Erismar or Gilson Macedo, at the IBAMA office in Ji-Paraná (☎ 421-4164). These officials may be willing to arrange 4WD transport from Ouro Prêto do Oeste, along Linhea 81 into the park, where there is rough accommodation in camps.

Estação Biológica Cuniã Lago do Cuniã, a biological reserve 110 km north of Porto Velho, on the Rio Madeira, contains the state's largest spawning area for fish and is renowned for its abundant birdlife. This reserve is accessible only by boat. Contact Douter Eurico, at the IBAMA office in Porto Velho, for details.

PORTO VELHO

Now capital of the young state of Rondônia, Porto Velho is rapidly losing its frontier feel. The streets have been paved, most of the Indians are dead and the forests are rapidly being felled. Nevertheless, 20th-century Porto Velho retains elements of the American Wild West: land-hungry cattle ranchers, fierce Indians, gold prospectors and desperados of all kinds.

The newspaper headlines tell the story, with articles ranging from the gold strike to border cocaine-trafficking, from poaching to conflicting land claims settled at gunpoint.

History

During the 17th and 18th centuries, Portuguese bandeirantes in pursuit of gold and Indian slaves crossed the lines drawn by the Treaty of Tordesillas and entered what is now known as Rondônia, to roam the Guaporé and Madeira river valleys. Since the Spanish were incapable of defending themselves from these incursions, the occupation was officially sanctioned in lofty Latin terms, which meant that it was ignored. The Portuguese secured their new possessions by building the fortress of Principe da Beira (1783), at the confluence of the Mamoré and Guaporé rivers.

The Treaty of Tordesillas was kept more in the breach than the observance; the Portuguese continued to push west and occupy Bolivian lands. The Brazil-Bolivia Treaty of Friendship (1867) and the Treaty of Petrópolis (1901) addressed Bolivian grievances. The Bolivians ceded the region – known today as the state of Acre – in return for UK£2 million and the construction of a railway along the upper reaches of the Rio Madeira (to give landlocked Bolivia access to world rubber markets via the Amazon).

The Public Works Construction Company of London started work on a railway in 1872, but abandoned the project after two years, due to rampant disease and Indian attacks. These swampy jungle lands came to be known as the most hostile in the world.

In 1907, the North American company Jeckyll & Randolph began work on a 364-km railway from the vicinity of Vila do Santo Antônio do Rio Madeira to the Bolivian border town of Riberalta, on the Rio Mamoré. German, Jamaican and Cuban workers, and old Panama Canal hands, were brought in as labourers to do the job. The track was completed in 1912; however, this achievement claimed the lives of thousands of workers, who perished from malaria, yellow fever and gunfights.

Since the railway did not go as far as intended (above the rapids of Rio Mamoré at Riberalta) and the price of rubber had plummeted on the world market, the project was effectively useless. However, the towns of Guajará-Mirim and Porto Velho were founded at either end of the completed railway, which functioned sporadically until it was officially closed, in 1972.

Today the line is used only as a tourist novelty, from the Porto Velho end. Marcio Souza chronicles the whole brutal story in his book *Mad Maria* (published by Avalon in an English-language paperback edition), which is mandatory reading for anyone interested in how a small parcel of the 'Green Hell' was briefly conquered.

During WW II, when the Japanese occupation of Malaysia cut Allied rubber supplies, rubber production in the Amazon picked up briefly once again. In 1958 cassiterite (tin ore) was discovered. The mining of cassiterite and timber extraction now constitutes Rondônia's principal source of wealth, but other minerals – gold, iron, manganese and precious stones – are also found in the region.

In fact, Porto Velho is riding out the tail end of a gold rush. There are still a few gold shops along Avenida 7 de Setembro, all empty save for the old-fashioned powder scales in glass cases. The prospectors haven't seen much gold lately, but they're still dredging the rivers, dumping mercury as they go. Most of the town's food is still brought in from São Paulo, half a continent away.

Orientation

Porto Velho sits on the right-hand bank of the Rio Madeira, almost contiguous with the state of Amazonas. The Rio Madeira, a 3240-km-long tributary of the Amazon, is formed by the Mamoré and Abunã rivers.

Porto Velho's main street is Avenida 7 de Setembro, which stretches almost two km, from the riverfront docks and Madeira Mamoré train station to Avenida Jorge Teixeira.

The new capital is still a little raw – electric wires slump and dangle over muddy dirt roads, and street vendors fry up potatoes and plantains for passers-by, but the mining-supply shops and gun stores have been replaced by electronics stores, record shops and clothing markets. 'Compra-se ouro' signs indicate the few gold shops where prospectors still bring their gold powder to be weighed and sold. The powder is melted into bullion and smuggled out to avoid government taxes.

You can't fail to notice the appalling volume of distorted street music, which is brought to a crescendo by a cruising noisemobile, complete with a battery of eight giant loudspeakers mounted on the roof. We'd willingly have foregone the advertised 30% discount at a local clothing shop if the bloody machine had only stopped broadcasting immediately!

Information

Tourist Offices There is a Departamento de Turismo de Rondônia (DETUR) office (☎ 223-2276) at Avenida Padre Chiquinho 670, Esplanada das Secretarias. It's difficult to find and has limited resources. The office is open from 8 am to noon and 2 to 6 pm Monday to Friday.

The tourist office in the Prefeitura, opposite the cathedral, is a poor source of information.

IBAMA The state office of IBAMA (☎ 223-33607) is at Avenida Jorge Teixeira 3477, Bairro C E Silva. For details about national parks and ecological reserves in Rondônia, see the separate section in this chapter.

Money The main branch of the Banco do Brasil is on Avenida José de Alencar.

Post & Telephone The main post office is on Avenida Rogério Weber. The head office of TELERON, the state telephone company, is on Avenida Presidente Dutra.

Bookshop Livaria da Rose, at Avenida Rogério Weber 1967, has a reasonable selection of books (in English, French and German) for exchange. If you want a survey (in Portuguese) of the history of Rondônia, pick up a copy of *Kayan*, by Emanuel Pinto.

Estação Madeira-Mamoré & Museu Ferroviária

The original terminal of the Madeira-Mamoré railway is Porto Velho's main tourist attraction. For details about the history of this railway, see the History section for Porto Velho. Restoration work on the terminal and museum was completed in late 1993.

Housed in a huge train shed, the museum displays train relics, memorabilia, and photographs charting the construction of the railway and the history of the Madeira-Mamoré line. Completed in 1912, the railway quickly fell into disuse. By 1931 the private railway had been nationalised, and was abandoned in 1966. Railway buffs will also get a kick out of the *Colonel Church*. Built in 1872, this dinosaur was the first locomotive in the Amazon. The museum is open from 8 am to 5 pm Monday to Friday.

Train Trips In 1981, in tribute to its historical origins, the new state government reinstated 28 km of the famous Madeira-Mamoré railway. The Maria Fumaça steam locomotive chugs to and from Santo Antônio (seven km from Porto Velho) on Sunday between 9 am and 6 pm. A return ticket for this excursion costs US$1.50.

Museu Estadual

The State Museum, at the intersection of Avenida 7 de Setembro and Avenida Farquar, houses modest exhibits on the state's archaeology, mineralogy, ethnology and natural history. The museum is open on weekdays, from 8 am to 6 pm.

River Beaches

There are several river beaches near the city centre: ask at the tourist office for directions

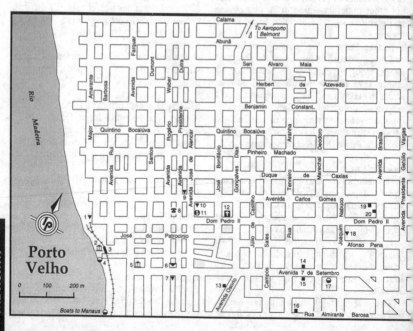

to **Areia Branca** (three km from town), and **Candeias** (20 km off BR-364; take the Linha Novo Brasil bus). The fishing village of **Belmont**, 20 km from Porto Velho, is a calm place to swim or fish.

Parque Circuito
If you are interested in seeing rubber trees, but aren't inclined to launch an expedition into the wilderness to do so, visit the Parque Circuito, on Avenida Lauro Sodré, four km from town on the way to the airport.

Organised Tours
Baretur and Plaktur, the tour agencies at the train-station docks, run daily one-hour booze cruises between 2 and 11 pm (US$2.50, excluding drinks), and excursions to the Santo Antônio rapids.

Festivals
Indian legends and traditions were so cor-

Old steam locomotive, Museu Ferroviário

rupted by Jesuit missionaries that the Indians circulated stories of the Virgin Mary visiting the Amazon. However, theatrical interpretations of authentic Amerindian legends, ritual dances and ceremonies are becoming popular among students in Porto Velho. Call the Teatro Municipal Secretária do Cultura (☎ 223-3836, ext 136) for information.

Along with the Northeastern settlers, folklore was also transplanted from the sertão to the jungle. The saints' days of Santo Antônio, São João and São Pedro are celebrated in June.

Places to Stay – bottom end
The best of the budget hotels is the friendly *Hotel Cuiabano* (☎ 221-4084), at Avenida 7 de Setembro 1180. Quartos cost US$5/8 for singles/doubles; apartamentos with fan cost US$10, single or double. Just across the street, the *Hotel Nunes* (☎ 221-1389) has double quartos for US$10 and apartamentos at US$15. A few metres away, the cheap and grungy *Hotel Sonora* (no phone) has coffin-sized quartos at US$6/8, and apartamentos for US$8/10. There's an on-and-off price war between these hotels; shop around before deciding on one, and check doors and windows for security.

The *Hotel Ouro Fino* (☎ 223-1101), at Avenida Carlos Gomes 2844, near the rodoviária, has clean but musty quartos (with

PLACES TO STAY	OTHER
13 Hotel Iara	2 Museu Ferroviária
14 Hotels Nunes & Sonora	3 Estaçào Madeira-Mamoré
15 Hotel Cuiabano	4 Booze Cruises
16 Hotel Regina	5 Museu Estadual
19 Hotel Vila Rica	6 Post Office
20 Hotel Seltom	8 Telephone Office
21 Hotels Ouro Fino &	11 Banco do Brasil
Amazonas	12 Catedral
	17 Buses to Airport &
PLACES TO EAT	Rodoviária
	22 Rodoviária
1 Restaurante Mirante II	
7 Night Food Stalls	
9 Master Pizza	
10 Genghis Khan	
18 Restaurant Ling	

To Guajará-Mirim

THE NORTH

fan) at US$10/15 a single/double. Next door, the *Hotel Amazonas* has quartos at US$4/8 and apartamentos for US$7/10.

Places to Stay – middle
The *Hotel Iara* (☎ 221-2127), on Avenida Osorio, has fairly ordinary single/double apartamentos with fan at US$10/15. Apartamentos with fridge, air-con and TV cost US$18/28. Better value, and more secure, is the *Hotel Regina* (☎ 224-3411), at Rua Almirante Baroso 1127. Spotless apartamentos with air-con, fridge and TV cost US$24/36.

Places to Stay – top end
The three-star *Hotel Seltom* (☎ 221-7535; fax 221-2900), at Avenida Brasília 2323, charges US$38/49 for singles/doubles. It's part of the same chain as the adjacent five-star *Hotel Vila Rica* (☎ 221-2333; fax 221-2900), Porto Velho's finest hotel. Singles/doubles here cost US$77/93.

Places to Eat
Porto Velho is not known for its haute cuisine, but a few decent restaurants have sprung up recently. The best place for fish is *Remanso do Tucunaré*, at Avenida Brasília 1506. Try the caldeirada of tucunaré and tambaqui.

Genghis Khan, at Avenida Carlos Gomes 714, has outdoor tables, friendly staff and specialises in Japanese food such as sukiyaki and noodle dishes. Across the road, *Master Pizza* has good pizzas and pastas. For Chinese food try *Restaurant Ling*, on Avenida Joaquim Nabuco.

Restaurante Mirante II serves fish dishes, and has an outdoor patio with a great view of the river. Unfortunately, this is sometimes shrouded in smoke; enjoy your meal as the forest on the opposite bank of the river burns before your eyes.

On Avenida Rogério Weber, near the corner of Avenida 7 de Setembro, you'll find some night food stalls with excellent, fresh chicken, meat and salad dishes.

Entertainment
Baretur has a popular floating bar at the docks – if you're up for beer and sweaty dancing, this is the place to go.

Getting There & Away
Air There are flights from Porto Velho to all major Brazilian cities. Major airlines with offices in Porto Velho include VASP (☎ 223-3755), at Rua Tenreiro Arenha 2326, Varig/Cruzeiro (☎ 221-8555), at Rua Campos Sales 2666, and TABA (☎ 221-5172), at Rua Prudente de Moraes 39.

An air-taxi company, TAVAJ (☎ 225-2094), operates three flights a week to Costa Marques.

Bus Porto Velho has bus connections to Rio Branco, Guajará-Mirim, Cuiabá, Humaitá and Costa Marques – services to Manaus have been suspended indefinitely. Driving conditions are generally poor (roads are often impassable during the wet season), so you should view schedules and trip times as optimistic approximations.

For Rio Branco, there are five daily departures (US$13, around 10 hours). There are eight buses a day from Porto Velho to Guajará-Mirim (US$10.50, around five hours), two of which (at 2 pm and midnight) run direct to Guajará-Mirim – buy tickets for these buses in advance, as they tend to fill up quickly.

Boat Boat services run between Porto Velho and Manaus. The US$65/95 fare for hammock/cabin accommodation on the four or five-day trip does include three meals a day, but you should take bottled water. The boats are small and the ride is long, so check out fellow passengers for unsavoury characters before committing yourself.

Most boats go directly to Manaus; others require transfer halfway down the Rio Madeira, at Manicoré. The trip takes anywhere from three days to a week, depending on the level of the water, the number of breakdowns and the availability of onward connections. One reader recommended taking a bus to Humaitá (203 km from Porto

Velho) and then catching a boat to Manaus – this shaves about 24 hours off the normal trip time.

Getting Around

To/From the Airport Aeroporto Belmont (☎ 221-3935) is seven km out of town. You can catch a bus to the city centre via the rodoviária from outside the airport. In the centre, a convenient bus stop for the bus to the airport is on Avenida 7 de Setembro, close to the budget hotels – buses leave from here hourly, on the half hour. The set price for a taxi from the airport to the city centre is US$13, but from the centre to the airport, it costs just US$10.

To/From the Rodoviária The rodoviária (☎ 221-2141) is about two km from the centre, on Avenida Jorge Teixeira. The 'Hospital de Base' bus runs to the rodoviária from Avenida 7 de Setembro, in the city centre.

AROUND PORTO VELHO

Santo Antônio, a small riverside settlement seven km from Porto Velho, is popular with the residents of Porto Velho, who come here to fish and swim. You can get here by boat (see the information on Organised Tours under Porto Velho). The fishing village of **Teotônio** (Km 23 off BR-364, 38 km from Porto Velho), situated by the longest waterfall on the upper Rio Madeira, is the site of an annual fishing championship, held in August and September.

Salto do Jirau is an impressive waterfall on the Rio Madeira, 132 km south-west of Porto Velho on BR-364. About 215 km down BR-364, south-west of Porto Velho and near the town of Abunã, is the **Cachoeira Três Esses**. Near this spectacular waterfall on the Rio Abunã are some Indian rock inscriptions.

VILHENA

Vilhena, at the border between Rondônia and Mato Grosso, is a good access point for a look at Brazilian frontier life. From Vilhena, take a bus east into Mato Grosso state, to Juina or further on to Fontanilhas. These are towns straight from the Wild West, complete with Indian wars, gold miners, rustlers and homesteaders. The real treat in the area is the route, north from Juina direct to Aripuanã, on a dirt road. There is an alternate route via Juruena, but it is not nearly as spectacular as the direct route, which passes through the mountains.

Just outside Aripuanã are the spectacular Dannelles Falls. A local guide may be able to take you on some longer hikes through the area, though it's rapidly being deforested. Note that trees marked with painted bands indicate disputed Indian territory, and you are well advised to stay out of these areas.

FORTE PRÍNCIPE DA BEIRA & COSTA MARQUES

Remote and little-visited Forte Príncipe da Beira, 170 river km south of Guajará-Mirim, was constructed between 1776 and 1783 on the eastern bank of the Rio Guaporé. The fort has 10-metre-high walls, with four towers, each holding 14 cannons (which took five years to carry from Pará). The fortress walls, nearly one km around, are surrounded by a moat and enclose a chapel, an armoury, officers' quarters, and prison cells in which bored convicts have scrawled poetic graffiti. Underground passageways lead from the fortress directly to the river. Nearby, there's a mini 'Meeting of the Waters', where the clear, dark Rio Baures flows into the murky, brown Rio Guaporé.

The region around Costa Marques has many Indian archaeological sites, inscriptions and cemeteries. Notable sites here are Pedras Negras and Ilha das Flores. For details about the Reserva Biológica do Guaporé, see the section on National Parks & Biological Reserves earlier in this chapter.

Getting There & Away

Air Regular flights between Porto Velho and Costa Marques are operated by the air-taxi company TAVAJ (☎ 225-2094 in Porto Velho).

Bus It's a long haul to the fort! There's one bus daily, at noon, from Porto Velho's rodoviária to Presidente Medici (around 10 hours). The next morning at 6 am, a bus leaves Presidente Medici for Costa Marques (around 12 hours). The trip costs US$30. This is as far as you can go by bus, and from there it's still 25 km to Forte Príncipe da Beira. West of Presidente Medici is a wild stretch of road, and the environmental destruction is heartbreaking. Because the land has been cleared and settled only recently, there's a significant risk of malaria and other tropical diseases.

Boat A preferable alternative to the bus may be to travel by boat up the Mamoré and Guaporé rivers from Guajará-Mirim. Boats ply this stretch of the river, making the trip from Guajará-Mirim to the military post at Forte Príncipe da Beira in two to three days. They then continue to Costa Marques, where food and accommodation are available. Enquire about schedules at the Capitânia dos Portos in Guajará-Mirim, but don't expect much help.

GUAJARÁ-MIRIM
Guajará-Mirim, on the Brazilian/Bolivian border, and its Bolivian counterpart, Guayaramerín, have gone through a reversal of roles in recent years. While the Brazilian town is now quiet and subdued by Brazilian standards, the Bolivian town is experiencing a boom since the upgrading of the roads from Porto Velho (on the Brazilian side) and Riberalta (on the Bolivian side). It's become very popular with crowds of Brazilians popping over the border for shopping. For a discussion of the history of Guajará-Mirim, see the History section for Porto Velho.

Visas
If you're entering Bolivia and require a visa, there is a Bolivian Consulate in Guajará-Mirim, at Avenida Costa Marques 495. It's open on weekday mornings. Have two photographs ready.

Museu Municipal
With a couple of old steam locomotives parked outside, the marginally interesting museum housed in the old train station on Avenida 15 de Novembro focuses on the history of the region and contains the remains of some of Rondônia's fiercely threatened wildlife. Particularly interesting are the huge anaconda (which stretches the length of the main salon) and a pathetically hideous turtle (which inhabits the aquarium area). The museum's collection of photographs has an especially intriguing portrayal of an Indian attack – or defence, depending upon your reference – taken in the 1960s.

The museum is currently closed for renovation, but you can see some of the displays by standing on your toes and peering through the windows.

Places to Stay
Guajará-Mirim is quite popular as a weekend destination, so it's worth ringing ahead to book a hotel if you're arriving on a weekend. The cheapest place in town is the *Hotel Chile* (☎ 541-3846), with single/double quartos at US$9/16 and musty apartamentos with aircon for US$18/24. The *Fenix Palace Hotel* (☎ 541-2326), centrally located at Avenida 15 de Novembre 459, has quartos at US$10/18 and apartamentos for US$18/30, including electric fan. Across the road, the popular *Hotel Mini-Estrela Palace* (☎ 541-2399) charges US$15/27 for single/double apartamentos with fan. The *Hotel Pousada Tropical* (☎ 541-3308) is quite comfortable, offering single/double apartamentos with air-con for US$25 (US$10/20 with fan).

More up-market, the *Alfa Hotel* (☎ 541-3121) charges US$24/36 for single/double apartamentos, breakfast included.

Places to Eat
Universally recommended as Guajará-Mirim's best restaurant, the *Oasis* is next door to the Hotel Mini-Estrela Palace. Across the road, *Pizzaria Stop Drink's* has a wide range of pizzas, and is popular at night – in fact, some of the clientele stop and drink all night!

Getting There & Away
Bus There are eight bus connections daily to Porto Velho (US$10.50, around 5½ hours),

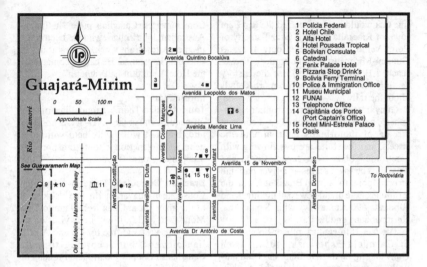

Guajará-Mirim

0   50   100 m

Approximate Scale

Rio Mamoré

See Guayaramerín Map

Old Madeira - Mamoré Railway

Avenida Quintino Bocaiúva
Avenida Leopoldo dos Matos
Avenida Mendez Lima
Avenida 15 de Novembro
Avenida Dr Antônio de Costa

Avenida Costa Marques
Avenida Constituição
Avenida Presidente Dutra
Avenida P. Menezes
Avenida Benjamin Constant
Avenida Dom Pedro

To Rodoviária

1 Polícia Federal
2 Hotel Chile
3 Alfa Hotel
4 Hotel Pousada Tropical
5 Bolivian Consulate
6 Catedral
7 Fenix Palace Hotel
8 Pizzaria Stop Drink's
9 Bolivia Ferry Terminal
10 Police & Immigration Office
11 Museu Municipal
12 FUNAI
13 Telephone Office
14 Capitânia dos Portos
    (Port Captain's Office)
15 Hotel Mini-Estrela Palace
16 Oasis

along an excellent road, commonly known – for what should be obvious reasons – as one of the 'Transcoca Highways'. Buses at 2 pm and midnight go direct to Porto Velho, without stopping, cutting around 1½ hours off the trip.

Boat It's possible to travel by boat up the Mamoré and Guaporé rivers to Costa Marques via Forte Príncipe da Beira. Enquire about schedules at the not-terribly-helpful Capitânia dos Portos (☎ 541-2208). For more details, see the Getting There & Away section for Forte Príncipe da Beira.

Crossing the Border Even if you're not planning to travel further into Bolivia, you can pop across the Rio Mamoré to visit Guayaramerín, which has cheaper accommodation than Guajará-Mirim. Between early morning and 6.30 pm, small motorised canoes and larger motor ferries cross the river from Guajará-Mirim every few minutes (US$1.50). After hours, there are only express motorboats (US$4 to US$5.50 per boat). You are permitted to travel back and forth across the river at will, but those trav-

elling beyond the frontier area will have to complete border formalities.

Leaving Brazil, you may need to have your passport stamped at the Bolivian Consulate in Guajará-Mirim before getting a Brazilian exit stamp at the Polícia Federal (☎ 541-2437) on Avenida Presidente Dutra, three blocks from the port in Guajará-Mirim. Once across the Rio Mamoré, pick up an entrance stamp at Migración (Bolivian Immigration) at the ferry terminal.

If you are planning to leave Bolivia from Guayaramerín, you must have your passport stamped at Migración, and again at the Polícia Federal in Guajará-Mirim, where you'll get a Brazilian entry stamp. Although officials don't always check, technically everyone needs a yellow-fever vaccination certificate to enter Brazil here. If you don't have one, there is a convenient and relatively sanitary clinic at the port on the Brazilian side. The medical staff use an air gun rather than a hypodermic needle.

GUAYARAMERÍN (BOLIVIA)

Guayaramerín, on the Rio Mamoré opposite the Brazilian town of Guajará-Mirim, is a rail town where the railway never arrived. The line that would have connected the Rio Beni town of Riberalta with the Brazilian city of Porto Velho was completed only as far as Guajará-Mirim just over the border – it never reached Bolivian territory! See the History section for Porto Velho for more details about the railway.

Guayaramerín retains a frontier atmosphere, but is growing quickly – a constant stream of motorbikes buzz around the streets, and the stores are overflowing with electronic goods from Japan, China and Taiwan. The town serves as a river port and an entry point to or from Brazil; it is also the terminus of the brand new road linking it and Riberalta, 90 km away, with Santa Ana, Rurrenabaque and La Paz.

The late 18th-century rubber-boom town of Cachuela Esperanza, 40 km from Guayamerín, on the Rio Beni, has been partially restored and is well worth a visit. Accommodation is offered in the *Canadian Hotel*, built around the turn of the century from imported Canadian pine. An Italian-Australian, John Zenari, who has been active in the restoration work, offers tours to Cachuela Esperanza. He can be contacted at the Hotel Litoral in Guayamerín.

Information

Tourist Office There's a tourist information office (of sorts) at the port – it has no literature, but staff will gladly help with some general information about transport and accommodation.

Brazilian Consulate There is a Brazilian Consulate in Guayaramerín, one block south of the main plaza. Open from 9 am to 1 pm Monday to Friday, it will issue visas on the same day. Visas are free for US and Australian citizens, but according to staff, Canadians must pay US$40 and French citizens $US50.

Money Cash US dollars can be changed at

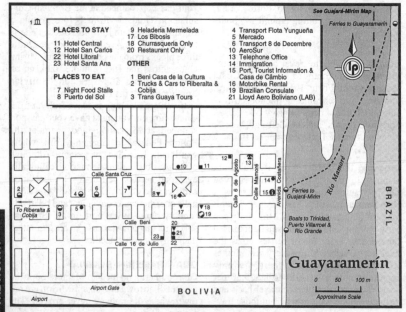

See Guajará-Mirim Map

PLACES TO STAY
11 Hotel Central
12 Hotel San Carlos
22 Hotel Litoral
23 Hotel Santa Ana

PLACES TO EAT
7 Night Food Stalls
8 Puerto del Sol

9 Heladería Mermelada
17 Los Bibosis
18 Churrasquería Only
20 Restaurant Only

OTHER
1 Beni Casa de la Cultura
2 Trucks & Cars to Riberalta & Cobija
3 Trans Guaya Tours

4 Transport Flota Yungueña
5 Mercado
6 Transport 8 de Decembre
10 AeroSur
13 Telephone Office
14 Immigration
15 Port, Tourist Information & Casa de Cámbio
16 Motorbike Rental
19 Brazilian Consulate
21 Lloyd Aero Boliviano (LAB)

Ferries to Guayaramerín

Calle Santa Cruz

Calle 6 de Agosto

Calle Mamoré

Avenida Costañera

To Riberalta & Cobija

Calle Beni

Calle 16 de Julio

Ferries to Guajará-Mirim

Rio Mamoré

B R A Z I L

Boats to Trinidad, Puerto Villarroel & Rio Grande

Guayaramerín

0   50   100 m

Approximate Scale

Airport Gate

Airport

BOLIVIA

THE NORTH

the Hotel San Carlos, at a good rate. Alternatively, exchange US dollars, bolivianos (abbreviated in this section to 'B') or Brazilian real with the cambistas who hang around the port area. In 1995, the going rate was B4.7 for US$1.

Places to Stay

The mellowest budget place to stay in Guayaramerín is undoubtedly the *Hotel Litoral*, near the airport. Private baths, refreshingly tepid showers and clean rooms are offered here for only B20 per person. Across the street, the quiet and shady *Hotel Santa Ana* (☎ 2206) offers similar amenities for the same price.

The *Hotel Central* (☎ 2042), on Calle Santa Cruz, costs B15 per person. It's a low-budget option, with shared baths and no double beds.

The *Hotel San Carlos* (☎ 2419), on Calle 6 de Agosto, is the up-market place in town, with a restaurant, TV, a sauna, air-conditioning, a billiards room and 24-hour hot water. Singles/doubles cost B100/150.

Places to Eat

Guayaramerín has two restaurants called 'Only' – and they both got it wrong! *Churrasqueria Only*, a barn-sized place with an extensive menu, is very popular with Brazilians. The smaller, more intimate *Restaurant Only* offers fish and meat dishes. Out of town is a very good restaurant: *Sujal*. Motorbike taxis will get you there for B1.5. On the plaza, *Los Bibosis* is a popular place for drinks and snacks, while *Heladeria Mermelada* has mountainous fruit and ice-cream creations. The *Puerto del Sol* is frequently recommended but we reckon it's grossly overrated: the food is only average and serious overcharging of foreigners is in effect.

Getting There & Away

Air Guayaramerín's airport, right at the southern edge of town, takes air safety seriously; prior to one of our visits, a bull had been mown down on the runway and the airport was closed for two weeks!

AeroSur (☎ 2201) has a daily flight (at 9 am) to Trinidad, with same-day connections to Santa Cruz, La Paz and Cobija. LAB flies four times a week to Cochabamba, twice weekly to Santa Cruz (on Thursday and Sunday) and twice a week to La Paz (on Tuesday and Saturday). The LAB office in Guayaramerín is not yet on the computer line, so book flights out of Guayaramerín elsewhere or risk not getting a seat.

Bus Most bus services to and from Guayaramerín (with the exception of services to Riberalta) operate only during the dry season – roughly from May to October. Trans Guaya Tours has two buses daily, at 7 am and 3 pm, to Riberalta (B10, two hours), a once-weekly (Wednesday) service to Cobija (B80, 14 hours) and three buses a week, on Wednesday, Friday and Sunday, to Trinidad (B110, 35 hours). Flota Yungueña has Wednesday, Friday and Sunday departures for Riberalta, Rurrenabaque and La Paz (B140, 36 hours).

Beware of bus companies cancelling trips: this may happen if tickets aren't sold out, with irate would-be passengers being given a lame excuse.

Boat From the port, ships leave frequently for Trinidad, five to seven days up the Rio Mamoré. For information regarding departures, the port-captain's office has a notice board which lists any activity into or out of town.

Hitching Camiones (trucks) to Riberalta leave from the main street, 2½ blocks west of the market, near the park. They charge the same as buses, and make the trip in less time. If you'd like to travel a bit more comfortably, cars (US$6) spare you exposure to the choking red dust that seems to get into everything. To Cobija, YPFB petrol trucks and a white Volvo freight carrier depart occasionally, from the same place.

Crossing the Border For information about onward travel into Brazil, see the Getting There & Away section for Guajará-Mirim.

Getting Around

You'll quickly discover that there are no automobile taxis in Guayaramerín, but then the town is so small that you can walk just about anywhere you'd like to go. There are motorbike taxis, which cost B1.5 anywhere around town. Those who want to do some exploring of the surrounding area can hire a motorbike from the main plaza for B10 per hour (negotiate a discount for daily rentals). Don't be tempted to take a swig of the stuff sold in Coke bottles on the street: it's motorbike petrol!

Acre

The state of Acre has become a favoured destination for developers and settlers, who have followed BR-364 and started claiming lands, clearing forest and setting up ranches. The issues of land ownership and sustainable forest use have caused major conflicts between the developers and the indigenous tribes and rural workers, mostly rubber-tappers, who are descended from settlers who arrived many decades ago. This conflict received massive national and international attention in 1988, with the assassination of Chico Mendes, a rubber-tapper and an opponent of rainforest destruction. For a discussion of Chico Mendes, see the section on Xapuri. For information about the history of Acre, refer to the History section for Porto Velho.

Most of the state operates two hours behind Brazilian standard time.

RIO BRANCO

Rio Branco, the capital of Acre state, was founded in 1882 on the banks of the Rio Acre, which is navigable via the Rio Purus to the Amazon. There's a relaxed and surprisingly cosmopolitan feel to this city, which has a few attractions close to the centre, and other points of interest, including intriguing religious communities, further afield.

Information

Tourist Office The Departamento de Turismo (☎ 223-1900), at Avenida Getúlio Vargas 659, is helpful. It's open from 8 am to 1 pm on weekdays.

Money The main branch of the Banco do Brasil is at Rua Acre 85. The exchange counter is open from 9 am to 1.30 pm Monday to Friday.

Post & Telephone The central post office is on Rua Epaminondas Jácome. The main office of Teleacre, the state telephone company, is on Avenida Brasil.

Casa do Seringueiro

This museum has a collection of photos, paintings, replicas of housing and utensils, portraying the life of a typical seringueiro (rubber-tapper). There is also a small area devoted to Chico Mendes.

The museum is open from 7 am to noon Tuesday to Friday, and sporadically from 4 to 7 pm on Saturday and Sunday.

Museu da Borracha

The collection in this museum is divided into sections relating to the archaeology, palae-ontology, ethnology and recent history of Acre. It's well worth a visit. The museum is open from 9 am to noon and 2 to 5 pm Tuesday to Friday, and from 4 to 7 pm on Saturday and Sunday.

Colônia Cinco Mil

The Colônia Cinco Mil (literally Colony of the 5000) is a religious community which follows the doctrine of Santo Daime, introduced in 1930 by Raimundo Irineu Serra, also known as Mestre Irineu. For more details about this cult, which is based on the sacred hallucinogenic drink called ayahuasca, see the section on Religion in the Facts about the Country chapter. Mestre Irineu founded the first centre at Alto Santo, seven km from Rio Branco. Various schisms amongst his followers led to the establishment of other centres, such as Casa de Jesus Fonte de Luz (in the Vila Ivonete district, three km from Rio Branco), Centro Fonte Luz Universal, or CEFLURIS (in the agricultural community of Côlonia Cinco Mil, 12 km from Rio Branco), and Ceú da Mapiá (a similar community, based at Mapiá, which is reached by a two-day boat trip from Boca do Acre, in Amazonas state).

Visits to Colônia Cinco Mil can be arranged through the Daimista family (ask for Raimundo or Marionete) at Kaxinawá, the Daimista restaurant in Rio Branco. The best time to make contact is on Wednesday morning, when they head out to the community for the main weekly festival. If you stay overnight, no fee will be charged, but you will be expected to share the cost of transport

Chico Mendes

Chico Mendes was born in 1944 at Seringal Cachoeira, in Acre, into a family descended from a rubber tapper. At an early age, he became interested in asserting the rights of rubber tappers to their lands. In the 1970s the Plano de Integração Nacional (PNI), an ambitious government plan to tame the Amazon, attracted developers, ranchers, logging companies and settlers into Acre. In 1975, Chico Mendes organised a rural workers' union to defy the tactics of violent intimidation and dispossession practised by the newcomers, who were destroying the forest and thus robbing the rural workers of their livelihood.

Mendes organised large groups of rural workers to form nonviolent human blockades around forest areas threatened with clearance, and soon attracted the wrath of developers, who were used to getting their way either through corrupt officials or by hiring pistoleiros to clear human impediments. These empates, or 'confrontational standoffs', proved effective in saving thousands of hectares of forest, which were set aside as *reservas extrativistas* where rural workers could continue to tap rubber and gather fruits, nuts and fibres.

International interest focussed on Mendes as a defender of the forests, but his role as a leader also made him a natural target for frustrated and infuriated opponents. Early in December 1988, he moved to establish his birthplace, Seringal Cachoeira, as an extractive reserve, defying the local landowner and rancher, Darly Alves da Silva, who disputed ownership of the land. On 22 December, Chico Mendes, who had received numerous death threats, momentarily left his bodyguards inside his house and stepped out onto the back porch. He was hit at close range by shots fired from the bushes, and died shortly afterwards.

For almost two years, there was much speculation about the murderers; although they were well known, the men were considered out of legal reach because of their connections with the influential landowners and corrupt officials of the region – a common arrangement in the frontierlands of Brazil. Intense national and international pressure finally brought the case to trial. In December 1990, Darly Alves da Silva received a 19-year prison term for ordering the assassination; his son, Darci, was given an identical sentence for pulling the trigger.

The verdict pleased rural workers, world opinion and the Brazilian government, which badly needed to demonstrate to Brazilians and foreigners a modicum of control in the Amazon region. But while the media spotlight moved on to other sensations, the murders continued. Documentation shows that this exhibition of justice was a rare flash in the media pan – of the hundreds of murders of union leaders and land-rights campaigners since the late 1970s, the only one that was thoroughly investigated and prosecuted was that of Chico Mendes.

Itamar Mendes, Chico's wife, was courted by 10 Hollywood producers to sell the film rights to her husband's story (*The Burning Season* was released in late 1994, directed by David Puttnam). International organisations made posthumous awards to Chico Mendes, and several parks in Brazil were named after him. In Xapuri, his house has been made into a commemorative museum. The rubber tappers and rural workers of the region are keen to keep up the pressure, not only to establish more extractive reserves throughout the Amazon region, but most importantly, to force the Brazilian government to enforce the laws governing the establishment of such reserves and to punish those who violate them.

In February 1992 the state appeals court in Rio Branco annulled the conviction of Darly Alves da Silva. For those who had hoped to see a glimmer of justice in Brazil, it was just another nail in the coffin. ■

THE NORTH

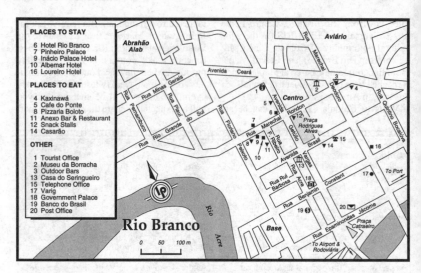

PLACES TO STAY

6   Hotel Rio Branco
7   Pinheiro Palace
9   Inácio Palace Hotel
10 Albemar Hotel
16 Loureiro Hotel

PLACES TO EAT

4   Kaxinawá
5   Cafe do Ponte
8   Pizzaria Boloto
11 Anexo Bar & Restaurant
12 Snack Stalls
14 Casarão

OTHER

1   Tourist Office
2   Museu da Borracha
3   Outdoor Bars
13 Casa do Seringueiro
15 Telephone Office
17 Varig
18 Government Palace
19 Banco do Brasil
20 Post Office

Rio Branco

0   50   100 m

and food. It's possible to visit the community independently at other times – a taxi from Rio Branco costs around US$12.

In the grounds of the Kaxinawá restaurant is a shop sponsored by the Fundação de Tecnologia do Estado do Acre (FUNTAC), a state organisation promoting sustainable use of forest products, which are sold here.

Horto Florestal

This municipal forest park in the Vila Ivonete district, three km from the centre, contains a selection of Amazon flora, a lake, and various paths which make a pleasant change from the traffic in the city centre. A taxi from the centre costs about US$3. The park is open daily from 8 am to 4 pm.

Lago do Amapá

This large, U-shaped lake eight km southeast of Rio Branco is a popular spot for swimming and boat excursions. A taxi from the city centre costs around US$7.

Parque Ecológico Plácido de Castro

In 1991 an ecological park was opened at Plácido de Castro, 94 km east of Rio Branco, on the Brazilian/Bolivian border. This park

offers good swimming at river beaches, and it's possible to take walks through the forests along the paths that were originally used by rubber-tappers.

There are five bus departures daily from Rio Branco to Plácido de Castro, where there's a hotel, the Hotel Carioca (☎ 237-1064), on Rua Juvenal Antunes, as well as various inexpensive pensões, some restaurants and even a danceteria.

Places to Stay

The *Albemar Hotel* (☎ 224-1938), at Rua Franco Ribeiro 99, has apartamentos at US$12/20 for singles/doubles, and a bar and restaurant in the same building. The manager speaks English. The *Loureiro Hotel* (☎ 223-1560), at Rua Marechal Deodoro 196, has apartamentos (without TV) at US$11.50/17 for singles/doubles; rooms with TV are more expensive.

The *Inácio Palace Hotel* (☎ 224-6397; fax 224-5726), at Rua Rui Barbosa 72, is an ugly building, but provides comfortable apartamentos. Single apartamentos with air-con and fridge are small, but good value at US$13.50. Larger rooms with fridge and air-con cost US$19/27 for singles/doubles.

The *Pinheiro Palace* (☎ 224-7191; fax 224-5726), across the street and under the same management, is a three-star luxury establishment. Apartamentos start at US$61/92.

The *Hotel Rio Branco* (☎ 224-1785; fax 224-2681), at Rua Rui Barbosa 193, has efficient service, bright decor, and neat apartamentos at US$49/65, with an excellent breakfast included.

If you're just passing through or have an early bus departure, the *Hotel Rodoviária*, opposite the rodoviária, has clean single/double quartos at US$6/8. The *Hotel Skina* (☎ 224-3731), nearby, is a more up-market rodoviária rest stop.

Places to Eat

Italian food seems to be the rage in Rio Branco. *Pizzaria Boloto*, on Rua Rui Barbosa, next to the Inácio Palace Hotel, has tables set out on a terrace and an outdoor video screen playing music videos. The *Anexo Bar & Restaurant* also does tasty Italian food, as well as regional dishes. *Casarão*, at Avenida Brasil 310, serves regional dishes and is popular with locals. *Cafe do Ponte*, on Avenida Getúlio Vargas, is a cute little place with good coffee, pastries and ice cream. Vegetarians can browse in the well-stocked health-food shop next to the Hotel Rio Branco. The *Kaxinawá* is described earlier, in the section on Colônia Cinco Mil.

Just over the bridge, on the riverfront, the *Caffé Crystal*, on Rua 24 de Janeiro, has pizzas, rodízio and a wide range of juices. There's live music here on Thursday, Friday and Saturday.

Entertainment

Tuesday is a big day in Rio Branco, with a football match in the afternoon and live music at Kaxinawá in the evening. The small square sandwiched between Avenida Ceará, Rua Marechal Deodoro and Rua Rui Barbosa, near the Kaxinawá restaurant, has several outdoor bars, which get crowded at night. There's often some live music here, as well.

Getting There & Away

Between October and June, when the rivers are at their highest and the roads are often impassable, the only viable transport options are plane or boat. We made it by bus to Brasiléia in mid-December, but it was a near thing – the bus spent a lot of the trip side-slipping through red sludge. Interest was added by a collection of prisoners on board, handcuffed to their seats, being escorted by what we assumed were plain-clothes police. From July to September, when the rivers are at their lowest, the roads are passable but river traffic is restricted.

Air There are flights between Rio Branco and Cruzeiro do Sul, Manaus, Porto Velho, Cuiabá, Rio and São Paulo. VASP (☎ 224-6585) is at Rua Marechal Deodoro 122, and Varig (☎ 224-2559) is close by, at Rua Marechal Deodoro 115. AeroSur (☎ 223-1350) flies to Puerto Maldonado (in Peru) a couple of times a week. There are also various air-taxi companies at the airport, such as TACEZUL (☎ 224-3242) and TAVAJ (☎ 224-5981).

Bus There are bus services between Rio Branco and Porto Velho (US$13, about 10 hours, four departures daily), Brasiléia (US$11, six hours, five departures daily), Xapuri, Plácido de Castro and Boca do Acre (in Amazonas state).

Boat To enquire about boats, either go direct to the port at the eastern end of Avenida Epaminondas Jácome or contact Paulo (☎ 223-1050). You might score a ride at the port; if there's a group of you, prices quoted for a 1½-day trip to Boca do Acre (Amazonas) are around US$65. From Boca do Acre, there is river traffic along the Rio Purus as far as the Amazon, and even to Manaus.

Getting Around

The airport, Aeroporto Internacional Presidente Medici (☎ 224-6833), is about two km out of town on AC-40, at Km 1. The rodoviária (☎ 224-1182) is also a couple of km out of town, at AC-40 No 1018 (in the Cidade Nova district).

From the airport, the bus marked 'Norte/Sul' runs via the rodoviária to the city centre. A taxi from the centre costs US$3 to the airport and about US$2 to the rodoviária.

XAPURI

Xapuri, 188 km south-west of Rio Branco, was founded in the late 19th century on territory formerly inhabited by the indigenous Xapuri, Latiana and Maneteri tribes. In 1902 it achieved historical fame as the site where Plácido de Castro proclaimed Acrean independence from Bolivia. In 1988, the town hit international and national headlines with the assassination of Chico Mendes, a rubber-tapper and an opponent of rainforest destruction.

Places to Stay & Eat

There are two inexpensive hotels on Rua Major Salinas – the *Hotel Veneza* (☎ 542-2397) and the *Santo Antônio Hotel* (☎ 542-2408). For places to eat in the centre of town, try the *Restaurante Eldorado*, on Rua Coronel Brandão, or *Pensão O Escadão*, on Rua 17 de Novembro.

Getting There & Away

There are three buses a day between Rio Branco and Xapuri (US$8, 3½ hours).

BRASILÉIA

The small town of Brasiléia lies on the Brazilian border with Bolivia, separated from Cobija (its Bolivian counterpart) by the Rio Abunã and the Rio Acre. Brasiléia has nothing to interest travellers, except an immigration stamp into or out of Brazil.

Visas

The Polícia Federal is two km from the centre; dress nicely. The office is open daily from 8 am to noon and 2 to 5 pm. For information on crossing the Brazilian/Bolivian border, see the following Getting There & Away section.

There is a Bolivian Consulate in Brasiléia,

Around Brasiléia

at Rua Major Salinas 205. It's open Monday to Friday from 8 to 11 am.

Places to Stay & Eat

If you're stuck in Brasiléia, try the *Hotel Fronteiras* (☎ 546-3045), near the church in the centre. Apartamentos cost US$10/12 for singles/doubles. The *Restaurant Carioca*, beside the hotel, serves drinks, chicken and beef dishes and standard prato feito (a veritable feast of Brazilian carbohydrates). Alternatively, there's the *Hotel Kador* (☎ 546-3283), at Avenida Santos Dumont 25, on the road between the international bridge and the Polícia Federal. Apartamentos cost US$10/15 for singles/doubles. *Pizzaria Ribeira* is just across the road.

Getting There & Away

From the rodoviária, four buses daily run to Rio Branco (US$11, six hours). Buses go to Assis Brasil in the dry season (roughly June to October); during the rainy season, you may be able to organise a ride with a truck; contact Transport Acreana in Brasiléia.

Crossing the Border If you're crossing to or from Bolivia, you'll have to get entry/exit stamps from Migración (Immigration) in Cobija and from the Polícia Federal just outside Brasiléia. A yellow-fever vaccination certificate is technically required to enter Brazil from Cobija, but there doesn't seem to be much checking done. There's no vaccination clinic in Brasiléia, so you'll have to track down a private physician if your health records aren't in order.

Since it's a rather long up-and-down slog from Cobija across the bridge to Brasiléia, you may want to take a taxi, but negotiate the route and the fare in advance. For about US$3.50, the driver will take you from Cobija to the Polícia Federal in Brasiléia, wait while you complete immigration formalities and then take you to the city centre or to the rodoviária. Going the other way, from the centre of Brasiléia, taxis try to charge double the price.

Alternatively, take the rowboat ferry (US$0.50 per person) across the Rio Acre to the landing in the centre of Brasiléia. From here it's about one km to the rodoviária and another 1.5 km to the Polícia Federal.

COBIJA (BOLIVIA)

The Bolivian border town of Cobija is linked to its Brazilian counterpart, Brasiléia, by the International Bridge. Founded in 1906 under the name of Bahia, Cobija experienced a boom as a rubber-producing centre during the 1940s. When the rubber industry declined, so did Cobija's fortunes, and the town was reduced to a forgotten hamlet of 5000 people. Today, Cobija's population has doubled, and the town has at least one claim to fame: with 1770 mm of precipitation falling annually, it is the rainiest spot in Bolivia.

There are now bus connections from Cobija to La Paz via Riberalta. Cobija is also the site of a new international airport, which has connections for the popular La Paz/Santa Cruz/Panama City/Miami flights. Hmmm?

Information

If you read Spanish, the best source of background information on this remote area will be the book *Pando es Bolivia*, by Alberto

Lavadenz Ribera, published in 1991. It outlines the history, development and official story of the entire Pando department, of which Cobija is the capital.

Brazilian Consulate For US citizens and others who need a visa to enter Brazil, there is a Brazilian Consulate (☎ 2110) on the corner of Calle Beni and Fernandez Molina. It's open from 8.30 am to 1 pm Monday to Friday.

Immigration Bolivian immigration is located in the Prefectural building, on the main plaza. The office is open from 9 am to 5 pm on weekdays and from 9 to 11 am on Saturday. The immigration officer is often taken with wanderlust, but he has trained his assistants to take you through the procedure. An exit stamp inexplicably costs B20.

Money Casa Horacio changes Brazilian real, bolivianos (abbreviated in this section to 'B') and US dollars cash, at official rates (B4.7 for US$1 in 1995), but won't change travellers' cheques. If you're changing money over the border in Brasiléia, be sure to check official rates before handing money to a shopkeeper.

Things to See

There are a few interesting things to see in the area, including rubber and brazil-nut plantations, a number of lakes and places to observe rainforest wildlife, but transportation is difficult and Cobija's hinterlands are not easily accessible.

A favourite retreat with locals is **Lago Bay**, a freshwater lake and picnicking and fishing site near the Rio Manuripi, about 150 km south of Cobija along the Chivé road. There are basic cabañas to rent if you want to stay there. Jeeps run there on weekends; otherwise, the return trip in a taxi will cost you around B60.

If you're really bored, take a look at the monument in front of the old hospital. It commemorates an apocryphal local youth who, during the Brazilian takeover of the Acre, shot a flaming arrow to light the fire that sent invading Brazilians fleeing back across the river.

Places to Stay

The friendly, Spanish-run *Hotel Prefectural* (☎ 2230), also known as the Hotel Pando, has nice breezy rooms with fan and private bath for B30 per person (B50 for a room with a double bed). Breakfast is included in the price. While you're there, say hello to their chatty parrots, and take a look at the immense anaconda and jaguar skins stretched across the reception area.

The *Residencial Frontera* is clean, but a bit overpriced, with quartos at B25 per person and apartamentos at B40/60 for singles/doubles. It's pleasant if you can get a room with a window onto the patio.

Still another option is the *Residencial Cocodrilo*, which charges B20/30 for clean (but far from opulent) singles/doubles.

Places to Eat

In the early morning, the market sells chicken empanadas, but that's about all in the way of prepared food. Nothing stays fresh very long in this stifling and sticky climate. There are, however, fresh fruits and vegetables and lots of tinned Brazilian products.

The *Restaurant La Esquina de La Abuela*, on Avenida Fernandez Molina, is Cobija's nicest restaurant, with outdoor tables. Fresh, well-cooked chicken and meat dishes cost B15. If you really want to pig out, finish off with an ice-cream sundae at *Heladeria Y Licoreria El Tucán*, across the road. On the same street, about five minutes' walk away from the city centre, is *Churrasqueria La Cabaína del Momo* (long names seem to be in vogue in Cobija). Here you can eat churrasco (B9) at tables on a raised balcony. The *Discoteca Restaurant Pachahuara*, Cobija's swinging nightspot, serves snacks, standard meals and parrillada.

Getting There & Away

Air AeroSur flies daily from Cobija to Trinidad, with same-day connections to La Paz and Santa Cruz. Next-day connections are available from Trinidad to Guayamerín,

Riberalta and San Borja. From La Paz, there are daily flights to Trinidad, with connections to Cobija. AeroSur (☎ 2230) has an office in the Hotel Prefectural.

LAB (☎ 2170), the Bolivian national airline, has an office on Avenida Fernandez Molina, near the Polícia Nacional base. LAB has two direct flights a week to and from La Paz, and another two flights weekly with stops in Riberalta, Guayamerín, Trinidad and Cochabamba. If you're on the LAB Fokker which flies this run, look for the golden plaque that hangs over the seat occupied by the Pope on his most recent visit to Bolivia.

On arrival at the airport, you may claim baggage immediately, but if you're walking the two km to the centre in Cobija's sticky heat, it's a good idea to collect your luggage from the LAB office in town.

Bus With the opening of the road to Riberalta, there's now a surface connection to La Paz. The bus to Riberalta (B50), leaves at 6 am daily and takes at least 12 hours. Connections can be made there for the 24-hour ride to La Paz. Purchase tickets at Trans Guaya Tours, near the Hotel Prefectural. Flota Cobija buses connect Cobija with the village of Porvenir, 30 km (about one hour) away. They depart at 11.30 am daily.

Details about bus connections from Brasiléia (Brazil) are given in the Getting There & Away section for Brasiléia.

Crossing the Border For information about crossing the border between Brasiléia (Brazil) and Cobija, see Crossing the Border in the Getting There & Away section for Brasiléia.

ASSIS BRASIL & IÑAPARI (PERU)

Although we haven't tried the route described here, locals reckon that access from Assis Brasil to Iñapari (Peru) is possible for the adventurous traveller. Unfortunately, Peru's Madre de Dios department has been a centre of operations for the Sendero Luminoso (Shining Path) guerrillas, drug-running, lawless gold digging and other renegade activities. If you do manage to get through, please write and let us know how it went!

Places to Stay & Eat
There's one hotel in Assis Brasil: the *Assis Brasil Palace Hotel* (☎ 548-1045), on Rua Eneide Batista. For places to eat in the town centre, try *Restaurante Seridó*, at Rua Valério Magalhães 62, or the *Bar & Restaurante Petisco*, on Rua Raimundo Chaar.

Getting There & Away
Crossing the Border The route involves taking a bus or a jeep from Brasiléia to Assis Brasil, 110 km west of Brasiléia. It may be simpler to complete Brazilian immigration procedures in Brasiléia.

Across the Rio Acre from Assis Brasil is the muddy little Peruvian settlement of Iñapari, where you must register your arrival in Peru with the police. From Iñapari, there is a road (of sorts) to Puerto Maldonado, which is accessible to Cuzco on the Peruvian road system but which is, for practical pur-

poses, impassable to all but pedestrian or motorbike traffic. You may be able to fly from Iñapari – there is an airport seven km from the village – to Puerto Maldonado on a Grupo Ocho cargo flight, but you shouldn't count on it.

CRUZEIRO DO SUL
Another option to reach Peru – and a decidedly bad idea, due to drug-running and Sendero Luminoso activity in the area – is to fly, or hitch on a truck (654 km along BR-364), from Rio Branco to Cruzeiro do Sul (in western Acre), and then fly from there to the Peruvian Amazon city of Pucallpa.

Places to Stay & Eat
In Cruzeiro do Sul, there are a couple of hotels – the *Plínio Hotel* (☎ 322-3445), at Boulevard Thaumaturgo 155, and *Sandra's Hotel* (☎ 322-2481), at Avenida Coronel Mâncio Lima 241. For places to eat in the town centre, try the *Restaurante Popular*, on Rua Joaquim Távora, or the *Zanzibar Bar & Restaurante*, at Avenida Getúlio Vargas 19.

Glossary

ABCD cities – refers to Brazil's industrial heartland; the cities of São André, São Bernardo, São Caetano and Diadema, which flank the city of São Paulo

abandonados – abandoned children

abertura – opening; refers to the process of returning to a civilian, democratic government which was begun in the early 1980s

afoxé – music of Bahia with strong African rhythms and close ties to the Candomblé religion

aguardente – firewater, rotgut; any strong drink, but usually cachaça

albergue – lodging house or hostel

álcool – car fuel made from sugar cane; about half the cars, and all new cars, in Brazil run on álcool

aldeia – originally a mission village built by Jesuits to 'save' the Indians, but now any small village of peasants or fisherfolk

andar – the verb 'to walk'; also used to denote the floor number in a multistorey building

apartamento – hotel room with a bathroom

arara – macaw

autódromo – racetrack; the one near Barra in Rio is the site of the Brazilian Grand Prix

automotriz – tourist train

avelã – hazelnut

azulejos – Portuguese ceramic tiles which have a distinctive blue glaze. You will often see them in churches.

bandeirantes – bands of *Paulistas* who explored the vast Brazilian interior while searching for gold and Indians to enslave. The bandeirantes were typically born of an Indian mother and a Portuguese father.

banzo – a slave's profound longing for the African homeland, which often resulted in a 'slow withering away' and death

barraca – any stall or hut, including those omnipresent food and drink stands at the beach, park etc

bateria – any rhythm section, including the enormous ones in samba parades

beija-flor – hummingbird; Beija-flor is also the name of Rio's most famous samba school

berimbau – fishing rod-like musical instrument used in the martial art/dance of capoeira

bicho de pé – parasite that burrows into the bottom of the foot and then grows until it is cut out. It's found near the beach and in some jungle areas.

bloco – a large group, which usually numbers in the hundreds, of singing Carnival revellers in costume. Most blocos are organised around a neighbourhood or theme.

boate or **boîte** – nightclub; refers to both the expensive joint and the strip joint

bogó – leather water-pouch typical of the sertão

bonde – cable car; tram/trolley

bossa nova – music that mixes North American jazz with Brazilian influences

boto – freshwater dolphin of the Amazon. Indians believe the boto has magical powers, most notably the ability to impregnate unmarried women.

Brazilian Empire – the period from 1822 to 1889, when Brazil was independent of Portugal but was governed by monarchy

Bumba Meu Boi – the most important festival in Maranhão; a rich folkloric event that revolves around a Carnivalesque dance/procession

bunda – an African word for buttocks

caatinga – scrub vegetation of the Northeast sertão

Cabanagem – the popular revolt that swept through Pará state in the 1830s until a large government force defeated the uprising and then massacred 40,000 of the state's 100,000 people

caboclo – literally, copper-coloured; a person of White and Indian ancestry

cachaça – Brazil's national drink: a sugarcane rum, also called *pinga* and *aguardente*. Hundreds of small distilleries produce cachaça throughout the country.

cachoeira – waterfall
café – means café da manha (breakfast) or just coffee
caipirinha – made from cachaça and crushed citrus fruit such as lemon, orange or maracujá
câmara – town council during colonial days
camisa-de-Vênus, camisinha – literally, cover or shirt of Venus; a condom
Candomblé – Afro-Brazilian religion of Bahia
canga – wrap-around fabric worn when going to and from the beach and for sitting on at the beach
cangaceiro – legendary bandits of the *sertão*
capanga – hired gunman, usually employed by rich landowners in the Northeast
capitania hereditária – hereditary province or estate. To settle Brazil at minimum cost to the crown, in 1531 the king of Portugal divided the colony into 12 capitanias hereditárias.
capivara (capybara) – the world's largest rodent; it looks like a large guinea pig and lives in the waters of the Pantanal
capoeira – martial art/dance performed to the rhythms of an instrument called the berimbau; developed by the slaves of Bahia
capongas – a freshwater lagoon
Carioca – a native of Rio de Janeiro
casa grande – plantation owner's mansion
casa de câmbio – money-exchange house
casal – married couple; also a double bed
castanha – brazil nut
catamarãs – typical boats of the Amazon
chapadões – tablelands or plateaux which divide river basins
churrascaria – restaurant featuring meat, which should be churrasco (barbecued)
Círio de Nazaré – Brazil's largest religious pilgrimage; takes place in Belém
cobra – any snake
collectivá – bed in a shared room or dorm-style accommodation
comunidades de base – neighbourhood organisations of the poor led by the progressive Catholic Church and inspired by liberation theology. They are involved in many struggles for social justice.

comida por kilo – pay-by-weight buffet
congelamento – freeze, as in a price freeze
coronel – rural landowner who typically controlled the local political, judicial and police systems; any powerful person
cruzeiro – former unit of national currency

delegacia – police station
dendê – palm oil; the main ingredient in the cuisine of Bahia
drogas do sertão – plants of the *sertão* such as cacao and cinnamon

Economic Miracle – period of double-digit economic growth while the military was in power during the late 1960s and early 1970s; now mentioned sarcastically to point to the failures of the military regime
Embolada – kind of Brazilian rap, where singers trade off, performing verbal jests, teasing and joking with the audience; most common in Northeastern fairs
EMBRATUR – federal government tourism agency
Empire – see Brazilian Empire
ENASA – a government-run passenger-shipping line of the Amazon
engenho – sugar mill or sugar plantation
escolas de samba – these aren't schools, but large samba clubs. In Rio the escolas have thousands of members and compete in the annual Carnival parade. Weekend rehearsals begin around November and continue until Carnival; they are open to the public.
Estado Novo – literally, New State; dictator Getúlio Vargas' quasi-fascist state, which lasted from 1937 until the end of WW II
estância hidromineral – spa, hot springs
exús – spirits that serve as messengers between the gods and humans in Afro-Brazilian religions

facão – large knife or machete
fantasia – Carnivalesque costume
farinha – flour made from the root of the manioc plant. Farinha was the staple food of Brazil's Indians before colonisation and remains the staple for many Brazilians today, especially in the Northeast and the Amazon.

favela – slum, shantytown

fazenda – ranch or farm, usually a large landholding; also cloth, fabric

ferroviária – railway station

ficha – token; due to inflation, machines (eg telephones) take tokens, not coins

fidalgos – gentry

figa – good-luck charm formed by a clenched fist with the thumb between the index and middle fingers. The figa originated with Afro-Brazilian cults but is popular with all Brazilians.

Filhos de Gandhi – Bahia's most famous Carnival bloco

fio dental – literally, dental floss. This is what Brazilians call their famous skimpy bikinis.

Flamengo – Rio's most popular football team; also one of Rio's most populated areas

Fluminense – native of Rio state; also the Rio football team that is Flamengo's main rival

forró – the music of the Northeast, which combines the influences of Mexico and the Brazilian frontier. The characteristic instruments used are the accordion, harmonica and drums.

frevo – fast-paced, popular music that originated in Pernambuco

FUNAI – government Indian agency

Fusca – a Volkswagen beetle, long Brazil's most popular car; they stopped making them in 1986

garimpeiro – a prospector or miner; originally an illegal diamond prospector

gaúcho – pronounced 'gaooshoo'; a cowboy of southern Brazil

gíria – slang

gringo – you don't have to be from the USA: any foreigner or person with light hair and complexion, including Brazilians, qualifies. It's not necessarily a derogatory term.

guaraná – an Amazonian shrub whose berry is believed to have magical and medicinal powers; also a popular soft drink

lemanjá – the god of the sea in Afro-Brazilian religions

igapó – flooded Amazon forest

igarapés – pools formed by the changing paths of the rivers of the Amazon

INPA – national agency for research on the Amazon

jaburú – giant white stork of the Pantanal with black head and red band on neck

jagunço – the tough man of the *sertão*

jangada – beautiful sailboat of the Northeast, usually made by the fisherfolk themselves with building techniques passed from generation to generation

jangadeiros – fishers who use jangadas

jeito (dar um jeito or **jeitinho)** – possibly the most Brazilian expression, jeito means finding a way to get something done, no matter how seemingly impossible. It may not be an orthodox, normal or legal way but is nonetheless effective in the Brazilian context. Jeito is both a feeling and a form of action.

jogo de bicho – a popular lottery, technically illegal but played on every street corner by all Brazilians, with each number represented by an animal. The banqueiros de bicho, who control the game, have become a virtual mafia and traditionally help to fund the escolas de samba. Many consider the jogo de bicho the most honest and trustworthy institution in the country.

Jogo dos Búzios – type of fortune-telling performed by a *pai* or *maê de Santo* throwing shells

Labour Code – labour legislation, modelled on Mussolini's system, which is designed to maintain government control over labour unions

ladrão – thief

lanchonete – stand-up snack bar. They are found all over Brazil.

lavrador – peasant, small farmer or landless farm worker

leito – super-comfortable overnight express bus

liberation theology – movement in the Catholic Church that believes the struggle for social justice is part of Christ's teachings

Literatura de Cordel – literally, Literature of String. Popular literature of the Northeast, where pamphlets are typically hung on strings. It is sold at markets where authors read their stories and poems.

maconha – type of marijuana

maê de Santo – female spiritual leader of Afro-Brazilian religions

maharajás – pejorative term for government employees getting rich from the public coffers; usually refers to army and police officers

malandro do morro – vagabond; scoundrel from the hills; a popular figure in Rio's mythology

mameluco – offspring of a White father and an Indian mother

manatee or **peixe-boi** – literally, cow fish; an aquatic mammal of the Amazon rivers that grows to 1.5 metres in length; now rare

Manchete – number-two national TV station and a popular photo magazine

Maracanã – football stadium in Rio; supposedly the world's largest, the stadium allegedly holds 200,000 but looks full with 100,000

maté – popular tea of southern Brazil

mestiço – a person of mixed Indian and European parentage

mineiro – miner; also a person from the state of Minas Gerais

mocambo – community of runaway slaves; small version of a quilombo

moço – waiter or other service industry worker

morro – hill; also used to indicate a person or culture of the *favelas*

motel – sex hotel with rooms to rent by the hour

mulatto – person of mixed Black and European parentage

novela – soap opera. Novelas are the most popular TV shows in Brazil. They are much funnier and have more insights than their American counterparts. From directors to actors to composers, many of Brazil's most talented and famous artists work on novelas.

NS – Nosso Senhor (Our Father), or Nossa Senhora (Our Lady)

O Globo – Brazil's number-one media empire. O Globo owns the prime national TV station and several newspapers and magazines.

Old Republic – period from the end of the Brazilian Empire in 1889 until the coup that put Getúlio Vargas in power in 1930. There were regular elections but only a tiny percentage of the population was eligible to vote.

Orixás – the gods of the Afro-Brazilian religions

pagode – today's most popular samba music

pai de Santo – male spiritual leader in Afro-Brazilian religions

pajé – shaman, witch doctor

palafitas – houses built on sticks above water, as in Manaus

paralelo – the parallel, semi-official exchange rate that reflects the currency's market value, not the government's regulated official value

Paruara – Amazon resident who came from Ceará

pau brasil – brazil-wood tree. It produces a red dye that was the colony's first commodity. The trees are scarce today.

Paulista – native of São Paulo

PCB – Communist Party of Brazil

pelourinho – stone pillar used as a whipping-post for punishing slaves

Petrobras – the government-owned oil company. Brazil's largest corporation is so powerful that it's referred to as a 'government within a government'.

pinga – another name for cachaça, the sugar cane brandy

pistoleiro – gun-toting henchman

Planalto – enormous plateau that covers a part of almost every state in Brazil

PMDB – the governing party, a loose coalition that encompasses a wide variety of ideologies and interests from far right to centre

posseiro – squatter

pousada – hotel

prato feito, prato do dia – literally, made plate, plate of the day; typically, an enormous and incredibly cheap meal

PT – Worker's Party. Brazil's newest and most radical political party. It came out of the massive strike waves of the early 1980s and is led by Lula. The PT's support is strongest in São Paulo and among industrial workers and the Catholic base communities.

PTD – Democratic Workers' Party; a social democratic party dominated by the charismatic populist Leonel Brizola

puxar – means pull, not push

quarto – hotel room without a bathroom

quilombo – community of runaway slaves. They posed a serious threat to the slave system as hundreds of quilombos dotted the coastal mountains. The Republic of Palmares was the most famous: it survived for most of the 17th century and had a population of as many as 20,000.

real – Brazil's unit of currency since 1994

rede – hammock

Revolution of '64 – the military takeover in 1964

rodízio – a smorgasbord with lots of meat (similar to a churrascaria)

rodoferroviária – bus and train station

rodoviária – bus station

sambódromo – the road and bleachers where the samba parade takes place on Rio's north side

senzala – slave quarters

sertão – drought-stricken region of the Northeast, known as the backlands. It has a dry, temperate climate, and the land is covered by thorny shrubs.

shiita – term derived from the Shiite Muslims of Iran, used to describe any zealot or radical, no matter their cause

suco – juice bar or juice

Terra de Vera Cruz – Land of the True Cross. This was the original but short-lived Portuguese name for the country. Generations of Portuguese believed Brazil was the work of the devil (who, according to common wisdom, was very active in the sinful colony).

terreiro – house of worship for Afro-Brazilian religions

travesti – transvestite; a popular figure throughout Brazil and considered by some to be the national symbol

Treaty of Tordesillas – agreement signed in 1494 between Spain and Portugal, dividing Latin America

trio elétrico – literally, a three-pronged electrical outlet; also a musical style that is a sort of electrified *frevo* played on top of trucks, especially during Carnival in Bahia

tropicalismo – important cultural movement centred in Bahia in the late 1960s

Tupi – the Indian people and language that predominated along the Brazilian coast at the time of the European invasion. Most animals and places in Brazil have Tupi names.

Umbanda – Rio's version of the principal Afro-Brazilian religion

vaqueiro – cowboy of the Northeast

várzea – Amazonian flood plain

Velho Chico – literally, Old Chico; the fond nickname for the great Rio São Francisco

violeiros – guitarists and guitar makers

zona da mata – bushland just inside the littoral in the Northeastern states

Index

ABBREVIATIONS

MAPS

TEXT

Map references are in **bold** type.

Abaís (Bah) 442
Academia Militar das Agulhas
  Negras (RJ) 220
accommodation 114, 117-119
Aceguá 136
Acre 653-671
afoxé 57
Afuá (Par) 600
Água Boa (Ror) 648
Agulha do Diabo (RJ) 216
air travel 129-136
  air travellers with special needs
    134-135
  airpass 139-141
  airport tax 141
  buying a plane ticket 133-134
  glossary 132-133
  reservations 141
  round-the-world tickets 131
  to/from Brazil 129-135
  within Brazil 139-141
Alagoas 482-492, **476, 477**
Albuquerque, Jerônimo de 564
Alcântara (Mar) 559, 569-571,
  570
Alcobaça (Bah) 462
Aleijadinho 58, 240, 242, 252,
  253, 254, 258, 260, 262
Alter do Chão (Par) 605-606
Alto da Sé (Per) 507
Alto de Moura (Per) 514
Alumar (Mar) 569
Álvares, Diego 418, 431, 433
Alves, Castro 416
Amado, Jorge 59, 441, 447, 448,
  449
Amanhecer, Vale do 362
Amapá 581, 608-614
Amazon 30-31, 578, 584
  jungle tours 628, 631-633
Amazon Basin (Min) 27
Amazon Monkey Jungle (Amz)
  628

Amazon River 27, 577, 597,
  602, 624
Amazonas 621-645
Anastácio (MGS) 396
Anchieta Palace (ES) 234
Anchieta, José de 236, 275
Andaraí (Bah) 472
Angelis, Doménico de 626
Angra dos Reis (RJ) 201,
  205-206
animals, *see* wildlife
animism, Indian 60
Antonina (Pan) 309-310
Aquidauana (MGS) 396-397
Aracaju (Ser) 478-481, **479**
Aracati (Cea) 544-545
Araguaia Park (Toc) 52
araucaria 32
architecture 59
Areia Branca (RGN) 533
Areia Branca (Ron) 657
Arembepe (Bah) 438
Aripuanã Park (MG) 52
Armação (Bah) 419
Armação (RJ) 228
Aroe Jari (MG) 378
Arpoador (RJ) 165
Arraial d'Ajuda (Bah) 458-459
Arraial do Cabo (RJ) 226-227,
  226
art 58
Artigas 136
Assis Brasil (Acr) 136, 670-671
Assis, Machado de 59
Assunção, Luís 537
Ataíde, Manuel da Costa 254
Atalaia Velha (Ser) 479
axé 57
Azeda (RJ) 229

babaçu 404
Bahia 405-474, **405, 477**
Baía da Ilha Grande (RJ) 206
Baía da Traição (Pab) 525
Baía de Guanabara (RJ) 201

Baía de Marajó (Mar) 584
Baía de Marajó (Par) 598
Baía de Paranaguá (Pan) 313
Baía de São Marcos (Mar) 559
Baía de Todos os Santos (Bah)
  430, 437, **429**
Baía do Guajará (Mar) 584
Baía do Sancho (Per) 518
Baía do Sol (Par) 595
Baía dos Golfinhos (Per) 518
Baía Formosa (RGN) 526
Baixio (Bah) 440
Balneário Camboriú (SC)
  327-329
Balneário do Lucena (Toc) 616
baloeiros (balloon makers) 79
bandeirantes 17-18, 242, 275,
  350, 366, 373, 465, 654
Bar Luis (RJ) 164
Barão de Melgaço (MG) 380
Bardot, Brigitte 228
bargaining 76
Barra Beach (Bah) 419
Barra da Itabapoana (RJ) 231
Barra da Lagoa (SC) 334
Barra da Tijuca (RJ) 159
Barra de Itariri (Bah) 441
Barra de Santo Antônio (Ala)
  491-492
Barra de São João (RJ) 230-231
Barra de São Miguel (Ala) 489
Barra do Camarajibe (Ala) 491,
  492
Barra do Cunhaú (RGN) 527
Barra do Garças (Toc) 618
Barra do Jacuípe (Bah) 438
Barra do Sahy (SP) 294
Barra dos Jangandas (Per) 505
Barra Grande (Bah) 446
Barra Velha (SC) 328
Barreira da Cruz (Toc) 618
Barreira do Inferno (RGN) 528
Barreirinhas (Mar) 571-572
Barro Branco (Bah) 472
Battle of Mbororé 351

684 Index

Thanks

Thanks also to those travellers who took the time and trouble to write to us about their experiences in Brazil. Writers (apologies if we've misspelt your name) to whom thanks must go include:

Mark Aitchison, Lualdi Alberto (I), Tom Alciere (USA), Steven Alexander, James Baker (USA), Mark Baker (USA), Susan Lowere Barbieri (USA), Andy Barnes (UK), Andrew Bartram (UK), Kalanit Baumhaft (USA), Maarten Bax, Felicity Bedford, Jan Bennink (Nl), Oliver Berls (D), P A Blackie, Toddy Blaich (SA) , Jacques Blanc (F), David Blatte (USA), L Bleeker (Nl), Stephen & Andre Brackman (UK), W Brauer (USA), Ashely Brown (Aus), Sandra Brown (Aus), Charlotte Callaghan (UK), Craig & Basia Coben (USA), Merle Conyer (Aus), Jeremy Coon (USA), Jack Cox (UK), Grant Crothers (Aus), Sowia Goureia Cruz, Alejandro Danzi, W Davidson (UK), Giovanna de Benedet (I), Olivier de Corta, Francoise Decherck (F), Oedo Denissen (Nl), Dirk Deschaumes (B), Eliete Dibo, Gordon Dinse (D), Tim Donovan (Aus), Patrick Emmerich (D), Don Fairweather (C), L Faller, Apollon Fanzeres Jr (USA), Lynne Fetterman (USA), Gustavo Fidalgo (USA), Stan Franczyk (USA), Nicolas Fujise (S), Peter Geiser (Nl), Patrik Gille-Johnson (S), Jimena Gomez-Paratcha, Kath Grieve (UK), Claudi Grinmis (USA), Sissel Gyrid Freim (N), Arthur Hawley (Aus), Julie Hassenmiller (USA), Konstautiuos Hatzisarrou (USA), Steve Heilig (USA), W J Hill (UK), Richard Hoath (C), Andreu Castellet Homet (Sp), Michel Homoui, Richard Hordern (UK), Paco Iglesias (Sp), Richard Jennen, Frank Jolles (SA), Martin Jones (USA), Toni Kaiser, Dorte Appel & Kildevang Kare (Dk), Herbert Klein, Kathy Klossner (USA), Steven Koenig (USA), Marianne Komst (Nl), Ingrid Koonen (Nl), Dr D Kumar (UK), David Last, Paul Lebailly (F), Jose Lomas (Sp), Andrea Loosen (D), Mette Lotus (Dk), Thomas Lovejoy (USA), Wijnand Loven (Nl), Ricardo Lurz, Kalevi Lyytikoinen (S), Joe & Lucy MacFarland, Elvira Manasi (UK), Marlo Morals Marques, Dr Wilson Marsilla, Axel Martens (Dk), Tony Marti (CH), Wilson Marvilla, James B Mathers (USA), Steven & Debra Meiers (USA), Mandy Melse (UK), Vanessa Melter (USA), Polly Moles, Dick Momsen (C), Al Monteiro (USA), John Moran (USA), Piedad Moreno (USA), Peter Morgan (UK), David Morris-Johnston (UK), Martin Mottram (UK), Nick Mundy (UK), Helena Nilsson (S), Conor O'Sullivan (UK), Louise Peres (D), Jonny Persey (UK), Paulo Philippidis (USA), Gary Pogson (UK), Carmen Poulin (C), Henrik Day Poulsen (Dk), Claire Puttick (UK), Viv Quarry, Wulf Quester (D), Joe Ragsdale (USA), Rodney Ramos (USA), Rejane Reis, Rita Reitz (Nl), Jeff Roach (Aus), Phillipe Raoul (F), V Ribano, Tomas Rohlin, Tony Rosenberg, Neal Ross (USA), Filip Rosselle (Nl), Beate Rupprecht (D), Lucy Sayres (UK), David Schein (USA), Dieter Schoop, Detlev Schrodi (D), Thilo Schultze (D), Linda Scott (USA), Keith Smith (USA), William la Soe (Nl), Christian Solenthaler (CH), Chaz Sowers (USA), Hans Stangerl (D), A Stradin, Dene Sykes (Aus), Julian Tang (UK), Steve Thompson (USA), Dr Lisinka Ulatowska (USA), Riccardo Ullio, Jens Ulmer (D), Lut van Damme (B), Geert van de Wiele (B), Kristi van Delm (B), Marian van den Hul (Nl), Ine & Marcel van der Berk (Nl), Emilie van Dooren (Nl), Sander van Kleef (Nl), Dr Mart van Roosmalen, Fred Vijver (Nl), Raphael Wache, Clive Walker, Amanda Walton (Aus), Marcus White (UK), Ken White (Aus), Andy Whittaker, Mark Wiermans (Nl), Ann Wright (UK), David & Jill Wright (UK), Jon Wunrow (USA)

Aus – Australia, B – Belgium, C – Canada, CH – Switzerland, D – Germany, Dk – Denmark, F – France, G – Greece, I – Italy, Irl – Ireland, Isr – Israel, J – Japan, N – Norway, Nl – The Netherlands, NZ – New Zealand, S – Sweden, SA – South Africa, Sin – Singapore, Sp – Spain, UK – United Kingdom, USA – United States of America

LONELY PLANET TV SERIES & VIDEOS

Lonely Planet travel guides have been brought to life on television screens around the world. Like our guides, the programmes are based on the joy of independent travel, and look honestly at some of the most exciting, picturesque and frustrating places in the world. Each show is presented by one of three travellers from Australia, England or the USA and combines an innovative mixture of video, Super-8 film, atmospheric soundscapes and original music.

Videos of each episode – containing additional footage not shown on television – are available from good book and video shops, but the availability of individual videos varies with regional screening schedules.

Video destinations include:
Alaska; Australia (Southeast); Brazil; Ecuador & the Galapagos Islands; Indonesia; Israel & the Sinai Desert; Japan; La Ruta Maya (Yucatan, Guatemala & Belize); Morocco; North India (Varanasi to the Himalaya); Pacific Islands; Vietnam; Zimbabwe, Botswana & Namibia.

Coming in 1996:
The Arctic (Norway & Finland); Baja California; Chile & Easter Island; China (Southeast); Costa Rica; East Africa (Tanzania & Zanzibar); Great Barrier Reef (Australia); Jamaica; Papua New Guinea; the Rockies (USA); Syria & Jordan; Turkey.

The Lonely Planet television series is produced by:
Pilot Productions
Duke of Sussex Studios
44 Uxbridge St
London W8 7TG
United Kingdom

Lonely Planet videos are distributed by:
IVN Communications Inc
2246 Camino Ramon, San Ramon
California 94583, USA

107 Power Road, Chiswick
London W4 5PL, UK

For further information on both the television series and the availability of individual videos please contact Lonely Planet.

PLANET TALK
Lonely Planet's FREE quarterly newsletter

We love hearing from you and think you'd like to hear from us.

When...is the right time to see reindeer in Finland?
Where...can you hear the best palm-wine music in Ghana?
How...do you get from Asunción to Areguá by steam train?
What...is the best way to see India?

For the answer to these and many other questions read PLANET TALK.

Every issue is packed with up-to-date travel news and advice including:

- *a letter from Lonely Planet founders Tony and Maureen Wheeler*
- *travel diary from a Lonely Planet author - find out what it's really like out on the road*
- *feature article on an important and topical travel issue*
- *a selection of recent letters from our readers*
- *the latest travel news from all over the world*
- *details on Lonely Planet's new and forthcoming releases*

To join our mailing list contact any Lonely Planet office.

Also available: Lonely Planet T-shirts. 100% heavyweight cotton (S, M, L, XL)

LONELY PLANET PUBLICATIONS
Australia: PO Box 617, Hawthorn 3122, Victoria
tel: (03) 9819 1877 fax: (03) 9819 6459 e-mail: talk2us@lonelyplanet.com.au

USA: Embarcadero West, 155 Filbert St, Suite 251, Oakland, CA 94607
tel: (510) 893 8555 TOLL FREE: 800 275-8555 fax: (510) 893 8563
e-mail: info@lonelyplanet.com

UK: 10 Barley Mow Passage, Chiswick, London W4 4PH
tel: (0181) 742 3161 fax: (0181) 742 2772 e-mail: 100413.3551@compuserve.com

France: 71 bis rue du Cardinal Lemoine – 75005 Paris
tel: 1 46 34 00 58 fax: 1 46 34 72 55 e-mail: 100560.415@compuserve.com

World Wide Web: http://www.lonelyplanet.com/

Guides to the Americas

Alaska – a travel survival kit
Jim DuFresne has travelled extensively through Alaska by foot, road, rail, barge and kayak, and tells how to make the most of one of the world's great wilderness areas.

Argentina, Uruguay & Paraguay – a travel survival kit
This guide gives independent travellers all the essential information on three of South America's lesser-known countries. Discover some of South America's most spectacular natural attractions in Argentina; friendly people and beautiful handicrafts in Paraguay; and Uruguay's wonderful beaches.

Backpacking in Alaska
This practical guide to hiking in Alaska has everything you need to know to safely experience the Alaskan wilderness on foot. It covers the most outstanding trails from Ketchikan in the Southeast to Fairbanks near the Arctic Circle – including half-day hikes, and challenging week-long treks.

Baja California – a travel survival kit
For centuries, Mexico's Baja peninsula – with its beautiful coastline, raucous border towns and crumbling Spanish missions – has been a land of escapes and escapades. This book describes how and where to escape in Baja.

Bolivia – a travel survival kit
From lonely villages in the Andes to ancient ruined cities and the spectacular city of La Paz, Bolivia is a magnificent blend of everything that inspires travellers. Discover safe and intriguing travel options in this comprehensive guide.

Canada – a travel survival kit
This comprehensive guidebook has all the facts on the USA's huge neighbour – the Rocky Mountains, Niagara Falls, ultramodern Toronto, remote villages in Nova Scotia, and much more.

Central America on a shoestring
Practical information on travel in Belize, Guatemala, Costa Rica, Honduras, El Salvador, Nicaragua and Panama. A team of experienced Lonely Planet authors reveals the secrets of this culturally rich, geographically diverse and breathtakingly beautiful region.

Chile & Easter Island – a travel survival kit
Travel in Chile is easy and safe, with possibilities as varied as the countryside. This guide also gives detailed coverage of Chile's Pacific outpost, mysterious Easter Island.

Colombia – a travel survival kit
Colombia is a land of myths – from the ancient legends of El Dorado to the modern tales of Gabriel Garcia Marquez. The reality is beauty and violence, wealth and poverty, tradition and change. This guide shows how to travel independently and safely in this exotic country.

Costa Rica – a travel survival kit
Sun-drenched beaches, steamy jungles, smoking volcanoes, rugged mountains and dazzling birds and animals – Costa Rica has it all.

Eastern Caribbean – a travel survival kit
Powdery white sands, clear turquoise waters, lush jungle rainforest, balmy weather and a laid back pace, make the islands of the Eastern Caibbean an ideal destination for divers, hikers and sun-lovers. This guide will help you to decide which islands to visit to suit your interests and includes details on inter-island travel.

Ecuador & the Galápagos Islands – a travel survival kit
Ecuador offers a wide variety of travel experiences, from the high cordilleras to the Amazon plains – and 600 miles west, the fascinating Galápagos Islands. Everything you need to know about travelling around this enchanting country.

Guatemala, Belize & Yucatán: La Ruta Maya – a travel survival kit
Climb a volcano, explore the colourful highland villages or laze your time away on coral islands and Caribbean beaches. The lands of the Maya offer a fascinating journey into the past which will enhance appreciation of their dynamic contemporary cultures. An award winning guide to this exotic fregion.

Hawaii – a travel survival kit
Share in the delights of this island paradise – and avoid its high prices – both on and off the beaten track. Full details on Hawaii's best-known attractions, plus plenty of uncrowded sights and activities.

Honolulu – a travel survival kit
Honolulu offers an intriguing variety of attractions and experiences. Whatever your interests, this comprehensive guidebook is packed with insider tips and practical information.

Mexico – a travel survival kit
A unique blend of Indian and Spanish culture, fascinating history, and hospitable people, make Mexico a travellers' paradise.

Pacific Northwest – a travel survival kit
Explore the secrets of the Northwest with this indispensable guide – from island hopping through the San Juans and rafting the Snake River to hiking the Olympic Peninsula and discovering Seattle's best microbrews.

Peru – a travel survival kit
The lost city of Machu Picchu, the Andean altiplano and the magnificent Amazon rainforests are just some of Peru's many attractions. All the travel facts you'll need can be found in this comprehensive guide.

Rocky Mountain States – a travel survival kit
Whether you plan to ski Aspen, hike Yellowstone or hang out in sleepy ghost towns, this indispensable guide is full of down-to-earth advice for every budget.

South America on a shoestring
This practical guide provides concise information for budget travellers and covers South America from the Darien Gap to Tierra del Fuego.

Southwest – a travel survival kit
Raft through the Grand Canyon in Arizona, explore ancient ruins and modern pueblos of New Mexico and ski some of the world's best slopes in Utah. This guide leads you straight to the sights, salsa and saguaros of the American Southwest.

Trekking in the Patagonian Andes
The first detailed guide to this region gives complete information on 28 walks, and lists a number of other possibilities extending from the Araucanía and Lake District regions of Argentina and Chile to the remote icy tip of South America in Tierra del Fuego.

Venezuela – a travel survival kit
Venezuela is a curious hybrid of a Western-style civilisation and a very traditional world contained within a beautiful natural setting. From the beaches along the Caribbean coast and the snow-capped peaks of the Andes to the capital, Caracas, there is much for travellers to explore. This comprehensive guide is packed with 'first-hand' tips for travel in this fascinating destination.

Also available:
Brazilian phrasebook, **Latin American Spanish** phrasebook, **Quechua** phrasebook and **USA** phrasebook.

Lonely Planet Guidebooks

Lonely Planet guidebooks cover every accessible part of Asia as well as Australia, the Pacific, South America, Africa, the Middle East, Europe and parts of North America. There are six series: *travel survival kits*, covering a country for a range of budgets; *shoestring guides* with compact information for low-budget travel in a major region; *walking guides*; *city guides, travel atlases* and *phrasebooks*.

Australia & the Pacific
Australia
Australian phrasebook
Bushwalking in Australia
Islands of Australia's Great Barrier Reef
Outback Australia
Fiji
Fijian phrasebook
Melbourne city guide
Micronesia
New Caledonia
New South Wales & the ACT
New Zealand
Tramping in New Zealand
Papua New Guinea
Queensland
Bushwalking in Papua New Guinea
Papua New Guinea phrasebook
Rarotonga & the Cook Islands
Samoa
Solomon Islands
Sydney city guide
Tahiti & French Polynesia
Tonga
Vanuatu
Victoria
Western Australia

North-East Asia
Beijing city guide
China
Cantonese phrasebook
Mandarin Chinese phrasebook
Hong Kong, Macau & Canton
Japan
Japanese phrasebook
Korea
Korean phrasebook
Mongolia
Mongolian phrasebook
North-East Asia on a shoestring
Seoul city guide
Taiwan
Tibet
Tibet phrasebook
Tokyo city guide

South-East Asia
Bali & Lombok
Bangkok city guide
Cambodia
Indonesia
Ho Chi Minh City city guide
Indonesian phrasebook
Jakarta city guide
Java
Laos
Lao phrasebook
Malaysia, Singapore & Brunei
Myanmar (Burma)
Burmese phrasebook
Philippines
Pilipino phrasebook
Singapore city guide
South-East Asia on a shoestring
Thailand
Thailand travel atlas
Thai phrasebook
Thai Hill Tribes phrasebook
Vietnam
Vietnamese phrasebook

Middle East
Arab Gulf States
Egypt & the Sudan
Arabic (Egyptian) phrasebook
Iran
Israel
Jordan & Syria
Middle East
Turkey
Turkish phrasebook
Trekking in Turkey
Yemen

Africa
Africa on a shoestring
Central Africa
East Africa
Trekking in East Africa
Kenya
Swahili phrasebook
Morocco
Arabic (Moroccan) phrasebook
North Africa
South Africa, Lesotho & Swaziland
West Africa
Zimbabwe, Botswana & Namibia

Mail Order

Lonely Planet guidebooks are distributed worldwide. They are also available by mail order from Lonely Planet, so if you have difficulty finding a title please write to us. US and Canadian residents should write to Embarcadero West, 155 Filbert St, Suite 251, Oakland CA 94607, USA ; European residents should write to 10 Barley Mow Passage, Chiswick, London W4 4PH; and residents of other countries to PO Box 617, Hawthorn, Victoria 3122, Australia.

Indian Subcontinent
Bangladesh
India
India travel atlas
Hindi/Urdu phrasebook
Trekking in the Indian Himalaya
Karakoram Highway
Kashmir, Ladakh & Zanskar
Nepal
Trekking in the Nepal Himalaya
Nepali phrasebook
Pakistan
Sri Lanka
Sri Lanka phrasebook

Central America & the Caribbean
Baja California
Central America on a shoestring
Costa Rica
Eastern Caribbean
Guatemala, Belize & Yucatán: La Ruta Maya
Mexico

North America
Alaska
Backpacking in Alaska
Canada
Hawaii
Honolulu city guide
Pacific Northwest USA
Rocky Mountain States
Southwest USA
USA phrasebook

Europe
Baltic States & Kaliningrad
Baltics States phrasebook
Britain
Central Europe on a shoestring
Central Europe phrasebook
Czech & Slovak Republics
Dublin city guide
Eastern Europe on a shoestring
Eastern Europe phrasebook
Finland
France
Greece
Greek phrasebook
Hungary
Iceland, Greenland & the Faroe Islands
Ireland
Italy
Mediterranean Europe on a shoestring
Mediterranean Europe phrasebook
Poland
Prague city guide
Scandinavian & Baltic Europe on a shoestring
Scandinavian Europe phrasebook
Slovenia
Switzerland
Trekking in Greece
Trekking in Spain
USSR
Russian phrasebook
Vienna city guide
Western Europe on a shoestring
Western Europe phrasebook

South America
Argentina, Uruguay & Paraguay
Bolivia
Brazil
Brazilian phrasebook
Chile & Easter Island
Colombia
Ecuador & the Galápagos Islands
Latin American Spanish phrasebook
Peru
Quechua phrasebook
Rio de Janeiro city guide
South America on a shoestring
Trekking in the Patagonian Andes
Venezuela

Indian Ocean
Madagascar & Comoros
Maldives & Islands of the East Indian Ocean
Mauritius, Réunion & Seychelles

The Lonely Planet Story

Lonely Planet published its first book in 1973 in response to the numerous 'How did you do it?' questions Maureen and Tony Wheeler were asked after driving, bussing, hitching, sailing and railing their way from England to Australia.

Written at a kitchen table and hand collated, trimmed and stapled, *Across Asia on the Cheap* became an instant local bestseller, inspiring thoughts of another book.

Eighteen months in South-East Asia resulted in their second guide, *South-East Asia on a shoestring*, which they put together in a backstreet Chinese hotel in Singapore in 1975. The 'yellow bible' as it quickly became known to backpackers around the world, soon became *the* guide to the region. It has sold well over half a million copies and is now in its 8th edition, still retaining its familiar yellow cover.

Today there are over 140 Lonely Planet titles in print – books that have that same adventurous approach to travel as those early guides; books that 'assume you know how to get your luggage off the carousel' as one reviewer put it.

Although Lonely Planet initially specialised in guides to Asia, they now cover most regions of the world, including the Pacific, South America, Africa, the Middle East and Europe. The list of *walking guides* and *phrasebooks* (for 'unusual' languages such as Quechua, Swahili, Nepali and Egyptian Arabic) is also growing rapidly.

The emphasis continues to be on travel for independent travellers. Tony and Maureen still travel for several months of each year and play an active part in the writing, updating and quality control of Lonely Planet's guides.

They have been joined by over 50 authors, 110 staff – mainly editors, cartographers & designers – at our office in Melbourne, Australia, at our US office in Oakland, California and at our European office in Paris; another five at our office in London handle sales for Britain, Europe and Africa. Travellers themselves also make a valuable contribution to the guides through the feedback we receive in thousands of letters each year.

The people at Lonely Planet strongly believe that travellers can make a positive contribution to the countries they visit, both through their appreciation of the countries' culture, wildlife and natural features, and through the money they spend. In addition, the company makes a direct contribution to the countries and regions it covers. Since 1986 a percentage of the income from each book has been donated to ventures such as famine relief in Africa; aid projects in India; agricultural projects in Central America; Greenpeace's efforts to halt French nuclear testing in the Pacific; and Amnesty International.

Lonely Planet's basic travel philosophy is summed up in Tony Wheeler's comment, 'Don't worry about whether your trip will work out. Just go!'